WOOD-WORKING

TOOLS, MATERIALS, PROCESSES

WILLIAM P. SPENCE

L. DUANE GRIFFITHS

American Technical Publishers, Inc.
Alsip, Illinois 60658

Library of Congress Catalog Number 81-67195
ISBN: 0-8269-4833-2

123456789-81-987654

Printed in the United States of America

Photo Credits

Section opening pages:
Evans Products Company (428, *bottom*), Robert H. Martin Company (570, *bottom*), Roseburg Lumber Company (500, *bottom;* 556, *bottom*), U.S. Forest Products Laboratory (500, *top*), Western Wood Products Association (570, *top left; top right*).

Preface

This book is designed as a text for general woodworking. It thoroughly covers both hand and machine woodworking. WOODWORKING: TOOLS, MATERIALS, PROCESSES includes basic skills and techniques suitable for a beginner, yet it includes sufficient depth in machine processes and techniques for use in advanced woodworking and cabinetmaking.

The many photographs clearly demonstrate the methods and practices being explained. Two-color illustrations also clarify techniques and procedures. The second color shows the major features of illustrations and thus helps learning.

WOODWORKING: TOOLS, MATERIALS, PROCESSES follows a logical learning sequence. After the introduction (Unit 1), it presents measurement systems, both customary and metric (Unit 2). Several units on project planning and design, including preparation of working drawings, follow (Units 3 to 5). Typical industrial drafting techniques show how final plans are prepared.

Safety is very important and is covered thoroughly (Unit 6). Specific safety suggestions are given also at the beginning of units that cover the use of tools.

The use of basic hand tools is covered, including use, care and sharpening (Units 7 to 14). Step-by-step procedures are given. The pictures are very helpful in showing how to hold and handle the tools.

The success of a project depends on the joining of wood. Joinery is discussed thoroughly and illustrated (Units 15 to 22). Types of fasteners and hardware are detailed (Units 23 and 24). Procedures for installing hardware and fasteners are covered also (Units 25 and 26). A unit on glues, adhesives and cements includes technical information on the types, advantages, disadvantages and proper uses of the most commonly used materials (Unit 27).

Several units cover in detail the operation of major stationary woodworking machinery (Units 28 to 38). This section illustrates and explains the proper way to set up machines, how to use guards, safety rules and operation procedures. Most units also include project suggestions.

Portable power tools are covered (Units 39 to 44). These units explain setup and operations. Safe operating procedures are stressed.

Construction techniques for furniture and cabinets are explained in the next section (Units 45 and 46). Seven units on finishing follow, beginning with the preparation of the raw wood. They cover filling, staining and finish coating (Units 47 to 53).

The next section studies wood as a raw material, logging, grading, veneering, plywood, particle board and hardboard (Units 54 to 60). It presents wood as a material of industry and some important manufacturing processes.

Forming curved wood members is studied (Unit 61). A unit on wood preservatives and fire retardants follows (Unit 62). Mass production is explained and illustrated to show how wood is formed into useful products (Unit 63). The unit on careers presents jobs in mass production, forestry and other wood-related industries (Unit 64).

The last section includes 30 recommended projects ranging from simple to complex.

Each unit clearly states objectives and lists important technical terms. The review questions check mastery of the material. Suggested activities expand learning about the subject presented.

A glossary at the end of the book gives a speedy reference for building a technical vocabulary.

The authors thank the individuals, organizations and companies that have contributed materials and advice during the preparation of this text.

William P. Spence
L. Duane Griffiths

Contents

page

Section 1
Planning for the Job vi
Unit
1 Introduction to Woodworking 2
2 Measurement Systems 8
3 Planning a Project 12
4 Designing a Project 19
5 Working Drawings 33
6 General Safety 48

Section 2
Using Hand Tools 56
Unit
7 Layout Tools 58
8 Handsaws 68
9 Hand Planes and Scrapers 78
10 Chisels, Gouges and Carving Tools 89
11 Sharpening Edge Tools 94
12 Files, Rasps and Forming Tools 104
13 Drilling and Boring Tools 110
14 Clamping Tools and Assembly Procedures 120

Section 3
Fastening Techniques 138
Unit
15 Wood Joints 140
16 Making Edge and Butt Joints 150
17 Making Miter Joints 155
18 Making Lap Joints 160
19 Making Dado and Rabbet Joints 162
20 Making Dowel Joints 165
21 Making Mortise and Tenon Joints 170
22 Making Dovetail and Box Joints 175
23 Fasteners 179
24 Hardware 190
25 Installing Wood Screws 208
26 Fastening with Nails 214
27 Glues, Adhesives and Cements 219

page

Section 4
Stationary Power Tools 230
Unit
28 Table Saws 232
29 Scroll Saws 262
30 Band Saws 270
31 Radial Arm Saws 283
32 Jointers 298
33 Planers 312
34 Shapers 320
35 Wood Lathes 332
36 Mortisers and Tenoners 349
37 Drill Presses 359
38 Stationary Sanding Machines 373

Section 5
Portable Power Tools 382
Unit
39 Portable Circular Saws 384
40 Reciprocating and Saber Saws 391
41 Portable Power Planes 398
42 Routers 401
43 Portable Drills 419
44 Portable Sanders 423

Section 6
Construction Techniques 428
Unit
45 Furniture Construction 430
46 Kitchen Cabinets and Plastic Laminates 441

Section 7
Finishing 454
Unit
47 Abrasives 456
48 Preparing Surfaces for Finishing and Sanding 460
49 Filling Wood Surfaces 466
50 Wood Stains 470
51 Varnishes, Enamels and Brushing Techniques 476
52 Lacquers and Spraying Techniques 485
53 Wipe-on Finishes 496

page

Section 8
The Woods Industry 500
Unit
54 Wood Science 502
55 Logging and Sawmill Industry 518
56 Grading Lumber 523
57 Veneers 528
58 Plywood 534
59 Particle Board 539
60 Hardboard 543
61 Curved Wood Members 546
62 Wood Preservatives and Fire Retardants 552

Section 9
Mass Production 556
Unit
63 Mass-production Manufacturing 558

Section 10
Careers in Woodworking 570
Unit
64 Careers 572

Section 11
Woodworking Projects 586
Unit
65 Projects 588

Glossary 618

Index 626

COLONIAL RECIPE BOX

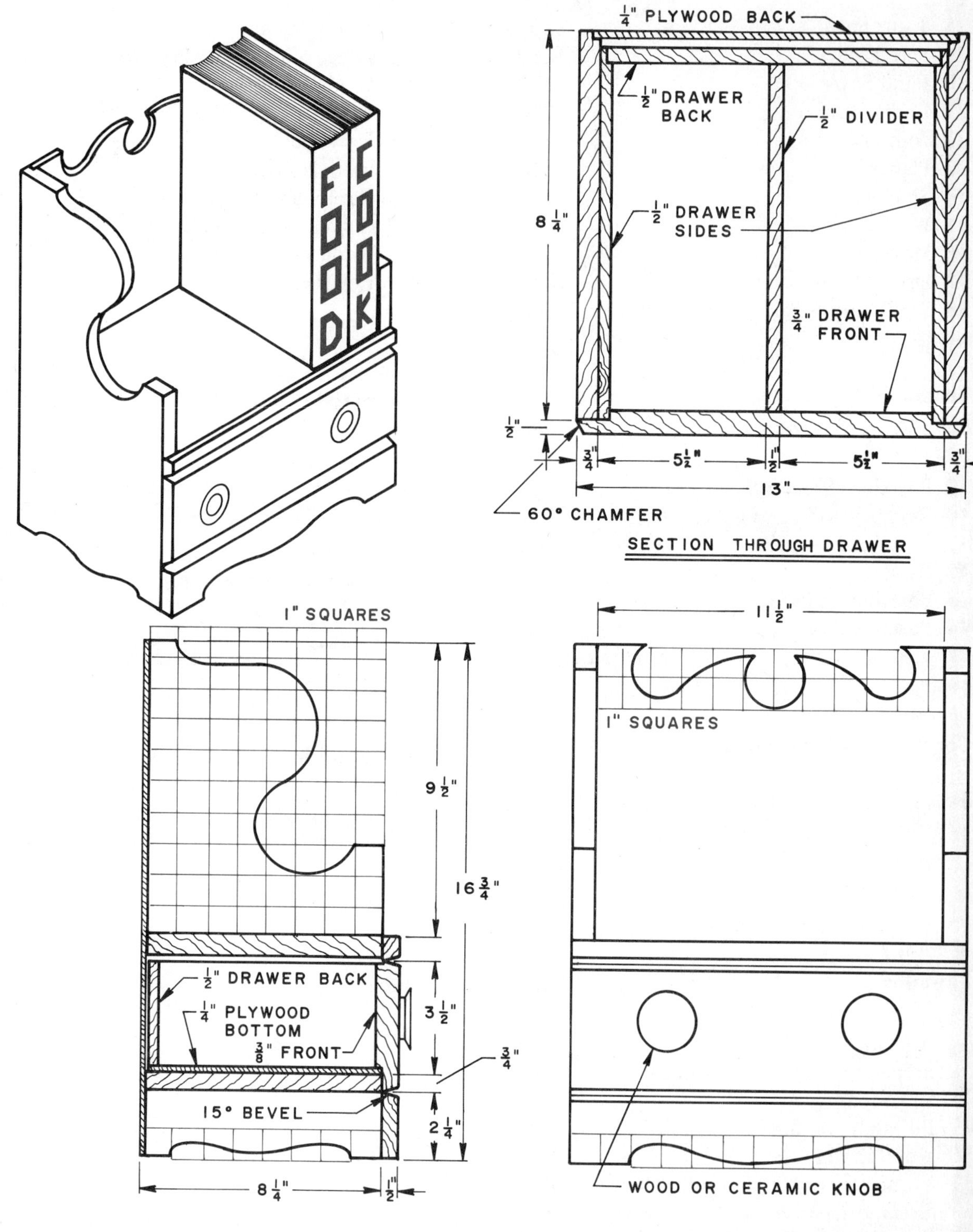

SECTION

1

Planning for the Job

1
Introduction to Woodworking

2
Measurement Systems

3
Planning a Project

4
Designing a Project

5
Working Drawings

6
General Safety

Any useful activity requires a certain amount of planning. This is true whether you are going on a trip or building. To plan a woodworking project you must have:

- A knowledge of design principles.
- The ability to use customary and metric measurement systems.
- The skill and knowledge to make working drawings.
- The ability to choose and to calculate the materials to be used.
- A knowledge of woodworking processes so that you can develop an orderly plan of procedure.
- An understanding of safety rules, which protect you and the people around you.

Section 1, Planning for the Job, presents the basic skills and principles you will need for planning a woodworking project.

UNIT

1

Introduction to Woodworking

Objectives

After studying this unit you should be able to:

1 Describe the importance of the woods industry in our economy.
2 Use this book properly.

The future of the woods industry is unlimited and is very important to our economy. The United States Department of Commerce reports that there are more than 42 thousand wood-related companies and organizations. These businesses pay more than $6 billion per year in salaries. This makes the woods industry fourth largest in the nation in terms of salaries paid to full-time employees. Together, these companies produce more than $22 billion in goods each year.

Wood is grown throughout the United States, Figure 1-1. It is used in thousands of ways, both in and out of our homes. Because of the high technology of today's woods industry, wood is used to make all types of cabinets, furniture, toys, buildings and paper products. New inventions and production methods are being developed.

Wood is selected for many products because of its advantages. It is well known for beauty and high strength, Figure 1-2. Wooden parts are made easily with hand tools or woodworking machinery. These shaped pieces then can be quickly joined with fasteners such as nails, screws or adhesives. Finished wood products are durable and will give many years of service.

The demand for wood is increasing. Imagine a wooden highway 1 foot thick, 24 feet wide and long enough to reach to the moon 230,000 miles away. By the year 2000, we will need that much wood *each year.* But because wood is a renewable resource, its future is quite bright. Through research we have learned to take better care of our growing forests, Figure 1-3. Trees once took almost a hundred years to grow to full size. Trees being planted today, however, can be harvested in 20 to 30 years. This will allow future generations to meet the high demand for wood and to continue using it as a raw material.

LEARNING ABOUT WOODWORKING

You can learn much by using this book. It will give you information that can be used to construct furniture, cabinets and many other wood products. You can refer to the glossary at the end of the book for meanings of words you do not understand. Unit 65 will suggest many projects to develop your skills.

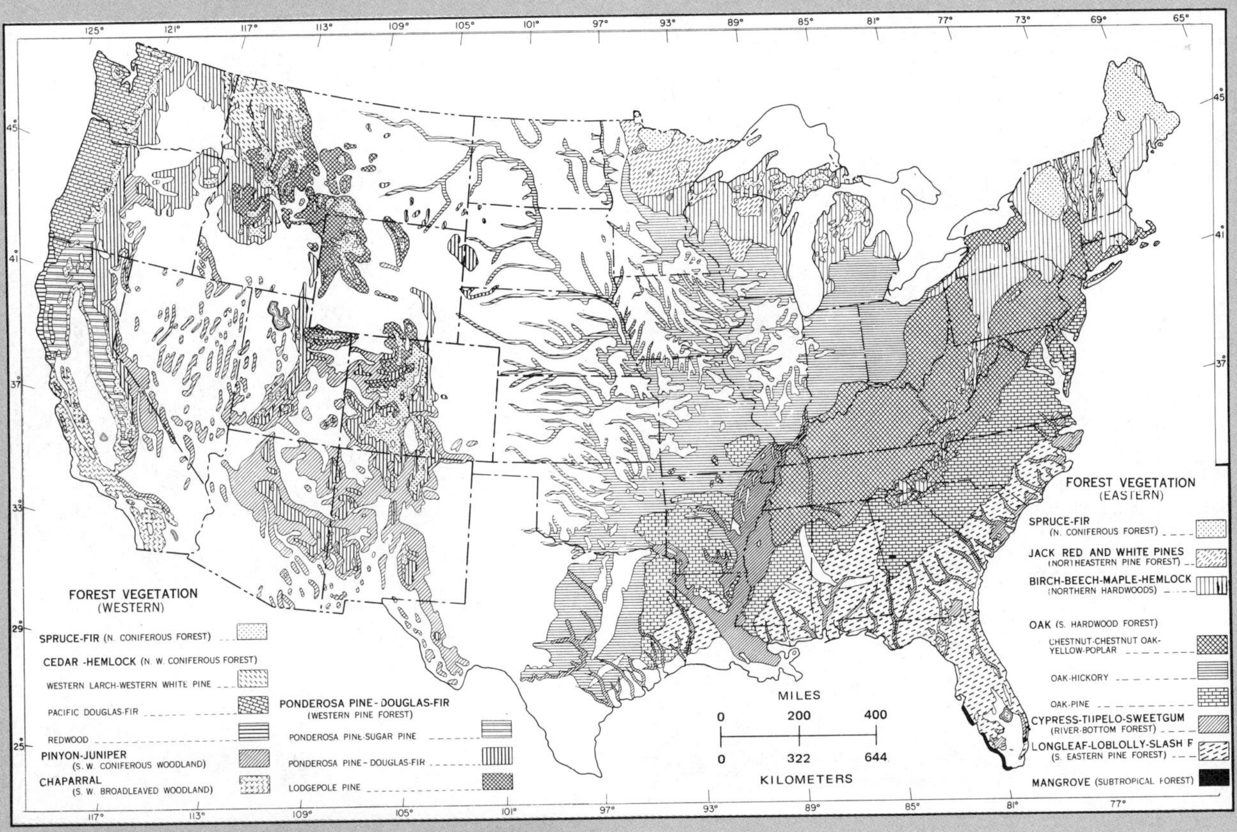

Figure 1-1
Trees are grown in most parts of the United States. Which trees are grown in your state? (U.S. Forest Service)

Figure 1-2
The laminated wood beams in this church are very strong to support the roof. They also create a beautiful building. (American Institute of Timber Construction)

Figure 1-3
Researchers have developed trees that grow quickly. Trees are started in a nursery before being planted in a forest. (Western Wood Products Association)

Figure 1-4
Planning your project is a very important part of woodworking.

Figure 1-5
A great deal of information is given on these grading stamps for plywood. Which grade should you use?

The major points to study in this book are:

1. *Planning projects and making simple drawings,* Figure 1-4. A skilled worker must know how to plan a job before starting work. Final design ideas are recorded in the form of working drawings. The drawings must be accurate and complete. Any mistakes made in the design probably will also be made on the project. Your plans should be complete enough that another woodworker could build your project using only your drawings.

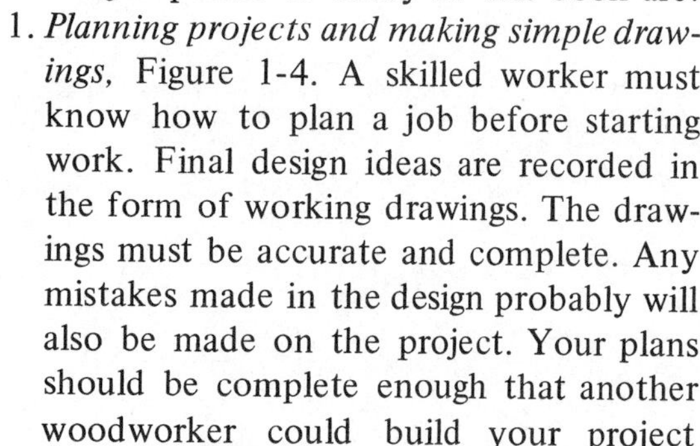

2. *Understanding quality and selection of wood and supplies,* Figure 1-5. Many kinds of wood and supplies are available. Each has desirable qualities and limitations. Selecting the proper supplies for each job is important. As a consumer, you should be able to examine wood products in stores and identify quality materials. Once purchased, these materials should be used properly. The best supplies will not last if they are handled incorrectly.
3. *Specifying and using hardware, fasteners, adhesives and other products of the woods industry,* Figure 1-6. People working in the woods industry must be able to select hardware, fasteners and adhesives. Because a properly constructed product requires the correct hardware, this knowledge is of great importance.

   There are hundreds of different types of hardware, including hinges, pulls and glides. Fasteners consist of nails, screws and bolts. Adhesives are sometimes called liquid fasteners because they are applied in a liquid form. When spread on the wood they form a strong joint.
4. *Using woodworking hand tools and machines properly and safely,* Figures 1-7 and

Figure 1-6
There are many different types of fasteners. A clamp nail is used as a fastener to strengthen a miter joint.

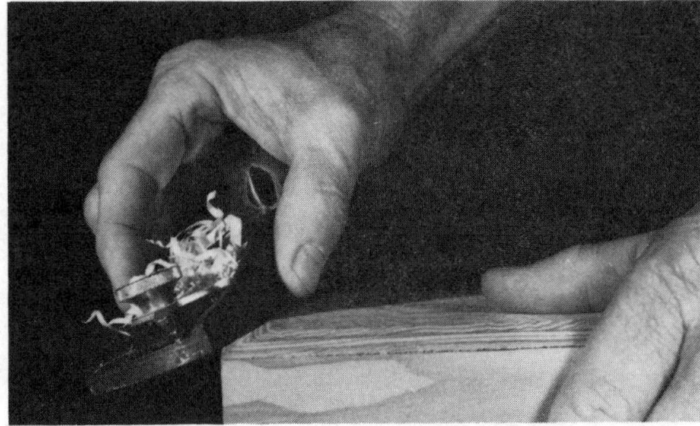

Figure 1-7
Hand tools can make fine, clean cuts. Entire projects as well as finishing cuts can be made with these tools. (American Plywood Association)

1-8. The safety of the worker and those around the worker is a top priority in industry. This text stresses the safe and proper way to assemble and use hand and power tools. Never perform any operation without knowing the safe procedure. This book will introduce you to the basic procedures. It will also cover some advanced operations.

5. *Preparing the surface of the wood and applying wood finishes,* Figure 1-9. No product, even if strongly constructed, is satisfactory unless it has a proper finish. The surface first must be properly sanded and cleaned. Many finishes are available to protect the wood. The woodworker must know the proper uses for each material. Proper application techniques also must be followed. Finishes can be brushed, sprayed or wiped on the wood.

Figure 1-8
Always follow the correct safety procedure when operating woodworking equipment.

Figure 1-9
The surface of this chair must be prepared carefully before a finish can be applied. (Southern Furniture Manufacturers Association)

Figure 1-10
One layer of light and dark wood is grown each year on a tree. By counting its rings, you can tell that this log is quite old. (U.S. Forest Products Laboratory)

Figure 1-11
Many joints were used to build this hutch. How many can you find? (Crawford Furniture Manufacturing Corporation)

6. *Knowing how wood grows and knowing its common properties,* Figure 1-10. Wood is made of millions of tiny cells. Knowledge about wood and its possible defects is important when selecting or rejecting material for your project. Defects include knots, decay, warp and other undesirable features. The properties of woods make some kinds more suitable than others for certain uses.
7. *Using proper joinery and construction techniques for furniture and cabinets,* Figure 1-11. Another key to a well-built wood product is the proper joining of parts. Deciding on the appropriate type of joint, fastener or adhesive is vital to the final success of the product. This book will provide construction techniques for furniture, kitchen cabinets and counter tops.
8. *Understanding mass-production principles and how a company is organized and operated,* Figure 1-12. Mass production has enabled more people to buy quality wood products. If produced one at a time, most wood products would be too expensive for many people to buy. Mass production

Figure 1-12
These table legs are being mass-produced on a spindle sander. (Stowell Wood Products)

also has produced many jobs for those who enjoy working with wood. An understanding of mass production will make you a better worker.

9. *Using the experience from your woodworking course to help you with career decisions,* Figure 1-13. Courses taken in school help prepare you for your career as an adult. The woodworking course you are taking will provide a wide variety of hand- and machine-tool experiences. You will find out if you enjoy woodworking. You may also want to take more courses to prepare for a career in woods.

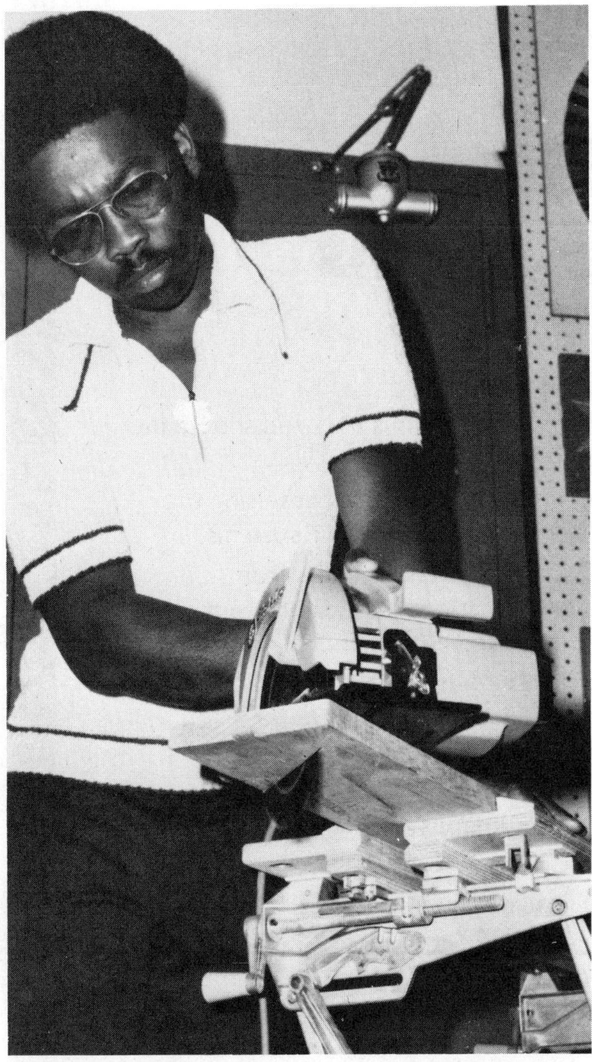

Figure 1-13
Woodworking offers many exciting careers. Working with wood is a fulfilling job. (Black & Decker Manufacturing Company)

REVIEW QUESTIONS

1 How many wood-related companies and organizations are there in the United States?
2 What is the yearly dollar value of wood products?
3 Name four uses of wood.
4 What are three advantages of wood?
5 Why will future generations also use wood as a raw material?
6 List five things that you can learn from this book.

SUGGESTED ACTIVITIES

1 Turn to the glossary at the end of the book and see how many terms you already know. Make a list of ten words you would like to know more about and write out their definitions.
2 Find a project at the end of the book you would like to make. Develop a plan for producing this project.

UNIT

2

Measurement Systems

Objectives

After studying this unit you should be able to:

1 Measure linear distances using the customary and metric systems.

2 Convert measurements from customary to metric and from metric to customary.

3 Measure using common fractions and decimal fractions.

Technical Terms

Customary system
Common fraction
Decimal fraction
Metric system
Meter
Millimeter

Accuracy in measuring is vital to the successful manufacturing of a product. Many wood products, such as furniture, cabinets, doors and windows, are mass-produced. The various parts making up one unit are made in different parts of the woodworking plant. Often they are made in two or more separate plants, which might even be in different states. The parts are brought together at a single assembly plant where they are joined together to produce a finished product. They must be made to exact sizes, or they will not fit together. This is why accurate measurements are vital.

Measuring in a straight line is called linear measure. There are two systems of linear measure in use. These are customary and metric.

THE CUSTOMARY SYSTEM

The inch is the basic unit in the *customary system.* Thirty-six inches equals a unit called a yard. This unit is not commonly used when designing wood products. All dimensions are usually stated in inches. The inch is divided into smaller parts, providing a system of fine measurement. There are two commonly used ways to subdivide the inch, common fractions and decimal fractions.

Common fractions divide the inch into 2, 4, 8, 16 and 32 parts. Shown as fractions, they would be written 1/2″, 1/4″, 1/8″, 1/16″ and 1/32″. The fractions are always stated in numbers divisible by 2. Study the rule in Figure 2-1. It is drawn larger than true size so the fine subdivisions can be seen. An actual-size rule is shown in Figure 2-2. Common fractions do not provide a great deal of accuracy. Some wood product manufacturers, therefore, use the decimal fraction.

Decimal fractions divide the inch into 10 and 100 parts. These are stated 0.10″ (one tenth of an inch) and 0.01″ (one hundredth of an inch). Study the decimal rule in Figure 2-3. It is drawn much larger than true size so the fine subdivisions can be seen. A rule of the actual size is shown in Figure 2-4. The decimal fraction system is more accurate than the common fraction method.

Thirty-six inches equals a unit called a yard. This unit is not commonly used when designing

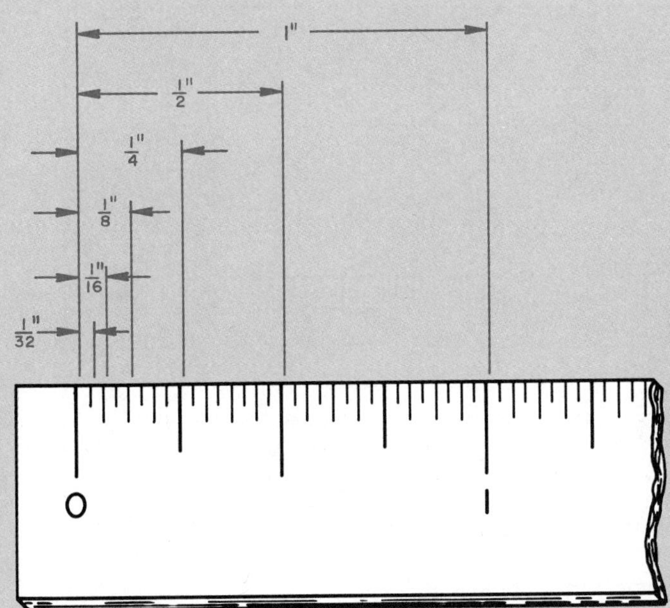

Figure 2-1
An inch divided into common fractions (drawing enlarged).

Figure 2-2
Actual size of a common fractional scale divided into one-sixteenth-of-an-inch increments.

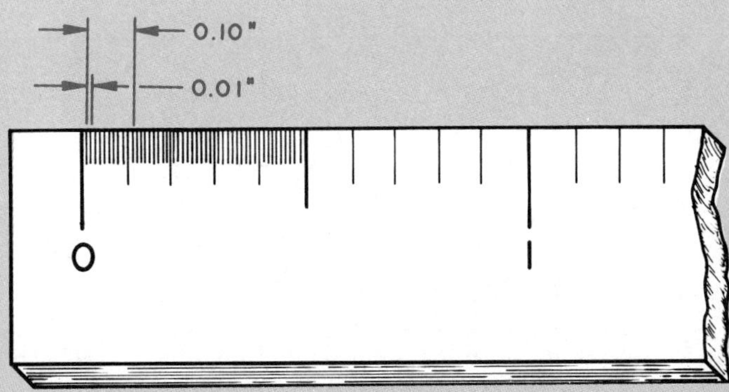

Figure 2-3
An inch divided into decimal fractions (drawing enlarged).

Figure 2-4
Actual size of a decimal fraction scale divided into tenths of an inch.

wood products. All dimensions are usually stated in inches.

THE METRIC SYSTEM

The *metric system* is a decimal system using the meter as the basic unit. A meter equals 39.37 inches, or slightly more than one yard.

The meter is divided into finer parts for precision measurement. The divisions are decimeters, centimeters and millimeters. These are based on the unit 10. There are 10 decimeters in a meter. There are 10 centimeters in a decimeter. There are 10 millimeters in a centimeter, Figure 2-5.

1 meter = 10 decimeters (dm)
1 decimeter = 10 centimeters (cm)
1 centimeter = 10 millimeters (mm)

or

1 meter = 10 decimeters
= 100 centimeters
= 1000 millimeters

Figure 2-5
Metric units of linear measure.

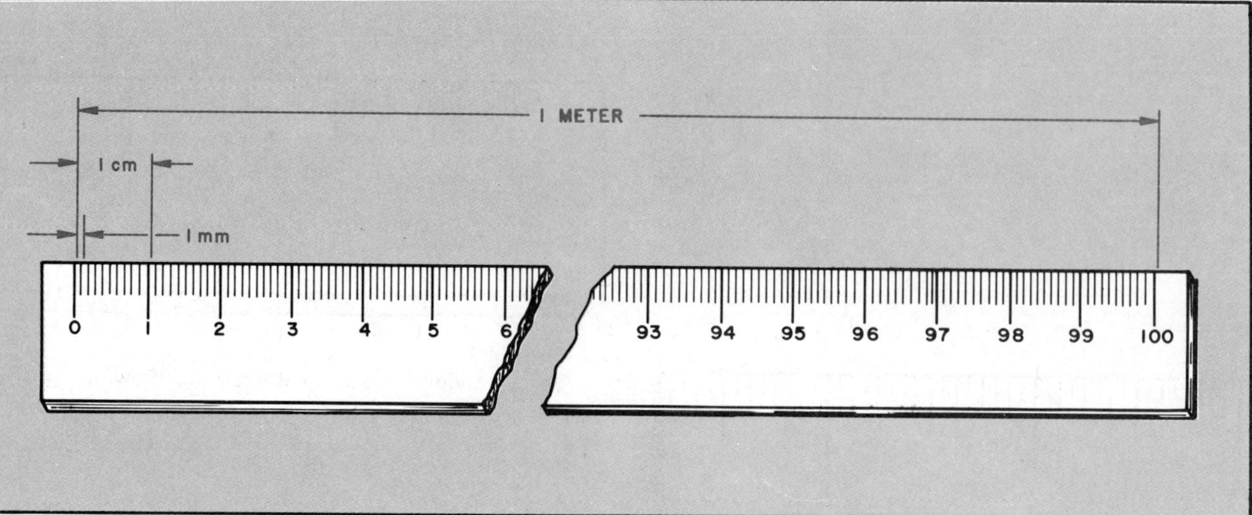

Figure 2-6
A meter divided into centimeters and millimeters. The centimeter and millimeter units shown are actual size.

FRACTIONAL INCHES TO MILLIMETERS

In.	mm	In.	mm	In.	mm	In.	mm
1/64	0.397	17/64	6.747	33/64	13.097	49/64	19.447
1/32	0.794	9/32	7.144	17/32	13.494	25/32	19.844
3/64	1.191	19/64	7.541	35/64	13.890	51/64	20.240
1/16	1.587	5/16	7.937	9/16	14.287	13/16	20.637
5/64	1.984	21/64	8.334	37/64	14.684	53/64	21.034
3/32	2.381	11/32	8.731	19/32	15.081	27/32	21.431
7/64	2.778	23/64	9.128	39/64	15.478	55/64	21.828
1/8	3.175	3/8	9.525	5/8	15.875	7/8	22.225
9/64	3.572	25/64	9.922	41/64	16.272	57/64	22.622
5/32	3.969	13/32	10.319	21/32	16.669	29/32	23.019
11/64	4.366	27/64	10.716	43/64	17.065	59/64	23.415
3/16	4.762	7/16	11.113	11/16	17.462	15/16	23.812
13/64	5.159	29/64	11.509	45/64	17.859	61/64	24.209
7/32	5.556	15/32	11.906	23/32	18.256	31/32	24.606
15/64	5.953	31/64	12.303	47/64	18.653	63/64	25.003
1/4	6.350	1/2	12.700	3/4	19.050	1	25.400

Figure 2-7
Use this chart to convert fractional inches to millimeters.

Stated in other terms, there are 10 decimeters in a meter, 100 centimeters in a meter and 1000 millimeters in a meter. A meter divided into centimeters and millimeters is shown in Figure 2-6. This is the true size of the millimeter and centimeter units.

The metric units are identified by symbols, Figure 2-5. They are written in lower-case letters.

Working drawings are dimensioned entirely in millimeters.

CONVERSION FACTORS

The United States currently recognizes the customary system as primary. We are moving to adopt the metric system as the primary system of measuring. While this change is in process, products will be manufactured using both systems of measurement.

Sometimes it will be necessary to convert a drawing from one system to the other. For example, all of a company's drawings are in inches.

MILLIMETERS TO DECIMAL INCHES

mm In.	mm In.	mm In.	mm In.	mm In.
1 = 0.0394	21 = 0.8268	41 = 1.6142	61 = 2.4016	81 = 3.1890
2 = 0.0787	22 = 0.8662	42 = 1.6536	62 = 2.4410	82 = 3.2284
3 = 0.1181	23 = 0.9055	43 = 1.6929	63 = 2.4804	83 = 3.2678
4 = 0.1575	24 = 0.9449	44 = 1.7323	64 = 2.5197	84 = 3.3071
5 = 0.1969	25 = 0.9843	45 = 1.7717	65 = 2.5591	85 = 3.3465
6 = 0.2362	26 = 1.0236	46 = 1.8111	66 = 2.5985	86 = 3.3859
7 = 0.2756	27 = 1.0630	47 = 1.8504	67 = 2.6378	87 = 3.4253
8 = 0.3150	28 = 1.1024	48 = 1.8898	68 = 2.6772	88 = 3.4646
9 = 0.3543	29 = 1.1418	49 = 1.9292	69 = 2.7166	89 = 3.5040
10 = 0.3937	30 = 1.1811	50 = 1.9685	70 = 2.7560	90 = 3.5434
11 = 0.4331	31 = 1.2205	51 = 2.0079	71 = 2.7953	91 = 3.5827
12 = 0.4724	32 = 1.2599	52 = 2.0473	72 = 2.8247	92 = 3.6221
13 = 0.5118	33 = 1.2992	53 = 2.0867	73 = 2.8741	93 = 3.6615
14 = 0.5512	34 = 1.3386	54 = 2.1260	74 = 2.9134	94 = 3.7009
15 = 0.5906	35 = 1.3780	55 = 2.1654	75 = 2.9528	95 = 3.7402
16 = 0.6299	36 = 1.4173	56 = 2.2048	76 = 2.9922	96 = 3.7796
17 = 0.6693	37 = 1.4567	57 = 2.2441	77 = 3.0316	97 = 3.8190
18 = 0.7087	38 = 1.4961	58 = 2.2835	78 = 3.0709	98 = 3.8583
19 = 0.7480	39 = 1.5355	59 = 2.3229	79 = 3.1103	99 = 3.8977
20 = 0.7874	40 = 1.5748	60 = 2.3622	80 = 3.1497	100 = 3.9371

Figure 2-8
Use this chart to convert millimeters to decimal inches.

If the company decides to manufacture products measured in millimeters it must convert inch measurements to millimeters. This is done with the help of conversion tables. In Figure 2-7 fractional inches are converted to millimeters. In Figure 2-8 millimeters are converted to decimal inches.

If a table is not available, inches can be converted to millimeters by multiplying by 25.4. One inch equals 25.4 millimeters.

As new products are designed and old products are redesigned, drawings will be made using millimeters so conversion will not be necessary at a later date.

REVIEW QUESTIONS

1 What are the differences between common fractions, decimal fractions and millimeters?
2 Into what units is a meter divided?
3 What is the linear relationship between a yard and a meter?
4 What are conversion tables?

SUGGESTED ACTIVITIES

1 Make a freehand sketch of the book rack in Figure 5-9. Replan it, converting the dimensions to millimeters. When converting, carry the sizes to one decimal place only.
2 After you convert to millimeters, convert to decimal fractions of inches. Place these dimensions above the metric dimensions. Record them in color. Convert them to two decimal places.
3 Practice measuring items found in the woodworking shop with both measuring systems. Measure the length of the workbench and a jack plane, the width of the jointer table and the thickness of a handsaw blade.
4 Measure the lines below. Record their lengths in common fractions, decimal fractions and millimeters.

UNIT

3

Planning a Project

Objectives

After studying this unit you should be able to:

1 Write a complete bill of materials.

2 Begin planning the steps of procedure.

3 Locate quality-control points.

4 Figure the number of board feet of solid stock in a project.

5 Figure the number of square feet of plywood, hardboard and particle board.

Technical Terms

Bill of materials
Plan of procedure
Quality-control points
Board foot
Nominal size
Random widths and lengths
Square

Before starting a woodworking project you must plan the entire job. Most things you do in your daily life need a plan. For example, if you are going on a trip you must plan what you want to take with you. You may even make a list. You will plan how to reach your destination and may mark the route on a map. The cost of the trip will have to be considered. You may have to decide when you will start and arrive.

Planning for a woodworking project is much the same. First you must decide what to build. Then you can make drawings in which every detail is specified. Determine the tools and materials. Finally, develop a step-by-step plan of procedure to follow throughout the job. A suggested planning sheet is shown in Figure 3-1.

THE WORKING DRAWING

First prepare a drawing of the project. It will help you to visualize the finished product. This unit explains how projects are designed. Unit 4 will discuss shop drawings. The size of the drawing will vary from project to project. A typical drawing is shown in Figure 3-1. Notice that each part is identified with a number.

THE BILL OF MATERIALS

After you complete the working drawing, prepare a *bill of materials.* The bill lists a description of each part, its size and its cost. When the cost of each part is known, you can find the total cost of the materials. Study the bill of materials in Figure 3-1. As in the working drawing, identify each part with a number. Give the finished size of each part. Use the finished sizes to figure the cost of each part. Because the part will be cut larger and shaped to the finished size, the price per unit must include a waste factor. Therefore, the cost is increased slightly to cover normal waste. Record the types of material and the price per unit.

The unit of measurement will vary, depending on the material. In Figure 3-1 the price for plywood is *per square foot* and for solid stock *per board foot.* The number of units is the number of square feet or board feet in the part. If there is more than one part, remember to multiply the

BILL OF MATERIALS						
NO. OF PIECES	NAME AND NUMBER OF PART	SIZE	MATERIAL	COST PER UNIT	NO. OF UNITS	COST OF ITEM
1	NO. 1 – TRAY FRONT	$\frac{3}{4}$" x 10$\frac{3}{4}$" x 12"	BIRCH PLY	$1.14	0.9	$1.03
1	NO. 2 – TRAY BACK	$\frac{3}{4}$" x 10" x 12"	BIRCH PLY	$1.14	0.8	$0.91
2	NO. 3 – LEGS	$\frac{3}{4}$" x 4$\frac{1}{4}$" x 11$\frac{3}{16}$"	SOLID BIRCH	$1.14	0.8	$0.90
4	NO. 4 – PADS	$\frac{1}{8}$" x $\frac{3}{4}$" x 3"	CORK	$2.00	0.06	$0.12
12	F. H. SCREWS	NO. 8 x 1$\frac{1}{2}$"	STEEL	$0.05	12	$0.60
				MATERIAL COST		$3.56

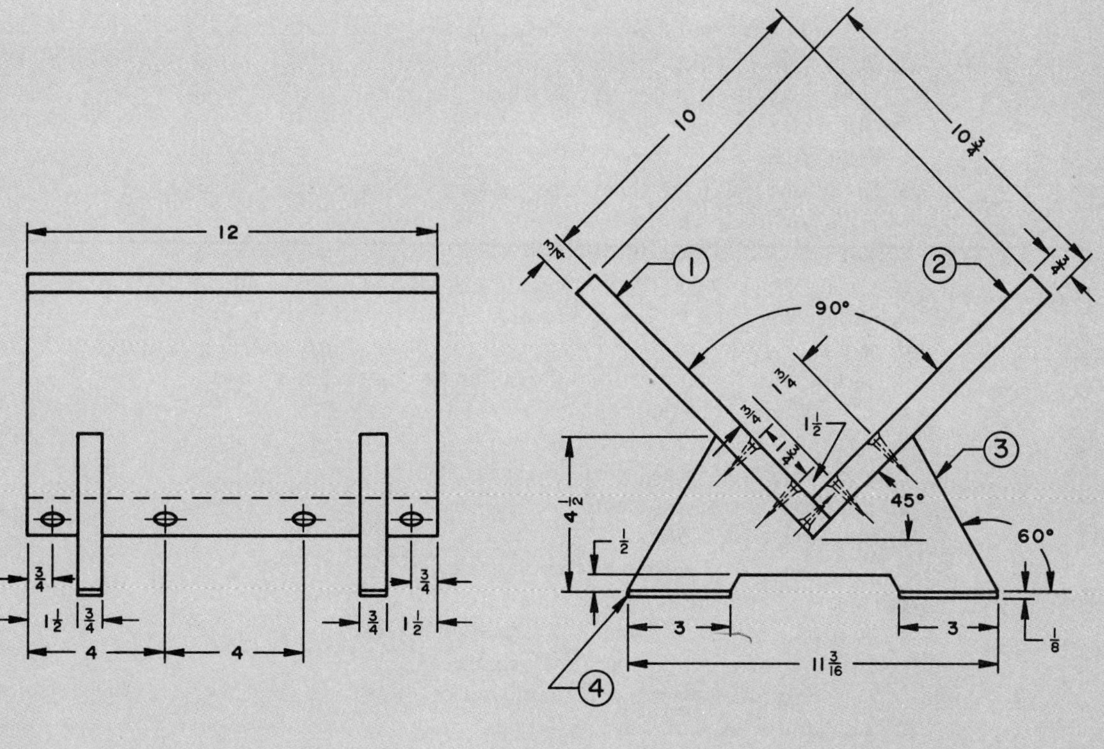

PROJECT: RECORD RACK
DESIGNER: BILL SPENCE
SCALE: $\frac{3}{8}$" = 1"

Figure 3-1
A typical working drawing and bill of materials for a small wood product.

PLAN OF PROCEDURE
(Project Planning Sheet)

Student's Name Chris Jones **Class** Wood II **Time** ____
Name of Project Record Rack

Tools and machines needed

1. ruler	5. drill press	9. T bevel
2. try square	6. twist drill	10. screwdriver
3. circular saw	7. countersink	11.
4. jointer	8. push drill	12.

Plan of Procedure

_______ 1. Lay out parts 1 and 2 on birch plywood. Keep grain on both pieces in the same direction.
_______ 2. Quality control—Have instructor check.
_______ 3. Cut to size.
_______ 4. Joint edges.
_______ 5. Locate and drill screw holes in part 2. Countersink holes.
_______ 6. Hand sand parts 1 and 2 with fine-grit abrasive.
_______ 7. Quality control—Have instructor check.
_______ 8. Locate, drill and countersink holes to hold part 3 to parts 1 and 2.
_______ 9. Drill anchor holes for screws in part 1. Fasten parts 1 and 2 with screws.
_______ 10. Secure stock for part 3. Grain should run horizontally when part is in assembled position.
_______ 11. Lay out the angles to be cut.
_______ 12. Quality control—Have instructor check.
_______ 13. Cut part 3 to size and shape.
_______ 14. Smooth the edges of part 3.
_______ 15. Hand sand part 3 with fine-grit abrasive paper.
_______ 16. Locate and drill anchor holes in part 3.
_______ 17. Join assembled parts 1 and 2 to part 3 with screws.
_______ 18. Resand lightly with fine-grit abrasive paper.
_______ 19. Quality control—Have instructor check.
_______ 20. Apply three coats of brushing lacquer.
_______ 21. Cut cork pads, part 4, to size.
_______ 22. Glue pads onto part 3.

Figure 3-2
A project-planning sheet.

DAILY WORK RECORD

Estimate of number of hours to build the project.____________________

Date started__________ Date completed __________

Total hours to build project____________________

Labor cost (hours x minimum wage)____________________

Record minutes worked each day

Date	Minutes	Date	Minutes	Date	Minutes
___	___	___	___	___	___
___	___	___	___	___	___
___	___	___	___	___	___
___	___	___	___	___	___
___	___	___	___	___	___
___	___	___	___	___	___
___	___	___	___	___	___
___	___	___	___	___	___

Figure 3-3
A project production-time estimate and record form.

number of units in one part by the number of parts. The *cost per item* is the *cost per unit* multiplied by the *number of units.* The material cost is the sum of all materials used, including waste. Some bills of materials include a finishing charge.

THE PLAN OF PROCEDURE

Study the drawing and develop a *plan of procedure.* This is your detailed list of the steps to follow while building your project. List the tools you will have to use. The list of tools will help you decide if you can make the project. Are the tools available in the shop? Do you know how to use them? If not, begin to read about them in the text and have your instructor show you how to use them when you are ready to begin.

Planning the procedure is difficult for the inexperienced woodworker. To plan well, you need to know the best ways to form wood into parts and how to assemble these parts. Your instructor will have to help you with your first planning efforts.

There is more than one correct way to plan a job. Study the plan of procedure in Figure 3-2 for the record rack. Part 3 could have been made before parts 1 and 2. Part 3, however, is more difficult to make and was therefore delayed.

When something goes wrong with your project, it can often be corrected if it is noticed in time. Early detection may save the entire project. This is why a plan of procedure includes quality-control points. Quality-control points are checkpoints to ensure that you are accurately completing each step of the plan before you proceed to the next step. Your instructor will advise you how to correct errors and when to proceed. As you complete each step on the plan of procedure, place a check in the space provided to the left of the step. This will help you keep a record of what you have finished.

The planning sheet has a place for you to estimate the number of hours to complete the project. Figure 3-3 is an example of a daily work record. When you actually finish the project, add up the minutes and divide by 60. This will give you the number of hours you needed to make the project. To get the labor cost of your project, multiply hours by the current minimum wage. The total cost of the project includes the cost of materials, finishing and labor.

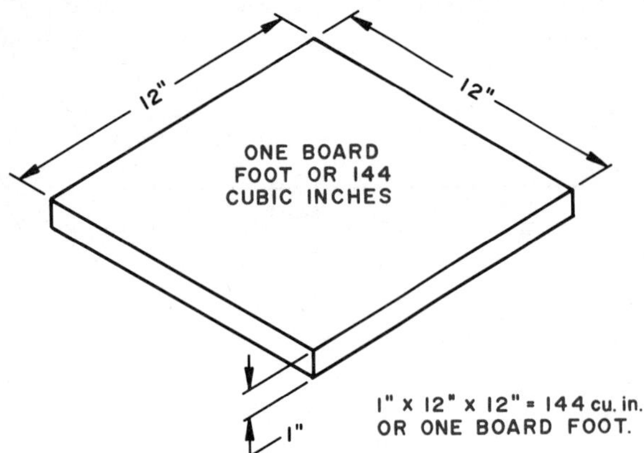

Figure 3-4
A board foot equals 144 cubic inches.

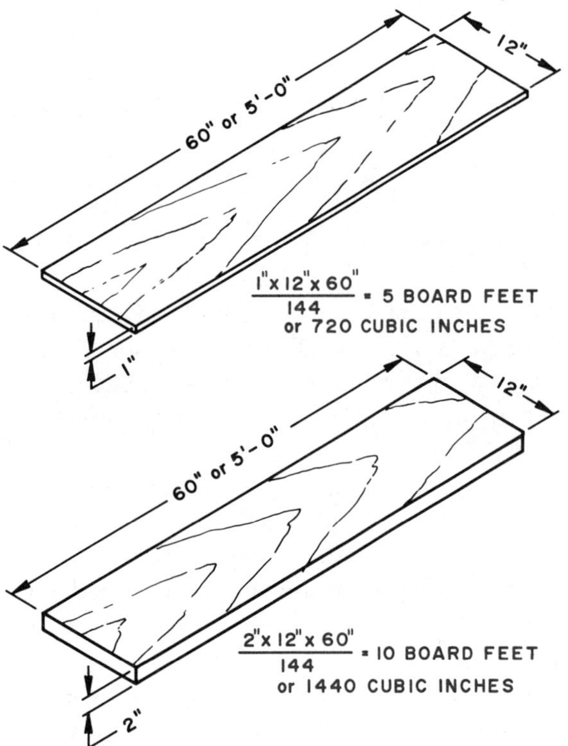

Figure 3-5
An increase in thickness increases the number of board feet.

BOARD FEET

The unit of measure for solid lumber is the *board foot.* It represents 144 cubic inches. A board foot is the unit used in pricing solid lumber. A typical board foot is 1 inch thick and 12 inches square, Figure 3-4. A 1″ x 12″ board 5′ long contains 5 board feet. A board 2″ x 12″ x 5′ contains 10 board feet, Figure 3-5.

Board feet can be calculated in several ways:

1. Multiply the number of pieces by thickness by width by length (all in inches) and divide by 144.
   Example: Four boards, 1″ thick, 5″ wide and 30″ long:

$$\text{board feet} = \frac{\text{no. of pieces} \times T'' \times W'' \times L''}{144}$$

$$= \frac{4 \times 1'' \times 5'' \times 30''}{144} = 4.2$$

2. Multiply the number of pieces by thickness by width (both in inches) by length in feet and divide by 12.

$$\text{board feet} = \frac{\text{no. of pieces} \times T'' \times W'' \times L'}{12}$$

$$= \frac{4 \times 1'' \times 5'' \times 2.5'}{12} = 4.2$$

3. Multiply the number of pieces by thickness by width by length (all in inches) by 0.007. This constant is found by converting 1/144 to a decimal. This will give a close approximation of the number of board feet.

$$\text{board feet} = \text{no. of pieces} \times T'' \times W'' \times L'' \times 0.007$$
$$= 4 \times 1'' \times 5'' \times 30'' \times 0.007$$
$$= 4.2$$

4. Multiply the number of pieces by thickness by width (both in inches) by length in feet by 0.083. This constant is found by converting 1/12 to a decimal.

$$\text{board feet} = \text{no. of pieces} \times T'' \times W'' \times L' \times 0.083$$
$$= 4 \times 1'' \times 5'' \times 2.5' \times 0.083$$
$$= 4.2$$

When figuring board feet use the *nominal size.* This is the size of the rough-sawed board. For example, a 1″ softwood board is sawed 1″ thick but is to be planed to 3/4″ before it is used. All 3/4″-surfaced boards are figured as 1″. Sometimes nominal sizes are given in quarters. Each quarter is 1/4″. For example, a 4/4 (four-quarter) board is 1″ thick. An 8/4 (eight-quarter) board is 2″ thick. Figure 3-6 shows the nominal and dressed thicknesses for various widths of softwoods. Softwoods also are cut to standard lengths from 8′ to 20′ in 2′ increments.

SOFTWOODS				
Nominal thickness		**Finished thickness**	**Nominal width (rough)**	**Finished width**
Quarters	**Rough inches**			
4/4	1	3/4 or less	2	1-1/2
5/4	1-1/4	1	3	2-1/2
6/4	1-1/2	1-1/4	4	3-1/2
8/4	2	1-1/2	5	4-1/2
10/4	2-1/2	2	6	5-1/2
12/4	3	2-1/2	7	6-1/2
14/4	3-1/2	3	8	7-1/4
16/4	4	3-1/2	9	8-1/4
			10	9-1/4

Figure 3-6
Nominal (rough) and finished thicknesses and widths of softwoods.

Calculating sizes of many pieces of softwood using a formula is slow. Tables that show the board feet for each size board are available. Using tables, such as the one shown in Figure 3-6, can save much time.

Rough-sawed hardwoods are generally found in the thicknesses shown in Figure 3-7. They are not sawed to standard widths or lengths. Each piece is cut as wide and long as possible. Hardwoods cut this way are referred to as *random widths and lengths.*

HARDWOODS		
Nominal thickness		**Finished thickness Surfaced 2 sides**
Quarters	**Rough inches**	
	3/8	3/16
	1/2	5/16
	5/8	7/16
	3/4	9/16
4/4	1	13/16
5/4	1-1/4	1- 1/16
6/4	1-1/2	1- 5/16
8/4	2	1- 3/4
12/4	3	2- 3/4
16/4	4	3- 3/4

Figure 3-7
Nominal (rough) and finished thicknesses of hardwoods.

Formulas for figuring sizes of many pieces of random-width-and-length stock are slow and difficult to use. To measure board feet, a board rule may be used. At the head and handle is a row of numbers. They represent lengths of boards. Running along the body are tables, like the one shown in Figure 3-8, that read in surface feet.

To use the rule you first must know the length of the board. Measure it with a tape rule. Then place the head on one edge and the body across the board. Read the number in the table that is in line with the length figure. This gives the surface area in feet. If the board is 1" thick the board feet is the same as the surface feet. If it is 2" thick the board feet is double the surface feet.

SQUARE FEET

Measure sheet stock, such as plywood, hardboard and particle board, in square feet. Figure square feet by multiplying the width by the length (both should be in either inches or feet).

The following is the formula for figuring square feet:

$$\text{square feet} = \frac{W'' \times L''}{144} \quad \text{or} \quad \frac{W' \times L'}{1}$$

Thickness is not considered. It is included in the cost of the material. A square foot of 1/4"-thick stock will cost less than a square foot of the same stock 3/4" thick.

BOARD FEET FOR SELECTED SIZES						
	Lengths in Feet					
T x W in inches	1	2	3	4	5	6
1 x 2	.16	.33	.50	.67	.83	1.00
1 x 3	.25	.50	.75	1.00	1.25	1.50
1 x 4	.33	.67	1.00	1.33	1.67	2.00
1 x 5	.42	.83	1.25	1.67	2.08	2.50
1 x 6	.50	1.00	1.50	2.00	2.50	3.00
1 x 7	.58	1.17	1.75	2.33	2.92	3.50
1 x 8	.67	1.33	2.00	2.67	3.33	4.00
1 x 9	.75	1.50	2.25	3.00	3.75	4.50
1 x 10	.83	1.67	2.50	3.33	4.17	5.00
1 x 11	.92	1.83	2.75	3.67	4.58	5.50
1 x 12	1.00	2.00	3.00	4.00	5.00	6.00

Figure 3-8
Tables like this are found on board rules.

REVIEW QUESTIONS

1 What is shown in a bill of materials?
2 How do you use a working drawing when you write a bill of materials?
3 What is the purpose of a plan of procedure?
4 What are quality-control points?
5 How many board feet are there in the problems below?
  one piece 1″ x 8″ x 7′0″
  five pieces 2″ x 5″ x 1′6″
  three pieces 1/2″ x 11″ x 2′0″
6 How many square feet are there in the problems below?
  one piece 1″ x 12″ x 6′0″
  three pieces 3/4″ x 6″ x 1′6″
  one piece 3/4″ x 48″ x 96″

SUGGESTED ACTIVITIES

1 Prepare a complete project-planning sheet for the kitchen knife holder, shown to the right. If you wish, redesign it and select your own sizes.
2 Prepare a bill of materials for the kitchen knife holder project.

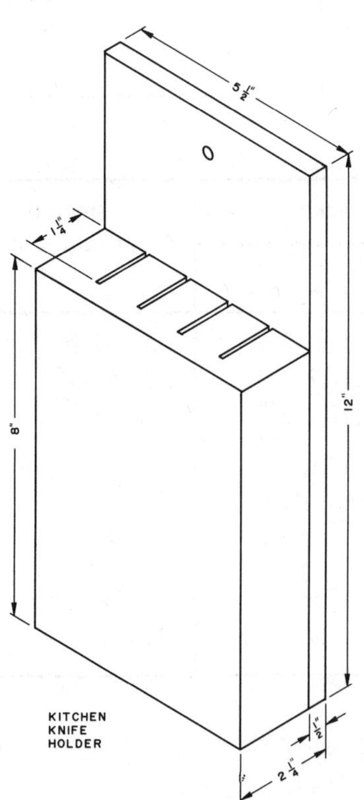

UNIT

4

Designing a Project

Objectives

After studying this unit you should be able to:

1 Understand what makes a good design.

2 Discuss the basic elements of design.

3 Recognize the basic principles of design as they apply to industrial products.

4 Follow the basic steps in the design process.

5 Use preferred metric design sizes.

Technical Terms

Function	Shape	Balance
Honesty	Mass	Proportion
Structure	Texture	Rhythm
Appearance	Color	Unity
Line		

Figure 4-1
A drop-lid desk designed in the style of the Queen Anne period, 1702-1714. (Hekman Furniture Company)

Many factors contribute to a good design. Design decisions are based on well-established principles. With experience a designer can combine, refine, vary and in some cases violate basic design principles. An object may be well designed, but not liked. Good design is not the same as personal likes and dislikes. Sometimes a creative design solution is not accepted simply because it is different from the usual solutions.

One way to learn more about design is to compare past and current styles. Furniture is an example. Some furniture designs of hundreds of years ago are still in use. These designs are regarded as classics, Figure 4-1. Furniture design, however, continues to change, Figure 4-2. Whether old or new, a design can be judged by qualities that do not change.

Figure 4-2
A design reflecting trends toward lightness and clean simple lines. (Paoli Chair Company)

QUALITIES OF DESIGN

Some qualities that a well-designed wood project should have follow.

Figure 4-3
A library carrel is designed to serve a specific function. (Library Bureau)

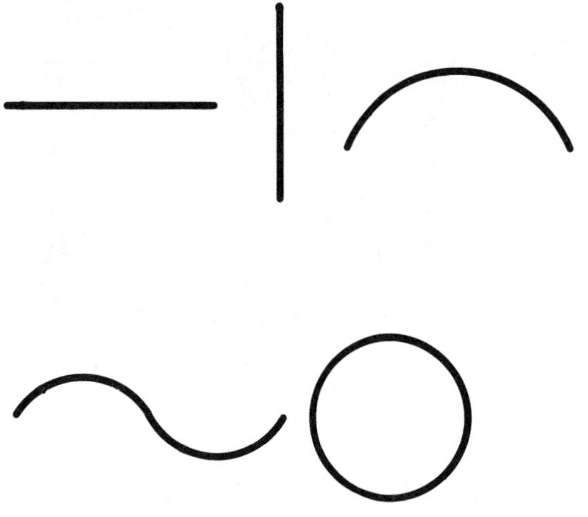

Figure 4-4
These are the basic lines used to design industrial products.

Figure 4-5
The designer of this table combined various line elements to produce an attractive, functional piece of furniture. (Knoll Associates, Inc.)

Function. The project must do the job it is designed to do, Figure 4-3. The *function* must show in the design.

Honesty. The materials used must show their own characteristics. A plastic drawer front made to look like expensive hardwood is not honest.

Structure. The *structure* of a project depends on its use. The project should be assembled so that it is strong enough to serve its intended purpose.

Appearance. The completed product must be pleasing to view as a whole. Such details as fasteners, wood grain and finish are parts of its *appearance.*

BASIC ELEMENTS OF DESIGN

In creating a design, the designer chooses and arranges certain elements. These elements include line, shape, mass, texture and color.

Line. An object is a combination of *lines.* The four basic lines are straight, curved, S-shaped and circular, Figure 4-4. These are combined in different ways to form the object, Figure 4-5.

Shape. The basic two-dimensional *shapes* are the square, the rectangle, the triangle and the circle, Figure 4-6. These shapes are made by different combinations of the basic types of lines.

Mass. The three-dimensional form of an object is its *mass.* The mass of the utility cabinet in Figure 4-7 is rectangular. Generally mass is the first element of a design to be noticed. Other elements are noticed later.

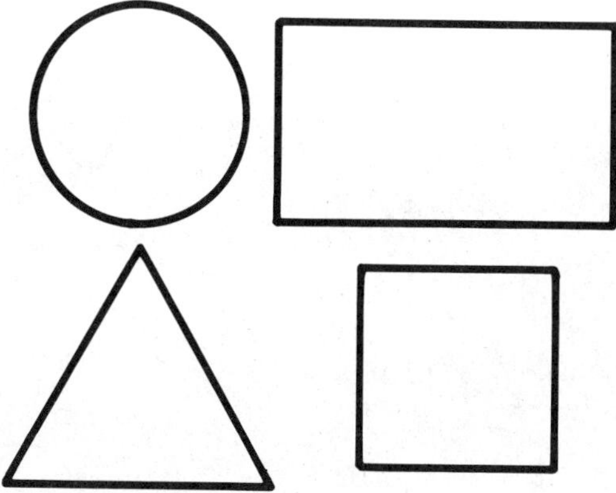

Figure 4-6
The basic two-dimensional shapes.

Figure 4-7
The mass of this cabinet is a rectangular solid. The drawers and drawer pulls are secondary elements of design. (Hekman Furniture Company)

Texture. The way the surface of an object feels when it is touched is called its *texture.* A glass table top has a texture different from that of a rough-surfaced wood panel. Some materials, such as glass, plastics and metal, are cool to the touch. They also convey a feeling of coolness, Figure 4-8. Wood and fabric convey a warm feeling, Figure 4-9.

Figure 4-8
A molded plastic chair gives an effect of coolness. (Knoll Associates, Inc.)

Figure 4-9
Wood and fabric combine to produce a warm effect. (Armstrong World Industries)

Figure 4-10
An example of formal balance. Right and left sides of this drawer unit are exactly the same. (Knoll Associates, Inc.)

Figure 4-11
An example of informal balance. The long section of short, overhead cabinets with heavy posts on the end balances the longer cabinet on the right side. (Coppes, Inc.)

Color. Feelings of warmth and coolness are also suggested by *color.* Red, orange and brown are considered warm colors. Blue and green are cool colors. The natural colors of woods are warm. They are sometimes changed by coloring the wood with stains.

Color is an important element of design. There are three primary and three secondary colors. The primary colors are red, yellow and blue. The secondary colors are orange, green and violet. The three secondary colors are made by mixing equal amounts of two primary colors. On the color wheel, each secondary color is halfway between the two primary colors that made it.

Colors opposite each other on the color wheel are called complementary colors. Colors near each other on the color wheel are called analogous colors. Generally complementary colors are better for product design.

Color can focus attention on one or more parts of an object. For example, a cabinet may be finished in white except for its larger doors, which are red. Red calls attention to the doors and makes them the dominant element of the design.

BASIC PRINCIPLES OF DESIGN

The basic principles of design are balance, proportion, rhythm and unity.

Balance. A product is in *balance* when its elements viewed as a whole appear to be of equal significance. No one feature dominates another, Figure 4-10.

Balance can be either formal or informal. Formal balance occurs when the left and right sides of an object are the same size or shape, Figure 4-10. Informal balance occurs when one-half of a product is different from the other, but because it is pleasing to the eye, it appears to be in balance, Figure 4-11. Elements on one side tend to balance different elements on the other side.

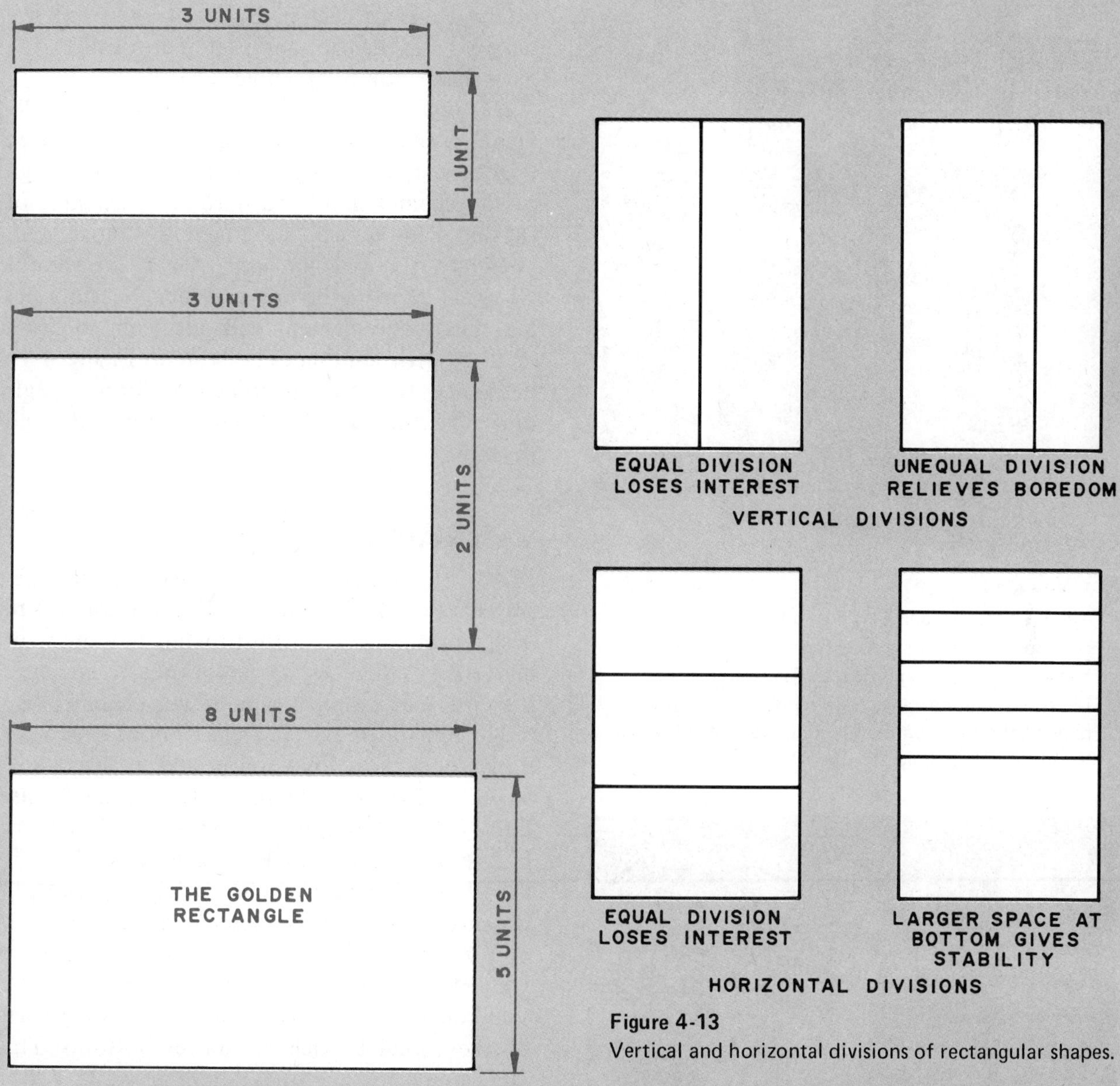

Figure 4-12
Pleasing rectangular proportions.

Figure 4-13
Vertical and horizontal divisions of rectangular shapes.

Proportion. The size relation of one part to another and of the parts to the whole is called *proportion.* Designers have found that a rectangular form is more pleasing to view than a square. Proportions of one to three and two to three are considered good. The golden mean rectangle is accepted as having the most pleasing proportions. Basically the rectangle is five units wide and eight units long, Figure 4-12.

A rectangle can be divided vertically and horizontally. If it is divided vertically, the design is more pleasing when the parts are unequal. The parts, however, should not be too different in size, Figure 4-13. If divided horizontally, the rectangle may have equal parts. But such a design tends to be monotonous. If the parts are not equal, the largest is usually at the bottom. This provides stability.

The parts of a product should be in proportion to the overall size. For example, the base

Figure 4-14
The base of the cabinet is not the same height as the top section. But it provides a sense of stability because it is wider and deeper. The solid doors increase the appearance of mass. The glass doors prevent the top from dominating the unit. (Hekman Furniture Company)

Figure 4-15
The vertical divisions of the shelf, the scrollwork along the edges and the repetitive recessed panels in the doors all give this shelving unit rhythm. (Coppes Inc.)

of the china cabinet in Figure 4-14 is not the same size as the top shelf unit. Yet together, the parts make a pleasing whole.

Rhythm. The orderly repetition of some element of the design is its *rhythm.* This element might be a shape, a line or a color. The design of the cabinet in Figure 4-15 is an example of rhythm. Rhythm can give a feeling of movement.

Unity. A design has *unity* when the various elements seem to belong together. If a product has unity, one element will not seem to be in conflict with another. The table in Figure 4-16 has unity. Its parts are joined to form a single unit. The table also has balance, proportion and rhythm.

MATERIALS

An experienced designer is aware of the types and sizes of stock materials. It is economical to design products that permit the maximum use of materials. A high waste factor greatly increases the cost. For example, you design a cabinet 48″ (1219 mm) high and 50″ (1270 mm) wide with a plywood back. Plywood is sold in sheets 48″ x 96″ (1219 x 2438 mm). The back will use only 50″ (1270 mm) of the 96″ (2438 mm), Figure 4-17. This will leave a piece 48″ x 46″ (1219 x 1168 mm). This piece represents a potential waste of 48 percent of the sheet. If you designed the case to be 48″ (1219 mm) wide, two backs can be cut from one sheet. Or you could use the waste portion for other parts of the product, such as drawer bottoms. This also would reduce the potential waste factor considerably.

The use of standard sizes, such as the full 48″ (1219 mm) of the plywood sheet, also can save labor costs. The 48″ (1219 mm) would not have to be cut. One manufacturing operation would be avoided. This would reduce the cost of the product.

FURNITURE SIZES

The size of furniture greatly varies. The pieces shown in Figure 4-18 are typical sizes.

Furniture and cabinets should fit the human body. They must be large enough for a person to use them comfortably. A chair, for example,

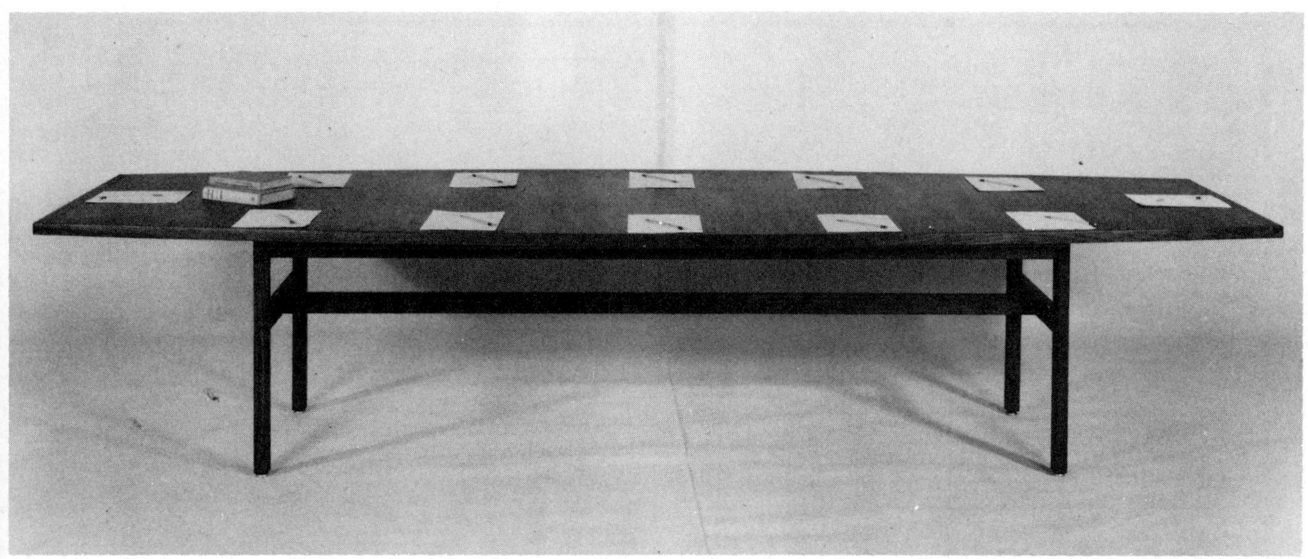

Figure 4-16
This conference table exhibits a sense of unity.
(Jens Risom Design, Inc.)

should be wide enough and the seat high enough from the floor to permit comfortable use. Base (lower) cabinets in a kitchen should be high enough to permit food preparation with minimum back strain. Wall cabinets should be sized so that a person of average height can reach the top shelf.

Studies have produced design data for the human body, Figure 4-19. They give information about the small, average and large sizes of the male and the female body. For example, the recommended height for the seat of a chair for the average male is 17" (432 mm). For the average female, it is 15.6" (396 mm). These average figures fit 80 percent of the population.

The sizes of kitchen cabinets vary slightly depending on the manufacturer. The recommended spacing of kitchen cabinets depends on where they are used. A wall cabinet should be 18" (457 mm) above a base cabinet. It should be 30" (762 mm) above a stove or range. This permits the installing of a hood on the bottom of the wall cabinet. A cabinet should be at least 24" (610 mm) above a sink. The highest shelf that most people can reach easily is 6' (1829 mm) from the floor.

Most base cabinets are built 34-1/2" (876 mm) high without the top. The height including the top is usually between 35-1/2" (902 mm)

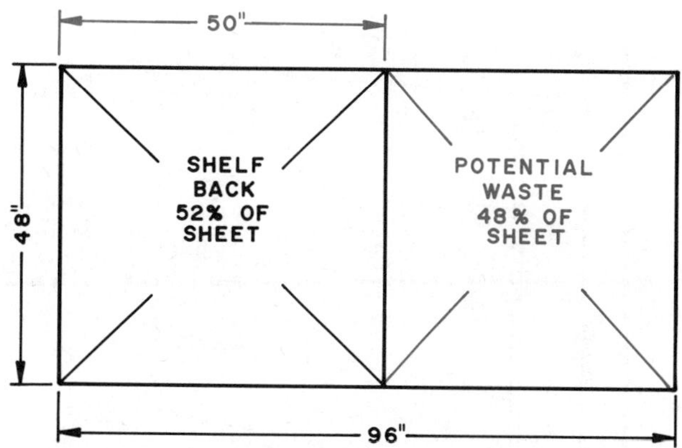

Figure 4-17
A designer must consider stock sizes of materials when selecting design sizes so that waste can be kept to a minimum.

and 36" (914 mm). Counters at which people sit to eat or work should be 30" to 36" (762 to 914 mm) high depending on the height of the stool to be used.

LETTERING

Occasionally a product will require lettering. One style frequently used is vertical Gothic, in capital letters. Letters and numerals in this style are shown in Figure 4-20. They can be copied the same size, enlarged or reduced.

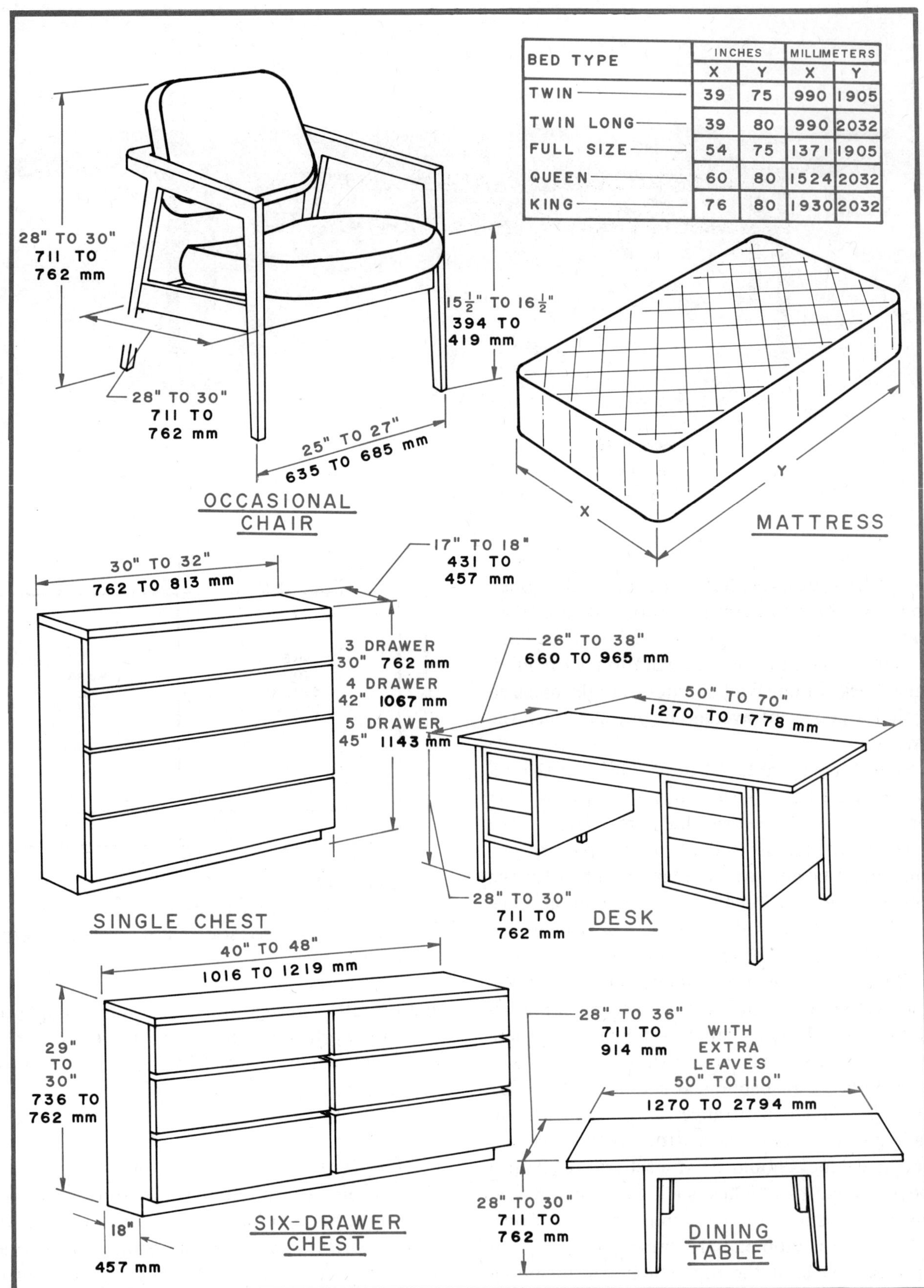

BED TYPE	INCHES X	INCHES Y	MILLIMETERS X	MILLIMETERS Y
TWIN	39	75	990	1905
TWIN LONG	39	80	990	2032
FULL SIZE	54	75	1371	1905
QUEEN	60	80	1524	2032
KING	76	80	1930	2032

Figure 4-18
Examples of furniture sizes used for selected products.

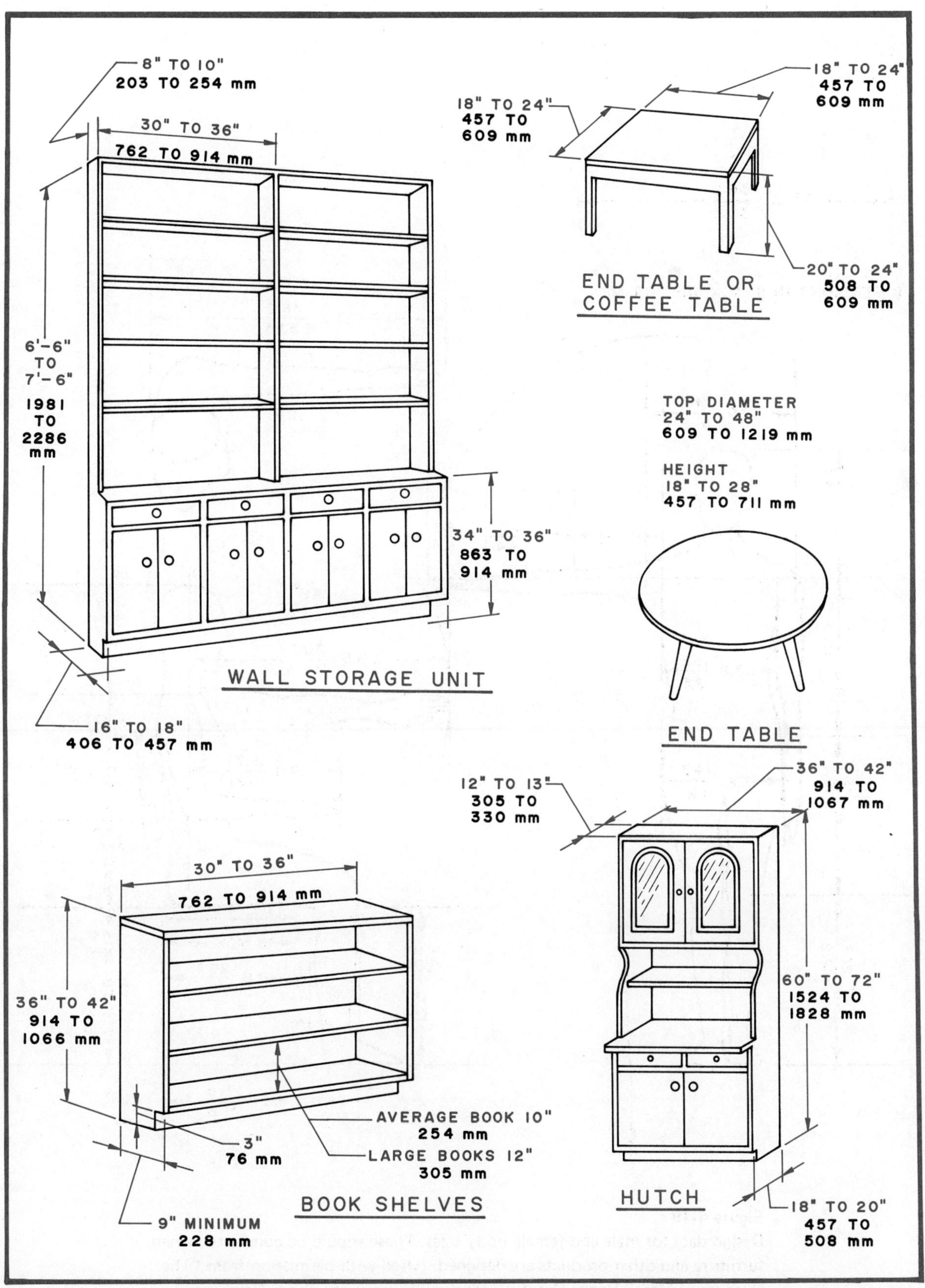
8" TO 10"
203 TO 254 mm
30" TO 36"
762 TO 914 mm
6'-6" TO 7'-6"
1981 TO 2286 mm
34" TO 36"
863 TO 914 mm
16" TO 18"
406 TO 457 mm
WALL STORAGE UNIT
18" TO 24"
457 TO 609 mm
18" TO 24"
457 TO 609 mm
20" TO 24"
508 TO 609 mm
END TABLE OR COFFEE TABLE
TOP DIAMETER
24" TO 48"
609 TO 1219 mm
HEIGHT
18" TO 28"
457 TO 711 mm
END TABLE
12" TO 13"
305 TO 330 mm
36" TO 42"
914 TO 1067 mm
60" TO 72"
1524 TO 1828 mm
18" TO 20"
457 TO 508 mm
HUTCH
30" TO 36"
762 TO 914 mm
36" TO 42"
914 TO 1066 mm
3"
76 mm
AVERAGE BOOK 10"
254 mm
LARGE BOOKS 12"
305 mm
9" MINIMUM
228 mm
BOOK SHELVES

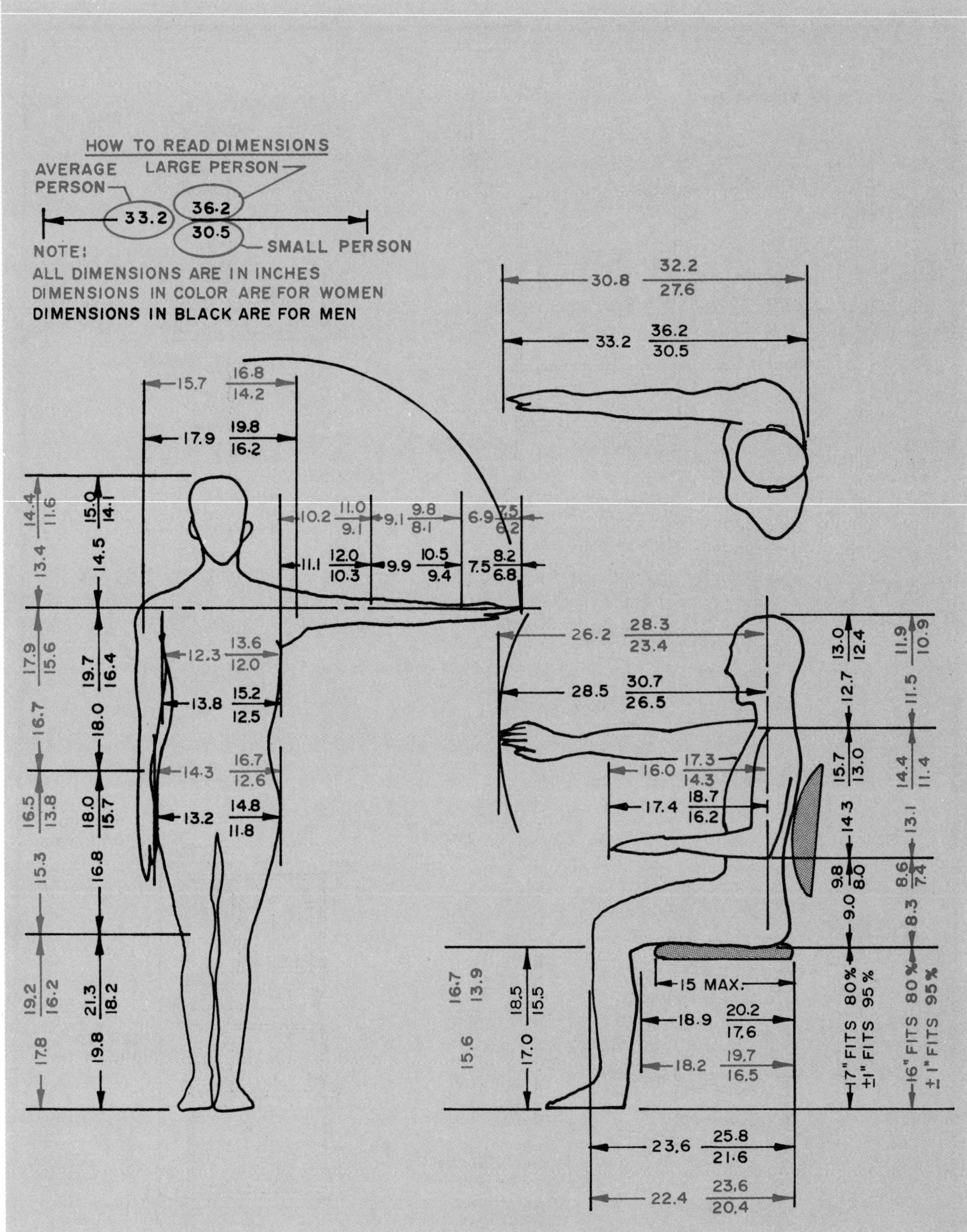

Figure 4-19

Design data for male and female body sizes. These should be considered when furniture and other products are designed. (Used with permission from "The Measure of Man," Henry Dreyfuss, Whitney Library of Design, New York.)

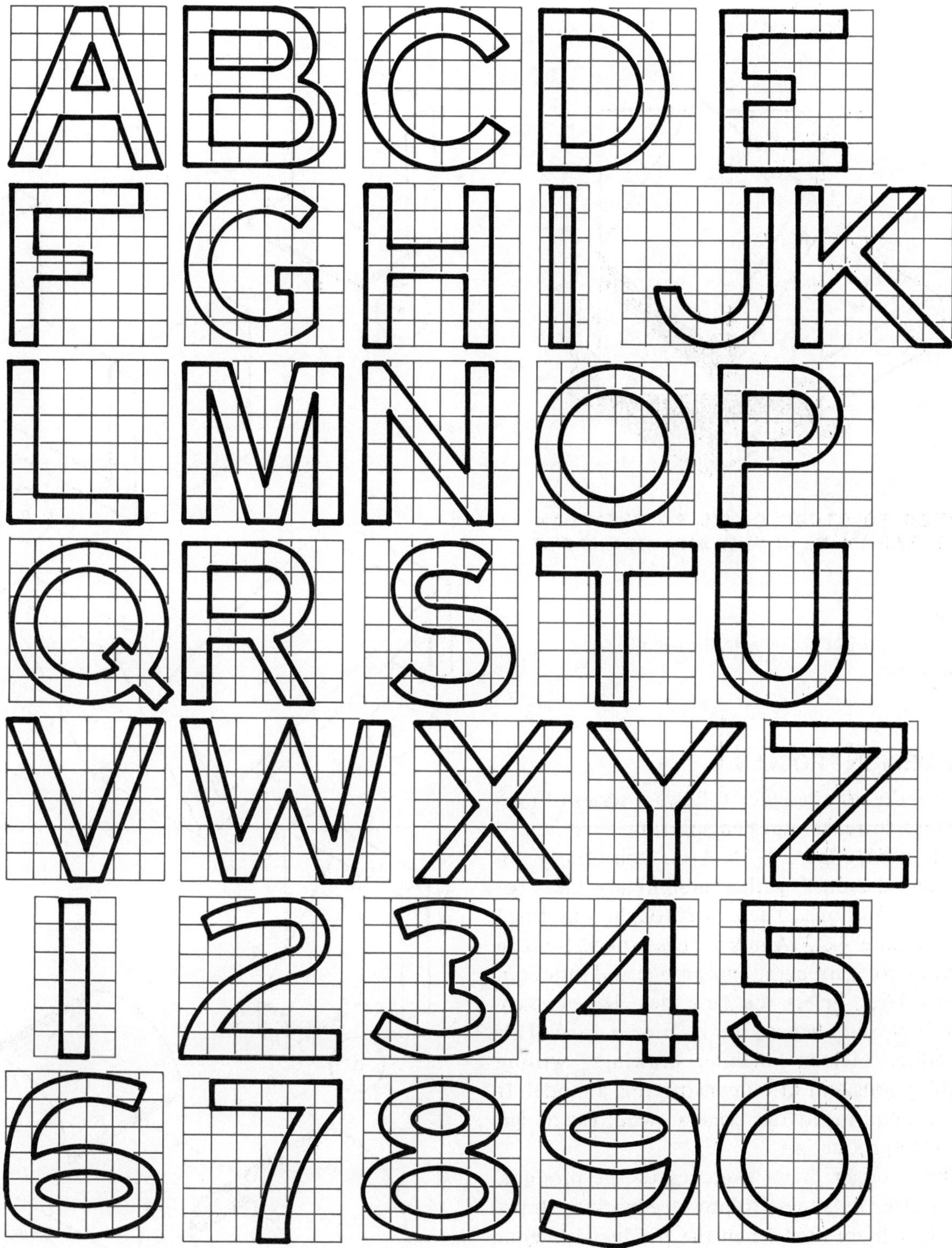

Figure 4-20
Examples of vertical Gothic lettering, which is frequently used in product design.

NEED TO STORE BOOKS SO THEY CAN
BE EASILY REMOVED AND REPLACED

Figure 4-21
A design project begins with the need to solve a problem.

THE DESIGN PROCESS

An industrial designer follows a series of logical steps to reach a design solution. First a need is presented, Figure 4-21. After you clearly understand the need, gather preliminary ideas for possible solutions. These are rough, unrefined ideas, Figure 4-22. Analyze these suggestions in terms of cost, strength, appearance and function, Figure 4-23. Select the best idea. If necessary modify it and then refine it, Figure 4-24. This procedure includes making drawings, writing specifications and often constructing a model. If the idea still meets the original need, the design goes into production.

The designer draws sketches of the product. The drafter uses these to produce working drawings, which are used when the product is manufactured. Unit 5 has details for making drawings.

MEASURE IN DESIGN

A product should be designed and made in one system of measure—either inches or millimeters. If the product is to be manufactured in

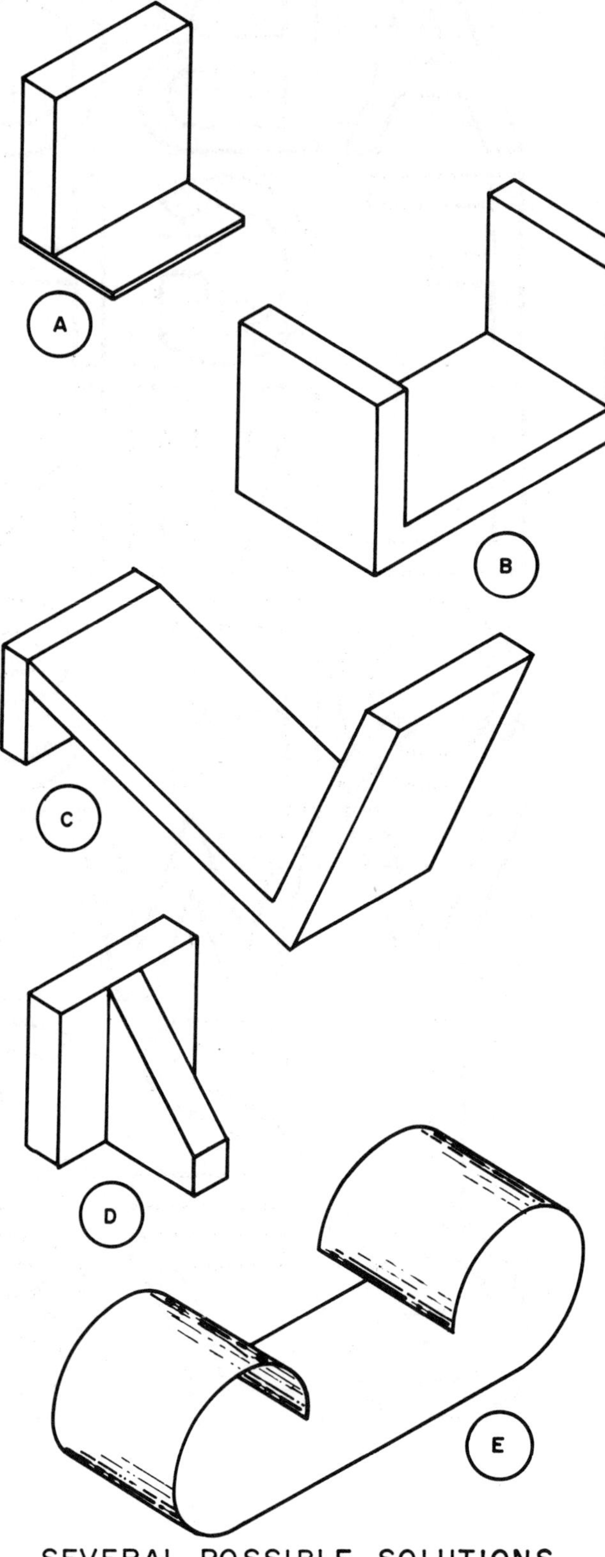

Figure 4-22
Possible solutions to the design problem are sketched.

ANALYSIS OF POSSIBLE SOLUTIONS

A Four pieces of material—two wood, two metal.
Assembly operation difficult.
This type often falls over.
Books fall if not pushed together.
Scratches table top.

B Three pieces of wood.
Heavy.
Two joints.
Books fall over if holder is not full.

C Three pieces of wood.
Heavy.
Two joints.
Will hold books without their falling regardless of number.

D Two pieces of wood.
One joint—difficult.
Will slide if more than a few books are in place.
Falls over easily.

E One piece of metal.
Complex metal-bending operation required.
Metal must have spring qualities, which increase cost.
Books will fall over unless holder is full.

Figure 4-23
Each proposed design solution is analyzed.

metric units, design it in metric units from the start. If it is to be manufactured in inches, design it in inches.

The metric system of linear measure is explained in Unit 2. When designing a product using millimeters as the unit of measure, try to have all sizes in even millimeters. Whenever possible, size the parts to the preferred design sizes. Preferred sizes simplify manufacturing. A table of preferred sizes is shown in Figure 4-25. Whenever possible, use the first choice. If for some reason this is not suitable, use the second and then the third choice.

A designer seldom would specify a dimension in tenths of a millimeter. This is a very precise measurement that generally is unnecessary. Hundredths of a millimeter would never be used in woodworking.

BEST SOLUTION MODIFIED

Design C uses no more material than the other designs and is not any more difficult to make. It has the advantage of holding a number of books up to its capacity without their falling over. It permits the removal of one book without moving other books. The design is stable, and the unit will not tip over. Suggestion: modify this design to lower the cost and simplify construction.

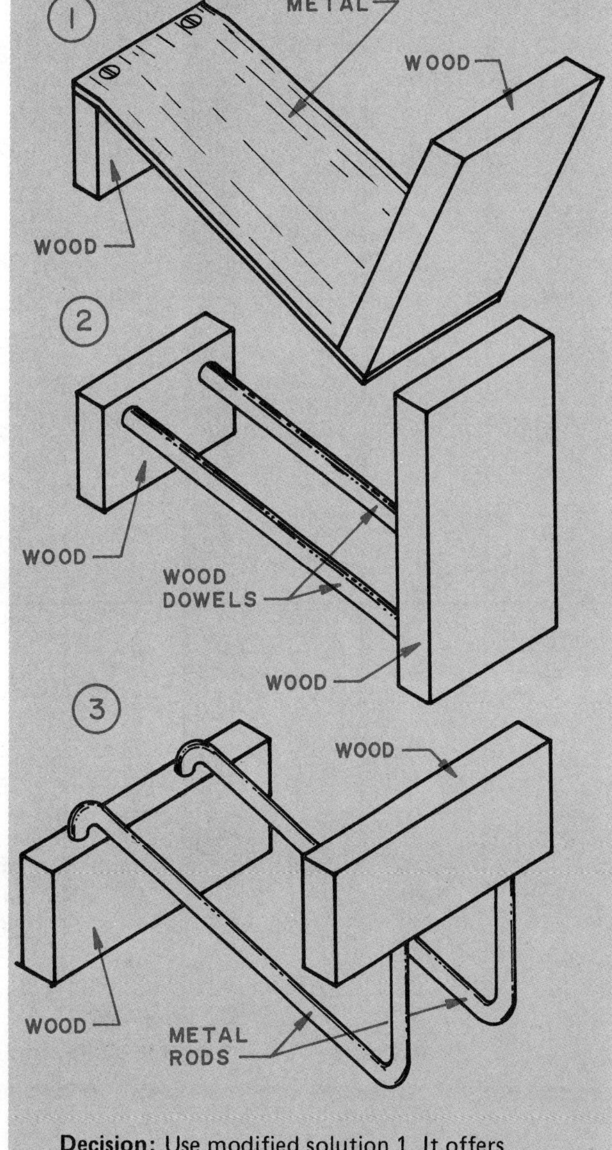

Decision: Use modified solution 1. It offers simplified manufacturing cost. It can produce a lightweight unit of good design at low cost.

Figure 4-24
The best solution is selected, refined and modified. A final design is chosen.

PREFERRED METRIC SIZES FOR ENGINEERING								
Sizes 1 mm to 10 mm			Sizes 10 mm to 100 mm			Sizes 100 mm to 1000 mm		
Choice 1st	2nd	3rd	Choice 1st	2nd	3rd	Choice 1st	2nd	3rd
1.0			10			100		
								105
	1.1			11		110		
								115
1.2			12			120		
								125
		1.3			13		130	
								135
	1.4			14		140		
								145
		1.5			15		150	
								155
1.6			16			160		
								165
		1.7			17		170	
								175
	1.8			18		180		
								185
		1.9			19		190	
								195
2.0			20			200		
		2.1			21		210	
	2.2			22		220		
					23		230	
		2.4			24		240	
2.5			25			250		
		2.6			26		260	
								270
	2.8			28		280		
								290
3.0			30			300		
		3.2		32			320	
					34			340
	3.5			35		350		
					36			360
		3.8		38			380	
4.0			40			400		
		4.2		42			420	
					44			440
	4.5			45		450		
					46			460
		4.8		48			480	
5.0			50			500		
		5.2		52			520	
					54			540
	5.5			55		550		
					56			560
		5.8		58			580	
6.0			60			600		
					62		620	
								640
		6.5		65			650	
								660
					68		680	
	7.0			70		700		
					72		720	
								740
		7.5		75			750	
								760
					78		780	
8.0			80			800		
					82			820
		8.5		85			850	
					88			880
	9.0			90		900		
					92			920
		9.5		95			960	
					98			980
10.0			100			1000		

Figure 4-25
A table of preferred metric design sizes.

REVIEW QUESTIONS

1 What qualities are present in a good design?
2 What is mass?
3 How does color affect reaction to a product?
4 How do the two types of balance differ?
5 What is meant by *proportion*?
6 How does unity influence cost?
7 What are preferred metric design sizes?

UNIT

5

Working Drawings

Objectives

After studying this unit you should be able to:

1 Make simple working drawings.

2 Produce drawings to customary and metric scales.

3 Use sections to describe product design.

4 Dimension working drawings using customary and metric units.

5 Make simple pictorial drawings.

6 Produce preliminary design sketches.

7 Explain the types of furniture drawings used in the industry.

Technical Terms

Working drawing	Phantom line
Visible line	Leader
Hidden line	Scale
Dimension line	Section
Extension line	Dimension
Centerline	Isometric drawing
Section line	Oblique drawing
Cutting-plane line	Design sketch
Break line	

After a product is designed and the design is accepted, *working drawings* are made. A woodworker must be able to make simple drawings to be able to assist in the design process. People working in manufacturing must be able to read drawings. Following is a brief discussion that will explain the major features of a drawing.

VIEWS

A product can be viewed from six basic positions. These are the top, the front, the bottom, the rear, and the right and left sides, Figure 5-1. To use these views to produce a working drawing, imagine they are projected on the surface of a glass box that surrounds the product. Then imagine the box is unfolded and laid flat. This

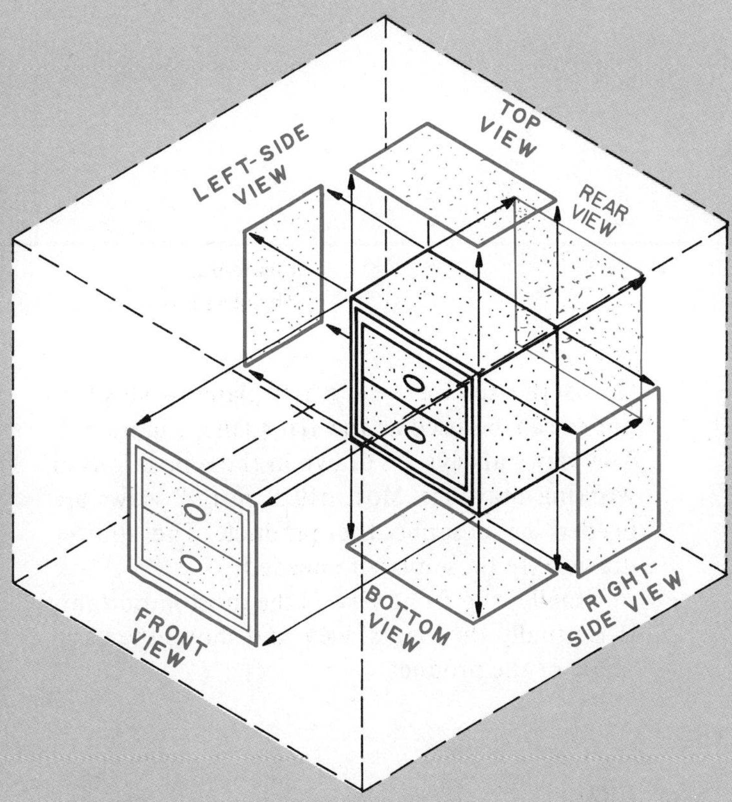

Figure 5-1
Six basic views used in working drawings.

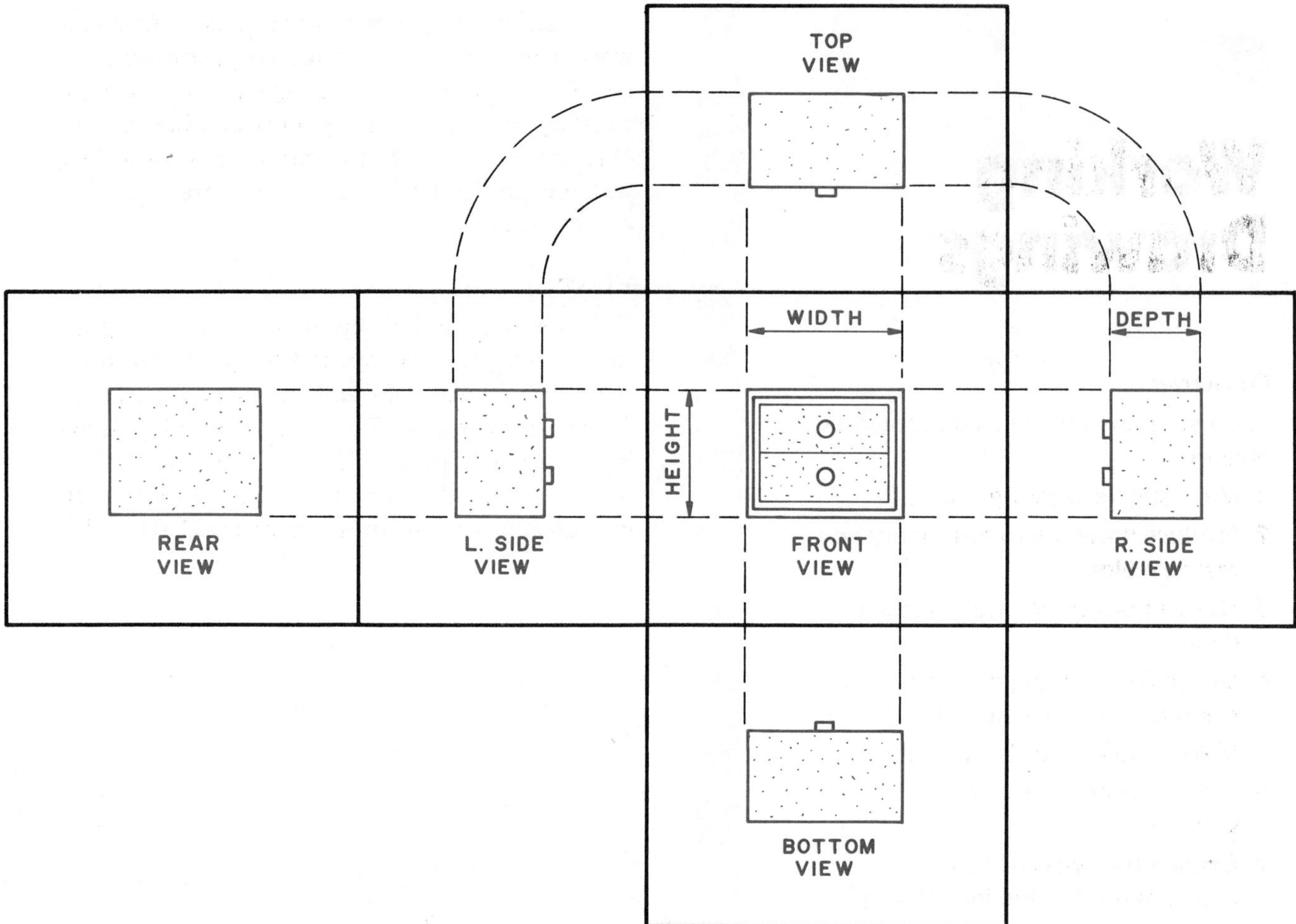

Figure 5-2
The glass box unfolded into a flat plane.

shows the six views on a flat plane. A sheet of paper can be used as the flat plane, Figure 5-2. The views always are drawn in these positions in working drawings. Most often, not all views are needed to describe the product. The drafter draws only those that are needed.

Usually, the front view is the most important. It is usually the longest view and shows the basic shape of the product.

LINE

To understand a drawing, a woodworker first must know line symbols. These are explained in Figures 5-3 and 5-4.

Visible line. Edges that you see when you look at the object are shown by *visible lines.*

Hidden line. Surfaces and edges that you cannot see are shown by *hidden lines.*

Dimension line. Size measurement and beginning and ending are shown by *dimension lines.*

Extension line. So that parts of the drawing can be dimensioned, they are extended out by *extension lines.*

Centerline. The centers of holes and arcs are located by *centerlines.*

Section line. The surface of a part that has been sectioned (cut in half) to show interior details has *section lines* drawn on it.

Cutting-plane line. The places where sections are cut through the object are indicated by *cutting-plane lines.*

Break line. The places where parts of an object are broken away and not drawn are indicated by *break lines.*

LINE SYMBOL AND ITS THICKNESS	USE OF LINE SYMBOL
CONSTRUCTION LINE	USED TO LAY OUT THE DRAWING.
VISIBLE LINE	USED TO SHOW ALL VISIBLE EDGES.
HIDDEN LINE	USED TO REPRESENT HIDDEN LINES.
DIMENSION LINE	USED TO SHOW SIZE.
CENTERLINE	USED TO SHOW THE CENTER OF SYMMETRICAL OBJECTS AND TO LOCATE CENTERS OF CIRCLES AND ARCS.
EXTENSION LINE	USED TO SHOW THE LIMITS OF DIMENSIONS.
SECTION LINING	USED TO SHOW SURFACES CUT IN A SECTION.
CUTTING-PLANE LINE	USED TO SHOW WHERE A SECTION CUT WAS MADE.

Figure 5-3
Line symbols.

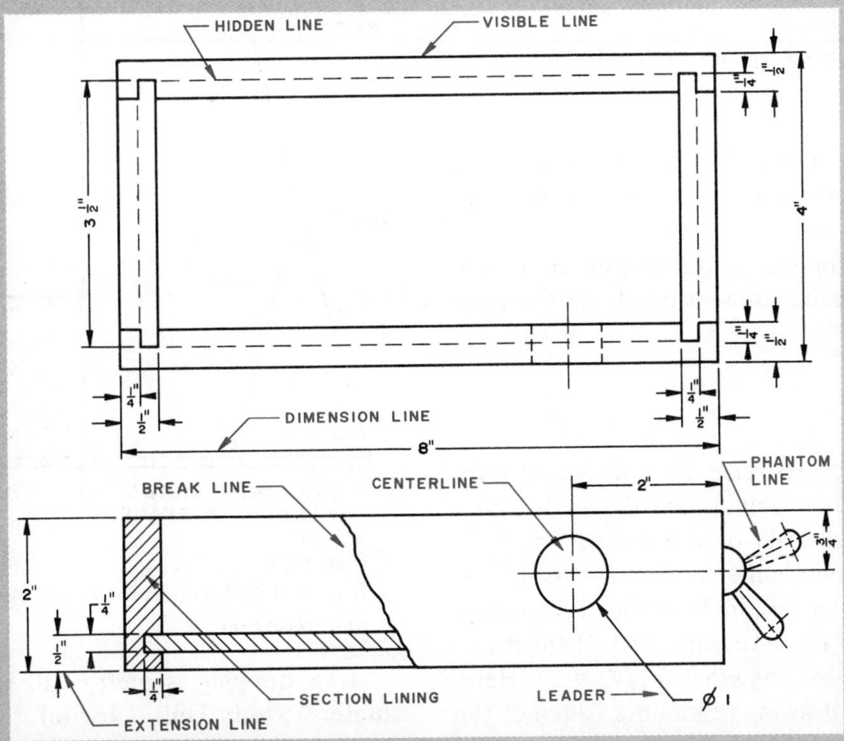

Figure 5-4
How line symbols are used in drawings.

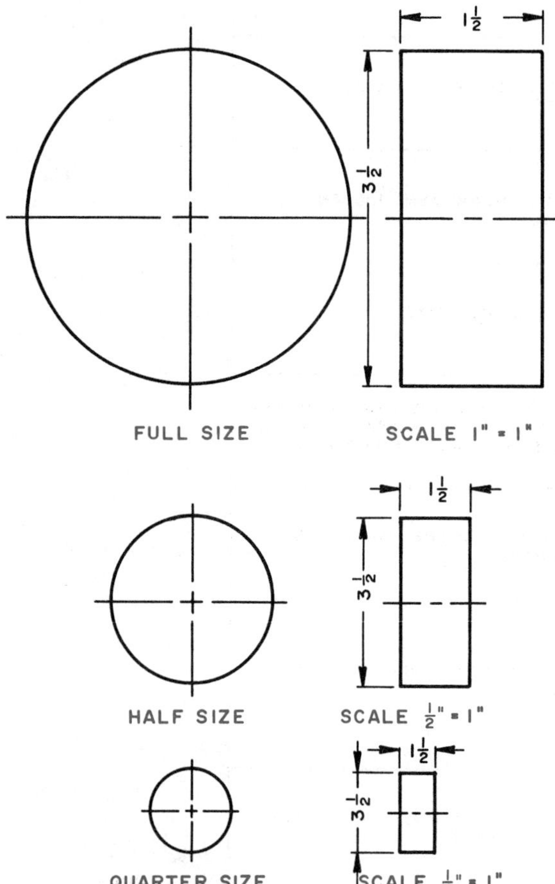

Figure 5-5
The size of a drawing depends on its scale.

Phantom line. The various positions to which a moving part can go are shown by *plantom lines.*

Leader. To connect a dimension or a note with the part being dimensioned, drafters use *leaders.*

SCALE

Scale describes the size an object is drawn. For example, some objects are drawn full-size. This is called full-scale or the scale 1″ = 1″. If the object is drawn half-size, the scale is 1/2″ = 1″. This means that 1/2 inch on the drawing represents 1 inch of the actual product. If the drawing is a quarter-size, the scale is 1/4″ = 1″. Here, 1/4 inch on the drawing represents 1 inch of the actual product. These are the scales most commonly used, Figure 5-5.

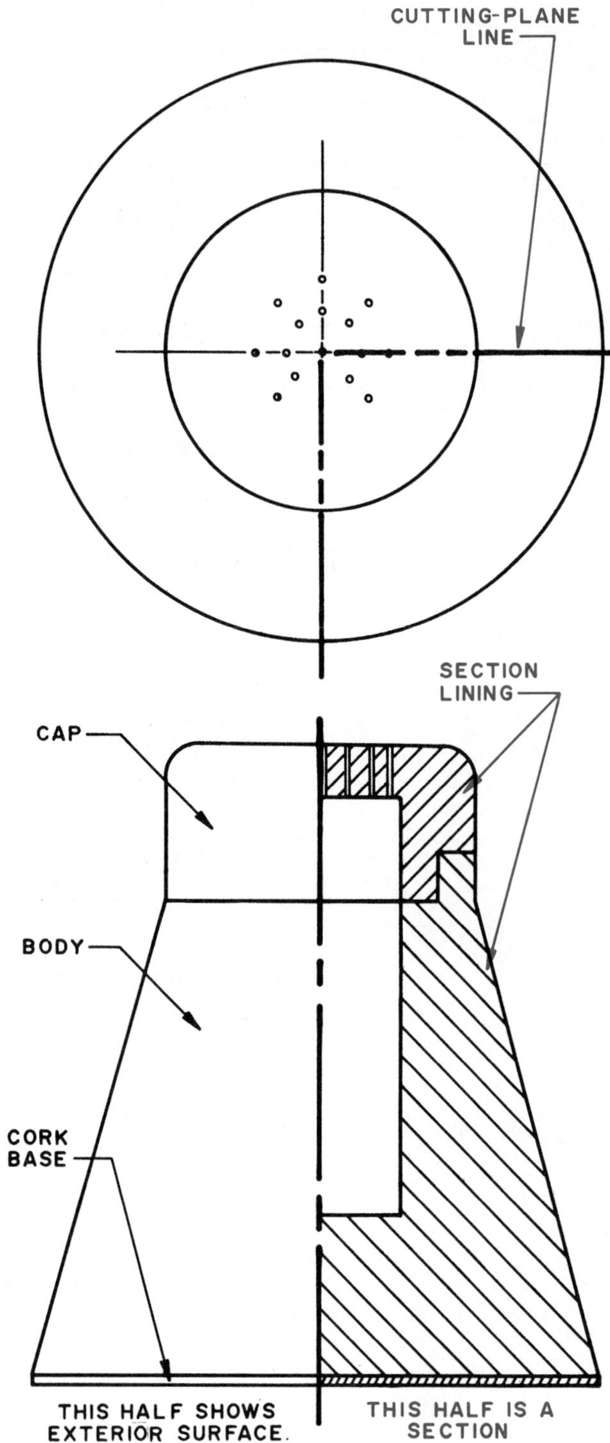

Figure 5-6
A typical half-section shows the inside details of a saltshaker.

If a drawing is metric, all sizes are in millimeters. Study Unit 2 for information on metric units. The principles of reading a metric drawing are the same as for reading a drawing in inches.

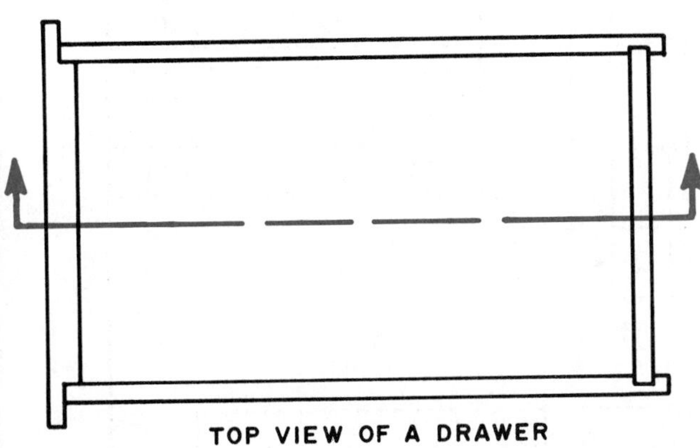

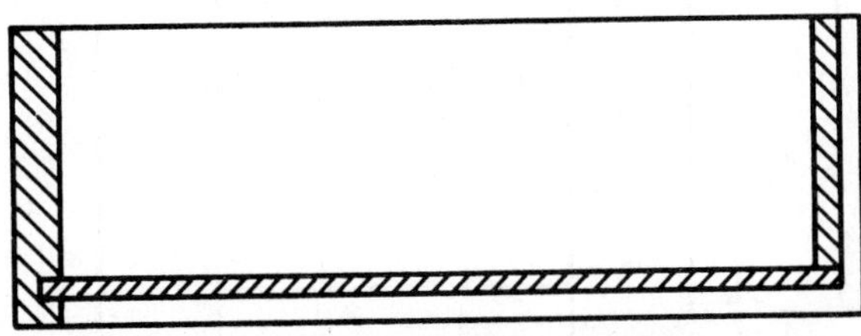

Figure 5-7
A typical full-section shows drawer-construction details.

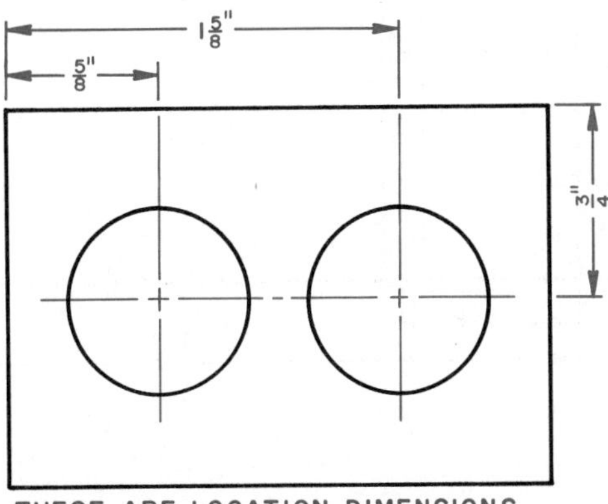

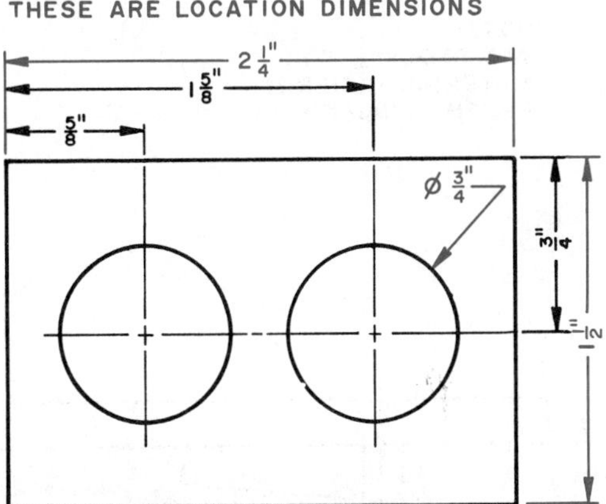

Figure 5-8
Drawings show location and size dimensions.

Metric drawings also are drawn to scale. Although many scales are possible, those most used in the design of wood products are 1:1, 1:2.5, 1:5 and 1:10. These read as follows. The 1:1 scale is full-size. One millimeter on the scale equals 1 millimeter on the product. The 1:2.5 scale has 1 millimeter on the drawing representing 2.5 millimeters. Other drawings follow this plan of reduction.

SECTION

Sometimes making an imaginary cut into an object helps show some hidden interior detail. A drawing that shows interior detail is called a *section.*

The most commonly used sections are half sections and full sections. A half section shows a product cut halfway through. Half sections are made when an object, such as the salt shaker shown in Figure 5-6, is symmetrical.

In the top view a section line shows where the imaginary cut was made. The front view contains the section. Notice the section lining drawn on all cut surfaces. This makes the surfaces stand out. Section lines slant in different directions on each part of the product. Figure 5-6 has three parts.

A full section is cut all the way through. Figure 5-7 shows a full section.

DIMENSIONS

Dimensions describe an object's size. Some dimensions locate things, such as the center of a hole. Others give sizes, such as the diameter of a hole. You can see location and size dimensions in Figure 5-8. Dimensions are placed on a drawing where the feature is visible. A hidden feature is seldom dimensioned. Each dimension is given only once, even though the distance may appear several times on various views.

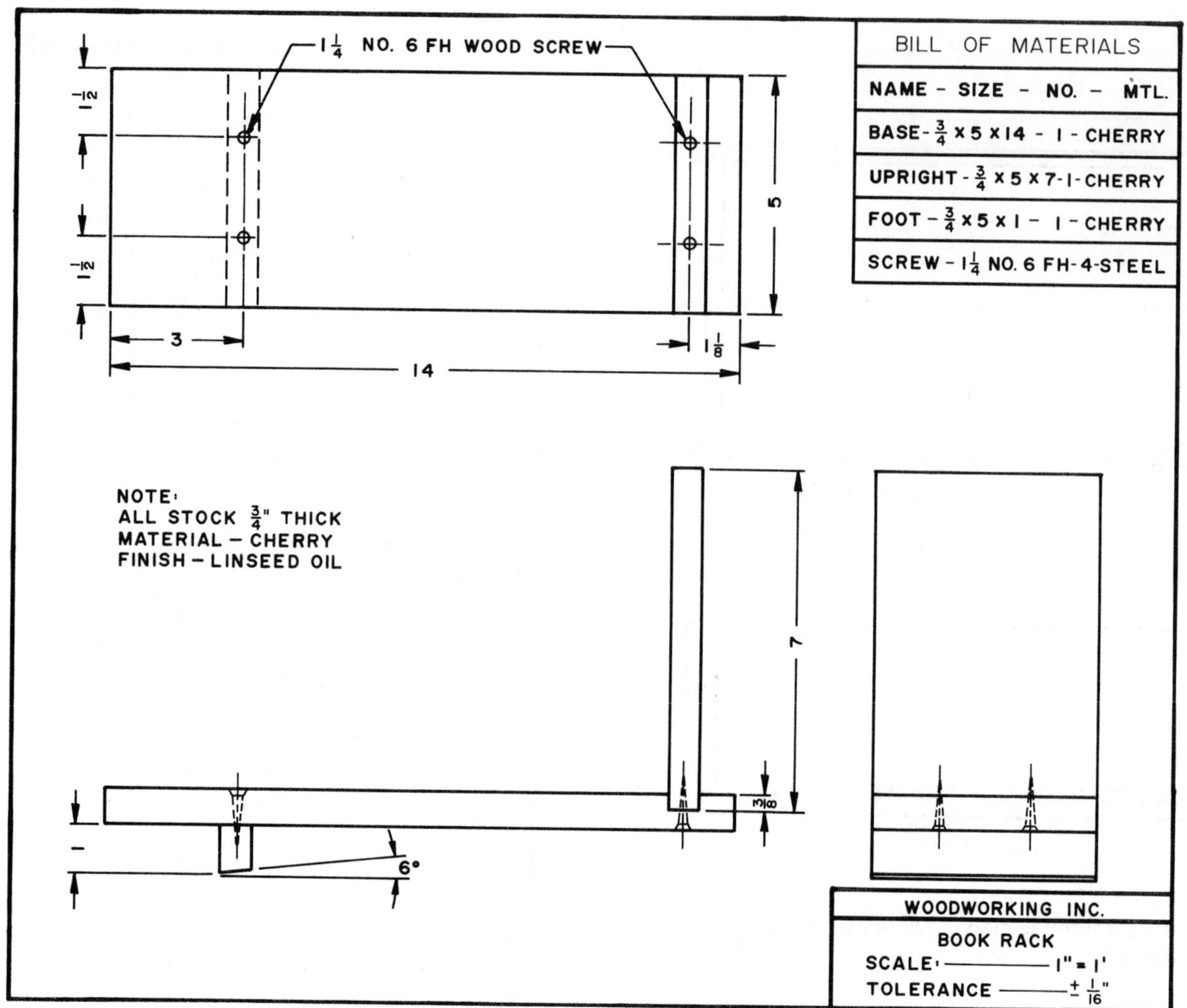

Figure 5-9

A typical working drawing with dimensions in inches.

Short distances have their dimensions placed near the object. The overall length is always placed on the outside of all dimensions. Study the dimensioned drawing in Figure 5-9. Then answer the following questions.

1. What size screws are used?
2. How thick is the wood?
3. Find two location dimensions. What are their sizes?
4. What is the size of the dado?
5. How wide is the bookholder?
6. How long is the bookholder?
7. How many books that are 1-1/2" (38 mm) thick will the bookholder hold?

You can see metric drawings in Figures 5-10 and 5-20. All dimensions are in millimeters. Metric drawings are dimensioned the same way as drawings using inches.

NOTES

There are some things about a product that you cannot find out from a drawing and its dimensions. More information is included in notes. Typical product notes deal with type of wood, finish and hardware and the scale of the drawing, Figure 5-9.

BILL OF MATERIALS

A bill of materials lists what is needed to build a product. Sometimes the list is part of a planning sheet. Often it is part of a working drawing, Figure 5-9. A bill of materials usually includes the name of the part, its size, the number needed to make one product and the material. The bill of materials is used to help figure the total cost of a product. The sizes of wood parts are listed in this order: thickness, width and length.

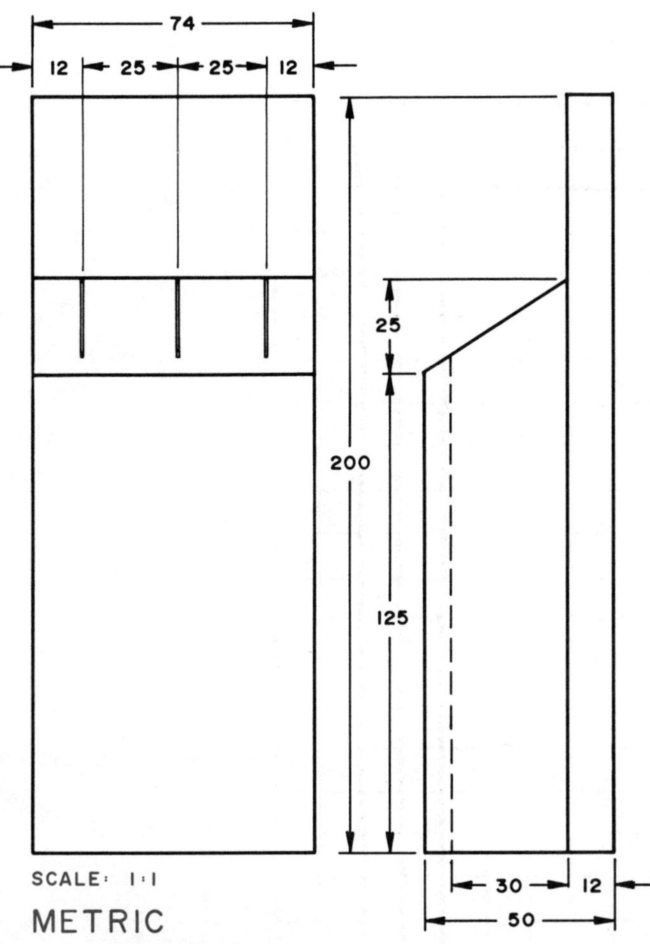

Figure 5-10
A typical working drawing with dimensions in millimeters.

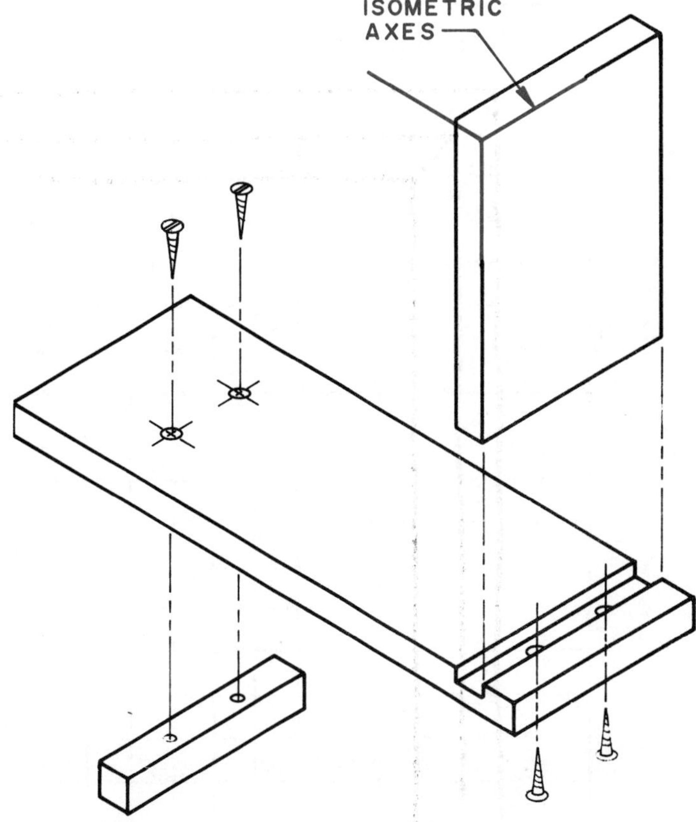

Figure 5-11
An isometric pictorial drawing showing an exploded view of a product.

PICTORIAL DRAWINGS

Sometimes a pictorial drawing helps to explain a working drawing. A pictorial drawing shows how products are put together. Figure 5-11 is a simple pictorial drawing of the product in Figure 5-9. Figure 5-11 shows all the parts. Arrows show how they fit together. This particular drawing is called an *isometric drawing* because it has equal angles between axes.

The *oblique drawing* is another type of pictorial drawing. It does not have equal axes, Figure 5-12. The front view is drawn the usual way while the side view is drawn at a 45° angle from the horizontal. Most often the horizontal and vertical dimensions are drawn true-size. The dimensions on the receding axis are drawn half-size.

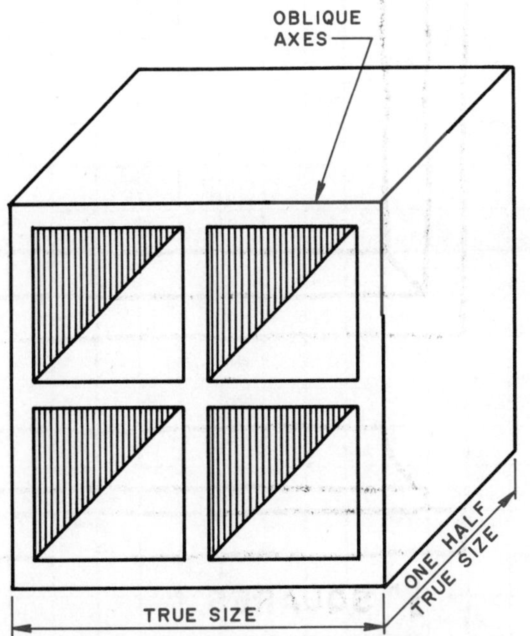

Figure 5-12
An oblique drawing of a furniture cube. This is known as a cabinet drawing.

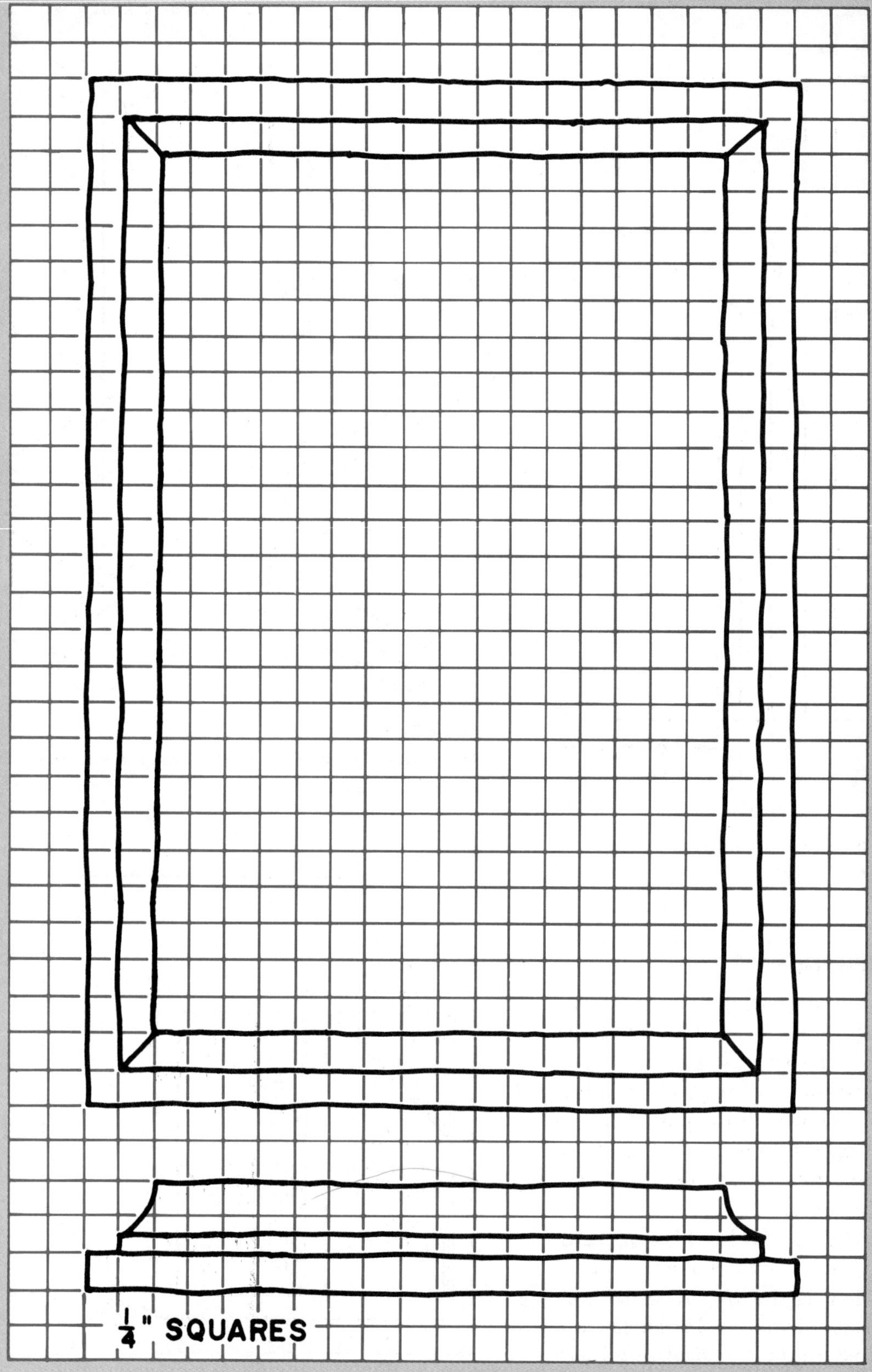

Figure 5-13
Graph paper helps when sketching product ideas.

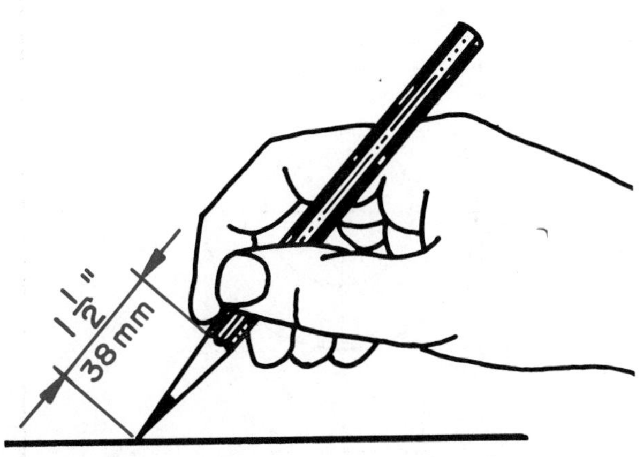
$1\frac{1}{2}$"
38 mm

Figure 5-14
How a pencil is held for sketching.

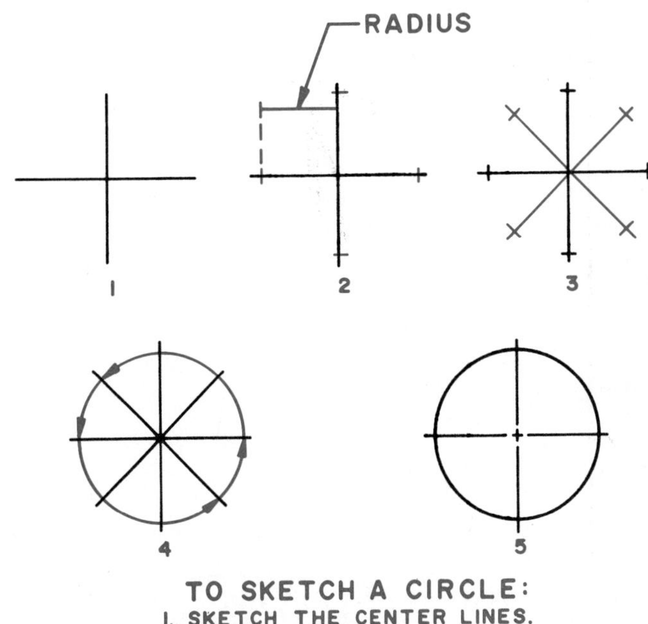
RADIUS
1
2
3
4
5
TO SKETCH A CIRCLE:
1. SKETCH THE CENTER LINES.
2. MARK THE RADIUS.
3. SKETCH SEVERAL OTHER DIA. AND MARK THE RADIUS.
4. LIGHTLY SKETCH THE CIRCLE THROUGH THE POINTS.
5. DARKEN THE CIRCLE.

Figure 5-16
Steps in sketching a circle.

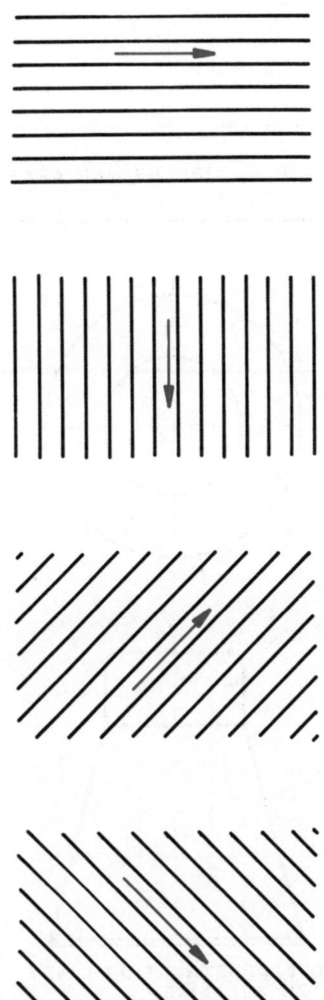

Figure 5-15
Directions for sketching horizontal, vertical and inclined lines for right-handed persons.

MAKING A DESIGN SKETCH

A *design sketch* is a simple drawing of a product. Usually, the first ideas about how a product will look, its size and construction details are worked out in a sketch. Most of the lines on a sketch are done freehand. A ruler can be used, however. Graph paper is also helpful. The grid of horizontal and vertical lines helps make the drawing, Figure 5-13.

Sketching Techniques

Use a pencil with a soft lead. Hold the pencil about 1-1/2" (38 mm) from the end, Figure 5-14.

Right-handed people sketch lines from left to right, Figure 5-15. Lines can be solid or a series of long dashes. Sketch vertical lines from top to bottom, Figure 5-15. Sketch inclined lines as shown in Figure 5-15. Left-handed persons often find it easier to sketch in the opposite directions. Circles can be sketched as shown in Figure 5-16.

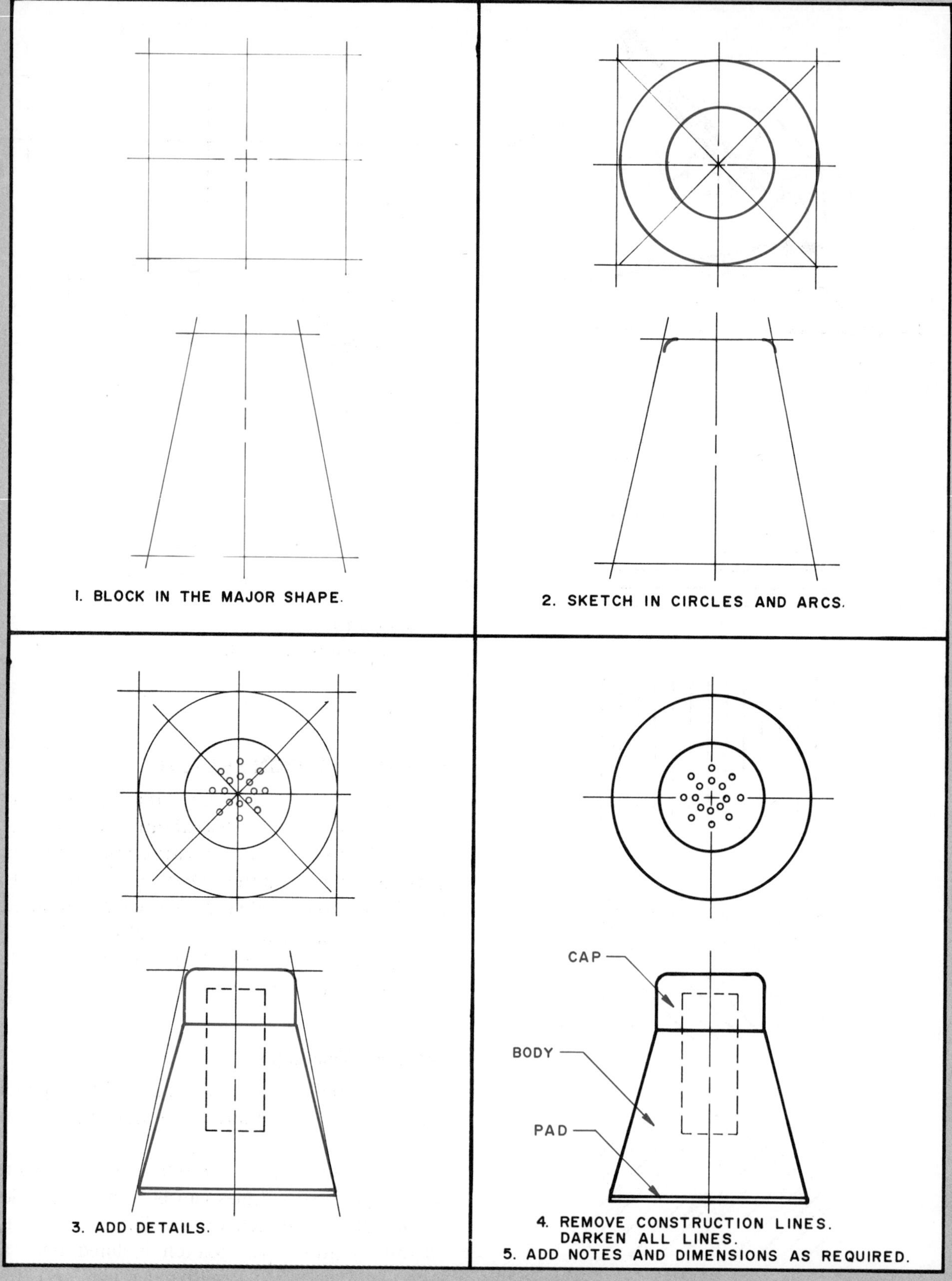
1. BLOCK IN THE MAJOR SHAPE.
2. SKETCH IN CIRCLES AND ARCS.
3. ADD DETAILS.
CAP
BODY
PAD
4. REMOVE CONSTRUCTION LINES.
DARKEN ALL LINES.
5. ADD NOTES AND DIMENSIONS AS REQUIRED.

Figure 5-17
Steps in making a working drawing.

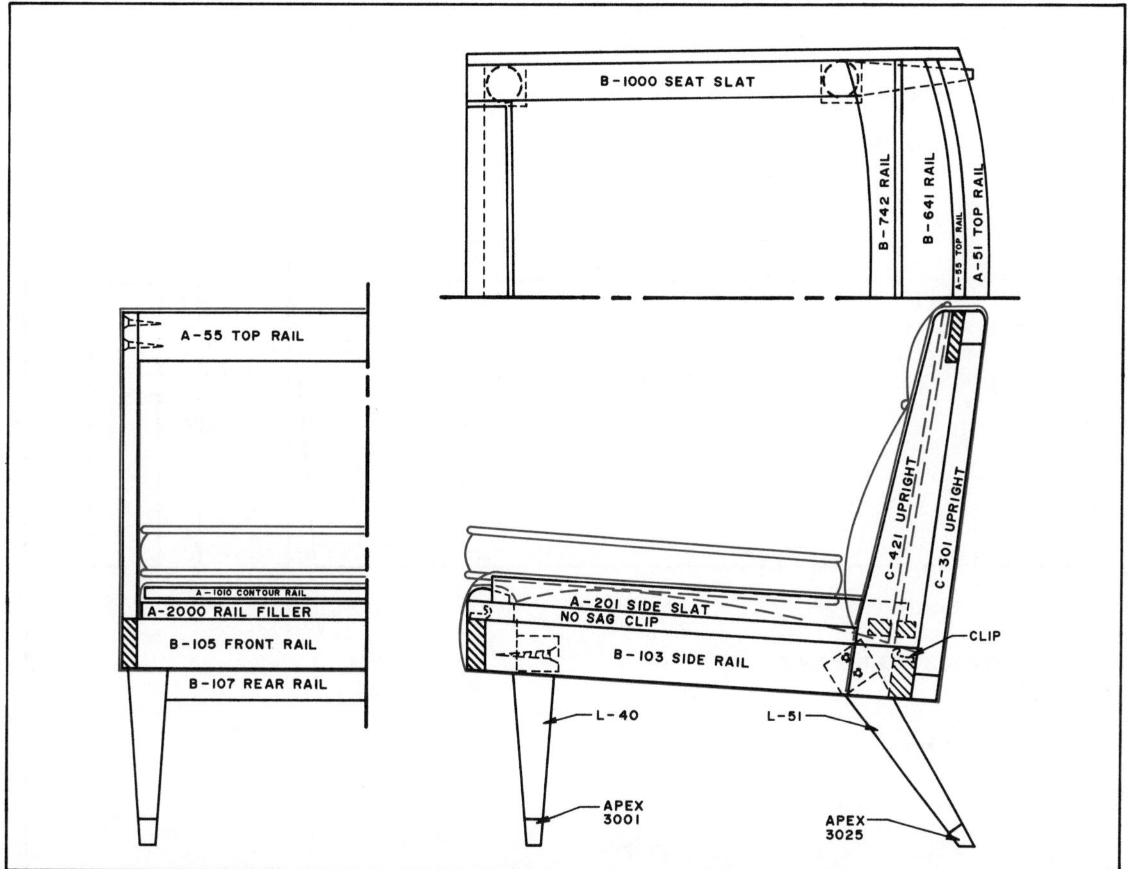

Figure 5-18
This furniture drawing shows the assembly of parts and the line of upholstery. This type of drawing usually is full-size. Each part is identified by number and has separate detail drawings made for its production.

Drawing Procedure

Follow these guidelines to make your design sketch:

1. Decide how many views are needed to show all details of the product.
2. Determine which scale to use. This depends on the size of the product and the paper available. In the furniture industry, full-size drawings often are used even if they are very large. If necessary, you can tape several pieces of paper together.
3. Locate the views on the paper. This is done by blocking in the major shape. Leave room between views for dimensions, Figure 5-17.
4. Block in the major shape and locate centerlines on the drawing.
5. Sketch all circles and arcs.
6. Add the details.
7. Remove unneeded lines.
8. Darken the remaining lines.
9. Add dimensions and letter notes.

DRAFTING IN THE CABINETMAKING INDUSTRY

The cabinetmaking industry is divided into millwork, fixture and furniture production. Millwork includes such products as doors and windows. Fixtures include such things as display shelving and merchandising display cabinets. Furniture production includes household and office units, such as chairs, tables and bedroom suites.

The basic drafting practices in these industries are the same as in other industries. The drafter should know how materials are processed and joined. Each company has drafting standards. The standards that follow are typical.

Full-size drawings are common. They are very large, Figure 5-18. This drawing was reduced to fit in this book, but the original was full-size. This is a production drawing. It shows the assembled unit and identifies each part. It is a guide to assembling the complete unit after each part is mass-produced.

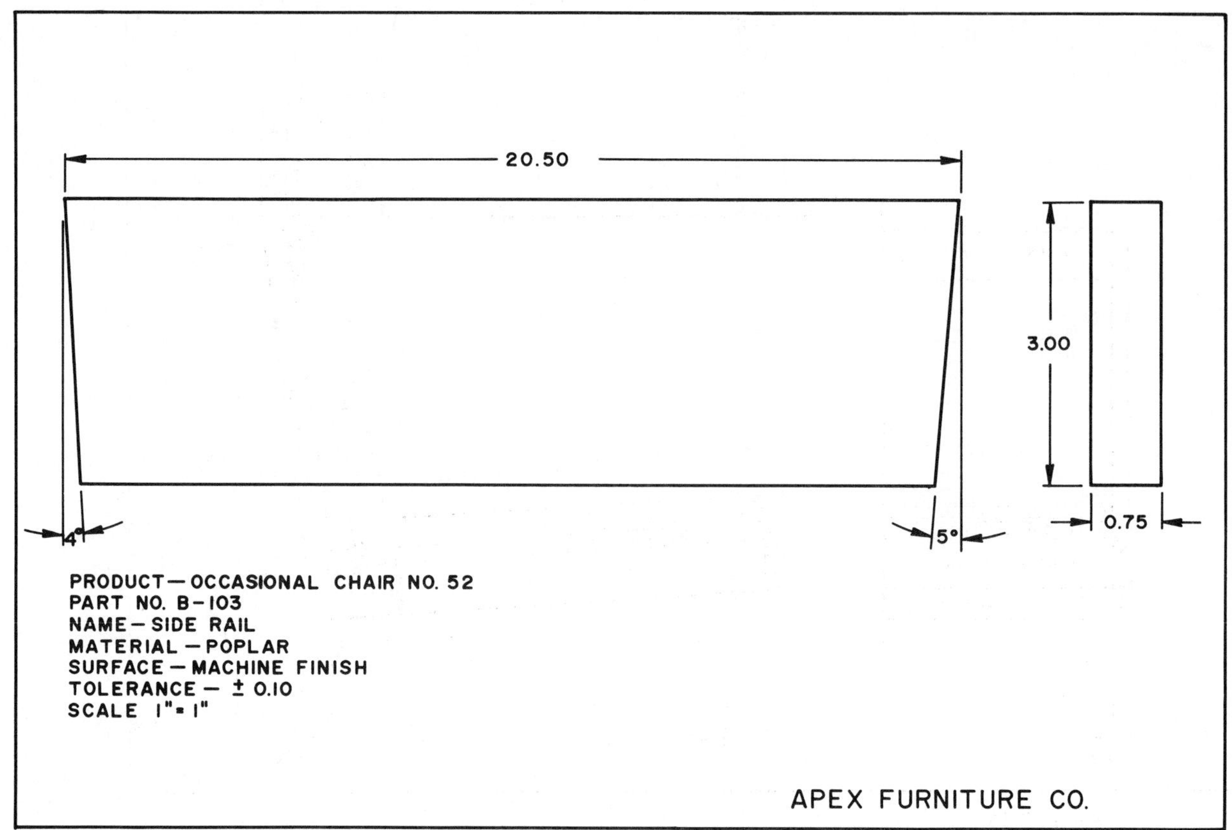

Figure 5-19
A typical detail drawing. This is a part of the chair shown in Figure 5-18. Can you find it on the production-assembly drawing?

Each part is drawn separately, Figure 5-19. Detailed drawings, such as this, are completely dimensioned. Workers who produce the parts must make them exactly as shown in the drawing. If they fail to do so, they will stall the assembly operation.

A common type of drawing for simple furniture is shown in Figure 5-20. Here, the front and side views of a table are given. A top view would be needed if the tabletop had an unusual shape. Because construction is simple, no sections are needed. An enlarged detail of the leg is drawn. Patterns for curves in the rails are laid out on a 10-mm grid. This drawing is all in metric measures. All dimensions are in millimeters.

Figure 5-21 shows a typical cabinet drawing. Cabinet drawings generally are full-size. To reduce the size of the drawing, portions of the cabinets are broken out. The dimensions show the actual size of the finished unit.

Another type of furniture drawing is shown in Figure 5-22. The table is symmetrical (same on both sides), so only half a front view is drawn. Because the table has a drawer, the drafter thought sections were needed. Thus, the project is seen directly from the front view.

The top view of the table is a particular type of drawing. The left half shows the wood top and the direction of the grain. It also shows the rail and the drawers below the top. They are drawn as though they were visible. It really presents two visible views, one drawn over the other. The right half of the top view shows the tabletop removed. It also shows the details of the rail and the drawer.

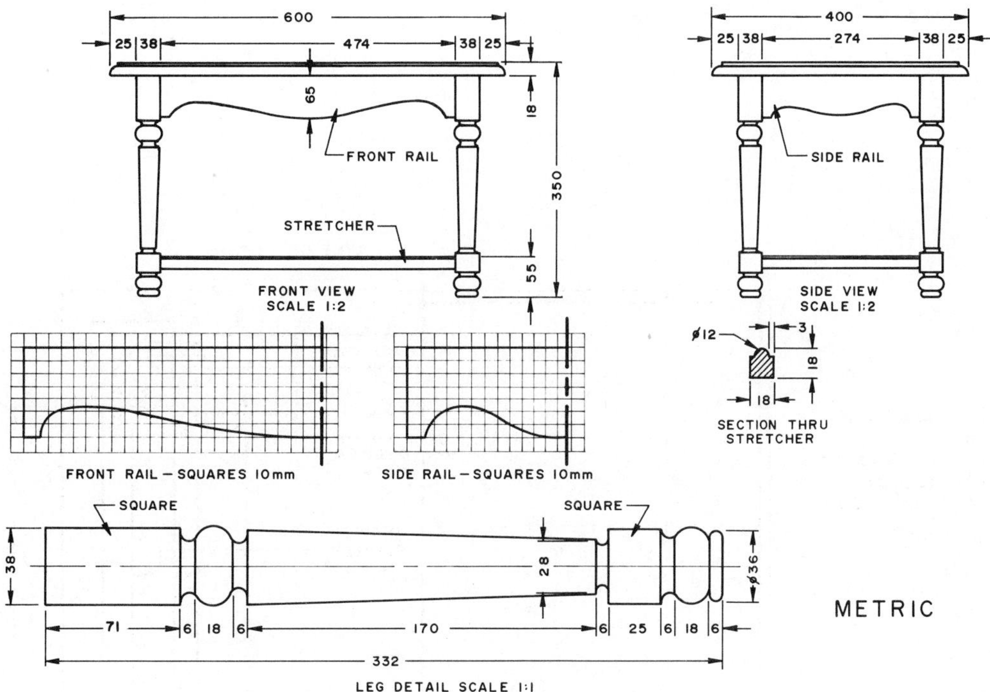

Figure 5-20
This metric production drawing shows part details and assembly information for a simple piece of furniture. This type of drawing usually is full-size.

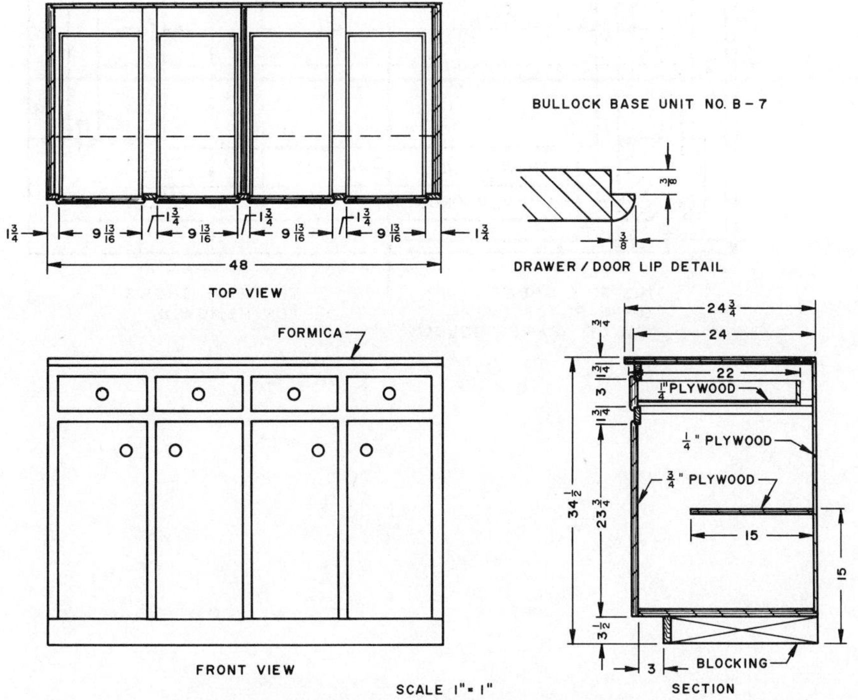

Figure 5-21
A typical wood-cabinet production drawing. Some companies prefer to draw this type full-size and use broken-out parts to reduce the size of the drawing.

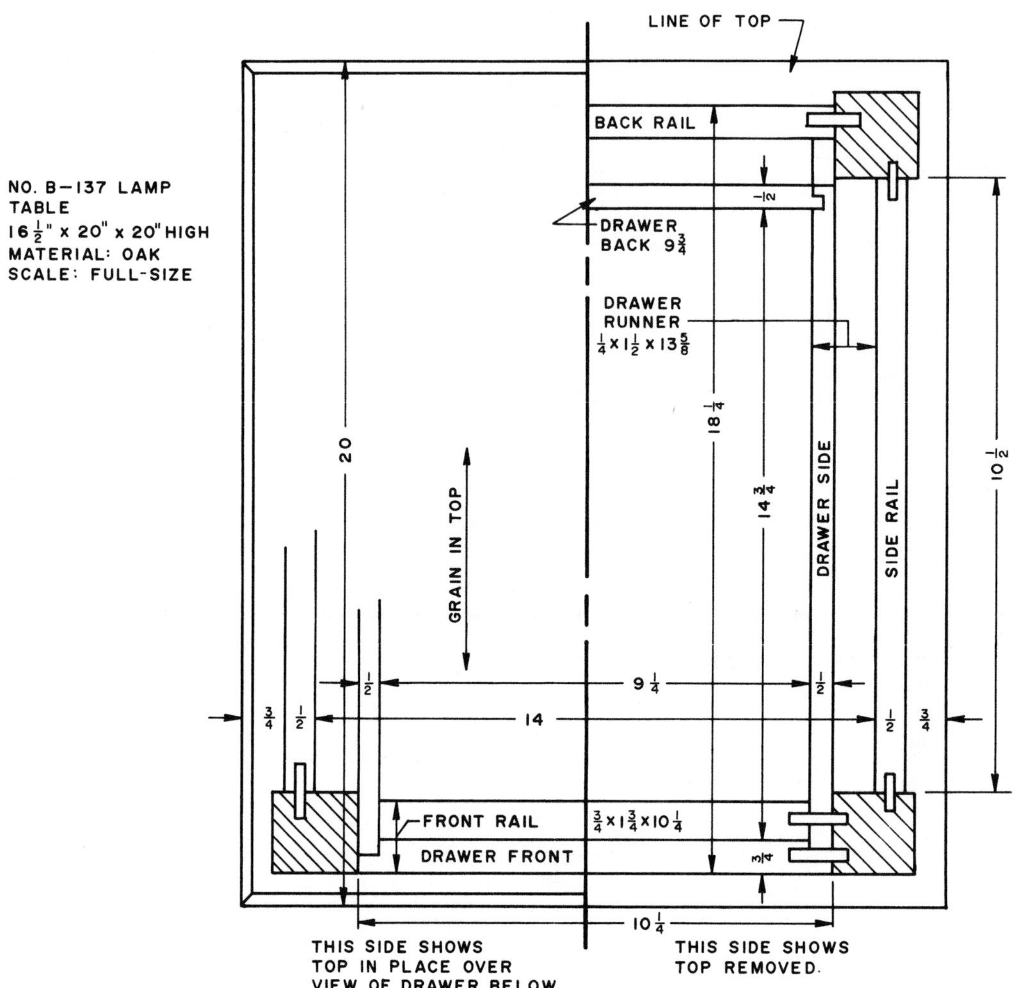

Figure 5-22

This production drawing shows part sizes and assembly information. Sections clarify details. This type of drawing often is full-size.

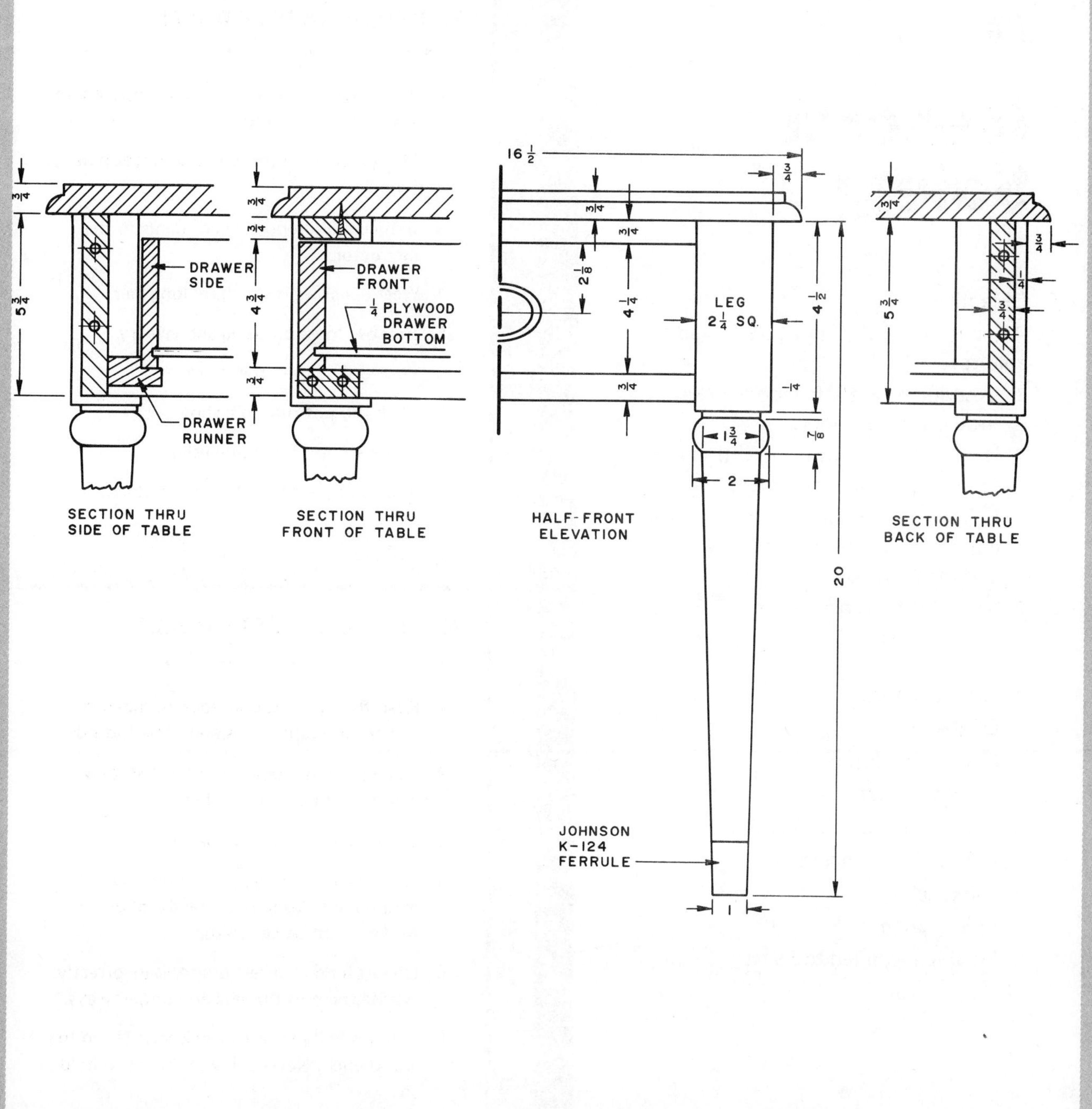

REVIEW QUESTIONS

1 Which views are shown on a working drawing?
2 Explain what is meant by *drawing to scale.*
3 What types of sections are used on working drawings?
4 What is the purpose of dimensions on a drawing?
5 What types of pictorial drawings are used? How do they differ?
6 What is the procedure for making a drawing?
7 What are the possible differences between furniture drawings?

UNIT

6

General Safety

Objectives

After studying this unit you should be able to:

1 Describe how a safe woodworker should act and work.

2 Dress safely for working with hand tools and power equipment.

3 Explain the importance of properly maintaining working areas, tools and machines.

4 Identify the types of fire extinguishers.

Technical Terms

OSHA

Eye protection

Ear protection

Classes of fires—A, B and C

A-B-C fire extinguisher

Kickback

Safety zone

Double-insulated tools

PERSONAL SAFETY RULES

1 Do not work in a shop without supervision or special permission.

2 Always wear approved eye protection in a shop.

3 Immediately report all accidents to the instructor.

4 Wear a hairnet if you have long hair.

5 Remove loose clothing and jewelry.

6 Wear only closed-toe shoes.

7 Walk (do not run) in a shop.

8 Learn to use fire extinguishers.

9 Wear a respirator if dust is a problem.

HAND-TOOL SAFETY RULES

1 Keep the floor around your workbench free from scraps, chips and other hazards.

2 When carrying tools, hold them so they will not injure you or others.

3 Store tools on the tool panel.

4 Keep hand tools sharp and properly maintained. A sharp, correctly adjusted tool will not be apt to slip.

5 Do not let coworkers use tools incorrectly. Advise them of the safe and proper ways.

6 Clamp small pieces of stock securely to the workbench. Never use your hands to hold stock.

7 Keep your balance by placing your feet solidly on the floor.

8 Do not force a small tool. Use a heavy-duty tool or take a lighter cut.

9 Always push a knife, chisel or any sharp hand tool away from you. Never place your hands or any part of your body in front of a tool.

10 Use a plastic or wooden mallet to drive chisels.

11 Be careful where you swing a hammer, mallet or hatchet.

12 Use the right tool for the job.

MACHINE SAFETY RULES

1 Make sure that only the operator and the helpers are inside the safety zone around the machine.

2 Ask the instructor to approve all special setups.

3 Keep the floor around the machines free of any material, including scraps.

4 Be certain that saws and cutters are sharp and properly installed. Do not change a cutter without permission.

5 When replacing saws or cutters, be certain that the power is off at the fuse or breaker box.

6 Be sure that all guards are in place and operating properly before turning on the power.

7 Remove all wrenches and other setup tools from the table before operating the machine.

8 Do not permit someone else to turn on a machine you are operating.

9 Ground all electric tools or use tools with double electrical insulation.

10 Do not use a tool with frayed wire or a defective switch.

11 Arrange cords on portable tools so they do not get caught in the machine or cause others to trip.

12 Do not use electric tools when inflammable gas or vapors are present.

13 Keep electrical cords away from hot, wet or oily places.

14 Notify the instructor immediately if a machine does not seem to be running properly.

15 Never talk to or distract a person who is operating a machine.

16 Examine all wood to be machined for knots, wane, splits, checks, twists and curly grain. Any of these defects can be a source of danger.

17 Get help when cutting long or wide boards and panels.

18 Operate machines at full speed before starting to feed material.

19 Do not feed material into a machine faster than it will cut easily nor so slowly that it burns the material. Take light cuts if possible.

20 Give your full attention to operating a machine.

21 Never make adjustments while machines are running.

22 In case of electrical power failure, turn off the machine and stand clear.

23 Turn off the power and wait until the cutting tool stops turning before leaving a machine.

FINISHING SAFETY RULES

1 Do not allow open flames, sparks or smoking.

2 Keep finishes and solvents in approved containers and stored in safety cabinets.

3 Ground your storage containers to prevent sparks.

4 Do not mix solvents or finishes together without your instructor's permission.

continued on page 50

FINISHING SAFETY RULES *(continued)*

5 Clean up all spills immediately.

6 Keep all containers covered.

7 Wear rubber gloves when working with harsh chemicals.

8 Apply finishes only in a well-ventilated area.

9 Wear a respirator while spraying.

10 Do not pour finishes down a sink drain.

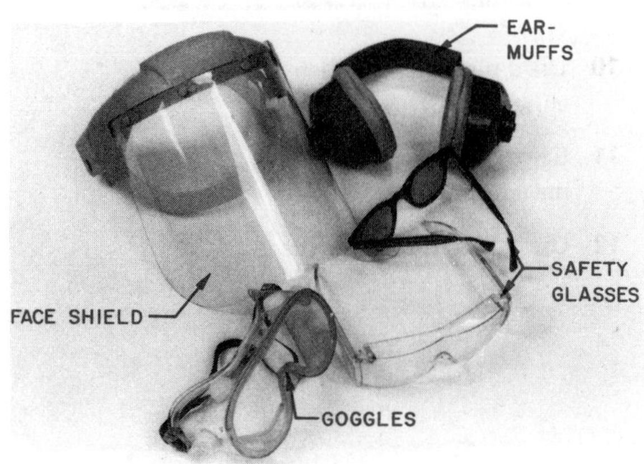

Figure 6-2
Different styles of protective clothing.

Figure 6-1
Industry workers follow many safety rules. OSHA manuals list these regulations.

Working safely is the responsibility of every woodworker. Otherwise, an accident probably will occur. Safety should be considered before starting any woodworking operation.

Industry has a rigid set of rules. These are federal laws that were established by the Occupational Safety and Health Act, better known as *OSHA*. Figure 6-1 shows various OSHA manuals. They provide many guidelines for workers. For example, they tell how machines are to be placed, which machines are to be guarded and what are acceptable noise levels.

You can imagine the danger of using hand tools and machines incorrectly. Because of sharp-cutting edges on tools and machines, accidents can easily occur. This book outlines procedures that will help you to work safely. Also ask your instructor about safety. Never start an operation with hand tools or machines if you have any doubt on how it should be done safely.

Some individuals hurry too much when they work. They are not careful. They are running and not thinking about their job. Thus, they may cause an accident. Think through every step before you start. Taking short cuts will lead to mistakes and injuries. You always must walk—*never* run—when working with woodworking equipment.

PROPER CLOTHING AND BEHAVIOR

The most important protective clothing guards the eyes and ears, Figure 6-2. Frequently, wood chips fly or hand tools slip. Protective clothing and safe work habits will help prevent accidents. You should wear *eye protection* at all times in the laboratory. Even if you are not working, you can get hit by a flying piece of material from someone else's work. Remember, your eyes cannot be replaced.

Machine noise also can hurt you. Wear ear protectors to help block out harmful noise. *Ear protection* is very important.

Clothing should be comfortable but not loose. Long, bulky sleeves, neckties and jackets can get caught in the moving parts of machines. Rolled-up or short sleeves are a must. In addition, remove *all* jewelry, such as a watch and rings. They

Figure 6-3
This woodworker is dressed for safety. He does not wear jewelry or long sleeves. He is wearing safety glasses and an apron to restrict loose clothing.

Figure 6-4
Long hair must be pinned up above the shirt collar. Note that the shirt sleeves are rolled up to the elbow.

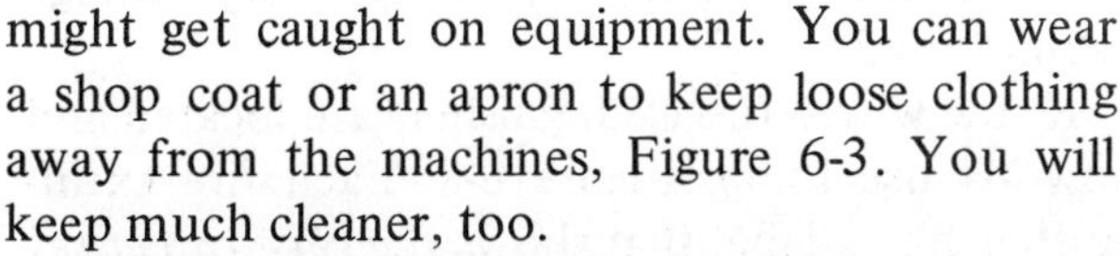

might get caught on equipment. You can wear a shop coat or an apron to keep loose clothing away from the machines, Figure 6-3. You will keep much cleaner, too.

Long hair should be pinned up or covered by a hairnet, Figure 6-4. Wear shoes that cover your entire foot. Many employers insist that their workers wear steel-toed shoes for protection.

Be on your best behavior. You or your friends can get injured in many ways. Horseplay can mean trouble. A well-meaning trick or prank often can spell disaster and injury. Do not speak to anyone who is performing an operation. This can distract the person and cause an accident.

SAFETY MAINTENANCE

Maintenance includes keeping work areas clean, equipment sharp and machines properly adjusted. Sawdust and wood scraps on floors and machines are a fire hazard and can cause a person to slip.

You must see that hand tools and machines are working properly. If there is a problem, call your instructor. Dull cutting tools require the stock to be forced into the cutter. This may cause the board to slip or create a kickback. Keep all cutting tools sharp. Sharp tools require less force to cut properly and are less likely to slip.

FIRE PREVENTION AND FINISHING SAFETY

Because wood and wood finishes burn easily, everyone must be responsible for reducing fire hazards. Good housekeeping is the best way to reduce the threat of fire. Keep the bottoms of machines cleaned out and scraps properly stacked. Figure 6-5 shows a scrap rack that holds short wood pieces.

Figure 6-5
A well-kept scrap rack.

Figure 6-7
Finishes and solvents must be stored properly.

Figure 6-6
Dirty rags must be placed in a safety trash can.

Finishing materials generally are flammable. Keep any high heat or open flame away from the finishing area. Never smoke in the woodworking or finishing area.

Dispose of used rags and solvents correctly in a covered container, Figure 6-6. Store finishes and solvents in safety cans in a safety storage cabinet, Figure 6-7.

Know where fire extinguishers are located and how to use them, Figure 6-8. Each fire extinguisher has a label that shows the *class* or *classes of fires* it can be used on.

Classes of fires are labeled *A, B* or *C.* Type A fire contains combustible materials such as wood, paper and most trash. Type B refers to finishing-type materials. Alcohol, paint and lacquer products are typical examples. Type C includes electrical equipment. Use the correct fire extinguisher for each type of fire. An *A-B-C fire extinguisher* can be used on all types of fire, Figure 6-8.

HAND-TOOL SAFETY

Most woodworking hand tools have sharp, exposed cutting edges. They should be handled and carried with the cutting edge pointing down,

Figure 6-8
Know how to use fire extinguishers. Notice that this extinguisher can be used on all classes of fires.

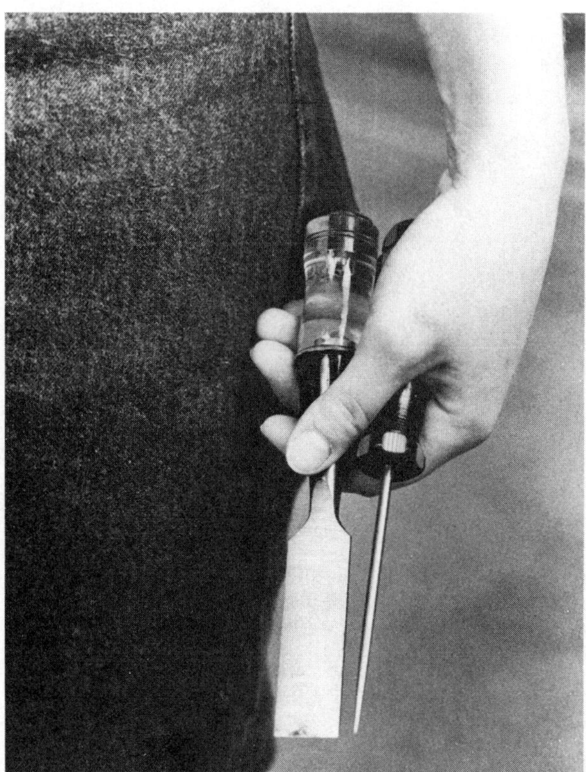

Figure 6-9
Carry hand tools with the cutting edge down.

Figure 6-9. Keep the edge sharp. Dull edges may cause the hand tool to slip from the stock when it is forced into the wood. Keep hands away from the cutting area. Always clamp the work in a vise or to the bench with clamps. This will leave both hands free to control the tools.

MACHINE SAFETY

The most important part of portable and stationary power tools is the safety guards. Check to see they are operating properly. *Never* remove guards without your instructor's permission. If possible, use some form of push stick and feather board, Figure 6-10. The feather board holds the wood piece against the fence. The push stick pushes the piece into the cutting tool. Always know where the cutting tool is located. Do not reach on top or over the far side of the blade or knives.

There is always a danger of a *kickback* when operating a power tool. The wood may be thrown back out of the machine. Never stand or work

Figure 6-10
Use a feather board and a push stick whenever possible.

Figure 6-11
Safety zones should be marked around each machine.

Figure 6-12
A double-insulated tool has a plastic housing.

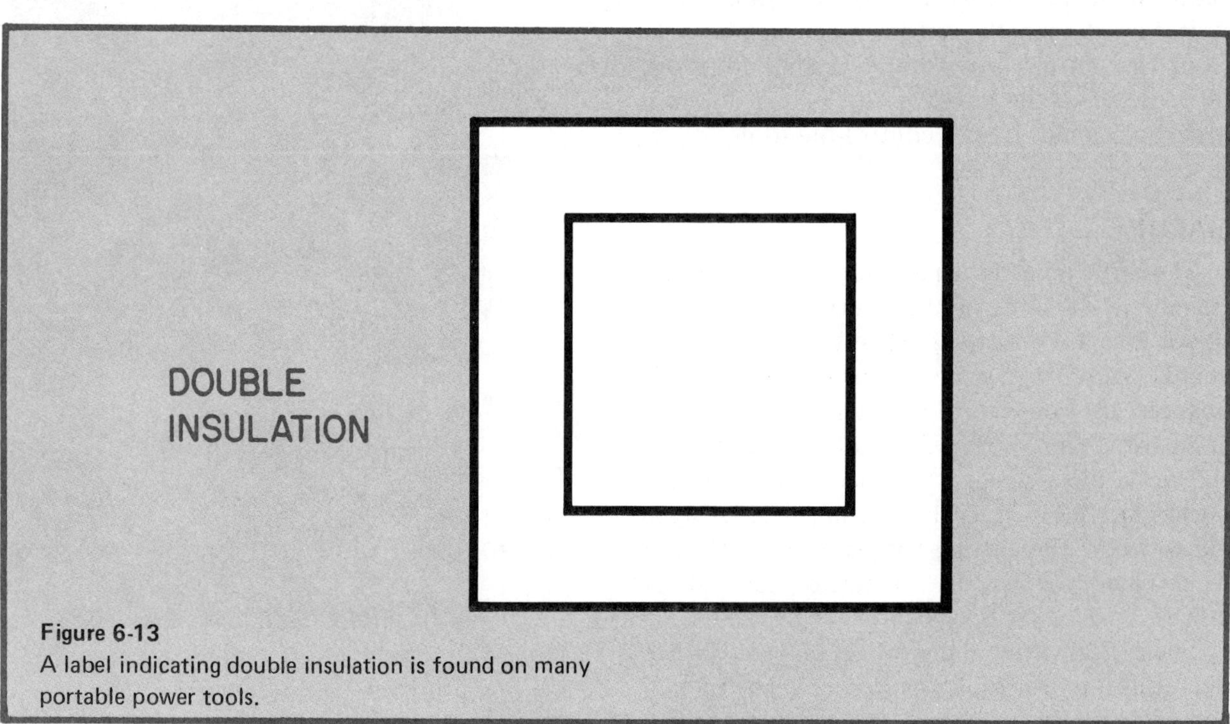

Figure 6-13
A label indicating double insulation is found on many portable power tools.

Figure 6-14
Always use a grounded receptacle for a three-prong plug.

directly behind the path of the cutting tool. If a kickback occurs, the board will strike anything or anybody in its path.

A *safety zone* should be marked around each machine, Figure 6-11. Only the operator and the tail-off person (helper) should be in this zone. Keep this area free of excessive sawdust and wood scraps.

Most power tools run on electricity. Electrical shock is always a danger. Stationary machines must be grounded to reduce this danger. Portable power tools often have plastic housings and may be double insulated, Figure 6-12. All double-insulated tools will have the label shown in Figure 6-13. Never operate any power tool in or around water. A portable power tool with a three-prong plug must be used with a grounded receptacle, Figure 6-14. Never use this tool unless it is properly grounded.

FIRST AID

You should report immediately any accident to your instructor. Even a small scrape on your skin or a tiny particle in your eye can lead to serious problems. When an injury occurs, your instructor will help you to get immediate attention from qualified help.

REVIEW QUESTIONS

1. Whom should you ask questions you have about safety?
2. When should you wear eye protection?
3. Why should you not speak to someone who is operating a machine?
4. What can happen if you use a dull tool?
5. Where should you keep used rags and solvents?
6. List the three classes of fire.
7. Which type of fire is each fire extinguisher designed to fight?
8. Which type of fire extinguisher can fight all fires?
9. Why is a safety zone marked around each machine?
10. What kinds of accidents should you report to your instructor?

SUGGESTED ACTIVITIES

1. Locate all fire extinguishers in your shop or laboratory. List which types of fires they are designed to fight.
2. Find and write down the telephone number of your local fire station. Post the number by the telephone.
3. Arrange for a nurse or another qualified person to talk to your class about first aid.

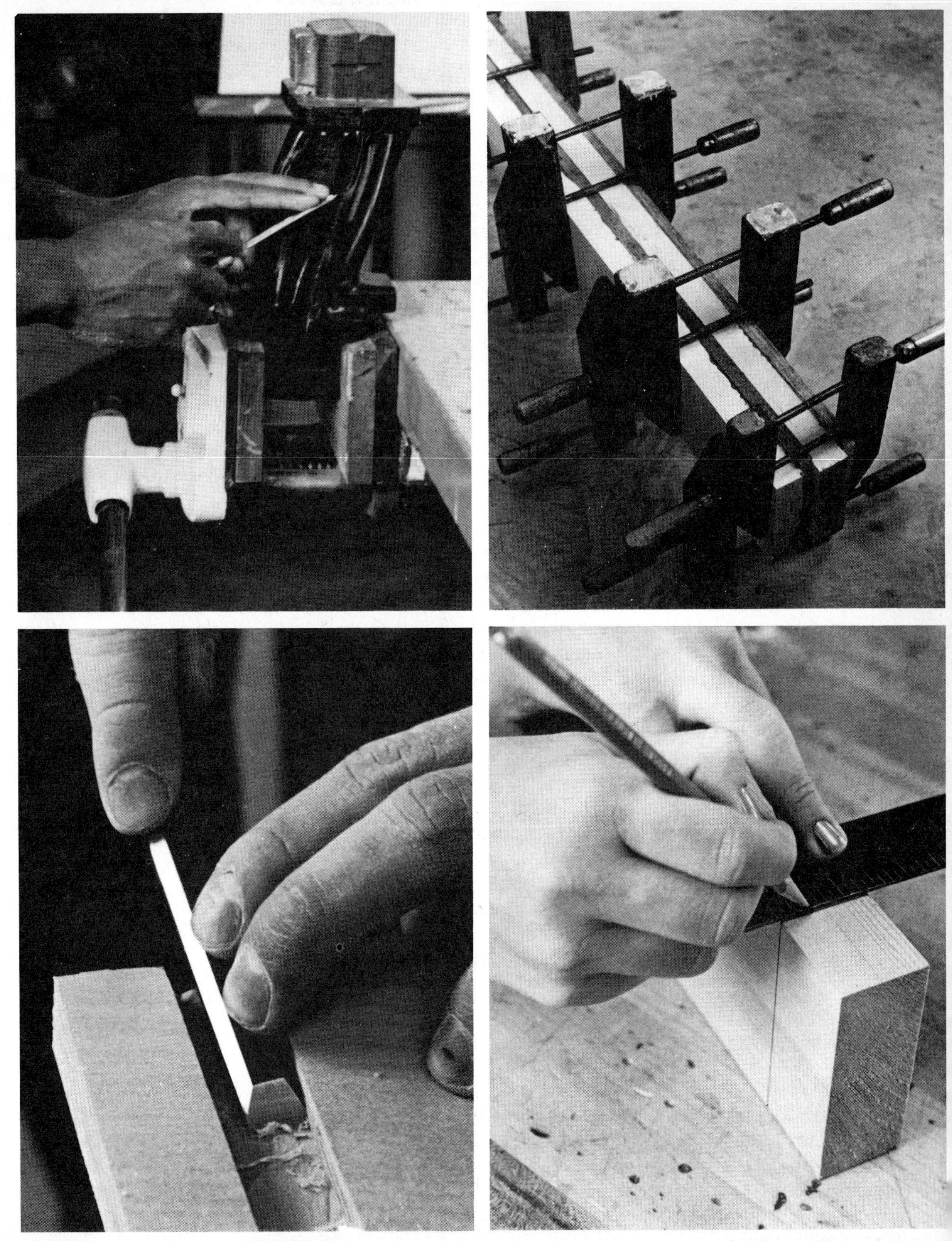

SECTION

2 Using Hand Tools

7
Layout Tools

8
Handsaws

9
Hand Planes and Scrapers

10
Chisels, Gouges and Carving Tools

11
Sharpening Edge Tools

12
Files, Rasps and Forming Tools

13
Drilling and Boring Tools

14
Clamping Tools and Assembly Procedures

As a woodworker you must be able to use hand tools skillfully. Your use of tools can make the difference between an amateur-looking project and one that looks professional.

Hand tools are usually the first tools you will purchase for home and hobby use. Although they cost less than power tools, hand tools can be expensive. If you maintain and store them properly, however, hand tools will last a lifetime. Tools properly used and cared for will be efficient, effective and safe.

Section 2, Using Hand Tools, shows the types and sizes of hand tools and how to use them skillfully and safely.

UNIT

7

Layout Tools

Objectives

After studying this unit you should be able to:

1 Identify and use tools for measuring linear distances.
2 Lay out square cuts.
3 Lay out angles.
4 Lay out circles, arcs and irregular curves.
5 Enlarge and reduce patterns.
6 Use templates to lay out duplicate parts.
7 Lay out a hexagon and an octagon.

Technical Terms

Bench rule	Compass
Folding rule	Trammel points
Tape rule	Irregular curve
Try square	Template
Framing square	Duplicate parts
Combination square	Hexagon
Marking gauge	Octagon
Protractor	Dividers
T bevel	

Before laying out the part you wish to make, you must select the stock. Examine all its surfaces for warp, cracks, splits and knots. These may ruin the part. Often a part can be laid out so the defects are cut away.

Lay out the part on the stock so that you have little waste. For example, if the stock has a good, straight edge, use it for one edge of your part, Figure 7-1. Do not lay out a part in the center of a board. When laying out on plywood, always work from an edge. If a pattern is laid out in the center of a sheet, a great deal of wood can be wasted, Figure 7-2.

Be certain to lay out the part so the wood grain runs in the direction desired. A long part will be stronger if the grain runs the long way.

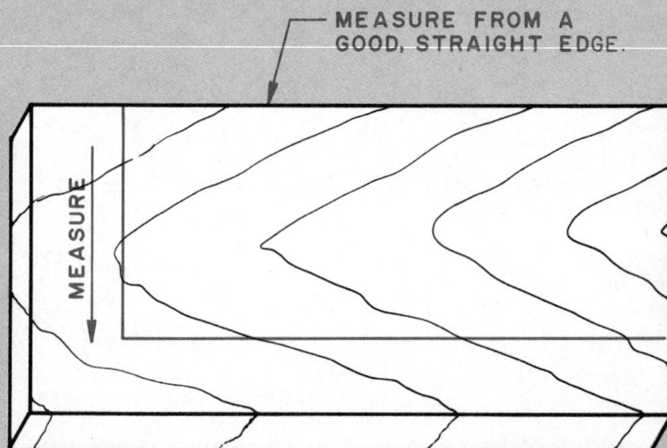

Figure 7-1
Begin a layout from a good edge of the board.

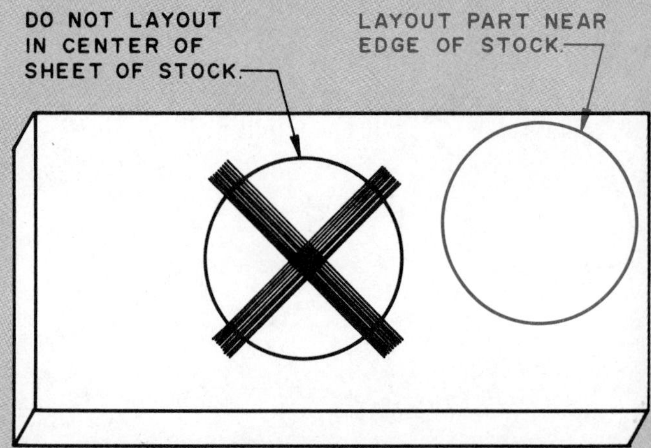

Figure 7-2
Lay out parts near the edges of sheets of material. This saves material and lowers costs.

MEASURING LENGTH

The bench rule, the folding rule and the tape rule are used for measuring length. *Bench rules* are made of wood or metal. They are available in 1-, 2- and 3-foot lengths, Figure 7-3. A wooden 1-meter rule is available.

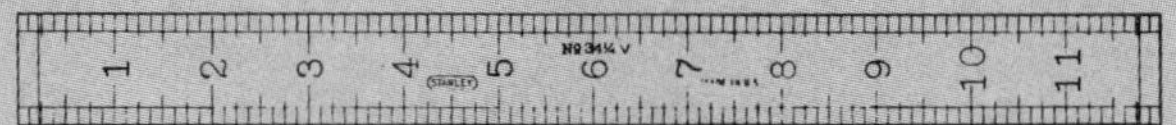

Figure 7-3
A 1-foot bench rule. (The Stanley Works)

A *folding rule* marked in inches is usually 6 feet long. Metric folding rules are available in 1- and 2-meter lengths. They are used for measuring longer distances, Figure 7-4.

A *tape rule* is a flexible steel band that rolls up inside a case. It has a hook on one end to place over the edge of a board. Tapes come in many widths and lengths. The most common lengths are 8, 10 and 12 feet and 2 and 3 meters, Figure 7-5. Many woodworkers prefer tapes 1 inch wide and 25 feet long for measuring long distances. Inch tapes also come in 50- and 100-foot lengths. Metric tapes are made in 15-, 20-, 25-, and 30-meter lengths.

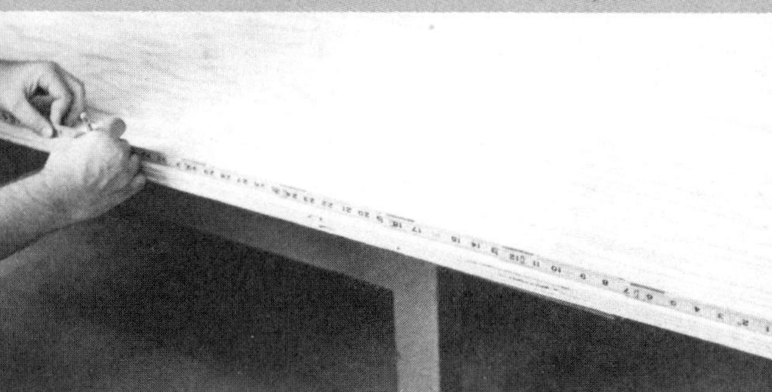

Figure 7-4
Measuring with a folding rule, *top*. Measuring with a steel tape rule, *bottom*.

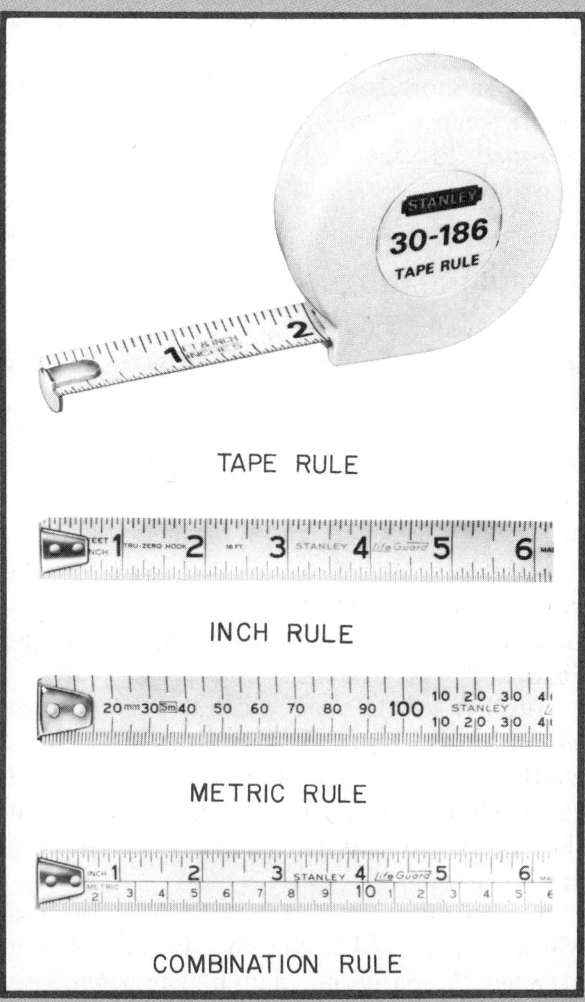

Figure 7-5
A tape rule is useful for measuring long lengths. An inch rule measures feet and inches. A metric rule measures millimeters. A combination rule measures inches or millimeters. (The Stanley Works)

Figure 7-6
Keeping the rule on edge when measuring increases accuracy.

Figure 7-7
When measuring width, keep the rule perpendicular to the edge.

The most accurate way to mark a length is to stand the rule on edge, Figure 7-6. Place the markings next to the board. Use a sharp pencil to draw a short, straight line. When you measure length, keep the rule parallel to the edge being measured, Figure 7-4. If it is not, the length will be wrong.

MEASURING WIDTH

To measure width, keep the rule perpendicular to the edge, Figure 7-7. Hold the side of the rule flush with the edge of the board.

Width also can be measured with a *try square* or *framing square.* To mark width using a square, draw a line across the stock, Figure 7-8. Hold the handle of the square firmly against the stock. Use the rule gradations on the blade of the square. Mark the width in several places. Connect the marks with the straight edge of the rule, Figure 7-9.

Another way to mark width is with a *combination square,* Figure 7-10. Set the blade to the width desired. Lock it in place. Place a pencil at the end. Holding the head against the board, slide the square and pencil down the board, Figure 7-11.

A *marking gauge* also may be used to mark widths, Figure 7-12. Set the distance desired between the head and the pin. The beam has a scale on it. Place the head against the edge of the stock. Turn the beam until the pin touches the stock. It will be at an angle of approximately 45°. Hold the head firmly against the stock and slide the gauge down the board, Figure 7-13. The

Figure 7-8
A try square or framing square can be used to measure width. Both can be used to draw a line perpendicular to the edge.

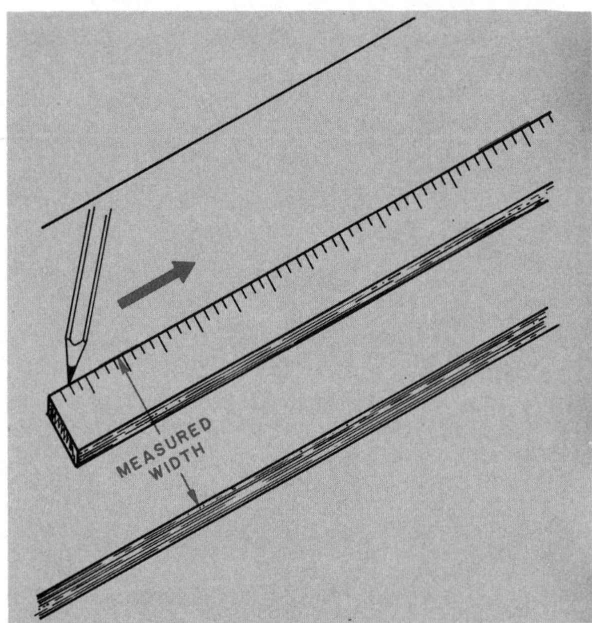

Figure 7-9
Mark the width in several places and connect these with a straightedge.

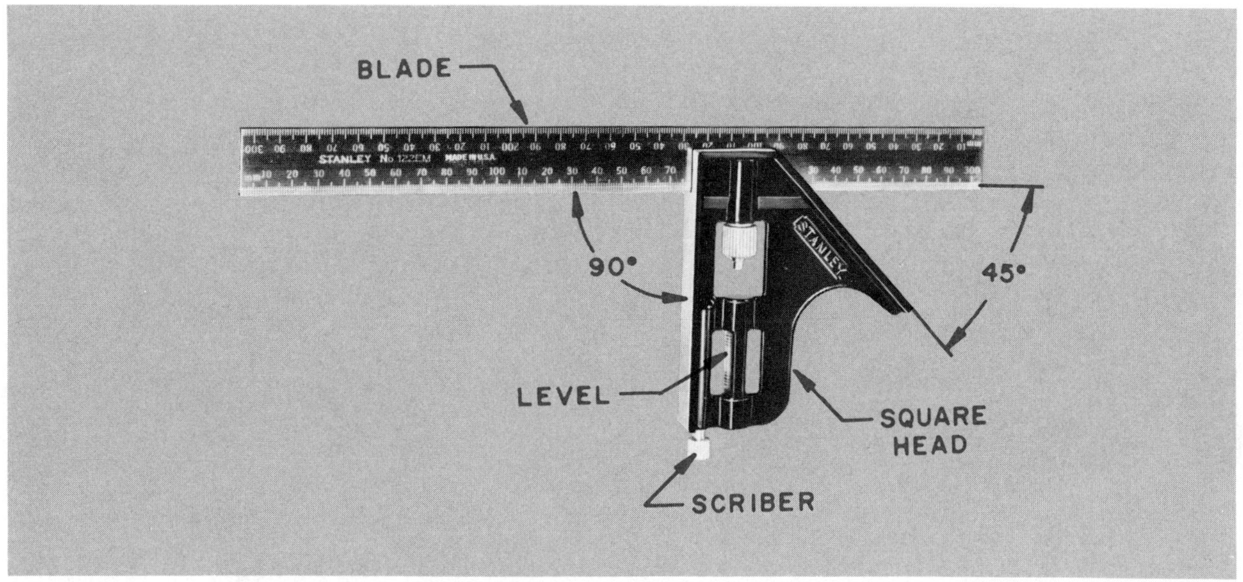

Figure 7-10
A combination square. (The Stanley Works)

Figure 7-11
A combination square is a good tool for measuring width.

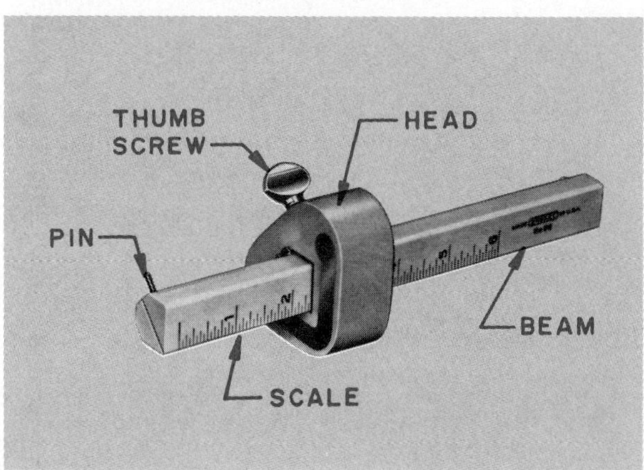

Figure 7-12
A marking gauge. (The Stanley Works)

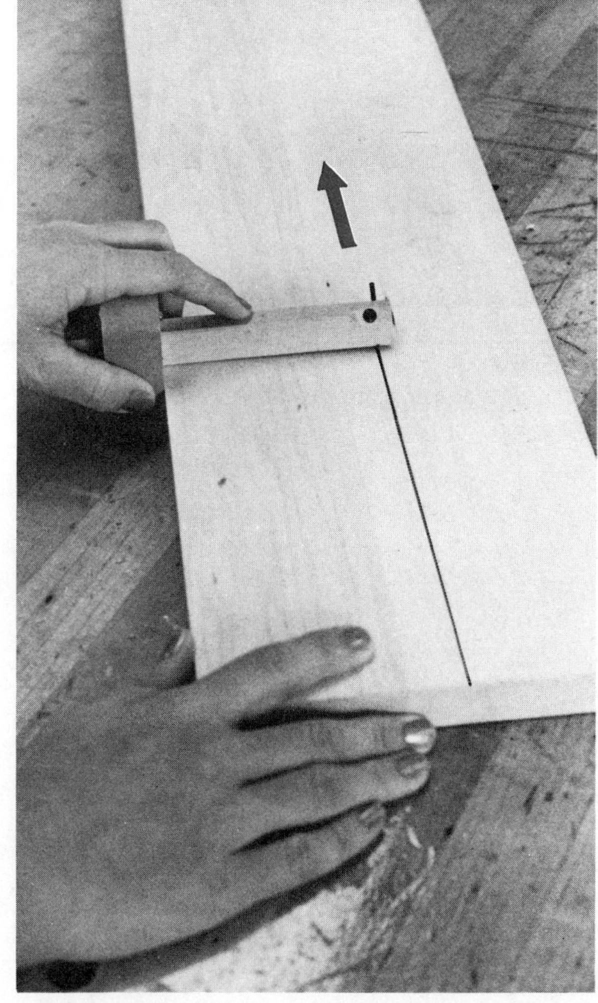

Figure 7-13
To use the marking gauge, slant the head and push it away from you.

Figure 7-14
Approximate widths can be marked using a finger as a guide.

Figure 7-16
A T bevel is used to lay out and transfer angles measured with a protractor.

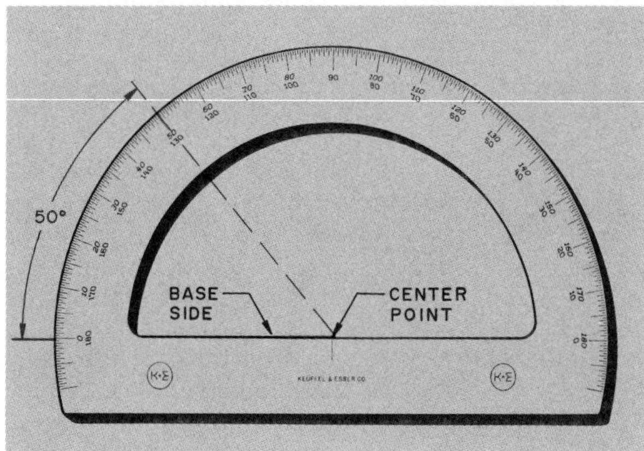

Figure 7-15
A protractor is used to lay out angles. (Keuffel & Esser Co.)

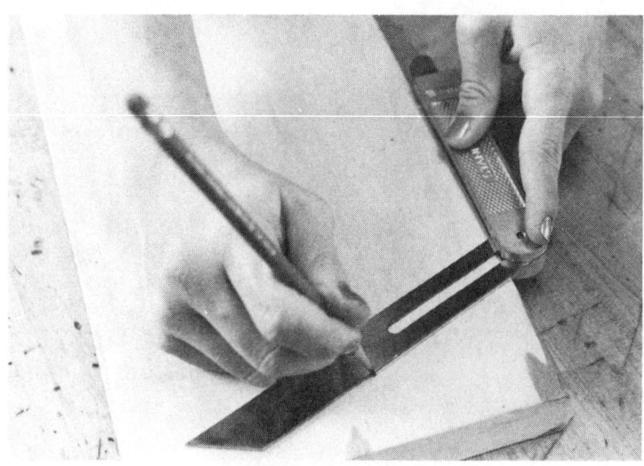

Figure 7-17
Laying out an angle with a T bevel.

pin leaves a shallow groove on the surface. This tool works best if you push it away from you. It is not recommended for marking across the grain.

A quick way to lay out an approximate width is using your finger as a gauge. Rest your middle finger against the edge of the stock and extend a pencil to the desired width. Holding the pencil firmly, slide your hand down the stock, Figure 7-14.

LAYING OUT ANGLES

Use a *protractor* to measure the size of angles. The protractor is divided into 180 degrees, Figure 7-15. To lay out an angle on a piece of stock, place the center point of the protractor on the point to be the corner and mark it. Place the base on one side of the angle. Count the number of degrees wanted. Place a mark there. Remove the protractor and connect the mark with the center point mark.

Use a *T bevel* to lay out and transfer angles. Use the protractor to set it for the desired angle, Figure 7-16. Lock the blade in place. Place the T bevel handle against the edge of the stock. The blade will cross the stock. Use a pencil to draw the angle, Figure 7-17. You also can use the T bevel to measure an angle and lay it out on another board, Figure 7-18.

LAYING OUT SQUARE CUTS

Use the try square, framing square and combination square to lay out square cuts. Place the handle firmly against the edge of the stock. The pencil marks along the blade. See Figures 7-19, 7-20 and 7-21.

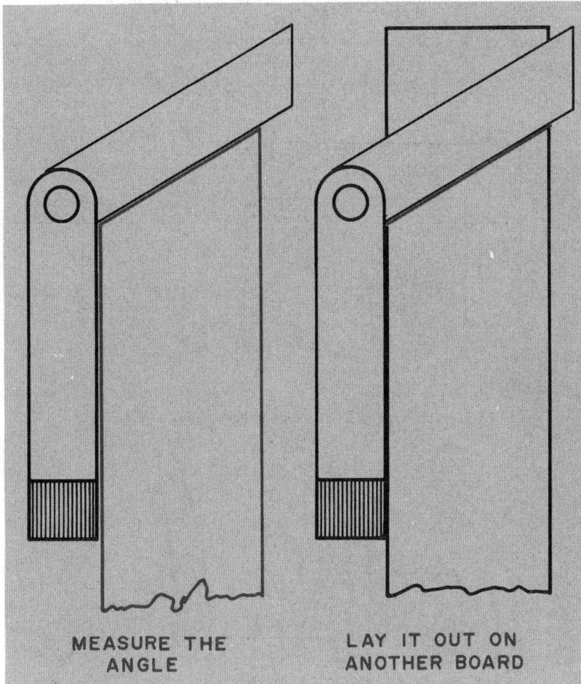
MEASURE THE ANGLE
LAY IT OUT ON ANOTHER BOARD

Figure 7-18
A T bevel is used to transfer angles.

Figure 7-19
A try square is used to lay out a square cut.

LAYING OUT REGULAR CURVES AND CIRCLES

Draw small circles and arcs with a *compass.* A compass has one leg with a point and one leg which holds a pencil or pencil lead, Figure 7-22. To draw a circle or arc, find the center of the circle with a square. Set the distance between the pin leg and pencil point equal to the radius. Place the pin leg on the center. Holding the compass at the top, rotate it in a clockwise direction. Slant it in the direction it is rotated.

Figure 7-20
The square cut can be marked on all sides of the board.

Figure 7-21
A combination square can be used to lay out a square cut.

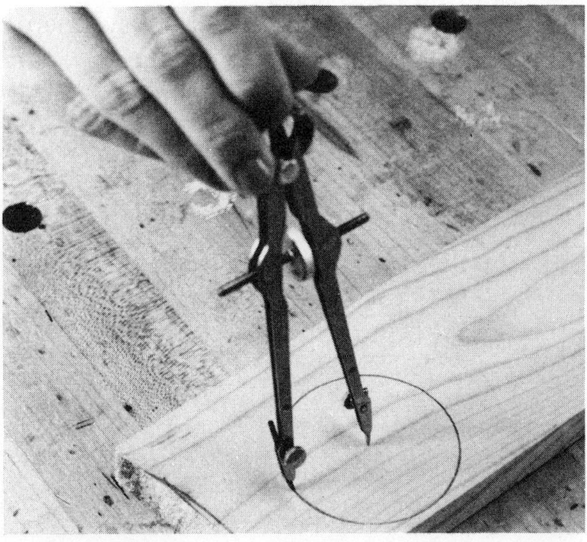

Figure 7-22
Small circles are laid out with a compass.

Draw large circles with *trammel points.* The points slide along a long beam. Set the radius of the circle or arc between the points. Hold one pin on the center. The other pin holds a pencil. Rotate the pencil around the center, Figure 7-23.

LAYING OUT A ROUNDED CORNER

Locate the center of the corner by measuring the radius from each corner, Figure 7-24. Place the pin leg of the compass on the center and draw the corner.

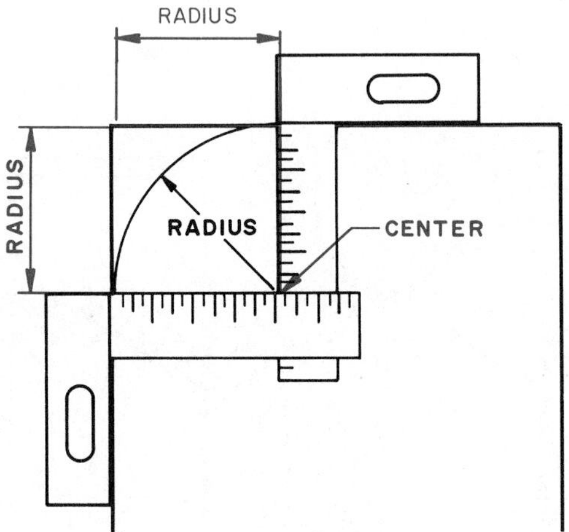

Figure 7-24
The radius is used to draw a rounded corner.

DRAWING IRREGULAR CURVES

Irregular curves do not have a fixed radius. Draw them with a tool called an *irregular curve.* There are many shapes and varieties of irregular curves, Figure 7-25.

Mark the desired curve with a series of points or a light freehand sketch. Move the irregular curve around these markings until it matches five or six points. Draw that part of the line. Move the curve around again and draw more parts of the line until the curve is complete, Figure 7-26.

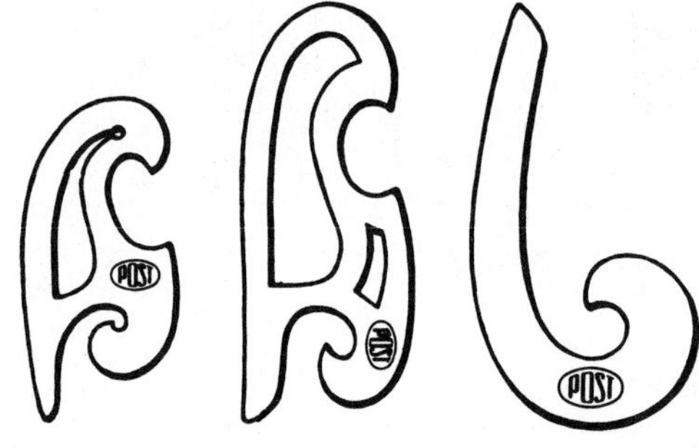

Figure 7-25
Common irregular curves. (Frederick Post Company)

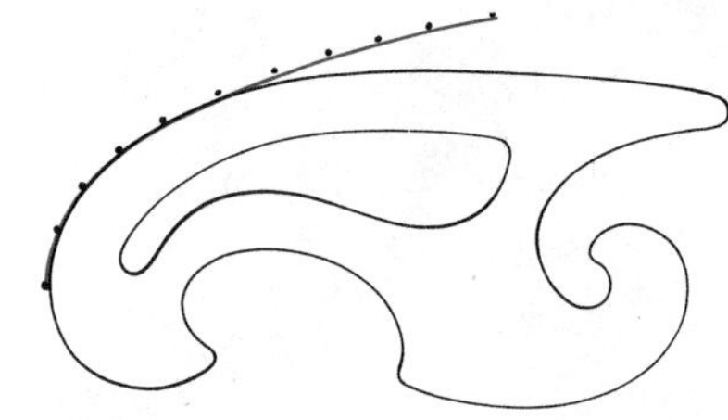

Figure 7-26
An irregular curve is drawn several points at a time, using the irregular curve tool.

USING TEMPLATES

You usually will lay out parts with irregular curves on heavy paper or cardboard. Trace the part onto the wood. Use tracing paper or cut out the cardboard or paper part and use it as a *template,* Figure 7-27. When a design is symmetrical (the same on each side of a centerline), draw only half the pattern. Use it to draw both halves of the design.

Figure 7-23
Large-diameter circles are laid out with trammel points.

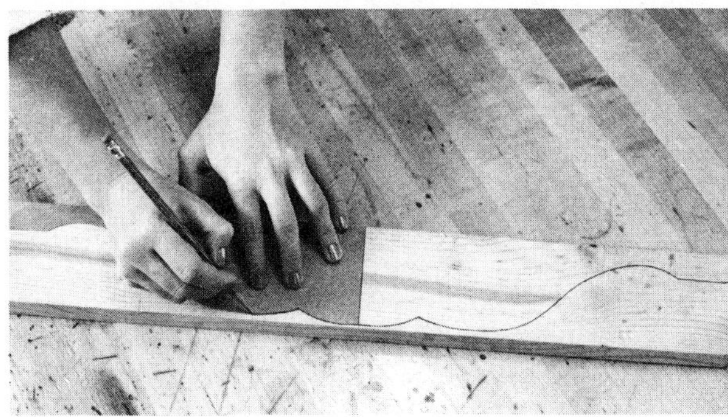

Figure 7-27
Only half a template is needed to lay out parts that are symmetrical.

ENLARGING AND REDUCING DESIGNS

You may find a design in a magazine or other source that you would like to enlarge. First decide how much you want to enlarge the design. Suppose you want to double its size. Draw a grid of 1/4" squares over the original design. To double the size, draw a grid of 1/2" squares on another piece of paper. Mark on the larger grid all points at which the design crosses the smaller grid, Figure 7-28. Connect these points to form the enlarged pattern. To reduce a design, draw a grid smaller than the one on the original design.

DIVIDING INTO EQUAL PARTS

Often you need to divide a board of odd width into several equal parts. The easiest way to do this is to lay a ruler across the board until the inch marks divide the space equally. For example, to divide a board into four equal parts, place the rule as shown in Figure 7-29. The zero is on one side and the 8" mark is on the other. Mark the 2", 4", and 6" locations. This divides the board into four equal parts.

LAYING OUT DUPLICATE PARTS

Many products have several parts that are the same size. You can save time and improve accuracy if you lay out the parts together. To make *duplicate parts,* carefully clamp the pieces of stock together. Mark the lengths or locations you will need. Mark all the parts at the same time, Figure 7-30.

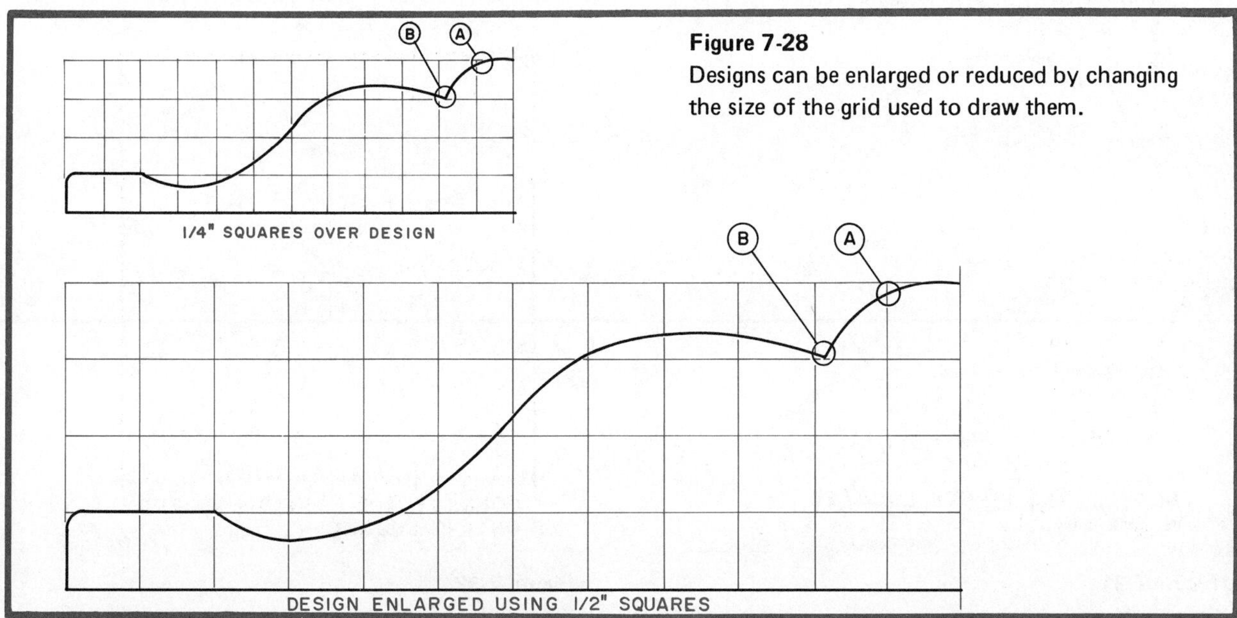

Figure 7-28
Designs can be enlarged or reduced by changing the size of the grid used to draw them.

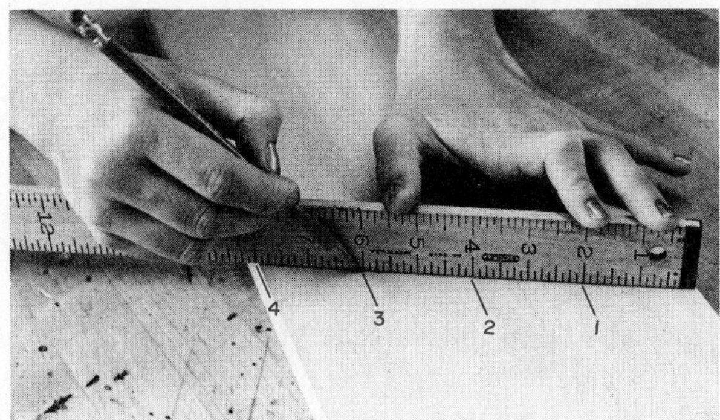

Figure 7-29
Dividing a board into four equal parts.

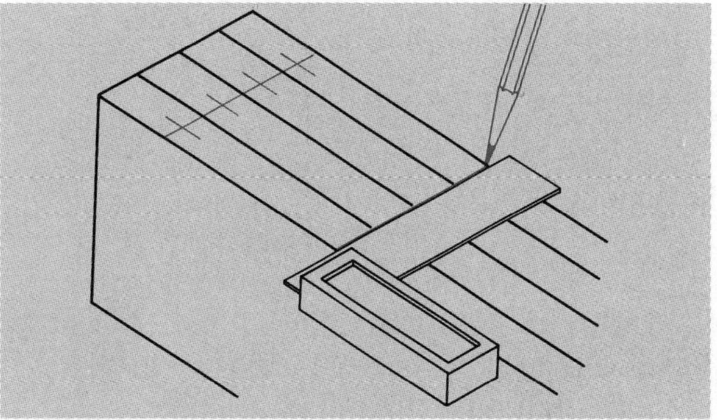

Figure 7-30
Lay out duplicate parts at the same time.

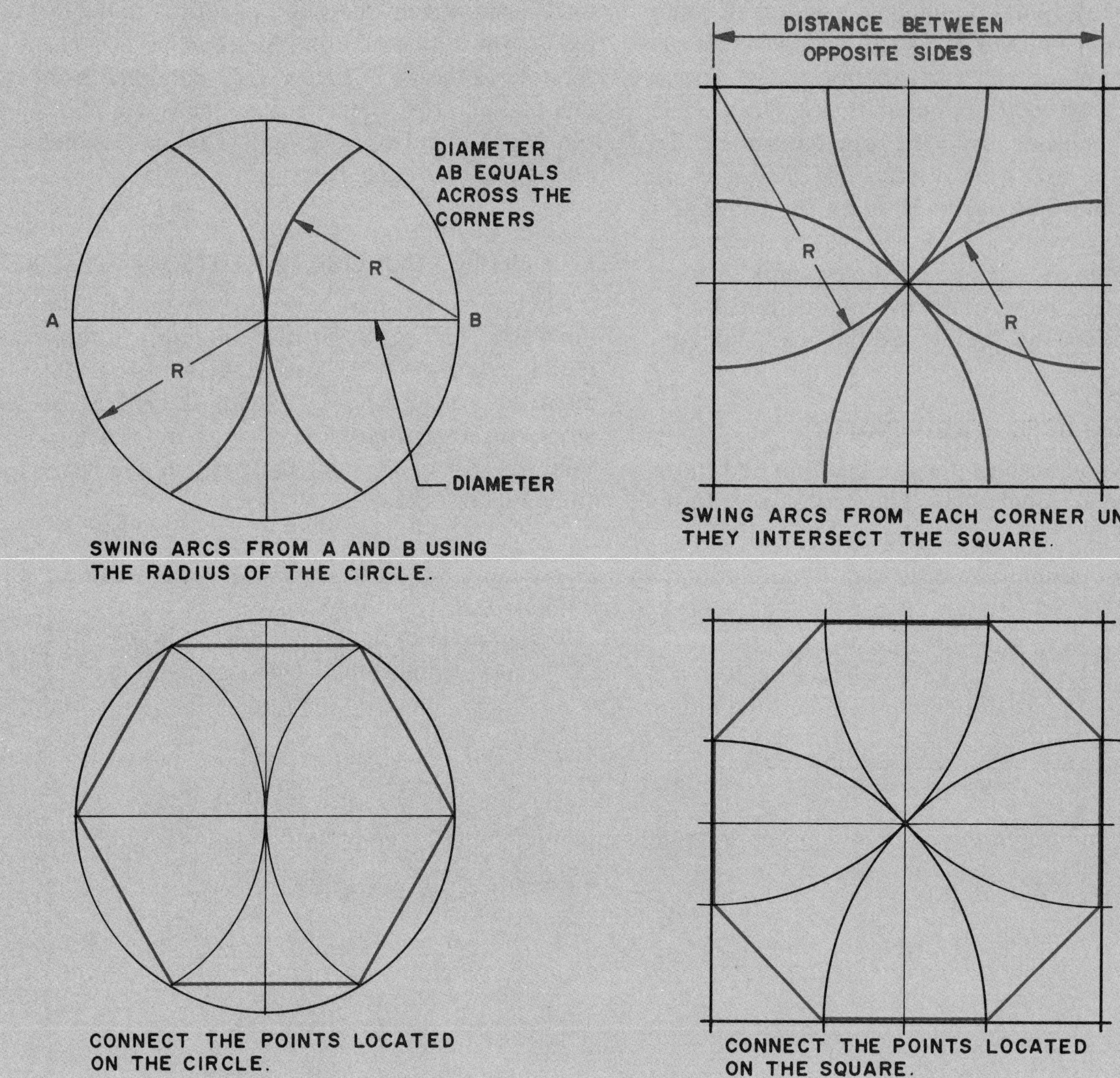
DIAMETER
AB EQUALS
ACROSS THE
CORNERS
R
A
B
R
DIAMETER
SWING ARCS FROM A AND B USING
THE RADIUS OF THE CIRCLE.
DISTANCE BETWEEN
OPPOSITE SIDES
R
R
SWING ARCS FROM EACH CORNER UNTIL
THEY INTERSECT THE SQUARE.
CONNECT THE POINTS LOCATED
ON THE CIRCLE.
CONNECT THE POINTS LOCATED
ON THE SQUARE.

Figure 7-31
Steps in laying out a hexagon.

Figure 7-32
Steps in laying out an octagon.

DRAWING A HEXAGON

A *hexagon* is a six-sided figure. Each side is the same length. To lay out a hexagon:

1. Draw a circle with a diameter equal to the distance from one corner of the hexagon to the other, Figure 7-31.
2. Swing arcs with the radius of the circle from opposite ends of the diameter.
3. Connect the points at which the arcs touch the circle.

DRAWING AN OCTAGON

An *octagon* is an eight-sided figure. Each side is the same length. To lay out an octagon:

1. Draw a square with sides equal in length to the distance across the octagon from one flat side to the other, Figure 7-32.
2. Locate the center of the square.
3. Set a compass to the distance from a corner of the square to the center. Swing an arc from each corner to intersect the sides of

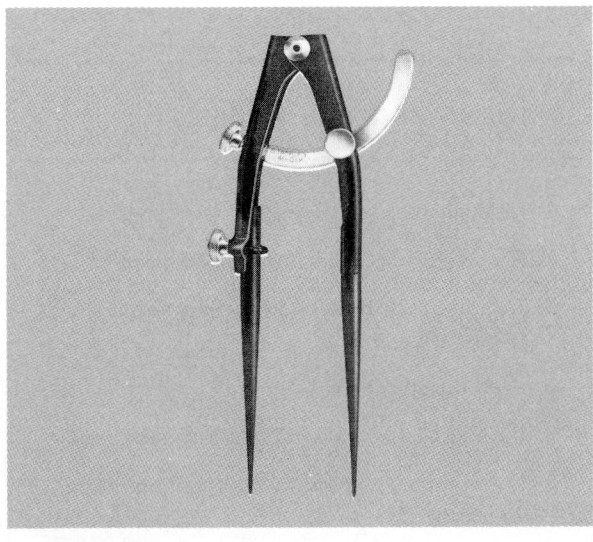

Figure 7-33
Dividers. (The Stanley Works)

the square. This locates the corners of the octagon.

4. Connect these points to form the octagon.

TRANSFERRING EQUAL DISTANCES

Dividers transfer a distance from one part to another. The divider is much like a compass but has metal points on both legs, Figure 7-33. To transfer a distance, first set the dividers on the distance to be moved. Then move the dividers to the new part and lightly push the points into the wood. This marks the desired distance, Figure 7-34.

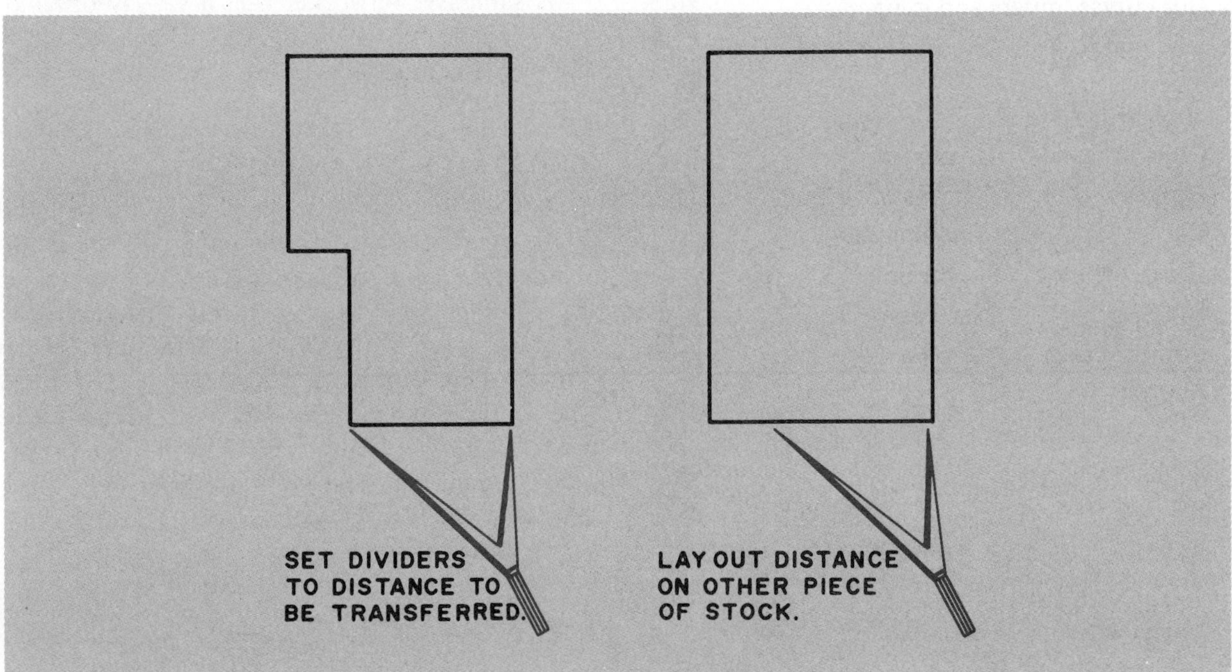
SET DIVIDERS
TO DISTANCE TO
BE TRANSFERRED.
LAY OUT DISTANCE
ON OTHER PIECE
OF STOCK.

Figure 7-34
Dividers are used to transfer distances from one part to another.

REVIEW QUESTIONS

1 What tools would you use to lay out linear distances?
2 How should you hold a rule when measuring a distance?
3 How are protractors used to lay out angles?
4 What tools are used to lay out square cuts?
5 What tools are used to lay out large and small circles and arcs?
6 How are irregular curves laid out?
7 How is the design for irregular parts enlarged or reduced?

UNIT

8

Handsaws

Objectives

After studying this unit you should be able to:

1 Identify the various types of handsaws.

2 Crosscut and rip stock.

3 Resharpen saw teeth.

4 Cut curves, miters and joints.

5 Saw metal.

Technical Terms

Crosscut saw	Backsaw
Ripsaw	Miter saw
Kerf	Dovetail saw
Crosscutting	Miter box
Ripping	Hacksaw
Compass saw	Coping saw
Keyhole saw	

HANDSAW SAFETY RULES

1 Hold all stock securely while it is being cut.

2 Keep your hands clear of the saw blade.

3 Avoid pushing heavily on the saw to force it to cut faster.

4 Keep the saw sharp.

5 Have someone help hold large or long pieces.

6 Keep the saw pointed toward the floor when you carry it.

A skilled woodworker uses a variety of handsaws. These must be used safely. The proper saw for each job must be selected carefully.

CROSSCUT SAWS AND RIPSAWS

A *crosscut saw* is designed to cut across the grain of a board. A *ripsaw* cuts with the grain. These two saws are used often. They appear to be identical, but their teeth are different. The teeth on a crosscut saw are like a series of sharp knives. This type of tooth easily slices through the wood fibers as the saw cuts across grain. Crosscut saws usually have 8 to 12 points per inch, Figure 8-1. The teeth are finer than those

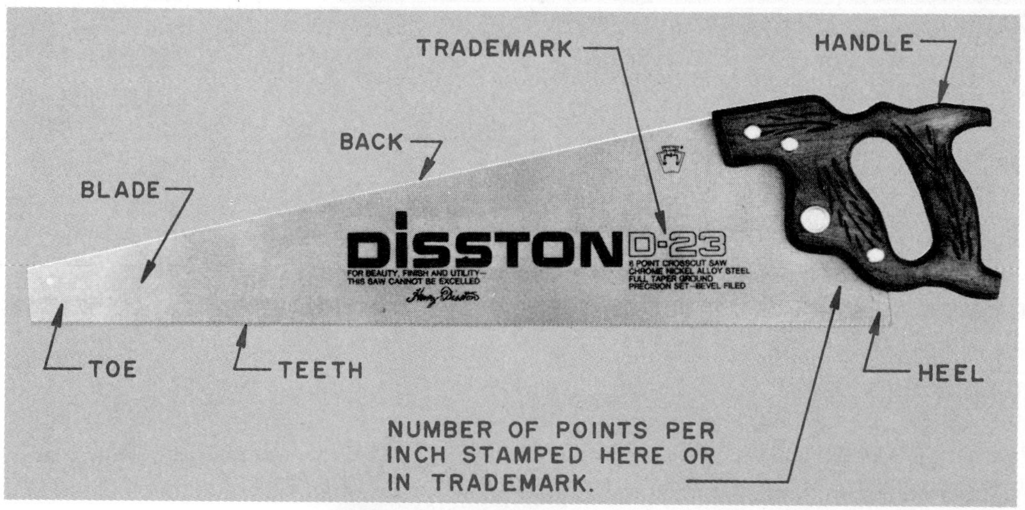

Figure 8-1
The parts of a handsaw. (Disston, Inc.)

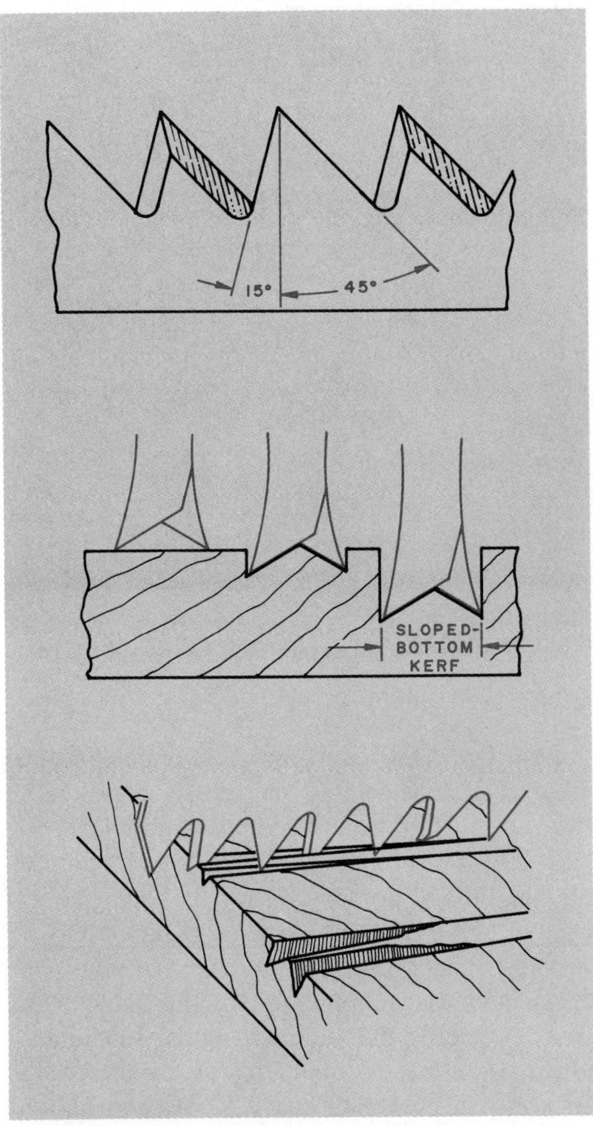

Figure 8-2
Crosscut saw teeth are like a series of sharp knives. The kerf is a groove made by the teeth of the saw.

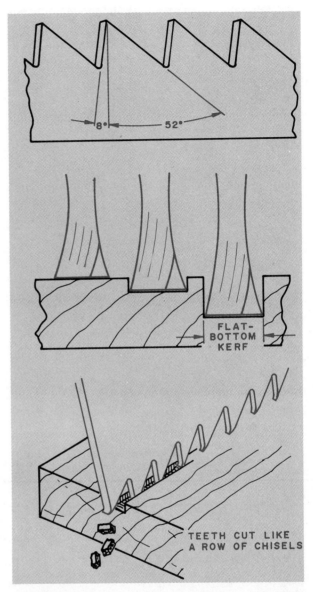

Figure 8-3
Ripsaw teeth are like a series of chisels.

on ripsaws. The teeth are set. This means that the teeth are bent alternately. One tooth is bent to the right, the next to the left. The set makes it possible for the saw to cut a *kerf* (groove) wider than the thickness of the blade, Figure 8-2. This keeps the wood from binding on the sides of the blade as it cuts.

A ripsaw usually has 5-1/2 to 8 points per inch. The teeth are like a series of chisels. They remove small chips of wood, Figure 8-3. The teeth are set.

Crosscut saws and ripsaws are usually 26″ (660 mm) long.

Crosscutting

To begin *crosscutting,* place the board on sawhorses so that it rests firmly. Use a square to draw a line across the board. If you are right-handed hold the saw in your right hand. Grasp the board in your left hand near the line. Place the teeth of the saw on the waste side of the line. Steady the blade of the saw with your left

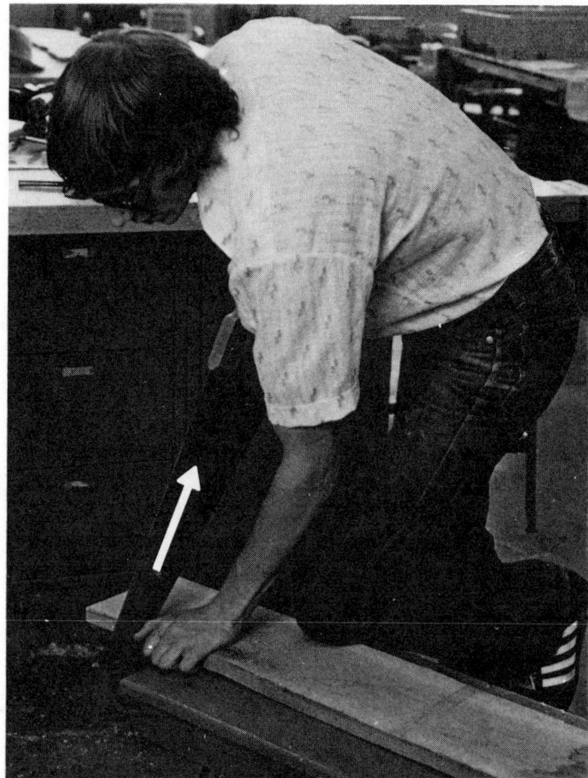

Figure 8-4
The proper position to crosscut a board.

Figure 8-5
A crosscut saw should be kept at a 45° angle to the board.

Figure 8-6
As you finish the cut, hold the end to be cut off.

thumb. Draw the saw toward your body several times, Figure 8-4. This will cut a small kerf in the board. Then, holding the saw at a 45° angle take long even strokes, pushing and pulling on the handle. Do not press down heavily. The saw will cut best with light pressure, Figure 8-5.

As you near the end of the cut, slow the stroke and use no pressure on the blade. With your left hand hold the end that is not supported, Figure 8-6. You might have someone hold it for you if it is long or heavy. If you do not hold the end, it will fall before the cut is finished, and the wood will splinter. Continue to cut with slow strokes until the cut is completed.

Ripping

Ripping is like crosscutting. It is difficult, though, to support the board while ripping it. Place the board on steady sawhorses and start cutting at one end. Hold the saw at a 60° angle to the board. If the kerf begins to bind the saw, place a wood wedge in it to hold it open, Figure 8-7. Always cut on the waste side of the line.

Sawing Plywood

A sheet of plywood has several layers. The grain of each layer alternates at right angles. Use a crosscut saw on plywood, because fibers must

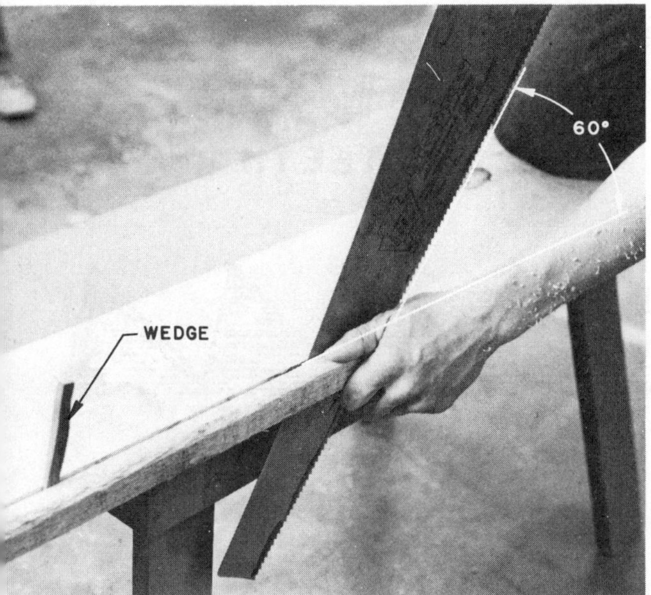

Figure 8-7
A ripsaw should be kept at a 60° angle to the board.

Figure 8-9
Always saw to the waste side of the line. (American Plywood Association)

Figure 8-8
Use extra support beneath plywood panels while they are being cut.

Figure 8-10
A saw being sharpened on a saw-filing machine.

be cut on every other layer. The crosscut saw, having a finer tooth, will give a smoother cut than the ripsaw.

Lay out the sheet of plywood to be cut. If the sheet is thin, it will tend to bow. Place several boards on sawhorses beneath the plywood sheet, Figure 8-8. Do not saw into the horses. Cut on the waste side of the line, Figure 8-9.

Sharpening a Handsaw

Handsaws usually are sharpened on a saw-filing machine driven by electricity, Figure 8-10. With the teeth up, clamp the saw blade in the machine. Adjust the angle at which the file meets

Figure 8-11
Adjusting a saw-filing machine.

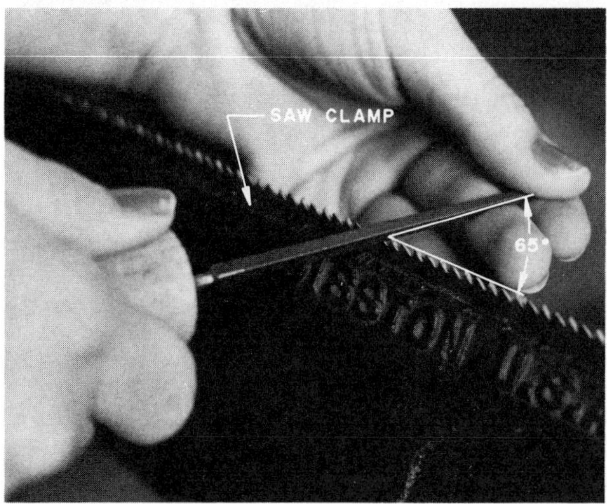

Figure 8-12
Crosscut saws are filed at an angle of 65°.

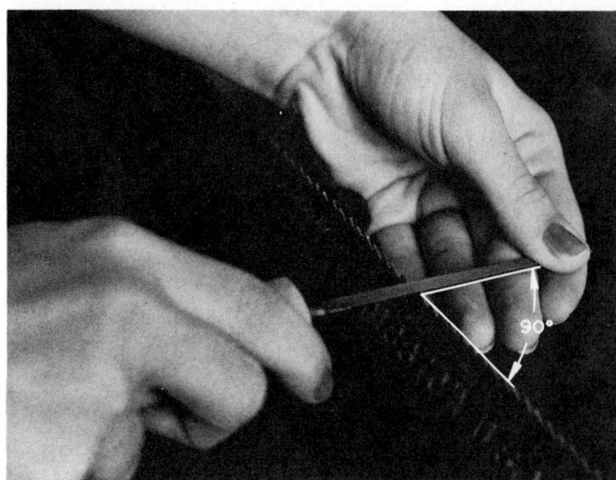

Figure 8-13
Ripsaws are filed at an angle of 90°.

Figure 8-14
This is how properly filed saw teeth should look.

the teeth. The machine then will automatically file alternate teeth, Figure 8-11.

You can also sharpen saws by hand. Hand-sharpening is difficult but is useful for a quick touch-up of the teeth.

1. Clamp the saw into a saw clamp or vise.
2. Hold the saw file in both hands. Place the file at the proper angle to the blade. For a crosscut saw, the angle is 65°, Figure 8-12. For a ripsaw it is 90°, Figure 8-13. Slant the file 10° to 15° below the horizontal.
3. Start filing from the toe of the saw. File toward the heel.
4. File with an even pressure. Give each tooth the same number of strokes. Raise the file from the tooth after each stroke.
5. File every other tooth this way. The alternate teeth have their cutting edges facing the other side of the saw, Figure 8-14. Turn the saw around and file the alternate teeth.
6. Set the teeth. Place the saw in the clamp. Adjust the saw set to bend each tooth the amount desired. Place the saw set on the first tooth at the toe. Bend it, Figure 8-15. Repeat this for every other tooth. Remove the saw from the clamp and turn it around. Set the other row of teeth.

COMPASS SAWS AND KEYHOLE SAWS

The *compass* and *keyhole saws* are much alike. The keyhole saw is smaller than the compass saw, Figure 8-16. Each saw has a tapered

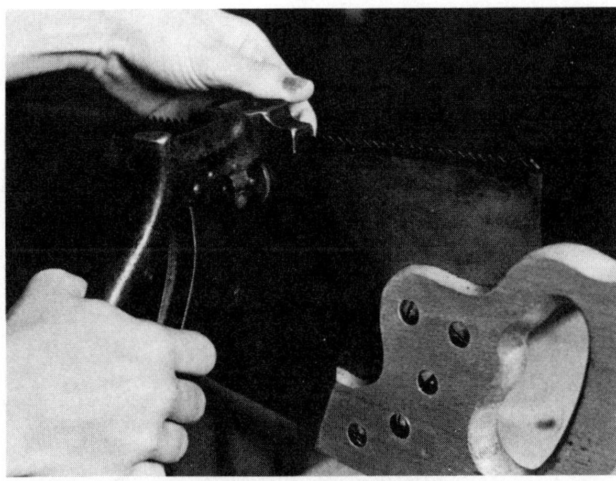

Figure 8-15
Alternate teeth are set by using a saw-setting tool.

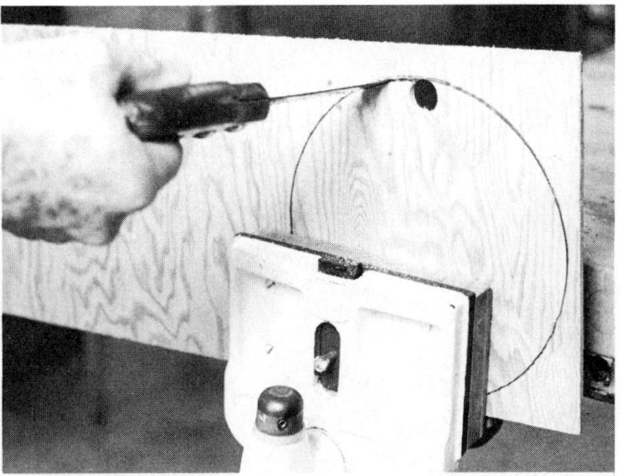

Figure 8-17
Compass and keyhole saws are used to saw internal curved edges.

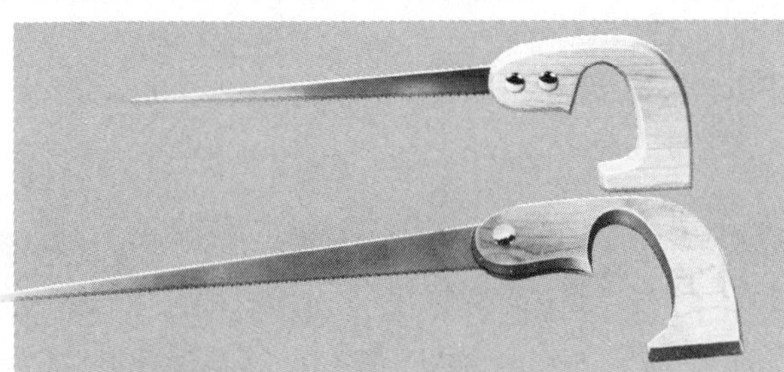

Figure 8-16
A keyhole saw is smaller than a compass saw. (Disston, Inc.)

blade. It ends in a point. This enables it to get into small places. The teeth of these saws are similar to those of a ripsaw.

A typical job is cutting a hole in the center of a piece of material. First bore a hole through the material. Then slide the tapered blade into the hole and make the cut, Figure 8-17.

BACKSAWS, MITER SAWS AND DOVETAIL SAWS

These saws are alike but differ in size, Figure 8-18. They have a thin metal blade with a strong

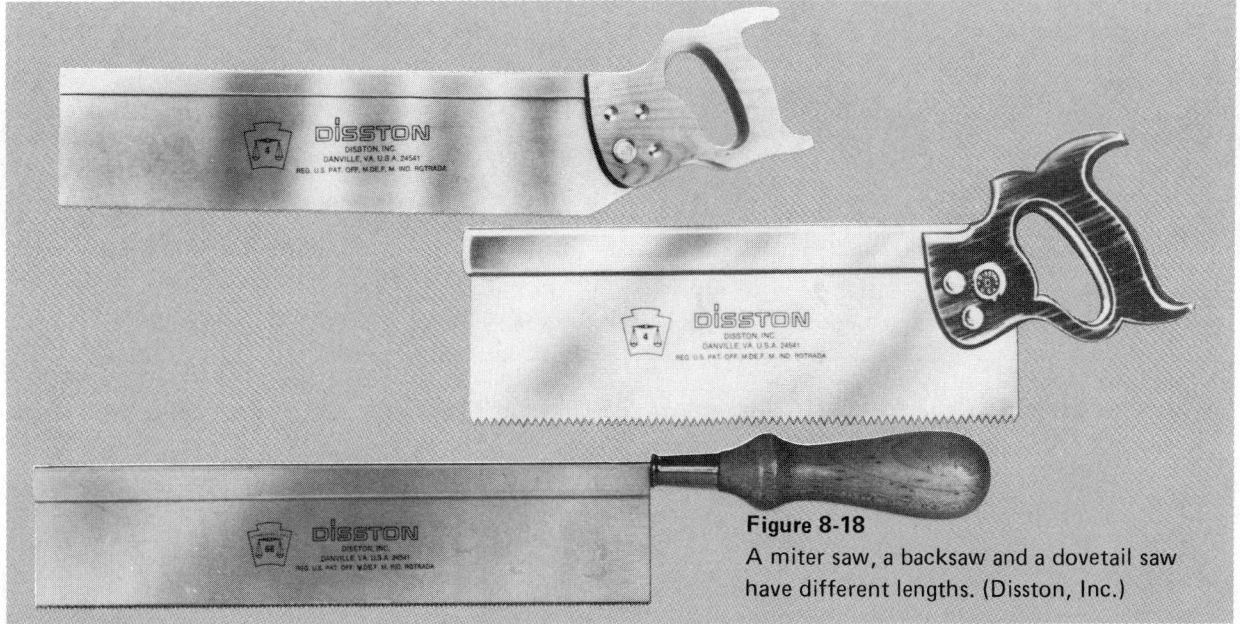

Figure 8-18
A miter saw, a backsaw and a dovetail saw have different lengths. (Disston, Inc.)

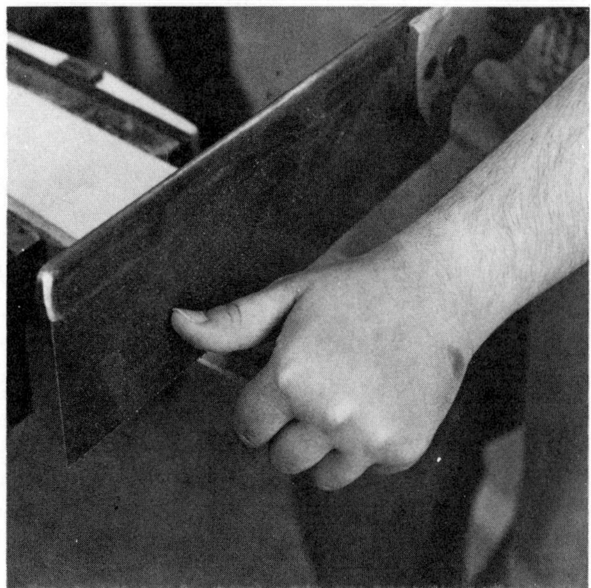

Figure 8-19
How to hold a backsaw when starting a cut.

Figure 8-21
A block of wood can serve as a guide to produce square cuts.

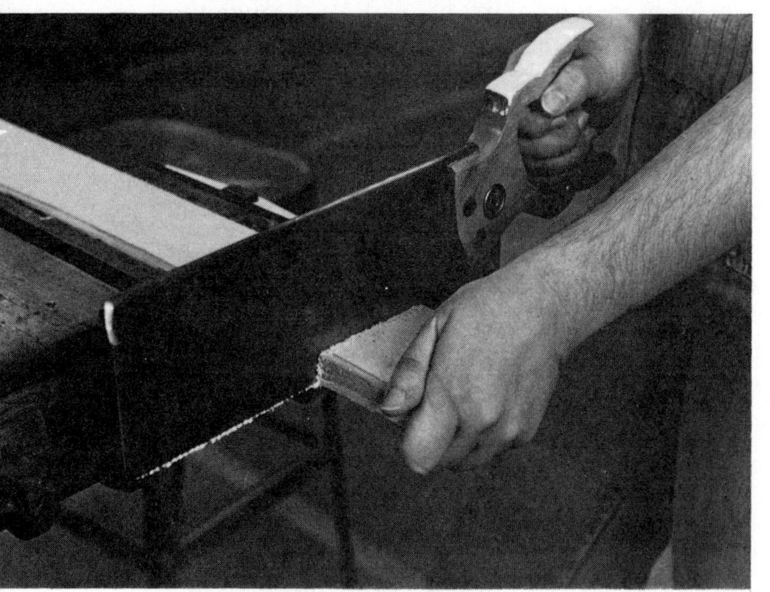

Figure 8-20
A backsaw is held in a horizontal position.

Figure 8-22
A miter box.

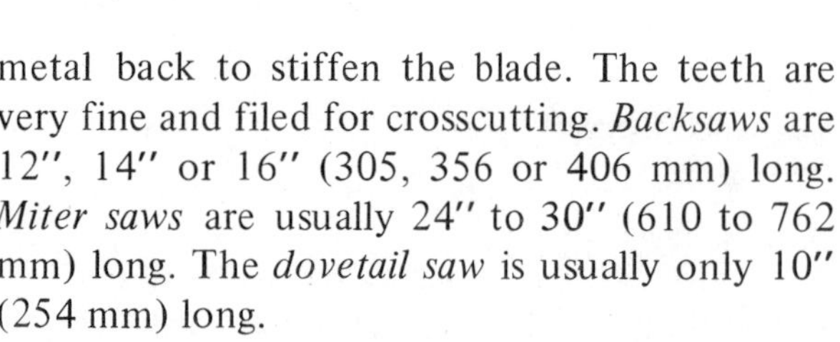

metal back to stiffen the blade. The teeth are very fine and filed for crosscutting. *Backsaws* are 12″, 14″ or 16″ (305, 356 or 406 mm) long. *Miter saws* are usually 24″ to 30″ (610 to 762 mm) long. The *dovetail saw* is usually only 10″ (254 mm) long.

These saws are made for fine, accurate cutting. Use the backsaw and the dovetail saw to hand-cut wood joints. Mark the wood and make the cut on the waste side of the line. Place the saw on the wood and pull it back a few times, Figure 8-19. Then push the saw back and forth in a nearly horizontal position, Figure 8-20. If you have difficulty getting a square cut, clamp a

Figure 8-23
A miter saw cuts in a horizontal position.

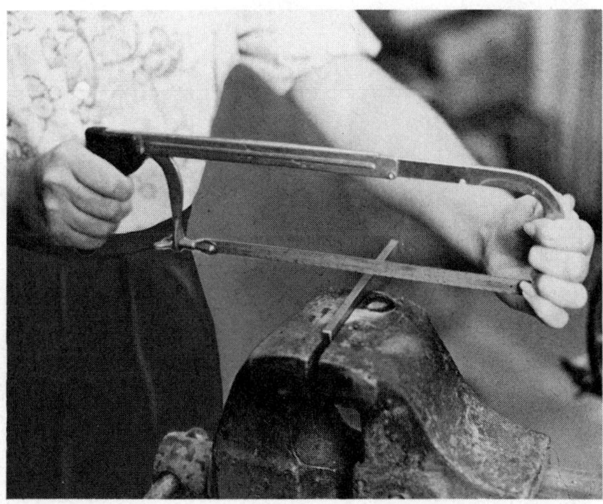

Figure 8-25
A hacksaw cuts in a horizontal position.

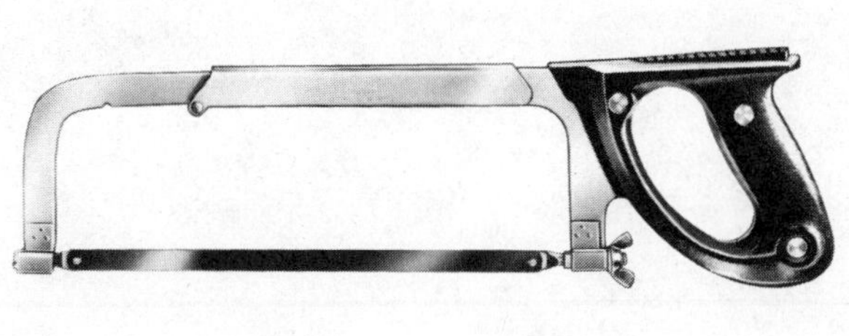

Figure 8-24
A hacksaw. (Disston, Inc.)

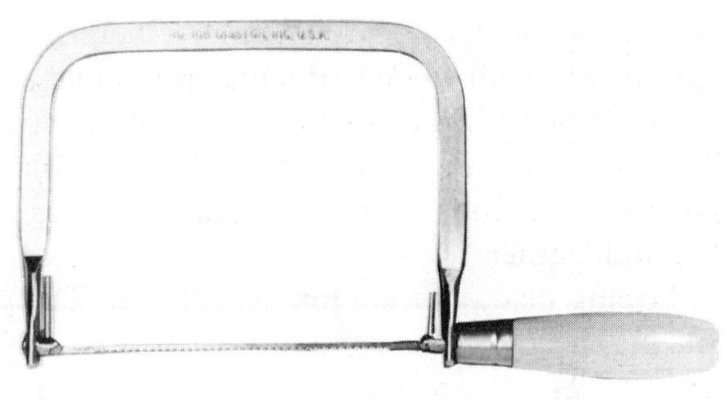

Figure 8-26
A coping saw. (Disston, Inc.)

block of wood along the line to use as a guide, Figure 8-21.

The miter saw is used in a *miter box,* Figure 8-22. The box holds the saw perpendicular to the table. The saw moves right and left to cut various angles, Figure 8-23.

THE HACKSAW

The *hacksaw* cuts metal. It has a metal frame and handle. The blades are removable, Figure 8-24. A variety of blades is available. Blades with fine teeth are used on thin metal. Those with larger teeth are used on thicker metal. The saw is used in the same way as the backsaw. It should be moved slowly at about 40 strokes per minute. A faster movement would produce heat and wear the blade, Figure 8-25.

THE COPING SAW

The *coping saw* is used to cut scrollwork in thin material. It has a U-shaped frame with a thin blade held between the ends of the frame by tension, Figure 8-26. Blades are usually 6-1/2" (165 mm) long. They are available in many

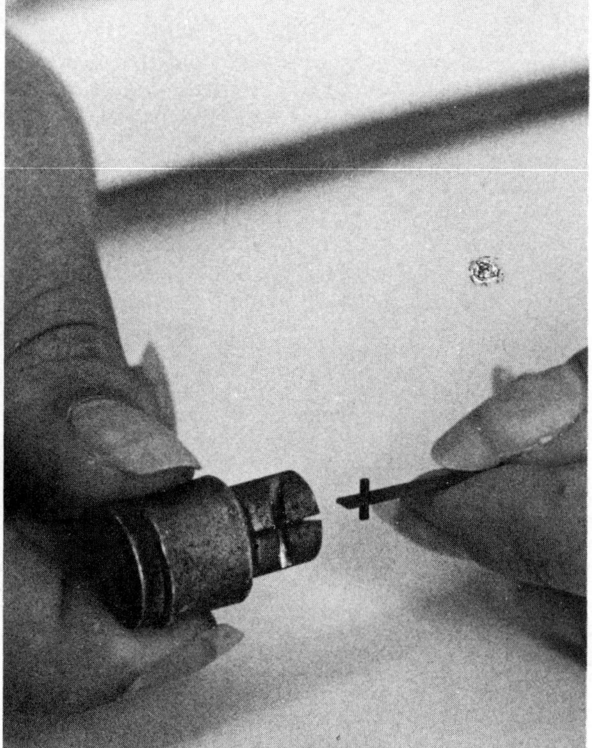

Figure 8-27
The pin ends of a coping saw blade fit into notches in the end of the saw frame.

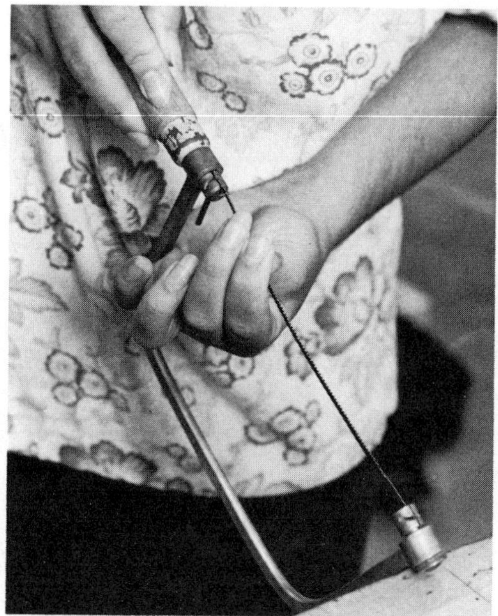

Figure 8-28
To insert a coping saw blade, press the ends of the frame together. Slip the pin end of the blade into the notches on the end of the saw frame.

thicknesses and have 15 teeth per inch. Blades for cutting both wood and metal are available. A Spyral® blade has teeth that look like a thread. The blade cuts in any direction. Spyral® blades cut materials such as wood, metal, plastics, rubber and leather.

Coping blades have a pin in each end. The pin fits into a slot on each end of the saw frame, Figure 8-27. To insert a blade, place one end in the slot. Place the frame against the workbench. Push the frame together to enable the other pin to go into its slot, Figure 8-28.

You can place work to be sawed vertically in a vise. When the work is mounted vertically, the saw teeth should point *away* from the handle. The saw will then cut on the push stroke. Make internal cuts by boring a hole through the waste portion of the wood. Remove the blade from the frame. Place the blade through the hole and put it back in the frame. Then cut as usual, Figure 8-29.

You also can saw work in a horizontal position. The edge to be cut must overhang the edge of the bench, Figure 8-30. When sawing work held horizontally, point the teeth of the saw *toward* the handle. A sawing jig can be built to help in horizontal cutting, Figure 8-31. Clamp the jig in a vise. Place the work on it and saw in the V slot, Figure 8-32.

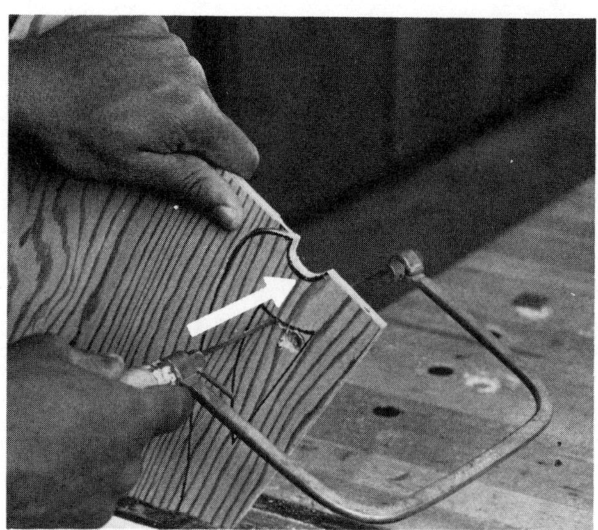

Figure 8-29
When work is held in a vertical position, the teeth should point away from the handle.

To start, make a few light cuts to get the blade into the wood. Then use full, steady strokes to guide the blade along the line. Keep the blade perpendicular to the work. Do not force the blade to cut. If it gets too hot, the blade will break. Keep the work positioned so that the part being cut is near the vise or saw bracket. This steadies the work. Sawing is easier, and there is less vibration. Move the work around as needed to reach the area being sawed.

Figure 8-30
When work is held in a horizontal position, the teeth should point toward the handle.

Figure 8-31
A shop-built jig for horizontal sawing with a coping saw.

Figure 8-32
Using the jig to support the work.

REVIEW QUESTIONS

1. What is the difference between a ripsaw and a crosscut saw?
2. How does a backsaw differ from a keyhole saw?
3. What is the first step in cutting into a board with a crosscut saw?
4. What is the primary use for a hacksaw?
5. How should sheets of plywood be supported to be cut to size?
6. What file angles are used to sharpen crosscut and ripsaws?
7. How is a new blade placed in a coping saw frame?

SUGGESTED ACTIVITIES

1. Prepare a wall chart illustrating the various types of saws. Explain the purpose of each.
2. Bring an old saw from home and practice sharpening it by lightly touching up the teeth.
3. Prepare a list of possible uses for each type of saw. Include as many different kinds of jobs as possible.
4. Using scrap stock, practice crosscutting and ripping. Try to make straight, square cuts.

UNIT

9

Hand Planes and Scrapers

Objectives

After studying this unit you should be able to:

1. Identify various kinds of hand planes.
2. Take apart and reassemble planes.
3. Smooth stock with a hand plane.
4. Check stock for squareness.
5. Plane chamfers, bevels and tapers.
6. Cut rabbets, dados and grooves.
7. Smooth a surface with a hand scraper.

Technical Terms

Smooth plane	Block plane
Jointer plane	Trimming plane
Fore plane	Bullnose rabbet plane
Jack plane	Rabbet
Plane iron	Rabbet plane
Frog	Router plane
Lever cap	Dado
Cap iron	Spokeshave
Chamfer	Cabinet scraper
Bevel	Hand scraper
Taper	

HAND PLANES AND SCRAPERS SAFETY RULES

1. Before planing, clamp the stock firmly to the workbench.
2. Keep both hands behind the cutting edge.
3. Keep the plane iron sharp.
4. Do not try to take too deep a cut.
5. Be very cautious of the sharp corners on the hand scraper.
6. Be sure the screwdriver does not slip when tightening or loosening the iron-cap screw.

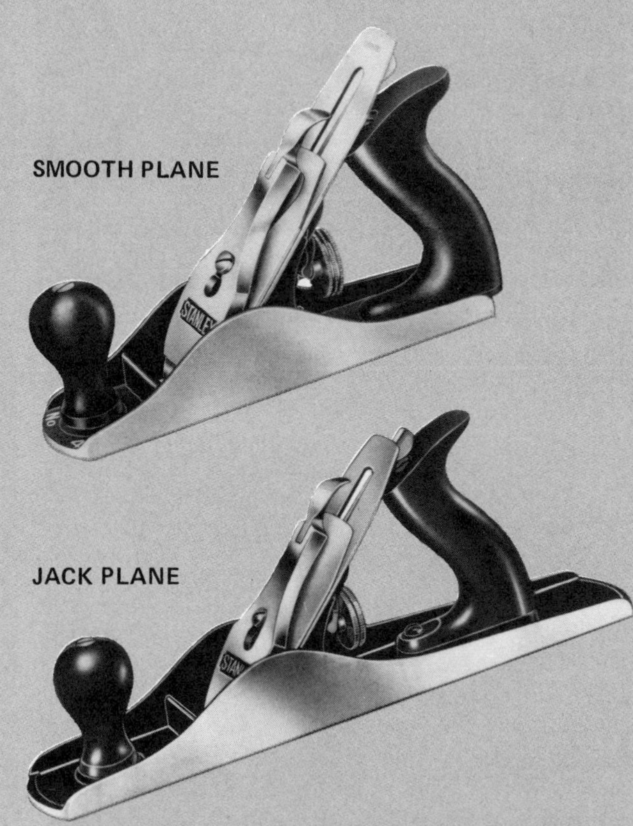

Figure 9-1
Smooth planes are usually 7″ to 9″ (178 to 229 mm) long. Jack planes are usually 14″ to 15″ (356 to 381 mm) long. (The Stanley Works)

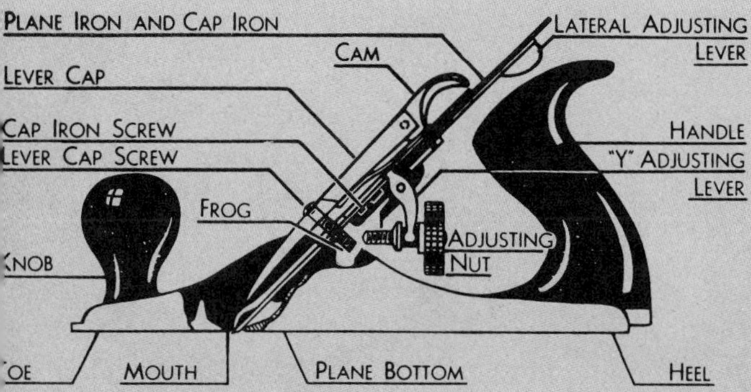

Figure 9-2
Parts of a hand plane. (The Stanley Works)

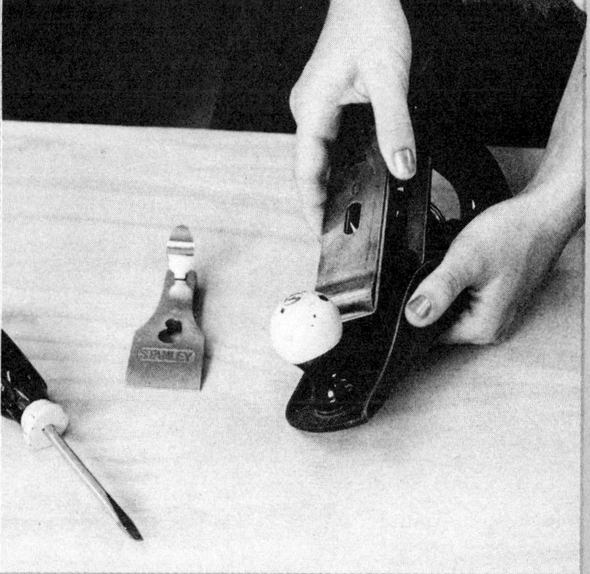

Figure 9-3
To clean the plane, remove the cap iron and the plane iron.

You often will need to plane the surface of a board. An edge may need to be squared or cut on an angle. A hand plane is the tool you need for these operations.

SMOOTH, JOINTER, FORE AND JACK PLANES

There are several types of planes. They are almost identical in appearance. The major difference is their length. The *smooth plane* is used for most general work, Figure 9-1. The *jointer plane, fore plane* and *jack plane* (Figure 9-1) are longer than the smooth plane. These longer planes are used for smoothing longer boards.

The plane uses a cutting action. The *plane iron* is the part of the tool that does the cutting. Adjust the depth of cut by turning the adjusting nut, Figure 9-2. The plane iron is held on the *frog* by the *lever cap.* The bevel on the plane iron faces down.

To operate a plane properly, make sure it is cleaned and sharpened regularly. To disassemble the plane, lift the cam and remove the lever cap. Then lift out the plane and *cap iron,* Figure 9-3. The cap iron is fastened to the plane with a bolt. Loosen the bolt with a screwdriver and swing the two pieces apart. Remove chips that have collected between the cap iron and the plane iron. Sharpen the plane iron.

To reassemble, slide the cap iron and plane iron together, Figure 9-4. The beveled edge of the plane iron faces away from the cap iron. Set

Figure 9-4
To reassemble, lay the cap iron across the plane iron, *top left.* Place the cap screw in the slot, swing the cap iron parallel with the plane iron and move it to within 1/16" of the cutting edge, *top right.* Tighten the cap screw, *bottom.*

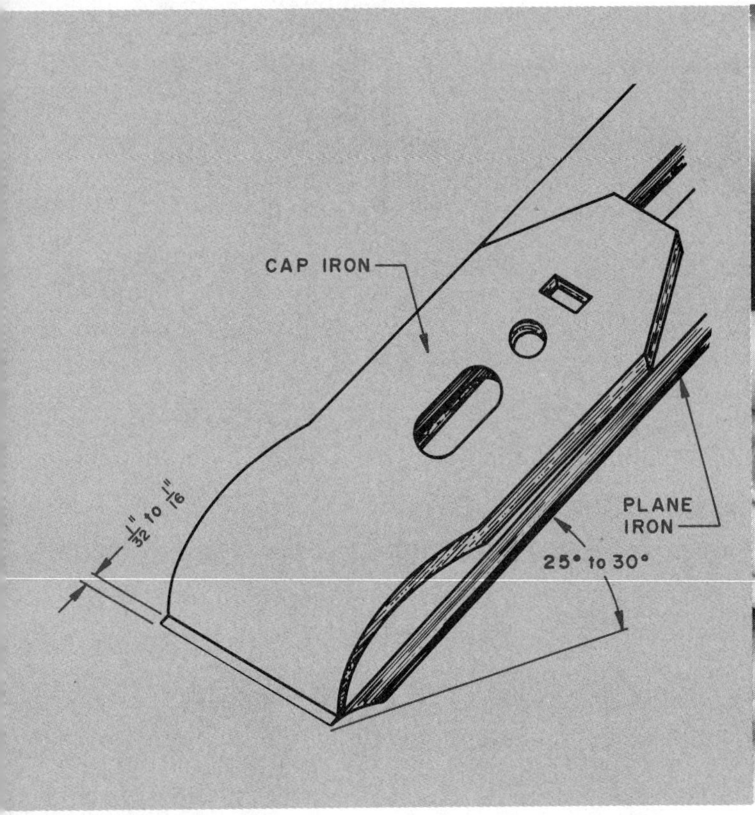

Figure 9-5
Adjust the cap iron so it is 1/32″ to 1/16″ (1 to 2 mm) from the cutting edge of the plane iron.

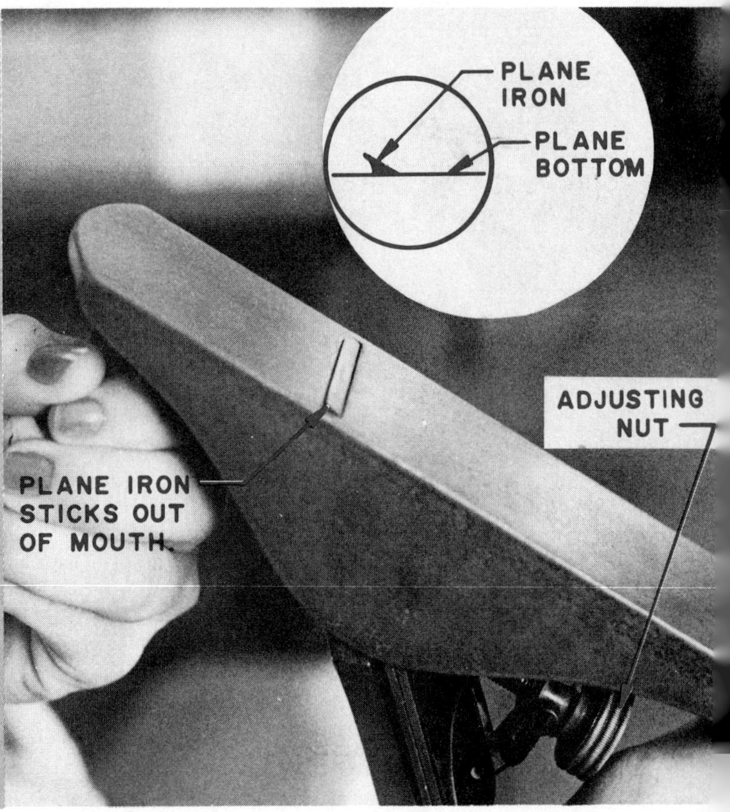

Figure 9-6
How far the plane iron extends from the mouth determines the depth of cut.

the cap iron about 1/16″ (2 mm) above the cutting edge of the plane iron, Figure 9-5. Tighten the screw holding them together. Now replace them on the frog. Place the screw on the cap iron into the hole in the frog. Replace the lever cap and close the cam. Be sure the cap iron fits tightly on the plane iron.

Two more adjustments must be made before the plane is ready for use. First, set the depth of cut by moving the adjusting nut, Figure 9-6. Try a very shallow cut at first. Set the cut deeper if needed. Never start with a deep cut. Second, adjust the plane iron laterally. The plane iron sticks out of the mouth in the bottom of the plane. Be sure the cutting edge is parallel with the edge of the mouth. If it is not, move the lateral-adjusting lever right or left until the cutting edge is parallel, Figure 9-7.

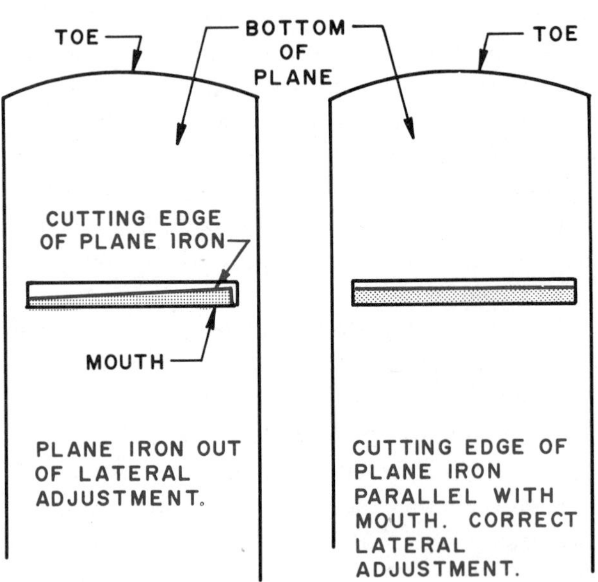

Figure 9-7
The cutting edge of the plane iron must be parallel with the front edge of the mouth.

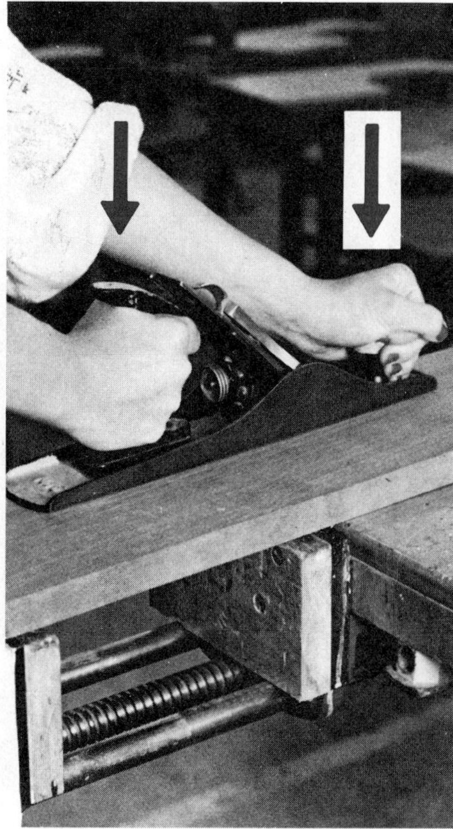
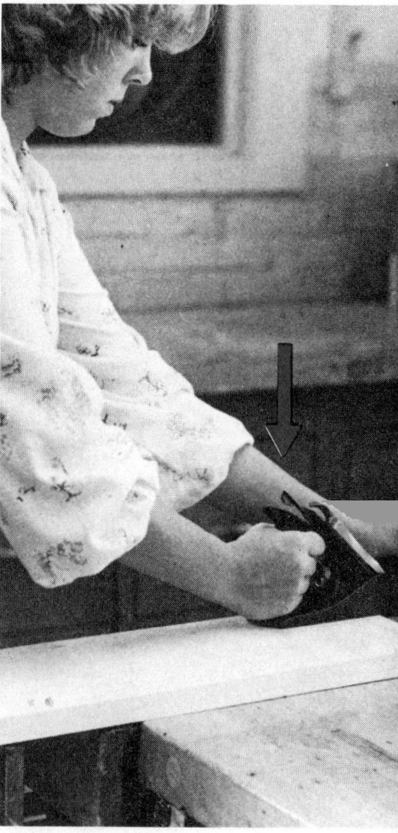

Figure 9-8
To plane a board, apply pressure on the knob, *left*; apply equal pressure on the handle and knob, *center.* Then apply pressure on the handle, *right.*

USING A PLANE

The following are some suggestions for using the plane:

1. Tightly clamp the board to be planed to the work table.
2. Adjust the depth of cut. Check the lateral adjustment.
3. If you are right-handed, hold the handle in your right hand. Hold the knob in the left hand. Place the toe of the plane on the edge of the board. Press on the knob and start to push the plane across the board, Figure 9-8.
4. As the plane goes across the board, place equal pressure on both the knob and the handle.
5. As the plane finishes its stroke, put more pressure on the handle and less on the knob.
6. Always plane with the grain. The direction of the grain usually can be found by examining the board. The grain rings point in the direction of the grain, Figure 9-9. If the grain is not clear, take a light cut. If the wood chips or becomes rough, change the direction of your cut.

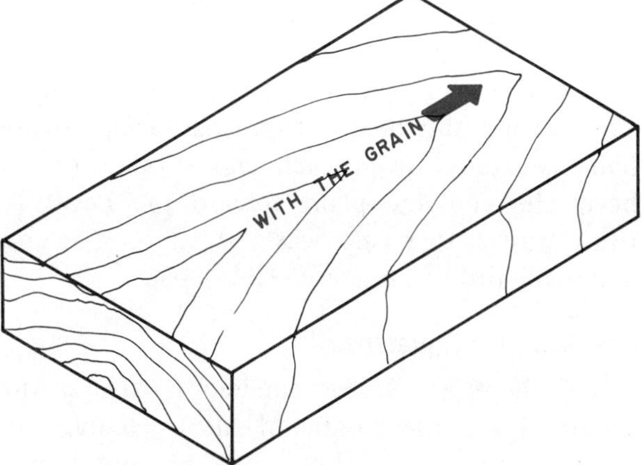

Figure 9-9
The grain rings point in the "with the grain" direction.

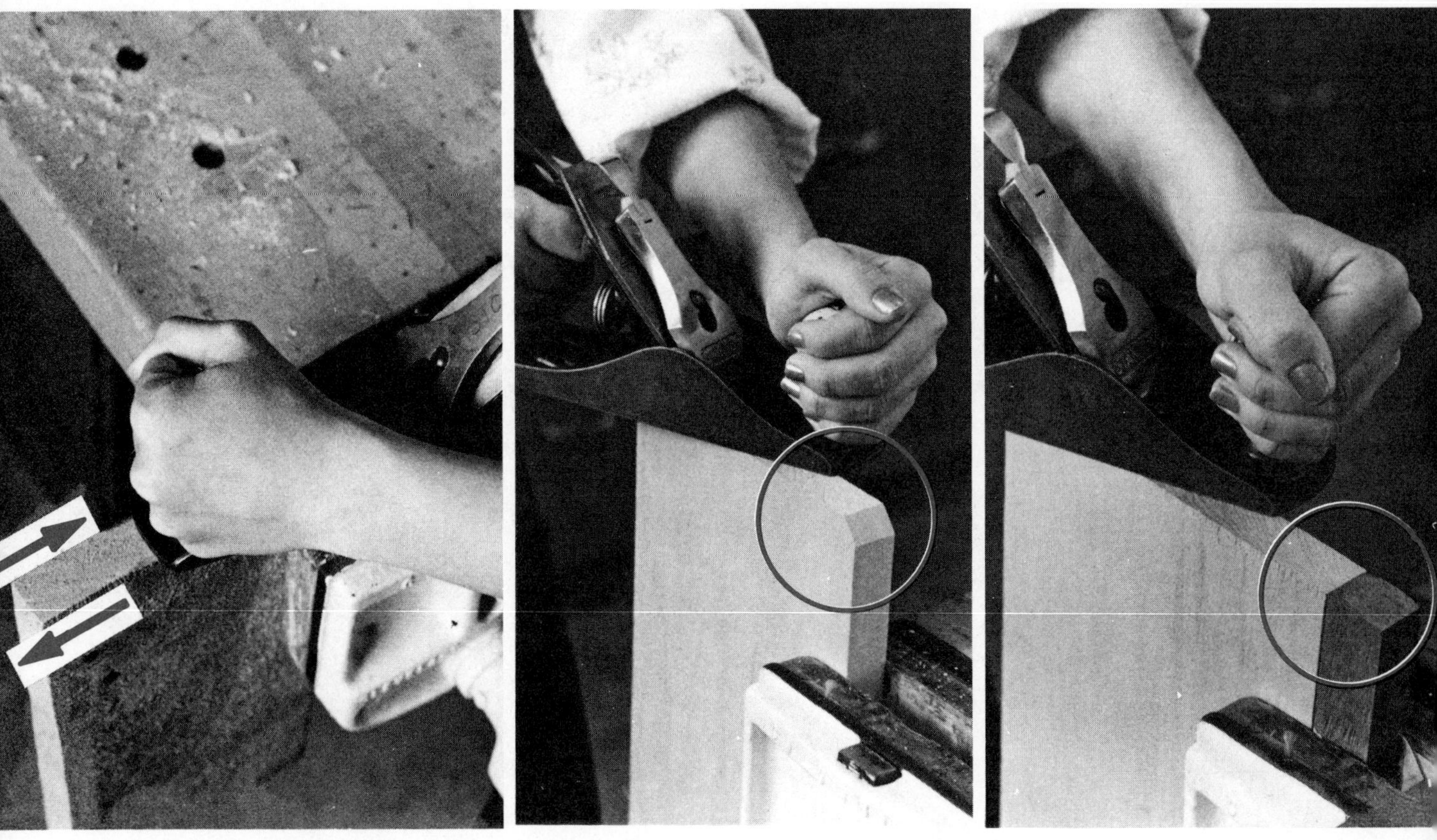

Figure 9-10
To plane end grain, plane halfway across from each side, *left*; bevel the end, *center*; or back up the edge with waste stock, *right*.

If you are careful, you can plane end grain. To prevent the board from splintering, plane halfway across from each end. You also can bevel the end and plane toward the bevel. A third way is to clamp waste stock on the end and plane onto it, Figure 9-10.

Checking for Squareness

To check stock for squareness, use a try square. Place the handle of the try square on the face of the board. Lower the try square until the blade touches the edge. By looking toward the light, you can tell whether the blade touches the edge squarely. If light shows, the other edge is high, Figure 9-11. Check the length of the edge for straightness by placing the blade of the try square on it, Figure 9-12.

Check the surface with the blade. Hold the board toward the light and place the blade firmly across it. Light will show through at low spots, Figure 9-13. Mark low spots with a pencil. Plane away wood surrounding the low spots. For larger boards, use a framing square or a straightedge that is as long as the board being checked.

Planing Chamfers, Bevels and Tapers

A *chamfer* is a slanted surface cut part-way down an edge. It usually forms a 45° angle. A *bevel* is a sloping edge that runs from one surface to the other. A *taper* is a gradual reducing of the width of a board from one end to the other. These cuts are shown in Figure 9-14.

To plane a chamfer, lay out the starting and stopping points of the slant. If it is a 45° chamfer, the line on the top and the line on the edge will be the same distance from the corner, Figure 9-15. Clamp the board firmly in a vise. Plane until the chamfered surface reaches the lines,

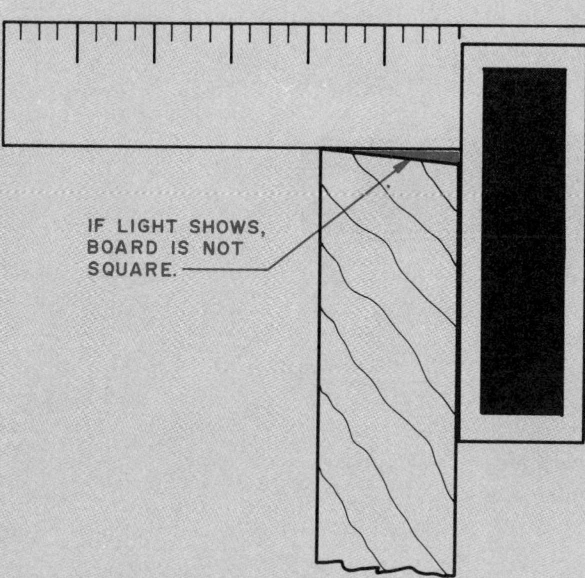
IF LIGHT SHOWS,
BOARD IS NOT
SQUARE.

Figure 9-11
Checking an edge for squareness. Look for light between the try square and the board. Light will show through in low places.

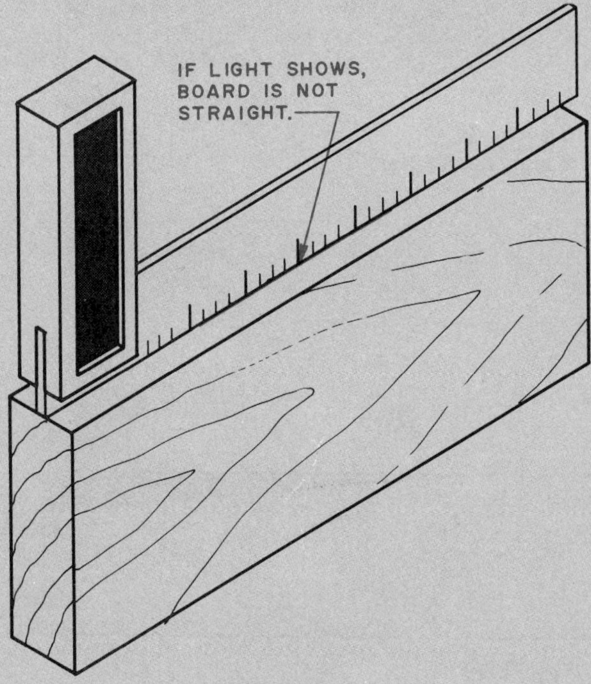
IF LIGHT SHOWS,
BOARD IS NOT
STRAIGHT.

Figure 9-12
Checking the length of an edge for straightness.

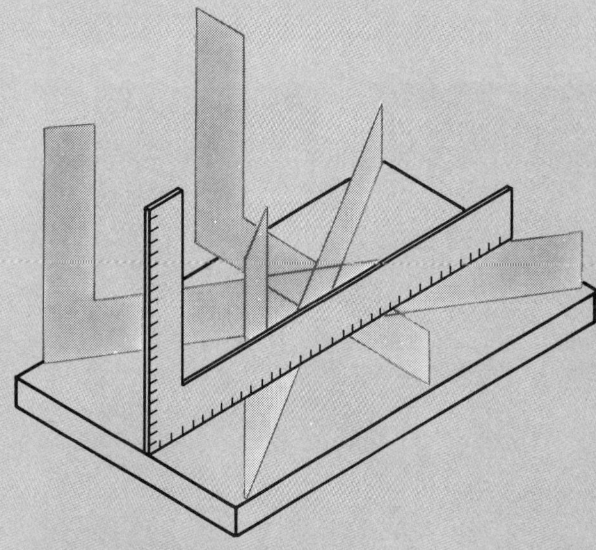

Figure 9-13
Use a try square or a framing square to check the surface for evenness. Check across diagonals as well as from side to side.

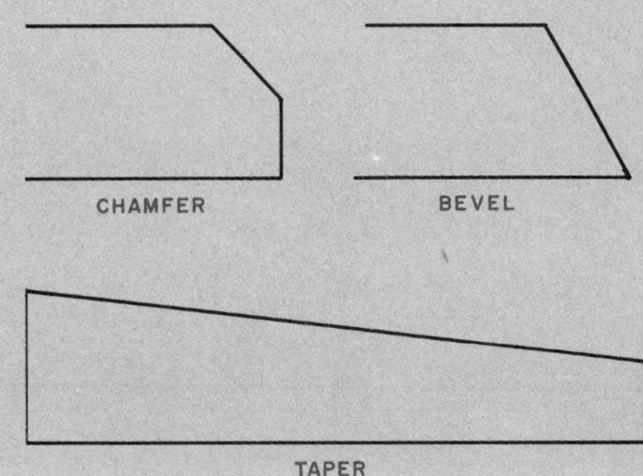
CHAMFER
BEVEL
TAPER

Figure 9-14
A chamfer, bevel and taper.

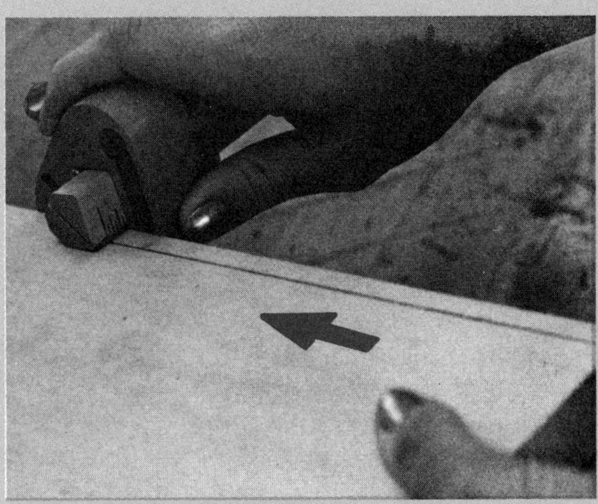

Figure 9-15
Use a marking gauge to lay out a chamfer.

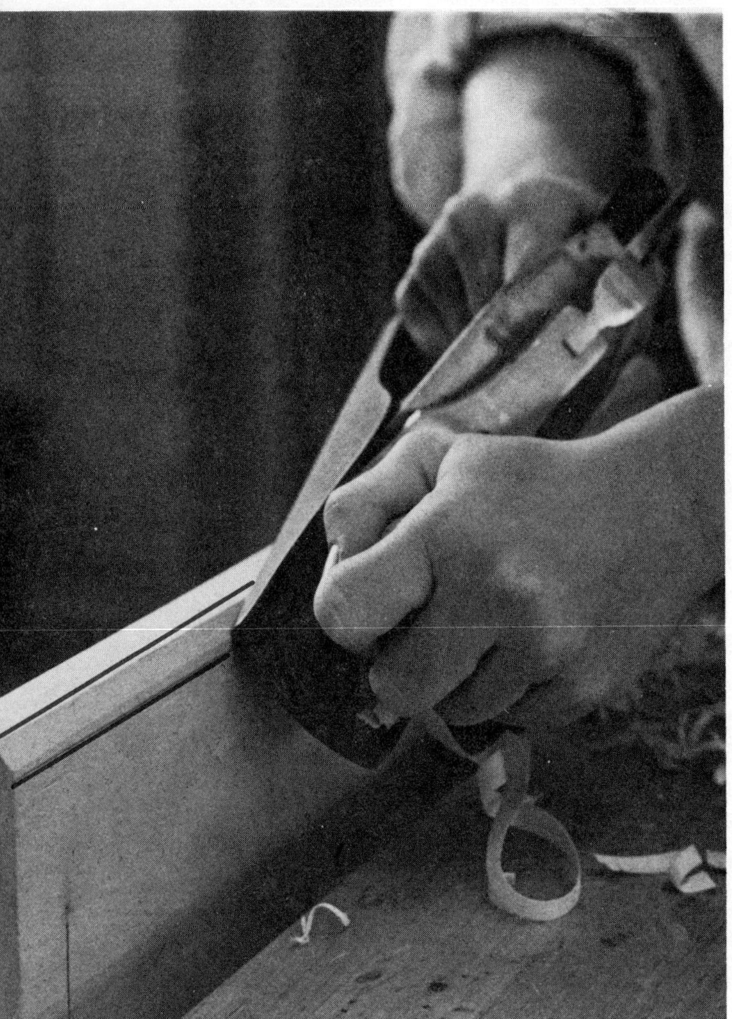

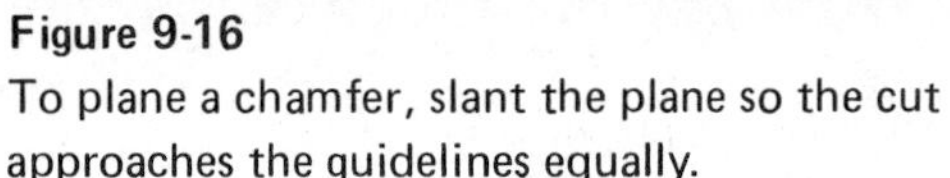

Figure 9-16
To plane a chamfer, slant the plane so the cut approaches the guidelines equally.

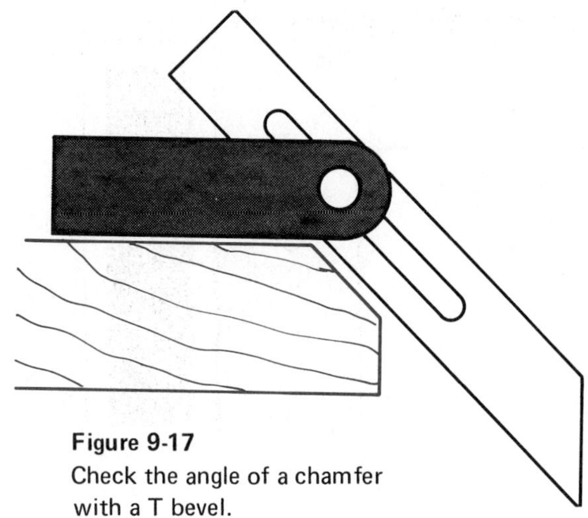

Figure 9-17
Check the angle of a chamfer with a T bevel.

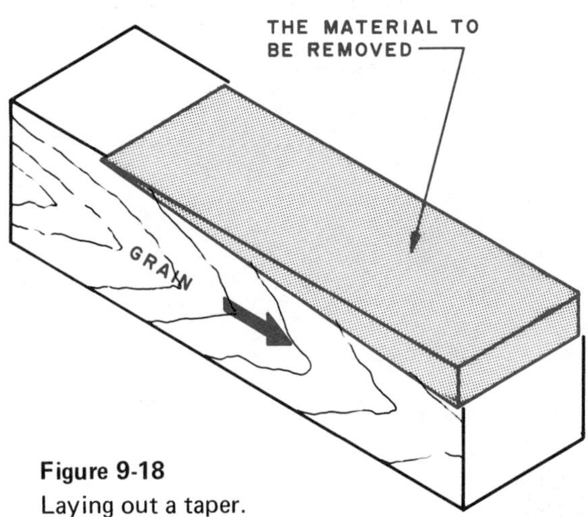

Figure 9-18
Laying out a taper.

Figure 9-16. Check the chamfer with a T bevel, Figure 9-17. Check the length for straightness with a framing square.

You can plane a bevel the same way as a chamfer. Only one edge, however, needs to be marked.

To plane a taper, mark its limits on the stock, Figure 9-18. Be certain the direction of the grain points toward the small end of the taper. If you are making several pieces with the same taper, clamp them together and plane them all at once. Plane toward the small end. Begin the first cuts near the end. Increase the length of the cuts as the taper develops, Figure 9-19. Check the surface for squareness with a try square.

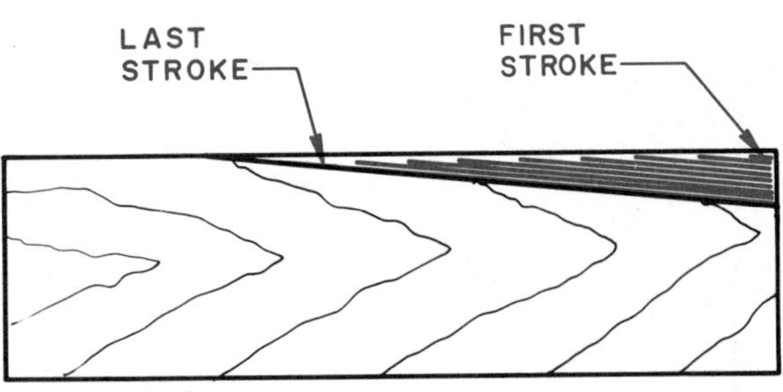

Figure 9-19
To plane a taper, begin at the smaller end. Increase the length of each stroke.

BLOCK PLANE

Use the *block plane,* Figure 9-20, to plane end grain. The angle of the block plane iron is lower than the angle of the smooth plane iron. The bevel on the plane iron of a block plane faces up, allowing it to cut fibers in end grain. It has no cap iron.

Hold the block plane in one hand. Rest your forefinger on the finger knob. Apply uniform pressure to the knob as the plane crosses the board, Figure 9-21.

Control the depth of cut by turning the adjusting nut. The lever cap holds the plane iron in place. You can remove the lever cap and plane iron by loosening the cam, Figure 9-20.

A *trimming plane* is a type of block plane. It is about 3″ (76 mm) in length. Hold the trimming plane in one hand by gripping the sides. You can use this plane for light modeling, sculpture and light finishing work, Figure 9-22.

Figure 9-21
Planing end grain with a block plane.

BULLNOSE RABBET AND RABBET PLANES

The *bullnose rabbet plane* is similar to the block plane, Figure 9-23. Because the cutting edge is near the front and sides of the bed, it can plane close to surfaces that meet at 90° angles.

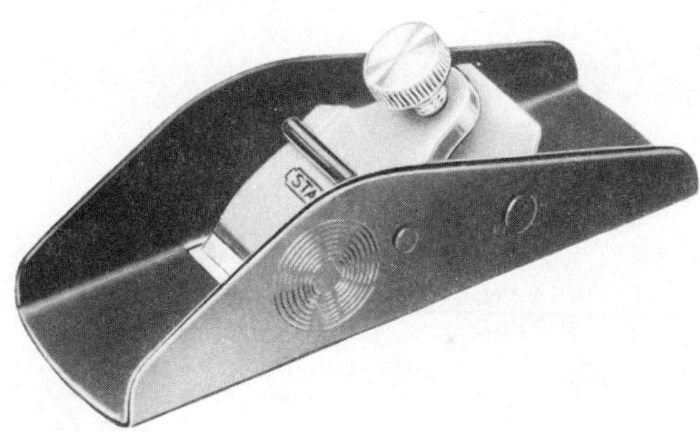

Figure 9-22
A trimming plane. (The Stanley Works)

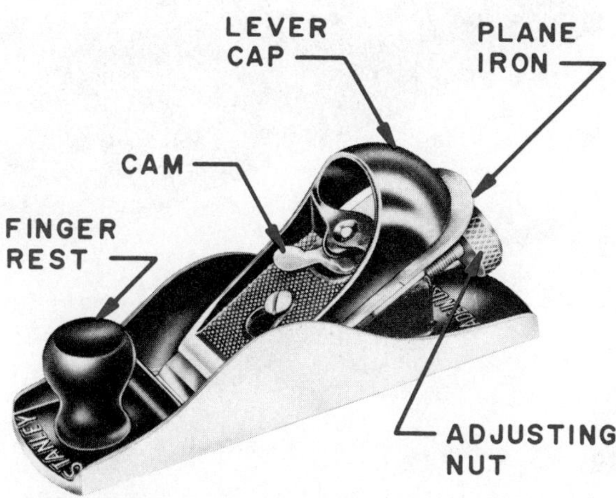

Figure 9-20
A block plane. (The Stanley Works)

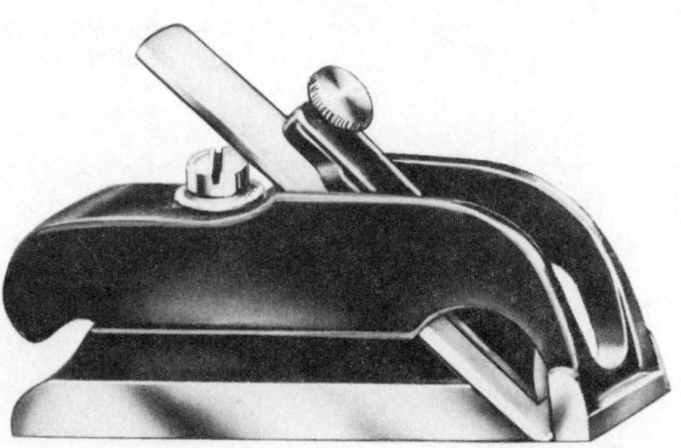

Figure 9-23
A bullnose rabbet plane. (The Stanley Works)

These L-shaped cuts on the edges of boards are called *rabbets,* Figure 9-24.

The *rabbet plane* is like the bullnose rabbet plane, but is larger, Figure 9-25. Its plane iron has two possible positions. One is near the front for bullnose work. The other is near the center of the plane for regular work. The rabbet plane is used to cut rabbets along the grain, Figure 9-26.

ROUTER PLANE

A *router plane* has a wide, flat bed and two handles, Figure 9-27. The cutter is a round bar with a flattened end much like a plane iron. Use a router plane to smooth the bottoms of *dadoes* (rectangular grooves cut across the grain) and other recessed areas in a board. Set the cutter to take a light cut. Hold the plane with both hands and push it across the board, guiding the cutter over the recessed area.

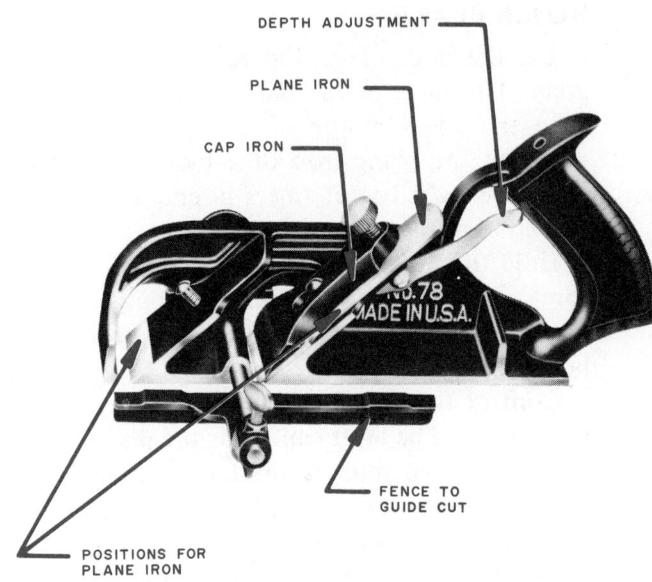

Figure 9-25
A rabbet plane. (The Stanley Works)

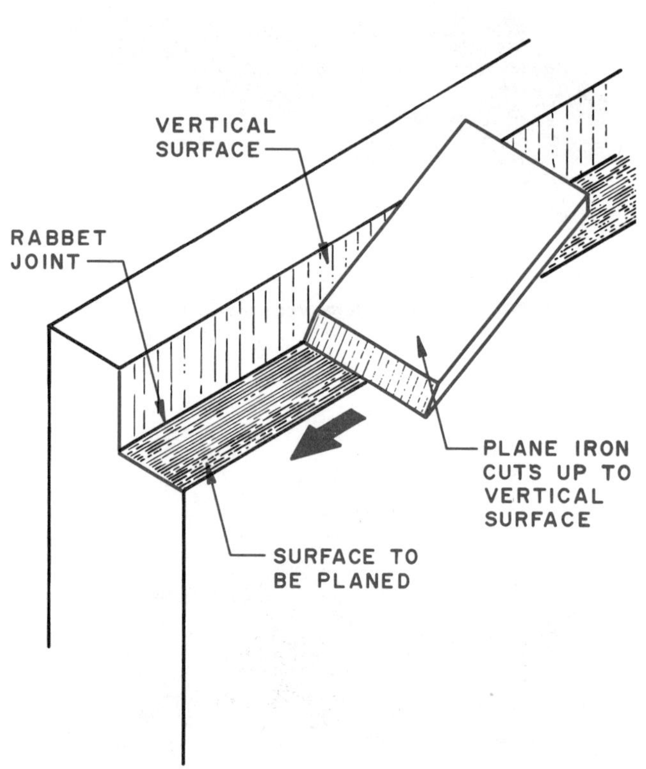

Figure 9-24
A bullnose rabbet plane will smooth a surface next to a vertical surface.

Figure 9-26
Hold the rabbet plane with both hands. Press tightly against the vertical face of the rabbet joint.

THE SPOKESHAVE

A *spokeshave* is a small, plane-like tool, Figure 9-28. The cutting edge is like a plane iron. Use it to shape objects with irregular surfaces, such as a sculpture. Hold the spokeshave with both hands and push it along the grain, Figure 9-29.

Figure 9-28
A spokeshave. (The Stanley Works)

CABINET SCRAPER

The plane iron often leaves minor ridges after it planes a surface. There are several ways to remove these ridges. One way is to dress the surface with a *cabinet scraper,* Figure 9-30. The cabinet scraper also can smooth knots and boards having irregular or cross grain.

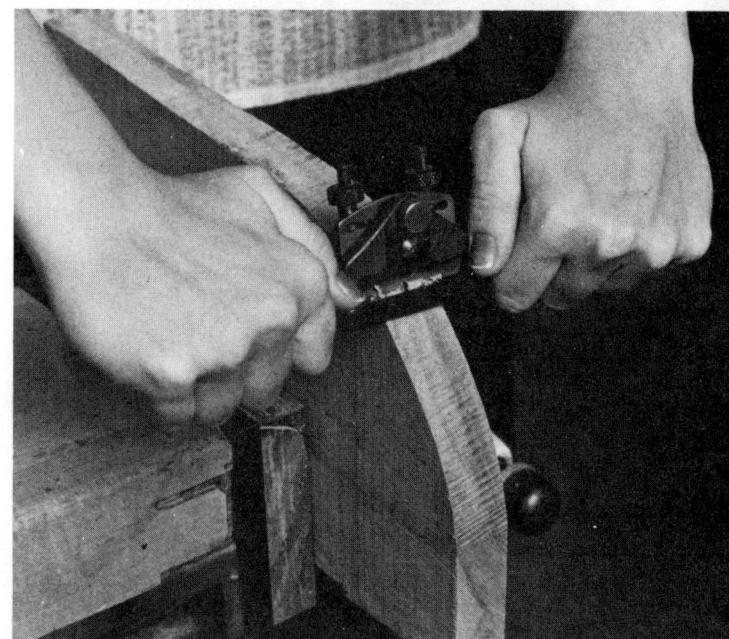

Figure 9-29
Use a spokeshave to smooth irregular surfaces.

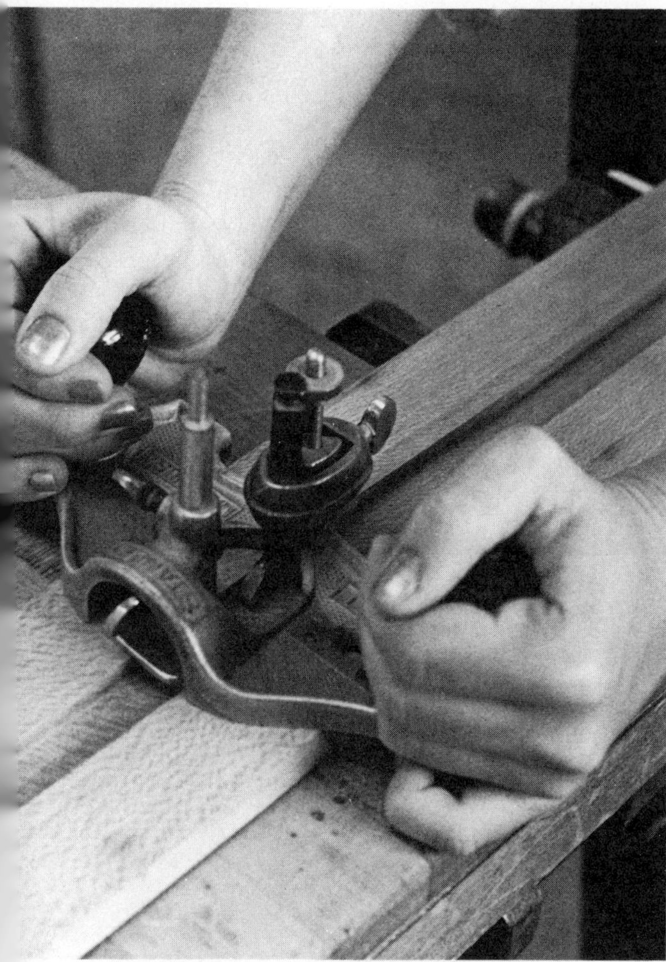

Figure 9-27
Use a router plane to smooth the bottom of a recessed area.

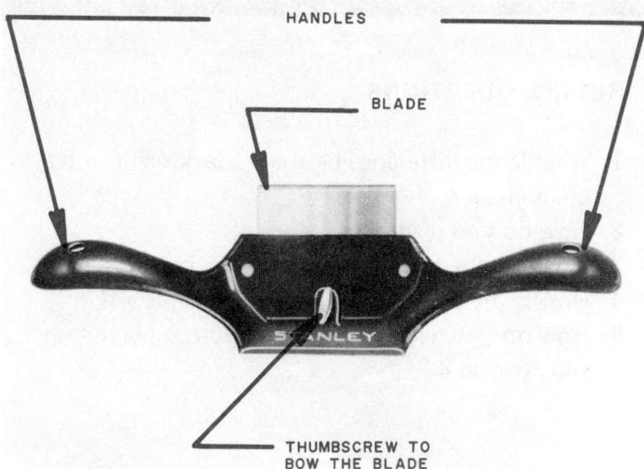

Figure 9-30
A cabinet scraper. (The Stanley Works)

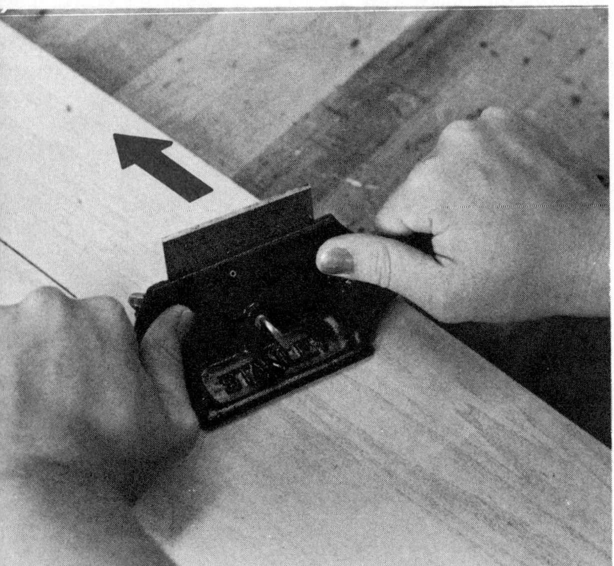

Figure 9-31
Push the cabinet scraper away from you.

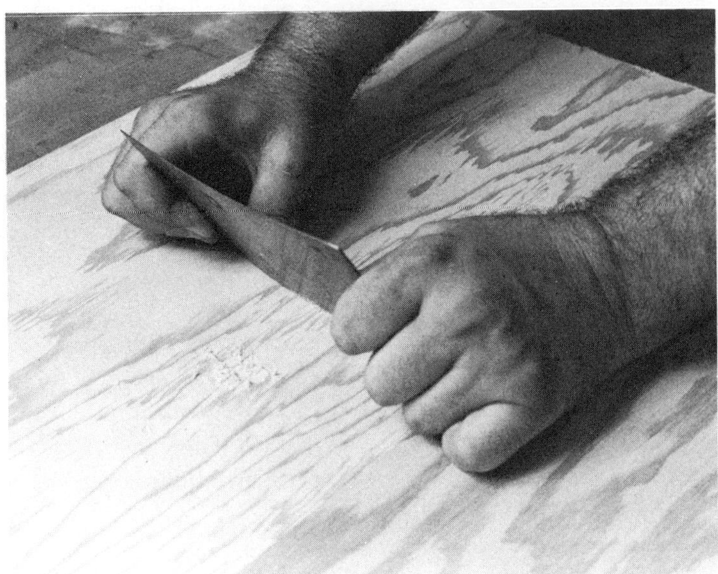

Figure 9-32
Hold the hand scraper with both hands. Slant it in the direction of your push.

A cabinet scraper does not cut into the wood. Instead, the beveled edge of the blade cuts a fine shaving when you press the cabinet scraper across the surface of the board.

Before using the cabinet scraper, replace the blade. Place the scraper frame on a flat surface. Slide in the blade until it rests on the flat surface. Lock the two screws that hold it in place. Tighten the thumb screw on the front of the frame. This will cause the blade to bow a little. Hold the cabinet scraper with both hands and push it away from you, Figure 9-31. Scrape with the grain.

The *hand scraper* is a thin blade of steel. It is used like the cabinet scraper, but you hold the blade in your hands, Figure 9-32. Slant the top of the scraper away from you, in the direction of your push.

REVIEW QUESTIONS

1 What is the difference between a jack plane and a block plane?
2 How do you plane end grain?
3 What are the steps for assembling a jack plane?
4 How is the depth of cut of a plane adjusted?
5 How do you decide which direction to plane face and edge grain?
6 Be sure the screwdriver does not slip when tightening or loosening the cap iron screw.
7 What is the difference between a bevel and a chamfer?

UNIT

10

Chisels, Gouges and Carving Tools

Objectives

After studying this unit you should be able to:

1 Identify the various types of chisels and gouges.

2 Make horizontal and vertical cuts with a chisel.

3 Smooth concave and convex surfaces with a chisel.

4 Cut straight, concave and convex grooves.

Technical Terms

Tang chisel

Shank chisel

Convex curve

Concave curve

Gouge

CHISELS, GOUGES AND CARVING TOOLS SAFETY RULES

1 Firmly clamp the stock to the workbench.

2 Keep both hands on the chisel behind the cutting edge, Figure 10-2. Never put your hand in front of the tool.

3 Always chisel away from yourself. Do not cut toward other people.

4 Do not chisel or gouge in crowded conditions.

5 Keep the tools sharp. See Unit 11 for sharpening instructions.

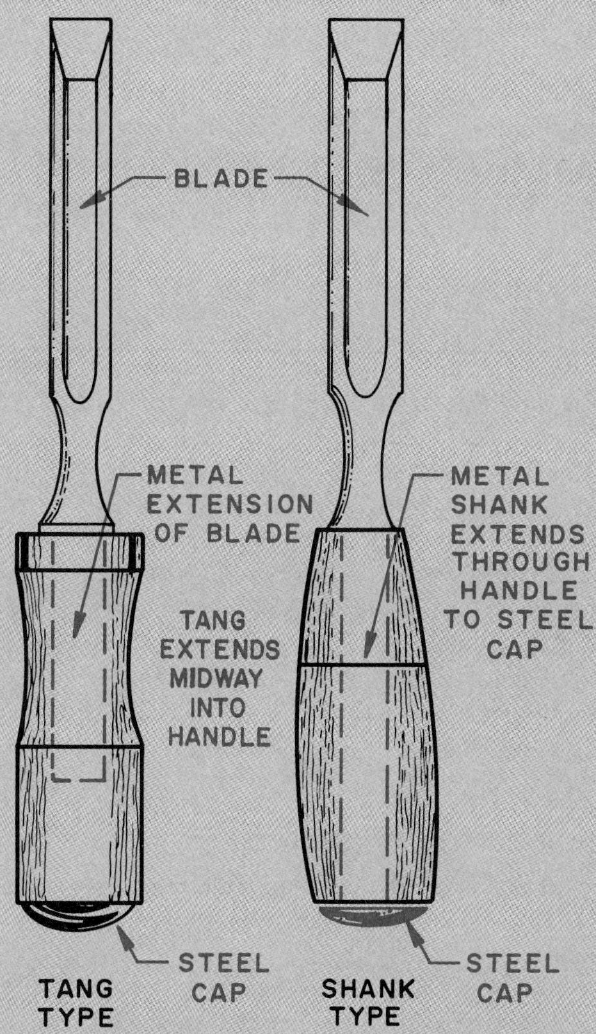

Figure 10-1
The tang and shank wood chisels.

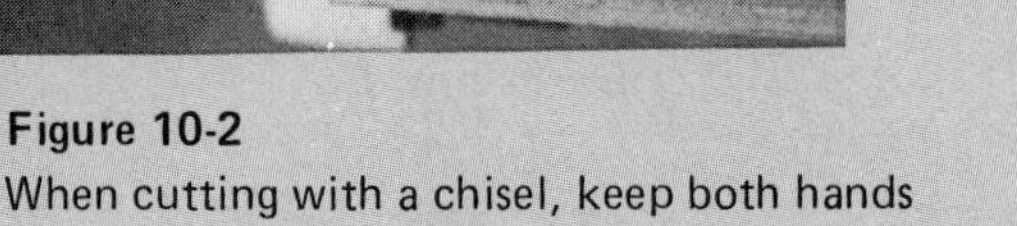

Figure 10-2
When cutting with a chisel, keep both hands on the tool. To cut flat work, keep the bevel up.

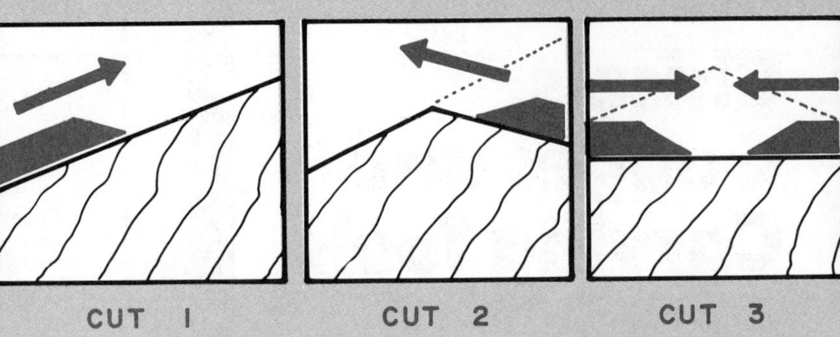

Figure 10-3
To cut across a board, work from each side toward the center.

Chisels, gouges and carving tools make accurate cuts, shapes and grooves. They also can produce surface decorations. You will have to practice to use these tools properly.

CHISELS

There are two types of chisels, Figure 10-1. The *tang chisel* blade extends midway through the wood or plastic handle. Use it for light-duty work, such as cutting using only hand pressure. The *shank chisel* has a metal shank forged as a continuation of the blade. The shank runs through the length of the handle to a steel cap. You can drive this type of chisel with a wood or plastic mallet. Never drive a wood chisel with a metal hammer.

Chisels are available in many widths. The common blade widths are 1/4″, 3/8″, 1/2″, 3/4″, 1″, 1-1/4″ and 1-1/2″.

HORIZONTAL CHISELING

Chiseling with the blade parallel to the work table is called horizontal chiseling. To chisel horizontally:

1. Fasten the stock to the bench.
2. Lay the chisel flat on the work. Be certain the bevel is up. Hold the blade in one hand and the handle in the other, Figure 10-2.
3. Push the chisel about halfway across the board, making a light cut. Then cut from the other side, Figure 10-3. If you cut across the board in one direction only, the edge will splinter.
4. Continue to make light cuts until the job is finished. Check your work for squareness with a try square.

VERTICAL CHISELING

Chiseling with the blade perpendicular to the work table is called vertical chiseling. To chisel vertically:

1. Fasten the stock to the bench.
2. Place the flat side of the chisel against the surface to be cut.
3. Hold the blade in one hand and the handle in the other. The hand on the blade controls the vertical movement of the chisel, Figure 10-4.
4. Push down on the handle. Restrain and control the downward movement of the chisel with the other hand.
5. Make short, paring strokes to remove thin layers of wood. If you use a mallet, strike the chisel very lightly, Figure 10-5. Never drive a chisel deeply into the wood. Do not try to remove a large piece in a single cut.

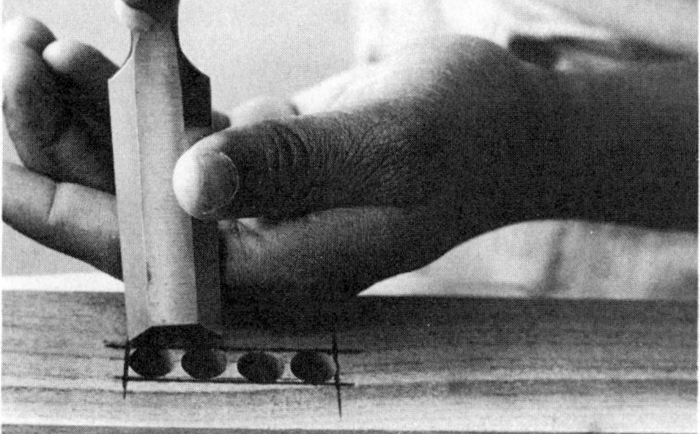

Figure 10-4
To chisel vertically, hold the blade in one hand and the handle in the other.

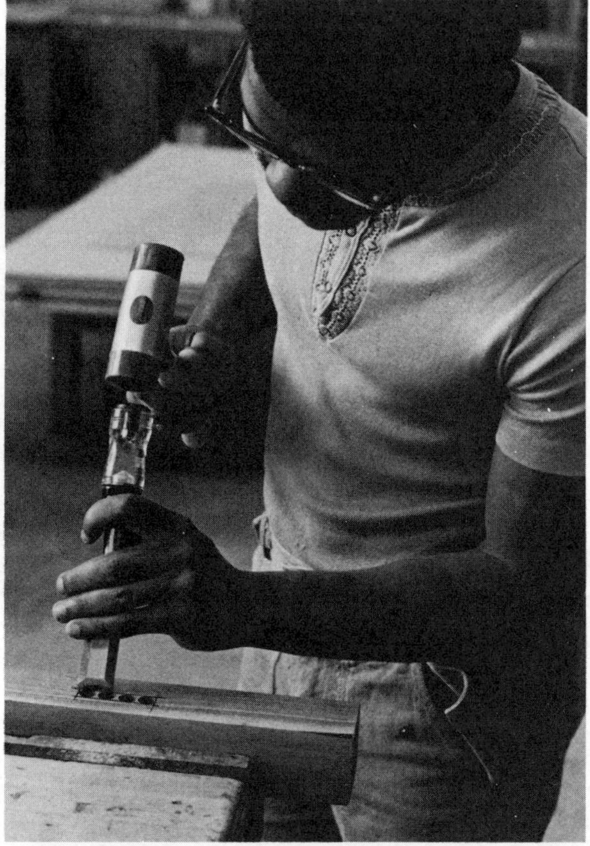

Figure 10-5
When using a mallet, strike the chisel lightly.

Figure 10-6
To smooth a convex curve, keep the bevel up and cut down the curve.

Figure 10-7
To smooth a concave curve, keep the bevel down and cut down the curve.

SMOOTHING CONVEX CURVES

Curves which bend outward are called *convex curves.* To smooth a convex curve:

1. Secure the stock in the vise.
2. Place the chisel flat on the stock with the bevel up.
3. Start at the top of the curve and take a light cut moving down the curve, Figure 10-6. Use your hand on the blade to restrain and control the stroke.

SMOOTHING CONCAVE CURVES

Curves which bend inward are called *concave curves.* To smooth a concave curve:

1. Secure the stock in the vise.
2. Place the chisel on the surface with the bevel down.
3. Start at the top of the curve and take a light cut down the curve, Figure 10-7. Use your hand on the blade to restrain and control the stroke.

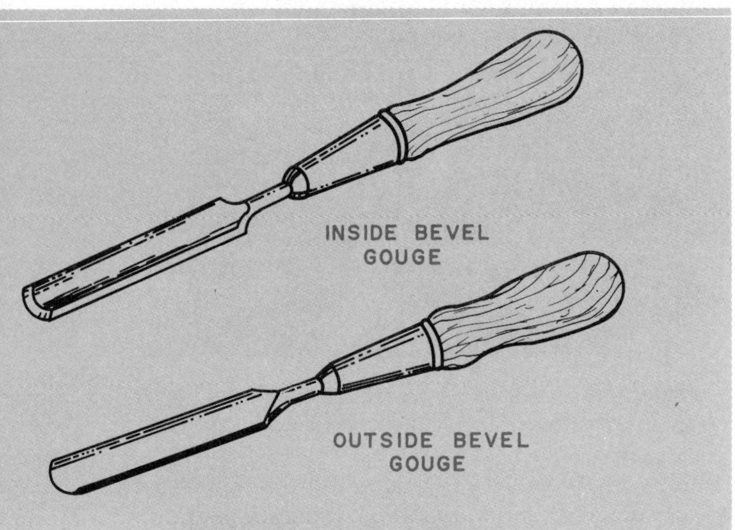

Figure 10-8
Gouges are made with inside and outside bevels.

GOUGES

A *gouge* is a type of chisel used to cut grooves. Because they are rounded, they make round-bottom cuts. The bevel of a gouge can be either on the inside or outside of the tool, Figure 10-8.

Gouges are available in various widths. The most common widths are 1/4″, 3/8″, 1/2″, 3/4″, 1″, 1-1/4″ and 1-1/2″.

CUTTING GROOVES

To make a groove in a board:

1. Fasten the stock to the bench.
2. Select the proper gouge. When cutting grooves, use the outside bevel gouge, Figure 10-9. When cutting the edge of curved stock, use the inside bevel gouge, Figure 10-10.
3. Hold the gouge with both hands.
4. Take shallow cuts in the direction of the grain. If the groove is not to go all the way across the board, finish the end with short strokes against the grain. A mallet can be used if needed.

Cutting grooves across the grain is difficult. For best results, rock the tool gently from side to side as you push it into the wood. You can use a plastic or wood mallet to help the cutting action.

Figure 10-9
Use an outside bevel gouge to cut a groove.

Figure 10-10
Use an inside bevel gouge to cut curved edges.

CARVING TOOLS

Carving tools are sold individually or in sets. They are usually very small, specialized chisels and gouges, Figure 10-11. To use carving tools:

1. Fasten the stock to the bench.
2. Handle carving tools in the same manner as described for chisels and gouges.
3. Keep both hands behind the cutting edge. Hold cutting tools with both hands, as explained for chisels and gouges, Figure 10-12.

STORAGE

When storing chisels and gouges, be certain that cutting edges are protected from damage. They can be stored in a wooden rack, with the cutting edge resting on wood, Figure 10-13. They also may be stored in a commercial storage box, Figure 10-14.

Figure 10-11
A set of woodcarving tools.

Figure 10-13
Wood chisels stored in a homemade wooden rack.

Figure 10-12
Use woodcarving tools for decorative carving. Keep both hands on the tool.

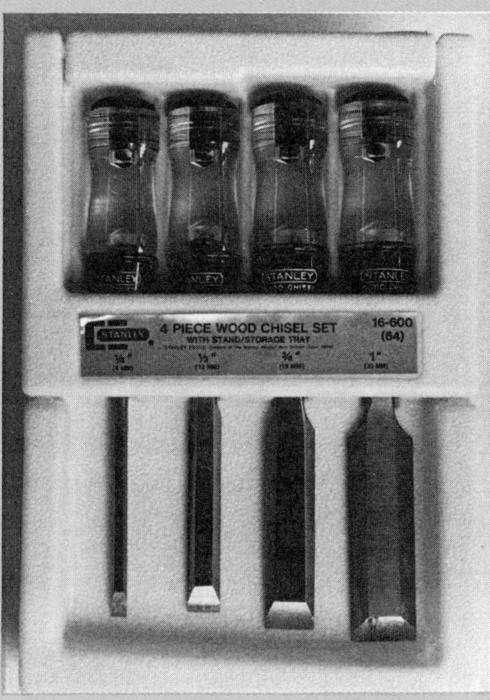

Figure 10-14
Wood chisels stored in a commercial plastic box.

REVIEW QUESTIONS

1 What is the difference between a tang chisel and a shank chisel?
2 In what position is the chisel bevel when cutting flat surfaces? Convex surfaces? Concave surfaces?
3 What type of gouge is used for cutting concave and convex grooves?
4 What are some common widths of chisel blades?
5 What are some common widths of gouges?
6 How should chisels and gouges be stored?

SUGGESTED ACTIVITIES

1 Prepare a series of photographs showing the proper way to cut stock with chisels and gouges. Mount them in a display and write an explanation below each.
2 Using scrap stock, cut a rabbet and a dado with a wood chisel.
3 Using scrap stock, cut a concave and a convex groove.

UNIT

11

Sharpening Edge Tools

Objectives

After studying this unit you should be able to:

1 Grind edge tools on an electric grinding wheel.

2 Hone edge tools on an oilstone.

3 Dress a screwdriver.

4 Sharpen a cabinet scraper.

Technical Terms

Electric grinder
Abrasive wheel
Wheel dresser
Oilstone
Silicon carbide
Aluminum oxide
Hone
Slip stone
India gouge slip
Drill-grinding gauge
Burnisher

SHARPENING EDGE TOOLS SAFETY RULES

1 Wear approved eye protection when using an electric tool grinder.

2 Replace chipped or cracked wheels before using a grinder.

3 Always use the grinder tool rest and keep it within 1/8" (3 mm) of the wheel.

4 Operate a grinder only with the wheel guards in place and properly adjusted.

5 Keep the grinding wheel clean.

6 Provide good lighting on the tool grinder.

7 Do not grind on the side of the wheels.

8 Test the sharpness of cutting edges on a piece of wood, not on your finger.

9 Hone away from the cutting edge when you are using a slip stone.

A sharp tool produces top quality work. A sharp tool is a safe tool. A dull tool is dangerous because it does not cut easily. Forcing a dull tool to cut could make it slip and cause injury.

ELECTRIC GRINDER

An *electric grinder* restores the edge of a cutting tool to its proper angle and shape. A grinder has two *abrasive wheels* mounted on the motor shafts, Figure 11-1. Metal guards around each wheel give protection from flying particles of metal. The guards also give protection in case the grinding wheel shatters. A grinder has a shield with a safety-glass window. The shield gives some protection, but you also should wear safety glasses or a face shield.

The pores in the grinding wheel clog with use. Clogging causes friction to develop between the clogged wheel and the tool. The friction heats

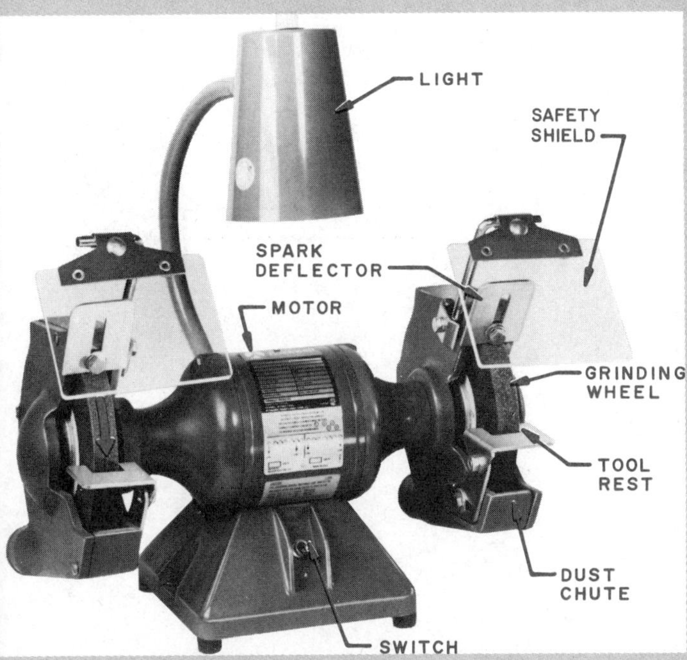

Figure 11-1
The parts of a tool grinder. The grinding wheel rotates toward the tool rest. (Rockwell International)

Figure 11-2
Use a wheel dresser to dress a grinding wheel.

the tool. If the tool turns dark blue, it means that the steel has lost its temper, or hardness, and will not stay sharp. Keep the grinding wheel clean by dressing it with a *wheel dresser,* Figure 11-2.

To grind tools, hold them on the grinder tool rest. Move them across the wheel freehand if you have had enough practice. Otherwise, use a grinding attachment, Figure 11-3. Adjust the grinding attachment to the angle required to grind the tool. Lock the tool onto the attachment. When the grinding wheel has reached its full operating speed, pass the tool across the wheel. Keep the tool moving against the wheel. Otherwise it will overheat. Remove the tool and let it air cool. If the tool is not too hot, dip it in water. This will quickly reduce the temperature. If the tool is too hot, the water may cause tiny cracks in the cutting edge. Some grinding wheels are run in water. This keeps both the tool and the wheel cool.

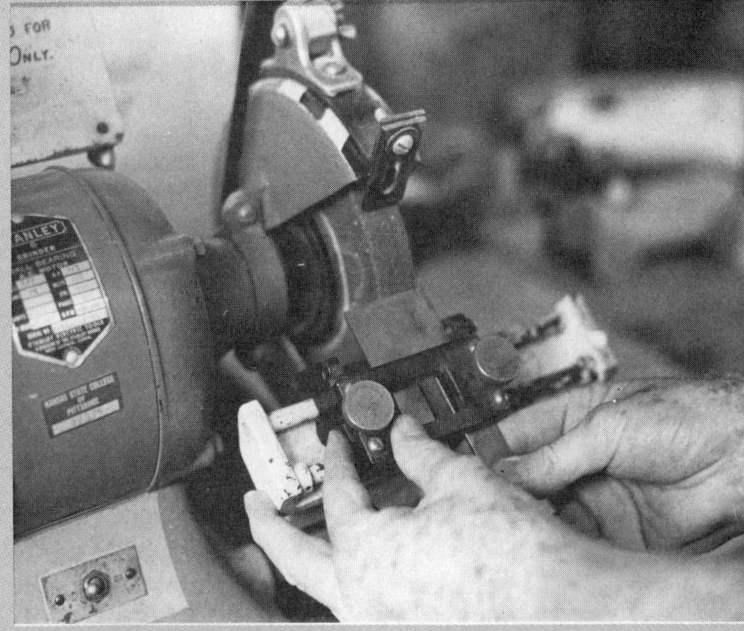

Figure 11-3
A grinding attachment holds plane irons, chisels and other bevel-edged cutting tools.

OILSTONE

An *oilstone* is a block of abrasive material. It is also called a whetstone. Use an oilstone after grinding to complete the sharpening of a cutting

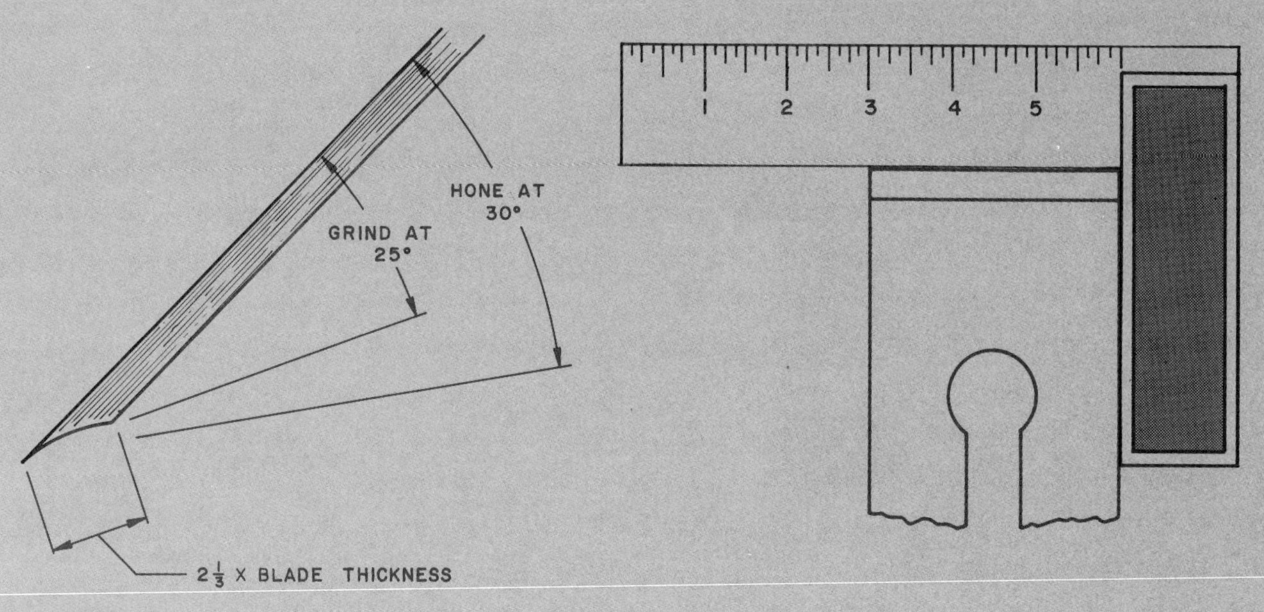

Figure 11-4
Grind the plane iron at 25° and hone it at 30°.

Figure 11-5
A try square checks the cutting edge for squareness.

tool. You can sharpen many tools on an oilstone without first using a grinder.

Oilstones are available in many sizes and degrees of coarseness. They usually are made from *silicon carbide* or *aluminum oxide*. An aluminum oxide stone is harder and tougher than a silicon carbide one. It is better for sharpening hard tool steels.

Before using the stone, lubricate it with a light oil such as motor oil. Oil helps keep the metal chips from clogging the stone. The stone then can produce a fine cutting edge. Wipe all the oil off the stone when you have finished using it. This keeps the oil from thickening and clogging the stone. Clean the stone occasionally with an oil solvent. Ammonia is a safe cleaner.

SHARPENING A PLANE IRON

Sharpening a plane iron takes two operations. First, grind the cutting edge to the proper angle and shape. Then use an oilstone to *hone* the edge to final sharpness. If the cutting edge is dull but not worn or nicked, it needs only to be honed. You should grind a plane iron only when it is worn out of shape.

Grind plane irons for jointer, fore, jack and smoothing planes at an angle of 25°. Hone them at an angle of 30°, Figure 11-4. This produces a concave surface. Check the cutting edge with a try square to be sure it is at a 90° angle to the side of the plane iron, Figure 11-5. If it is off a little, hold it perpendicular to an oilstone. Move it back and forth to remove the high spots, Figure 11-6.

After the plane iron has been ground square, place the bevel flat on a medium-fine oilstone. Put a few drops of oil on the stone. Raise the plane iron about 5° so that only the cutting edge touches the stone, Figure 11-7. Move the plane iron back and forth across the stone. You can angle it and slide it straight back and forth, Figure 11-8, or move it in a figure-8 pattern, Figure 11-9. Then lay the blade flat on the stone with the bevel up, Figure 11-10. Move it back and forth. This action removes a wire edge formed by the first honing action. Next, raise the plane iron up and again hone it on a fine oilstone.

Figure 11-6
Square the cutting edge of the plane iron by lightly dressing it on an oilstone.

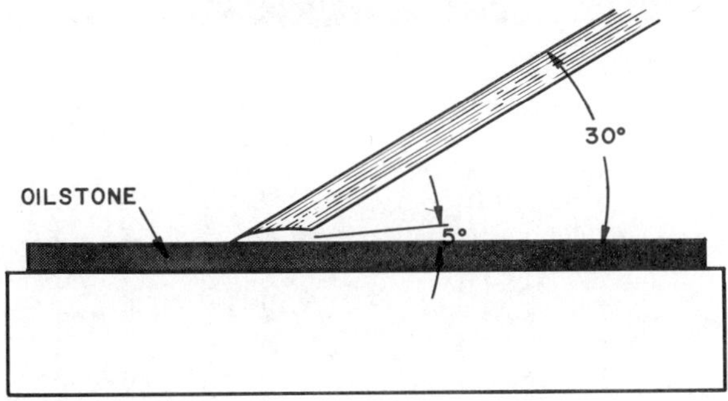

Figure 11-7
Raise the plane iron 5° above the surface of the oilstone as you sharpen it.

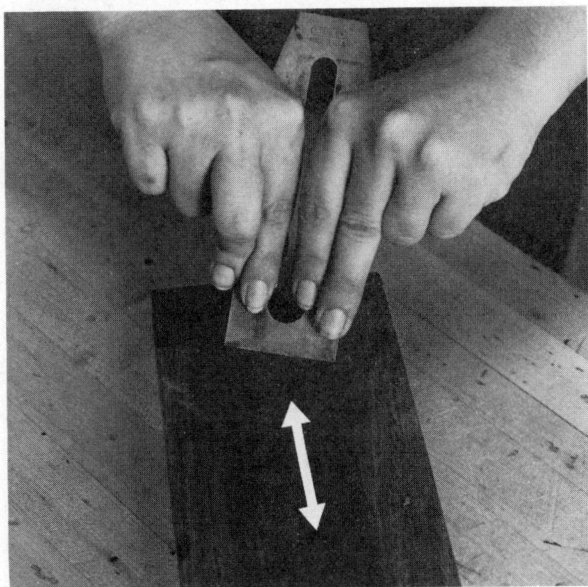

Figure 11-8
Slant the plane iron on the oilstone and slide it straight back and forth.

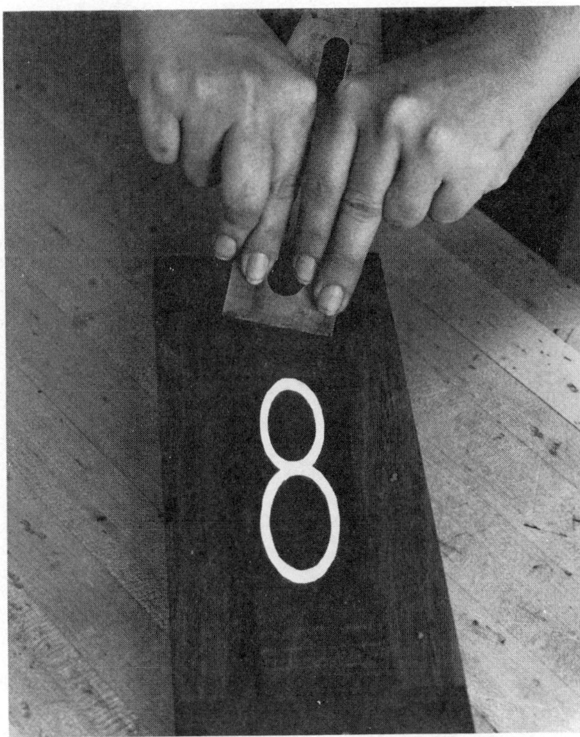

Figure 11-9
The plane iron can be moved in a figure-8 pattern as it is sharpened on an oilstone.

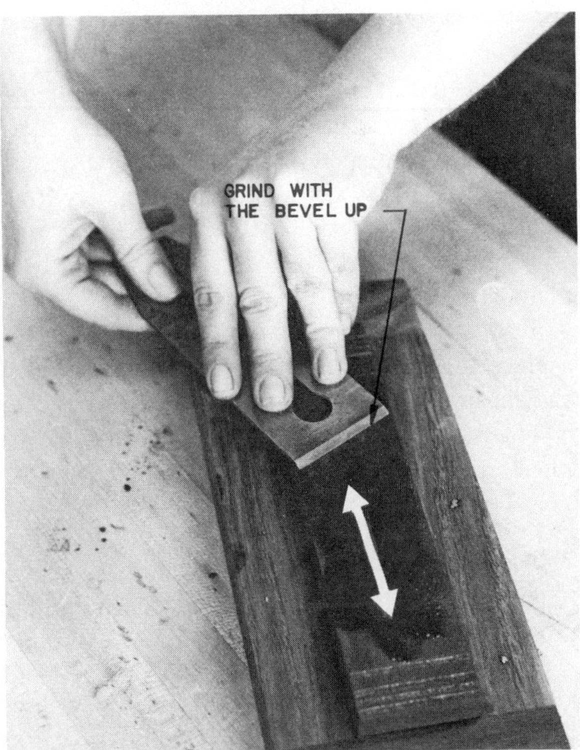

Figure 11-10
The side of the plane iron opposite the bevel lies flat on the oilstone when sharpened.

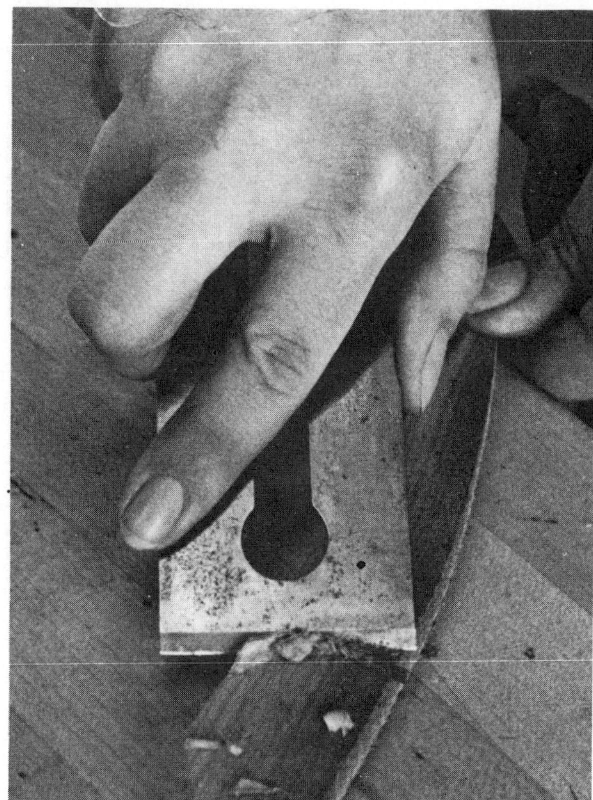

Figure 11-11
Test a plane iron for sharpness by seeing if it will cut fine shavings with slight pressure.

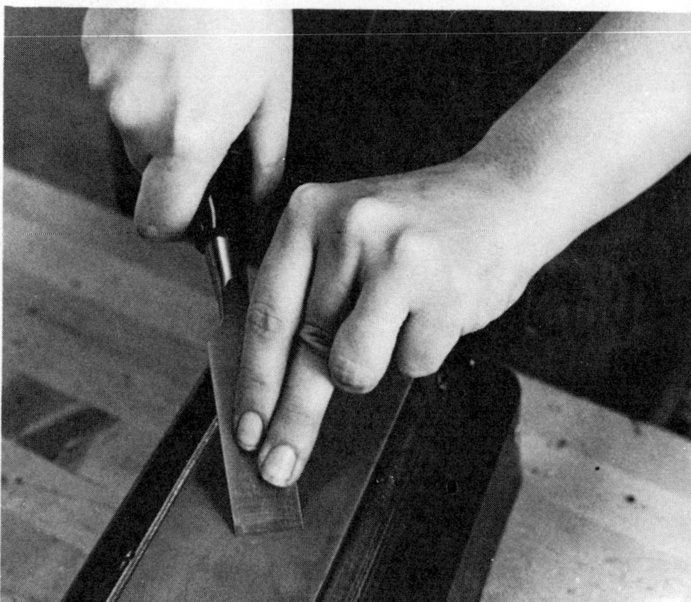

Figure 11-12
Hone a wood chisel on an oilstone.

Then lay it flat and hone it again. After doing this several times the blade should be very sharp. After it is sharp, you may want to hone the corners lightly. This will make them slightly lower than the center of the cutting edge. The corners will not leave marks on the board as it is being planed.

To test for sharpness, try the cutting edge on a piece of wood. The plane iron should cut fine shavings with little pressure, Figure 11-11.

The plane irons for block, bullnose and rabbet planes are ground at an angle of 27°.

SHARPENING CHISELS

Grind chisels at an angle of 25°. Sharpen them in the same way as plane irons, Figure 11-12.

SHARPENING WOOD-TURNING TOOLS

Sharpen wood-turning tools in the same way as plane irons. The angles for grinding and honing are slightly different, Figure 11-13. Because

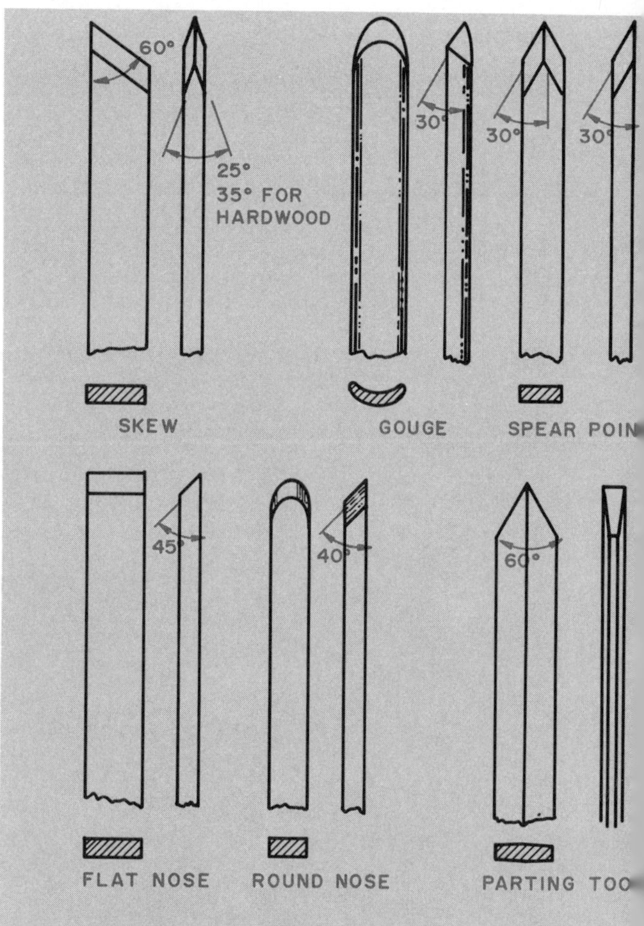

Figure 11-13
The drawing shows correct angles for grinding the cutting edges of wood-turning tools.

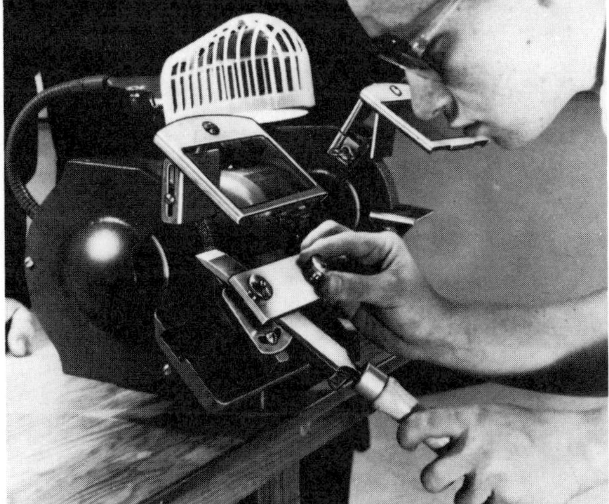

Figure 11-14
An edge-tool grinding attachment helps sharpen a wood-turning tool. (Rockwell International)

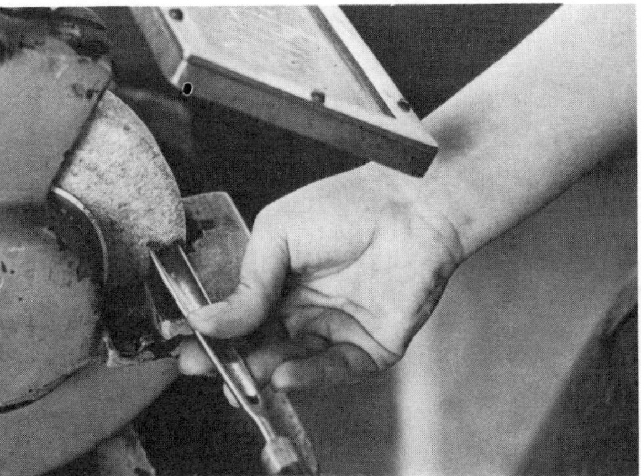

Figure 11-16
Place the worn cutting edge of a gouge perpendicular to the side of the grinding wheel.

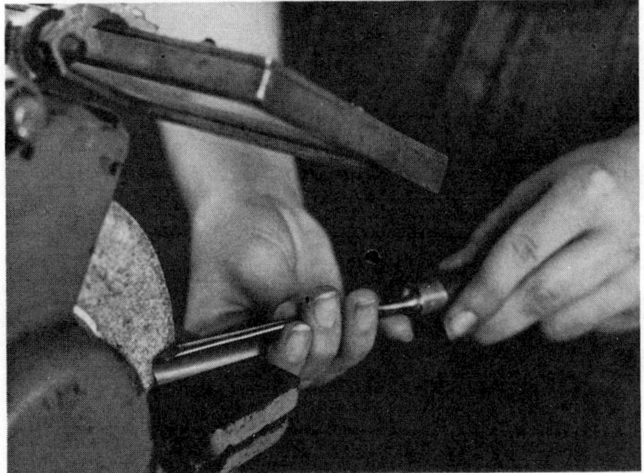

Figure 11-15
Grind a gouge on the side of the grinding wheel. Be sure to hold it on a tool rest.

some have bevels at angles to the side of the tool, you must adjust the grinder tool attachment, Figure 11-14.

SHARPENING GOUGES AND CARVING TOOLS

Grind gouges on the side of the grinding wheel at an angle of 30°, Figure 11-13. Pressure against the side of the wheel should be light. Move the tool rest so that the gouge is resting on it, Figure 11-15.

If the cutting edge is badly worn or chipped, it must be ground square. Place it flat against the side of the grinding wheel, Figure 11-16.

After grinding the gouge, hone it. Use a *slip stone* on the inside bevel to remove the burr, or wire edge, Figure 11-17. Use an *India gouge slip* to hone the outside bevel.

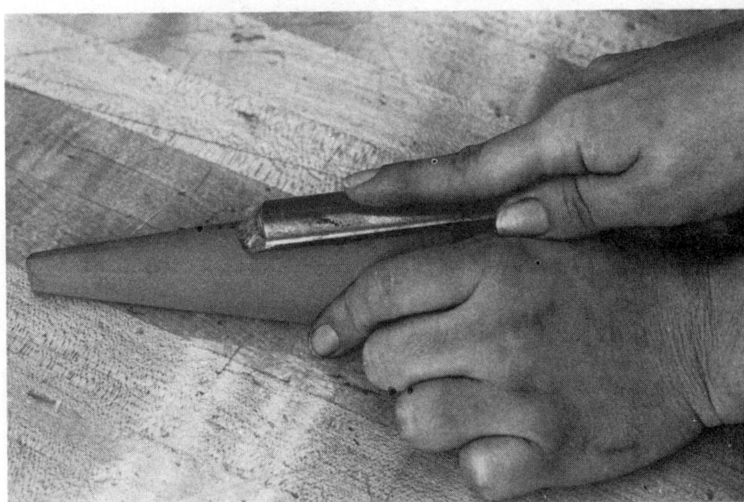

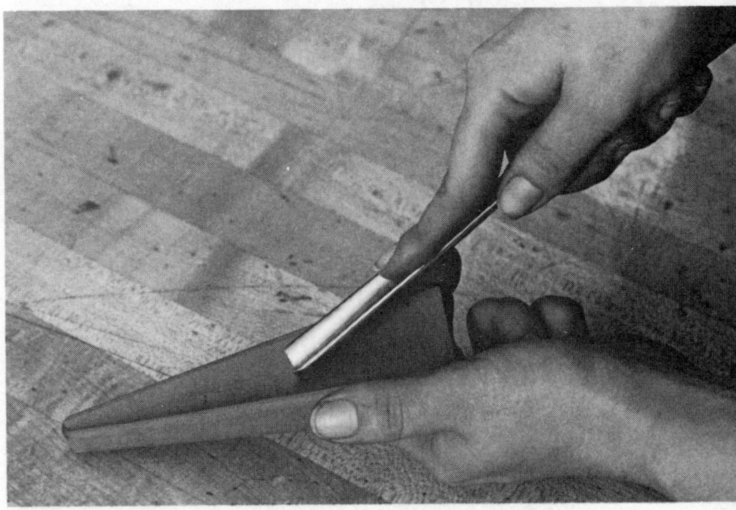

Figure 11-17
To hone a gouge, use a slip stone to remove the burr on the inside bevel, *top.* Use an India gouge slip to hone the outside bevel, *bottom.*

Figure 11-18
Hone each side of a pocket knife on an oilstone.

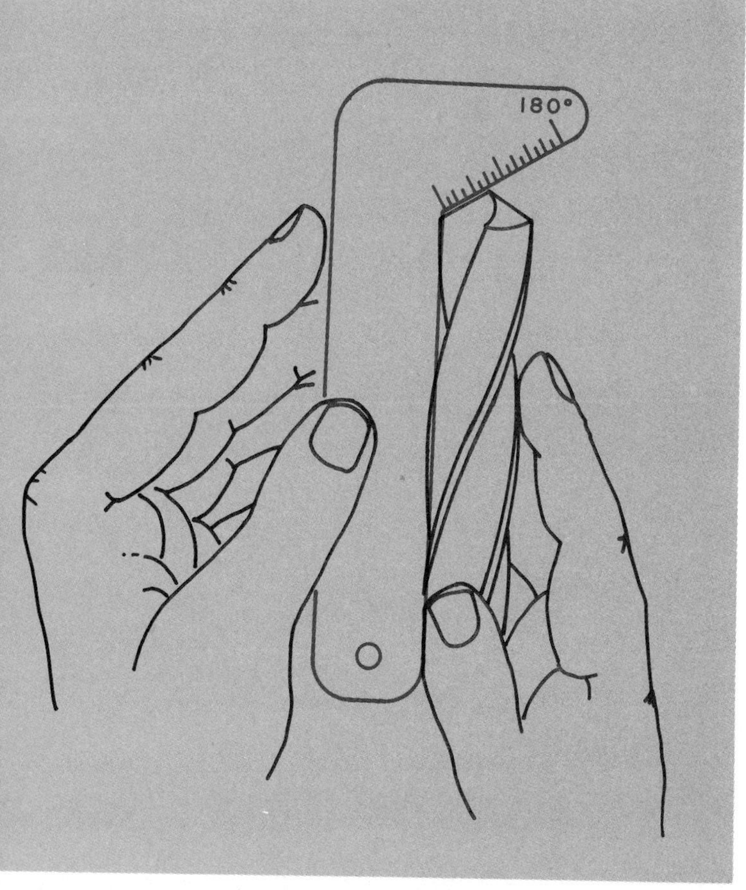

Figure 11-19
A drill-grinding gauge measures the angle of the cutting lips of a twist drill.

SHARPENING POCKET KNIVES

Grind pocket knives at an angle of 25°. The blade should be ground from both sides on a fine wheel. Hone the blade by laying it flat against an oilstone and then raising it 25°. Hone from both sides, Figure 11-18.

Figure 11-20
A drill-grinding attachment holds the drill at the proper angle for grinding. (Clausing Corp.)

SHARPENING TWIST DRILLS

Sharpen twist drills by grinding on a very fine wheel. Grind at an angle of 118°. Check the angle with a *drill-grinding gauge,* Figure 11-19.

You can grind twist drills freehand but it is difficult to get the correct angle. A better way is to use a drill-grinding attachment, Figure 11-20. It holds the drill at the proper angle as it is fed into the side of the grinding wheel and rotated.

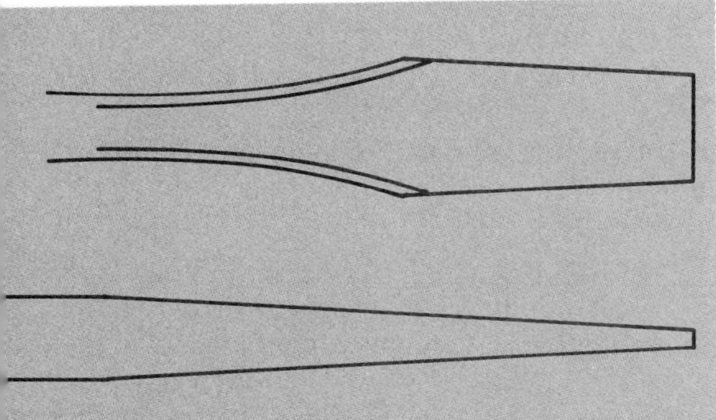

Figure 11-21
The tip of the screwdriver must be flat and square.

Figure 11-22
The tip of a screwdriver that is not heavily worn can be restored to shape by squaring the end and the face on an oilstone.

DRESSING A SCREWDRIVER

The tip of a screwdriver should be flat on the bottom, Figure 11-21. The sides of the tip should be flat or slightly concave. If a screwdriver is slightly worn, adjust it by honing on an oilstone, Figure 11-22. If it is badly worn or chipped, you must grind the screwdriver to shape. Grind the tip square on the side of the grinding wheel. Recondition the face of the tip on the front of the wheel. This produces the slight concave surface, Figure 11-23.

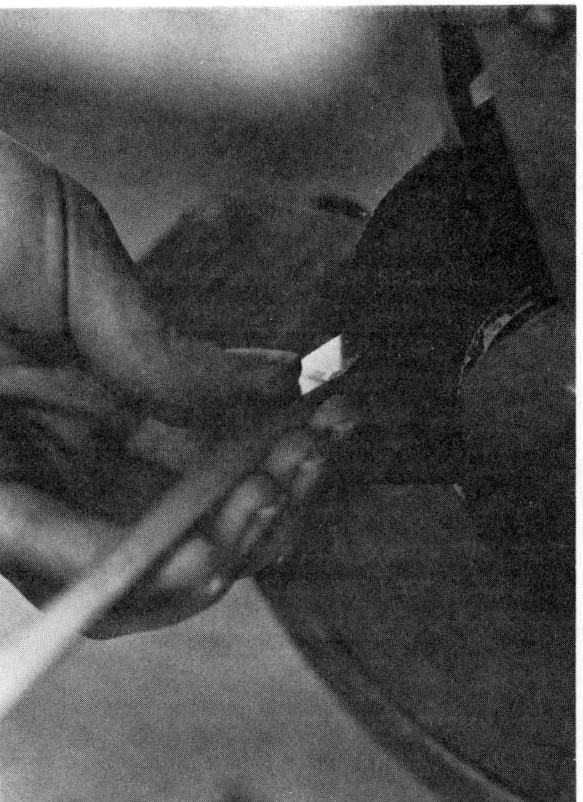

Figure 11-23
To grind a screwdriver, square the end on the side of the grinding wheel, *top*. Then grind the tip to the proper thickness on the front of the wheel, *bottom*.

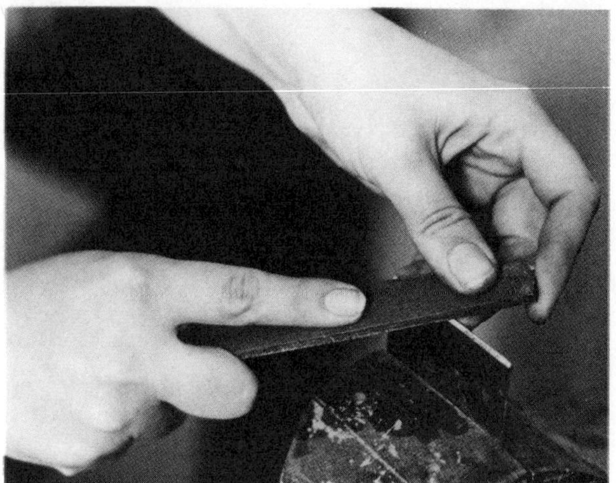

Figure 11-24
Restore a cabinet-scraper blade to shape by filing.

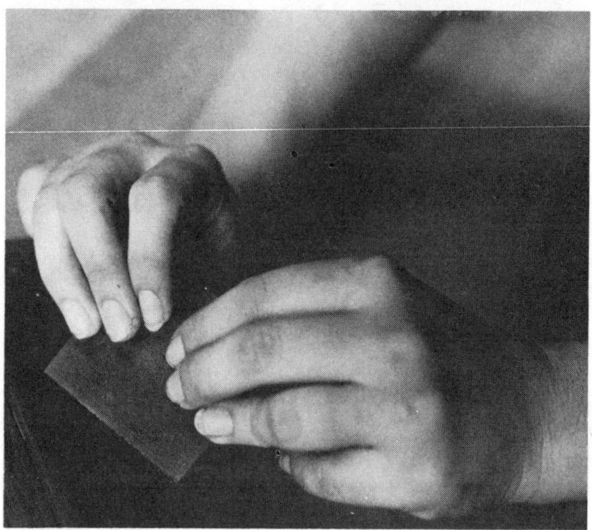

Figure 11-25
Sharpen a cabinet-scraper blade on an oilstone after it has been filed.

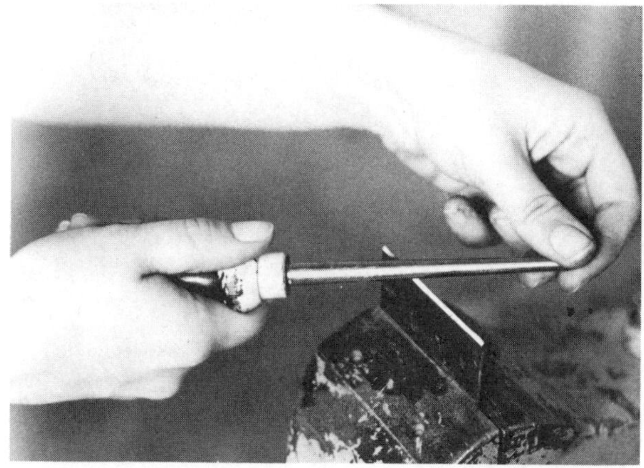

Figure 11-26
A burnisher forms a burr on the newly sharpened edge of a cabinet-scraper blade.

SHARPENING A SCRAPER

To sharpen a scraper, clamp the blade in a vise. Then file the edge at a 35° angle, Figure 11-24. Sharpen the edge on an oilstone, Figure 11-25. Form the burr by placing a *burnisher* flat on the 35° surface. Raise the handle of the burnisher 5°. Press down on the burnisher as you slide it across the sharp edge, Figure 11-26. Be careful not to let the burnisher slip as you move it across the cutting edge.

SHARPENING AUGER BITS

To sharpen an auger bit, file the lips and the spurs, Figure 11-27. File the lips as shown in Figure 11-28. File the spurs only on the inside, Figure 11-29. Use a small, fine, triangular file or an auger bit file. Keep the spurs and the lips the same size.

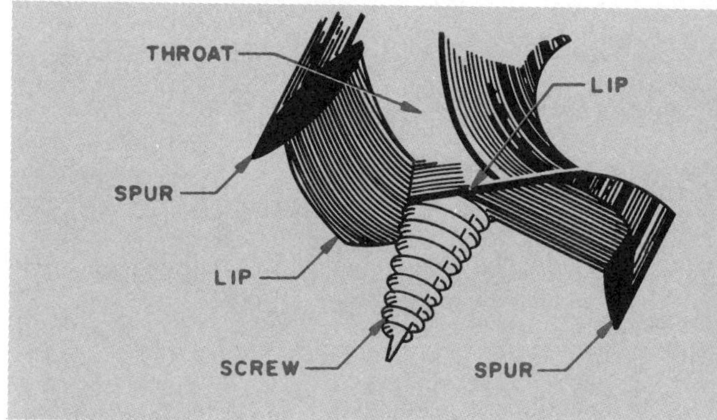

Figure 11-27
The cutting parts of an auger bit.

Figure 11-28
Use a small triangular file to file the lips of an auger bit.

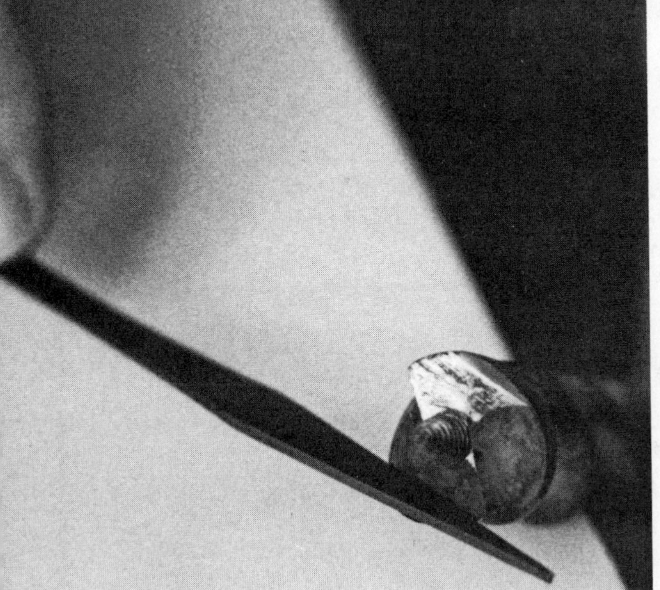

Figure 11-29
Use an auger bit file to file the spurs of an auger bit.

DRESSING A COUNTERSINK

To dress a countersink, use a fine stone or file. Hone each cutting edge lightly, Figure 11-30.

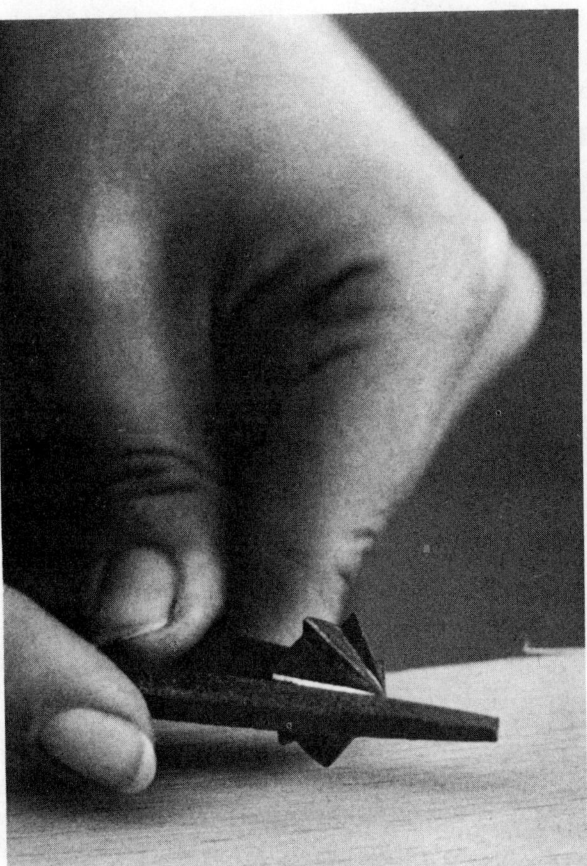

Figure 11-30
Sharpen the cutting edges of a countersink by lightly filing or honing them on the face.

REVIEW QUESTIONS

1. What device is used to restore a badly worn edge tool to its original cutting shape and angle?
2. Why should a grinding wheel be dressed frequently?
3. What tool is used to hone a cutting edge?
4. Why is oil used on an oilstone?
5. What is the proper angle for the bevel of a jack plane iron?
6. How should you test a cutting edge for sharpness?
7. What tools are used to hone the inside and outside bevels on gouges?
8. What parts of an auger bit are sharpened?
9. What is the proper angle for the cutting edge of a twist drill?

SUGGESTED ACTIVITIES

1. Bring worn tools from home and recondition them. Practice on old, less valuable tools before working on more valuable tools.
2. Recondition the tools in your shop.

UNIT

12

Files, Rasps and Forming Tools

FILES, RASPS AND FORMING TOOLS SAFETY RULES

1 Never use a file or rasp without a handle on the tang.

2 Secure stock firmly to the workbench before starting to file.

3 Keep both hands on the file or rasp.

4 Do not file stock near someone. A file could strike someone if it slips.

5 Make sure that the file or rasp does not slip off the work, causing you to strike your hand against it.

Objectives

After studying this unit you should be able to:

1 Identify various types of files, rasps and forming tools.

2 Clean, maintain and properly store files.

3 Smooth stock with files and rasps.

4 Smooth stock with perforated forming tools.

Technical Terms

File	Rasp
Single cut	File card
Double cut	Perforated-blade tool

A *file* smooths surfaces and edges that cannot be smoothed with cutting tools. The parts of a file are shown in Figure 12-1. A handle should always cover the tang. The tang is sharp and can cause injury if it is not covered. The most common file shapes used in woodworking are in Figure 12-2. Files come in lengths ranging from 4″ to 18″. Length measures from the heel to the point. The most popular sizes are 6″, 8″, 10″ and 12″.

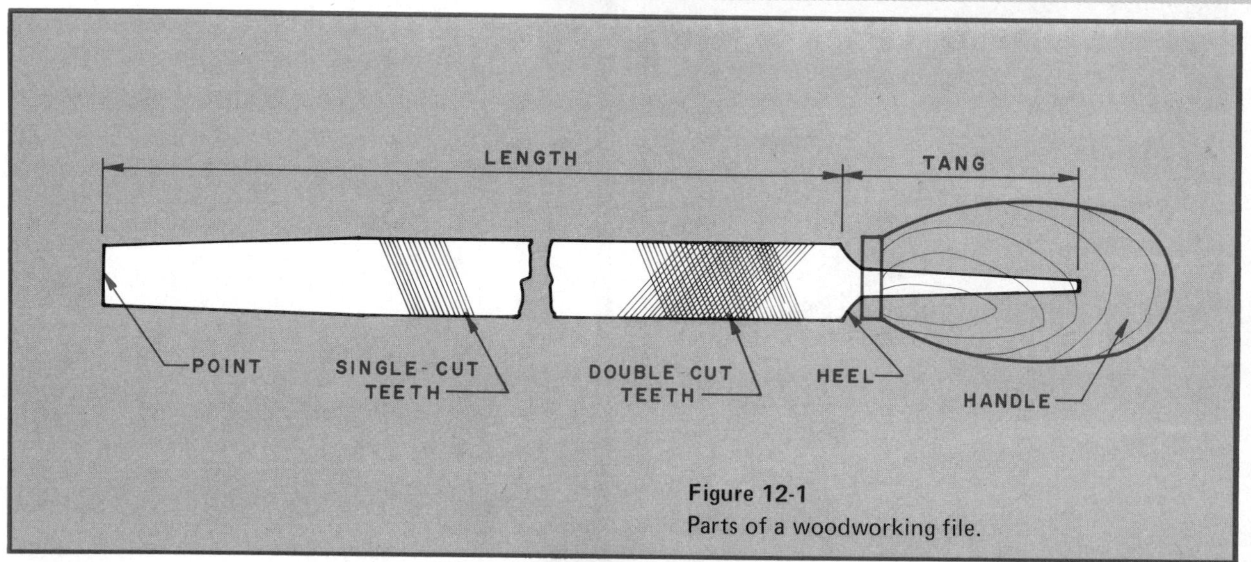

Figure 12-1
Parts of a woodworking file.

Files have *single-cut* and *double-cut* teeth. The single cut has one row of teeth cut on a diagonal, Figure 12-1. The double cut has a second row of teeth cut across the first row, Figure 12-1. Each row is a single, long tooth. The teeth are on a diagonal so the file will have a shearing cut. Files are specified by degree of coarseness of the teeth. The degrees, from rough to fine, are coarse, bastard, second cut and smooth, Figure 12-3.

Wood *rasps* look like files. Their difference is in their teeth. The teeth form individual points, Figure 12-2. Rasps are made in flat, half-round and round shapes. The degrees of roughness are coarse, bastard, second cut and smooth. The most common lengths are 6″, 8″, 10″ and 12″.

Do not use wood files to smooth metal. Files designed for smoothing metal can be used on wood. They tend to clog quickly, however, and must be cleaned often.

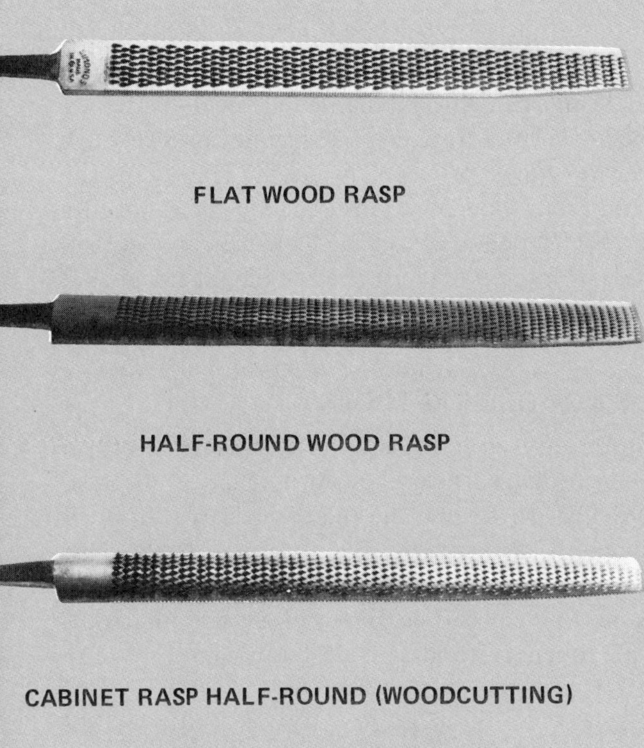

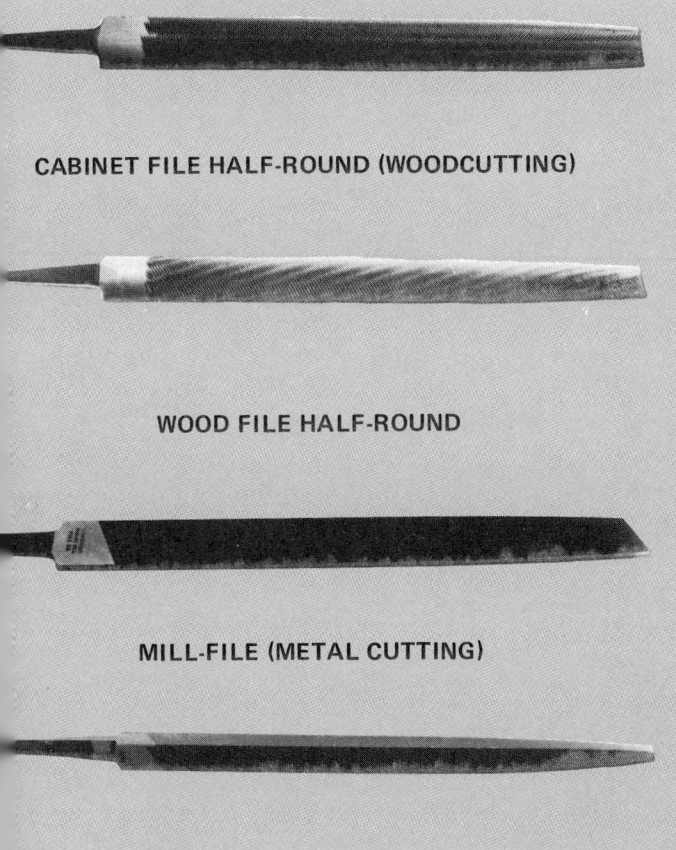

Figure 12-2
Common shapes of woodworking files and rasps. (Simonds Cutting Tools)

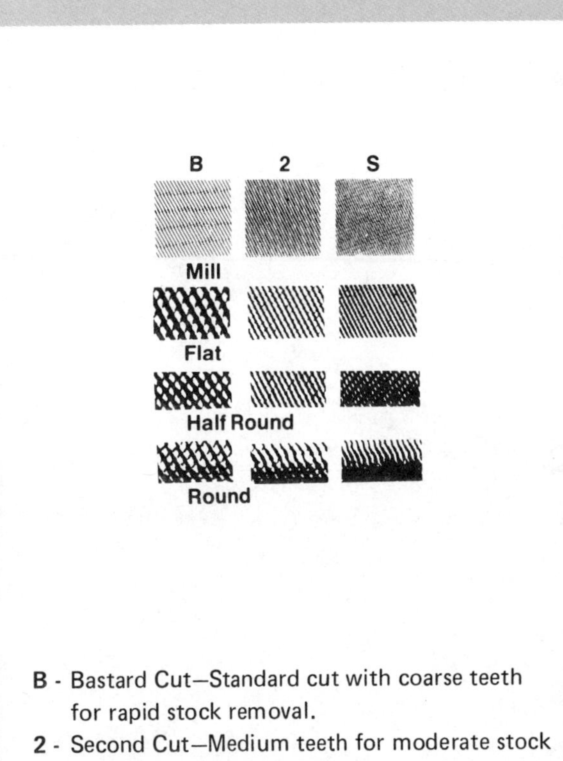

Figure 12-3
Teeth patterns and degrees of coarseness. (Simonds Cutting Tools)

CLEANING AND MAINTAINING FILES AND RASPS

Files and rasps are cleaned with a *file card.* A file card is a short, metal-bristle brush that removes chips from the teeth, Figure 12-4. You should clean files often, Figure 12-5. Clean files cut fast and smooth.

When storing or using files, make sure they do not rest on one another or on other metal tools. Keep them dry.

PERFORATED-BLADE FORMING TOOLS

Each of the forming tools in Figure 12-6 has teeth formed in a thin, perforated metal blade. *Perforated-blade tools* work in the same way as files and planes. They smooth wood, plastics, copper, aluminum, tile, laminated countertops and mild steel. The hardened steel blade has razor-sharp cutting edges. Shavings pass through the openings between the teeth. This keeps the tool from clogging. You use very little pressure to get the tool to cut. Dull blades are replaceable. Common blade styles are file, plane, pocket plane, shaver and round.

USING FORMING TOOLS

A rasp is very rough. Use it to smooth only a very rough surface. The rasp removes material quickly. It works the piece near its finished shape. Use a coarse file to smooth the rasp marks. Use a finer file to finish the job. Then sand the piece. Perforated-blade forming tools can rough cut and smooth. You can use one in place of a file.

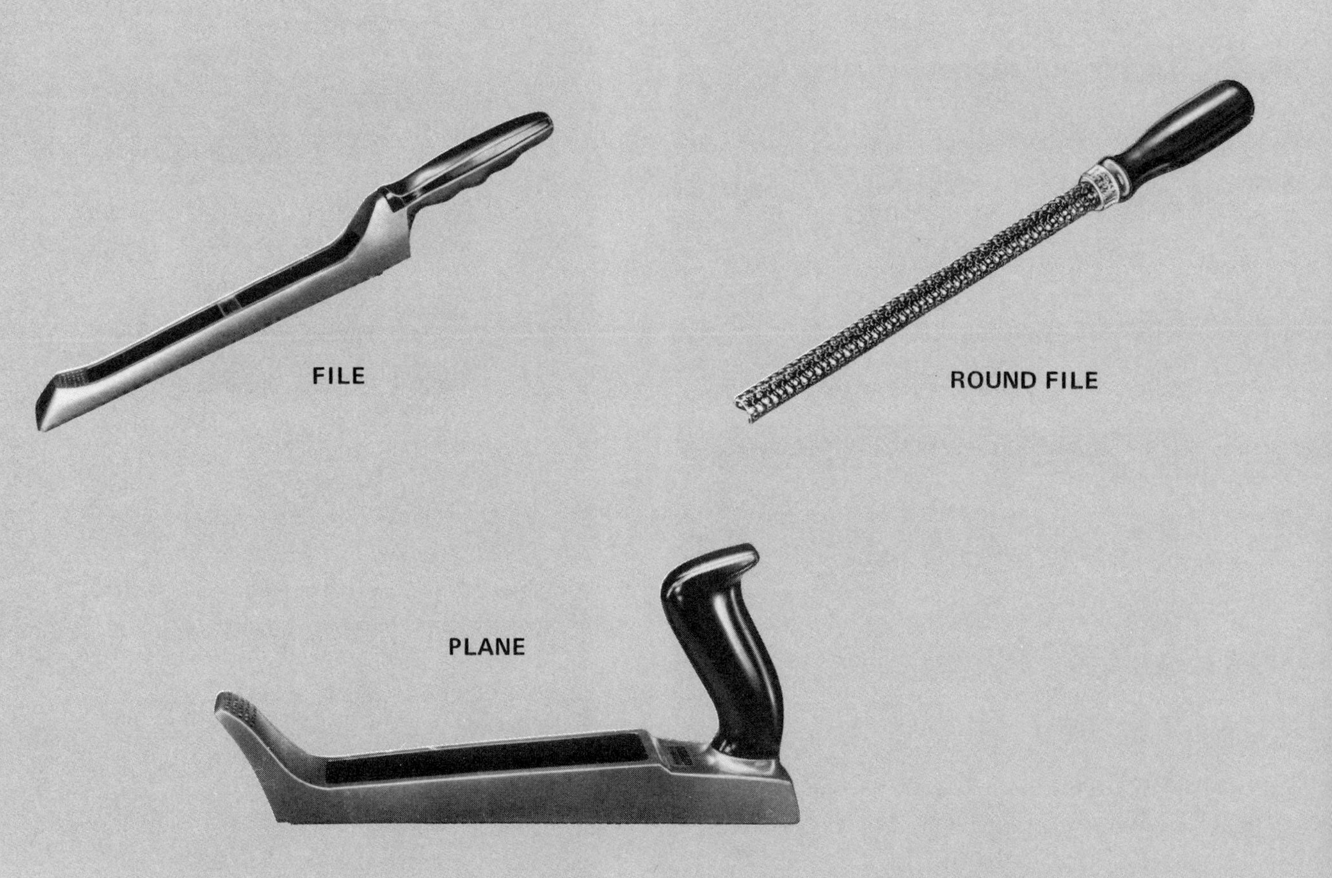

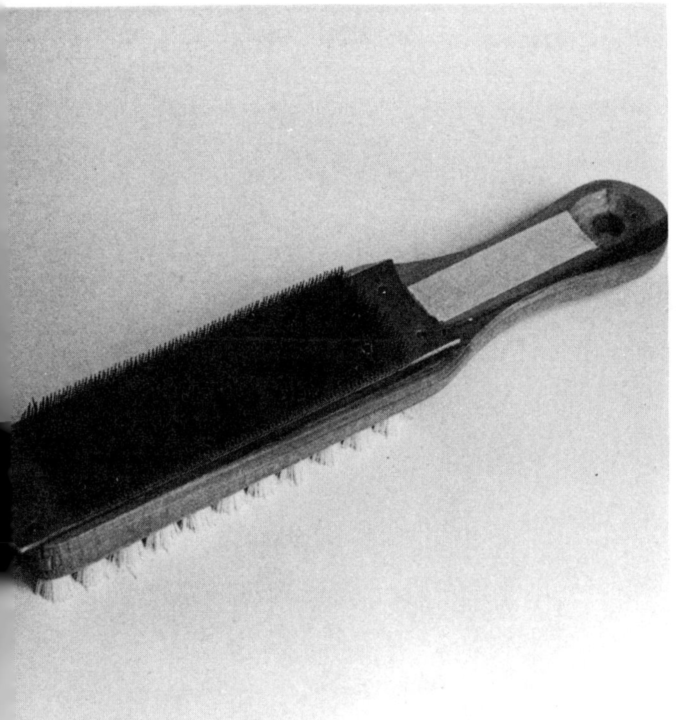

Figure 12-4
A file card cleans file teeth.

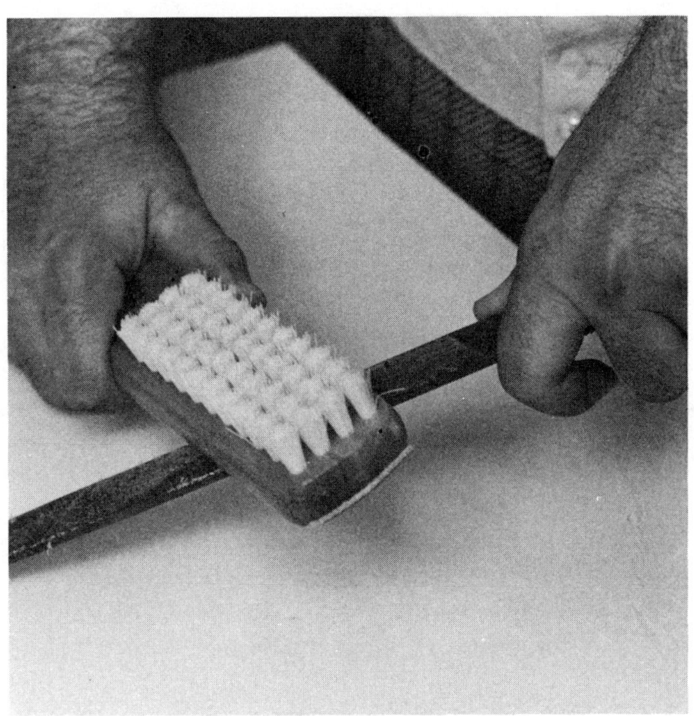

Figure 12-5
Brush across the file to clean the teeth.

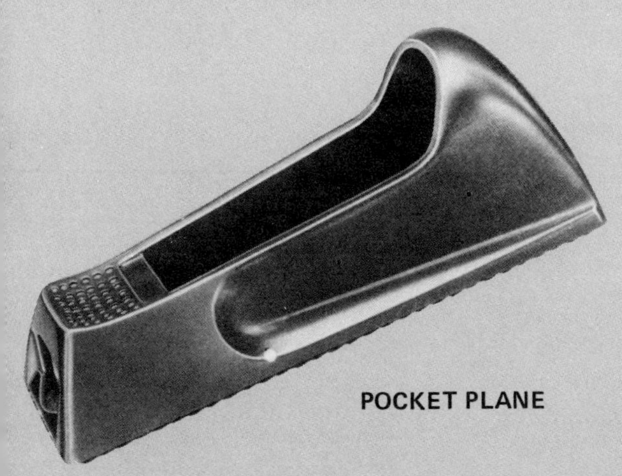

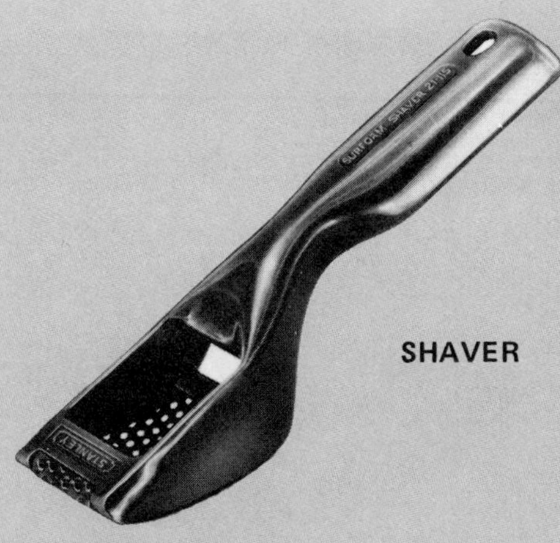

Figure 12-6
Common types of perforated-blade forming tools. (The Stanley Works)

USING FILES AND RASPS

To use a file or rasp:

1. Select the appropriate file shape and coarseness. Usually, you will choose a bastard or a second cut. Use a flat file for flat and convex curves. For concave curves use a half-round file. Use round files for small curves.
2. Fasten the stock to the bench.
3. Push the file diagonally across and forward along the surface, Figure 12-7. The sliding movement produces a shearing cut and does not split the opposite edge. Clean the file often. Plywood edges split more easily than solid wood. Be careful when filing them.
4. File convex curves downward, Figure 12-8. File concave curves downward, Figure 12-9.
5. Finish dressing the surface with a smooth file.
6. Check the edge for squareness with a try square in the same way as if you were using a plane.

Also follow these procedures when you use perforated-blade forming tools, Figures 12-10 to 12-12.

Figure 12-8
File convex curves with the flat side of the file. Push the file down the curve.

Figure 12-7
Filing a flat edge. Keep the file flat on the wood.

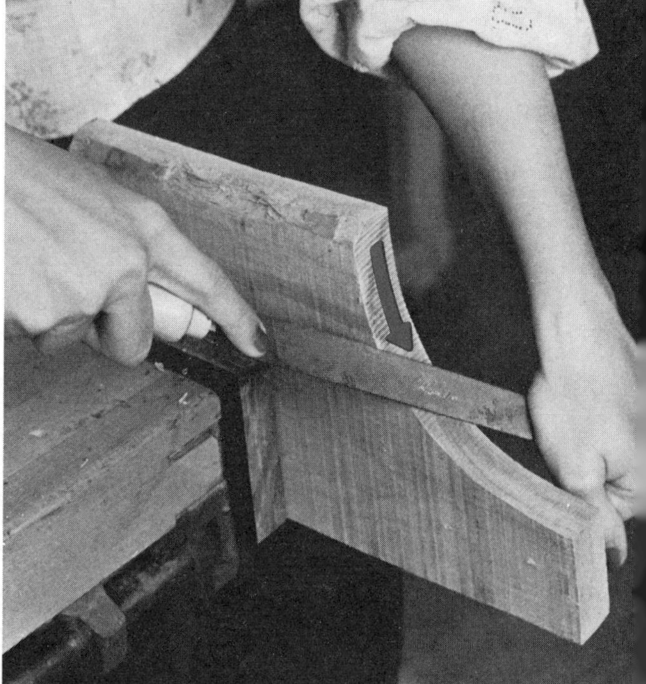

Figure 12-9
File concave curves with the rounded side of the file. Push the file down the curve.

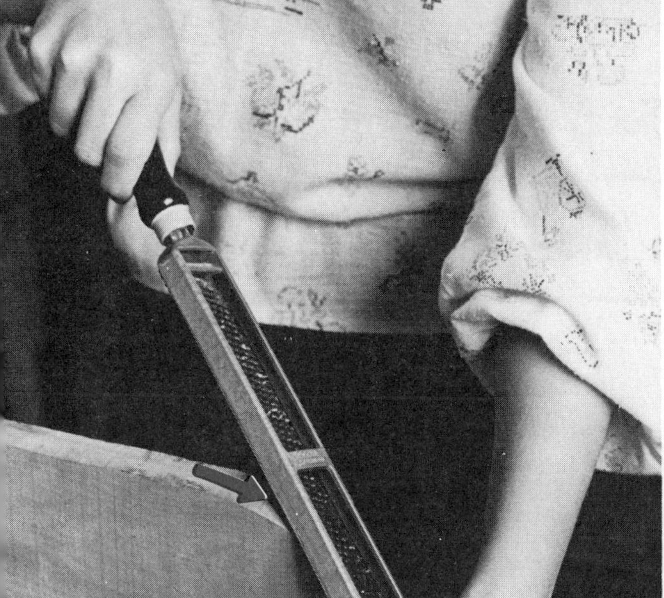

Figure 12-10
Smooth a convex edge with a flat, file-type perforated-blade forming tool.

Figure 12-11
Smooth a convex edge with a pocket plane-type perforated-blade forming tool.

Figure 12-12
Smooth a flat edge with a plane-type perforated-blade forming tool.

REVIEW QUESTIONS

1 How can you tell a file from a rasp?
2 What is the difference between a single-cut and a double-cut file?
3 What do you do with a file card?
4 Why do perforated-blade forming tools seldom clog?
5 What are the common shapes of files?
6 What are the common types of perforated-blade tools?
7 In what direction do you file concave and convex surfaces?

SUGGESTED ACTIVITIES

1 Prepare a list of the different types and shapes of files and rasps in the shop.
2 Using scrap stock, practice smoothing a square end, a concave surface and a convex surface.
3 Check the files in the shop. Clean those that are clogged.

UNIT

13

Drilling and Boring Tools

Objectives

After studying this unit you should be able to:

1. Identify each tool that drills or bores holes.
2. Bore holes through stock to a fixed depth.
3. Drill holes in wood.
4. Countersink and counterbore holes.
5. Bore holes near the opposite face of the stock.

Technical Terms

Drill	Bit gauge
Bore	Counterbore
Auger bit	Countersink
Feed screw	Expansive bit
Spur	Forstner bit
Lip	Twist drill
Dowel bit	Hand drill
Brace	Push drill
Chuck	

DRILLING AND BORING TOOLS SAFETY RULES

1. Clamp the work firmly to the workbench.
2. Secure drills and bits tightly in the chuck.
3. Keep both hands behind the drill point.
4. If drilling through stock, keep a scrap block below so that the drill does not burst through.
5. Keep the drill or bit out of the brace or hand drill when walking around the shop.
6. Do not drill or bore holes if other persons are nearby.
7. Do not press hard on a drill or bit to try to speed up the cutting process.

Many woodworking projects require holes to be cut in the stock. You can *drill* or *bore* these holes. A hand drill or a push drill will drill holes smaller than 1/4" (6 mm) in diameter. An auger bit or a Forstner bit will bore holes 1/4" (6 mm) in diameter and larger. Use an expansive bit in a brace to bore holes from 5/8" to 3" (16 to 76 mm) in diameter.

AUGER BIT

Two types of *auger bits* are available—single twist and double twist, Figure 13-1. A double-twist bit removes chips from the cutter at the faster rate. A single-twist bit is heavier and more durable.

The *feed screw* centers the auger bit on the point chosen for the hole, Figure 13-2. Then it enters the wood, pulling the auger into the board. The knife-like *spurs* cut the wood fibers in a circle. The *lips* act like chisels to gouge the wood away inside the circle cut by the spurs. The twist carries the chips out of the hole. The tang fits into the chuck on the brace.

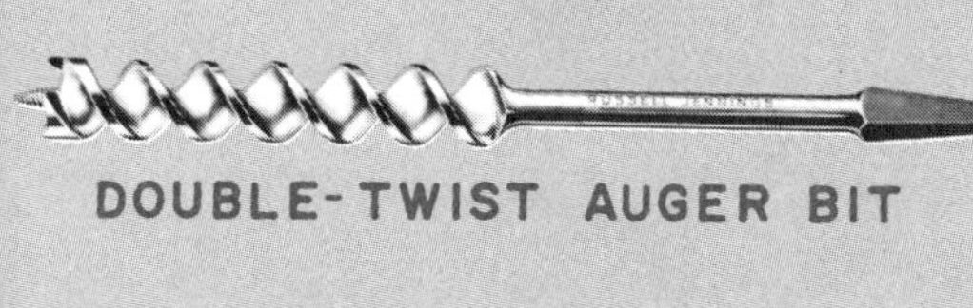

Figure 13-1
Double-twist and single-twist auger bits. (The Stanley Works)

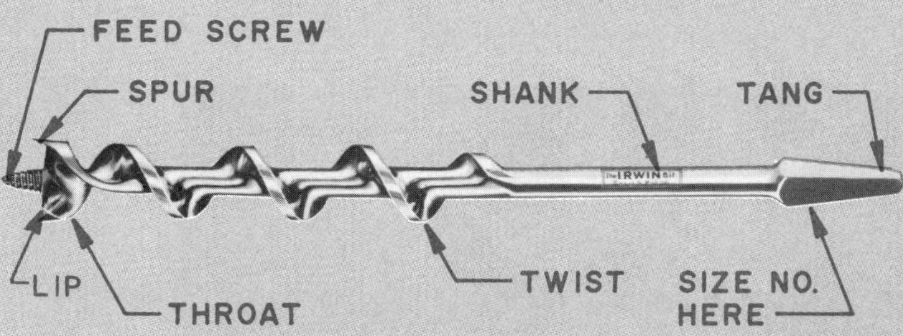

Figure 13-2
The parts of an auger bit. (Irwin Auger Bit Co.)

Figure 13-3 shows three types of feed screws. The pitch of the feed screw determines how fast the bit bores through the wood. For general work, use an auger that has a medium-pitch feed screw. A screw with a steep-pitch thread cuts fast. A fast screw requires more strength to turn. A fine screw has a low-pitch thread. It takes a light cut and turns easily, but is slow to bore a hole.

Auger bits are available in diameters from 1/4" to 1-1/2". On customary measure bits, the size is stamped on the tang in 16ths. For example, the number 8 on the tang means the diameter is 8/16". Auger bits vary in length from 5" to 7".

Auger bits also are available in metric sizes. Diameters are given in millimeters. Sizes range from 6 to 38 mm. Below is a comparison between inch and millimeter bit sizes.

Millimeter Bit Sizes	Inch Bit Sizes
6	
	1/4
8	5/16
	3/8
10	
	7/16
12	
13	1/2
14	
	9/16
16	5/8
	11/16
18	
19	3/4
20	
	13/16
22	
	7/8
24	15/16
25	1
	1-1/16
28	
	1-1/8
30	1-3/16
32	1-1/4
	1-5/16
35	1-3/8
	1-7/16
38	1-1/2

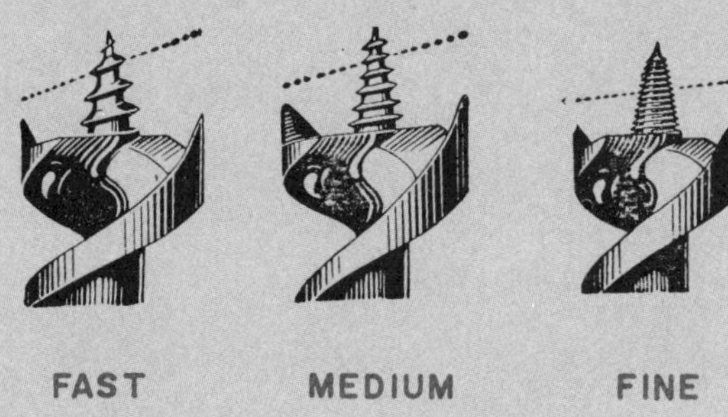

Figure 13-3
Types of auger bit screws. (Irwin Auger Bit Co.)

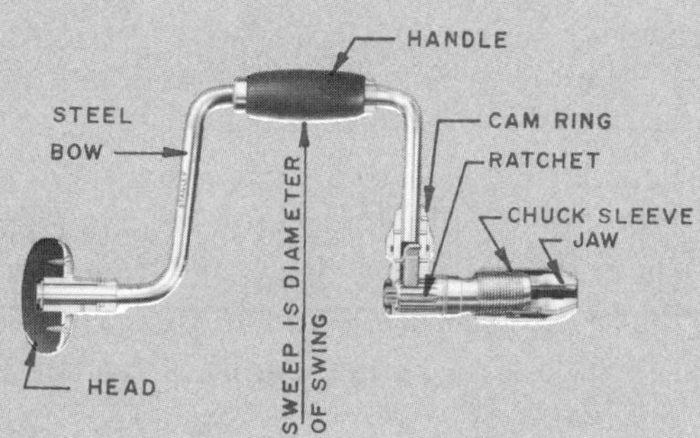

Figure 13-4
The parts of a ratchet brace. (The Stanley Works)

A *dowel bit* is a special auger bit. It is short, usually only 5-1/2" long. Sizes of dowel bits range from 1/4" to 1/2". Dowel bits are useful when a short bit is needed. For instance, see Unit 20 on making a dowel joint.

BRACE

A *brace,* Figure 13-4, holds and turns the auger bit so that it bores into the wood. The *chuck* holds the tang of the auger bit. The sweep of a brace determines its size. The sweep is the diameter of the circle formed by the handle as a hole is bored. Common sweeps are 8", 10" and 12". The ratchet allows boring in corners where a full swing with the handle is impossible.

Figure 13-5
Carefully locate the centers of holes.

Figure 13-6
Punch the centers with an awl. This helps to get the auger bit started in the center.

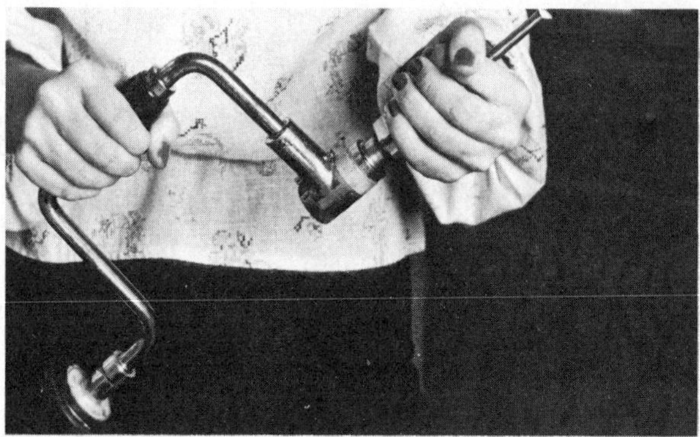

Figure 13-7
Place the auger bit tang in the chuck of the brace. Tighten the bit in place by rotating the outer shell of the chuck.

BORING HOLES WITH AN AUGER BIT

To bore a hole:

1. Lay out the location of the hole, Figure 13-5.
2. If the wood is hard, make a punch mark at the center location, Figure 13-6.
3. Secure the wood to a workbench.
4. Place the auger bit in the brace. Tighten the chuck around the tang, Figure 13-7.
5. Place the feed screw in the punch mark. If the hole is to be perpendicular to the face of the board, use two try squares as guides, Figure 13-8.

   You also can use a boring fixture. A boring fixture is a wood block with a bored hole that is perpendicular to the surface, Figure 13-9. The hole keeps the auger bit perpendicular to the work. Notice how the centerlines are drawn to the base of the fixture.
6. Hold the head of the brace in your right hand and the handle in your left, Figure 13-10. Turn the handle clockwise.
7. Do not bore all the way through the board. If you do, the auger bit will splinter the back side. To prevent this, place a piece of scrap on the back and bore into it, Figure 13-11. You can use another approach. Bore until the feed screw comes through the back. Remove the bit and finish boring the hole from the other side, Figure 13-12.

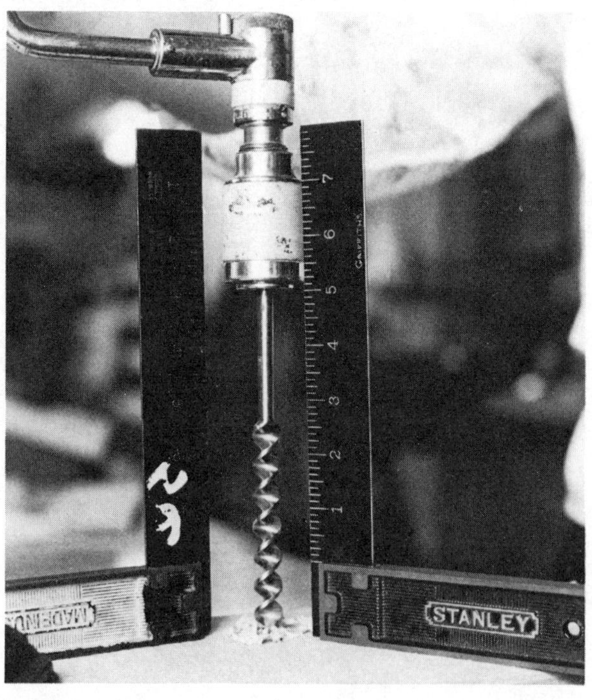

Figure 13-8
A try square keeps a bit perpendicular to the work piece.

Figure 13-9
A shop-made boring fixture helps to bore perpendicular holes.

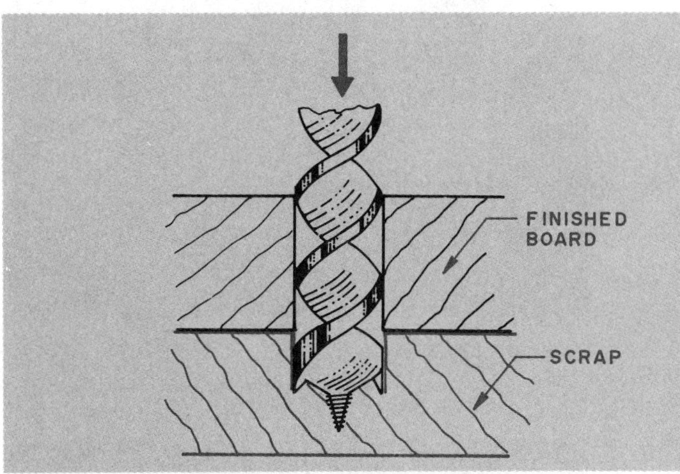

Figure 13-11
When boring through a piece of wood, bore into a scrap board beneath it.

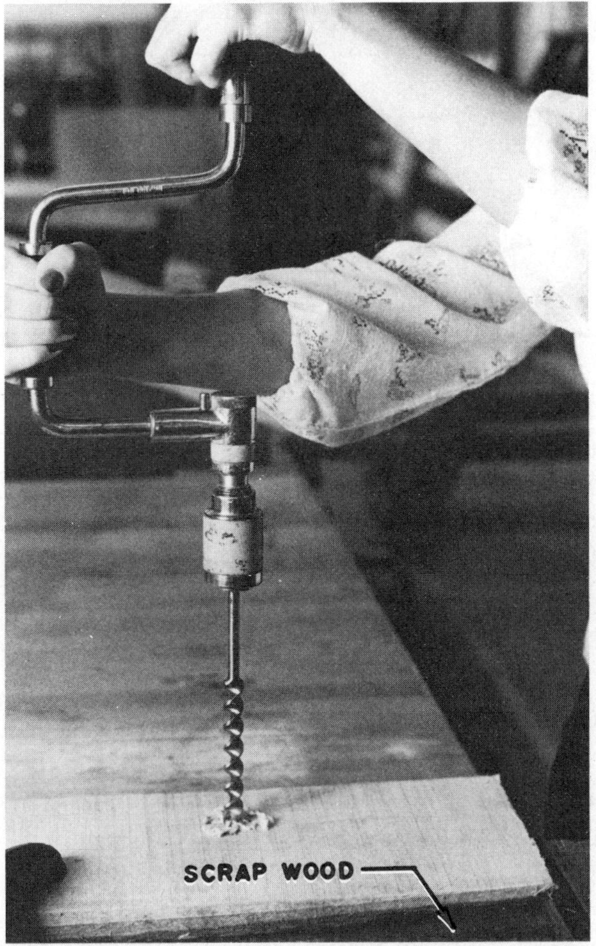

Figure 13-10
Right-handed persons hold the knob in their left hand and rotate the brace with their right. Rotate the brace clockwise.

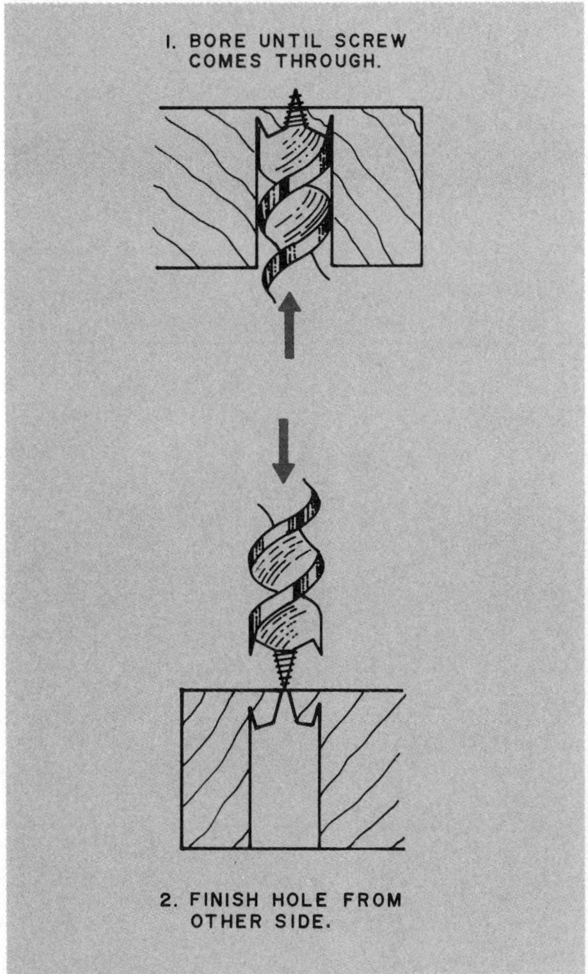

Figure 13-12
Another way to bore a hole completely through stock.

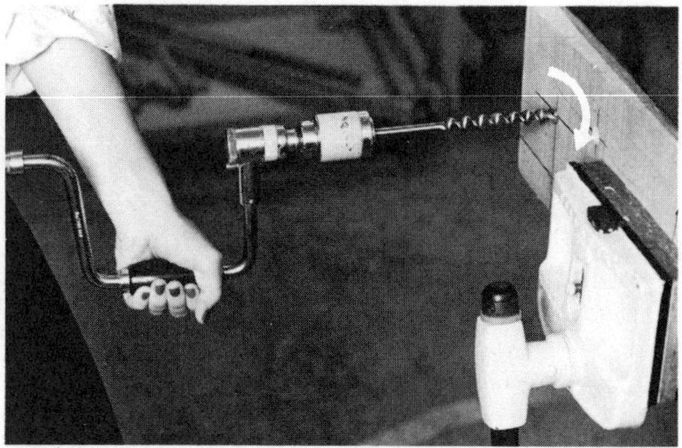

Figure 13-13
Boring a hole while holding the brace horizontally.

Figure 13-14
A bit stop controls the depth to which a hole is bored.

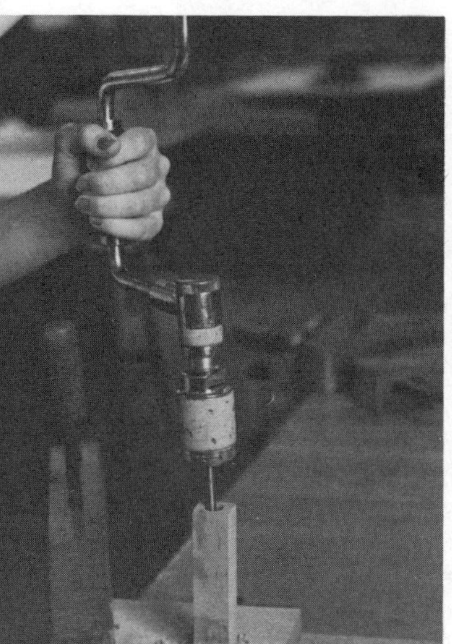

Figure 13-15
A wood block or a piece of tape make good depth stops.

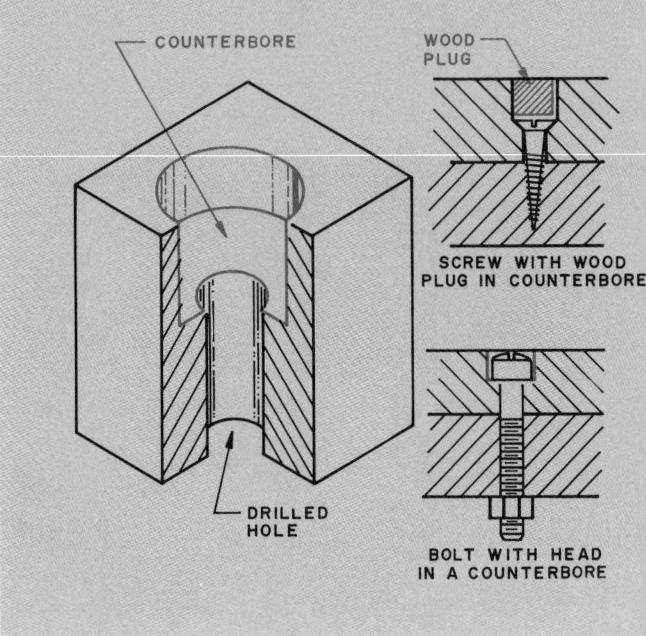

Figure 13-16
A counterbored hole.

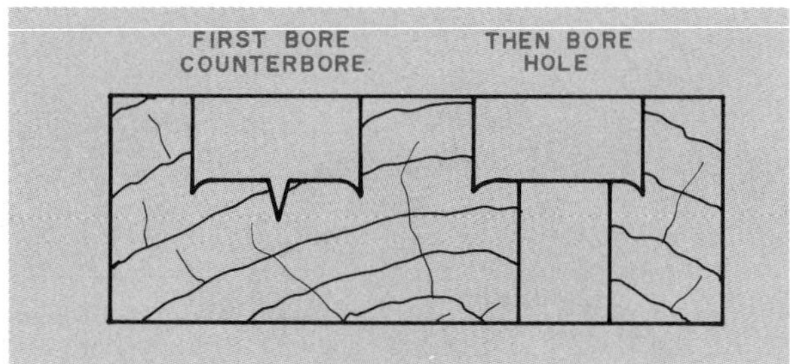

Figure 13-17
How to counterbore a hole.

Sometimes you may find it easier to bore holes while holding the brace and the bit horizontally, Figure 13-13. If the hole will be perpendicular, you can use a try square to line up the auger bit with the face of the board.

Review the procedure for sharpening auger bits in Unit 11.

BORING TO A FIXED DEPTH

To begin this process, place a *bit gauge* on the auger. Bit gauges come in several types. One type is shown in Figure 13-14. Measure the depth of the hole from the lip to the bottom of the bit gauge. Bore the hole in the usual way until the foot of the gauge lightly touches the wood.

You can make a simple bit gauge by slipping a piece of wood over the auger, or you can use a piece of tape, Figure 13-15. Let the length of the bit needed to bore the hole stick out.

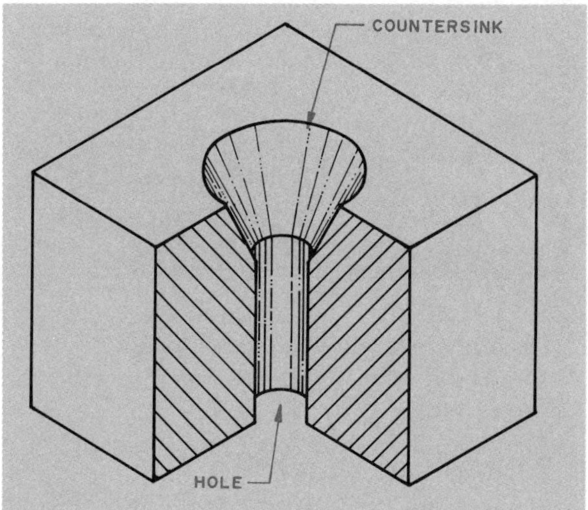

Figure 13-18
Section view of a hole with a countersink.

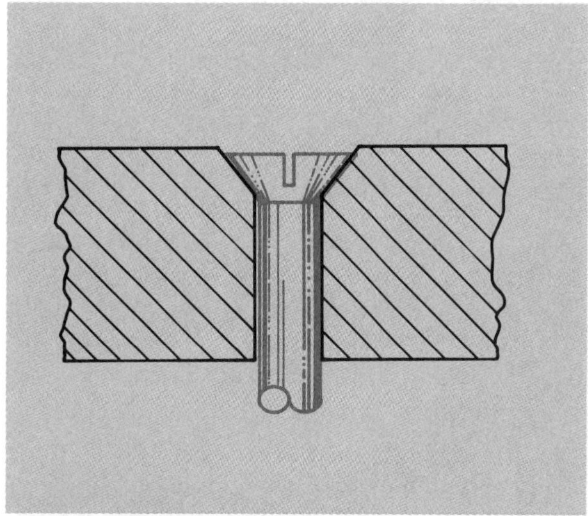

Figure 13-20
Cone-headed fasteners fit into countersinks.

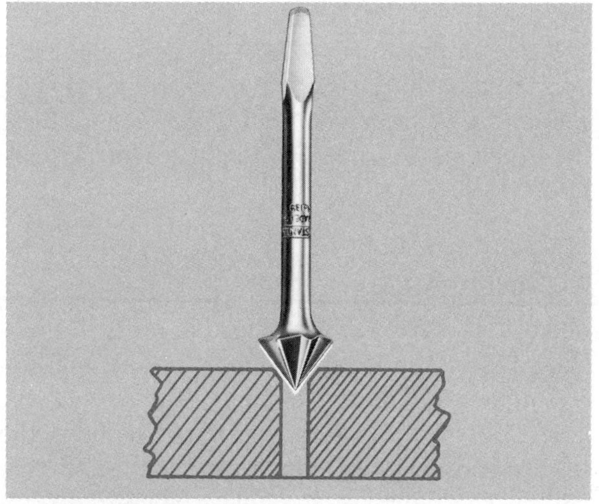

Figure 13-19
A countersinking tool forms a countersink.
(The Stanley Works)

Figure 13-21
Form the countersink after you bore the hole.

COUNTERBORE

A *counterbore* is a large-diameter hole that is bored over a smaller hole, Figure 13-16. You use counterbores if you wish to place the head of a bolt flush with or below the surface of a board. You also use them when you are installing wood plugs to cover screw heads.

To counterbore, first bore the larger-diameter hole to the desired depth, Figure 13-17. Then bore the smaller-diameter hole. If you bore the small hole first, you will not be able to center the bit for the larger hole.

COUNTERSINK

A *countersink* is a cone-shaped depression that is cut into the top of a hole, Figure 13-18. The tool that forms the tapered hole also is called a countersink, Figure 13-19. Holes that are countersunk receive fasteners that have cone-shaped heads, such as wood screws. The head fits into the countersink and is flush or slightly below the surface, Figure 13-20.

To countersink a hole, first bore the hole. Then place the countersink tool in the hole and rotate it as if you were boring a hole, Figure 13-21.

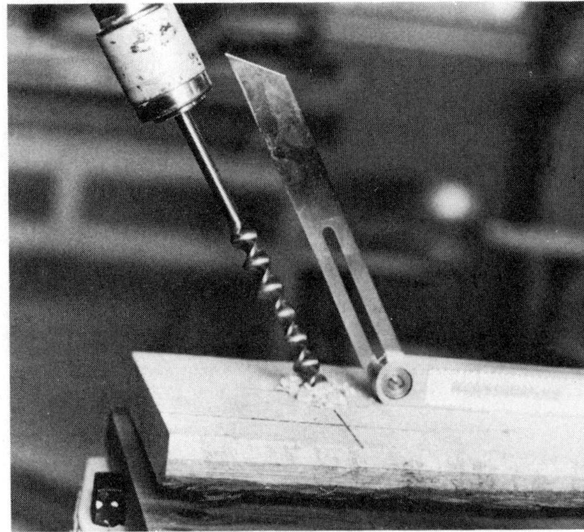

Figure 13-22
A T bevel can line up holes that will be bored on an angle.

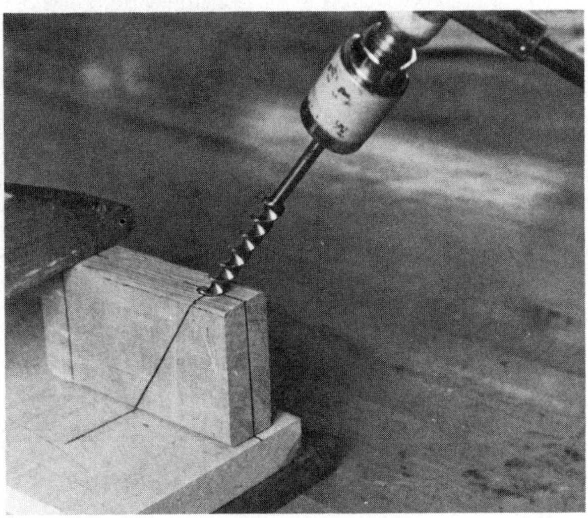

Figure 13-23
A shop-made jig can bore many holes that have the same angle.

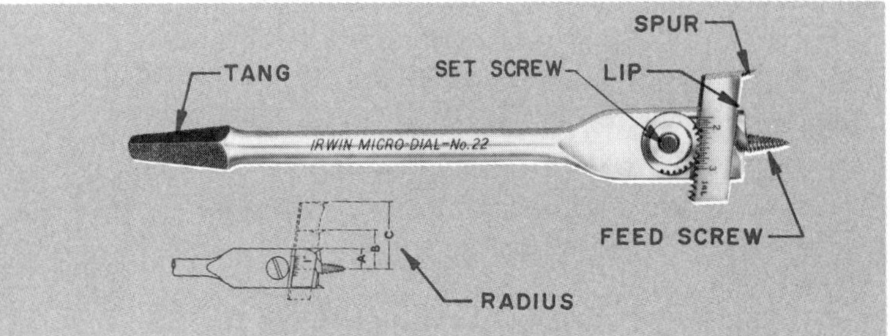

Figure 13-24
The parts of an expansive bit. (Irwin Auger Bit Co.)

Figure 13-25
When boring a hole through stock with an expansive bit, back up the stock with a piece of scrap wood.

BORING AT AN ANGLE

To bore a single hole at an angle, set the T bevel on the desired angle. Locate the center of the hole. Bore in the usual manner, keeping the auger parallel with the blade of the T bevel, Figure 13-22.

When boring several holes on an angle, use a boring jig. A boring jig is a block of wood with a hole bored at the desired angle. Clamp it on the stock as a guide for the auger bit, Figure 13-23.

EXPANSIVE BIT

An *expansive bit* has a feed screw and only one spur and lip. The spur and lip make up a single, adjustable unit. To adjust the size of the hole, loosen the set screw and then move the spur toward or away from the feed screw, Figure 13-24. The radius of the hole is measured from the spur to the center of the feed screw. The tool has a scale to help you set the radius. For accuracy, check the radius with a ruler.

Use the expansive bit in the same way as you would an auger bit. For the best results, back up the board with a piece of scrap and bore into the scrap, Figure 13-25.

FORSTNER BIT

A *Forstner bit* bores shallow holes with flat bottoms. It can bore close to the opposite face of a board without splitting through, Figure 13-26.

The Forstner bit does not have a feed screw or a twist. It has a pin end that helps you locate the bit, Figure 13-27. The lips remove the wood.

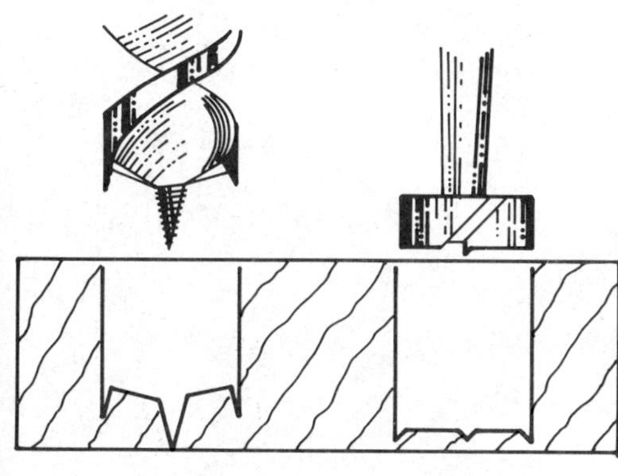

Figure 13-26
Use a Forstner bit to bore a hole close to the opposite face.

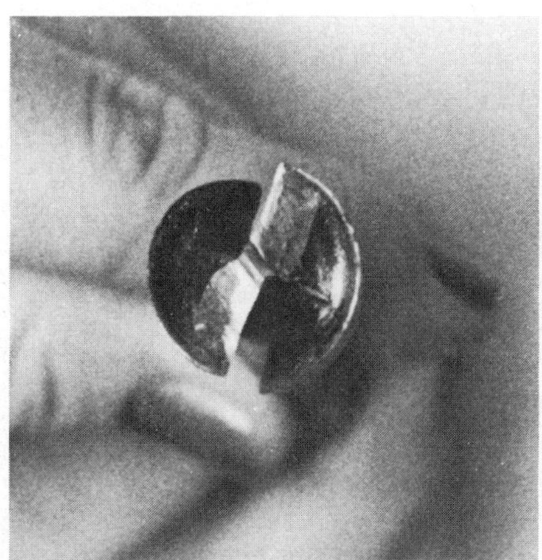

Figure 13-27
A Forstner bit has a pin center and no spurs.

Figure 13-28
Boring a hole with a Forstner bit.

Use a Forstner bit to bore end grain, Figure 13-28.

Forstner bits are available in diameters from 1/4″ to 2″. The size is marked on the tang in 16ths of an inch.

To use a Forstner bit:

1. Locate the center of the hole.
2. Punch a small pin mark at the center.
3. Place the pin in the hole and the bit flat on the board.
4. Rotate the brace carefully until the cutting edge cuts a circle.

If the wood is hard, you may have difficulty in keeping the bit in place. To correct this, start the hole with an auger bit. When the spur cuts a circle, remove the auger bit and use the Forstner bit, Figure 13-29.

Figure 13-29
Steps in boring a hole with a Forstner bit.

TWIST DRILL

A *twist drill* drills holes in wood, metal or plastics. Many sizes are available in both customary and metric measures. Generally, they run from 1/32″ to 1/2″ in 1/64″ increments. The most popular sizes are from 1/16″ to 1/4″. Bits are available in metric sizes. They range from 1 to 13 mm. They have two cutting lips and a spiral flute that carries cut chips out of the hole. The bit's shank is round, Figure 13-30. The shank is designed to fit into a hand drill. The chuck of a brace does not hold twist drills adequately.

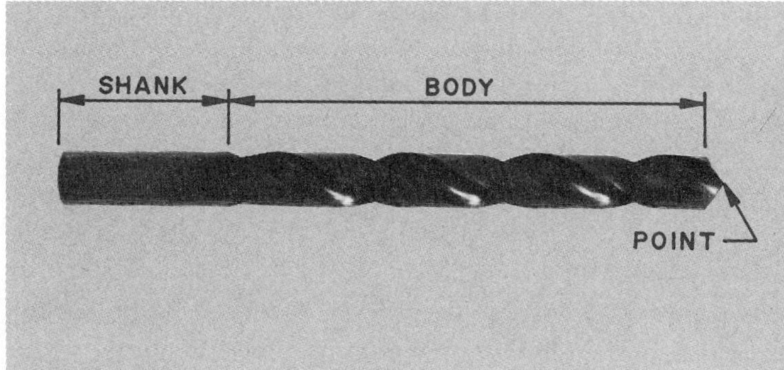

Figure 13-30
Parts of a straight-shank twist drill.

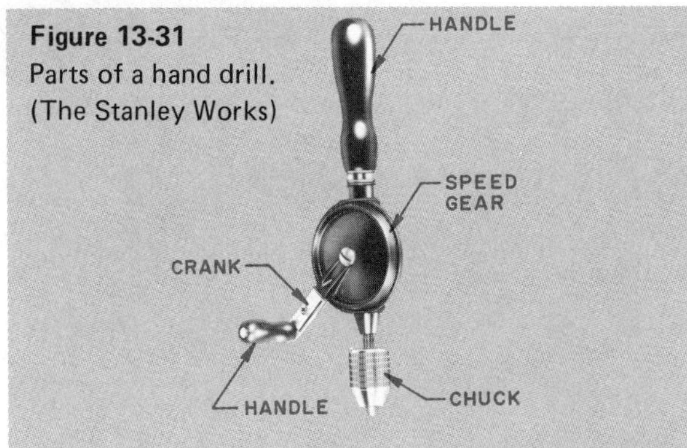

Figure 13-31
Parts of a hand drill. (The Stanley Works)

Figure 13-32
Tighten the twist drill in the chuck of the hand drill.

Figure 13-33
Turn the hand drill handle clockwise.

USING A HAND DRILL

Hand drills have a chuck with jaws that hold the round shank of a twist drill. You rotate the chuck by turning the crank, Figure 13-31. A hand drill's size is determined by the largest diameter drill that the chuck will hold. Common sizes are 1/4″ and 3/8″.

To insert a twist drill, open the chuck by turning the outside collar. Hold the crank tightly so that it will not turn. Place the twist drill all the way into the chuck and tighten the chuck, Figure 13-32.

To drill holes, first locate the center. A punch mark at the center helps to get the twist drill started in the right place. Hold the hand drill at the angle the hole should be and turn the crank clockwise, Figure 13-33. If the depth of the hole is important, you can place a piece of tape on the twist drill to show when the desired depth has been reached.

You can use a dowling jig to help drill holes perpendicular to the wood. Notice the depth stop clamped to the twist drill, Figure 13-34.

USING A PUSH DRILL

Push drills drill small-diameter holes in wood. They are fast. You can operate one with only one hand, Figure 13-35.

The drill points used with a push drill have two cutting lips and a straight flute, Figure 13-36. The points have special shanks that slip into a catch in the chuck. To insert a drill point, slide it into the chuck and rotate the drill point until it snaps in place. To remove the point, push up on the outside of the chuck. This will release the point. Typical sizes of drill points range from 1/16″ to 11/64″ in increments of 1/64″.

To use the push drill, place the point on the center location of the hole. Push down on the handle. This causes the chuck to rotate clockwise. A strong spring in the handle will force it back to the original position when the downward pressure is released. This causes the chuck to rotate counterclockwise. Push down again, Figure 13-37. This repeated motion rotates the point into the wood.

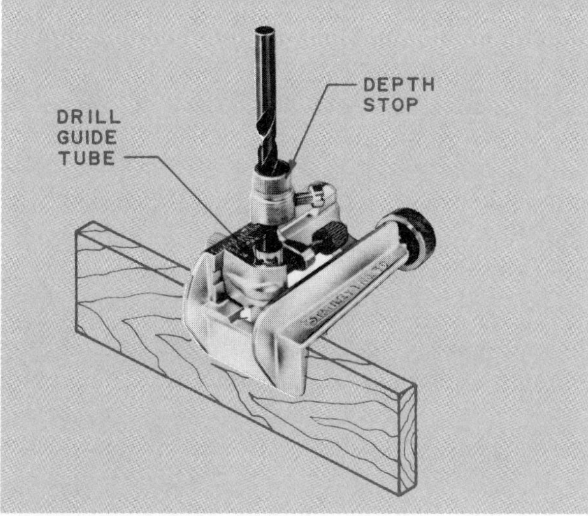

Figure 13-34
Drilling a perpendicular hole with a doweling jig. (The Stanley Works)

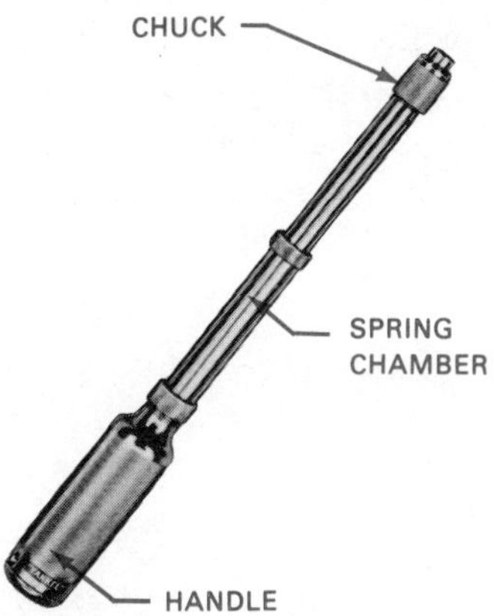

Figure 13-35
A push drill. (The Stanley Works)

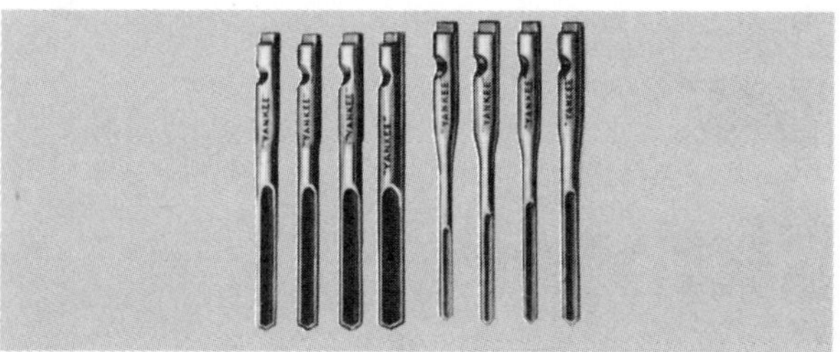

Figure 13-36
Drill points for a push drill. (The Stanley Works)

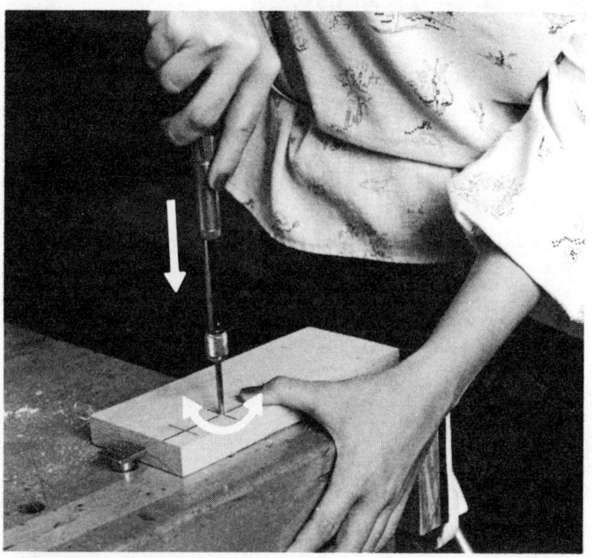

Figure 13-37
Operate a push drill by pushing down on the handle and then raising it.

REVIEW QUESTIONS

1 What is the difference between a bored hole and a drilled hole?
2 How are the sizes of auger bits shown on the tool?
3 What is the purpose of the auger bit screw?
4 What metric auger bit sizes are nearest the following inch sizes: 1/4", 1/2", 3/4", 1"?
5 What purpose does a brace serve?
6 How do you keep the auger bit from splitting out the stock as it comes through the board?
7 How do you bore a hole to a fixed depth?
8 What is the difference between a countersink and a counterbore?
9 What is the special purpose of a Forstner bit?
10 How does an expansive bit differ from an auger bit?
11 In what sizes are twist drills available?

SUGGESTED ACTIVITIES

1 Prepare a list of the different types of shop tools used for drilling and boring holes.
2 Using scrap stock, perform the following operations. Bore a 1/2" hole through stock with a 3/4"-diameter counterbore. Bore a hole to within 1/16" of the other side. Drill a 1/4"-diameter hole and countersink it.
3 Using an expansive bit, bore the following diameter holes through a piece of scrap stock: 1-1/2", 2", 2-3/4".

UNIT

14

Clamping Tools and Assembly Procedures

Objectives

After studying this unit you should be able to:

1 Identify clamping and assembly tools.
2 Recognize basic industrial assembly devices.
3 Set up your project for subassembly and final assembly.
4 Assemble stock face-to-face and edge-to-edge.
5 Clean glue joints.
6 Assemble cabinet and furniture frames.

Technical Terms

Hand screw	Spring clamp
C clamp	Web clamp
Face-to-face assembly	Corner clamp
	Miter vise
Bar clamp	Stapling machine
Edge-to-edge assembly	Nailing machine
	Trial assembly
Piling clamp	Adhesive spreader
Press screw	Subassembly

After the parts of a product are manufactured, assembly begins. There are a number of standard hand-operated clamps and other assembly tools. Some products, especially mass-produced furniture and millwork, require special clamping devices. Hand-operated clamping devices are too slow for mass production, and the chance for error is large. Hand clamps are quite satisfactory for school use, however.

STANDARD HAND-OPERATED CLAMPING TOOLS

The *hand screw* has parallel wooden jaws. To adjust it grip the two handles and spin the clamp like a propeller, Figure 14-1. When clamping, keep the jaws parallel, Figure 14-2. Clamp sizes are specified by number. The larger the number, the larger the clamp. Some common hand screw sizes are:

No.	Jaw Length	Jaw Opening
5/0	4″	2″
4/0	5″	2-1/2″
3/0	6″	3″
2/0	7″	3-1/2″
0	8″	4-1/2″
1	10″	6″
2	12″	8-1/2″
3	14″	10″
4	16″	12″
5	18″	14″

C clamps have a metal, C-shaped frame and a threaded shaft. They also are called carriage clamps. Use them for *face-to-face assembly* and general assembly work. The clamping surfaces are metal and may mar wood surfaces. Place pieces of scrap wood between them and the finished wood surface, Figure 14-3.

Some common sizes of C clamps are:

Opening	Depth
2″	1-3/4″
3″	2-1/4″
4″	2-1/2″
6″	3-1/8″
8″	3-3/4″
10″	4″
12″	4-1/4″

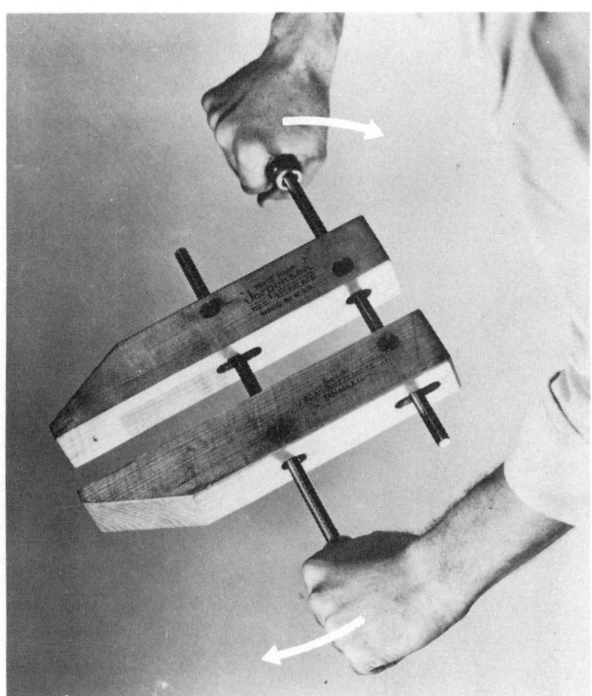

Figure 14-1
Open or close hand screws by holding the handles and spinning them. (Adjustable Clamp Co.)

Figure 14-2
Wood hand screws have parallel clamping jaws. (American Plywood Association)

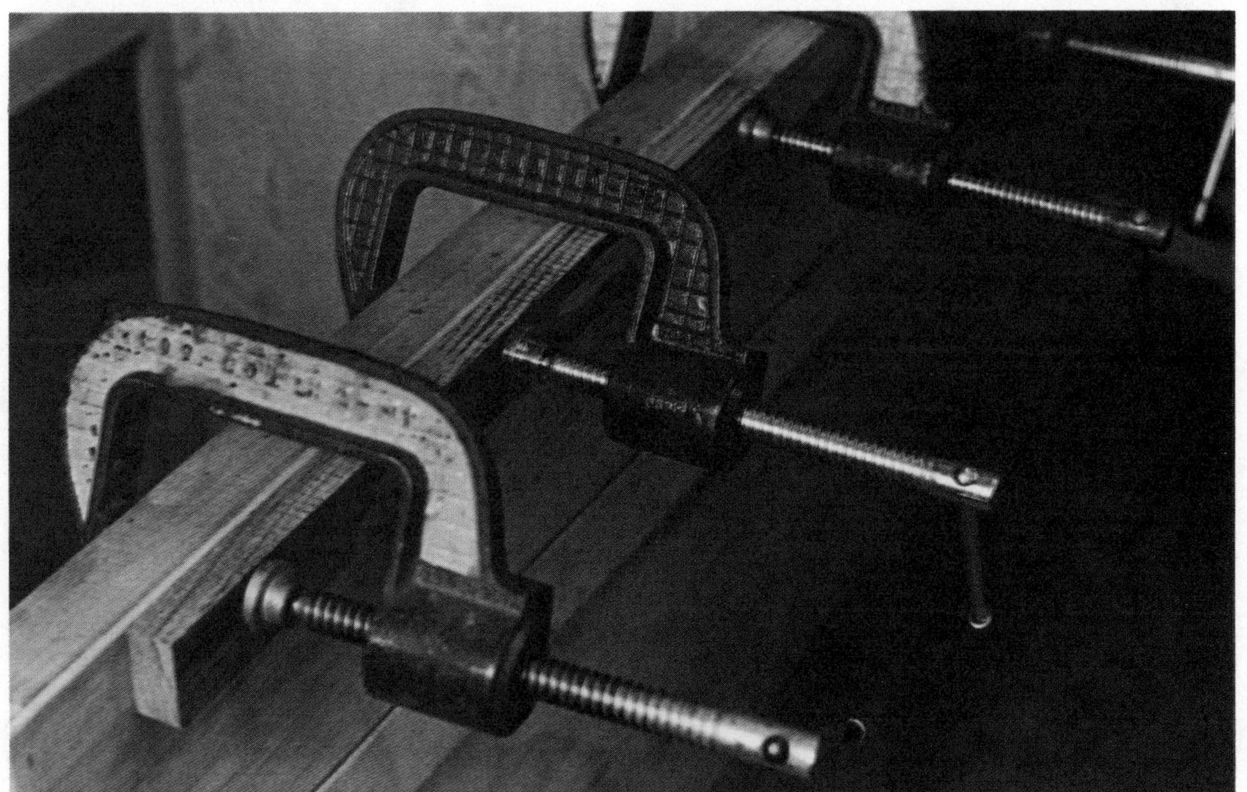

Figure 14-3
Use C clamps for general assembly work.

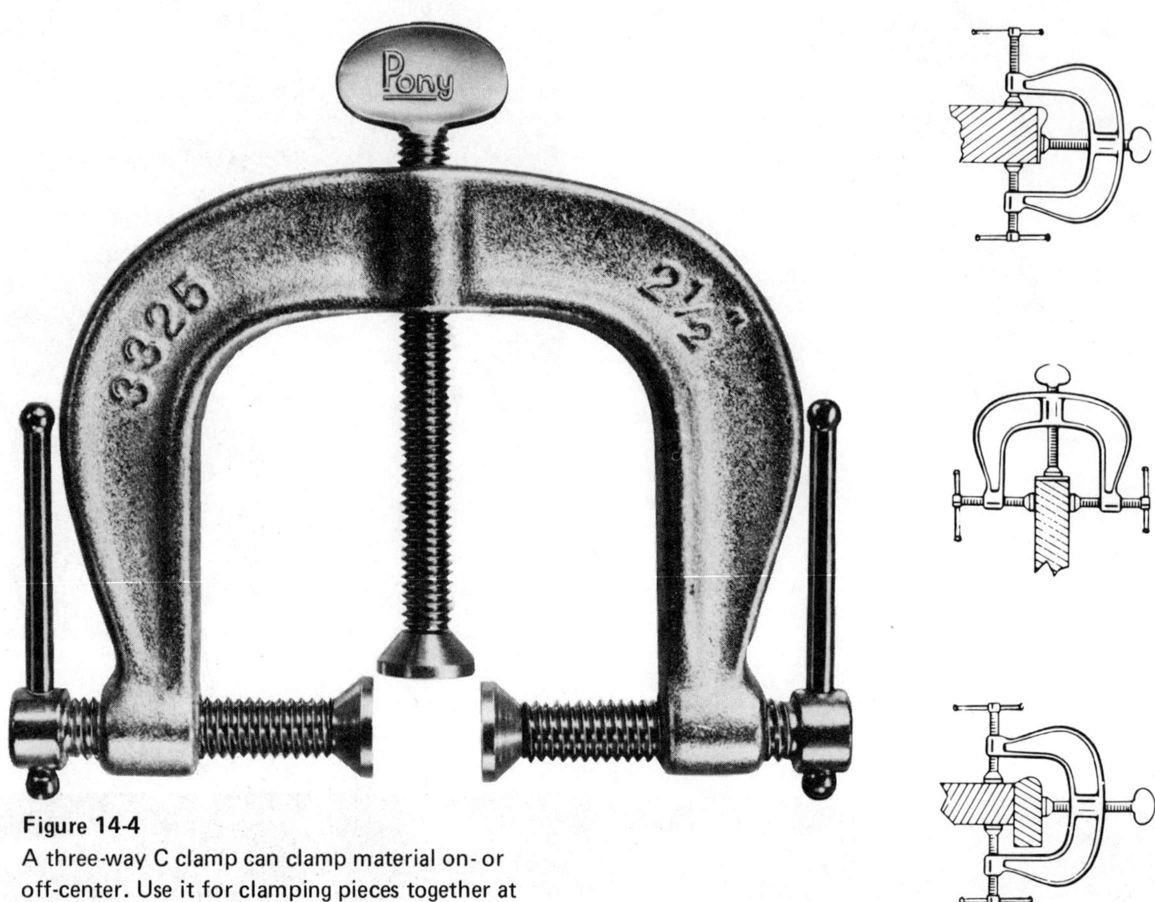

Figure 14-4
A three-way C clamp can clamp material on- or off-center. Use it for clamping pieces together at right angles. (Adjustable Clamp Co.)

A three-way C clamp clamps right angles. This clamp permits the clamping pressure to be either on- or off-center, Figure 14-4.

The double-C leverclamp uses leverage to produce a clamping action, Figure 14-5. The clamp is self-adjusting. Place the upper jaw on the work and squeeze the clamp lever. The clamp automatically adjusts the lower jaw to fit tightly. Close the clamp lever to lock the jaws in position. Adjust the amount of clamping pressure with the adjusting screw. Release the clamp by opening the clamp lever.

A *bar clamp,* also called a cabinet clamp, is a long, metal bar with an adjustable foot. Pressure is applied by a foot operated by a screw. Bar clamps may have a single or a double bar, Figure 14-6. Use bar clamps for *edge-to-edge assembly* of boards. You also can use them in cabinet assembly, Figure 14-7.

Short bar clamps are available in lengths of 6″, 12″ and 18″, Figure 14-8. Long bar clamps are available in lengths of 2′, 3′, 4′, 5′ and 6′. Use blocks of scrap wood between the clamp feet and the product to prevent marring the wood.

A bar-type *piling clamp,* Figure 14-9, has two sets of jaws facing in opposite directions. The jaws permit each layer of wood to be clamped from below and above. The clamp under the layer clamps it from below. The clamp above the layer clamps it from above. The piling clamp reduces buckling. It also removes the need for spacer strips between glued layers.

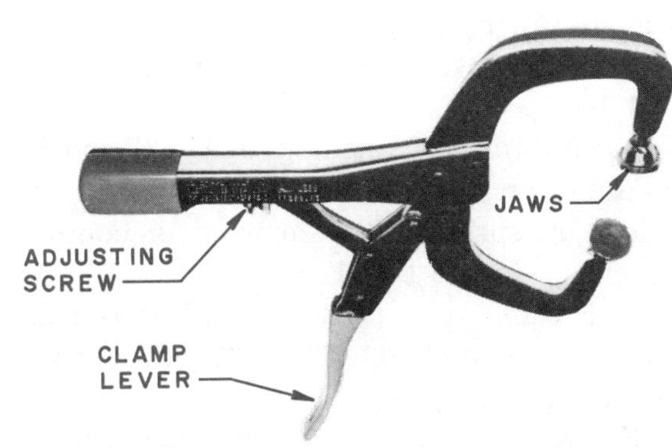

Figure 14-5
A double-C clamp, called a Lever Wrench®. (Leverage Tools, Inc.)

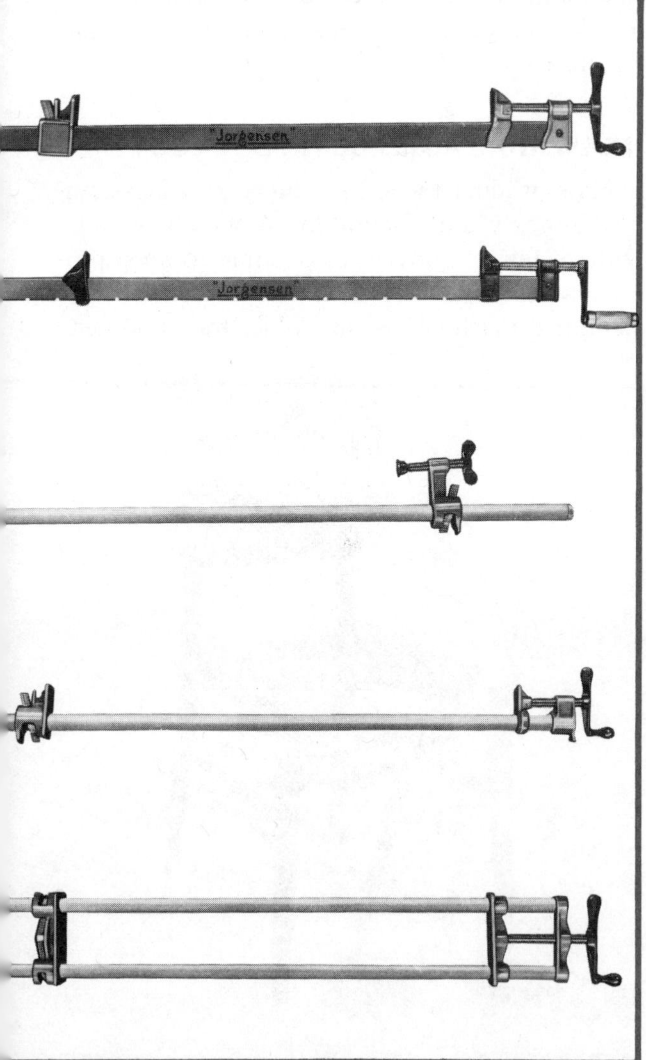

Figure 14-6
Types of bar clamps. (Adjustable Clamp Co.)

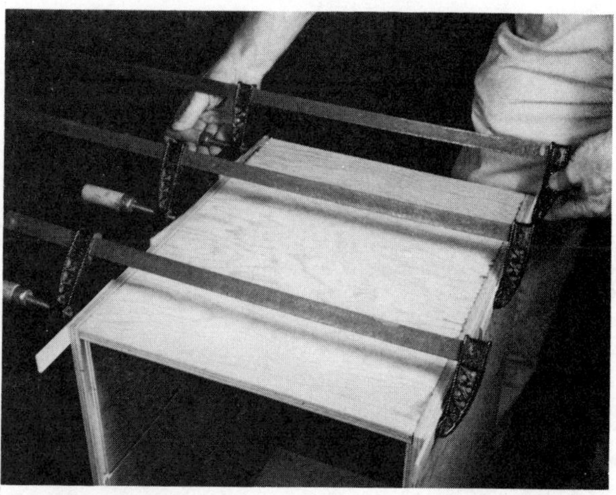

Figure 14-7
Use bar clamps for clamping long products. (American Plywood Association)

Figure 14-8
Short bar clamps. (Adjustable Clamp Co.)

Figure 14-9
A bar-type piling clamp holds a layer of wood from above and below. (Adjustable Clamp Co.)

Figure 14-10
Use press clamps to apply pressure over large surfaces. (Adjustable Clamp Co.)

Press screws help make veneer press frames and many other gluing jigs. They are easy to install and to remove during job change-overs, Figure 14-10.

Spring clamps have openings of 1″, 2″ and 3″. They apply pressure with a torsion spring in the handle. This spring keeps them under continuous pressure, Figure 14-11.

A *web clamp* can hold objects of irregular shape. It is a nylon band, 1″ to 3″ wide, running through a clamping device. It is like a car seat belt, Figure 14-12. Place the band around the irregular object and tighten the clamp. A ratchet holds the web tight, Figure 14-13.

The *corner clamp* and *miter vise* hold mitered corners while they are glued or nailed. The corner clamp holds stock up to 3″ wide, Figure 14-14. The miter clamp holds stock up to 4″ wide, Figure 14-15.

INDUSTRIAL ASSEMBLING DEVICES

Mass produced wood products must be assembled quickly and accurately. Assembly is done with as few employees as possible to keep production costs low. A wide variety of industrial clamping machines is available for producing

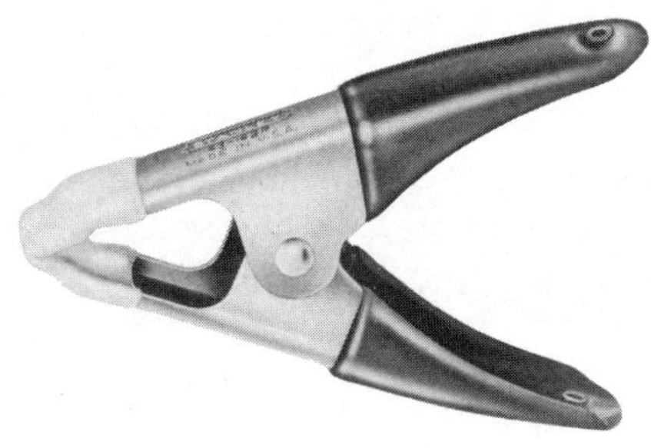

Figure 14-11
A spring clamp. (The Stanley Works)

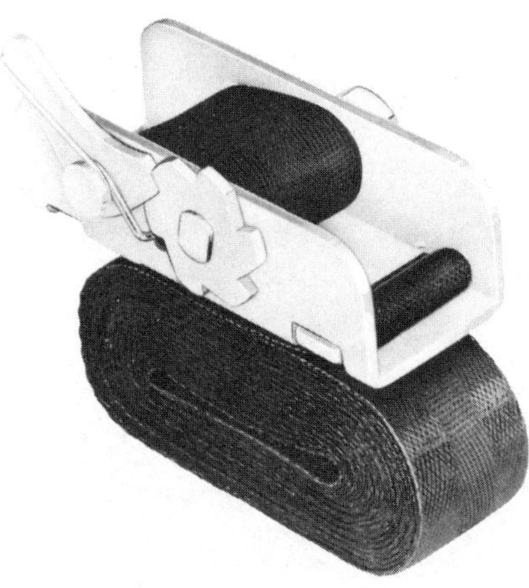

Figure 14-12
A web clamp. (The Stanley Works)

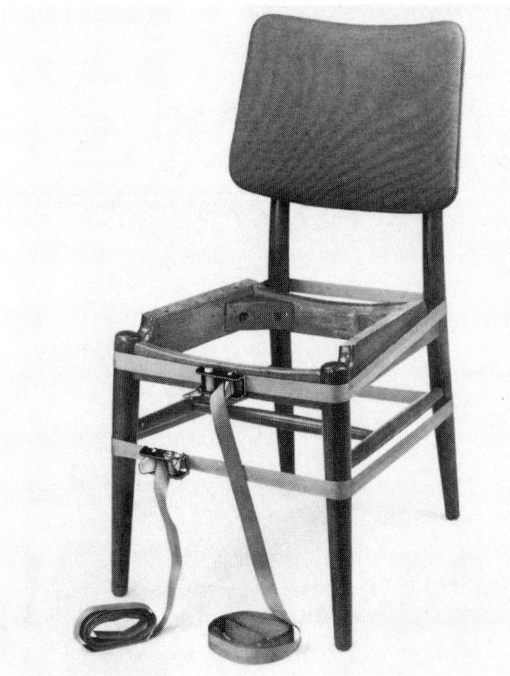

Figure 14-13
A web clamp holds irregularly shaped objects. (Adjustable Clamp Co.)

Figure 14-14
Corner clamps hold mitered corners.

Figure 14-15
A miter vise holds miters while they are nailed or screwed together

wood products. Most clamping machines operate by compressed air. Air-powered machines and tools are called pneumatic.

A headboard and cabinet clamping machine is shown in Figure 14-16. One jaw is stationary. The other jaw is a combination setup and pressure jaw. To use this machine, place the furniture unit between the jaws. Turn the handwheel to lock the setup between the jaws. The pressure jaw moves when air flows into an air cylinder.

A two-way clamping machine is shown in Figure 14-17. You would use it to assemble case ends, mirrors, face frames, case doors and bases. Notice the wood frame being assembled in the clamp. Hand cranks close the long jaws on the unit. Two air cylinders apply the main pressure. Air cylinders at the ends of the long jaws then apply end pressure.

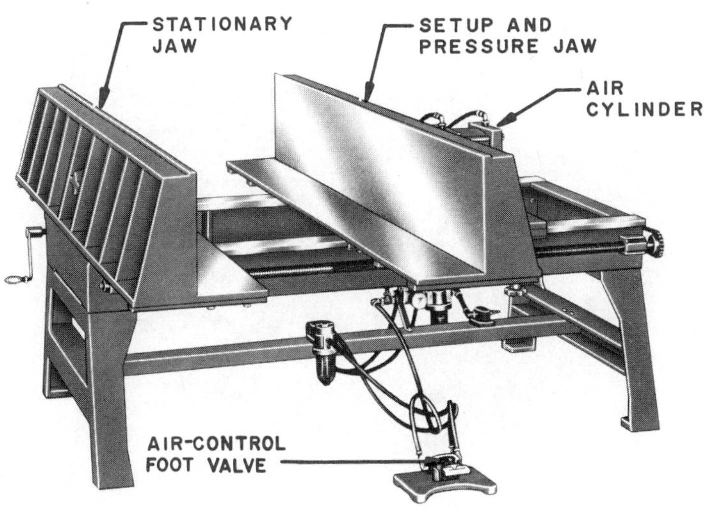

Figure 14-16
A headboard and cabinet clamping machine. (J. M. Lancaster, Inc.)

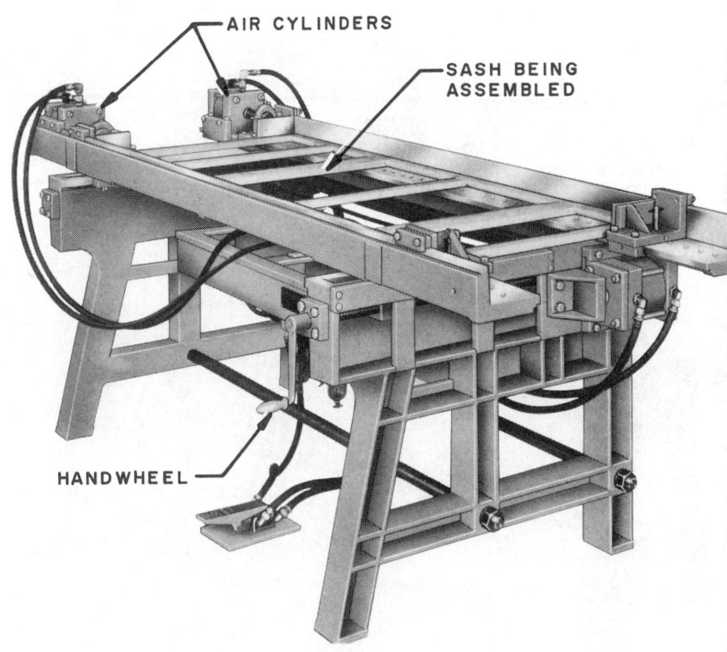

Figure 14-17
This two-way clamping machine applies pressure from the sides and the ends. (J. M. Lancaster, Inc.)

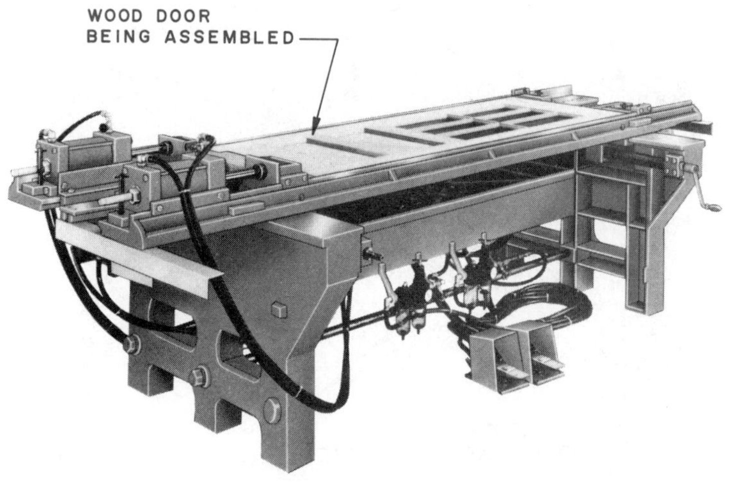

Figure 14-18
A door and sash clamping machine uses two-way clamping action. (J. M. Lancaster, Inc.)

A two-way door and sash clamping machine is shown in Figure 14-18. It operates in the same manner as the unit in Figure 14-17. It has two foot controls. This makes it possible for you to use a clamp on each side of the machine. It can be inched closed from either side. Assemble the door or sash on the frame of the machine, or partially assemble them elsewhere and lay the pieces on the machine for final assembly.

Another machine assembles a variety of drawers, Figure 14-19. It is useful for holding kitchen cabinet drawers while they are stapled together. An operator can assemble 80 to 100 drawers per hour. If drawers are glued, a glue-spreading machine is used.

A high-frequency assembly machine uses electrodes to quickly draw and apply glue, Figure 14-20. To use this assembly machine, clamp the units to be assembled in the machine. Place the electrodes about 1/4" over the glue line. Close the lid by pressing a button. This activates the electrodes that cure the glue. If the electrodes touch the work, they will burn it. The output of radio waves through the electrodes cures the glue.

Figure 14-19
A drawer assembly machine. (J. M. Lancaster., Inc.)

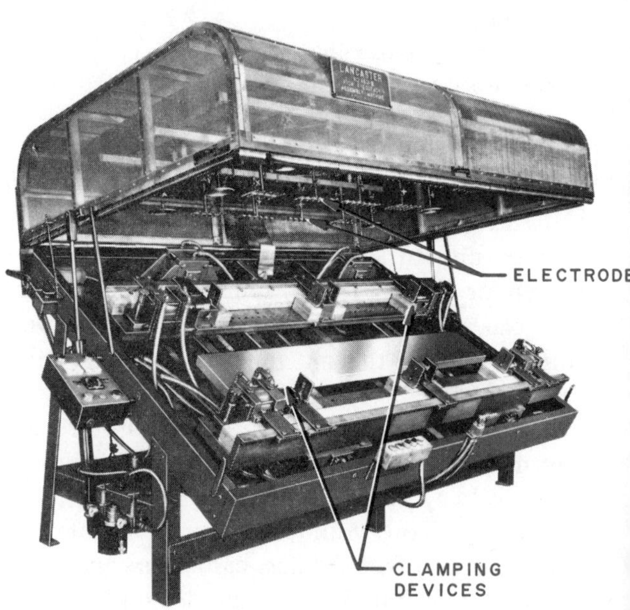

Figure 14-20
A high-frequency assembly machine uses radio waves to cure the glue. (J. M. Lancaster, Inc.)

A chair clamping machine assembles chairs. The machine shown in Figure 14-21 assembles dining room chairs. The setup and pressure jaws apply pressure to the back of the chair. The jaws apply pressure low on the chair leg to press the stretchers between the legs and to press the joints in the seat area. The side clamping assembly holds the chair squarely in the front of the clamp. It applies pressure to the front joints.

Case goods are clamped with a revolving case-clamping machine, Figure 14-22. Place the pre-assembled case between the setup and pressure jaws. The setup jaw closes on the case, binding it between the two jaws. The pneumatic jaw brings the case under pressure. The entire assembly can be revolved to make it easy to reach all sides of large cases.

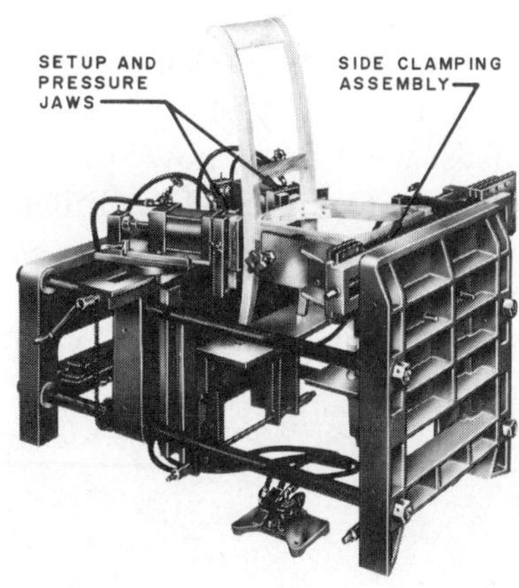

Figure 14-21
A chair assembly machine designed for dining room chairs. (J. M. Lancaster, Inc.)

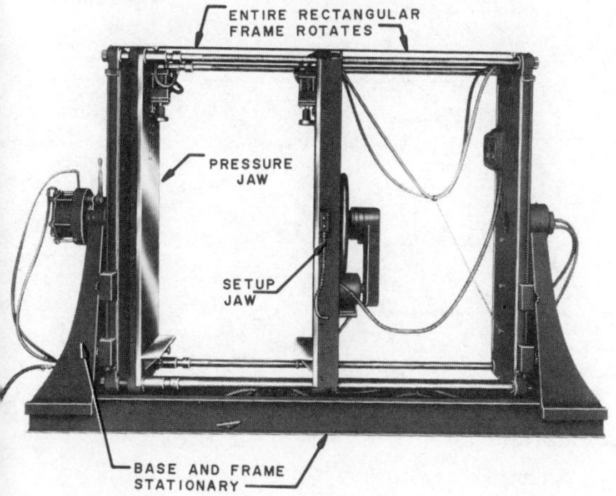

Figure 14-22
A revolving case clamping machine. (J. M. Lancaster, Inc.)

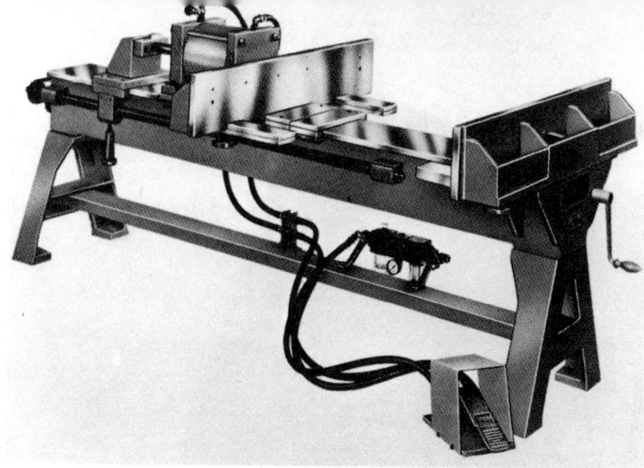

Figure 14-23
A frame assembly machine for upholstered furniture. (J. M. Lancaster, Inc.)

The machine shown in Figure 14-23 assembles frames for upholstered furniture. It can hold frames for straight chairs, barrel-back chairs, straight sofas and curved sofas, Figure 14-24. A larger clamping machine for chairs, sofas, cabinets and tables is shown in Figure 14-25. This machine can hold an entire sofa, applying pressure on the ends, front and back.

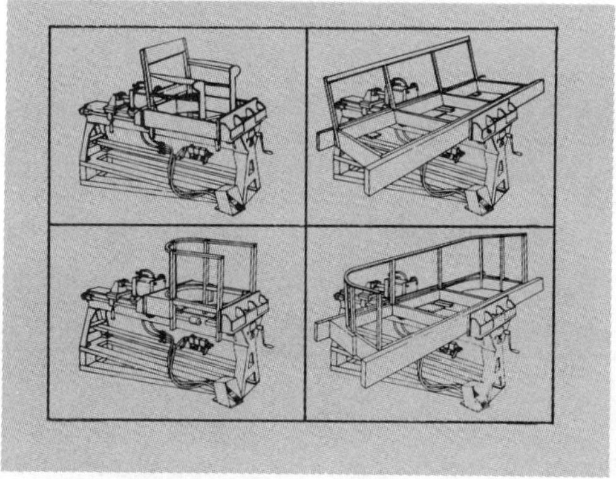

Figure 14-24
The upholstered-furniture machine can assemble a variety of frames. (J. M. Lancaster, Inc.)

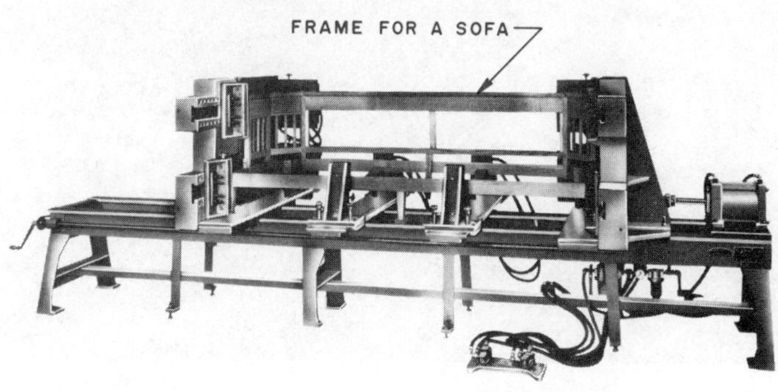

Figure 14-25
Large assembly machines for upholstered furniture can assemble an entire sofa frame. (J. M. Lancaster, Inc.)

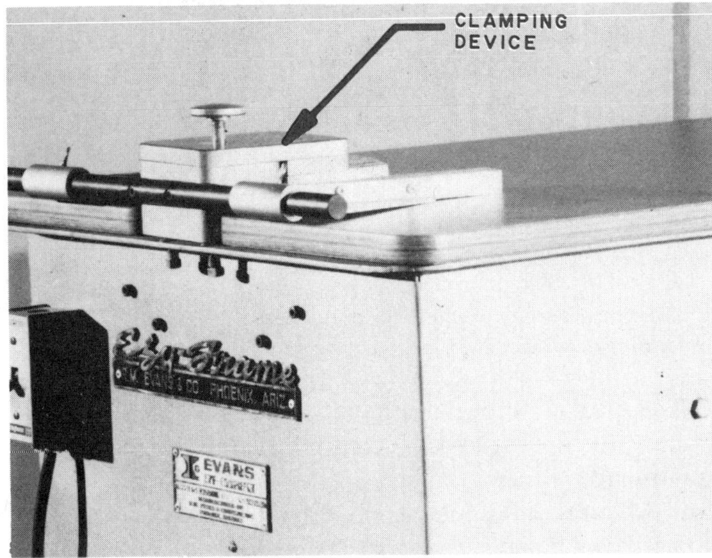

Figure 14-26
Individual parts of furniture frames are drilled and countersunk on this drilling table. The frame clamp holds the work to the table. (Evans Rotork, Inc.)

Figure 14-27
Furniture frames are assembled, clamped and fastened with glue and screws on this assembly table. The assembler is using a pneumatic screwdriver. (Evans Rotork, Inc.)

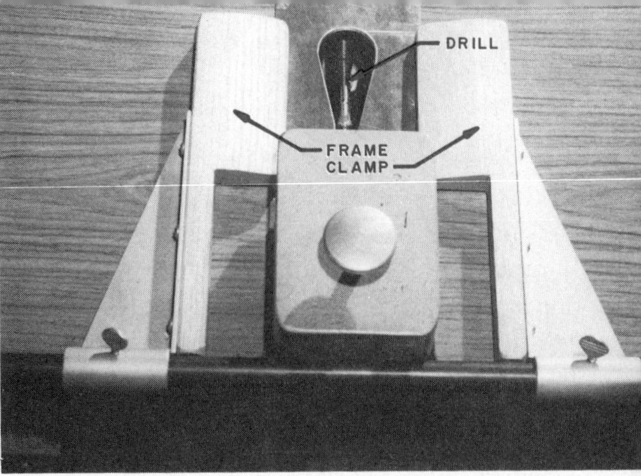

Figure 14-28
The clamping device on the drilling table holds the frame as it is being drilled and countersunk. Notice the drill below the table. (Evans Rotork, Inc.)

The frame assembly-system machine is a drill table, Figure 14-26, an assembly table, Figure 14-27, and a portable, pneumatic screwdriver in one unit. The drill table drills countersunk holes in the ends of frame parts. A clamp unit, shown in Figure 14-28, holds the part against the table. The drill moves up from below, drilling and countersinking, Figure 14-29. The drilled parts are positioned for assembly on the assembly table. Air cylinders clamp them to the table. A power screwdriver drives the screws, Figure 14-30.

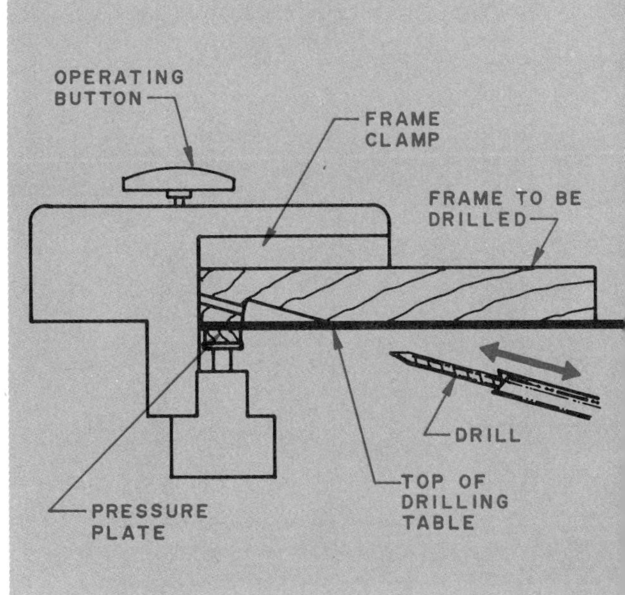

Figure 14-29
A cross section of the drilling table. The frame clamp holds the frame to the table. The drill moves up from below. (Evans Rotork, Inc.)

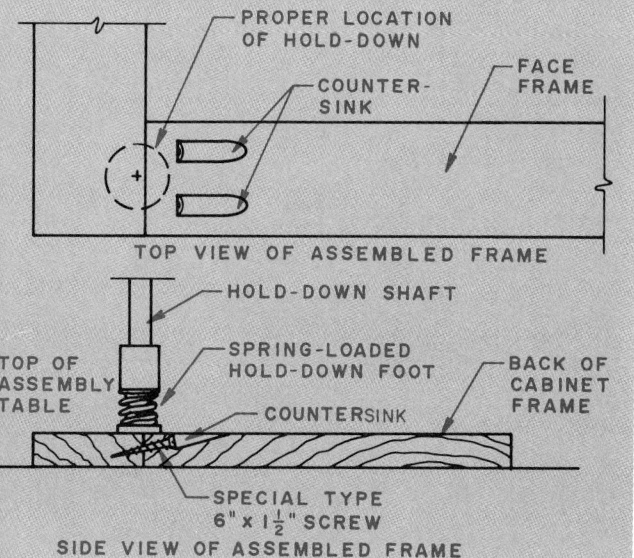

Figure 14-30
The assembly table clamp holds frame parts. A pneumatic screwdriver drives the screws. (Evans Rotork, Inc.)

A conveyor-type clamp carrier helps glue board edges to form panels, Figure 14-31. An automatic glue applicator applies the glue, Figure 14-32. This equipment performs the same operations as hand-operated bar clamps. The stock lays upon each row of clamps. An air wrench tightens the clamps. A foot holds the center of the panel to the clamp to prevent buckling, Figure 14-33. The assembler rotates the clamped panel down and away from the operator. After one revolution, the glued panels are ready to be removed, Figure 14-34.

Figure 14-31
A panel-clamping device for edge-gluing boards to produce panels. (James L. Taylor Manufacturing Co.)

Figure 14-32
A glue spreader. (James L. Taylor Manufacturing Co.)

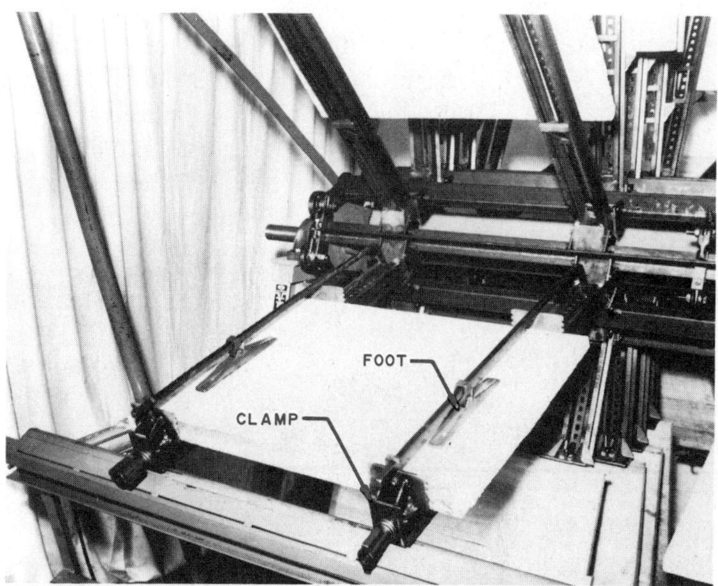

Figure 14-33
The edge clamps pull the glued edges together. The feet hold the panel firmly to the clamp. (James L. Taylor Manufacturing Co.)

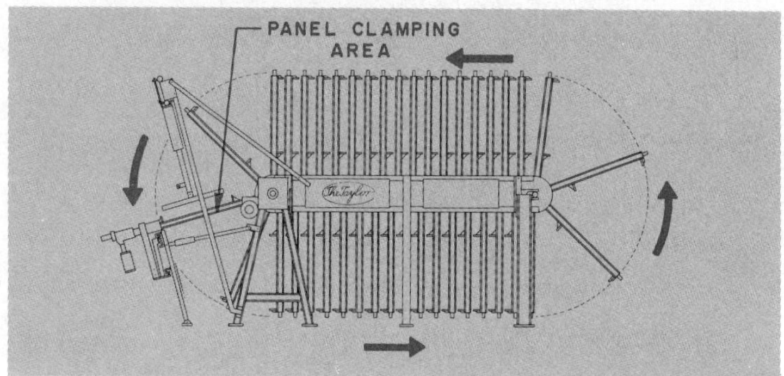

Figure 14-34
The glued panels dry as they rotate away from the operator. (James L. Taylor Manufacturing Co.)

STAPLES AND POWER NAILS

Wood production plants use power *stapling machines* and *nailing machines*. Many specially-designed machines are available. Some machines are portable and move about the product. Others are stationary, and the assembled parts move about the machine.

Figure 14-35 shows a portable pneumatic stapling machine fastening mattress springs to a wood frame. A cartridge inside the machine holds the staples. A portable pneumatic tacker is shown in Figure 14-36. It can join plywood dust barriers in a cabinet. It drives 1/8″ to 1/2″ staples.

The automatic nailing machine shown in Figure 14-37 is assembling a shipping crate. It drives specially-designed nails. A nailing machine that drives a thin nail is shown in Figure 14-38. It nails thin wood overlays and plastic molding.

Figure 14-35
A pneumatic stapling machine fastens mattress springs to the wood frame. (Bostitch Textron)

Figure 14-36
A portable pneumatic stapler fastens plywood dust panels in a cabinet. (Bostitch Textron)

Figure 14-37
A shipping crate being assembled on an automatic nailing machine. (Auto-Nailer Company)

Figure 14-38
This air-operated, automatic nailing machine nails wood overlays and plastic molding. Air cylinders activate both the nailing head and the clamping device. (Auto-Nailer Company)

ASSEMBLY PROCEDURES

Each assembly job requires careful study. Clamping devices must be adapted and adjusted for each job. Some products are easy to clamp. Others require special preparation.

The different parts being assembled should have the same moisture content. If all the stock is kiln-dried and stored in the same place, the moisture content should be the same. In addition, the moisture content of the product must be about the same as the moisture content of the environment where the finished product will be used. Air moisture varies throughout the United States. It ranges from 4 or 5 percent in northern states to 12 or 13 percent in coastal areas. Eight percent is an average moisture level for furniture used in homes. Moisture content more than 15 percent requires a special type of glue. See Unit 25 for more information on glues and adhesives.

Following assembly procedures, you sand the parts before assembling them. Separate pieces are easier to sand than assembled products, especially those with inside surfaces.

Before applying glue for the final assembly, put the parts together when they are dry. This is called a *trial assembly,* Figure 14-39. Set the clamps and pull all joints closed. Check joints for a tight fit. A joint with irregular openings will not be strong. It also will show a glue line after it is dry. After you have checked the trial assembly, open the clamps and lay them aside where they can be reached easily. Preset the clamps to save time. Because some glues dry quickly, your product must be assembled and checked quickly.

Know the drying time of the glue you will use. Some glues dry so quickly that it is impossible to assemble the entire product at one time. In this case, plan to assemble only those parts that can be clamped in the time available. After the glue in one portion has dried, assemble the next pieces.

Remember, the time available before a glue dries includes application time plus assembly time. A brush or roller often is used in small, hand-assembly operations.

Adhesive spreaders control the thickness of the adhesive layer. They speed the application process. A small adhesive spreader for edge gluing is shown in Figure 14-40. The unit controls

Figure 14-39
Assembling a product before glue is applied is called a trial assembly. Check the joints for proper fit.

Figure 14-40
An adhesive spreader for edge gluing. The large roller rotates in the adhesive. (Black Brothers Co., Inc.)

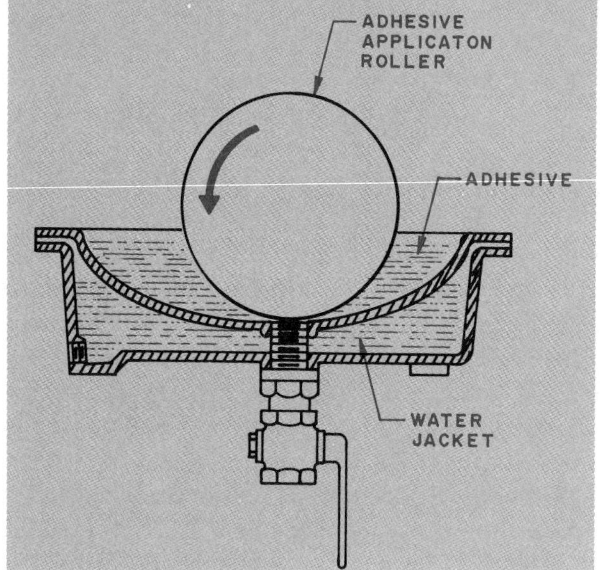

Figure 14-41
A cross section of an adhesive spreader. A jacket filled with cold water controls the temperature of fast-setting adhesives. Hot water is used to control hot, slow-drying adhesives. A thermostat controls the temperature. (Black Brothers Co., Inc.)

the temperature of the glue. A constant temperature prolongs the life of the glue in the machine, Figure 14-41. A face-coating spreader is shown in Figure 14-42. It quickly and uniformly applies adhesives to many kinds of materials.

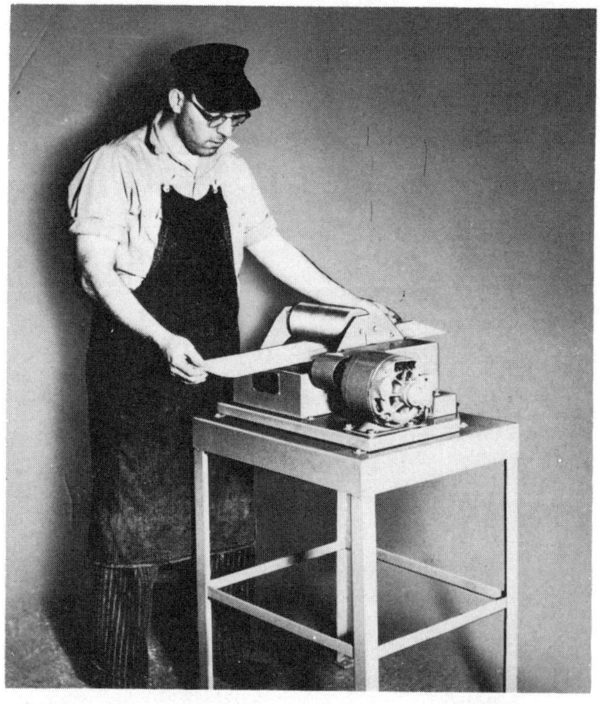

Figure 14-42
This unit applies adhesive to the face of stock. It can be used to coat wood, hardboard, particle board, cardboard, veneer, plastics and other flat stock. (Black Brothers Co., Inc.)

Check the assembly after tightening the clamps. Use a try square to check for squareness, Figure 14-43. Check rectangular or square parts by measuring their diagonal. Each diagonal will measure the same if it is square, Figure 14-44.

Arrange the assembly area carefully. Everything you need should be close at hand. Be sure to include clamps, a mallet, scrap blocks, glue, a glue applicator, a scraper to remove excess glue and a work table. Glue should dry at a normal

Figure 14-43
After the unit is glued and clamped, check it carefully for squareness.

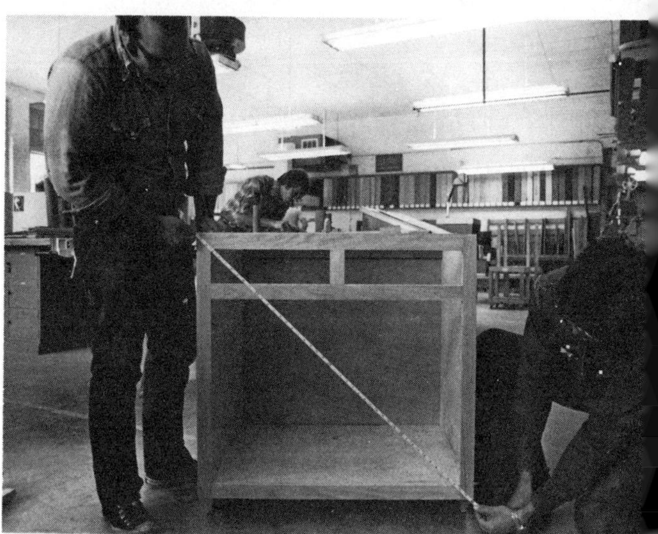

Figure 14-44
Rectangular products can be checked for squareness by measuring diagonals.

room temperature, about 70° Fahrenheit (21° Centigrade). Your work area should be heated or cooled to this temperature.

Use saw horses or special racks to hold clamps when assembling large products. Bar clamps are the most difficult to secure. All bar clamps must be held horizontally. Be sure all clamps are level. A clamping table is shown in Figure 14-45.

Assemble prefinished wood on a padded table, Figure 14-46. Work carefully so the finish is not damaged.

Figure 14-45
A glue bench.

Figure 14-46
Assembling the sides of a desk. Notice that the work table is heavily padded. (Armstrong World Industries)

FACE-TO-FACE ASSEMBLY

To assemble material face-to-face:

1. Make a trial assembly. Set the hand screws to the proper size.
2. Place the stock face up on the gluing table. Brush a thin layer of glue on both pieces.
3. Place the pieces on edge on the bench top and move them together.
4. Place two or more hand screws on one side. The number needed depends on the length of the boards. Tighten the screws until the joint closes. Do not overtighten, Figure 14-47.
5. Turn the boards over and place two or more hand screws on the other side. Make certain the joint is closed.
6. Remove excess glue.

Figure 14-47
Use hand screws to hold stock face-to-face.

EDGE-TO-EDGE ASSEMBLY

To assemble parts edge-to-edge:

1. Make a trial assembly. Check the joint to see if it is tight. Set bar clamps to the proper size. Space the clamps about 24" (610 mm) apart.
2. Apply a thin layer of glue to each edge. Be certain the surface is completely covered, Figure 14-48.
3. Place the pieces against the bars of the clamps. Tighten the clamps until the joint closes. Do not overtighten. Overtightening will reduce the glue in the joint. It will also cause the boards to buckle. Mark the time and date the job was glued, Figure 14-49.
4. Place one or more clamps across the top of the boards between the bottom clamps. This will prevent buckling. Tighten until firm, Figure 14-50.
5. Check the pieces from the side for flatness. If the boards touch the bars they are flat.
6. Remove excess glue.
7. Store the assembly so the bar clamps remain parallel. Improper storing could cause the assembly to dry twisted.

CLEANING GLUE JOINTS

After tightening the clamps, remove the glue that has been forced out of the joint. If permitted to dry on the surface, the glue will seal the wood surface. When the product is stained, the stain will not go through the glue to the wood surface. Glue joints will show even if a clear finish is used.

To remove the excess glue, let it dry until it becomes semihard and is like jelly. Scrape it off with a metal scraper, Figure 14-51.

Figure 14-48
Apply a thin layer of glue to each edge.

Figure 14-49
Tighten the clamps until the joints close. Do not overtighten.

Figure 14-50
Place one or more clamps on the other side.

Figure 14-51
Remove excess glue from the joint.

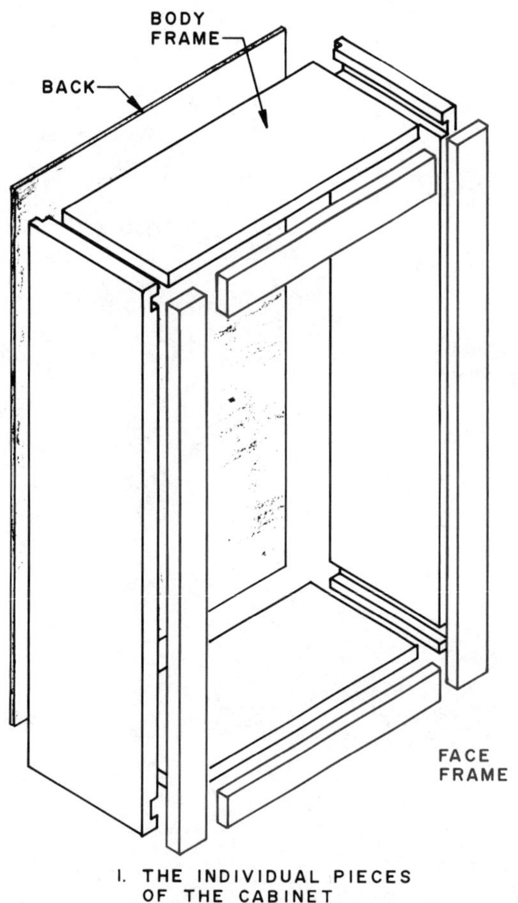

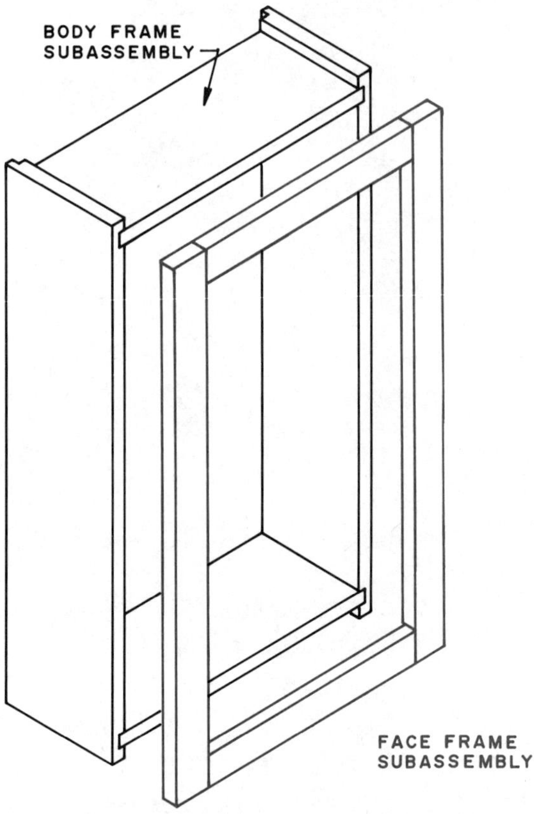

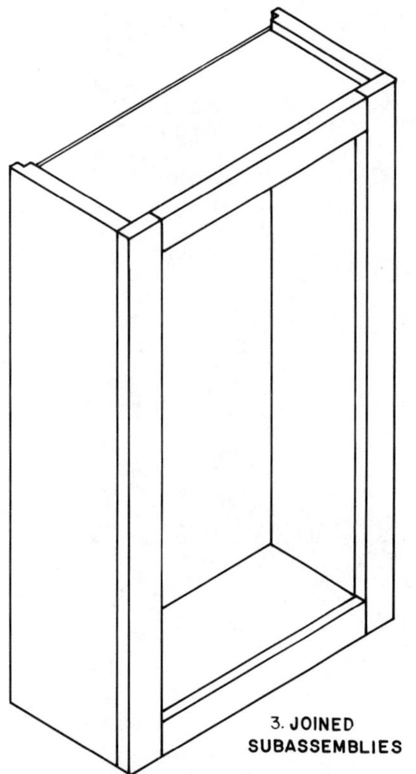

Figure 14-52
A product is formed from several subassemblies.

ASSEMBLING CABINETS AND FURNITURE FRAMES

The key to a good assembly is planning. Decide which parts will be *subassemblies.* A subassembly is a few related parts of a product glued together and allowed to dry. The face frame in Figure 14-52 is a subassembly.

After you identify the subassemblies, plan how they will come together for final assembly. Final assembly might take several steps. Figure 14-52 shows the pieces of a cabinet. The assembly will be in three steps. The face frame subassembly of rails and stiles will be assembled and dried. Then the top, bottom and sides will be assembled. After this subassembly is dry, the back and face frames will be fastened to the top-bottom-side subassembly. A glued subassembly is shown in Figure 14-53.

Remember, as you assemble a product, check to see that it is square and free of twist. Store the assembled product so that it is free of strain while drying. A good assembly job can be ruined by careless storage.

REVIEW QUESTIONS

1 What is the difference between a hand screw and a bar clamp?
2 What are some sizes of C clamps?
3 How does a spring clamp keep pressure on the stock?
4 What type of clamp should you use to make picture frames?
5 What is the maximum acceptable moisture content in wood when using conventional adhesives?
6 What is a trial assembly?
7 How should you remove excess glue from a joint?

SUGGESTED ACTIVITIES

1 Practice assembling some typical joints without glue.
2 Visit a local wood-product plant. Make a list of the assembly devices used. Take photos of these and prepare a display.
3 Glue scrap stock together. Clean only half the joint. After the glue has dried, stain the joint. Notice the difference between the cleaned and uncleaned joint.

Figure 14-53
A glued subassembly. (Adjustable Clamp Co.)

SECTION

Fastening Techniques

15
Wood Joints

16
Making Edge and Butt Joints

17
Making Miter Joins

18
Making Lap Joints

19
Making Dado and Rabbet Joints

20
Making Dowel Joints

21
Making Mortise and Tenon Joints

22
Making Dovetail and Box Joints

23
Fasteners

24
Hardware

25
Installing Wood Screws

26
Fastening with Nails

27
Glues, Adhesives and Cements

Permanent assembly of a wood product depends on the joints and fasteners used. As a skilled woodworker you must be familiar with all of the joints and fasteners used in wood products. You will make better choices when you know the advantages, disadvantages and sizes of fasteners. As you learn about different joints, you will be able to choose, lay out and cut them quickly and accurately.

Section 3, Fastening Techniques, introduces the basic wood joints and mechanical fasteners. It also shows how to lay out joints and cut them with hand tools. This section also tells you how to install mechanical fasteners and how to use glues and adhesives.

UNIT

15

Wood Joints

Objectives

After studying this unit you should be able to:

1 Select the best joint for a specific need.

2 Identify the basic joints used in wood products.

Technical Terms

Butt joint	Scarf joint
Dowel	Finger joint
Edge joint	Mortise-and-tenon joint
Miter joint	Box joint
Compound miter	Dovetail joint
Dado joint	Corrugated fastener
Groove joint	Clamp nail
Rabbet joint	Skotch® fastener
Corner joint	Teenut® fastener
Lap joint	

Selecting which wood joints to use is part of a designer's work. There are many kinds of joints, Figure 15-1. Each has advantages and disadvantages. As designers decide on joints, they consider the following factors.

Strength. Some joints are stronger than others. The joint selected must fit the job it is supposed to do. Joints must not separate during use.

Appearance. Sometimes the joint should be hidden. A joint not visible is called a blind joint. Sometimes a joint is exposed so that it becomes part of the overall design.

Cost. A complicated joint is costly to cut. Is it worth the cost? Would metal fasteners give acceptable results for less money?

Difficulty. Select the simplest joint that will do the job.

Assembly. Ease of assembly influences the cost and time of production. Can the product be assembled easily and accurately?

Quality. A low-cost product often has joints that are not the best but that are the least costly. What is the quality of the product that you will be making?

Disassembly. Is the product one that will be taken apart for shipping? Knocked-down furniture has many joints that can be easily assembled. This feature makes it easy to move the product from a store to a home.

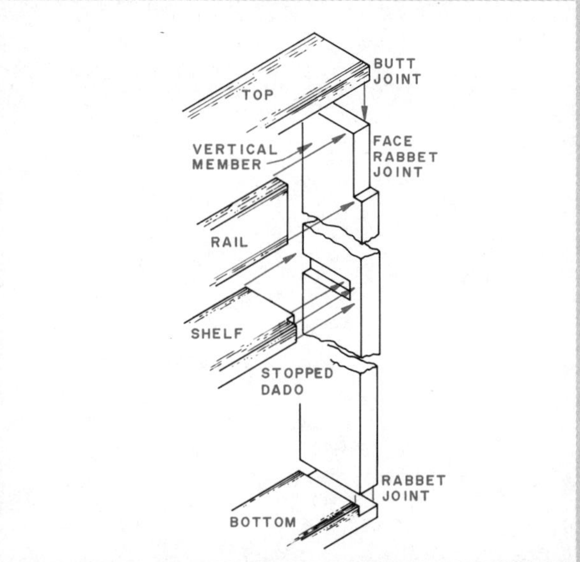

Figure 15-1
Many different joints are used in furniture construction. (Hekman Furniture Company)

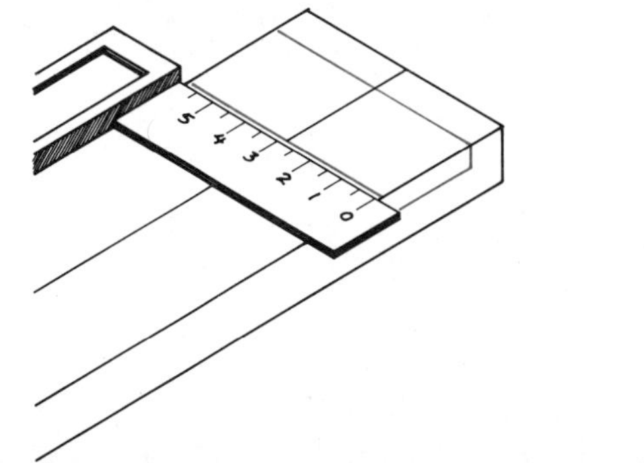

Figure 15-2
Lay out joints on mating parts at the same time.

GENERAL CONSIDERATIONS

The strength of a joint depends on a good fit. The contact area between joining pieces must be smooth and flat. This is necessary for maximum contact of glued surfaces.

The direction of the wood grain influences the choice of the joint. Wood is strongest in the with-the-grain direction. The more edge and face grain in the joining surfaces, the stronger the joint will be.

The pieces to be joined should be cut to their finished sizes before the joints are cut.

Lay out the joints on mating pieces at the same time, Figure 15-2. Use a sharp pencil or knife. Accuracy requires a thin line. Lay out all joints of the same kind together.

Mark matching parts of a joint with matching numbers or letters. Mark these numbers or letters on the faces to be glued. This will assure that you will put the proper pieces together. You will make fewer mistakes if you make all measurements from the same end.

Following are descriptions of the commonly used wood joints and fastening devices. Instructions on how to cut the joints with hand tools are in Units 17 through 21. Joints can also be cut with power tools. Power tool operation is covered in later units.

BUTT JOINTS

The *butt joint* is probably the easiest to make, but it is not as strong as other types. One of the butting surfaces is end grain. This makes joining by gluing ineffective. To achieve needed strength, some type of fastener or other reinforcement is needed. Nails and screws can be used to strengthen this joint, Figure 15-3. Other metal fasteners, such as clamp nails and corrugated fasteners, also can be used, Figures 15-18, 15-19, 15-20. A glue block can be used to strengthen a butt joint.

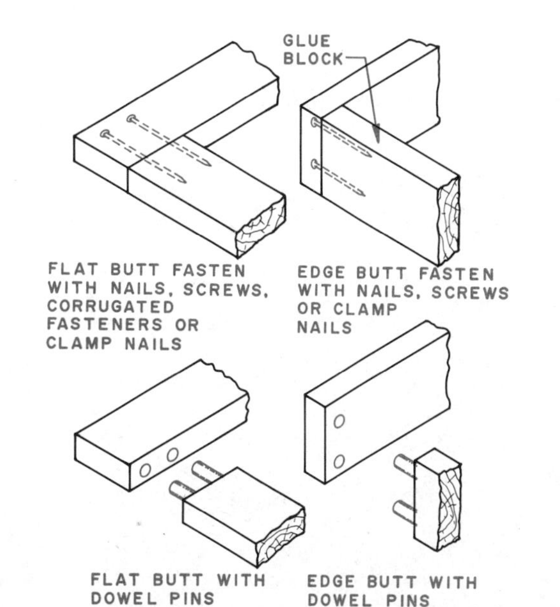

Figure 15-3
Typical end butt joints.

You can use wood *dowels* to strengthen a butt joint. They not only strengthen the joint but help align the joining members.

Use butt joints to form frames and box corners, Figure 15-4. They often are used in cabinet construction. Join chair and table rails with doweled butt joints, Figure 15-5.

Figure 15-4
Butt joints can be glued and nailed. (American Plywood Association)

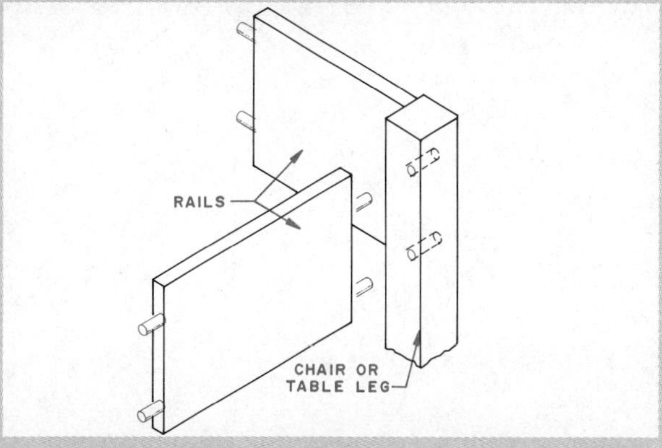

Figure 15-5
Dowels join rails and legs.

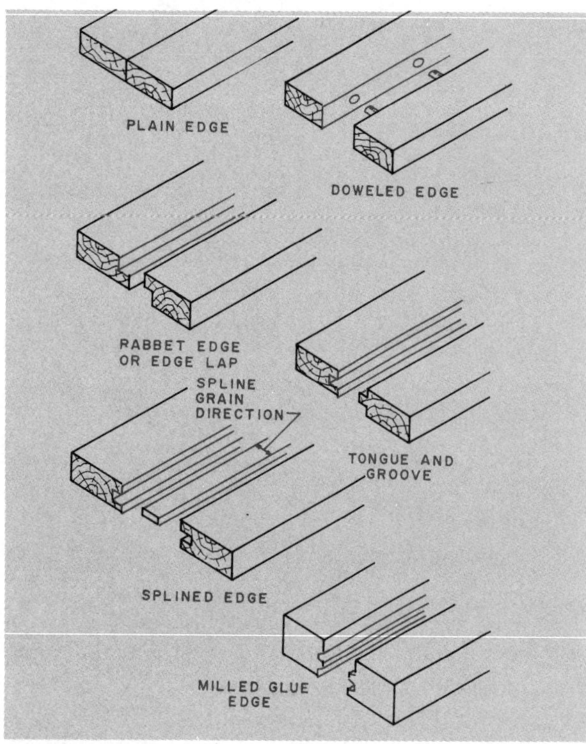

Figure 15-6
Typical edge joints.

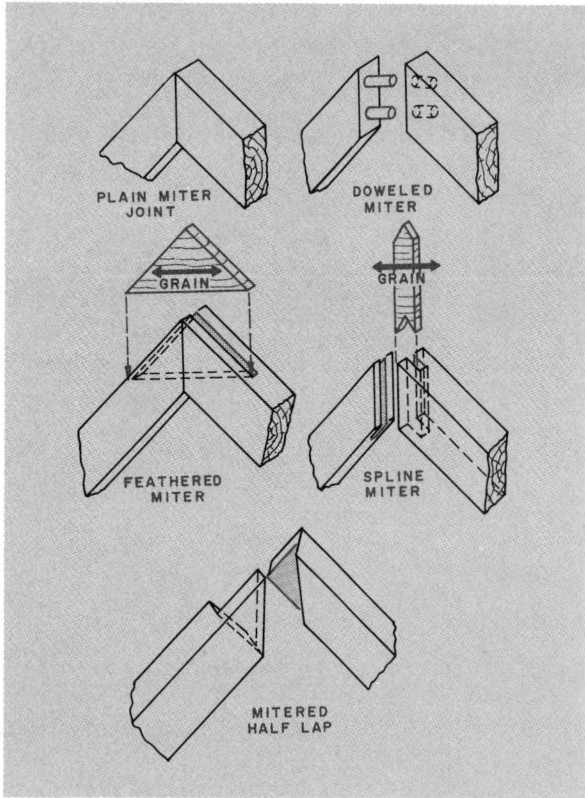

Figure 15-7
Common types of flat miter joints.

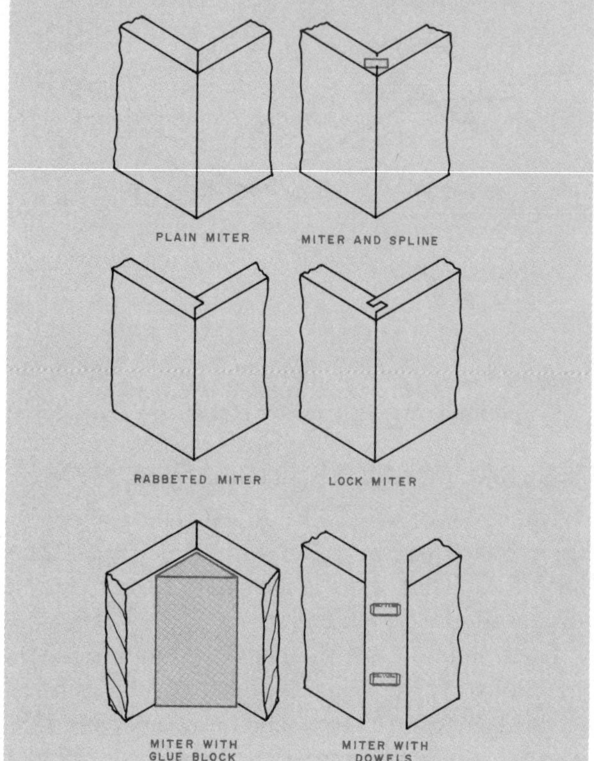

Figure 15-8
Typical edge miter joints.

EDGE JOINTS

Edge joints usually are held by glue. If you glue a plain edge joint properly, it will be stronger than the wood itself. You may want to use wood dowels. Dowels help align the pieces when gluing and add to the strength. Carefully square the edges so that they fit tightly together. Gaps between the boards weaken the joint.

The spline type of joint is very strong. Notice that the grain of the spline runs across the spline. The edge lap and tongue and groove types of joints help align the pieces and provide additional gluing surface, Figure 15-6. The wedge-shaped tongue and groove joint provides additional gluing surface, aligns the joint and strengthens it.

You also can use corrugated metal fasteners. Use them for rough work when appearance is not critical. The millwork industry uses the milled glue joint.

MITER JOINTS

A *miter joint* is much like a butt joint. The main difference is that the members are cut on a 45° angle. This produces a joint that has no end grain showing.

The miter joint is a weak joint because both surfaces are end grain. This joint requires the same types of fasteners as those used for butt joints.

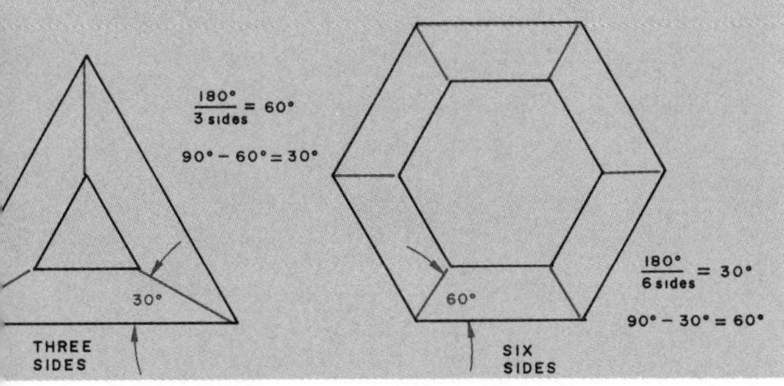

Figure 15-9
How to find miter angles on polygons.

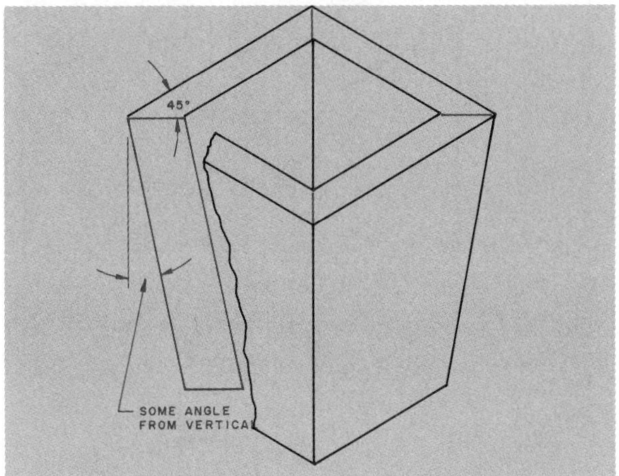

Figure 15-10
A compound miter slopes two ways.

Use miter joints in making picture frames and facing strips on cabinets.

Common ways to join flat miters are shown in Figure 15-7. You can join the mitered half lap entirely by gluing since it has face grain exposed in the joint.

Typical edge miter joints are shown in Figure 15-8. They use the same methods of fastening as flat miter joints.

The polygon miter and compound miter are variations of the 45° miter. Polygon miters are those cut on angles other than 45°. To find what angle you should cut the miter, divide 180° by the number of sides and subtract the answer from 90°, Figure 15-9. The most commonly used polygon miters are:

Three sides	=	30°
Four sides	=	45°
Five sides	=	54°
Six sides	=	60°
Seven sides	=	64.3°
Eight sides	=	67.5°

A *compound miter* forms products that have a tapered shape. The joint is a combination miter and bevel cut, Figure 15-10.

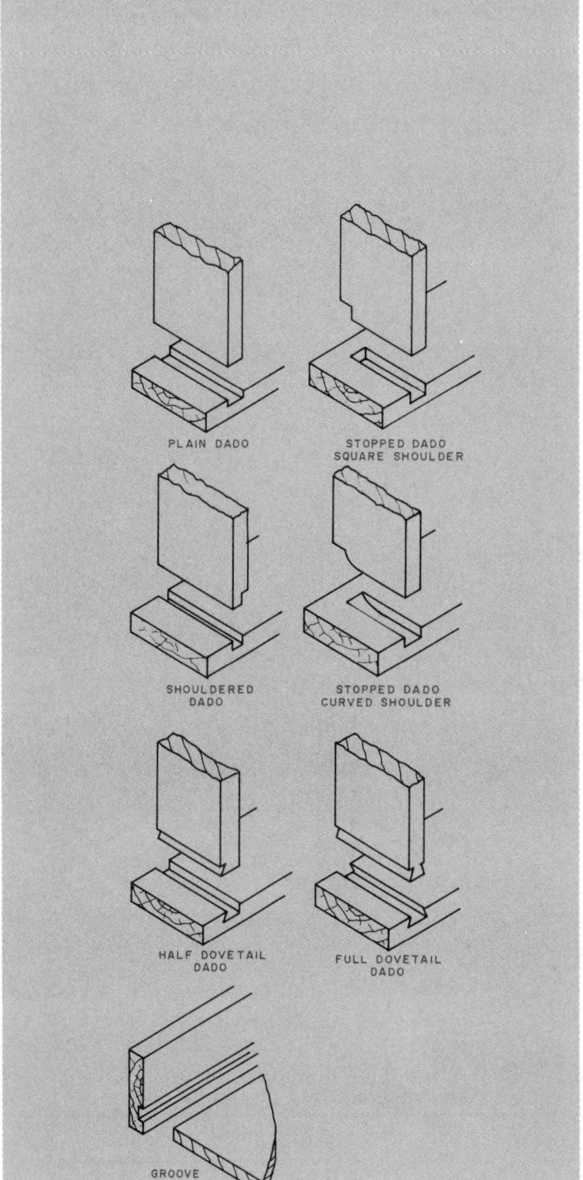

Figure 15-11
Groove and dado joints.

DADOES AND GROOVES

A dado is a rectangular slot cut across the grain of a board. Use the *dado joint* for holding the ends of shelves, cabinet sides and bottoms and partitions or dividers. It is a strong joint but must be cut so the members fit snugly. The edge of the dado provides a lip on which a shelf can rest. It also helps align members as they are assembled, Figure 15-1.

There are many variations of the dado. Examples are shown in Figure 15-11. The through dado is exposed to view when assembled. If this is not desired, a blind, or stopped, dado can be used. The dado can be used with a rabbet joint. The rabbet should be one-half to two-thirds of the width of the board on which it was cut. The

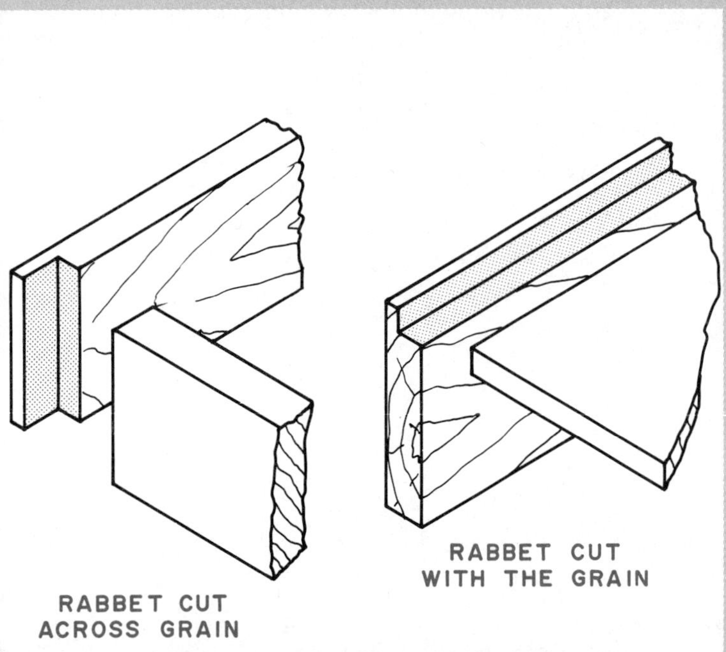

Figure 15-12
End and edge rabbet joints.

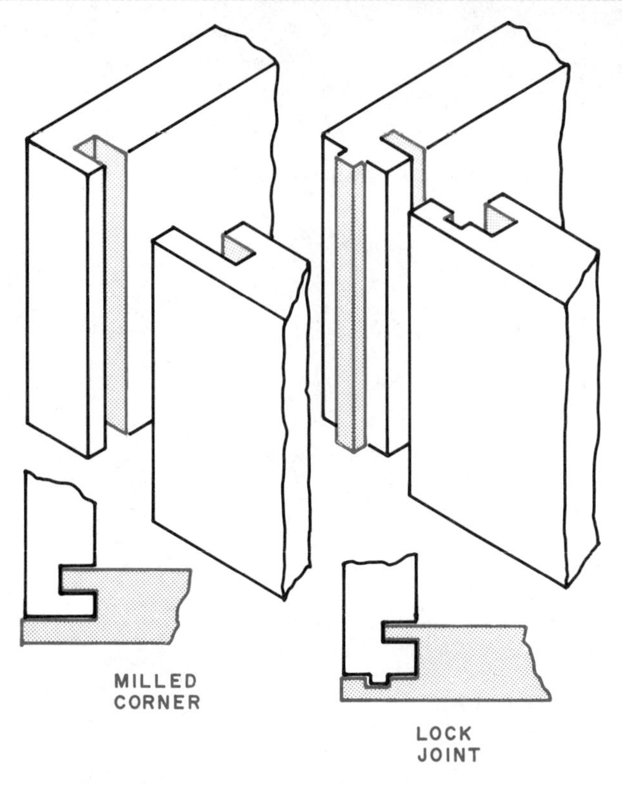

Figure 15-13
Special corner joints.

dovetail dado is strong but difficult to cut with hand tools.

Dadoes on solid lumber usually are cut to a depth of half the thickness of the board. Dadoes in 3/4" (19 mm) plywood should be only 1/4" (6 mm) deep. If the dado is cut deeper, too many plies of veneer will be cut, thus weakening the board.

Join dadoes by gluing. For additional strength, nail the glued joint or join it with screws. You usually do not need clamps when the joint is fastened with glue plus nails or screws.

A groove is a rectangular slot cut with the grain. A *groove joint* frequently is used to hold panels. A drawer bottom usually is set in a groove. Grooves most often are cut to a depth of half the thickness of the board. Panels set in grooves, such as drawer bottoms, often are not glued. The assembled unit, the drawer, is thus permitted to expand and contract around the bottom of the unit. This prevents the wood from cracking or buckling.

RABBET JOINTS

Use *rabbet joints* for forming corners. You also can use them for holding the backs in cabinets.

A rabbet joint is much like a dado or a groove. The cut is along the end or edge of the board, forming an L-shape. Commonly used rabbet joints are shown in Figure 15-12.

The recess cut is usually about two-thirds of the thickness of the board. For example, this would be a 1/2" (13 mm) cut in a 3/4" (19 mm) thick board.

You can assemble the rabbet joint with glue. Then strengthen it by nailing or by using wood screws.

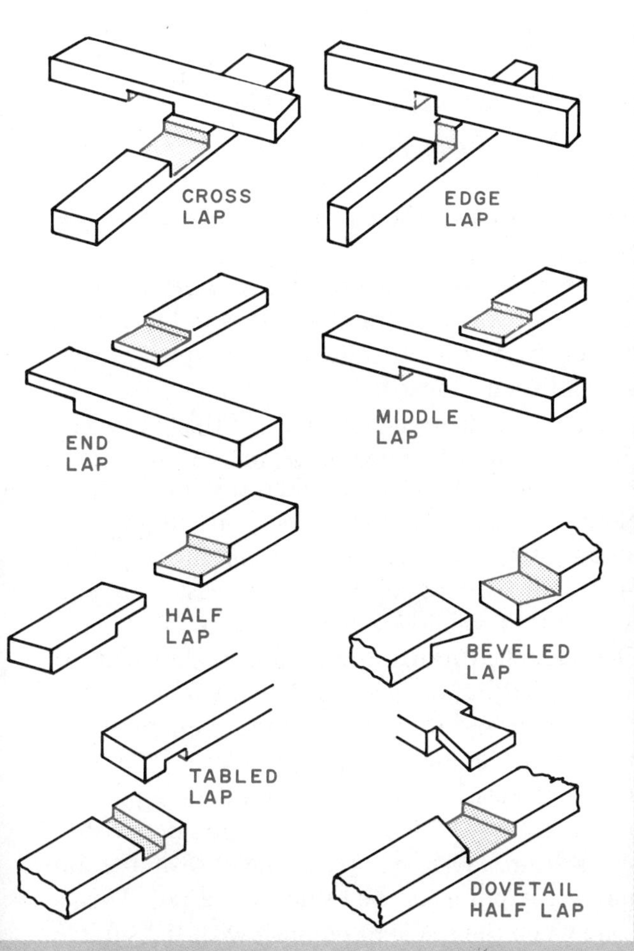

Figure 15-14
Typical lap joints.

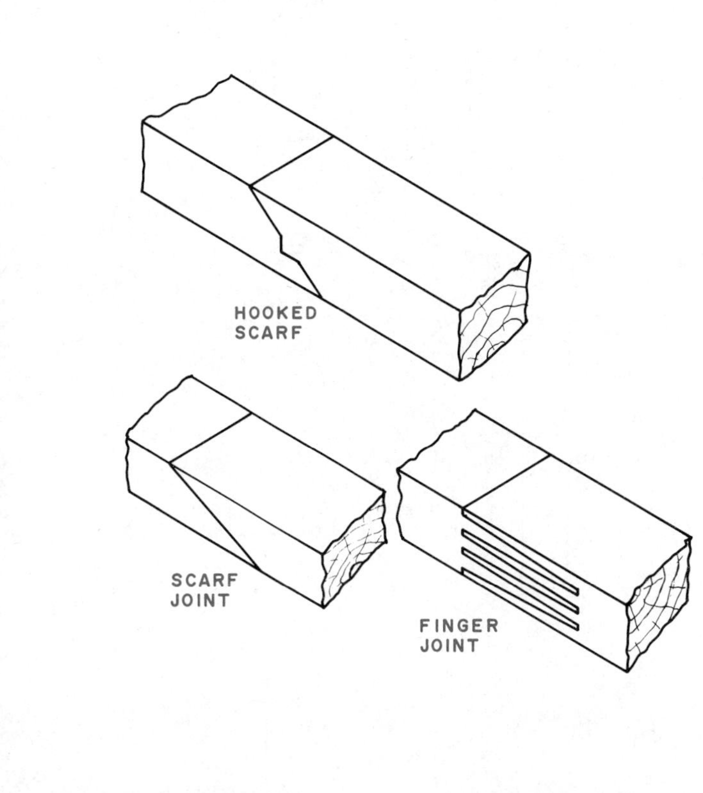

Figure 15-15
Scarf and finger joints.

Notice the rabbet combined with the dado forming a shouldered dado in Figure 15-11.

CORNER JOINTS

A variety of *corner joints* are used to join wide boards at 90° corners. The rabbet, Figure 15-12, the edge butt, Figure 15-3, and the miter, Figure 15-7, are three types used. Combinations of dado and tongue joints are shown in Figure 15-13.

LAP JOINTS

Cut a *lap joint* when two pieces of wood are joined so that their surfaces will be flush. Use the half lap to splice two pieces. Use the end lap to form a corner (as in a miter joint). Use the cross lap when two pieces cross. Join an end member to a crossmember with the middle lap. Common lap joints are shown in Figure 15-14. You usually will make a cut one-half the thickness of each member. Secure the joints by gluing. Add nails or screws as needed.

END-TO-END JOINTS

Two commonly used joints that unite two boards end to end are *scarf* and *finger joints,* Figure 15-15. The scarf joint is cut at a low angle to provide maximum gluing surface. Sometimes it is strengthened by adding dowels.

The finger joint is widely used in the construction industry. The joint is cut with special, powered cutters. It is used to join short pieces of wood to form longer pieces. The joint is then glued. This joint is as strong as or even stronger than the original board.

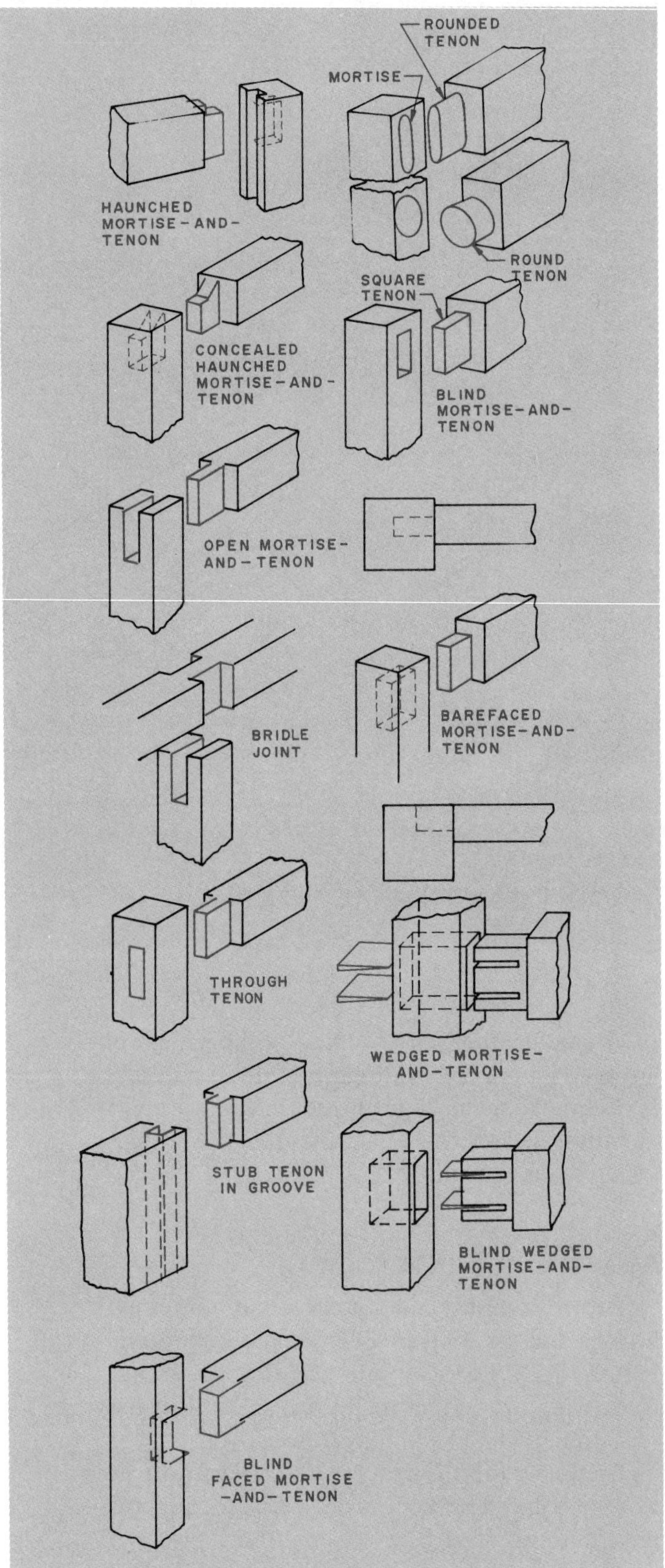

Figure 15-16
Mortise-and-tenon joints.

MORTISE-AND-TENON JOINTS

The *mortise-and-tenon joint* is one of the more difficult joints to make with hand tools. It also is one of the strongest joints for joining end grain to edge grain.

The mortise-and-tenon joint is widely used to join crossmembers—for example, a rail to the leg of a chair or table. It is used in high-quality cabinet and frame construction.

There are many adaptations of this joint. The common ones are shown in Figure 15-16.

The blind mortise-and-tenon joint is completely hidden. The shoulders cut around the tenon and cover the edges of the mortise. The open mortise-and-tenon joint is easier to cut. It is useful when joining members at corners. The haunched mortise-and-tenon is designed for frames that have a panel. The haunch on top fits in the panel groove in the side rail. The stub joint has a short tenon that fits in a long groove. A plywood panel is held in the remaining portion of the groove. It does not have shoulders at top or bottom. The barefaced mortise-and-tenon places the tenon on one side of the rail. This is done when the rail is to be flush with the surface of the leg.

The tenon should be as large as possible without reducing the strength of the matching member. Usually it is about half the thickness of the piece upon which it is cut. The length of the tenon should be a minimum of two and one-half times its thickness.

BOX AND DOVETAIL JOINTS

The *box joint* joins corners. It is a decorative joint and often is chosen for that reason. If properly made, it glues tightly to form a strong corner, Figure 15-17.

The *dovetail joint* is both strong and decorative. It is difficult to cut with hand tools because of the angles and close fit required. Machine cutting of dovetails is discussed in the power tool units of this text.

Several variations of the dovetail joint are in common use, Figure 15-17. The half-blind dovetail provides a strong corner. The joint is hidden from the front. It is widely used on quality furniture for drawer construction. The stopped

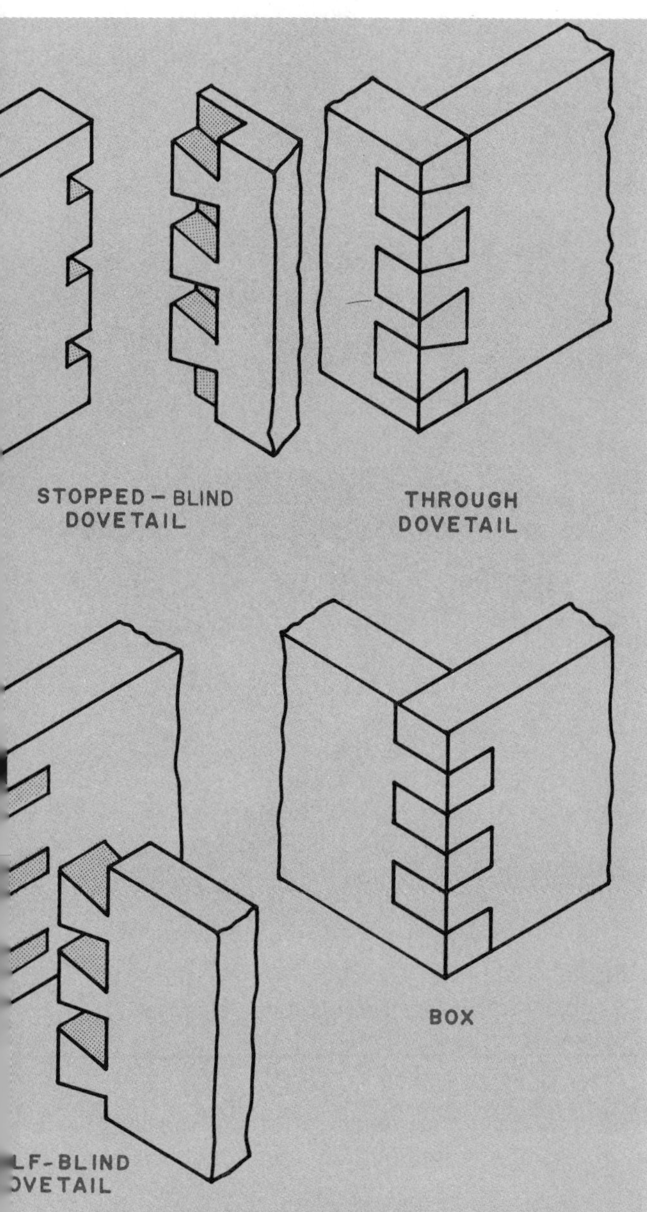

Figure 15-17
Typical dovetail and box joints.

blind dovetail forms a corner where the joint is completely hidden. The half-blind and stopped blind joints are very hard to make with hand tools. The through dovetail serves the same purpose as the box joint. Because its elements are wedge shaped, it is stronger.

METAL AND PLASTIC FASTENING DEVICES

In addition to wood joints, there are a number of metal fasteners used in forming joints. Three types are the *corrugated fastener,* Figure 15-18, the *clamp nail,* Figure 15-19, and the *Skotch*®

Figure 15-18
Corrugated fasteners strengthen joints.

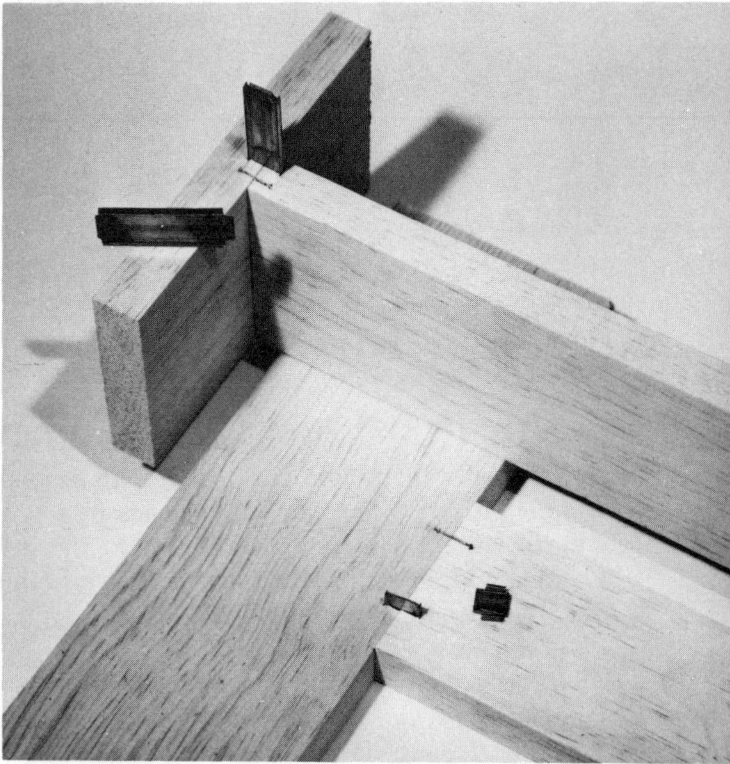

Figure 15-19
Clamp nails join a variety of joints. (Knape & Vogt Manufacturing Co.)

Figure 15-20
Skotch® fasteners strengthen butt and edge joints.

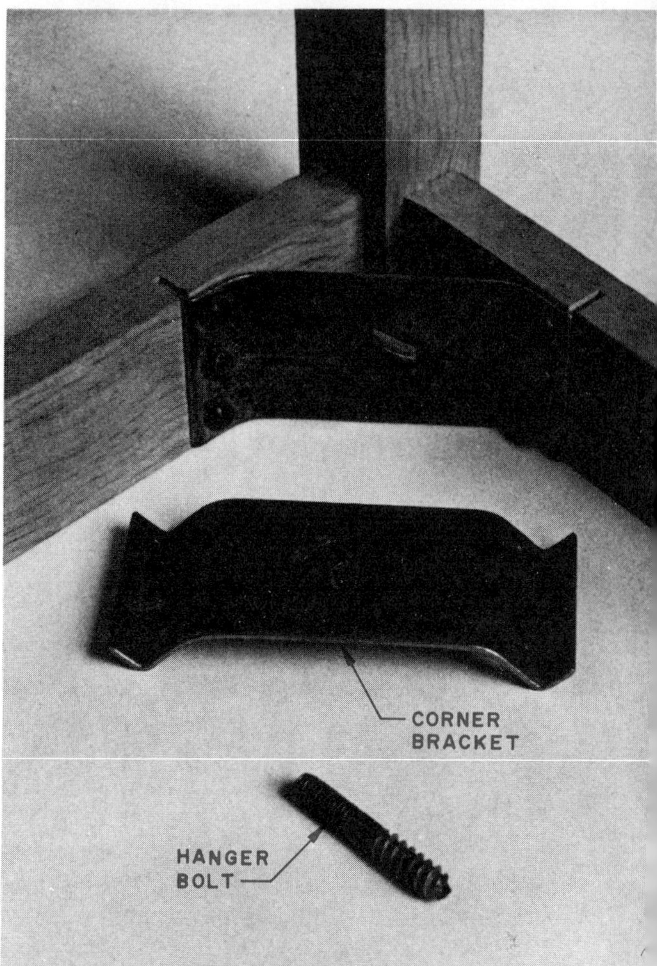

Figure 15-21
A corner bracket and hanger bolt can join rails to legs.

fastener, Figure 15-20. In addition, you sometimes will want to join rails to legs with a metal corner bracket. Set the bracket ends in a saw kerf in the rail. Secure the bracket to the rail with wood screws. Screw a hanger bolt into the leg and secure it to the corner bracket with a nut, Figure 15-21.

You sometimes will join legs with a hanger bolt and *Teenut® fastener,* Figure 15-22. Hammer the Teenut® fastener into the cabinet. Screw the hanger bolt into the wood leg. Then screw the other end of the bolt into the Teenut® fastener, Figure 15-23.

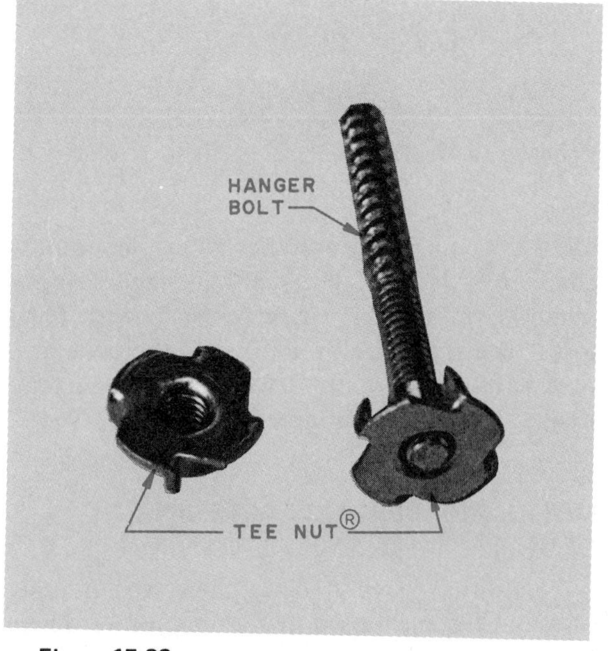

Figure 15-22
A hanger bolt and Teenut®.

Metal clips fasten rails to table tops. Set them in a kerf in the rail. Fasten the other end to the top with a wood screw, Figure 15-24.

Plastic miter dowels sometimes are used to join mitered corners. Bore holes into the mitered faces parallel with the surfaces of the boards. Then coat the mitered faces and dowel holes with glue, insert the dowels and join the faces, Figure 15-25.

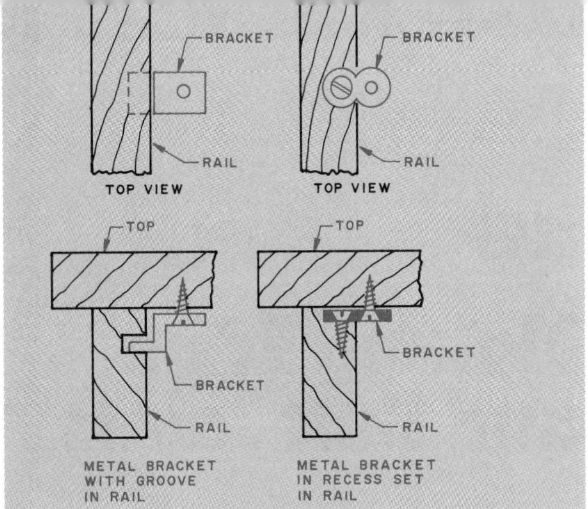

Figure 15-24
Join table tops to the rails with metal clips.

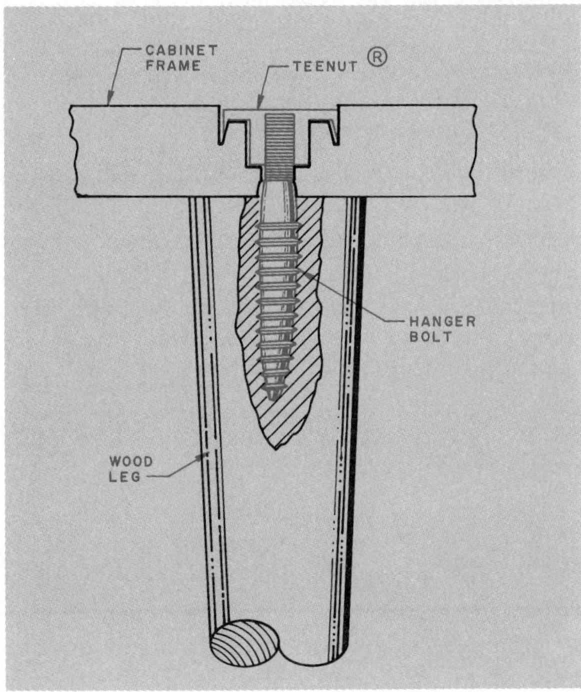

Figure 15-23
Join wood legs to cabinet frames with a hanger bolt and Teenut®.

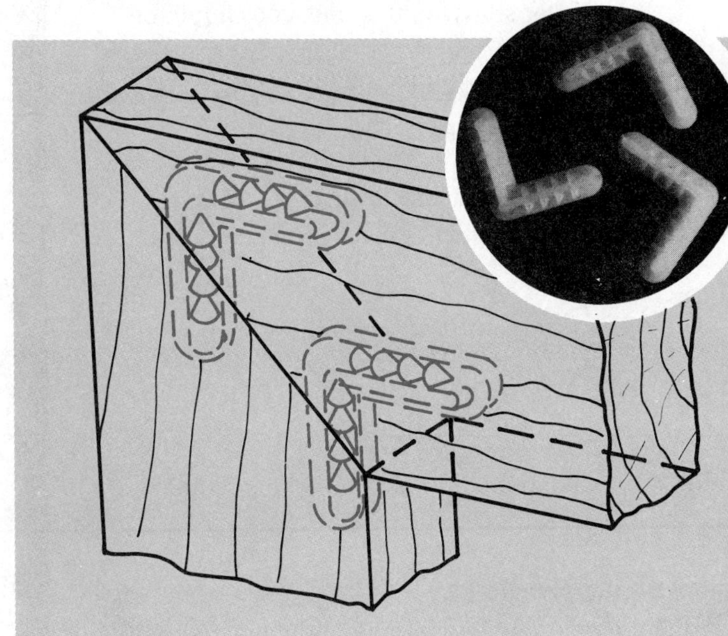

Figure 15-25
Plastic dowels can strengthen miter joints.

REVIEW QUESTIONS

1 What factors must a designer consider when selecting the joints to be used in a product?
2 How are butt joints held together?
3 Why are dowels sometimes used in edge joints?
4 What types of joints can be cut in the edges of boards that are to be glued together?
5 What is the difference between a dado and a groove?
6 How are panels held in a rabbet joint?
7 What ways are used to assemble lap joints?
8 Why is a mortise-and-tenon joint stronger than a butt joint?
9 How do box joints and dovetail joints differ?

SUGGESTED ACTIVITIES

1 Make a wall chart illustrating the different kinds of joints.
2 Analyze the furniture in the shop. Make a list of the joints used in each piece.

UNIT

16

Making Edge and Butt Joints

Objectives

After studying this unit you should be able to:

1 Lay out and cut a butt joint.

2 Make edge joints.

Technical Term

Glue block

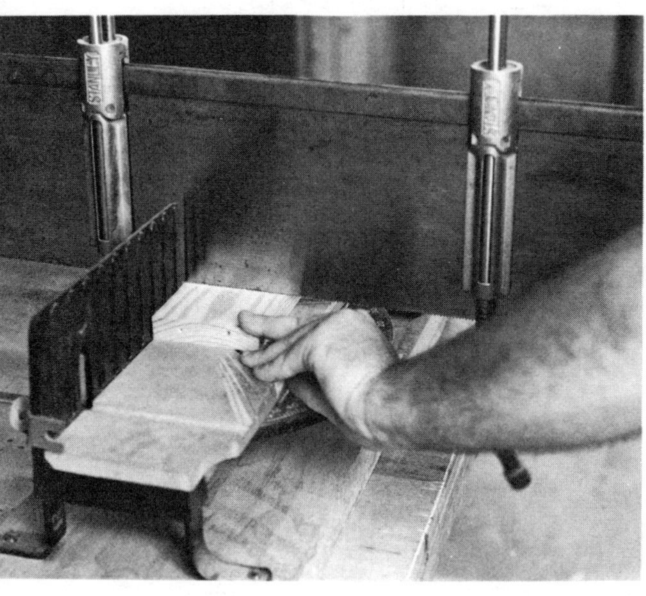

Figure 16-1
A miter box cuts square ends for forming butt joints.

Figure 16-2
Butt joints can be held by nails.

The joining members for a butt joint must be square. The joining surfaces should be smooth and straight for a tight joint. The most accurate way to hand cut the end grain is with a miter box. It holds the saw on a 90° angle. The miter saw has a fine tooth and makes a smooth cut, Figure 16-1. The edge or face of the board must be planed smooth to produce a tight joint. If the stock was power planed, the surface or edge is probably smooth enough for a joint.

BUTT JOINTS

Butt joints can be joined with nails, screws, corrugated fasteners, clamp nails or dowels. To nail a joint, hold two boards together so they are firm and steady, Figure 16-2. A bench vise will help steady the boards. If the board is thin, the nail can be driven through it into the end grain. If the board is thick, drill a hole into the side grain, Figure 16-3. The hole should be slightly smaller in diameter than the nail. The drill hole guides the nail through the grain, prevents splitting of the wood and makes hammering the nail easier.

When using wood screws, drill through the first piece. The hole diameter should be the same as or slightly larger than the screw diameter. If you want the screw head to be flush, countersink the drilled hole, Figure 16-4. Then fasten the screws in place, Figure 16-5.

A corrugated fastener has notched edges slanting toward its center. This helps pull two pieces of wood together. To fasten with corrugated fasteners, place both pieces flat on the workbench. Clamp one to the top with a hand screw. Hold the other next to it and drive the fastener across the joint into both pieces, Figure 16-6.

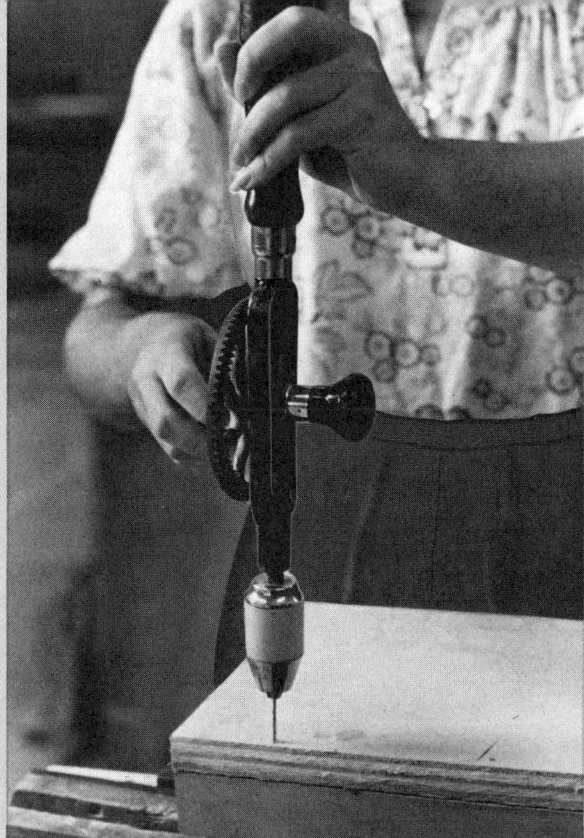

Figure 16-3
Before you nail through thick wood, drill holes slightly smaller in diameter than the nails.

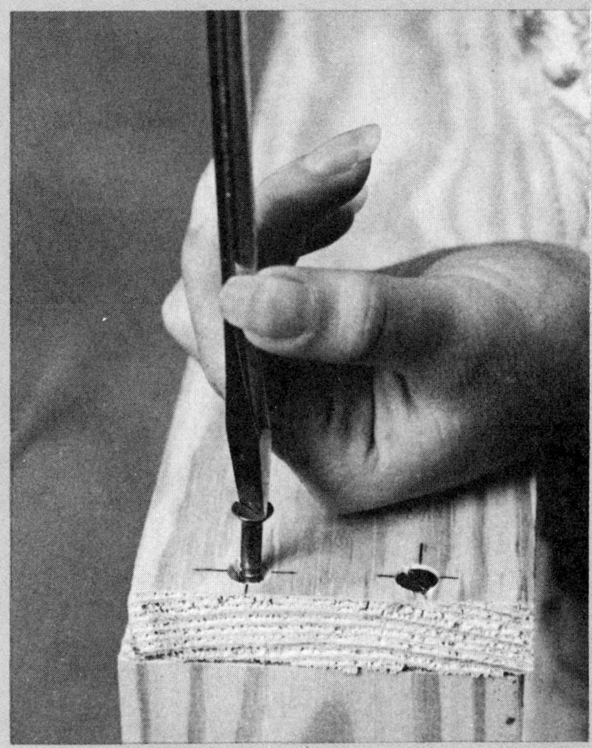

Figure 16-5
A butt joint made with wood screws.

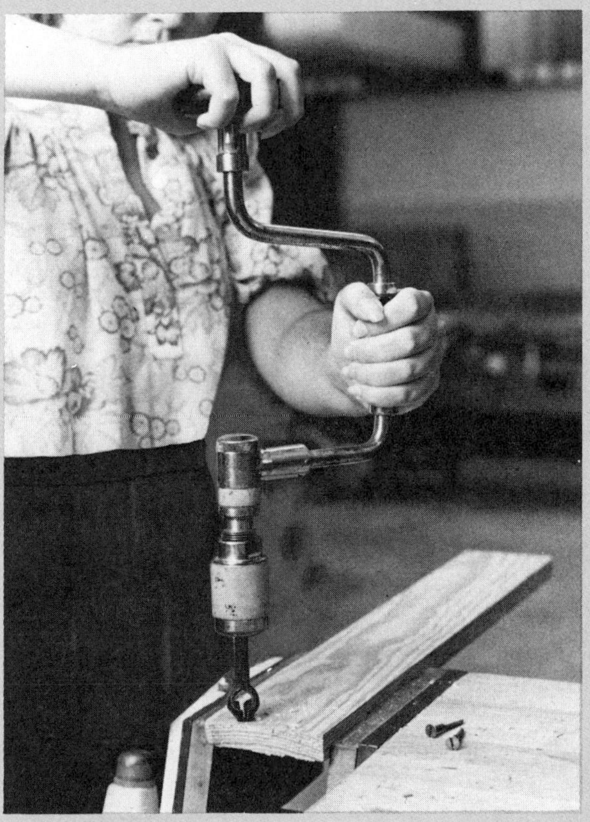

Figure 16-4
Countersink holes to receive wood screws.

Figure 16-6
Corrugated fasteners can be used to form a butt joint if appearance is not important.

Figure 16-7
Skotch® fasteners are used to join butt and edge joints.

SAW KERFS

Figure 16-8
Cut saw kerfs in each board to receive a clamp nail.

You also can use Skotch® fasteners to join butt and edge joints. Drive the nail-like legs into the face of the wood while you hold the joint together, Figure 16-7.

To fasten with clamp nails, cut a narrow kerf in each board to receive the nail, Figure 16-8. The clamp nail is tapered to help pull the two pieces of wood together. Drive the nail with a hammer while you hold the joint together, Figure 16-9.

A *glue block* strengthens a butt joint. After assembling the joint, apply glue to the surfaces of the corner. Then apply glue to the glue block. Press into place and hold briefly until the glue sets, Figure 16-10. The glue block may be any length.

For a long joint you may want to use several short pieces.

Figure 16-9
A butt joint or an edge joint can be joined with clamp nails.

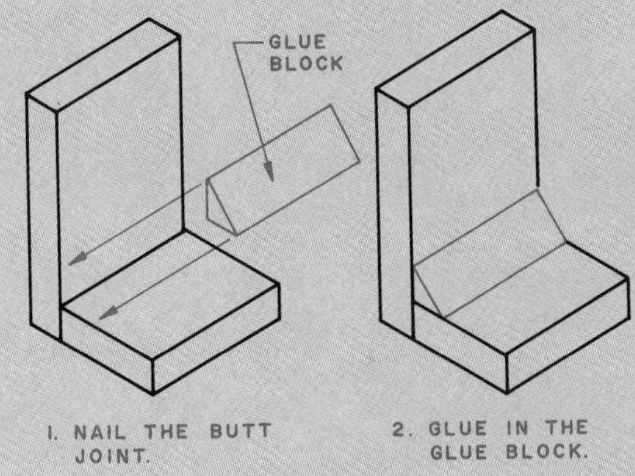
GLUE BLOCK
1. NAIL THE BUTT JOINT.
2. GLUE IN THE GLUE BLOCK.

Figure 16-10
Glue blocks make butt joints stronger.

EDGE JOINTS

Edge joints are difficult to make with hand tools. You need considerable skill in planing long edges to achieve good results.

First lay the pieces to be joined on the workbench. Mark the edges to be joined on the face of the boards, Figure 16-11. Use chalk or light pencil marks. Do not mark so hard that you groove the surface of the board.

Place the two edges to form a joint in a vise. Place the face surfaces out, Figure 16-12. In this way, a tight joint will be formed even if the edges are a little out of square with the face. Plane these together until they are square and straight, Figure 16-13. Check with a try square and framing square. (Refer to Unit 9 for squaring techniques.) Then remove the boards and place them together. Hold them up to the light to see if they fit tightly, Figure 16-14. Light will show through any low areas. Plane the high areas very carefully. Recheck for fit. When you get a tight fit, the joint is ready for gluing. (Refer to Unit 14 for assembly information.)

How to make doweled-edge joints is shown in Unit 20.

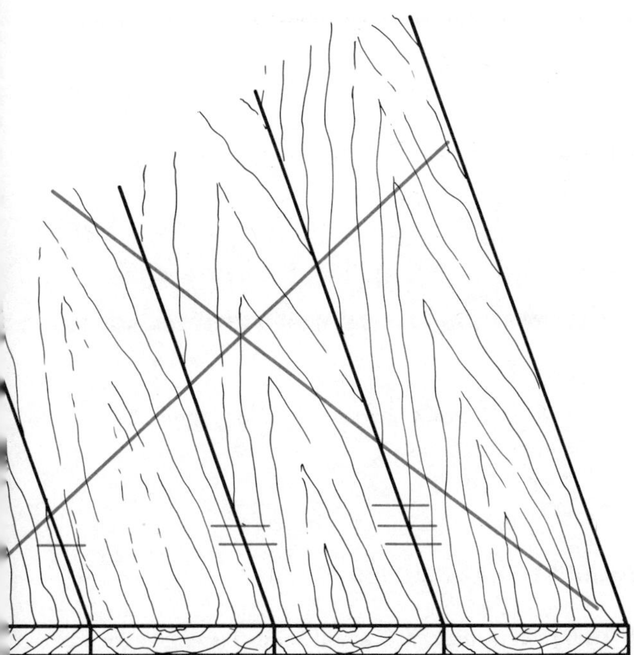

Figure 16-11
Boards joined edge to edge must be marked so they can be assembled after planing.

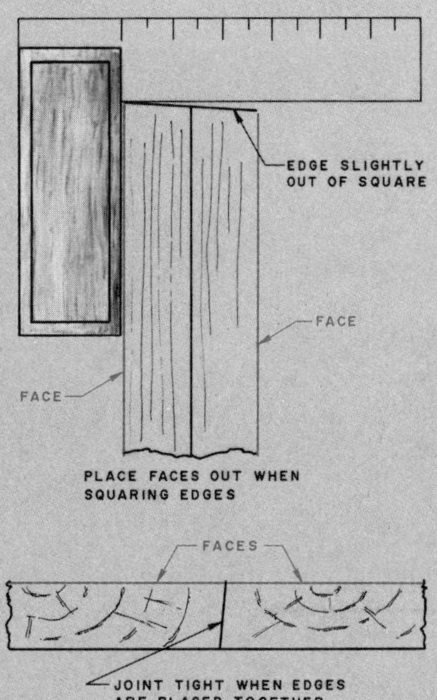

Figure 16-12
Plane both edges to be joined at the same time, so errors in squaring will not cause a poor joint.

Figure 16-13
Planing edges to form an edge joint.

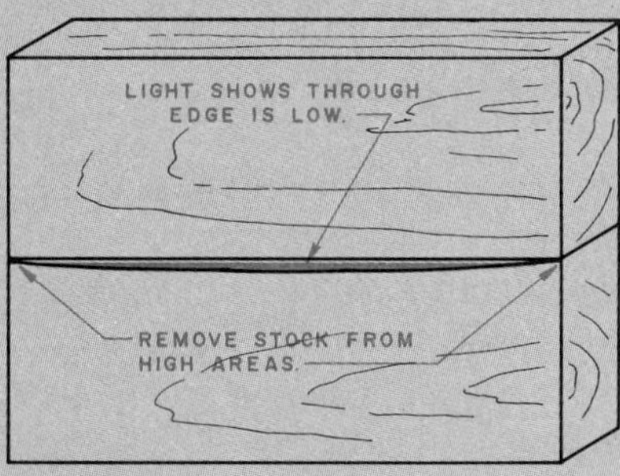

Figure 16-14
Place the edges to be joined together, and hold up to the light to check for fit.

Figure 16-15
Edge rabbets can be cut with a rabbet plane.

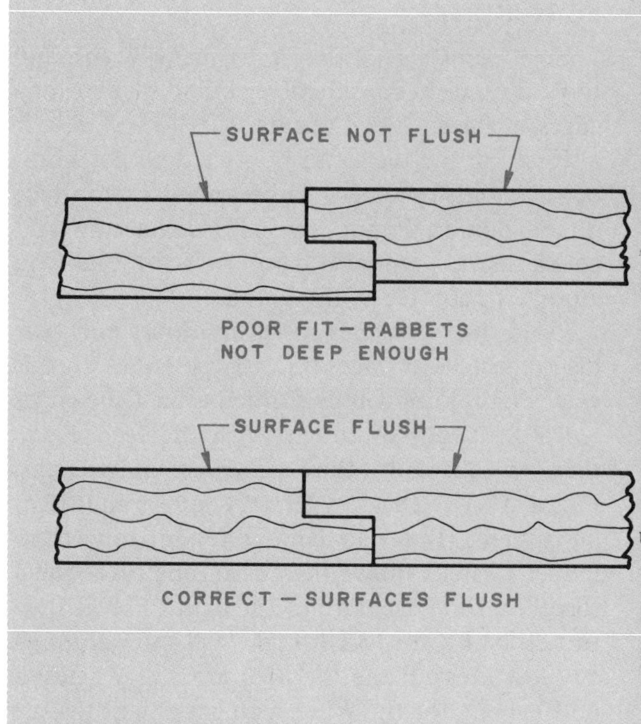

Figure 16-16
Rabbet-edge joints should be cut deep enough to form a flat surface on the panel.

The rabbet-edge lap can be hand cut with a rabbet plane, Figure 16-15. First match and square the surfaces as explained for plain-edge joints. Then set the rabbet plane to cut half the width of the edges to be joined. Plane until you reach the desired depth. The correct depth can be marked with a marking gauge, Figure 16-16. Remember, the rabbet is on the top face of one piece but on the bottom of the other.

When you reach the marked depth, place the two boards together on a flat surface. Check to see if the surfaces of the boards are flat, Figure 16-16.

Tongue and groove joints and spline-edge joints usually are not cut with hand tools. The circular saw is most frequently used. (Refer to Unit 26 for details.)

REVIEW QUESTIONS

1 What is the best way to hand cut end grain to form a butt joint?
2 How do you prepare a butt joint that is to be joined with wood screws?
3 How does the clamp nail pull the two parts of the joint together?
4 What is a glue block?
5 Why are edge joints difficult to make?
6 How do you mark the stock when laying out an edge joint?
7 How do you check boards to be edge jointed for squareness?

SUGGESTED ACTIVITIES

1 Using scrap stock, make butt joints fastened with screws, nails, corrugated fasteners, clamp nails and dowels.
2 Using scrap stock, make edge joints with dowels and tongue and grooved edges.

UNIT

17

Making Miter Joints

Objectives

After studying this unit you should be able to:

1 Set up a miter box to cut wood on angles.

2 Cut and assemble flat miter joints.

3 Set up and cut a compound miter.

4 Fasten miter joints.

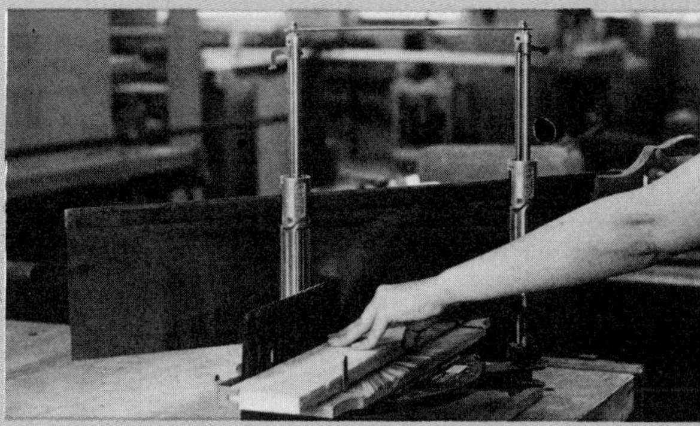

Figure 17-1
Use a miter box to cut wood on angles.

Many wood products have joints formed by two pieces meeting at an angle. These joints are called miters. Miters often are used to form a frame. This might be a picture frame or a frame on the front of a cabinet.

CUTTING MITERS

The easiest way to make a plain, flat miter is by using a miter box. A scale of degrees on the miter box helps you adjust your saw to any angle. By releasing a lock lever on the miter box, you can swing the saw to the angle needed. The clamping device that holds the saw is notched at commonly used angles, such as 45°. The notches permit the saw to have a firm, locked position for cutting on these angles, Figure 17-1.

Set the saw to the desired angle. Then place the wood against a support known as the fence. Slide it under the saw. Set the wood so that the saw cuts on the waste side of the guide mark, Figure 17-2.

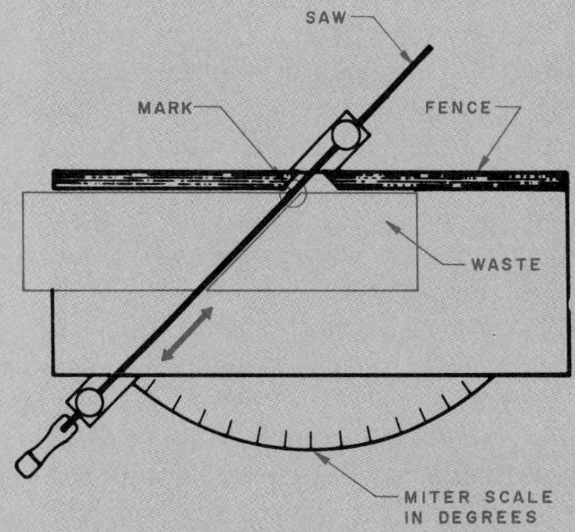

Figure 17-2
How to set the miter box to cut on an angle.

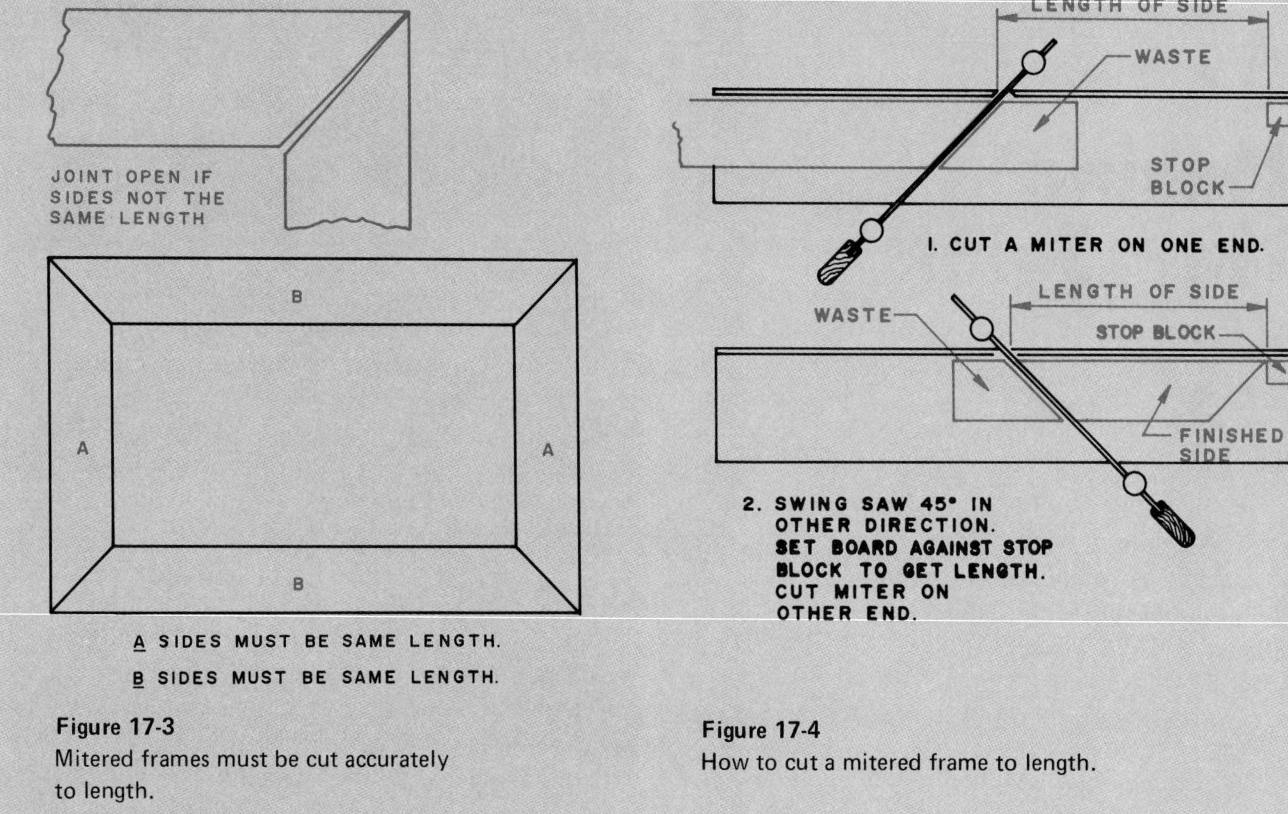
JOINT OPEN IF SIDES NOT THE SAME LENGTH
B
A
A
B
A SIDES MUST BE SAME LENGTH.
B SIDES MUST BE SAME LENGTH.
LENGTH OF SIDE
WASTE
STOP BLOCK
1. CUT A MITER ON ONE END.
LENGTH OF SIDE
WASTE
STOP BLOCK
FINISHED SIDE
2. SWING SAW 45° IN OTHER DIRECTION.
SET BOARD AGAINST STOP BLOCK TO GET LENGTH.
CUT MITER ON OTHER END.

Figure 17-3
Mitered frames must be cut accurately to length.

Figure 17-4
How to cut a mitered frame to length.

Hold the wood firmly against the fence when you are ready to cut. Then move the saw back and forth across the wood. Do not push down on the saw when you cut. If it is properly sharpened, it will cut easily. Its own weight provides the downward pressure.

When you are about to saw through the board, slow the cut so the saw eases through the bottom. Cutting too fast at this point could split the edges of the miter at the bottom.

Miters are cut for various types of frames. To succeed in making a frame, you must be sure to cut the correct length of each piece. The pieces on opposite sides of the frame must be the same length. If they are uneven, the miter joint will not close, Figure 17-3.

When you mark the length of frame sides, place the marks on the outside edge. Measure the lengths carefully. One way to get accurate lengths is to put a stop on the fence of the miter box. A hand screw can serve as a stop. Set the distance between the saw and the stop equal to the outside length of the frame. When the distance is set, cut a miter on one end of the board. Then swing the saw 45° in the other direction. Place the mitered end against the stop and cut the miter on the other end, Figure 17-4.

If a miter box is not available, a miter can be cut by using a piece of wood as a guide. First mark the 45° angle on the face of the board to be mitered. A combination square is the best tool for this job, Figure 17-5. Then clamp the wood block along your guide line. Cut the board with a backsaw, and use the block to keep the saw square, Figure 17-6.

If a miter is slightly off, a correction can be made. Clamp the two sides tightly together and then cut through the joint with a backsaw. This cut will make the frame a little out of square but usually not enough to do any harm, Figure 17-7. The miter can also be adjusted slightly by planing the high edge with a block plane.

Cut edge miters in the same manner as flat miters. Most miter boxes can be used to cut stock up to 3-1/2" (89 mm) high, Figure 17-8. It is difficult to cut edge miters on wide boards by hand. As a result, they usually are cut with power saws.

Figure 17-5
To cut a miter without a miter box, mark the desired angle with a combination square.

Figure 17-6
Clamp a wood block along the miter line to guide the saw as it cuts the angle.

Polygon miters are miters cut on angles other than 45°. You can cut them by using a miter box in nearly the same way as described for flat miters. The only difference is the angle setting of the saw. Unit 15 has details about polygon miters.

Compound miters usually are cut with a circular power saw. You can cut them, however, with a miter box. In the normal manner, set the miter saw on the angle wanted and place the board against the fence. Place a wedge on the table to hold the board on the angle the miter is to be cut, Figure 17-9. With this setup, you can cut the miter at an angle to the bottom of the board.

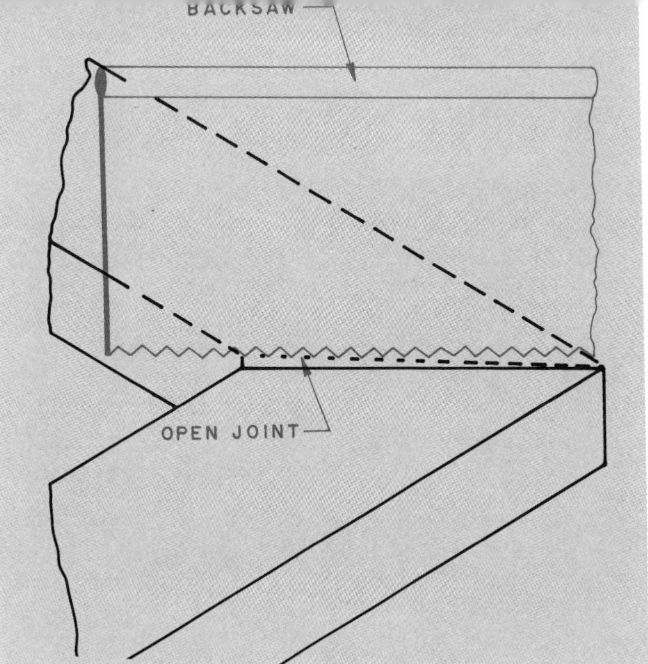

Figure 17-7
Use a backsaw to cut through a poorly fitting miter to improve the fit.

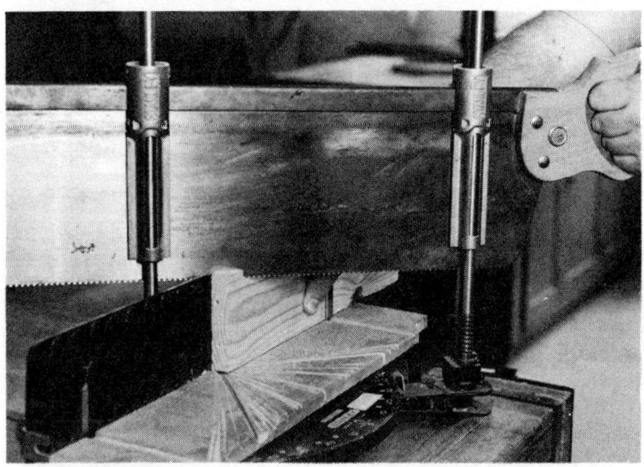

Figure 17-8
Short-edge miters can be cut on a miter box.

Figure 17-9
Compound miters can be cut by raising the end of the board as the miter is sawed.

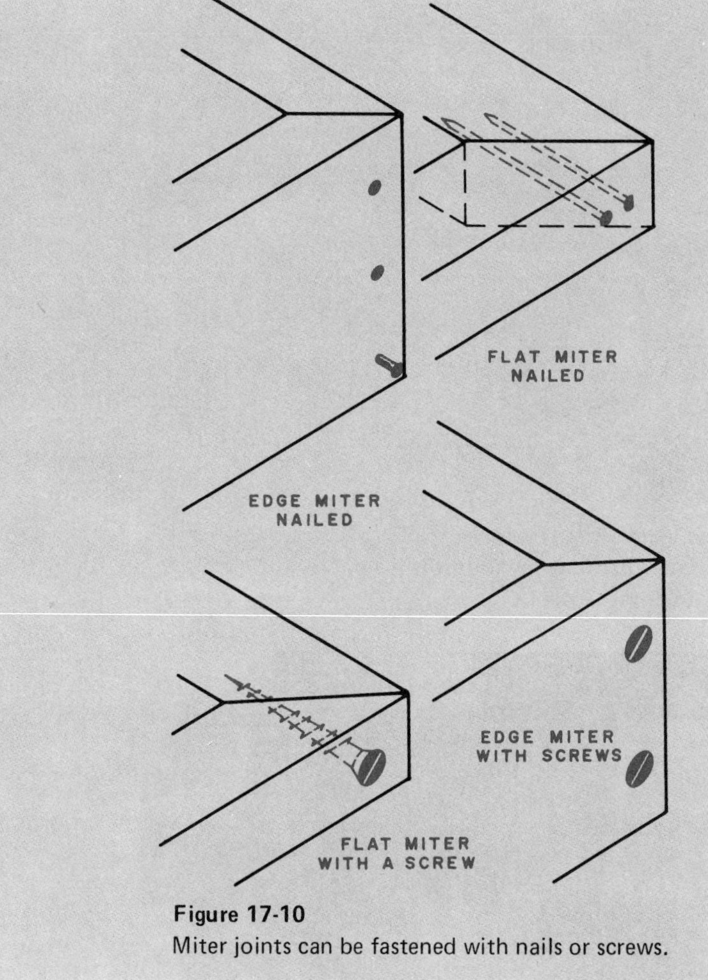

Figure 17-10
Miter joints can be fastened with nails or screws.

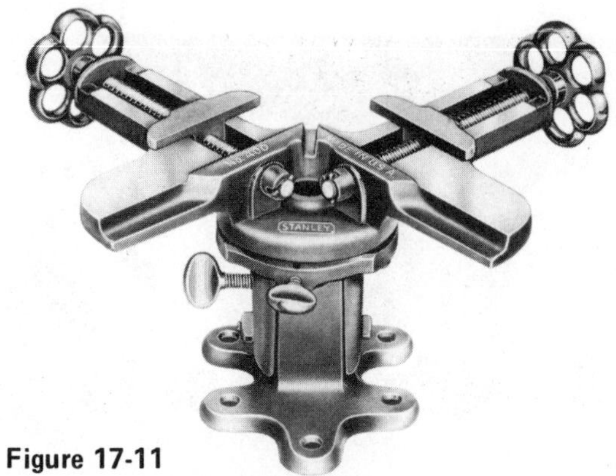

Figure 17-11
A miter vise. (The Stanley Works)

Figure 17-12
The miter vise holds the pieces of the frame as they are nailed or screwed together.

FASTENING MITERS

Miters, like butt joints, need some type of fastening device. Nails and screws often are used. To join a miter with nails, clamp the two boards together on the workbench. Then drive the nails perpendicular to the outer edge, Figure 17-10. Finishing nails often are used. To help prevent the boards from splitting, you can drill small holes through the first piece. The holes should be smaller than the diameter of the nail.

You also can use wood screws. Drill holes the same diameter as the screw in the first piece. Countersink the opening. Drill a small-diameter hole into the second piece. Clamp the two pieces together on a bench top, and install the screws.

A miter vise helps assemble a miter joint, Figure 17-11. This tool holds each piece firmly as the joint is fastened with nails or screws, Figure 17-12.

The parts of a miter joint can be glued before they are assembled. Glue will not hold the joint without other fasteners, but it does stiffen the joint.

Metal corrugated fasteners often are used to hold flat miters. The joint is clamped together on the workbench. The fasteners are hammered in perpendicular to the joint, Figure 17-13.

Short clamp nails also are used to fasten flat miters, Figure 17-14. Long clamp nails join edge miters. A saw kerf is cut in the face of the miter to help install clamp nails, Figure 17-15.

Long edge miters also are joined with plastic dowels. Holes are drilled into each miter parallel to the face of the board. Glue fastens the dowels and the joint, Figure 17-16.

Flat and edge miters also may be joined with wood dowels. Refer to Unit 20 for information on dowel joints.

Figure 17-13
Flat miter joints can be assembled with corrugated fasteners.

Figure 17-14
Clamp nails can join flat miter joints.

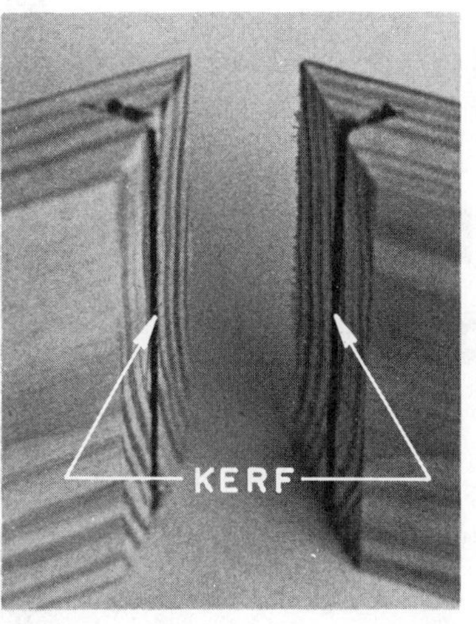

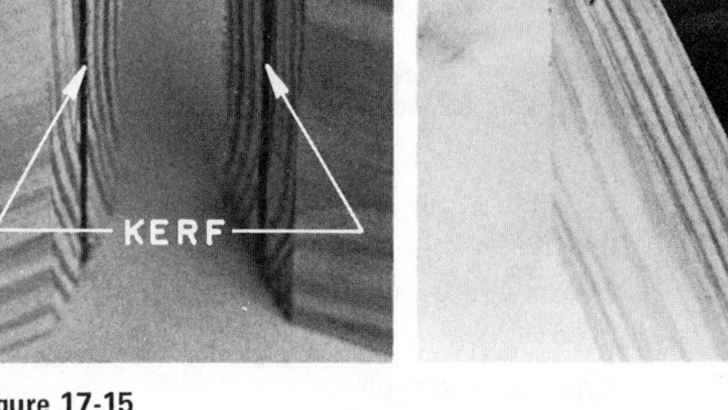

Figure 17-15
Long clamp nails are used to join edge miter joints.
A kerf can be cut into the miter to install clamp nails.

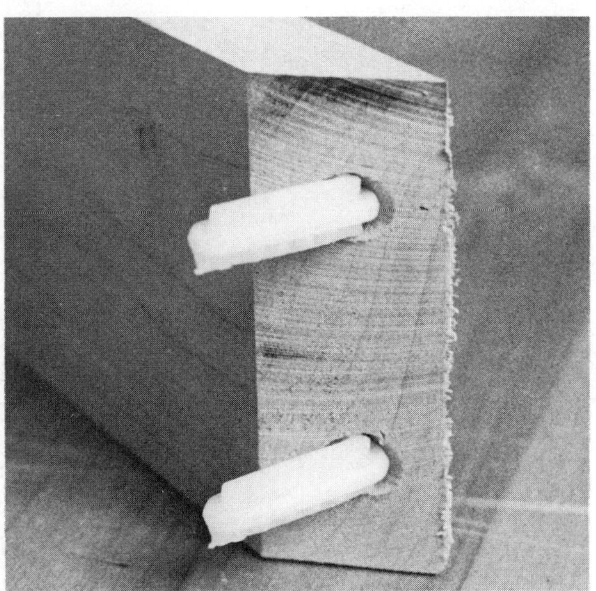

Figure 17-16
Plastic dowels can fasten edge miters.

REVIEW QUESTIONS

1. How can you tell when a miter box is set on a particular angle?
2. Why should the opposite sides of a product being mitered be the same length?
3. How can you correct a miter that is slightly off the 45° angle?
4. What is needed to cut a compound miter on a miter box?
5. What tool is useful for holding the parts of a miter together for assembling purposes?
6. What metal fasteners often are used to hold flat miters?

SUGGESTED ACTIVITIES

1. Cut several miters out of scrap materials.
2. Assemble the miters with nails, screws and corrugated fasteners.

UNIT

18

Making Lap Joints

Objectives

After studying this unit you should be able to:

1 Lay out a lap joint.
2 Cut a lap joint.
3 Assemble a lap joint.

Make a lap joint by cutting the same amount from each piece of wood. When the joint is assembled, the faces should be flush.

To make a hand-cut lap joint, first lay it out on the stock. Place the members that form the joint side by side. Mark the width on both pieces, Figure 18-1. Use a sharp, hard-lead pencil or a knife. Then with a marking gauge mark the depth of the joint. A properly laid-out cross lap is shown in Figure 18-2. Another way to lay out the width is to clamp the members in position. Use their edges to mark the width, Figure 18-3.

Figure 18-1
Lay out both sides of a lap joint. Mark the width.

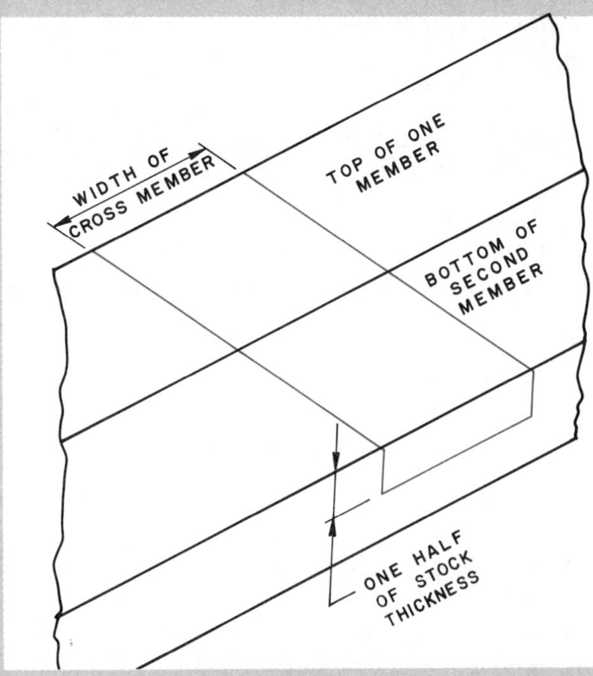

Figure 18-2
A properly laid-out cross lap joint.

Figure 18-3
The layout is more accurate if you use a knife to locate the joint.

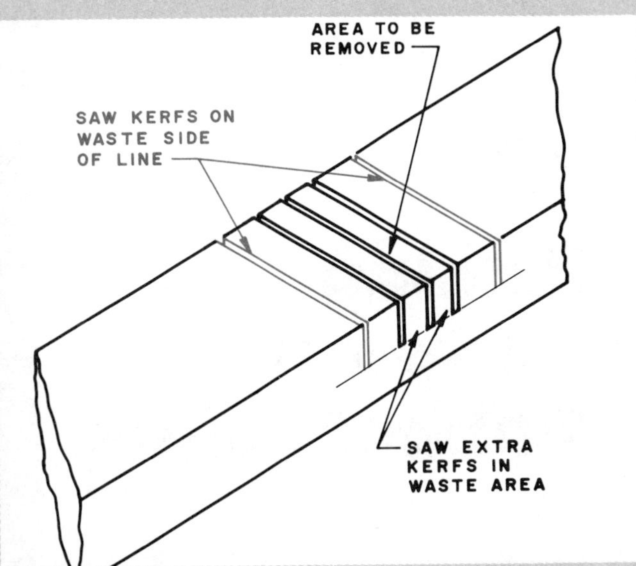

Figure 18-5
Saw on the waste side of the line.

Figure 18-4
Make the shoulder cuts with a miter box.

Figure 18-6
Remove the wood between the shoulder cuts with a chisel.

Next, make the shoulder cuts on the face. Use a miter box to make accurate cuts, Figure 18-4. Cut on the waste side of the line. If the board is wide, take several cuts in the center of the waste portion. Cut to the depth line, Figure 18-5. You also can clamp a square block beside the layout line. Use the block as a guide. Cut the shoulder with a backsaw or a dovetail saw.

Now clamp the stock to the workbench. Use a wood chisel to remove the waste material. Chisel until the bottom of the cut is flat, Figure 18-6. Trial assemble the joint. Carefully chisel away material until the surfaces of the lap joint are flat.

These procedures are the same for any kind of lap joint.

REVIEW QUESTIONS

1. How deep is a lap joint cut?
2. What is the best way to make the shoulder cuts?
3. How do you remove the stock between the shoulder cuts?

SUGGESTED ACTIVITIES

1. Using scrap materials, lay out, cut and assemble a cross lap joint.
2. Find examples of different kinds of lap joints in your home or shop.

UNIT

19

Making Dado and Rabbet Joints

Objectives

After studying this unit you should be able to:

1 Lay out and cut a dado.

2 Lay out and cut a rabbet.

Before laying out the joints, check to see that all boards are cut to their finished sizes. Surfaces and edges must be square.

CUTTING A DADO JOINT

To make a dado, first lay out its width, Figure 19-1. Use a sharp, hard-lead pencil or a knife.

Figure 19-1
Lay out the width of the dado with a try square.

Figure 19-2
Check the width with the part to fit in the dado.

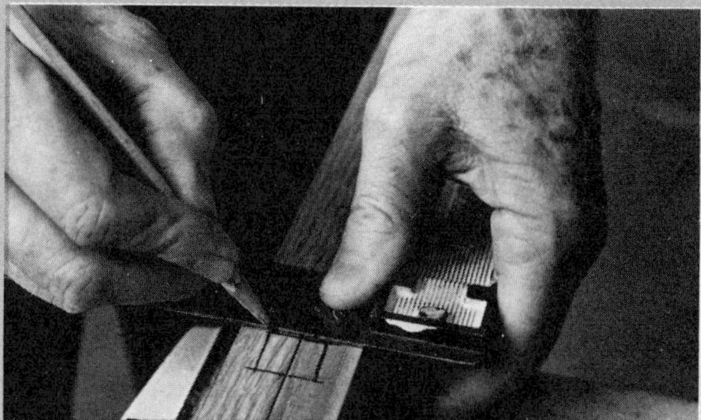

Figure 19-3
Mark the depths of dadoes in matching parts at the same time.

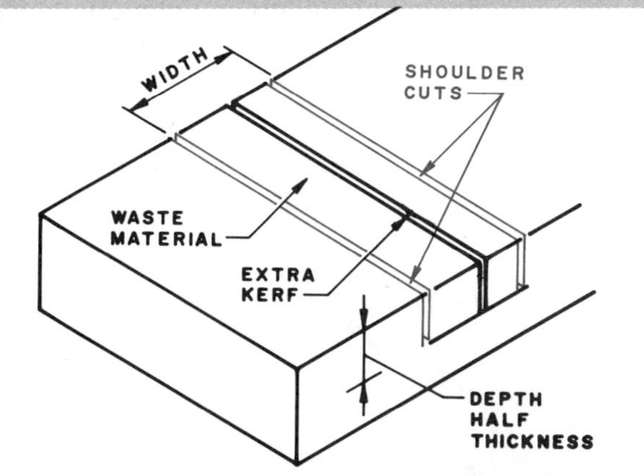

Figure 19-4
This drawing shows a dado joint laid out. Shoulder cuts are on the waste sides of the lines.

The line is the outside edge of the joint. The line should be faintly visible when the joint is cut. As a check, stand the board to fit in the dado on the width marks, Figure 19-2.

Next mark the depth. The depth usually is half the thickness of the board. For projects in which the dadoes must line up, as in a bookcase, mark both sides at the same time, Figure 19-3. Use a marking gauge to mark the depth. A finished layout is shown in Figure 19-4.

For accuracy, make the shoulder cuts with a miter box. Cut on the waste side of the line. Cut so that the line marking the width is faintly visible. Cut to the depth line. You may want to make an extra cut in the center of the waste material, Figure 19-4. This will help you remove the waste.

If a miter box is not available, make the shoulder cuts with a backsaw. Clamp a square block of wood along the line of the joint. The block guides the saw, Figure 19-5.

Now, clamp the board to the workbench with a hand screw. Chisel out the waste material, Figure 19-6. (Review Unit 10.) If a router plane is available, use it to smooth the bottom of the dado, Figure 19-7.

CUTTING A RABBET JOINT

To make a rabbet joint, lay out the boards as you did for the dado. Mark the line on the face with a try square. Mark the depth and the end lines with a marking gauge, Figure 19-8. The

Figure 19-5
A miter saw makes the shoulder cuts. A wood block clamped on the line guides the saw.

Figure 19-6
Remove the wood from the dado with a wood chisel. Clamp the board tightly to the workbench.

Figure 19-7
Use a router plane to smooth the bottom of the dado.

Figure 19-8
A marking gauge marks the depth of a rabbet joint.

depth usually is two-thirds the thickness of the board. A finished layout is shown in Figure 19-9.

Make the shoulder cut on the miter box. You also can use a square block and a backsaw. Cut the depth with a backsaw or a chisel. If you use a chisel, cut several saw kerfs in the waste to the full depth of the rabbet. Remove the waste with a chisel as you did for the dado joint.

With a backsaw, you can make the cut freehand, but it is difficult to get the cut square. Build a cutting fixture to steady the saw. One type of fixture is shown in Figure 19-10. Clamp the fixture to the board in a vise. Make the cut by sawing in the normal vertical position. Then adjust the fit by trimming the surface with a wood chisel.

Both dado and rabbet joints can be cut with power tools. These operations are described in a later unit.

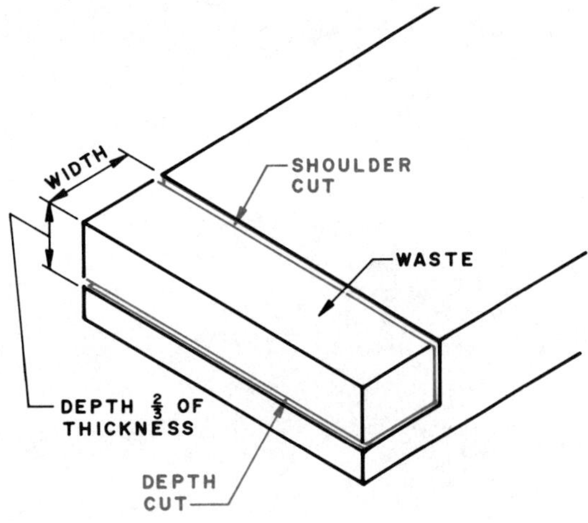

Figure 19-9
The drawing shows a rabbet joint laid out.
The shoulder and depth cuts are on the waste side of the line.

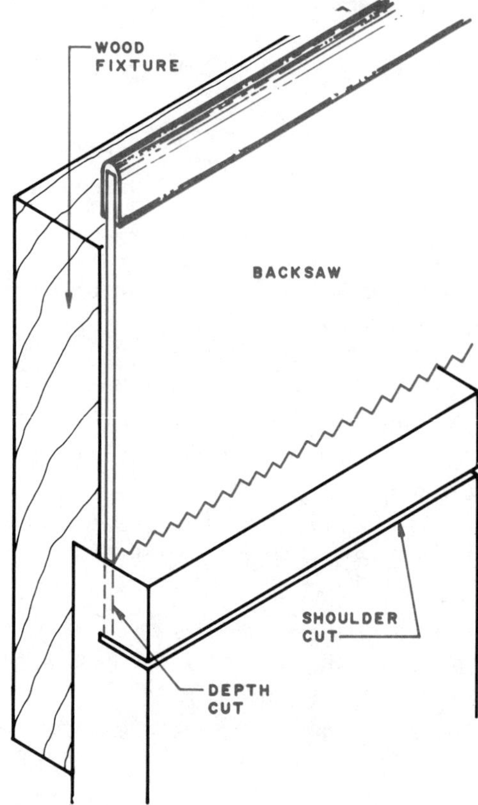

Figure 19-10
You can build a wood fixture to help you make the depth cut on a rabbet joint.

REVIEW QUESTIONS

1 What are the steps in laying out a dado?
2 How do you make the shoulder cuts on a dado?
3 How do you cut short rabbets with hand tools?

SUGGESTED ACTIVITIES

1 Using scrap stock, lay out and cut a dado.
2 Using scrap stock, lay out and cut a short rabbet.

UNIT

20

Making Dowel Joints

Objectives

After studying this unit you should be able to:

1 Lay out and construct dowel joints on legs, rails and miters.

2 Lay out and construct edge-to-edge dowel joints.

Technical Terms

Dowel pin

Doweling jig

Dowel center

Dowels are round, wooden pins used to align and strengthen various joints. They are commonly used with butt, miter and edge joints. Dowels usually are made of birch or maple.

Dowels are available in 36″ lengths. They range in diameter from 1/8″ to 1/2″ by 1/16ths and from 1/2″ to 1″ by 1/8ths. *Dowel pins* cut to standard lengths are also available. Typical lengths are 1-1/2″, 2″, 2-1/2″ and 3″. Some dowels have a spiral groove cut on the surface. This helps the excess glue and air to escape as the joint is clamped, Figure 20-1.

The diameter of the dowel should be half the thickness of the wood. For example, a 3/8″ diameter dowel would be used in a piece of wood 3/4″ thick. The spacing of dowels is a matter of judgment. On long edge joints they should be 4″ to 6″ (102 to 152 mm) apart. On a small butt joint two dowels usually are enough. The farther apart the dowels are placed in a butt joint, the stronger the joint is formed.

The dowel should be long enough to go into the wood at least two and one-half times its diameter. A 3/8″ dowel should therefore enter the wood 15/16″. The total dowel length would

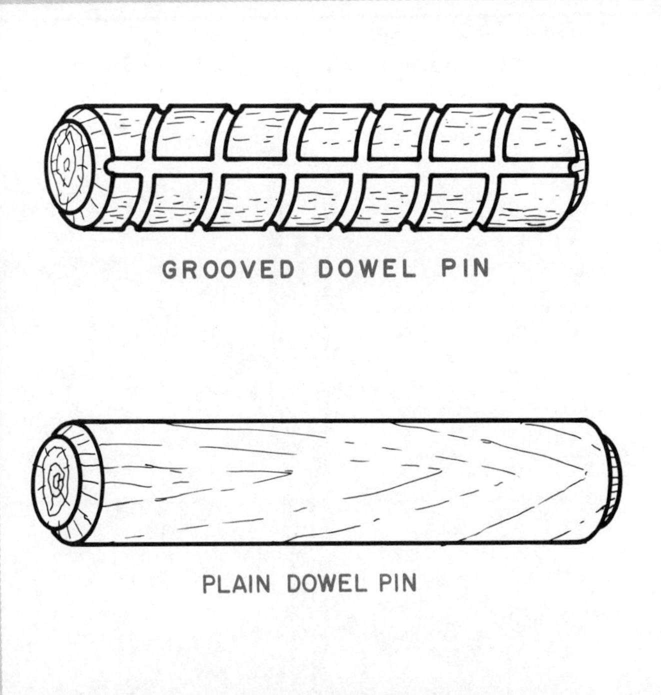

Figure 20-1
Two types of dowel pins.

be 1-7/8″. The holes bored to receive the dowels should be about 1/8″ deeper, Figure 20-2. This provides a place for the excess glue.

After cutting the dowel to length, you remove the sharp edges. A dowel should have a slight bevel. This can be cut with a knife, a pencil sharpener or a special tool designed for this purpose, Figure 20-3. The cone end helps get the dowel started into the hole.

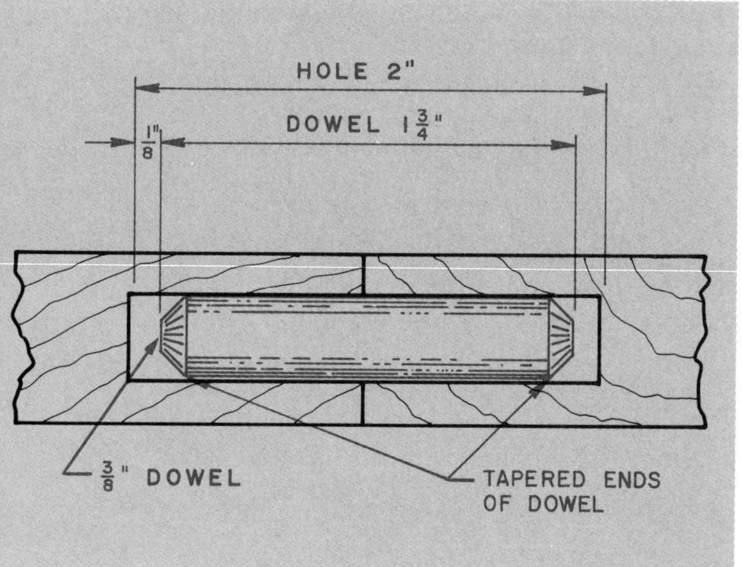

Figure 20-2
A section through a dowel joint in a board 3/4″ thick.

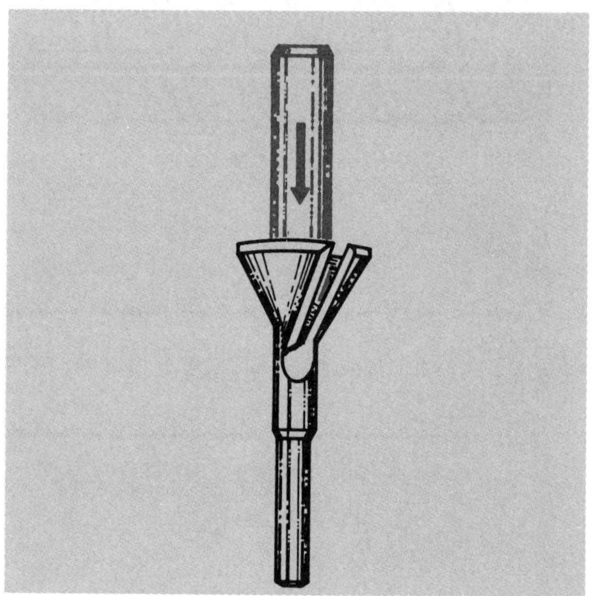

Figure 20-3
Bevel dowels with a dowel pointer.

LAYING OUT EDGE JOINTS

Locate dowels by marking their centers. This placement must be made accurately so that the boards to be joined come together properly.

One way to do this is to mark the pieces to be joined at the same time. Place the boards together in a vise with the faces out. Mark the face with chalk. Locate the position of each dowel by drawing a line across the edge with a square, Figure 20-4. Then set a marking gauge half the thickness of the board. Mark each center from the face side, Figure 20-5.

Now select an auger bit the same diameter as the dowel pin. To drill an accurate hole, use a *doweling jig.* A doweling jig clamps on the edge of the board. It has a hollow tube that is centered over the center mark on the edge. The doweling jig holds the auger perpendicular to the edge. Put a depth stop on the auger so the hole is the correct depth, Figure 20-6. You also could use a twist drill with the doweling jig.

Place the dowels in the holes and assemble them dry. This will give you a chance to make corrections. Be certain to assemble with the face sides up. In this way the surface of the boards will be flush even if the holes miss the center of the boards a little, Figure 20-7.

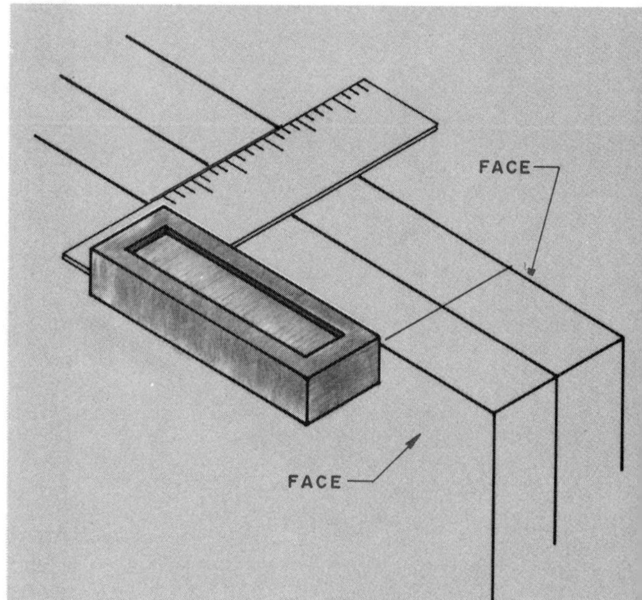

Figure 20-4
Lay out the dowel locations on both edges at the same time.

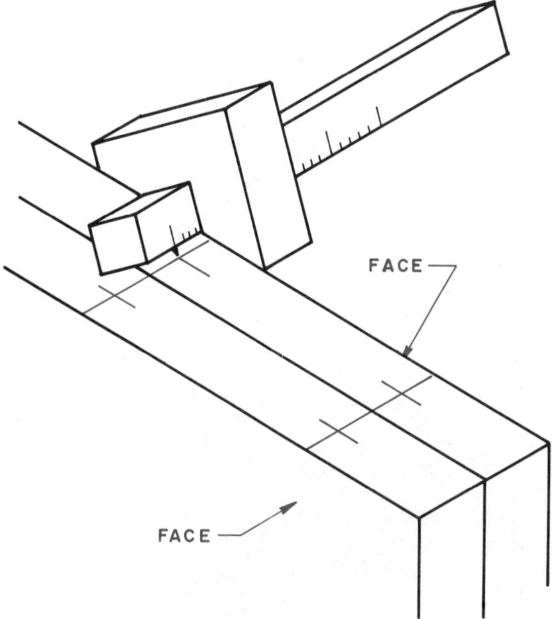

Figure 20-5
Measure the centers of the dowel locations from the face of each board.

Figure 20-6
Bore dowel holes with a doweling jig. Control the depth of the hole with a bit stop.

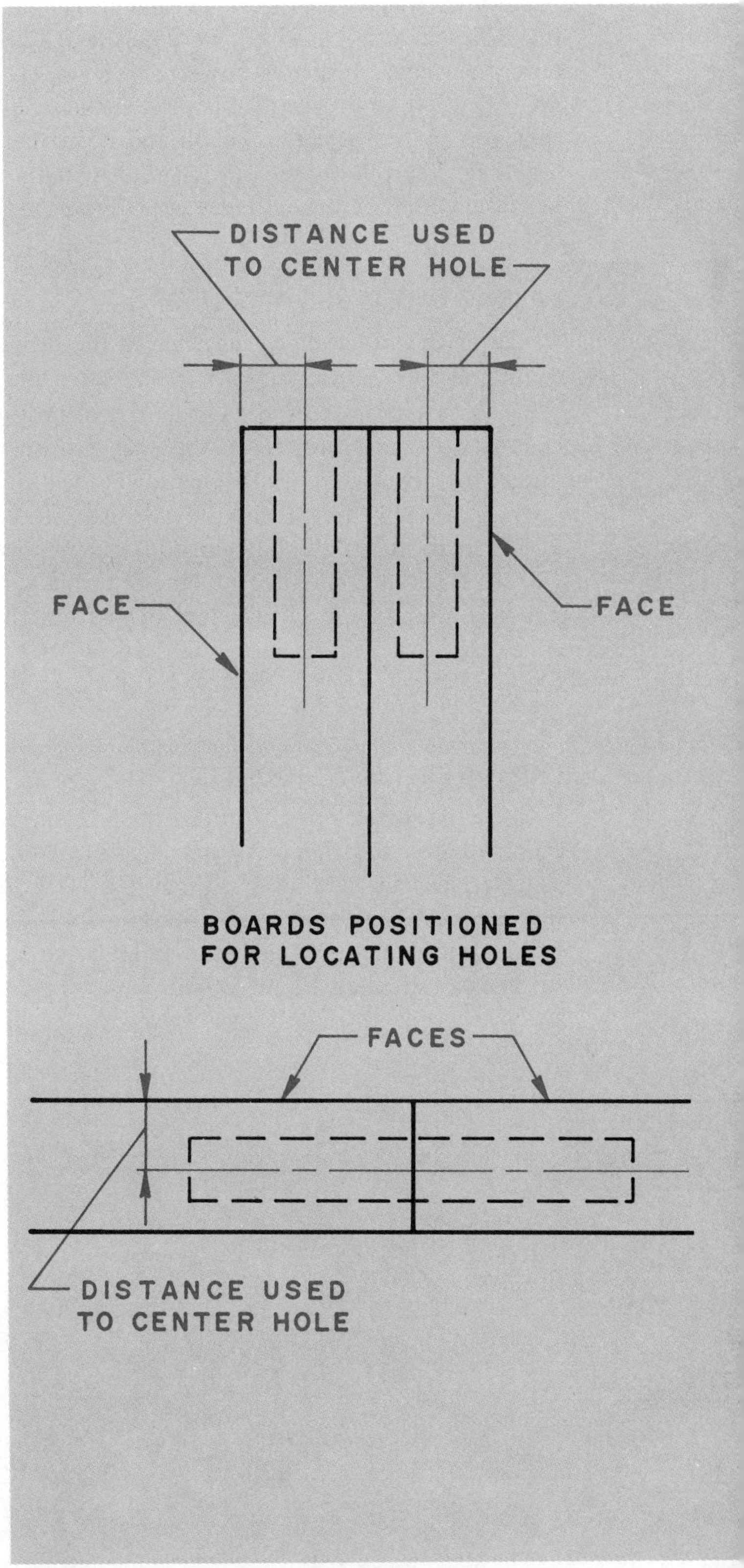

DISTANCE USED
TO CENTER HOLE

FACE

FACE

BOARDS POSITIONED
FOR LOCATING HOLES

FACES

DISTANCE USED
TO CENTER HOLE

Figure 20-7
If holes are located from the faces of the board, the joint will assemble with the faces flush.

Another way to mark dowel joints is to mark the holes in one piece as just described. Then bore the holes. Insert a *dowel center* in each hole. Place the two boards on a flat surface, line them up in the proper position and push them together. The pin on the dowel center will mark the hole centers on the other piece, Figure 20-8.

LAYING OUT RAILS AND LEGS

Clamp the rail and leg together so the dowel centers can be located on both at the same time. Mark the locations with a try square. Locate the centers by measuring from the face (finished outer) surface, Figure 20-9. The dowel locations in the rail will be in its center. These are marked with a marking gauge. The locations in the leg will be a distance equal to half the rail thickness plus the amount the rail will be set in from the edge of the leg. This is usually 1/8″ to 1/4″ (3 to 6 mm), Figure 20-10.

LAYING OUT MITER JOINTS

Place the surfaces of the miters flush together. Clamp tightly together with the faces out. Mark as described for edge miters, Figure 20-11. Bore the holes with an auger and doweling tool. Remember to bore the holes perpendicular to the surface of the miter, Figure 20-12.

Figure 20-8
Dowel centers can locate dowel holes.

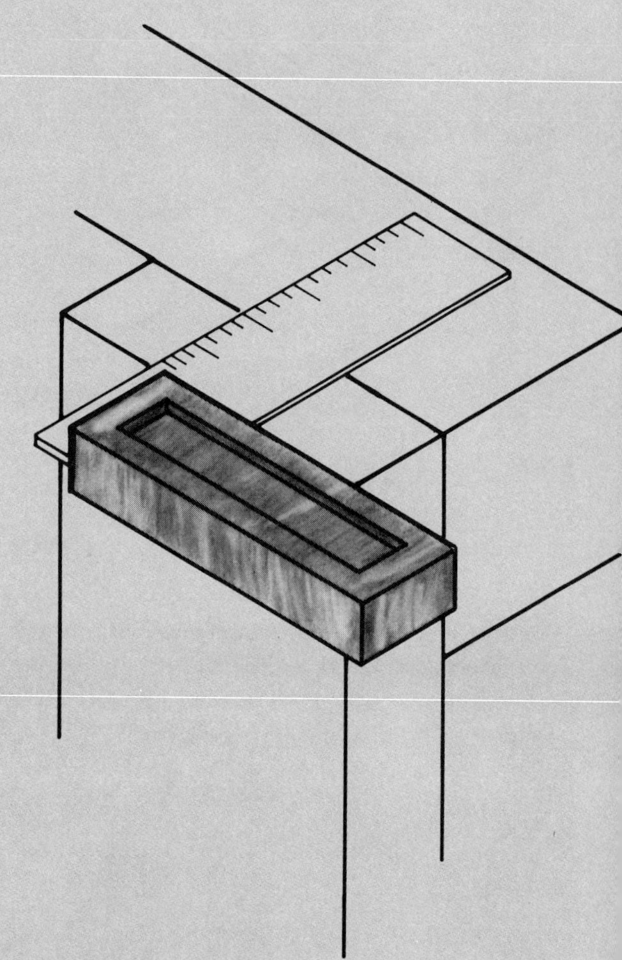

Figure 20-9
Clamp rails and legs together and mark dowel holes on both at the same time.

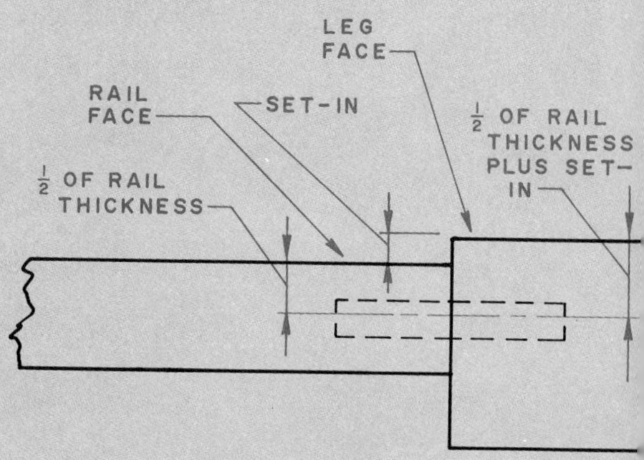

Figure 20-10
Locate dowel holes from the finished surface (face) of the rail and leg.

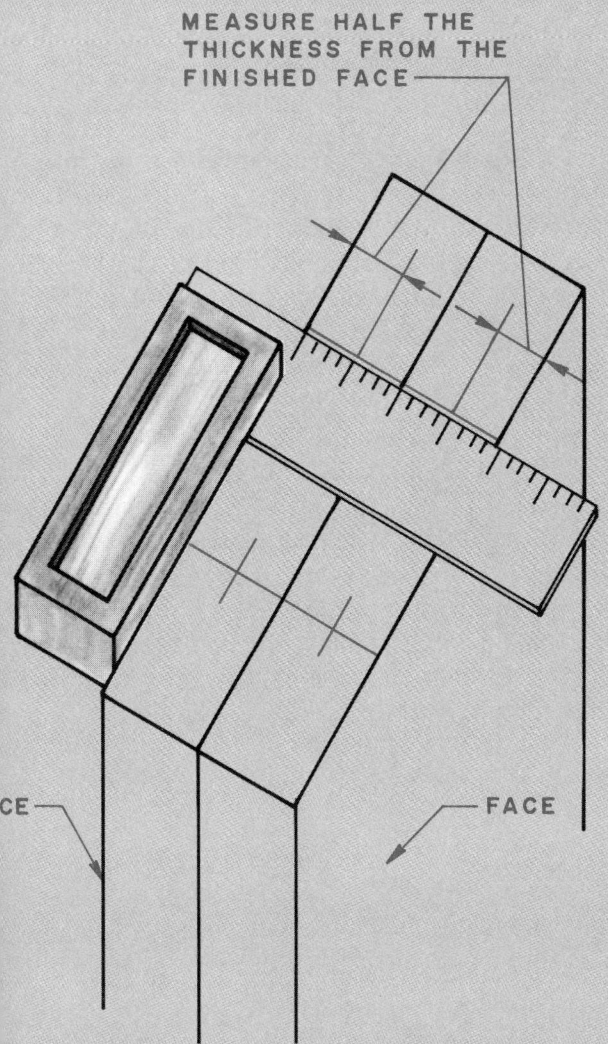
MEASURE HALF THE
THICKNESS FROM THE
FINISHED FACE
CE
FACE

Figure 20-11
How to lay out a doweled miter joint.

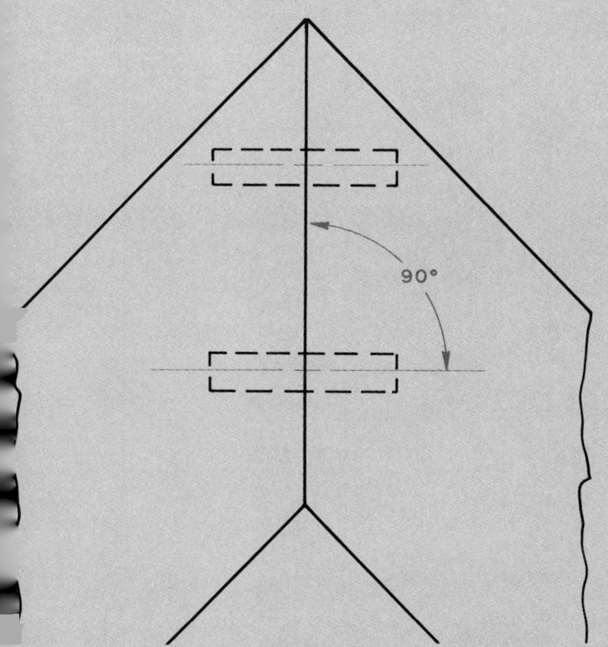
90°

Figure 20-12
Bore dowel holes perpendicular to the mitered face.

REVIEW QUESTIONS

1 What are the standard lengths of dowel pins?
2 How do you decide the diameter of the dowel to use?
3 How deep should a dowel be placed into the wood?
4 Why are dowel holes bored deeper than the length of the dowel pin?
5 Why are dowel pins beveled on each end?
6 How does the doweling tool help produce a dowel joint?
7 Why should a dowel joint be assembled dry before it is glued?

SUGGESTED ACTIVITIES

1 Using scrap stock, lay out and cut an edge-to-edge dowel joint.
2 Using scrap stock, lay out and cut a dowel joint to join a rail to a leg.
3 Using scrap stock, lay out and join a miter with a dowel joint.

UNIT

21

Making Mortise and Tenon Joints

Objectives

After studying this unit you should be able to:

1 Lay out and cut a mortise.

2 Lay out and cut a tenon to match the mortise.

Technical Terms

Mortise

Tenon

A *mortise* is a rectangular opening cut into wood. A *tenon* is a projecting part designed to fit into a mortise. The mortise and the tenon make a strong joint. For maximum strength, lay out and cut each part of the joint accurately.

LAYING OUT THE MORTISE

Cut the mortise no closer to the end of a part than 1/2″ (13 mm). Cut it no closer to the face of a part than 5/16″ (8 mm). If possible, increase these distances to 3/4″ and 7/16″ (19 and 11 mm). The mortise should be about 1/8″ (3 mm) deeper than the length of the tenon, Figure 21-1.

Cut the mortise before you cut the tenon. It is easier to adjust the size of the tenon than to adjust the size of the mortise.

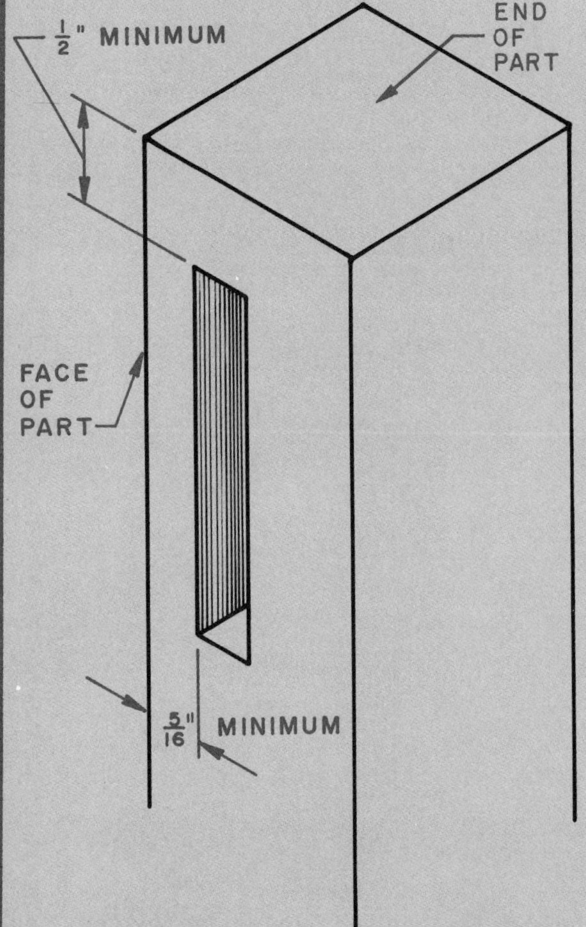

Figure 21-1
Minimum spacing for a mortise.

To lay out the mortises for assembling legs and rails, first mark on each leg the surfaces that are to be faces. A face is a finished surface that will not have a mortise. In most cases, each leg will have two mortises.

Clamp the four legs together and lay out the length of the mortise on all legs, Figure 21-2. Set a marking gauge to mark the edge nearest the face. Set a second marking gauge to mark the other side of the mortise. Make both marks from a finished face, Figure 21-3. Then turn the legs and mark the mortises on the other inside surface. A properly marked mortise will look like the drawing in Figure 21-4.

To cut the mortise, position a doweling jig over the marked area. Select an auger bit that is about 1/16″ (2 mm) smaller in diameter than the width of the mortise. Place a bit stop on the auger to control the depth of cut. Clamp the leg

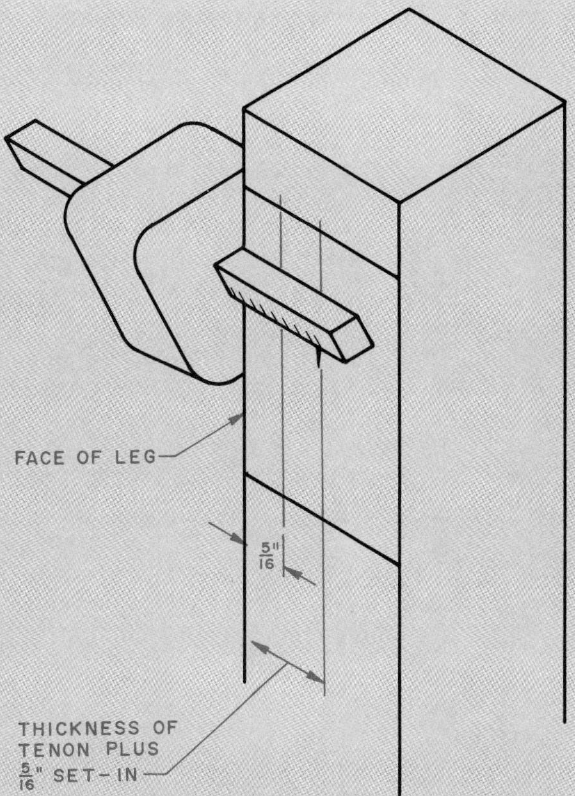

Figure 21-3
Locate the width of the mortise with a marking gauge.

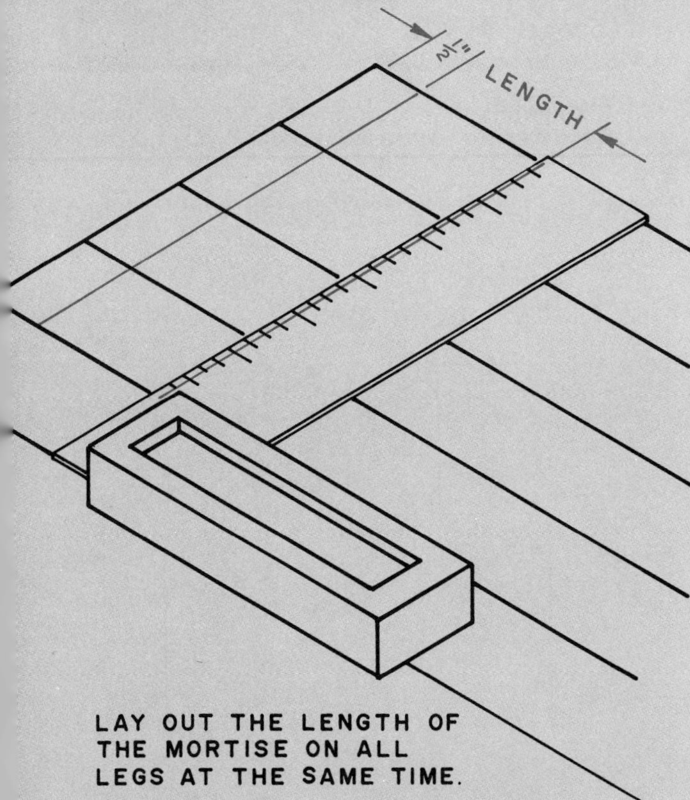

Figure 21-2
Lay out all mortises together.

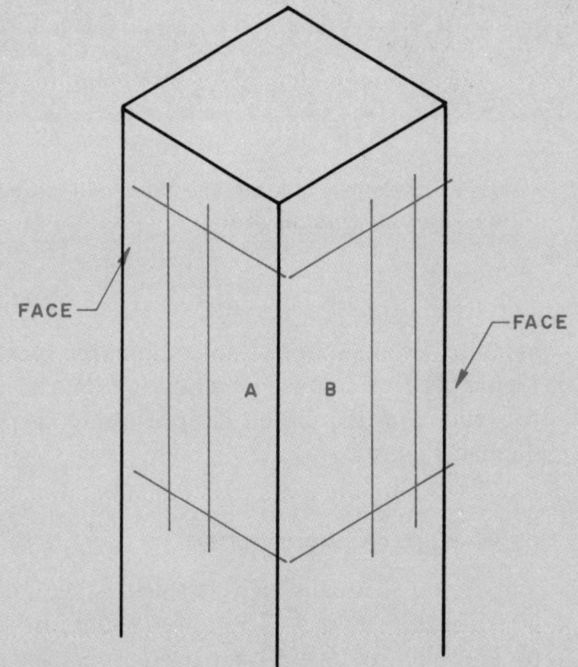

Figure 21-4
The layout for a pair of mortises on a table leg.

Figure 21-5
Use a doweling jig to locate the holes for a mortise. A bit stop controls the depth.

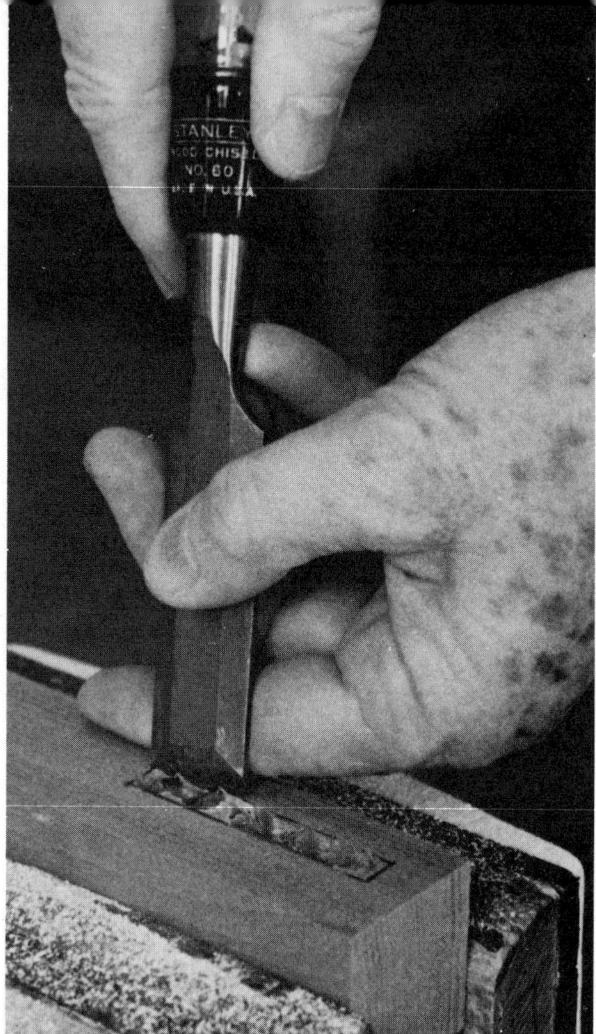

Figure 21-6
Cut the mortise with a wood chisel.

in a vise. Bore a series of holes along the mortise, Figure 21-5. Remove the wood left in the mortise with a wood chisel. Keep the sides perpendicular, Figure 21-6.

LAYING OUT THE TENON

A tenon is usually half as thick as the rail on which it is to be cut. The tenon should be 1/2″ to 3/4″ (13 to 19 mm) narrower than the width of the rail. The length should be two and one-half times the thickness, Figure 21-7.

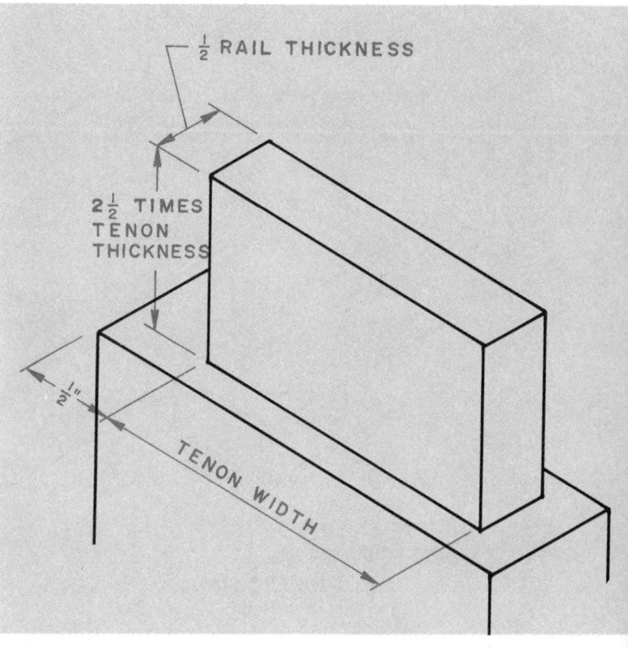

Figure 21-7
Recommended proportions for a tenon.

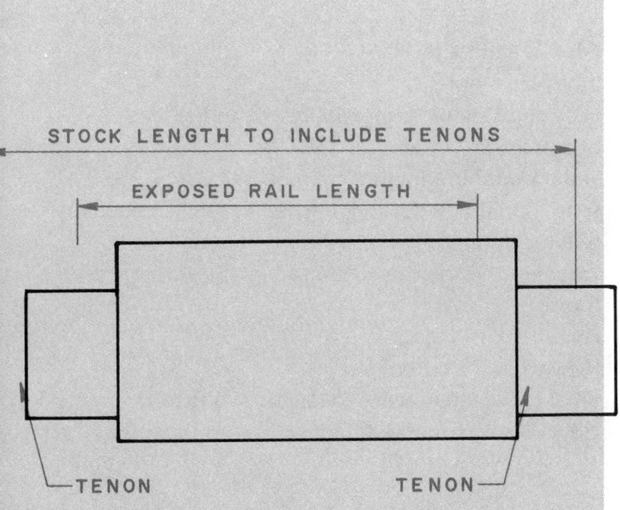

Figure 21-8
The stock length includes the exposed rail plus the two tenons.

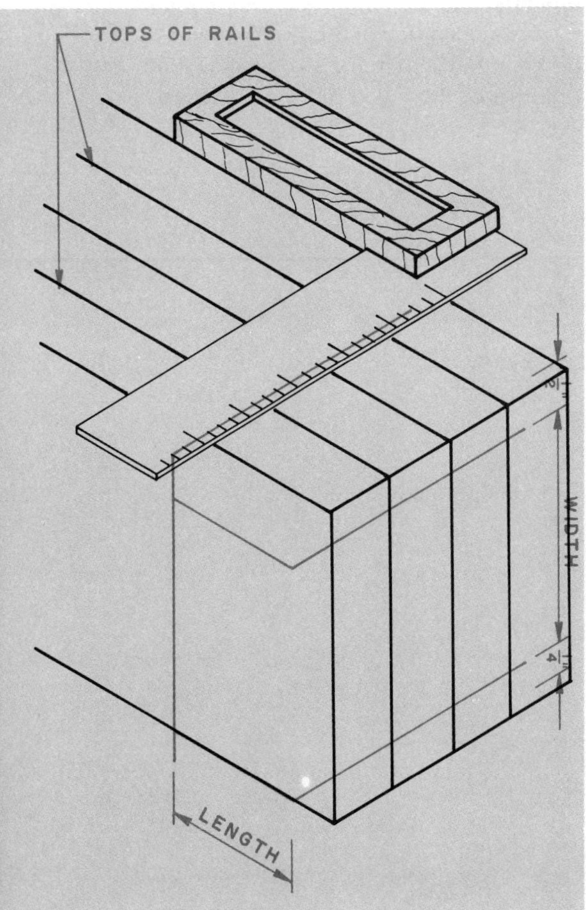

Figure 21-9
Lay out the length and the width of a tenon on all parts at one time.

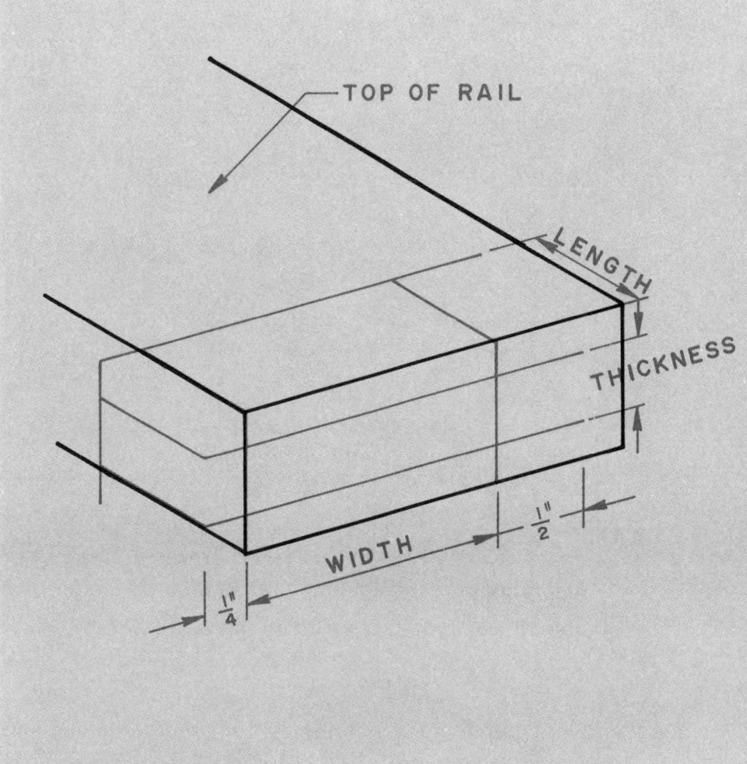

Figure 21-10
A finished layout for a tenon.

Cut the rails to their finished size before making the tenons. The length of the rails should be equal to the length of the exposed section of the rail plus the lengths of the two tenons, Figure 21-8.

To lay out the tenons, clamp the rails together. Mark the length and the width. The top of the tenon should not be closer than 1/2″ (13 mm) to the top of the rail. If the tenon were 3/4″ (19 mm) narrower than the rail, the bottom of the tenon would be 1/4″ (6 mm) from the bottom of the rail, Figure 21-9.

Unclamp the rails. Finish marking the length and the width on all pieces. Then mark the thickness, using a marking gauge. Figure 21-10 shows a tenon completely laid out.

To cut the tenon, make the shoulder cuts first. These must be square with the face of the rail. Use the miter box for accuracy. Cut on the waste side of the line. (Review Units 18 and 19 for these techniques.) Make the shoulder cuts on all four sides. Do not cut below the depth mark.

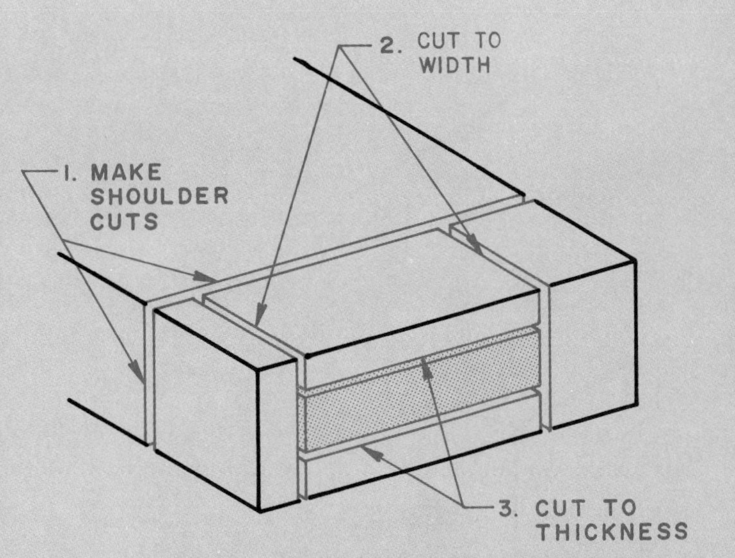

Figure 21-11
Steps in cutting a tenon. Cut on the waste wood.

Figure 21-12
A finished mortise and tenon.

This weakens the tenon. Then use a backsaw to cut the width and the thickness, Figure 21-11. Build a jig as described in Unit 20 to guide your cuts.

Once the tenon is cut, try it in a mortise, Figure 21-12. Trim it with a chisel until it fits snugly. You should be able to pull the tenon out by hand. If it is too tight, you may not be able to insert the tenon in the mortise after it is wet with glue. The glue will be wiped from the tenon. This will make a starved glue joint.

After trimming the tenon, mark it with a letter or number. Mark the same letter or number near the mortise. These marks will identify the mortises and tenons to be glued together.

REVIEW QUESTIONS

1. What is a mortise?
2. What is a tenon?
3. How close should a mortise be cut to the face of a board?
4. How deep should you cut a mortise?
5. Why should you cut the mortise before its matching tenon?
6. What are the steps in cutting a mortise with hand tools?
7. How thick is a tenon?
8. How wide is a tenon?
9. What is the recommended length of a tenon?
10. How do you trim the tenon to fit into the mortise?

SUGGESTED ACTIVITIES

1. Using scrap, lay out a mortise and a matching tenon. Cut the mortise and then the tenon. Trim so they fit properly.
2. Find examples in your home or shop of the different kinds of mortise-and-tenon joints. Prepare drawings of those you think are practical.

UNIT

22

Making Dovetail and Box Joints

Objectives

After studying this unit you should be able to:

1 Lay out and cut a dovetail joint.

2 Lay out and cut a box joint.

Technical Terms

Box pin

Template

Dovetail

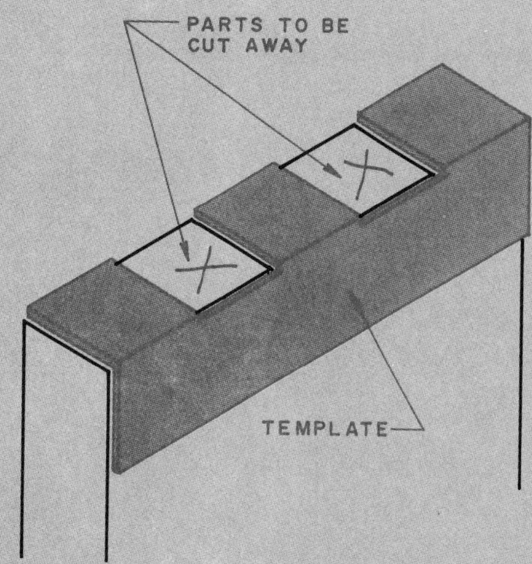

Figure 22-1
Use a template to mark the pins for a box joint.

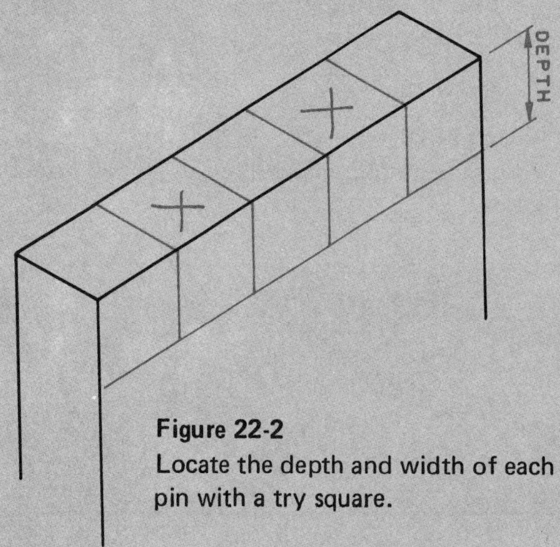

Figure 22-2
Locate the depth and width of each pin with a try square.

Dovetail and box joints are difficult to make using hand tools. They have to be laid out with extreme care and cut with great accuracy. After you cut a dovetail or a box joint, you must work skillfully with a wood chisel to get the joint to fit properly. If you cut these joints by hand, you often will need to build special fixtures for spacing the cuts and guiding the saw.

LAYING OUT A BOX JOINT

The sizes of *box pins* vary. In a typical joint the pins would be the same thickness as the wood. This equal thickness produces a square pin. The pins should all be the same size.

Make a *template* for laying out the pins accurately. This can be strong cardboard or metal. Put an *X* on the places where the wood is to be cut away, Figure 22-1. Next, locate the depth. The depth is the thickness of the piece that forms the corner, Figure 22-2.

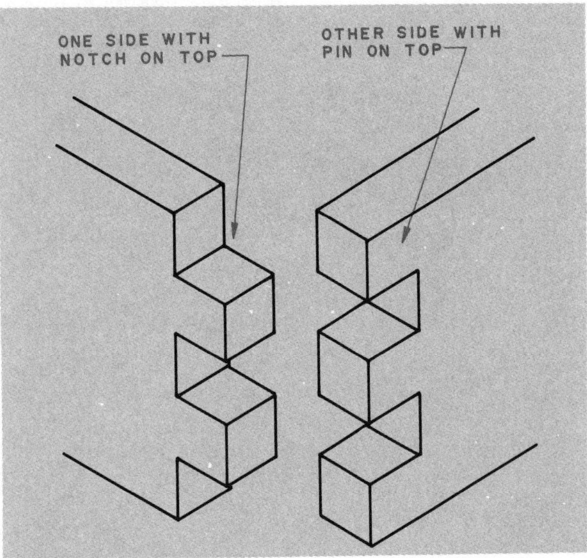

Figure 22-3
Alternate notches and pins on the top of each mating piece.

Figure 22-4
A box joint can be cut with a dovetail saw.

When you mark the joints on boards, remember to alternate the pins and notches. On one piece a pin starts on the top edge. On the second piece a notch is on the top edge, Figure 22-3.

Cut the joint with a backsaw or a dovetail saw, Figure 22-4. You can make the cuts freehand, but a wood fixture will help you keep the saw perpendicular, Figure 22-5. Be certain to saw on the waste side of the line, Figure 22-6.

After sawing the sides of the pins, make the horizontal cuts with a coping saw. Straighten and smooth the pins with a wood chisel. As you smooth the pins for a corner, try to assemble them. Carefully remove excess material. Mark each fitted corner with letters so they can be assembled. A finished joint is in Figure 22-7.

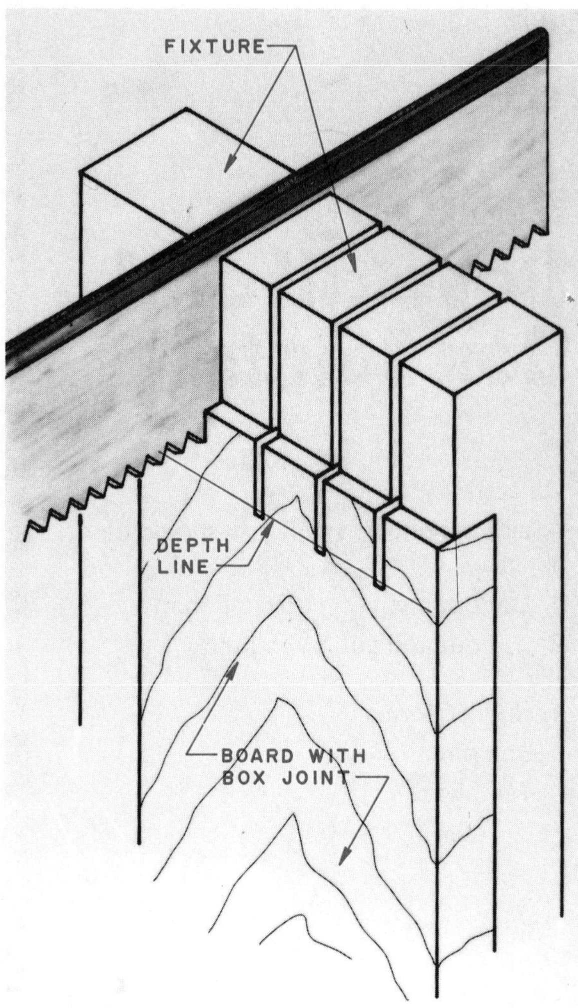

Figure 22-5
When you cut box joint pins, a fixture helps steady the saw.

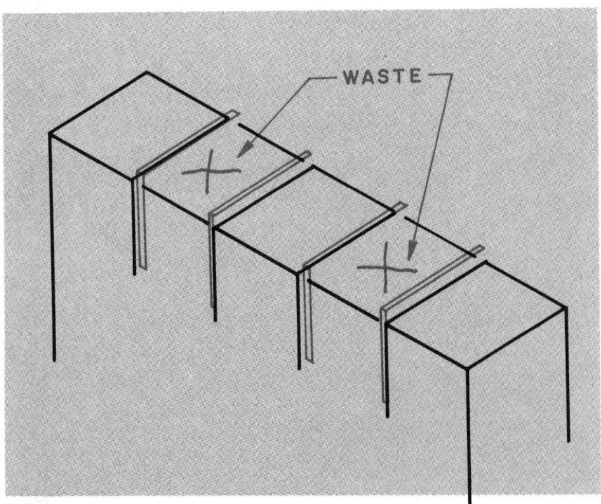

Figure 22-6
Saw on the waste side of the pin lines.

Figure 22-7
A cut and assembled box joint.

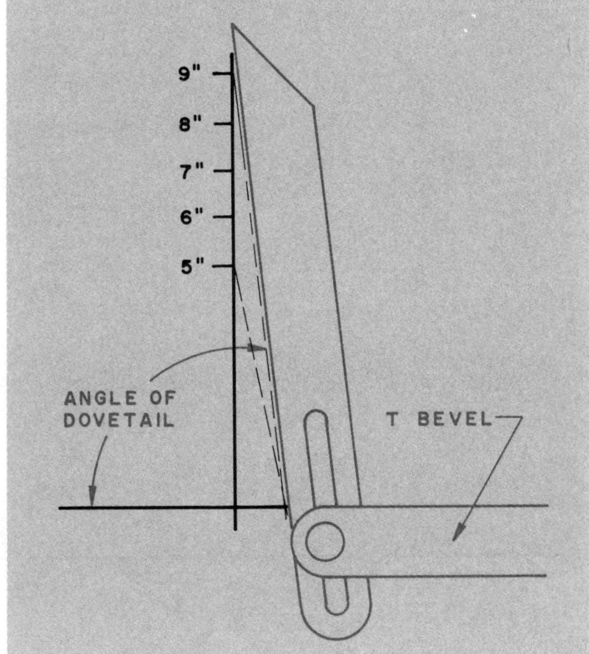

Figure 22-8
How to select the angle for the dovetail.

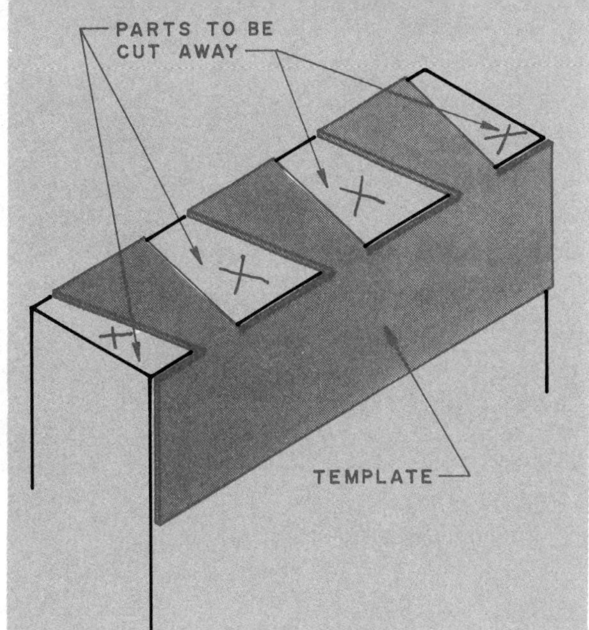

Figure 22-9
Mark dovetail pins with a template.

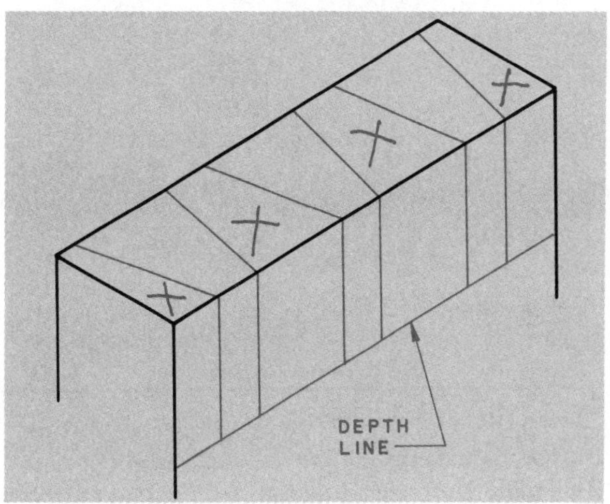

Figure 22-10
Draw the dovetail, mark the depth and connect the two with a try square.

LAYING OUT A DOVETAIL JOINT

This discussion will be limited to the through *dovetail.* The procedures for a dovetail joint are the same as for the box joint. But, the dovetail joint is more difficult because the pins are cut on angles.

To make a dovetail joint, first select an angle for the dovetail. The angle should not be too acute. An acute angle is one less than 90°. Generally, use an angle of about 80°. To lay out the angle, draw on a piece of paper two lines perpendicular to each other. Mark off either 5″, 6″, 7″, 8″ or 9″ (127, 152, 178, 203 or 229 mm) on the perpendicular. Then measure a point more than 1″ (25 mm) from the perpendicular line. Connect this point with any of the numbers. Each connection produces a usable angle, Figure 22-8. Take the angle off the drawing with a T bevel. Use it to lay out the dovetails on a cardboard or metal template. The dovetail pin is usually 1/4″ (6 mm) wide at the small end.

To lay out a series of dovetails, start with a half pin at the top of the wood and lay out the full pins with the template. Mark the pins to cut away, Figure 22-9. It is best if the joint also stops on half a pin at the end of the piece of wood. Measure the depth of the pins. Draw lines from the angled marks on the end of the board perpendicular to the depth mark, Figure 22-10.

Figure 22-11
Cutting a dovetail joint with a dovetail saw.

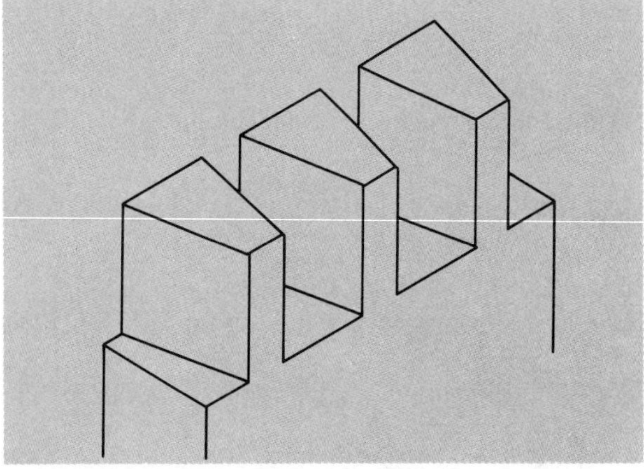

Figure 22-12
Cut and smooth the dovetail pins to finished size.

Then cut these dovetails, Figure 22-11, and smooth them to their finished size, Figure 22-12. To mark the other dovetail, stand the cut joint on the board it is to join, Figure 22-13.

Cut these pins the same way as described for box joints. A fixture to guide the saw is very helpful.

After the dovetails are cut, try to put them together, smoothing them until they fit properly, Figure 22-14.

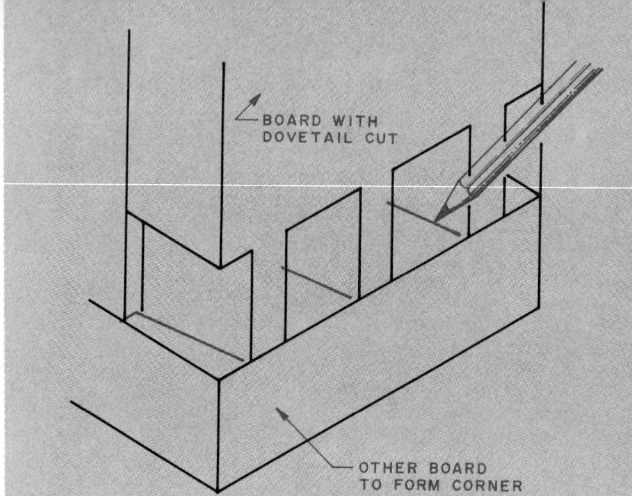

Figure 22-13
Place the cut dovetail pins on the other corner board and mark the pins on it.

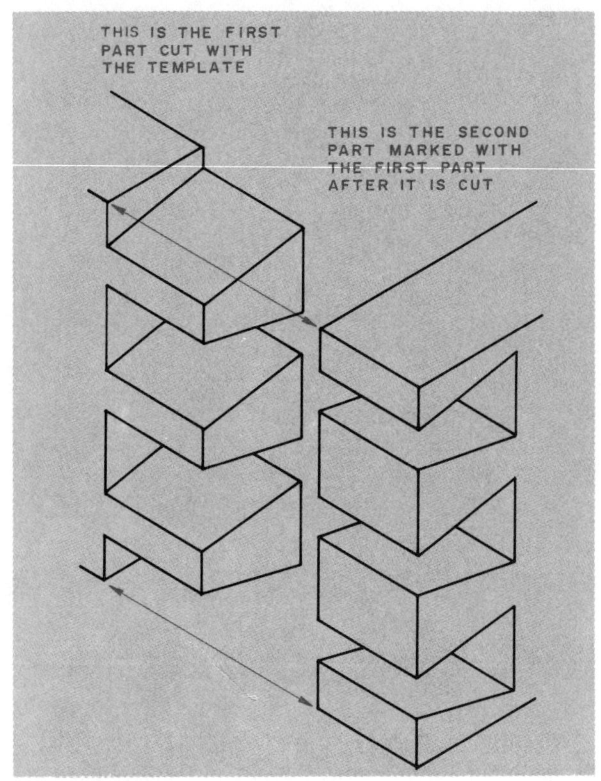

Figure 22-14
A finished set of through dovetails.

REVIEW QUESTIONS

1 Why are dovetail joints difficult to cut with hand tools?
2 What sizes are the pins on a box joint?
3 How can a template help lay out a box joint?
4 What hand tools are used to cut a box joint?
5 How does a dovetail joint differ from a box joint?
6 How do you start laying out a dovetail joint?

SUGGESTED ACTIVITIES

1 Lay out a dovetail joint on scrap stock. Cut and fit it carefully.
2 Lay out a box joint on scrap stock. Cut and fit it carefully.

UNIT

23

Fasteners

Objectives

After studying this unit you should be able to:

1 Recognize the common types of fasteners used in making wood products.

2 Select the best fastener for the job.

3 Order fasteners by clearly identifying them.

Technical Terms

Brad	Lag screw
Penny	Stove bolt
d	Dowel screw
Wire gauge number	Clamp nail
Wood screw	Upholstery tack
Phillips	Chevron
Pozidriv®	Screw eye
Clutch head	Toggle bolt
Robertson	Hollow wall anchor
Power nailer	Masonry anchor
Power stapler	Plastic screw anchor
Hanger bolt	Anchor plate

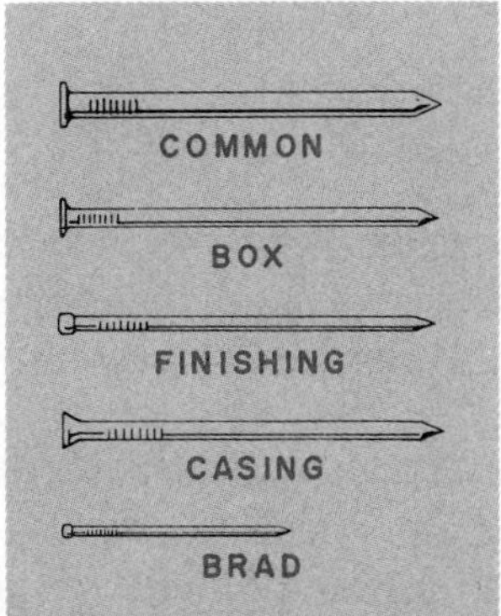

Figure 23-1 The types of nails commonly used for fastening wood. (Northwestern Steel and Wire Company)

The purpose of a fastener is to hold two or more members together. A variety of fasteners are available. The most familiar types are nails and screws. But power nailers and staplers are increasing in use. In industrial production they have largely replaced the conventional nail or screw.

In selecting a fastener for a particular use, consider these factors:

1. Strength. Will it hold the loads and pressures put on it?
2. Security. Will it remain attached to the wall or object?
3. Cost. Can you afford the extra costs per unit of some fasteners?
4. Installation. Is the fastener easy to install?
5. Skill. Or does it require skill and special training to install?
6. Equipment. Can you afford the cost of equipment, such as a power nailer, to install some fasteners?
7. Appearance. If the fastener will show on the wood, which kind would look best?

GENERAL-PURPOSE NAILS

Most nails are made from mild (soft) steel or aluminum. Bright steel nails have no surface finish. They usually are uncoated and used for inside work. Coated, galvanized or aluminum nails are made for exterior work or for places where moisture is present.

There are many types of nails. Each type has special features. The most widely used are common, box, finishing and casing nails and *brads,* Figure 23-1.

Use common nails for general carpentry work. The thick heads and large bodies of common nails make them good for heavy construction. Box nails look like common nails, but they are more slender and have thinner heads. Use a box nail when you think a common nail would split the board. Many contractors use box nails for house construction. Finishing nails and brads are the same diameter as box nails, but they have small, rounded heads.

Use finishing nails or brads when you want the nail head hidden. Drive the head below the surface of the wood with a nail set and then fill

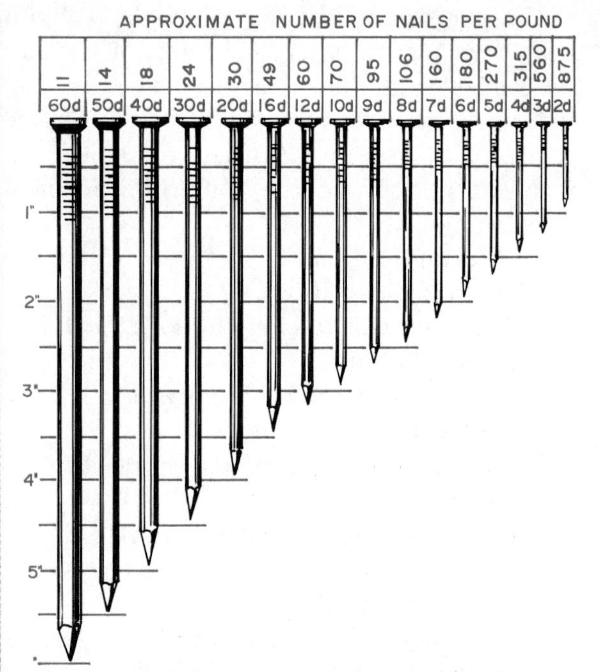

Figure 23-2
Sizes and weights of common nails.

NAIL LENGTHS AND DIAMETERS

Size	Length	American Steel Wire Gauge Number: Common	Box and Casing	Finishing
2d	1"	15	15-1/2	16-1/2
3d	1-1/4"	14	14-1/2	15-1/2
4d	1-1/2"	12-1/2	14	15
5d	1-3/4"	12-1/2	14	15
6d	2"	11-1/2	12-1/2	13
7d	2-1/4"	11-1/2	12-1/2	12-1/2
8d	2-1/2"	10-1/4	11-1/2	12-1/2
9d	2-3/4"	10-1/4	11-1/2	12-1/2
10d	3"	9	10-1/2	11-1/2
12d	3-1/4"	9	10-1/2	11-1/2
16d	3-1/2"	8	10	11
20d	4"	6	9	10
30d	4-1/2"	5	9	
40d	5"	4	8	

Figure 23-3
Lengths and diameters of common, box, casing and finishing nails.

the hole. Brads are shorter than finishing nails, usually measuring less than 1" long. Use them to nail thin material. Casing nails are thicker than finishing nails and have a small cone-shaped head. They are designed for heavy jobs where the nail head is not to show. For example, you would use casing nails to fasten the trim on the outside of a house.

Nail Sizes

Nails are sized by the *penny*. The symbol for penny is the lowercase letter *d*. For example, a 2d nail is called a 2-penny nail. It is 1" long. For each penny the length increases 1/4". A 3d nail is 1-1/4" long. How long is a 6d nail? Sizes of commonly used nails are in Figure 23-2. Notice that as the nail gets longer, the wire diameter increases. Nail diameters are specified by the American Steel *wire gauge number*. The wire numbers and decimal equivalents are in Figure 23-3. Brads have wire gauges from 12 to 20.

Nails are sold by the pound. Obviously, there are more nails in a pound of 6d nails than in a pound of 12d.

Special-Purpose Nails

Many nails are designed for special uses, Figure 23-4. Some nails have greater holding power because they have screw, spiral or annular threads, Figure 23-5. Once you drive these nails into place, removing them is difficult. You can pull out smooth nails easily.

Nails may be coated with cement to increase holding power. Others are hot-dipped galvanized, enameled or zinc-plated to resist rust.

Special-purpose nails are available in a variety of metals that includes copper, brass, bronze, monel and stainless steel.

WOOD SCREWS

A *wood screw* serves much the same purpose as a nail. But a screw has greater holding power than a nail. In addition, it can be easily removed and replaced.

The most commonly used screws have slotted flat, oval and round heads. Install these with a flat blade screwdriver. But several other types of screw heads are available. These are the *Phillips,*

POLE BARN—RING SHANK
COMMON—RING SHANK
FLOORING—SCREW SHANK
DRY WALL—RING SHANK
SIDING NAILS
SHINGLE NAILS
DOUBLE-HEAD SCAFFOLD
FLOORING
ROOFING LARGE HEAD
COUNTER SUNK (SINKERS)
PLASTERBOARD
LATH

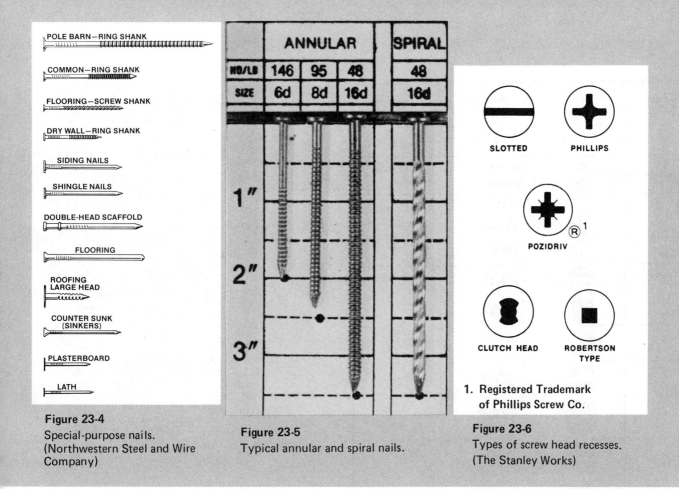

Figure 23-4
Special-purpose nails. (Northwestern Steel and Wire Company)

	ANNULAR			SPIRAL
NO./LB	146	95	48	48
SIZE	6d	8d	16d	16d

1″
2″
3″

Figure 23-5
Typical annular and spiral nails.

SLOTTED
PHILLIPS
POZIDRIV®[1]
CLUTCH HEAD
ROBERTSON TYPE

1. Registered Trademark of Phillips Screw Co.

Figure 23-6
Types of screw head recesses. (The Stanley Works)

Pozidriv®, *clutch head* and *Robertson* types, Figure 23-6. These screws require screwdrivers with tips shaped to fit their recesses. They reduce the possibility of the screwdriver slipping off the head of the screw. They help drive the screw straight. They are valuable especially for power-operated screwdrivers. (See Unit 25 for more information.)

Wood Screw Sizes

Wood screw size is specified by length and diameter. To determine length, measure from the part of the head that is flush with the wood surface to the tip of the threaded end, Figure 23-7. The diameter is the width of the wire between the head and the threads.

Wood screws are made in lengths from 1/4″ to 6″, Figure 23-8. The diameter is given in wire gauge sizes. These screw sizes range from gauge 0 to 24. The larger the screw size or gauge number, the larger the diameter, Figure 23-9.

Every screw is made in several diameters. For example, a 1″ flat head screw is made in gauge numbers from 4 through 14. A number 4 screw

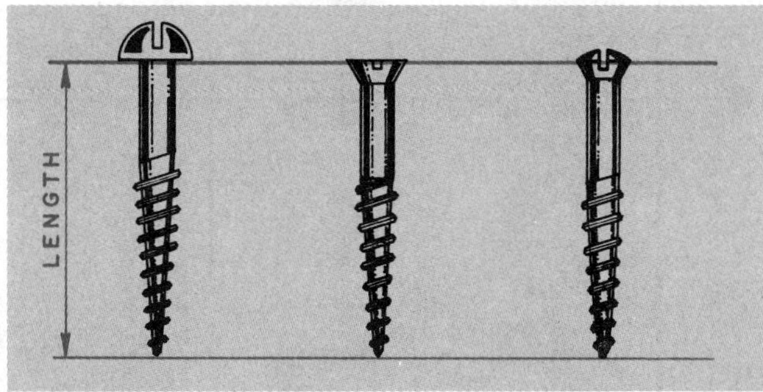

Figure 23-7
The length of a wood screw is the portion that enters the wood.

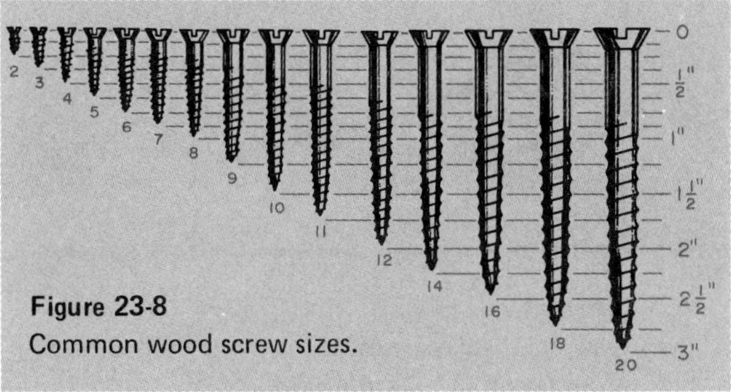

Figure 23-8
Common wood screw sizes.

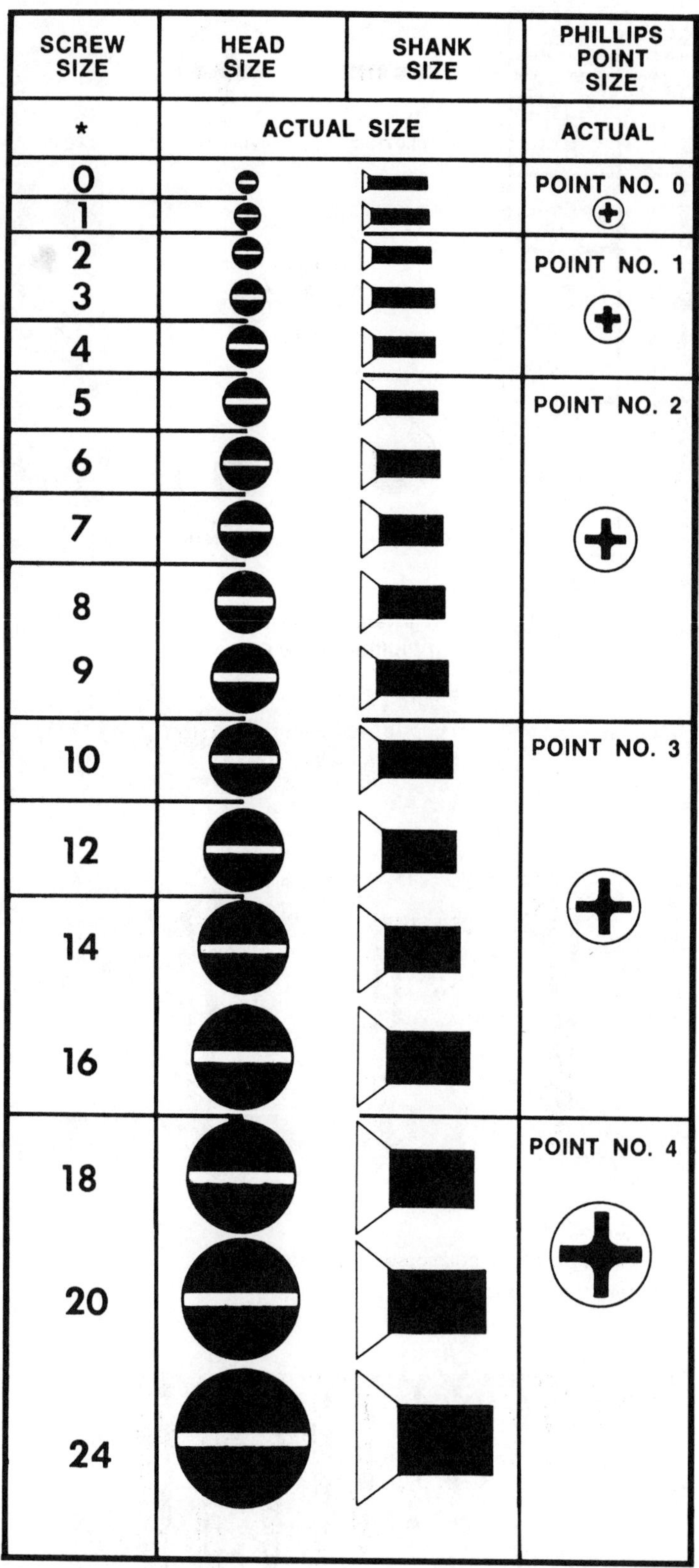

SCREW SIZE
HEAD SIZE
SHANK SIZE
PHILLIPS POINT SIZE
*
ACTUAL SIZE
ACTUAL
0
1
2
3
4
5
6
7
8
9
10
12
14
16
18
20
24
POINT NO. 0
POINT NO. 1
POINT NO. 2
POINT NO. 3
POINT NO. 4

Figure 23-9
Head and shank sizes for regular and Phillips head wood screws. (The Stanley Works)

TYPICAL DIAMETERS FOR FLAT AND ROUND HEAD WOOD SCREWS[1]

Length	Diameter (Wire Gauge Number)
1/4"	2, 4
3/8"	2, 3, 4, 5, 6
1/2" and 5/8"	2, 3, 4, 5, 6, 7, 8
3/4", 7/8" and 1"	4, 5, 6, 7, 8, 9, 10, 11, 12
1-1/4"	4, 5, 6, 7, 8, 9, 10, 11, 12, 14, 16
1-1/2"	6, 7, 8, 9, 10, 11, 12, 14, 16
1-3/4"	6, 8, 9, 10, 12, 14, 16
2"	8, 9, 10, 12, 14, 16
2-1/4"	10, 12, 14
2-1/2"	8, 9, 10, 12, 14, 16
3"	10, 12, 14, 16

[1] Phillips steel screws follow almost exactly the same sizes.

Figure 23-10
Common lengths and diameter numbers of flat and round head wood screws.

has a small diameter (0.112"). The number 14 screw has a large diameter (0.242"). Typical sizes of flat and round head wood screws are listed in Figure 23-10. The difference in diameter from one gauge to another is 0.013". The decimal sizes for the various screw diameters are listed in Figure 23-11.

Most wood screws are made from mild steel. They have no surface finish. Other wood screws are made from aluminum and brass. Some are plated with chromium, nickel or blued steel.

Use flat head screws in places where you do not want the head to show. Round or oval head screws are more attractive than flat heads, so use them when you want the head to show. Plated screws are used with hardware. For example, brass-colored hinges should have matching brass-colored screws.

To order wood screws, give the type of head, type of screwdriver slot, length, diameter, material and finish. For example, a 2" x no. 12-slotted FHB-steel screw is 2" long, has a number 12 diameter and a slotted flat head, is unfinished and made from steel. Screws usually are sold by the gross (144). They are packaged one gross per box, Figure 23-12.

SIZES OF WOOD SCREW DIAMETERS (in inches)																	
Wire Gauge Number	0	1	2	3	4	5	6	7	8	9	10	11	12	14	16	18	20
Decimal Size	.060	.073	.086	.099	.112	.125	.138	.151	.164	.177	.190	.203	.216	.242	.268	.294	.320
Fractional Size	1/16	5/64	3/32	7/64	1/8	1/8	9/64	5/32	11/64	3/16	13/64	13/64	7/32	1/4	9/32	19/64	21/64

Figure 23-11
The decimal and fractional sizes of wood screw wire gauge numbers.

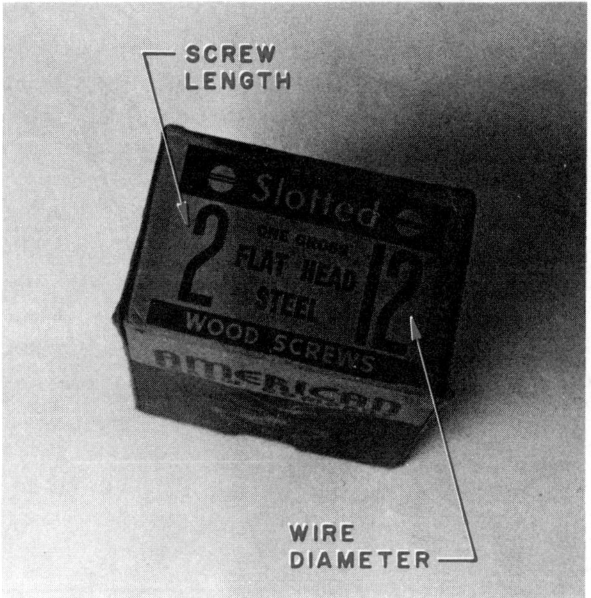

Figure 23-12
Information on wood screws is given on each box.

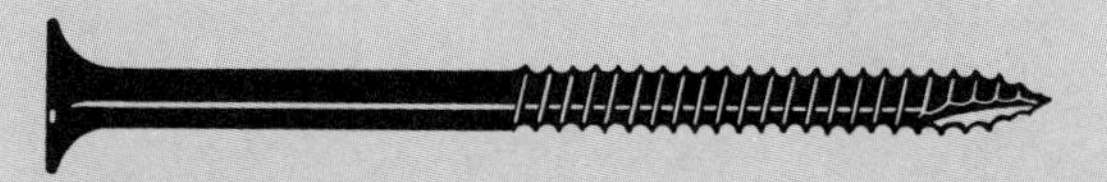

Figure 23-13
A special-purpose screw designed for face framing cabinets. (Equality Screw Company)

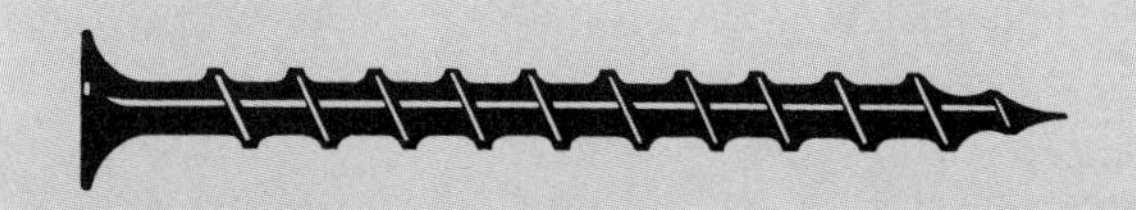

Figure 23-14
A special-purpose screw designed for use in particle board. (Equality Screw Company)

Special-Purpose Screws

Many screws have threads designed for the rapid assembly of cabinets and furniture. A face framing screw has a Phillips head and a special auger point, Figure 23-13. The auger point drills the screw directly into the wood. You do not need to drill a pilot hole first. In addition, the face framing screw can be driven without splitting the wood. It has a dry lubricant that helps installation. When you make frames, this screw can replace nuts and bolts and Teenuts®.

Another special fastener is designed for particle board, Figure 23-14. Notice the widely spaced threads. Special screws for assembling cabinets and installing hinges and other hardware are also available.

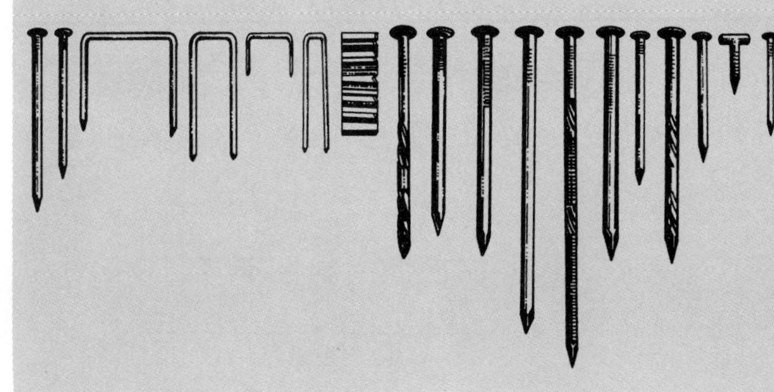

Figure 23-15
Typical staples and nails used in power machines. (Auto-Nailer Company)

POWER-DRIVEN STAPLES AND NAILS

Power-driven staples and nails come in a variety of styles. Staples vary in width, length and wire size. Nails can have a smooth wire or spiral and annular threads, Figure 23-15. Both *power nailers* and *power staplers* are used in the assembly of different kinds of wood products.

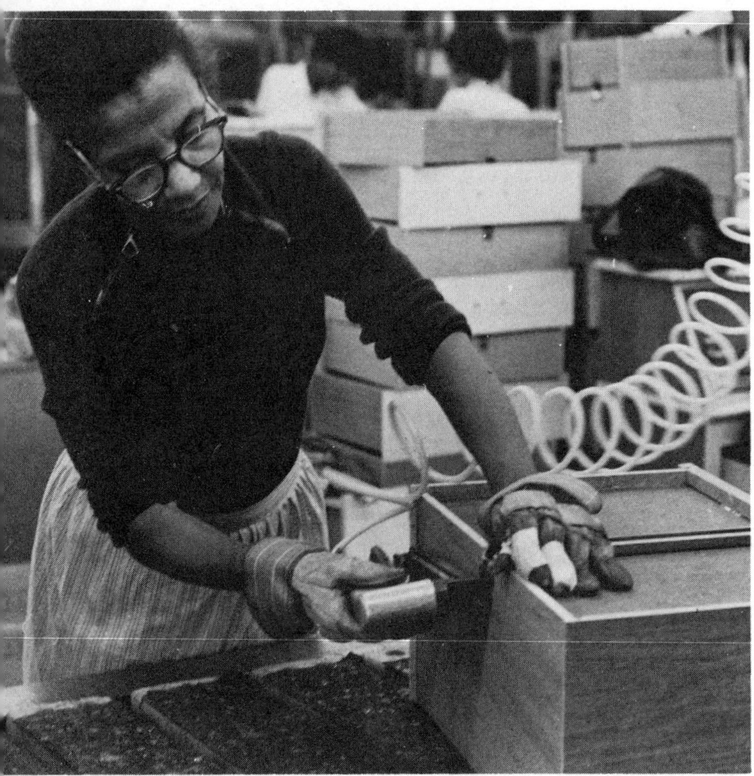

Figure 23-16
A power stapler used to assemble a drawer. (Auto-Nailer Company)

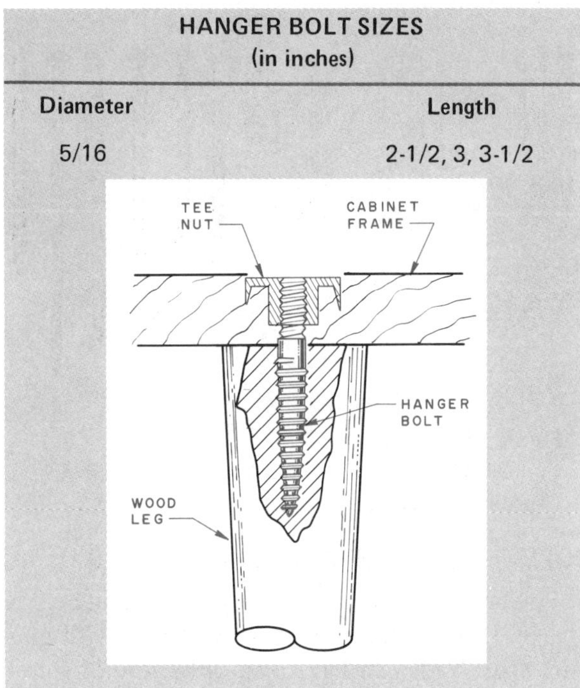

HANGER BOLT SIZES (in inches)

Diameter	Length
5/16	2-1/2, 3, 3-1/2

Figure 23-17
Hanger bolts join legs to a wood or metal furniture frame.

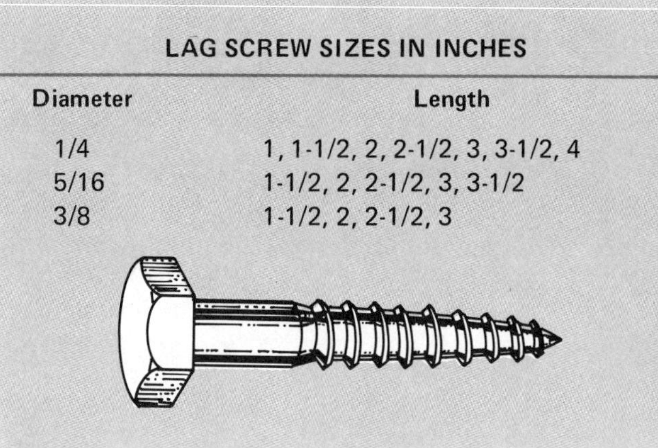

LAG SCREW SIZES IN INCHES

Diameter	Length
1/4	1, 1-1/2, 2, 2-1/2, 3, 3-1/2, 4
5/16	1-1/2, 2, 2-1/2, 3, 3-1/2
3/8	1-1/2, 2, 2-1/2, 3

Figure 23-18
Common lag screws.

Figure 23-16 shows a metal drawer runner being stapled to a wood drawer.

Power-driven fasteners are thrust into the wood under high air pressure. In many cases fasteners are coated with dry cement to increase their holding power. An operator must be careful to keep eyes protected and hands away from machinery parts. A major disadvantage of power nailers and staplers is that the fasteners are almost impossible to remove. A mistake is not easy to correct.

OTHER FASTENING DEVICES

Other fastening devices join wood and metal parts. A *hanger bolt* joins legs to a furniture frame, Figure 23-17. *Lag screws* have either square or hexagonal heads and must be driven with a wrench, Figure 23-18. Use them for heavy construction. Lag screws are available in lengths from 1″ to 6″ and diameters from 1/4″ to 1/2″. *Stove bolts* fasten metal parts to wood products. Often washers are used to increase the surface bearing on the wood, Figure 23-19. *Dowel screws* are threaded on both ends. They join two wood members such as a leg to a frame, Figure 23-20.

Corrugated and Skotch® fasteners join butt and edge joints, Figure 23-21. You can use them for joints that are not visible or when appearance is not important. Butt and edge joints put together with these fasteners are not as strong as other joints. (Refer to Units 16 and 17.)

SIZES OF FLAT AND ROUND HEAD STOVE BOLTS
(in inches)

Length	Diameter
1/2	1/8, 3/16, 1/4
3/4	1/8, 3/16, 1/4, 5/16
1	1/8, 3/16, 1/4, 5/16
1-1/4	1/8, 3/16, 1/4, 5/16
1-1/2	1/8, 3/16, 1/4, 5/16
2	3/16, 1/4, 5/16
2-1/2	3/16, 1/4, 5/16
3	3/16, 1/4, 5/16

Figure 23-19
Typical sizes of stove bolts.

SIZES OF CORRUGATED FASTENERS

3/8″[1] x 4	3/8″ x 5
1/2″ x 4	1/2″ x 5
5/8″ x 4	5/8″ x 5
1/4″ x 5	3/4″ x 5
3/4″ x 5	

[1] depth of fastener

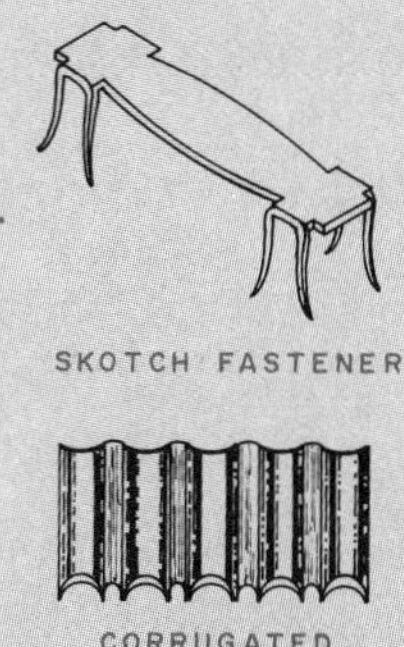

Figure 23-21
Corrugated and Skotch® fasteners join butt and edge joints.

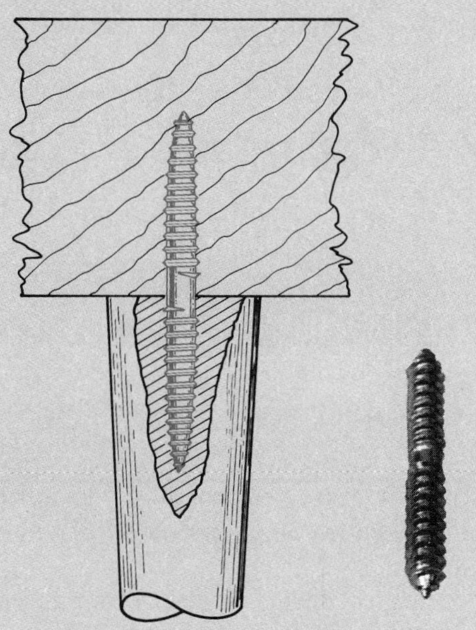

Figure 23-20
Dowel screws hold legs to wood frames.

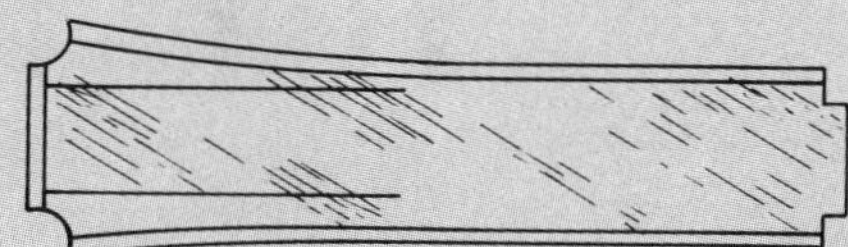

Figure 23-22
A clamp nail.

UPHOLSTERY TACK SIZES
(in inches)

Length	3/8	7/16	1/2	9/16	5/8	11/16	3/4
Size Number	3	4	6	8	10	12	14

Figure 23-23
Common sizes of upholstery tacks.

Clamp nails also join wood members, Figure 23-22. Drive them into saw kerfs cut in the wood. (Refer to Units 16 and 17.)

Upholstery tacks secure fabric to a frame. Figure 23-23 shows the sizes available.

Chevrons look like corrugated fasteners and work in a similar way. They have teeth that are nailed into the wood, Figure 23-24. Chevrons join miter joints. They are 3/8″ deep and are sold by the hundred.

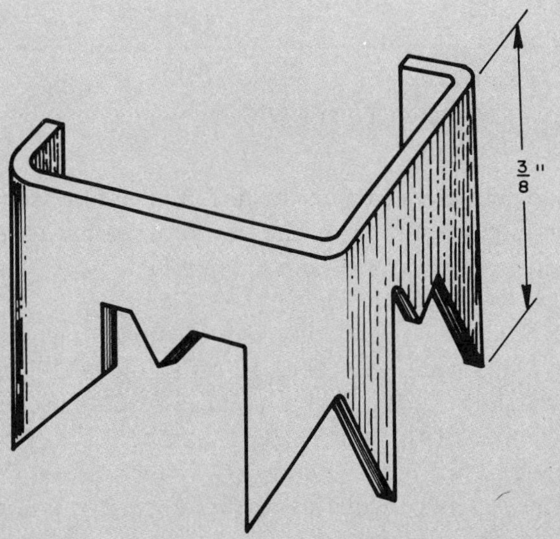

Figure 23-24
Chevrons connect flat miter joints.

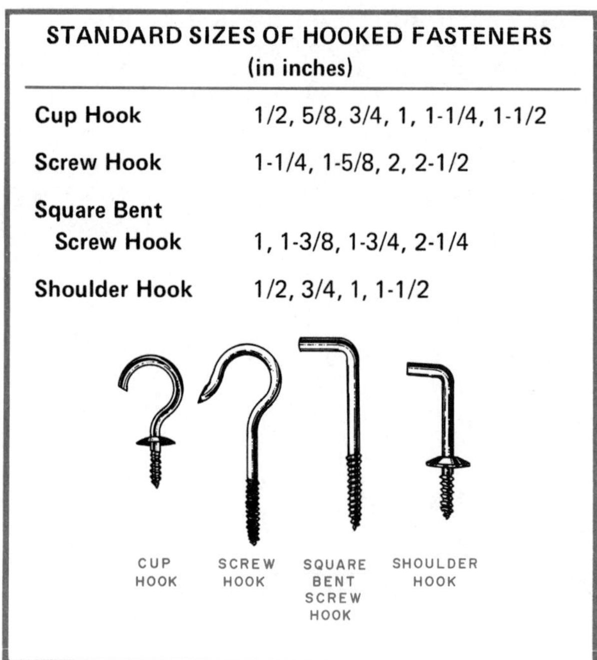

STANDARD SIZES OF HOOKED FASTENERS (in inches)

Cup Hook	1/2, 5/8, 3/4, 1, 1-1/4, 1-1/2
Screw Hook	1-1/4, 1-5/8, 2, 2-1/2
Square Bent Screw Hook	1, 1-3/8, 1-3/4, 2-1/4
Shoulder Hook	1/2, 3/4, 1, 1-1/2

Figure 23-25
Typical sizes of hook fasteners.

SIZES OF SCREW EYES

Medium Eye	Small Eye
106	206
108	208
110	210
112	212
114	214
	216

MEDIUM EYE
SMALL EYE

Figure 23-26
Common sizes of screw eyes.

There are a number of different hook fasteners. Most common are the cup hook, screw hook, square bent screw hook, shoulder hook and screw eye, Figure 23-25.

Screw eyes have two size openings, medium eye and small eye. They are available with long and short screw shanks. You can specify a screw eye size with a three digit number. The first digit indicates medium eye (1) or small eye (2). The last two digits are the wire gauge number. Sizes are in Figure 23-26.

Metal plates strengthen a joint or assist in a joining operation. Because metal plates are not attractive, use them only when they will not be seen. Flat head screws hold the metal plates on the wood, Figure 23-27.

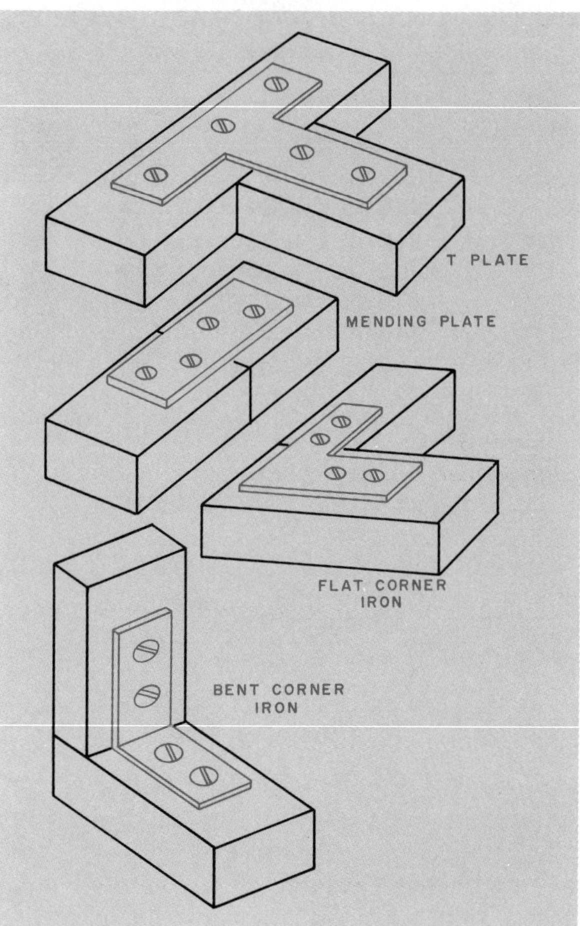

Figure 23-27
Metal plates strengthen joints.

Several kinds of devices fasten cabinets and other objects to a wall. These include the toggle bolts, hollow wall anchors, masonry anchors, plastic screw anchors and anchor plates.

To install a *toggle bolt,* begin by drilling a hole large enough for the toggle to slide into the wall. When the toggle enters the wall cavity, a spring forces it open, Figure 23-28. Sizes are shown in Figure 23-29. You must attach a hook or object to the toggle bolt while you are installing it. If you take out the screw after it has been inserted, the toggle drops off inside the wall.

Install *hollow wall anchors* the same as toggle bolts. Insert the anchor in a drilled hole, Figure 23-30. As you screw the bolt into the anchor, the end bends to form a foot that rests on the inside wall surface, Figure 23-31. Sizes are shown in Figure 23-32. Because of this anchor, the screw can be removed and reinserted.

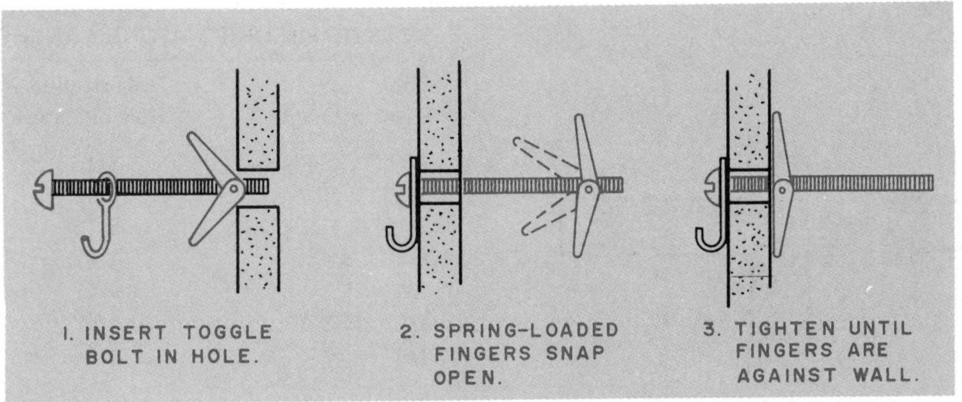

1. INSERT TOGGLE BOLT IN HOLE.
2. SPRING-LOADED FINGERS SNAP OPEN.
3. TIGHTEN UNTIL FINGERS ARE AGAINST WALL.

Figure 23-28
How to install a spring toggle bolt.

SPRING TOGGLE BOLT SIZES
(in inches)

Bolt Size	Drill Size
1/8 x 2	1/2
1/8 x 3	1/2
1/8 x 4	1/2
3/16 x 2	5/8
3/16 x 3	5/8
3/16 x 4	5/8
3/16 x 6	5/8
1/4 x 3	3/4
1/4 x 4	3/4

Figure 23-29
Typical sizes of spring toggle bolts. (ITT, Phillips Drill Division)

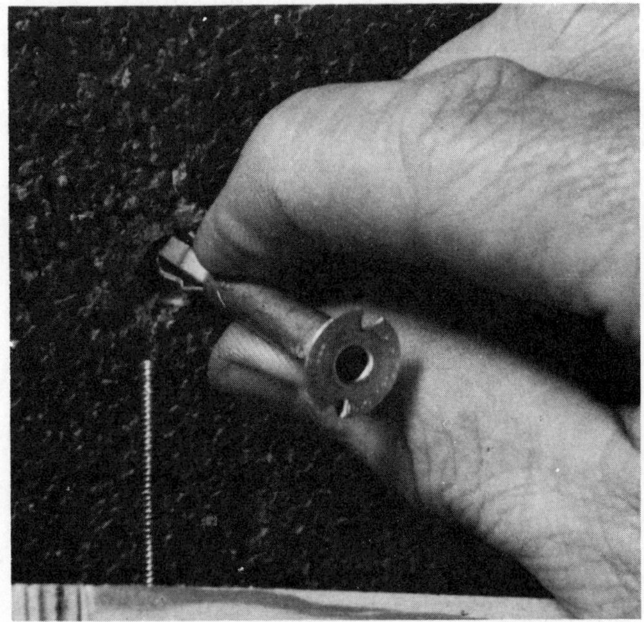

Figure 23-30
A hollow wall anchor is inserted in a drilled hole in the wall. (American Plywood Association)

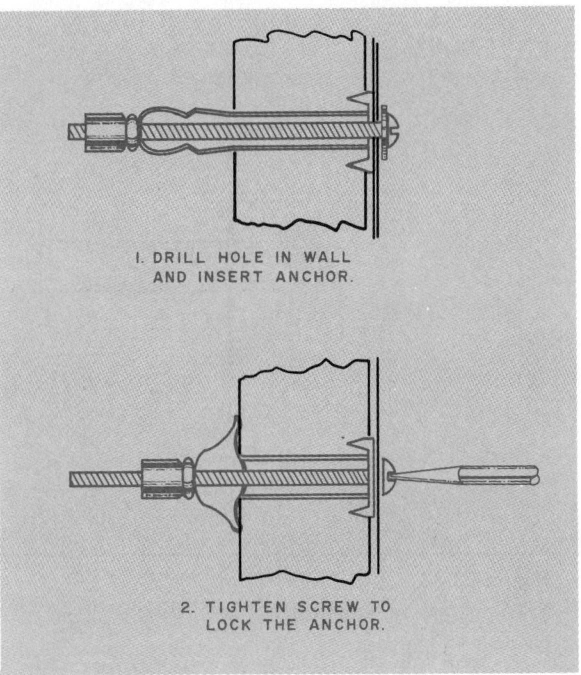

1. DRILL HOLE IN WALL AND INSERT ANCHOR.
2. TIGHTEN SCREW TO LOCK THE ANCHOR.

Figure 23-31
Installing a hollow wall anchor.

HOLLOW WALL ANCHOR SIZES

Size	For Material Thickness
1/8 XS	0″ to 1/4″
1/8 S	1/8″ to 5/8″
1/8 L	5/8″ to 1-1/4″
3/16 S	1/8″ to 5/8″
3/16 L	5/8″ to 1-1/4″

Figure 23-32
Typical sizes of hollow wall anchors. (ITT, Phillips Drill Division)

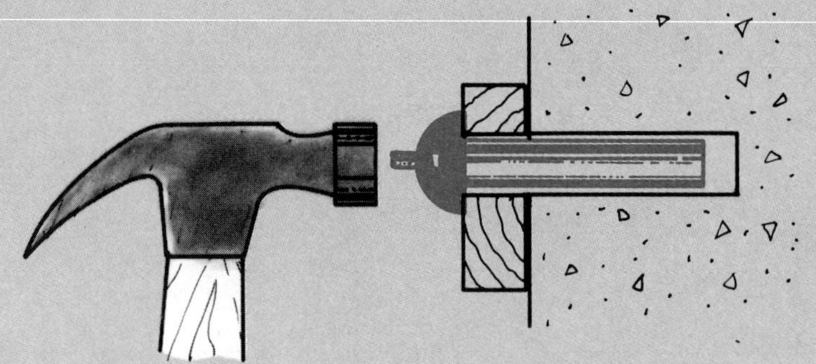

1. DRILL A HOLE IN THE MASONRY. INSERT THE PIN-GRIP ANCHOR THROUGH THE MATERIAL TO BE FASTENED TO THE WALL. STRIKE THE PIN WITH A HAMMER.

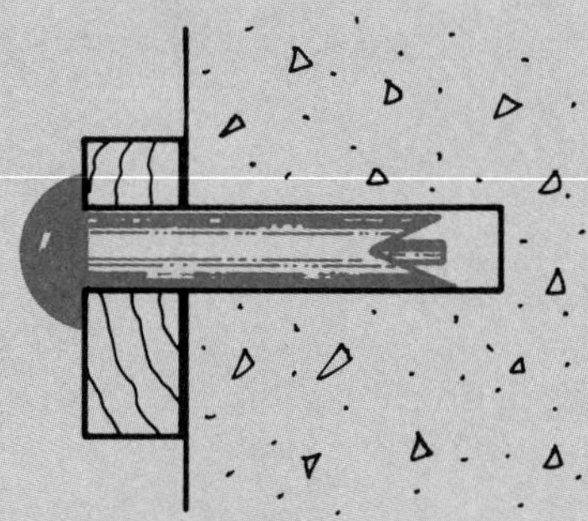

2. THE PIN EXPANDS THE END OF THE ANCHOR, WEDGING IT INTO THE SIDES OF THE HOLE.

Figure 23-33
Set a pin-grip masonry anchor by hitting the pin with a hammer.

SIZES OF PIN-GRIP MASONRY ANCHORS

Size Diam. x Length	Drill Size for Hole in Masonry
3/16" x 3/4"	3/16"
3/16" x 1"	3/16"
3/16" x 1-1/4"	3/16"
1/4" x 3/4"	1/4"
1/4" x 1"	1/4"
1/4" x 1-1/4"	1/4"
1/4" x 1-1/2"	1/4"

Figure 23-34
Typical sizes of pin-grip masonry anchors.

SIZES OF LEAD CALKING ANCHORS

Bolt Size[1]	Drill Size
No. 6 - 32	5/16"
No. 8 - 32	5/16"
No. 10 - 24	3/8"
No. 12 - 24	1/2"
1/4" - 20	1/2"
5/16" - 18	5/8"
3/8" - 16	3/4"
1/2" - 13	7/8"
5/8" - 11	1-1/8"
3/4" - 10	1-1/4"

[1] Bolt diameter and number of threads per inch.

Figure 23-35
A lead calking anchor set in masonry is shown with sizes of lead calking anchors. (ITT, Phillips Drill Division)

Masonry anchors fit into a hole drilled into solid masonry. To install a pin-grip masonry anchor, you must first attach the anchor to the object or material that you want held to the wall. Then strike the pin end with a hammer. This causes the pin to spread the end of the anchor and bind the anchor to the masonry, Figure 23-33. Sizes are shown in Figure 23-34.

Lead calking anchors install machine screws and bolts in masonry. Place the anchor in the hole drilled and use a tool to hammer the bolt in place. The bottom of the anchor flares out and binds it to the sides of the hole. Typical sizes are in Figure 23-35.

Plastic screw anchors are placed in a hole drilled in any solid material. As you drive the screw into the anchor, the sides of the anchor expand to fit tightly against the hole, Figure 23-36. Typical sizes are in Figure 23-37.

Use the Phillips nylon anchor in both solid and hollow materials, Figure 23-38. Install it in wood, concrete, plaster, metal, tile, block or mortar. It has five head styles. To install a Phillips nylon anchor, drill a hole the same size as the anchor, then insert the anchor and drive the screw with a hammer.

Fasten *anchor plates* to the wall with a black mastic or epoxy cement. The plate has holes in it. Push the plate onto the mastic until the mastic comes through the holes. The bolt in the center of the plate is ready for use after the adhesive has dried, Figure 23-39.

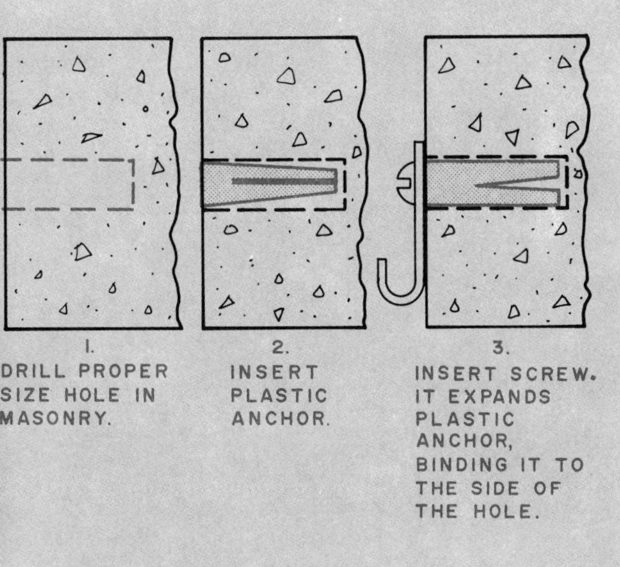

Figure 23-36
Installing a plastic screw anchor.

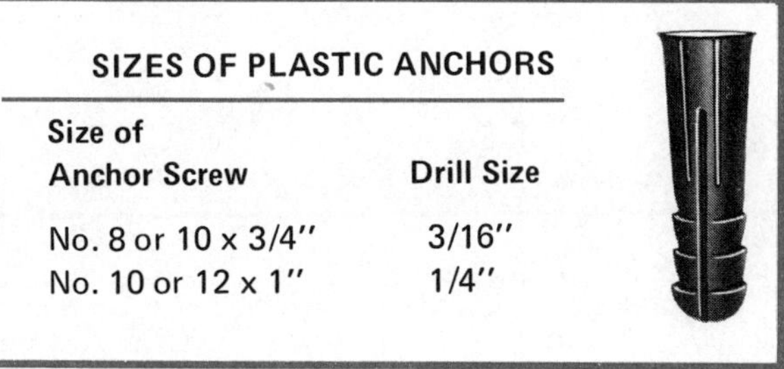

SIZES OF PLASTIC ANCHORS

Size of Anchor Screw	Drill Size
No. 8 or 10 x 3/4″	3/16″
No. 10 or 12 x 1″	1/4″

Figure 23-37
Sizes of plastic screw anchors. (ITT, Phillips Drill Division)

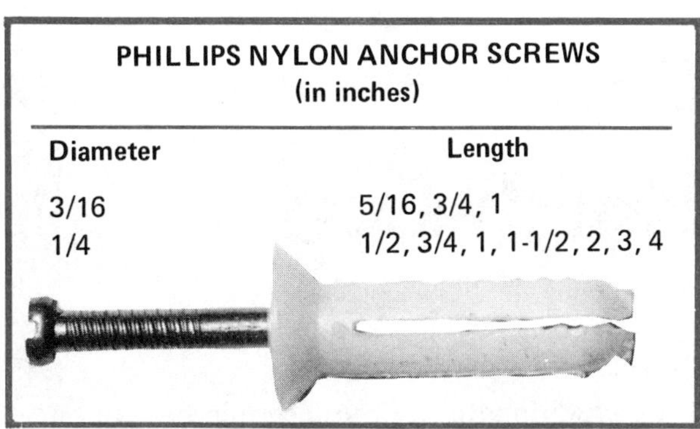

PHILLIPS NYLON ANCHOR SCREWS
(in inches)

Diameter	Length
3/16	5/16, 3/4, 1
1/4	1/2, 3/4, 1, 1-1/2, 2, 3, 4

Figure 23-38
A nylon anchor. (ITT, Phillips Drill Division)

Figure 23-39
An anchor plate secured to the wall with an adhesive. (American Plywood Association)

REVIEW QUESTIONS

1 What factors should you consider when you select fasteners?
2 What kinds of nails are available?
3 What does the term "penny" mean?
4 How does a wood screw differ from a nail?
5 What are the common types of wood screw heads?
6 When you order wood screws, what information must you give?
7 How do you drive staples into wood products?
8 Describe other metal fasteners used in wood products.

SUGGESTED ACTIVITIES

1 Build a wall chart showing all the various types of fasteners you can find. Check with local hardware stores to find other fasteners not mentioned in the text.
2 Lay a variety of fasteners on a table. Number each one. Then see who in the class can identify correctly the largest amount.

UNIT

24

Hardware

Objectives

After studying this unit you should be able to:

1 Recognize the common types of hardware for wood products.
2 Install hardware.

Technical Terms

Drawer pull	Glide
Hinge	Caster
Door track	Ferrule
Catch	Support
Lock	Bracket
Drawer guide	

Figure 24-1
The knobs on this cabinet are at the open edge of the door.

Choosing hardware for a wood product is important. Hardware should enable the unit to function well. For example, a drawer slide should permit the drawer to move easily. Hardware should reflect the style of the furniture. Colonial furniture should have hardware designed for that period. The hardware should be of good quality. It should be strong enough for the job. It should resist tarnish and rust. It also should be free of surface blemishes, roughness and other defects.

KNOBS AND DRAWER PULLS

The position of the hardware on furniture is a part of the design. On some doors, the knobs are near the edge that opens, Figure 24-1. This makes opening the door easy. On others, they are in the center of each door, Figure 24-2. This provides balance in the overall design.

Figure 24-2
The door pulls are in the center of each door.

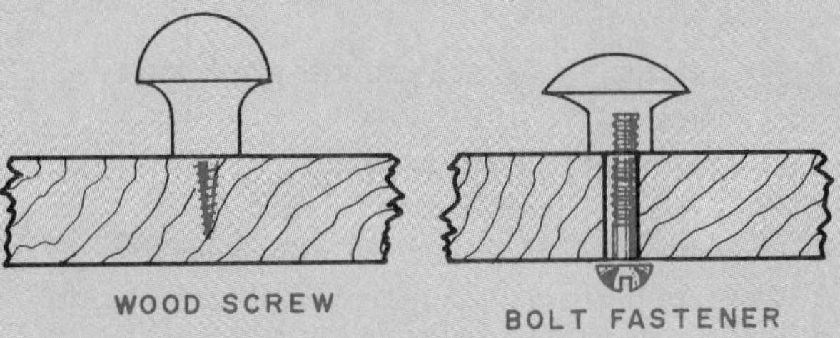

Figure 24-3
Fasten knobs with a wood-screw fastener or a bolt-type fastener.

Figure 24-4
These knobs and pulls have an antique English finish. (Amerock Corporation)

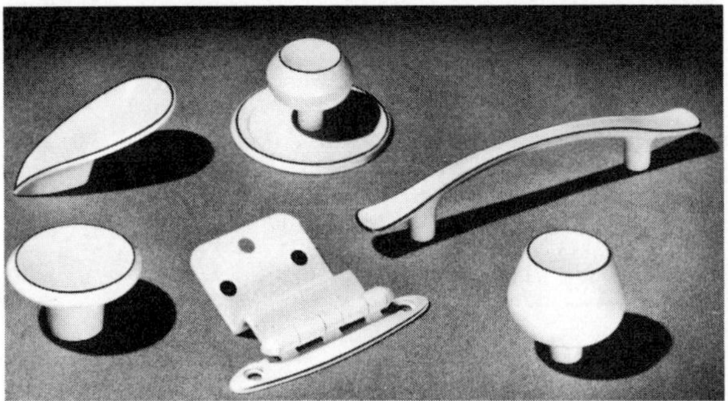

Figure 24-5
A hinge, knob and drawer-pull set with a white finish and a gold accent stripe. (Amerock Corporation)

Generally, knobs fasten to doors or drawers in two ways, Figure 24-3. One type of knob has a thread like that of a wood screw. Install this knob like a wood screw. (Refer to Unit 25.) The other type of knob has internal threads that serve as a nut. It is held in place by a small-diameter bolt. To install this knob, drill a hole the same size as the bolt. Figures 24-4 and 24-5 show knobs of different design.

Fasten *drawer pulls* to the drawer front with two bolts or wood screws, Figure 24-6. Drill the bolt holes the proper distance apart. Then the bolts will screw into the threaded pull. Locate the holes squarely so that the pull will not slant. Figures 24-7 and 24-8 show types of drawer pulls. Notice that pulls and knobs are in matching sets.

Rolling and sliding doors have finger cups instead of pulls or knobs. Set the cups into the door, Figure 24-9. This permits the doors to slide past each other.

Figure 24-6
Installing drawer knobs and pulls. (American Plywood Association)

Figure 24-7
Drawer pulls with matching hinge in an antique design. (Amerock Corporation)

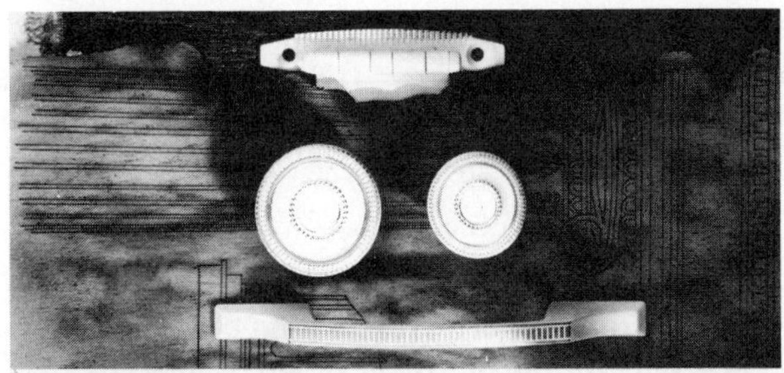

Figure 24-8
A drawer-pull and knob set reflecting the designs of ancient Rome. (Amerock Corporation)

Figure 24-9
Sliding doors have finger cups and recessed pulls. (American Plywood Association)

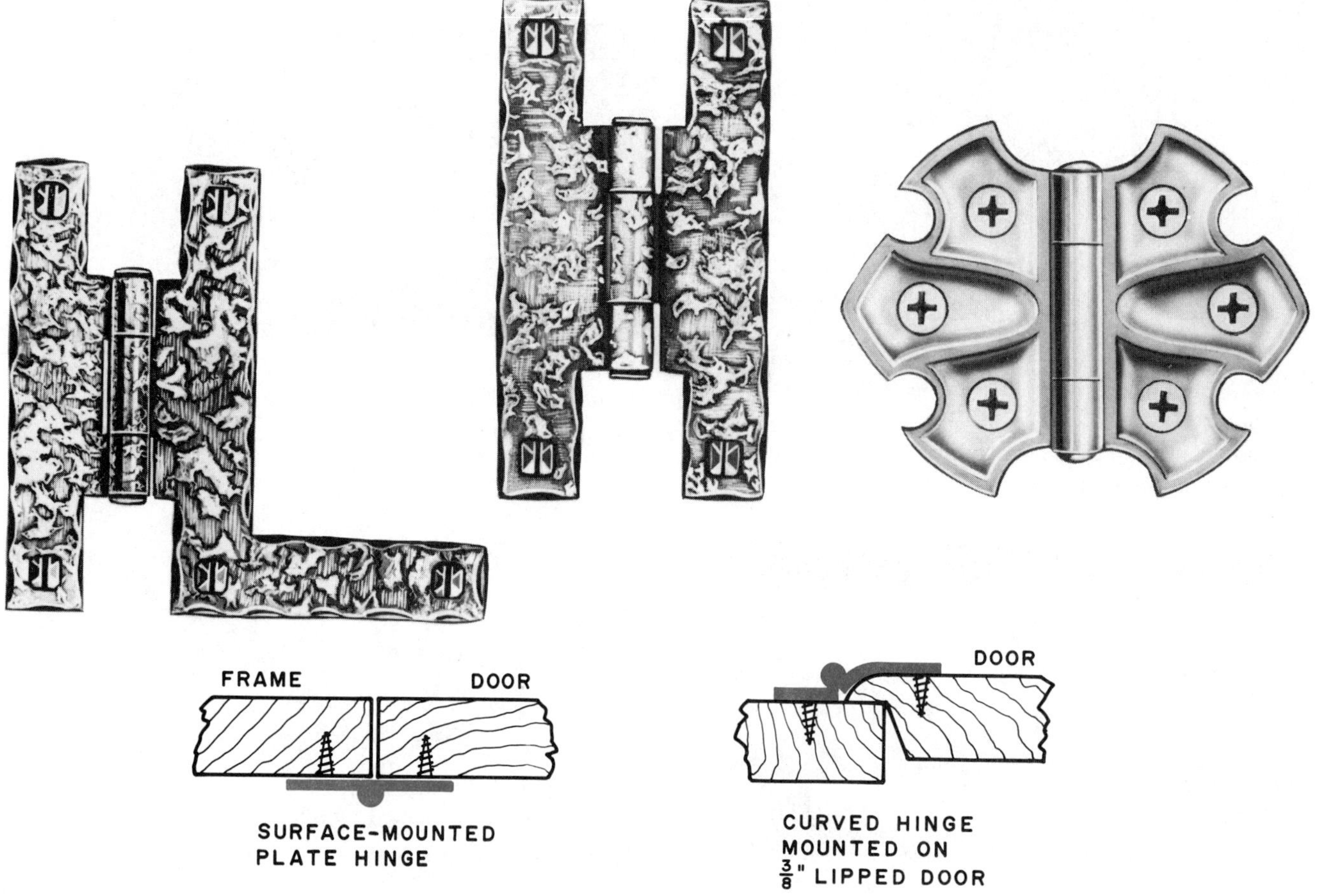

Figure 24-10
Decorative surface-mounted hinges. (The Stanley Works)

CABINET HINGES

Hinges fasten doors to frames. Hinges permit a door, lid or other part to swing open and shut.

Surface-mounted hinges. These hinges are decorative and intended to be seen, Figure 24-10. Fasten them with wood screws. The screws have the same design as the hinge. For example, an antique copper hinge will have screws with antique copper heads, Figure 24-11.

To install surface-mounted hinges, measure their locations. Fasten the hinges to the door. Place the door in the frame. Fasten the hinges to the frame with one screw in each side of the hinge. Then open and close the door. If it moves easily, install the other screws. The barrels, or the parts containing the pins, should line up, Figure 24-12.

Butt hinges. These are plain or swaged. Plain-hinge leaves are straight. Swaged-hinge leaves are slightly offset. This permits the leaves to come closer together, Figure 24-13.

Install the butt hinge so that it is hidden except for the barrel. The leaves are recessed into the edge of the door and the edge of the frame. This recess is called a gain, Figure 24-14.

To install butt hinges, measure the distance each hinge is to be from the top and the bottom of the door. Usually these are the same. Mark the length of the hinge from the top and the bottom of the door. Place the door next to the frame and transfer the marks to the frame. Remove the door. Square the marks across the edge of both door and frame. Place a hinge on the edge. Let it stick out the needed distance. Mark the depth along the edge of the hinge. Mark the depth of cut needed to set one hinge leaf into the door and the frame. The depth is different for swaged and plain hinges. Refer to Figure 24-14.

Figure 24-11
Installing surface-mounted hinges. (American Plywood Association)

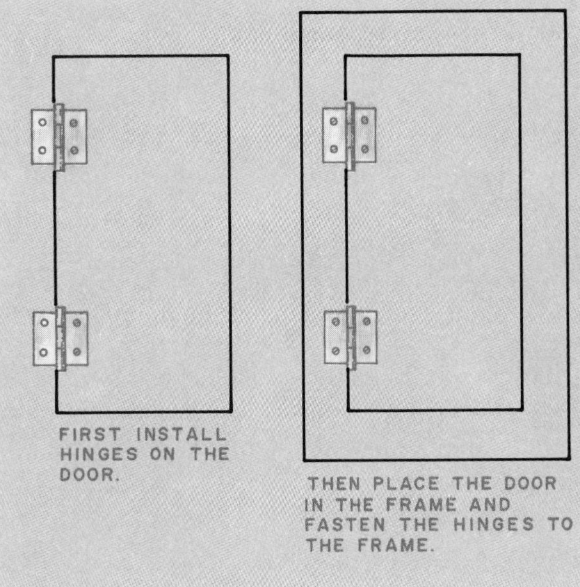

FIRST INSTALL HINGES ON THE DOOR.
THEN PLACE THE DOOR IN THE FRAME AND FASTEN THE HINGES TO THE FRAME.

Figure 24-12
Steps in installing surface-mounted hinges.

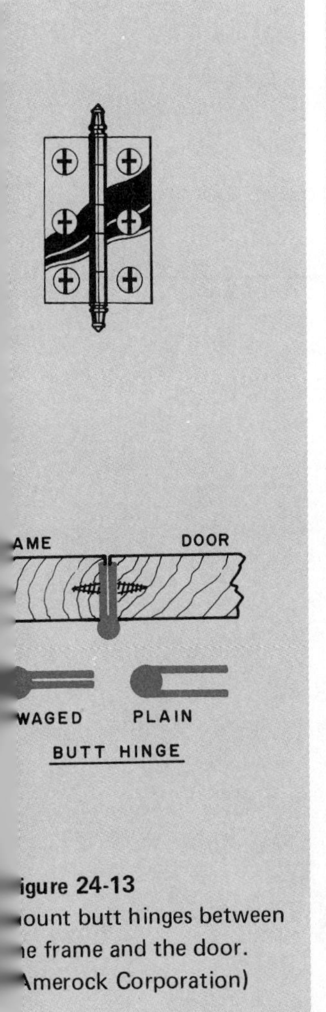

igure 24-13
ount butt hinges between ne frame and the door. merock Corporation)

DOOR
① TO TOP OF HINGE
LENGTH OF HINGE
FRAME
DOOR
② TRANSFER MARKS TO FRAME.
DOOR
③ DRAW LINES ON EDGE.
DOOR
④ PLACE HINGE ON EDGE AND MARK DEPTH.
DOOR
⑤ MARK DEPTH EQUAL TO ONE-HALF THICKNESS OF HINGE LEAVES. THIS DIFFERS FOR SWAGED AND PLAIN HINGES.
DOOR
⑥ CUT THE GAIN.
DOOR
⑦ INSTALL THE HINGE IN THE GAIN.

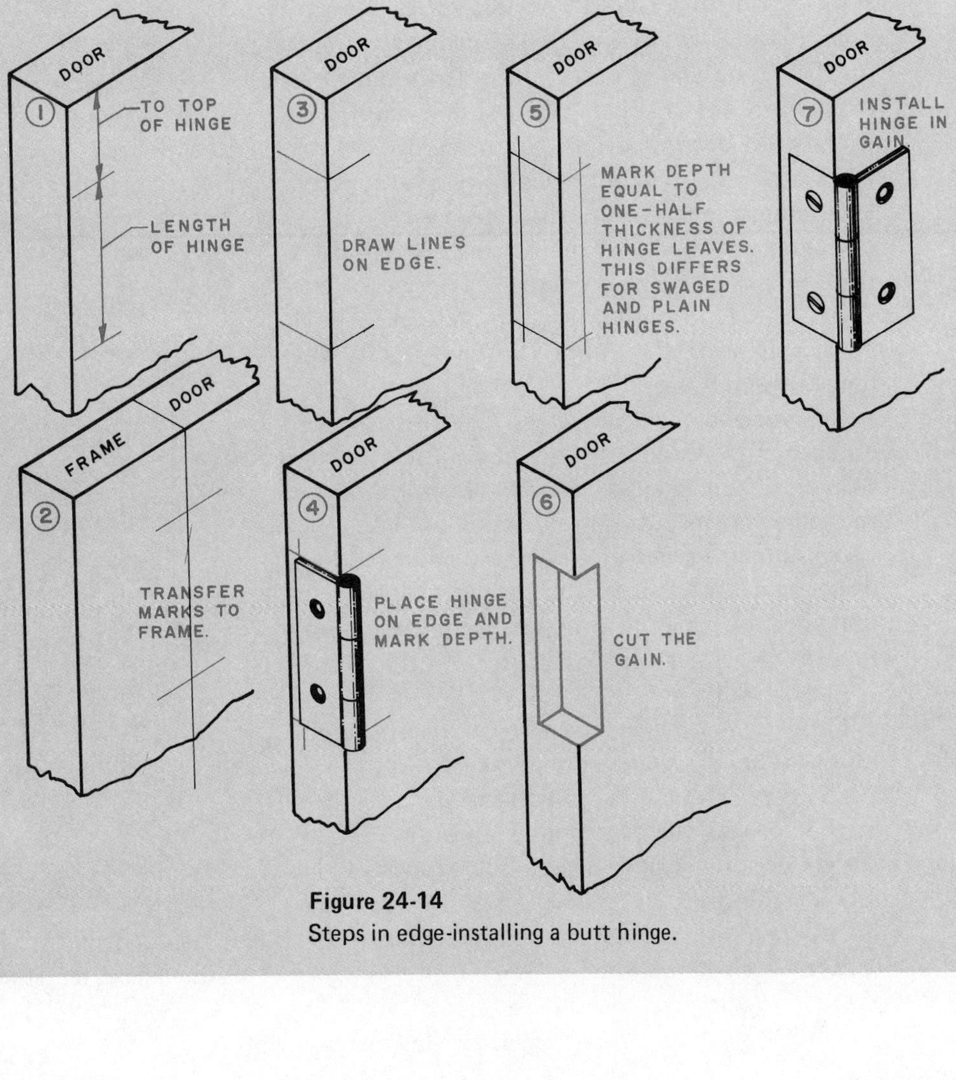

Figure 24-14
Steps in edge-installing a butt hinge.

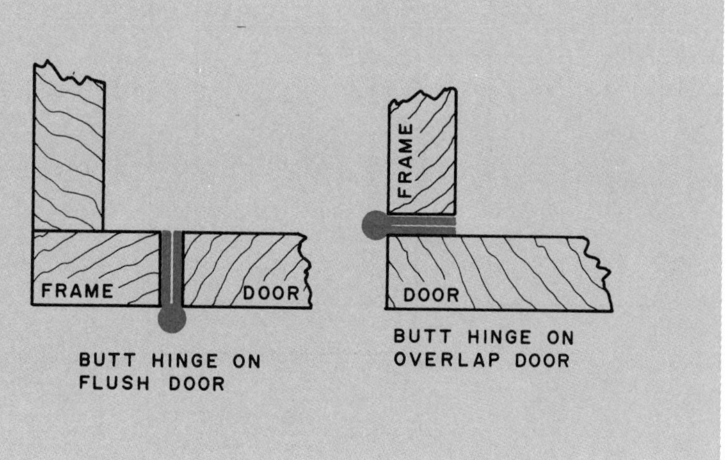

Figure 24-15
Butt hinges can install flush and overlapped doors.

Cut the gain with a wood chisel or an electric router. Position the hinge in the gain and drill the pilot holes. Install the screws. When installed, the hinge should be flush with the surface of the edge, Figure 24-15. Install the hinge on the frame and close the door. It should close easily without binding. If the door binds, the gain is too deep. Place a piece of cardboard beneath one leaf. If the door is too far away from the frame, trim the gain a little deeper.

Figure 24-16 shows another way to mount a butt hinge. Cut a dado across the edge of the door. The dado should be deep enough to hold both leaves of the hinge. Surface-mount the hinge on the frame.

Continuous or piano hinges. Use this type on doors or drop leaves that require more strength than individual hinges can give. Install them in the same way as butt hinges, Figure 24-17.

Nonmortising hinges. Use these hinges to join doors that fold as they open, Figure 24-18. Fasten the top and bottom leaves to one door. Fasten the larger center leaf to the other door, Figure 24-19.

Concealed wrap-around hinges. These hinges fasten doors of veneer core plywood, Figure 24-20. The design permits you to install the screws in the face of the plywood, Figure 24-20. The design permits you to install the screws in the face of the plywood. This gives a stronger hold than when the screws are in the edge of the veneer.

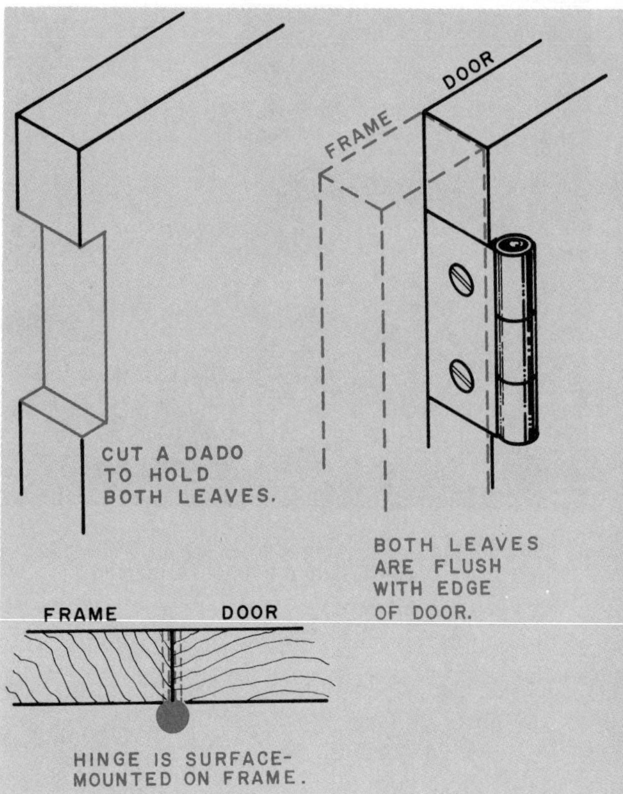

Figure 24-16
A dado cut in the door can receive a butt hinge.

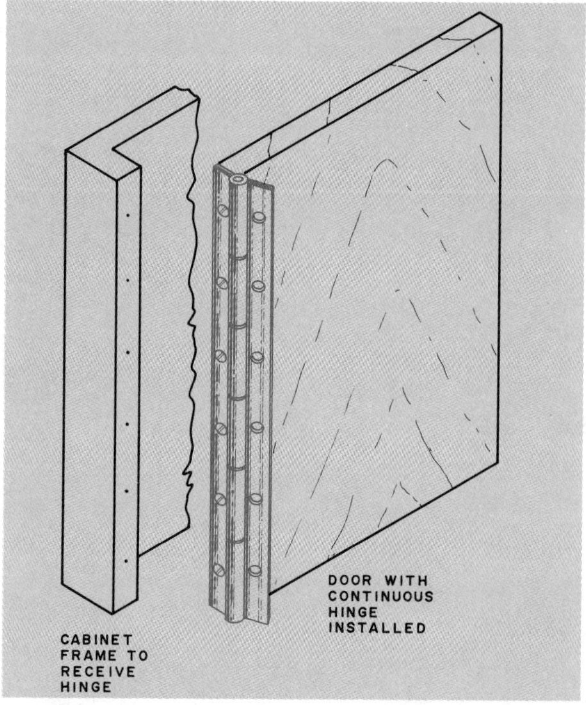

Figure 24-17
Continuous hinges run the entire length of the door.

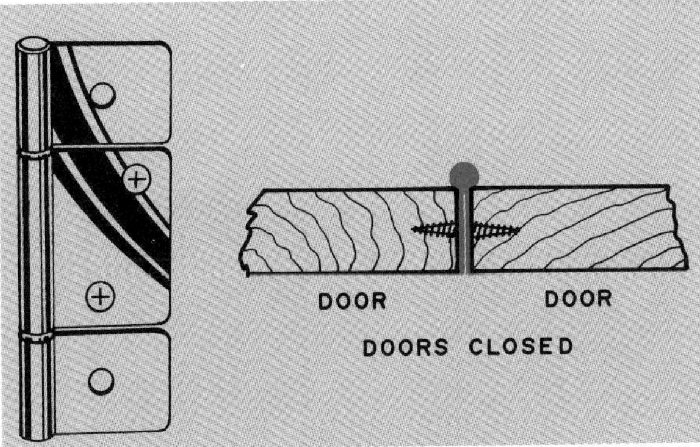

Figure 24-18
How to install a nonmortising cabinet hinge. (Amerock Corporation)

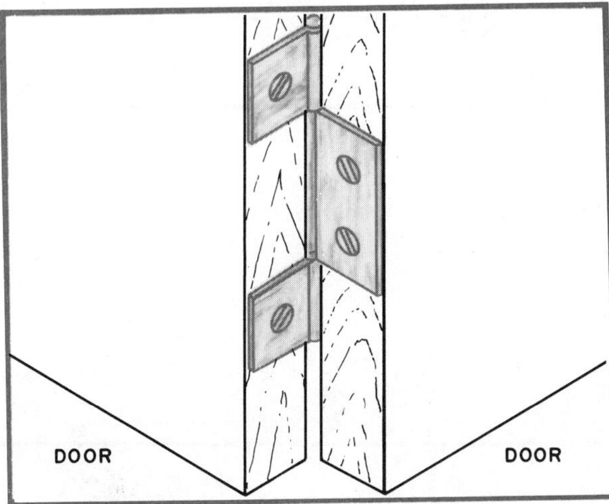

Figure 24-19
The nonmortising cabinet hinge joins folding cabinet doors.

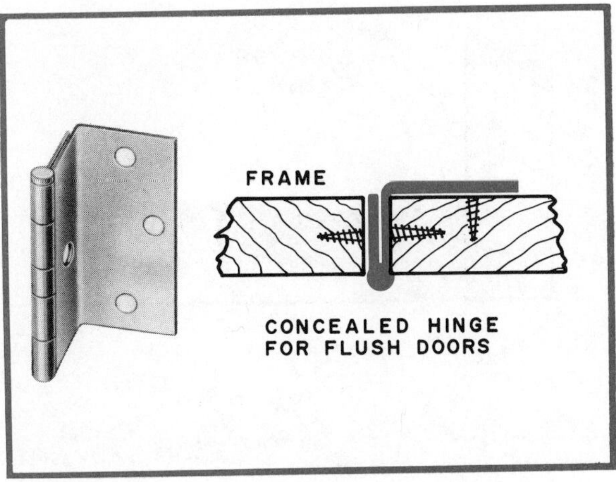

Figure 24-20
How to install a concealed wrap-around hinge. (The Stanley Works)

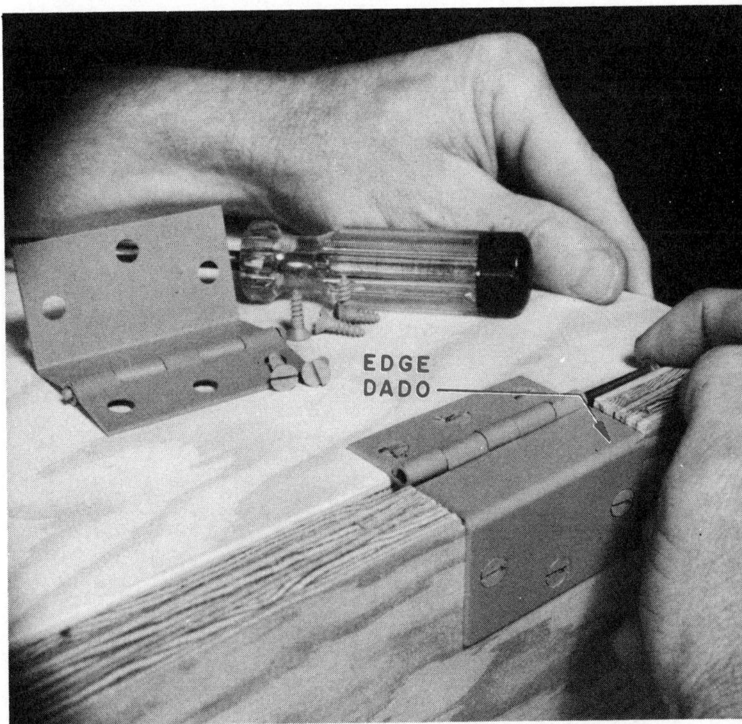

Figure 24-21
Set the concealed wrap-around hinge in a dado in the door. (American Plywood Association)

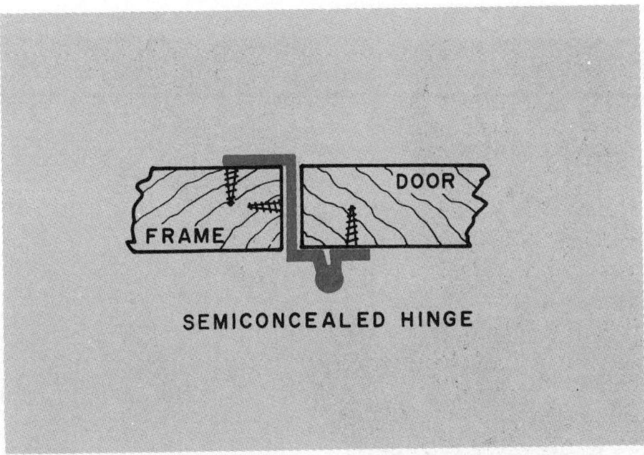

Figure 24-22
Mount a semiconcealed hinge on the surface of a square-edge door.

To install a concealed wrap-around hinge, first cut a dado in the edge of the door. The depth of the dado should equal the diameter of the barrel, Figure 24-21.

Semiconcealed hinges. This type is designed for use on square-edged flush doors, Figure 24-22. The screws enter the face of both door and frame.

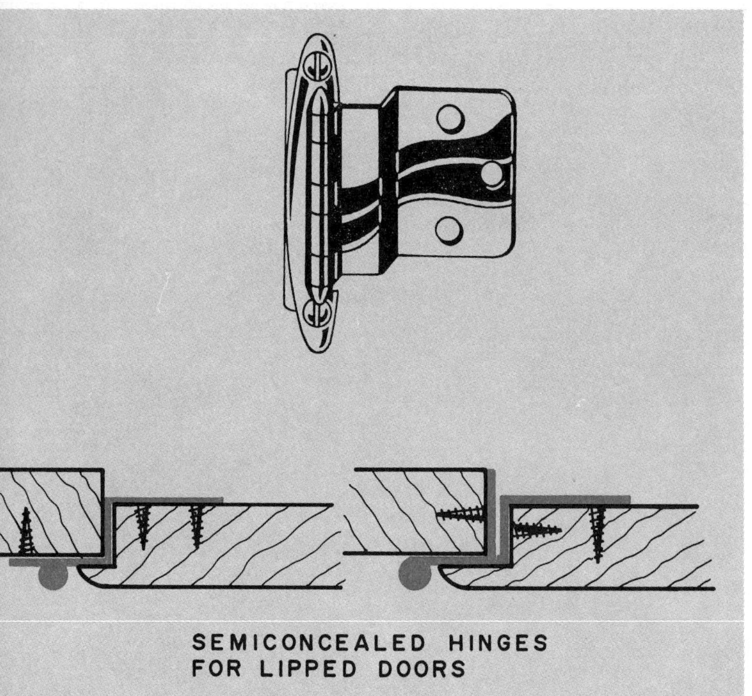

Figure 24-23
These semiconcealed hinges are for mounting lipped doors. (Amerock Corporation)

Figure 24-24
Mounting a semiconcealed hinge on the inside of the lipped door. (American Plywood Association)

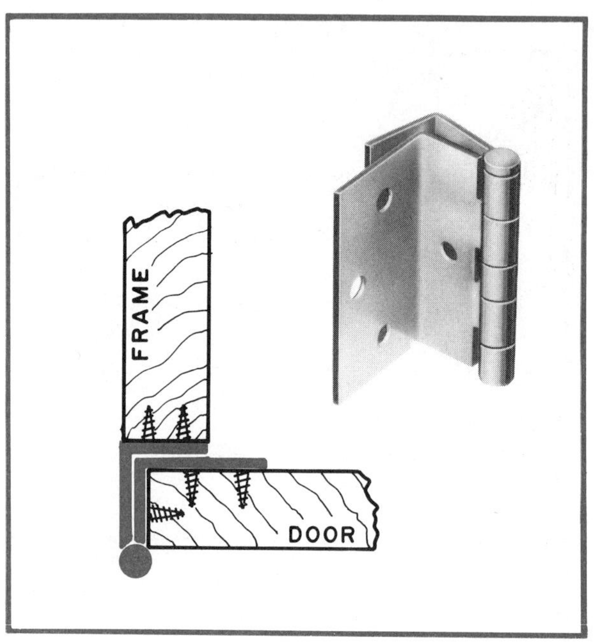

Figure 24-25
This hinge for overlay doors permits the door to open 180°. (The Stanley Works)

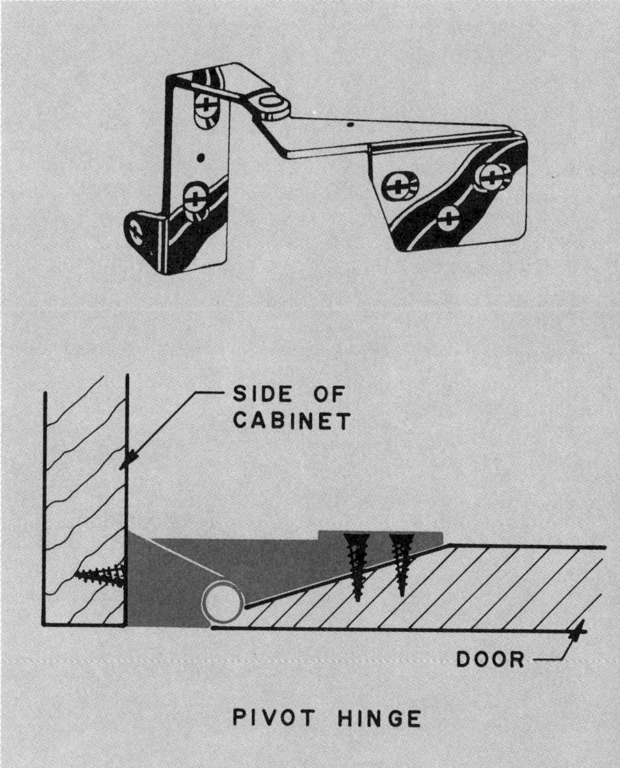

Figure 24-26
Use a pivot hinge to mount doors on cabinets without a faceframe. (Amerock Corporation)

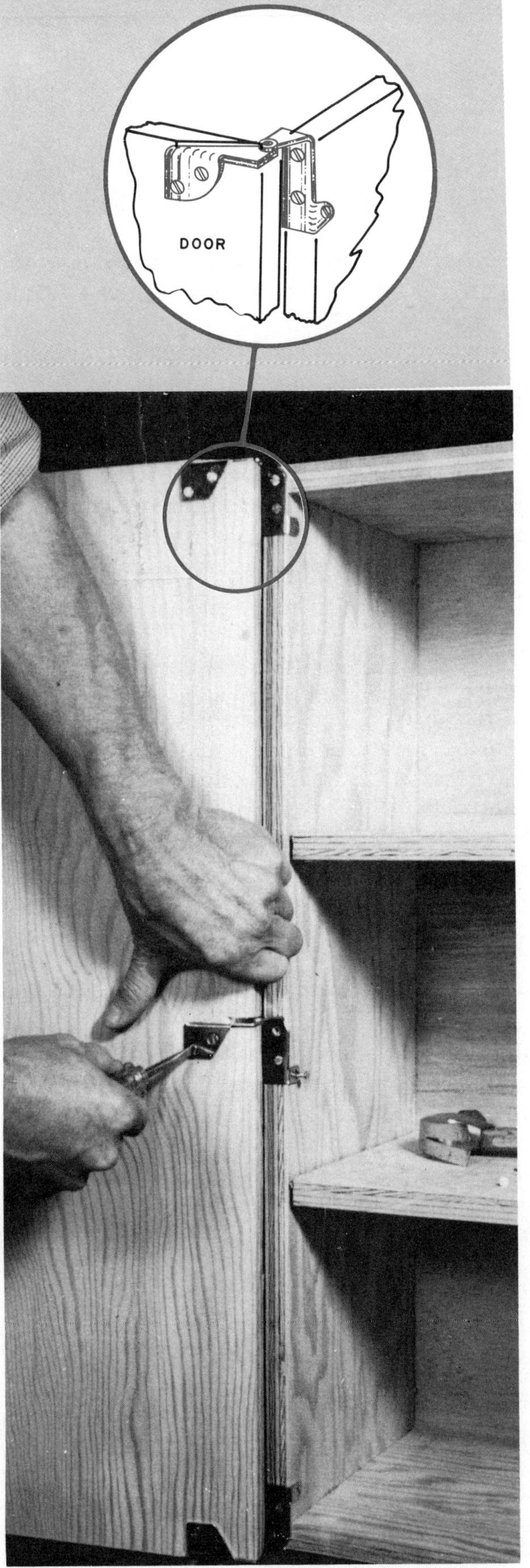

Figure 24-27
Mounting a pivot hinge for an overlay door. (American Plywood Association)

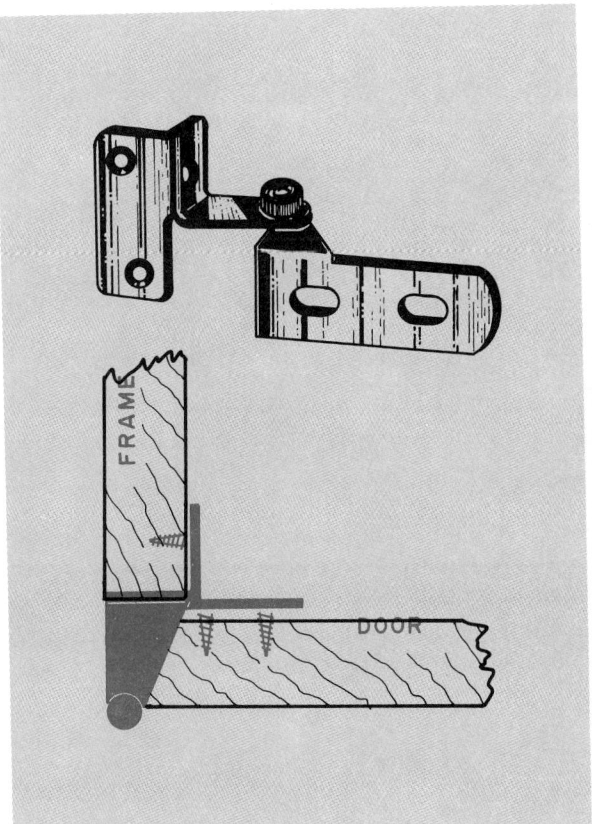

Figure 24-28
A pin hinge can fasten to the frame or to the cabinet partition.

Use a semiconcealed hinge for lip doors. Figure 24-23 shows two types. First fasten the hinge to the door. Set the door in place on the frame. Square the frame with the cabinet. Install one screw in each exposed leaf. If the door moves without binding, install the other screws, Figure 24-24.

Another type of semiconcealed hinge for overlay doors permits the door to open 180°, Figure 24-25.

Pivot hinges. These mount doors on cabinets without a faceframe, Figure 24-26. The door covers the edge grain of the frame sides. Make a small-angle cut at the top and the bottom of the door. Fasten the hinge to the inside face of the door and to the edge and face of the side of the cabinet, Figure 24-27.

Pin hinges. Fasten a pin hinge to the frame or a vertical cabinet partition, Figure 24-28. It permits the door to swing all the way around to the

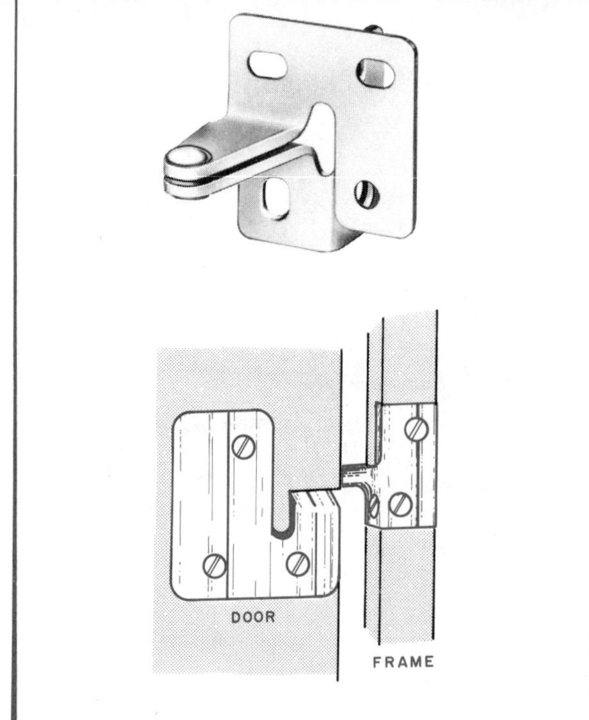

Figure 24-29
Another style of pin hinge requires a slot to be cut in the door. (The Stanley Works)

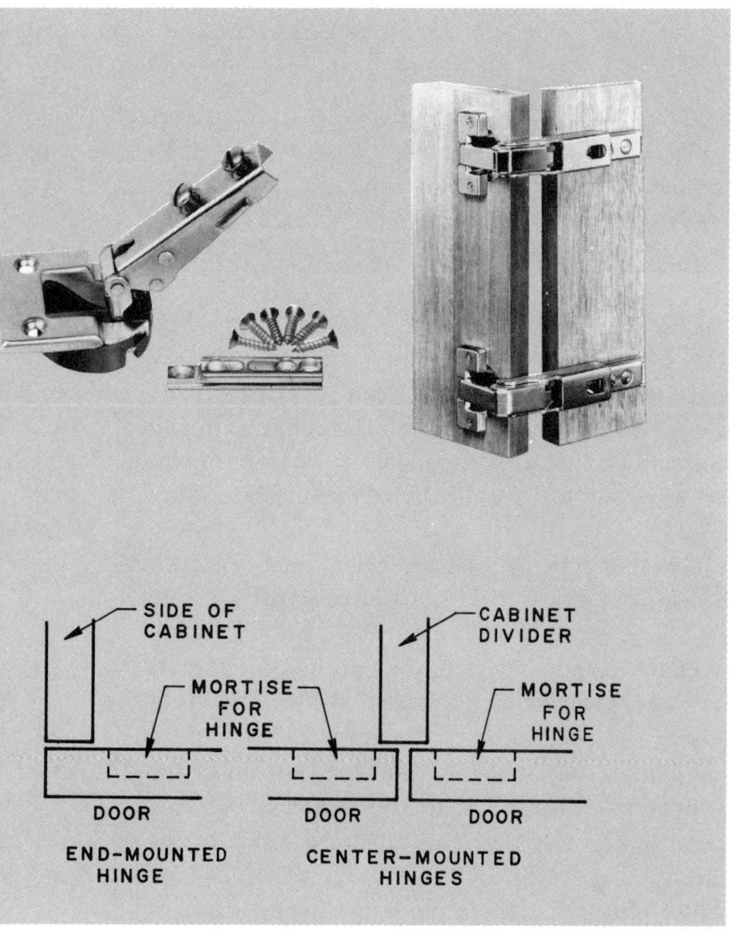

Figure 24-30
Two types of concealed hinges. (The Stanley Works)

side of a cabinet. Set the arm on the door portion of the hinge in a slot cut in the door, Figure 24-29.

Concealed hinges. To fasten overlay doors, set the hinges into holes bored in the edge of the door, Figure 24-30.

HARDWARE FOR ROLLING AND SLIDING DOORS

Mount rolling doors on a metal *door track* and rollers. Fasten the track inside the top of the cabinet. Fasten the rollers to the door with screws. Keep the bottoms of the doors in line with a metal or plastic guide, Figure 24-31.

Sliding doors have a wood, metal or plastic track. Most sizes will carry quarter-inch plywood, hardboard or glass doors. Set the track in a groove cut in the top and bottom parts of the cabinet, Figure 24-32. Notice the space above the doors in the track. The space permits you to lift the doors out of the bottom groove.

Another type of hardware is a plastic track with raised rails, Figure 24-33. Cut a groove in the top and the bottom of the doors. Fasten the track directly to the cabinet or make it recessed, Figure 24-34.

A single track that can be bent around corners is available for tambour, or flexible, sliding doors. These doors are made of wood members with grooves cut in the ends. The grooves ride on the plastic track. Heavy canvas glued to the inside face of the wood members provides the flexibility needed to turn the corner, Figure 24-35.

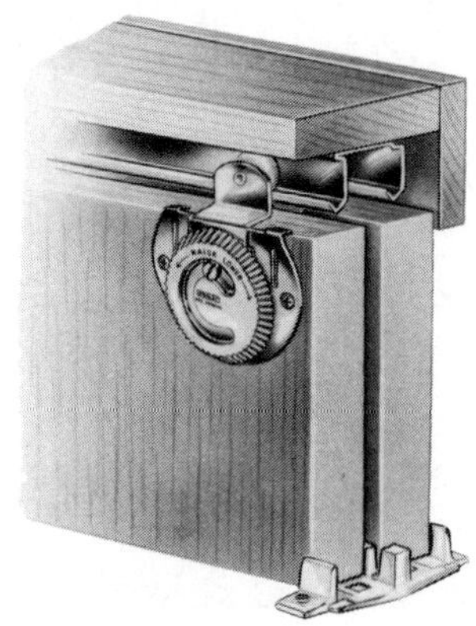

Figure 24-31
Mount rolling doors on a metal track. (The Stanley Works)

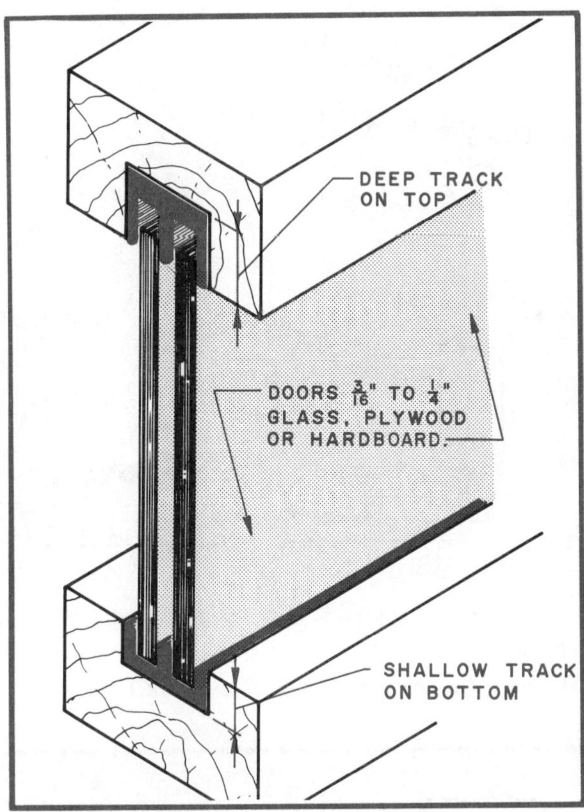

Figure 24-32
Sliding doors can run on wood or plastic tracks.

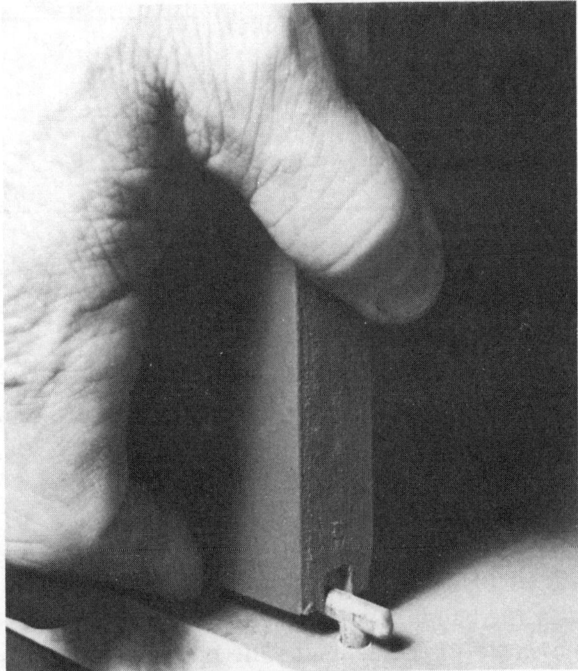

Figure 24-33
Sliding doors can run on the bottom edge of a plastic rod. (American Plywood Association)

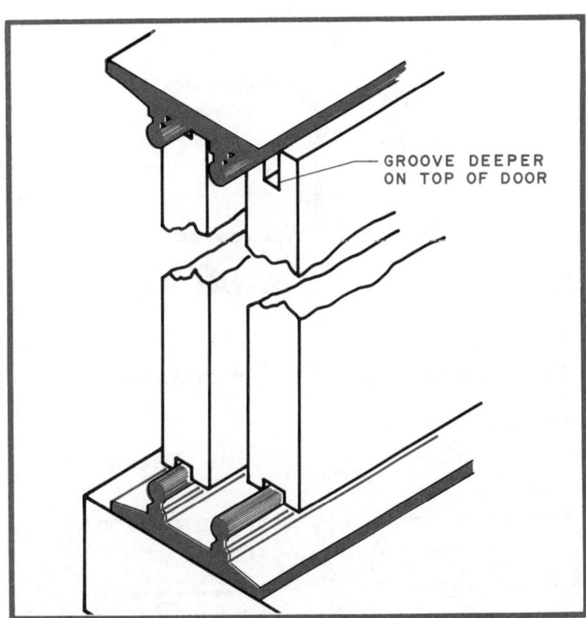

Figure 24-34
A double plastic track with raised rails.

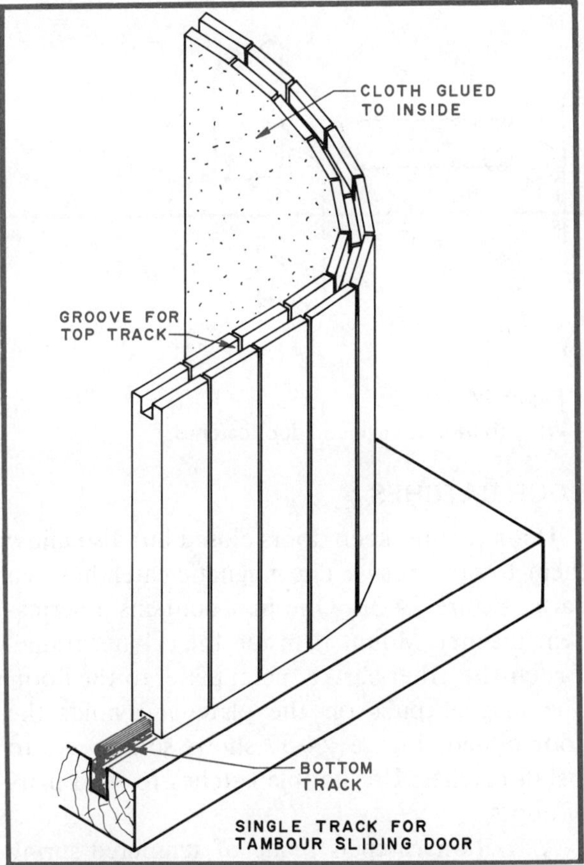

Figure 24-35
Single plastic tracks can carry tambour sliding doors around corners.

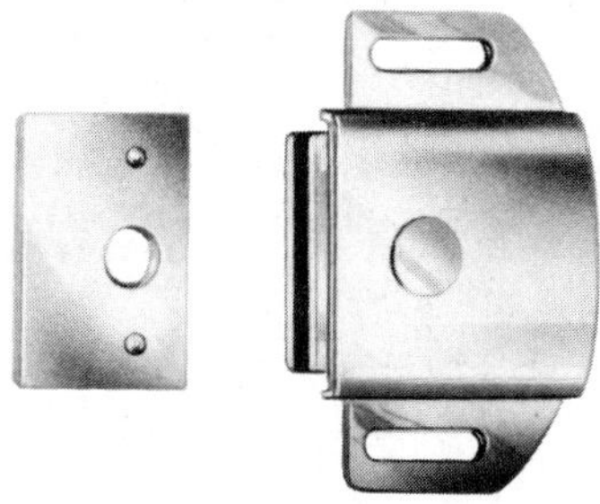

Figure 24-36
A magnetic door catch. (The Stanley Works)

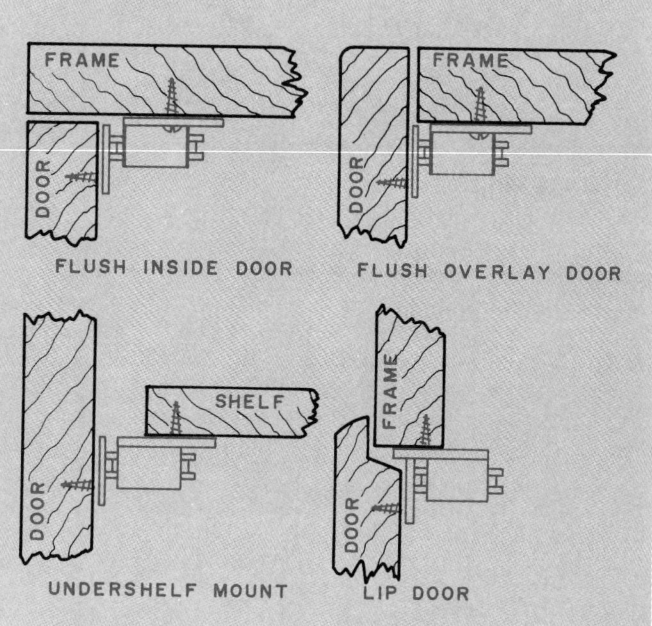

Figure 24-37
Ways to mount magnetic door catches.

DOOR CATCHES

Door *catches* keep doors closed but also allow them to open easily. The magnetic catch has two parts, Figure 24-36. One part contains a permanent magnet. Mount it inside the cabinet frame. Fasten the other part, a metal plate, to the door. The magnet pulls on the plate and holds the door closed. Figure 24-37 shows some ways to install catches. Use double catches to hold pairs of doors.

A friction catch is made of tempered spring steel. Mount the spring part on the cabinet frame or on a shelf. Mount the strike on the door, Figure 24-38.

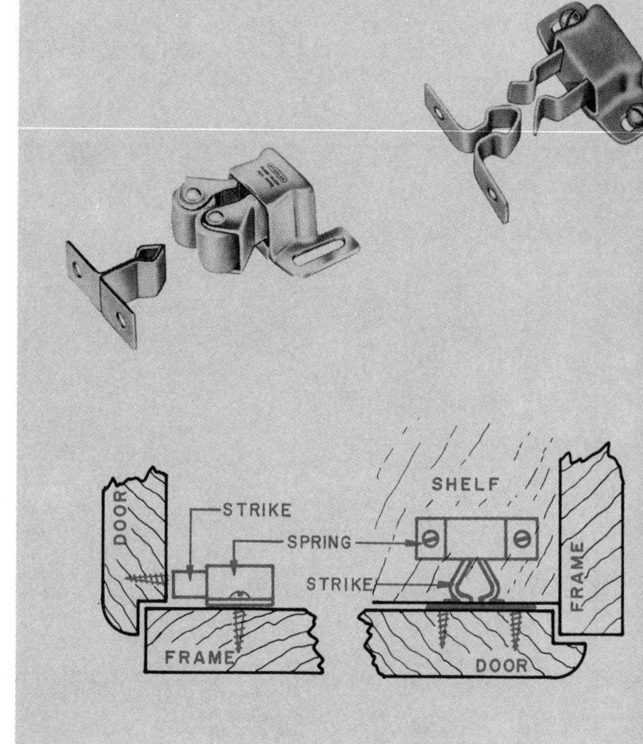

Figure 24-38
Friction door catches. (The Stanley Works)

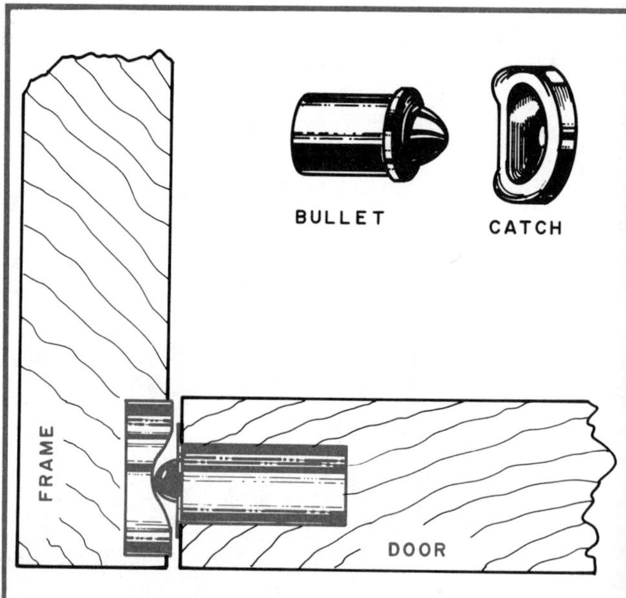

Figure 24-39
A bullet-type door catch.

A bullet-type friction catch uses a spring-loaded ball as the holding device. Set the unit with the ball in a hole drilled in the door. Fasten the strike to the cabinet. The ball slips into the recess in the strike, Figure 24-39.

Figure 24-40 shows a roller catch. Mount the roller on the door.

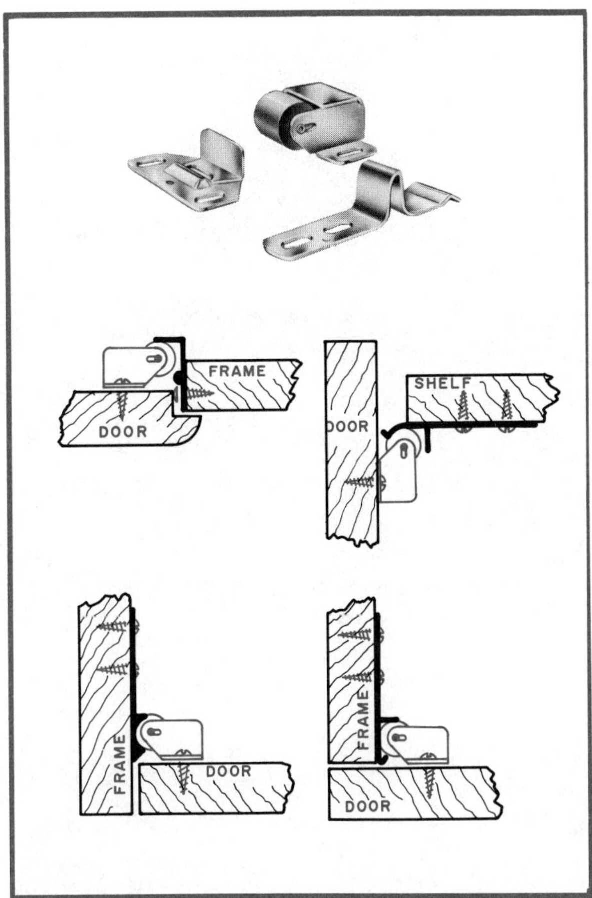

Figure 24-40
A roller-type door catch. (The Stanley Works)

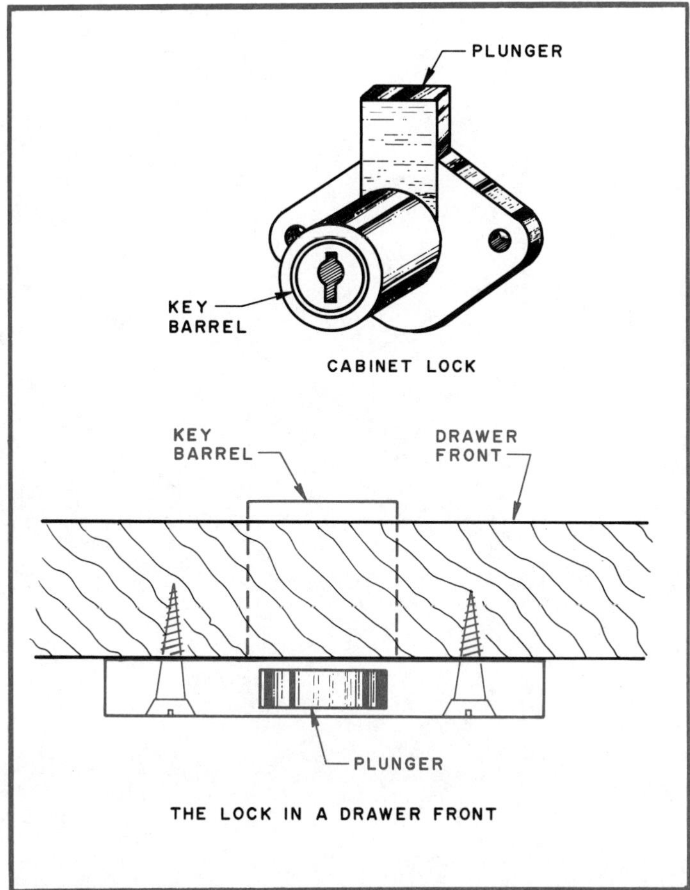

Figure 24-41
A typical furniture lock.

LOCKS

A variety of cabinet *locks* is available. Figure 24-41 shows one type. To install it, bore a hole through the drawer front or cabinet door. Insert the lock barrel in the hole from inside the unit. Screw the lock barrel to the drawer or door.

DRAWER GUIDES

Commercial *drawer guides* are either side or center guides. The side guide mounts the metal channel on the side of the cabinet. The runner mounts on the side of the drawer. The runner moves on metal rollers. Drawers with side guides operate easily. They can carry heavy loads and not bind. Before making the drawer, be sure you know what clearance you must keep between the cabinet casing and the drawer side. Leave room for the metal guide, Figure 24-42.

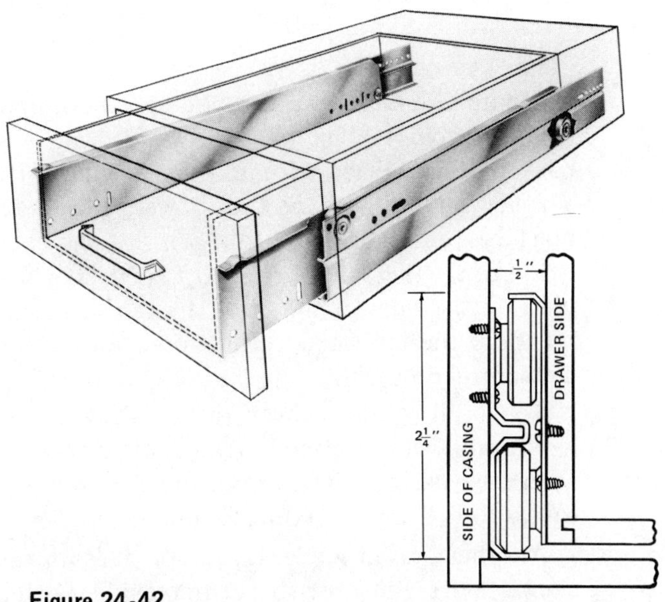

Figure 24-42
Metal drawer guides with rollers. (Knape & Vogt Manufacturing Co.)

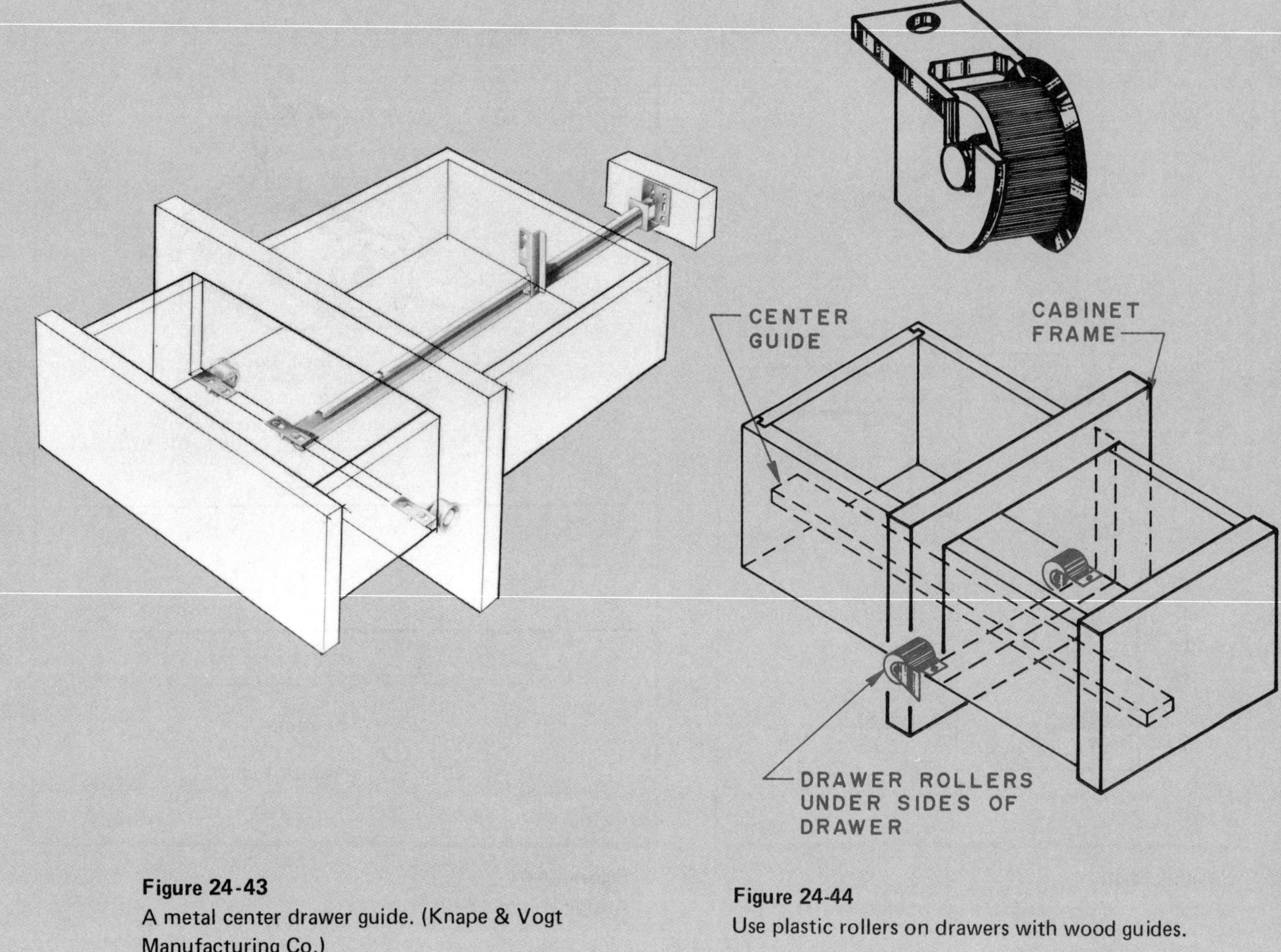

Figure 24-43
A metal center drawer guide. (Knape & Vogt Manufacturing Co.)

Figure 24-44
Use plastic rollers on drawers with wood guides.

Figure 24-43 shows a center, or monorail, guide. Fasten the metal track to the rail and back of the cabinet. Mount a metal guide with a roller on the back of the drawer. The track must be perpendicular to the front of the cabinet. Locate the roller guide so that it does not bind on the sides of the track. Fasten small side rollers to the faceframes. The wood sides of the drawer roll on them.

To improve the movement of drawers on wood runners, use plastic tack inserts or rollers. Insert the tacks in the drawer runner. Fasten the rollers to the cabinet frame, Figure 24-44.

Another drawer guide has plastic pads for the drawer sides and a plastic center guide. Fasten the rail to the cabinet frame. Fasten the guide to the drawer, Figure 24-45.

GLIDES, CASTERS, FERRULES

Place furniture *glides* on the bottoms of legs. The glides raise the legs off the floor and keep the edges of the legs from splitting. The glides help you slide furniture along the floor. They protect the floor from the pressure centered on the leg.

Many types of glides are available. Some have a pin center. Nail this type into the end of the leg, Figure 24-46.

Casters have small wheels. Fasten them to the bottoms of cabinets and other furniture. One type has a pin inserted into a metal socket. The socket is in a hole bored in the leg. The caster slips into the socket. Another type has a plate. Fasten the plate with wood screws to the bottom of the furniture, Figure 24-47.

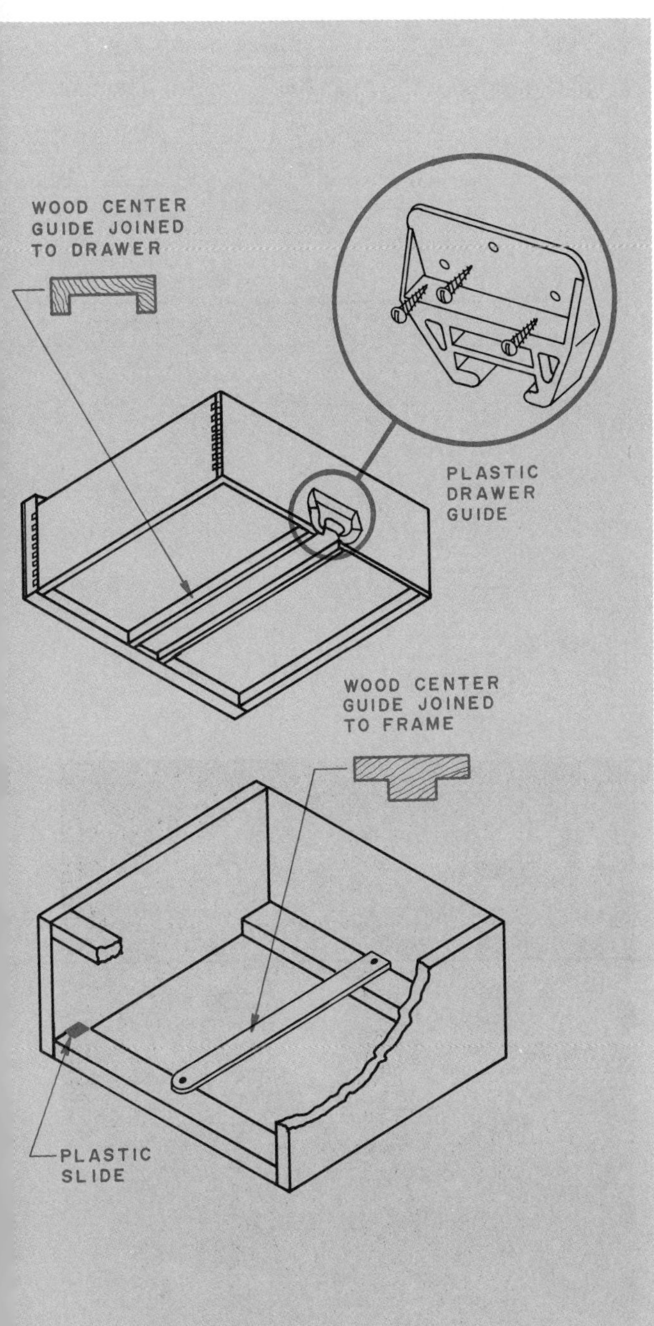

Figure 24-45
Plastic guides designed to slide on wood center guides.

Figure 24-46
Typical furniture glides. (Brodhead-Garrett)

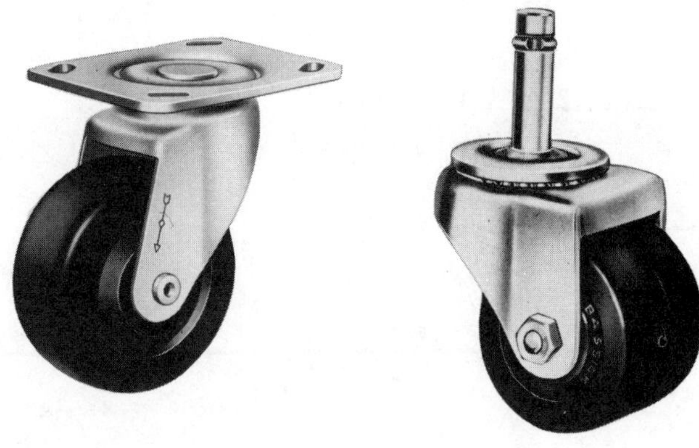

Figure 24-47
Two types of casters. (Brodhead-Garrett)

Ferrules are tapered metal cylinders. Use ferrules on the ends of legs. They give the ends a finished look and protect them from splitting. Some ferrules are available with glides attached. They are sold in various sizes. Before designing legs, you should know what sizes of ferrules you can buy, Figure 24-48.

Figure 24-48
A metal ferrule for a round leg. (Brodhead-Garrett)

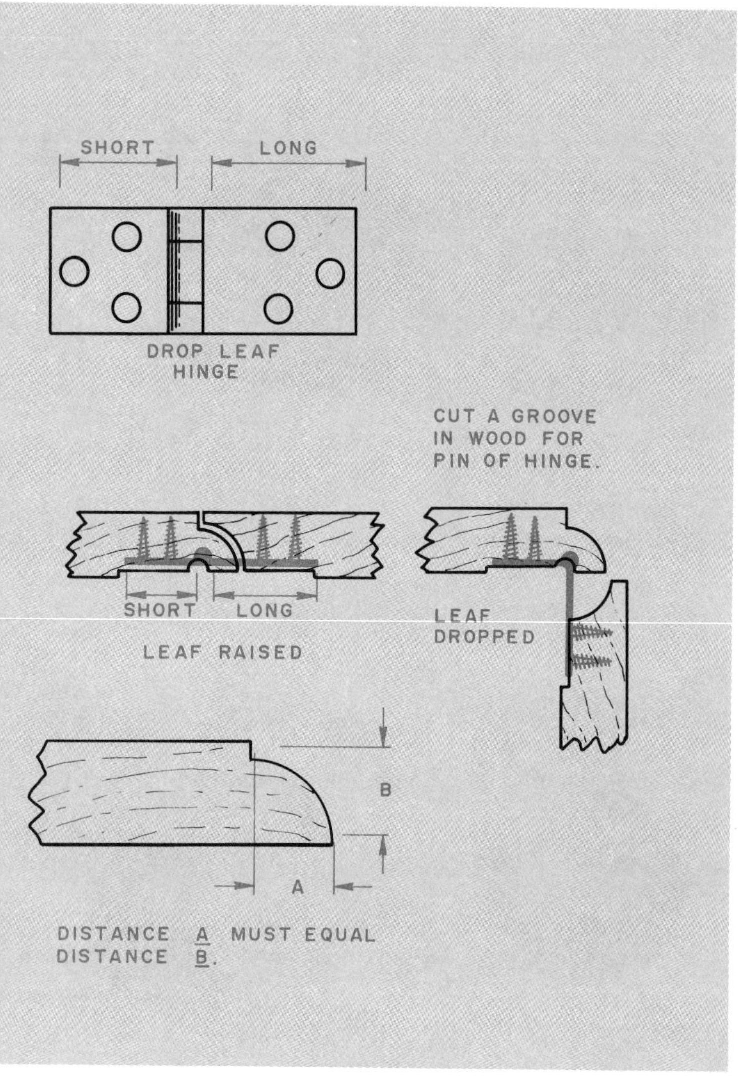

Figure 24-49
A drop-leaf hinge with a rule joint.

SUPPORTS

A drop-leaf table needs a *support* for its movable leaves. Figure 24-49 shows a drop-leaf hinge and an example of the properly shaped edge. This edge is called a rule joint. The hinge permits the leaf to fold down, exposing the attractive, shaped edge. The hinge does not provide support for the leaf. Instead, use a drop-leaf support, Figure 24-50. These supports are available in 8″ and 10″ lengths. Screw the supports to the table apron and to the drop leaf.

Another way to support a drop leaf is to use a wood wing. The wing swings out under the leaf to support it when it is in a raised position, Figure 24-51.

Dimension A (inches)	Dimension B (inches)	
	8″ Size	10″ Size
1-1/2	2-1/16	3-1/2
2	1-11/16	3-1/4
2-1/2	1-3/8	2-13/16

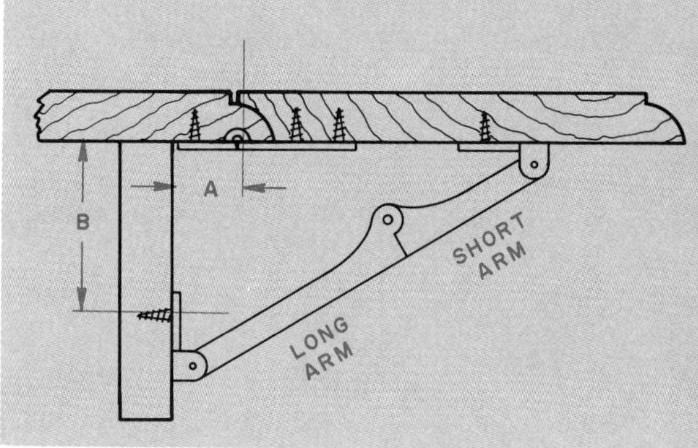

Figure 24-50
A drop-leaf support. (The Stanley Works)

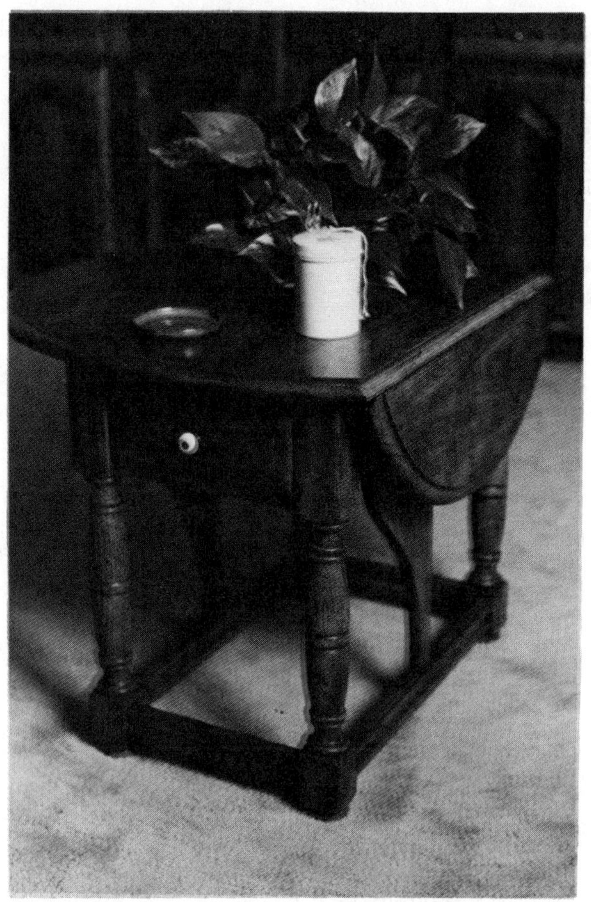

Figure 24-51
A movable wood wing can hold a drop leaf.

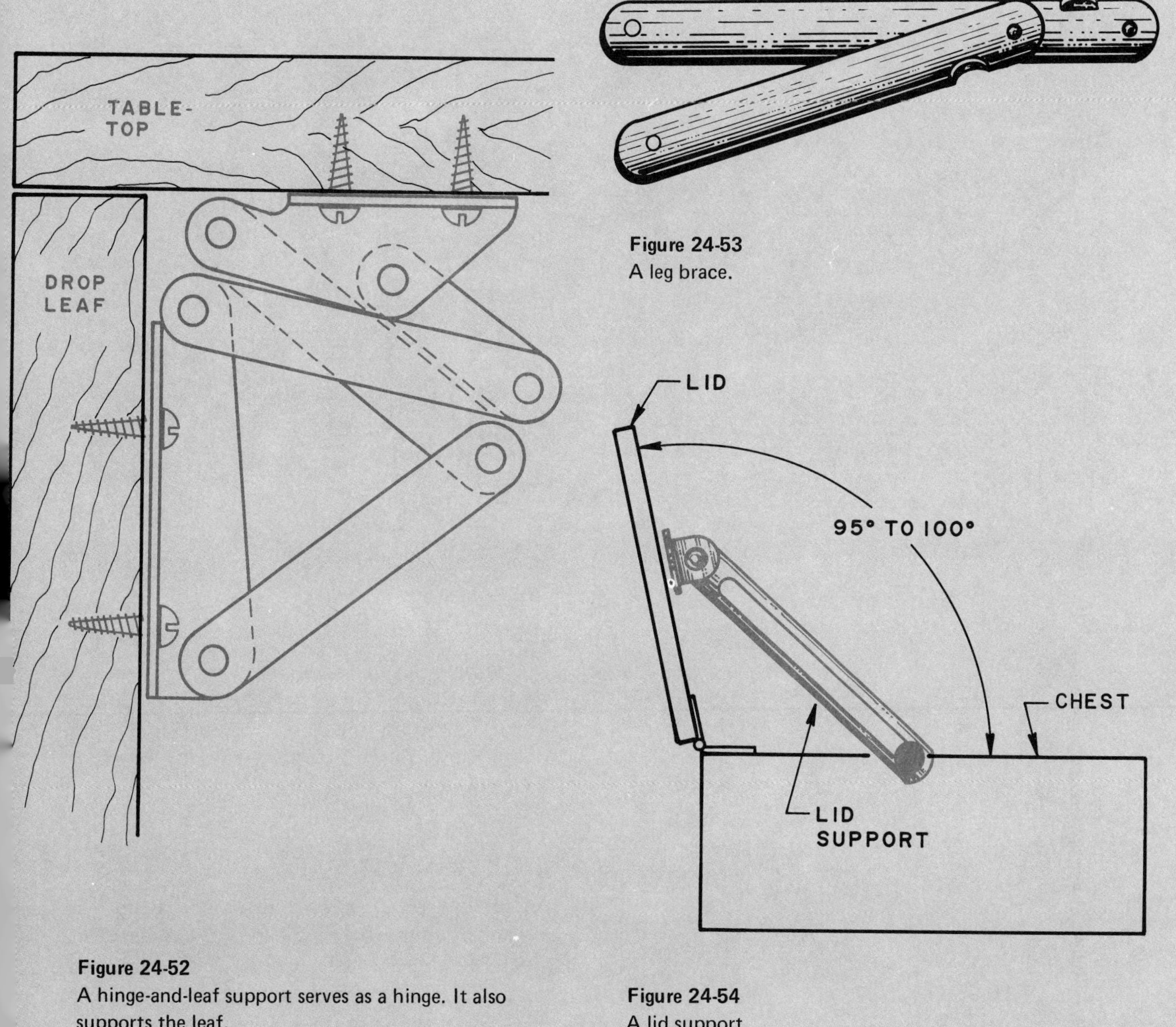

Figure 24-53
A leg brace.

Figure 24-52
A hinge-and-leaf support serves as a hinge. It also supports the leaf.

Figure 24-54
A lid support.

The hinge-and-leaf support enables a drop-leaf table to have square edges, Figure 24-52. This unit serves as a hinge. It also supports the leaf in a horizontal position. When the leaf is in a down position, there is little gap between the top and the dropped leaf.

Use a leg brace on furniture when the legs must fold up. A card table is an example. Use wood screws to fasten the brace to the table, Figure 24-53.

Use a lid support to hold lids on chests. The support permits you to open the lid and let it lean back. It prevents the lid from falling over, Figure 24-54.

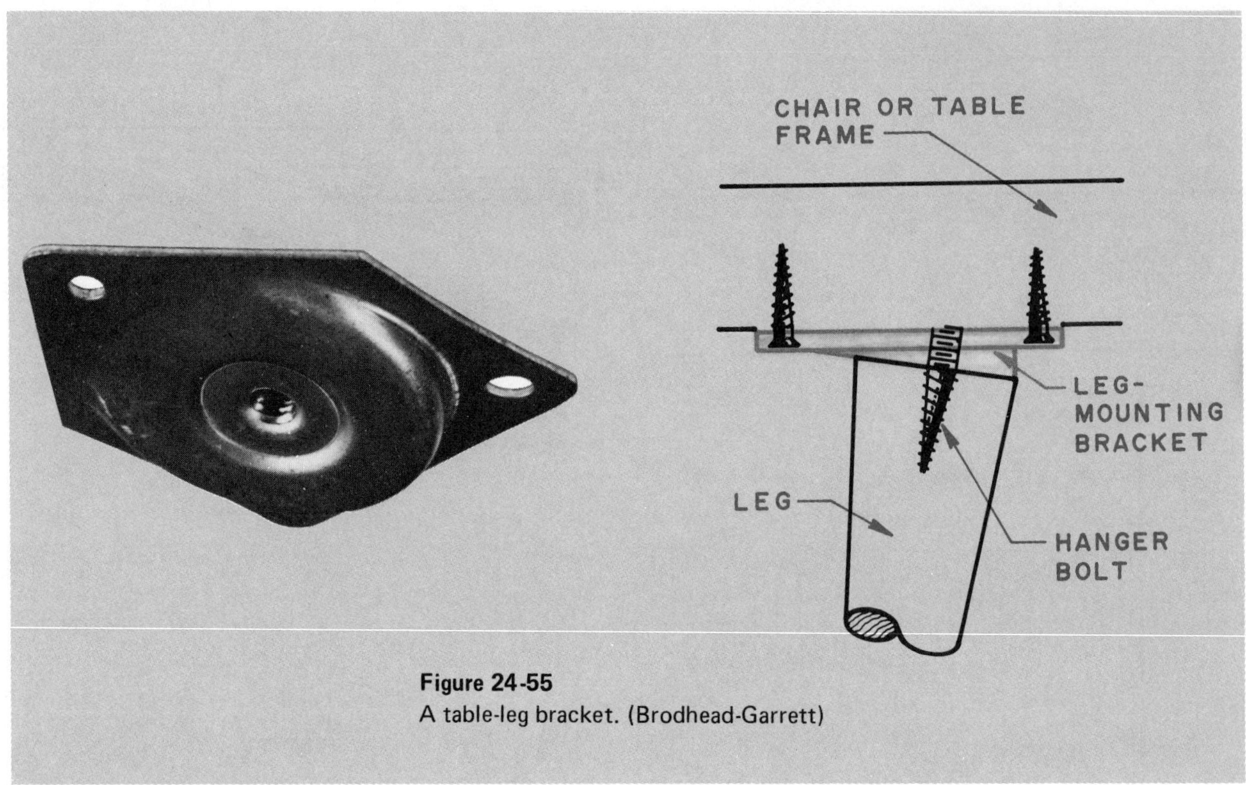

Figure 24-55
A table-leg bracket. (Brodhead-Garrett)

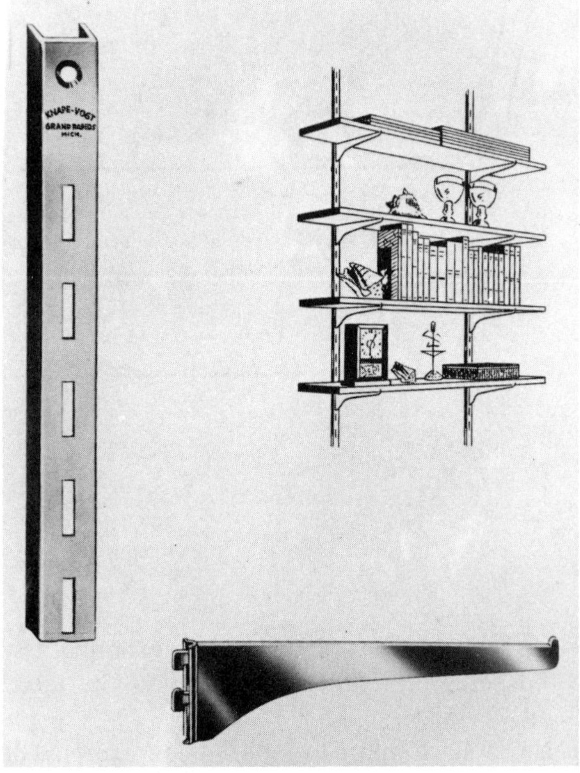

Figure 24-56
These shelf brackets fasten to the wall. (Knape & Vogt Manufacturing Co.)

LEGS

A variety of mass-produced legs is available. These are round, square and turned to different designs. They are made of wood and metal. Fasten them to the furniture with a leg mounting bracket, Figure 24-55.

SHELF BRACKETS

Use shelf *brackets* to adjust shelves to different heights. One type has slotted standards into which the bracket fits, Figure 24-56. The standards are available in lengths up to 144″. The brackets are available in widths up to 20″.

Another type has a standard that may be recessed or surface-mounted. Shelf clips fit into the openings in the standard. The standard fits on the sides of the cabinet and supports the shelf from the ends, Figure 24-57.

MOLDINGS

Moldings are packaged as a set for one door or drawer, Figure 24-58. Apply moldings with glue or brads.

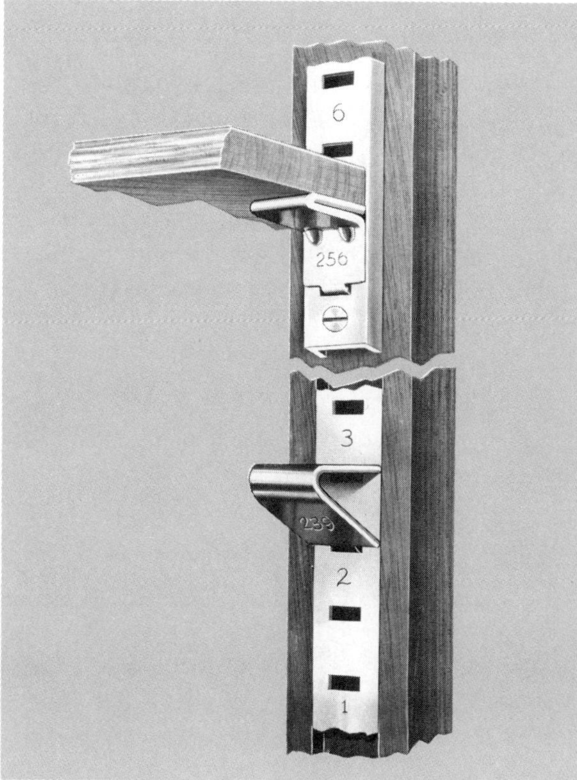

Figure 24-57
The top standard is surface-mounted. The lower standard is recessed. (Knape & Vogt Manufacturing Co.)

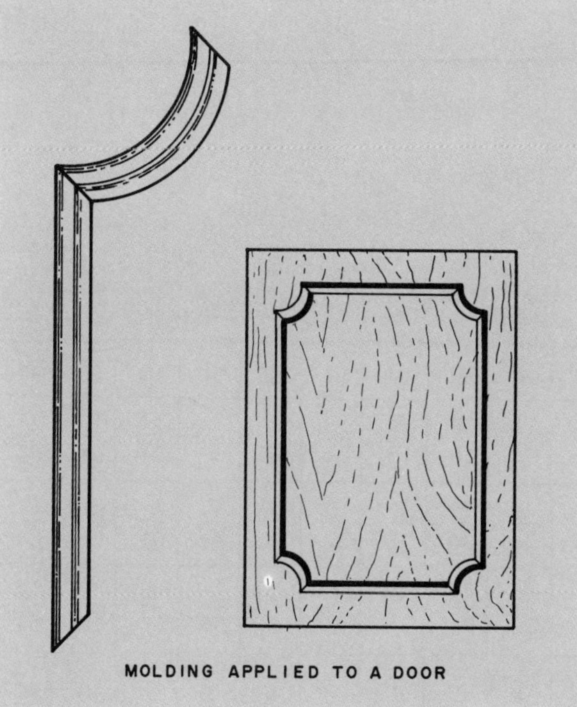

Figure 24-58
Glue or tack factory-produced wood molding to cabinet drawers and doors.

REVIEW QUESTIONS

1. What factors affect the choice of hardware for a particular product?
2. How are knobs fastened to doors?
3. What different types of hinges are available?
4. What is the difference between a surface-mounted hinge and a concealed wrap-around hinge?
5. What type of hinge is used on lipped doors?
6. How do sliding doors work?
7. What types of door catches are in common use?
8. Describe several types of drawer guides.
9. Why are glides used?
10. Why are ferrules used on chairs?

SUGGESTED ACTIVITIES

1. Visit a local hardware store. Which of the hardware items discussed in the text are sold there? Write a report describing the items not mentioned in the text. Make a sketch of each item.
2. Install two different kinds of hinges on scrap.

UNIT

25 Installing Wood Screws

Objectives

After studying this unit you should be able to:

1 Install wood screws correctly.

2 Counterbore and countersink wood screws.

3 Identify various screwdriver tips.

Technical Terms

Shank hole
Pilot hole
Root diameter
Screwdriver
Screwdriver bit
Ratchet screwdriver
Plug cutter
Wood button

Wooden members to be joined by screws must have holes to receive the shank and threaded portions of the screw, Figure 25-1. The hole for the shank portion, called the *shank hole,* must be the same diameter as the shank. The screw must slide through the shank hole without binding. Shank diameters for various wood screws are listed in Figure 25-2.

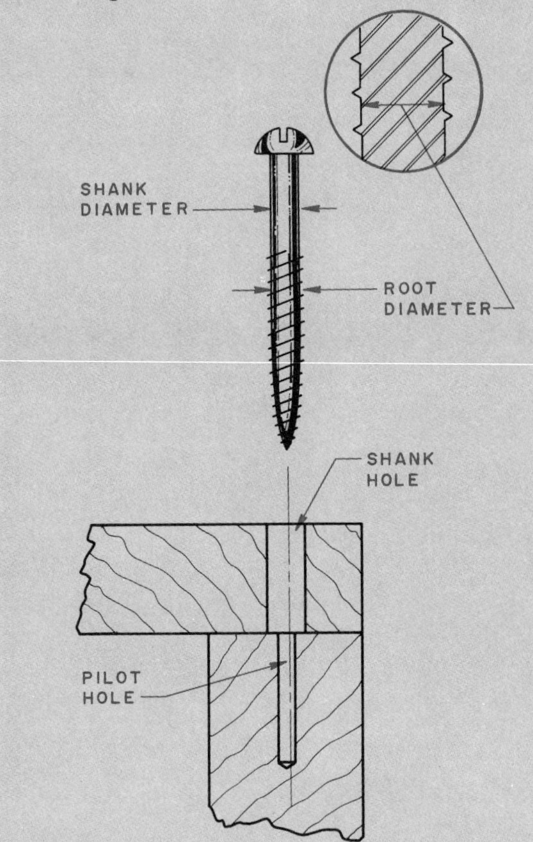

Figure 25-1
Properly driven screws require a pilot and a shank hole.

Screw Gauge No.	0	1	2	3	4	5	6	7	8	9	10	11	12	14	16	18	20
Shank Hole Hard & Softwood	$\frac{1}{16}$	$\frac{5}{64}$	$\frac{3}{32}$	$\frac{7}{64}$	$\frac{7}{64}$	$\frac{1}{8}$	$\frac{9}{64}$	$\frac{5}{32}$	$\frac{11}{64}$	$\frac{3}{16}$	$\frac{3}{16}$	$\frac{13}{64}$	$\frac{7}{32}$	$\frac{1}{4}$	$\frac{17}{64}$	$\frac{19}{64}$	$\frac{21}{64}$
Pilot Hole Softwood	$\frac{1}{64}$	$\frac{1}{32}$	$\frac{1}{32}$	$\frac{3}{64}$	$\frac{3}{64}$	$\frac{1}{16}$	$\frac{1}{16}$	$\frac{1}{16}$	$\frac{5}{64}$	$\frac{5}{64}$	$\frac{3}{32}$	$\frac{3}{32}$	$\frac{7}{64}$	$\frac{7}{64}$	$\frac{9}{64}$	$\frac{9}{64}$	$\frac{11}{64}$
Pilot Hole Hardwood	$\frac{1}{32}$	$\frac{1}{32}$	$\frac{3}{64}$	$\frac{1}{16}$	$\frac{1}{16}$	$\frac{5}{64}$	$\frac{5}{64}$	$\frac{3}{32}$	$\frac{3}{32}$	$\frac{7}{64}$	$\frac{7}{64}$	$\frac{1}{8}$	$\frac{1}{8}$	$\frac{9}{64}$	$\frac{5}{32}$	$\frac{3}{16}$	$\frac{13}{64}$
Auger Bit Sizes for Plug Hole			3	4	4	4	5	5	6	6	6	7	7	8	9	10	11

Figure 25-2
Recommended drill sizes for wood screws, in inches.

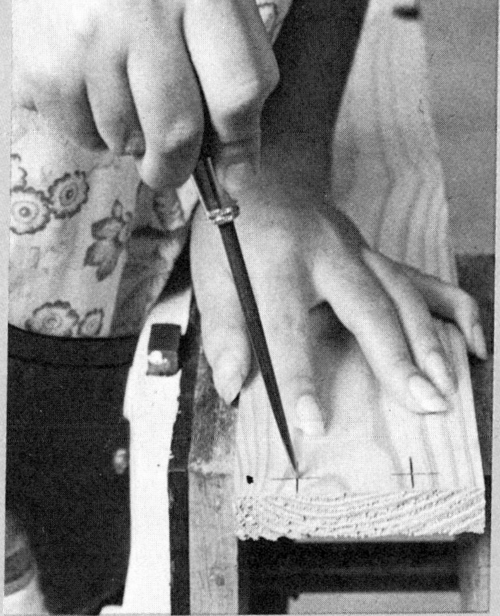

Figure 25-3
Center punch the location of each hole before drilling.

Figure 25-4
Drill the shank hole the same diameter as the shank diameter of the screw.

Figure 25-5
Center punch the pilot hole.

The hole for the threads is called a *pilot hole.* The size of the pilot hole varies depending upon the wood. In softwood, it is about 60 to 70 percent of the *root diameter,* the diameter of the screw inside the thread. In hardwood, pilot holes should be 80 to 90 percent of the root diameter. For most work, select the drill to be used for the pilot hole by holding the drill against the threads and estimating its size. For more accurate work, use the table of recommended sizes shown in Figure 25-2. Drill pilot holes in softwood about half the length of the threaded portion of the screw. In hardwood, drill the same length as the threaded portion.

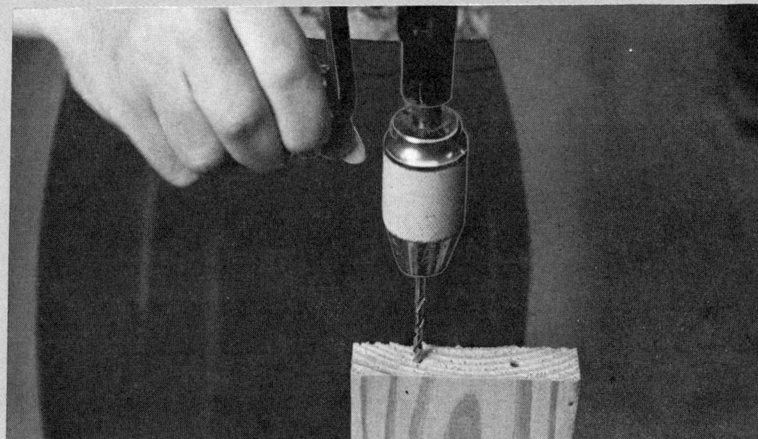

Figure 25-6
Drill the pilot hole.

DRILLING HOLES FOR WOOD SCREWS

To prepare holes for screws:

1. Mark the location of each screw. Use a center punch or awl, Figure 25-3.
2. Select a drill the same size as the shank diameter of the screw. Drill the shank holes, Figure 25-4.
3. Place the board with the shank hole over the second piece. Mark the location of the pilot hole with an awl, Figure 25-5.
4. Remove the top board. Select the proper size drill for the pilot hole. Drill to the proper depth, Figure 25-6.
5. If a flat head screw is used, countersink the shank hole, Figure 25-7. Enlarge the hole until it is the same size as the diameter of the screw head. Check this by placing the screw head in the countersink, Figure 25-8.

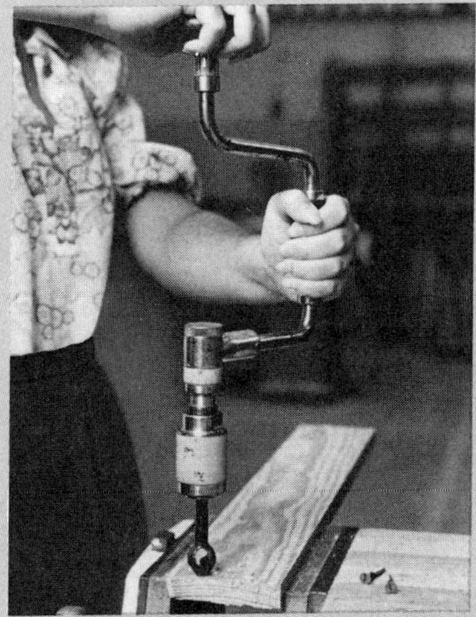

Figure 25-7
Countersink for flat head screws.

Figure 25-8
Check the diameter of the countersink with the head of the screw.

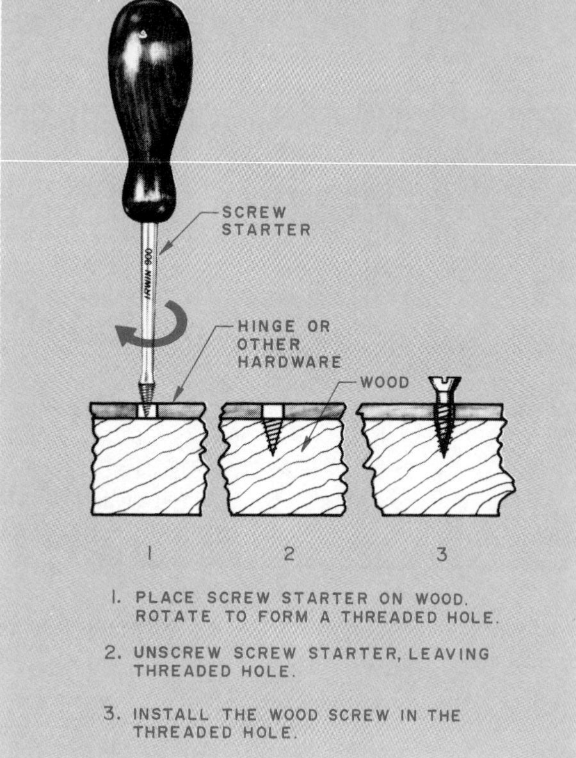
SCREW
STARTER
HINGE OR
OTHER
HARDWARE
WOOD
1
2
3
1. PLACE SCREW STARTER ON WOOD. ROTATE TO FORM A THREADED HOLE.
2. UNSCREW SCREW STARTER, LEAVING THREADED HOLE.
3. INSTALL THE WOOD SCREW IN THE THREADED HOLE.

Figure 25-9
A screw starter can be used instead of pilot and shank holes for short screws. (Irwin Auger Bit Company)

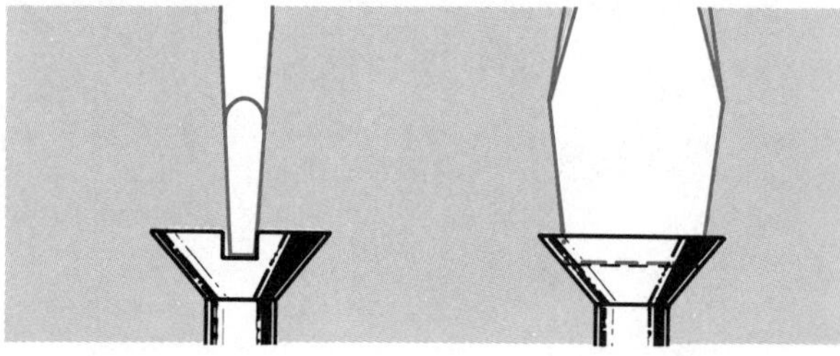

Figure 25-10
The tip of the screwdriver should be nearly the same size as the slot in the head of the screw.

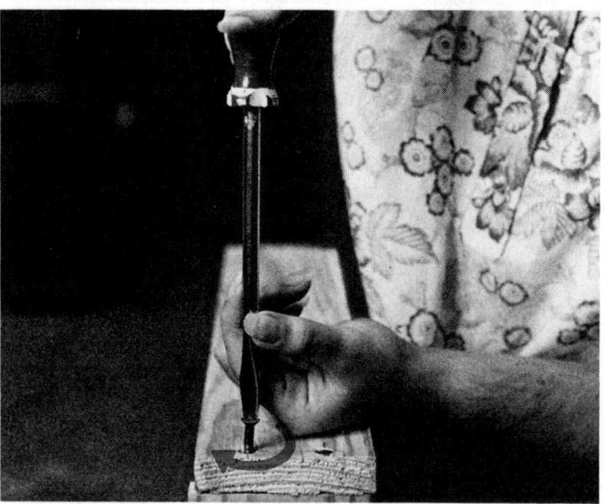

Figure 25-11
To drive a screw, turn the screwdriver handle clockwise.

If an oval head screw is used, only half the head enters the wood. Such screws often set themselves in softwood without countersinking. In hardwood, some countersinking of oval head screws is necessary.

You can prepare holes for short screws, often used on cabinet hinges, with a screw starter, Figure 25-9. Place the point of the tool where the screw is to go. Turn the handle, screwing the end into the wood. Unscrew the tool from the wood. Insert the screw in the threaded hole. When securing hardware, hold the metal part in place and form the screw hole through the hole in the hardware. You also can use the screw starter to mark points for drilling shank and pilot holes.

INSTALLING SCREWS

To insert screws in the holes you have drilled:

1. Place the boards with prepared holes together. Slide a wood screw through the shank hole into the pilot hole.
2. Select the proper size *screwdriver.* For slotted-head screws, the width of the screwdriver tip should be almost as wide as the screw diameter. The tip should be square on the end so it fills the slot, Figure 25-10.
3. Drive the screw in place by turning the screwdriver clockwise, Figure 25-11.

You can drive screws more quickly and easily with a *screwdriver bit* in a brace, Figure 25-12, or a *ratchet screwdriver,* Figure 25-13. The screwdriver bit has a tip like a standard screwdriver. It is held in a brace. Bits with tip widths of 3/16", 1/4", 5/16" and 3/8" are available. To operate a ratchet screwdriver, push down on the handle. The ratchet makes the blade rotate. A spring in the handle automatically returns the blade to the driving position after each stroke. You can change the direction of rotation by moving a button below the handle.

Whatever screw-installation tool you use, a screw will drive more easily if you coat the threads with soap, wax or paraffin. For example, brass screws are soft and can twist in two if not properly installed. To prevent this, be certain the shank and pilot holes are the proper sizes. Lubricate the threads. Drive in a steel screw and remove it. Install the screw in the prepared hole.

Different types of wood require different

Figure 25-12
A screwdriver bit in a brace will drive screws quickly.

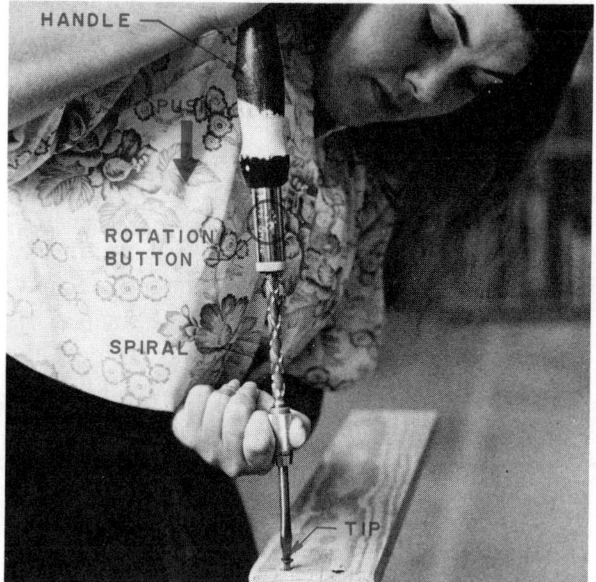

Figure 25-13
Drive screws with a spiral ratchet screwdriver by pushing down on the handle.

screw sizes and types. Plywood is made of several layers of wood. For satisfactory plywood joining with wood screws, use the sizes shown in Figure 25-14. Screws used in solid wood should be long enough so that two-thirds of their total length will go into the second part. End grain has less screw-holding power than face grain. Therefore, screws in end grain should be longer than those in face grain. Finally, screw diameters vary with the thickness of wood. Use small-diameter screws in thin boards. Thicker boards require larger screws. With practice, you soon will be able to judge which size and type of screw to use.

SETTING SCREWS BELOW THE SURFACE

Sometimes you may want to hide the heads of wood screws. To do this, set the screws below the wood's surface and cover the opening. Three common coverings are a paste-type wood filler, wood plugs and wood buttons, Figure 25-15.

Wood plugs can be made with a *plug cutter,* Figure 25-16. A plug cutter is a hollow drill that removes round discs from boards. Cut the plug

RECOMMENDED WOOD SCREW SIZES FOR JOINING PLYWOOD

Plywood Thickness	Screw Sizes
3/4"	1-1/2" No. 8
5/8"	1-1/4" No. 8
1/2"	1-1/4" No. 6
3/8"	1" No. 6
1/4"	3/4" No. 4

Figure 25-14
Recommended screw sizes for joining plywood.

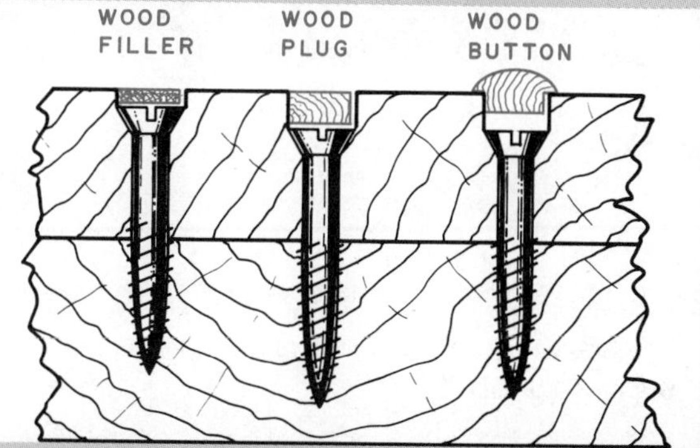

Figure 25-15
Heads of screws can be hidden.

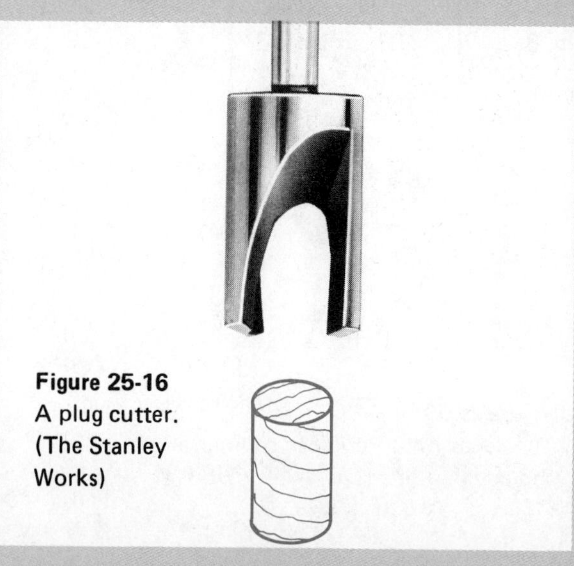

Figure 25-16
A plug cutter. (The Stanley Works)

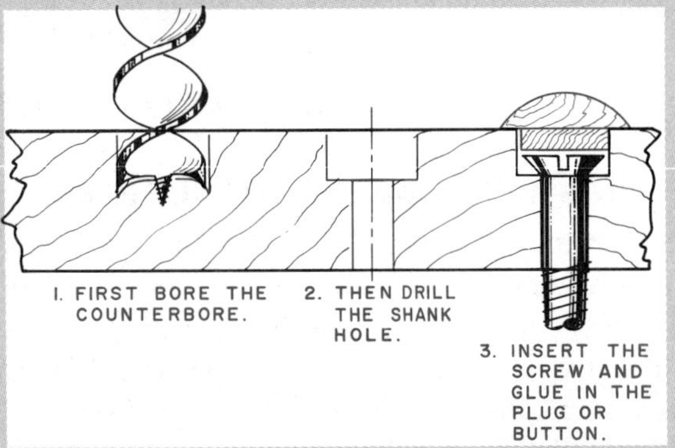

Figure 25-17
Steps to form a counterbore.

SCREW SIZE

1/2" x No. 5	1-1/4" x No. 8	1-1/2" x No. 14
3/4" x No. 6	1-1/4" x No. 9	1-1/4" x No. 8
3/4" x No. 7	1-1/4" x No. 10	1-3/4" x No. 10
3/4" x No. 8	1-1/4" x No. 12	1-3/4" x No. 12
1" x No. 6	1-1/4" x No. 14	2" x No. 10
1" x No. 7	1-1/2" x No. 8	2" x No. 12
1" x No. 8	1-1/2" x No. 10	2" x No. 14
1" x No. 10	1-1/2" x No. 12	2-1/2" x No. 12

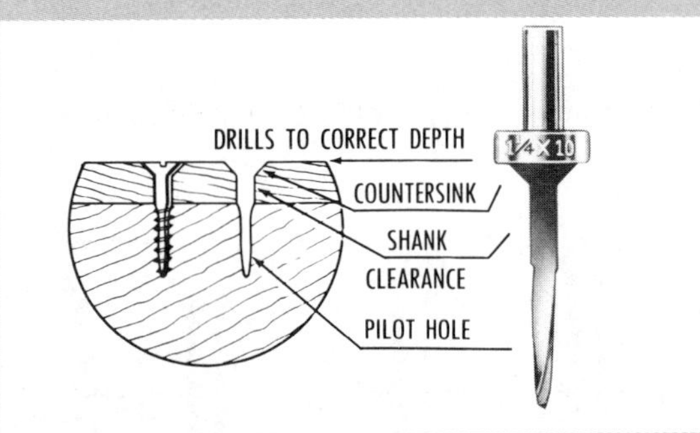

Figure 25-18
The Screw-Mate® drill and countersink. (The Stanley Works)

SCREW SIZES

3/4" x No. 6	1-1/2" x No. 8	1-3/4" x No. 10
1" x No. 6	1-3/4" x No. 8	2" x No. 10
3/4" x No. 8	1" x No. 10	1-1/2" x No. 12
1" x No. 8	1-1/4" x No. 10	2" x No. 12
1-1/4" x No. 8	1-1/2" x No. 10	1-1/2" x No. 14

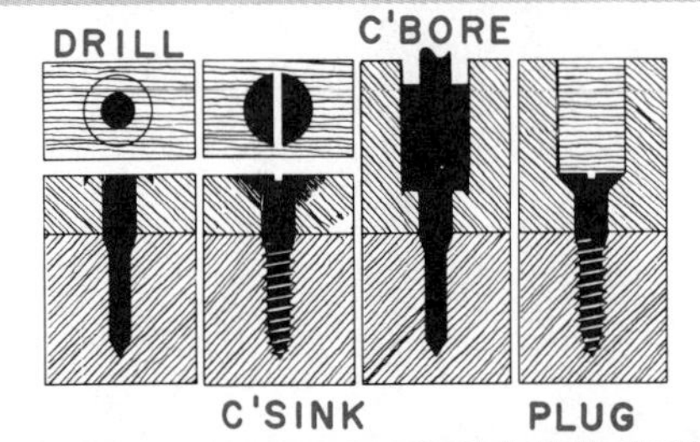

Figure 25-19
The Screw-Sink® drill can countersink and counterbore. (The Stanley Works)

from the same type of wood used for your project. Plugs should be about 3/8" (10 mm) deep. After installing the screw, apply glue to the plug and push it into the hole. The grain of the plug should be similar to the surrounding wood. Align the grain of the plug with the grain of the surrounding piece. Place the plug so that it extends slightly above the surface of the wood. When the glue is dry, trim the plug so it is even with the surface.

Wood buttons are manufactured in many sizes. The most common sizes are for 3/8" and 1/2" holes. Buttons also are available in various woods. Oak, birch, maple, walnut and mahogany buttons are common.

The recess into which the screw head is placed is called a counterbore. Make the counterbore before drilling the shank hole. To counterbore, use a large-diameter twist drill or an auger bit, Figure 25-17. See Unit 13 for information on types of drill bits.

If you need to countersink a large number of holes, use a special drill bit called the Screw-Mate®. It drills the pilot hole and shank hole and countersinks in one operation, Figure 25-18. You can counterbore many holes quickly with a Screw-Sink® drill bit. It drills the pilot and shank holes and counterbores in one operation. It also can countersink, Figure 25-19. Screw-Mate® and Screw-Sink® bits are available for many screw lengths and diameters. The bits have round shanks for use in hand or electric drills.

SCREWDRIVERS

There are many kinds of screwdrivers. Each type has a different tip. The most common tips are cabinet, standard, clutch head and Phillips, Figure 25-20. Specify cabinet and standard screwdrivers by giving the length of the blade from the tip to the handle. Common sizes include 3", 4", 6", 8" and 10". The width of the tip is related to the length of the blade. Phillips screwdrivers specify the point size by numbers. The most frequently used point sizes are No. 0, 1, 2, 3 and 4. The 0 point is about 1/8" in diameter. The No. 4 point is 3/8" in diameter. Other types used for driving special fasteners include the Pozidriv® and Robertson tips.

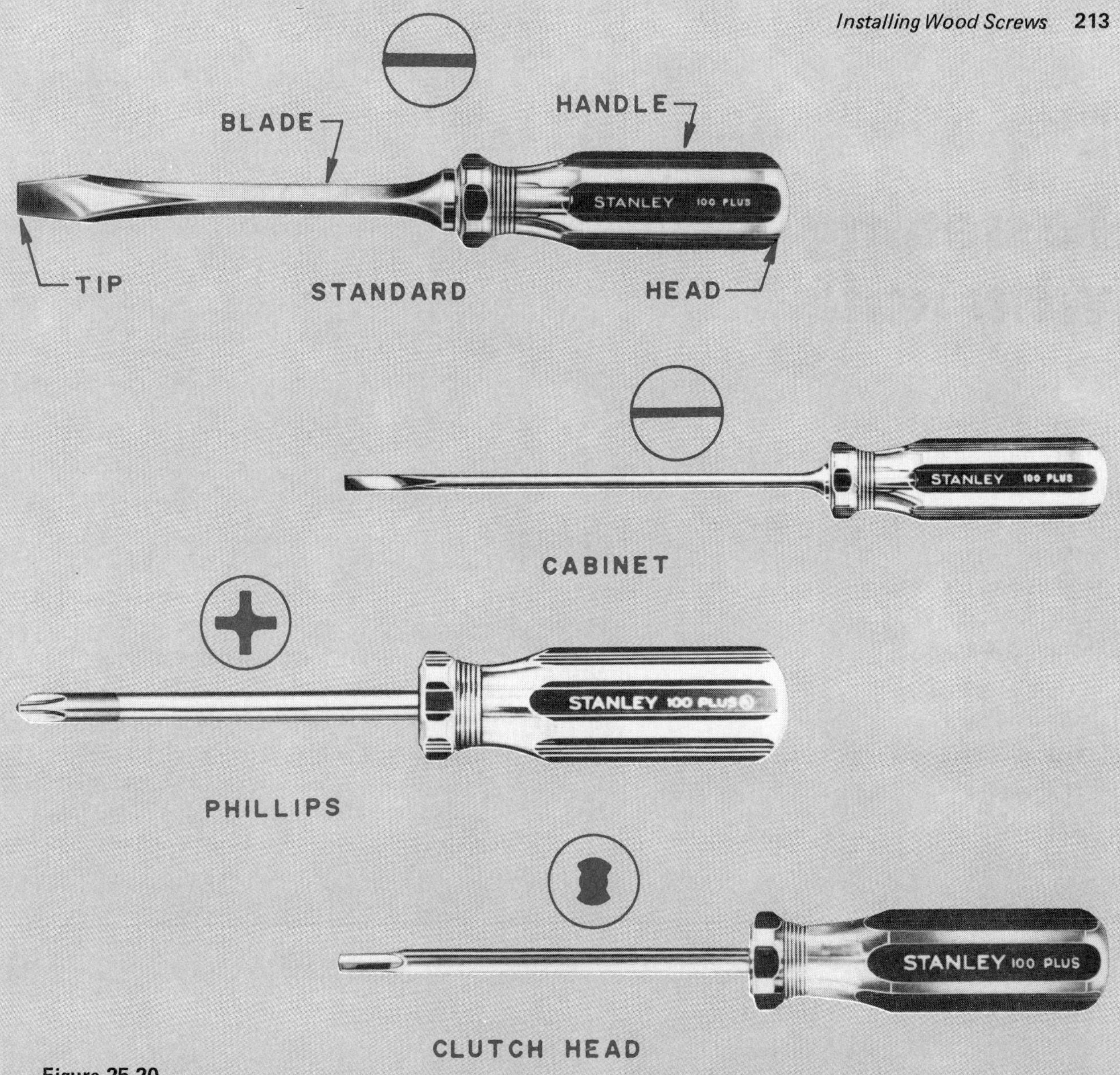

Figure 25-20
Some common types of screwdrivers. (The Stanley Works)

REVIEW QUESTIONS

1. Why are shank and pilot holes drilled before installing a screw?
2. What is the recommended diameter of the pilot hole?
3. Why are flat head screws countersunk?
4. How deep should an oval head screw be countersunk?
5. How does a screwdriver bit differ from a screwdriver?
6. How does the blade of a ratchet screwdriver rotate?
7. What can you do to help a screw drive more easily in hardwood?
8. How can you hide a screw head?
9. How does a counterbore differ from a countersink?
10. What are some common sizes of screwdrivers?

SUGGESTED ACTIVITIES

1. Using scrap stock, practice installing wood screws.
2. Practice making setting screws in counterbores and countersinks.

UNIT

26

Fastening with Nails

Objectives

After studying this unit you should be able to:

1 Identify tools used to drive and pull nails.

2 Drive and set nails.

Technical Terms

Claw hammer
Ripping claw
Hammer face
Nail set
Knurled
Toenailing

There are many types of nails available. Each serves a particular purpose. Unit 23 described different kinds of nails and some of their uses.

Nailing is one of the easiest and fastest ways to join wood together. However, nailed joints are not as strong as those that are fastened with glue or screws.

NAILING TOOLS

The *claw hammer* is available with ripping and curved claws, Figure 26-1. Use the curved claw for most general work. It is best for pulling nails. The *ripping claw* is designed to pry apart pieces of wood that have been nailed together. Carpenters frequently use it.

The *hammer face* can be either flat or slightly convex (curved outward). The convex face permits you to drive a nail near the surface of the wood with less chance of leaving hammer marks on the surface.

Hammers have wood, fiberglass and steel handles. The heads are made of high-quality steel. Common weights of curved claw hammers are 7, 13, 16 and 20 oz. Ripping hammers usually weigh from 22 to 28 oz. Most hammers are 13″ to 16″ long.

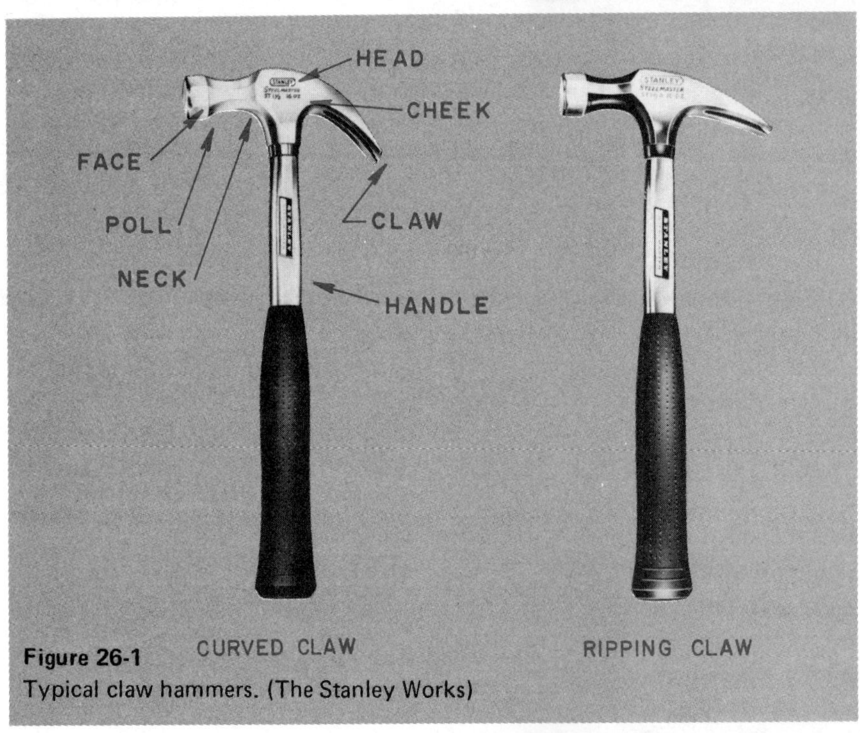

Figure 26-1
Typical claw hammers. (The Stanley Works)

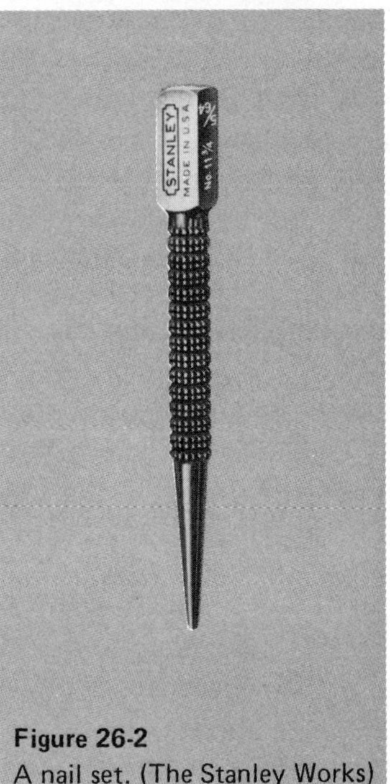

Figure 26-2
A nail set. (The Stanley Works)

The *nail set* sinks the heads of nails below the surface of the wood. It has a cupped end that helps keep it from slipping off the nail. The common diameters of points are 1/32", 1/16", 3/32", 1/8" and 5/32". The body is *knurled* (grooved) to keep it from slipping when being used, Figure 26-2.

DRIVING NAILS

Select the proper size hammer. For most cabinet and carpentry work, use a 13 oz. curved claw hammer. Use the 7 oz. hammer for driving brads.

Hold the nail in one hand. Place the point at the spot where the nail is to be driven. Strike the head of the nail a few short, easy blows to set the nail in the wood, Figure 26-3. This is a wrist movement, Figure 26-4. Let go of the nail and finish driving it into the wood. Use full strokes. Learn to swing the hammer using the arm from the elbow. The elbow serves as a hinge. Hold the hammer at the end of the handle. As the hammer approaches the nail the wrist bends slightly. Swing with easy, steady strokes. Keep the hand holding the hammer on a level with the head of the nail being driven. A series of sharp taps usually is better than very heavy blows.

When nailing wood of different thicknesses, always nail the thin piece of wood to the thicker piece. Do not nail into knots or other defects. If the nail follows the grain, remove it and put it somewhere else or drill a hole.

If a casing or finishing nail is being used, the head usually is set below the surface, Figure 26-5. Stop driving the nail when the head is almost flush with the surface. Place a nail set on the head, Figure 26-6. Strike the nail set with the hammer. Use a wrist movement. The tip of the

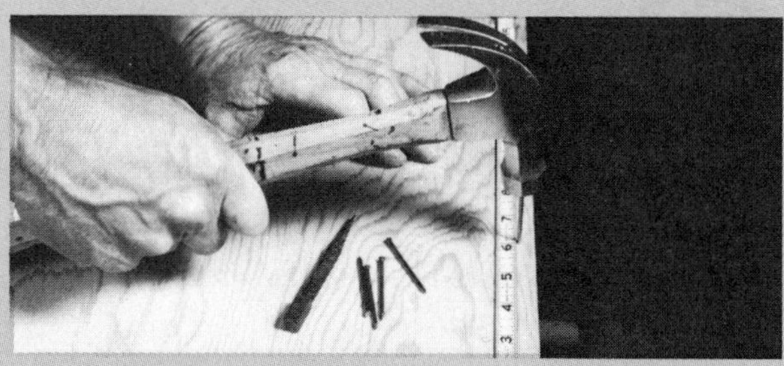

Figure 26-3
Strike the nail solidly but not too hard. (American Plywood Association)

Figure 26-4
Drive the nail with a full, even stroke.

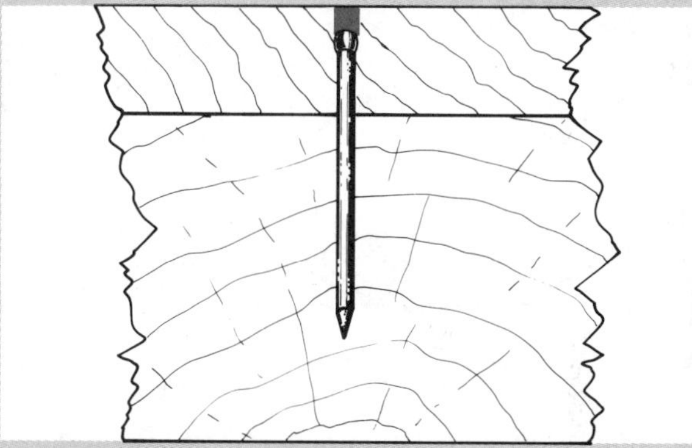

Figure 26-5
Finishing and casing nails usually are set below the surface and covered with a filler.

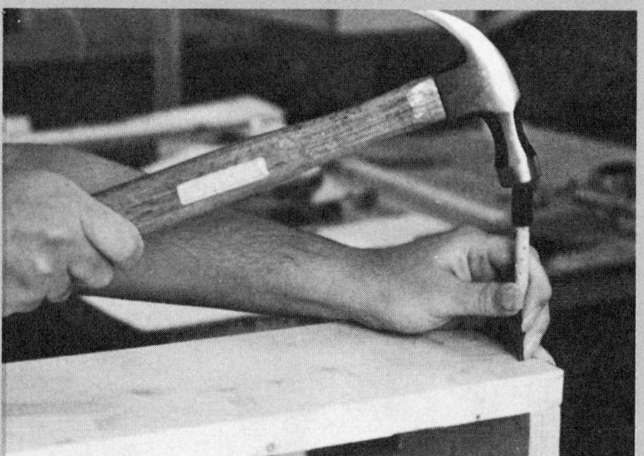

Figure 26-6
Setting a finishing nail using a nail set.

Figure 26-7
Drill holes to prevent nails close to the edge of a board from splitting the wood. (American Plywood Association)

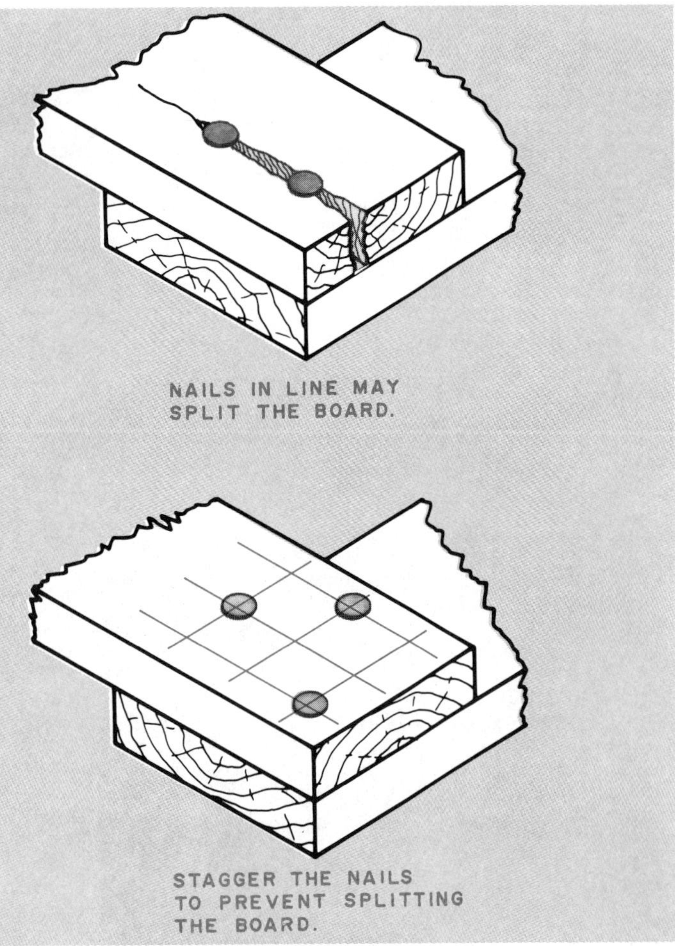

NAILS IN LINE MAY
SPLIT THE BOARD.
STAGGER THE NAILS
TO PREVENT SPLITTING
THE BOARD.

Figure 26-8
Stagger the nails to help avoid splitting the board.

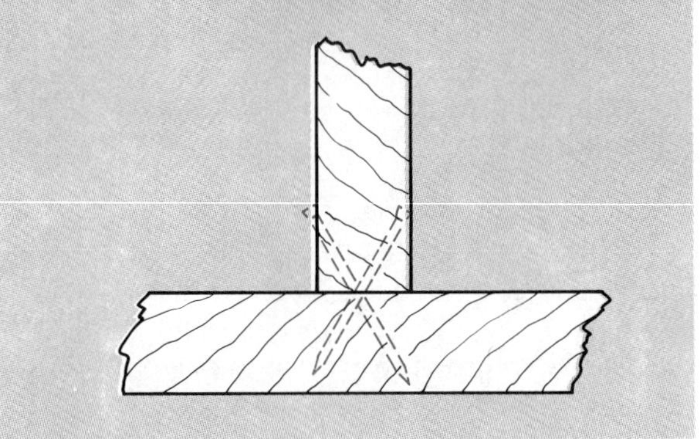

Figure 26-9
Toenailing butt joints helps increase the strength of the joint.

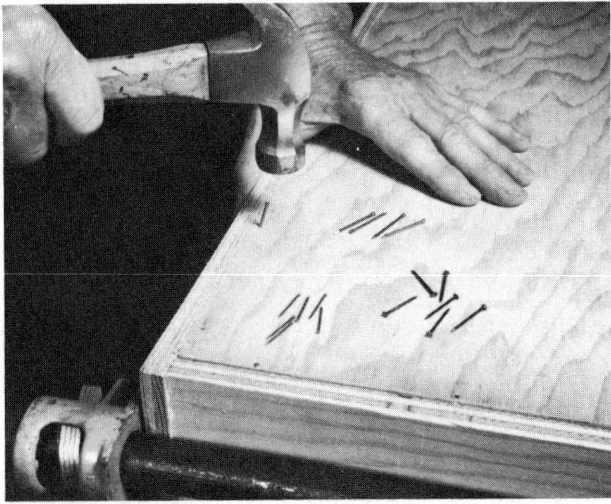

Figure 26-10
A cabinet back is face nailed to the sides. (American Plywood Association)

nail set should be slightly smaller than the diameter of the head of the nail.

Fill the nail hole with a wood filler.

PLACING NAILS

Under most conditions nails should be placed at least 3/4" (19 mm) from the edge of the board. If they are closer, the wood is likely to split. Holes close to the edge can be predrilled. The hole should be slightly smaller than the diameter of the nail, Figure 26-7.

If you have to nail where the wood may split, consider using a nail with a smaller diameter. A box nail can substitute for a common nail. Little holding power is lost. A shorter, thinner finishing nail will give more holding power than a larger one that splits the wood.

When placing nails, stagger the nailing pattern. Do not line up two nails along the grain. They will be likely to split the wood, Figure 26-8.

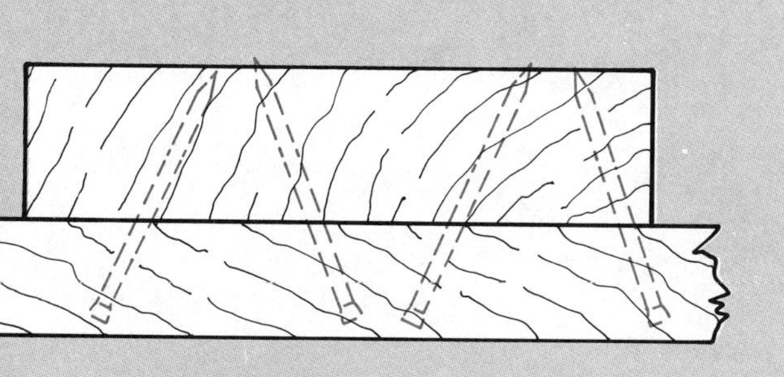

Figure 26-11
Increase holding power by slanting the nails in opposite directions.

Splitting can be reduced by blunting the point of the nail. Either strike the point with a hammer or cut it off.

Toenailing helps increase the holding power of a nail, Figure 26-9. Drive the nails at an angle of 30° from the vertical. Stagger them from each side so they do not hit each other.

Most nailing is face nailing. Drive the nail into the work at a right angle, Figure 26-10. You can increase holding power by alternately slanting the nails, Figure 26-11.

Use staples much as you use nails. The unit in Figure 26-12 is fastening a plywood back on a cabinet. The staple is driven by striking the stapler head with a rubber mallet.

Clinching nails can increase holding power. Drive the nails through both pieces of wood. Bend over the ends that are sticking through, so that they are at a 90° angle to the grain of the wood. A single bend provides extra strength. A double bend is even stronger. It also buries the sharp point, which could be harmful, Figure 26-13. Pliers help form the first bend of a double bend clinch.

PULLING NAILS

If a nail bends it is best to remove it, instead of trying to straighten it. It may not drive straight after it has been bent.

Use a curved claw hammer to pull a nail. Slip the claws under the head of the nail. Place a piece of wood or metal on the surface next to the nail. Pull back on the hammer handle, and let the head press on the wood or metal scrap,

Figure 26-12
Staples serve the same purpose as face-driven nails. (American Plywood Association)

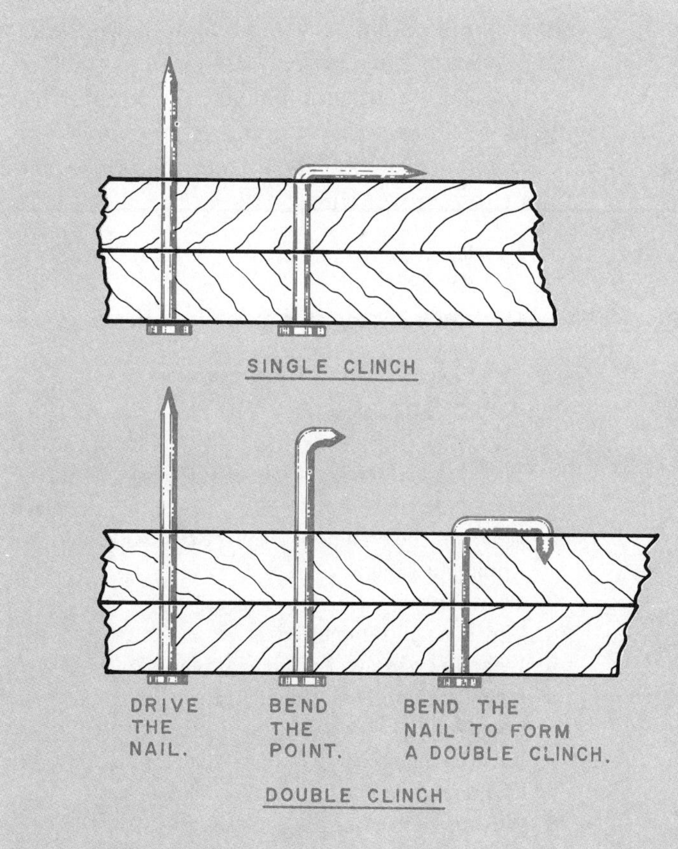
SINGLE CLINCH
DRIVE THE NAIL.
BEND THE POINT.
BEND THE NAIL TO FORM A DOUBLE CLINCH.
DOUBLE CLINCH

Figure 26-13
Clinching nails greatly increases their holding power.

Figure 26-14. This will reduce surface marring. You can pull the nail with less effort if the pressure is on the end of the hammer handle.

The nail may pull out far enough so that leverage is lost. Then place a thick block of wood under the head of the hammer. This gives new leverage. It also reduces the possibility of breaking the hammer handle. Pull back on the handle to continue pulling the nail, Figure 26-15.

Figure 26-14
Place a thin piece of wood or metal under the head of the hammer to prevent damage to the surface of the wood.

RELATED FACTORS

When you use nails for fastening, keep the following points in mind.

Nails hold better in face grain than in end grain.

The longer the nail, the greater the holding power.

The larger the diameter of the nail, the greater the holding power.

The surface of the nail influences holding power. Galvanized nails, cement coated nails and nails grooved in either a spiral or a ring pattern have more holding power than smooth nails.

A dense wood, such as oak, has greater holding power than softer wood, such as pine.

Nails in dry wood have greater holding power than those in wet wood.

Figure 26-15
To increase the leverage when pulling a nail, use a large block of wood under the head of the hammer.

REVIEW QUESTIONS

1 What is the difference between ripping and curved claws?
2 What are the common weights of curved claw and ripping hammers?
3 What job is done with a nail set?
4 Why is a nail set knurled?
5 What size hammer is used to drive brads?
6 How far should nails be placed from the edge of a board?
7 What is done to keep nails driven close to the edge of a board from splitting it?
8 Why are nails placed in a staggered pattern?
9 What can you do to a nail to reduce the chance of splitting a board?
10 What is meant by toenailing?
11 Why are nails sometimes clinched?
12 What can you do to protect the surface of the board when pulling a nail?
13 When pulling a nail, what can be done to get more leverage?

SUGGESTED ACTIVITIES

Using scrap stock, perform the following nailing operations.

1 Face nail and clinch.
2 Face nail and double clinch. Use four nails.
3 Nail a 3/4" (19 mm) piece to a 2" (51 mm) piece. Use four nails.
4 Drive a 6d nail halfway into 2" (51 mm) stock. Try to remove the nail.
5 Drive a 4d finishing nail into 2" (51 mm) stock. Set it below the surface.

UNIT

27

Glues, Adhesives and Cements

Objectives

After studying this unit you should be able to:

1 Describe the importance of mechanical and specific adhesion.
2 List the major types of bonding agents and the advantages of each.
3 Explain the proper procedure for edge-gluing panels.
4 Use technical terms as they pertain to bonding agents.

Technical Terms

Bonding agent
Glue
Adhesive
Cement
Mechanical adhesion
Specific adhesion
Hot animal glue
Chilled joint
Liquid hyde glue
Casein glue
Blood albumin
Thermoplastic
Polyvinyl
Aliphatic resin
Alpha cyanoacrylate
Hot melt
Thermoset
Urea-formaldehyde
Resorcinol-formaldehyde
Phenol-formaldehyde
Melamine-formaldehyde
Epoxy
Contact cement
Mastic
Edge-to-edge glue joint
Skinning over
Starved joint
High-frequency radio energy

Glues, adhesives and cements are *bonding agents.* They hold wood joints together. *Glues* are made from natural materials. *Adhesives* are synthetic materials. *Cements* are rubber-based.

Sometimes, bonding agents are used with mechanical fasteners, such as screws, nails and staples. The primary purpose of a mechanical fastener is to hold a joint together long enough for the bonding agent to dry, Figure 27-1. After curing, the bonding agent becomes the major holding device for the joint. Because glues, adhesives and cements have a high holding power, few mechanical fasteners are required.

DEVELOPMENT OF THE GLUE LINE

A glue line develops when a bonding agent is spread on a surface and then comes into contact with another surface. This causes the bonding agent to enter the wood pores and harden. This is called *mechanical adhesion.* Mechanical adhesion is not the only bonding force in a glue line. Materials also are bonded by specific adhesion.

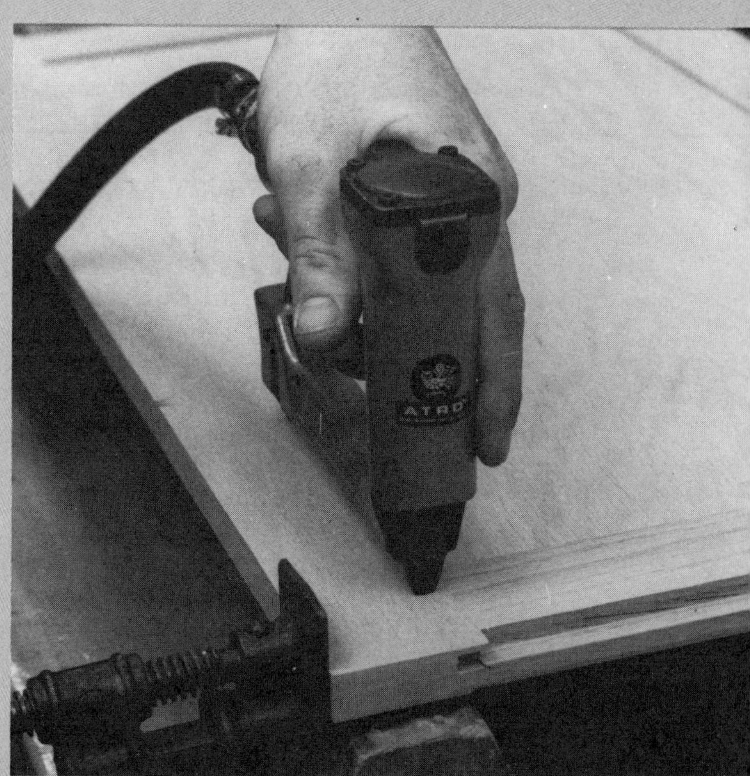

Figure 27-1
An air stapler shoots staples to help hold a joint together until the bonding agent dries.

Specific adhesion allows materials without any pores, such as glass, rubber and plastic, to be bonded. It works by the attraction of unlike electrical charges. Every material has electrical charges. The charges in the glue are attracted by positive (+) and negative (−) charges on the surface of the material. Bonding agents and wood thus are molecularly attracted to each other. Specific adhesion is the strongest holding force in a joint or a glue line. Face grain or edge grain must be present for specific adhesion to take place.

A miter is the weakest of all joints. This is due to little specific adhesion. A bonding agent can flow into the miter's hundreds of open-end grain pores to form mechanical adhesion. But because mechanical adhesion is a weak holding force, the miter can be broken easily. To strengthen this end-grain-to-end-grain joint, you should reinforce the joint. The face grain of a spline or a dowel can unite with the face grain of the mitered piece through specific adhesion. This makes the joint very strong.

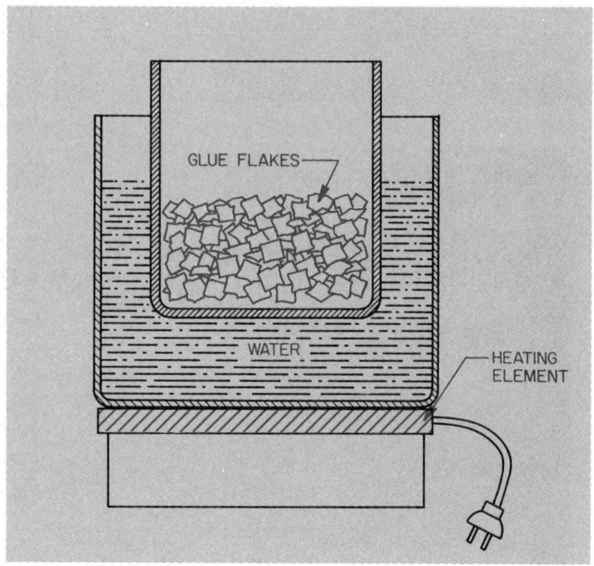

Figure 27-2
A glue pot is used to melt the solid animal glue.

Figure 27-3
Mix casein glue with water to a creamy consistency.

GLUES

Glues are made from animal and vegetable products. Glues used to be more popular than they are today. They mostly have been replaced by adhesives and cements, which have superior qualities.

1. *Hot animal glue* was once popular with furniture makers. It can still be purchased in the form of dry powder or flakes. The raw glue is placed in a heated glue pot where it is melted, Figure 27-2. Then the glue is applied to a surface and solidifies or hardens as it cools.

   Hot animal glue must be applied and assembled quickly. If allowed to cool before assembly, a chilled joint will occur. A *chilled joint* has low mechanical and specific adhesion and is very weak.
2. *Liquid hyde glue* is a newer form of animal glue. It is a ready-to-use liquid. The major advantage of liquid hyde glue is that it develops a dark glue line for darker-colored woods, such as walnut and cherry. Liquid hyde also is noted for its gap-filling qualities. It will fill small cracks and chips.
3. *Casein glue* is made from dried milk curds and is sold as a powder. It stains certain types of woods. A nonstaining type is available. Casein is mixed with water to form a thick cream, Figure 27-3. A small amount can be hand-mixed with a stirring stick in a plastic or glass container. Industry frequently uses a power mixer for larger quantities. Before it can be applied to the wood, the mixture must set for 15 minutes. This allows the necessary chemical action to occur in the casein.

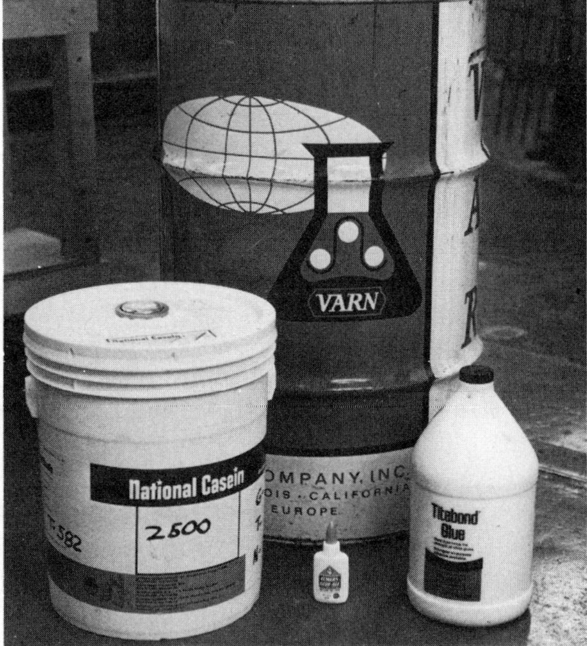

Figure 27-4
Polyvinyls are available in several different quantities.

Figure 27-5
Any bonding agent left on the surface or rubbed into the pores of the wood will prevent the stain from penetrating.

Casein glue is considered water-resistant. It can be used out-of-doors but should be kept under cover. The glue will weaken if exposed to a great deal of moisture. One major advantage of casein is that it can be applied at very cold temperatures. Casein will harden as long as the temperature is above freezing. The length of time it must be left in the clamps increases as the temperature gets colder. Being able to harden in cold temperatures makes casein desirable for construction work. A disadvantage is that casein dulls cutting tools quickly.

4. *Blood albumin, vegetable and fish glues* are also bonding agents. The blood albumin and vegetable glues are sometimes used to make interior plywood. Fish glues are used on packing tapes and for sealing shipping boxes.

ADHESIVES

Adhesives are the most popular bonding agents. Adhesives can be divided into thermoplastics and thermosets. Each division has its own properties.

Thermoplastics

Thermoplastics make up the largest division and are used most frequently with woods. Most thermoplastic adhesives are resistant to moisture. They should not be used, however, on projects that may be exposed to very wet conditions. Because all thermoplastic adhesives soften with heat, do not use them on lathe turnings. A sunken joint will develop when friction melts the glue during the sanding and polishing operation. There are four commonly used types of thermoplastics.

1. *Polyvinyl* adhesives usually are referred to as white glues. Because they are so popular, polyvinyls are available in many sizes. The do-it-yourself person may select a small squeeze bottle. Industry workers use large barrels, Figure 27-4.

   Polyvinyl adhesives have many advantages. They are premixed, ready to use and easy to apply. A minimum of 30 minutes clamping time is required. The glued-up stock should not be worked for 24 hours. After drying, the adhesive produces a colorless glue line. It then should be removed from the wood surface. Any leftover bonding agent on or in the wood will not allow the stain to penetrate, Figure 27-5. Polyvinyl adhesives cure by the loss of moisture. It is important that the wood being bonded has a moisture content between 6 and 12 percent. Any wood drier or wetter than this will have a very weak glue line.
2. *Aliphatic thermoplastic resin* is another form of polyvinyl resin. It is identified by its yellow color. It is superior to other polyvinyl resins because it is stronger, more heat resistant and not affected by lacquer finishes. Lacquers sometimes dissolve standard

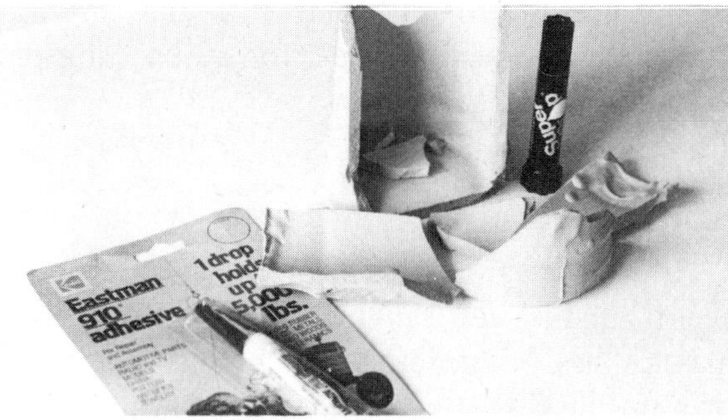

Figure 27-6
"Superglues" are used primarily on nonporous material, such as this piece of ceramic pottery.

Figure 27-7
Hot melts are available in several different shapes for gluing many materials.

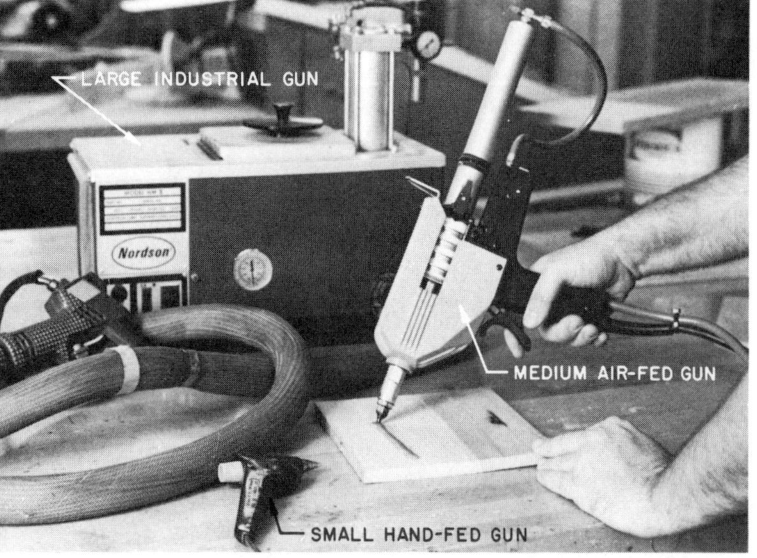

Figure 27-8
Hot melt applicators are available in many different models.

polyvinyls and cause a sunken joint. Aliphatic resin does not discolor the finish. Because of its advantages, most woodworkers prefer aliphatic over polyvinyl.

3. *Alpha cyanoacrylate* usually is called "superglue." Although it is a thermoplastic, it is not designed for porous materials. It works well with metals, certain plastics and other dense materials, Figure 27-6.

   Alpha cyanoacrylate is best known for its rapid drying time and extra-strong glue line. Full strength, however, is not reached for 24 hours. Do not get this adhesive on your skin. If you do, it will glue your skin to anything you touch. Use fingernail polish remover (acetone) or other recommended solvents to soften the adhesive.

4. *Hot melts* are relatively new to the wood field. They glue just about any type of material. Hot melts are sold in several solid forms, Figure 27-7. A different form is recommended for different plastics, particle board, softwoods and hardwoods.

   Hot melts first are heated with a special applicator. There are many applicator models, Figure 27-8. The applicators apply the bonding agent in a hot, molten form. Only one of the surfaces is glued. Once the hot melt is spread, the two pieces being glued should be brought together quickly. The adhesive may become chilled and not develop full mechanical and specific adhesion. Pressure can be applied with clamps, or the glue line can be handheld. Depending on the type of adhesive, pressure can be released after three seconds to three minutes. The very short clamp time is an advantage in using hot melts.

   Hot melts have several disadvantages. One is that a wide glue line usually develops. If the joint is exposed, the glue line will be very noticeable. Also, hot melts are not very strong. They are very poor for edge gluing. They are best, however, for applying an overlay or other pieces to furniture or cabinets.

Thermosets

Thermosets generally are more expensive but have several desirable qualities. Because there is a chemical reaction when they are mixed, they are resistant to water and do not soften when heated. Some thermosets are more resistant to moisture and heat than others. There are four common types of thermosets.

1. *Urea-formaldehyde* is purchased in a powdered form. Water changes the raw powder into a liquid and starts a chemical reaction. The clamp time is six hours. This time can be decreased by using either higher drying temperatures or radio-frequency glue-drying equipment. Although other adhesives can be used, urea-formaldehyde is recommended for this type of equipment. Urea-formaldehyde is more moisture resistant than polyvinyl. It is not waterproof. It has very poor gap-filling qualities. Glue joints must fit well because urea will not fill in any gaps.
2. *Resorcinol-formaldehydes* are expensive. They can be used in very harsh conditions. Most woodworkers select a resorcinol when a waterproof glue line is needed, Figure 27-9. A wooden boat may be glued strongly together with this adhesive.

   Resorcinols are purchased in two containers. A liquid resin is in one container. A catalyst is in the other. After the two substances are measured, they must be stirred. Any resorcinol placed on the surface of a board will stain the wood a dark reddish-brown. The excess can be scraped off, but a dark glue line will remain. As with urea-formaldehyde, a long clamp time is recommended.
3. *Phenol- and Melamine-formaldehyde* are used only in industry. Phenol resin is used for making exterior plywood. Melamine is added to other adhesives to improve overall properties, Figure 27-10. Because it is very expensive, melamine rarely is used by itself.
4. *Epoxy* usually is not used with woods. As with resorcinol, the epoxy resin and catalyst are packaged separately and need to be mixed together, Figure 27-11. Although it produces one of the strongest glue joints, epoxy is too costly for most common applications. Some furniture refinishers use epoxy for regluing wooden joints that have been saturated with hardened glue.

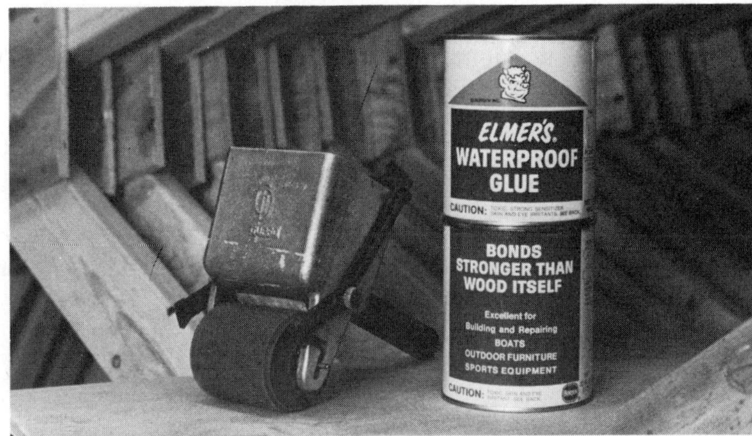

Figure 27-9
Resorcinol is an excellent adhesive for an out-of-doors application, such as these roof trusses.

Figure 27-10
Melamines are sometimes used with urea and sawdust to make molded wood-flour products.

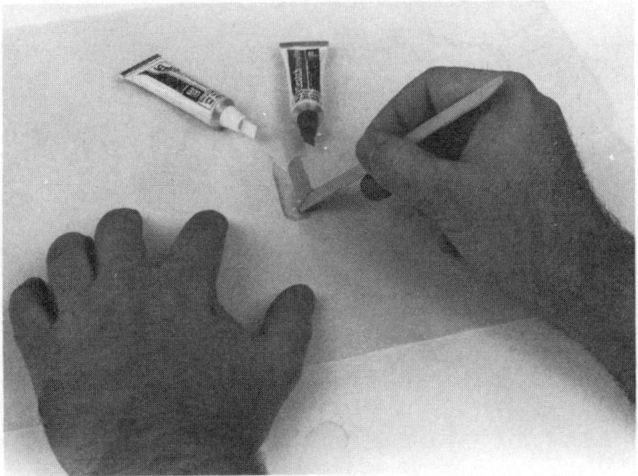

Figure 27-11
Epoxy should be thoroughly mixed on a piece of wax paper.

CEMENTS

Cements usually are made of rubber suspended in a liquid. Most types are either flammable or nonflammable mixtures. Nonflammable varieties will not start a fire and are recommended for home and school use.

1. *Contact cement* is the most common type of cement used with wood. It glues down veneer, plastic laminates and other surface decorations. The cement is applied to both surfaces of the glue joint, Figure 27-12.

Figure 27-12
Contact cement is applied to both the plastic laminate and the particle board.

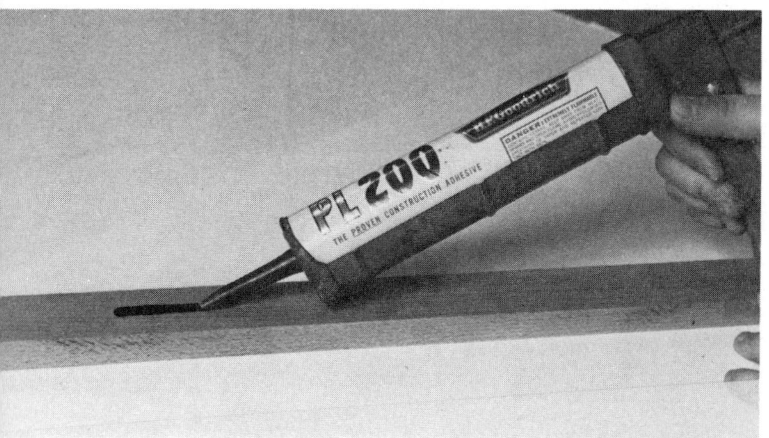

Figure 27-13
Mastics are applied with a caulking gun.

Surfaces that have been glued with contact cement should not be allowed to touch until the cement is completely dried. When the two pieces are brought together, they stick immediately. Neither piece can be easily moved or shifted afterwards.

2. A *mastic* is a very thick contact cement used in building construction. This bonding agent may be applied with a calking gun, Figure 27-13. Many contractors use mastics to glue plywood sheathing and subflooring to joists. This makes an extra strong building.

GLUING PROCEDURE

Solid lumber is glued edge to edge to make panels. Panels are used for the top, sides and other parts of furniture. Pieces are also glued edge to face, end to edge and in other combinations when being assembled for projects. Refer to Unit 14 for additional information on clamping tools and assembly procedures.

Edge-to-Edge Gluing

An *edge-to-edge joint* is the most common type of glue joint. Many of the same gluing techniques also can be applied for other glue joints. The proper procedure is as follows.

1. Select the material to be glued. One face should be jointed smooth while the opposite surface may be planed and still have some rough places. The stock should be left as thick as possible.

   When gluing panels of solid stock, pieces should be no wider than 4" (102 mm). Stock wider than this will cup. Cupping is a warping of the board. Ripping a wide board into narrow strips and then regluing them will reduce this problem.

   The edges to be glued must be straight and true. Generally, the edge is run over a jointer to achieve this smooth surface. A fine saw cut edge also will work. Many experts feel that a dull jointer or any action causing a machine burn will greatly weaken the joint. Whichever method is used, there should be no space along the entire glue line when the edges of the two boards are brought together.

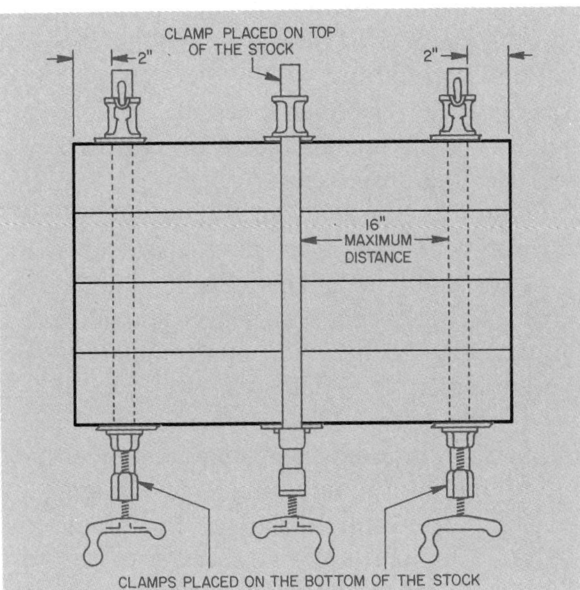

Figure 27-14
Clamps must be positioned properly to develop a strong glue line.

2. Select the clamps needed to apply pressure to the stock. Start by setting up the clamps to be placed on the bottom side of the panel. The maximum distance between the clamps should be 16″ (406 mm). A clamp also must be placed within the first 2 inches (51 mm) of each end of the panel, Figure 27-14.
3. Move the adjustable jaws of the bar clamps so that the boards can be laid on the clamps. The grain of each strip of wood should be running in the same direction. The end grain of every other board must be reversed, Figure 27-15. This prevents the panel from cupping.
4. Turn all boards except one on their edges. Run a bead of glue on each edge that is standing up. Then spread the glue so that the entire surface is covered. Use either your finger or a glue brush, Figure 27-16. Industry frequently uses a glue spreader. The entire surface must be covered.

   Only one surface of the glue joint is coated with the bonding agent. Coating one edge will produce a stronger glue joint than if both edges are coated. Applying adhesive on both surfaces does not allow specific adhesion to take place fully.

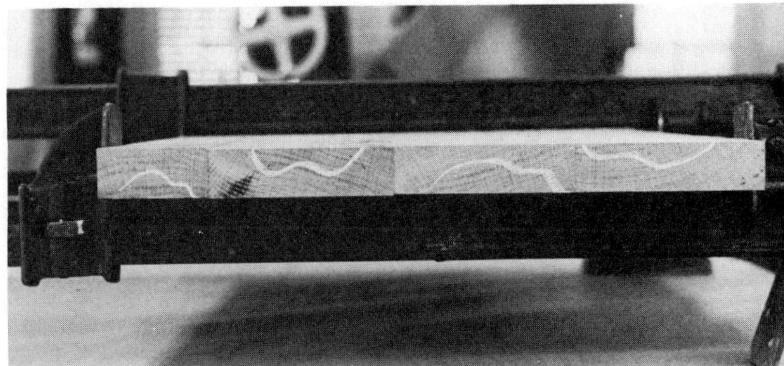

Figure 27-15
The reversed end grain is marked with a piece of chalk for easy identification.

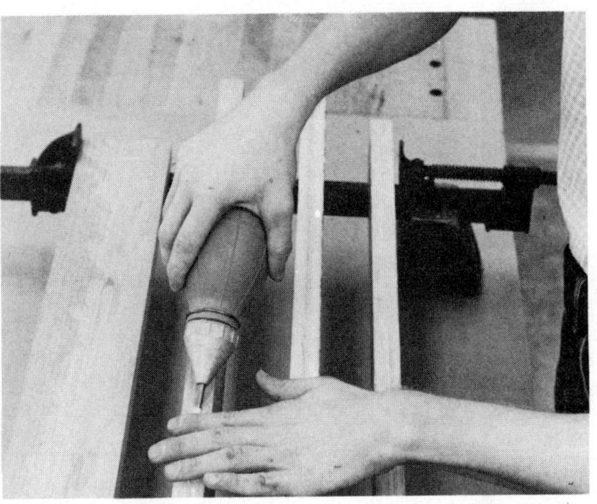

Figure 27-16
Applying glue and spreading it over the entire surface.

5. Let the boards set for the recommended open time. Each glue and adhesive has a recommended open time. This is the period of time from the application of glue to the stock until the boards are brought together. Open time must be as short as possible. A long open time will cause the bonding agent to skin over. *Skinning over* happens when the top surface of the exposed glue starts to dry. Skinning over reduces the mechanical and specific adhesion.
6. Bring the boards back together. The time after the boards are together and before clamps are applied is called closed time. Some adhesives require a longer closed time than others. Dense wood, such as hard maple, will develop a stronger joint if a longer

Figure 27-17
Boards must be pushed against the bar clamps as pressure is applied.

Figure 27-18
C clamps will help hold the panel flat.

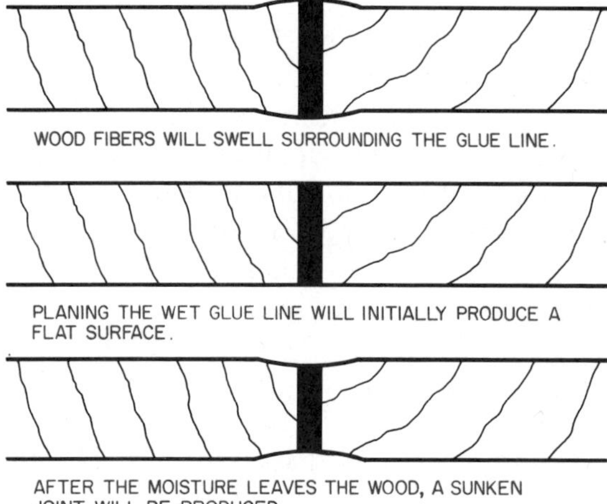

WOOD FIBERS WILL SWELL SURROUNDING THE GLUE LINE.
PLANING THE WET GLUE LINE WILL INITIALLY PRODUCE A FLAT SURFACE.
AFTER THE MOISTURE LEAVES THE WOOD, A SUNKEN JOINT WILL BE PRODUCED.

Figure 27-19
A sunken joint is caused when the boards are planed before the glue has completely cured.

closed time is used. Improper closed time will produce a *starved joint.* The glue will be squeezed out of the glue line before it can enter the opposite surface.

7. Start applying light pressure with clamps after the proper closed time has passed. Begin on the far end and slightly tighten each clamp as you come to it. Push down on each glue joint as the pressure is applied. If many boards are being glued, you may need someone to help you apply pressure. The boards must be flat against the bars of the clamps, Figure 27-17.
8. Place additional clamps on the top surface of the board. Applying pressure only on the bottom side of the panel will cause the stock to cup upward. Clamps on the top surface will pull in the opposite direction of the bottom clamps and balance the pulling force.
9. Go back and place additional pressure with the clamps. Too much pressure will squeeze the glue out and create a starved joint. The correct pressure generally is between 125 and 150 pounds per square inch. Most woodworkers can apply this amount of pressure using only one hand to tighten the clamps.
10. You may also apply C clamps to the ends of the panel, Figure 27-18. When clamped to a straight piece of wood, the panel will be held perfectly flat. Wax paper should be used under the boards to keep the boards from sticking together.
11. Maintain clamp pressure for the recommended time. Taking the clamps off too early will greatly weaken the glue line. Mark the panel with the time and date of gluing. This will tell you when you can take the clamps off.

Do not attempt to plane a glued panel for at least 24 hours. Planing the board before this time will create a sunken joint. A sunken joint is caused by planing off the surrounding fibers of the glue joint while they are still swollen from the liquid glue, Figure 27-19. When the moisture from the glue has evaporated from the wood, the panel will have a groove formed on each side of the glue line.

CABINET ASSEMBLY

Cabinets that are glued together require a few additional steps. Always assemble the piece first without any glue. This is called dry assembly. Check for proper fit and make any needed corrections. Because there are many parts, have an assistant help with the work. Tops, bottoms and other parts usually are dadoed into the sides. Apply the selected bonding agent to all dados and assemble. As the bar clamps are being applied, place a straight scrap board across the entire width of the side, Figure 27-20. This will aid in pulling in the dado when pressure is applied. The clamps should be parallel with the member they are clamping. If pressure is applied at an angle, the case will be pulled out of square. Always check for squareness before the glue has set.

Figure 27-20
A properly assembled case. Note the straight boards applied between the clamps.

TIPS FOR GLUING

Here are some good tips to follow when gluing:

1. Stock should be glued and clamped as soon as possible after it has been cut and surfaced. Newly released stresses within sawn boards will cause them to warp as they are being stored.
2. The fit of a joint is quite important. Too tight a fit on a mortise and tenon or a dowel joint will cause a starved joint. If the fit is too loose, the adhesive will not bridge the space between the pieces. The joint should be cut so that the pieces will slide together with slight hand pressure. If a mallet must be used to drive the joint together or if the joint falls apart when picked up, the fit is not good.
3. Instructions come with the bonding agent. Read them carefully. Usually, instructions are printed on the container. Open, closed and clamping times are given. Suggested temperature ranges also are given. If this information is not available, the glue or adhesive manufacturer can provide it.
4. The surface to be glued must be kept clean. Any material such as grease, wax or dried glue will have a poor effect on the joint. Handle the boards as little as possible and keep the machine tops clean.
5. Adhesives that contain pigments are available. Although all glue that remains on the surface should be removed, colored pigments may allow any leftover adhesive to blend into the finish. Industry often uses this technique for production reasons.

   Fluorescent dyes also are added to bonding agents to cause the adhesives to glow when exposed to black light. After they are marked with chalk under the black light, bring the glued piece back into natural light. Then you can easily sand it off.
6. Wood should stay at least 48 hours in the laboratory before it is machined and glued together. Stock will change dimensions and possibly warp as temperatures change. If glued too soon, a panel may come apart and warp.

PORTABLE ELECTRONIC GLUE WELDER

Sometimes glued stock cannot remain in the clamps for long. Most conventional glues and adhesives should have clamp pressure applied for approximately 24 hours. If several pieces need to be glued, they will require many clamps.

The ideal solution to short clamping time is the use of an electronic glue welder. With this machine, one set of clamps can provide enough holding force. Glued-up assemblies can be turned out in as short a time as one minute.

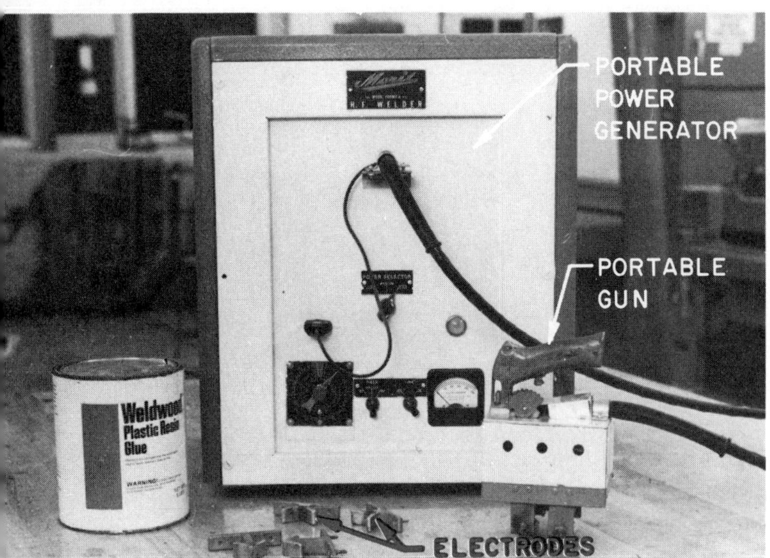

Figure 27-21
The electronic glue welder consists of a power generator, portable gun and various sets of electrodes.

The glue welder is a generator inside a cabinet that contains all necessary electronics and a portable gun for directing *high-frequency radio energy,* Figure 27-21. Different-sized units can glue different thicknesses of material. The larger the welder, the thicker the stock it can glue.

The welder works by generating a short-length high-frequency radio signal like that of a ham radio set or a citizens band. The frequency usually ranges from 3 to 27 megacycles. This means that the direction of the signal is reversed 3 to 27 million times per second.

Although different bonding agents can be used, urea-formaldehyde is used more than 90 percent of the time. This thermoset adhesive responds well to dielectric heating. Standard polyvinyls can be applied but will not develop their maximum holding strengths. Animal glues and caseins should not be used.

The purpose of the welder is to bring concen-

Straight electrodes are used for flat panels.

Inverted electrodes are used for inside corners.

Outside electrodes are used for exposed corners.

Figure 27-22
Select the electrode shape that will best match the glue line.

trated radio-frequency energy to the glue line. This energy excites the adhesive molecules and heats the bonding agent to its polymerizing temperature. This is about 200° F (93° C) for most adhesives. Heating the glue line cures the adhesive almost instantaneously. Although most assemblies can be immediately machined, full strength will not develop for 12 to 24 hours.

To operate the glue welder, apply the adhesive to the stock and clamp the boards together. Select the electrode that best fits the shape of stock being glued, Figure 27-22. The flat electrodes are used for edge-to-edge gluing. Angle electrodes are available for corner work.

After the machine has been turned on, apply the electrodes so that they lay across the glue line. Pull the trigger on the gun and hold it in for 3 to 5 seconds. The length of time will be determined by trial and error. Keep the gun in place until the adhesive stops boiling. Most welders have a tuner on the gun to magnify the energy. After you pull the trigger, move the tuner to the right or left to achieve maximum power. This can be determined by watching the power meter on the machine cabinet. Relocate the gun 3" to 6" (76 to 152 mm) down the glue line and repeat the process. The entire length of the glue line must be covered.

Safety is a must when operating the welder. Do not pull the trigger unless the electrodes are against the stock. You should not hold the stock with your hands while using the welder because an electrical short can develop. Do not touch the metal bar clamps while operating the gun.

REVIEW QUESTIONS

1 Define *mechanical* and *specific adhesion.*
2 What is used to heat hot animal glue?
3 List one major advantage of liquid hyde glue.
4 Why should casein glue be allowed to set for 15 minutes after it has been mixed?
5 Why is casein glue considered good for construction work?
6 Interior plywood is sometimes bonded with what type of glue?
7 When should thermoplastic adhesives not be used?
8 What is a sunken joint and why does it occur?
9 Polyvinyls often are known by what other name?
10 Aliphatic resin can be identified by what color?
11 What will happen if alpha cyanoacrylate gets on your skin?
12 Are hot melts known for their high holding-strengths?
13 The chemical reaction developed by thermoset adhesives gives them what two desirable qualities?
14 Which bonding agent is recommended for use with radio-frequency glue-drying equipment?
15 If a waterproof glue is required, what adhesive is most likely to be selected?
16 Which adhesive is used for making exterior plywood?
17 Why are epoxies rarely picked for gluing woodworking projects?
18 Is flammable or nonflammable cement recommended for home and school use?
19 How are most mastics applied?
20 What is the widest board that should be used in gluing up a solid panel?
21 Sketch the top view of a panel that is 18" (46 mm) wide by 36" (91 mm) long. Next indicate the spacing and the location of the necessary clamps.
22 Why should the bonding agent be applied to only one surface of a glue joint?
23 Define a starved joint.
24 How does a glue welder cure a glue line?
25 What should you keep your hands away from when you use a glue welder?
26 Make a list of all the bonding agents in this unit. List several advantages and applications of each.

SUGGESTED ACTIVITIES

1 Select a piece of furniture at home and sketch how the various pieces probably were clamped together during assembly.
2 Go to a local lumberyard or hardware store and list all the different bonding agents you can find. Indicate the brand name and type of bonding agent.
3 Glue two pieces of wood together edge to edge. Next glue another two end grain to end grain. Try breaking each over the corner of a workbench. Which is stronger? Why?

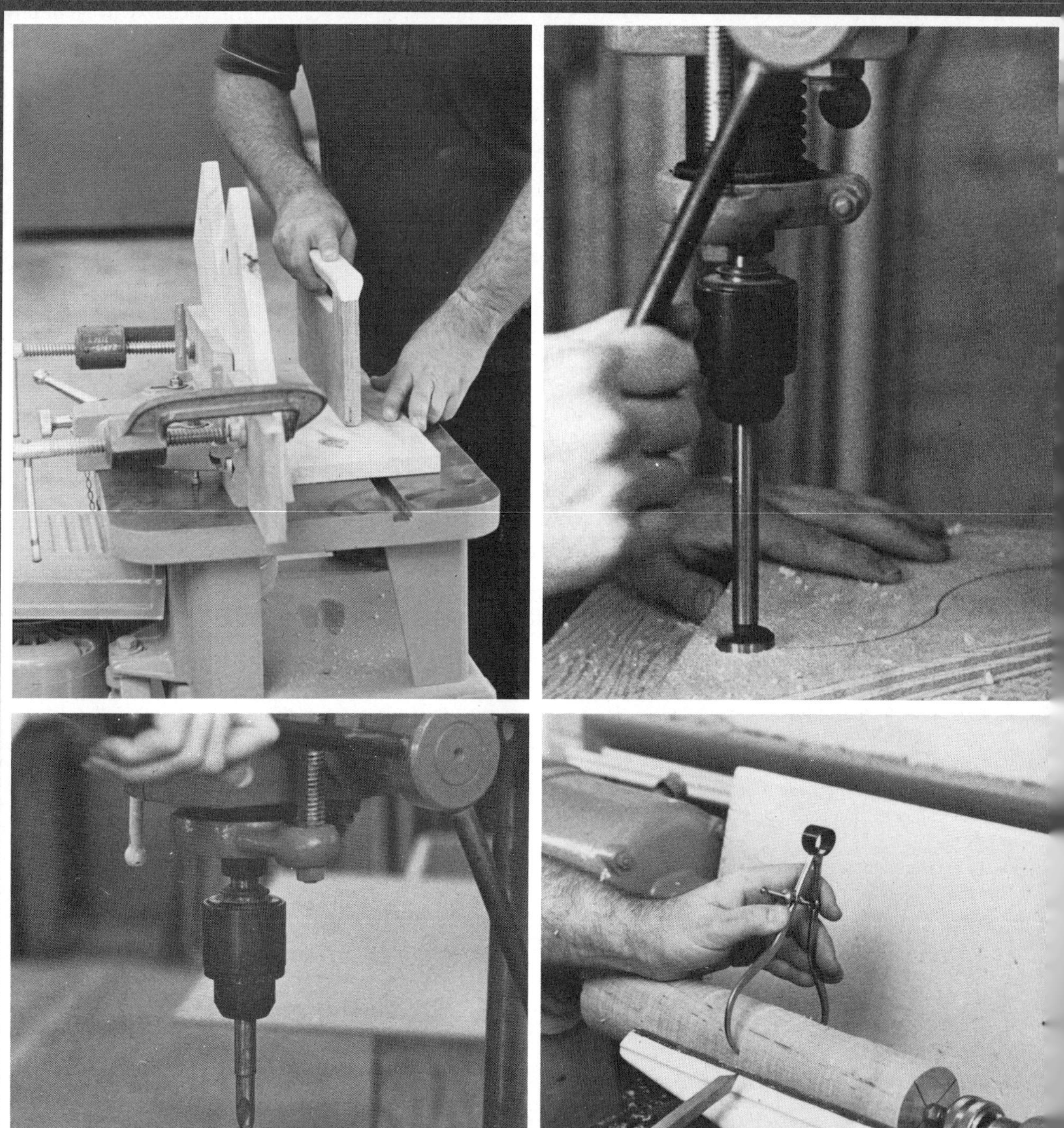

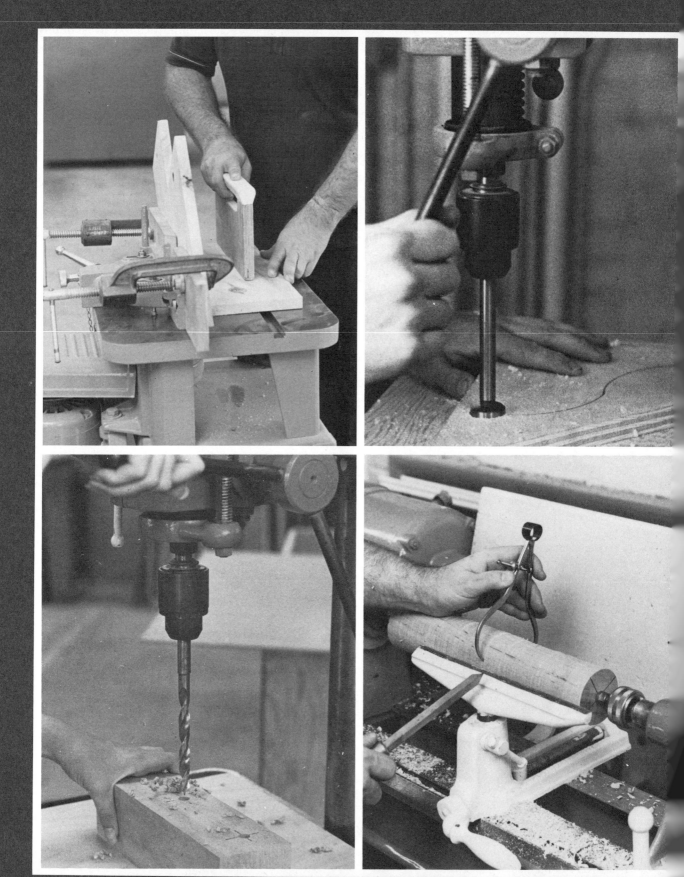

SECTION

4

Stationary Power Tools

28
Table Saws

29
Scroll Saws

30
Band Saws

31
Radial Arm Saws

32
Jointers

33
Planers

34
Shapers

35
Wood Lathes

36
Mortisers and Tenoners

37
Drill Presses

38
Stationary Sanding Machines

Stationary power tools greatly reduce the amount of labor needed to make wood projects. Stationary power tools are becoming very popular, especially in the woods industry. Although they are expensive, they are more accurate and faster than hand tools.

You must consider safety first when you use any power equipment. Because machines cut so rapidly, you must follow safety rules exactly. Placing your hands in the wrong spot or disregarding operating procedures may cause a serious accident.

Section 4, Stationary Power Tools, will help you learn safe working habits. When you can safely operate power tools, you can build almost any project. You will be able to surface rough lumber to shape. With machines you can easily cut plywood, particle board and other panels to size. Then you will be able to make joints, spindles and molded edges. Finally you can sand all pieces quickly to prepare them for finishing.

UNIT

28 Table Saws

Objectives

After studying this unit you should be able to:

1 Identify the major parts of a table saw and understand its basic adjustments.
2 List the different types of circular saw blades.
3 Do crosscutting and ripping operations.
4 Make special cuts, such as grooving and cove moldings.

Technical Terms

Panel saw
Gang ripsaw
Rip fence
Miter gauge
Ways
Trunnions
Splitter
Antikickback fingers
Carbon steel blade
Carbide-tipped blade
Spring set
Hollow-ground body
Stop rod
Push stick
Feather board
Tapering fixture
Dado head
Blind dado
Tenoning fixture
Cove cut
Molding head

GENERAL TABLE SAW SAFETY RULES

1 During all operations, keep your fingers out of the 4" (102 mm) safety margin. (Refer to Figure 28-1.)

2 When cutting dados or rabbets, never place your hands on top of the board when it is directly over the blade.

3 Stand to the left or the right side of the saw blade. Never stand directly behind it because of a possible kickback.

4 Use the guard whenever possible.

5 Set the saw blade to approximately 1/8" (3 mm) above the stock being cut.

6 If the stock is warped, check with your instructor before cutting.

7 Never attempt to clear away scraps or loose stock while the blade is turning.

8 Never reach over the blade to pick up cut stock.

9 Never rip stock without using the rip fence. Never crosscut without using the miter gauge.

10 Do not cut cylindrical stock on the table saw.

11 After using the saw, turn off the power and lower the saw blade below the tabletop.

One of the most useful pieces of equipment in woodworking is the table saw, Figure 28-1. The machine makes a variety of cuts and joints. The table saw also is known as the circular saw and the variety saw.

The size of a table saw is determined by the largest diameter of blade that safely can be mounted on the saw. Popular blade sizes are 10" to 18" (254 to 458 mm).

Although the table saw is a general-purpose machine, many specialized models are available. These include the *panel saw,* Figure 28-2, and the *gang ripsaw,* Figure 28-3. A panel saw cuts

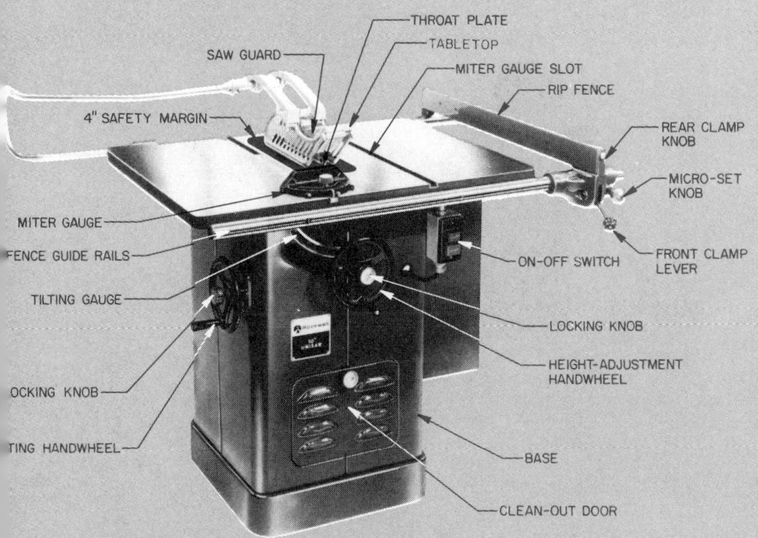

Figure 28-1
Major parts of the table saw. (Rockwell International)

Figure 28-3
Gang ripsaws cut a large number of wood strips. Machines have many saw blades mounted above the table. (Stetson-Ross)

Figure 28-2
Panel saws are industrial machines that cut plywood and particle board sheets. (Rodgers Machine Corporation)

CROSSCUTTING SAFETY RULES

1 Keep a minimum of 6" (152 mm) of stock in contact with the miter gauge.

2 When using the rip fence as a stop for cutting pieces to length, use a clearance block. At any other time, move the rip fence out of the way.

3 Make sure that the edge of the stock placed against the miter gauge is straight. Make sure that the face positioned against the tabletop is flat.

RIPPING SAFETY RULES

1 Remember that the shortest piece of lumber that can be ripped is 10" (254 mm).

2 Use a push stick when ripping stock to a width of less than 6" (152 mm).

3 Make sure that the wood that fits against the rip fence is straight. See that the face positioned against the table is flat.

4 Keep in mind that the narrowest stock that can be ripped is 3/8" (10 mm).

5 Push the stock completely past the saw blade before you release it.

6 When helping to "tail-off," never pull on the board being ripped.

Figure 28-4
Large table saws with a sliding table are used in industry. (Rockwell International)

sheets of plywood and particle board. A gang ripsaw cuts a piece of lumber into narrow strips with one pass through the machine. Industry often uses large commercial table saws, Figure 28-4. Large panels can be cut easily on the sliding table.

TABLE SAW TERMINOLOGY

The top of the table saw is mounted on a base, Figure 28-1. These two parts must be constructed out of heavy steel or cast iron. The machine lasts much longer if all its components are heavy and absorb vibration. If you use the saw for cutting plywood panels, you will need to support the stock on a large table, like the one shown in Figure 28-5. New models may have sliding tables to help cut large panels.

Adjust the depth of cut by raising or lowering the saw blade. To raise or lower the blade, turn the height-adjustment handwheel. The handwheel is on the front of the base. In the center of the handwheel is a locking knob. It locks the blade so that it will not change the depth of cut while the saw is running.

Some cuts require the blade to be tilted at an angle. A handwheel on the side of the base tilts the blade. A tilting gauge is mounted on the front of the saw. It shows the approximate angle at which the blade is tilted, Figure 28-1.

The metal straightedge you use to rip a board is the *rip fence*. When fastened to the table with the fence clamp lever, the surface of the fence aligns with the blade. A well-made rip fence has two clamps to hold it to the fence guide rail. One clamp secures the front of the fence. The other clamps the back. You can adjust the fence for ripping various widths of stock by sliding the fence to the left or the right along the fence guide rails. Make small adjustments by pushing in and turning the micro-set knob before tightening the fence clamp handle, Figure 28-6.

The *miter gauge* assists in most crosscutting. Usually you place the miter gauge in the slot on the left side of the blade. You can complete some operations, however, by using the slot on the right. Certain saws have T-shaped slots to help hold the miter gauge, Figure 28-7. When pulled away from the table, the miter gauge will not fall to the floor.

Figure 28-5
Use a saw with a wide table for cutting up large panels.

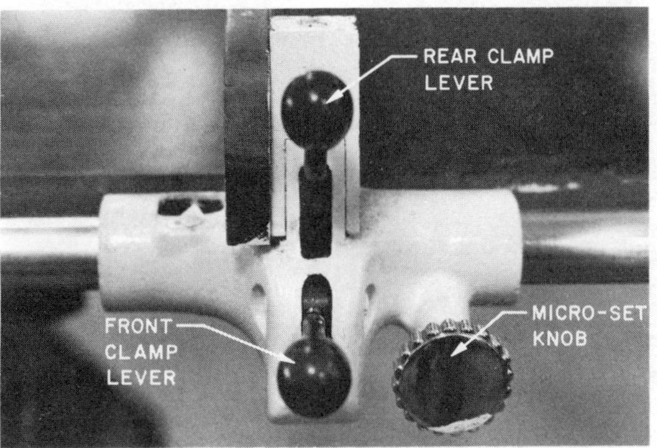

Figure 28-6
A micro-set knob makes small adjustments on the rip fence.

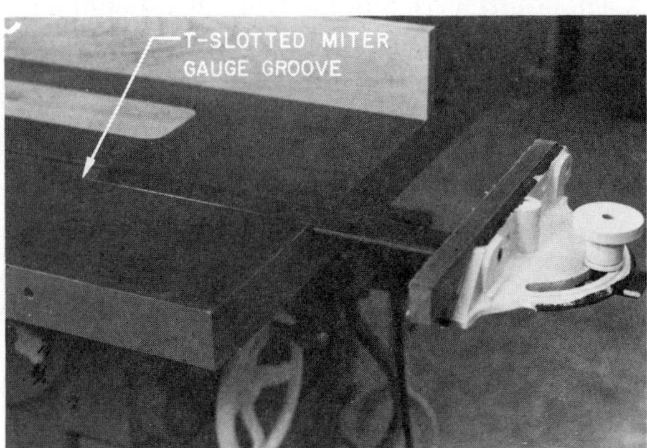

Figure 28-7
A T-slotted miter gauge groove prevents the miter gauge from falling.

The internal workings of the saw are located under the table. *Ways* and *trunnions* raise, lower and tilt the blade, Figure 28-8. The blade is mounted on a threaded shaft called the arbor. A collar and a hexagon-shaped arbor nut hold the blade on the arbor. Either a belt drive or a direct drive motor supplies power to the arbor. The throat plate is placed in the opening in the table. Dado and molding heads require a special throat plate with an extra-wide slot.

The cutting tool used on a table saw usually is a circular saw blade. As the blade turns, the

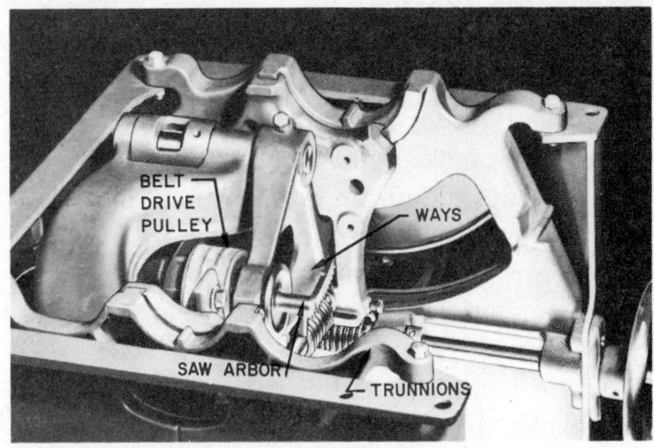

Figure 28-8
Ways and trunnions direct the movement of the saw blade. (Rockwell International)

tips of the teeth produce a cutting arc, or circle. The arc, or circle, helps locate many cuts and accessories.

SAW GUARDS

Use the saw guard whenever possible. Very few cuts require removing the guard. You always should provide a guard for the blade. Before turning on the power, see that the guard is working properly.

Parts of a standard guard include the blade shield, the *splitter* and the *antikickback fingers*, Figure 28-9. The blade shield is mounted on top of the blade and covers its sides. When used in the lowered position, the blade shield keeps your hands away from the blade. Accidents, however, can occur if you do not follow safety rules.

The splitter is mounted directly behind the blade. As the blade cuts a kerf, the splitter keeps the kerf open so that the wood does not pinch the blade. The wood's pinching the saw may cause the stock to kick backward off the table. Thus, you can get seriously injured.

Antikickback fingers hold the board down firmly if a kickback occurs. The sharp fingers bite into the wood if the board moves back toward you.

Guards come in a variety of styles. New saws always are equipped with a guard. You can purchase custom guards for older saws. You also can purchase one for special cuts, Figure 28-10.

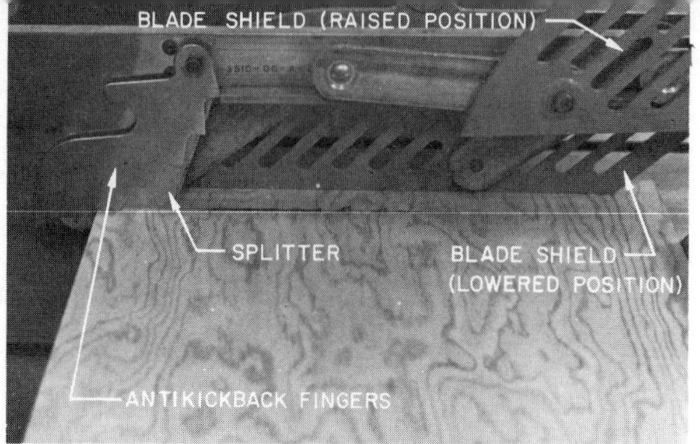

Figure 28-9
Major parts of a saw guard include the blade shield, the splitter and the antikickback fingers.

Figure 28-10
A special guard gives good visibility.

BLADE SELECTION

You must select a saw blade before making a cut. Different blades make different kinds of cuts. Many blades make only one kind of cut. Other blades make many kinds of cuts.

Saw blades either are made entirely of carbon steel or have a body of carbon steel with carbide inserts for teeth, Figure 28-11. Carbide is a harder material than carbon steel. It stays sharper longer. It easily cuts hard materials, such as plastic laminates and particle board. Carbon steel blades dull rapidly when cutting these materials. But, you need expensive, professional equipment to sharpen carbide-tipped blades, Figure 28-12. Sharpening carbon steel blades is less expensive. You use hand-filing techniques, Figure 28-13.

You can get either type of blade in many tooth styles:

1. Crosscut blades cut across the grain, Figure 28-14. The shape of the teeth forms a sharp angle that cuts cleanly across the wood fibers.
2. Rip blades cut with the grain, Figure 28-15. The deep gullets remove sawdust much faster than the crosscut blade and allow for

Figure 28-11
A carbon steel saw blade and a carbide-tipped saw blade.

Figure 28-12
Carbide-tipped blades require professional sharpening equipment. (Foley Manufacturing Company)

Figure 28-13
Hand-filing can sharpen steel blades.

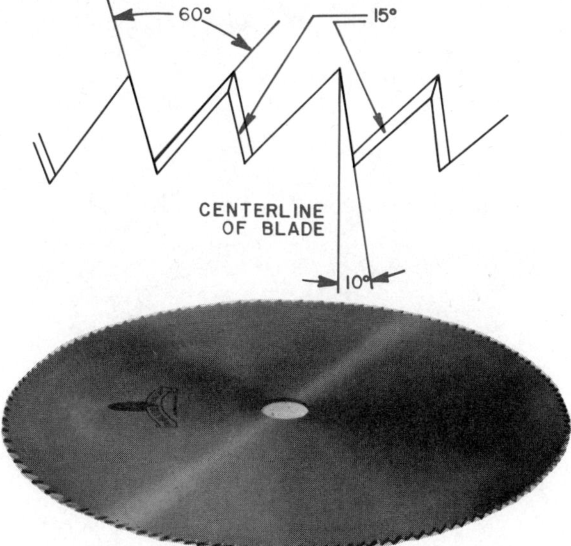

Figure 28-14
A crosscut blade has teeth that are alternately filed to a sharp bevel.

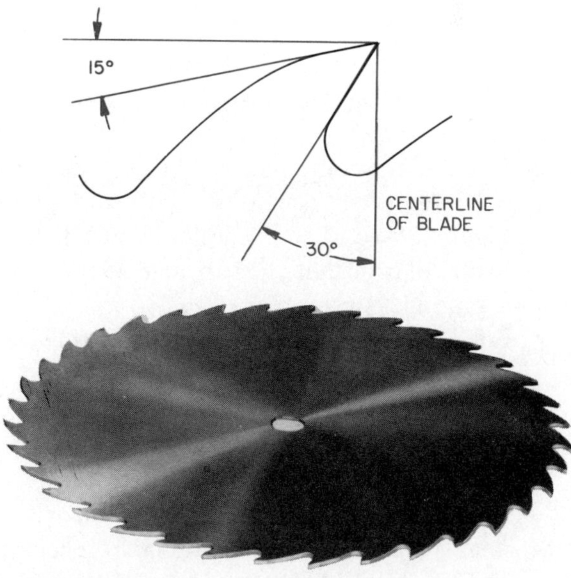

Figure 28-15
Ripsaw blades have teeth that lie flat on the top cutting edges.

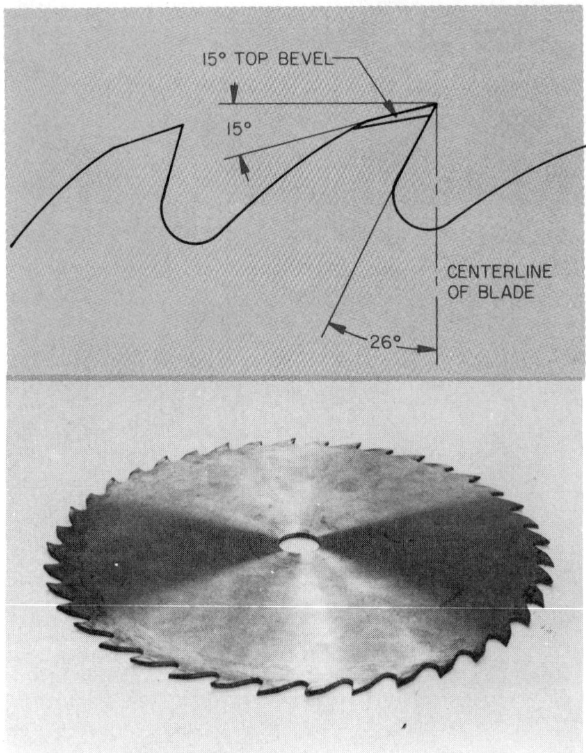

Figure 28-16
A rough-cut combination blade has teeth that are filed to a sharp bevel but are shaped like those on a rip blade.

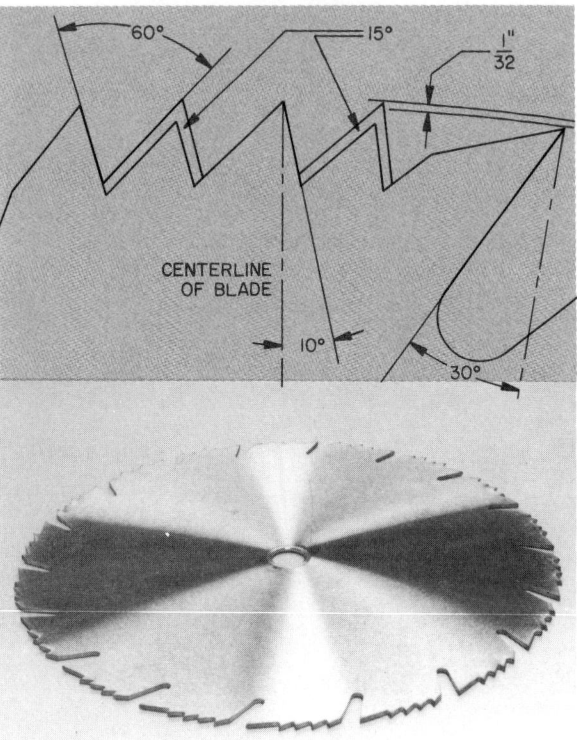

Figure 28-17
Four-tooth combination blades have several sets of teeth that contain two shapes. Four of the smaller teeth are alternately filed to a bevel. The one raker tooth has a flat top.

a faster feed speed. The blunt-shaped teeth create a rough cut, particularly when used to crosscut.

3. Rough-cut combination blades do fast cutting either across or with the grain, Figure 28-16. The blade looks like the rip blade, except that the top edge of the teeth is ground to a sharp angle.
4. Four-tooth combination blades do fine cutting across or with the grain, Figure 28-17. This efficient blade produces a good cut.
5. Specialty blades cut certain kinds of material, Figure 28-18. The most common specialty blade is the plywood blade. Its small teeth are shaped to a sharp top bevel. The plywood blade makes one of the finest cuts.

Each carbon steel blade requires a set to provide clearance for the saw body. Setting the teeth usually provides the clearance. *Spring set* is the most common. In spring set, every other tooth bends slightly to one side. The other teeth bend or are set to the opposite side of the blade. The set teeth make a groove, or kerf, wider than the thickness of the saw body, Figure 28-19. When the set wears off, the body will rub on the wood. You then will have difficulty feeding stock into the blade. A worn blade will burn the stock and kick the board toward you.

The *hollow-ground body* creates another type of clearance, Figure 28-20. The sides of the saw are ground on a taper. This makes the body thin. One advantage of this style is that it produces a thin kerf that reduces waste. A disadvantage is that a support hub is left around the center of the saw, limiting the depth of cut. Blades with a hollow-ground body and a four-tooth combination tooth style often are called planer blades.

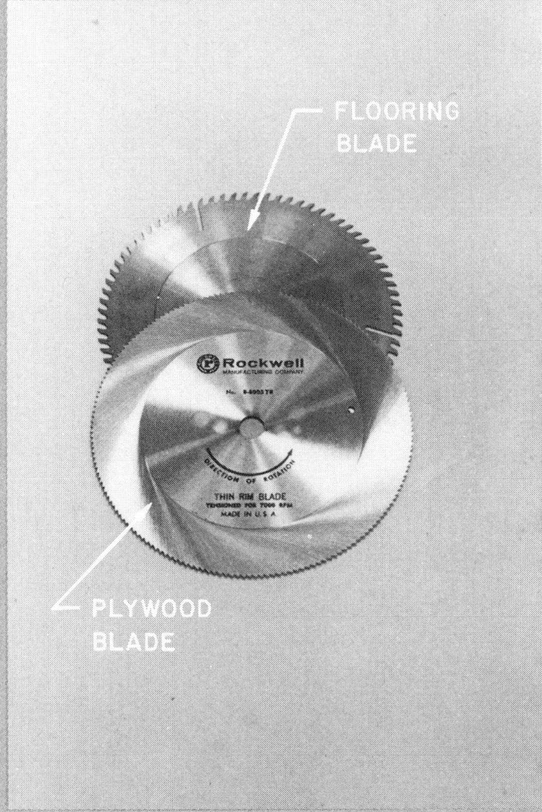

Figure 28-18
A plywood blade and a flooring blade are specialty blades.

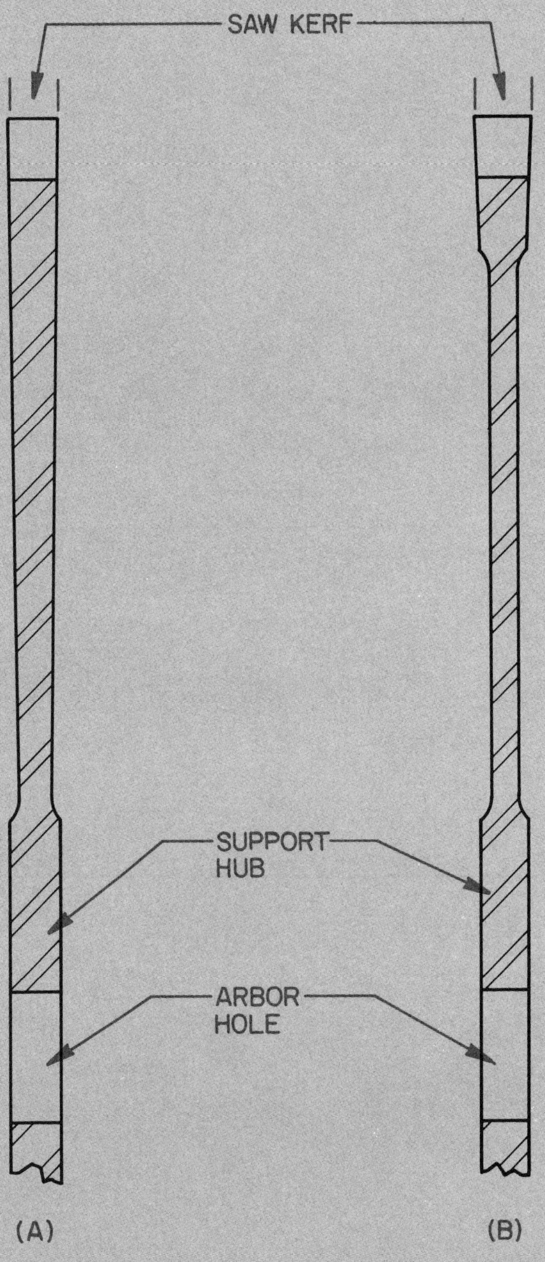

Figure 28-20
A hollow-ground style allows clearance for the body. Style *A* is used on high speed steel. Style *B* is used on carbide-tipped blades.

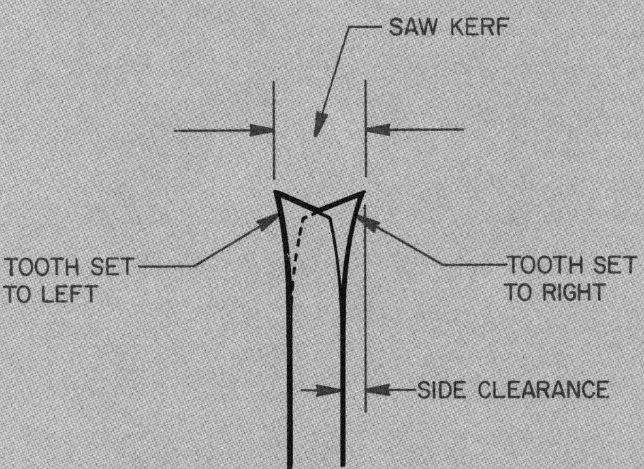

Figure 28-19
Spring set provides clearance for the body of the saw.

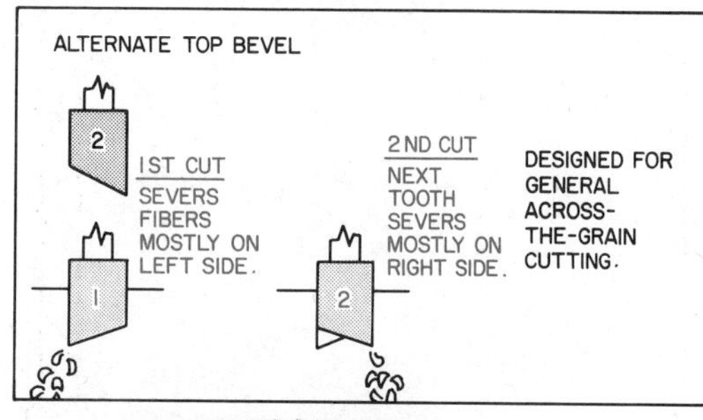

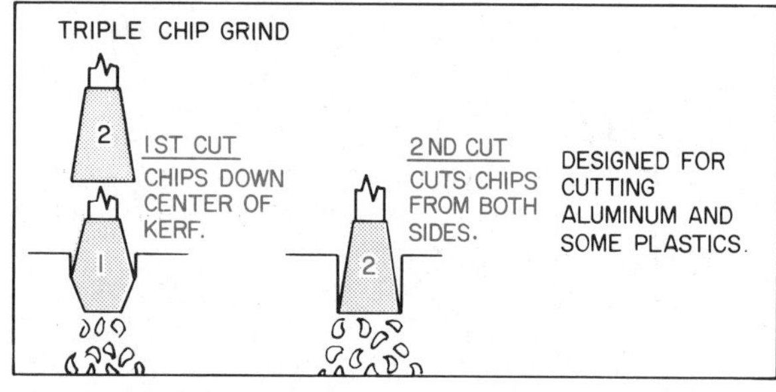

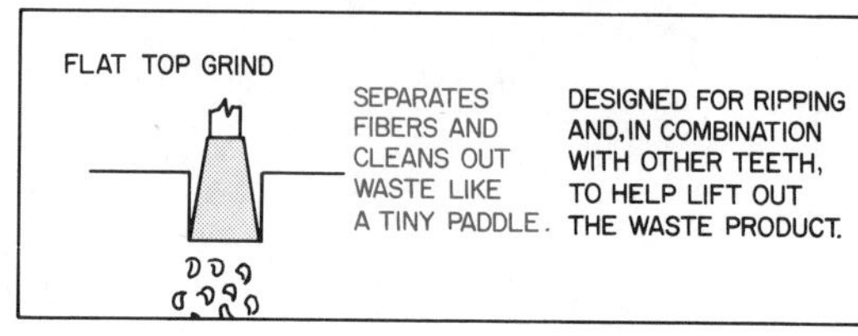

ALTERNATE TOP BEVEL

SEVERS FIBERS MOSTLY ON LEFT SIDE.

NEXT TOOTH SEVERS MOSTLY ON RIGHT SIDE.
DESIGNED FOR GENERAL ACROSS-THE-GRAIN CUTTING.

TRIPLE CHIP GRIND

CHIPS DOWN CENTER OF KERF.

CUTS CHIPS FROM BOTH SIDES.

FLAT TOP GRIND
SEPARATES FIBERS AND CLEANS OUT WASTE LIKE A TINY PADDLE.
DESIGNED FOR RIPPING AND, IN COMBINATION WITH OTHER TEETH, TO HELP LIFT OUT THE WASTE PRODUCT.

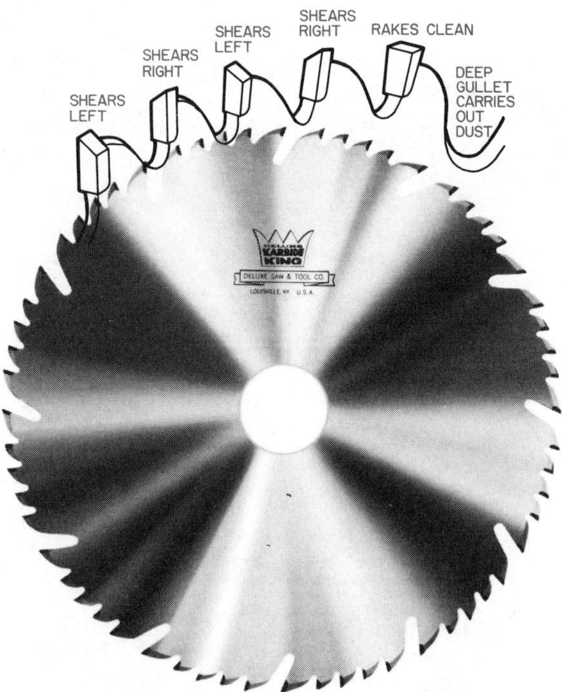

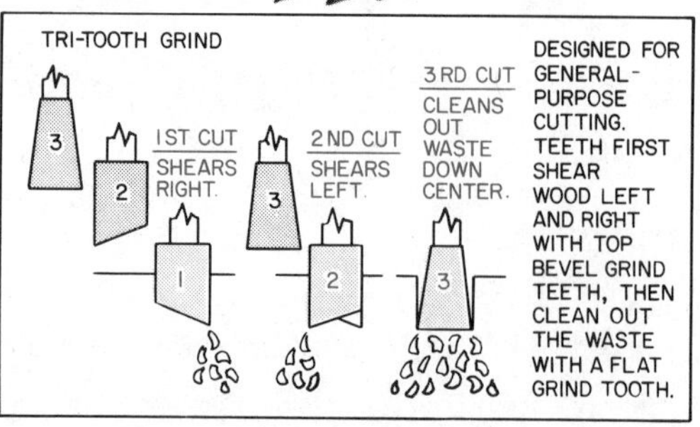

SHEARS LEFT
SHEARS RIGHT
SHEARS LEFT
SHEARS RIGHT
RAKES CLEAN
DEEP GULLET CARRIES OUT DUST

TRI-TOOTH GRIND

SHEARS RIGHT.

SHEARS LEFT.

DESIGNED FOR GENERAL-PURPOSE CUTTING. TEETH FIRST SHEAR WOOD LEFT AND RIGHT WITH TOP BEVEL GRIND TEETH, THEN CLEAN OUT THE WASTE WITH A FLAT GRIND TOOTH.

Figure 28-21
Several terms apply to teeth shape in carbide-tipped blades. (Deluxe Saw and Tool Company)

Carbide-tipped and carbon steel blades come in many of the same styles. Manufacturers sometimes use different terms to describe the parts of the blade, Figure 28-21. Selection of tooth styles would be similar to that of the high-speed steel blade.

CHANGING A BLADE

You must choose and install the correct blade style for your job. If the correct blade is not already on the saw arbor, you must change the blade. To replace and install a blade:

1. Disconnect the power. Unplug the machine or switch off the electricity at the power panel on the wall. This will keep the machine from accidentally being turned on.
2. Remove the guard and the throat plate that covers the opening in the saw table. This will expose the arbor and the existing saw blade.
3. Hold a piece of scrap wood against the front of the blade to keep it from turning.
4. Loosen the arbor nut by pulling the handle of the wrench toward the front of the machine, Figure 28-22. Be careful that the wrench does not slip. If it does, you might hit your finger on the saw blade.
5. Place your middle finger on the end of the arbor. Unscrew the nut until it slides on your finger, Figure 28-23. This will prevent the nut from dropping down into the sawdust at the bottom of the base. Remove the stabilizing collar and the blade. Place the blade on a piece of wood or heavy cardboard. Laying the blade on the metal table or striking it against other metal objects will dull it.
6. Install the proper blade on the arbor with the manufacturer's name facing out and at the top of the arbor. The teeth must point toward you. If the brand stamp is up, the blade will cut a true circle. Continue the operation by replacing the stabilizing collar and hand-tightening the nut.
7. To finish tightening the arbor nut, force a piece of wood against the blade. Quickly jerk the wrench handle toward the rear of the saw.

Figure 28-22
A board wedges against the blade as you pull the wrench toward yourself.

Figure 28-23
A finger placed on the end of the arbor catches the nut.

8. Replace the throat plate. Check for free rotation of the blade. When the guard is in proper position, and the power is turned back on, you can start to saw.

CROSSCUTTING

Use a miter gauge to do crosscutting. The miter gauge slides in either of the two grooves cut in the top of the table. You will use the left groove most often.

Never crosscut stock freehand. Always hold stock against a miter gauge. This will prevent the stock from binding the saw and throwing the board toward you.

A minimum of 6" (152 mm) of stock must come in contact with the miter gauge. On most saws a board must be at least 10" (254 mm) in length to crosscut safely. If you attach a board covered with a fine abrasive paper to the miter gauge, the stock is less likely to slip, Figure 28-24. Do not place your hands within the 4" (102 mm) safety margin surrounding the blade, Figure 28-1.

To cut a board to length:

1. Move the rip fence so that it will not get in the way of the cutting.
2. Check the accuracy of the miter gauge's setting. Do this by turning over the miter gauge and sliding it into the miter gauge groove. With a 90° cut, there should be no space between the face of the gauge and the rip fence guide rail, Figure 28-25.
3. Set the depth of cut so that the blade is 1/8" (3 mm) higher than the thickness of the piece being cut.
4. Lower the guard over the blade.
5. Square the first end by cutting off a small piece, 1/4" to 1/2" (6 to 12 mm) long. To do this, place the material against the miter gauge. Hold the stock to the miter gauge with your right hand, Figure 28-26. You should support extra-wide material with your left hand. This will apply pressure toward the miter gauge.
6. Slide the gauge and the stock past the rotating blade. Feeding should be smooth and continuous.
7. Move the board away from the path of the blade when the stock has completely cleared the blade. Pull the gauge and board back to the starting position. Turn the power off. Do not remove the scraps until the blade has stopped completely. Then push off scraps with a wood stick.

Figure 28-24
The abrasive paper on the front of the miter gauge prevents stock from slipping.

8. End-for-end the board. Measure the desired length. Make a V-shaped mark in pencil at the desired length. Align the mark with a saw tooth that is set to the right, Figure 28-27. If the ends of the board will be exposed, you may need to cut the board 1/16" (2 mm) longer than the finished length. This will allow for extra stock being sanded off.
9. Repeat the same procedure as for cutting the first end. Never reach over the blade to clear waste material until the blade has stopped completely.

Crosscutting Duplicate Parts

When constructing a project, you often may need several pieces of the same length. You can cut them on a table saw, using a miter gauge and a clearance block clamped to the rip fence. The clearance block usually is a piece of scrap material at least 3/4" (19 mm) thick. You must clamp the block onto the rip fence so that the cut pieces between the blade and the fence do not bind. Always use a clearance block with the rip fence as a stop for crosscutting.

To crosscut duplicate parts:

1. Set the rip fence in position by measuring the desired length of stock between the tooth set to the right and the clearance block placed against the fence.

Figure 28-25
Aligning the miter gauge with the rip fence guide rails.

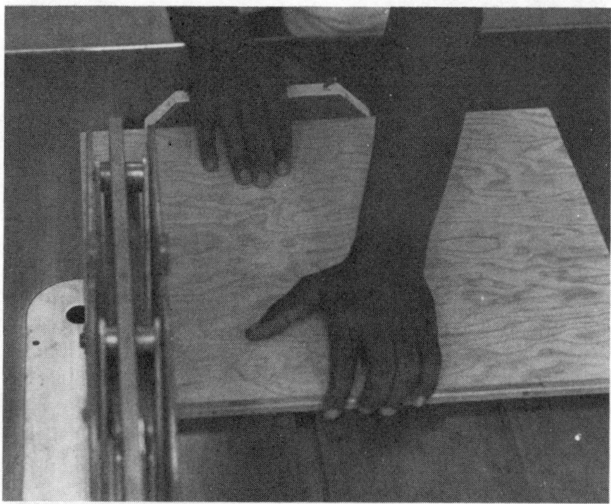

Figure 28-26
When crosscutting, your hands should be in this position.

Figure 28-27
Align the mark on the board with the saw tooth set to your right.

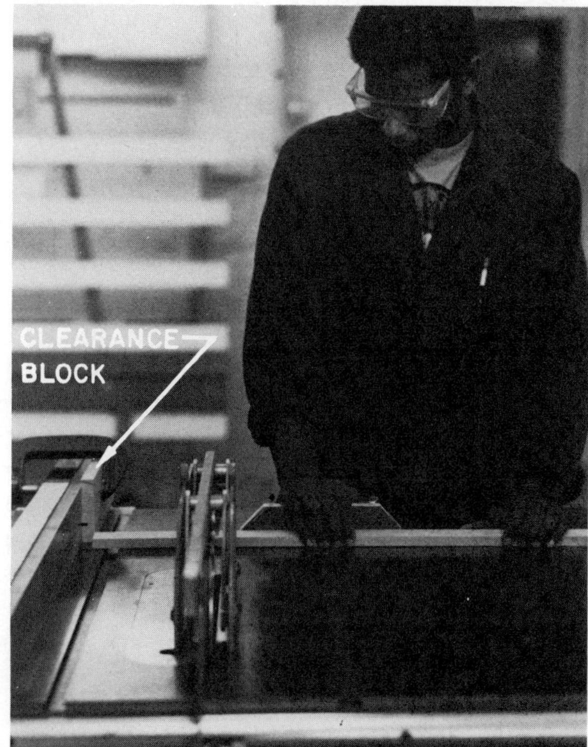

Figure 28-28
A clearance block clamped to the rip fence prevents kickbacks.

2. Clamp the clearance block to the front side of the fence. It must clear the blade. Place the miter gauge in the groove to the left of the blade.
3. Lower the guard over the blade.
4. Place the stock against the miter gauge and the square end against the clearance block, Figure 28-28. Hold the stock tight to the miter gauge. Slide it forward into the saw to complete the cut. You can cut longer lengths with the miter gauge in the right-hand groove.
5. Occasionally turn off the saw to clear the cut pieces off the table. Do not clear pieces while the blade is turning. Remember, turn off the saw when clearing pieces.

Figure 28-29
Stop rods can be attached to the miter gauge.

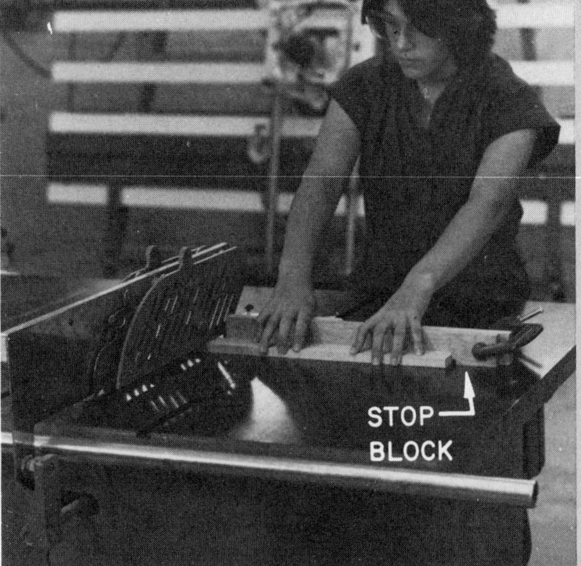

Figure 28-30
A long board and a stop block attached to a miter gauge works well for crosscutting.

Crosscutting Long Pieces

You can measure and cut each long piece separately by using only a miter gauge. But you may want to use a faster method. You can:

1. Install a *stop rod* in the miter gauge. Use the L-shaped end as a stop, Figure 28-29.
2. Attach a long board to one or two miter gauges. To cut duplicate lengths, clamp a stop block to the board the desired distance away from the blade, Figure 28-30. Place the square end against the stop block, Figure 28-31. Always lower the guard over the blade before starting the motor.

Figure 28-31
A shop-made sliding table. *The guard is removed only for illustrative purposes. Do not do this without help from your instructor.*

CUTTING LARGE PANELS AND WIDE BOARDS

Plywood, hardboard and particle board are purchased in 4′ x 8′ (1200 x 2400 mm) or larger panels. For larger sizes, use the rip fence for cutting both with and across the face grain. A tail-off person, or helper, must assist with handling and cutting the material, Figure 28-32.

As with cutting wide lumber, you will push mostly with your right hand. Pushing with your left will cause a kickback. Keep the stock against the rip fence to produce a straight cut. Your tail-off person should not pull on the panels. Panels

Figure 28-32
Cutting large panels requires the help of a tail-off person.

provide only minimal support. They only keep the piece flat on the table.

You may construct a sliding table, Figure 28-31. A sliding table is ideal for crosscutting strips of wide stock after they have been ripped.

By reversing the miter gauge, you can crosscut wide pieces. Woodworkers prefer this method when no other attachments are available, Figure 28-33.

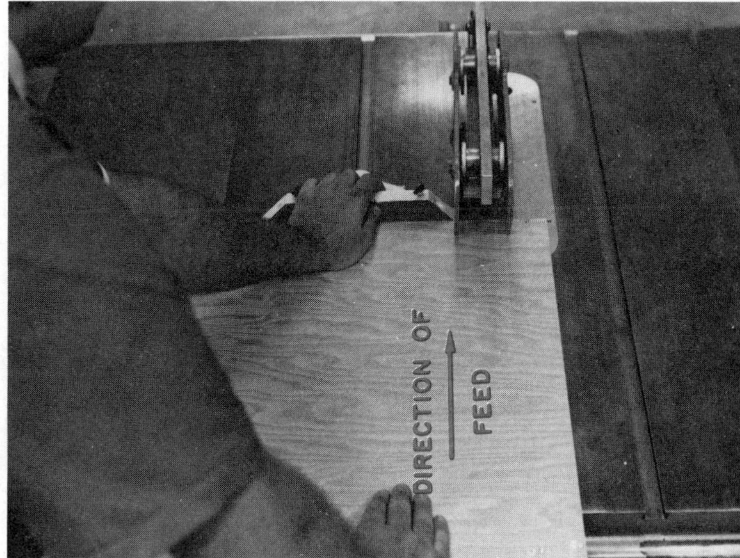

Figure 28-33
Reversing the miter gauge for cutting extra-wide stock.

RIPPING

A table saw is one of the best woodworking machines for ripping stock to width. When stock is ripped it must have a flat surface against the table and a straight edge against the rip fence. Otherwise the stock will bind the saw and kick back. You must see that the guard is in place and that all other safety rules are followed. In all ripping operations a minimum of 10″ (254 mm) of stock must be in contact with the rip fence. If stock is shorter than this, cut it with the bandsaw.

Ripping Wide Stock

Follow this procedure when ripping stock 6″ (152 mm) and more in width:

1. Place the stock beside the blade. Raise the blade until it is approximately 1/8″ (3 mm) above the thickest portion of the board.
2. Position the rip fence to the right of the saw blade. Measure the desired distance between the rip fence and the saw tooth set to the right, Figure 28-34. Allow at least 1/16″ (2 mm) more than the finished width for smoothing the edge on the jointer.
3. Lower the guard over the blade.
4. Stand to the right or the left of the blade. If a kickback occurs, the board will not strike you.
5. Grasp the end of the board with your right hand and push forward. Use your left hand only to guide the stock against the fence. Pushing forward with your left hand will cause the board to move away from the fence. Keep both hands at least 4″ (102 mm) from the blade.
6. Feed the material through the saw at a smooth, steady rate. Listen to the sound of the saw as it cuts. The sound should be lower than it was before you started the cut. If the feed rate is too fast, the saw will sound very low. This is a signal that the saw has become overloaded. If the saw sounds only slightly different, your feed rate is too slow. Continuing at this rate will overheat the blade, burn the wood and possibly ruin the blade.

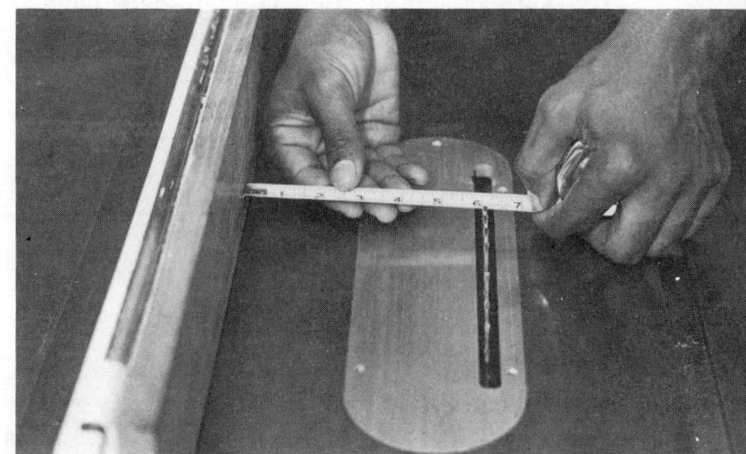

Figure 28-34
Setting the rip fence to the correct position. *The guard is removed so you can see the relationship between the ruler and the rip fence.*

7. Push forward with your right hand to complete the cut, Figure 28-35. Pushing with your left hand on the far side of the blade will pinch the blade and cause a kickback.
8. Allow the stock to fall to the floor as you complete the cutting. If this is not possible, a tail-off person standing at the rear of the saw can catch the boards. Never reach over the blade to support or retrieve the stock.
9. Always cut boards more than 4′ (1200 mm) in length with the aid of a tail-off person.

Ripping Narrow Stock

Rip any stock less than 6″ (152 mm) in width with a *push stick.* A push stick keeps your hands away from the blade. To rip narrow stock:

1. Set up the saw as suggested for ripping wide stock. Your hands should come no closer than 4″ (102 mm) from the blade as you feed the material.
2. Lower the guard into place.
3. Hold a push stick in your right hand to guide the stock past the blade. If the stock is very narrow, use a second push stick in your left hand to guide the board against the rip fence, Figure 28-36. Keep the second push stick in front of the blade to prevent the kerf being pinched closed.

RESAWING STOCK

Resawing a piece of thick stock produces two or more thin boards. This ripping process saves material. For example, a board 1″ (25 mm) thick may be resawed into two pieces slightly less than 1/2″ (13 mm) thick.

Resawing is a ripping operation. You should follow this procedure:

1. Cut from both edges of a piece if it is wider than the cutting capacity of the saw. Because the blade does not come out the top of the wood, you can remove the standard guard. When possible, leave the guard in place or use a specially designed guard.
2. Adjust the ripping fence so that the board is cut into the desired pieces.
3. Adjust the height of the blade to 1/8″ (3 mm) higher than half the width of the stock. If the board is very dense, or if the saw does not have enough power to make deep cut, raise the blade only to 1/2″ (1 mm). After cutting both edges, continu to raise the blade by 1/2″ (13 mm) unti the board is cut in half. Making too deep cut in one pass will cause the blade to ove heat and to lose its tension. This may rui the blade.
3. Position a *feather board* so that its fa finger is immediately behind the fron tooth of the blade, Figure 28-37. If th feather board goes farther forward, the ke will close. This may cause a kickback. feather board is a wood member that hol stock to the fence. You can make one b making multiple saw cuts with a bandsa The end of the device is cut on a 30° angl Figure 28-38.
4. Use a push stick to feed the stock into th blade. The feather board helps keep th board against the rip fence.
5. Complete the cut on one edge. Then tu the board end-for-end while keeping th same side against the rip fence. Saw the se ond edge.
6. If the board is wider than the cutting c pacity of the saw, finish the cut with handsaw or a band saw.

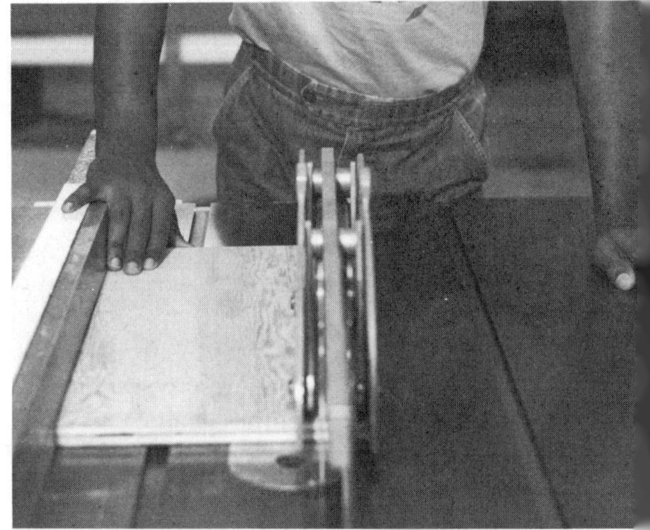

Figure 28-35
Push only with your right hand toward the end of the cut.

SAWING AFTER A PATTERN

A miter gauge and a rip fence cut square- or rectangular-shaped pieces. A table saw also cuts triangles, pentagons, hexagons and other multi-sided figures. Use a table saw particularly when you need to make a number of identical multi-sided pieces. To cut multisided pieces:

1. Clamp an auxiliary fence to the rip fence. Position the auxiliary fence so that the stock can slide under it, Figure 28-39.

Figure 28-36
Using push sticks keeps the hands away from the blade. *Notice that the guard is missing so that you can see the relationship between push sticks and the blade.*

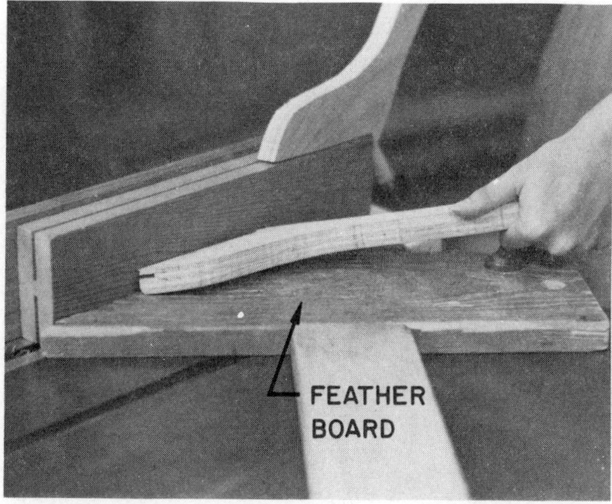

Figure 28-37
Use a feather board and push sticks when resawing. *With the guard removed, you can see the relationship between the push sticks and the blade.*

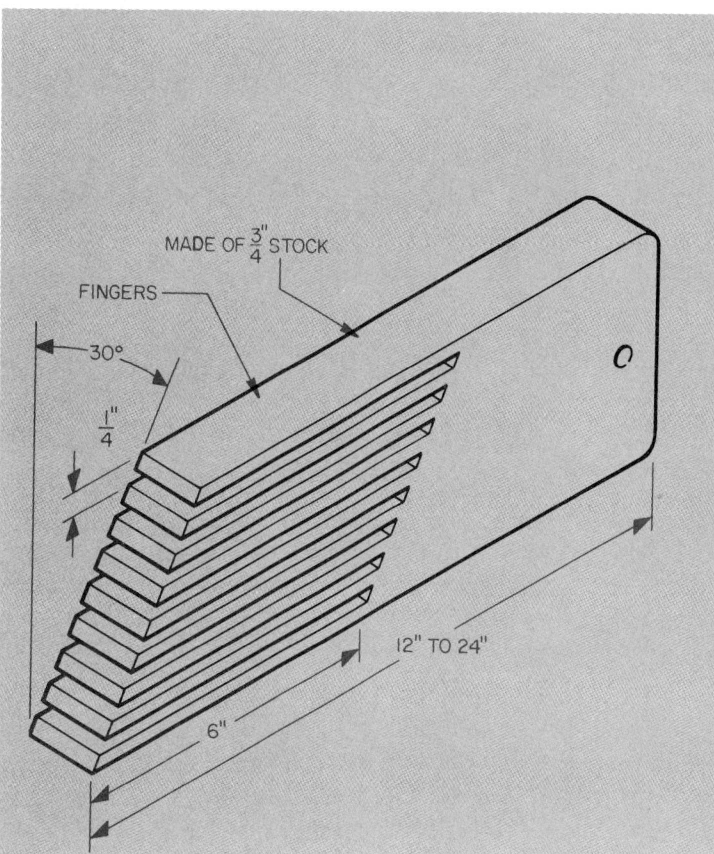

Figure 28-38
Make a feather board by cutting saw kerfs 6" (152 mm) long and placing them 1/4" (6 mm) apart.

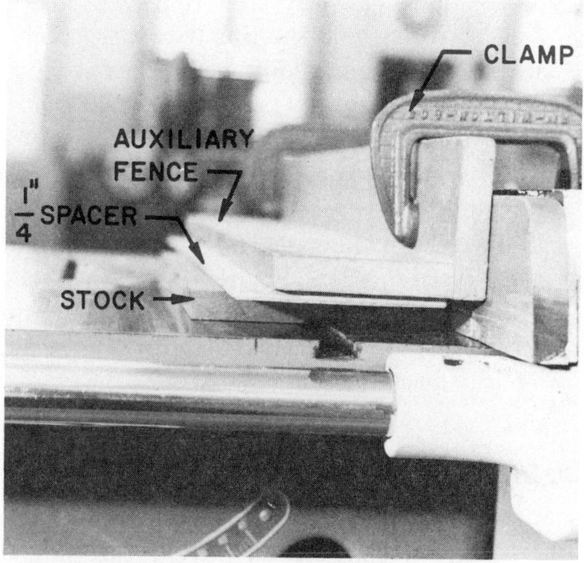

Figure 28-39
A 1/4" (6 mm) spacer sets the clearance for the auxiliary fence.

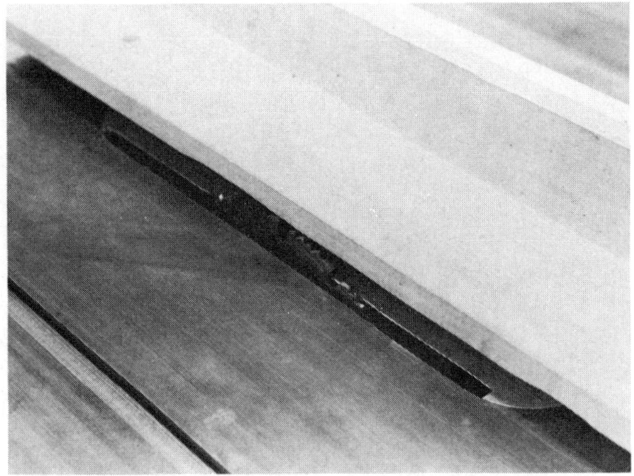

Figure 28-40
The blade is positioned directly under the auxiliary fence. *The guard has been removed so that you can see the relationship between the auxiliary fence and the blade.*

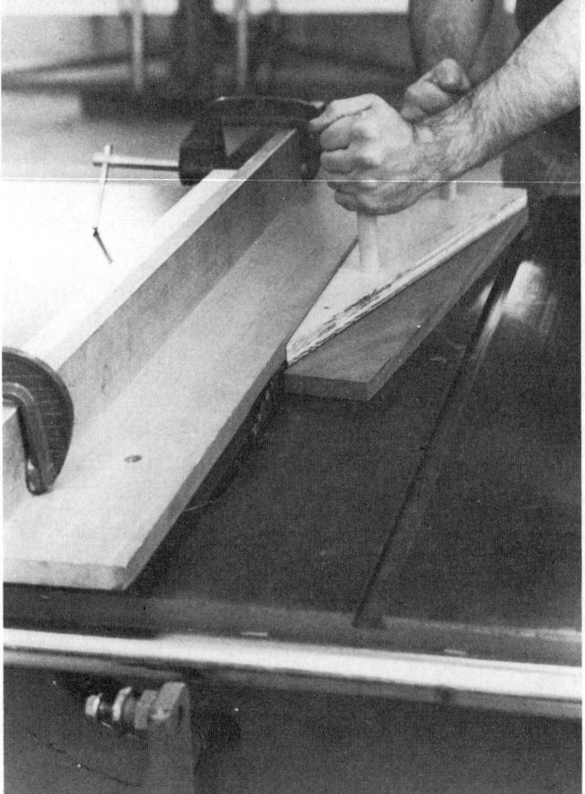

Figure 28-41
Slide the pattern against the auxiliary fence. *The guard has been removed so that you can see the relationship between the pattern and the blade.*

2. Move the rip fence so that the teeth set to the left are even with the outside edge of the auxiliary fence. Raise the blade so that the cutting arc is just under the bottom of the auxiliary fence, Figure 28-40. If you have a special guard, use it.
3. Make an exact duplicate of the finished piece out of 3/4″ (19 mm) hardwood plywood or dense particle board. Drive three or more 1″ (25 mm) screws through the pattern so that the screw tips stick out on the bottom. File the tips to a sharp point. Sharpened points easily penetrate the stock to be cut.
4. Position the pattern over the stock. Drive the screw points into the board with a mallet.
5. Slide the pattern against the fence to cut the piece to shape, Figure 28-41. Any stock that extends past the pattern will be cut off. Stop the saw after cutting a few pieces. Clean away the scraps.

CUTTING TAPERS

A tapered board has one end wider than the other. Use an adjustable *tapering fixture* if you want to make many sizes of tapers.

Adjust the legs of the tapering fixture to the same distance as the desired taper per foot. Measure this distance between the inside of the two legs 12″ (305 mm) from the hinged end of the fixture, Figure 28-42. For example, a 1″ per 12″ (25 mm per 305 mm) taper would require the legs to be 1″ (25 mm) apart measured 12″ (305 mm) from the hinge.

You also can set the taper fixture by sighting. Lay out the taper on the stock. Place the taper fixture and the board against the rip fence. Move the leg of the fixture and the rip fence until the layout line on the board aligns with the path of the saw blade. You can do this best by sighting down the layout line and moving the leg in or out until the line is parallel to the blade, Figure 28-43. Move the guard in place and cut the board using the ripping procedure.

You can cut a four-sided taper by using a two-stepped taper fixture. Each taper size requires a custom-made fixture, Figure 28-44. You should use the same techniques as for the one-sided taper, Figure 28-45. Cut the first two adjoining sides of the stock on the step closest to the leg of the fixture. This is equal to *W* in Figure 28-44. Cut the remaining sides by placing the end of the stock on the second step. This is equal to *2W* in Figure 28-44.

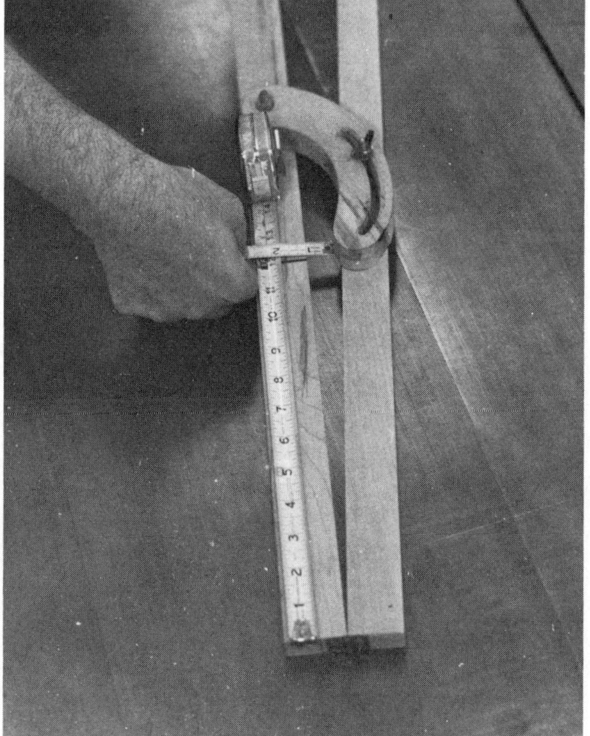

Figure 28-42
Adjusting the shop-made tapering fixture.

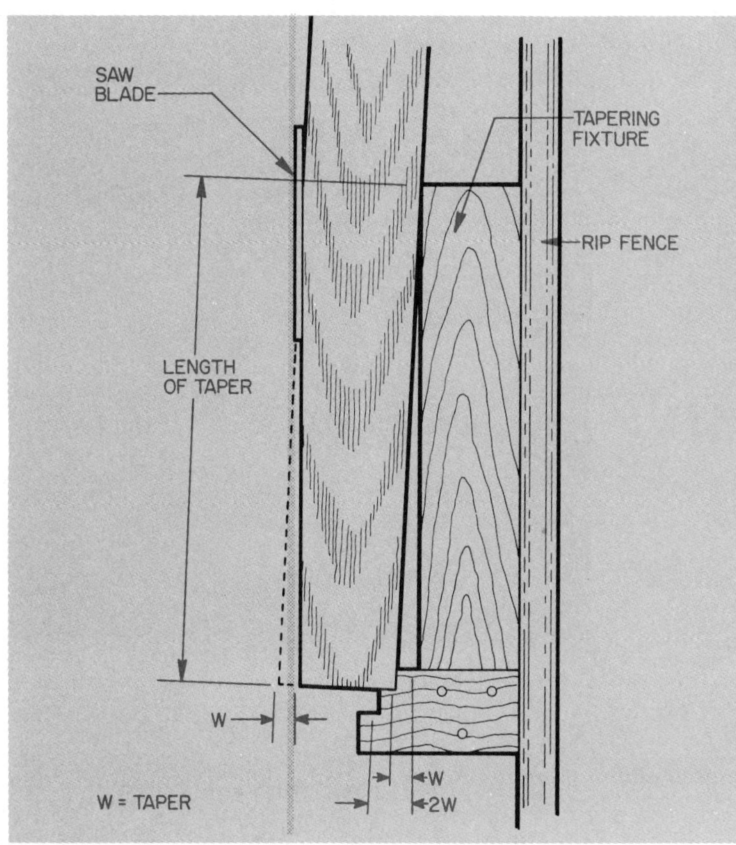

Figure 28-44
A tapering fixture for a four-sided taper.

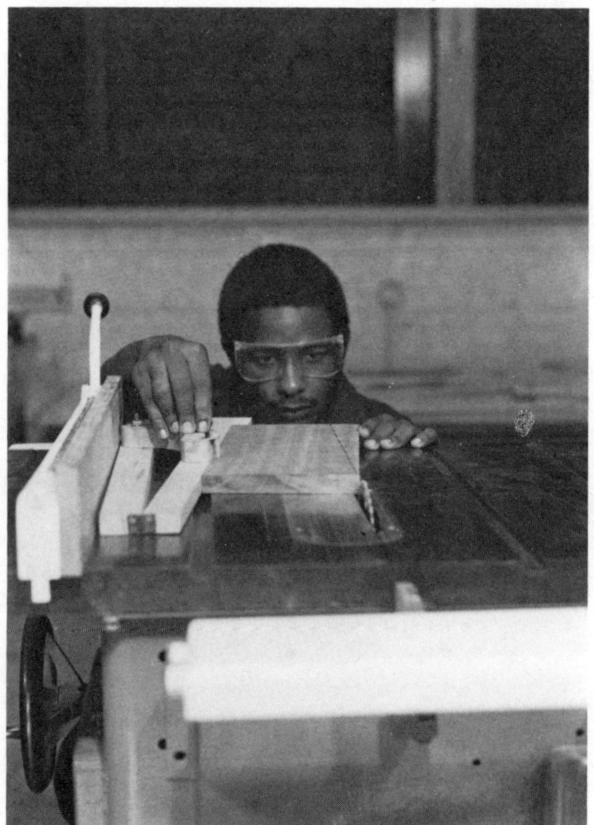

Figure 28-43
Sighting method of setting tapering fixture. Be certain to replace the guard before cutting. *Here, the guard has been removed so that you can see the relationship between the layout line and the blade.*

Figure 28-45
Cutting the first taper on the first step of the fixture. *The guard has been removed so that you can see the relationship between the board and the blade.*

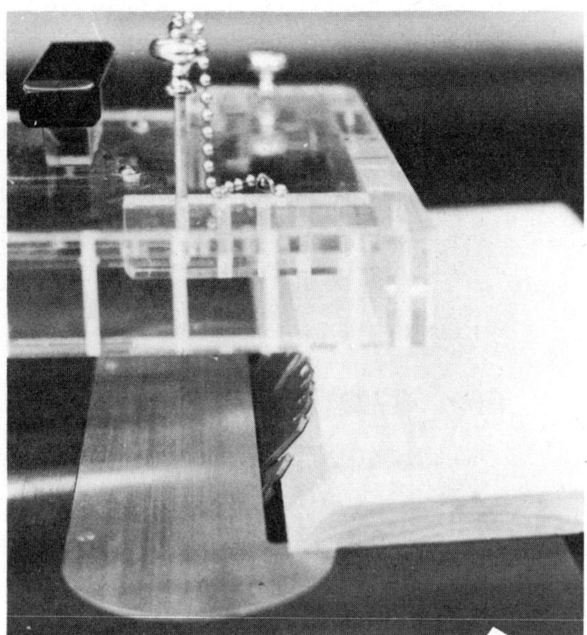

Figure 28-46
Cutting a bevel with the blade tilted.

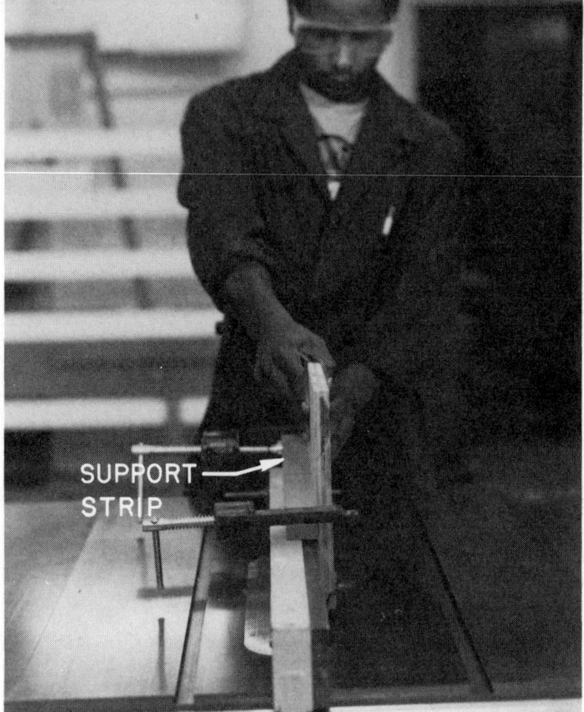

Figure 28-47
A support strip keeps the stock from slipping down into the table. *The guard has been removed so that you can see the relationship between the board and the blade.*

CUTTING BEVELS AND CHAMFERS

With the blade in a tilted position, you can make both a bevel and a chamfer, Figure 28-46. Making these cuts is either a crosscutting or a ripping operation. You do a ripping operation when the rip fence is used as a guiding device. You do a crosscutting operation when you use a miter gauge for sawing across the grain.

You must set the blade angle accurately when cutting bevels for a joint. Always check the angle by cutting a piece of scrap and measuring it with a combination square or T bevel. Never rely on just the tilting gauge of the saw for an accurate measurement.

By standing the stock on end, you can cut bevels and chamfers that are more than 45° on faces of boards. Set the saw blade to the complement of the angle. Clamp a support strip to the back of the stock. A complement is the desired angle subtracted from 90°. For example, to cut a 75° angle, first subtract 75° from 90°. The difference is 15°. Thus, 15° is the complement of 75°. Position the blade to this setting. Lower the guard before turning on the power. By resting the strip against the top of the rip fence, you will keep the stock from dropping into the opening of the throat plate, Figure 28-47.

CUTTING MITERS

A table saw cuts miters well. Using a miter gauge, you can cut angles accurately and easily. You can produce many different types of miters.

Cutting Flat Miters

Flat miters, such as those used for a picture frame, frequently are cut at a 45° angle. Four pieces cut at this angle will make a square or a rectangle. If a larger number of sides are required, you will need to set the miter gauge at a different angle. To determine an angle, use this formula:

$$90^\circ - (180 \div \text{Number of sides in the piece})$$

Therefore, to determine the angle for a six-sided top:

$$180 \div 6 = 30$$
$$90 - 30 = 60$$

The miter gauge would be set at 60°.

To cut a flat miter, follow this procedure:

1. Use one or two miter gauges to cut the miters. To save time, have two miter gauges with one angled to the right and the other to the left.
2. Cut the first end of all boards using the miter gauge set to the right. Check the accuracy of the cut with a protractor.

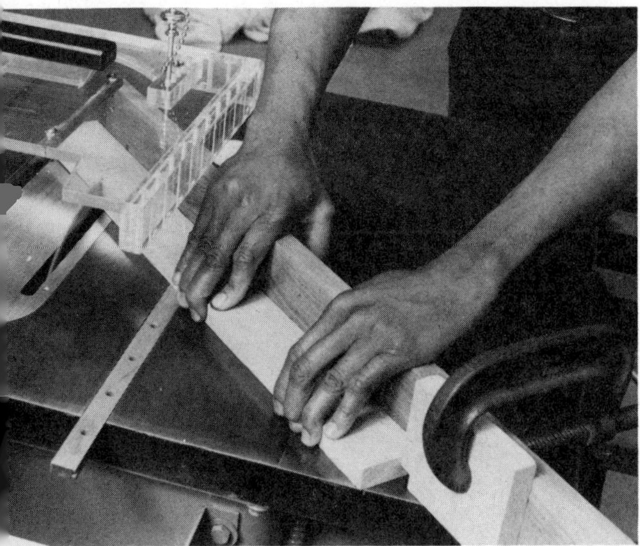

Figure 28-48
A stop block helps when cutting all pieces the same length.

Figure 28-49
Opposite sides of a mitered frame must be exactly the same length.

3. Install a board on the face of the second miter gauge to act as a fence. To this board, clamp a stop block the desired distance from the blade.
4. Butt the previously cut mitered corner against the stop block. Cut the remaining end, Figure 28-48.
5. Make sure that the opposite sides of any mitered piece are exactly the same length. Check the lengths and angles before assembling them, Figure 28-49.

Keep the guard over the blade as in any crosscutting operation.

Cutting a Compound Miter

Compound miters also are known as hopper joints or beveled miters. They are used in projects such as decorative flower boxes, Figure 28-50.

When cutting compound miters, refer to the table in Figure 28-51. Adjust the miter gauge and tilt the blade to the given angles. Always cut two pieces of scrap stock to check the fit and the appearance of the joint. The top and bottom edges often are beveled so that they appear parallel to the ground.

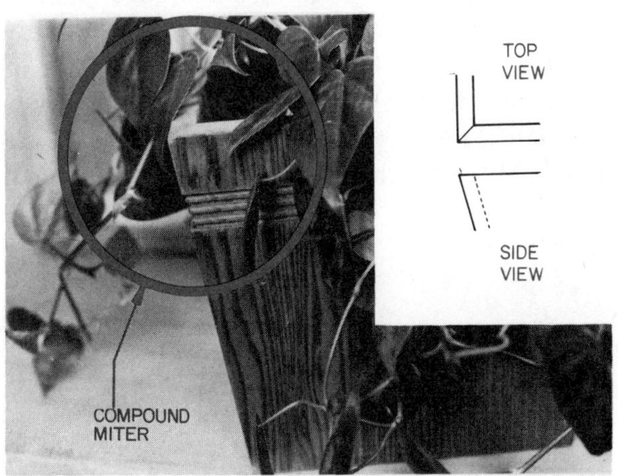

Figure 28-50
A compound miter used on a flower box.

Front View	4 Sides		6 Sides		8 Sides	
Work Angle (Degrees)	Blade Tilt (Degrees)	Arm Setting (Degrees)	Blade Tilt (Degrees)	Arm Setting (Degrees)	Arm Setting (Degrees)	Blade Tilt (Degrees)
5	44-3/4	5	29-3/4	2-1/2	22-1/4	2
10	44-1/4	9-3/4	29-1/2	5-1/2	22	4
15	43-1/4	14-1/2	29	8-1/4	21-1/2	6
20	41-3/4	18-3/4	28-1/4	11	21	8
25	40	23	27-1/4	13-1/2	20-1/4	10
30	37-3/4	26-1/2	26	16	19-1/2	11-3/4
35	35-1/4	29-3/4	24-1/2	18-1/4	18-1/4	13-1/4
40	32-1/2	32-3/4	22-3/4	20-1/4	17	15
45	30	35-1/4	21	22-1/4	15-3/4	16-1/4
50	27	37-1/2	19	23-3/4	14-1/4	17-1/2
55	24	39-1/4	16-3/4	25-1/4	12-1/2	18-3/4
60	21	41	14-1/2	26-1/2	11	19-3/4

Figure 28-51
Table for cutting compound miters.

Reinforcing Miter Joints

A table saw can cut many different reinforced miters, Figure 28-52. These include the slip feather, the spline, the lock and the housed.

Glue together slip feather without any reinforcement. Then construct a special holding fixture and use it to cut a diagonal groove across each corner. After making the slot, glue a wooden key in the slot, Figure 28-53.

Use a spline on long miters or bevels, such as the corners for a speaker cabinet. First cut a bevel by tilting the blade. Then cut a groove along the entire length of the bevel for the spline to fit into. Use the rip fence and a blade tilted to the correct angle to make this cut, Figure 28-54.

A lock miter and a housed miter also reinforce a miter joint. The shape of the miter cut actually provides enough face and edge grain to make a strong glue joint. A lock miter requires many setups on the saw and is selected for its decorative features. Make housed miters when you must miter two pieces of different thicknesses. Miter the thin piece at 45°. After you cut the shoulder on the thickest member, miter it at 45°.

Figure 28-52
Different miters cut on a table saw—lock miter, housed miter, spline miter and slip feather miter.

Figure 28-53
Cutting a slip feather with a shop-made fixture.

Figure 28-54
Cutting a groove for a spline miter. ***The guard has been removed so that you can see the relationship between the blade and the board.***

CUTTING GROOVES AND DADOES

Three types of grooves—the dado, the plough or gain and the rabbet—are common in constructing furniture and cabinets, Figure 28-55. The dado is a rectangular groove, cut on the face of a board, that runs across the grain. The plough or gain is similar to the dado except that it runs with the grain. Rabbets are rectangular cuts made on an edge or end.

These cuts are made with a *dado head.* A standard dado head contains two types of cutting tools. These are the outside cutters and the inside chippers, Figure 28-56.

The outside cutters make a smooth cut with a minimal amount of chipping. They look like a standard four-tooth combination blade. A dado set contains two cutting blades. Each makes a cut 1/8" (3 mm) wide. They are mounted together to make a groove 1/4" (6 mm) wide.

The inside chippers remove any material between the outside cutters. Common sizes of chippers are 1/16", 1/8" and 1/4" (2, 3 and 6 mm). Always use them with two outside cutters.

Another type of cutting tool is the adjustable dado head, Figure 28-57. The cutters on this tool are mounted on an angle. You can adjust the pitch of the dado head for different widths of grooves.

Mounting the Dado Head

A combination of outside cutters and chippers cut dadoes and grooves. The width of cut is determined by the combination of parts. For example, two outside cutters, 1/8" (3 mm) each, plus two 1/8" (3 mm) inside chippers make a 1/2" (13 mm) groove.

To mount a dado head:

1. Turn off the power. Remove the guard and the throat plate. Take off the blade. Store it properly.
2. Select the outside cutters and the inside chippers to make up the desired width of cut.
3. Mount one outside cutter on the arbor. Place the first inside chipper on the arbor. Position the chipper next to the outside cutter so that the swagged tooth of the chipper is centered in the gullet of the outside cutter, Figure 28-58. Not doing this will cause serious damage to the dado head. Too large a dado will be cut.

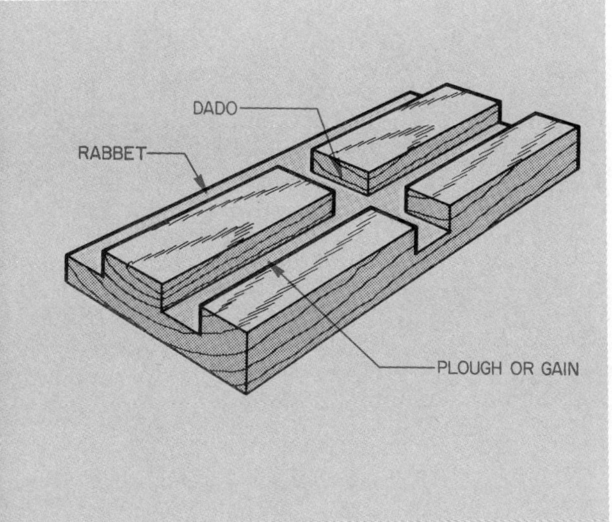

Figure 28-55
Different forms of grooves.

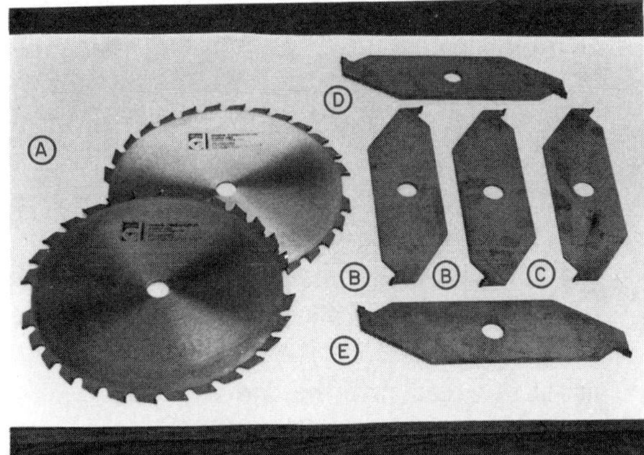

Figure 28-56
Parts of a dado head include (A) outside cutters; (B) 1/8" chipper; (C) 1/16" chipper; (D) 3/8" chipper; (E) 1/4" chipper.

Figure 28-57
An adjustable dado easily makes different widths of grooves.

Figure 28-58
Position the tooth of the inside chipper in the gullet of the outside cutter.

4. If you are using other inside chippers, space them evenly around the arbor before installing the last outside cutter, Figure 28-59. This will prevent the dado head from running out of balance and causing wear on the arbor bearings. Mount the last outside cutter. Position it so that the outside chipper tooth also is in one of the tooth gullets of the cutter. If space allows, place the stabilizing collar on the arbor. Tighten the arbor nut to secure the dado head.
5. Insert a throat plate that has a wide slot opening. The larger opening raises the dado head above the saw table surface.

A custom throat plate also can be made from wood. If the slot in the throat plate is the same width as the dado head, the stock is less likely to chip, Figure 28-60. A custom throat plate is helpful particularly when dadoing plywood, which tends to chip during sawing.

Making a Through Dado or Groove

Use the miter gauge, the rip fence or a combination of both to cut dadoes and grooves. Ploughs usually are made with just the rip fence. Wide boards require both the miter gauge and the rip fence. If you dado a pair of sides, the rip fence is an excellent stop for making matched cuts.

To make a through dado:
1. Mount the dado head.
2. Raise the head to the desired height, Figure 28-61. Position the rip fence and the miter gauge.
3. Install a guard to cover the top of the dado head. Do not use a guard with a splitter, because the board will not be cut into.
4. Cut a dado on a scrap piece of stock to check the accuracy of the setup. You may need to add a few paper washers between the inside chippers to make the cut wider, Figure 28-62. If you use paper washers, place them evenly between the chippers. Bunching the paper washers together in one spot will hold the individual chippers too far apart. This will leave a ridge of wood.
5. Slowly feed the stock over the cutters. The dado head removes lots of material and needs time to cut the wood. Never place your hands directly over the cutter. If you need to hold the stock down, use a push stick on top of the dado head, Figure 28-63. If there seems to be a problem, do not draw the stock back over the dado head while it is still turning. Turn off the machine and hold the board steady until the cutter stops turning.

Figure 28-59
Evenly space the inside chippers.

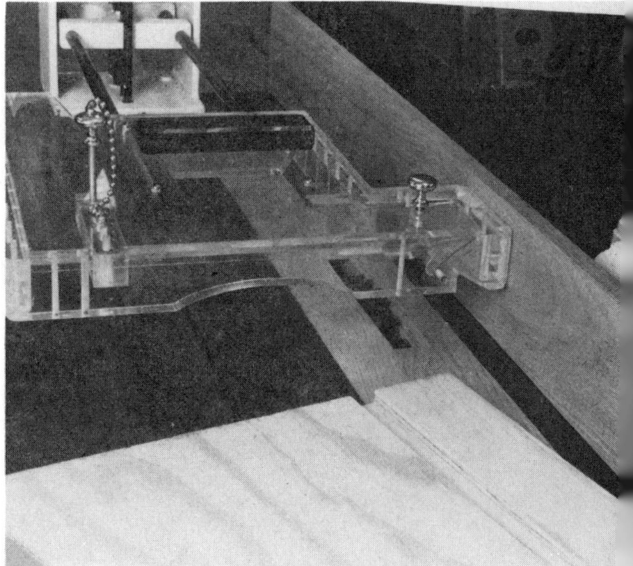

Figure 28-60
A custom throat plate leaves no space between it and the dado head.

Making a Blind Dado or Groove

Use a *blind dado* or groove on products where an exposed dado joint would be unattractive.

To cut a blind dado or groove:

1. Disconnect the power.
2. Remove the guard and install the dado head.
3. Mark the starting and stopping points of the cut on the wood. Because the layout line will be against the table surface during cutting, use a square to transfer the points of the dado to the top side of the board, Figure 28-64. These marks will help install the stop blocks on the rip fence.

Figure 28-61
Use a scrap piece of plywood to set the height of a dado head. Disconnect the power.

Figure 28-62
Paper washers help make odd-sized dadoes.

Figure 28-63
Never place your hands directly over the top of the dado head. ***The guard has been removed so that you can see the push stick.***

Figure 28-64
Laying out stopped dadoes.

4. Raise the dado head to the desired height and move the rip fence against the head. Use a pencil and a square to mark lightly on the fence the points at which the teeth of the dado head surface and go down into the throat plate, Figure 28-65. These marks will signal the beginning and the end of the cutting arc.
5. Move the rip fence the desired distance from the cutter. Lower the dado head. For the right side of a project, place the stock so that its front mark is aligned with the rear mark on the rip fence. Clamp a stop block against the back edge of the stock.
6. Lower the special guard over the dado head.
7. Raise the dado head back to the correct height. Clamp a stop block on the table to position the miter gauge. The front of the miter gauge should be in a straight line from the stop block. This will keep the stock from kicking back if it moves away from the fence. Using the miter gauge, pivot the stock off the stop block and onto the rotating head, Figure 28-66. Feed the board across the dado head. If more than one set of stopped dadoes are to be cut, dado all right sides before taking down the setup.
8. For the left side of the project, lower the head and remove the stop block used for the right sides. Align the back mark on the board with the front mark on the rip fence. Clamp a stop block on the rip fence against the leading edge of the board. Raise the dado head back to the correct height.
9. Butt the board against the rip fence and feed the stock with the miter gauge. When the front edge of the board reaches the stop block, have an assistant turn off the saw, Figure 28-67. Hold the board stationary until the head no longer turns. The board then can be removed safely from the saw.

Cutting a Rabbet

A rabbet is a rectangular groove cut on a face and edge or an end of a board. Often, a single saw blade cuts a rabbet if a dado head is not available or if a small number of rabbets need to be cut.

Figure 28-65
Marking the beginning and the end of the cutting arc.

The procedure for making a rabbet with a saw blade is:

1. Use a square to lay out the cut on one end of the stock. Number the lines, Figure 28-68. Mark the end of the board that will come in contact with the blade first. The layout lines provide a guide for adjusting the rip fence and the height of the blade.
2. Because the blade will not cut all through the stock, remove the standard guard to make the cut. Use a special guard.
3. Adjust the height of the blade so that the top of the cutting arc is the same height as the second layout line.
4. Position the rip fence so that the saw tooth set to the left is even with the first layout line, Figure 28-69.
5. Place the board on its edge with the saw kerf opposite the rip fence. Make the first cut. Feed the board over the blade with a push stick. Never place your hands on top of the stock while it is over the blade.
6. Readjust the height of the blade so that the cutting arc is even with the top of the first saw kerf. Move the rip fence so that the set of the tooth to the right is the same distance as the second layout line. Let the waste fall to the outside of the blade, not between the blade and the rip fence, Figure 28-70. Waste left between the blade and the rip fence will cause a kickback.

Figure 28-66
Pivoting the stock onto the rotating head.

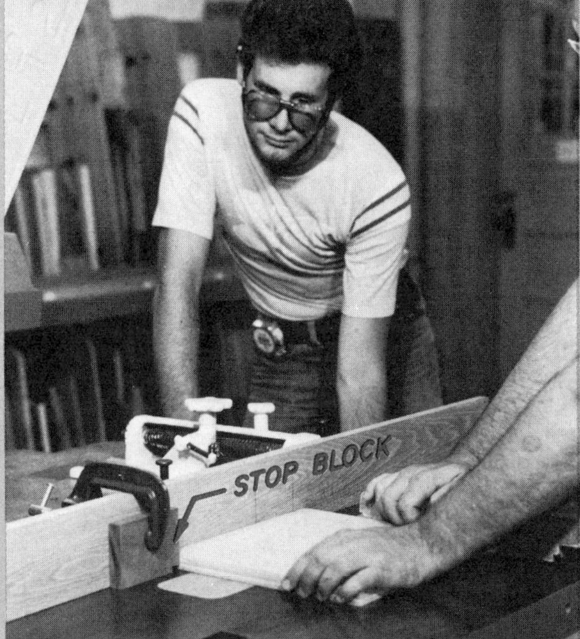

Figure 28-67
Do not move the stock until the dado head stops rotating.

Figure 28-68
Lay out the rabbet and number the marks.

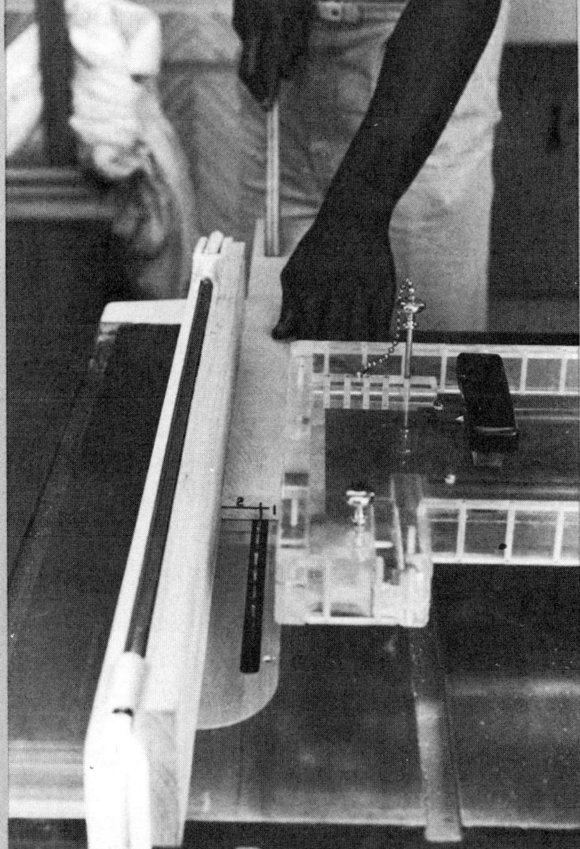

Figure 28-69
Setup for cutting a rabbet.

Figure 28-70
Making the second cut with the use of an elevated feather board.

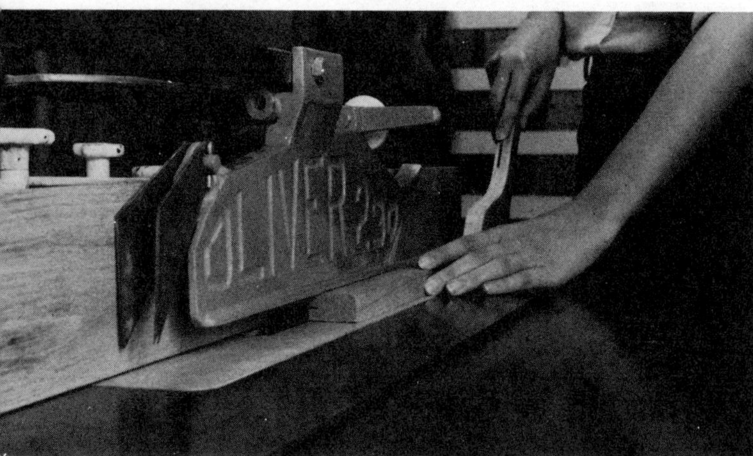

Figure 28-71
Cutting a rabbet with a dado head.

Figure 28-72
Laying out a tenon.

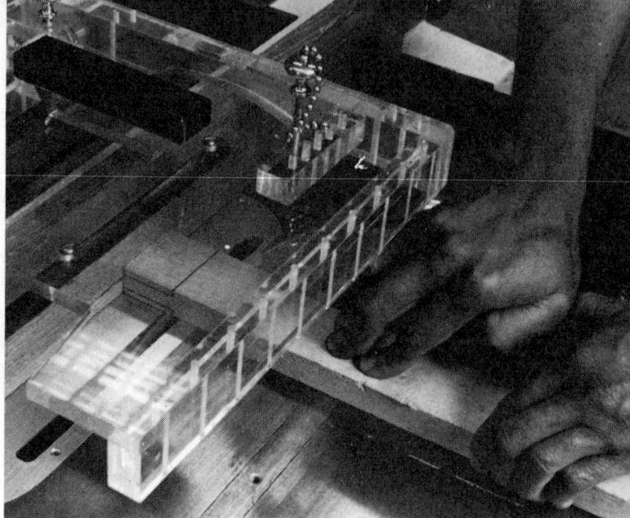

Figure 28-73
Cutting the shoulder cuts.

Figure 28-74
A commercial tenoning fixture for making the check cuts. Make sure that waste falls to the outside of the blade. *The guard has been removed so that you can see the relationship between the blade and the board.*

7. Make the remaining cut using a push stick.

Many times it is better to cut the rabbet using a dado head. The major advantage is that a dado head can cut a rabbet with only one pass over the saw. If you use a dado head, follow the same setup procedure as in making a through dado. Cover the rip fence with a piece of wood to prevent the blade from cutting into the metal fence, Figure 28-71.

CUTTING TENONS

Tenons can be cut with a circular saw or a specialized piece of equipment called a tenoner. Before making the tenon on the table saw, you must cut the mortise. The tenon is cut to fit the mortise.

To cut a tenon with a circular saw:

1. Surface all material to the same thickness. If the material is different thicknesses, you will cut different sizes of tenons.
2. Use a square to lay out the shoulder and cheek cuts on one piece, Figure 28-72.
3. Set up the shoulder cuts first. Raise the blade to the desired height. Set the length of the tenon by measuring between the rip fence and the tooth set to the left. The fence acts as a stop and sets the tenon

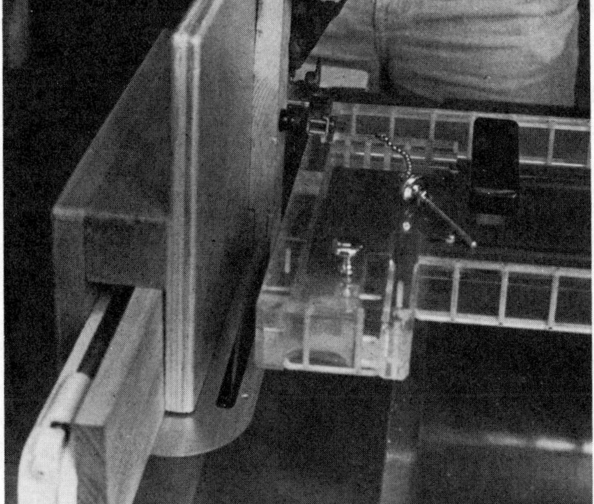

Figure 28-75
A shop-made tenoning fixture for making the cheek cuts.

Figure 28-76
Using a dado head for making a tenon. ***The guard has been removed so that you can see the relationship between a dado head and a board.***

length. These cuts can be made with the special guard in place.

4. Make the two shoulder cuts using a miter gauge and the rip fence as a guide, Figure 28-73.
5. Make the cheek cuts with a commercial *tenoning fixture*, Figure 28-74, or a shop-made tenoning fixture, Figure 28-75. Never make a cheek cut without using one of these fixtures to secure the stock.

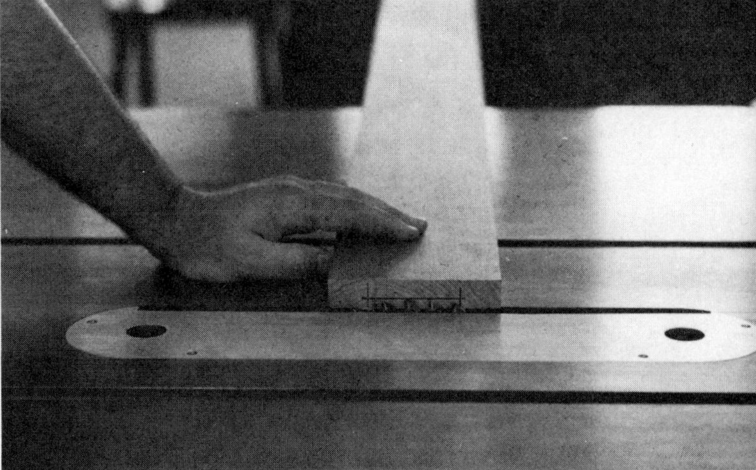

Figure 28-77
Adjusting the height of the blade for a cove cut. Note layout of cove.

6. Raise the blade so that it will cut up to the shoulder cut. Set the tenoning fixture so that the waste will fall to the outside of the blade.
7. Cut one side and turn the board around so you can finish the remaining side.
8. If more than one tenon will be made, try the fit of the joint on the mortise after the first two cheek cuts are made. This allows for adjustments to be made before you cut all of the pieces.

A tenon also may be cut using a dado head, Figure 28-76. This may be the best method if the tenons are short or few in number.

1. Install a dado head as wide as needed for the job. You may need to make multiple cuts to produce a cut wide enough.
2. Set the head to the correct height. Use the rip fence as a stop. Use the miter gauge with the single-blade technique.

COVE CUTTING

A *cove cut* is a decorative cut that can be made with a table saw. Industry workers use a large commercial molder, but you can use a circular saw.

To make a cove cut:

1. Lay out the desired cut on the end that will come in contact with the blade first.
2. Place the layout next to the blade. Raise

the blade to the correct height, Figure 28-77. Use a stiff, fine-tooth blade. An outside cutter from a dado head works quite well.

3. Set an adjustable parallel rule to the same width as the cove layout, Figure 28-78. If a parallel rule is not available, make a cardboard template.
4. Angle the rule until the far tooth of the blade just touches the right arm of the parallel rule and the tooth closest to you meets the left arm. This gives the angle for the auxiliary wooden fence.
5. Clamp the auxiliary fence on the downward side of the blade. Because you will feed the material at an angle, the fence will help you keep the stock in contact with the blade.
6. Lower the blade so that only 1/8" (3 mm) is above the table. Never attempt to take the full depth of the cut in one pass.
7. Use a special guard to cover the blade.
8. Position the material against the fence and start to feed the stock into the revolving blade. Use a push shoe to guide the stock over the top of the blade. Do not place your hands on top of the blade, Figure 28-79.
9. Continue to raise the blade by 1/16" (2 mm). Run the stock over the saw each time after the blade is raised.
10. Make the last pass when the blade has been raised to the finished height. Hand sand the rotary saw marks.

Figure 28-78
Establishing the angle of the auxiliary fence with a parallel rule.

Figure 28-79
Cutting a cove with a push shoe.

CUTTING MOLDINGS

Molding heads are used on a circular saw. A molding head is a cutting tool made of a solid metal body. Shaper-type knives are attached to the molding head, Figure 28-80. Knives are available in a variety of patterns. You can change them easily to produce different shapes of moldings and joints. Some brands of molding heads have more than 40 differently shaped knives.

Cutting moldings is a dangerous operation. Use a molding head with great care.

Draw the desired pattern on the end of a piece of stock. Then select the proper knives. Depending on the style of molding head, you will need one to three knives. Heads that use three knives produce the smoothest surface. All knives mounted in the head must be the same shape. After inserting the knives into the head, securely tighten the Allen screws. Occasionally stop the saw and retighten the Allen screws. Vibration from cutting can loosen the cutters.

Use the same procedure for the molding head you use for the dado head. Keep these points in mind. Cover the fence of the rip fence with a thick board if you use only the outside portion of the knives. If the stock must be in a vertical position for cutting, attach a tall piece of plywood to the rip fence for additional support. Use a throat plate with a wide opening. Use a push stick whenever possible. You must have a special guard. Do not place your hands over the top of the cutter.

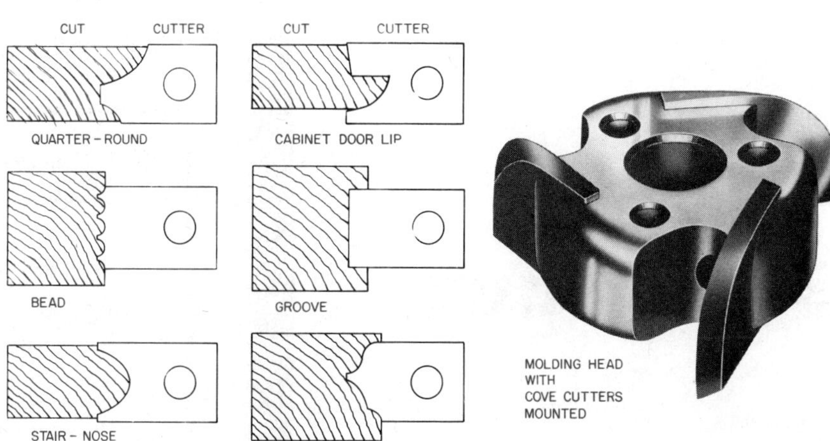

Figure 28-80
A molding head consists of a solid body with three knives. (Rockwell International)

REVIEW QUESTIONS

1 List two other names of the table saw.
2 Name two types of industrial saws. What is the purpose of each?
3 How is a blade raised and lowered and locked into position?
4 Define *ways* and *trunnions.*
5 Name the parts of a standard saw guard. What does each part do?
6 What are the five types of carbon steel blades?
7 Which direction do you move the wrench when loosening the arbor nut?
8 How high above the stock should you position the blade?
9 What is a clearance block? Why is it used?
10 Name three methods of crosscutting long pieces.
11 What is the shortest piece of stock that can be ripped?
12 Any stock to be ripped less than ___" in width requires the use of a push stick.
13 Where should a feather board be positioned for resawing?
14 Sketch the position of the auxiliary fence when sawing after a pattern.
15 What are the two methods for setting the adjustable tapering fixture?
16 How can a 15° bevel be cut on the face of a board?
17 At which angle would the miter gauge be set if you were making a twelve-sided figure?
18 At which angles would the miter gauge and saw blade be set if you were cutting a four-sided compound miter? The sides will angle 15°.
19 Which joint frequently is selected when two pieces of different thicknesses are to be mitered?
20 Which two cutting tools do you use in a standard dado head?
21 How are the inside chippers spaced around the saw arbor?
22 Name the two methods of cutting rabbets.
23 Which is cut first for a tenon: the shoulder or the cheek cut?
24 What do you use to determine the angle of the auxiliary fence when cutting a cove?
25 If the stock is held in the vertical position when using a molding head, what should be attached to the rip fence?

SUGGESTED ACTIVITIES

1 Name all the parts of your table saw. With your instructor's help, remove the throat plate. Watch the ways and trunnions as the handwheels turn.
2 Lay out a one-sided taper. With the adjustable tapering fixture, cut the taper to pattern.
3 Construct a small bookshelf using the table saw. Try a variety of cuts, including the blind dado, the rabbet, the cove cut and the taper.

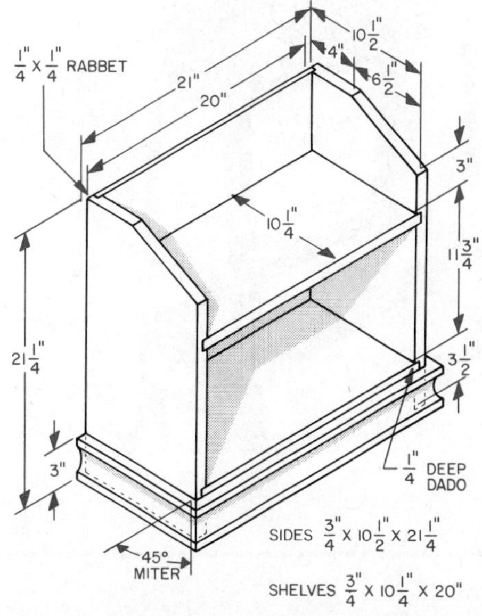

UNIT

29

Scroll Saws

Objectives

After studying this unit you should be able to:

1. Identify major parts and understand their function.
2. Install a blade and make machine adjustments.
3. Cut external and internal curves.
4. Understand basic marquetry.

Technical Terms

Overarm	Internal curve
Pitman	Saber sawing
Spring-loaded pulley	Marquetry

Figure 29-1
Major parts of a scroll saw. (Rockwell International)

SCROLL SAW SAFETY RULES

1. Keep hands away from the path of the blade.
2. Disconnect the power whenever the blade is being changed.
3. Be sure the upper hold-down is resting lightly on the top face of the stock.
4. Be sure the surface placed against the table is flat.

The scroll saw, also called the jig saw, is designed for cutting curves of all diameters. Its thin and narrow blade can easily cut very small curves. It is not recommended for making long, straight cuts.

Two models of scroll saws are available. The bench-type model is used for light to medium cutting, Figure 29-1. Heavy commercial models can make deep cuts on larger boards, Figure 29-2.

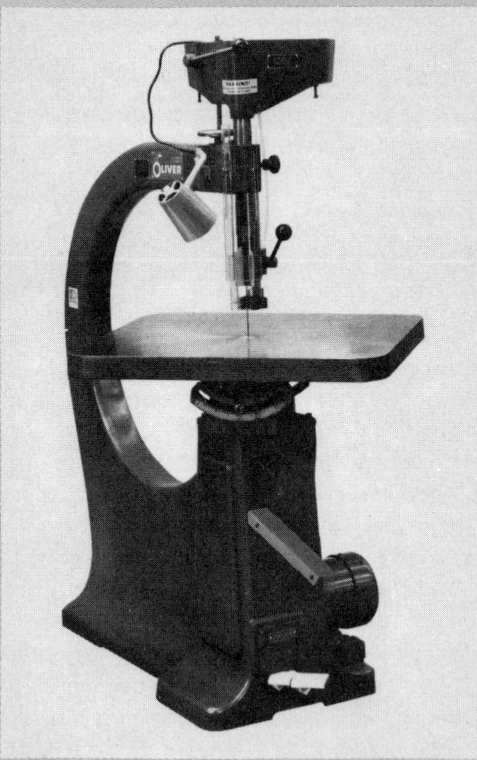

Figure 29-2
A commercial scroll saw. (Oliver Machinery Company)

Figure 29-3
Spring-loaded pulley for adjusting the cutting speed. The belt guard has been removed for illustration purposes only. ***Do not operate the saw without the belt guard in place.***

SCROLL SAW TERMINOLOGY

The major machine parts of the scroll saw are shown in Figure 29-1. It is primarily a framework, called the *overarm,* suspended over a cast iron table. The distance from the front of the blade to the front of the overarm determines the size of the saw. Most scroll saws are 24″ (600 mm) long.

The scroll saw cuts by moving a blade in an up-and-down motion. This motion is produced by the drive unit. The drive unit consists of a motor and a *pitman.* The motor is located under the overarm. A V belt connects it to the pitman. The pitman produces the up-and-down motion.

The blade is held between the upper chuck, found on the end of the tension sleeve, and the lower chuck, found below the table. The tension sleeve pulls the blade tight and keeps it from kinking. An upper guide post behind the blade prevents the blade from twisting.

The rate at which the blade moves up and down can be regulated for different types of cuts. Some scroll saws change speed with cone pulleys mounted on the motor and pitman. A belt connects the two and is moved to one of the grooves on the pulleys to change speeds. When the belt is on the largest pulley on the motor, the machine runs fast. If it is moved to a smaller pulley, it runs slower. See Figure 37-6. Speeds are more easily changed with scroll saws that have a *spring-loaded pulley,* Figure 29-3. By turning a speed-adjustment crank on the front of the table, the motor can be moved forward or backward. Turn the crank only when the belt guard is on and the motor is running. The spring-loaded pulley mounted on the motor keeps tension on the belt. As the motor slides forward, the pulley closes and the inside diameter of the pulley gets larger. This action increases cutting speed.

Material Cut	Width In.	Teeth Per Inch	Blade Full Size
Steel ■ Iron Lead ■ Copper Aluminum	.070	32	
Pewter Asbestos Paper ■ Felt	.070	20	
Steel ■ Iron Lead ■ Copper Brass	.070	15	
Aluminum Pewter Asbestos	.085	15	
Wood	.110	20	
Asbestos ■ Brake Lining ■ Mica Steel ■ Iron Lead ■ Copper Brass Aluminum Pewter	.250	20	
Wood Veneer Plus Plastics Celluloid Hard Rubber Bakelite Ivory Extremely Thin Materials	.035	20	
Plastics Celluloid	.050	15	
Bakelite	.070	7	
Ivory ■ Wood	.110	7	
Wall Board Pressed Wood Wood ■ Lead Bone ■ Felt Paper ■ Copper Ivory Aluminum	.110	15	
Hard and Soft Wood	.110	10	
	.187	10	
	.250	7	
Pearl ■ Pewter Mica	.054	30	
Pressed Wood Sea Shells	.054	20	
Hard Leather	.085	12	

Figure 29-4
There are many different blades to select from. (Rockwell International)

BLADE SELECTION AND MOUNTING

Scroll saw blades vary in length, width, thickness and number of teeth per inch. Blades should be changed for different materials and for various types of cuts. Narrow blades should be used for cutting small curves, while wider blades are selected for larger radii. Use the chart in Figure 29-4 to select the correct blade for the material being cut. Some blades are designed to cut wood, others to cut plastics, ivory, metal, paper, felt, leather and asbestos. Use a fine blade or one with many teeth for cutting thin material. It also will give a smooth cut. A coarse, thick blade should be used for thicker material. It will produce a rough surface.

To cut these various materials, the speed of the saw can be varied from 650 to 1750 revolutions per minute (rpm). The harder the material, the slower the cutting speed. Softwood is cut at a high rpm, while plastics are sawed at a very low rpm.

Once the proper blade is selected, it must be correctly installed on the scroll saw. The following are guidelines for mounting scroll saw blades:

1. Unplug the machine and remove the throat plate. Clamp the blade in the lower chuck with the teeth pointing downward. The teeth also should face forward toward the front of the saw. If the chuck has a thumbscrew to hold the blade, tighten the blade by hand, Figure 29-5. A guide board helps align the blade, Figure 29-6.
2. Move the shaft of the motor by hand until the lower chuck is at its lowest position.
3. Loosen the adjustment knob and move the tension sleeve so that the upper chuck is within 1" (25 mm) of the top of the blade, Figure 29-7. For thinner and narrower blades, the distance should be increased to 1-1/2" (38 mm). Too little tension or too thin a blade on thick stock will make it difficult to keep the blade cutting on the line. This is called drift, Figure 29-8.
4. Pull the upper chuck down over the top end of the blade. Insert it about 1/2" (13 mm) into the chuck. Tighten the clamp.
5. Find the blade-support disc located on the bottom of the adjustable guide. By turning the support you can align a groove of the correct width with the blade, Figure 29-9. The groove should allow the blade to move freely but keep it from twisting as the stock is turned. If the teeth rub against the guide, select the next larger size. The groove should touch only the back portion of the blade and not rub on the sides of the teeth. When installed correctly, the back of the blade also will rest against the support roller. Move the roller in or out until it touches the blade.
6. Turn the motor over by hand. Observe the operation of the blade. If all is running properly, replace the throat plate in the table.

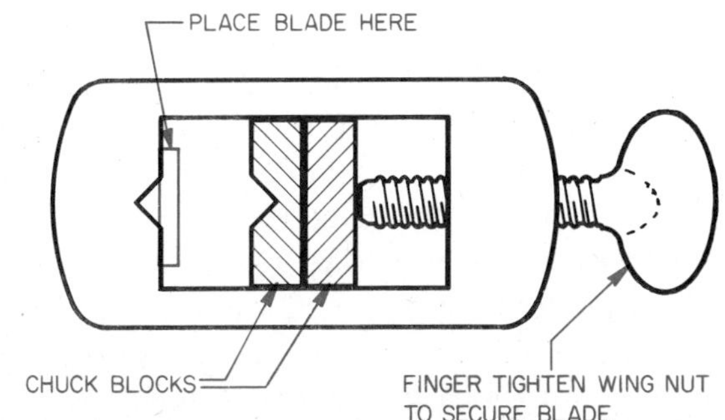

Figure 29-5
It is important to insert the blade in the proper slot in both blade chucks.

Figure 29-6
A guide board assists with aligning the blade. *Unplug the scroll saw for this operation.*

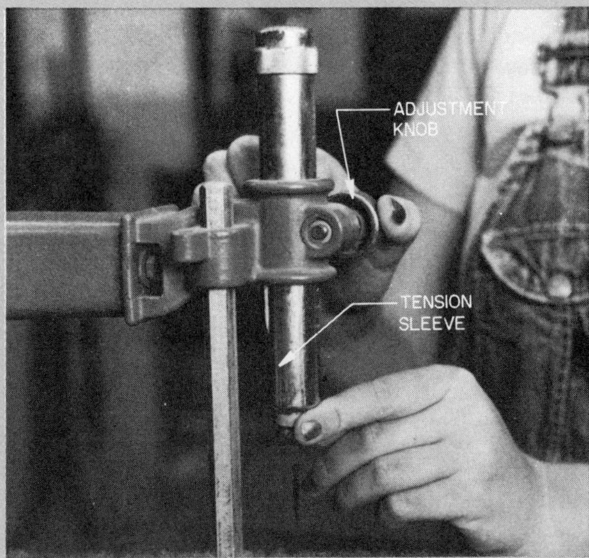

Figure 29-7
Adjusting the tension sleeve. *Unplug the scroll saw for this operation.*

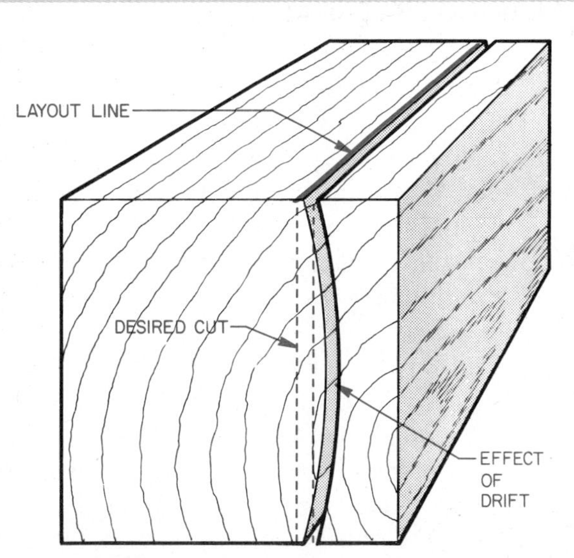

Figure 29-8
Drift causes the blade to wander away from the layout line.

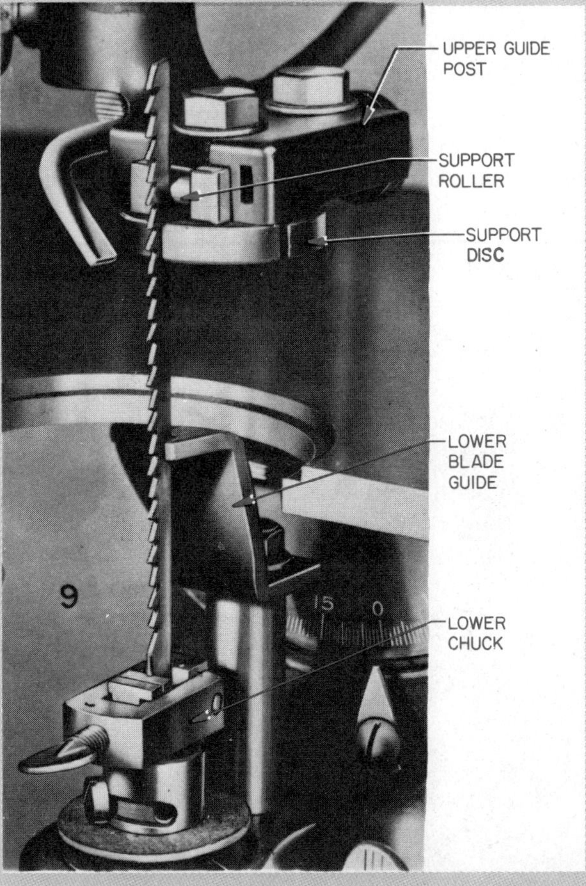

Figure 29-9
The support disc keeps the blade from twisting. (Rockwell International)

CUTTING EXTERNAL CURVES

To make external curves:

1. Mark the pattern on the stock.
2. Select the correct blade for the job and install it according to the directions given earlier. Set the upper hold-down to rest lightly on the top face of the stock, Figure 29-10.
3. Set the speed by either changing the belt position or by turning the speed-adjustment crank.
4. Plan the best path for the blade to follow. Ideally, the entire pattern is cut with one continuous motion. If the shape has any sharp curves, relief cuts must be made. Relief cuts are short cuts made in the waste from the outside edge up to 1/32" (1 mm) of the layout line, Figure 29-11. These cuts will prevent the blade from twisting.
5. Feed the stock slowly. Scroll saws do not cut material as rapidly as a band saw. If a piece of stock is advanced too rapidly, the blade will break. The operator should move the stock even slower when cutting small curves or thick stock.
6. Always cut on the waste side of the line. If the blade does accidentally work across the layout line, back the stock up and recut by staying on the outside of the pencil mark, Figure 29-12. Do not apply side pressure on the blade to bring it back on the line. This action will break the blade. Hold the board firmly to the table to prevent it from bouncing up and down.
7. Keep your hands out of line with the blade. Keep them on one side or the other so they will not touch the blade if you slip.

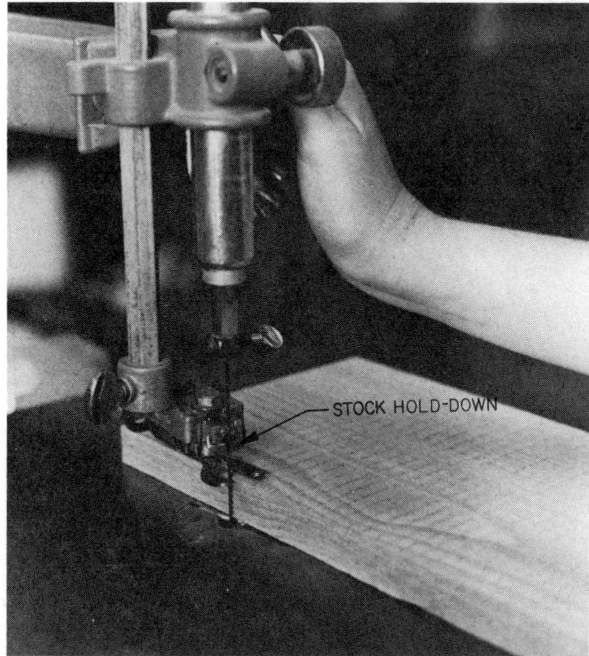

Figure 29-10
Adjusting the guidepost.

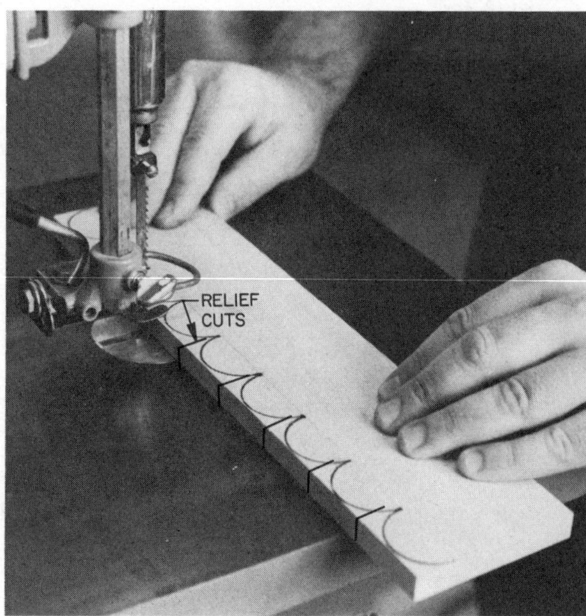

Figure 29-11
Relief cuts allow the material to be cut without binding the blade.

Figure 29-12
Correcting a wrong cut by backing the blade up and recutting on the waste side of the layout line.

CUTTING INTERNAL CURVES

Some cuts must be made that are totally within the edges of the board. Since the shape cannot be cut by starting at an outside edge, a different procedure must be followed. To make an *internal curve*:

1. Bore a hole in the waste portion of the stock. The hole should be large enough so that the blade can be threaded easily through the stock. Position the hole close to the layout line, Figure 29-13.
2. Unplug the machine. Raise the guidepost all the way up and remove the saw blade.
3. Position the stock so that the hole is immediately over the lower chuck. Feed the blade through the hole and install the blade, Figure 29-14.
4. Cut the stock to pattern. After the cutting is complete, shut off the power and loosen the top of the blade from its chuck. Slide the board up and off the blade.

SABER SAWING

The scroll saw can also work as a *saber saw.* This operation requires removing the arm and attaching a blade guide below the table.

A special blade held only by the lower chuck is also required, Figure 29-15. Insert the blade with the teeth pointing forward toward the operator and down. This leaves the remaining end unattached and unsupported. Saber saw blades are stiffer and wider than most scroll saw blades. The heavier blade used with the blade support makes deep cuts possible. Internal cuts also can be made easily because the stock can be lowered onto the blade after a hole has been bored.

Figure 29-13
Placement of the bored hole for an internal cut.

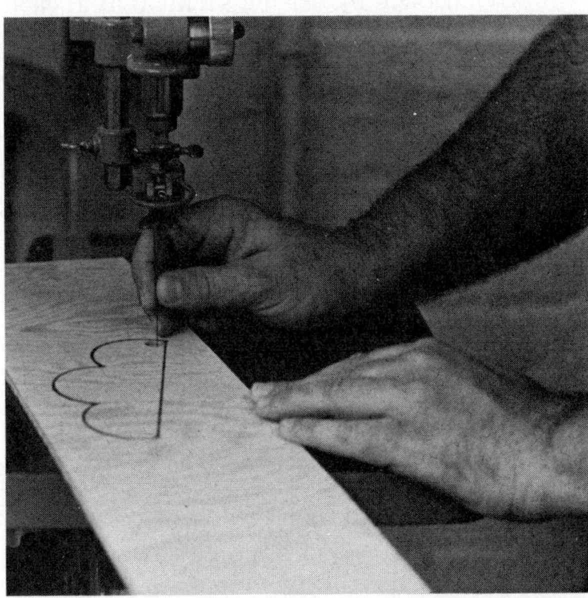

Figure 29-14
Installing a blade through the hole in the waste portion of the stock. *Unplug the scroll saw for this operation.*

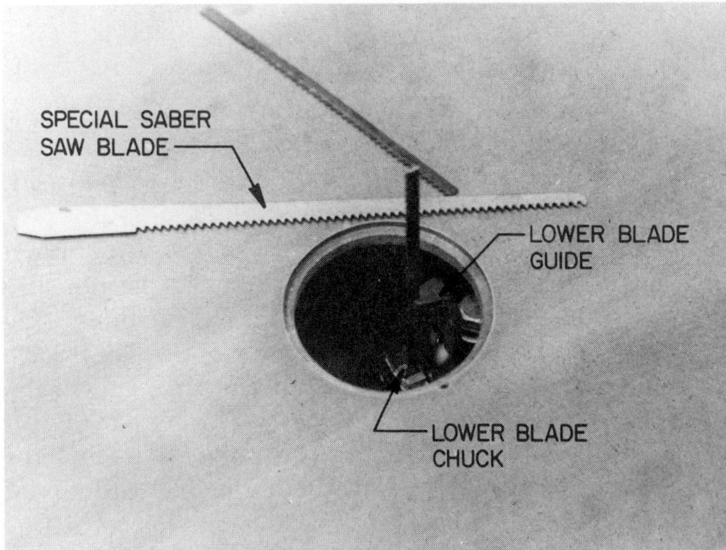

Figure 29-15
Setup necessary for saber sawing.

MARQUETRY SAWING

The art of *marquetry* is very old and is not practiced a great deal today. Marquetry is cutting out figures or pictures from different colored woods and placing them together. As a craft it can produce very beautiful products. To produce marquetry:

1. Stack two boards, one on top of the other. Attach them by driving small brads at each corner, Figure 29-16. More contrast is achieved when a light wood, such as maple, and a dark wood, such as walnut, are selected.
2. After drawing the design, tilt the table and upper guide 2°.
3. Bore a small hole in the stock along the layout line. Install a very fine, thin blade through this hole and cut exactly on the line. If you leave the line, keep cutting forward. Backing up and recutting to the line will cause a crack between the finished pieces.
4. Separate the two pieces of wood. Remove the section of dark wood. Replace with the light-colored wood of the same shape. If cut correctly, the two pieces of wood will fit together exactly, Figure 29-17. The remaining two pieces may also be placed together for an opposite effect.

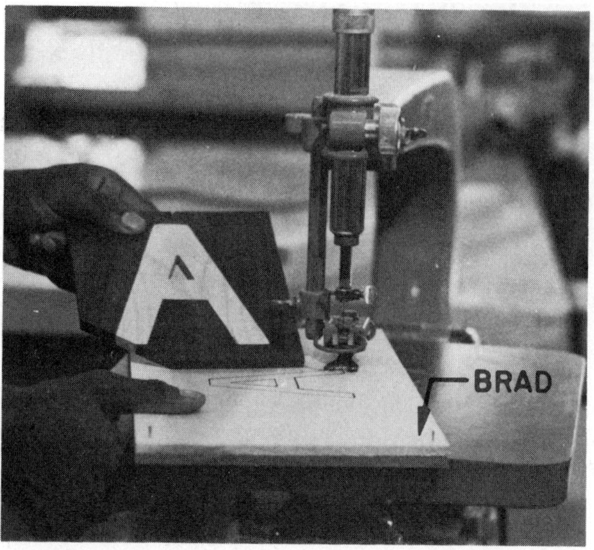

Figure 29-16
Marquetry sawing. A small brad is used in each corner. Note the visual aid.

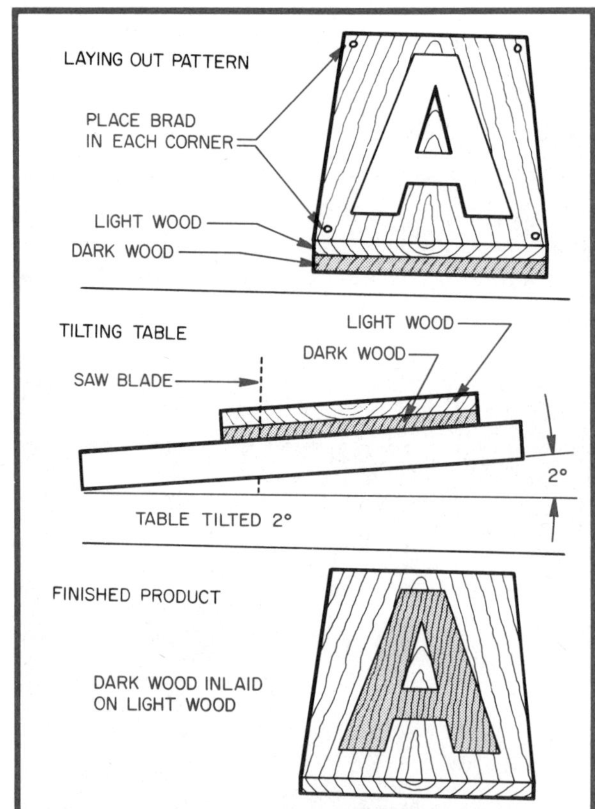

Figure 29-17
The three steps in producing marquetry include laying out the desired pattern and attaching the two boards with brads; tilting the table and cutting out the pattern; inserting the dark-colored piece in the tapered light-colored wood.

SANDING AND FILING

When you cut irregular curves very accurately, little sanding is required. What excess stock there is, however, can be filed and sanded using the scroll saw.

Scroll saw files can be clamped in the lower chuck, Figure 29-18. By running the saw at a low rpm, the excess stock can be removed without a great deal of chipping. A sanding attachment can also be used in the same way, Figure 29-19.

Filing and sanding attachments require the stock to be run without the standard throat plate. Smoother cuts and smaller pieces can be worked if an auxiliary table is made. A hole the same shape as the file or sander is made through which the tool is inserted.

Figure 29-18
Special files are used to remove rough edges.

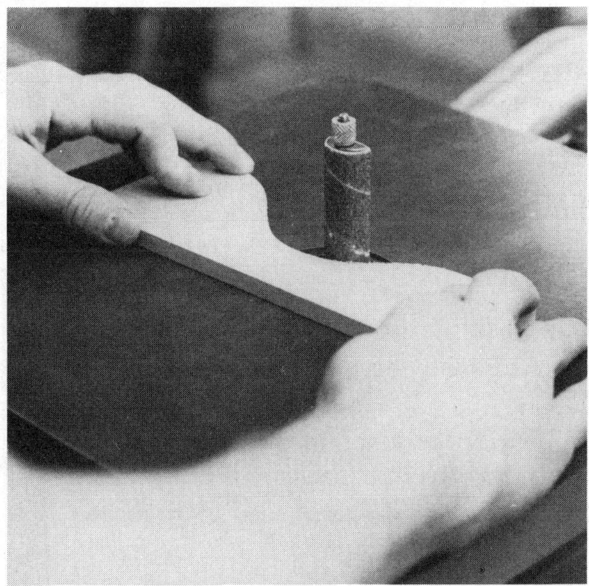

Figure 29-19
Sanding can be done with a special attachment.

REVIEW QUESTIONS

1 What does the pitman do on a scroll saw?
2 Name two ways to change the speed of the scroll saw.
3 List four different ways in which scroll saw blades vary.
4 How is the tension sleeve adjusted for most blades?
5 Where is the upper hold-down position before cutting begins?
6 Relief cuts are used for what purpose?
7 Why is a hole bored before an internal cut is made?
8 What is the advantage of saber sawing?
9 At what angle should the table be tilted for marquetry?
10 How can excess stock be removed from an edge with a scroll saw?

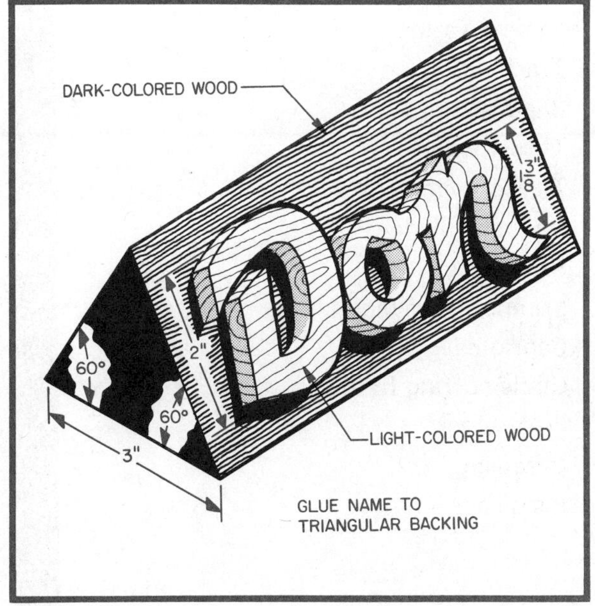

SUGGESTED ACTIVITIES

1 Inspect your scroll saw and check to see what adjustments can be made.
2 After unplugging the power, practice installing a blade.
3 Write your name on a board and cut out the pattern. After sanding the edges make it into a nameplate.

UNIT

30

Band Saws

Objectives

After studying this unit you should be able to:

1 Identify the function of machine parts on the band saw.

2 Install a blade and properly adjust the guides.

3 Coil a band saw blade for easy storage.

4 Cut both large and small curves or circles.

5 Make straight cuts using the rip fence, pivot block or miter gauge.

Technical Terms

Tracking
Band saw tire
Thrust wheel
Tension handwheel
Coiling a blade
Relief cut
Compound sawing
Cabriole leg
Circle-cutting fixture
Pivot block
Resawing
Inside corner

BAND SAW SAFETY RULES

1 Keep your hands and fingers out of the 4" (102 mm) safety margin around the blade. Refer to Figure 30-1.

2 Keep the upper adjustable guide no more than 1/4" (6 mm) above the stock.

3 Make sure the stock has at least one flat surface before you place it against the table.

4 Before backing out of a cut, turn off the power and allow the blade to come to a complete stop.

5 Use relief cuts when shaping curves that are narrower than the cutting capacity of the blade.

6 Cut cylindrical stock only while it is supported with a V block and miter gauge.

7 If the blade should break while cutting a board, turn the band saw off immediately. Apply the brake if there is one. Stand away from the right of the machine and tell your instructor about the break.

8 Disconnect the power before changing or working around any cutting tool.

A band saw cuts curved and irregularly shaped pieces, Figure 30-1. This machine is available in a number of sizes. Large band saws are called head rigs. Saw mills use them for cutting long, straight boards from logs, Figure 30-2.

Band saws with narrower blades are used for general manufacturing purposes.

BAND SAW TERMINOLOGY

The blade is held between two cast-iron or sheet-metal wheels. One wheel is mounted below the table and the other above. Each has a door guard that must be kept closed whenever the blade is moving, Figure 30-1. A motor drives the bottom wheel. The upper wheel is the idler wheel. It guides the blade above the table. This wheel puts tension on the blade by moving up or down a column. The wheel also can be tilted in or out to keep the blade centered on the wheels. This is called *tracking*, Figure 30-3.

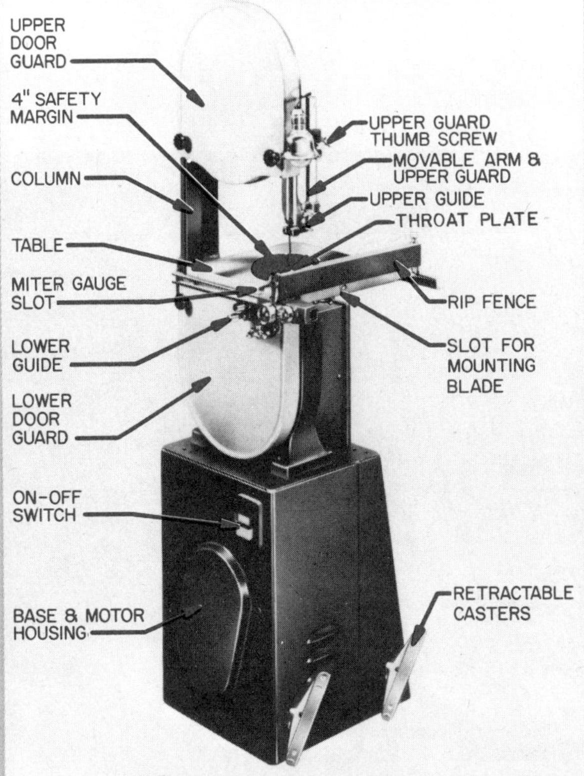

Figure 30-1
Major parts of a band saw. (Rockwell International)

Figure 30-2
Head rigs are the largest of all band saws. (Roseburg Lumber Co.)

The wheels are covered with rubber *band saw tires* to prevent the saw teeth from being damaged. Tires are available in many styles. Most machines have a plain rubber strip cemented to the metal wheels. Commercial band saws have removable tires reinforced with a metal core.

You can determine the size of the band saw by measuring the diameter of the wheel. A saw with a wheel 36″ (914 mm) in diameter is called a 36-inch saw. It will cut to the center of a circle 72″ (1829 mm) in diameter. Saws as small as 10″ (254 mm) and as large as 42″ (1067 mm) are available.

The table normally is mounted perpendicular to the blade. For cuts that require a bevel or chamfer, you can tilt the table up to 45° to the right and sometimes 5° to the left, Figure 30-4.

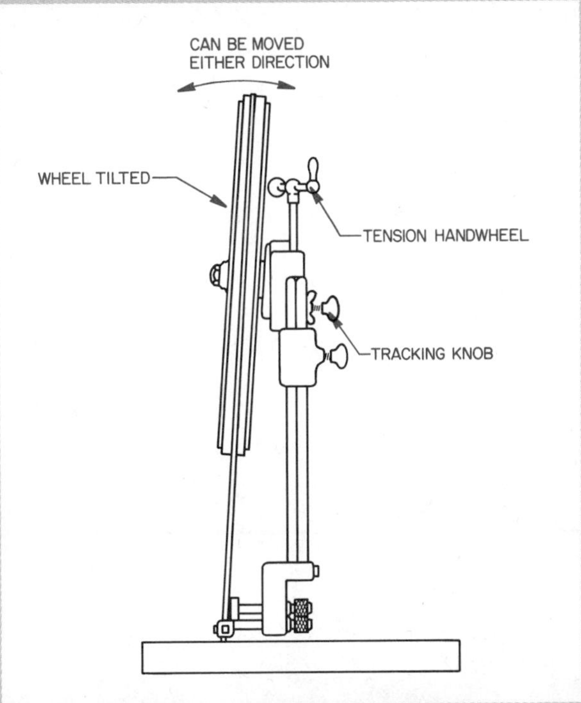

Figure 30-3
Tracking keeps the blade centered on the wheels.

Figure 30-4
Cutting a bevel with the table tilted to the right.

A slot in the top allows the blade to slide to the wheels. A throat plate covers the opening in the table that the blade runs through. Larger saws have two tables. The table surrounding the blade can tilt, but a smaller, auxiliary table remains stationary. The smaller table supports extra-wide stock.

The blade must run straight and true. This is accomplished by a set of guides mounted on a movable arm above the table and another set located permanently below the table. Both sets of guides are made up of pins and a wheel, Figure 30-5. Pins on each side of the blade keep the blade from twisting. The *thrust wheel* is directly behind the blade. When stock is being cut, it pushes the blade against the thrust wheel. This keeps the blade from being pushed off the wheels.

Sometimes the blade needs to stop quickly. Some band saws have a foot-operated brake for this purpose. First turn off the power and then step on the brake pedal.

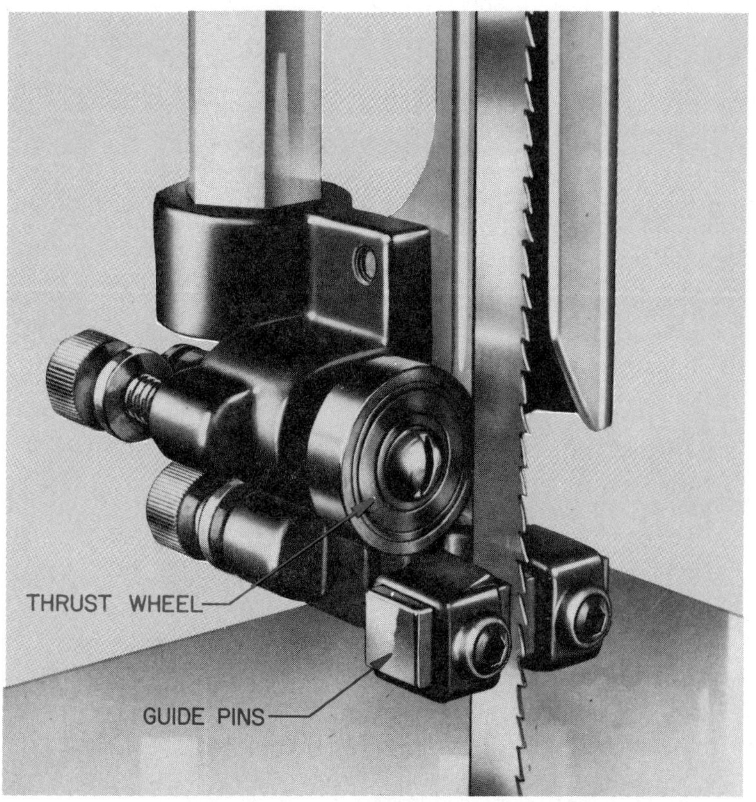

Figure 30-5
Parts of a band saw guide. (Rockwell International)

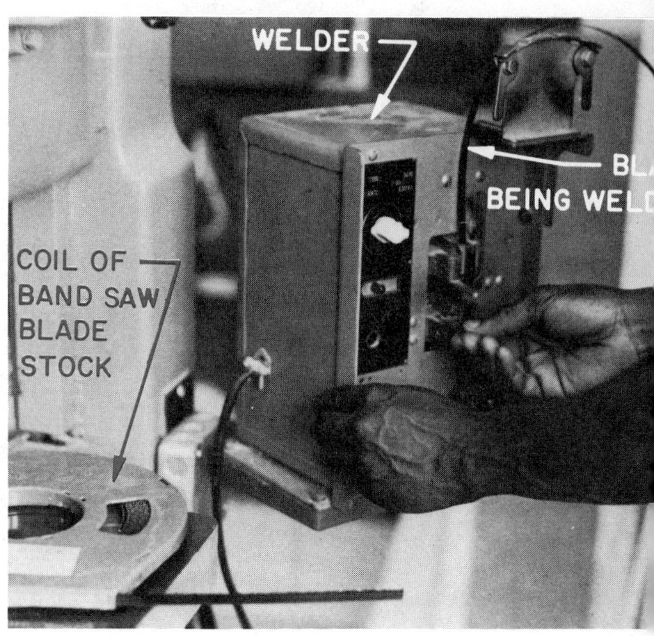

Figure 30-6
Use a band saw welder to weld the ends of the blade together.

BAND SAW BLADES

Band saw blades are made from steel bands that have teeth cut into one edge. Band saw blade stock is sold in long coils of 100′ (30,480 mm) or more. After the band has been cut to the desired length, the ends of the blade are welded together to form a closed loop, Figure 30-6.

Blade widths, types of set and tooth styles vary considerably, Figure 30-7. The wider the blade, the straighter the cut will be. A narrow blade cuts smaller curves. The most common blade for general-purpose wood cutting is 3/8″ (10 mm) wide, with four hook-teeth per inch. Band saw blades are designed to be disposable. Throw them away when they become dull.

Changing a Band Saw Blade

Band saw blades often need to be changed when different types of cuts are to be made or when a blade breaks or becomes dull. To mount a blade:

1. Shut off the power at the switch box. Open or remove the guard doors to expose the top and bottom wheels. Remove the throat plate in the table. To remove the blade, lower the upper wheel by loosening the

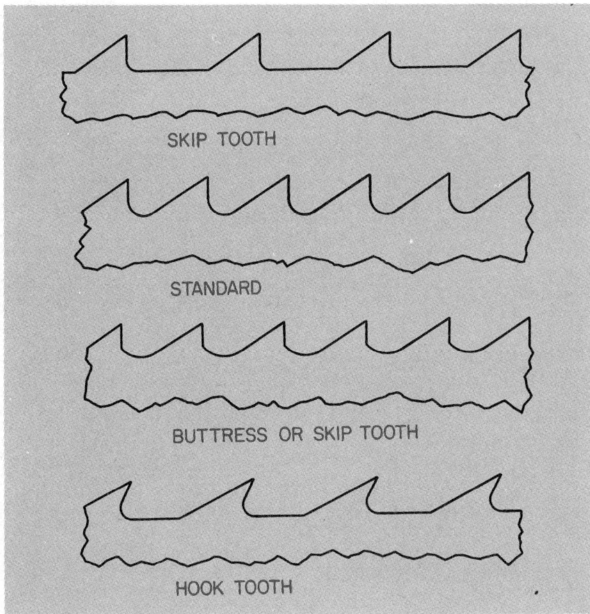

Figure 30-7
Band saw blade stock is available in different tooth styles.

tension handwheel, Figure 30-8. Holding the blade on the sides with both hands, slide it forward off the wheel and out through the slot in the table.

2. Select the new blade and place it on the two wheels. Make certain that the teeth are pointing forward and down toward the table.
3. Back the upper and lower guides off so that they clear the blade.
4. Tighten the tension handwheel until the blade is tight between the two wheels. Set the blade to the proper tension, or it will not saw straight or stay on the wheels. Some band saws have an indicator for the operator to determine the proper tension, Figure 30-9. For band saws without an indicator, the operator must rely on "feel" to set the tension. When pushed on the side, the blade should not deflect more than 1/8" to 1/4" (3 to 6 mm). Narrow blades require more tension than wide blades. Too little tension causes the blade to hit against the side of the saw guide. The blade also may tend to lead, or veer, to one side of the cut. Too much tension will cause the blade to break.
5. Spin the wheels by hand and note the position of the blade on the top wheel. It should be centered on the tire. If the blade is not running in the center, turn the tracking knob in or out as the wheel is turning, Figure 30-8. Improper tracking will cause the blade to come off the wheels and to rub on the guides. Refer to Figure 30-3.
6. Stop the blade and move the guide pins until they are immediately behind the gullets of the teeth. Place a piece of paper on

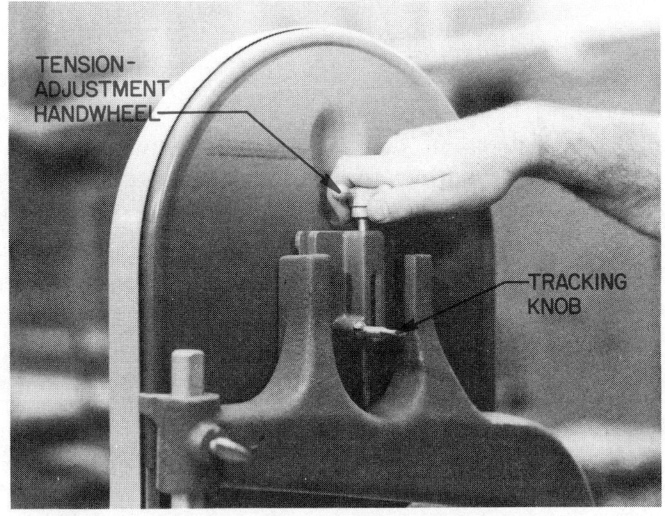

Figure 30-8
Adjustments for installing a blade.

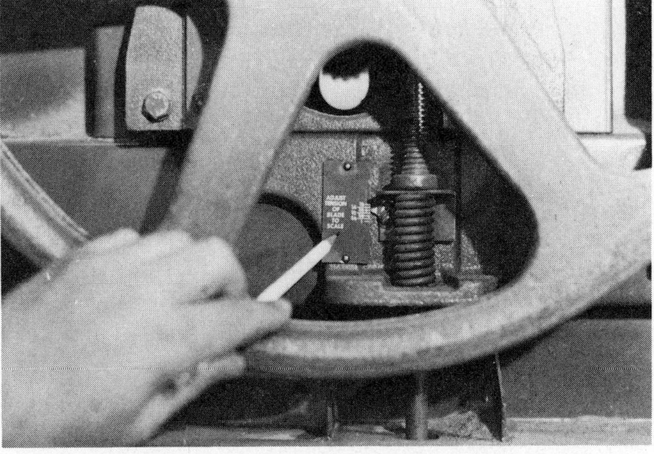

Figure 30-9
Blade tension indicator. *Power must be turned off.*

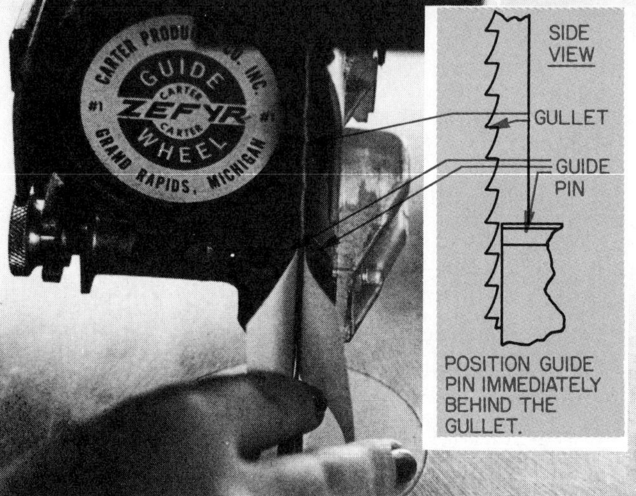

Figure 30-10
Use two pieces of paper to adjust the guide pins. *Power must be turned off.*

each side of the blade. Push the pins until they touch the paper next to the blade. Lock the pins on both guides in this position, Figure 30-10.

7. Adjust the thrust wheel until there is a space of 1/32″ (1 mm) between it and the back of the blade. The bearing should not turn when the blade is not cutting. Cutting stock will cause the blade to move back against the thrust wheel where it will be supported. Repeat the process for the other guide under the table. Replace the throat plate. Turn the wheel by hand to see if the blade is tracking correctly. If not, adjust the tracking knob.
8. Replace the guards and turn on the power. Make some trial cuts with a scrap piece of stock. Check to see that the blade is cutting properly.

Coiling the Blade

Band saw blades need a large storage space unless they are first coiled. *Coiling a blade* reduces the diameter of the blade for easier handling. Follow this procedure:

1. Position the blade with the teeth pointing away from the work and the bottom of the coil touching the floor. Place your foot on the blade and grasp each side with your thumbs pointing upward, Figure 30-11A.
2. With your thumbs on the back of the blade, push the top of the blade down. Twist the sides of the blade so that the teeth point to the sides, Figure 30-11B.
3. As you bend over, your hands should cross to continue making the coils. Finish the

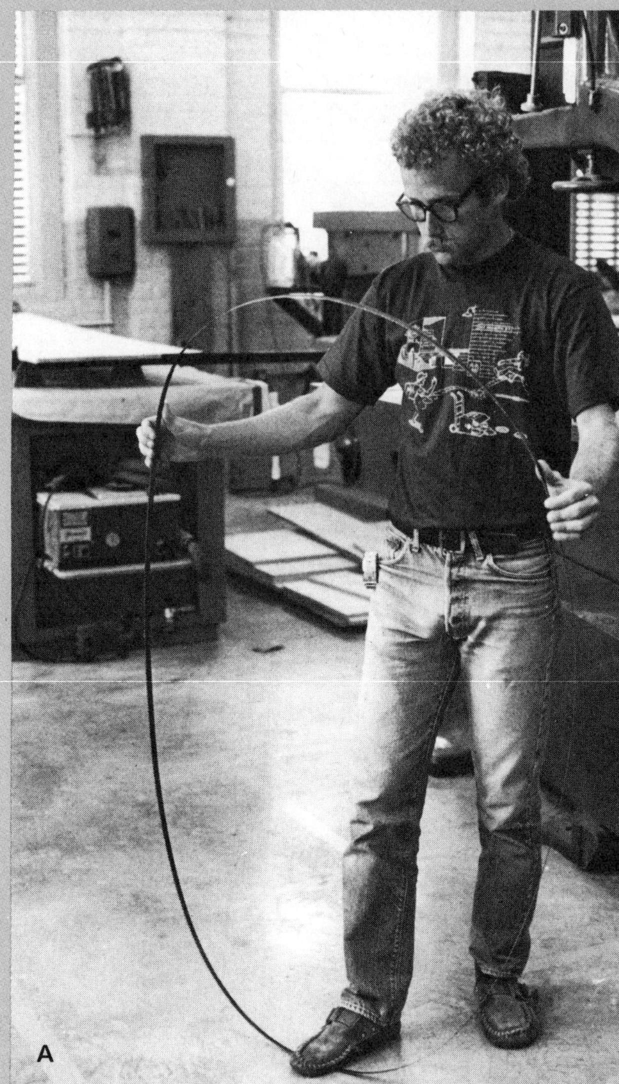

Figure 30-11
Procedure for coiling a band saw blade. Note the position of the operator's hands in each photograph.

B

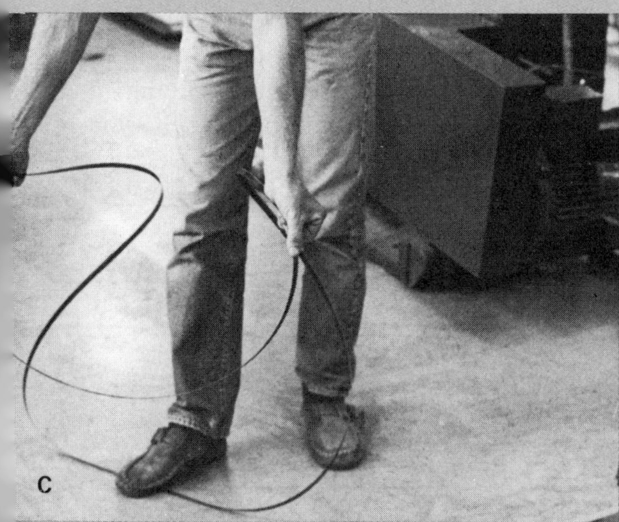
C

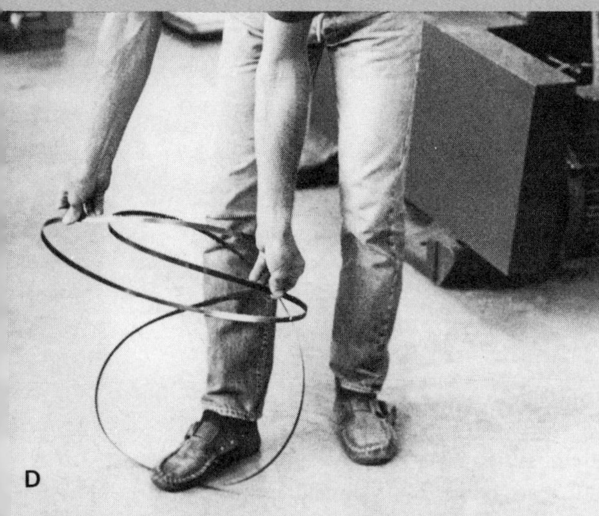
D

task by moving your palms to the front until they face forward, Figure 30-11C.

Practice this procedure until the individual steps can be performed smoothly and continuously, Figure 30-11D.

CUTTING CURVES

Curves usually are cut freehand. This requires a great deal of skill developed through much practice on the part of the operator.

Large Curves

To cut curves larger than 6″ (152 mm) in diameter:

1. Lay out the pattern on the surface of the stock. Select the side of the board that allows the stock to pivot without hitting the column, Figure 30-12.
2. Adjust the upper guide so that it is no more than 1/4″ (6 mm) above the thickest portion of the stock, Figure 30-13. This will keep the blade from drifting away from the layout line. It is also a safety feature.

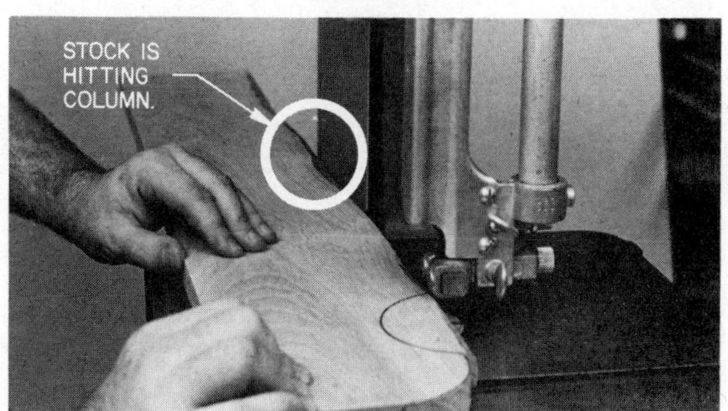

Figure 30-12
Lay out the pattern on the correct side of the board to avoid hitting the column.

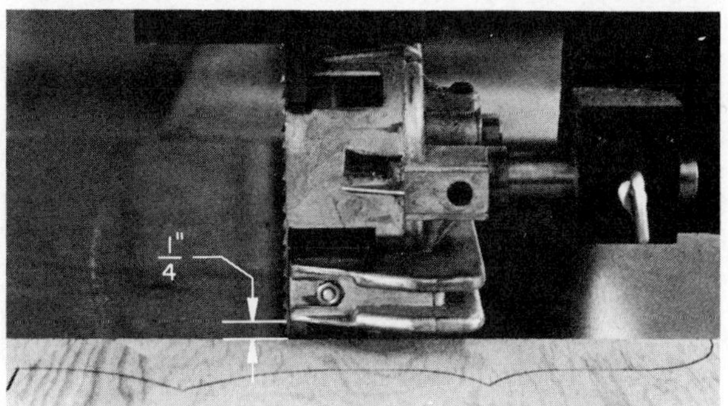

Figure 30-13
Adjusting the upper guide.

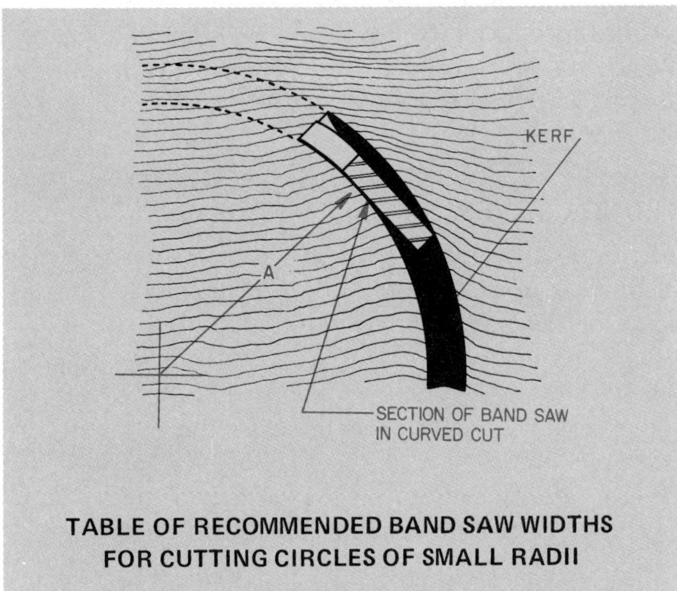

TABLE OF RECOMMENDED BAND SAW WIDTHS FOR CUTTING CIRCLES OF SMALL RADII

Width of Saw Blade		Minimum Radius (A) To Be Cut	
Inches	Millimeters	Inches	Millimeters
1/8	3	3/8	10
3/16	5	1/2	13
1/4	6	3/4	19
3/8	10	1-1/2	38
1/2	13	2-1/4	57
5/8	16	3	76
3/4	19	4-1/2	114
7/8	22	6	152
1	25	8	203

Figure 30-14
Recommended radii for different widths of blades. Note that the back of the blade will rub against the kerf when the radius becomes too small.

3. Study the pattern to be cut and select the best path for the blade to follow. If more than one curve is required by the layout, make the shortest cuts first. For shaping inside corners, cut up to the corner, turn off the power, brake the blade to a stop, and back out of the cut. Complete the pattern by cutting from the opposite direction.
4. Feed the stock into the blade as rapidly as it will efficiently cut the board. If fed too fast, the blade will cut roughly and may break. If fed too slowly, the blade will burn the stock and wear the set off of the teeth.

Small Curves

When the curve is smaller than what the blade can cut with a single pass, you must take other steps to cut the stock to pattern. The back of a wide blade will rub against the saw kerf as the stock pivots back and forth. Figure 30-14 gives recommended minimum radii that can be cut with various blade widths. To cut small curves:

1. Make *relief cuts* in the waste portion of the board. These small cuts make sawing sharp curves easier. Place the relief cuts in spots where the back of the blade otherwise would rub the kerf.
2. Cut within 1/32" (1 mm) of the layout lines. When the curve is cut, the scrap parts will come loose and prevent the blade from bending, Figure 30-15. Do not cut curves less than 1" (25 mm) in diameter on a band saw. Instead, drill a hole the desired diameter.
3. Do not push the scraps off the table with your hands while the saw is running. If scraps are in the way, remove them with a push stick.

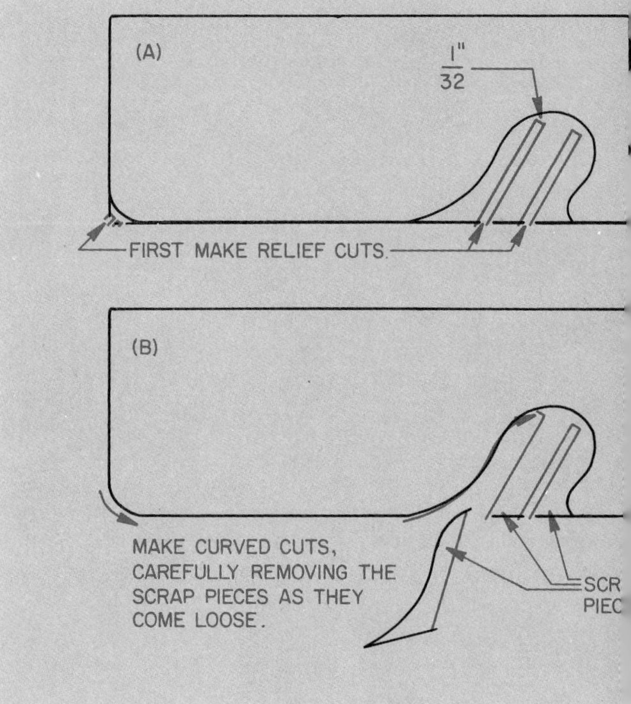

Figure 30-15
Cut sharp curves by first making the relief cuts and following the layout lines to cut the curve.

COMPOUND SAWING

Compound sawing is a technique for making decorative pieces on the band saw. Two adjoining surfaces are cut to a pattern on a square or rectangular piece of material. The resulting piece will have compound curves that blend together to form a graceful part. A *cabriole leg* is an example of compound sawing, Figure 30-16. To make compound cuts:

1. Make a full-size, cardboard template of the curves desired.
2. Trace around the template on the first surface and cut the stock to pattern, Figure 30-17A. Use a narrow blade so that few, if any, relief cuts have to be made.
3. Use masking tape to secure the scrap pieces to the parent piece, Figure 30-17B. Draw around the template on the adjoining side. If you are cutting a cabriole leg, mark the second side simply by using the same area of the side already cut, Figure 30-17C.

Figure 30-16
Cabriole legs are used on furniture.

Figure 30-17
Procedure for compound sawing.

A Laying out pattern.

B Taping stock back together.

C Laying out second cut.

D Cutting the second side.

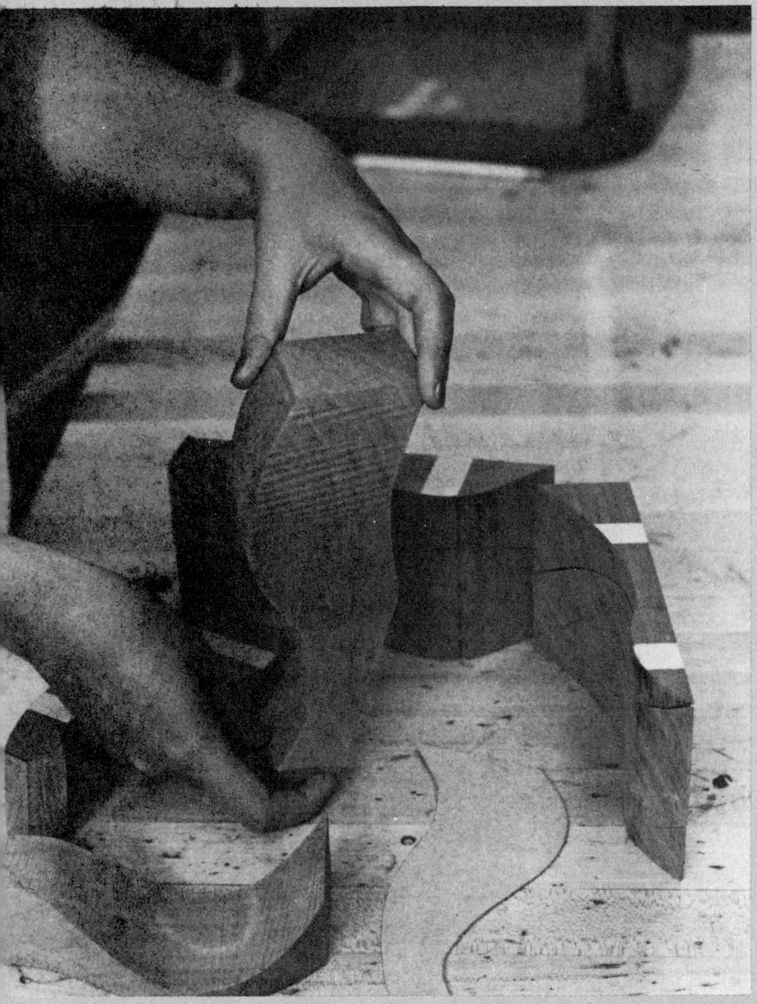

E Finished product.

Figure 30-17 (continued)

4. Cut the remaining side, Figure 30-17D. Finish the piece by hand-scraping and sanding the surface, Figure 30-17E.

CUTTING CIRCLES AND CIRCULAR SEGMENTS

One way to cut a true radius is to use freehand techniques, Figure 30-18. This method requires a considerable amount of skill to achieve a smooth, even cut. The freehand technique requires that each piece be laid out with a pattern or compass.

Use a *circle-cutting fixture* to cut true circles. You can buy a commercial fixture, Figure 30-19, or make a device in the shop, Figure 30-20. Make the circle-cutting fixture by fastening a piece of plywood that will cover the table to the right of the blade. Attach a center or pivot point to the plywood auxiliary top. You can make a point by filing the tip of a wood screw and screwing it in from the bottom side of the fixture. The location of the point is important. Fix it on a line even with the leading edge of the teeth of the blade. If it is offset to either the

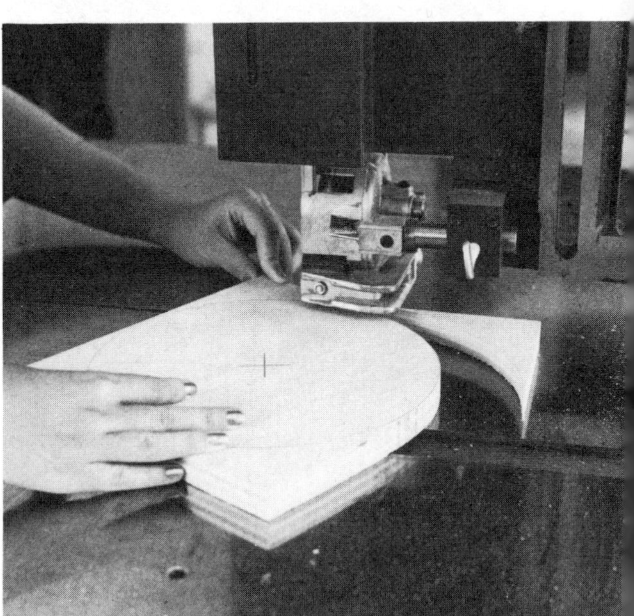

Figure 30-18
Freehanding a circle. Note the position of the operator's hands.

front or back, you cannot cut a true circle. The distance of the pivot point from the right side of the blade should equal the radius of the circle. Fixtures with a movable point permit you to cut different sizes of circles.

To cut circles using a fixture:

1. Cut square pieces of stock at least 1/4" (6 mm) larger than the diameter of the circle.
2. Mount the circle-cutting fixture on the band saw and check the location of the pivot point. Remember that the radius should be equal to the distance of the pivot point from the blade. Adjust the upper guide to 1/4" (6 mm) above the stock to be cut.
3. Center the stock over the top of the pivot point. Tap lightly on the top surface with a mallet. The point will sink into the bottom side of the stock.
4. Turn on the power and place a finger over the center to hold the stock against the fixture.
5. Rotate the stock into the blade until the disc is cut, Figure 30-21. You can cut segments of a circle and rounded corners with a similar fixture, Figure 30-22.

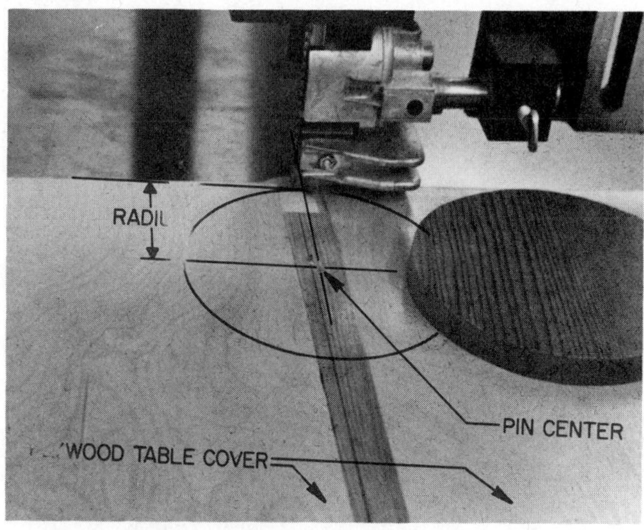

Figure 30-20
Shop-made circle-cutting fixture. Align the center point with the tips of the teeth.

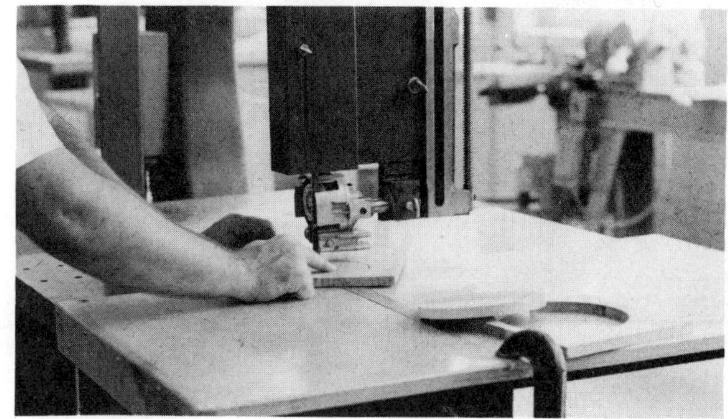

Figure 30-21
Cutting stock with a circle fixture.

Figure 30-19
Commercial circle-cutting fixture. (Rockwell International)

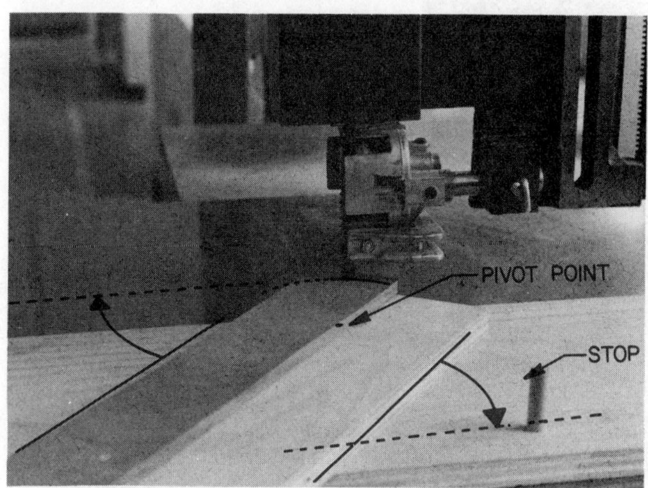

Figure 30-22
Rounding a corner.

Figure 30-23
Ripping with a commercial fence.

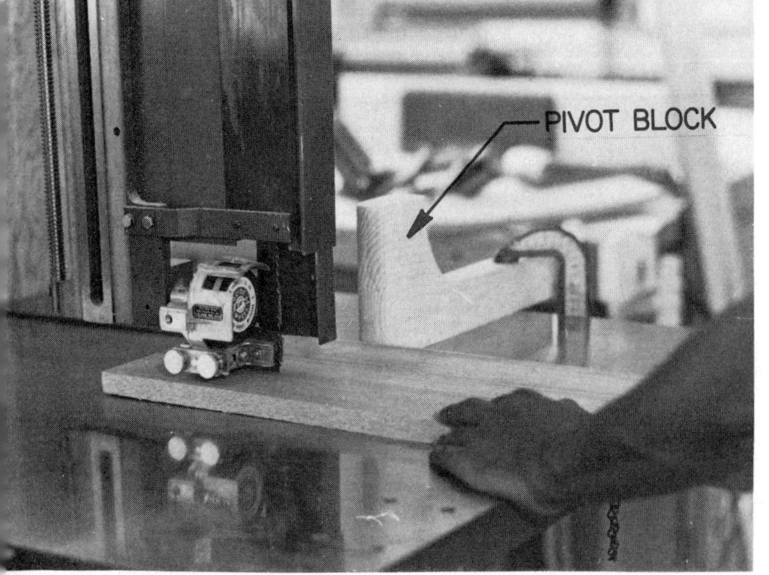

Figure 30-24
Ripping with a pivot block.

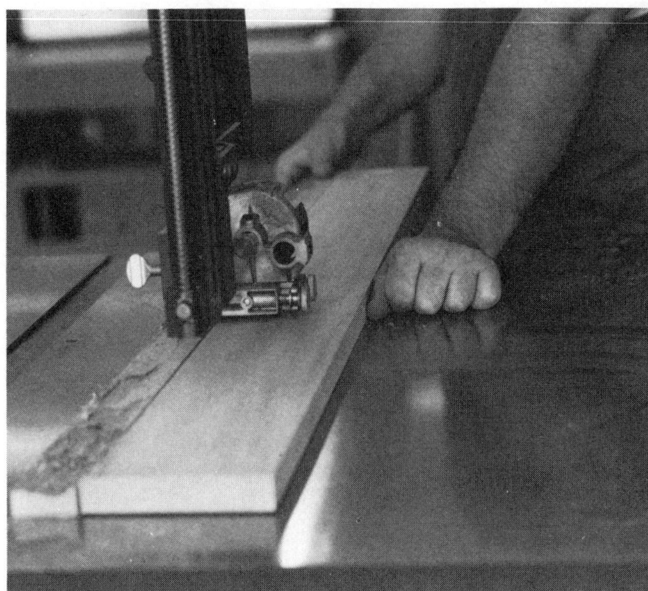

Figure 30-25
Freehand ripping.

MAKING STRAIGHT CUTS

Although the primary purpose of the band saw is to cut curves, it also makes straight cuts. In most cases, however, select a radial-arm saw or a table saw to make these cuts. But a band saw does have some advantages. There is no danger of kickbacks. The band saw can cut thinner kerfs and thicker boards. Make all straight cuts with as wide a blade as possible. There are three methods of ripping stock.

Using a ripping fence. Most band saws have a commercial rip fence. Place a smooth or straight edge of the stock against the fence. Place a flat surface against the table. Use a push stick on narrow stock, Figure 30-23.

Using a pivot block. Use a pivot block also to rip material. This method has an advantage over the rip fence. You can move the trailing end of the stock to the right or left. This allows you to saw a straight line even if the blade is leading. Leading causes the blade to move to one side or the other. You can correct this by moving the trailing end of the stock in the direction opposite the lead, Figure 30-24.

Freehand ripping. For freehand ripping, first scribe a line on the stock. Place your left hand on the table and use the side of your thumb as a guide. Your right hand feeds the stock into the blade, Figure 30-25.

Figure 30-26
Resawing with a pivot block.

Figure 30-27
Commercial resawing fixture.

RESAWING

Resawing is cutting thick stock into thinner boards. For resawing, the band saw has advantages over the table saw. The band saw removes less stock from the board because the kerf is thinner. The band saw can make the cut in one pass. The table saw often requires at least two passes.

To resaw, use a wide blade. Guide the stock with a pivot block or rip fence, Figure 30-26. Large commercial saws have resaw attachments, Figure 30-27.

Figure 30-28
A hole in each corner will allow you to turn the board when the blade reaches the corner.

CUTTING SQUARE INSIDE CORNERS

The band saw can cut square *inside corners.* You can use two methods. One method requires that you bore a hole in each corner. Turn the board when the blade reaches the holes, Figure 30-28.

Another method is to use only the blade to turn the corner. First, cut up to the layout line. To turn the corner, back up the stock approximately 1″ (25 mm) and make another cut to the side of the original cut, Figure 30-29. Repeat this process until a notch is cut wide enough for the blade to turn the corner.

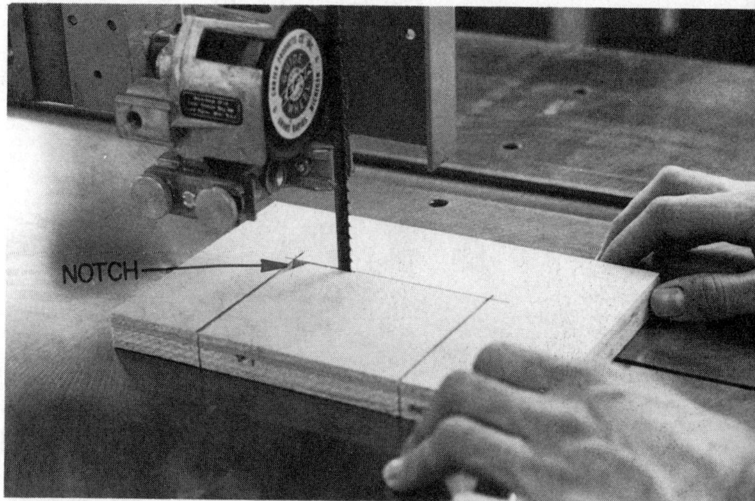

Figure 30-29
Cut a notch to allow the blade to turn.

CROSSCUTTING

A major advantage of crosscutting with a band saw is that you can cut short pieces. If cutting freehand would not be safe, use a miter gauge. You can cut circular stock, such as dowel pins, to length by using a miter gauge. Hold the stock with a V block, Figure 30-30.

Never attempt to saw circular pieces without a V block. The downward cutting action of the blade will tend to spin the board out of your control.

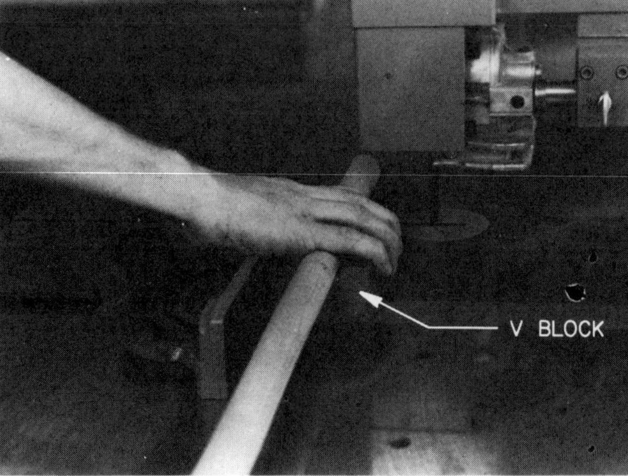

Figure 30-30
Crosscutting circular stock with a miter gauge and a V block.

REVIEW QUESTIONS

1 How do you determine the size of a band saw?
2 Sketch a set of blade guides on a band saw. Include side guides, thrust wheel and blade.
3 How far above the surface of the board should the upper guide be?
4 Sketch a set of small curves, and indicate where relief cuts should be made.
5 On which surfaces of the stock do you trace the template when you make a compound cut?
6 Where should you place the center point when you are using a circle-cutting fixture?
7 What is meant by sawing to a pattern?
8 What are three methods of cutting straight lines?
9 Why is a pivot block often used for ripping and resawing stock?
10 Sketch two methods of cutting inside corners.
11 What should you use to hold a dowel pin when you are cutting it to length?

DARK-COLORED WOOD 1/2" THICK
LIGHT-COLORED WOOD 3/8" THICK
ATTACH TO HOUSE OR DOOR WITH BRASS ROUND HEAD WOOD SCREWS.
1/2"
4"
20-30°
1/2"
1"

SUGGESTED ACTIVITIES

1 Draw a straight line near the edge of a scrap board. Practice cutting to the outside of this line, using the freehand ripping technique.
2 Select your house or apartment numbers from the picture shown in Unit 7. Draw them on a board and cut each with a band saw. Fasten them on a backing board and finish them with the desired finish.
3 Inspect your band saw to see what type of tires are mounted on the wheels. Ask your instructor to disconnect the power first.
4 Coil an old band saw blade so that it can be easily stored.
5 Check the guides on your band saw. Are they positioned correctly? Is the blade set at the proper tension?
6 Install a circle-cutting fixture on the band saw. Set the center point to cut a disc with a 2" (51 mm) diameter. After cutting four discs, use them as wheels to make a wooden toy.

UNIT

31

Radial Arm Saws

Objectives

After studying this unit you should be able to:

1 Identify all major parts of the radial arm saw and understand their functions.

2 Make basic adjustments and install a saw blade.

3 Crosscut, rip and dado stock.

4 Perform special cuts such as horizontal cutting.

Technical Terms

Single arm

Arm track

Chop saw

Antikickback fingers

Out-rip

In-rip

Horizontal cutting

RADIAL ARM SAW SAFETY RULES

1 Keep your hands at least 4" (102 mm) from the blade.

2 Always check that the guard is adjusted properly for each cut.

3 When crosscutting, hold the stock with your left hand and pull the saw with your right hand.

4 Do not cross your arms while crosscutting.

5 Be sure that surfaces placed against the fence and table are straight and flat.

6 Cut only one piece of stock at a time.

7 When ripping, feed stock from the correct direction.

8 Use a push stick when ripping stock less than 6" (152 mm) in width.

9 Use the in-rip position for ripping stock less than 6" (152 mm) in width. Always apply pressure primarily between the blade and fence.

10 Upon completing any cut, return the saw to the farthest position at the rear of the arm.

11 Disconnect the power before changing a blade or other cutters.

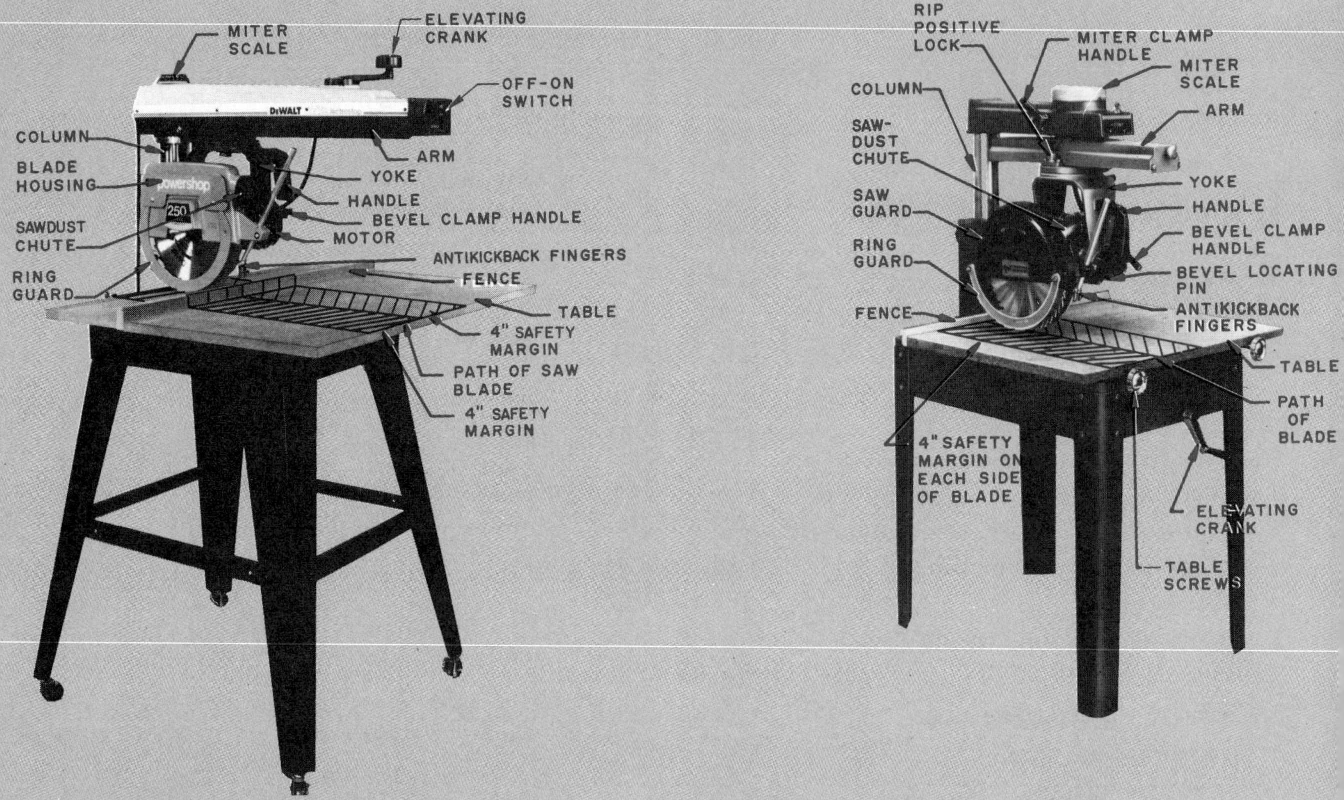

Figure 31-1
A single-arm radial arm saw is one of the most common types used. (DeWalt, Inc.)

Figure 31-2
The arm track radial arm saw can cut extra wide miters. (Rockwell International)

The radial arm saw, or cut-off saw, is one of the best machines for cutting boards to length. It originally was designed for crosscutting. But through the years, many improvements have widened its use.

There are two major types of radial arm saws. They are the *single arm,* Figure 31-1, and the *arm track,* Figure 31-2. Both types are used chiefly for crosscutting and ripping. With the proper attachments, however, a radial arm saw also can be used for boring, sanding and scroll sawing, Figure 31-3. There are special machines for each of these activities. But if the machines are not available, the radial arm saw is a good substitute.

A major advantage of crosscutting with the radial arm saw is that you can hold the stock stationary as the saw moves across the board. The saw rotates toward the fence and helps hold the wood against it. This prevents kickbacks. Holding the stock against the stationary fence also eliminates the possibility that the stock will slip to one side. Such slipping easily may occur during crosscutting on a table saw. Another advantage is that the blade enters the stock from the top surface. This makes it easier to align the saw blade with the layout line, Figure 31-4.

Another good machine for cutting stock to length is a *chop saw.* This saw is used often in industry. The blade of a chop saw automatically goes up and down when the operator steps on a foot pedal, Figure 31-5. This leaves both hands free to move the material to the left or right.

RADIAL ARM SAW TERMINOLOGY

The blade and motor travel as a unit on a horizontal arm called a track. Two styles of tracks are available for radial arm saws. A single overhead arm is the most common, Figure 31-1. The arm track is a newer design and enables you to cut larger miters, Figure 31-2. A good-quality saw will have a ball bearing track for moving the motor unit easily.

Figure 31-3
Many different attachments are available for the radial arm saw. They include (A) a drill chuck; (B) a sanding drum; and (C) a scroll saw device. (DeWalt, Inc.)

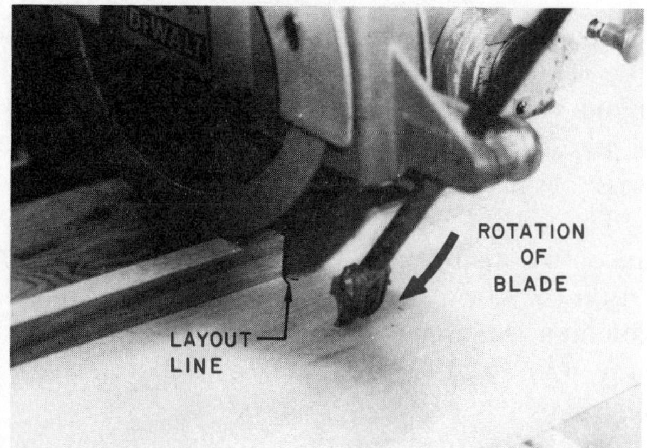

Figure 31-4
Because cutting starts from the top side of the stock, layout lines are easily seen.

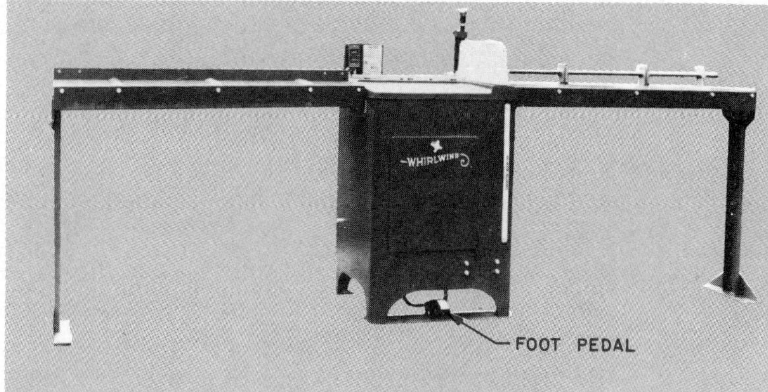

Figure 31-5
A chop saw only cuts boards to length. The blade saws up and down and is operated by a foot pedal. (Simplec Manufacturing Company, Inc.)

Figure 31-6
A radial arm saw in the miter position.

The track is mounted on a vertical column that can be turned to various angles for cutting miters, Figure 31-6. An elevating crank usually is mounted on top of the saw to raise and lower the column for different depths of cuts.

The motor and blade are housed in a metal frame called the yoke. A handle is attached to the yoke. Always use the handle to push or pull the blade along the track. You can rip stock by moving the yoke to the 90° position, Figure 31-7. Other adjustments can be made by tilting the motor to the right or left a maximum of 90°, Figure 31-8. Cut bevels and chamfers this way. The positive stops and swivel clamps are the parts that release or secure the arm, yoke and motor. A scale of degrees at these adjustment points allows you to set the blade to the desired angle.

The ring guard consists of a blade housing, sawdust chute and *antikickback fingers.* You can move all of these parts to various positions to protect you from injury. Each type of cut requires different adjustments.

The table and fence are the parts of the radial arm saw that should be replaced most often. Each is made from wood and is cut when the saw is used. A large number of cuts can remove much of the fence and table. These cuts can create a problem because the stock to be cut must always sit flat and straight. A heavily cut fence or table should also be replaced to lessen the chance of accident.

Most saws have two threaded shafts. The one

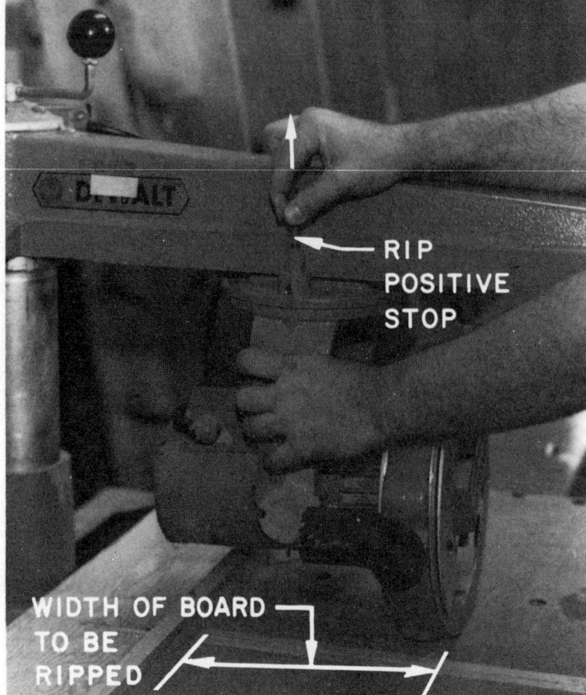

Figure 31-7
Setting the saw in the ripping position.

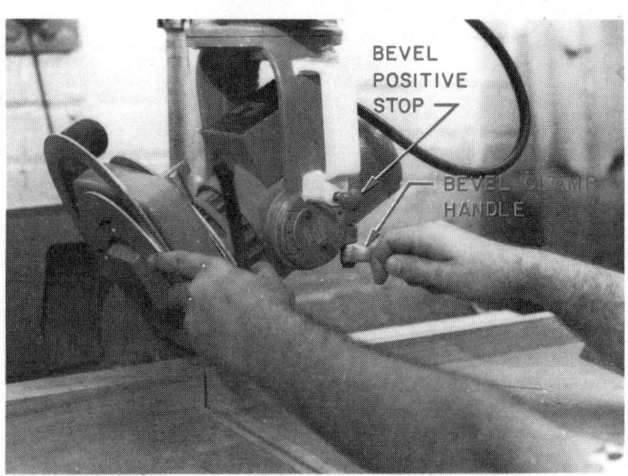

Figure 31-8
Setting the radial arm saw to cut a bevel.

to the left of the motor is the saw arbor. It holds the saw blade and such parts as a dado head or a molding head. On the opposite end of the motor is the auxiliary shaft. Router bits and other accessories may be attached to it.

The size of a radial arm saw is based on the maximum diameter of blade that can be mounted on the saw arbor within the guard. The most common size is 10" (254 mm). Industry, however, uses 18" (457 mm) blades–and even larger ones.

The length of the arm is also considered when determining the size. This is because the arm length determines the maximum width of board that the saw can cut. Some overhead arm tracks

Figure 31-9
An extra-long arm allows large panels to be cut to any size. (DeWalt, Inc.)

Figure 31-10
Hold the arbor with a wrench and move the arbor nut wrench downward. *Disconnect power for this operation.*

have extra long arms for cutting wide panels of plywood or other stock, Figure 31-9.

SELECTING AND MOUNTING A SAW BLADE

Both radial arm and table saws use the same blade styles. (Refer to Unit 28 for further details.) For general purposes, a four-tooth combination will cut satisfactorily. Use different styles if you will be doing a great deal of one type of cutting.

To remove the saw blade:

1. Switch the power off at the breaker box and remove the ring guard.
2. Raise the blade so that the teeth do not extend below the surface of the table. This will allow the blade to slide off the saw arbor once the arbor nut is removed.
3. Use a wrench provided with the saw to hold the arbor stationary, Figure 31-10. Some saw arbors are secured by inserting a locking pin. Do not wedge a piece of wood under the blade unless there is no other way to secure the blade. A wedge will rack, or bend, the saw out of alignment when you apply pressure with the arbor nut wrench.
4. Put a wrench on the arbor nut, Figure 31-10. Move the wrench in the direction that the saw rotates when cutting or in the direction that the teeth point. When the nut is loose, unscrew it by hand.
5. Remove a washer and then the blade. The blade must be stored away from other metal objects to prevent damage to the saw teeth.

Figure 31-11
The teeth should point in the same direction as the rotation arrow. *Disconnect power for this operation.*

To install a new blade:

1. Mount the new blade on the arbor with the teeth at the top of the blade pointing forward. Some saws have an arrow indicating the direction of rotation. The teeth should point in that same direction, Figure 31-11.
2. Hold the arbor securely and tighten the arbor nut by moving the wrench opposite the direction of rotation. Then install the blade guard and check to see that it is adjusted properly. Do not use the saw unless the guard is working correctly.
3. Lower the blade so it is no more than 1/16″ (2 mm) below the top of the table. If a groove for the blade is not already cut into the table, turn on the power and lower the rotating blade into the table. Keep pushing the saw against the column. Once the blade is 1/16″ (2 mm) below the table, pull the saw out, making the groove. Cut a wide scrap and check for squareness with a framing square.

CROSSCUTTING

The radial arm saw is the best machine for crosscutting boards to length. Short stock as well as long boards can be cut accurately. When sawing, observe the proper safety margin. This means that you should keep your hands a minimum of 4" (102 mm) from the blade. The procedure to follow for crosscutting is:

1. Set the miter scale pointer on 90°. If you are making an accurate cut, cut a piece of scrap board at least 1" (25 mm) thick and 6" (152 mm) wide. Check the board with a framing square. The piece should be square not only across the width but also along the thickness, Figure 31-12. If it is not square, adjust the saw according to instructions in the operator's manual.
2. Use the elevating crank to lower the saw blade 1/16" (2 mm) below the surface of the table. If the depth is less than 1/16" (2 mm), the stock will not be cut completely. If the blade is more than 1/16" (2 mm) below the table, it will cut too deeply and break the table.
3. Set the blade housing so that the bottom surface is parallel with the saw table. Position the antikickback fingers approximately 1/8" (4 mm) above the stock, Figure 31-13.
4. Decide whether to cut the stock to either the left or the right side of the blade. The preferred method is to use the left hand to hold the stock on the left side of the blade and pull on the handle of the saw with the right hand, Figure 31-14. The other method is to position the stock on the right side of the blade. Then hold the stock with the right hand and pull the saw with the left hand. Never cross your arms during cutting.
5. Place the stock against the fence and align the layout mark with the saw blade. Push the motor all the way back to the column and turn on the power.
6. Feed the rotating blade slowly into the stock. As the blade enters the wood, it may speed up by itself and cause the saw to jump forward. You can control this action by firmly gripping the handle and guiding the blade into the stock. Be especially care-

Figure 31-12
Check squareness of a cut from two directions.

Figure 31-13
The antikickback fingers and the saw guard must enclose the blade.

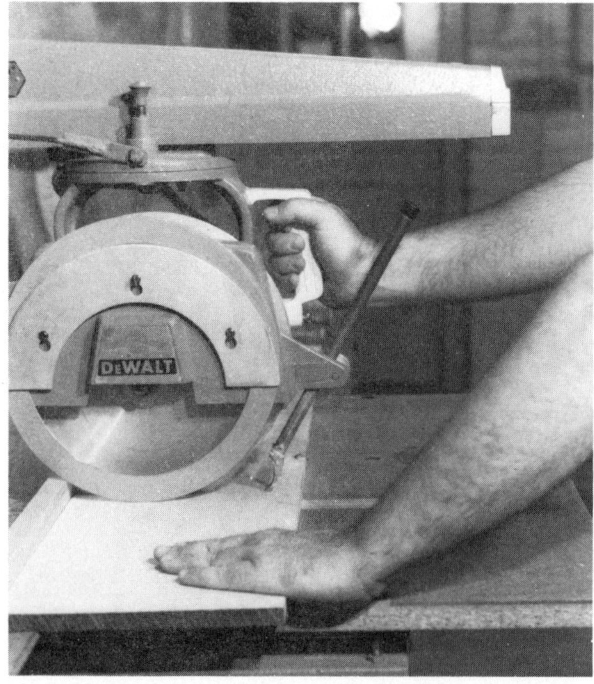

Figure 31-14
Hands properly positioned for operating the saw.

Figure 31-15
Use a rabbeted stop block when cutting duplicate pieces.

ful when cutting wood that is hard or extra thick. Pull the saw forward until the cut is through the stock.

7. Return the saw to the column and turn off the power.

CROSSCUTTING DUPLICATE AND WIDE PIECES

If you want to cut more than one piece to the same length, install a stop block. Clamp a shop-made rabbeted stop block to the fence for this purpose, Figure 31-15. The rabbeted corner of the stop block will reduce the buildup of sawdust. This is important because sawdust may cause the board to be cut short. You also can use commercial stops, Figure 31-16.

To cut stock to the same lengths, use the following procedure:

1. Cut the first end off squarely and then mark the desired length. Align this mark with the stopped saw blade and install a stop block for the squared end.
2. Make certain that the stock is against the stop block. Then cut the second end. Remeasure the length to check for accuracy. Reset the stop block if the length of the board is incorrect.
3. If the stop is positioned accurately, continue cutting all other duplicate pieces.

Use a stop block also to crosscut a board that is wider than the stroke length of the saw. For this type of cut, position the stock in front of the blade and install a stop block on the squared end opposite the saw blade. Make the first cut by pulling the blade to the front of the track. After returning the blade to the column, turn over the board and butt the same end up against the stop block. Then make the second cut. If the end against the stop block was square, the two cuts should meet in the middle of the board, Figure 31-17.

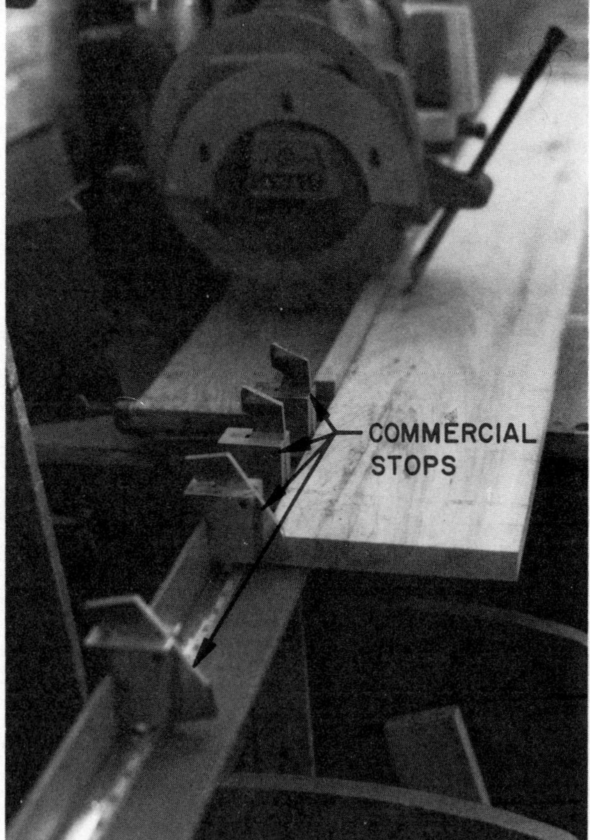

Figure 31-16
Commercial stops offer a choice of several sizes.

Figure 31-17
Cut extra-wide stock by sawing from both edges.

Figure 31-18
Setting the saw in the rip position.

RIPPING

Ripping stock on the radial arm saw can be dangerous unless you follow the safety rules exactly. Use a table saw for ripping if one is available. Your hands may get dangerously close to the blade during some ripping operations.

To rip a board:

1. Raise the blade and pull the saw to the end of the track. This will give easy access to the necessary adjustment handles. Then release the swivel clamp and lift the rip positive lock. Next, turn the motor yoke so the blade is parallel with the fence, Figure 31-18.
2. Position the blade according to the width of your stock. Wide stock is cut best by rotating the blade to the right. This is called the *out-rip* position, Figure 31-19. Moving the blade to the left will place it in the *in-rip* position, Figure 31-20. The in-rip position is preferred when ripping narrow stock. When the blade is set for ripping, a locating pin will automatically lock into position. Finish securing the saw blade by tightening the swivel clamp.
3. Measure the desired width between the fence and the saw tooth closest to the fence. Lock the blade into position with the rip lock, Figure 31-21.
4. Lower the blade so that it is 1/16″ (2 mm) below the table surface. If a groove for the blade is not already cut in the table, you may have to make one. To do this, turn on the power and then lower the rotating blade into the table. Be careful not to cut into the table more than 1/16″ (2 mm).
5. Adjust the front edge of the ring guard so it is no more than 1/4″ (6 mm) above the stock. Set the antikickback fingers on the back of the guard 1/16″ (2 mm) below the top of the board. Move the sawdust chute so it shoots the chips away from you.
6. Always feed the stock *against* the rotation of the blade. The blade must turn with the teeth rotating toward you, Figure 31-22. The blade will grab and throw out stock fed from the wrong direction. A serious accident could occur.
7. Turn on the power and feed the board slowly into the blade. Keep the stock against the fence and push only on the side of the board that is between the blade and the fence. Never place your hands in the path of the blade. Use a push stick to guide stock past the blade when cutting boards less than 6″ (152 mm) wide, Figure 31-23. Never allow your hands to pass under the motor or come closer than 4″ (102 mm) to the blade.

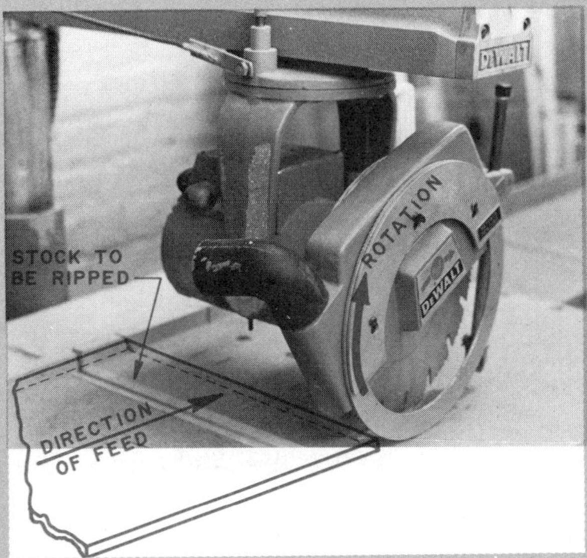

Figure 31-19
The saw set in the out-rip position.

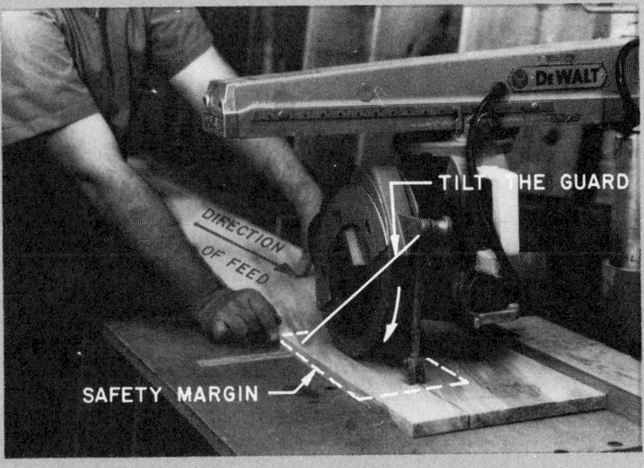

Figure 31-22
Always feed the board against the rotation of the blade.

Figure 31-20
The saw set in the in-rip position.

Figure 31-21
The rip lock secures the saw blade to the arm.

Figure 31-23
Use a push stick when ripping narrow stock.

CUTTING FLAT MITERS

There are three common methods of cutting flat miters with a radial arm saw. The first method requires no special attachments to be fastened to the saw.

1. Release the miter clamp handle. Pull up on the miter positive lock and move the arm to the right, Figure 31-24. If you want to cut a 45° angle, position the blade by moving the arm to a slot that the miter positive lock will fit into. Finish securing the arm by tightening the miter clamp handle. You can cut angles more or less than 45° by moving the arm along the miter scale pointer. There are no slots for the positive lock to fit into for cutting these angles. Secure the saw into position by pressing down the miter clamp.
2. If a groove is not already cut into the table and fence, first screw in the rip lock and turn the power on. Lower the rotating blade into the table to a depth of 1/16″ (2 mm). Then hold the handle and pull the blade out, making the desired groove. Check the accuracy of the setting by making a trial cut on a piece of scrap. This procedure is the same as that for crosscutting. Measure the cut with a protractor. After the correct angle has been established, cut the first end of all pieces to be mitered, Figure 31-25.
3. Using the same techniques as before, move the blade to the left to the desired angle. Clamp a stop block on the fence the proper distance from the blade. Finish by cutting all pieces to the correct length.

Use a second method when you want to cut a large number of miters. This method also allows the blade to remain in the 90° position, which keeps the fence and table from being cut.

1. Cut all pieces to the exact length by using a stop block. Then clamp a shop-made V fixture on the table top to position the material to be mitered. Center the path of the saw blade on the point of the V, Figure 31-26.
2. Saw the first end by pushing the stock against the left side of the V fixture and butting the end to be cut against the bottom of the V, Figure 31-27.

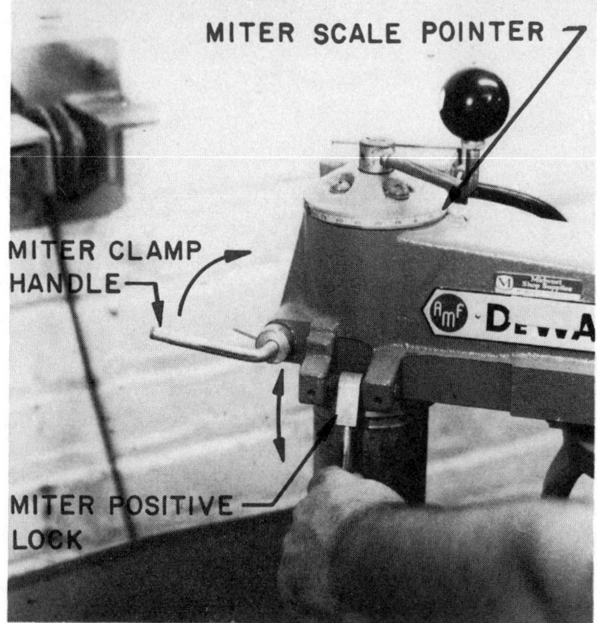

Figure 31-24
Setting the arm in the miter position.

Figure 31-25
Cutting the first end of the miter using the first method.

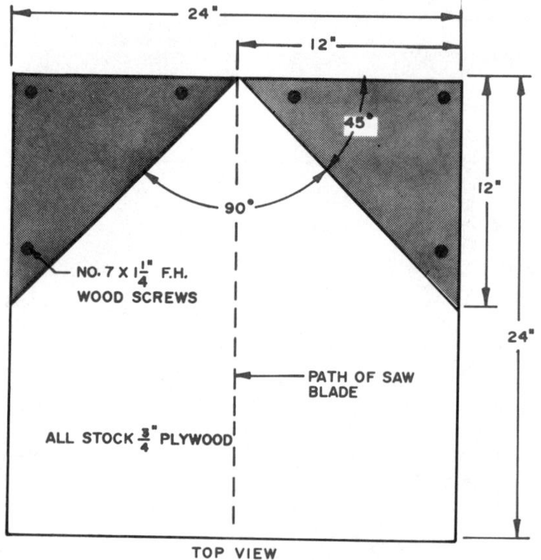

Figure 31-26
A V fixture for cutting miters.

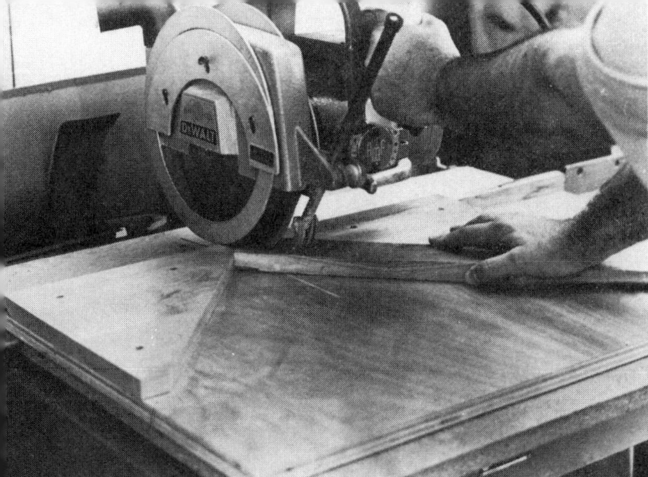

Figure 31-27
Cutting the first end of a miter using the second method.

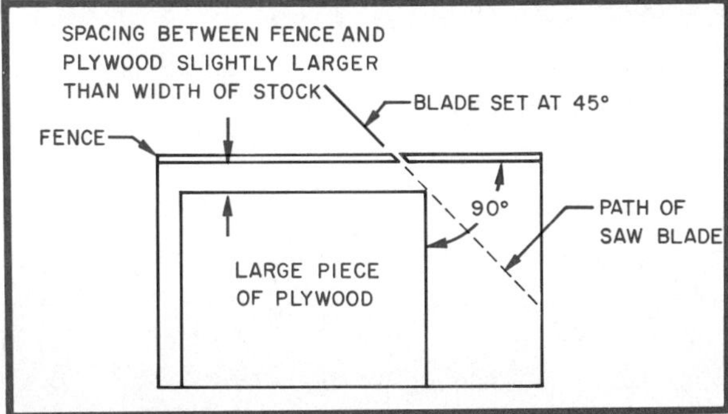

Figure 31-28
Proper setup for cutting miters using the third method.

3. Cut the other end while holding the stock against the right side of the fixture.

The third method provides a way of cutting the stock to length while making a miter. With this method, you do not need to precut stock to finished length before mitering.

1. Swing the arm to the right in the 45° position. Then clamp a large piece of squared plywood to the table at a right angle to the permanent fence, Figure 31-28. The space between the fence and the plywood should be slightly more than the width of the stock. This spacing allows the stock to slide between the fence and the plywood.
2. Place the stock against the side of the plywood and push the end to be cut against the permanent fence. Turn on the power and miter the first end, Figure 31-29.
3. Cut the second end by positioning the stock against only the permanent fence. Install a stop block on the permanent fence to help cut the proper lengths, Figure 31-30.

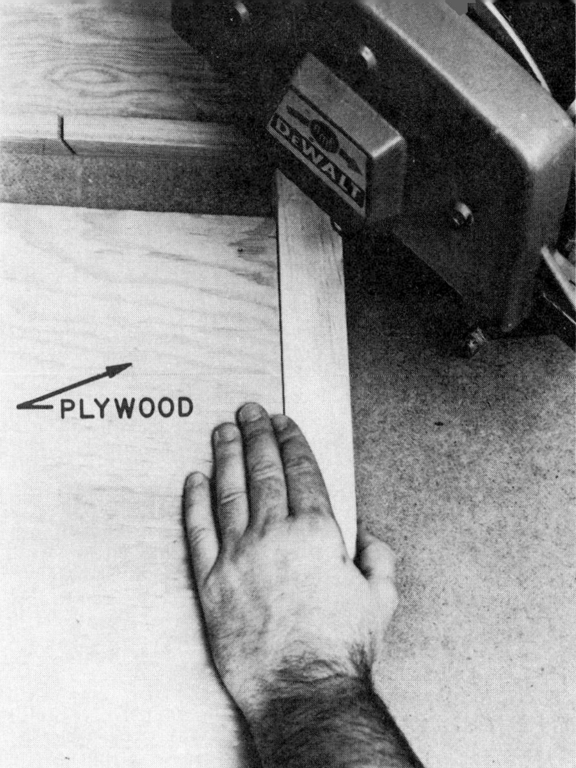

Figure 31-29
The first end is cut using the third method. *The side ring guard has been raised for illustration purposes only.*

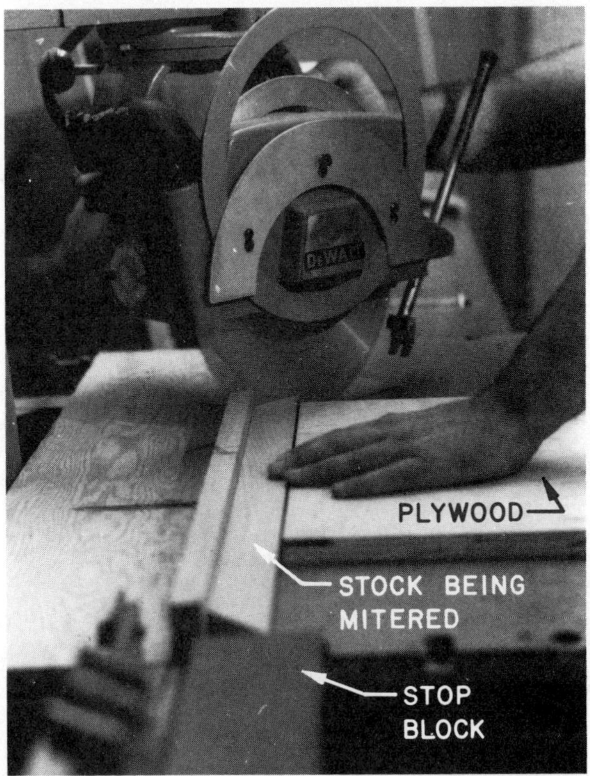

Figure 31-30
Cutting the second end using the permanent fence. *The side ring guard has been raised for illustration only.*

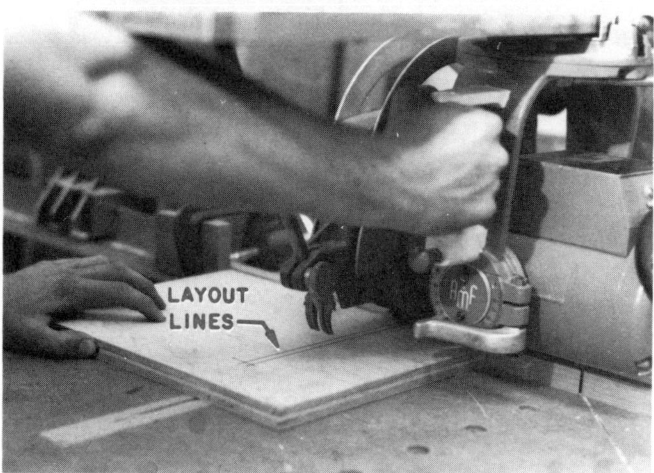

Figure 31-31
Layout lines can be seen easily when cutting dadoes.

Figure 31-32
Stop the dado exactly on the layout line.

DADOING

The radial arm saw is an excellent machine for cutting dadoes. It often is preferred over the table saw because the dadoes can be cut from the top surface. Dadoing on this surface allows the layout lines to be clearly seen, Figure 31-31.

A radial arm saw uses the same type of dado head as a table saw. Install the head the same way on both kinds of saw. (Refer to Unit 28 for further details on installation.) Make certain that the teeth are pointing downward and that the dado head rotates freely in the guard before turning on the power.

After properly installing the dado head, you can set up the saw for cutting blind dadoes. To make this type of cut:

1. Mark layout lines for dadoes on one set of sides of the boards to be cut. After marking the depth of the desired groove on the end of one of the boards, bring the dado head to this same level.
2. Position the marked board on the table so the stopped portion of the dado is away from the fence. If you want to cut several identical blind dadoes, install a stop block on the fence to assure that all cuts will be alike.
3. Bring the head to full speed and feed the saw slowly into the work. To maintain control, grip the handle.
4. Be sure to stop cutting the dado exactly on the layout line, Figure 31-32.

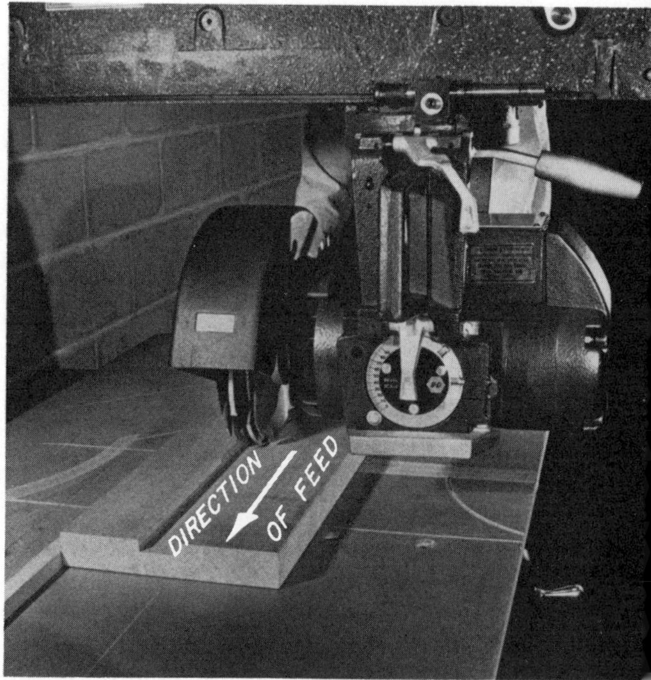

Figure 31-33
Making a gain with the dado head in the rip position. (DeWalt, Inc.)

5. Cut all identical dadoes before resetting the stop block for the next cut.

The dado head can make other types of cuts. For example, such cuts as rabbets and gains can be made by placing the motor in the rip position, Figure 31-33. You should use a table saw, however, to make these types of cuts.

HORIZONTAL CUTTING

Some cuts can best be made when the blade is in a horizontal position. Sawing in this manner is called *horizontal cutting.* To perform horizontal cutting:

1. Raise the column so that the blade will clear the table when it is pivoted to one side. Then release the bevel locking pin and loosen the bevel clamp handle, Figure 31-34. Now move the blade into the horizontal position.
2. Make sure that the bevel locking pin has shifted into the indexing hole. Finish securing the head by tightening the bevel clamp handle.
3. Determine whether you will need an auxiliary table on top of the regular saw table. This higher table will elevate the stock so that the end of the arbor can clear the regular table, Figure 31-35. The back edge of the stock must be supported by an additional fence.
4. Decide on the desired depth of your cut. The horizontal position at which the stock is held determines the depth. As long as you keep your hands 4" (102 mm) from the blade, you can make deeper cuts by moving the board closer to the saw arbor. Never move the board when the blade is touching the stock.

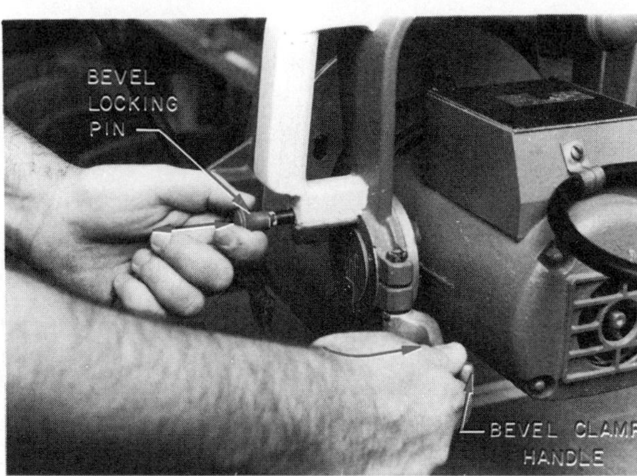

Figure 31-34
Setting the blade into the horizontal cutting position.

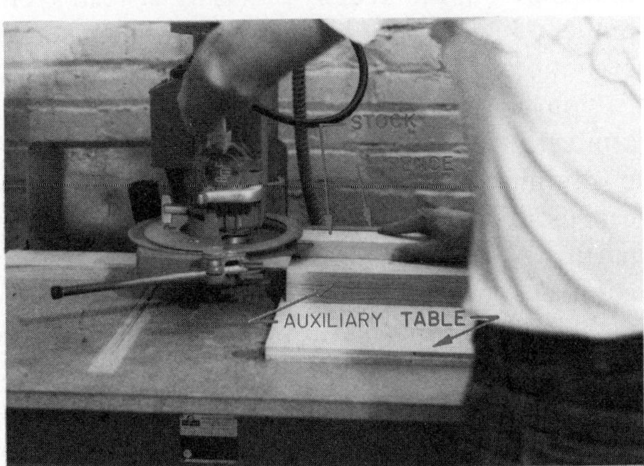

Figure 31-35
An auxiliary table raises the stock off the table.

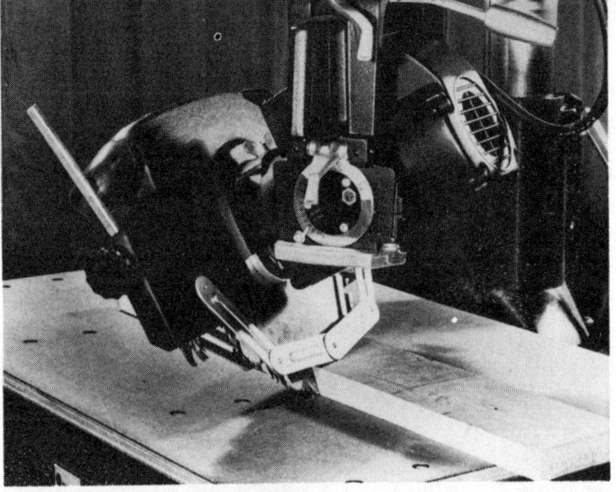

Figure 31-36
A compound miter can be cut on a radial arm saw. (DeWalt, Inc.)

Figure 31-37
A lap joint cut with the aid of a stop block.

SPECIAL CUTS

The radial arm saw can make many other types of cuts. These cuts are classified as either joinery or decorative types. Other machines can make similar cuts, but many operators prefer this saw.

Joinery cuts include elaborate miters, Figure 31-36; lap joints, Figure 31-37; tongue and

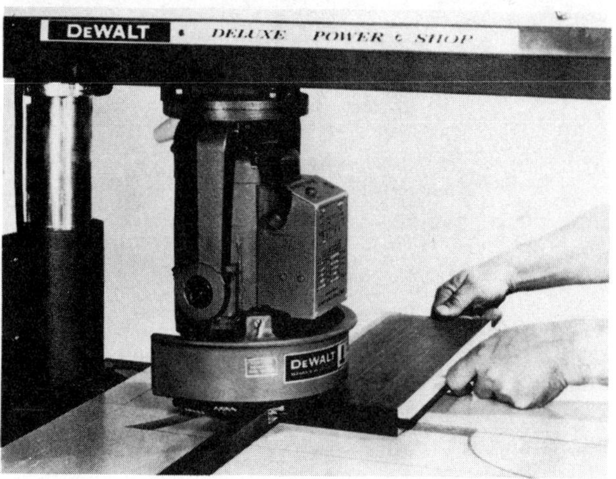

Figure 31-38
Making tongue and groove joints with the dado head in the horizontal position. Note the special guard. (DeWalt, Inc.)

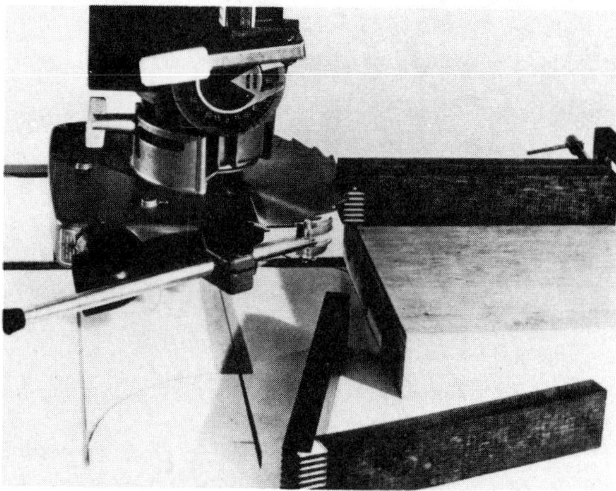
Figure 31-39
A box joint is cut in the horizontal position. (DeWalt, Inc.)

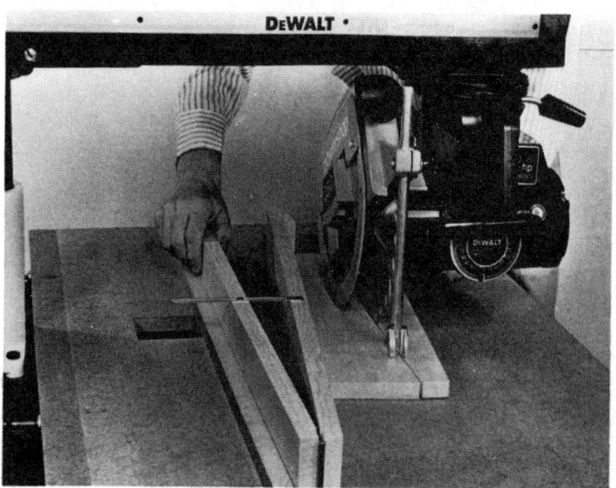

Figure 31-40
A taper is cut with a tapering fixture. (DeWalt, Inc.)

Figure 31-41
Producing curved decorations by making a series of kerfs. (DeWalt, Inc.)

groove, Figure 31-38; box joints, Figure 31-39; and tapers, Figure 31-40. All can be cut accurately because the layout lines are visible.

Decorative cuts are many and varied. They are limited only by what can be done safely and by the imagination of the operator. You can produce curved decorations by making many closely spaced kerfs, Figure 31-41. Other decorative cuts include the saucer cut, Figure 31-42, and the similar cove cut, Figure 31-43. You can cut moldings on the radial saw using special techniques, Figure 31-44. A molding head allows even more elaborate decorative cuts.

You can use many attachments on the radial arm saw, Figure 31-3. By removing the blade and positioning the motor vertically in the yoke, you can move the threaded auxiliary shaft into the cutting position. Special adapters permit you to connect router bits, sanding drums and other attachments to this shaft. You also can attach a scroll saw accessory to the threaded auxiliary shaft, Figure 31-3. When you use this accessory, keep the motor in the horizontal position. A sanding disc or molding head mounted on the saw arbor makes other special cuts.

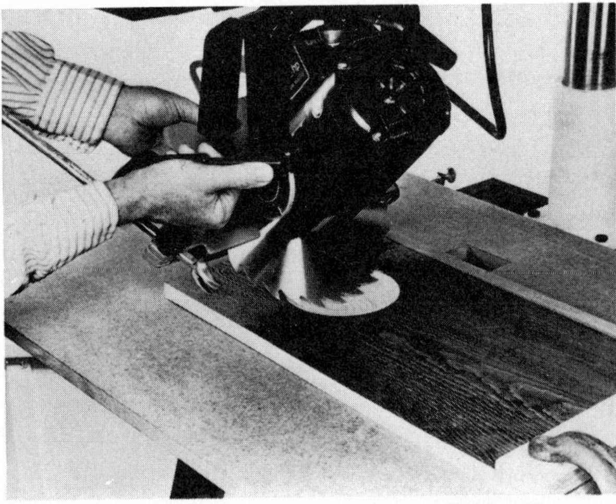

Figure 31-42
A saucer cut is made by pivoting the blade back and forth as light cuts are made. (DeWalt, Inc.)

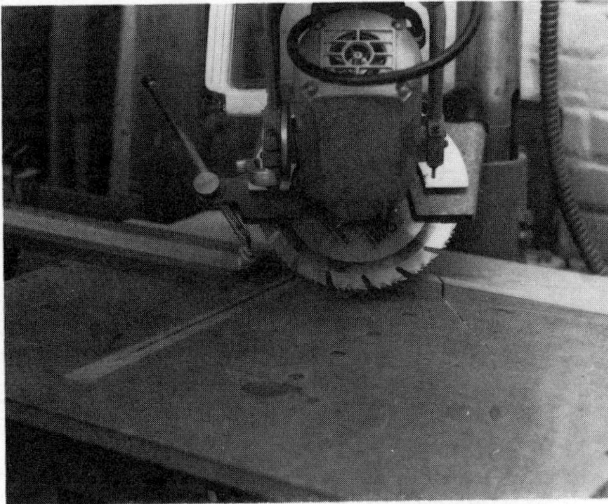

Figure 31-43
The blade correctly angled for making a cove cut.

Figure 31-44
Moldings are made with several cuts. (DeWalt, Inc.)

REVIEW QUESTIONS

1 What are the two major types of radial arm saws?
2 Why is it desirable to have the saw blade enter the stock from the top surface?
3 What are the two threaded shafts called and what is attached to each?
4 Which direction should the teeth point when mounting a different saw blade?
5 What is the safety margin on the radial arm saw?
6 How should the parts of a blade housing be adjusted for crosscutting?
7 From which direction should you feed the stock when ripping?
8 How is the saw positioned when cutting miters using the first method?
9 Sketch the fixture for cutting miters used in the second method.
10 When cutting miters by the third method, is it necessary to precut stock to finished length before mitering?
11 If several identical blind dadoes are to be cut, what should you install on the fence?
12 What is horizontal cutting?
13 List five special cuts that can be made with the radial arm saw.

SUGGESTED ACTIVITIES

1 Inspect your radial arm saw and identify all the major parts.
2 With the assistance of your instructor, adjust the saw for cutting a bevel, ripping wide stock, ripping narrow stock, cutting a miter and for horizontal cutting.
3 Make a frame for a photograph or mirror. Use any of the recommended methods for cutting miters.
4 Design and cut a piece of molding as shown in Figure 31-44. Use it to decorate the frame that you make.

UNIT

32

Jointers

Objectives

After studying this unit you should be able to:

1 Identify the various parts and understand the basic adjustments of a jointer.

2 Describe the procedure for jointing face, edge and end grain of stock.

3 Square stock from rough lumber.

4 Perform decorative and joinery cuts.

Technical Terms

Facer
Uniplane®
Cutterhead
Gib
Incline ways
Stopped chamfer
Stop block
Rabbeting arm
Taper
Spade foot

JOINTER SAFETY RULES

1 Never let fingers come within the 4" (102 mm) safety margin. Refer to Figure 32-10.

2 Use the guard at all times unless rabbeting.

3 Never take a cut deeper than 1/16" (2 mm) without special permission from the instructor.

4 Do not joint stock less than 10" (250 mm) in length.

5 Use a push stock when edge jointing stock that is less than the height of the jointer fence.

6 Do not edge joint wood that is less than 1" (25 mm) wide.

7 Do not face joint stock thinner than 1/2" (13 mm).

8 Do not joint material with loose knots, nails or other foreign material.

9 Disconnect the power before changing or working around any cutting tool.

The jointer (Figure 32-1) is an important and basic piece of equipment for processing wood. It is most often used to smooth or plane the edges and faces of boards. This machine also can cut rabbets, bevels, tapers and other shapes. Manufacturing firms that surface a large amount of lumber may select a *facer* in place of a jointer. The facer automatically feeds the stock across the cutter as it is being surfaced, Figure 32-2. A *Uniplane*® is somewhat like a jointer and can be used for surfacing very small pieces, Figure 32-3.

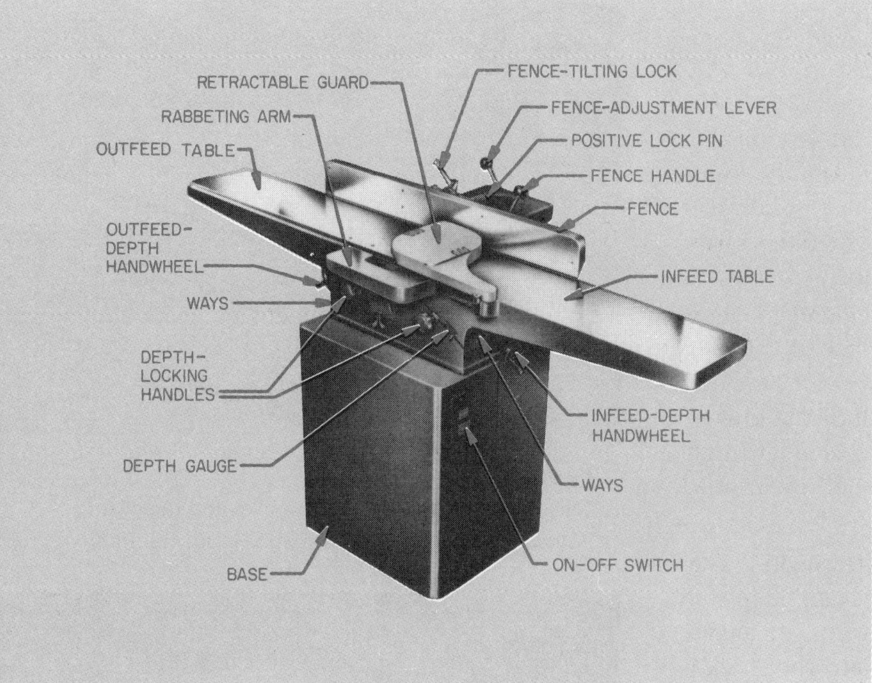

Figure 32-1
Major parts of a jointer. (Rockwell International)

Figure 32-3
A Uniplane® is capable of surfacing very small and thin material. (Rockwell International)

SPRING-LOADED FINGERS

JOINTER-TYPE CUTTERHEAD

PORTER

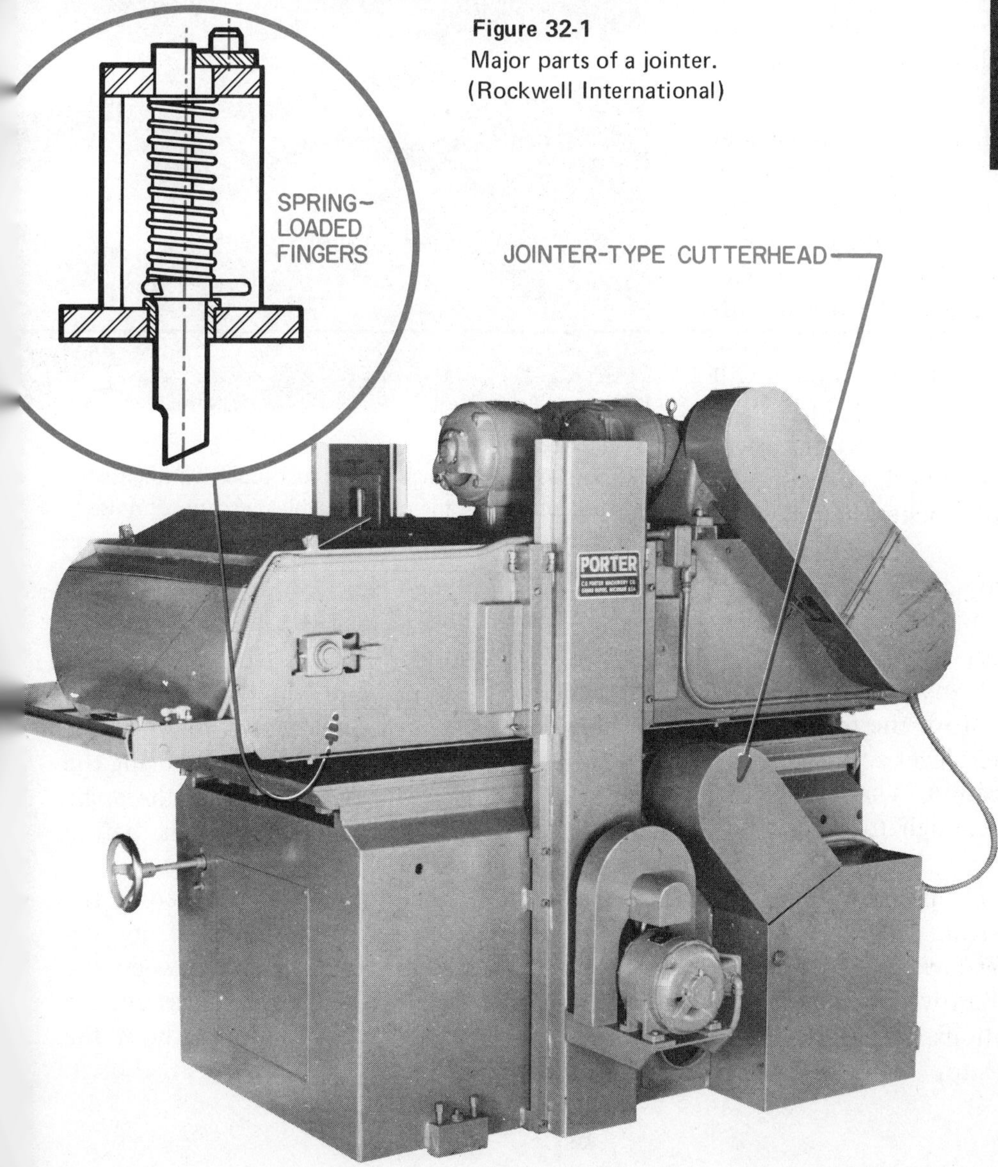

Figure 32-2
A facer is used in industry. The machine automatically feeds the material over the cutterhead with spring-loaded fingers. (C. O. Porter Machinery Co.)

JOINTER TERMINOLOGY

The *cutterhead* and the knives are responsible for cutting the stock as it is fed across the jointer. The cutterhead is made up of a solid steel cylinder that holds three or more flat knives. Each knife is held securely in a slot by a *gib* and locking nuts, Figure 32-4. The jointer most often has three knives. Industrial models may have up to six.

Jointers are sized by the length of the knives. The knife size determines the widest board that can be jointed. Sizes range from 6" (152 mm) to 24" (610 mm).

Located on each side of the cutterhead is a table, Figure 32-1. These two tables can be moved up or down on a set of *incline ways,* or angled adjustable castings. The table where the stock is first placed is called the front, or infeed, table. A rear, or outfeed, table located on the opposite side of the cutterhead is designed to support the stock after it has been jointed.

On most jointers both tables are raised and lowered separately with their own handwheels. Each table has a handwheel adjustment for this purpose. The distance the infeed table is below the cutting arc is equal to the depth of cut. The outfeed table must be exactly even with the cutting arc or tips of the knives, Figure 32-5. If the table is above the tips of the knives, a taper will be cut, Figure 32-6. When the outfeed table is too low, the trailing end of the board will be sniped off. When adjusted both tables should be secured with the depth-locking handles before the power is turned on.

A fence mounted on top of the tables further supports the stock. It should be as long as possible for maximum support. For safety purposes the fence can be moved anywhere along the width of the cutterhead. Move the fence by releasing the fence-adjustment lever and sliding the fence to the desired position. The cutterhead should be exposed only enough to surface the material.

To produce a bevel or chamfer, the fence can be tilted to the left or right. Tilt the fence by loosening the fence-tilting lock and pulling out on the positive lock pin. Positive stops are found at the 45° and 90° positions, Figure 32-7. The fence will automatically stop when it reaches these two angles. It cannot be moved again until the positive lock pin is pulled out. Other angles are possible and can be roughly set by using the attached angle gauge. No matter what the angle is, always tighten the fence-tilting lock before turning on the power.

A retractable guard is provided to cover the cutterhead. The guard is kept under spring tension so that the board may pass between the fence and the edge of the guard. Unless cutting rabbets, never operate the jointer without the guard in working order.

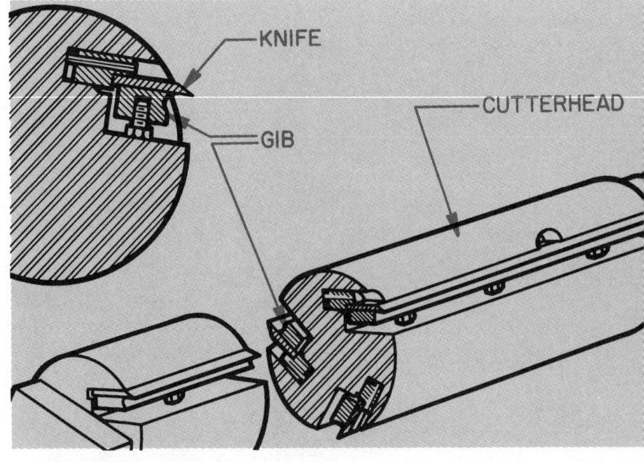

Figure 32-4
The cutterhead contains the knives and the gibs to hold them in place. (Powermatic Houdaille, Inc.)

Figure 32-5
The tips of the knives should just touch a straightedge when placed on the outfeed table. *Disconnect power before attempting this operation.* (Rockwell International)

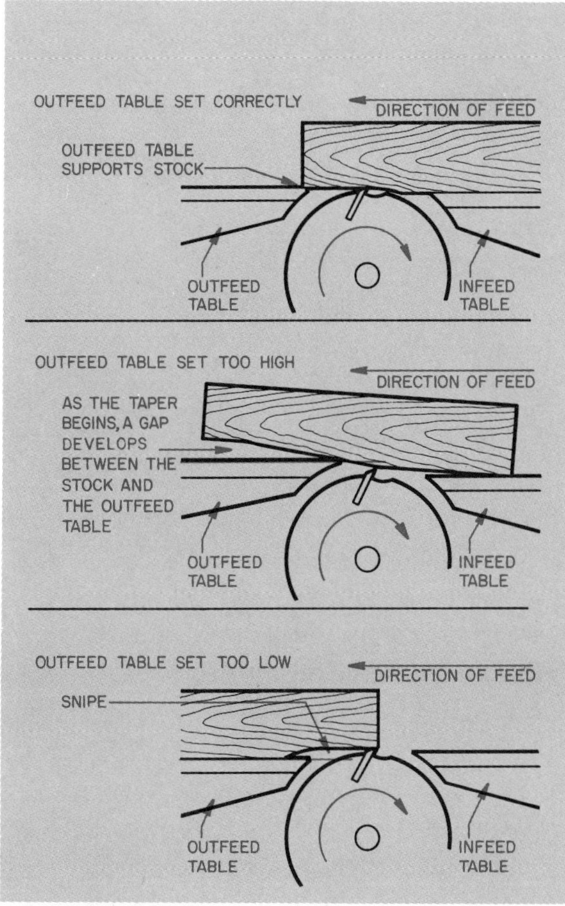

Figure 32-6
Correct setting of the outfeed table is important. A taper or sniped end will be cut if the outfeed table is not set even with the cutting arc.

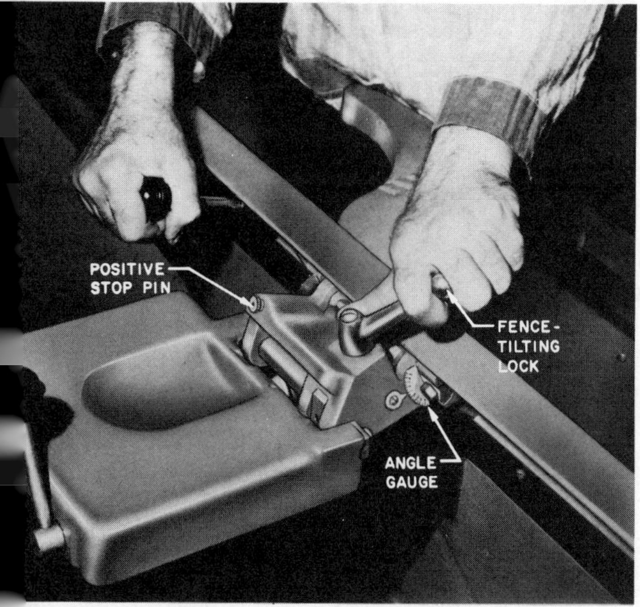

Figure 32-7
Tilting the fence for jointing bevels. (Rockwell International)

OPERATING THE JOINTER

The rotary cutting principle on the jointer removes material. As the cutterhead rotates and stock is fed forward, the cutterhead shaves the wood off, forming small arcs in the board, Figure 32-8. These small ridges are called mill marks. Mill marks can be decreased by feeding the wood slowly, by having more knives mounted in the cutterhead, by rotating the cutterhead at a higher speed, or by selecting a cutterhead of a larger diameter. Slowing the feed rate is the most practical method of reducing rough mill marks.

A jointer is a very safe machine if you keep your hands out of the safety margin. The safety margin is within 4" (102 mm) directly above and to each side of the cutterhead, Figure 32-9. If a kickback does occur or if your hands should slip, you will not be close to the cutterhead.

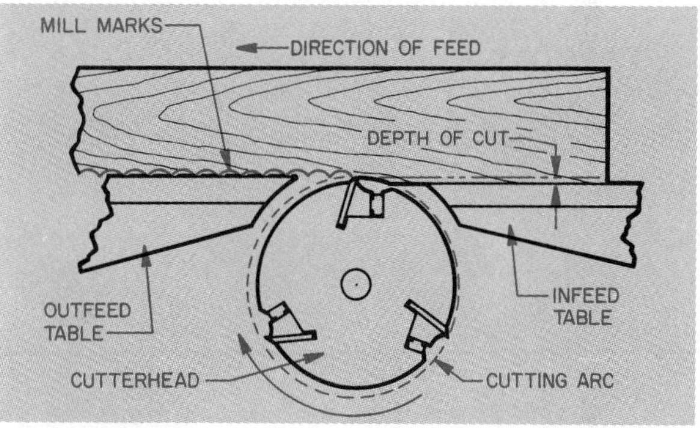

Figure 32-8
The jointer removes stock by the rotary cutting process.

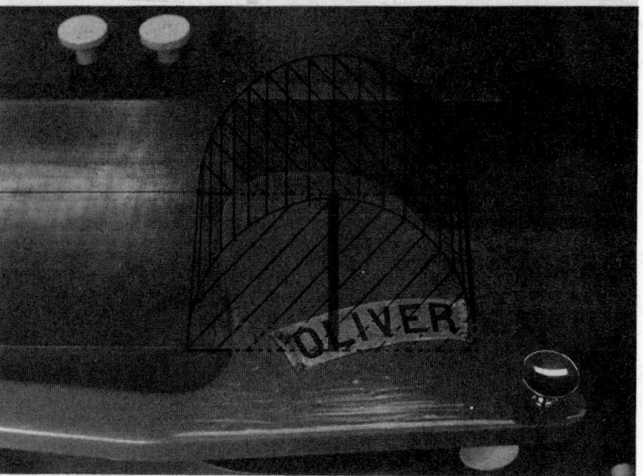

Figure 32-9
Never place your hands within the 4" (102 mm) safety margin.

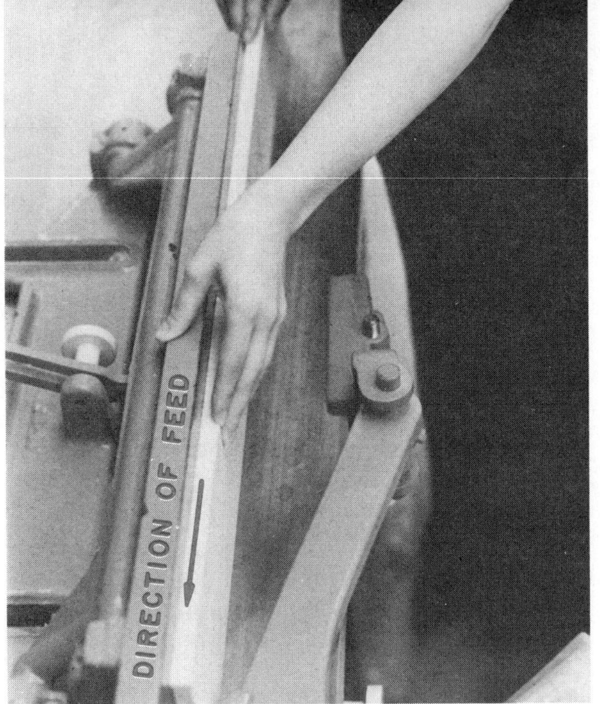

Figure 32-10
Stock must be kept against the fence and infeed table.

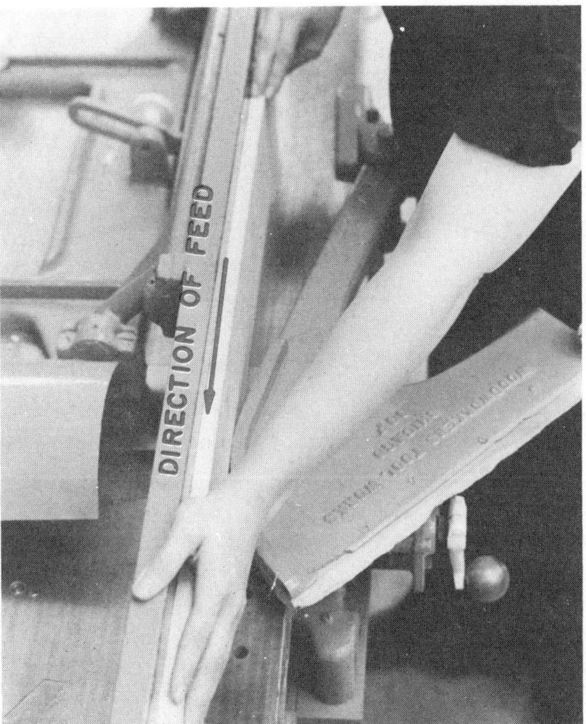

Figure 32-11
Keep both hands out of the safety margin.

A major problem in feeding material over the cutterhead is keeping an even amount of pressure on the stock. If the right procedure is not followed, the stock will tend to rock up off the table. Beginners must practice until the board will lie flat on both tables throughout the jointing operation.

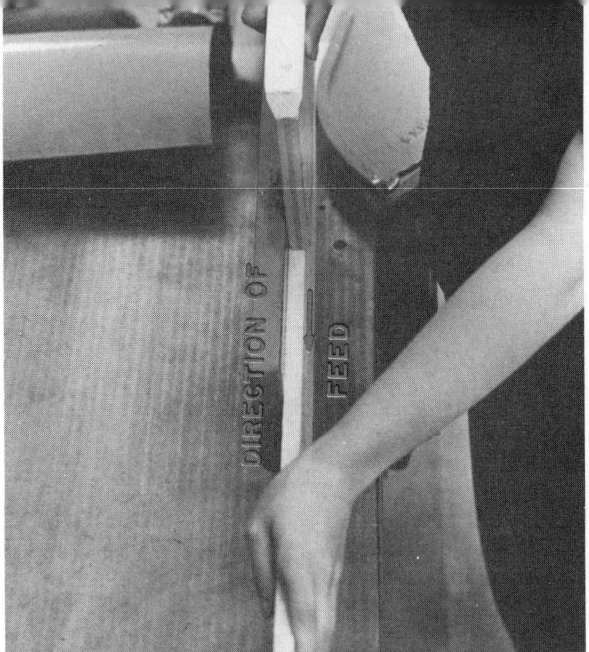

Figure 32-12
Clear the stock of the cutterhead with a push shoe. Keep the board against the fence.

To feed a piece of stock across the jointer:

1. Adjust the depth by first releasing the infeed depth-locking handle. Turn the infeed-depth handwheel until the depth gauge reads 1/16″ (2 mm).
2. Stand to the left of the infeed table. Place the board against the infeed table on the fence. Hold the board against the fence with your left hand. The grain should point to the front of the infeed table. Start to feed the stock forward by pushing with your right hand. Under no circumstances hook your right thumb over the end of the trailing edge of the board.
3. Be certain to keep your hands out of the safety zone. Divide the feeding process into three distinct parts. First, feed the board over the cutterhead keeping your hands behind the safety zone, Figure 32-10. After the stock moves past the front of the outfeed table, stop and remove your left hand from the board. Lift it well above the cutter and place it on the leading edge of the board, Figure 32-11. To finish the feeding process, continue pushing the material forward until your right hand reaches the safety zone. With a push stick or push shoe hooked over the trailing end of the stock, guide the board across the cutterhead, Figure 32-12. Be very careful not to rock the board off the table when you shift your hands.

FACE JOINTING

The purpose of face jointing is to produce a flat smooth face. Before jointing the face, however, check it for warp. The first kind of warp is cup. The cupped side, or hollow side, should be placed face down on the jointer table to keep the stock from rocking off the table as it is being jointed. The other kind of warp is wind, or twist. This defect can be detected by first placing the board on a flat surface. If the board rocks when opposite corners are pushed downward, the board is in wind. Stock with wind should not be jointed.

To face joint cupped or flat stock:

1. Position the stock with the grain pointing toward the front end of the infeed table. Place cupped side down. Place a push shoe on the trailing end. Never attempt to surface the face without a push shoe.
2. Hold the stock against the table and fence with your left hand. Do not pass your hand over the cutterhead, even though it is covered by the board. Observe the safety zone. When your left hand reaches the safety zone lift it up and over the cutter. Place it down on the board on the other side of the cutter. Stop pushing the board when you move your hand. Most of the pushing should be done with your right hand and the push shoe, Figure 32-13.

Because most boards to be face jointed are wide, only light cuts should be taken to prevent overloading the jointer. Never remove more than 1/16" (2 mm). A light cut will also reduce surface chipping if the board is accidentally jointed against the grain. If stock has been run against the grain, reverse the stock and run it in the opposite direction.

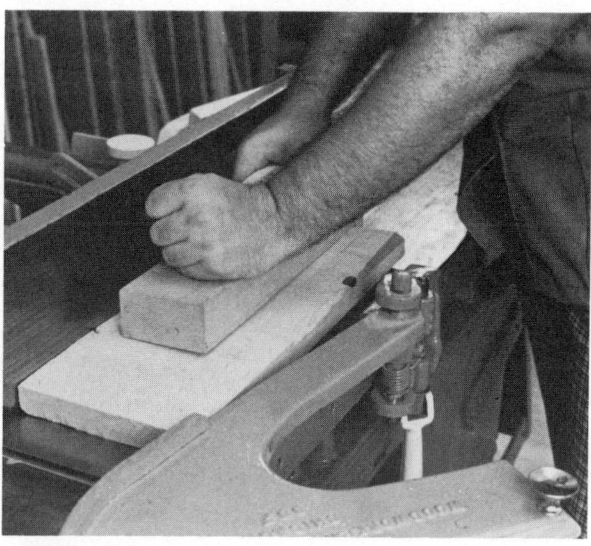

Figure 32-13
Use a push shoe for face jointing.

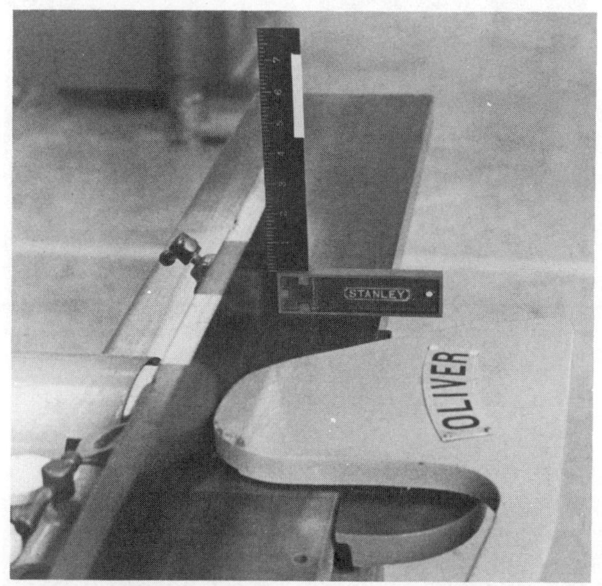

Figure 32-14
A square is used to align the fence with the table.

EDGE JOINTING

Edge grain can be jointed if there is one flat face to place against the fence. If an edge is very crooked, it should be straightened. Scribe a line along the edge to be jointed and then cut to the line with a band saw. The board can then be jointed to produce a smooth straight edge.

To edge joint a piece of stock:

1. Move the fence until the correct amount of the cutter is exposed. Lock it securely in position. With a square check that the fence angle is 90° to the table, Figure 32-14. Set the depth of cut a maximum of 1/16" (2 mm).
2. Place the board on the table to check edges for squareness. Generally, select the straightest edge for jointing. If one edge is convex and the other is concave, joint the convex edge. The grain should be pointing toward the front of the jointer.

Figure 32-15
Use a push block to guide the material over the cutterhead.

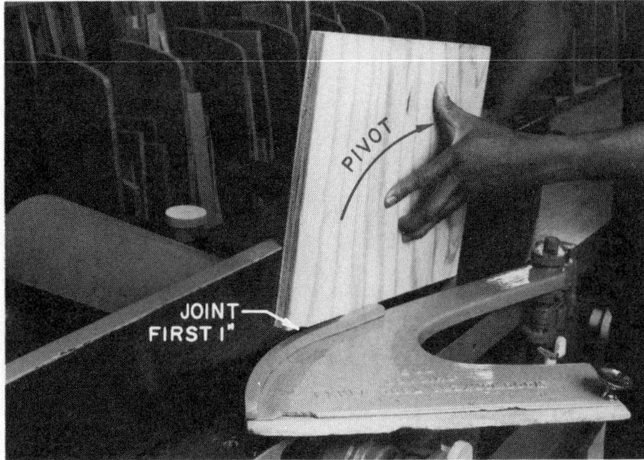

Figure 32-16
Pivot the board off the cutterhead after jointing 1″ (25 mm).

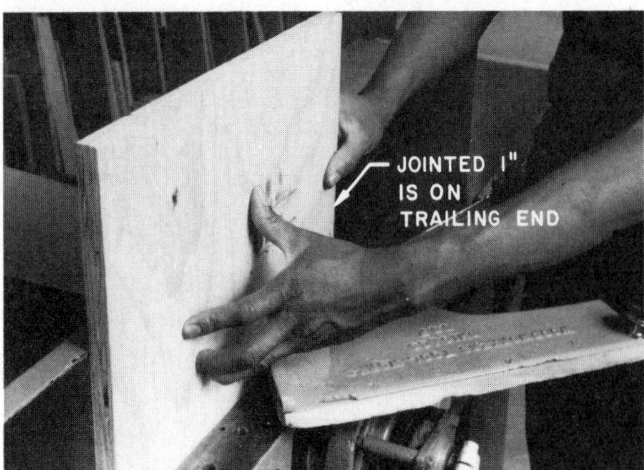

Figure 32-17
Taking the final pass for jointing plywood. The first 1″ (25 mm) joint in Figure 32-18 is now on the trailing end of the board.

3. Hold the stock firmly against the fence with your left hand. If the board accidentally tilts away from the fence as it is being fed, a bevel will be cut. Next, place your right hand on the trailing end of the board and push forward, Figure 32-15. Always use a push block when the stock is narrower than the height of the fence.
4. Keep your hands out of the safety zone. When the leading end of the stock is fed onto the outfeed table, stop feeding the board and move your left hand to the leading end of the board.
5. Hold the stock flat against the outfeed table to produce a straight cut. If a gap develops between the board and the outfeed table the cut will not be straight.

JOINTING END GRAIN AND EDGES OF PLYWOOD

Accurately jointing end grain is not easy. The ends of wood fibers are difficult to cut. The board also has a tendency to chip out on the trailing end. For these reasons end grain and plywood are rarely jointed. They usually are cut on the tablesaw with a fine tooth blade and then hand sanded.

If it is necessary to joint end grain or plywood:

1. Move the fence to expose a minimum amount of the cutterhead. Set the depth of cut to remove a small amount of material. About 1/32″ (1 mm) is a good starting point. Joint 1″ (25 mm) off of the leading corner. Lift the front corner off the cutter using the back corner as a pivot, Figure 32-16.
2. Reverse the board and joint the edge in a normal manner. Because the corner on the end of the board is already jointed, the cutter will not touch it, Figure 32-17.

   Another way to prevent the trailing end from chipping out is to start feeding the material over the cutterhead as when jointing edge grain. When the trailing end is near the cutterhead, stop pushing the stock forward and butt a 10″ (250 mm) or longer scrap piece against the trailing end of the

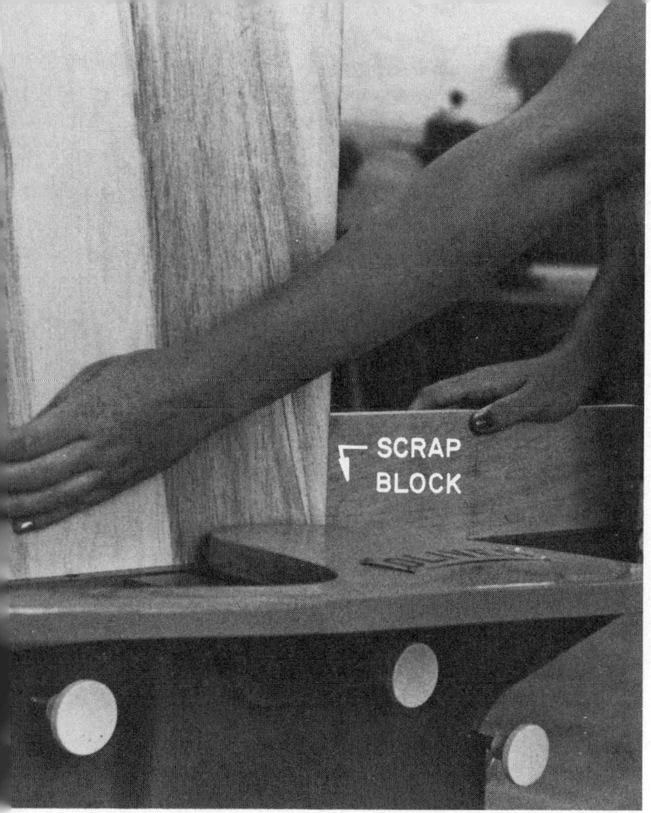

Figure 32-18
Backing up end grain with a scrap prevents chipping.

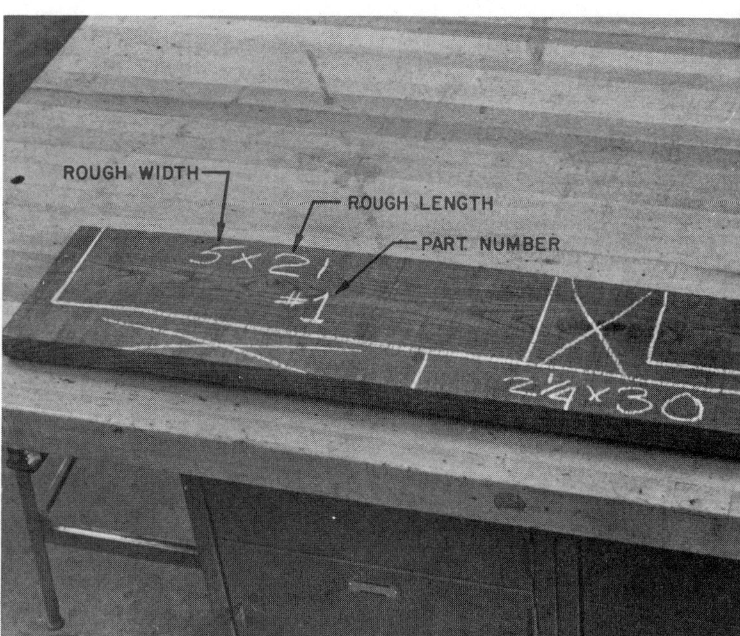

Figure 32-19
Mark out the pieces with a piece of chalk.

board, Figure 32-18. Continue feeding the board by pushing the scrap piece with your right hand. With your left hand keep the stock positioned against the fence.

SQUARING STOCK

Squared material is required for just about all woodworking projects. Few pieces of furniture or cabinets would fit together without the stock being square. To check for squareness measure the edges and faces with a square to see if a 90° angle is formed. Checking for squareness also requires the woodworker to be certain that all surfaces are parallel. This can be done by measuring at several locations along the board to see if the dimensions are identical.

To square a rough board use the following procedure:

1. Select a long, rough piece of stock from the storage area. With a piece of chalk lay out the board. Locate the pieces by considering the amount of waste, defects and the grain desired. The length of each individual piece should be 1″ (25 mm) longer than the finished dimension, Figure 32-19. Cut the stock to rough length using the radial-arm saw or a handsaw.

Figure 32-20
Sighting down a board to determine flatness of the face.

2. Determine the flattest surface of the rough stock. This can be found by placing the board on the jointer table and noting which surface rocks the least. Long boards need to be checked for flatness by sighting down the face of the stock, Figure 32-20. Joint the flattest surface smooth and true. Then place this surfaced face against the jointer fence and joint an edge straight.

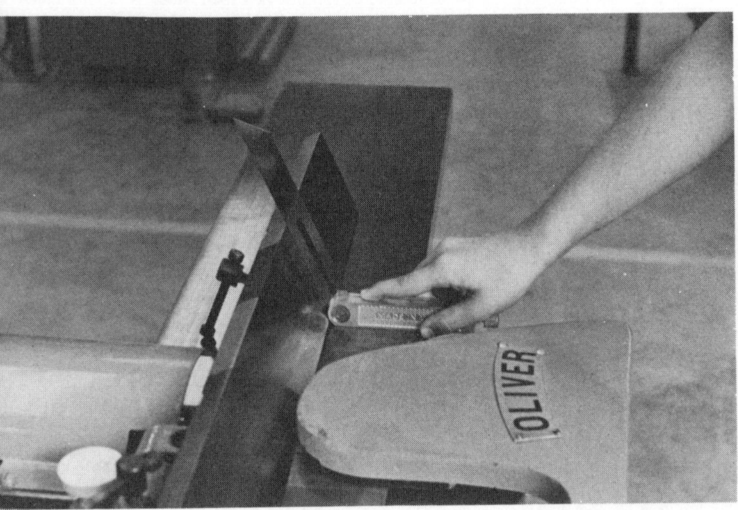

Figure 32-21
Setting the fence at an angle for cutting a bevel.

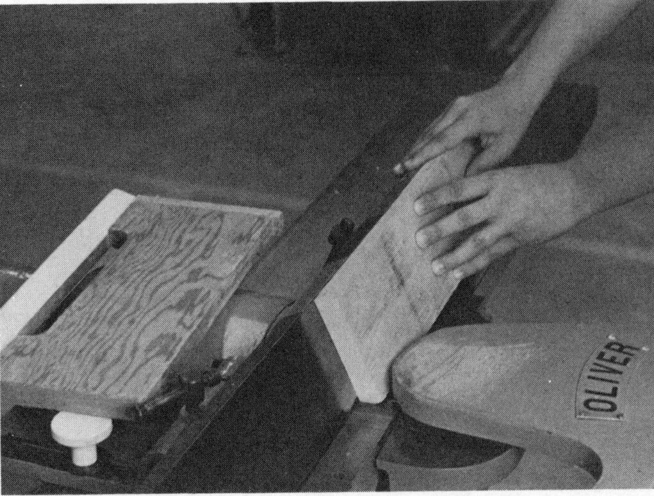

Figure 32-22
Hold the stock firmly against the fence when cutting bevels.

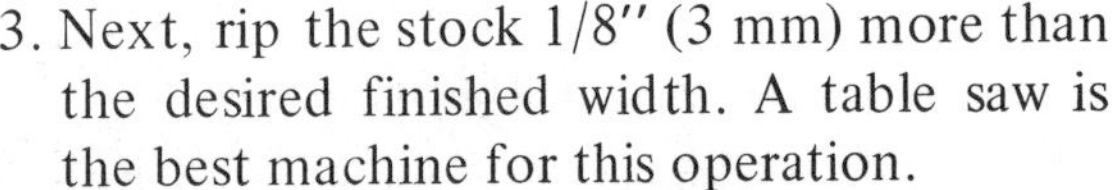

3. Next, rip the stock 1/8″ (3 mm) more than the desired finished width. A table saw is the best machine for this operation.
4. Place the jointed surface face down on the bed of the planer and remove enough material to get the second face parallel with the first. Then begin planing equal amounts off each surface until the board is the desired thickness. This will prevent the board from warping. Warping occurs if most of the material removed is planed only from one surface.
5. Return to the jointer and set the depth of cut to 1/16″ (2 mm). By taking two passes, the 1/8″ (3 mm) left on the second edge by the tablesaw can be removed.
6. Use the tablesaw or the radial arm saw to cut approximately 1/2″ (13 mm) off the first end of the board. Mark the finished length and crosscut the second end. If a large number of identical pieces are to be cut, set up a stop on the saw.

JOINTING BEVELS AND CHAMFERS

Jointing bevels and chamfers is very similar to edge jointing. The major difference is that the fence is tilted to a desired angle. A gauge is located on the fence so that an approximate angle can be set. For accurate cuts use a sliding T bevel to set the correct angle, Figure 32-21. Once the fence is set, joint a piece of scrap and check the cut with the same T bevel.

For sharp angles do not attempt to joint the entire edge in one pass. Set the depth of 1/16″ (2 mm) and make the first pass, Figure 32-22. Determine at this point whether an additional cut is needed or whether the depth should be readjusted to less than 1/16″ (2 mm).

Take care when guiding the board on a tilted fence. The board will tend to slide down the fence. This gives an angle that is less accurate and is very dangerous. Angling the fence to the right instead of the left will help reduce this problem.

STOPPED CHAMFERING

Stopped chamfers are sometimes used as decorative cuts on furniture parts, Figure 32-23. The procedure to follow is:

1. Set the desired depth on the infeed table. Lower the outfeed the same amount. Because most outfeed tables do not have a depth gauge, you must find the depth some other way. Place blocks of wood of equal thickness on each table, Figure 32-24. Use a level on top of the blocks to see when the outfeed table is on the same plane as the infeed table.

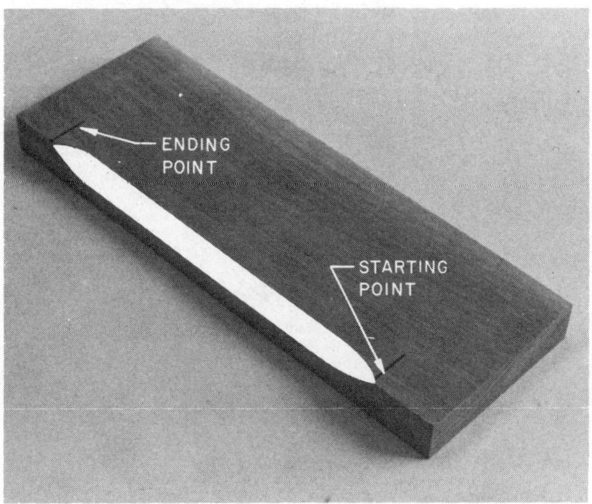

Figure 32-23
Stopped chamfers can be used as decorative cuts.

2. Tilt the fence to the desired angle. Move the fence over until a minimum of the cutter is exposed.
3. Lay out the starting and stopping points of the chamfer as pictured in Figure 32-23. Place the board over the cutterhead and match the starting point of the chamfer with the far side of the cutting arc next to the lip of the outfeed table. Clamp a *stop block* on the fence next to the trailing end of the stock.
4. Move the stock forward so that the other layout line is immediately over the lip of the infeed table. Butt a stop block next to the leading end of the fence and clamp it into position.
5. Turn on the power and place the trailing end of the stock against the stop block on the infeed side. For maximum safety have an assistant pull back the guard a small amount so the stock can pivot onto the cutter, Figure 32-25. Do not pull the guard back any farther than necessary. When the board is lowered and touching the table, release the guard.
6. Using a push shoe, guide the stock over the cutter until it comes to rest against the far stop block, Figure 32-26. Have an assistant turn off the power while you hold the stock against the table and fence. Hold the stock in position until the cutter stops.

Figure 32-24
A level aids in setting the infeed and outfeed tables to the same depth. *Disconnect power before attempting this operation.*

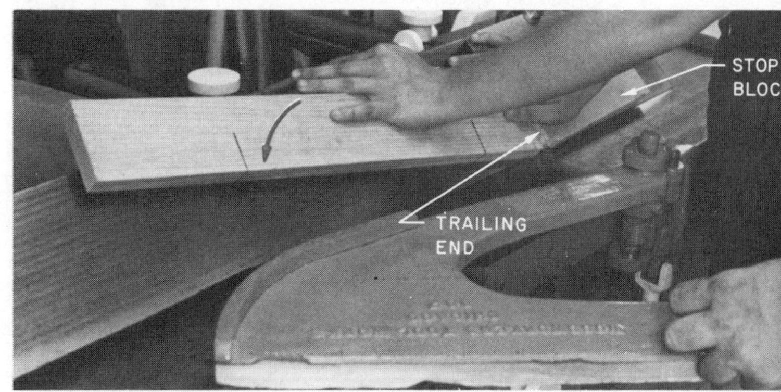

Figure 32-25
Pull the guard back only to allow the stock to be pivoted onto the cutterhead. *Keep hands out of the safety margin area.*

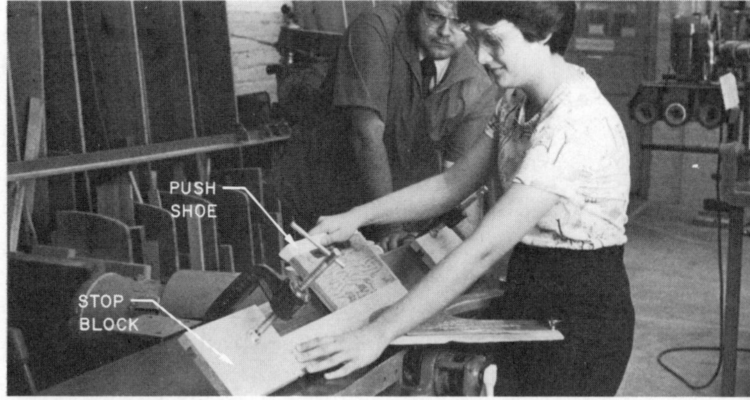

Figure 32-26
An assistant should turn the power off while the operator holds the chamfered board completely still. *Do not remove the board until the cutter has stopped turning.*

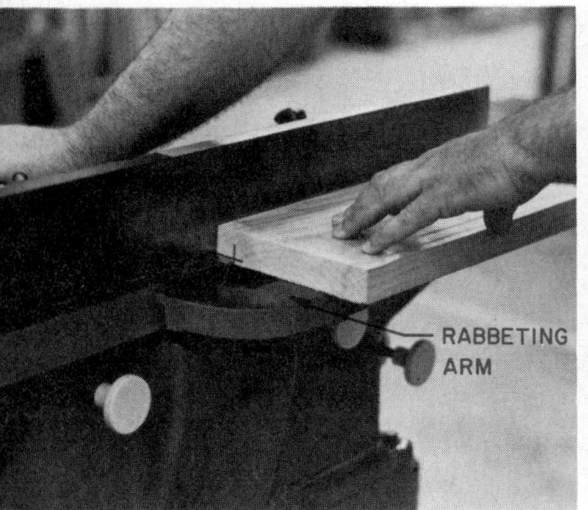

Figure 32-27
Adjusting the fence for producing a rabbet. Note the rabbeting arm supporting the stock.

Figure 32-28
Use a push block to guide the material over the jointer. The guard is removed for a rabbet cut. You must keep your hands out of the 4" (102 mm) safety margin.

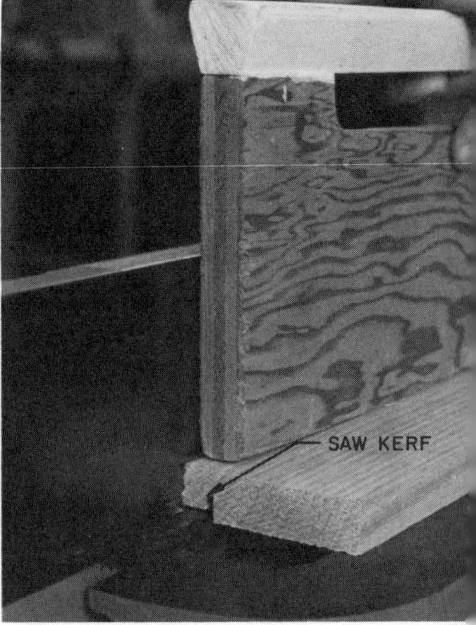

Figure 32-29
A saw kerf will reduce chipping on the shoulder of a rabbet.

CUTTING RABBETS

Cutting rabbets with a jointer requires little sanding. A *rabbeting arm* must be attached to the infeed table for the jointer to be used safely for this operation. The arm keeps the stock level with the jointer tables as the board is pushed across the cutterhead. Some jointers do not have rabbeting arms and should not be used for rabbeting.

To cut rabbets on this machine:

1. Swing the guard out of the way. This is one of the few jointer operations that requires the guard be removed. Lay out the rabbet on the end of the board that touches the cutterhead first.
2. Move the fence over until the exposed width of the cutter is the same as the width of the rabbet, Figure 32-27.
3. Divide the depth of the rabbet in half and lower the infeed table this amount. Start the jointer and guide the stock over the cutter. Always use a push block. Do not allow your hands to get within the safety margin, Figure 32-28.
4. Reset the depth of cut to the finished depth and run the board again.

To be certain the grain will not be torn along the face of the board, make a saw kerf with the tablesaw along the face of the rabbet before it is cut on the jointer, Figure 32-29. This is particularly important when rabbeting plywood.

CUTTING TAPERS

Although *tapers* can be cut on other machines, the jointer is one of the best pieces of equipment for making this cut. A taper produced by the jointer will be smooth and straight. Very little sanding will be needed in comparison to the tapers cut with the tablesaw or bandsaw.

Short Tapers

For cutting tapers shorter than the infeed table these steps should be followed:

1. Lower the infeed table the amount of the taper. This is equal to the total material removed from the small end on one side of the taper. For example, if a board 3" (76 mm) wide is to be tapered to 2-7/8" (73 mm) the depth of cut would be set to 1/8" (3 mm).
2. Scribe a line around the stock at the beginning of the taper. Do not attempt to cut a taper shorter than 10" in length. Place the layout line on the lip of the outfeed table. Clamp a stop block to the fence at the trailing end of the stock. Move the fence over to expose a minimum of the cutterhead.
3. Turn on the power and have an assistant pull the guard back a small amount to allow the stock to be pivoted onto the cutter. Release the guard once the stock meets the outfeed table, Figure 32-30. Place the trail-

Figure 32-30
Pivot the stock off the stop block onto the cutterhead. Never allow your hands to be placed in the safety margin.

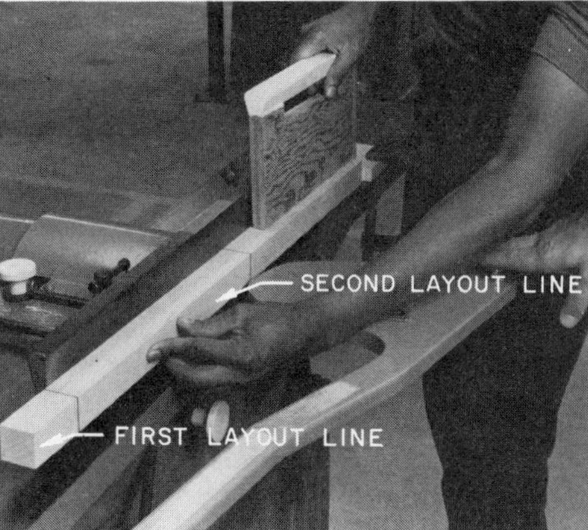

Figure 32-31
The first half of the taper is cut by using a push block. Allow the guard to cover the cutterhead when the stock first touches the outfeed table.

Figure 32-32
Cutting the second half of the long taper. Release the guard once the stock is pivoted onto the outfeed table.

ing end against the stop and table. Slowly lower the stock onto the cutter. Push the stock across the cutter with a push block much the same as when jointing an edge.

4. Feed the material over the jointer with a push block. The taper can be finished by hand sanding the jointed edge out to the layout line.

Long Tapers

Tapers longer than the infeed table must be cut by a different procedure than short tapers. To cut a long taper:

1. Make the layout of the taper on one piece of stock. Then divide the length of the taper in half and scribe a second line around the material at the halfway point, Figure 32-31. Divide the depth of the taper in half and set the jointer to this depth. Move the fence over to expose a minimum of the cutterhead.
2. Place the stock over the cutter so that the point at the second layout line is on the lip of the outfeed table. Install a stop block at the trailing end. Cut the first portions of the taper on all sides, Figure 32-31.
3. Leave the cutting depth the same. Place the first layout line over the lip of the outfeed table and feed the board over the jointer using a push block, Figure 32-32. This will produce the finished taper.

Figure 32-33
A stop block is placed at the trailing end of the stock. Note the finished spade-foot leg. Power has been turned off.

Stopped Tapers

Like a stopped chamfer, a stopped taper is generally a decorative type of cut. Most often it is used for legs on tables and chairs. It is frequently called a *spade foot.* Do not attempt this operation without a sharp, heavy-duty jointer.

To cut a stopped taper:

1. Lay out the cut by drawing a line completely around the beginning and ending points of the taper, Figure 32-38. Determine the

Figure 32-34
With a push block, guide the board over the cutterhead. The guard has been pulled back to show the cutterhead.

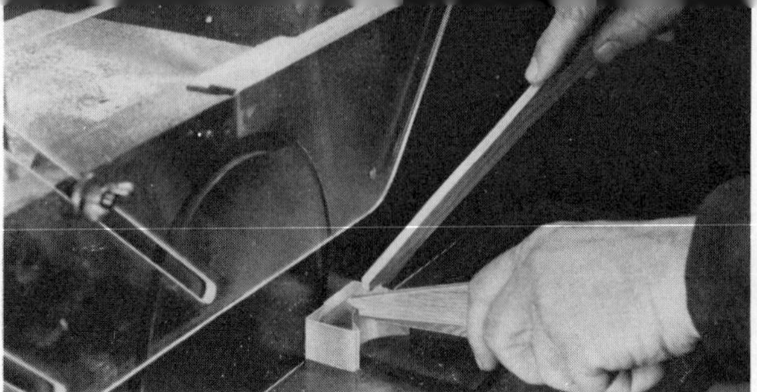

Figure 32-35
Small pieces of plastic can be planed using the Uniplane®. The shield has been raised so you can see the piece of plastic being cut. (Rockwell International)

maximum depth of the cut at the smallest end of the taper. Set the infeed table to this depth.

2. Move the fence forward to expose a minimum of the cutterhead. Align the layout line at the beginning of the taper with the lip of the outfeed table. Position a stop block at the trailing end of the piece of stock, Figure 32-33.
3. Remove the stock and turn on the power. Have an assistant pull the guard back just to allow the stock to be lowered down onto the outfeed table. Place the trailing end against the stop block and pivot the board onto the cutter. Release the guard when the board touches the table.
4. Push the board over the jointer with a push block. Cut up to the second layout line. Hold the stock completely stationary and have an assistant turn off the power.
5. After the cutter has come to a complete stop, clamp a stop block at the leading end of the stock.
6. Remove the stock and cut the other three sides, Figure 32-34. Always allow the cutterhead to come to a complete stop each time before removing the material from the tables. The remaining end may be tapered with the band saw and sanded to finished size.

UNIPLANE®

The Uniplane® is a machine that performs cuts much like that of the jointer. See Figure 32-3. The cutter, however, is mounted in a vertical position, and the stock is held against the vertical fence and on a horizontal table.

There are several advantages to the Uniplane®. The circular cutter rotates within the vertical fence and exposes only a 3/8″ (10 mm) portion of the knives. This not only minimizes the exposure to the cutter but also allows extremely small pieces to be planed, Figure 32-35. The downward cutting action into the table also prevents kickbacks. As little as 1/64″ (.4 mm) can be removed from large and small pieces of stock.

The Uniplane® cutterhead leaves rotary mill marks because of the circular motion of the knives. This may be objectionable on edge or face grain.

OPERATING THE UNIPLANE®

To operate the Uniplane®:

1. First, set the desired depth of cut. It is not recommended to remove more than 1/32″ (1 mm) in one pass. The depth setting can be changed with the micro-set adjustment knob that is located on the front of the machine. Each mark on the depth scale is equal to 1/64″ (.4 mm).
2. Check that the clear plastic shield slides up and down easily on the alignment screws. This guard must always rest on top of the stock to protect the operator, Figure 32-36.
3. Use a push shoe or push sticks if your hands will come closer than 4″ (102 mm) to the cutter, Figure 32-37. A miter gauge will assist with planing end grain, Figure 32-38.
4. Turn on the machine and feed the material forward. A smooth steady feeding action is recommended. Small pieces should be fed at a slower rate. If your hands come within the 4″ (102 mm) safety margin, pause and pick up a push stick to continue feeding the material.

Some Uniplanes® are equipped with a carbide cutterhead. These types of knives allow plastics, particle board and other abrasive materials to be planed.

Figure 32-36
As the stock is fed past the cutter the plastic shield must rest on top of the board. (Rockwell International)

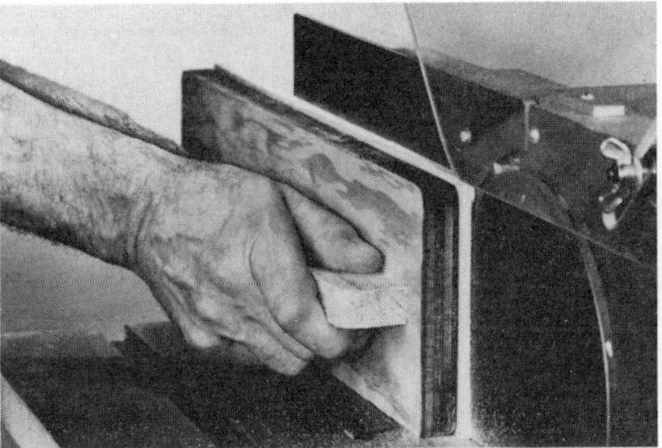

Figure 32-37
Use a push shoe to keep hands a minimum of 4" (102 mm) from the cutter. (Rockwell International)

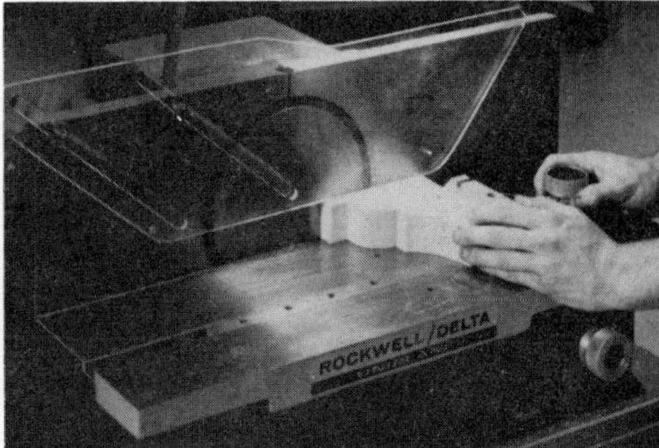

Figure 32-38
A miter gauge is used to assist with end grain jointing. (Rockwell International)

REVIEW QUESTIONS

1. Sketch the cutterhead assembly, including the solid steel cylinder, knives, gibs and locking nuts. Label all parts.
2. Where should the outfeed table be positioned in relation to the tips of the knives?
3. What is the positive lock pin, and what is its purpose?
4. Explain the rotary cutting process. How can mill marks be reduced?
5. What is the safety margin surrounding the cutterhead?
6. Should stock in wind be jointed?
7. What machine should be used for straightening a crooked edge?
8. Why is it difficult to joint end grain and edges of plywood? What are two methods of preventing the trailing end from chipping out?
9. List in order the surfaces that are cut, jointed or planed when squaring a board. (For example: end, end, face . . .)
10. What tool should be used when setting the fence for jointing accurate bevels?
11. Sketch a stopped chamfer.
12. What must be attached to the jointer for rabbets to be cut?
13. If a short taper is to be made where the board is 2-3/8" (60 mm) wide at the start of the taper and 2-1/2" (50 mm) wide at the small end of the taper, how should the depth of cut be set?
14. Describe the layout procedure for cutting a taper longer than the infeed table.
15. A stopped taper is sometimes called a ____ foot.
16. What safety features are built into the Uniplane®?
17. How should the plastic shield be adjusted?

SUGGESTED ACTIVITIES

1. Identify the major parts of your jointer. With the help of your teacher find out which parts are adjustable and what kinds of adjustments can be made.
2. After your teacher has disconnected the power, pull the guard back and inspect the cutterhead. Can you see how mill marks are made?
3. With a piece of wood at least 3" (76 mm) wide and 12" (305 mm) long practice cutting a short taper. Have your teacher check your setup before you turn on the power.
4. Make a stool using the spade-foot design.

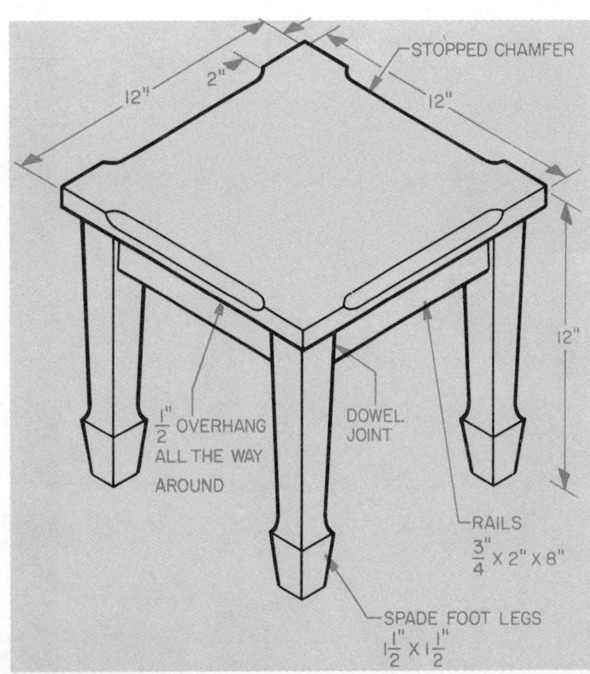

UNIT

33

Planers

Objectives

After studying this unit you should be able to:

1 Identify the major parts of the planer and describe their functions.

2 Follow the correct procedure for surfacing stock.

3 Name defects caused by the planer.

Technical Terms

Double surfacer
Abrasive planer
Depth scale
Infeed roller
Outfeed roller
Corrugated infeed roller
Chip breaker
Pressure bar
Dust hood
Backing board

PLANER SAFETY RULES

1 Never let your fingers come within the 4" (102 mm) safety margin in front of the infeed of the machine, Figure 33-1.

2 Stand to one side of the machine to avoid kickbacks or flying chips.

3 Figure the maximum depth of cut as 1/16" (2 mm) less than the thickest portion of the stock.

4 Never surface a board across the grain or the end grain.

5 Unless special permission is given by your instructor, do not surface stock that is less than 2" (51 mm) longer than the distance between the center of the infeed and outfeed rollers.

6 Use a backing board with stock less than 3/8" thick.

7 Feed one board at a time, unless the planer has a sectional corrugated feed roller.

8 If a board becomes stuck in the planer, apply forward pressure on the stock. If this does not help, turn off the power. After the cutter has come to a complete stop, lower the bed and remove the board. Notify your instructor.

9 Never look into the machine while the cutterhead is turning.

10 Disconnect the power before changing or working with any cutting tool.

The planer, or surfacer, is a single-purpose machine. It surfaces material to a desired thickness or width. You rarely will use it to do anything else.

There are two basic types of planers—abrasive and knife types. Knife-type planers have either a single or a double cutterhead. A single-head planer has only one cutterhead that planes the top surface of the stock, Figures 33-1 and 33-6. A *double surfacer* has two cutterheads and planes both top and bottom surfaces with one pass through the machine, Figure 33-2. One cutter-

Figure 33-1
The major parts of a single planer. (Oliver Machinery Company)

Figure 33-2
A double surfacer planes both the top and bottom surfaces. (Oliver Machinery Company)

head is located above the bed and the other below, Figure 33-3.

An *abrasive planer* has a large abrasive belt that removes material from the surface of a board, Figure 33-4. A very coarse abrasive is glued to the belt. The most common size is 36 grit. The width of the belt determines the size of the abrasive planer. Sizes vary from 12″ to 106″ (305 to 2692 mm). You easily can change the belt when it becomes worn or when you want a different grit size, Figure 33-5. Adjust for depth of cut or rate of feed as you would on a standard knife planer.

Abrasive planers have several advantages over knife planers. These include less noise, no chipping or grain tear-out, deeper cuts with one pass, wider cutting capacities, lower maintenance cost and less danger of kickback. An abrasive planer is similar in appearance to a wide-belt sander. It is much heavier, however, than a wide-belt sander and can take deeper cuts.

KNIFE-TYPE PLANER TERMINOLOGY

The planer is a heavy and expensive woodworking machine. One reason for its high cost is the need for heavy castings that absorb vibrations.

The cutterhead looks like the head of the jointer. Most conventional heads have three or four knives evenly spaced around the steel cylinder, Figure 33-6. Much research has been done on cutterhead design. New heads with carbide knives are now available. Carbide knives stay sharp a long time but are expensive. Other styles have knives arranged in various patterns around the cutterhead to reduce noise, Figure 33-7.

When surfacing stock, feed it across the bed and under the cutterhead. To adjust the planer for various thicknesses of stock, raise or lower the bed with the height-adjustment handwheel. Check the height of the bed on the *depth scale*. The widest piece of stock that you can feed across the bed determines the size of the ma-

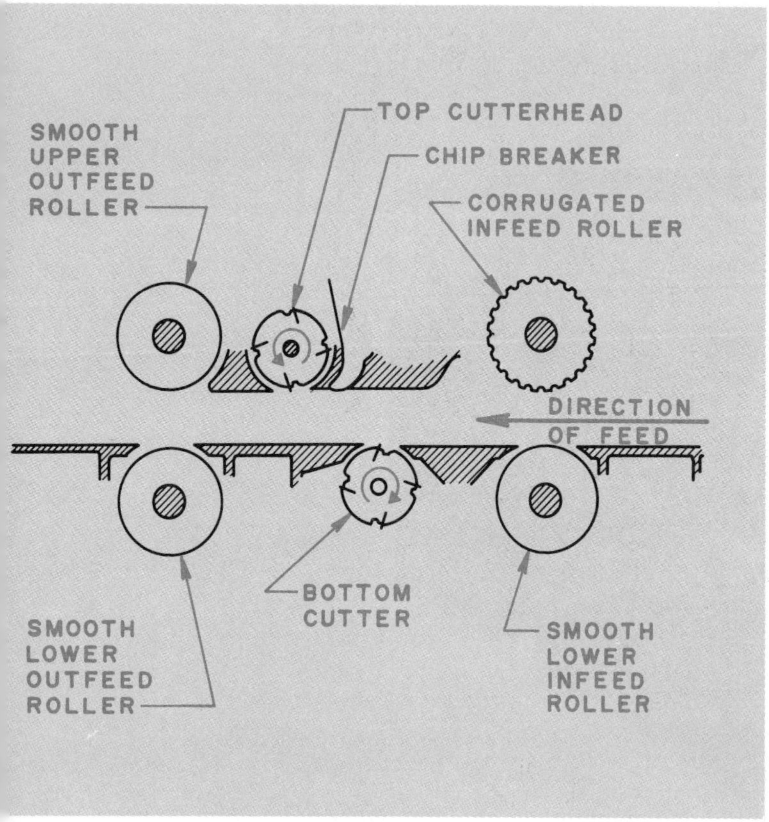

Figure 33-3
A double surfacer has two driving mechanisms and two cutterheads.

Figure 33-4
An abrasive planer removes material with a heavy sanding belt. (Timesaver, Inc.)

Figure 33-5
A belt being changed in an abrasive planer.

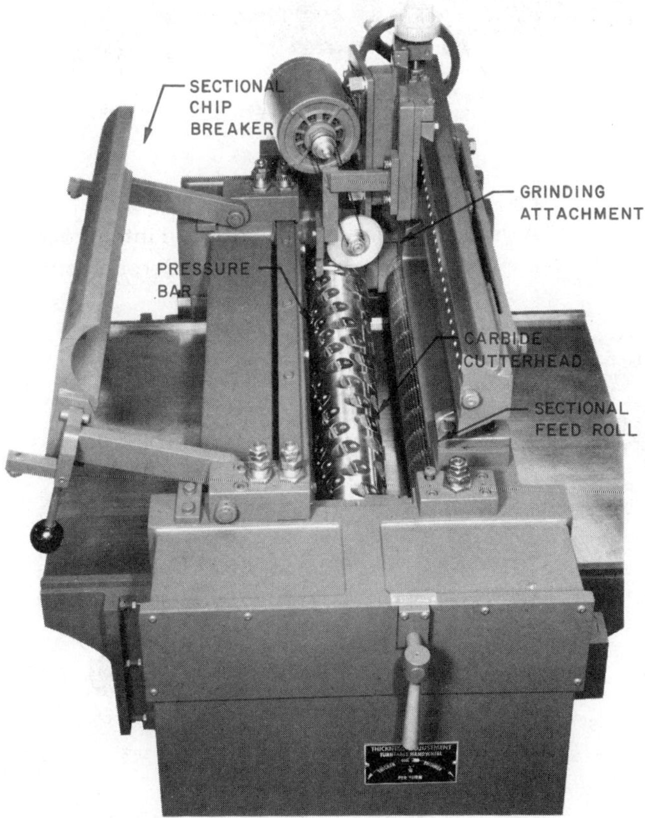

Figure 33-7
A new style of cutterhead with individual carbide teeth. (Oliver Machinery Company)

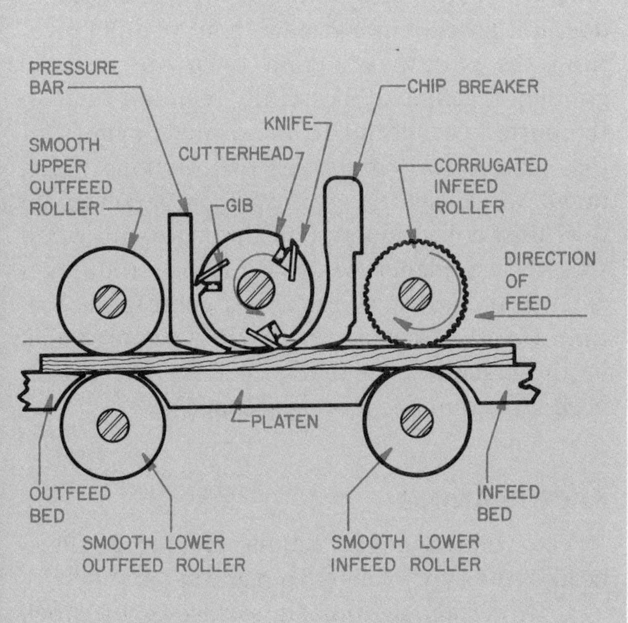

Figure 33-6
The major internal working parts of the single planer.

chine. Planer sizes range from 12″ to more than 60″. The most common widths of planers are 16″ to 30″ (407 to 762 mm).

Material feeds automatically through the planer. Two smooth, bottom rollers located slightly above the bed aid feeding. *Infeed* and *outfeed rollers* pull the stock through the machine. On some planers, these rollers are adjusted up and down with a bottom roller handle. More space may be placed between the bottom of the stock and the top of the bed. Extra space is needed when you are planing boards that have not been jointed smoothly before planing.

The first top roller to grip the stock is the *corrugated infeed roller.* This power-driven roller is spring-loaded, so it can adjust to variations in thickness of rough stock. Corrugated infeed rollers are available as a single roller or in sections. A sectional corrugated infeed roller allows two

Figure 33-8
A sectional, spring-loaded corrugated infeed roller is made in several parts. (Ex-Cell-O Corporation)

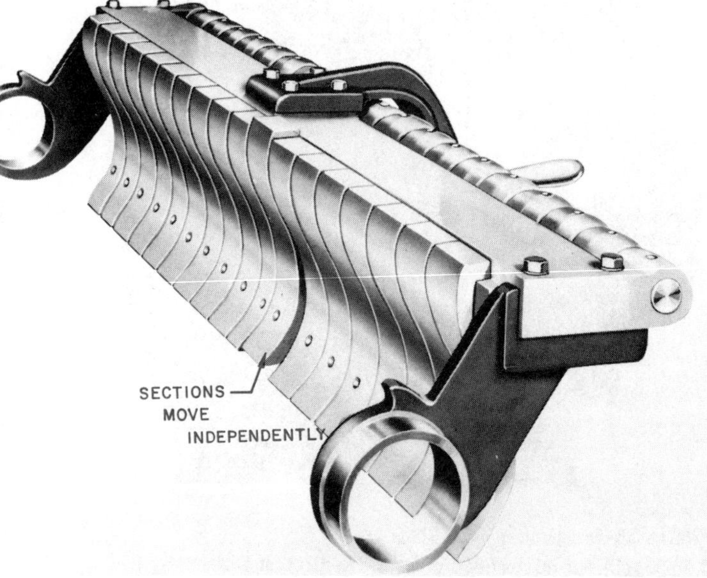

Figure 33-9
A sectional chip breaker is used with a sectional corrugated infeed roller. (Ex-Cell-O Corporation)

or more thicknesses of material to be planed at the same time, Figure 33-8. Each section can move up as much as 5/16″ (8 mm). Planers with solid rollers should be fed one board at a time.

The *chip breaker* is located behind the corrugated infeed roller. The chip breaker breaks off the long splinters of wood that form as the cutterhead rotates. Machines with sectional corrugated infeed rollers have sectional chip breakers, Figures 33-7 and 33-9. A sectional chip breaker adjusts for various thicknesses in the stock.

Immediately behind the cutterhead is the *pressure bar,* Figure 33-6. The pressure bar is spring-loaded and moves up and down as a single unit. It applies downward pressure on the board to keep it from vibrating. Unless the pressure bar rests on top of the board, deep mill marks will be made.

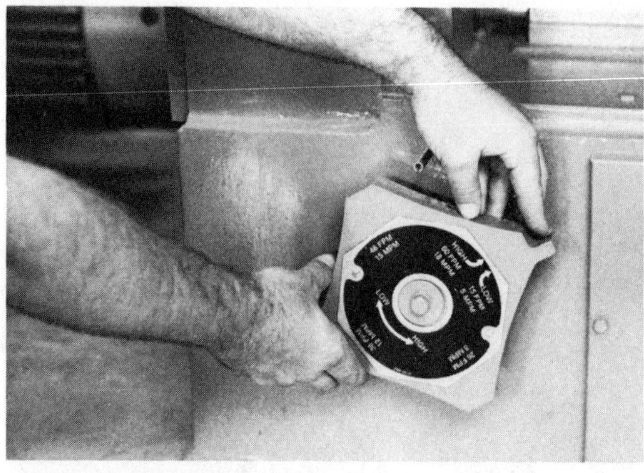

Figure 33-10
The adjustable feed-control wheel regulates the rate a board travels through the machine. Turn this wheel only when the machine is running.

Many machines have a handwheel that adjusts the speed at which the board passes through the machine, Figure 33-10. The faster the feed rate, the more boards can be surfaced in a period of time. Mill marks, however, will be deeper at fast speeds. Use a fast feed speed for rough, beginning cuts. Make finishing cuts and all cuts on hard materials at a slower speed. Do not adjust the speed unless the motor is on.

A good planer has a knife-grinding attachment, a dust hood and a brake. Mount the knife grinder directly on the machine when sharpening knives, Figures 33-1 and 33-7. If your planer does not have a knife grinder, remove dull knives from the cutterhead, grind them on a special grinding machine and carefully remount them in the cutterhead. Refer to the owner's manual of the planer for sharpening instructions. Each brand varies slightly. A *dust hood* is connected to a dust-collection system that sucks up wood shavings. A planer without a hood produces a great deal of dust. A brake is a good safety feature. Use the brake when a board becomes stuck in the machine. A brake will bring the cutterhead to a complete stop in seconds.

FACE PLANING

The following instructions are for a single-head, knife-type planer. To plane stock:

1. Be certain the bottom surface of the stock is flat. Cupped boards flatten as they pass under the rollers but will return to their cupped shape when they leave the machine.

A board with a crook or twist also will not plane properly. If a board is not flat, run the board over a jointer to flatten the surface before planing.

2. Measure the thickest part of the board and subtract 1/16" (2 mm). Set the planer to this measurement. For example, if a board measures 1" (25 mm) thick, the planer should be set to 15/16" (24 mm). Set the height of the bed with the height-adjustment handwheel. Set the depth gauge to this dimension.
3. Position the board with the grain pointing toward you. Place the flat surface of the board down on the bed. The face to be planed faces up.
4. Turn on the power and feed the material into the machine. Although the planer is a safe machine, a kickback may occur. Stand to one side of the bed so that if a board is kicked out you will not be injured, Figure 33-11. Check to see that no one is in the path of the board in front of the machine.
5. Watch the board as it feeds into the machine. It may lead to one side or the other. Try to straighten the board with a quick jerk to the opposite side. Also, a piece occasionally will become stuck in the machine. Apply pressure on either end to assist with the feeding. If this does not help, turn off the power and allow the cutter to stop completely. Use a brake if one is available. Lower the bed and remove the stock. Set the depth gauge for a more shallow cut and feed the board again. Do not use a hammer on the stock or reach into the planer to free the board.
6. Support the bottom of the trailing end as the board starts into the machine. With long boards, failure to do this will damage the planer. Do not place your hands on the bottom side of the board. They may become pinched between the board and bed.
7. Always remove equal amounts of material from both surfaces of the board. Removing all of the material from one side will cause the board to cup.
8. Very long boards require an assistant to help support the stock. This person should hold the boards as they leave the machine.

Figure 33-11
Stand to one side when feeding stock.

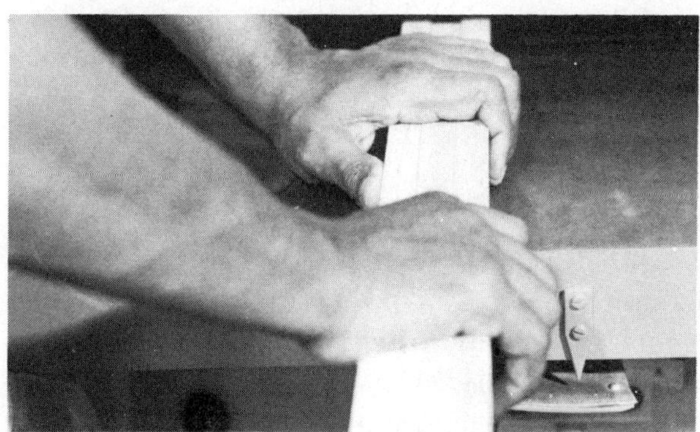

Figure 33-12
Keep boards together as you plane the edges.

A tail-off person will speed up the planing by catching boards as they come out of the planer.

EDGE PLANING

A planer also can surface the edges of boards. Use a planer when you need a large number of pieces of the same width. Only planers with a sectional corrugated feed roller can plane edges. To surface the edges of boards:

1. Joint one edge straight and true on the jointer.
2. Place at least three boards side by side with the grain pointing toward you. Do not attempt this operation unless a minimum of 2-1/4" (472 mm) of stock is against the bed.
3. Tightly hold the boards together as they

Figure 33-13
A piece of plywood makes a good backing board.

are fed into the machine, Figure 33-12. Continue to grip the portion of the boards extending out of the planer until the boards are in the machine completely.

4. Have a tail-off person hold the boards together as they leave the planer so they do not spread apart. If this is not done, the individual pieces will tilt to one side and a bevel will be cut.

FACEPLANING THIN STOCK

Some projects require stock thinner than 3/8" (10 mm). You can plane material as thin as 1/8" (3 mm) if you use a *backing board.* Without a backing board placed under such thin stock, the cutter will come dangerously close to the platen.

A backing board is a flat piece with two parallel faces. It must be at least 4" (102 mm) longer than the stock to be surfaced, Figure 33-13. A high grade of 3/4" (19 mm) hardwood plywood is recommended.

Place the stock on top of the backing board and measure the total thickness of both pieces. Subtract 1/16" (2 mm) and set the planer to this depth. Run both pieces through the planer until the stock is the desired thickness.

MAJOR DEFECTS

Surfacing boards on a correctly adjusted planer is easy. With use, however, the machine becomes out of adjustment. An incorrectly set planer will make rough, uneven cuts. Each brand of planer adjusts differently. Read your operator's manual for specific information.

Figure 33-14 lists some major defects and suggests how they can be corrected. Practice using the planer to become familiar with these defects and their remedies.

Defect	Causes	Remedies
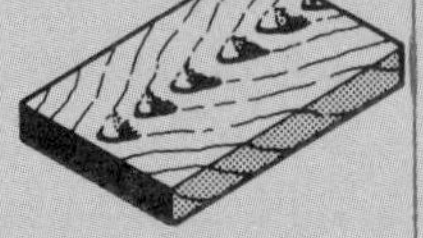	1. Running board in wrong direction 2. Grain direction change	1. Run board w the grain. 2. Run board a slowest feed speed.
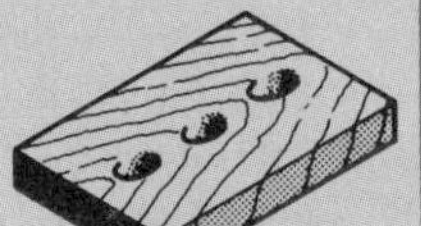	Resin deposits on rollers	Clean rollers with solvent
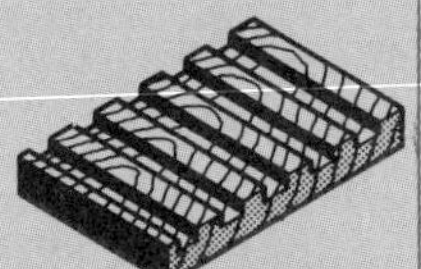	Too much pressure on corrugated feed roller	Reduce pres on the roller
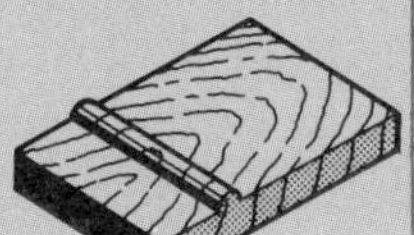	Lower infeed rollers set too high	Bring the lo infeed roller down.
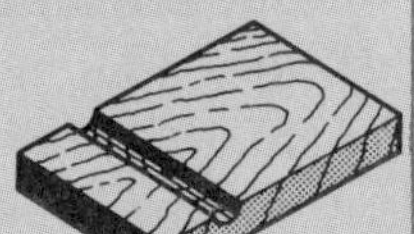	Too much pressure on roller	Reduce pres on top rolle and pressure bar.
	Bed not parallel with the cutterhead	Adjust bed.
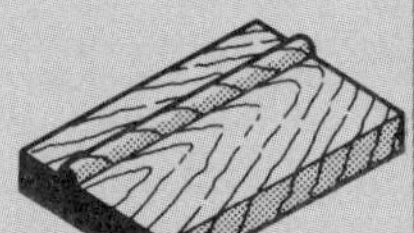	Cutters have nicks.	Regrind cutterhead.

Figure 33-14
Major defects and suggested remedies.

OPERATING HINTS

Keep the following hints in mind when operating a planer:

1. Scrape excess glue from all glue joints before planing. Glue will dull the knives.
2. Use stock that is at least 2″ (51 mm) longer than the distance between the bottom rollers. Planers will vary from model to model. Pieces as short as 1″ smaller than the distance between the bottom rollers can be planed if they are butted one against another, Figure 33-15. The last board must be long enough to clear the machine by itself.
3. Feeding boards in the same spot of the bed each time will dull the knives in that area very quickly. Feed boards in different places along the bed. Use the full width of the cutterhead to plane.
4. If you are surfacing several boards of different thicknesses, set the depth of cut to the thickest piece. Plane it to the next-thickest board. Continue this procedure for all of the remaining boards. Surfacing each board separately takes a considerable amount of time.

Figure 33-15
Feeding short boards. Note that the last board to be fed, board 3, is longer.

REVIEW QUESTIONS

1 What is the difference between a single and a double planer?
2 List three advantages of the abrasive planer.
3 Sketch and label the major internal parts of the planer. Include the bottom rollers, corrugated roller, chip breaker, cutterhead, pressure bar and upper outfeed roller.
4 What is the major advantage of a sectional corrugated feed roll?
5 What does a pressure bar do?
6 Should cupped or twisted stock be planed? Why or why not?
7 Why should equal amounts of material be removed from each surface of the board?
8 List the procedure for freeing a board that has become stuck in the machine.
9 What will happen if boards are not held together when planing edges?
10 Boards that are ____″ (____ mm) and thinner must be placed on a backing board to be face planed.
11 Sketch three defects that can be produced by the planer. Label and list causes and remedies for each.
12 How can the minimum length of a board that can be fed through a planer be determined?
13 Where should the operator stand when feeding stock through the planer?

SUGGESTED ACTIVITIES

1 Inspect the outside of your planer and name as many parts as you can.
2 Determine the shortest board that can be fed through your planer.
3 Using scrap stock, practice planing faces and edges. Follow the rules listed in the safety section.
4 Using a backing board, surface a piece of wood to 1/4″ (6 mm).
5 Have your instructor open the planer and identify the major internal parts.

UNIT

34

Shapers

Objectives

After studying this unit you should be able to:

1 Adjust the major parts of a shaper.
2 Mount the cutter and establish the direction of feed.
3 Shape straight edges and ends.
4 Shape curved pieces.

Technical Terms

Single-spindle shaper	Stack molding
Double-spindle shaper	Starting pin
Molder	Ring guard
Fence	Pattern shaping

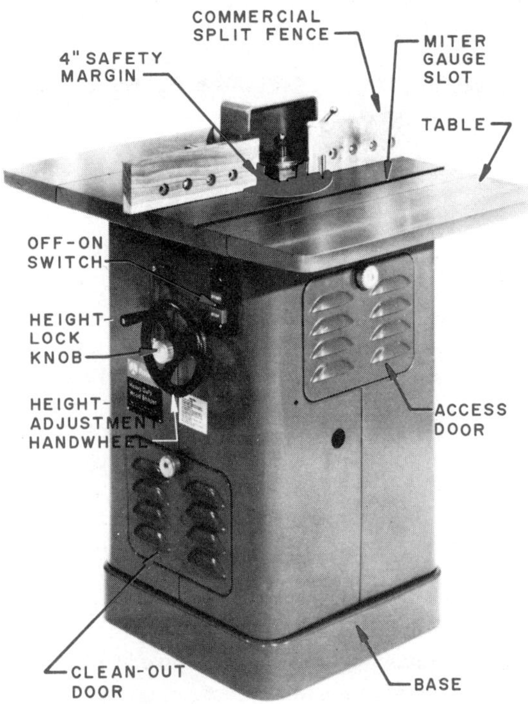

Figure 34-1
Major machine parts of the shaper. The safety zone is 4" (102 mm) around the cutter. (Rockwell International)

SHAPER SAFETY RULES

1 Disconnect the power before changing or working around any cutting tool.
2 Keep your hands and fingers outside the 4" (102 mm) safety margin surrounding the cutter. Refer to Figure 34-1.
3 Always use feather boards, other hold-downs or appropriate guards.
4 Use a push stick whenever possible.
5 Be certain that the cutter always rotates against the direction from which the stock is fed.
6 If possible, mount the shaper knife so that the major portion of the cutting is done on the bottom surface of the stock.
7 Always allow the cutter to reach full speed before starting a cut.
8 Use stock at least 2" (51 mm) wide and 10" (254 mm) in length when edge shaping.
9 Use stock at least 10" (254 mm) wide when shaping end grain.
10 Never move the stock backwards. If you need a different setting, pivot the stock away from the cutter and remove it from the table.
11 Take light cuts to prevent overloading the machine.
12 Keep cutters sharp.
13 Do not use cutters that are cracked or chipped.

The shaper, Figure 34-1, makes decorative cuts on both straight and curved surfaces. It also shapes such joints as rabbets and small grooves.

Most shapers are *single-spindle shapers.* One threaded shaft rotates a cutter. A *double-spindle shaper* sometimes is used in industry, Figure 34-2. The two spindles usually have the same shape of cutters mounted. The two cutters rotate in opposite directions. This allows the operator

Figure 34-2
A double-spindle shaper rotates in two directions. (Oliver Machinery Company)

Figure 34-3
Industry uses a molder to shape wood. (Mattison Machinery Company)

always to cut with the grain to prevent chipping the wood. Industry also uses a *molder* to make shaper-type cuts, Figure 34-3. The machine automatically feeds the boards past the cutterheads. Four to eight spindles shape all four surfaces of the stock with one pass through the molder.

SHAPER TERMINOLOGY

As the shaper cuts the stock, the stock moves over the top of a heavy cast iron table, Figure 34-1. The table is stationary and has a rectangular slot for the miter gauge. It also has several sets of threaded holes. One set of holes fastens the fence to the table, another set of tapered holes holds the guide pin, and one hole attaches the ring guard, Figure 34-4.

Figure 34-4
The shaper table has several holes to hold pins.

Figure 34-5
A shop-made wooden fence.

Figure 34-6
Interchangeable spindles come in several sizes.

The *fence* is a very important part of the shaper. Use it when you want to shape a straight edge. All styles of fences have an infeed and an outfeed side. When you feed stock, place it against the infeed fence. The stock moves past the cutter. The outfeed fence supports the stock as the cut is finished. A commercial split fence comes as standard equipment with the shaper, Figure 34-1. It is designed so that the two fence halves can move back and forth independently of one another. This is particularly important when the entire edge of the board is being removed and the fences are offset. Another style is a shop-made wooden fence. You can make it any length and height to support the stock. The two fence halves form a straight line, Figure 34-5. Secure either style of fence to the table with the fence studs, Figure 34-4.

The shaper cutters rotate on a spindle at speeds ranging from 5000 to 10,000 rpm. Many machines have interchangeable spindles of 1/2″, 5/8″, 3/4″, 1″ and 1-1/8″ in diameter, Figure 34-6. The most common spindle size for small cutters is 1/2″ (12 mm). There is a 4″ (102 mm) safety margin around the spindle, Figure 34-1. You must not put your hands within this area.

A height-adjustment handwheel moves the cutter up and down. When the height is correct, a height lock knob secures the spindle in position, Figure 34-7.

A motor in the base of the shaper drives the spindle. Most shapers have a reversing switch that controls the direction of rotation of the cutter. The cutter can run clockwise or counterclockwise, Figure 34-8. This allows stock to be fed from either direction.

A large spindle hole in the center of the table holds the table rings. These rings extend above the table top and help guide stock, Figure 34-9. Always use a ring guard or other style of guard as an additional safety device, Figure 34-10.

SHAPER CUTTERS

There are many styles of shaper knives and cutters, Figure 34-11. The most common type of shaper cutter is a three-lip style. This style are available with either high-speed steel or carbide tipped cutters, Figure 34-12. You easily can sharpen high-speed steel cutters on an oilstone,

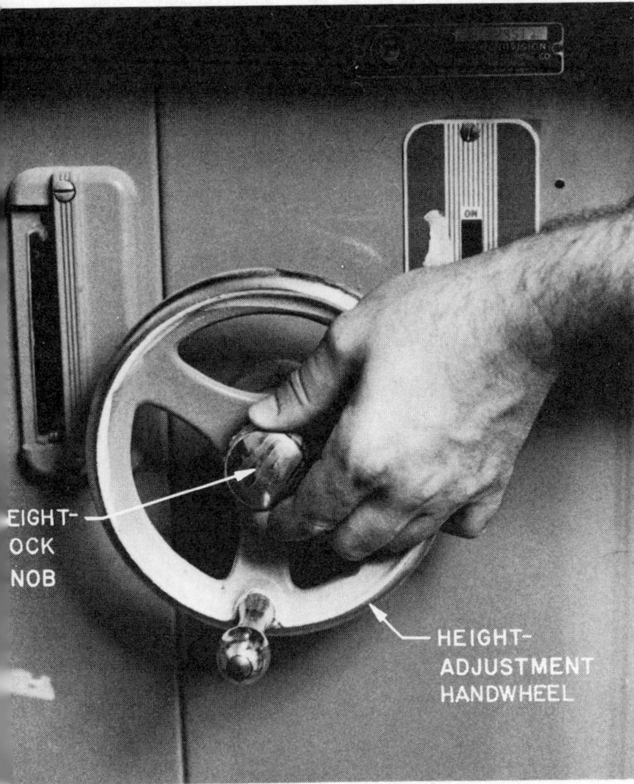

Figure 34-7
Securing the spindle with the height-lock knob.

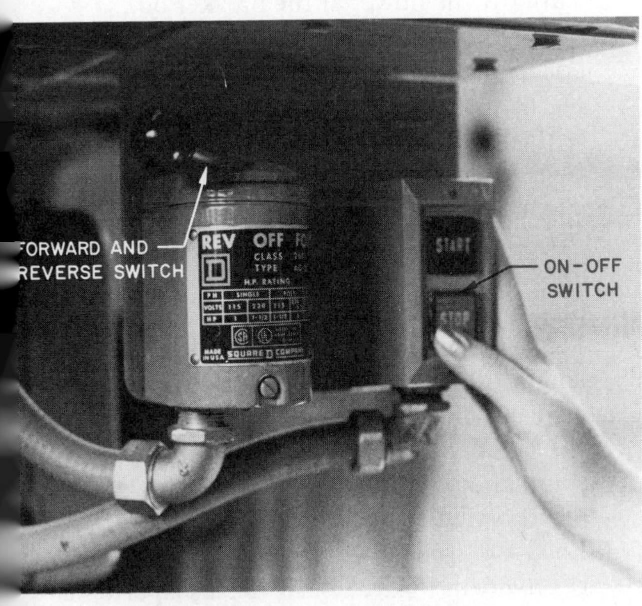

Figure 34-8
The shaper is turned off. Once the spindle has stopped, the forward and reverse switch can be used to change the direction of rotation.

Figure 34-9
Table rings ride against the stock to control the depth of cut. *The guard has been removed so you can see the table ring.*

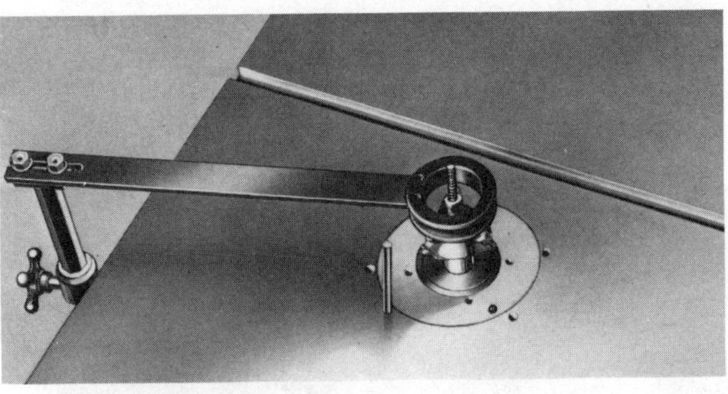

Figure 34-10
A ring guard forms a barrier on top of the cutter. (Rockwell International)

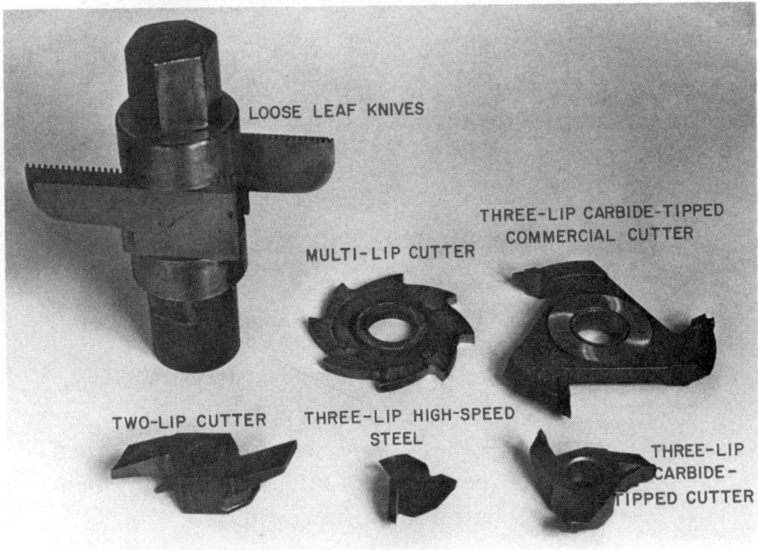

Figure 34-11
Shaper cutters are available in many styles.

Figure 34-12
Three-lipped shaper cutters come in many standard patterns. (Rockwell International)

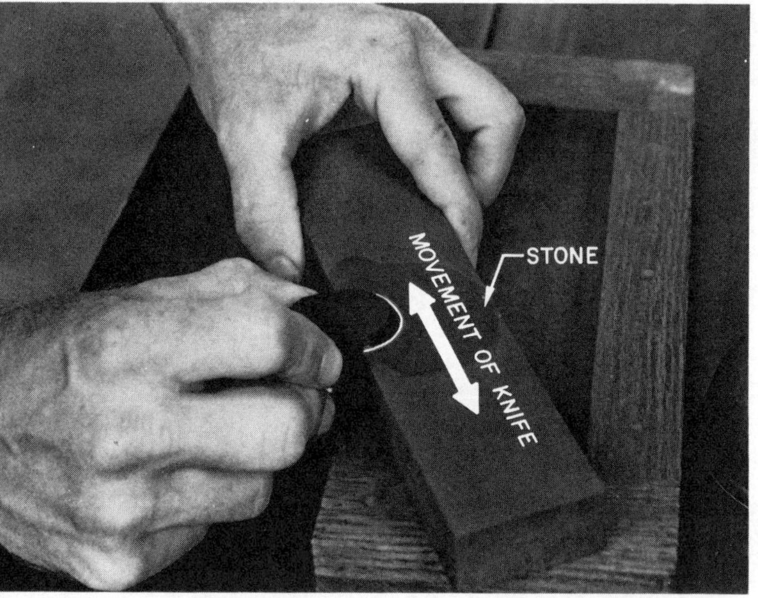

Figure 34-13
Sharpening the back side of a shaper knife on a flat oilstone.

Figure 34-13. Carbide requires professional sharpening equipment. For this reason high-speed steel cutters are often preferred.

Another shaper cutting tool is the loose leaf knife. These cutters are strips of steel with teeth ground into their top edges. The teeth fit into

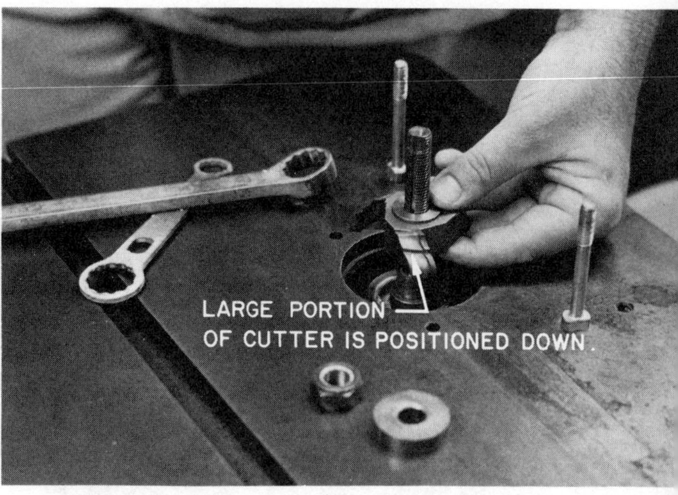

Figure 34-14
Place the cutter on the spindle so that it will cut from the bottom side. *Disconnect the power before attempting this operation.*

a keyed collar that is mounted on top of the knives. Most setups contain two knives custom ground to a particular shape. Industry selects this style of cutter because the knives can be ground to any shape needed.

MOUNTING THE CUTTERS

The first step in setting up the shaper is installing the cutter. Follow this procedure:

1. Turn off the power at the breaker box.
2. Select the desired cutter or cutters. Place a collar on the spindle. Then place the cutter on top of this collar. Position the cutter with the largest portion down to allow cutting from the bottom side of the board, Figure 34-14. This is much safer than having a large part of the cutting tool exposed above the stock.
3. Slip another collar on top of the cutter. Some shapers have a groove milled into the length of the spindle to hold a keyed washer. Place this washer immediately on top of the last collar to keep the spindle nut from spinning loose, Figure 34-15. Screw the nut on the spindle and tighten it by hand.
4. Lock the spindle with a spindle lock, if one is provided, Figure 34-16. On a shaper with no spindle lock, hold the top portion of the spindle with a special wrench. Place a wrench on the spindle nut. Tighten it by turning the wrench to the right, Figure 34-17.

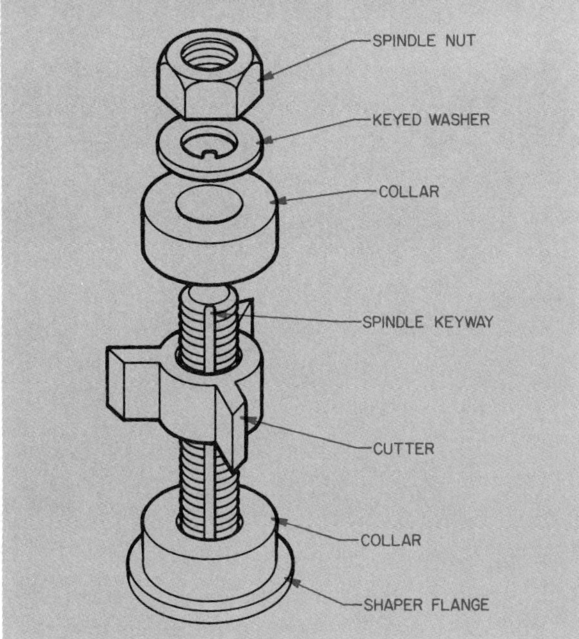

Figure 34-15
Spindle assembly.

DETERMINING DIRECTION OF FEED

One of the most common causes of shaper accidents is feeding the stock from the wrong direction. The cutter must always rotate so that the sharp edge of the cutter strikes the board first. The bevel edge of the cutter trails behind the leading cutting edge, Figure 34-18.

Quickly turn the motor on and off to determine the direction of rotation. If it is not correct, reverse the direction of rotation with the reversing switch. If there is no reversing switch, turn over the cutter. Change the direction of rotation only when the spindle is not turning. Stock must be fed against the rotation of the cutter to prevent a kickback. If you feed a board with the rotation, it will be thrown out of your hands. Always use a push stick on narrow stock in case a kickback occurs.

SHAPING A PORTION OF THE EDGE

Shaping only a part of the edge of stock leaves a small amount of the original surface uncut, Figure 34-19. The uncut part of the edge must be straight and true to act as a guide along the fence. It will also be part of the finished edge. Stock less than 10" (254 mm) long should not be cut on the shaper. Follow these steps to shape part of an edge.

1. Turn off the power at the breaker box.
2. Select the cutter to be used. Place it at the edge of the board that is to be cut and

Figure 34-16
Engaging the spindle lock.

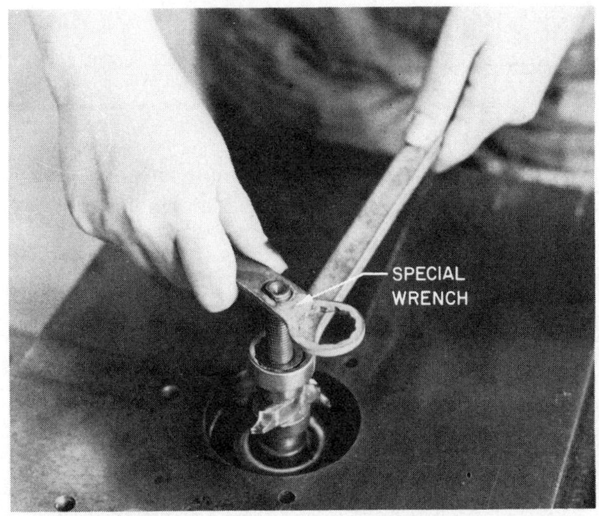

Figure 34-17
The special wrench secures the spindle. *Disconnect the power before attempting this operation.*

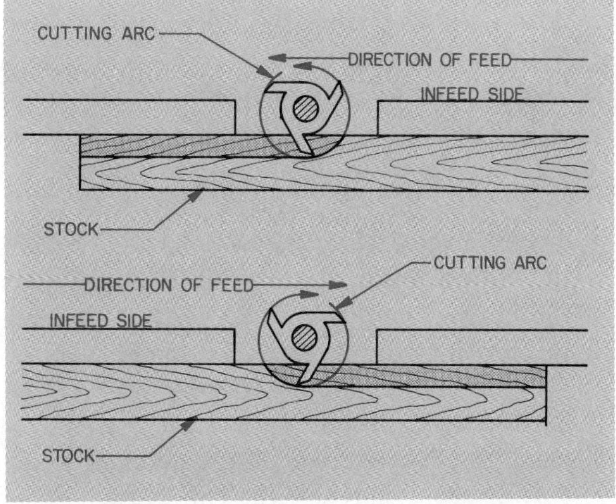

Figure 34-18
Direction of feed will depend on rotation of cutter and how it is placed on the spindle.

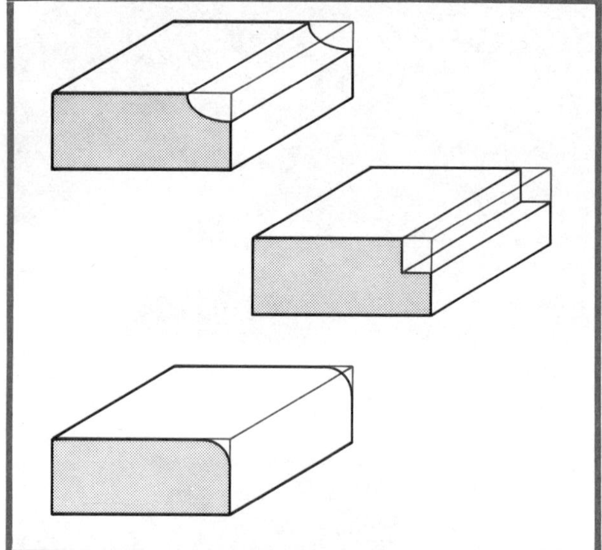

Figure 34-19
Examples of shaper cuts that require only a portion of the edge be removed. Colored lines indicate the original edge.

against the end that will be fed into the cutter. Trace the cutter shape to show where it will be cut.

3. Mount the cutter on the spindle. If possible, position the cutter so that it will cut from the bottom side of the board, Figure 34-14. Remember to mount it so that the sharp edge will strike the board first, Figure 34-18.
4. Place the fence on top of the table. If you use a commercial split fence, align the two sides with a straightedge, Figure 34-20. A wooden fence, such as the one shown in Figure 34-5, is recommended because the infeed and outfeed sides are already aligned.
5. Position the board to be cut on the infeed side of the spindle. Raise the spindle to the proper height. The cutter should align with the pattern previously traced on the end of the board, Figure 34-21. Secure the spindle by locking the height-adjustment handwheel.
6. Set the depth of cut. Rotate the cutter by hand and locate the farthest point of the cutting arc, Figure 34-22. This is the point at which the cutter will extend the farthest beyond the fence. If you are making a deep cut or using a small shaper, take two or more light cuts. Do not try to do the whole cut in one pass through the shaper. Move the fence into position until the correct amount of the knife extends beyond the fence. At this point the shape of the cutter will match the layout line that you drew on the stock. Fasten the fence securely with the fence studs.

Figure 34-20
Using a straightedge to align the two halves of a split fence. *Disconnect the power before attempting this operation.*

7. Finish the setup by installing feather boards, Figure 34-23. A feather board is a piece of wood that has many saw kerfs cut in one end. When clamped to the table and fence they hold the stock in position. Mount feather boards as close to the cutter as possible. Never shape stock without having these safety devices in place.
8. Rotate the cutter by hand to see that everything is clear. Then turn on the power. Let the shaper reach full speed. Feed the stock across the shaper with a push stick. Remember to keep your hands outside the 4" (102 mm) safety margin.
9. Use a slow, steady feeding rate. Feeding the stock too fast will cause chip-out and will overload the shaper. Feeding the stock too slowly will burn the stock and overheat the cutter.

SHAPING AN ENTIRE EDGE

Some patterns require shaping the entire edge, Figure 34-24. This way of shaping requires the use of the split fence. Stock must be at least 10" (254 mm) long. To shape an entire edge:

Figure 34-21
Aligning the cutter with the layout mark. *Disconnect the power before attempting this operation.*

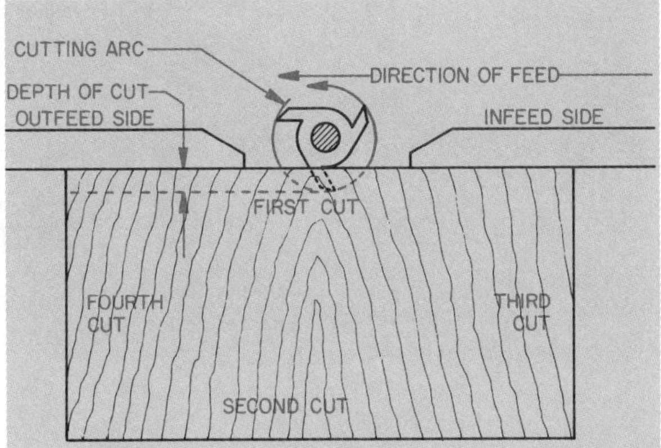

Figure 34-22
The distance the cutting arc extends beyond the fence is equal to the depth of cut.

1. Follow the same setup procedure that you followed for shaping a portion of the edge.
2. When you set the depth of cut, move the fence so that the cutting arc of the shaper knife aligns with the layout line. Fasten the infeed side of the fence tightly to the table, Figure 34-25.
3. Start the shaper and allow it to reach full speed. Then feed a 10" (254 mm) or longer scrap piece across the cutter. Stop the feed when the leading edge of the board goes past the near end of the outfeed fence. Hold the board firmly against the table and turn off the power. Do not move the stock until the cutter has come to a complete standstill.
4. Move up the outfeed table to the shaped edge, Figure 34-26. You do this with the depth-adjustment knob. Then lock the out-

Figure 34-23
Feather boards must be used with the fence. Note that a push stick is being used.

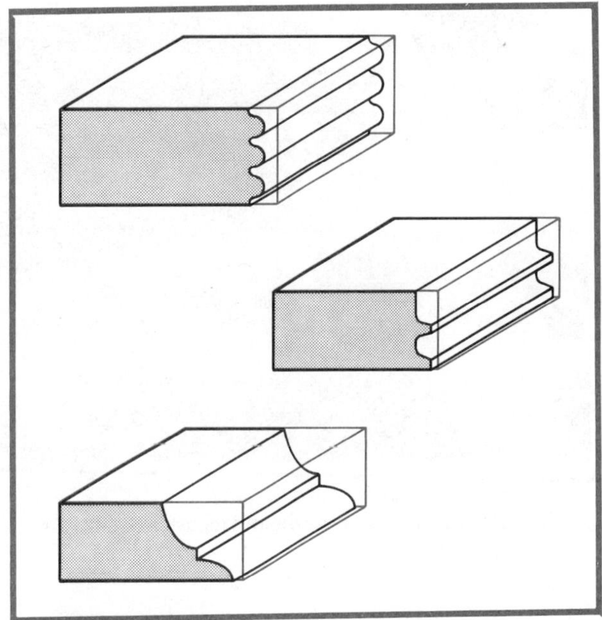

Figure 34-24
Examples of shaper cuts that require the entire edge be removed. Colored lines indicate the original edge.

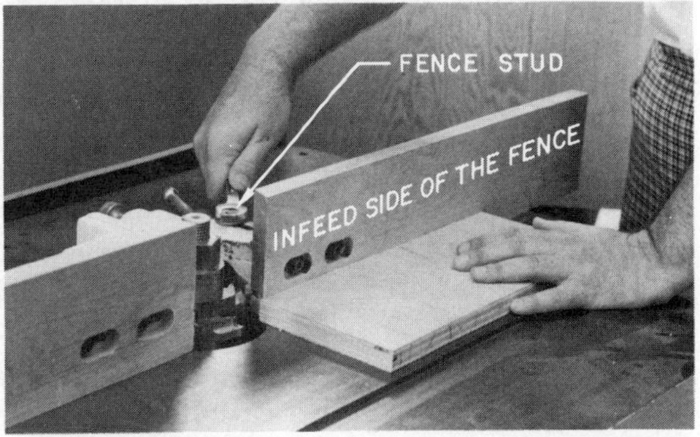

Figure 34-25
Securing the infeed side of the fence. *Disconnect the power before attempting this operation.*

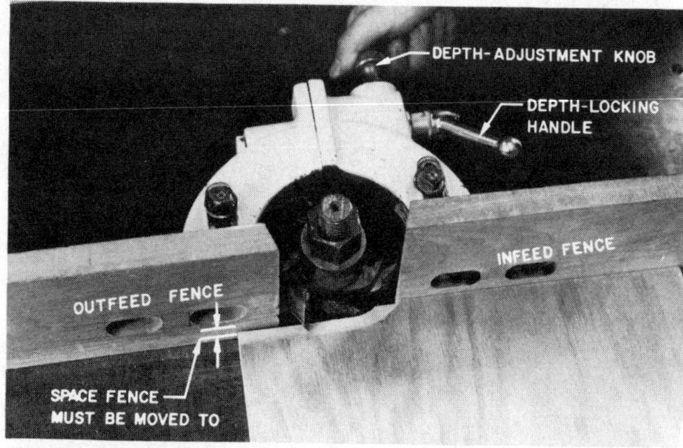

Figure 34-26
Moving the outfeed side of the fence with the depth-adjustment knob. *Disconnect the power before attempting this operation.*

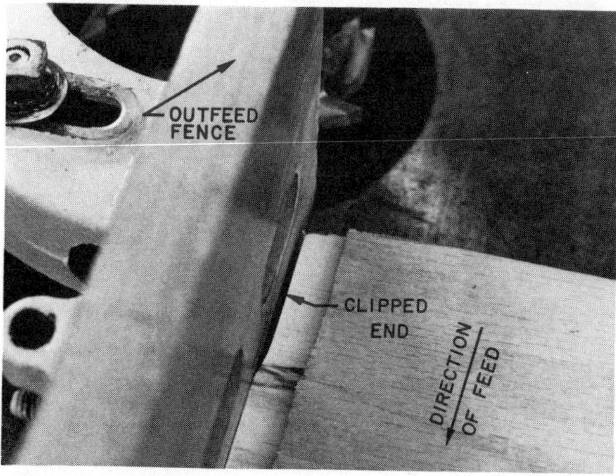

Figure 34-27
Clipped end is caused by the outfeed fence set too deep.

feed table in place with the depth-locking handle. Secure the outfeed side of the fence with the remaining fence stud.

5. Install the feather boards as close to the cutter as possible.
6. Run the first piece of stock and check the cut. If the board hits the lip of the outfeed fence, move the outfeed fence back. If the end of the trailing edge is cut too deeply, move the outfeed fence out, Figure 34-27.

Some shaper patterns require two or more cutters, Figure 34-28. This is called *stack molding.* On small shapers the first and second cuts will have to be made in two separate operations. With a heavy-duty shaper both cutters can be mounted on the spindle at the same time. The full edge can be made with one pass.

Figure 34-28
Stack molding is done with two or more cutters. Cutter number one shapes the top portion of the stock. Cutter number two shapes the bottom.

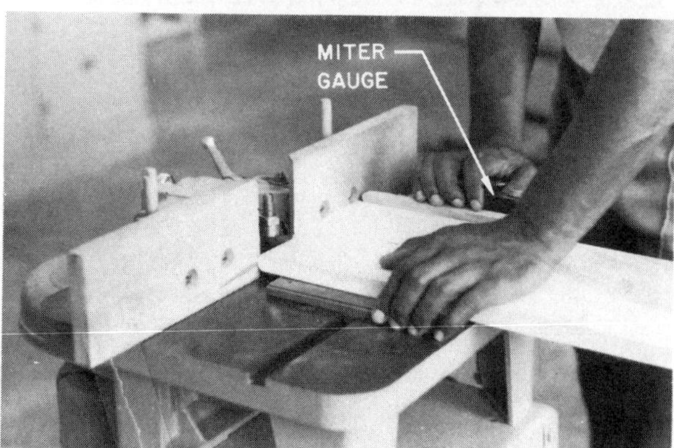

Figure 34-29
Shaping the end grain with a miter gauge. *Guard has been removed so you can see the cut.*

SHAPING END GRAIN

Shaping end grain is more difficult than shaping edge grain because the ends of the wood fibers are exposed. As the cutter rotates, it must cut across the cell walls rather than slicing along their sides. This can cause the fibers to chip at the end of the cut.

Always shape the ends before shaping the edges. This way any chipping on the corners can be cut away as the edges are cut. When shaping end grain, do not run boards less than 10″ (254 mm) long. Short boards may be caught in the opening between the fence halves. If possible, use a miter gauge to help guide the material along the fence, Figure 34-29. You can buy a special miter gauge that holds the stock down securely, Figure 34-30.

SHAPING WITH COLLARS

When you want to curve the edges of a piece of stock or shape inside edges, use a contact collar rather than the fence to guide the stock.

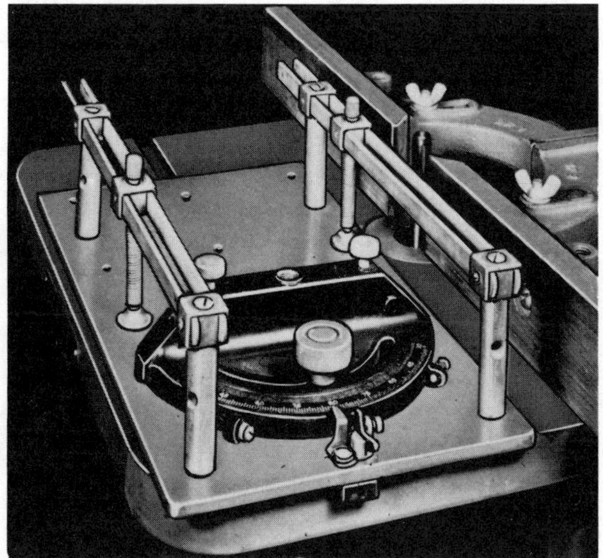

Figure 34-30
A commercial miter gauge with hold-downs.
(Rockwell International)

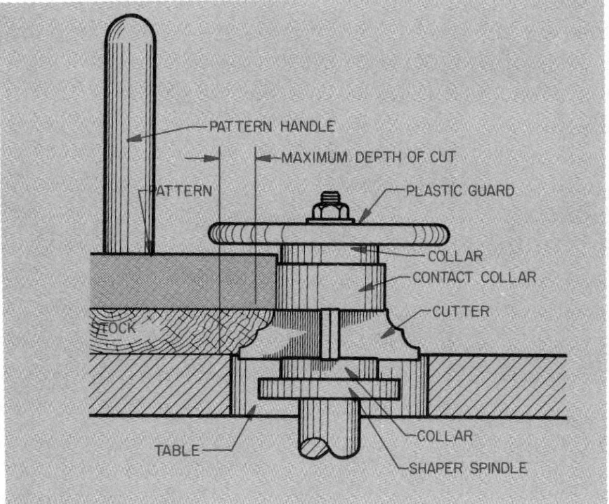

Figure 34-31
The amount the cutter extends over the contact collar will determine the maximum depth of cut. *The guard has been left off for illustration.*

Figure 34-32
Solid steel contact collars will ride against the stock. *Disconnect the power before attempting this operation.*

Mount the contact collar on the spindle along with the cutter. Guide the wood against the collar. The amount the cutter extends beyond the contact collar determines the depth of cut, Figure 34-31.

Two kinds of contact collars can be used. Solid steel collars are the least expensive, Figure 34-32. A solid steel collar may burn the edge of the stock and cause it to turn brown. Keeping the collars smooth and shiny will minimize burning.

To avoid burning completely, use a ball bearing collar. The outside of the bearing does not turn at the same high rpm as the spindle when the stock is brought in contact with it. It allows the stock to move at a slow, steady pace without burning.

The procedure for shaping a portion of an edge with a collar is:

1. Turn off the power at the breaker box.
2. Select the desired cutter and appropriate contact collar. The desired amount of cutter knife should extend beyond the collar. The amount the cutter extends beyond the contact collar will equal the depth of cut. You may first want to use a large-diameter collar to take a light cut. Then, after taking the first pass, put on a smaller-diameter collar to make the finish cut. This procedure will not overwork the shaper and will produce a quality cut.
3. Determine whether the contact collar should be mounted below or above a single cutter or between two cutters. For most shapes it is best to place the contact collar above the cutter. This puts the cutter below the top surface of the stock and protects the operator to a greater degree. Secure the assembly with the spindle nut and adjust the height of the spindle.
4. Install the tapered *starting pin* in the appropriate hole on the infeed side of the cutter, Figure 34-4. Position stock against this pin and then move it into the rotating cutter. Without the starting pin, a kickback will occur.

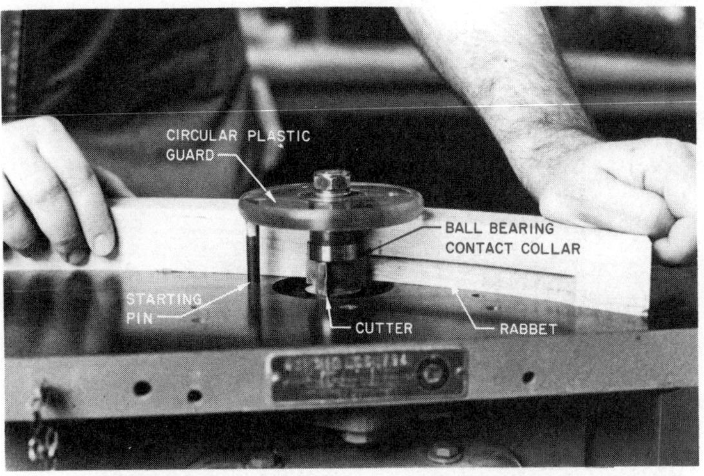

Figure 34-33
A circular plastic guard forms a protective barrier above the cutter. Motion has been stopped so that you can see the cutter.

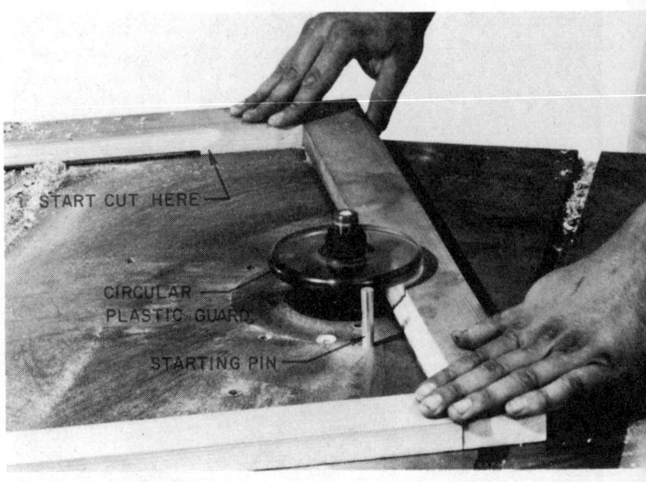

Figure 34-34
The starting pin should not touch the stock once shaping has begun. Note where the cut began. (Rockwell International)

5. Mount some type of extra guard. You cannot use a fence or feather boards in this procedure. A circular plastic guard is often used. Place it on top of the contact collar and secure it with the spindle nut, Figure 34-33. Some woodworkers select a *ring guard,* Figure 34-10.
6. Make sure the edge is smooth and true before shaping it. Any irregular or low spots will be reflected in the shaped edge.
7. Start the shaper and allow it to reach full speed. Bring the stock against the starting pin and pivot it into the cutter. There is extreme danger of a kickback as the cut begins. The cutting tool should first contact the stock 3/8″ to 1/2″ (10 to 13 mm) from the corner. If the cutter touches the corner of the board first, the board will be thrown out of your hands.
8. Swing the board away from the starting pin after the cut is started, Figure 34-34. Do not hold the board against both the pin and the collar. Continue feeding the stock along the edge until you reach the starting point. Pivot the stock when you come to a corner. When the cut is finished, slide the stock away from the contact collar and cutter.

PATTERN SHAPING

One method of producing curved pieces with shaped edges is called *pattern shaping.* A pattern allows the entire edge to be shaped. This method produces identical pieces quickly and accurately.

A pattern used to produce a small number of pieces is made from hardwood, such as maple, Figure 34-35. If a large number of pieces are to be shaped, use heavy, dense hardboard, plastic or metal to make the pattern.

When you have determined the size of the pattern, cut it out on the band saw or scroll saw. Follow the layout line very carefully. Smooth the edges to remove all irregularities. Accuracy is important because the shaped stock will be exactly like the pattern.

Mount the pattern on top of or underneath the raw stock. For safety reasons, it is better if the stock is on the bottom and handles are attached to the pattern. If a great deal of material has to be removed, cut the stock to a rough shape on the band saw.

Fasten the piece to be shaped to the pattern with screws driven through the pattern. File the screw points to a wedge shape. The wedge should align with the grain of the stock being shaped and be approximately 1/8″ (2 mm) in length.

Follow the same procedure for pattern shaping as was followed for cutting with collars. All sides usually are shaped. Therefore, you must start the cut in the middle of one of the sides and make a continuous cut completely around the stock, Figure 34-36. Do not start on a corner. Once the cut is started with the help of the starting pin, continue rotating the stock until all four edges are shaped. Be cautious when turning corners because the cutter may grab the stock.

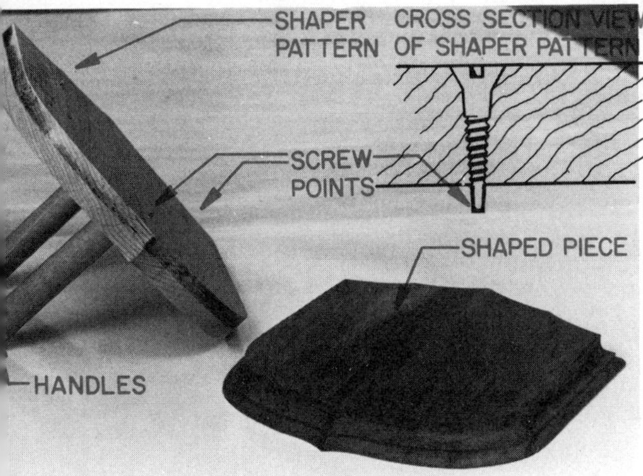

Figure 34-35
Dense hardwood works quite well for a shaper pattern.

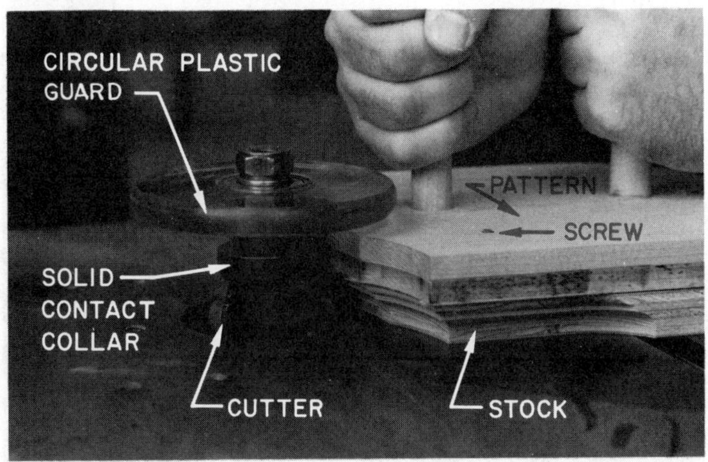

Figure 34-36
Shaping an entire edge by using a pattern and contact collar.

REVIEW QUESTIONS

1 Why does industry use a double-spindle shaper?
2 What is the major difference between a commercial split fence and a shop-made wooden fence?
3 Sketch the top view of a shaper with a cutter properly positioned. Include the infeed and outfeed fences and the direction of feed.
4 How are the infeed and outfeed sides of a commercial split fence adjusted when removing only a portion of an edge?
5 What are feather boards? What are they designed to do?
6 Sketch the proper position of the fence when shaping the entire edge. Include the infeed and outfeed fences, the cutter and the stock being shaped.
7 Should you first shape the end grain or the edge grain? Why?
8 How is the depth of cut determined when shaping with collars?
9 What guard must you use when shaping with collars or pattern shaping?
10 Where should the cutter first touch the stock when performing pattern shaping?

SUGGESTED ACTIVITIES

1 Inspect your shaper and name all of the major parts.
2 Use the stack molding technique to design your own molding. Combine two or more cutter shapes.
3 With the help of your instructor, set up the shaper to remove the entire edge. Be certain to use feather boards.
4 Make a pattern for a plaque. With the direct supervision of your instructor, cut the plaque using the shaper. Be certain you use all suggested safety features.

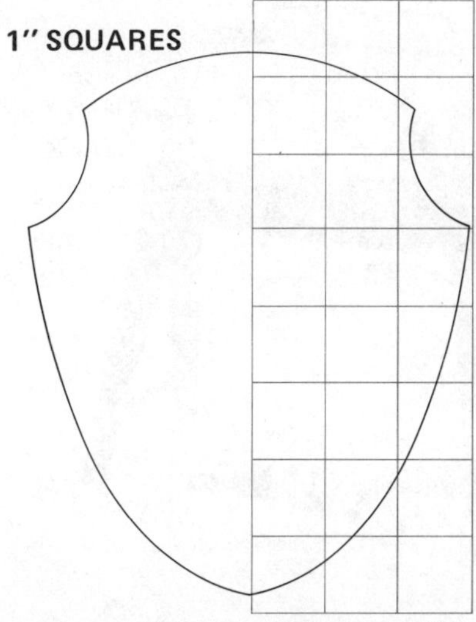

UNIT

35

Wood Lathes

Objectives

After studying this unit you should be able to:

1 Identify the major parts of the lathe and understand the basic adjustments.

2 Select and use the proper lathe chisels.

3 Turn a cylinder, taper, bead, cove and V.

4 Make faceplate turnings.

Technical Terms

Spindle lathe	Lathe shield
Automatic lathe	Cutting method
Patternmaking lathe	Scraping method
Inboard	Outboard
Headstock	Split turning
Tailstock	Duplicator
Lathe chisels	French Polish

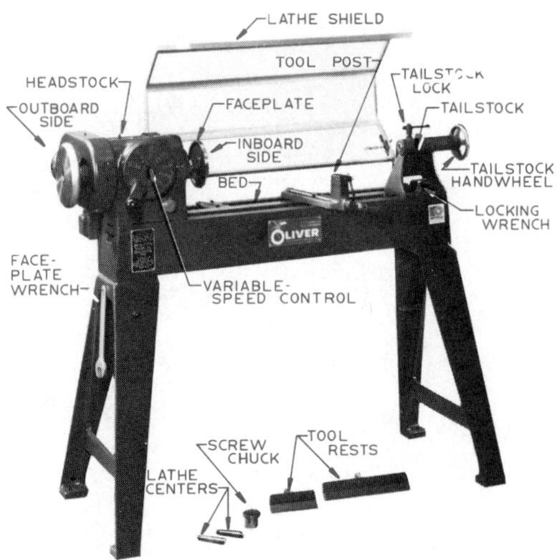

Figure 35-1
A spindle lathe is used to make several different types of turnings. Note that the lathe shield is in the open position. *Only leave the shield in this position when the stock is not rotating.* (Oliver Machinery Company)

WOOD LATHE SAFETY RULES

1 Check to see that stock is free of cracks, knots or poor glue joints.

2 Lock the tailstock, tool rest and tool post securely before turning on the power.

3 After centering the stock and positioning the tool rest, rotate the stock by hand.

4 Position the tool rest 3/8" (10 mm) or less from the stock.

5 Position the tool rest 1/8" (3 mm) above the lathe centers.

6 Stand to one side of the lathe when turning on the power.

7 Rotate rough stock at the slowest possible speed.

8 Turn stock down to a cylinder before using higher speeds.

9 Hold all lathe chisels firmly with both hands.

10 Rotate large-diameter turnings only at slow speeds.

11 Change speeds gradually to prevent the turnings from spinning off the lathe.

12 Use the calipers only when the stock is not turning.

13 Remove the tool post when stock is being sanded or polished.

Figure 35-2
An automatic lathe produces spindles rapidly. Note the hopper feeder. (Stowell Wood Products)

Figure 35-3
A custom set of knives is ground for each shape of spindle. (Stowell Wood Products)

A lathe is used to produce external turnings such as table legs. It can also produce internal turnings such as bowls. It can sand, bore holes and be used for finishing processes. Model builders, patternmakers, small shops and school laboratories generally use a *spindle lathe*, Figure 35-1. A spindle lathe requires a highly skilled operator to control the shaping process.

Furniture and other high-production manufacturers usually choose an *automatic lathe*, Figure 35-2. An automatic lathe does not require a high degree of skill to operate. The automatic lathe has a large set of knives. They rotate at high speed while the stock revolves slowly into the knives, Figure 35-3. When a spindle is changed for one with a different shape or size, another set of knives also is ground and installed.

Patternmaking shops may use a specialized spindle lathe. It is called a *patternmaking lathe*, Figure 35-4. A patternmaking lathe has a compound rest to hold the cutting tools. This type of tool holder can make very accurate cuts.

Figure 35-4
A patternmaking lathe is capable of making accurate cuts. (Oliver Machinery Company)

Figure 35-5
The live center can be removed from the headstock with a knockout rod.

SPINDLE LATHE TERMINOLOGY

A square piece of wood called a turning square is mounted between two centers. The center on the motor side of the lathe is called the live center. It is located on the *inboard* side of the *headstock*. The live center fits into a hollow tapered spindle. It can be removed from the spindle by tapping the end with a knockout rod, Figure 35-5.

The *tailstock* contains the other center. This is called the dead center. The tailstock can be moved along the bed and secured into position to hold different lengths of turnings.

The dead center can be either a cup or cone style, Figure 35-6. The cup is preferred because it does not sink into the end of the stock. It also can be lubricated. A ball bearing frequently is built into the dead center so that it rotates with the stock. This eliminates friction and burning.

The size of the lathe is the maximum length of stock that can be turned between the two centers and the swing. Swing is the largest diameter of stock that can be turned on the lathe. A common-size lathe has a swing of 12″ (305 mm) with a 36″ (914 mm) bed. Some lathes have a gap-bed to allow for larger diameter turnings, Figure 35-7.

Lathe chisels are laid on top of a tool rest while the turning is being shaped. Lengths vary from 4″ to 48″ (102 to 1219 mm). The most common shape is a straight bar. L-shape rests can be used for faceplate turning. Rests come in different lengths and shapes. The tool rest is held in position by the tool post, Figure 35-8. To run long spindles it is necessary to move the tool post to several locations along the bed or to use a long tool rest.

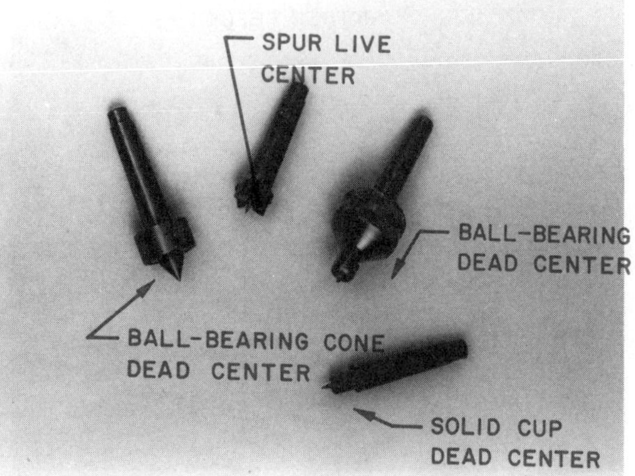

Figure 35-6
Several different centers are used in the lathe: ball bearing cone dead center, spur live center, ball bearing cup center and solid cup dead center.

The speed of the live center is controlled either by a stepped pulley or by a variable speed device. A variable-speed headstock is preferred because the turning speed can easily be changed. Speeds range from 300 to 3600 rpm.

A *lathe shield* should be used to prevent flying pieces of wood and chisels from striking the operator. When the stock is rotating, the shield must be in the closed position, Figure 35-7.

LATHE CHISELS

Lathe chisels are designed to be used with the spindle lathe. They have long handles and blades to control the cut. The handles provide leverage to prevent the chisel from being thrown from the lathe. Most of the tools can make more than one type of cut.

The major chisels are shown in Figure 35-9. There are six types.

1. *Gouges* are available in a variety of widths. The common sizes are 1/4″, 3/8″, 1/2″, 3/4″ and 1″ (6, 10, 13, 19 and 25 mm). These chisels are used primarily for roughing a square piece into a round cylinder. They also can be used to turn cove cuts and other circular shapes.
2. *Skews* are also available in the same widths as the gouges. A skew is ideal for making smooth finishing cuts and for forming beads or Vs.
3. *Square noses,* similar to hand chisels, are used for the same jobs as the skews.

4. *Spear points* can be used for the same type of cuts as the skew. Sometimes they are preferred because they have two cutting edges. They can cut from either direction without turning over the chisel.
5. *Round noses* shape coves and make smooth circular shapes. The body of the round nose is flat; the gouge is curved. Wide round-nose chisels are used for smoothing operations. Narrower chisels cut concave shapes. Common widths are 1/2", 3/4" and i" (13, 19 and 25 mm).
6. *Parting tools* can mark off distances and cut to specified depths.

MEASURING DEVICES

Turnings require that diameters be measured and distances be laid out along their lengths.

Outside and inside calipers are used to measure critical diameters. The legs of an outside

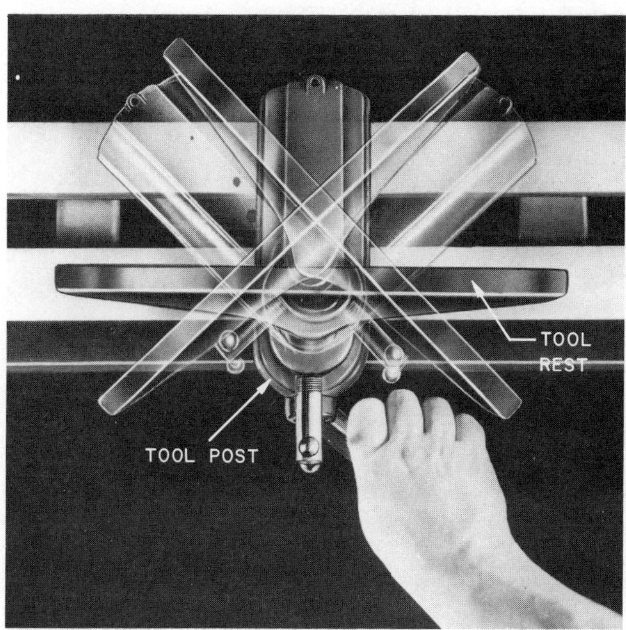

Figure 35-8
The tool rest can be moved to many different positions. (Rockwell International)

Figure 35-7
A gap-bed allows larger diameter turnings to be made. Note that the lathe shield is in place for turning. (Rockwell International)

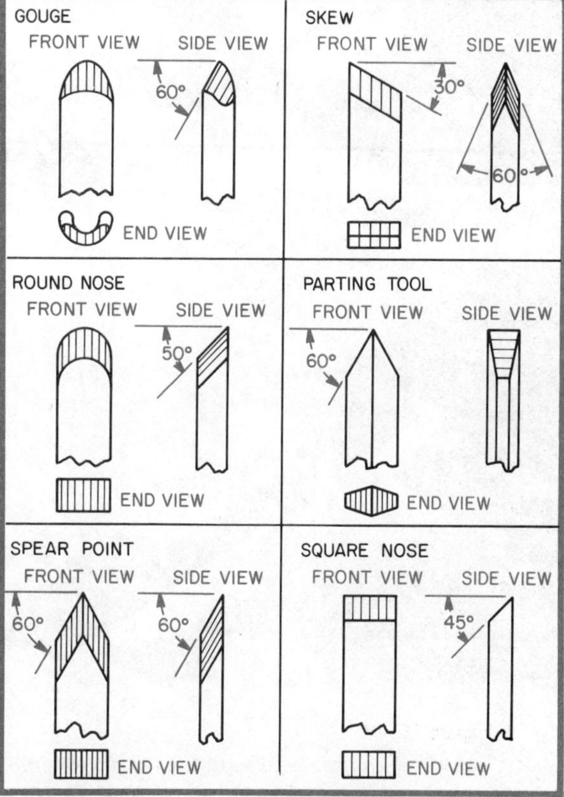

Figure 35-9
Major lathe turning chisels. The top, edge and end views are shown.

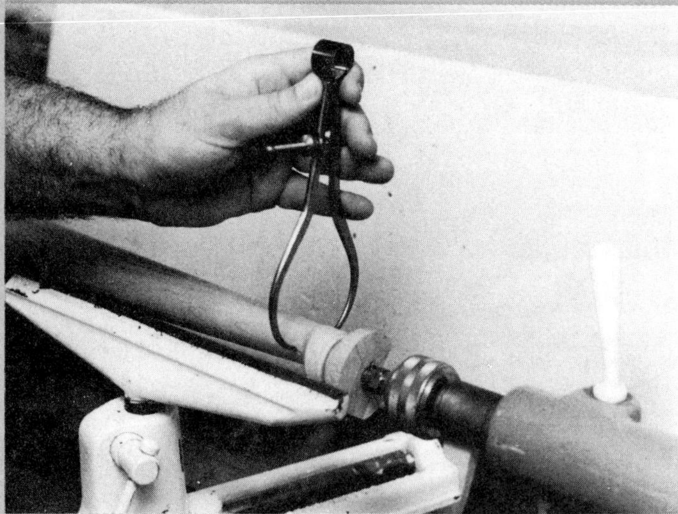

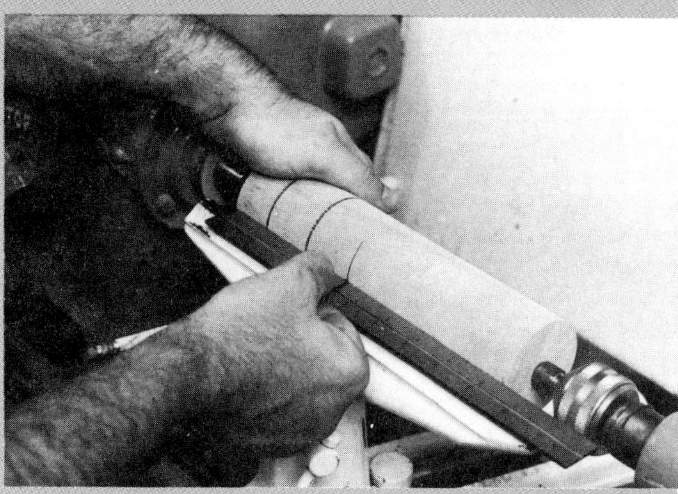

Figure 35-10
Measuring devices used with the lathe. *Use only when stock is not turning.* Outside calipers for measuring spindle diameters, *top*. Inside calipers for measuring internal diameters, *center*. Steel ruler for transferring measurements, *bottom*.

caliper curve in for measuring the overall diameters of spindles, Figure 35-10A. The legs of inside calipers curve out. They are used for measurements on the inside of fruit bowls and other internal diameters, Figure 35-10B. To use either type of caliper, first adjust the legs to the desired distance. Check to see if the diameter on the turning is the same as that set on the caliper.

A ruler is placed on the tool rest to transfer longitudinal measurements. Mark the distances on the surface with a pencil, Figure 35-10C. Do not bring any of these measuring devices in contact with the lathe project while it is turning.

AUXILIARY LATHE EQUIPMENT

Various accessories can be used with the lathe. A steady rest will support long small-diameter turnings from flexing and breaking as they are turned, Figure 35-11. The support area is located in the middle of the turning or next to the area being shaped.

Screw chucks and faceplates are used for turning stock on the face grain. These pieces come in many diameters. They are designed to screw on the headstock spindle, Figure 35-12. A screw chuck has one permanent center screw. The larger faceplate holds the stock on with standard flathead wood screws.

Drill chucks are used with the tailstock. The chuck holds the drill bit while a drill pad supports the turning. The stock is placed on the

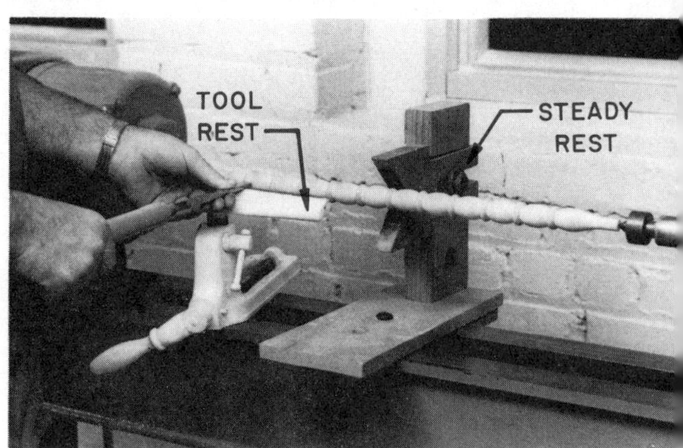

Figure 35-11
A steady rest is used to support long slender turnings. *Guard has been removed so you can see the steady rest.*

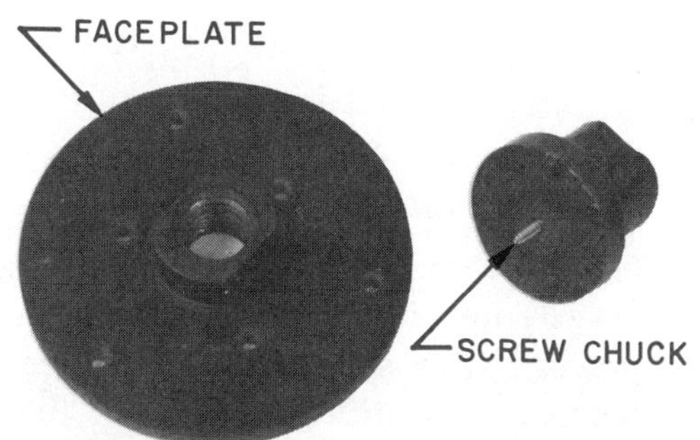

Figure 35-12
Faceplates and screw chucks are used to attach stock to the lathe.

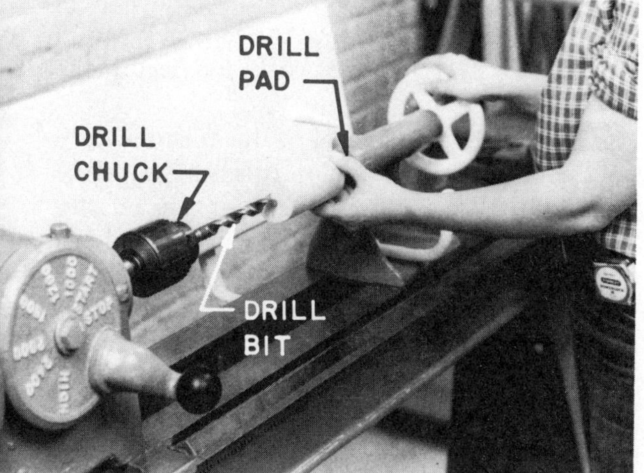

Figure 35-13
A drill chuck and pad allow holes to be bored in the end of stock. *Guard has been removed so you can see the operation.*

drill pad, and the handwheel of the tailstock is slowly advanced to feed the bit into the stock, Figure 35-13.

Sanding drums can be mounted on the lathe for sanding curves, Figure 35-14. Disc sanding can also be done on the lathe with a shop-made disc. It can be mounted on the headstock with a faceplate and a support table fastened to the tool post.

METHODS OF STOCK REMOVAL

Stock can be removed from the turning by either cutting or scraping. Cutting requires more skill. Cutting is done with the gouge, skew and parting tool. The key to using the *cutting method* is to hold the tool at an angle with the handle lower than the tip of the chisel. The stock will be removed in the form of thin shavings, Figure 35-15.

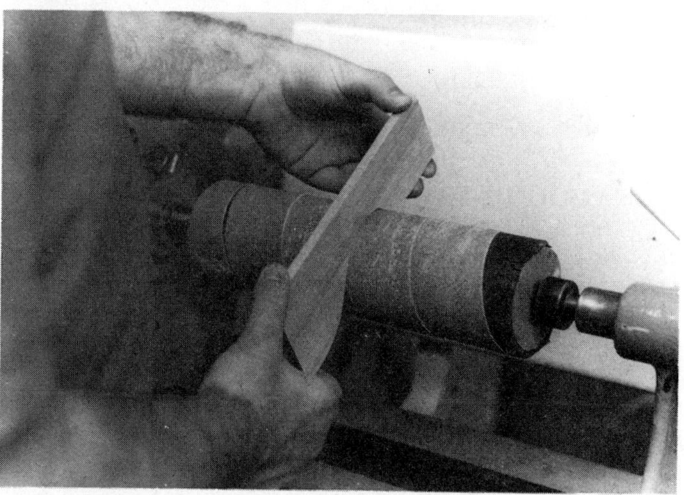

Figure 35-14
A shop-made spindle sands inside curves. *Guard has been removed so you can see the operation.*

The *scraping method* uses any of the cutting chisels plus the round nose and spear point. Chisels are held so that the handle is parallel with the floor. Waste is removed in the form of small particles of fine sawdust, Figure 35-16. This method is more accurate and simpler. A beginning wood turner should use the scraping method.

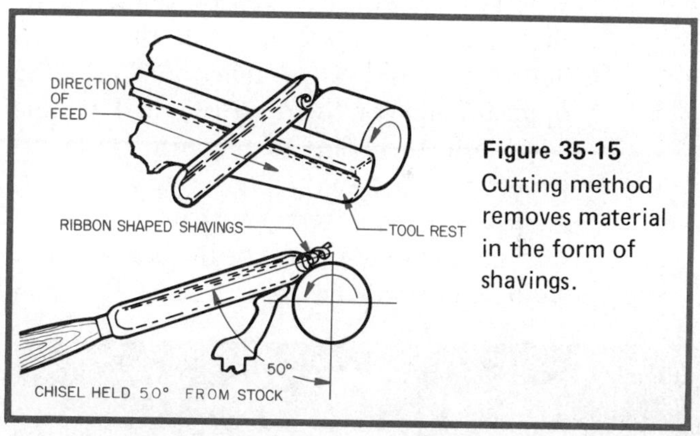

Figure 35-15
Cutting method removes material in the form of shavings.

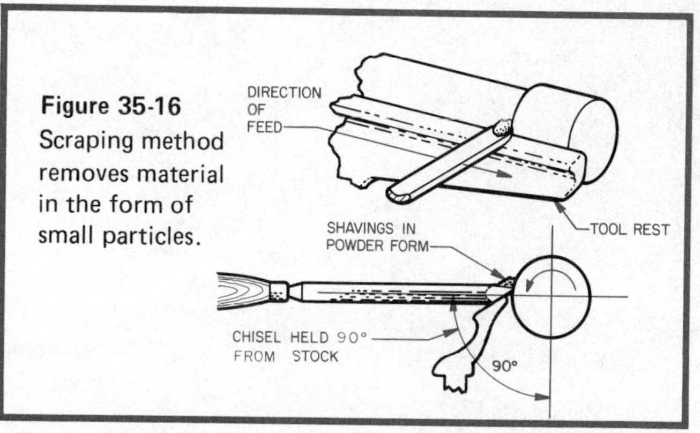

Figure 35-16
Scraping method removes material in the form of small particles.

MOUNTING A TURNING SQUARE

A square must first be mounted on the lathe before any turning can be done. The procedure is as follows:

1. If the ends of the finished piece will be exposed, cut the squared stock 1" (25 mm) longer than the finished length. Make the square at least 1/4" (6 mm) larger than the largest diameter of the turning. When the diameter of the turning exceeds 2-1/2" (64 mm), remove the corners, making an octagon. Use a hand plane, jointer or table saw.
2. Mark the center of both ends by drawing diagonal lines to opposite corners. With a backsaw or band saw, cut shallow grooves on these diagonal lines on the end that will be against the live center, Figure 35-17. Locate the spurs of the live center in the saw kerfs and tap the end of the center into the stock with a mallet, Figure 35-18. Place an *X* beside the groove filed in the live center. This will enable you to recenter the work exactly as it was mounted on the lathe the first time. See Figure 35-18. If the stock is hard, drill an 1/8" (3 mm) hole into the opposite end for the dead center. The hole will allow the point of the dead center to penetrate the stock.
3. Adjust the tool rest so that it is 1/8" (3 mm) above the point of the dead center. Adjustment will be easier now rather than waiting until the stock covers the centers. Move the tool rest out of the way so that it will not interfere with the mounting process. The shaft of the live center is tapered to match the taper on the inside of the hollow spindles. Pushing it in by hand will secure it into position.
4. Slide the live center in the spindle of the headstock. Place the stock between the centers. Make certain the filed nick is in the correct place. Move the tailstock within 1" (25 mm) of the work and secure the tailstock to the bed.
5. Rotate the handwheel of the tailstock until the dead center is firmly gripping in the stock. Release the handwheel one quarter of a turn and lock it into position. If a solid dead center is used, it will be necessary to stop the lathe occasionally and apply oil or beeswax to the point of the dead center. This will reduce friction between the dead center and the stock. Be careful, however, about using too much lubricant. Move the tool rest into position so that a maximum of 1/8" (3 mm) is between the stock and the front edge of the tool rest, Figure 35-19. It must also be 1/8" (3 mm) above the center of the stock. Hand-rotate the stock so that it will not strike the tool rest. Before turning the power on, be certain that all corners of the turning square clear the rest.

Figure 35-17
Cutting diagonals with a backsaw.

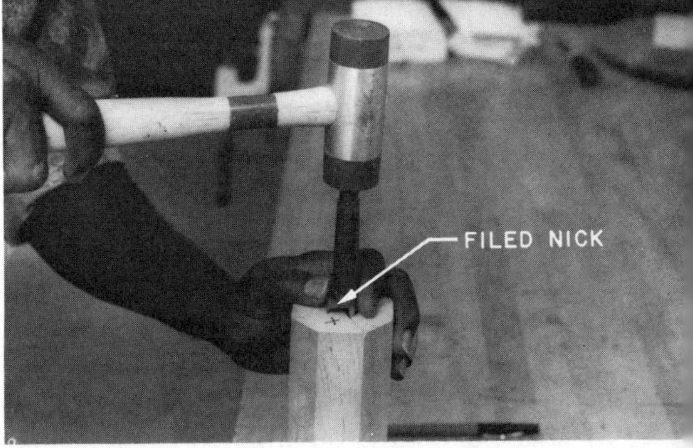

Figure 35-18
A mallet is used to drive the live center into the stock. An *X* is placed on the end to relocate the center later.

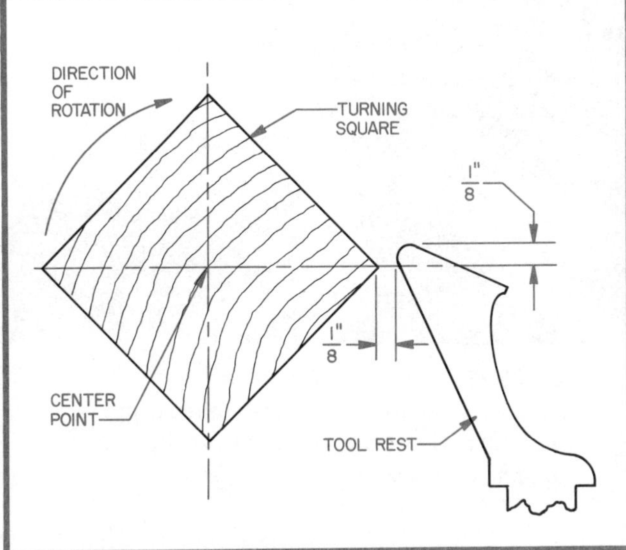

Figure 35-19
Position the tool rest 1/8" (3 mm) above and 1/8" (3 mm) away from the turning square.

TURNING A CYLINDER

Turning can begin once the stock has been properly mounted on the lathe. Generally, no matter what the pattern, the first step is to shape the turning square into a cylinder. When turning a cylinder:

1. Rotate the stock at about 600 rpm. This minimizes chipping and the danger of losing control of the chisels.
2. Place a skew on its edge and nick the corners of the square every 2" (51 mm). This will prevent long slivers from flying off as the square is turned, Figure 35-20.
3. Select the widest gouge that can be controlled for the initial cut. Hold the gouge by grasping the end of the handle with your right hand. The tip of the chisel is controlled with your left. Hold the body of the chisel between your thumb and index finger. The depth of the cut can be controlled by sliding the index finger along the edge of the tool rest, Figure 35-21. Place the chisel firmly on the tool rest.
4. Determine the direction of your cut. When moving the gouge to make a cut to the right, lower the handle below the tool rest and roll it to the right. This will expose only a small portion of the edge of the gouge to the stock and will give superior cutting results. Roll the gouge to the left when moving it toward the left.

Begin the cutting by bringing the gouge into contact with the stock approximately 1" (25 mm) from the headstock end. Move the chisel to the right. Continue to work toward the tailstock and stop the cut 1" (25 mm) from the dead center in the tailstock. Do not try to remove too much stock with one cut. The remaining 1" (25 mm) on each end can be turned by moving the chisel from the center of the spindle. Never begin the cutting on the end, because of the possibility of catching the wood with the chisel. This would throw the chisel from the lathe. When working

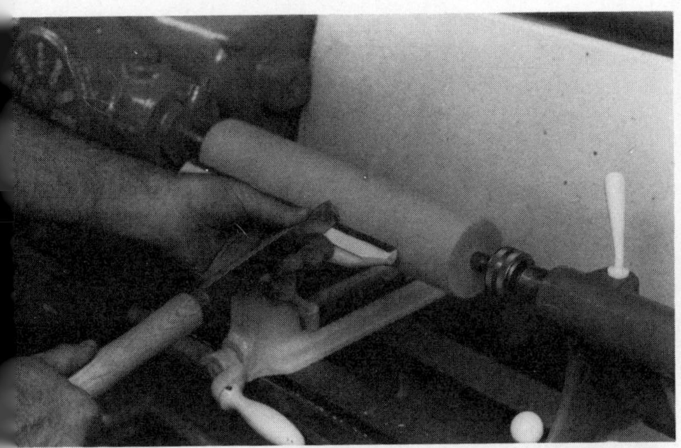

Figure 35-20
Placing a skew on its edge, nick the turning every 2" (51 mm). *Guard has been removed so you can see the operation.*

Figure 35-21
Controlling the gouge by using the scraping method. *Guard has been removed so you can see the operation.*

on the ends, do not touch the live and dead centers with the chisel.

5. Turn the power off frequently and move the tool rest in toward the stock. No more than 3/8" (10 mm) should be between the turning and the tool rest. Inspect the stock and check to see if any flat sides are still present. If the stock is not completely round, turn on the power and continue to round the turning.
6. Set a pair of outside calipers to 1/16" (2 mm) more than the desired diameter. The last 1/16" (2 mm) is left for the purpose of sanding.
7. Use a parting tool to cut the stock to the desired depth every 2" (51 mm). This will act as a gauge for cutting to the correct diameter, Figure 35-22. Turn off the power and let the turning come to a stop before checking the diameter with the calipers.
8. Use a large skew to level the turning down to the grooves made by the parting tool. A skew will give a much smoother cut than a gouge.
9. Increase the speed of the lathe to improve the quality of cut. For stock less than 3" (76 mm) in diameter, a speed of 1200 rpm is recommended. When using the cutting method, hold the skew at a 60° angle and cut in the middle of the cutting edge. Roll the chisel slightly on its edge and start cutting from the headstock end on the top of the cylinder, Figure 35-23. Be careful not to catch the end of the turning or to let the heel of the skew touch the stock.

   For the scraping method, hold the skew flat on the tool rest. Bring the entire cutting edge against the stock. This method is suggested for beginners. With either method, check the diameter frequently, using outside calipers. Use the calipers only when the stock is not turning.
10. Continue cutting the stock until the diameter matches the caliper setting. Remove the last 1/16" (2 mm) with abrasive paper. Remove the tool post and tool rest and turn the lathe on at 2000 rpm. First use a 100-grit abrasive paper and sand all major defects, Figure 35-24. Hold the folded abrasive on the underside of the stock and move it from side to side. Do not wrap the paper around your fingers. After the major marks have been removed, use finer grits through 220.
11. Measure the finished length of the cylinder. Scribe a pencil mark around the stock at the two end points. This can be done by holding a pencil on the tool rest and rotating the stock by hand, Figure 35-25.
12. Use a parting tool to turn down the stock on each pencil mark. Turn each end until a 1/4"- (6 mm-) diameter stock remains, Figure 35-26. If a depth greater than 3/8" (10 mm) is to be cut, make the groove wider by making a second cut to the side of the first cut. This will prevent the chisel from overheating.
13. Remove the stock from the lathe and cut the two ends off with a back saw.

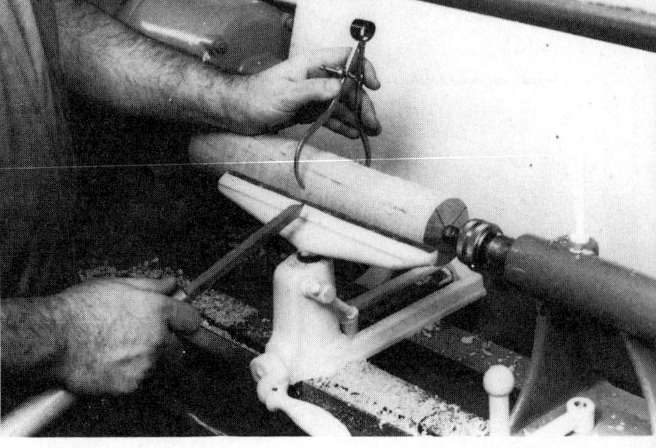

Figure 35-22
Use a parting tool to cut in to the desired depth. Check with a pair of calipers. *Lathe turning must not be rotating when you are using the calipers.*

Figure 35-23
A skew will smooth a rough cylinder. *Guard has been removed so you can see the operation.*

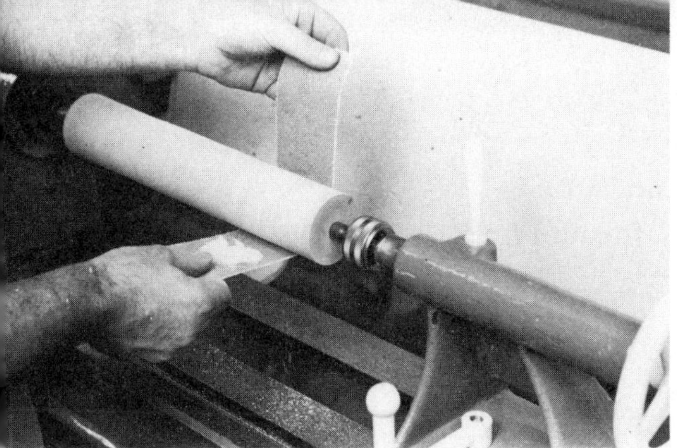

Figure 35-24
The last 1/16" (2 mm) is removed with abrasive paper. *Guard has been removed so you can see the operation.*

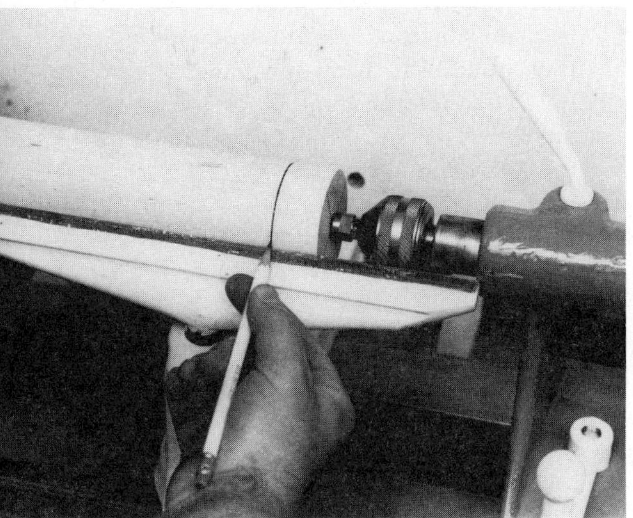

Figure 35-25
Mark the end of the finish turning with a pencil. *With the power off, turn stock by hand.*

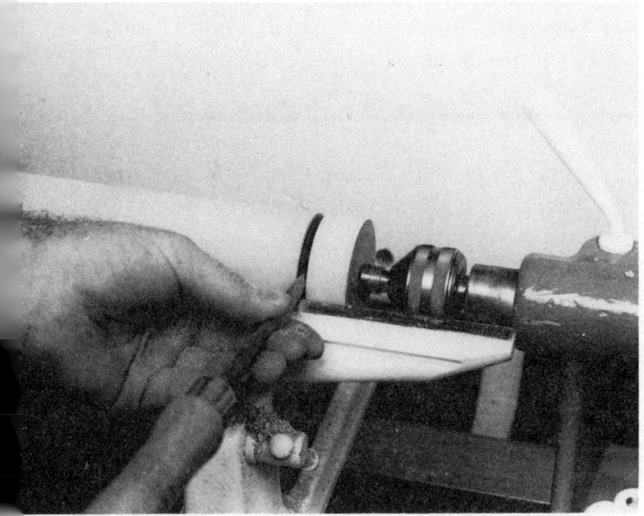

Figure 35-26
A parting tool is used to turn the stock to length. *Guard has been removed so you can see the operation.*

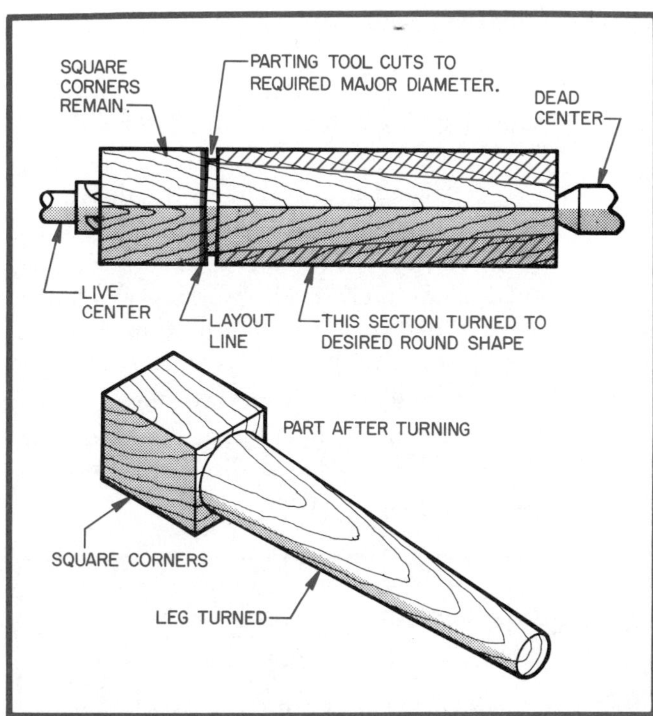

Figure 35-27
Procedure for turning a spindle with a square corner.

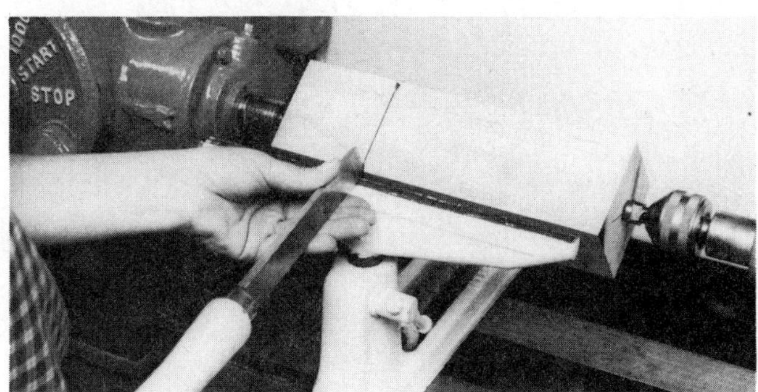

Figure 35-28
Use a skew to nick the corners. *Action has been stopped and guard removed so you can see position of chisel.*

Cutting Square Corners

After a turning square is made, square corners can be cut.

1. Lay out the location of the corners by scribing a pencil mark around the stock, Figure 35-27. Use a square for transferring the lines to all sides.
2. Set the outside calipers to 1/16" (2 mm) more than the finish diameter to allow for sanding.
3. Turn the work at 600 rpm or less. While turning, place a skew on the stock's edge and nick the corners on the pencil mark.

This will cut the wood fibers and keep the shoulder from tearing out later, Figure 35-28.

4. Use a parting tool to cut to the depth set on the calipers. Place the parting tool so that the groove it makes is exactly on the edge of the nicks made by the skew. Make the cut wider if the depth is more than 3/8" (10 mm).
5. Use a round nose to remove the stock up to the cut made by the parting tool. Use the scraping technique. Be careful not to cut the square shoulders.

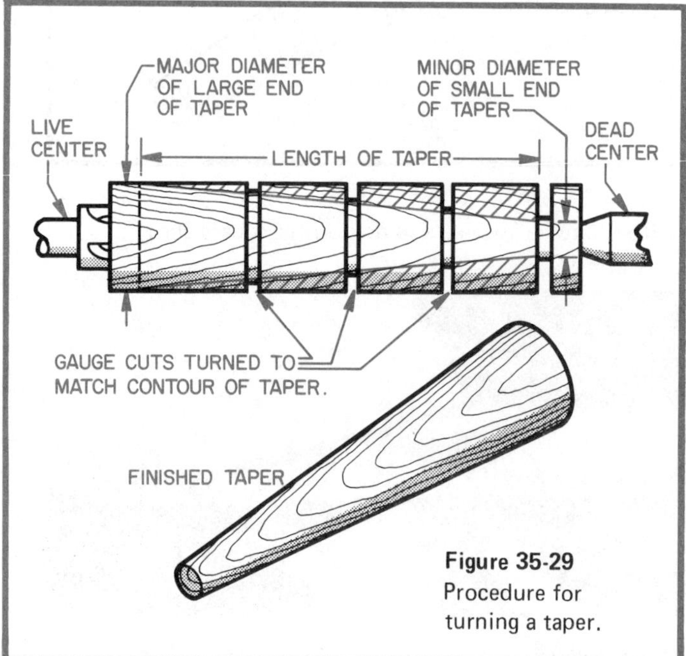

Figure 35-29
Procedure for turning a taper.

Figure 35-30
A gouge is used to rough out a taper. *Guard has been removed so you can see the operation.*

Cutting Tapers

To turn a taper:

1. Turn the stock down to a cylinder. The diameter should be equal to the largest diameter of the taper. Lay out the length of the taper with a ruler and a pencil, Figure 35-29.
2. Use a parting tool to cut down one end of the spindle to the smallest diameter of the taper.
3. Lay out several points approximately 1" (25 mm) apart between the end points of a long taper. These measurements can be determined from the drawing. A gouge can then be used to turn down the cylinder to rough diameter, Figure 35-30.
4. Smooth the cut with a skew. Sand to the finished diameters.

Making Concave, or Cove, Cuts

To make cove cuts:

1. Lay out the two end points and the center line of the cove, Figure 35-31. Using a parting tool, cut down to the smallest diameter in the middle of the cove.
2. Take a round-nose chisel and complete the cut, using a scraping action. Keep the chisel flat on the tool rest and pivot it back and forth, Figure 35-32.

Making Convex, or Bead, Cuts

To make a bead:

1. Turn the stock to a rough cylinder 1/16" (2 mm) larger than the diameter of the

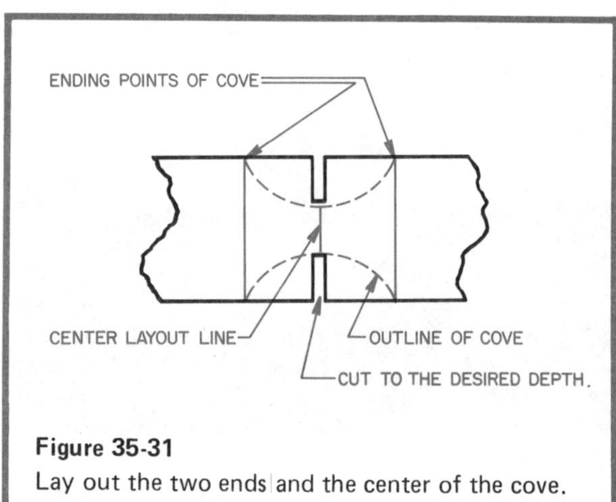

Figure 35-31
Lay out the two ends and the center of the cove.

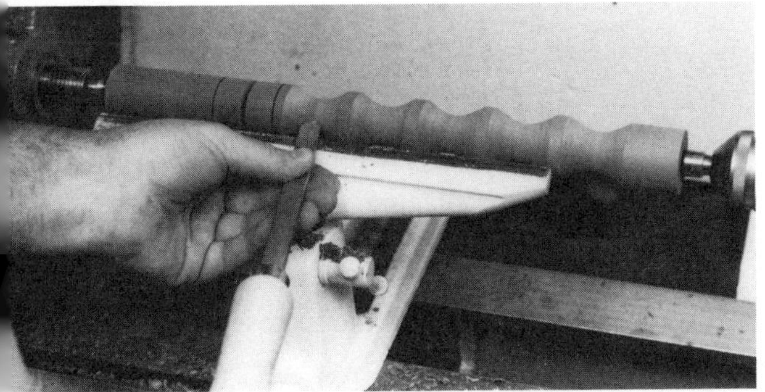

Figure 35-32
Using a round nose to form a cove. Note the cove that has been laid out to the left of the cuts. *Guard has been removed so you can see the operation.*

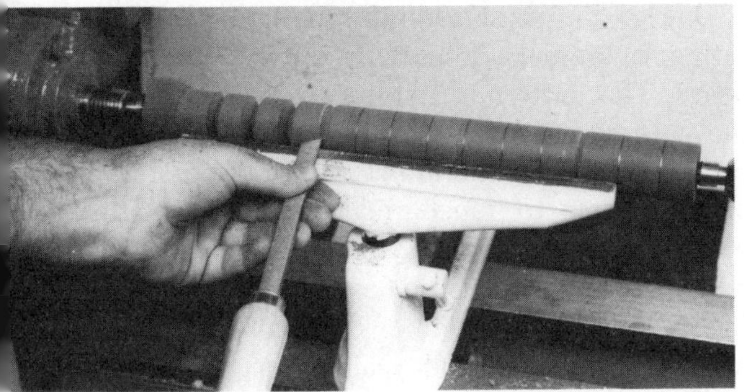

Figure 35-33
A skew is used to cut the shoulders of a bead. *Guard has been removed so you can see the operation.*

center of the bead. Lay out the beginning and ending points of each bead. Use the toe of the skew to make a shallow V cut on each pencil mark. The skew is laid flat on the tool rest and fed straight into the stock, Figure 35-33. Check the depth with a pair of outside calipers.

2. Finish shaping by rounding over the corner with a spear point. Place the spear point flat on the tool rest, Figure 35-34. Small beads can be cut with a specialty chisel called a beading tool. Commercial beading tools are available from 1/8" to 5/8" (3 to 16 mm) in width, Figure 35-35.

Making V Cuts

To cut a V:

1. Rough out the cylinder. Mark the center point and the two ends of the V by scribing pencil lines around the turning.
2. Place the skew flat on the tool rest. Feed the chisel into the rotating stock to the desired depth. A wide V may require pivoting the tool to the left and right, Figure 35-36.

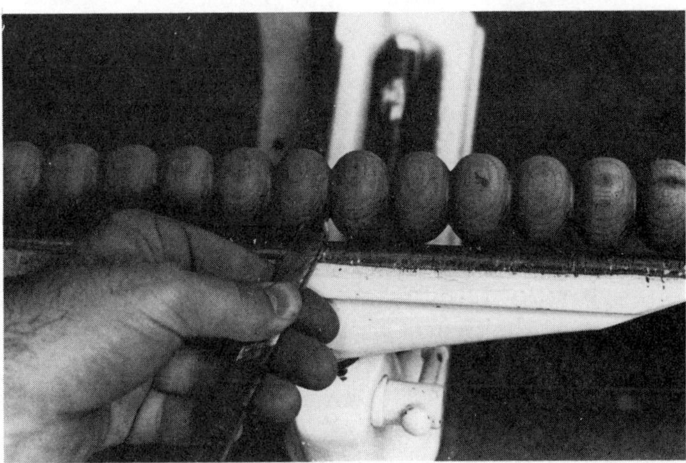

Figure 35-34
The spear point rounds the corners over to form a bead. *Action has been stopped and guard removed so you can see the position of chisel.*

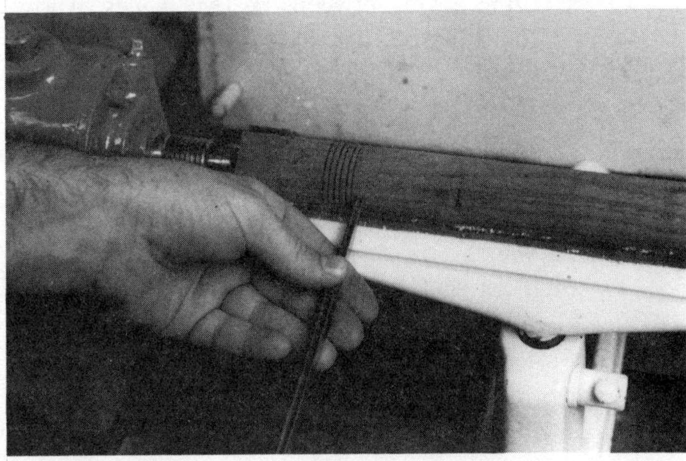

Figure 35-35
A beading chisel forms beads rapidly. *Action has been stopped and guard removed so you can see position of chisel.*

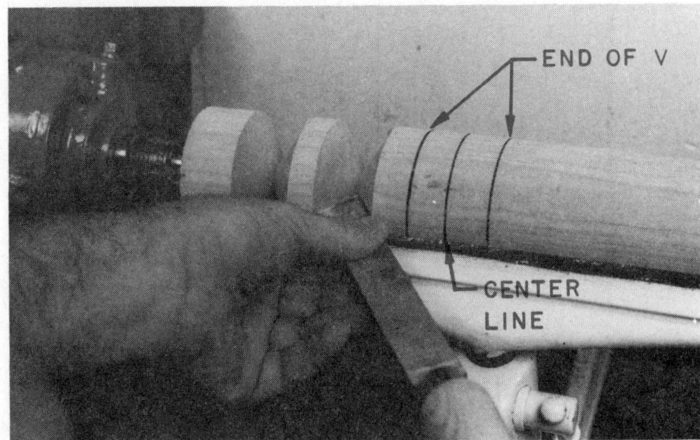

Figure 35-36
Cutting a V with a skew. Note the V marked out to the extreme right. *Action has been stopped and guard removed so you can see position of chisel.*

MAKING A SPLIT TURNING

Split turnings are made when three-quarter-, half- and quarter-columns are required, Figure 35-37. Frequently, half-columns are used on the front of furniture when the back of the turning must be flat. Quarter and three-quarter split turnings are used to decorate corners.

To make a split turning:

1. Make two pieces of stock approximately 3" (76 mm) longer than the finished length and one-half the desired thickness of the turning square.
2. Apply adhesive to both pieces of wood. Before clamping together, place a glossy magazine cover between the two pieces. Allow the adhesive to cure for a minimum of 24 hours.
3. Place a screw at each end of the stock to reinforce the glue joint, Figure 35-38. Be careful not to place the screws too close to the center of the square. You do not want to hit them with a chisel.
4. Turn the glued stock following the normal procedure.
5. Remove the screws from the stock. Split the turning by placing a wide chisel exactly on the glue line and striking the end with a mallet, Figure 35-39.
6. Scrape away the paper and excess glue.

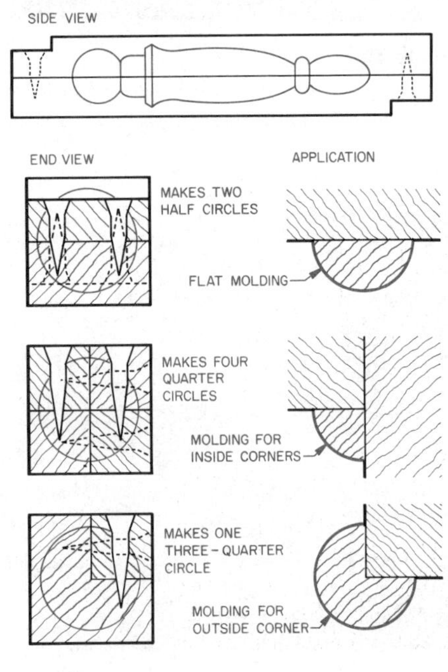

Figure 35-37
Split turnings can be made that are halves, quarters and three-quarters.

DUPLICATING SPINDLES

Turning only one spindle to a pattern is rare. Most pieces of furniture require two or more identical turnings.

One of the most common methods of duplicating is to make a pattern out of thin cardboard. This pattern is first drawn full-size. Shape the pattern by cutting the layout in half along the center line of the drawing. Use the first half of the pattern to transfer major reference points onto the roughed-out cylinder, Figure 35-40. Next, cut the second half of the pattern along the outline of the spindle. This half of the pattern can then be held against the turning to check the progress of the shaping, Figure 35-41. When the spindle is turned to the desired shape, it will match the contour of the pattern.

A *duplicator* is another method of producing identical turnings, Figure 35-42. This lathe attachment is fastened to the lathe bed. A template cut from hardboard is made to the exact profile or outline of the turning. Some duplicators require a spindle to be used as a pattern.

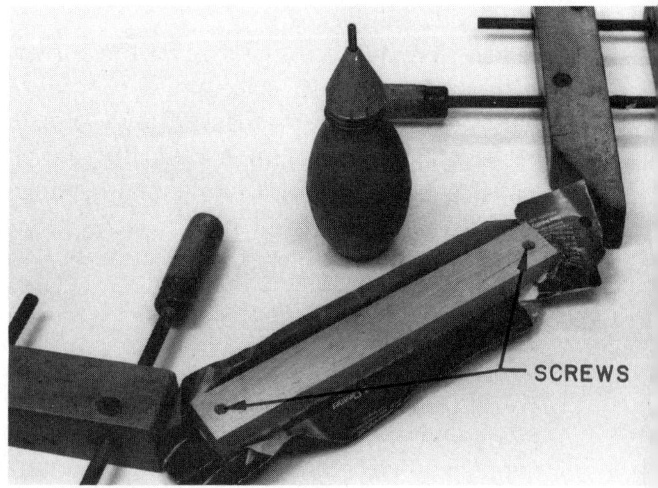

Figure 35-38
After the adhesive has cured, clamps are removed and screws inserted in the waste portion of the split turning.

A turning square is mounted between the lathe centers. As the stylus of the duplicator traces the template or spindle, the cutting tool duplicates its motion and shapes the turning.

FACEPLATE TURNING

Faceplate turning is used when the face as well as the edge of the stock is to be turned. A fruit bowl is an example of this type of product.

The tailstock is seldom used in faceplate turning. This is the major difference between faceplate turning and spindle turning. A faceplate also is used to secure the stock to the headstock.

Most faceplate turning requires thin pieces of stock to be glued together to form a large block. Make certain that the glue joints are of the highest quality. Continue with the following procedure to finish the turning:

1. Cut the glued-up stock to a circle with a band saw. The circle should be at least 1/4" (6 mm) larger in diameter than the finished size.
2. Center the faceplate on the bottom of the turning by first scribing a circle equal to the diameter of the faceplate. Align the faceplate with this circle. Select and install screws with a shank size the same diameter

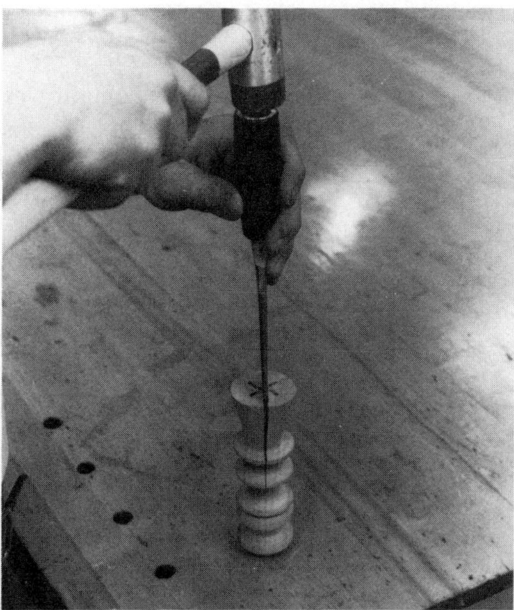

Figure 35-39
A wide chisel is used to split the finished turning.

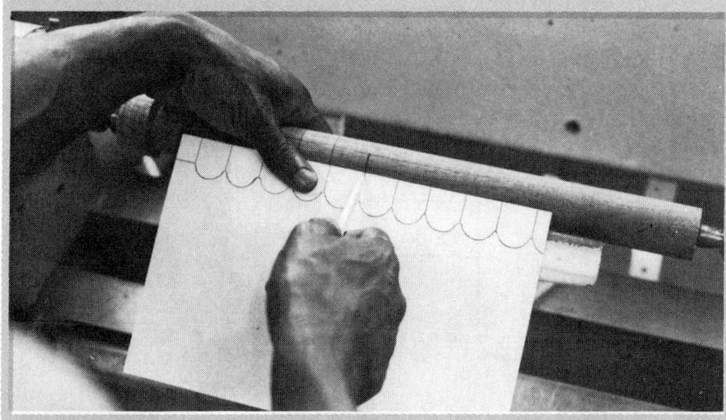

Figure 35-40
A cardboard template is used to transfer key reference points. *Stock is rotated by hand and power is off.*

Figure 35-41
A template is used to check the contour of the turning. *Stock is rotated by hand and power is off.*

Figure 35-42
A duplicator produces identical turnings. *Guard has been removed so you can see the operation.* (Rockwell International)

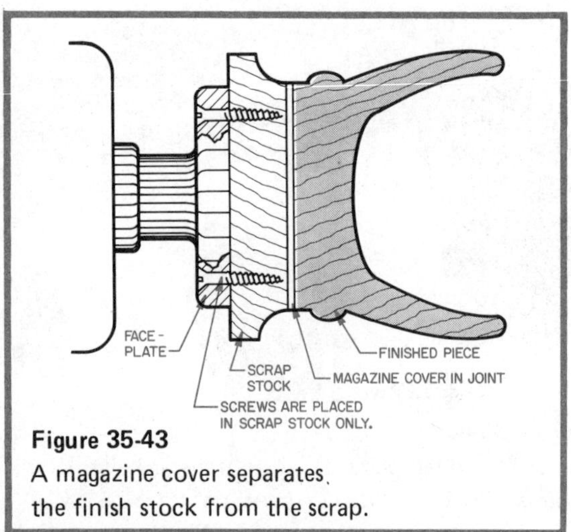

Figure 35-43
A magazine cover separates the finish stock from the scrap.

Figure 35-45
Shape the edge of the turning first. *Guard has been removed so you can see the operation.*

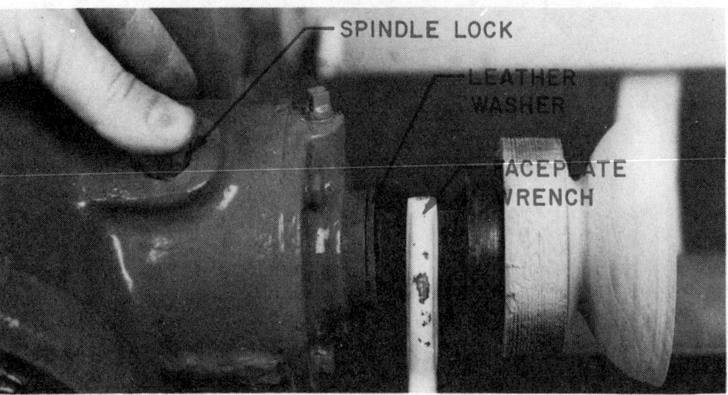

Figure 35-44
The faceplate should be screwed all the way on while the spindle lock is held down.

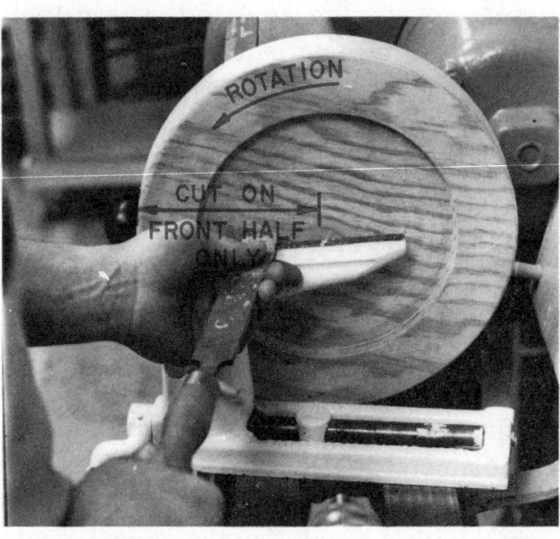

Figure 35-46
Use only the front half of the tool rest to prevent losing control of the chisel. *Action has been stopped and guard removed so you can see position of chisel.*

as the holes in the faceplate. Use several screws to secure the faceplate.

3. Glue a scrap piece of stock to the bottom of the turning block if you do not want screw holes in the bottom surface of the finish turning. Screws from the faceplate can then be placed into this waste material, Figure 35-43. A glossy magazine cover must be placed in the glue joint so that the two pieces can be later separated with a flat wood chisel when the turning is finished. Because this may produce a weak glue line, use the tailstock to support the turning while shaping the edge.
4. Place a leather washer between the spindle and the faceplate. This will allow the faceplate to be removed easily from the lathe if it becomes stuck. Remove the live center and screw the faceplate onto the spindle of the lathe. The faceplate must be screwed all the way on with the faceplate wrench, Figure 35-44. The spindle lock keeps the spindle from turning while the faceplate is tightened.
5. Start turning by using a scraping action along the edge of the stock. Run on a slow speed until the stock is round. Most of the shaping can be done either with a round nose or a gouge chisel, Figure 35-45.
6. Position the tool rest across the face. Turn only on the front half of the tool rest, Figure 35-46. Turning on the far side of the tool rest will cause the chisel to be thrown from the lathe. Keep the tool rest within 1/8″ (3 mm) of stock or as close as is possible.
7. Use a template and a pair of inside calipers to check the depth of cut frequently. The

work should not be turning when you are checking for correct size.

8. Remove the tool rest. Sand the outside and inside of the turning. Sand on the front side so that work is turning down on the abrasive paper. Make certain all defects are sanded before removing the stock from the faceplate.

Chucking

Some products require that the bottom surface be turned also. To do this:

1. Turn the bowl with a piece of scrap glued to the bottom side.
2. Separate the turning from the scrap glued to the bottom of the bowl. Make a recessed block to hold the turning. The hollowed-out area in the recessed block should be no more than 1/16" (2 mm) larger than the outside diameter of the turning. This will allow for a tight fit, Figure 35-47.
3. Press the turned piece into the block. If the recessed block was made a little too large, place paper shims around the perimeter of the hollowed-out area of the recessed block to provide a tight fit. Check the fit again.
4. Turn the lathe on at a slow speed so that the turning will not come loose, Figure 35-48. Shape the bottom surface, using standard turning techniques.

Because the turning is held in place by the outside edge, it is called outside chucking. Inside chucking holds the turning from the inside surface.

Outboard Turning

Faceplate turning generally is done on the bed side of the headstock or the inboard side of the lathe. There are times, however, when larger diameters are to be turned.

Most lathes also can turn large-diameter faceplate-type projects on the opposite side of the headstock, or *outboard* side. If stock is mounted on this side of the lathe, a floor stand is used to hold the tool rest. It is placed on the floor and moved into position much as when a tool post is used, Figure 35-49.

Use the scraping techniques and revolve the turning at the slowest possible speed.

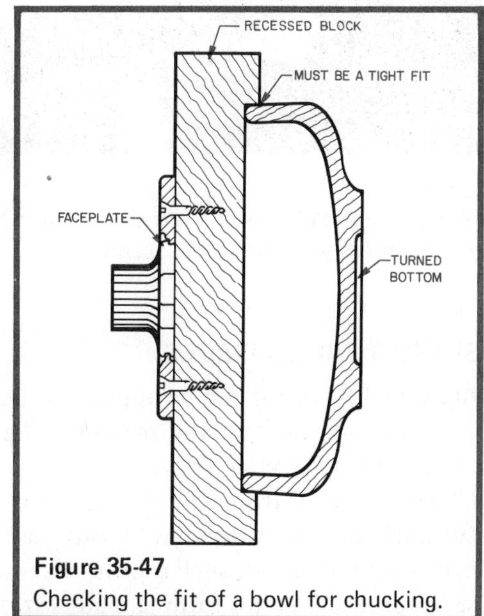

Figure 35-47
Checking the fit of a bowl for chucking.

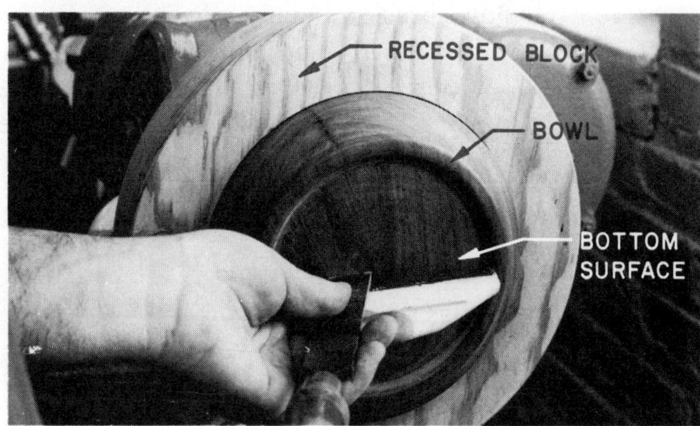

Figure 35-48
Inside chucking allows the bottom surface to be turned. *Action has been stopped and guard removed so you can see the position of chisel.*

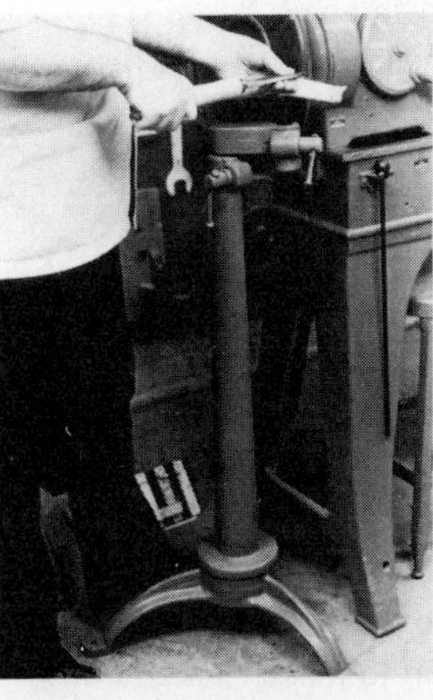

Figure 35-49
Outboard turning is performed with the aid of a floor stand. *Action has been stopped and guard removed so you can see the position of chisel.*

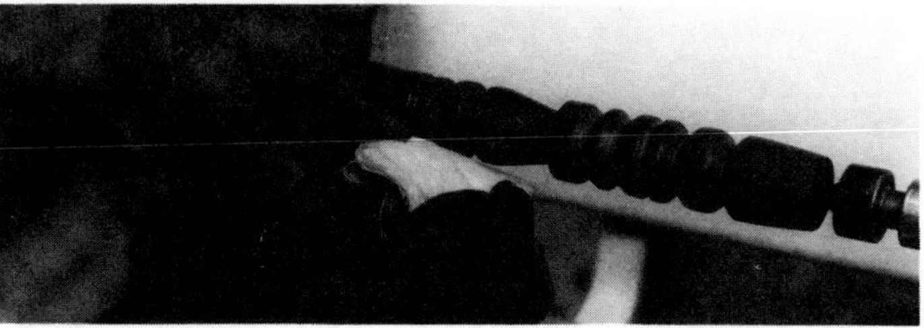

Figure 35-50
Applying French Polish with a soft cloth. *Guard has been removed so you can see the operation.*

FINISHING TURNED PIECES

A high quality finish can be applied while the piece is still mounted on the machine. This is commonly called a *French Polish.*

1. Clean all dust from the lathe, floor and turning. Lay a cotton cloth out flat and brush a light coat of shellac onto the middle section. Fold it to form a pad with the shellac area facing out. Turn the lathe on to a slow speed and apply a light coat, Figure 35-50. After the shellac is worked in, place a few drops of boiled linseed oil on the cloth and continue rubbing it into the stock.
2. Distribute the mixture evenly over the entire area of the turning by moving the soaked cloth from side to side. If any of the finish should accumulate in one area, use denatured alcohol to soften the buildup.
3. Allow the finish to dry over night and apply a second coat the next day. Repeat the process four or five times or until the desired luster is obtained.

If a turning is to be used around food, use a finish approved by the Food and Drug Administration. Apply the finish with a soft cloth until the surface is totally saturated. Buff with a clean cloth to bring out a soft luster.

Paste wax is another finish that is satisfactory for turning. This simple method requires that wax be rubbed on the surface. Allow it to dry for 10 to 15 minutes. Take a soft cloth and buff the surface while the turning is rotating at a slow speed.

Other finishes that give various effects can be applied to lathe turnings. Royal 1-2-3® finish is a popular product that gives a high luster surface. It can be wiped on with a soft cloth.

REVIEW QUESTIONS

1. Name the different types of centers used on the lathe. Where are they mounted?
2. Sketch the major lathe chisels and label each.
3. Describe the two methods of removing stock on the lathe.
4. Where should the tool rest be positioned?
5. Which chisel is used to rough out a cylinder?
6. Why is a cylinder turned down to 1/16″ (2 mm) more than the finished diameter?
7. Which chisel is used to nick the corners when turning a piece with square corners?
8. Sketch the way a cove cut should be laid out.
9. Name two ways of shaping beads.
10. What are split turnings?
11. How can a pattern be used to make duplicate spindles?
12. Center the faceplate on the bottom of the turning by first scribing a circle ____ to the diameter of the faceplate.
13. What surface on a fruit bowl is turned by chucking?
14. Why is the outboard side of the lathe used?
15. What two liquids are used to make French Polish?

SUGGESTED ACTIVITIES

1. Inspect your lathe and name the major parts. With the help of your teacher make the basic adjustments.

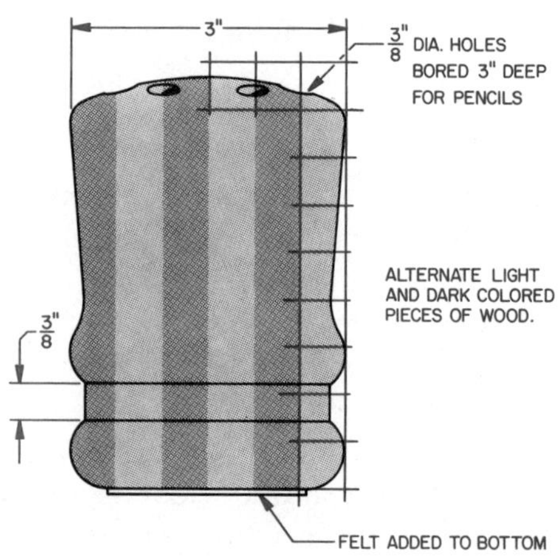

2. Design a pencil holder and turn it on the lathe.
3. Design a fruit or nut bowl and turn it with a scrap piece glued to the bottom. Make a recessed block and turn the bottom surface, using outside chucking.

UNIT

36

Mortisers and Tenoners

Objectives

After studying this unit you should be able to:

1 Identify the major parts and understand the basic adjustments of the mortiser and tenoner.

2 Set up the mortiser and operate it correctly.

3 Identify the major cutting stations on a tenoner.

Technical Terms

Chisel mortiser	Single-end tenoner
Chain mortiser	Double-end tenoner
Reciprocating chisel mortiser	Tenoning heads
Mortising chisel and bit	Cope head

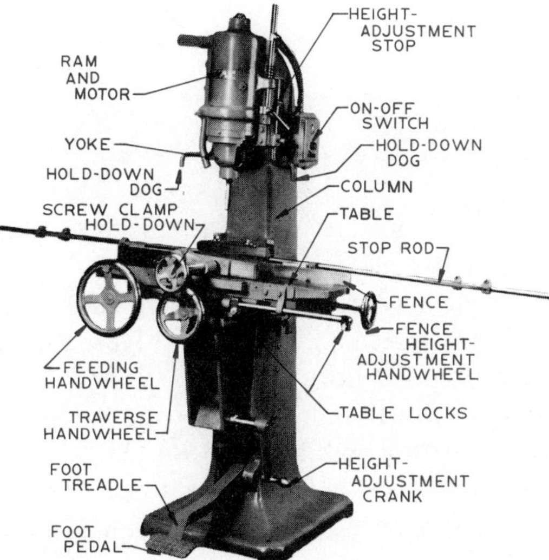

Figure 36-1
Major machine parts of a hollow chisel mortiser. (Oliver Machinery Company)

CHISEL MORTISER SAFETY RULES

1 Disconnect the power before changing chisels.

2 Keep hands out from under the chisel when operating the machine.

3 Securely clamp stock to the table.

4 Keep feet clear from under the foot pedal.

TENONER SAFETY RULES

1 Do not touch the cutters unless the power has been disconnected.

2 Keep hands out of the 4" (102 mm) safety margin. Refer to figure 36-4.

3 Do not back up the stock through the cutters.

4 Securely clamp stock to the moving table.

5 Use boards a minimum of 10" (254 mm) in length.

One of the oldest and most common methods of joining a horizontal board to a vertical member is with a mortise and tenon joint. This is a superior production method and is a sign of quality craftsmanship. Mortise and tenon joints are found on furniture, cabinets and millwork.

A mortiser, Figure 36-1, punches square holes, which form the mortise portion of the joint. First a bit bores a round hole as it enters the stock. A square chisel surrounding the bit then shaves the corners to form 90° angles. This is completed in one stroke of the machine. Many schools use a drill press with a mortising attachment in place of a mortiser. This method does a very adequate job.

Figure 36-2
A single-end tenoner shapes one end of the board at a time. (Oliver Machinery Company)

The tenoner, Figure 36-2, is used to make high-quality tenons. Because the tenons can be varied easily in size, they are made after the mortises are punched. The tenon is basically a rectangular peg that fits into the rectangular mortise. Although the table saw can be used to shape tenons, the tenoner cuts at a much faster rate. The tenoner will be discussed toward the end of this unit.

MORTISERS

There are three types of mortisers. A *chisel mortiser* uses a square chisel to produce the mortise. It is the most common of all the mortisers. A *chain mortiser* has a cutting tool that appears similar to a small chain saw, Figure 36-3. It makes a rounded bottom mortise. The *reciprocating chisel mortiser* has a flat, solid bar with teeth on the cutting end, Figure 36-4. As the bar vibrates back and forth, a mortise is cut, Figure 36-5. The reciprocating chisel is becoming more popular.

Chisel Mortiser Terminology

There are many parts to a chisel mortiser,

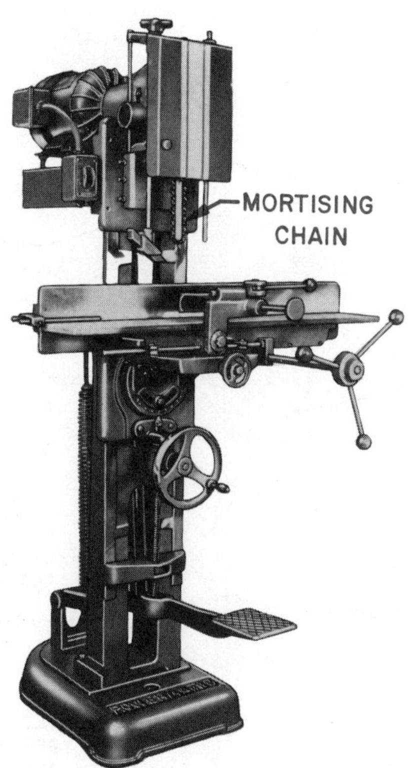

Figure 36-3
A chain mortiser with a chain-saw-type cutting tool. (Powermatic Houdaille, Inc.)

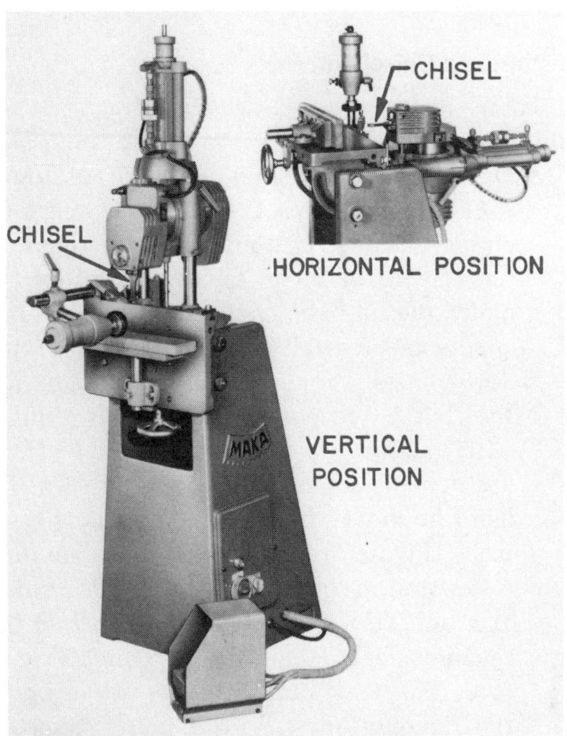

Figure 36-4
A reciprocating chisel mortiser in the vertical and horizontal position. (Danckaert Woodworking Machinery Company)

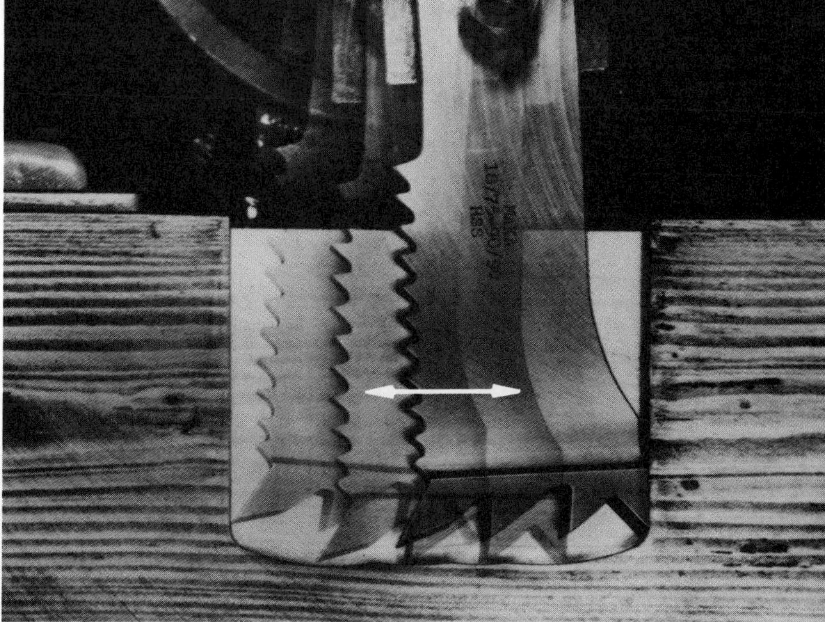

Figure 36-5
The reciprocating chisel moves back and forth very rapidly. (Danckaert Woodworking Machinery Company)

Figure 36-6
Tilting the table for punching a mortise on an angle. (Oliver Machinery Company)

Figure 36-1. Stock to be mortised is clamped on the mortiser table with the screw clamp hold-down. This table can move in six directions. The in and out movements of the table are for centering the chisel across the thickness of the board. The traverse handwheel controls these movements. The table also is moved from left to right with the feeding handwheel. This is how the length of the mortise is cut. To vary the depth of the cut, the table can be raised and lowered with the height adjustment crank. Some tables can be tilted up to a 45° angle for angular cuts, Figure 36-6.

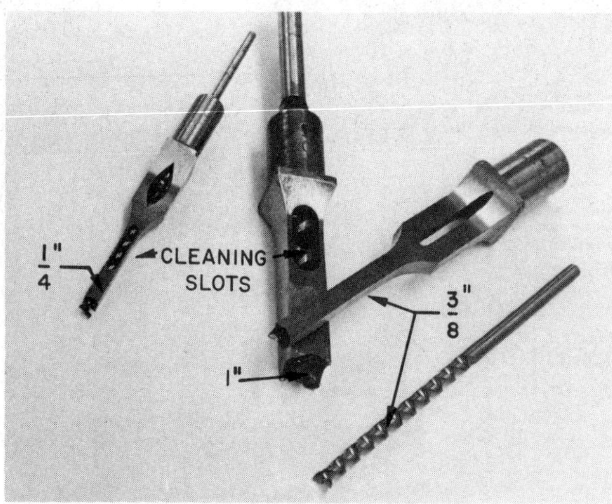

Figure 36-7
Chisels and bits are available in several sizes.

The *mortising chisel and bit* are held in a ram that also contains the drive motor. These components move up and down as a unit with either a foot treadle or an automatic power drive unit. The foot treadle is the most common on small mortisers and requires the operator to step down on the foot pad to bring the chisel into the stock.

Mortising Chisels

A square, hollow chisel and an auger-type bit are the cutting tools used with a hollow chisel mortiser. Sizes range from 1/4″ to 2 1/2″ square (6 to 64 mm), Figure 36-10. The most common chisel is 3/8″ (10 mm) in width. It is used for making mortises in 3/4″ (19 mm) thick material. Various lengths are also available.

The body of the chisel is hollow to allow a mortising bit to revolve inside. A mortising bit is shaped somewhat like an auger drill bit but does not contain a lead screw on the tip. The bit extends below the end of the chisel and has a flared end of the same diameter as the outside of the chisel. Thus the bit removes most of the wood first. The square corners of the chisel then trim the hole into a square shape.

The cutting edge of the chisel is sharpened on the inside. It shears off the wood fibers in the edges of the round hole bored by the bit. A slot is cut into the side of the body of the chisel to remove wood chips from the rotating bit, Figure 36-7. Either a single or a double cleaning slot may be found in the chisel.

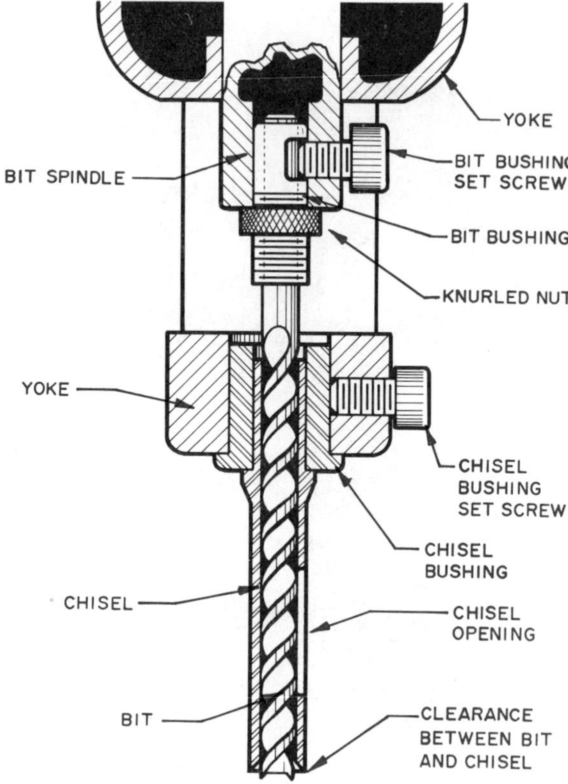

Figure 36-8
Major parts for the head of a chisel mortiser.

Installing a Chisel and Bit

To install a mortiser chisel and bit:

1. Turn off the power at the breaker box.
2. Determine the desired width of the mortise. Choose a chisel, bit, bit bushing and chisel bushing of the same size. Place a scrap piece of wood on the table directly under the mortising head. This will cushion an unexpected fall if the chisel or bit slips during installation.
3. Insert the bit bushing in the bit spindle with the open side toward the set screw. Tighten the set screw a couple of turns by hand to hold the bushing temporarily in place, Figure 36-8. The chisel bushing then is inserted in the yoke along with the chisel and bit. Turn the slot of the chisel so the opening faces opposite the direction of feed. This is so that the chips will not hide the layout lines as the chisel removes material.

Some mortisers and drill presses with mortising attachments have a drill chuck in place of a bit bushing, Figure 36-6. Use a chuck key in all three holes of the chuck to tighten the bit.

4. Place a dime between the shoulder of the chisel and the bottom of the chisel bushing, Figure 36-9. This will later establish the clearance between the end of the bit and the tip of the chisel. Bits larger than 3/4" (19 mm) in width require more clearance. The flared end of the bit must not rub against the sharpened end of the chisel. If too small a clearance is provided, the bit will rub, dull and burn the chisel.
5. Push the bit and chisel as far up into the yoke as it will go. Tighten the bit bushing set screw in the side of the spindle securing the bit and the bit bushing.
6. Remove the dime and push the shoulder of the mortising chisel up against the bushing. Because the bit has been previously locked into position, the desired amount of clearance will be given between the bit and chisel. Always turn the bit by hand before the power is turned on to check for adequate clearance.

Figure 36-9
A dime is used as a spacer to establish the final clearance between the tip of the chisel and the end of the bit. ***Disconnect the power before performing this operation.***

7. Place a try square against the fence of the mortiser and the side of the chisel. Move the chisel until it is square with the fence, Figure 36-10. Finish tightening the chisel bushing set screw with a wrench.

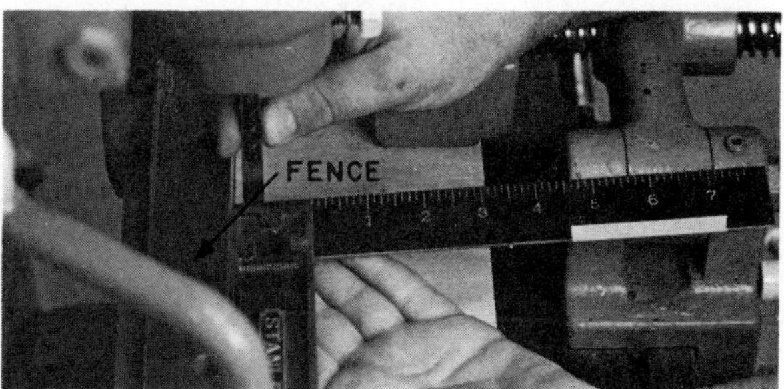

Figure 36-10
Squaring the chisel with the fence. ***Disconnect the power before performing this operation.***

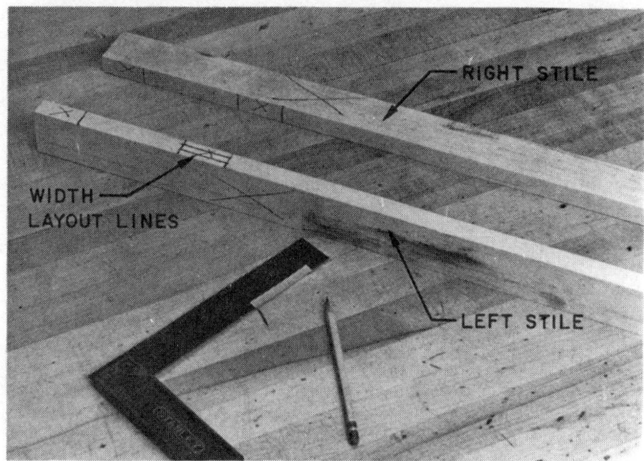

Figure 36-11
Properly marked right and left stiles.

Adjusting the Chisel Mortiser

To adjust the mortiser:

1. Square all stock to finished dimensions. It is very important that every piece be of the same thickness.
2. Lay out the width and length of the mortise on a sample piece, Figure 36-11. The mortises are usually centered on the edge of the board.
3. Mark the outside face of each piece to receive a mortise with an *X*. This surface is placed away from the fence, or facing the operator. When you follow this procedure, the mortise will be the same distance from the face on all pieces.
4. Mark the depth of the mortise on the end of the stock. The depth should be 1/8" (3 mm) deeper than the length of the tenon. This will provide a space for the excess glue and also will allow for the roughness left at the bottom of the mortise.

Figure 36-12
Moving the height adjustment crank with the foot treadle all the way down. *Disconnect the power before performing this operation.*

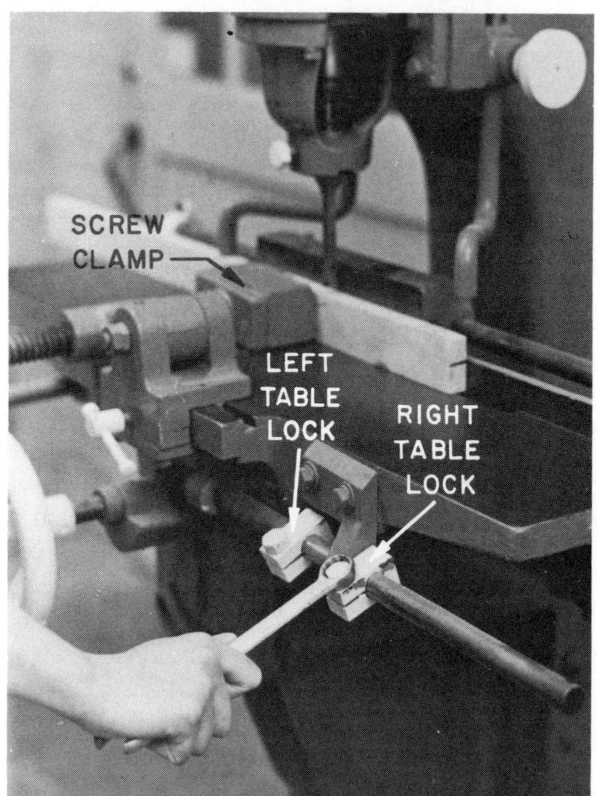

Figure 36-13
Tightening down the table lock. *Disconnect the power before performing this operation.*

5. Step on the foot pedal and lower the chisel to its lowest point. Place the stock on the table. Adjust the table height so the bottom of the chisel is aligned with the depth layout mark, Figure 36-12. If a mortise is to be cut all the way through the stock, place a scrap piece under the stock before adjusting for depth of cut. This will protect the chisel points and the table as the chisel breaks through the stock.
6. Position the marked mortise directly in front of the screw clamp hold-down and tighten the screw clamp. Secure the table lock for the right side of the table, Figure 36-13. The table locks are stops that determine how far to the right and left the table can be moved. Move the handwheel so the table moves to the left side of the mortise. Tighten the remaining table lock. The two table locks will give the starting and stopping points of each identical mortise.
7. Move the stock over until the width layout lines are directly below the chisel. Depress the foot pedal again until the chisel is approximately 1/8" (3 mm) above the stock. Match the chisel with the mortise location marks by moving the table in or out with the traverse adjustment wheel.
8. Position the stop rods before the screw clamp is loosened to locate the next pieces to be mortised. The stock is butted against the stop rods when it is first placed on the table. Finish the setup procedure by placing the hold-down dogs on top of the stock. The hold-down dogs hold the stock against the table when the chisel is drawn out of the board.
9. Punch all mortises in the same location on the board before changing any settings. Often pieces with mortises are cut in pairs. The stop rods must be moved in order to change from right to left sides of a facing or frame.

Punching a Mortise

To punch a mortise:

1. Make the first cut at the extreme right mortise marks. Move the table to the far left and punch the other side of the mortise, Figure 36-14.

2. Move the feeding handwheel to skip a space equal to less than the width of the chisel and work back across the mortise, Figure 36-15. If the mortise is punched without leaving any space, the chisel will be bent to the side of the previous cut. This will cause the chisel to bend or break.
3. Center the bit over each remaining section to be cut and remove the stock. All identical mortises should be punched with the existing setup.

Figure 36-14
Start punching the mortise by lowering the chisel first on the right and then on the left.

MORTISING ON A DRILL PRESS

Many small shops and school laboratories use a mortising attachment on a drill press, Figure 36-16. More setup time is required, but high-quality mortises can be produced.

Select a chuck speed of 900 to 1000 rpm to rotate the bit. Mount the fence to the table and the yoke on the head of the drill press. Follow the instruction manual with the mortising attachment as to how to finish the setup. It will be very similar to the instructions already given on the mortiser. Most drill presses do not have stop rods or table locks. This means that each mortise must be marked out individually. The chisel also is lowered with a hand-feed lever in place of a foot treadle.

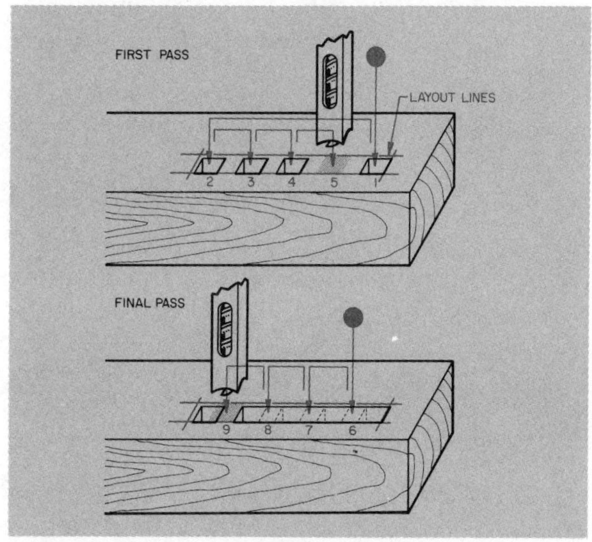

Figure 36-15
To prevent bending the chisel, make the first pass leaving a small amount of stock between each punch. The remaining material is removed with the final pass.

TENONER

A tenon can be cut with a table saw or radial arm saw. This method is commonly used in school laboratories and is described in Units 28 and 31. Although very accurate when set up correctly, a tenon cut with a saw requires a great deal of time.

Industry frequently cuts tenons on a machine called a tenoner. This piece of woodworking equipment produces tenons very rapidly and should be used for producing many identical pieces.

Two major types of tenoners are used to produce furniture and cabinet components. A *single-end tenoner* is used in small cabinet shops. See Figure 36-2. This machine shapes only one end at a time.

A *double-end tenoner* shapes both ends with

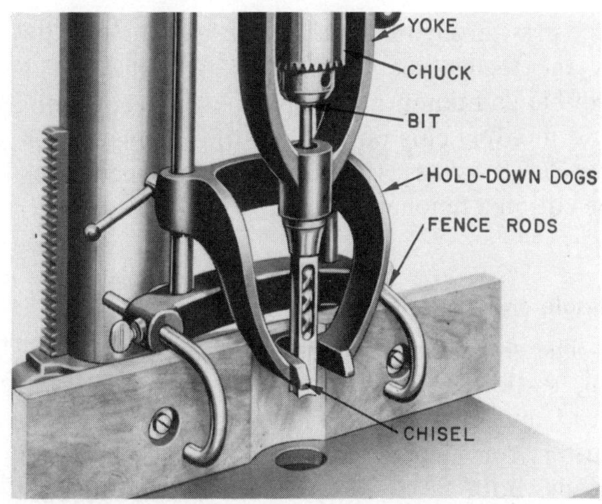

Figure 36-16
Mortising attachment installed on a drill press. (Rockwell International)

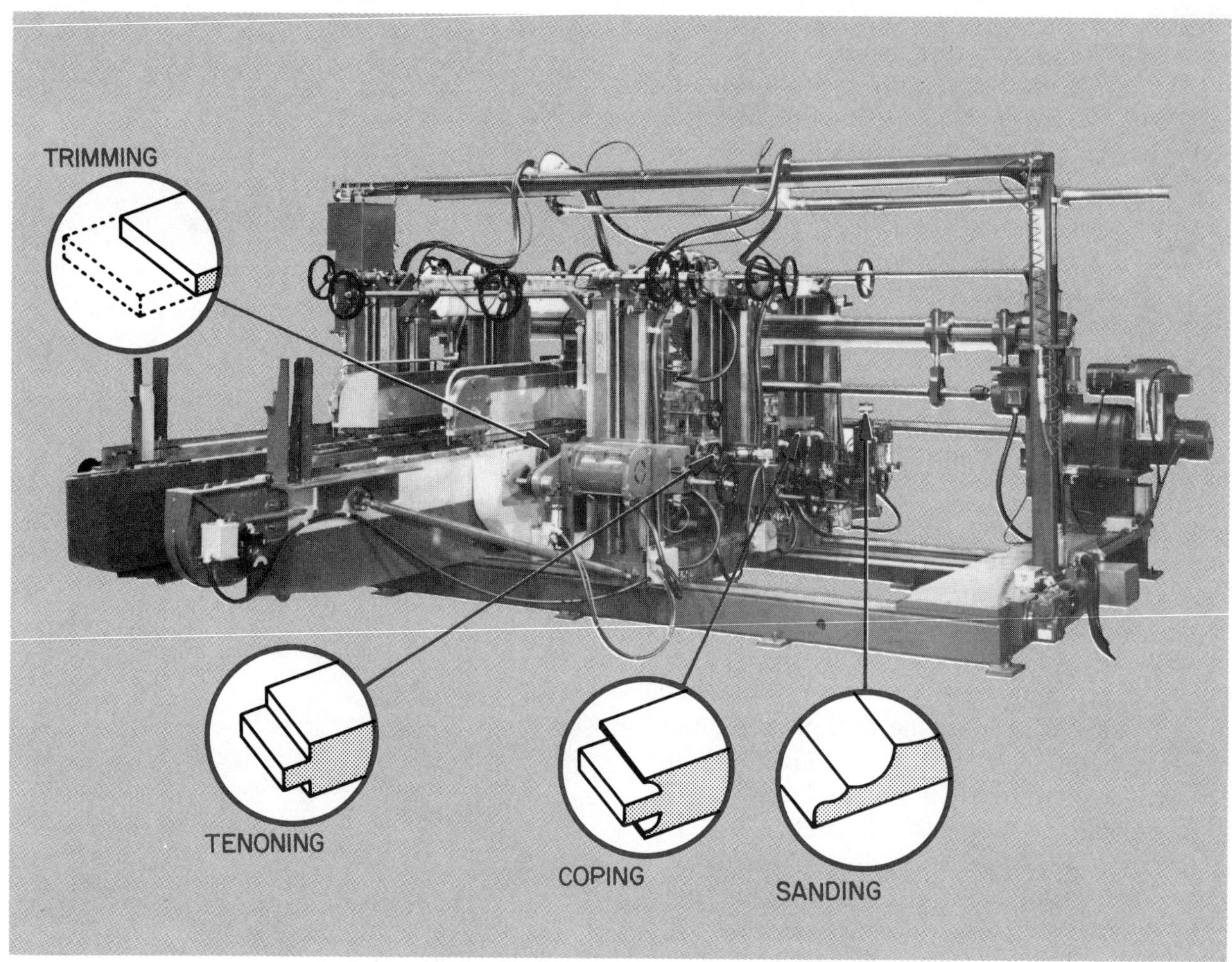

Figure 36-17
A double-end tenoner shapes both ends at once.
(Jenkins Kohler—General Corporation & Co.)

one pass through the machine, Figure 36-17. This is the fastest method of making tenons. The double-end tenoner also can be used to cut dados and molding cuts on the face of each piece. Figure 36-18 shows several different shapes that can be cut on a tenoner.

Single-end Tenoner Terminology

The single-end tenoner has three major shaping stations. These are *tenoning heads, cope head* and cut-off saw, Figure 36-19. The first cutters for shaping a tenon are called tenoning heads. Both heads are used for cutting tenons. The heads produce the cheek and shoulder cuts, Figure 36-20. On most tenoners these cutters can be raised and lowered as well as moved in or out. These adjustments allow for varying the thickness and height of the cut. The horizontal adjustment also is used to make offset shoulders on tenons.

If the tenon requires a molded shoulder, coped heads are used. Cope spindles are mounted in a vertical direction to allow the heads to be raised and lowered. On a plain tenon with square shoulders, the cope heads are not used and are moved out of the way.

The last cutting unit on a tenoner is the cut-off saw. Generally, stock to be run on a tenoner is cut only to rough length. To complete the shaping process, the saw cuts the pieces to their finished length, Figure 36-21. If the stock is cut to finished length before the tenon is shaped, the cut-off saw is not used.

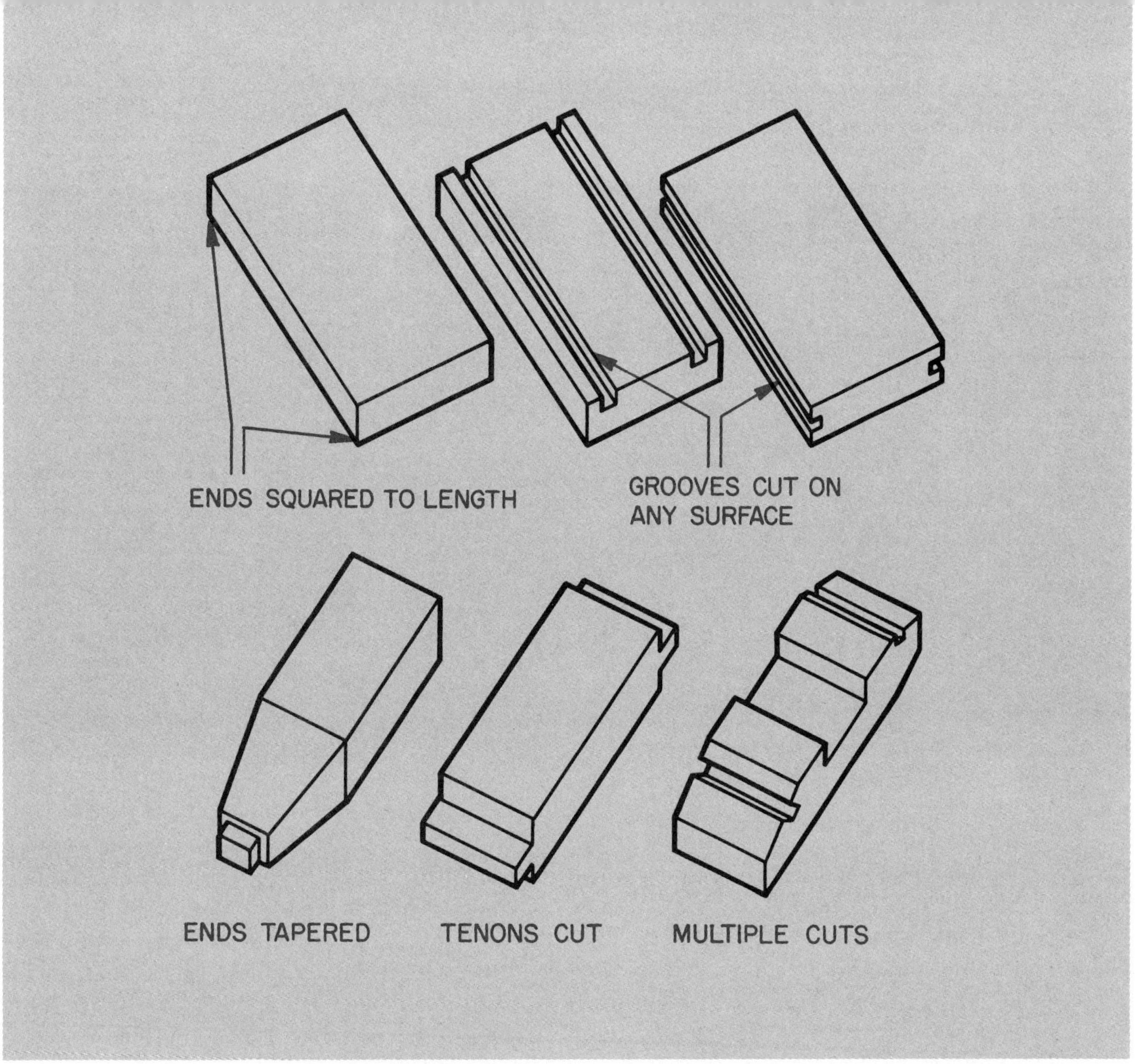

Figure 36-18
Different types of cuts made with a tenoner.

Figure 36-19
The three stations of a single-end tenoner include tenoning heads, cope head, cut-off saw.

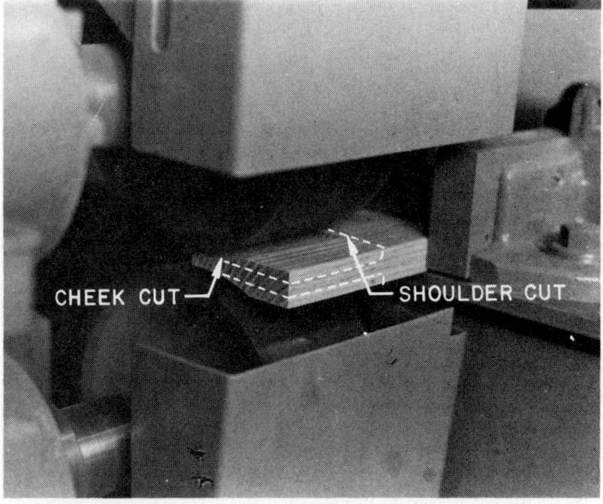

Figure 36-20
The tenoning heads make a plain tenon.

Figure 36-21
Cutting the tenon to finished length.

Cutting a Tenon on a Single-end Tenoner

To cut a tenon, the stock is first cut to finished width and thickness. It is then clamped to the heavy, moving table. The operator pushes the table forward through the three cutting stations. Once the stock has cleared the saw, it is unclamped, moved out of the way, and the table is pulled back to the beginning position. The opposite end is then shaped. After the first piece is cut the distance between the two shoulders must be checked. The measurement must be accurate for the frame to be the correct size when assembled.

REVIEW QUESTIONS

1 What two parts make up the cutting tool for the chisel mortiser?
2 Name the three types of mortisers.
3 List the different directions the mortiser table can be moved.
4 What is the most common width for a mortise on 3/4'' (19 mm) stock?
5 How is the clearance established between the chisel and bit?
6 Why are mortises punched 1/8'' (3 mm) deeper than the length of the tenon?
7 Which stop must be changed when making right and left sides?
8 Name the two types of tenoners.
9 List the three cutting stations on a single-end tenoner.

SUGGESTED ACTIVITIES

1 Inspect your mortiser or mortising attachment and list all the major parts.
2 Punch a mortise that is 3/8'' (10 mm) wide and 1-1/2'' (38 mm) long. If a tenoner is available, cut a tenon to fit. If you do not have one, cut the tenon on the table saw. Check it for the correct fit.

UNIT

37

Drill Presses

Objectives

After studying this unit you should be able to:

1 Identify major parts and understand the basic adjustments of a drill press.

2 Identify the primary drill bits and boring tools.

3 Bore through and stopped holes.

4 Make specialty holes such as angular, multiple and counterboring.

Technical Terms

Horizontal boring machine
Multi-spindle boring machine
Drill chuck
Quill
Through hole
Drill pad
Drill press vise
Stopped hole
Pocket hole
V block

DRILL PRESS SAFETY RULES

1 Keep hands and fingers out of the 4" (102 mm) safety margin surrounding the boring tool.

2 Clamp small work and all metal pieces to the drill press table or in a drill press vise.

3 Remove the chuck key before turning on the power.

4 Clamp cylindrical stock in a V block.

5 Disconnect the power before changing or working near any cutting tool.

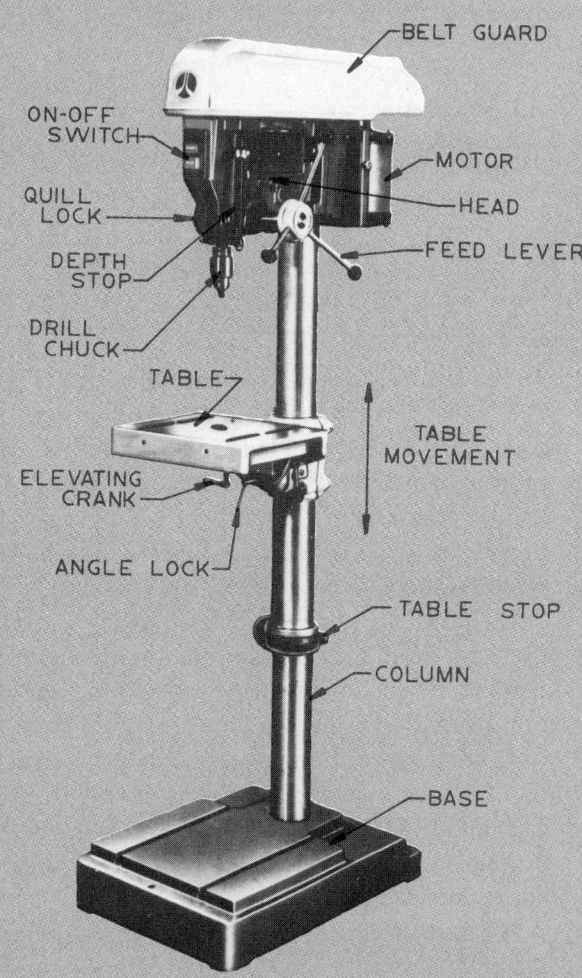

Figure 37-1
Major parts of a floor-model drill press. (Rockwell International)

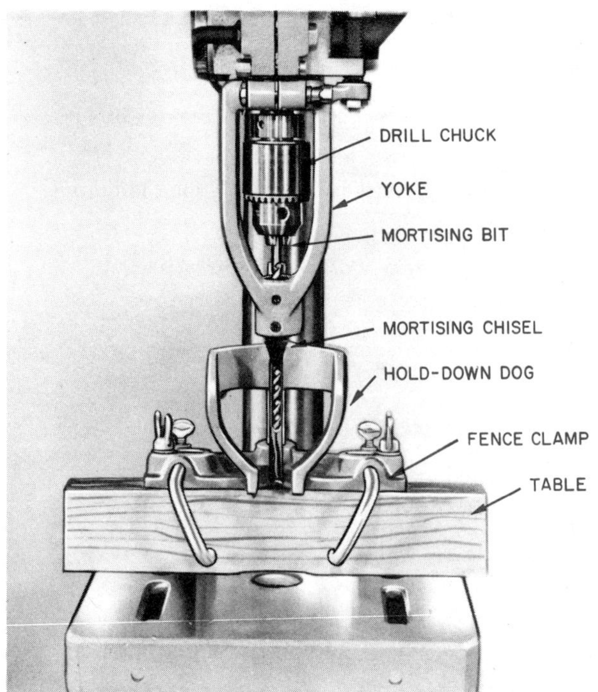

Figure 37-2
A mortising attachment installed on a drill press. It is used to bore square holes for joints called mortises. (Rockwell International)

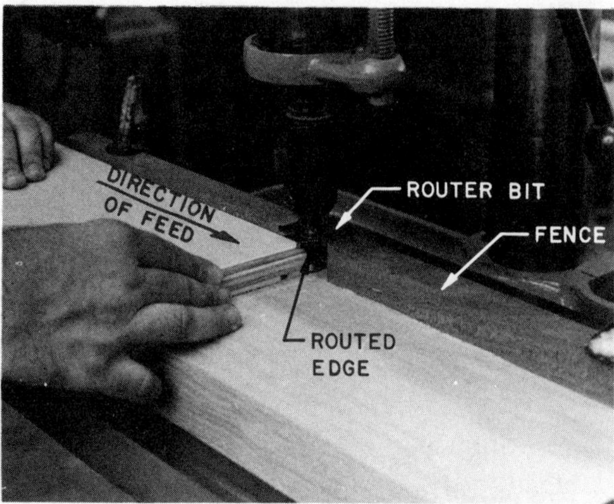

Figure 37-3
An auxiliary table and fence is installed for routing. The router bit shapes edges on the board. *The guard has been removed and action stopped so you can see this operation. Do not operate a drill press unless the guard is in place.*

The primary function of a drill press, Figure 37-1, is to bore holes. It can, however, perform other operations. For example, a square hole or mortise can be cut on a drill press with a mortising attachment, Figure 37-2. Large drill presses can also be used as routers, Figure 37-3. Drum sanding accessories are also available.

In industry, other types of machines are also used to bore holes. Two commonly used machines are the horizontal boring machine and multi-spindle boring machine.

A *horizontal boring machine* has one or more drill bits in a horizontal position, Figure 37-4. This allows the board to be placed on its face for boring on an edge or end. Dowel joints generally are made with this machine.

A *multi-spindle boring machine* can bore many holes with one stroke of the spindles, Figure 37-5. The *drill chucks* can be positioned wherever a hole is required. The drill bits usually are fed into the stock with a foot pedal.

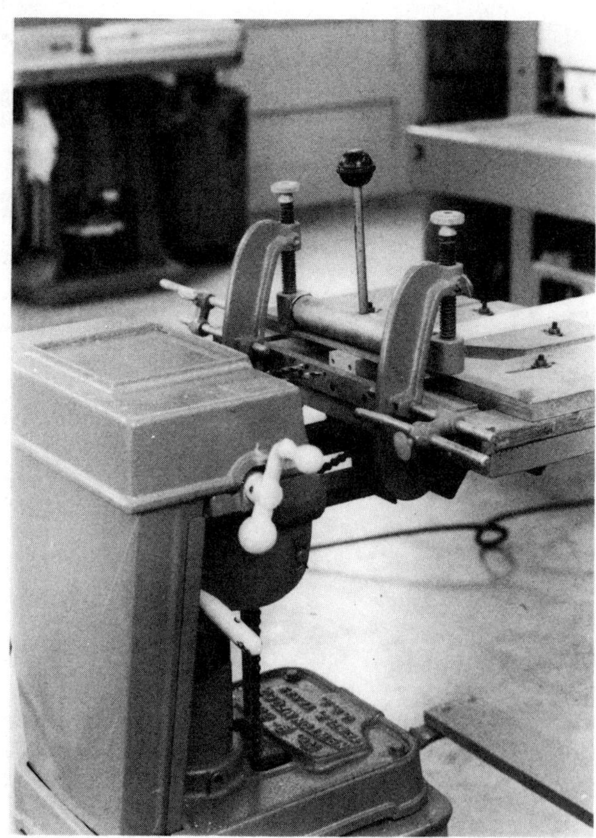

Figure 37-4
A horizontal boring machine is used to make dowel joints. Two holes are bored at one time.

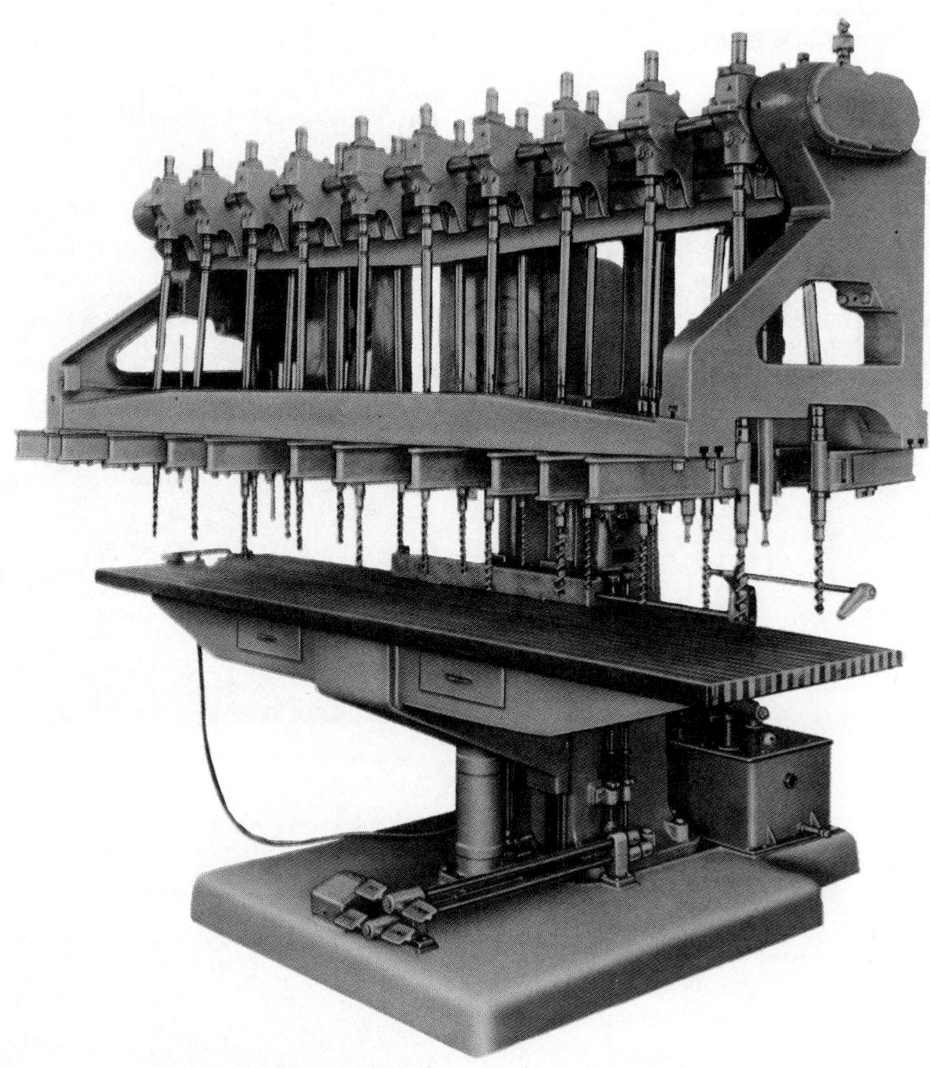

Figure 37-5
A multi-spindle boring machine has many drill bits. (B. M. Root Company)

DRILL PRESS TERMINOLOGY

The major parts of the drill press are the base, table and head, Figure 37-1. A steel column separates these three parts and allows the table to be moved up or down. The length of the column determines whether the machine is a bench or floor model. Bench models must be placed on a table, while the base of a floor model rests on the floor.

The head is made up of a motor and a spindle unit. The motor is mounted on the rear of the machine and powers the spindle. The spindle unit is made of a *quill* and a spindle. The quill moves the spindle up or down. The chuck is attached to the spindle. The spindle rotates the chuck. General-purpose drill presses have a 1/2" (13 mm) chuck located on the end of the spindle. This chuck will allow a maximum drill bit shank size of 1/2" (13 mm) in diameter.

There are two major methods of regulating speed. Some machines have step pulleys, which contain three or more different pulley diameters.

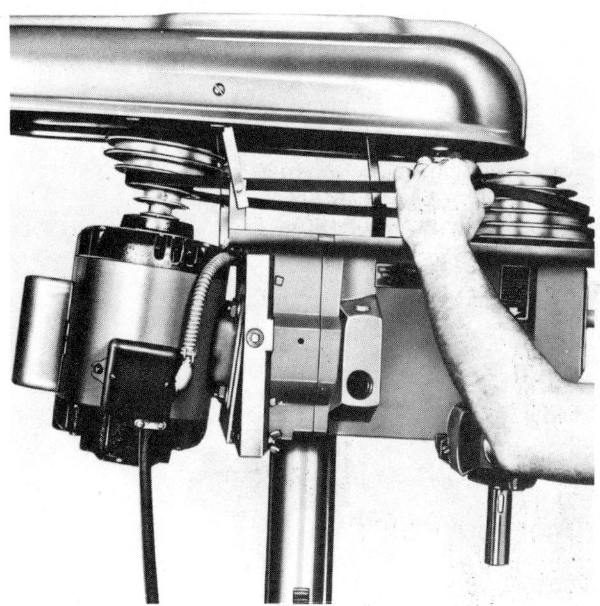

Figure 37-6
Changing the chuck speed on a step pulley. *Disconnect power before attempting this operation.* (Rockwell International)

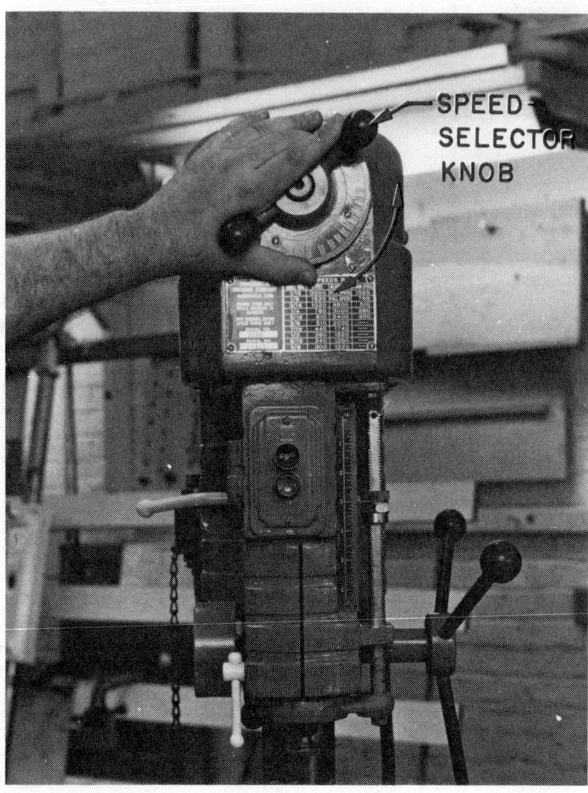

Figure 37-7
The speed on a variable-speed drill press can be changed only when the power is on.

Moving the belt to a different level changes the chuck speed, Figure 37-6. The larger the diameter of the motor pulley, the faster the chuck turns.

Other drill presses have variable-speed, spring-loaded pulleys. To change speeds while the motor is running, turn the speed selector knob, Figure 37-7. Do not move the speed selector knob unless the motor is on. This system, with its broader range of speeds and greater ease in changing spindle rpm, is preferable to the step pulley.

The size of a drill press is twice the distance from the center of a drill bit in the chuck to the front of the column, Figure 37-8. A common size is 15" (381 mm).

Figure 37-8
Determine the size of a drill press by doubling the distance from the tip of the bit to the front of the column.

OPERATING THE DRILL PRESS

The drill bit can be lowered with the feed lever located on the side of the head, Figure 37-1. A spring returns the quill to the highest position. When several holes are to be bored, a depth stop can limit the travel of the feed lever and chuck, Figure 37-9. Certain operations require

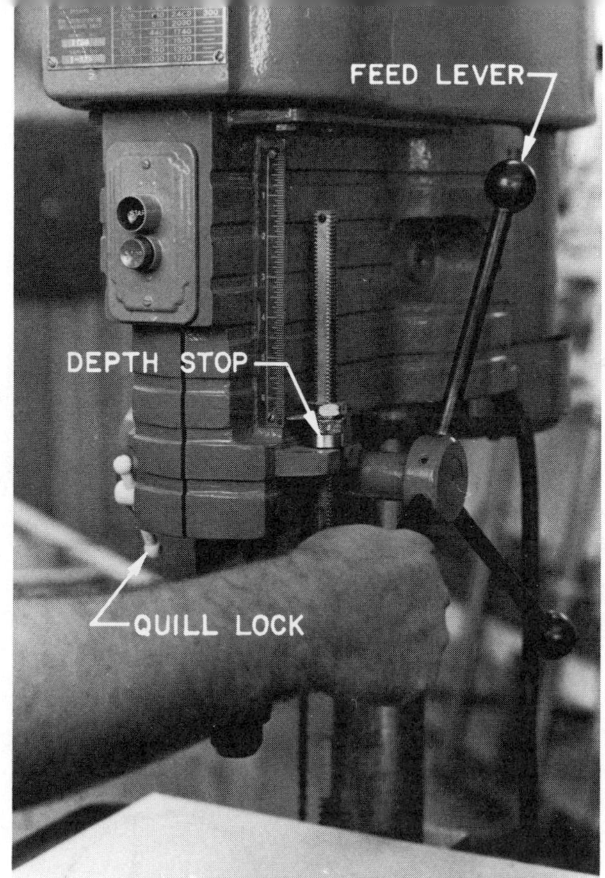

Figure 37-9
A depth stop limits the depth of the hole.

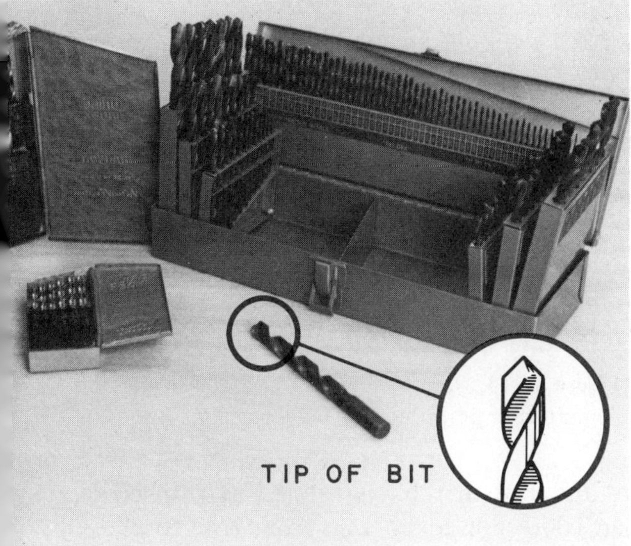

Figure 37-10
Twist drills are stored in a drill index.

the quill to be locked in a stationary position. A quill lock will secure the quill, Figure 37-9. The chuck is lowered to the desired level, and the quill lock is tightened to secure the quill.

The total distance the chuck travels downward is the stroke length. Most drill presses have

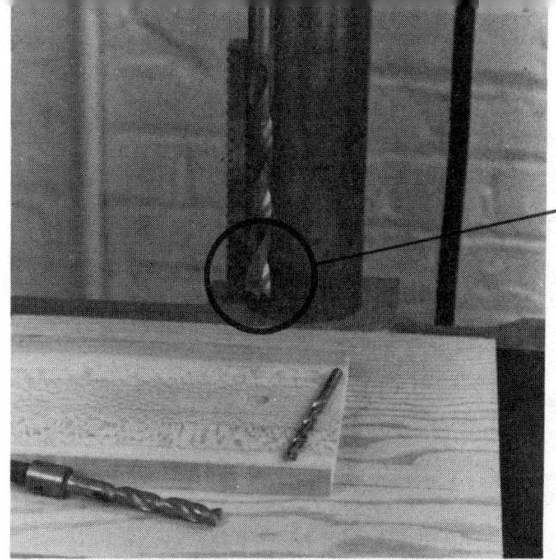

Figure 37-11
A spur bit bores a very clean hole.

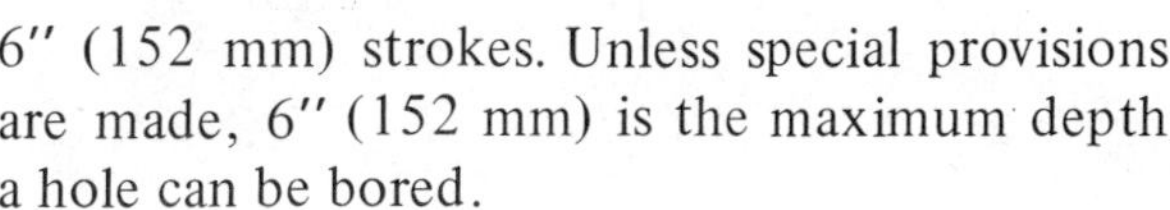

6″ (152 mm) strokes. Unless special provisions are made, 6″ (152 mm) is the maximum depth a hole can be bored.

DRILL BITS AND DRILLING TOOLS

Many drilling tools and bits are available. Each piece has a different function. It is important to choose the best bit or tool for the job at hand.

Twist Drills

Straight-shank twist drills are generally used for holes smaller than 1/2″ (13mm). They can be used for making holes in wood, plastic and metal. Standard twist drills are stored in a metal storage box called a drill index, Figure 37-10. Indexes can be purchased with bit diameters from 1/32″ to 1/2″ and from 1.0 mm to 13.0 mm. Inch sizes increase in diameter by 1/64″ and metric sizes increase by 0.5 mm. Standard length twist bits are called jobbers length. Other lengths are also available.

The tip of the twist bit is ground to 118°. The body of the bit is wrapped with a spiral groove. As the bit cuts into the stock, chips push their way up along the grooves and onto the top surface of the board. If the grooves become clogged, it is important to back the twist bit out of the hole and to allow the chips to fall free.

Spur Bits

Spur bits are similar in shape to twist bits, but the tip is ground differently, Figure 37-11. The very tip forms a brad point, which resists following the grain of the wood. If the grain is hard, the twist drill may be pulled to one side.

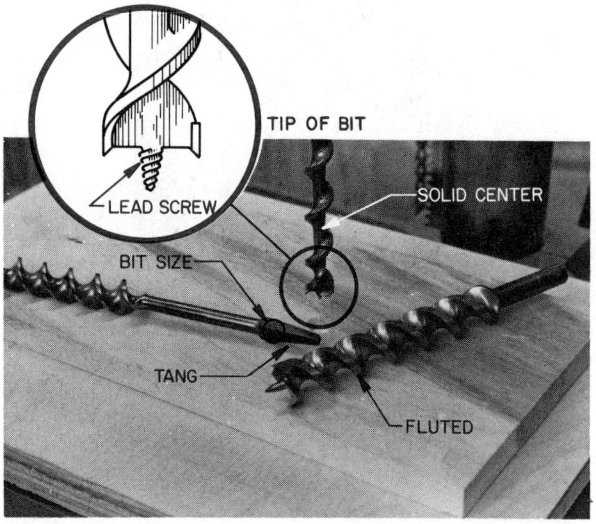

Figure 37-12
Auger bits require the work to be clamped to the table.

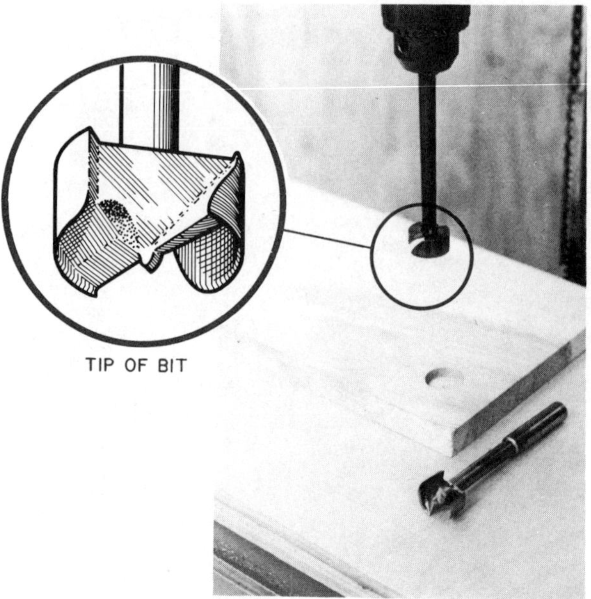

Figure 37-13
Forstner bits require the work to be clamped to the table.

Two cutting lips are ground on the outside edge of the tip to give a smooth, clean cut. Because they cut clean and bore straight, spin bits are good for boring dowel holes. Sizes vary from 3/16″ to 1-1/4″ by 1/32″.

Auger Bits

Auger bits with straight shanks are designed for use in a drill press, Figure 37-12. An auger bit with a tang should be used only in a hand-operated brace, never in a drill press. Straight-shank auger bits are widely used in multi-spindle boring machines.

A threaded brad point at the tip of the bit feeds the bit automatically into the board. This feature requires the stock to be clamped or fastened to the table. Body styles include fluted and solid centers. Fluted bits bore smoother holes, but the solid-center style is much stiffer.

Sizes are stamped on the shank by the number of sixteenths measured in the diameter. For example, a 7/8″ bit will have a 14 stamped in the metal of the shank. Sizes range from 1/4″ to over 1″.

Forstner Bits

Straight-shank Forstner bits are used in the drill press. They are used when flat-bottom holes are needed, Figure 37-13. The sharp lips of the bit give a smooth cut. Because of the style of its tip, the Forstner bit is rotated at a speed less than 1000 rpm. Sizes range from 1/4″ to 2″.

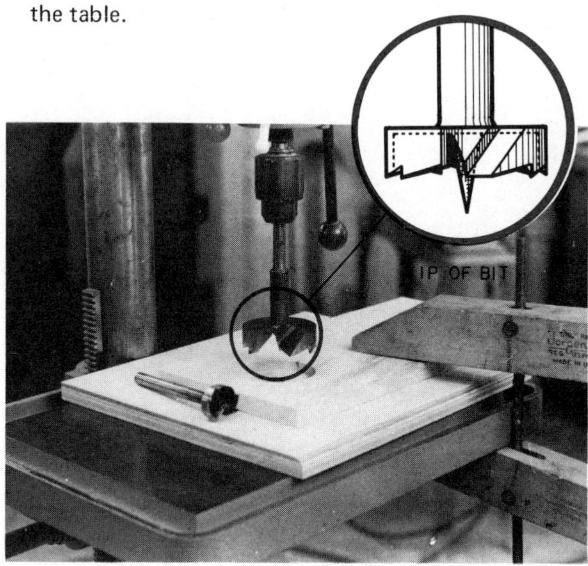

Figure 37-14
A multi-spur bit bores large holes rapidly.

Multi-spur Bits

Multi-spur bits also can bore flat-bottom holes, Figure 37-14. The teeth on the multi-spur bit, however, are ground into the outer lips, allowing it to bore at a faster rate than the Forstner bit. Although the teeth appear as if they would make a rough cut, the multi-spur bit is well known for its smooth, clean cutting action. Sizes range from 1/2″ to 4″.

Spade Bits

A spade, or speed, bit is a third kind of drill used to bore flat-bottom holes, Figure 37-15. Their long centering points leave a tapered hole on the bottom. Because their cutting blades are thin, spade bits overheat easily and should not be used for heavy cutting. Sizes range from 1/4″ to 2″.

Hole Saws

Hole saws consist of a drill bit and a saw unit, Figure 37-16. They make large-diameter holes in a variety of materials. A 1/4″ twist drill first bores into the wood, guiding the saw. The rim of the saw has many small teeth that cut a circular groove. After cutting through the board, turn off the drill press. The plug produced from the hole can then be removed from the inside of the saw. Sizes range from 9/16″ to 6″.

Circle Cutters

Circle cutters are also used to make large-diameter holes, Figure 37-17. A cutting arm can be adjusted for circles varying from 1-1/8″ to 8-3/8″ (29 to 213 mm). The arm is secured with an Allen wrench. A 1/4″ bit serves as a guide for the swinging cutter arm. To use this cutter, clamp the board to the working surface to prevent the bit from grabbing the stock and throwing it off the table. The cutter should rotate no faster than 500 rpm. After boring as far as you can from one direction, turn the board over and bore from the other side.

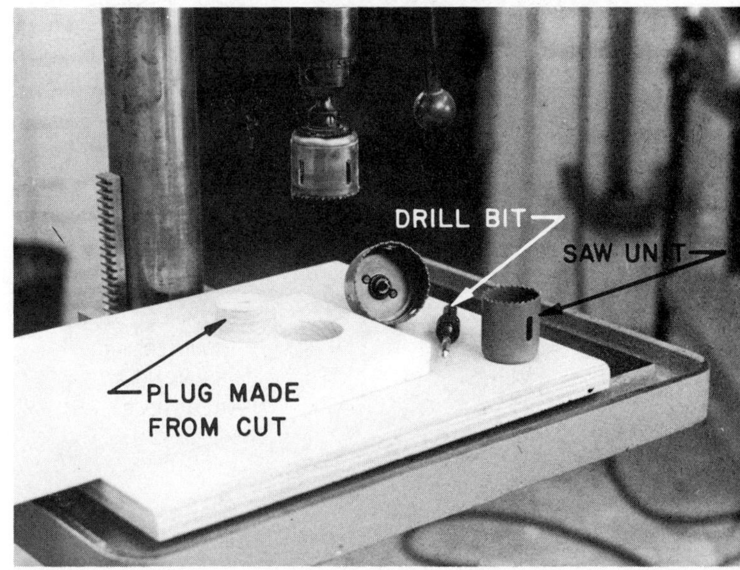

Figure 37-16
Hole saws actually saw a circular-shaped plug.

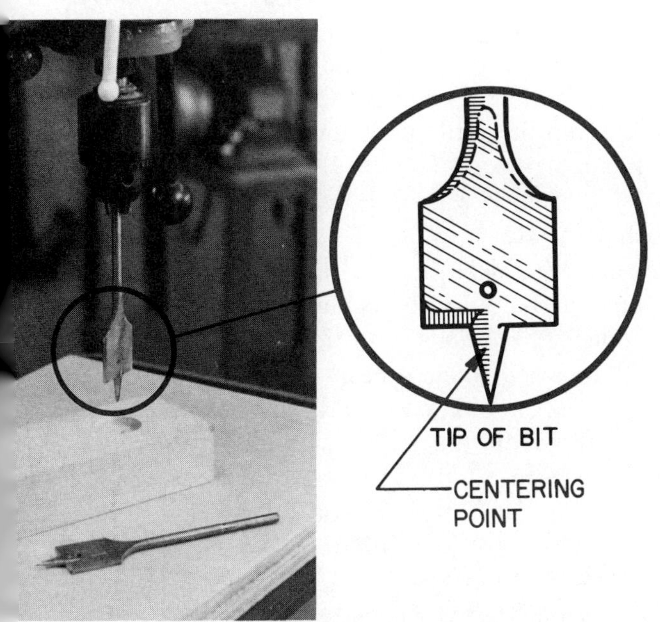

Figure 37-15
A spade bit is designed to make large-diameter holes.

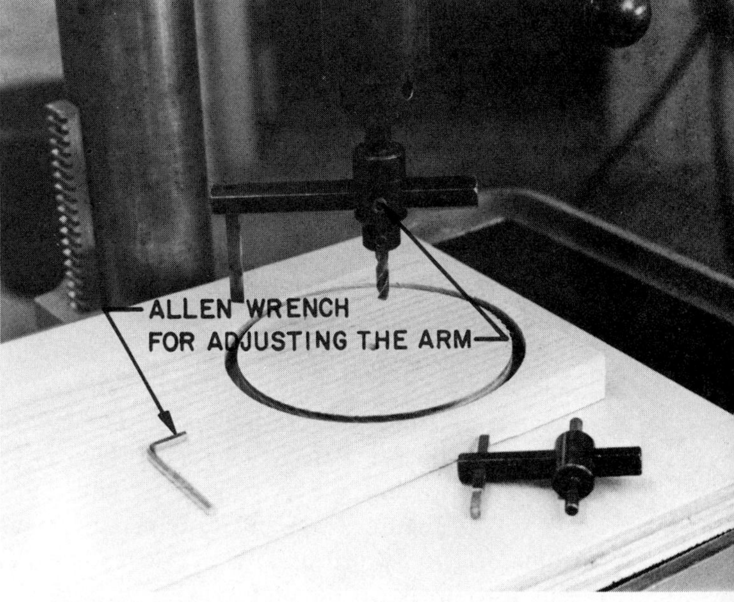

Figure 37-17
Circle cutters make the largest holes.

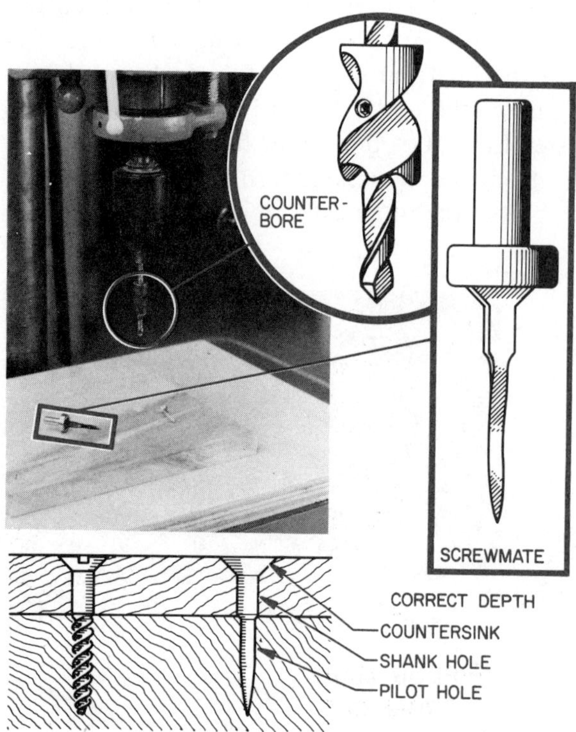

Figure 37-18
Counterbores are frequently used for wood screws.

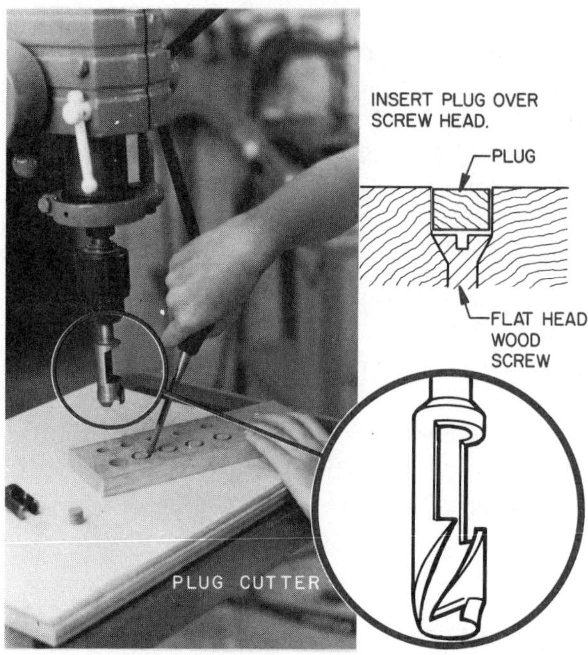

Figure 37-19
A plug cutter makes plugs to cover up screw heads.

Counterbore and Countersink

Counterbores are sometimes fastened to twist bits so that two holes can be bored at one time. Screw holes can be bored rapidly with this arrangement, Figure 37-18. Screwmates® bore the countersink, shank and pilot hole all in one stroke of the bit. They are sold to match various screw sizes.

A countersink is a bit that bores a tapered hole to match the bottom of a flathead wood screw. Use it only after the shank hole for the screw has been bored.

Plug Cutters

When flathead wood screws are used on outside surfaces, the heads of the screws should be covered. If a counterbore hole is the correct diameter for the screw head, a wooden plug can be inserted into this hole. A plug cutter will shape this plug, Figure 37-19. Plug diameters range from 3/8" to 1" (10 to 25 mm). A hand chisel is used to break off the plug.

BORING THROUGH HOLES

Most holes made in wood are bored completely through the stock. These are called *through holes.* The drill press is excellent for this task. It will produce a straight, high-quality hole.

When the bit breaks through the bottom surface of the stock, it will drill into the surface of the table. If a drill press has a hole already drilled through the center of the table, align this hole with the path of the bit. This will prevent accidental drilling into the tabletop. A *drill pad* or scrap piece of stock should also be placed on the table to protect it. If this is not done, the table surface will become so marred with holes that the stock will split out on the bottom side when the drill breaks through. Woodworking bits will be seriously damaged if the cutting edge comes into contact with the metal table.

To bore through holes:

1. Use a square to mark the position of the hole on the stock with two center lines, Figure 37-20. The point at which the layout lines intersect will be the center point of the hole. Sometimes this point is marked with an awl, which gives an indentation to serve as a starting guide for the drill bit.
2. Select the correct bit and place it in the drill chuck. Turn the outer sleeve of the chuck by hand until the bit is held in the chuck. The chuck is tightened on the drill

using a chuck key. The key is placed into each of the three holes on the chuck and turned to tighten the chuck jaws around the drill. Remove the chuck key once the bit is secured.

3. Determine the best speed for the type of bit and the material to be drilled. A general rule for determining speed is that the harder the material to be bored, the slower the bit should rotate. Metal and plastic require a speed of less than 1000 rpm. Hardwoods, such as maple, should be bored at a slower speed than softwoods, such as pine. Another general rule concerns the size of the bit. The larger the diameter, the slower the speed. See Figure 37-21 for recommended speeds. The operator should listen to the bit and observe the cutting action. The sound should not be a high piercing noise. Rough cutting action or a whining noise indicate that the rotational speed should be slowed down. Waste should be removed in the form of smooth chips.
4. Lower the feed lever until the bit is just below the top surface of the drill pad. Lock the quill in this position with the quill lock. Screw the depth stop down until it rests against the flange on the side of the drill press, Figure 37-9. Release the quill lock and allow the chuck to return to the upper position.
5. Clamp the piece of material to the table if necessary. Small boards may twist out of the operator's hands. Large-diameter bits also require the stock to be clamped to the table. Metal stock, especially sheet metal, needs to be secured. A *drill press vise* is made for holding small parts, Figure 37-22.
6. Turn on the power and slowly lower the bit until it is 1/4″ (6 mm) above the top surface of the stock. Move the board until the layout lines are centered under the bit.
7. Feed the drill bit at a slow, even pace by turning the feed lever. If the stock is fed too fast, the bit may grab the stock, which will produce a rough surface. If fed too slowly the bit will burn the material. For deep holes, remove the bit from the stock several times to allow the chips to fall free.

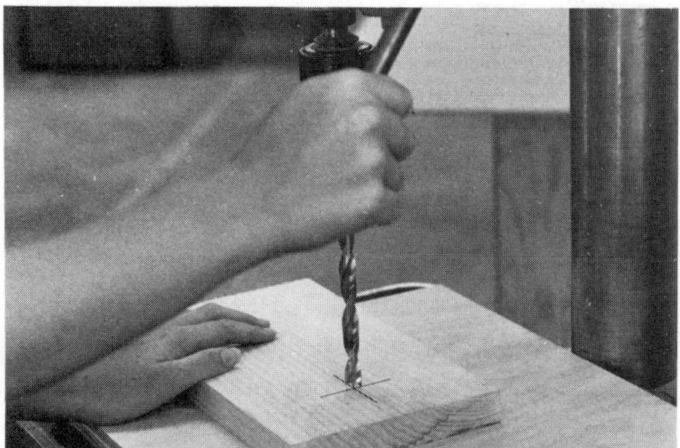

Figure 37-20
Properly marked center.

DRILL SPEEDS	
Diameter of Bit	**Revolutions per Minute (rpm)**
1/4″ and smaller	Full speed
5/16″ - 1/2″	1500 - 3000
5/8″ - 1″	1000 - 1500
1-1/4 - 2″	1000 - 500
2″ and larger	500 and smaller

Figure 37-21
Because each piece of wood is different, these speeds are only approximate. Use the speeds given here as a beginning point. Through experimentation, they should be adjusted faster or slower. A clear chip should be formed.

Figure 37-22
A vise is used to clamp metal pieces.

8. Draw the bit out of the stock when the depth stop reaches the flange. The depth stop prevents the bit from drilling any deeper. Position the next hole under the bit and repeat the procedure.

BORING STOPPED HOLES

Stopped holes do not extend all the way through the stock. A drill bit enters the board on the top surface and stops before it reaches the bottom surface. Dowel and pilot-screw holes are examples of stopped holes. Certain bits cannot be used for stopped holes. For example, an auger bit has a tapered lead screw, which may break through the opposite face. Bore a stopped hole as you would a through hole. The depth must be set differently, however. Mark the desired depth on one end of the board and place it next to the bit. Lower the bit to this level and tighten the quill lock, Figure 37-23. Adjust the depth stops and release the quill lock. Feed the bit into the stock until the depth stop reaches the flange. This will produce a hole of the desired depth.

Figure 37-23
Aligning the end of the bit with the depth mark.

BORING EXTREMELY DEEP HOLES

Sometimes holes that are deeper than one stroke of a standard drill must be bored. A special procedure must be used for such holes.

If possible, the piece requiring a deep hole should be made in sections. The sections can be bored using a standard drilling procedure. They are then assembled to produce the finished depth.

Two other methods can also be used. One requires the use of a special bit, or extension. Many woodworkers prefer to use a spur bit with a steel rod brazed to the end of the bit shank and a portable drill. This is not an accurate method because the long bit may drift to one side.

The second method will bore holes twice the length of the stroke of the drill press:

1. Bore the first hole in the stock as far as the bit will reach.
2. Make a boring fixture by boring a hole of the same diameter as the finish hole into the middle of a scrap piece of wood. Clamp the board to the table.
3. Lower the table to the combined distance of the stock and the bit. Place a straight dowel of the same diameter as the bit in the chuck. Lower the chuck approximately 1″ (25 mm) and center the hole in the fixture under the dowel, Figure 37-24.

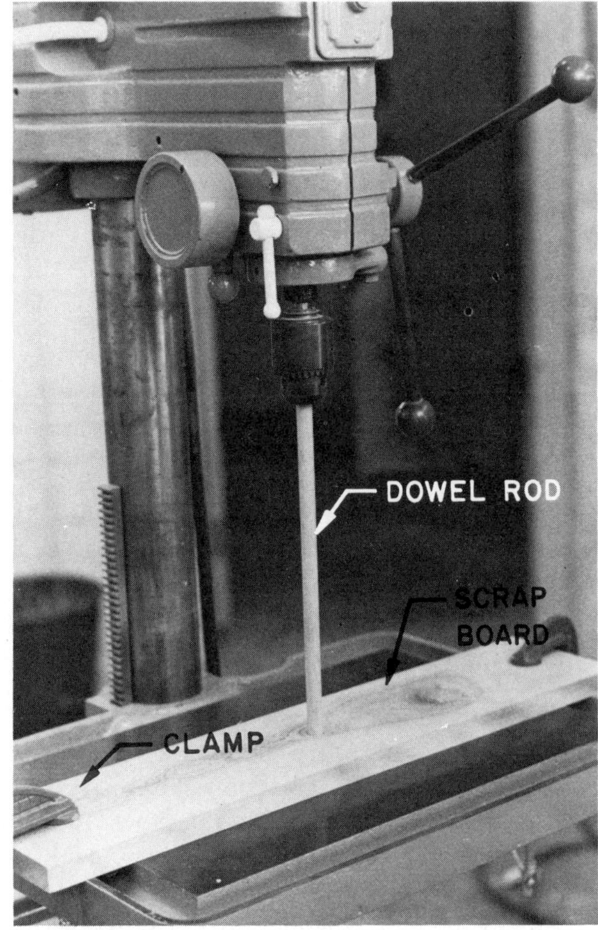

Figure 37-24
Centering the scrap board under the chuck.

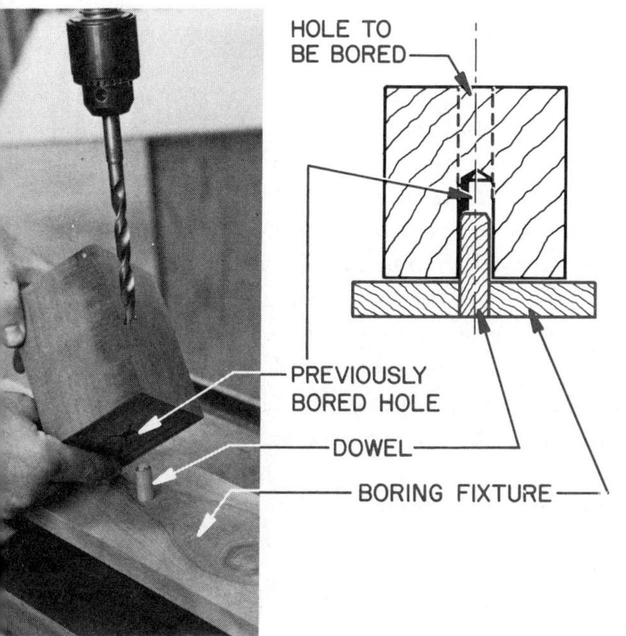

Figure 37-25
The previously drilled hole is placed over the dowel pin.

Figure 37-26
Last step in boring a deep hole.

4. Remove the dowel from the chuck and replace the bit. Insert a short section of the dowel into the hole of the fixture clamped on the table. Position the previously bored hole in the stock over the top of the dowel pin, Figure 37-25.

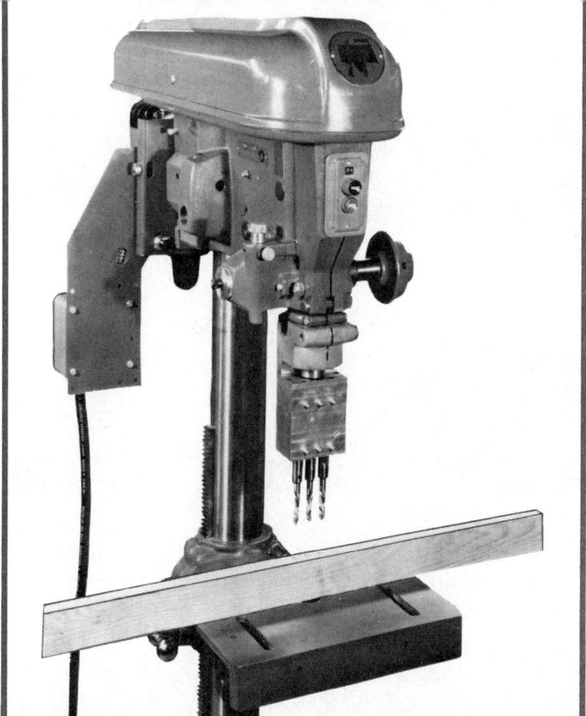

Figure 37-27
A drill head mounted on a standard drill press. (Forest City Tool Company)

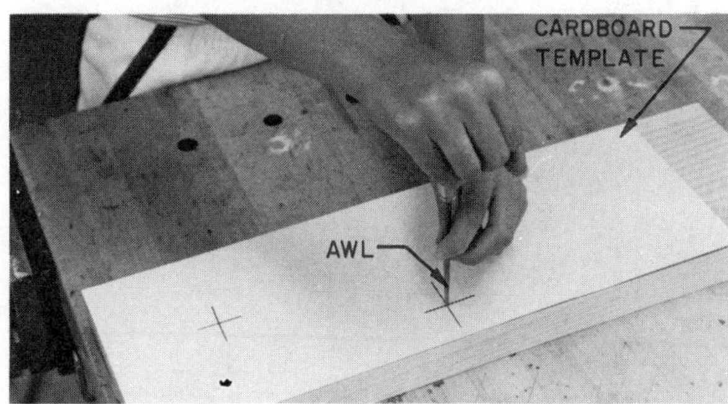

Figure 37-28
Using a cardboard template for marking holes.

5. Finish the hole by boring from the opposite end until the bit breaks through the end of the first hole, Figure 37-26.

BORING MULTIPLE HOLES

Quite often a series of holes of the same size are required. Industry accomplishes this task with a multi-spindle boring machine, Figure 37-5, or a drill head mounted to a drill press, Figure 37-27. The same result can be achieved with a special setup of a drill press and a single drill bit.

A metal or cardboard template can be placed over the top of the stock. Use an awl to mark the hole centers, Figure 37-28. Bore the holes one at a time. If used many times the template may eventually wear out.

Figure 37-29
The dowel is moved from hole to hole in the fence. The holes in the stock will be the same distance apart as those in the fence.

Figure 37-30
Boring holes in a straight line with the peg method.

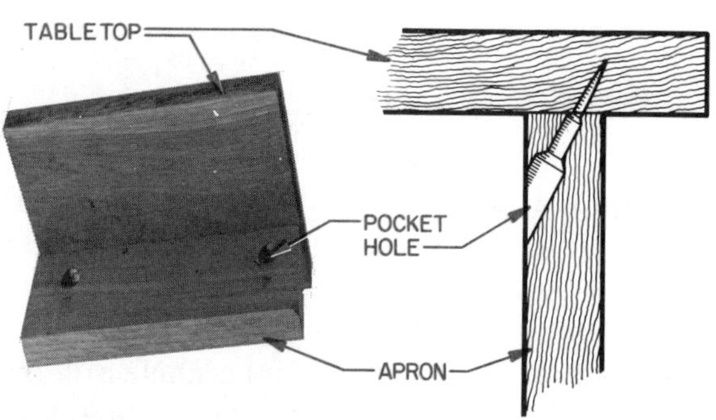

Figure 37-31
Angular holes used to fasten tabletops are called pocket holes.

A more sophisticated method uses a fence clamped to the table of the drill press. Previously, holes have been bored in the face of the fence. The fence holes are the same distance apart as the holes will be on the spacing desired. Place a dowel in one hole at a time, and butt the end of the stock up against it, Figure 37-29. After each hole is drilled, move the dowel pin to the next hole, slide the board to touch the pin and drill another hole. Holes in the board will be the same distance apart as the holes in the fence.

Evenly spaced holes can be made with a stop-peg method, Figure 37-30. This is a good method for making holes for adjustable shelving. Position the front edge of the fence so that the center of the bit is the desired distance away. Clamp the pin block so that the center of the pin is the same distance from the drill bit as the desired space between the holes. Measure and bore the first hole. Slide the stock along the fence until the pin can be pushed into the first hole. This will situate the board for the next hole. Drill one hole at a time.

BORING ANGULAR HOLES

Holes that enter the stock at an angle other than 90° require the table to be tilted. (Not all drill presses tilt, so an auxiliary table may have to be constructed.) A *pocket hole* used for attaching table tops is a good example of this type of hole, Figure 37-31. A Forstner bit is good for boring angular holes. To bore angular holes:

1. Tilt the table to the desired angle by releasing the angle lock. Use a T bevel against the bit and table as a guide, Figure 37-32.
2. Clamp the stock securely to the table and feed the bit gradually into the stock, Figure 37-33.

COUNTERBORING

Some applications have screw heads and bolt heads set below the top surface. This requires two holes to be bored with the same center. The process is called counterboring.

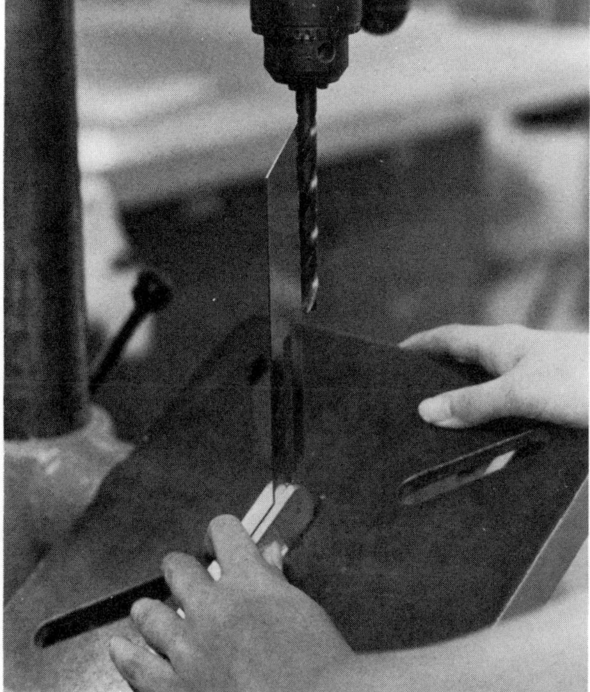

Figure 37-32
A sliding T bevel is used to set the table. *Disconnect the power before attempting this operation.*

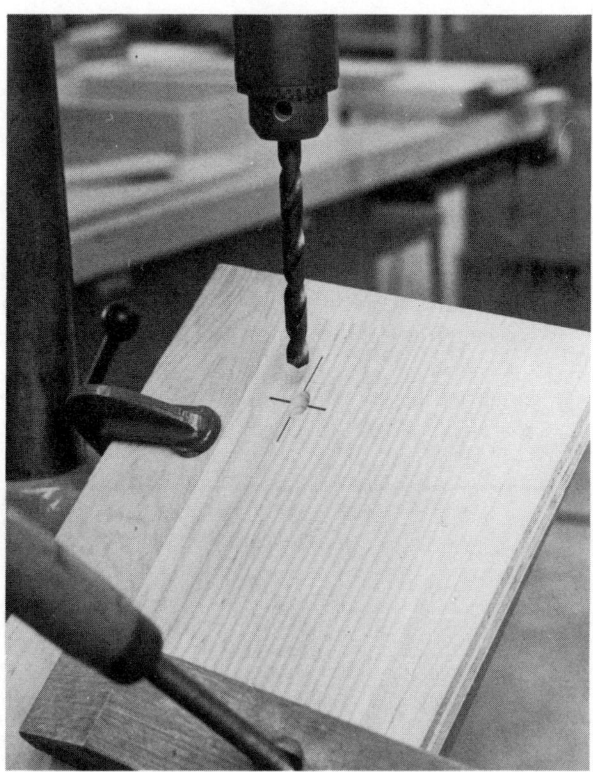

Figure 37-33
Boring an angular hole.

Always bore the larger hole first. If you do not, there will be no material to guide the centering of the larger bit, Figure 37-34. Some specialized bits drill both holes with one plunge of the chuck, Figure 37-18.

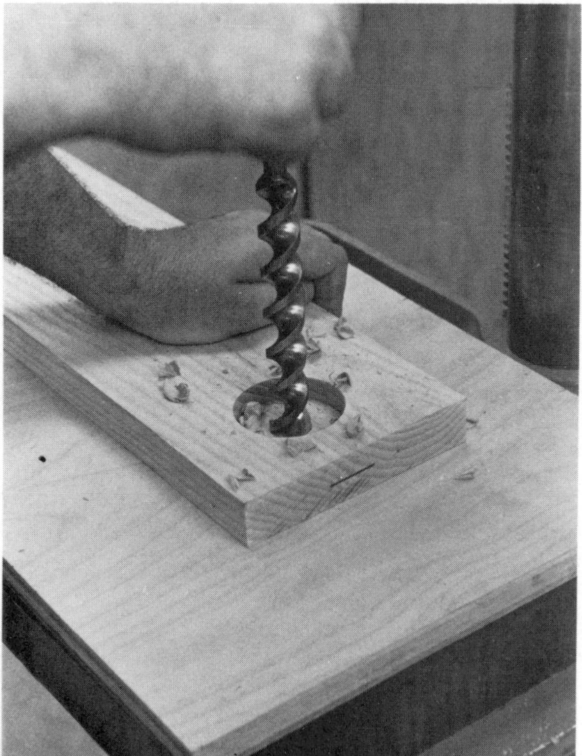

Figure 37-34
Counterboring requires the larger hole to be bored first.

Figure 37-35
A V block assists in holding circular stock.

BORING CIRCULAR STOCK

Lathe turnings, dowel pins and other circular shapes should not be bored without a special holding device. Due to the curved shape, the stock may turn during the drilling operation. A simple *V block* cut on a table saw should be used to cradle the work piece, Figure 37-35.

SANDING WITH A DRILL PRESS

A drill press can be used as a spindle sander by attaching a sanding drum to the chuck. The drum should be turned at a speed between 1000 and 2000 rpm. Reduce the speed if burning occurs. A sanding drum can be made in the shop by wrapping a cloth-backed abrasive around a wood cylinder. Commercial heads using manufactured sanding cones are also available.

To receive maximum use from the drum, use the whole surface. Start by building an auxiliary table. Make a hole in the center a little larger in diameter than the drum. The chuck can then be raised and lowered, Figure 37-36. After a section of the abrasive is used, that portion can be lowered below the table surface. The quill lock secures the drum at the desired level.

Figure 37-36
An auxiliary table allows the drum to be raised and lowered.

REVIEW QUESTIONS

1 What type of hole does the horizontal boring machine make?
2 List the two methods of regulating the speed on the drill press.
3 How is the size of a drill press determined?
4 Which device is used to secure the quill at a desired height?
5 What is the name of the storage box in which twist drills are kept?
6 What advantage does the spur bit have over the twist drill?
7 Name two types of bits that can be used to make flat-bottom holes.
8 Name two types of bits that could make a 6" (152 mm) diameter circle.
9 What purpose does the drill pad serve?
10 What safety precaution should be taken before drilling small boards and pieces of metal?
11 Name the device that is used to set the depth when boring a stopped hole.
12 List three methods of making multiple holes.
13 How is a pocket hole made?
14 How is cylindrical stock held on the drill press?

SUGGESTED ACTIVITIES

1 Inspect your drill press and name all the major parts.
2 Counterbore two holes in a piece of scrap. Ask your teacher to give you the location and dimension of the holes.
3 Practice using the drill press by constructing a set of coasters. Use 1/4" (6 mm) plywood.

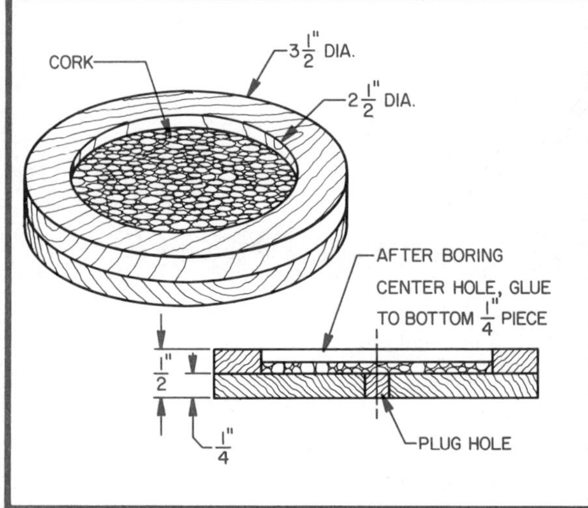

UNIT

38

Stationary Sanding Machines

Objectives

After studying this unit you should be able to:

1 Identify the major parts of a sanding machine and make the basic adjustments.

2 Describe the types of sanding machines.

3 Sand surfaces safely and correctly.

Technical Terms

Disc sander
Cleaning stick
Oscillating spindle sander
Stationary belt sander
Wide belt sander
Stroke sander
Edge sander
Pneumatic-headed sander

GENERAL SANDER SAFETY RULES

1 Keep fingers outside the 4" (102 mm) safety margin.

2 Keep the stock against the table.

3 Do not operate a sander if the abrasive paper is loose, torn or loaded.

4 Make special holding fixtures for sanding small pieces.

5 Apply firm pressure on the stock. Excessive pressure will tear the abrasive material.

DISC SANDER SAFETY RULES

1 Follow general sander safety rules.

2 Sand only on the downstroke side of the disc.

SPINDLE SANDER SAFETY RULES

1 Follow general sander safety rules.

2 Change spindles only when the power is off.

SMALL STATIONARY BELT SANDER SAFETY RULES

1 Follow general sander safety rules.

2 Make adjustments on the belt only when the power is off.

WIDE BELT SANDER SAFETY RULES

1. Follow general sander safety rules.
2. Do not reach into the machine or open the guard doors while the belt is turning.
3. If the belt tears or if stock becomes stuck in the machine, push the emergency-stop button.
4. Release the pressure on the contact roller only after the belt has stopped turning.
5. Make certain the belt is tracking correctly before feeding any boards.

STROKE SANDER SAFETY RULES

1. Follow general sander safety rules.
2. Position stock solidly before sanding.
3. Do not apply excessive pressure with the pressure block.

EDGE SANDER SAFETY RULES

1. Follow general sander safety rules.
2. Feed material squarely into the belt. If the stock vibrates, move it away from the belt and refeed.

Wood can be quickly and smoothly removed with a sanding machine. Although hand-sanding also is useful, sanding machines are faster and can remove more material at a time.

There are many kinds of sanding machines. Stationary sanding machines usually perform one type of sanding job. Manufacturing plants and schools may have several specialized sanding machines. Sanding machines often are available with other woodworking machines, such as lathes and drill presses.

ABRASIVE TYPES AND SIZES

Sanding machines use different types of abrasives and different grit sizes. Garnet and aluminum oxide are common abrasives. Grit sizes, or diameters of the abrasive particles, range from 36 to 180. Figure 38-1 shows some common grit sizes. The smaller the grit number, the larger the size of the abrasive used. Rough sanders use 36 to 80 grit. Finishing sanders use 100 to 180 grit.

DISC SANDERS

A *disc sander* has a metal disc covered with abrasive paper. The disc rests on a table and is motor-driven. The size of the sander is rated by the diameter of the disc. Sizes range from 12″ to 36″ (305 to 914 mm), Figures 38-2 and 38-3. The larger the disc, the wider the stock that can be sanded.

Use a disc sander for rough shaping, sanding end grain and making outside curves. You rarely

SIZES OF GRITS FOR ABRASIVES ON SANDING MACHINES

	Garnet and Aluminum Oxide Grit Size	Approximate Size of Abrasive
FINE (Belt, Stroke, Edge Sanders)	180 150 120	
MEDIUM (All Sanders)	100 80 60	
COARSE (Abrasive Planer, Disc)	50 40 36	

Figure 38-1
Sanding belts, discs, sleeves and drums come in a variety of sizes.

Figure 38-2
A small, 12″ (305 mm), disc sander with a miter gauge. (Rockwell International)

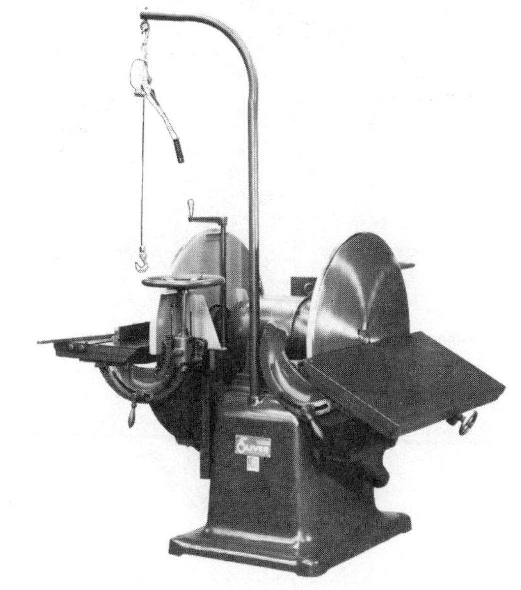

Figure 38-3
A large, 36″ (914 mm), commercial disc sander with two tables. (Oliver Machinery Company)

will use it for finishing because the circular motion of the disc and the coarse abrasive do not produce a smooth, finished surface. Most often, 36 or 60 grit abrasive paper is used on disc sanders. As a board is brought in contact with the rotating abrasive, scratches are made across the grain.

Replacing the Abrasive

When the paper has become worn or loaded with pitch, replace it. Try scraping the paper from the disc with a putty knife. If scraping does not work, unscrew the metal disc and soak it in water.

Use a *cleaning stick* to remove pitch build-up, Figure 38-4. Bring the stick against the turning disc and move it from side to side. This will increase the life of the abrasive paper.

Apply new abrasive paper either with a special stick cement or with polyvinyl adhesive. Bring the stick adhesive in contact with the clean, spinning disc. The spinning action spreads the bonding agent. Turn off the power. Press a fresh disc of abrasive paper against the newly glued surface. When using the polyvinyl adhesive, remove the clean disc from the sander. Coat the disc with the bonding agent. After positioning the abrasive paper on the disc, place the unit in a press until it dries. Figure 38-5 shows the supplies you need to mount abrasive paper on a disc.

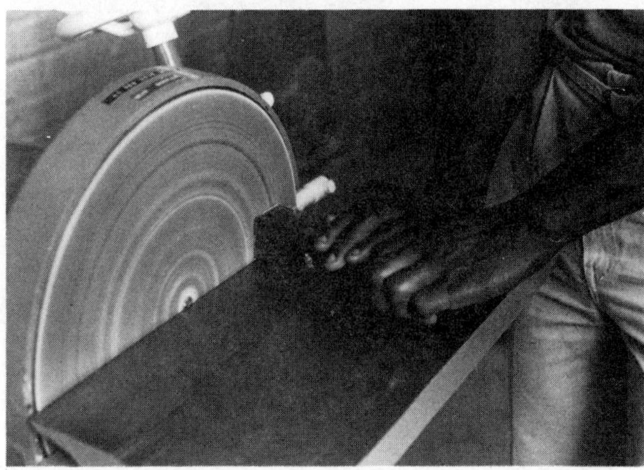

Figure 38-4
A cleaning stick removes resin between disc changes.

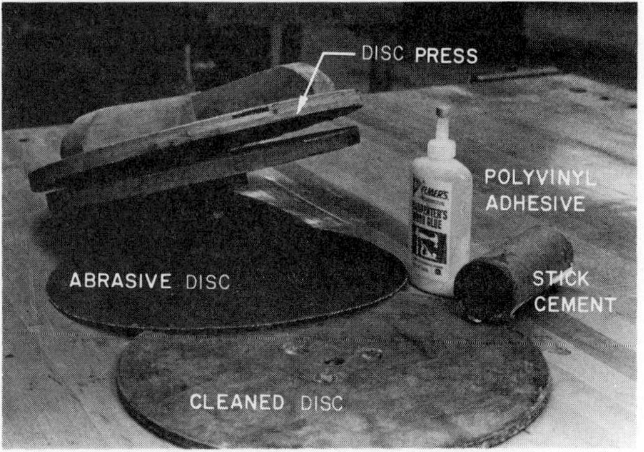

Figure 38-5
Supplies needed for recovering the disc.

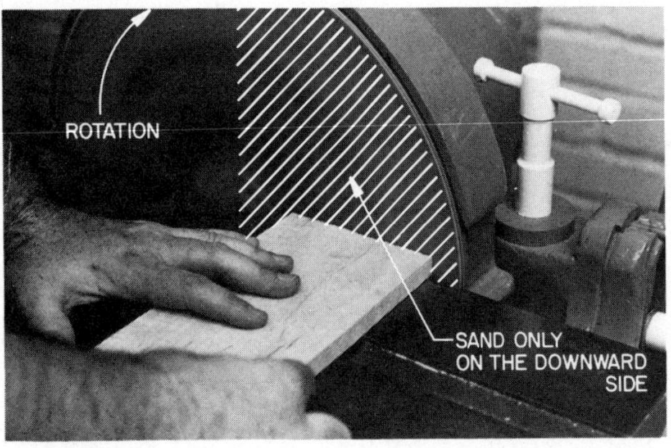

Figure 38-6
Sand only on the downward side of the disc.

Figure 38-7
A table in the tilted position for sanding bevels and chamfers. (Rockwell International)

Figure 38-8
Sanding up to the layout line.

Figure 38-9
A table saw can be used as a disc sander. *The guard has been removed and the action stopped so you can see the disc. Do not operate a table saw unless the guard is in place.*

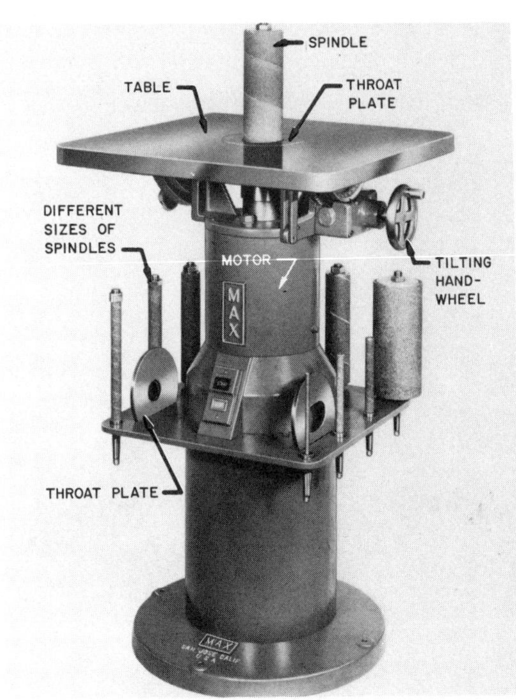

Figure 38-10
Major parts of a spindle sander. (Max Manufacturing Company)

Using the Disc Sander

Always sand on the downward side of the rotation, Figure 38-6. If you sand the board on the upward side, sanding dust will be thrown in your face and the stock will be thrown from the table.

Most stationary disc sanders have a grooved table for a miter gauge, Figure 38-2. Use the miter gauge as a guide when sanding end grain. Some tables also tilt for sanding bevels and chamfers, Figure 38-7. Because of the sander's deep cross-sanding marks, most surfaces sanded on the disc sander require additional hand-sanding.

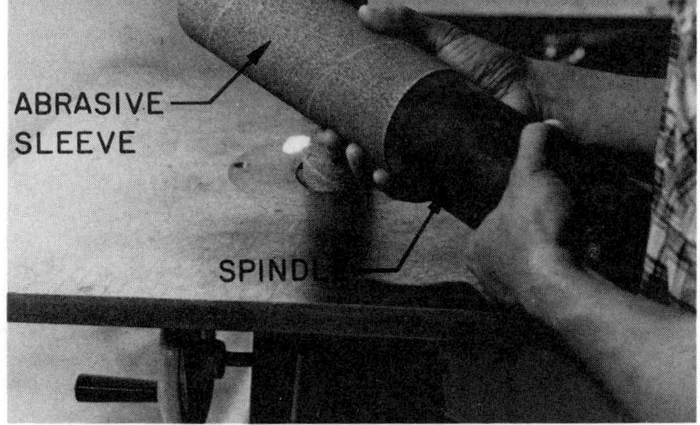

Figure 38-11
Replacing an abrasive sleeve on a spindle.

Figure 38-12
Use the largest-diameter spindle that will fit the curve. Note the layout lines.

Sanding wide boards requires a special procedure. As the disc turns, it removes more material toward the outer rim of the disc than toward the center. This is because the outer surface of the disc rotates at a faster speed than the center.

If you want to make a square edge, draw a layout line on the top surface of the board. Sand up to the line, Figure 38-8. Press harder on the side of the board near the center of the disc than on the side near the outside. Keep the board moving from side to side at all times to make use of the entire downward side of the disc. If you hold the stock in one position, the board will burn and load the abrasive paper in that area with waste.

Although the disc sander removes material quickly, do not remove too much material at one time. Sand gradually down to your layout line. Sanding very large amounts of wood will overheat the abrasive paper and shorten its life. The edge being sanded also is likely to burn.

You can also use a radial arm or table saw as a disc sander, Figure 38-9. The abrasive-covered metal disc has a center hole with the same diameter as the arbor of the saw. Place the disc on the arbor. As with the disc sander, remove stock only on the downward side of the rotation.

Figure 38-13
Using a drill press as a spindle sander.

SPINDLE SANDER

The spindle sander has a revolving spindle, table and motor, Figure 38-10. Abrasive paper is wrapped around the spindle, or an abrasive sleeve is slipped over the top, Figure 38-11. Abrasive sleeves are available in various degrees of coarseness. Common grit sizes are 80 and 100.

Use a spindle sander primarily to finish inside curves. Some models have tilting tables for sanding chamfers or bevels. Unlike the disc sander, the spindle sander revolves parallel to the table. This causes sanding scratches that are parallel to the grain. Do not use the spindle sander to remove large amounts of material or for sanding outside curves.

The spindle sander is easy to operate. Choose the correct spindle size. Different spindle diameters sand different sizes of curved edges. Use the largest spindle that will fit the curve, Figure 38-12. A smaller spindle diameter will make small dips on the sanded surface. Place the stock on the table and push it against the spindle. Keep the stock moving at all times.

Many machines have spindles that move up and down as they rotate. These are called *oscillating spindle sanders.* The oscillating action distributes the use of the abrasive over a large area, so the abrasive lasts longer.

You also can sand inside curves with a sanding drum on a drill press or lathe, Figure 38-13. Follow the procedure for a spindle sander.

SMALL STATIONARY BELT SANDERS

Use small *stationary belt sanders* for general-purpose sanding. This sander works well for sanding face, edge and end grain. It also can sand outside curves, Figure 38-14. A flat platen is located immediately behind the abrasive belt. The platen is a backing for the belt so that the belt will not stretch out of shape and tear. Grit sizes vary from 60 to 220. A general-purpose size is 100.

The belt can be placed in three positions. Stock edges and ends are sanded with the belt in the vertical position, Figure 38-15. Use the horizontal position for sanding faces of small boards, Figure 38-16. The belt in a slanted position can sand surfaces with angular cuts.

There are different ways of guiding stock. Like the disc sander, the belt sander has a grooved table for a miter gauge. Use the gauge as an additional guide when you feed stock across the belt.

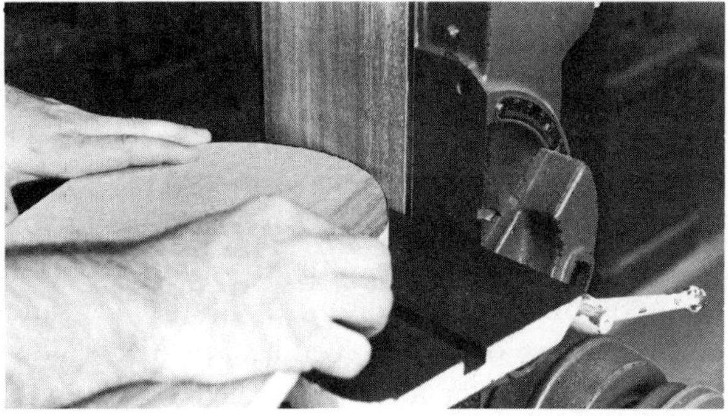

Figure 38-14
Sanding an outside curve. Note that a layout line is necessary.

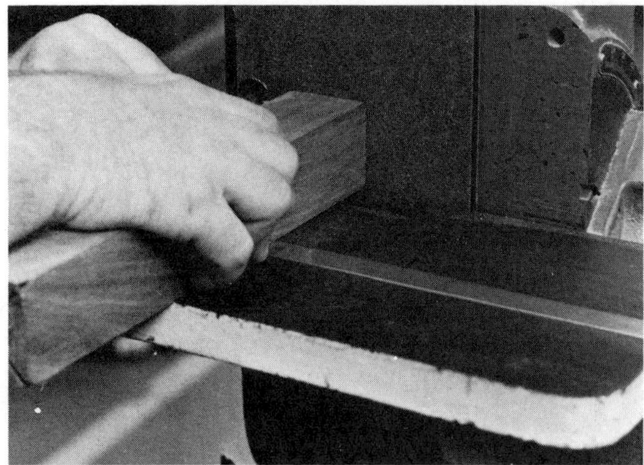

Figure 38-15
Sanding end grain with the belt in the vertical position.

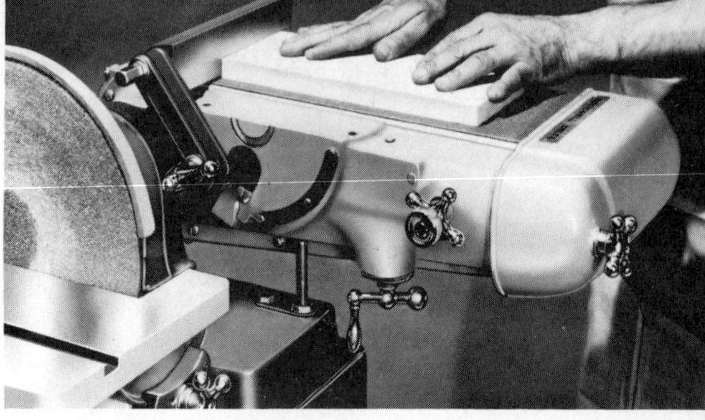

Figure 38-16
A small belt sander in the horizontal position. (Rockwell International)

Figure 38-17
A small belt sander has a horizontal table and a belt 1" (25 mm) wide. (Rockwell International)

Belt sanders smaller than the one shown in Figure 38-16 can do many of the same things larger sanders do, Figure 38-17. They have the advantage of being able to sand smaller curves. Some woodworkers also like to sharpen pocket knives and other tools on small belt sanders.

WIDE BELT SANDERS

Use a *wide belt sander* for finishing flat material, Figure 38-18. This sander looks like an abrasive planer but is of a lighter construction, Figure 38-19. A wide belt sander shallow cuts, so a heavy feed belt, steel rollers and large motor are not necessary. Plywood panels, large cabinet and furniture parts and doors are frequently sanded with this type of sander.

The major parts of the wide belt sander are a contact roller, idler roller, endless feed belt, table and platen, Figure 38-20. Place the stock on the endless belt to feed it through the sander.

Figure 38-18
Wide belt sanders are used for the faces of flat panels. This model has three heads for fine, medium and coarse abrasives. (Timesaver, Inc.)

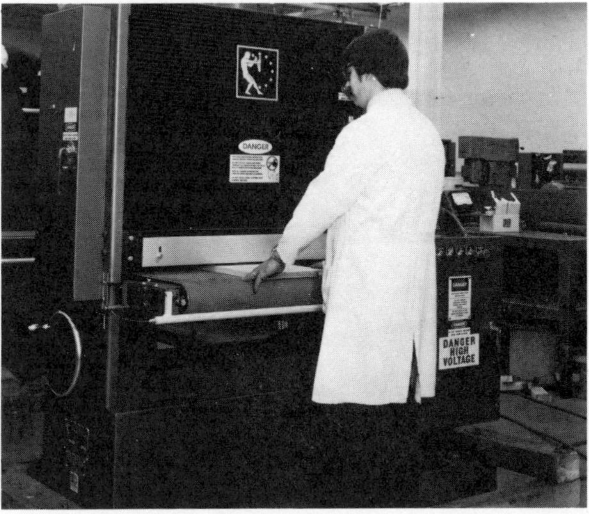

Figure 38-19
This wide belt sander has one head. (Timesaver, Inc.)

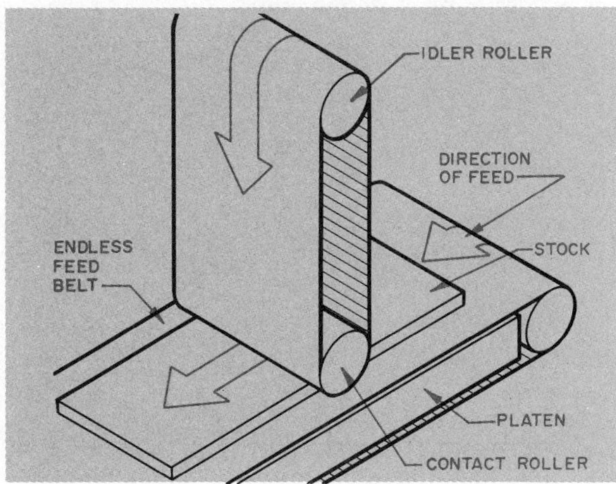

Figure 38-20
The major parts of a wide belt sander.

Figure 38-21
Mounting a belt on a wide belt sander.

Most sanders have adjustable feed rates to control how fast the feed belt turns. The contact roller pushes the belt against the top surface of the stock as it passes over the platen. The idler roller keeps tension on the belt. Set the depth of cut as you would on a knife-type planer. The higher the table, the deeper the cut. Take only light cuts.

The size of the sander is determined by the width of the belt. Sizes vary from 6″ to 106″ (152 to 2692 mm). The larger the size, the wider the stock that can be sanded. Popular sizes are 30″ and 36″ (762 and 940 mm). Belts are easy to change on a wide belt sander, Figure 38-21. Each manufacturer has a different way of mounting belts. Usually, make the first passes through the sander with an 80- or 100-grit belt. These passes remove a great deal of material but leave deep scratch marks. Use finer belts, 150 to 180 grit, for finishing stock. Rub a cleaning stick across the moving belt to remove most of the resin buildup. Finally, it is important to store the belts properly when they are not in use, Figure 38-22.

Figure 38-22
Store belts on a rack when not in use.

STROKE SANDERS

Use a *stroke sander* for sanding flat surfaces, Figure 38-23. This machine requires much skill to operate. An inexperienced operator may sand deep grooves into the surface.

An endless belt removes material with the assistance of a pressure block. A fine belt, usually 120 or 150 grit, is best for the stroke sander. Place the stock on the shuttle table. The table moves back and forth. To bring the abrasive belt in contact with the stock, push the pressure block down against the back side of the moving belt. Keep the block moving at all times to keep the boards level, Figure 38-24. To sand stock that is wider than the sanding belt, move the table in and out as you move the block along the length of the stock. Practice will give you the coordination you need to keep both hands working together.

The stroke sander can do other sanding operations. You can sand internal curves on the open pulley at the end of the sander. You also can sand decorative molding with a custom-made pressure pad. The pad should fit against the molding exactly, Figure 38-25.

EDGE SANDERS

Use an *edge sander* for sanding edges and end grain, Figure 38-26. Mount the endless abrasive belt in the vertical position. Select a fine, 120- or 150-grit belt. Place the stock on the horizontal table. Bring the board against the moving belt. Some edge sanders also have an exposed pulley that can sand large curves.

PNEUMATIC-HEADED SANDERS

A *pneumatic-headed sander* has a rotating, cylindrical air blatter covered with a cloth abrasive sleeve, Figure 38-27. Use it for sanding short, straight edges and inside curves. Inflate the air blatter with a tire-type valve stem to the desired firmness. The more air pressure applied, the harder the tube becomes. A fully inflated head will sand edges perpendicular to the tube. The less air pressure applied, the rounder the finished surface. For rough sanding that removes much material, use 80- or 100-grit abrasive sleeves. For a finished surface, use 120- or 150-grit sleeves.

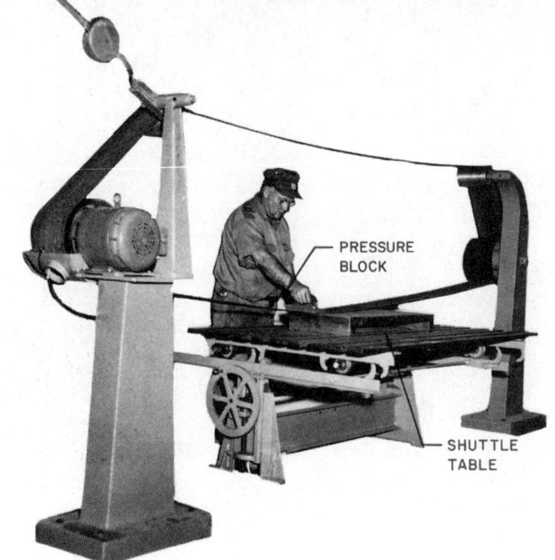

Figure 38-23
Use a stroke sander to sand large, flat surfaces. (Beach Manufacturing Company)

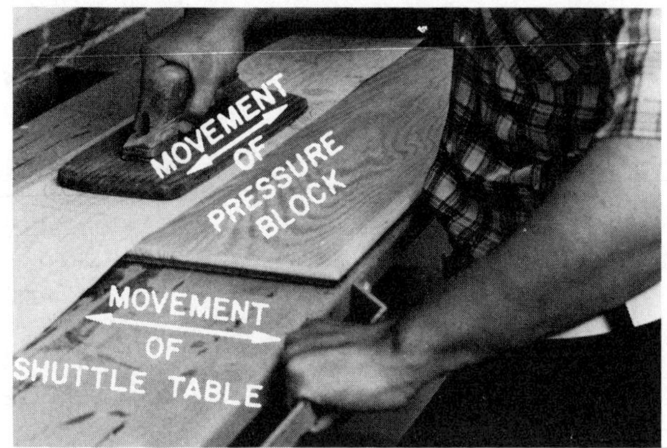

Figure 38-24
Using a pressure block to bring the belt in contact with the work.

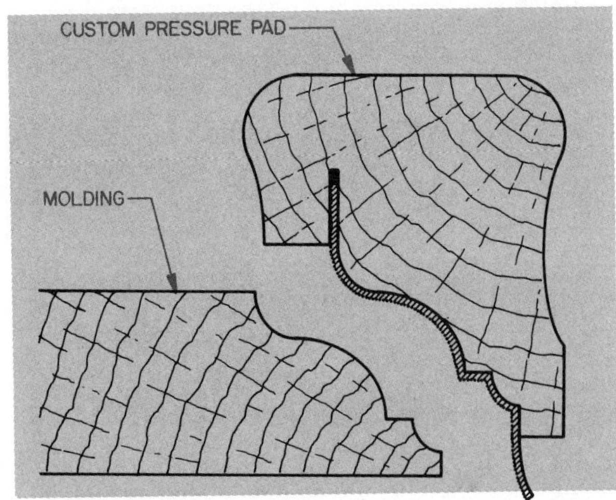

Figure 38-25
Use a custom-made pressure block for sanding decorative molding.

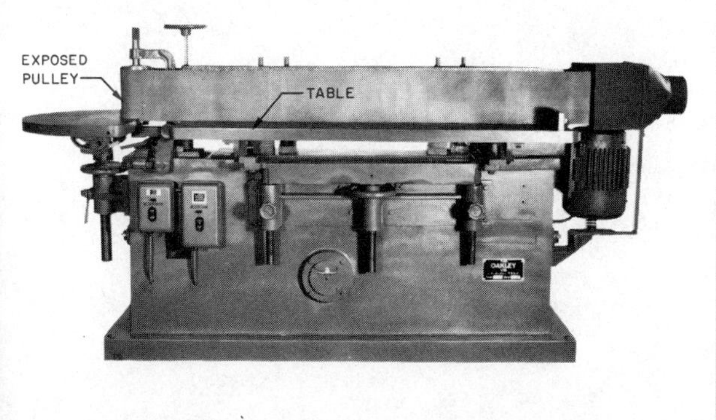

Figure 38-26
Use an edge sander to sand straight stock. You also can use the exposed pulley for sanding curves. (Oakley Company)

Figure 38-27
A pneumatic-headed sander has an abrasive sleeve wrapped around an inflated air blatter. (Ekstrom Carlson & Co.)

REVIEW QUESTIONS

1 What types of surfaces can a disc sander finish?
2 Which side of the sanding disc should you use?
3 What types of surfaces can a spindle sander finish?
4 What is an oscillating spindle sander?
5 A small stationary belt sander has three belt positions. What are these positions?
6 Sketch the major parts of a wide belt sander.
7 How are decorative moldings sanded with a stroke sander?
8 What types of surfaces can an edge sander finish?

SUGGESTED ACTIVITIES

1 Identify the sanding machines in your shop. What size grit is used with each machine?
2 If you cut your name or house number using the pattern in Unit 7, use your sanding machines to smooth the edges.

SECTION

5

Portable Power Tools

39
Portable Circular Saws

40
Reciprocating and Saber Saws

41
Portable Power Planes

42
Routers

43
Portable Drills

44
Portable Sanders

Portable power tools cut like stationary machines, but are easy to move. This is an advantage when stock is too large to be cut on table saws, jointers or other machines. Because they are light in weight, portable power tools are easy to use on the job site and away from the shop. In addition, portable power tools cost less than stationary equipment.

Section 5, Portable Power Tools, will help you develop your tool skills. This section will explain how to use each portable power tool safely and properly.

UNIT

39

Portable Circular Saws

Objectives

After studying this unit you should be able to:

1 Identify the major parts of a circular saw and make basic adjustments.

2 Crosscut and rip stock.

3 Make pocket cuts.

Technical Terms

Worm-gear drive

Four-tooth combination blade

Pocket cut

Panel saw

PORTABLE CIRCULAR SAW SAFETY RULES

1 Unplug the cord when changing blades.

2 Clamp small pieces to a workbench or sawhorse.

3 Hold the saw securely with both hands.

4 Keep your hands outside the 4" (102 mm) safety margin, Figure 39-10.

5 Keep the cord away from the cutting area.

6 Always check to see that the guard is working. Never use a saw without a working guard.

7 Do not reach underneath the stock during cutting.

8 Do not stand directly in the line of the saw.

9 Retract the guard only with the retracting handle.

The portable circular saw, Figure 39-1, is a multipurpose machine that is easy to use. It is used for cutting lumber for houses and other buildings. Because it is portable, it can make many different types of cuts. It often is used in the woodworking shop to make cuts on large pieces of material, Figure 39-2.

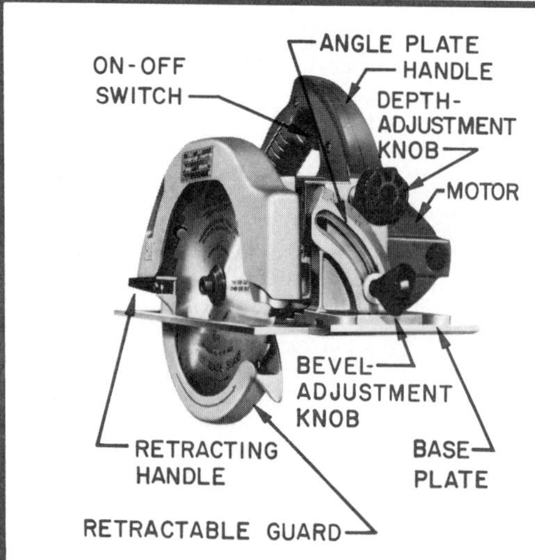

Figure 39-1
Major parts of a portable circular saw. (Milwaukee Electric Tool Corp.)

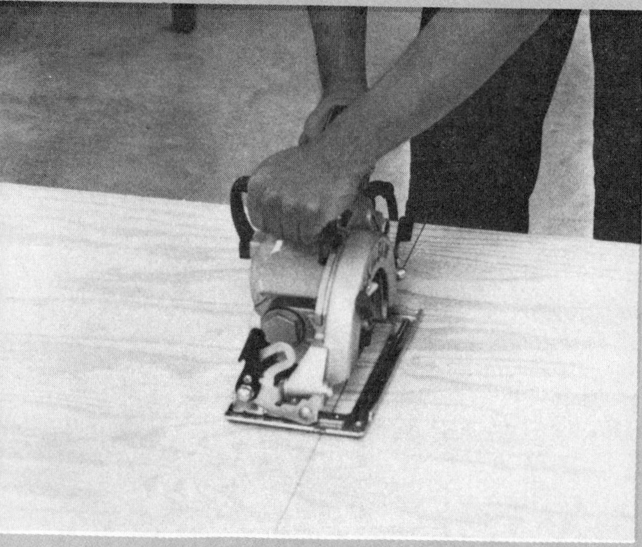

Figure 39-2
A large sheet of plywood is cut easily with a portable circular saw.

PORTABLE CIRCULAR SAW TERMINOLOGY

An electric motor powers the saw, Figure 39-1. Even with large motors, the blade can be pinched in the saw kerf. A friction clutch helps reduce damage to the motor when this occurs. It allows the motor to keep turning while the blade comes to a stop. Heavy saws have *worm-gear drives*, Figure 39-3. This special gear arrangement gives the saw a great deal of power. Worm-gear drive saws frequently are used in heavy construction work.

The handle of the circular saw houses the on-off switch. Control the portable saw with both hands, Figure 39-4. Do not cover the motor vents with your hand. This will stop the flow of air through the motor and cause it to overheat.

Adjust the base plate to set the angle of the blade and the depth of the cut. The bottom of the plate slides on the top surface of the stock. Keep the plate in contact with the stock at all times.

One of the most important parts of the saw is the retractable guard. It covers the portion of the blade that extends below the base plate. The guard is spring-loaded and slides out of the way when cutting stock. You also can move the guard with the retracting handle. The tension on the spring returns the guard to its original position when cutting is completed, Figure 39-5. Never operate the saw unless the guard is working properly.

Two major adjustments should be made on the saw. The depth-adjustment knob raises and lowers the base plate. Adjust the base plate each time you cut a different thickness of material. The bevel-adjustment knob tilts the base plate for cutting bevels and chamfers.

The size of a portable circular saw is determined by the largest-diameter saw blade that can be used on the saw. Portable circular saw sizes range from 4" (102 mm), for cutting wall paneling, to 18" (457 mm), for sawing bridge timbers. The most common saw is 7-1/4" (184 mm). This saw has a cutting depth of 2-1/2" (64 mm). The ampere rating of the motor also may be considered when determining size. The higher the ampere rating, the deeper the cutting capacity of the saw. Most cuts can be made by a saw that has a motor size of 10 amperes.

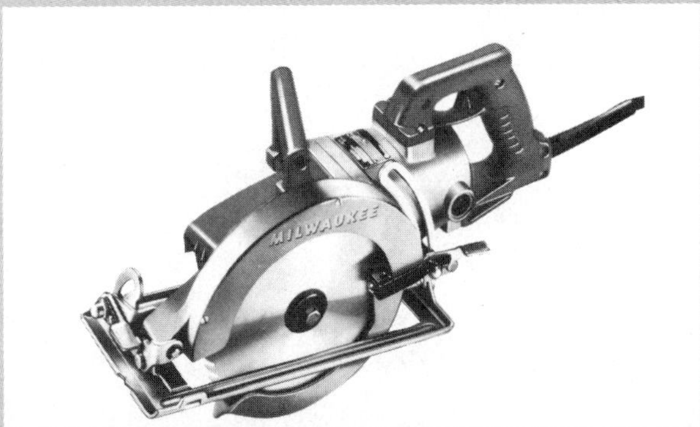

Figure 39-3
Carpenters use worm-drive portable circular saws. (Milwaukee Electric Tool Corp.)

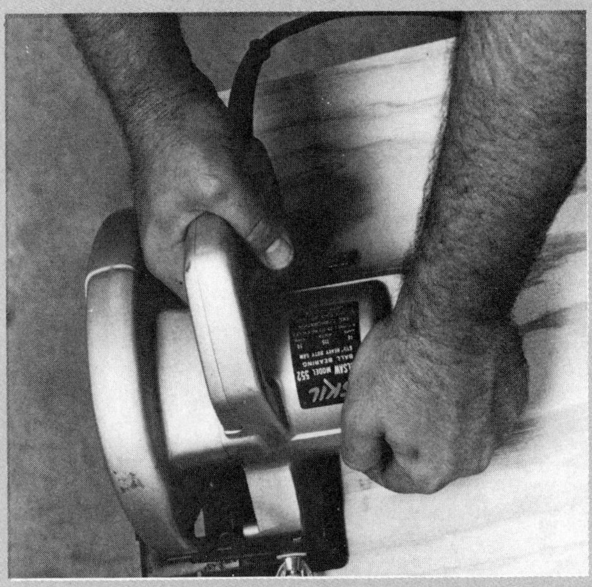

Figure 39-4
Control the saw with both hands and keep them clear of the blade.

Figure 39-5
Immediately after the saw clears the stock, the retractable guard covers the blade.

Figure 39-6
A blade lock secures the saw shaft. Move the wrench as indicated. *Unplug the power cord before attempting this operation.*

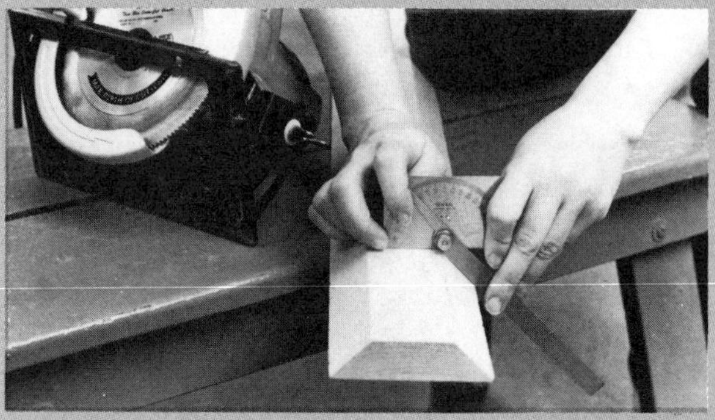

Figure 39-7
Checking a bevel cut with a protractor. Note that the base is tilted.

Figure 39-8
Long boards can be positioned on sawhorses without the use of clamps.

BLADE SELECTION AND INSTALLATION

Like the table saw, the circular saw can use a variety of blades. Use a *four-tooth combination blade* for crosscutting or ripping. You can use a plywood blade to make very fine cuts. Carpenters often use a rough-cut combination blade for framing work. Many portable circular saws now are equipped with carbide-tipped saw blades.

When installing a blade, always unplug the saw. Because the blade is close to the switch, accidents can occur easily. Many portable saws have blade locks to secure the saw shaft, Figure 39-6. If you use a saw without a blade lock, wedge it against a scrap board to keep the blade from turning. To loosen the arbor bolt, move your wrench in the direction the teeth point. Remove the blade and replace it with a new one. The teeth must point in the direction the saw rotates. Some saws have an arrow on the guard to indicate the direction of rotation. Replace the arbor bolt and tighten with a wrench.

CROSSCUTTING

To crosscut a board:

1. Unplug the saw. If the wrong blade is mounted on the saw, change to the correct style. Place the saw on top of the stock and loosen the depth-adjustment knob. Set the depth of the blade 1/8" (3 mm) below the bottom surface of the board.
2. Set the blade at the correct angle. Do not rely entirely on the angle plate on the saw. For accuracy, first set the blade according to the angle plate. Test-cut a piece of scrap at this setting and check it with a square or protractor. Set the protractor to the desired angle and place it on the cut, Figure 39-7. If space appears between the protractor and the board, readjust the angle plate.
3. Place the good face of the material to be cut down. The saw cuts on the upward swing. Any chipping or splinters will occur on the top or back side of the stock.
4. Draw a layout line on the back of the material where the cut is to be made. After clamping the stock down, plug in the saw. Large pieces can lie flat on the saw horses without being clamped, Figure 39-8.

5. Place the base plate on the stock and align the blade with the layout line. Most saws have a notch on the front of the base plate to guide you. The blade is correctly positioned when the side of the notch aligns with the layout line, Figure 39-9. Be certain the blade is not touching the stock.
6. Turn the power on and begin the cut slowly. The retractable guard will move out of the way as the blade cuts into the stock.
7. Support the waste side of the stock with one hand as you near the end of the cut, Figure 39-10. If the waste is twisted and the saw kerf closes, a kickback may occur. Never allow your hands to come within the 4″ (102 mm) safety margin. Waste shorter than 4″ (102 mm) does not need to be supported.
8. Do not lay down the saw until the blade has stopped turning.

RIPPING

Use the same basic procedure to rip stock, with a few exceptions. To rip stock:

1. Unplug the cord.
2. Adjust the saw for correct depth. Adjust the angle of the base plate.
3. Because you rip along the grain, you must hold the stock differently. Use a pair of saw horses. If you are ripping a long board, clamp the stock with one end of the board extending over the end of the saw horse, Figure 39-11. Plug in the cord.
4. Align the blade with the layout line and start the saw. As the blade comes close to

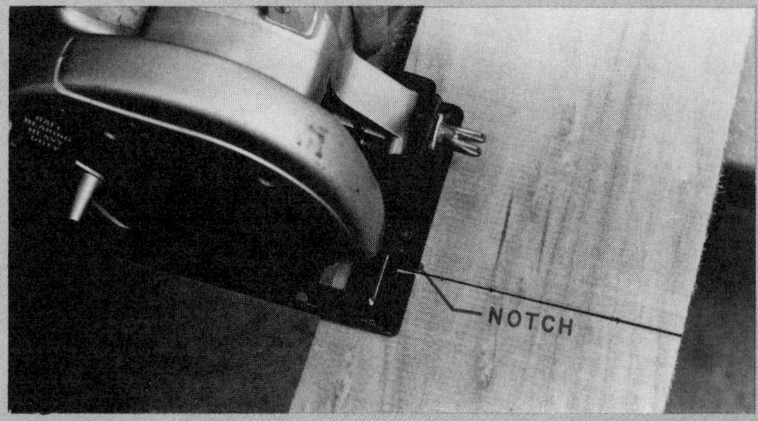

Figure 39-9
Before turning on the power, align the notch in the base plate with the layout line. *The blade must not touch the board before the motor is running.*

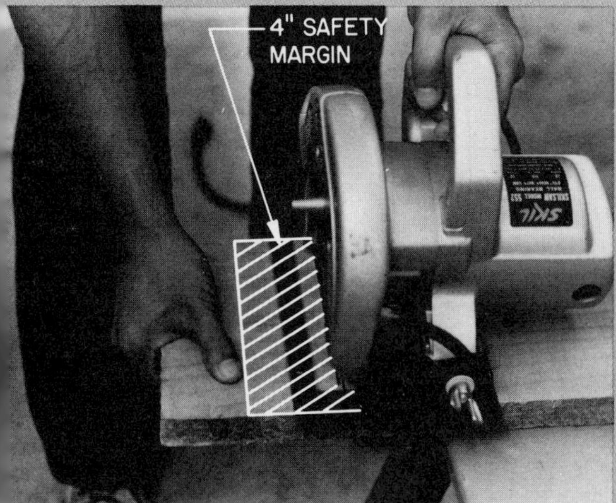

Figure 39-10
Support the waste as the saw nears the end of the cut.

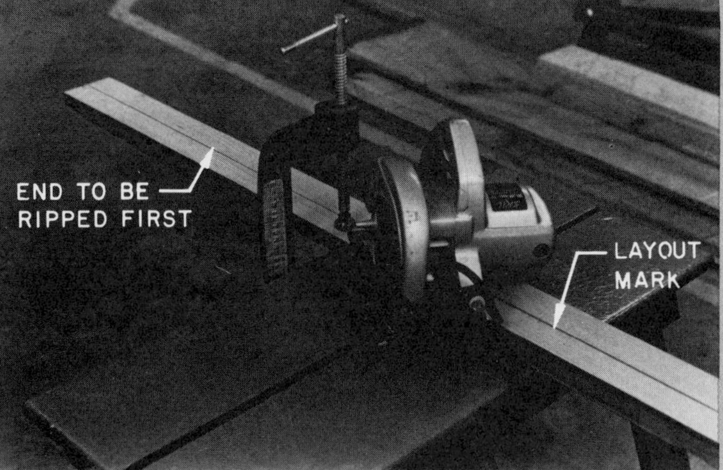

Figure 39-11
Extend the board over the end of the sawhorses for ripping.

Figure 39-12
Clamp one side of the ripped stock to the first sawhorse and continue cutting.

Figure 39-13
An adjustable fence helps you cut a long board.

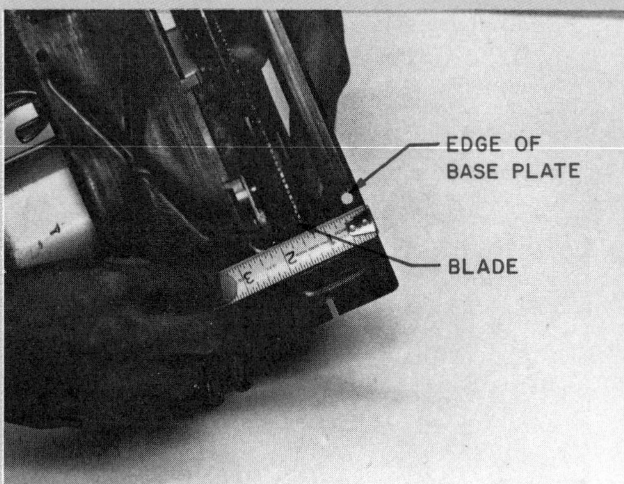

Figure 39-14
Measuring the distance between the blade and the edge of the base plate. *Disconnect the power cord before attempting this operation.*

the first saw horse, stop the saw. Before moving the saw, turn off the power and allow the blade to come to a complete stop.

5. Move the board so the blade can saw between the two saw horses. Before you turn on the power, make sure the blade turns freely in the saw kerf. Turn on the power and saw until the blade reaches the second saw horse, Figure 39-12.
6. Move the board so the uncut end extends over the second saw horse. Finish ripping the remaining portion of the board. If the board pinches the blade, push a small wedge of scrap into the kerf to hold it open.

Many saws have an adjustable fence, Figure 39-13. The fence keeps the blade running parallel with the edge. Layout lines are not necessary with an adjustable fence.

CUTTING PLYWOOD

Plywood must be cut straight and square. A skilled operator can cut material freehand with precision. Beginners may need to use a straight-edge to achieve the same results. To cut plywood:

1. Draw a layout line where the cut is to be made. Measure the distance between the outside of the blade and the edge of the base plate, Figure 39-14.

Figure 39-15
Sliding the base plate along the straightedge.

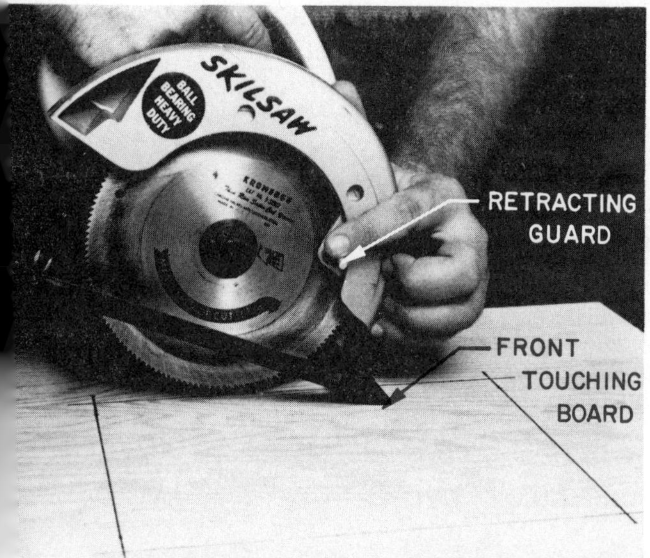

Figure 39-16
Tilt the saw on the front of the base plate. Note the safe position of the hands. *The blade must not touch the board before the motor is running.*

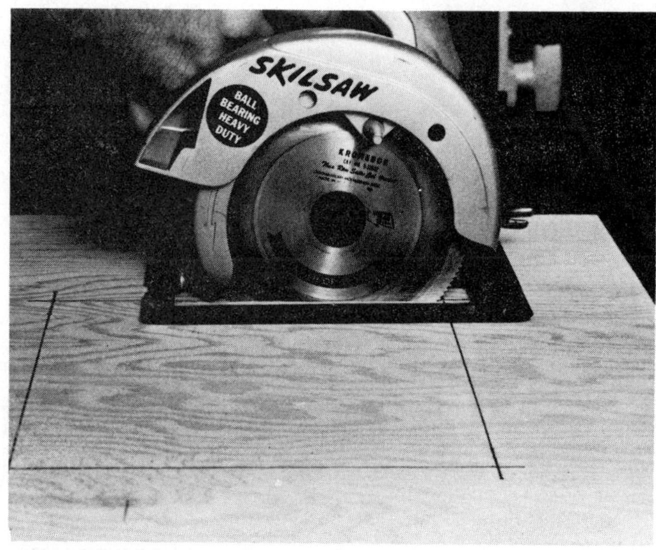

Figure 39-17
Sawing up to the layout line for a pocket cut.

2. Clamp a straightedge on the stock at a distance from the layout line equal to the distance found above.
3. Place the edge of the base plate against the straightedge and begin cutting the plywood. Sliding the base plate along the straightedge produces a straight cut, Figure 39-15.

POCKET CUTS

Pocket cuts are internal holes in stock. They do not begin at an outside edge. To make pocket cuts with a portable circular saw:

1. Mark out the desired shape. Pull the guard out of the way with the retracting handle to expose the blade.
2. Tilt the saw on the front of the base plate, Figure 39-16. Align the blade with the layout line.
3. Pivot the saw further up on the front of the base plate. Make certain the blade is clear of the stock.
4. Turn on the power and slowly lower the rotating blade straight down into the stock. When the plate is flat against the stock, move the saw forward. Stop the saw when the saw kerf is even with the intersecting layout line, Figure 39-17. Do not remove the saw until the blade stops completely.
5. Repeat the process for the other sides. Finish the pocket cut with a hand saw.

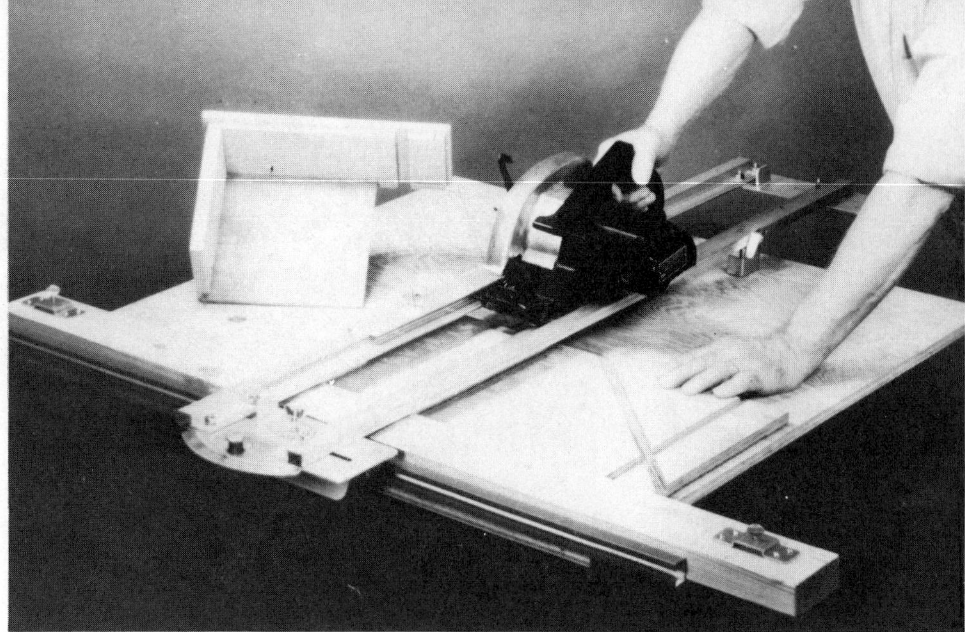

Figure 39-18
Little skill is needed to make straight cuts with a commercial fixture. (Brett-Hauer Co. Inc.)

COMMERCIAL FIXTURES

A commercial fixture helps an unskilled operator make very straight cuts with a portable circular saw, Figure 39-18. Mount the saw on the fixture track and position the stock under it. Simply pull the saw forward, producing the desired cut. You also can make dados with this fixture.

Use a *panel saw* to crosscut or rip large panels of plywood and particle board, Figure 39-19. It is mounted on an inclined table and requires little floor space. For crosscutting, hold the panel in a stationary position and move the saw downward on the track. You can rip by rotating the saw so the blade is parallel to the bottom fence. Lock the saw to the track at the desired distance from the fence. Slide the panel along the fence past the saw blade.

REVIEW QUESTIONS

1 How can you determine the size of a portable circular saw?
2 Where should you place your hands when operating the saw?
3 What is the purpose of the retractable guard?
4 How should you set the angle to the saw blade? How can you check the adjustment for accuracy?
5 How is the saw blade aligned with the layout line?
6 On what should you place stock when ripping long boards?
7 What guide can help you cut plywood accurately?
8 An internal hole cut with a portable circular saw is called a ______ ______.

SUGGESTED ACTIVITIES

1 Inspect your portable circular saw and name all the parts.
2 The next time you cut a plywood panel or crosscut a long board, use the portable circular saw. Ask your instructor for permission first.

UNIT

40

Reciprocating and Saber Saws

Objectives

After studying this unit you should be able to:

1 Identify the major parts of saber and reciprocating saws and make adjustments.
2 Crosscut and rip stock with these saws.
3 Cut curves.
4 Make internal cuts.

Technical Terms

Saber saw
Reciprocating saw
Adjustable rip guide
Internal cut
Plunge cut

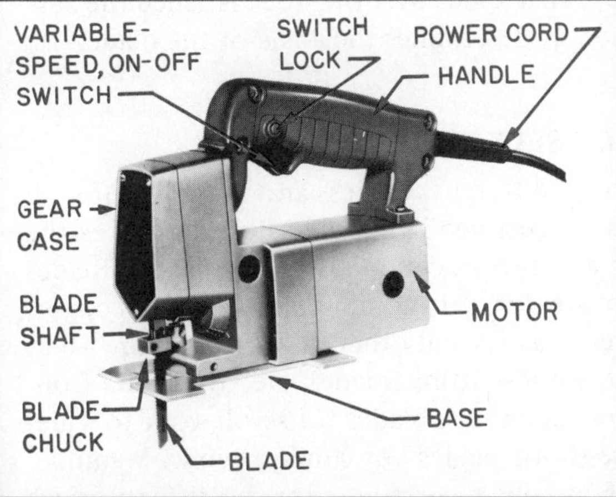

Figure 40-1
Major parts of a saber saw. (Milwaukee Electric Tool Corp.)

RECIPROCATING AND SABER SAWS SAFETY RULES

1 Unplug the cord when installing the blade.
2 Use the correct saw blade for the job.
3 Clamp small stock before cutting.
4 Keep the cord away from the cutting area.
5 Keep hands out of the 4" (102 mm) safety margin, Figure 40-8.
6 Do not make a plunge cut on stock more than 1/4" (6 mm) thick.
7 Hold the saw securely by the handles.
8 Do not reach under the stock during cutting.

A portable tool often selected for cutting curved pieces is the *saber saw,* Figure 40-1. A *reciprocating saw* is similar to the saber saw and can cut curves in heavy materials, Figure 40-2. Both portable saws can do the same work as the stationary scroll and band saws. When using stationary power tools, you are limited to stock that is small enough to feed across the machine table.

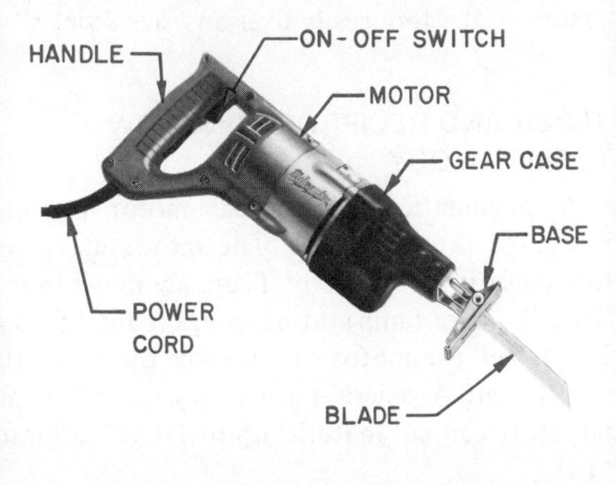

Figure 40-2
Major parts of a reciprocating saw. (Milwaukee Electric Tool Corp.)

RECIPROCATING SAW BLADES	Blade Type	Length	Teeth per Inch	Applications
CARBIDE-TIPPED				
	Carbide-Tipped	4"	6	For cutting fiberglass and similar materials and all types of wood. Tooth configuration provides rapid cutting for production use.
	Carbide-Tipped	6"	6	
ALL-PURPOSE WOOD AND COMPOSITION CUTTING				
	General Purpose	6" 12"	7 7	For general roughing-in work. Resists embedded nails. Also cuts heavy gauge non-ferrous metal tubing. Ideal for tree pruning.
	Skip Tooth, Fast Wood Cutting	6" 12"	3 3	More efficiently cuts up to ¾" thick plywood, plastics, has extra space for chip clearance.
	Deluxe Fast Cutting Wood	6"	6	For fast roughing-in work in wood without nails. Long blade life.
	Flexible-Back Wood and Composition	6" 12"	6 6	For cutting wood without nails, plaster, asphalt, builders "Transite" and cast aluminum. For inaccessible flush cuts in wood, use 12" blade.
	Nail-Embedded Wood Cutting	4" 6"	10 10	For cutting nail-embedded wood, asbestos, plaster, plywood and insulating wood.
	Down Cutting	6"	10	For down-cutting in wood with nails where smooth edges are desired.
	Fine Wood Cutting	4" 6"	18 18	Especially useful for opening wood boxes and crates with nails. Removing wood siding and shingles.
	Pocket Cutting	4 3/32"	6	For making pocket cuts in wood, plaster and similar materials.
	Double Edge	4 5/16"	6	For making pocket cuts in wood, plaster and similar materials. Cuts in both directions without removing blade from material—an EXCLUSIVE B&D feature.
	Offset Flush Double Edge	4¼"	6	For making flush cuts in corners and other tight spots in wood, plaster and similar materials.
	Plaster Cutting Blade	6" 4¼"	5 5	For cutting plaster, plasterboard, and other abrasive materials.
SCROLL CUTTING WOOD AND COMPOSITION				
	Fast Cutting Scroll	3⅝"	6	High-speed steel blades give long blade life. For fast cutting small radius holes and irregular cuts in wood, plaster and similar materials.
	Wood & Composition Scroll Cutting	3⅝"	6	For cutting small radius holes and irregular cuts in wood, plaster and similar materials.

When using the saber or reciprocating saw, you can move the tool easily over any size stock.

SABER AND RECIPROCATING SAW TERMINOLOGY

A pneumatic or electrical motor provides power to the saw blade. The motor makes up the majority of the body. There are many motor sizes. Ampere (amp) ratings range from 2.5 to 4. The larger the motor, the thicker the stock the saw can cut. A general-purpose saw has a 3.5 amp rating. It can cut material up to 1-1/2" (38 mm) thick.

The gear case changes the circular motion of the motor to the up-and-down action of the blade. The blade chuck holds the blade. The metal plate that slides over the stock is called the base or shoe. It determines the angle of the blade.

BLADE SELECTION

Many different blades are available for all types of cutting. This wide selection makes the saber and reciprocating saws very useful. Blades are made for cutting aluminum, brass, copper, leather, plastics and other materials, Figure 40-3. Many wood-cutting blades are available, from narrow, fine-tooth blades for scroll work to wide, coarse-tooth blades for lumber work. Manufacturers usually suggest uses for the different saws they make. Although most blades will fit many brands of saws, some blades can be used only with certain models.

SABER SAW BLADES	Blade Type	Length (in.)	Teeth per Inch	Applications
CARBIDE-TIPPED				
	Carbide-Tipped	3″	6	For cutting fiberglass and similar materials and all types of wood. Tooth configuration provides rapid cutting for production use.
HIGH-SPEED METAL CUTTING				
	Coarse-Set Tooth, Metal Cutting	3″	14	Cuts steel—16 gauge to 10 gauge. Cuts 3/32″ to 3/16″ aluminum, copper, brass. Cuts plastics, asbestos, Fiberglas, etc. ½″ to ¾″ rigid conduit, 1/0 stranded cable and 3/16″ buss bar.
	Coarse-Set Tooth, Metal Cutting	3″	18	Cuts ferrous metals from ⅛″ to ¼″ thick; non-ferrous (aluminum, copper, brass, etc.) from 1/16″ to ⅛″; will cut pipe and tubing from 3/64″ to ⅛″ wall thickness.
	Medium-Set Tooth, Metal Cutting	3″	24	Cuts ferrous metals from 1/16″ to 3/16″ thick; Non-ferrous metals under 1/16″ thick. Suitable for pipe and tubing under 3/64″ wall thickness.
	Fine-Set Tooth, Metal Cutting	3″	32	Cuts steel—22 gauge to 13 gauge. For cuts under 3/32″ in aluminum, copper, brass. Cuts plastics, slate, formica, Fiberglas. Also ½″ to ¾″ thin-wall conduit.
ALL-PURPOSE WOOD AND COMPOSITION CUTTING				
	Hollow-Ground, Fine-Tooth, Wood-Cutting	3″	10	Deluxe series for faster, smooth scroll cuts in wood up to ¾″ thick. Precision-hollow-ground. Excellent for pocket cutting.
	Hollow-Ground, Medium-Tooth, Wood-Cutting	3″	7	Deluxe series for faster, smooth scroll cuts in wood up to ¾″ thick. Precision-hollow-ground. Excellent for pocket cutting.
	Hollow-Ground, Coarse-Tooth, Wood-Cutting	3″	5	Deluxe series for faster, smooth scroll cuts in wood up to ¾″ thick. Precision-hollow-ground. Excellent for pocket cutting.
	Knife Punch Blade	1″		Especially useful to signmakers for scroll cutting all types of paperboard materials. Excellent for making intricate pocket cuts in vinyl floor tiles for inlay work.
	Knife Edge Blade	3″		For smooth, fast cuts in leather, rubber, cork and other composition materials.
	Fine-Tooth, Hi-Speed Steel, Hollow-Ground, Wood-Cutting	4	10	For fine finish scroll cutting in wood, plywood, Masonite, plastics etc. Also for ⅛″ to ½″ soft aluminum, brass. Maximum cut in wood—3″ thick.
	Coarse-Tooth (Narrow) Hi-Speed Steel, Hollow-Ground, Wood-Cutting	4	6	For faster scroll cutting in wood, plywood, Masonite, etc. Maximum cut—3″ thick.
	Coarse-Tooth (Wide), Hi-Speed Steel, Hollow-Ground, Wood-Cutting	4	6	For fast "production" cutting. Handles wood and plywood up to 3″ thick. Also cuts Masonite. Stays sharp longer. Saws through a 2 x 4 at 45°.
	Fine-Set Tooth, Hi-Speed Steel, Wood-Cutting	4″	10	For scroll cutting in wood, plywood, Masonite, plastics, etc. Maximum cut in wood—2″. Set tooth designed for excellent side-cutting action.
	Coarse-Tooth, Plaster-Cutting	3⅝″	9	For coarse, fast cuts in plaster, plasterboard and other highly abrasive materials.
	Coarse-Set Tooth, Hi-Speed Steel, Wood-Cutting	4″	6	Set tooth designed for excellent side-cutting action.
	Coarse-Tooth, Wood-Cutting	3″	7	Makes fast cuts in wood, plywood, composition boards, etc.
	Fine-Tooth, Wood-Cutting	3″	10	For smoother cuts in wood, plywood, composition boards, etc.
	Coarse-Tooth Hollow-Ground	3″	7	For fast, very smooth cuts in wood, plywood, composition boards, etc.
	Flush Coarse, Wood-Cutting	3″	7	Very accurate flush cuts in corners and other tight spots permitted by projecting cutting area. Cannot be used with No. 3155.
	Double-Edge Coarse, Wood-Cutting	3″	7	Makes fast pocket cuts up to ¾″ thick in wood, composition boards, etc. Exclusive: cuts forward and backward. Cannot be used with No. 3155.
	Double-Edge Fine, Wood-Cutting	3″	10	
	Scroll Fine, Wood-Cutting	2½″	10	Makes intricate cuts, as small as ⅛″ radius, up to ½″ in wood, plastics, etc.
	Skip-Tooth, Wood-Cutting	3″	5	More efficiently cuts up to ¾″ thick plywood, plastics, etc. due to extra space for chip clearance.
	Coarse-Tooth, Wood-Cutting	6″	4	For coarse cuts in wood over 2″ thick. Also suitable for plastics and composition boards.
	Medium-Tooth, Wood-Cutting	6″	7	For smoother cuts in wood over 2″ thick.

Figure 40-3

Blade selection charts for saber and reciprocating saws. (Black & Decker Manufacturing Co.)

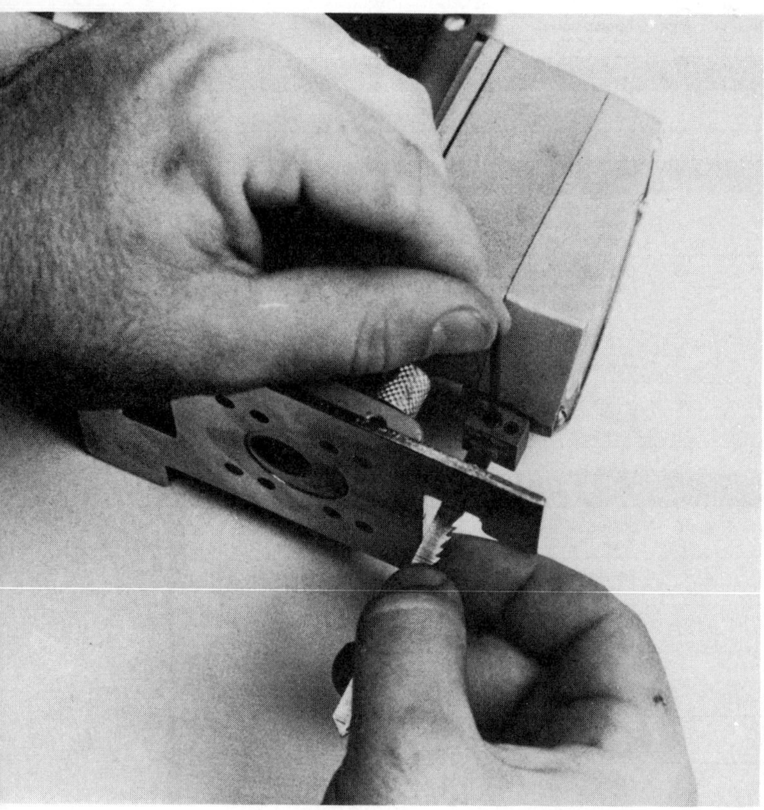

Figure 40-4
Using an allen wrench to secure the blade. *Disconnect power before attempting this operation.*

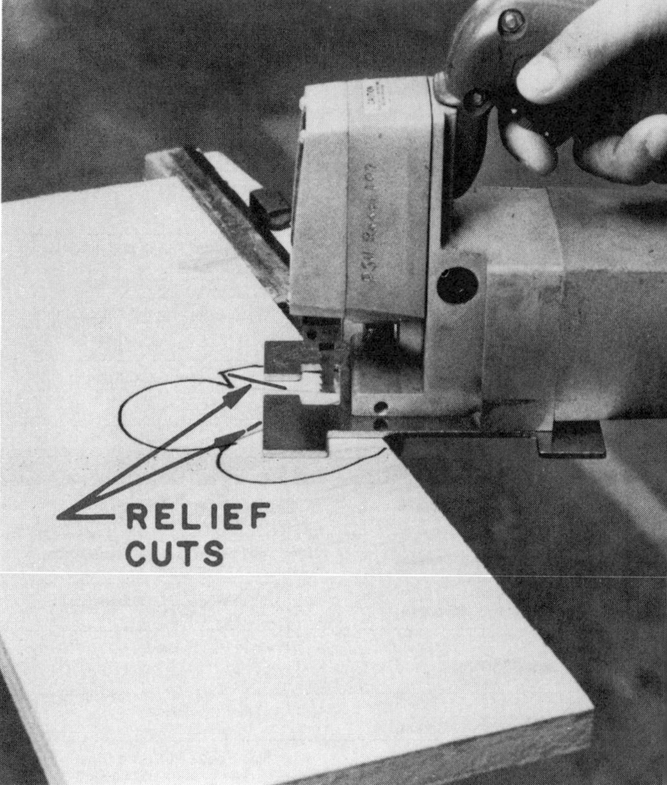

Figure 40-5
Make relief cuts before cutting small curves.

USING A SABER SAW

A saber saw is easy to use. Always follow the safety rules. To use the saber saw:

1. Unplug the cord. Select the proper blade. Insert the blade in the chuck with the teeth facing forward and down. There are several ways of tightening the chuck, depending on the model. Some saws require the use of a screwdriver while others need an Allen wrench, Figure 40-4.
2. Secure the stock with a clamp or bench vise. The up-and-down motion of the blade will cause small pieces of stock to vibrate as they are being cut. Because the blade goes through the board completely, do not place anything immediately below the layout line. You may need to cut a portion of the board, move it and reclamp the stock, so you do not cut into the top of the workbench. Because the saw cuts on the upward stroke, more chipping will occur on the top side of the board. When cutting paneling, plywood or other easily-chipped materials, place the best side down.
3. Lay out the pattern to be cut and plan the cutting procedure. Make relief cuts when cutting small curves, Figure 40-5.
4. Hold the handle of the saw with your right hand. Hold the stock on the saw with your left hand. Do not place your hands within 4″ (102 mm) of the blade. When the base is flat on the stock, turn the power on. Make sure the blade is not touching the board when the motor starts. Apply light, forward pressure to begin sawing. Pushing the saw too hard will break the blade. Keep the base against the stock at all times. Continue until the cut is complete.

Figure 40-6
Use both hands to control the reciprocating saw. Here, metal conduit is being sawed with a metal-cutting blade. (Rockwell International)

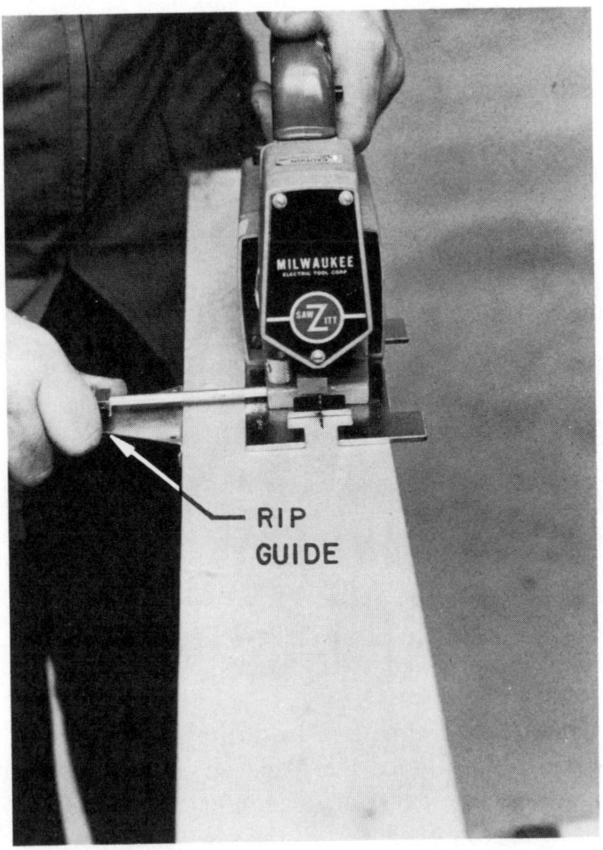

Figure 40-7
No layout line is required when a rip guide is used.

USING A RECIPROCATING SAW

Operation of the reciprocating saw is similar to the saber saw. Follow the same safety and setup procedure. Because the reciprocating saw is large, hold it with both hands, Figure 40-6. Many blades are coarse and may make the saw jump. Apply light, downward pressure to prevent this.

GUIDING METHODS

The most common method of guiding saber and reciprocating saws is to use freehand techniques. Even crosscutting and ripping can be done freehand. Use an *adjustable rip guide* to rip unusually long boards and to crosscut many short boards, Figure 40-7.

To make a bevel, adjust the base to the desired angle. Check the angle by cutting a piece of scrap and measuring the cut with a protractor. Guide the saw freehand or with a fence, Figure 40-8.

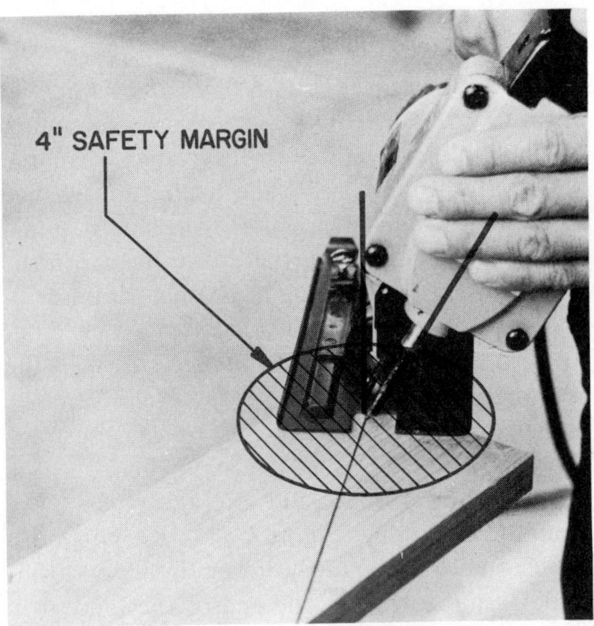

Figure 40-8
A bevel cut is made with the blade in the tilted position.

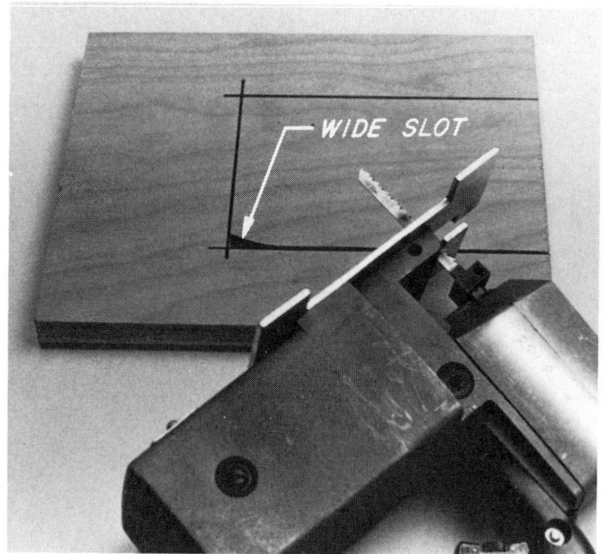

Figure 40-9
A wide slot lets you turn the saw around a corner.

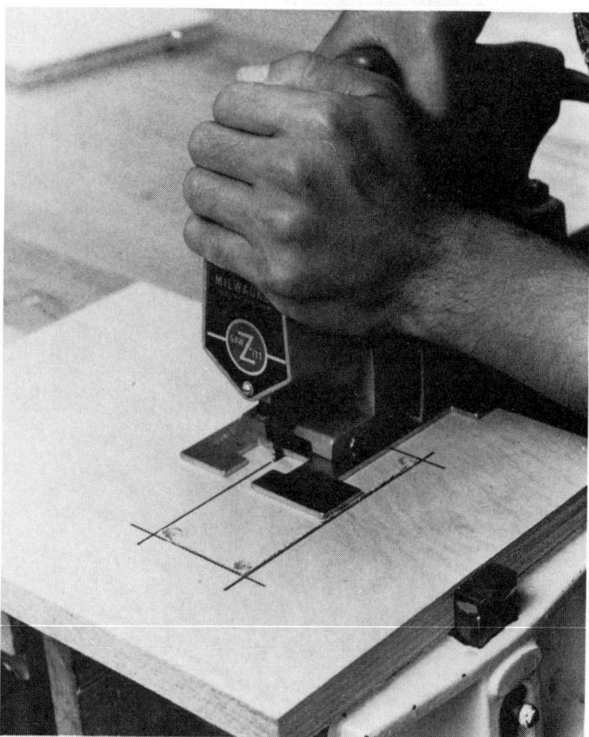

Figure 40-10
Making an internal cut.

Use the slot method to turn a square corner, Figure 40-9. Place the blade on the layout line and start the cut. Cut to an intersecting line and back up the blade. Bring the saw forward again, but cut to the side of the previous saw kerf. Repeat this procedure until you make a wide slot. Turn the blade and cut around the corner.

INTERNAL CUTTING

One way to make an *internal cut* or a pocket cut is to drill a hole in each corner. The diameter of the hole should be slightly larger than the width of the blade. Slip the blade through one of the holes and start to cut, Figure 40-10. When the blade comes to a corner, turn the saw in the hole and continue cutting in another direction.

You can make internal cuts in stock 1/4" (6 mm) and thinner with a *plunge cut*. Tilt the saw upon the front of the base. Make sure the blade is clear of the stock. The blade must not touch the stock as you adjust it. Turn on the power. Lower the blade into the stock away from the layout line, Figure 40-11. Keeping both hands on the saw, slowly lower the base until it is flat on the stock. The end of the blade will cut through the material. Figure 40-12 shows how to make a plunge cut with a reciprocating saw.

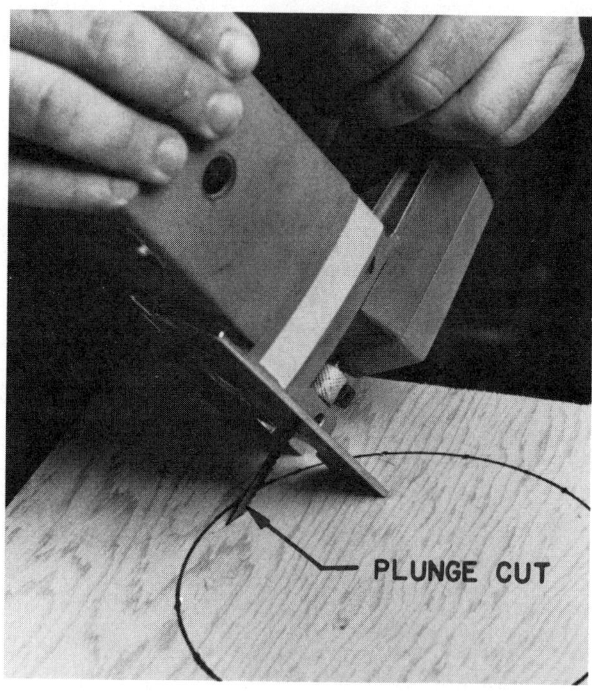

Figure 40-11
Start a plunge cut away from the layout line. *The blade must not touch the board before the motor is running.*

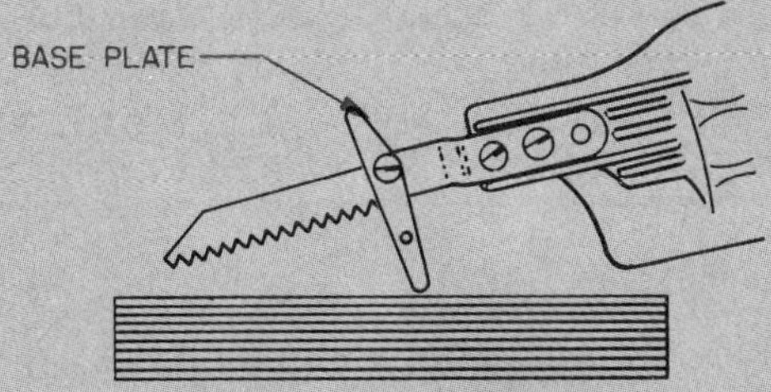
BASE PLATE
1. PIVOT SAW BACK ON ITS BASE PLATE.

2. TURN ON POWER AND SLOWLY ROCK BLADE INTO STOCK.

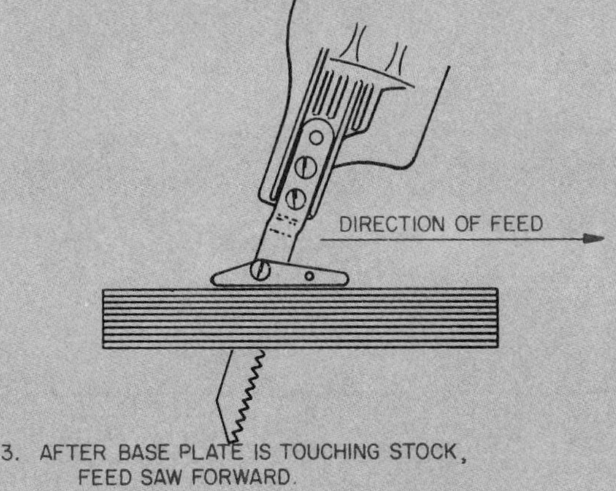
DIRECTION OF FEED
3. AFTER BASE PLATE IS TOUCHING STOCK, FEED SAW FORWARD.

Figure 40-12
Steps in making a plunge cut with a reciprocating saw.

REVIEW QUESTIONS

1 What is the major advantage of saber and reciprocating saws over scroll and band saws?
2 How close can your hands come to the blade?
3 What are relief cuts used for?
4 How can you stop the jumping action of a reciprocating saw?
5 When should you use an adjustable rip guide?
6 What is one way to cut a square corner?
7 What is one way to make an internal cut?

SUGGESTED ACTIVITIES

1 Inspect your saber and reciprocating saws and name the major parts.
2 With a saber or reciprocating saw, cut out the year your class will graduate. Mount it on a board.

CLASS OF
1988

UNIT

41

Portable Power Planes

Objectives

After studying this unit you should be able to:

1 Identify major parts of a portable power plane and make its basic adjustments.

2 Plane edges at a 90° angle.

3 Make bevels and chamfers.

Technical Terms

Bed

Spiral cutter

Chip deflector

Motor-ampere rating

PORTABLE PLANE SAFETY RULES

1 Unplug the cord when changing cutters.

2 Clamp down small pieces to a workbench or sawhorse.

3 Hold the plane securely with the handle and motor housing.

4 Keep the cord away from the cutting area.

5 Never reach underneath the stock to support it.

6 Remove a maximum of 1/16″ (2 mm) with each pass.

7 Keep hands beyond the 4″ (102 mm) safety margin. Refer to Figure 41-5.

8 Leave the plane on the stock until the cutter has stopped turning.

A portable power plane, Figure 41-1, is used for many planing operations. It makes cuts similar to those made by a jointer or hand plane. But the portable power plane is used primarily for planing the edges of boards.

The portable plane is small and light. It moves easily over the top of the stock. As a result, it is easier to smooth the edges of large pieces with

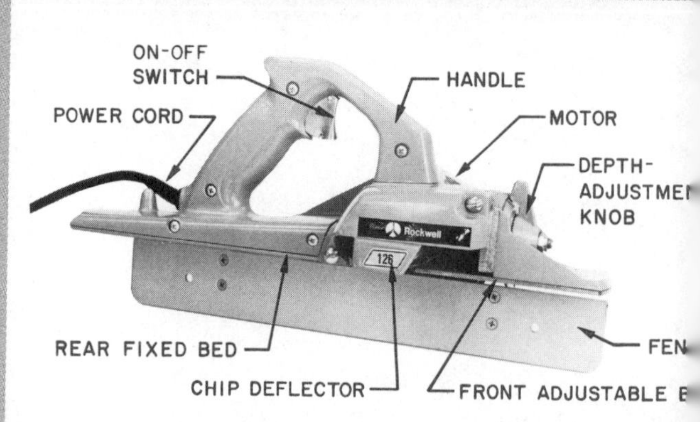

Figure 41-1
Major parts of a portable power plane. (Rockwell International)

a portable power plane than with a jointer. Carpenters often use a portable power plane for trimming large doors, Figure 41-2.

PORTABLE POWER PLANE TERMINOLOGY

The *bed* (bottom) of the plane rests on the stock to be smoothed. The bed has two sections, the front adjustable bed and the rear fixed bed, Figure 41-1. The front adjustable bed is set at the desired depth of cut by a depth-adjustment knob. After the plane's *spiral cutter* has cut the stock to the desired depth, the rear fixed bed supports the machine on the edge of the stock.

Both sections of the bed are attached to a fence. The normal position of the fence is 90° to the bed. But the fence adjusts to angles ranging from 45° to 90°. This feature allows the plane to cut chamfers and bevels, Figure 41-3. When planing the face of narrow stock, the fence moves along the side of the board, Figure 41-4. The portable power plane also has a *chip deflector.* It catches pieces of stock that have been cut.

The size of the portable power plane is determined by the *motor-ampere rating* and the length of the bed. Small machines have a 2.5-ampere motor with a 7-1/2" (191 mm) long bed. Commercial models have motors up to 10 amperes and an 18" (457 mm) bed. These planes are designed for working large stock.

OPERATION OF A PORTABLE PLANE

To operate a portable power plane:

1. Unplug the cord before making any adjustments. Adjust the front bed for the depth of cut. Large models may cut up to 1/16" (2 mm) with one pass. Small planes should be set to cut no more than 1/64" (0.5 mm). If you want a cut deeper than the maximum allowable depth, make more than one pass.
2. Check the angle between the fence and the bed with a square, if the fence is to be used. Clamp the stock to a workbench or sawhorse to prevent the board from moving when the machine passes over the stock. Make sure that clamps or the vise on the bench are not in the way of the plane.
3. Plug in the plane and place the front part of the bed on the stock. Arrange the cord

Figure 41-2
A portable plane easily planes the edge of a large door.

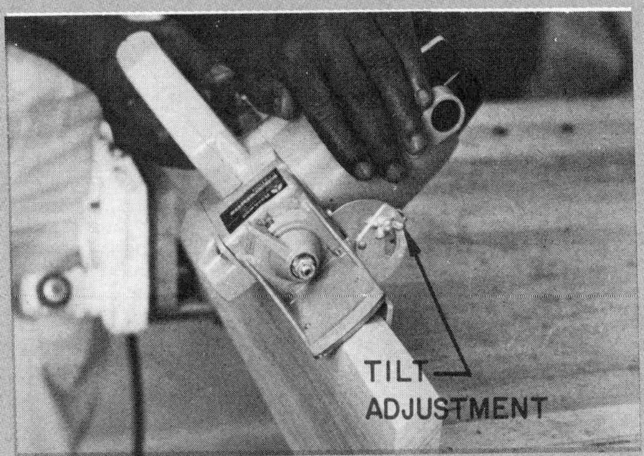

Figure 41-3
By tilting the fence, a bevel or chamfer can be shaped.

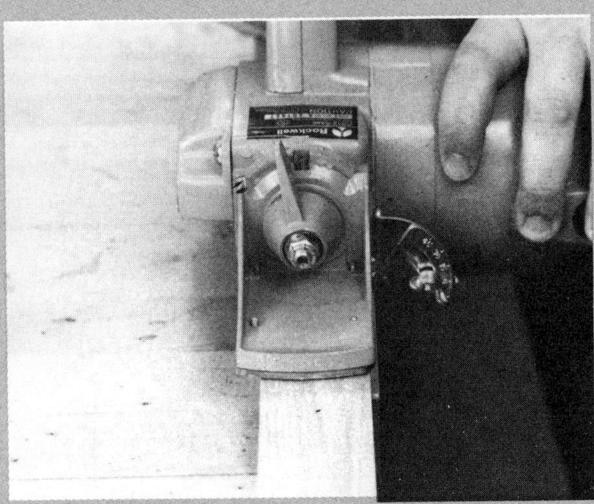

Figure 41-4
The face of narrow stock can be planed.

so it will not come in contact with the cutter. For your protection, hold the plane handle with your right hand, Figure 41-5. Steady the plane further by holding the motor housing with your left hand. Do not block the motor's vents. If the vents are blocked, the motor will overheat.

4. Keep the cutter away from the board as you prepare to operate the plane. Then press the switch and let the motor reach full speed. Next, guide the machine over the stock. Move the plane at a speed that allows it to cut cleanly. If it is pushed too fast, the plane will make mill marks. If it is pushed too slowly, the cutter may burn the wood. As long as you hold in the switch, the cutter will turn. When the switch is released, the cutter will coast to a stop. Keep the fence against the side of the stock to assure an accurate cut, Figure 41-6.

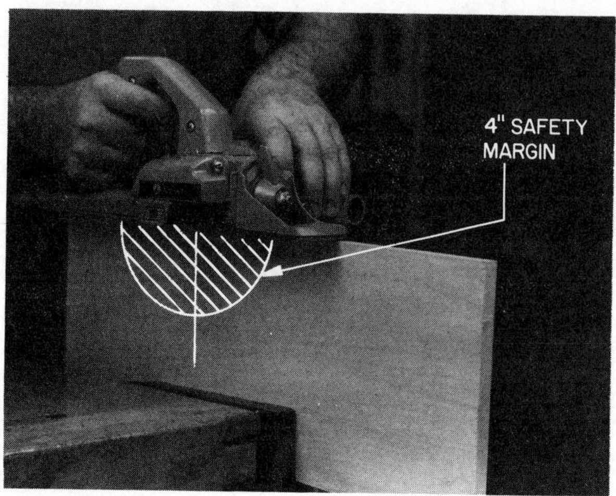

Figure 41-5
Hold the plane by the handle and motor housing.

5. Wait for the cutter to stop before taking the plane from the stock at the end of the cut. Put down the plane only after the cutter has stopped.

A carbide cutter may be installed on the portable power plane to cut hard abrasive materials, Figure 41-7. Carpenters frequently use this auxiliary cutter on hardboard, particle board and plastic laminates.

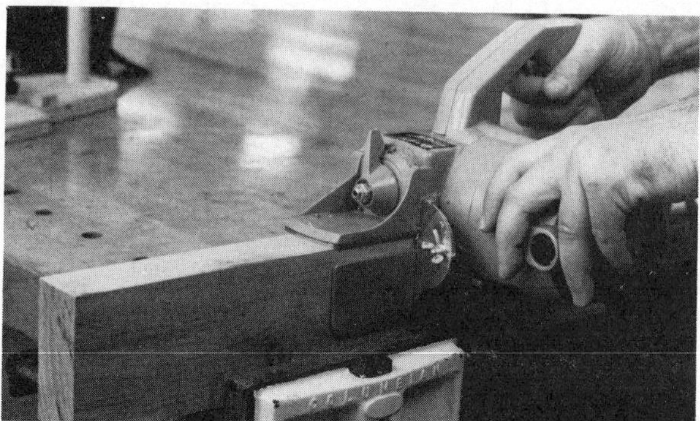

Figure 41-6
Keep the fence against the stock at all times.

Figure 41-7
A carbide cutter allows the planing of particle board.

REVIEW QUESTIONS

1 What advantages do portable power planes have over jointers?
2 How should you hold the plane for safe operation?
3 How is the size of a plane determined?
4 Why should you clamp the stock before planing it?
5 What type of cutter is recommended for planing hardboard, particle board and plastic laminates?

SUGGESTED ACTIVITIES

1 Inspect your portable power plane and name all the parts.
2 Select a long board from your scrap rack and practice planing a straight edge, a bevel and a chamfer.

UNIT

42

Routers

Objectives

After studying this unit you should be able to:

1 Identify the major parts of routers and understand basic adjustments.
2 Know the primary router bits and how they are installed.
3 Make decorative and joinery cuts on the portable router and pin router.
4 Construct fixtures for the portable router and pin router.

Technical Terms

Portable router
Pin router
Panel router
Numerically controlled router
Pilot
Commercial straight guide
Dovetail fixture
Dovetailer
Pin router fixture

PORTABLE ROUTER SAFETY RULES

1 Unplug the cord when changing bits.
2 Clamp down small pieces to a workbench.
3 Hold the router securely by both handles.
4 Never reach underneath the stock to support it.
5 Take only light cuts to prevent overloading the machine.
6 Move the router in a counterclockwise direction when making a cut.
7 Do not rest the router against your body.

PIN ROUTER SAFETY RULES

1 Disconnect the power when changing router bits.
2 Move the guard into place before turning on the power.
3 Always lower the table to the bottommost position before lowering the bit for the first time.
4 Feed stock against the rotation of the cutter.
5 Keep your hands at least 4" (102 mm) away from the router bit.

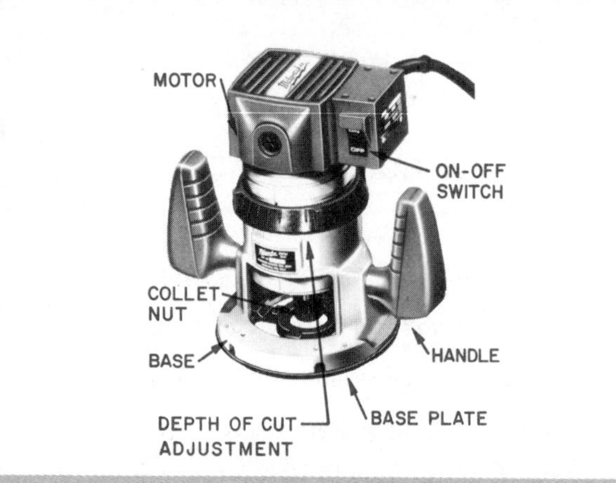

Figure 42-1
Major parts of the portable router. (Milwaukee Electric Tool Corp.)

Figure 42-2
A pin router is used to make heavy cuts. (Danly Machine Corporation and Onsrud Corporation)

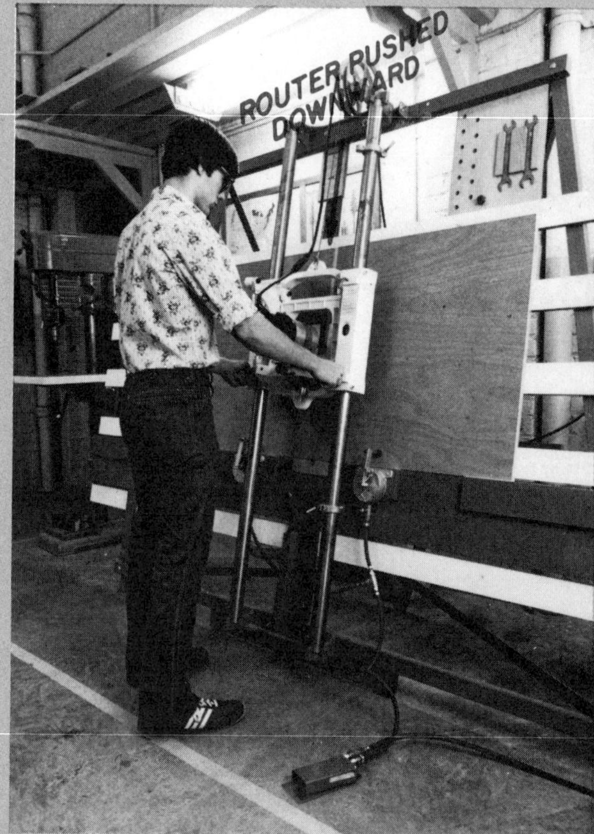

Figure 42-3
A panel router makes vertical cuts with the stock clamped to the inclined table.

Figure 42-4
Sliding the stock along the panel router fence produces horizontal cuts.

The *portable router,* Figure 42-1, is one of the most useful woodworking machines. It is used to shape joints and make decorative cuts. The cuts are of a high quality and require little sanding.

The portable router will be emphasized in this unit. Industry, however, often uses stationary routers. The *pin router* is a popular stationary router, Figure 42-2. It is very useful for making

Figure 42-5
A punched paper tape controls the movement of the router.

Figure 42-6
Routers are available in many sizes and styles.

grooves and cutting out irregular shapes. A pin mounted in the table serves as a guide. A template runs against the pin to shape pieces to size. Stock also may be run against the fence.

A *panel router* is a stationary device to which a portable router is attached, Figure 42-3. Stock usually is clamped to the table and the router is moved across the stock. For horizontal cuts the router can be locked in a stationary position and the stock slid across the fence, Figure 42-4. Because the router is mounted on a vertical track it makes straight cuts. These machines are used primarily for making dadoes and rabbets but can make other decorative designs.

A *numerically controlled router,* or N.C. router, is a stationary router guided by a coded paper tape. Code holes are punched in the tape to control the movement of the cutting tool, Figure 42-5. The hole pattern in the tape raises and lowers the router bit and moves the table. The N.C. router is used in mass production jobs, including furniture manufacturing.

PORTABLE ROUTER

The portable router is a very simple machine. It can be broken down into two major components. The power unit is the motor that holds the bit. The base controls the depth of cut and slides along the surface being routed, Figure 42-1.

Router motors are available in many sizes and cutting speeds, Figure 42-6. Size is indicated by the horsepower (hp) rating. Motors range from 1/4 to more than 5 hp. Speeds range from 15,000 to 30,000 rpm. You use the small routers for light cuts, such as trimming plastic laminates or inlay work. You use large routers to make large dadoes and cuts that remove a lot of material. A good general-purpose size for most projects is 1 hp.

The threaded shaft of the motor extends beyond the bottom of the motor housing. The inside of the shaft tapers toward the top. A split sleeve, called a collet, is inserted into the shaft. The collet fits over the shank of the bit and secures it in the motor unit when the collet nut is tightened. Collets can be purchased in 1/4″, 3/8″ and 1/2″ sizes to fit various sizes of router bit shank diameters.

You adjust the depth of cut of the router bit by moving the base unit up or down within the

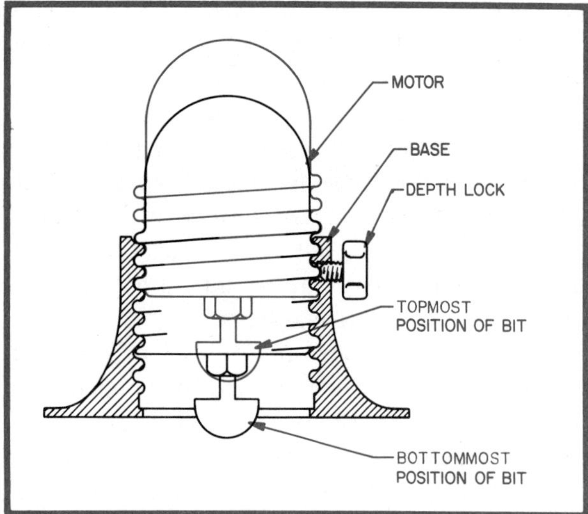

Figure 42-7
Regulate the depth by sliding the motor up and down within the base.

motor housing, Figure 42-7. A locking device on the base secures the motor in position.

Router Bits

The router can make many different cuts because of the great variety of router bits available. In addition, most of the bits can be purchased in several sizes.

There are three main parts to a router bit. These are the shank, cutting edge and *pilot,* Figure 42-8. Not all router bits have a pilot. Bits are available with 1/4", 3/8" and 1/2" diameter shanks. The most common size for portable routers is 1/4". The desired pattern is ground into the cutting edge. Most router bits are manufactured with the shank and cutting edge as one piece. Others are available that are made as individual pieces that can be interchanged to make different setups. The pilot is located on the bottom of the cutting edge. The pilot controls the horizontal depth of the cutter. Either a solid or a ball-bearing pilot can be used. The ball bearing has advantages over the solid type–it will not burn the wood as the bit rotates at fast speed.

Router bits are made from two types of metals, carbon steel and carbide. Most styles can be purchased in either material. Carbon steel bits are the least expensive and the easiest to sharpen,

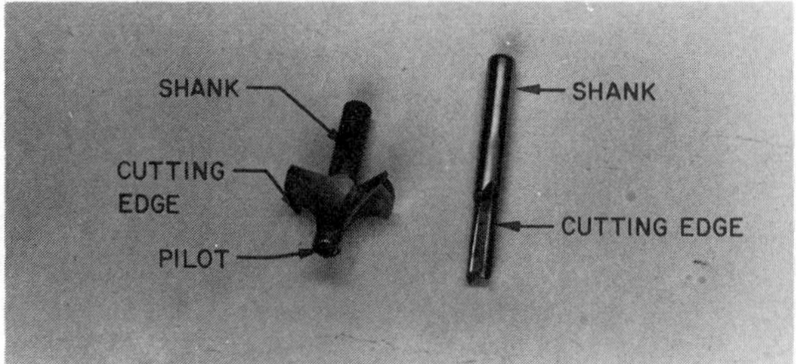

Figure 42-8
Major parts of router bits. Note that the bit on the right does not have a pilot.

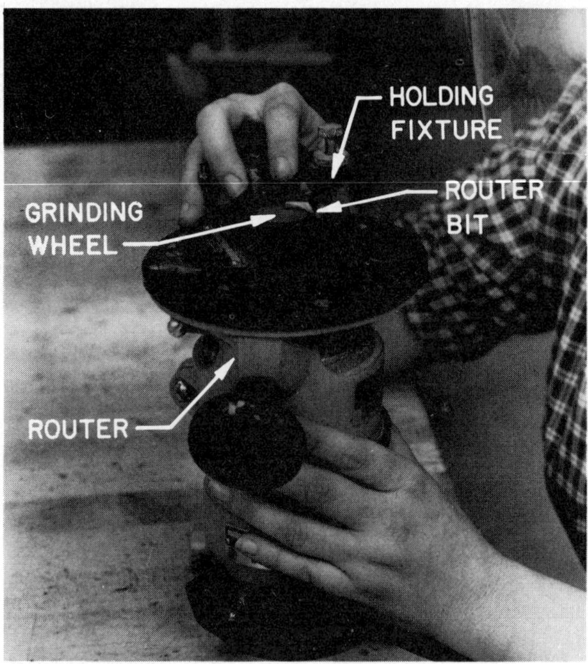

Figure 42-9
A router can sharpen carbon steel router bits.

Figure 42-9. With a carbide tip you can cut hard, dense materials, such as plastic laminates and particle board. A carbide tip will keep a sharp cutting edge longer than a carbon steel tip.

Decorative bits shape edges or make irregular internal cuts. Descriptions of some decorative bits follow.

Rounding over bits are available in many radii. They shape a rounded edge, Figure 42-10. A pilot the same diameter as the bottom of the cutter controls the depth of cut.

Beading bits are shaped similarly to rounding over bits. The pilot, however, is smaller in diam-

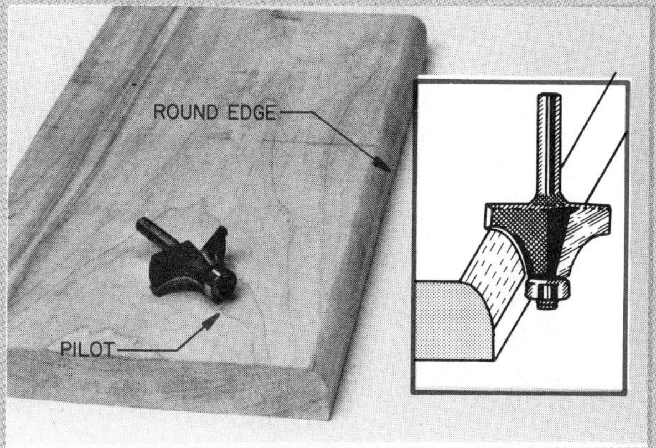

Figure 42-10
Rounding over bit. Note the ball-bearing pilot.

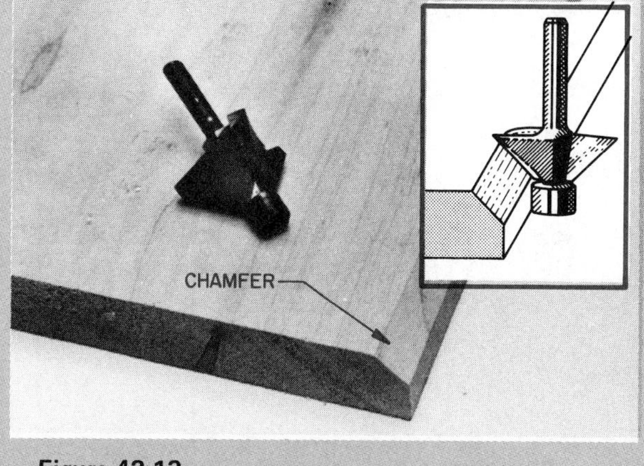

Figure 42-13
A chamfer bit.

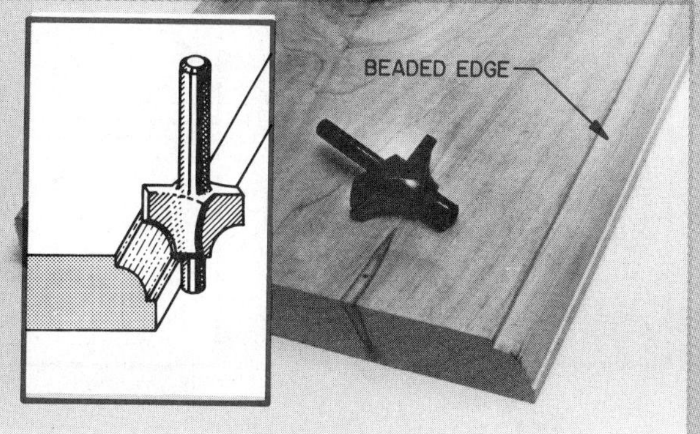

Figure 42-11
A beading bit.

Figure 42-14
A cove bit.

Figure 42-12
A roman ogee bit.

Figure 42-15
A core box bit.

eter than the bottom portion of the cutter, Figure 42-11.

Roman ogee bits produce one of the most highly figured edges of all common router bits. They are popular for use on edges of tabletops, Figure 42-12. A pilot is mounted on the bottom of the bit.

Chamfer bits cut a 45° bevel on an edge, Figure 42-13. These bits have a pilot.

Cove bits cut a concave shape into the corner of a board, Figure 42-14. A pilot is mounted on the bottom of the bit.

Core box bits produce the same shape as the cove bit produces, Figure 42-15. The core box

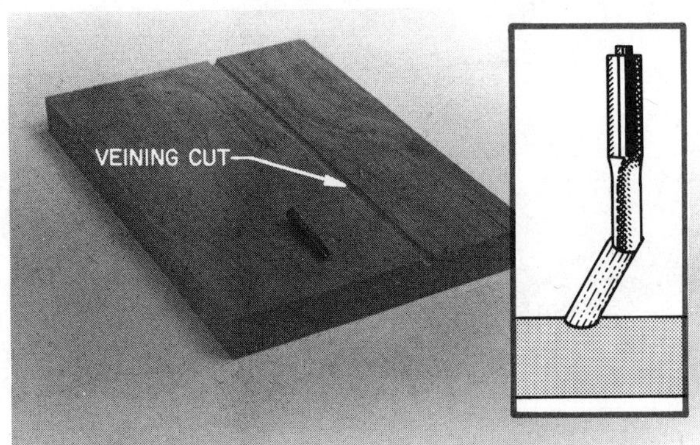

Figure 42-16
A veining bit.

bit, however, does not have a pilot. You use a core box bit to make a rounded groove on the face of a board.

Veining bits make very small rounded-bottom grooves. They are different from core box bits because of the smaller diameter and the longer cutting edge, Figure 42-16.

V-grooving bits are used to highlight areas, Figure 42-17. The sides of the groove are at a 45° angle.

The following bits are used primarily for joinery. When set up and guided correctly, accurate joints can be produced.

Straight bits are available in many diameters and two styles, Figure 42-18. A cutting edge is located on the side of the cutter as well as on the bottom. This edge location allows boring into the stock as well as cutting on the edges. The two styles of straight bits are single and double flute. A single flute has one cutting surface and

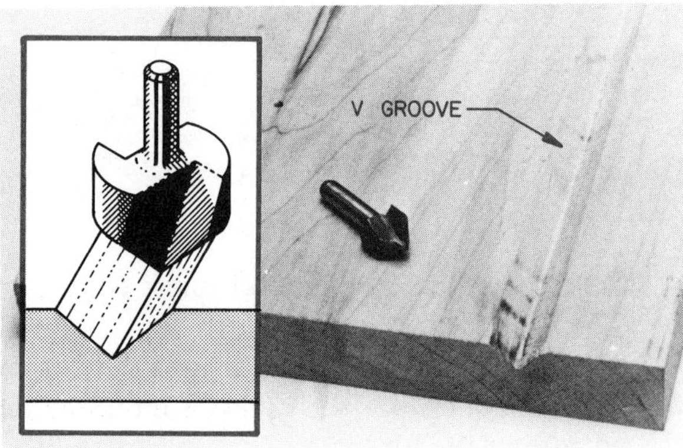

Figure 42-17
V-grooving bit.

is the stronger of the two. It is less likely to break. The double flute has two cutting surfaces and will give the smoother cut. Grooves frequently are made with these bits.

Rabbeting bits are used to cut different sizes of rabbets, Figure 42-19. A pilot controls the depth of the cut.

Dovetail bits usually are used only to make dovetail joints, Figure 42-20.

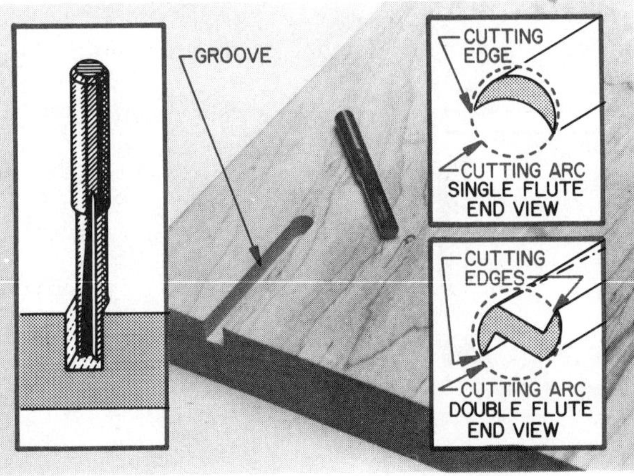

Figure 42-18
A straight bit is available in either a single or double flute style.

Installing a Router Bit

Follow these steps to install a router bit:

1. Unplug the router from the electrical outlet. Select the proper router bit and collet.
2. Slide the collet into the tapered hole in the motor shaft. After making certain that the collet is clean, insert the shank of the bit a minimum of 1/2" (13 mm) into the collet. Use the wrenches provided with the router to tighten the collet nut, Figure 42-21. Adjust the vertical height of the router bit by rotating the motor unit while holding the base. Secure the base with the locking handle.
3. Install the proper guiding device if the bit you are using does not have a pilot.
4. Clamp a scrap piece to the workbench and make a trial cut. Make any adjustments of the router bit before cutting the finished piece.

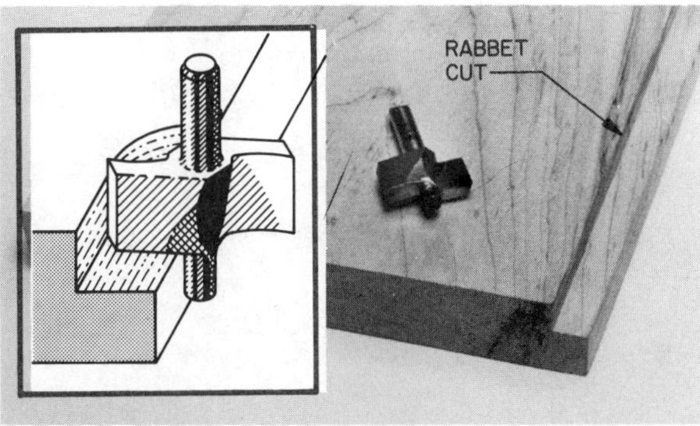

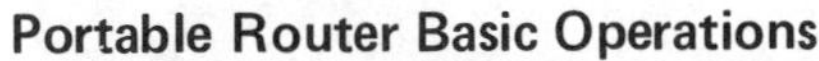

Figure 42-19
A rabbeting bit.

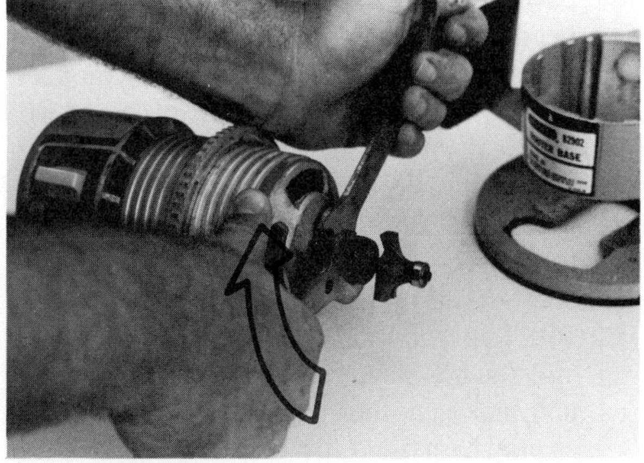

Figure 42-21
Tightening a collet nut. Pull up on the right wrench while holding the left wrench stationary. *Unplug the power cord before attempting this operation.*

Portable Router Basic Operations

No matter how the router bit is guided, you should follow these rules for safe router use.

To operate a router:

1. Keep the cord free of the path of the bit. Do not let it hang over the top of the board that is being shaped.
2. Hold the router securely with both hands on the handles at all times. When the power is turned on, the machine will tend to twist out of your hands.
3. Move the router in a counterclockwise direction, Figure 42-22. This motion causes the bit to rotate into the stock for a proper cutting action.
4. Keep the router moving at all times once cutting begins. A deep burn will occur on the edge of the board if the router is allowed to rest in one place or if too much pressure is applied, Figure 42-23. These

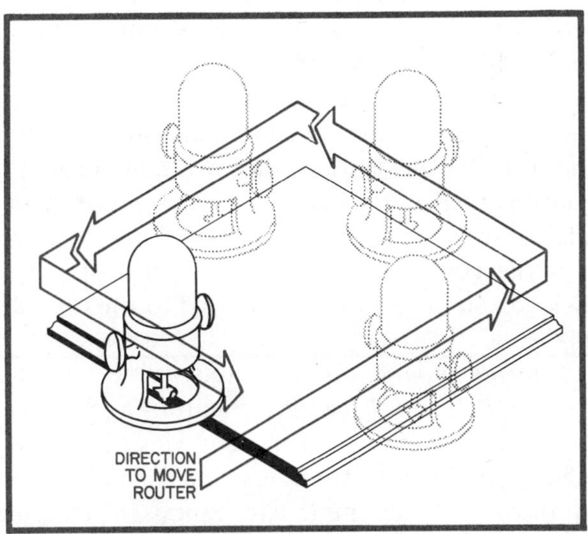

Figure 42-22
Move the router in a counterclockwise direction.

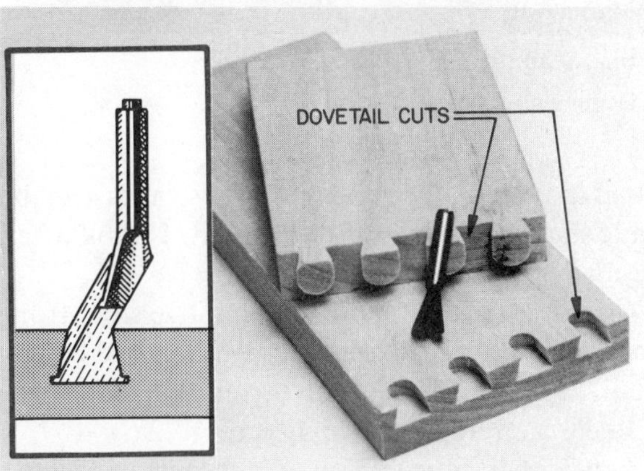

Figure 42-20
A dovetail bit.

Figure 42-23
A solid pilot can burn the wood if not fed properly.

burns are almost impossible to sand out. Feeding a router too fast will cause a rough cut and overwork the router. If you feed the router too slowly, the bit and wood will overheat and burn. The correct speed can be determined through practice and by listening to the sound of the motor as the router is cutting.

5. Make several light cuts rather than one deep cut. This will increase the life of the router and the bit. Then reset the depth of the cut and make another pass. Three or four passes may be needed for deep cuts.

Guiding the Router

You can guide a router in several different ways.

Piloted router bits. You most commonly use bits with piloted ends when you shape an edge, Figure 42-24. A smooth, solid pin or ball bearing on the bottom of the bit rides on the outside of the board to control the horizontal depth. You can not vary the depth of the cut when bits have pilots permanently attached to the cutter. The edge of the board must be perfectly true because it is the guide that the pilot runs against. Any nicks or bumps will be transferred to the routed edge.

Straight guides. Most routers come with a *commercial straight guide,* Figure 42-25. This device clamps to the base and rides along the edge of the board. It is adjustable and can move in or out to accommodate various distances.

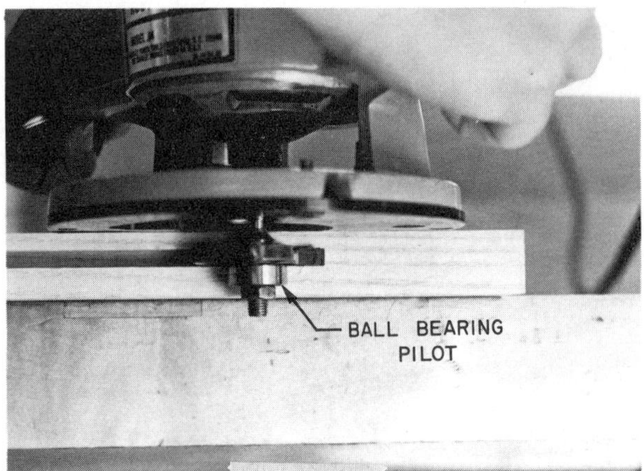

Figure 42-24
Guiding a router with a piloted router bit.

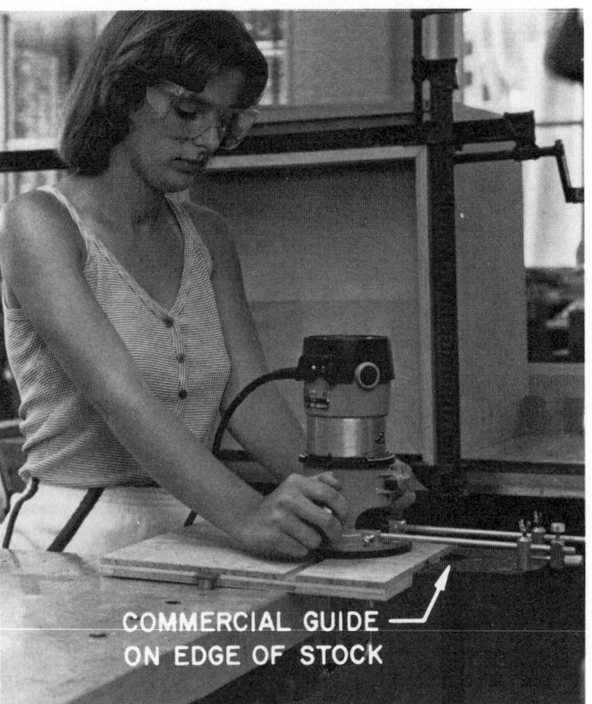

Figure 42-25
Guiding a router with a commercial straight guide.

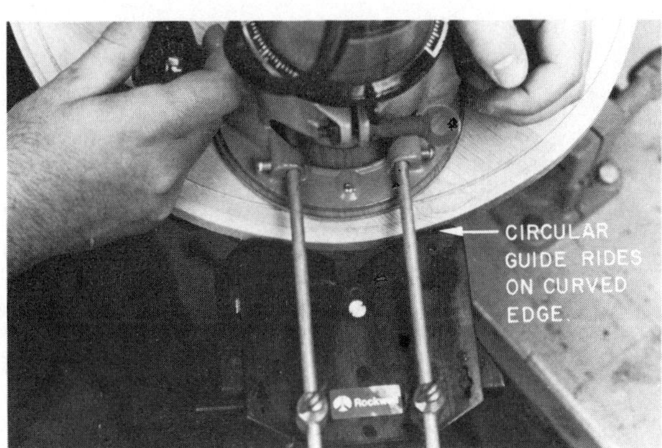

Figure 42-26
Using a circular guide.

When you use bits without pilots, cuts can be made across the face of the board. Dados often are made with a straight guide.

Circular guides. You can remove the front plate on the straight guide to rout a curved edge, Figure 42-26. Adding a pivot pin will allow you to make a circular groove, Figure 42-27.

Fabricated fence. You can use a fabricated fence to cut straight grooves or dados, Figure 42-28. You must position the wooden fence pre-

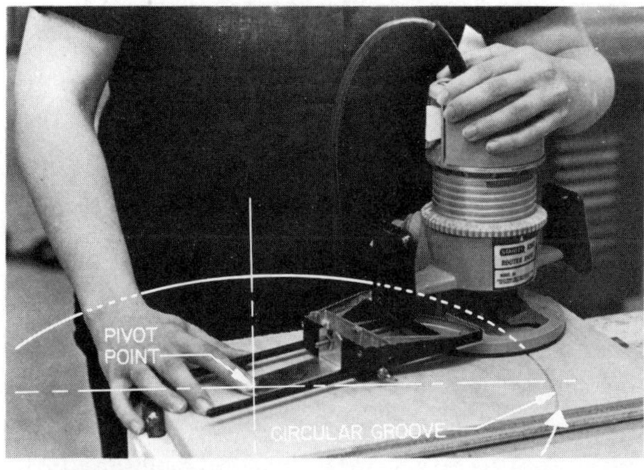

Figure 42-27
Adding a pivot point to the straight guide.

Figure 42-28
A wooden fence used for making straight grooves. *A* is equal to the distance from the edge of the router bit to the edge of the base plate.

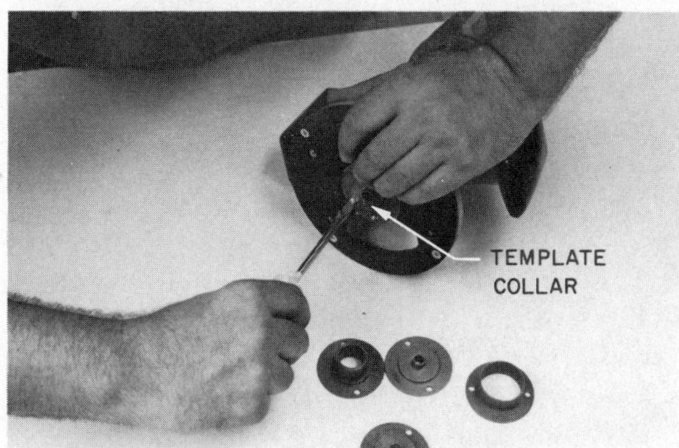

Figure 42-29
Installing a template collar. *Unplug the power cord before attempting this operation.*

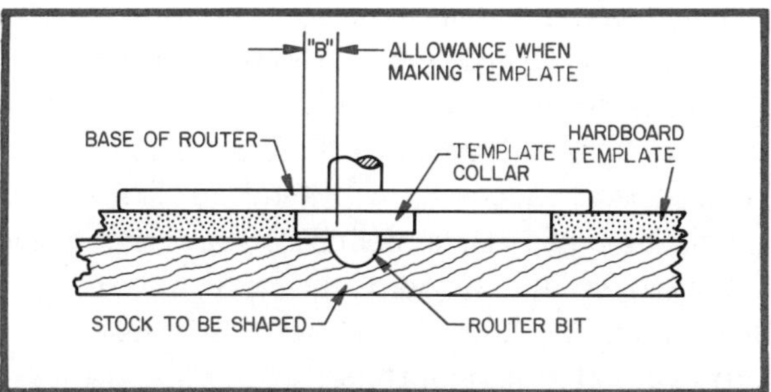

Figure 42-30
The template must be made larger than the pattern to be routed. This amount is equal to *B*.

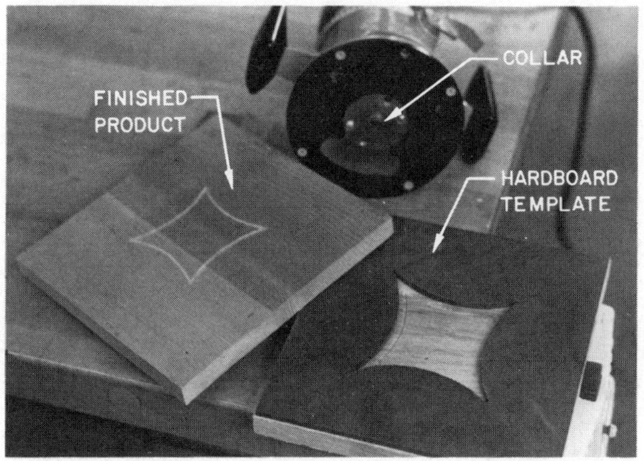

Figure 42-31
Guiding the router with a template and collar.

cisely. Place the fence so that the distance from the edge of the cutter to the fence equals the distance from the outside of the base plate to the edge of the cutter.

Template and collar. To use a template, first attach a collar to the router base, Figure 42-29. Make the template by laying out the desired pattern on tempered hardboard or a dense hardwood. The pattern must be the same size as the finished design plus the clearance between the bit and the outside of the template collar, Figure 42-30. You must smooth out any low or high spots on the edge of the template with a hand file. If you do not do this, these areas will show up on the finished product.

Use a bit without a pilot to cut the desired shape. You can use a straight bit to cut completely through the stock. Use veining bits to make decorative cuts, Figure 42-31.

Freehand. You can use a router equipped with a veining or core box bit to make a sign, Figure 42-32. Guide the router by hand. Set the bit no deeper than 1/4" (6 mm). If it is set any deeper than this, the cutter will tend to follow the grain. You can use a stencil or draw the design freehand on the wood to make a pattern for a sign. You will have to practice to make smooth, professional looking letters.

Joinery with a Router

A router often is selected to shape parts for joints because it makes a very smooth cut. It works well when shaping plywood because the cutter usually will not chip the wood.

Use the following procedures when making joints.

Dadoes and grooves. Select a straight shank bit the same diameter as the width of the dado. For dadoes where a same-size bit is not available, select the closest smaller size and make two cuts. You can guide the router with a commercial straight guide or a custom guide. A commercial straight guide can be set up quickly, but there is a tendency to push it away from the guiding edge of the stock. You can counteract this tendency by adding a longer auxiliary wood fence to the commercial guide, Figure 42-33.

You can make another style of custom fence by gluing a strip of plastic laminate to the bottom of a straightedge fence. The laminate should extend beyond the edge of the fence approximately 1" (25 mm) farther than the distance from the edge of the router base plate to the outside of the cutter, Figure 42-34. Install a carbide-tipped bit of the same diameter as the width of the dado. Place the router base against the fence and cut the laminate. The bit will trim the plastic to the correct width.

You can now place the custom fence on the board to be dadoed. Position the fence by placing the outside edge of the plastic laminate against the inside layout line of the dado. Clamp the guide to the stock with C clamps and cut the dado, Figure 42-35.

Before you store the guide, mark it with the size of the router and the bit diameter, Figure 42-36. This will save time when dadoes of the same size are to be made again. Each width of dado will require construction of a different guide.

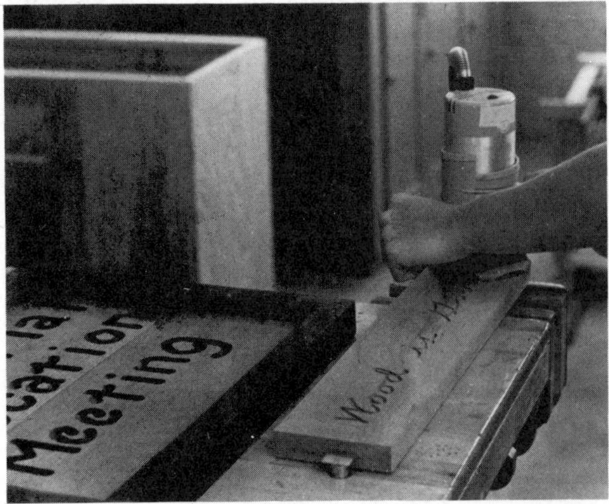

Figure 42-32
Freehanding with a router.

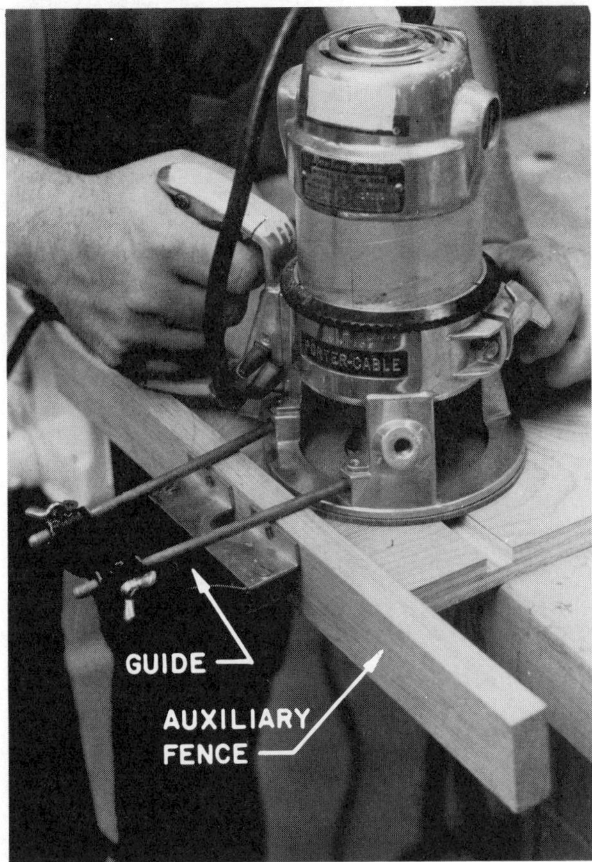

Figure 42-33
A guide with an auxiliary wooden fence.

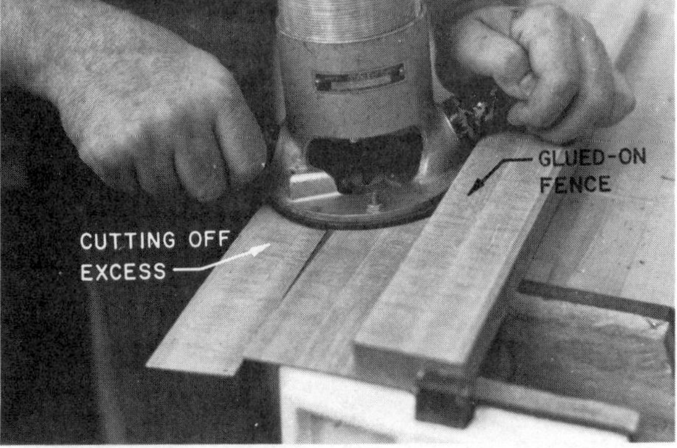

Figure 42-34
Constructing a custom fence by trimming laminate to size.

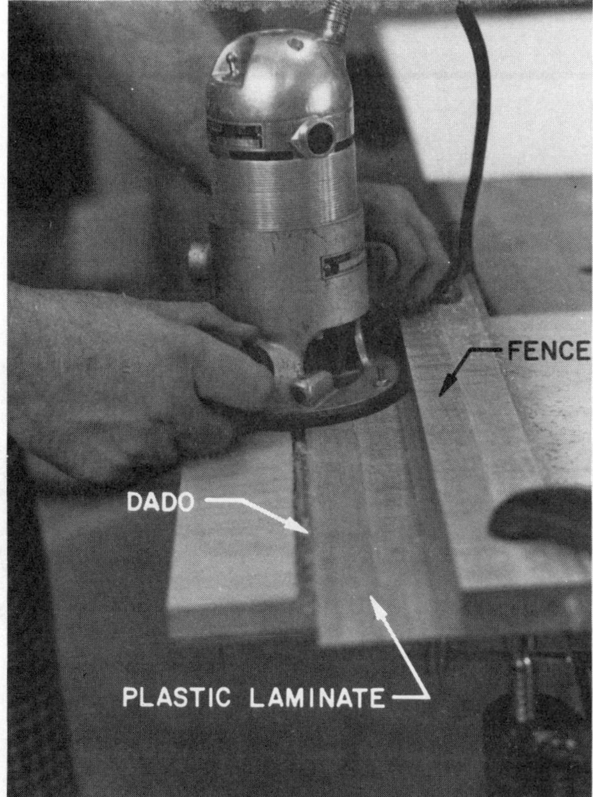

Figure 42-35
The custom fence automatically aligns the straightedge.

Figure 42-36
Marking the custom fences assures that they may be reused.

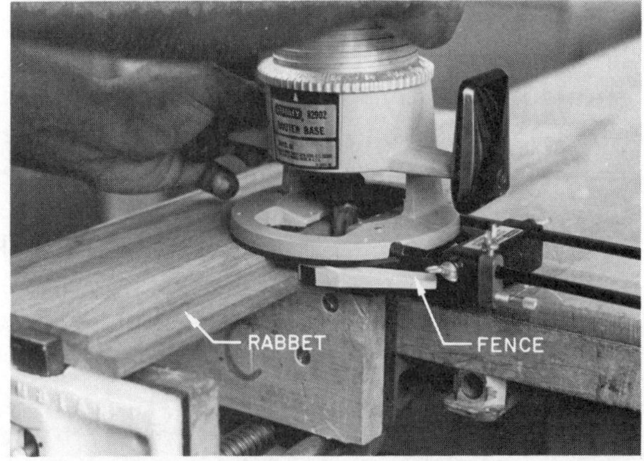

Figure 42-37
Cutting a rabbet with a commercial fence.

Rabbets. Cut rabbets with a rabbeting bit with a pilot end. If you do not have a rabbeting bit or if a smaller rabbet is required than you can shape with an available bit, use a straight bit with a commercial straight fence, Figure 42-37.

Mortises. Mortises require a straight bit the same diameter as the width of the tenons. Most 3/4″ (19 mm) stock has mortises that are 3/8″ (10 mm) wide. You must be sure to center the cut on the stock. You can guide the router either by a commercial guide or by attaching it to an auxiliary table. Because mortises usually are cut on narrow edges, you will have to steady the router when using the commercial guide. You can do this by clamping a board on each side of the piece of stock to make a wider base, Figure

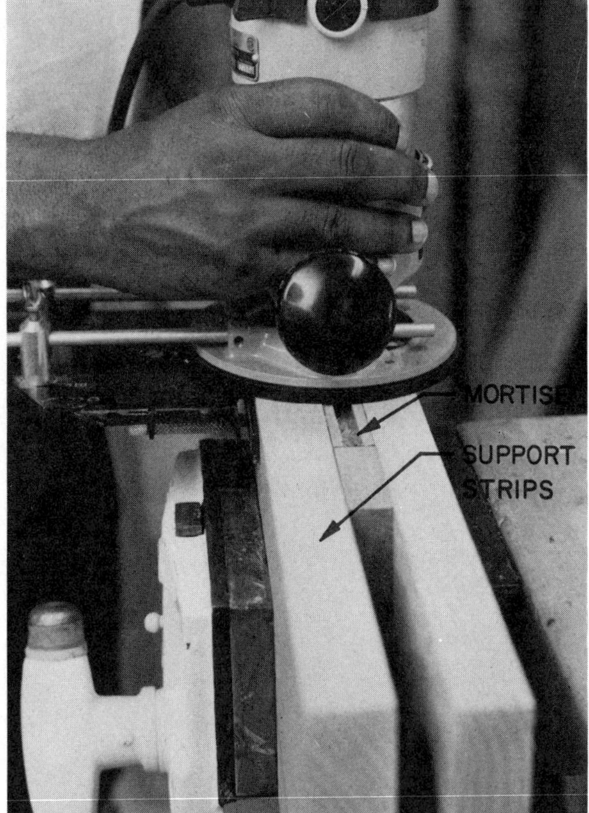

Figure 42-38
Two strips of wood help support the router.

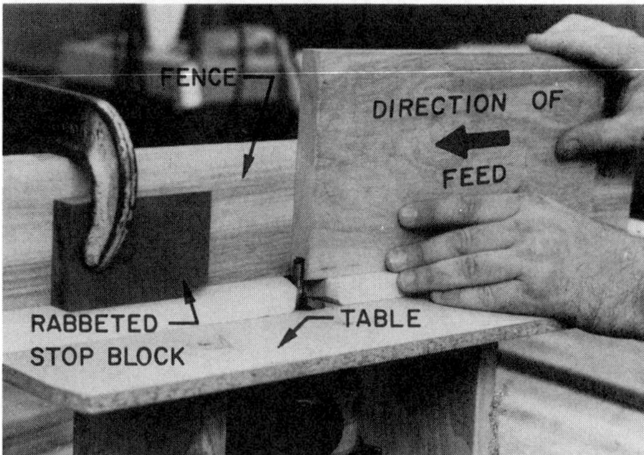

Figure 42-39
A router table can be used for cutting mortises.

42-38. To start the cut, pivot the bit down into the work. This is called a plunge cut.

An auxiliary table also can be used to make exposed mortises on the ends of boards, Figure 42-39. After the bit is installed in a portable router, attach the router to the bottom of the table. Adjust the fence so that the mortise will be centered on the edge of the stock. Clamp a stop block to the fence to ensure correct length of the mortise. Feed the stock against the rotation of the bit.

The bit will produce rounded corners in the mortise. You must round the corners of the tenon to match or make the tenon narrower to fit inside the mortise's rounded corners. If the mortise is more than 3/4" (19 mm) deep, divide the depth in half and make the mortise in two passes to reduce the chances of breaking the bit.

Dovetail joints. Multifinger dovetails are used frequently for drawer joinery on well-constructed furniture. They make a very attractive and strong joint.

Dovetails can be made either with a router *dovetail fixture* or with a commercial *dovetailer.* Commercial dovetailers perform the cutting procedure in one operation, Figure 42-40. This machine is used when hundreds of joints are to be

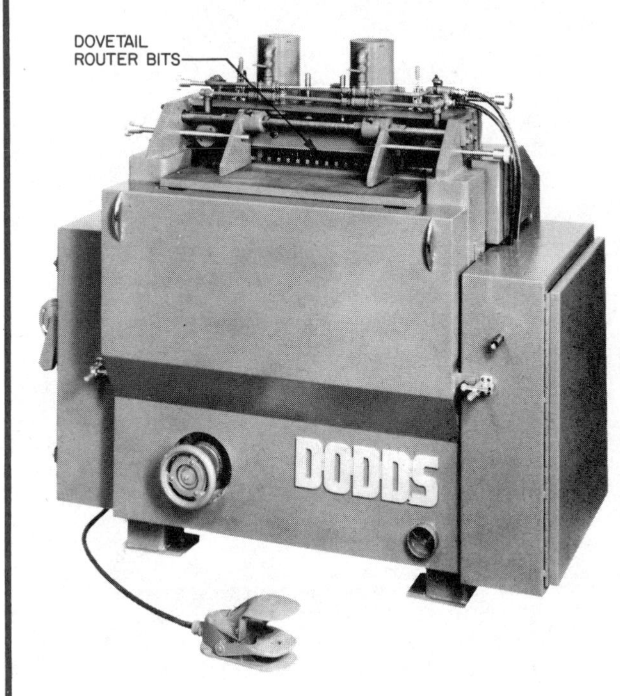

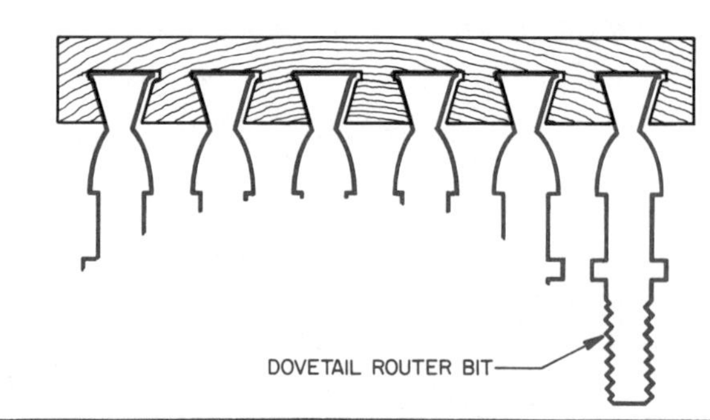

Figure 42-40
An automatic dovetailer cuts all dovetail parts with one pass through the machine. (Dodds Inc.)

Figure 42-41
Setting the depth of a dovetail bit. *Unplug the power cord before attempting this operation.*

made. When a limited number of joints are required, use a dovetail fixture, following this procedure:

1. Surface and square all material for the drawer to the exact specified thickness. Surface at least two pieces of scrap to the same dimensions. One piece of scrap should match the drawer sides. The other should match the drawer front.
2. Screw the template guide to the base of the router. Insert the dovetail bit through the bottom of the guide and tighten the collet nut.
3. Adjust the bit exactly 9/32" (7 mm) below the base. A fixture will aid in this setting, Figure 42-41.
4. Mount the dovetail fixture on the workbench. A woodworking vise works well for this purpose.
5. Clamp the piece of scrap that you prepared to match the side of the drawer on the front of the fixture in a vertical position. The inner face of the drawer side must be facing out. The drawer side should extend approximately 1/2" (13 mm) above the top surface of the fixture, Figure 42-42.
6. Insert the scrap front of the drawer with the groove for the bottom facing up. Place it under the top bar of the fixture. Locate the board by placing it against the indexing pin on the top of the fixture and the drawer side. Tighten the hold-down knobs, Figure 42-43.

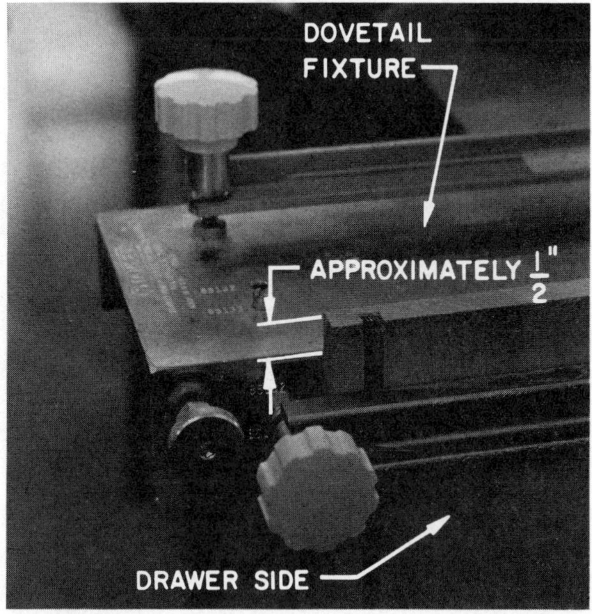

Figure 42-42
Positioning the drawer side.

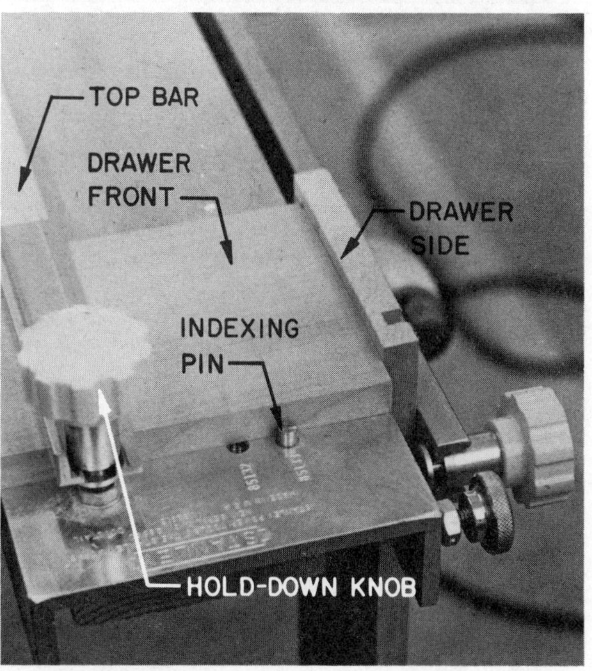

Figure 42-43
Permanently positioning the drawer front.

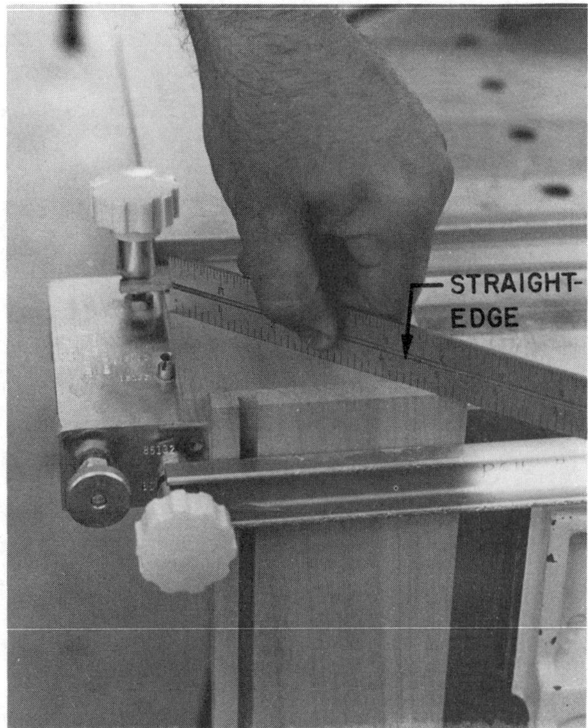

Figure 42-44
Permanently positioning the drawer side.

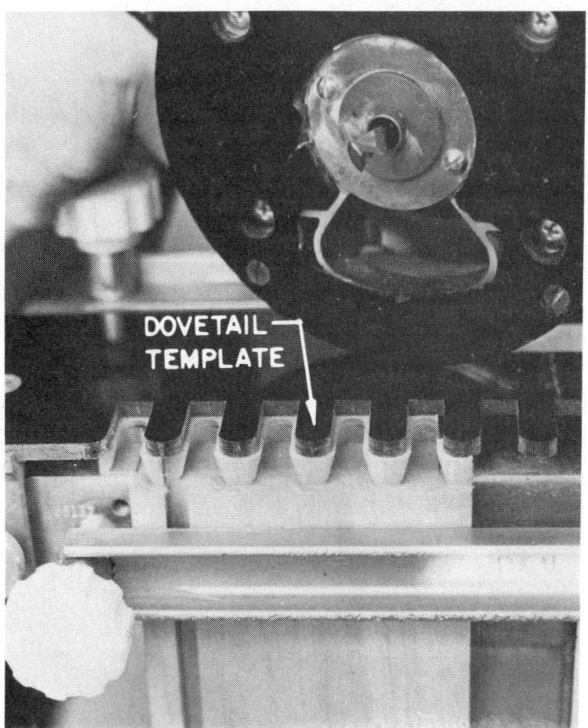

Figure 42-45
Properly cut dovetails. A flush drawer front and side joined with a dovetail.

Figure 42-46
This drawer front is flush with the drawer sides.

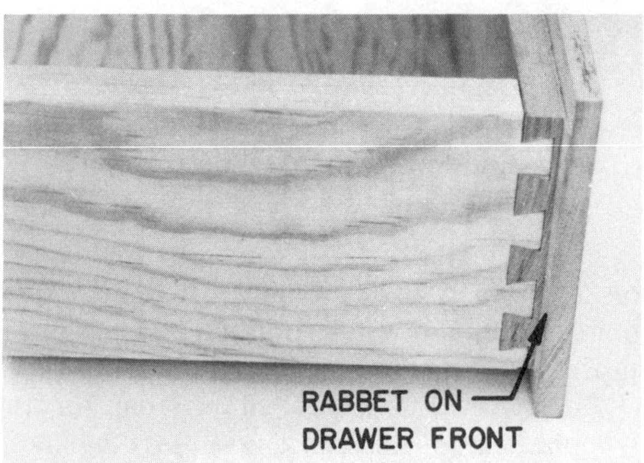

Figure 42-47
A rabbeted drawer front joined to the side with a dovetail.

7. Reposition the scrap drawer side so that the end that extends above the fixture is flush with the top surface of the drawer front. Before clamping the drawer side in place, push it against the indexing pin on the front of the fixture, Figure 42-44.
8. Place the dovetail template over the top of the setup. Tighten the knobs, once the template rests on top of the stock.
9. Position the router on top of the template. Rotate the dovetail bit by hand to check that the bit will not cut into the fixture. Plug in the cord and make a trial cut on the scraps, Figure 42-45. Do not raise the router base off the template. This action will cut the template and ruin the fixture.
10. Check the fit of the two pieces before cutting any additional stock, Figure 42-46. If

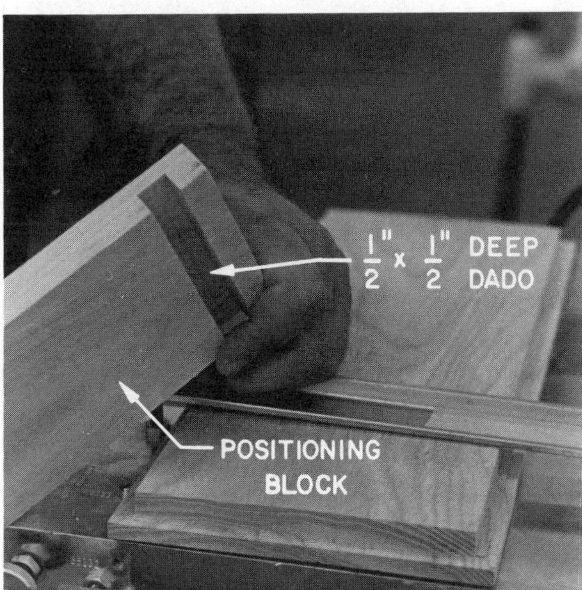

Figure 42-48
A positioning block is cut first.

the pieces are too loose, lower the bit 1/64" (.5 mm). Correct too tight a fit by raising the bit 1/64" (.5 mm).

Another adjustment to consider is the alignment of the drawer side with the end of the drawer front. If the side is not flush with the end of the drawer front, turn the template nuts located on the front of the template in a clockwise direction. When the side extends beyond the end of the drawer front, turn the same nuts counterclockwise.

When you have determined the cause of the poor fit, make small adjustments. Only one adjustment should be made for each trial cut. The pieces must meet exactly before you start to cut finished pieces.

Dovetails for rabbeted drawer fronts. You must follow a different procedure to cut dovetails on a rabbeted drawer front, Figure 42-47. The rabbet on the edges prevents the drawer front from sliding far enough forward on the dovetail fixture.

1. Make a positioning block with a dado that is 1/2" x 1/2" (13 x 13 mm), Figure 42-48. Place the rabbeted drawer front face down on top of the fixture. Locate the front by pushing the board against the indexing pin and into the groove of the positioning block, Figure 42-49.

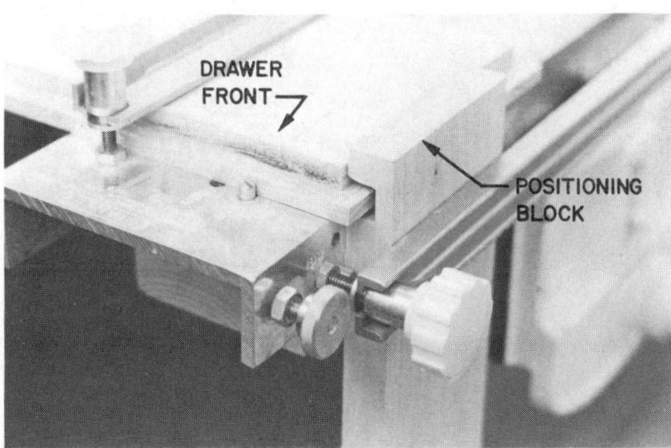

Figure 42-49
Positioning the rabbeted drawer front with the help of the positioning block.

Figure 42-50
Shaped drawer front.

2. Remove the positioning block and place the template in the normal position. Cut the dovetails, Figure 42-50.
3. Cut the drawer side by clamping the board to the fixture in the vertical position with the inner side of the drawer facing out. The height to which the drawer side should extend above the top surface of the fixture can be established by clamping a scrap piece the same thickness as the drawer front to the top of the fixture. Position the drawer side flush with the top surface of the scrap.
4. Place the template over the top of the fixture. Rout the drawer side in the normal manner.

Figure 42-51
The router-shaper consists of a table, column and power head. *The guard has been removed so you can see the router bit.* (Rockwell International)

Figure 42-53
Fixture clamps work well to secure the stock to the fixture. *The guard has been removed so you can see the router bit.*

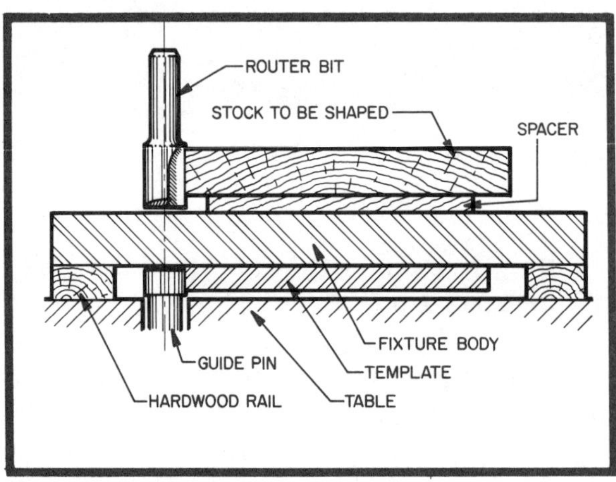

Figure 42-54
Major parts of a pin router fixture.

PIN ROUTER

Pin routers are available in two sizes. A small router-shaper is designed for light cutting. This kind usually is available in a school laboratory, Figure 42-51. Large commercial models are used in industry and are capable of heavy cuts, Figure 42-2.

Both sizes of pin routers have an adjustable table, a column and a power head. Stock moves across the table while the router bit is held firmly in the power head. The depth of cut is adjusted differently on various models. Consult the owner's manual for further deatils on the adjustments.

Routing to a Pattern

A pin router can shape curves and contours, Figure 42-52. Start the process by constructing a *pin router fixture.* Use tempered hardboard for the pattern, which will be attached to the bottom of the fixture. Carefully cut the full-size pattern with a scroll or band saw. Smooth the edges of the pattern with a fine file. Any irregularities will be reflected in the finished product.

To complete the fixture, laminate the pattern to the bottom of a piece of 3/4" (19 mm) hardwood plywood. The piece of plywood must be large enough to support the hold-down devices, Figure 42-53. Attach the stock to the top of the plywood with screws, fixture clamps or other devices. Once cutting begins, the material being shaped must not shift or move on the fixture. You can attach a bottom hardwood rail to the bottom of the fixture body to reduce friction and eliminate buildup of dust, Figure 42-54. You can attach a spacer on top of the fixture body to save wear and tear on the fixture. You may want to attach handles to minimize fatigue and im-

Figure 42-52
Curves can easily be cut once a fixture is constructed. *The guard has been removed so you can see the router bit.* (Rockwell International)

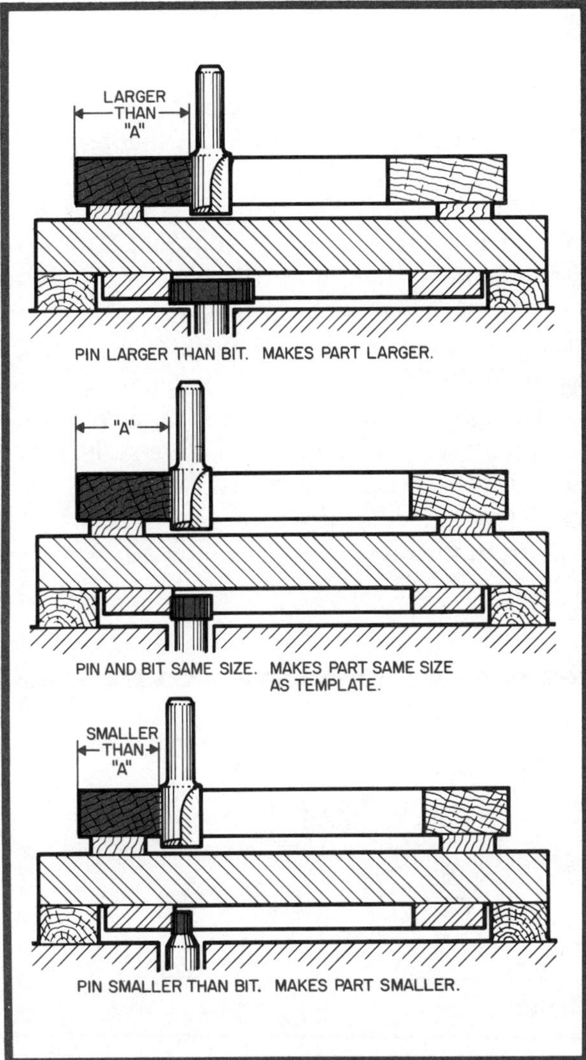

Figure 42-55
Changing the pin size affects the size of the finished part.

prove safety, Figure 42-53. You should not move your hands within 4" (102 mm) of the router bit.

Many router bits can cut a pattern. You will cut out most products initially with a straight bit. A common size is 1/2" (13 mm). Some bits have a spiral flute to help remove dust. Larger or smaller pins may be used to adjust the finished size of the product, Figure 42-55.

If the product is to be cut out completely, place the fixture on the router table and adjust the depth of cut. The bit should extend no farther than 1/8" (3 mm) below the top of the spacer. Lightweight router-shapers may require two or three passes to cut through the stock. Take no more than a 1/4" (6 mm) cut in one pass. If the cut is not to be made completely through the board, set the bit for the desired depth of cut.

To cut out the product, first adjust the plastic guard to cover the router bit. Position the fixture against the pin. Hold the fixture still, and plunge the router bit into the stock. As the fixture rotates around the pin, the finished product will take shape. Always move the fixture against the direction the bit rotates. Moving with the rotation will cause the fixture to be thrown by the bit. Be very careful when coming to the end of an internal cut. The waste piece may be grabbed by the bit.

At the end of the cut return the router bit to the top position or lower the router table. Remove the finished product. Some products may require additional shaping by using a rounding over or other decorative bit to ease the corners.

Straight Cuts

The pin router also works well for shaping dadoes, gains or straight decorative cuts. It produces a high-quality cut that is difficult to reproduce on other machines.

Guide the stock against a fence. This can be either a commercial stepped fence or a shop-made wooden fence. The commercial fence comes with the machine, Figure 42-56. Use a

Figure 42-56
A commercial fence can be used as a guide for making straight cuts. *The guard has been removed so you can see the router bit.* (Rockwell International)

Figure 42-57
A wooden fence works well for making grooves and other internal cuts. *The guard has been removed so you can see the router bit.*

wooden fence whenever you cut a portion of the edge or make an internal cut, Figure 42-57.

To rout a straight cut, first install the desired bit. After adjusting the depth of cut, lock the power head or table into position. Finish the set-up by clamping the fence to the table. Attach a commercial fence with screw studs. The shop-made wooden fence is held in position with C clamps. Adjust the plastic guard so that the stock just passes under it. Turn on the power and feed the stock forward. Always feed against the rotation of the cutter. Use a push stick whenever possible. Keep your hands at least 4" (102 mm) away from the bit. If the stock moves away from the fence, a straight cut will not be produced.

REVIEW QUESTIONS

1. What controls the numerically controlled router?
2. How is the depth of the router bit adjusted?
3. Router bits come in what three shank diameters?
4. What purpose does the pilot on a router bit serve?
5. How far should the shank of the router bit be inserted into the collet?
6. In which direction should the router be moved when shaping an edge?
7. What is one method of guiding a router when making a dado?
8. How much larger should a template be than the desired routed pattern?
9. A sign can be made by using which guiding method?
10. How can a rabbet be made with a router?
11. Name two methods of guiding a router when making a mortise.
12. To what depth is the dovetail router bit set when using a dovetail fixture?
13. Sketch a fixture to be used on a pin router to shape a wall plaque. Include all safety features.
14. What size of pin would you select if you used a 1/2" (13 mm) bit to rout a piece to the same size as the pattern?
15. What is attached to the pin router table to make a straight cut?

SUGGESTED ACTIVITIES

1. Inspect your portable router and pin router and name all the major parts.

2. Draw the name of your school or club on a piece of wood and use the portable router to trace around the letters. Spraypaint the routed area and then sand off any overspray that is not in the recessed area. The paint will help make the letters stand out. Apply a clear finish over the entire board.

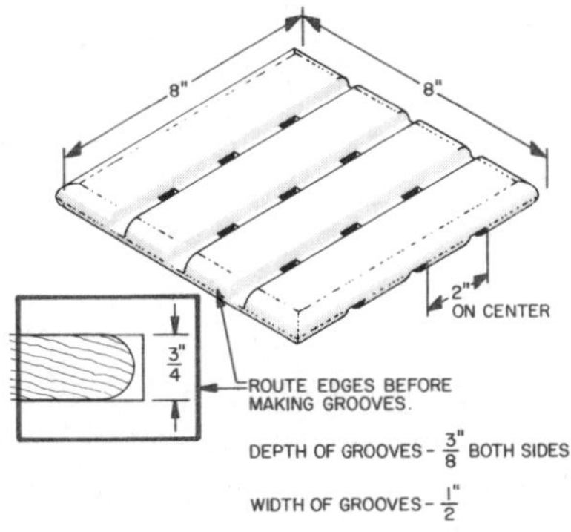

3. Use the portable router or pin router to make a trivet.

UNIT

43

Portable Drills

Objectives

After studying this unit you should be able to:

1 Identify the major parts of the portable drill and make the basic adjustments.

2 Install a drill bit.

3 Bore both through holes and stopped holes.

Technical Terms

Pistol-grip handle
T handle
Variable speed
Reversing switch
Pneumatic drill

PORTABLE DRILL SAFETY RULES

1 Always unplug the drill before changing bits or tightening the chuck.

2 Always remove the chuck key after installing the drill bit.

3 Clamp down small pieces of stock. Do not hold stock by hand.

4 Grip the drill with both hands to maintain control.

5 Keep the cord clear of the bit drilling area.

6 Keep fingers and clothing away from the drill bit.

The portable power drill, Figure 43-1, is one of the most useful tools for woodworking. One reason for its popularity is that it can use many accessories, Figure 43-2.

PORTABLE DRILL TERMINOLOGY

A portable drill has a chuck attached to a motor. Figure 43-1 shows the key parts of the drill.

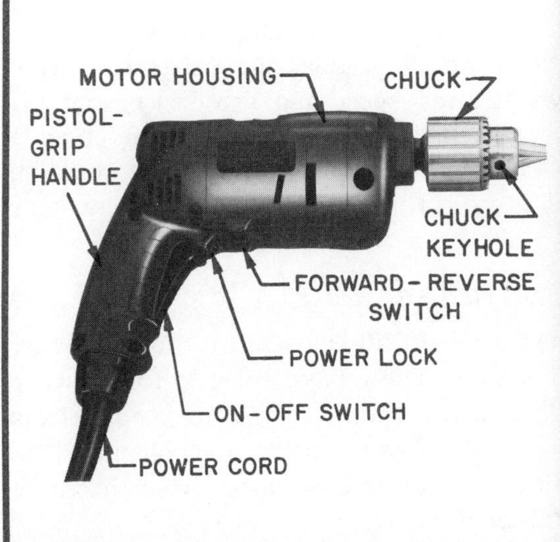

Figure 43-1
Major parts of a portable drill with a pistol-grip handle. (Milwaukee Electric Tool Corp.)

Figure 43-2
Many accessories can be used with the portable drill.

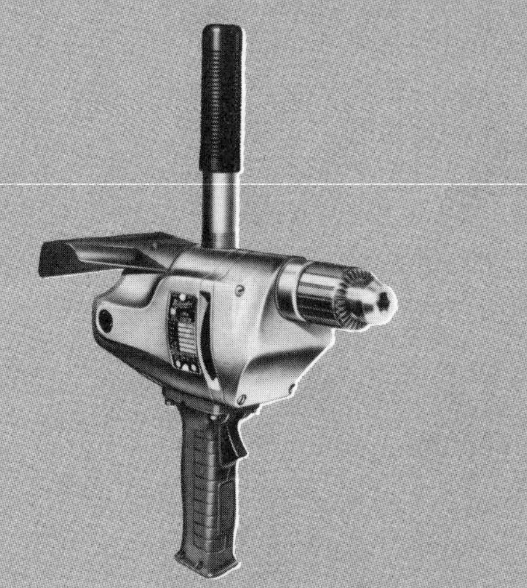

Figure 43-3
Large drills have a T handle. (Milwaukee Electric Tool Corp.)

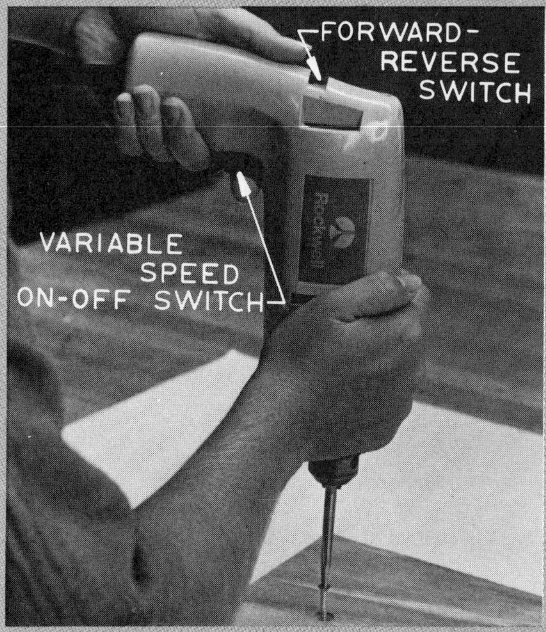

Figure 43-4
Variable speed drills allow you to install screws easily.

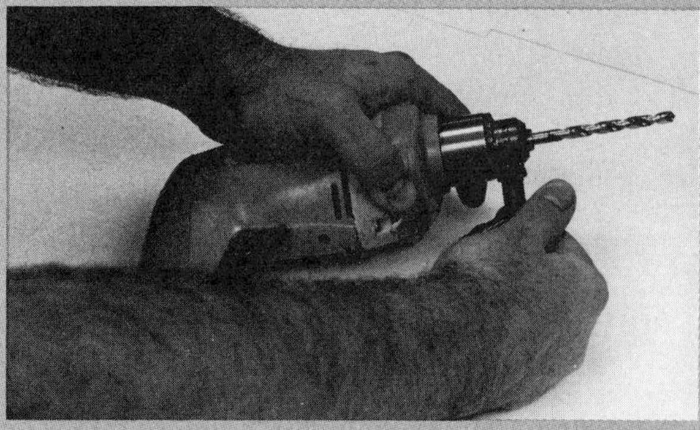

Figure 43-5
Use a chuck key to secure the drill bit. *Unplug the cord before attempting this operation.*

The housing surrounds the motor and contains the handle and the power switch. Small drills have a *pistol-grip handle.* Large drills have a *T handle,* Figure 43-3.

Drill sizes depend on the sizes of their chucks. The most common chuck sizes for woodworking are 1/4″, 3/8″ and 1/2″ (6, 10 and 13 mm). The size is determined by the maximum diameter of the shank of a bit that will fit into the chuck. A 1/4″ (6 mm) drill will accept a bit with a shank diameter no larger than 1/4″ (6 mm).

Quality portable drills have heavy-duty, break-resistant plastic housings. Plastic is an excellent insulator and will prevent electrical shock. Drills with metal housings must have a third wire in the power cord to serve as a ground. Do not use a drill of this type unless it is properly grounded.

The on-off switch usually has a power lock. It locks the switch in the "on" position. The drill will run without your holding the switch. Grinding and other operations require this feature. Do not lock the power on if there is any danger that the attachment mounted in the chuck will grab the work. This might cause the work or the drill to be thrown out of control.

Variable speed drills allow you to change the rotational speed of the chuck. You can install screws at a fast speed and also drill in metal or concrete at a slow speed, Figure 43-4. Do not overload the motor when it is at a slow speed. This quickly will burn out the motor.

A *reversing switch* changes the direction of rotational speed of the chuck. You can install screws at a fast speed and also drill in metal or change the reversing switch unless the chuck is at a complete stop. After using the reversing switch, turn it to the forward position.

BORING HOLES

The portable drill is a safe tool to use. There are, however, a few basic rules to follow. Grip the drill firmly by the handle to keep it from slipping out of your hands. Keep hands, hair, clothing and power cords away from the rotating drill bit.

To bore a hole in wood, follow this procedure:

1. Check that the cord is not plugged in. Select the correct bit to bore the hole. You usually will use a twist bit. Refer to Unit 36

Figure 43-6
Use an awl to mark the center of the hole.

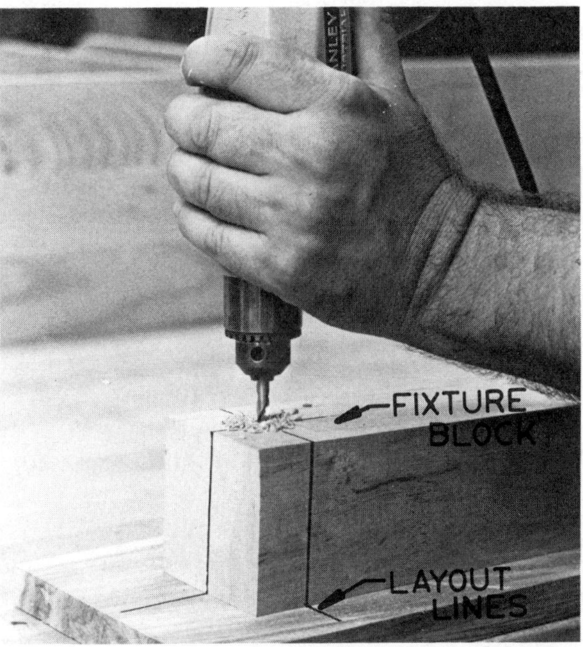

Figure 43-7
A fixture block positions the drill bit.

for information on other types of drill bits. Insert the shank of the bit at least 1" (25 mm) into the chuck and finger-tighten it. Use the chuck key to secure the bit. After placing the chuck key in the chuck keyhole, turn it in a clockwise direction to tighten the jaws of the chuck, Figure 43-5. (Turn it counterclockwise to remove the bit.) For larger-diameter bits, use the chuck key in all three chuck keyholes. This will tighten the jaws and prevent the bit from spinning within the chuck. Remove the chuck key.

2. Mark the center point of the desired hole with two intersecting lines. If the drill bit must be precisely located, use an awl to mark the center point, Figure 43-6. The small starting point made by the awl will help you locate the tip of the drill bit.
3. Plug in the drill and position the bit over the marked center point. The bit's angle to the surface depends on the angle of the hole to be bored. If the bit's angle to the wood must be very accurate, use a drill fixture block. A fixture block is a wooden block with a hole bored through it at the angle desired. This permits boring many holes at an identical angle, Figure 43-7. Commercial fixtures are available to aid in aligning the bit with the surface of the stock, Figure 43-8. Many holes, such as those for wood screws, need not be bored with the fixture block. Estimate the angle by eye.
4. Start the bit slowly into the work when using drills that have a variable speed motor. For standard motors, start the hole by using light but firm pressure.
5. Apply full power by pulling back all the

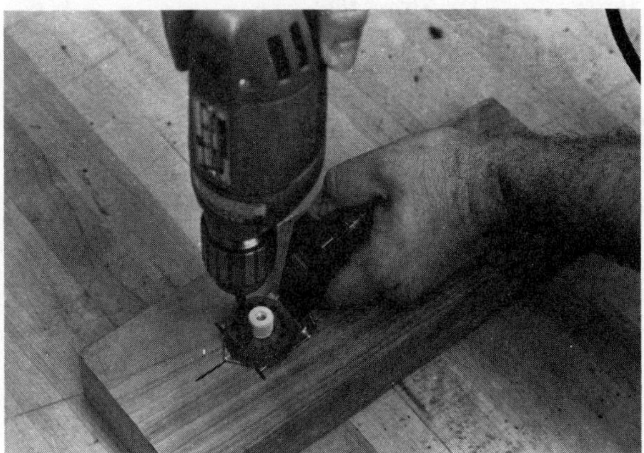

Figure 43-8
A commercial fixture is helpful for boring holes that must be perpendicular to the surface.

way on the trigger as you continue to bore the hole. When drilling deep holes, withdraw the rotating bit occasionally to remove the chips.

6. Reduce the speed and the pressure just before breaking through the opposite surface. This will minimize the chance of the bit's breaking through and splintering the wood. If a back-up board is clamped to the bottom surface, splintering will be avoided, Figure 43-9.

Sometimes you will want to bore stopped holes. You then need to know how far to feed the bit into the stock. Mark on the outside edge of the board the depth of the hole. Place the bit on the side of the stock. Align the end of the bit with the layout line. Wrap a piece of tape around the portion of the bit extending above the top of the board. You can now bore the hole to the correct depth. Bore into the wood until the tape meets the top of the board. Be careful not to let the tape touch the stock.

Figure 43-9
Clamp a back-up board to the stock to avoid any splintering on the bottom surface.

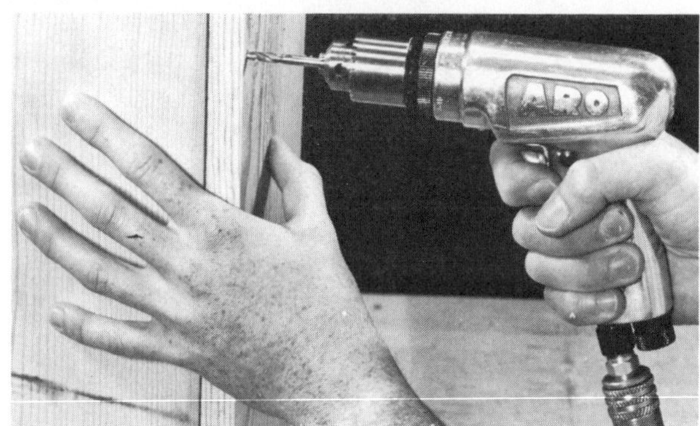

Figure 43-10
Pneumatic drills are becoming popular. (The Aro Corporation)

PNEUMATIC DRILLS

Some drills are powered by a pneumatic, or air, motor rather than by an electric motor, Figure 43-10. Each has its advantages. The *pneumatic drill* is powered by compressed air and requires a compressor. Tools powered by air run cooler and generally last much longer, Figure 43-11. Pneumatic motors are smaller, more compact and lightweight. Electric motors, however, usually are less expensive. They run from any conventional 110-volt outlet.

Figure 43-11
Pneumatic screwdrivers run cooler even when a great deal of power is required. (The Aro Corporation)

REVIEW QUESTIONS

1 What determines the size of drills?
2 What is an advantage of a variable speed drill?
3 Why is a reversing switch needed?
4 How far should the shank of a drill bit be inserted into the chuck?
5 What tool can you use to make a small starting point for the drill bit?
6 What is the purpose of a fixture block?
7 List three advantages of a pneumatic drill.

SUGGESTED ACTIVITIES

1 Inspect your portable drill and name each part. What size is the drill? Does the drill have a reversing switch?
2 Practice boring both through holes and stopped holes. Have your instructor specify the dimensions.

UNIT

44 Portable Sanders

Objectives

After studying this unit you should be able to:

1 Identify the major parts of a portable sander and make basic adjustments.

2 Install sanding belts and paper.

3 Operate portable belt and pad sanders.

Technical Terms

Portable belt sander
Dustbag attachment
Orbital pad sander
Vibrating pad sander
Straight-line pad sander
Pneumatic sander
Disc sander

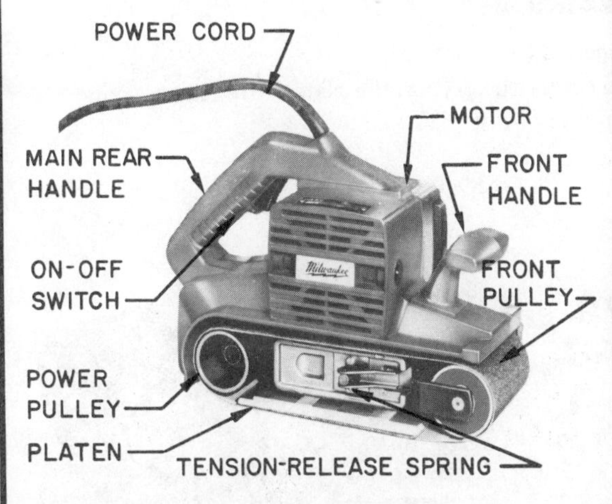

Figure 44-1
Major parts of a portable belt sander. (Milwaukee Electric Tool Corp.)

PORTABLE SANDER SAFETY RULES

1 Unplug the cord when you change belts.

2 Clamp small pieces of stock to a workbench.

3 Hold the sander securely by both handles.

4 Keep the cord away from the sanding area.

5 Never set a machine on a workbench with the belt still moving.

6 Make sure that the switch is off before plugging in the power.

Wooden parts should be sanded both before and after assembly. You can sand these pieces with power-driven equipment, either stationary or portable. You can also hand-sand them using a block wrapped with abrasive paper. Power-driven sanding is faster than hand-sanding but the equipment can be expensive. Hand-sanding with a sanding block produces good results but takes a great deal of time.

Portable sanders are fast and efficient. Their small size permits you to move them around easily. *Portable belt sanders* remove material quickly. Portable pad sanders are designed for fine-finish sanding.

PORTABLE BELT SANDERS

Use a portable belt sander to remove mill marks and other deep-surface scratches from flat areas, Figure 44-1. The sander has a small sanding belt held between two rollers. The width and length of the belt determine the size of the sander. Common sizes are 3″ x 21″, 3″ x 24″ and 4″ x 24″ (76 x 533, 76 x 610 and 102 x 610 mm).

Belts have an arrow printed on the inside of the backing, Figure 44-2. The arrow indicates the direction of rotation. Rotate the belt to the rear of the sander. If you run the belt in the opposite direction, the splice where the two ends of the belt come together will separate. The size

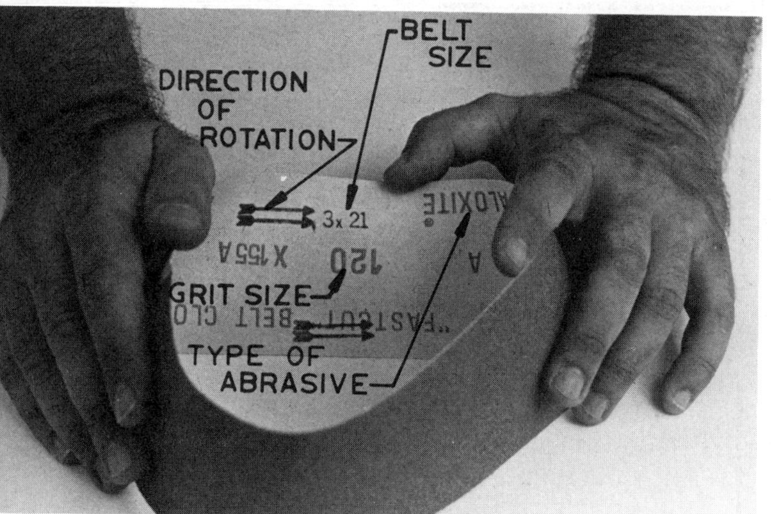

Figure 44-2
Information is printed on the backing of the sanding belt.

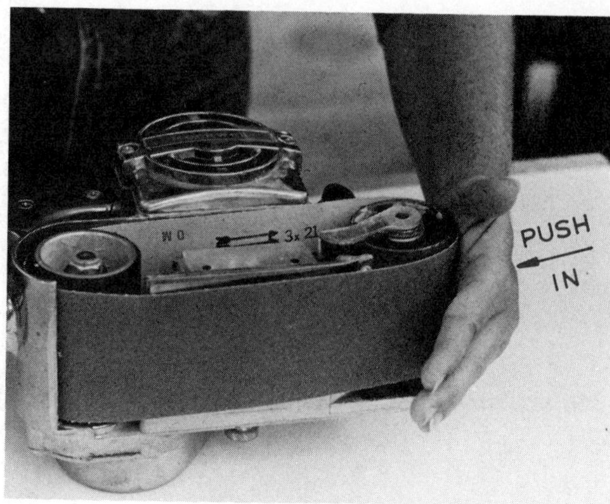

Figure 44-3
To take the tension off the belt, push in on the front pulley, or push down the tension-release spring. *Unplug the sander before attempting this operation.*

of the belt and the type of abrasive are also printed on the backing.

Install belts on the sander by pushing in on the front pulley, Figure 44-3, or by pushing down the tension-release spring. Different models of machines will operate differently. Follow instructions in the owner's manual.

After placing the belt over the pulleys and releasing the tension spring, pull and release the on-off switch to run the motor in short bursts. Check to see if the belt is running on the platen. If it drifts to one side, you must track it. Tracking means running the belt and turning the belt-tracking adjustment knob, Figure 44-4. Do not turn the adjustment knob unless the motor is on. When the belt runs centered on the platen, the sander is ready to use.

Some belt sanders are available with *dustbag attachments.* This accessory vacuums the fine sanding dust as you sand the board, Figure 44-5. This attachment reduces the sanding dust in the air and on the project. The bag may get in the way when you are sanding the inside of cabinets and other enclosed areas. Empty the dustbag when it is full.

The belt sander can damage the wood surface unless you use it correctly. Moving the sander in the wrong direction or applying incorrect pressure will make the sander dig into the wood. The grooves will show when you apply the finish.

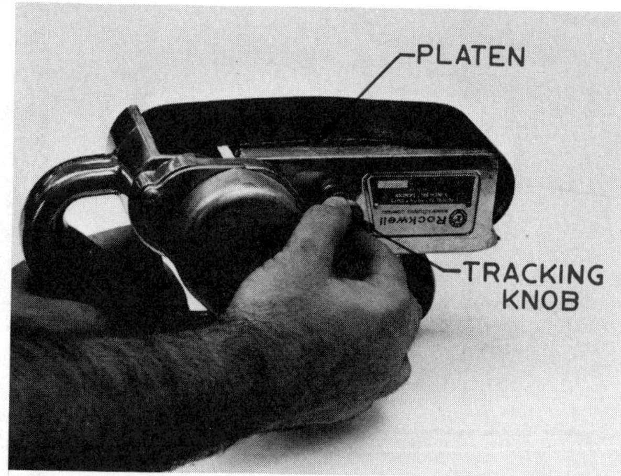

Figure 44-4
To center the belt on the platen, turn the tracking knob in or out.

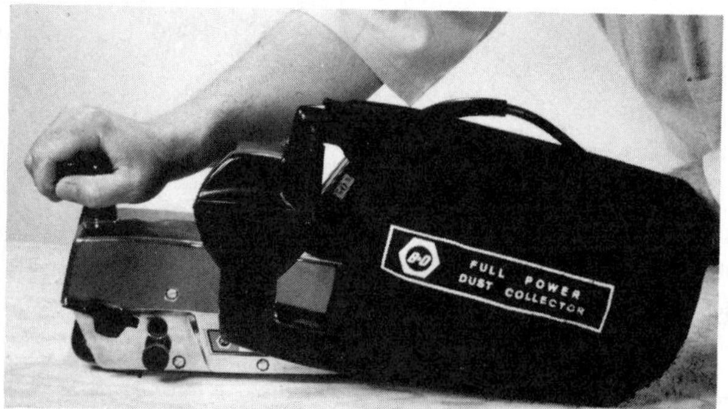

Figure 44-5
A dustbag collects most of the sanding dust. (Black & Decker Manufacturing Co.)

Follow this procedure when you are using the belt sander:

1. Unplug the cord. Select and install a belt with the correct grit for the job. A coarse grit, 60 or 80, will remove much material quickly. But it will also leave coarse, deep scratches in the wood surface. A 100-grit belt is a general-purpose size. Finer belts, 120 to 150, do not cause such deep scratches in the surface, but they cut at a slower rate.
2. Position the cord where it will not interfere with the operation. Be sure that the switch is off before plugging the sander in. When the switch is turned on, the sander will tend to pull away from you. Control the machine by holding onto the handles.
3. If possible, clamp the stock to a workbench. Sanding on a vertical surface is difficult. You can sand vertical parts by laying them flat on a workbench top before you assemble them. Clamp the stock to the workbench with either the bench vise or wood-screw clamps. Otherwise the sander will throw the work off the bench.
4. Place the sander flat on the stock and turn on the switch, Figure 44-6. Be ready to move the machine immediately. If you stop the movement, the machine will dig into the stock. If you allow the sander to lean to one side, it will damage the wood.
5. Establish a pattern like that in Figure 44-7. Move the sander in the direction of the grain. Sanding across the grain will make deep scratches that are difficult to remove. Be careful when you are sanding plywood. The top veneer is thin, and the sander can cut through it quickly, exposing the inner plies. Keep the sander moving. Sand the entire surface.
6. Do not apply any downward pressure. The weight of the sander gives enough pressure. Applying more will overload the motor. The belt will dig into the surface and make deep scratches that will show when you apply the finish.

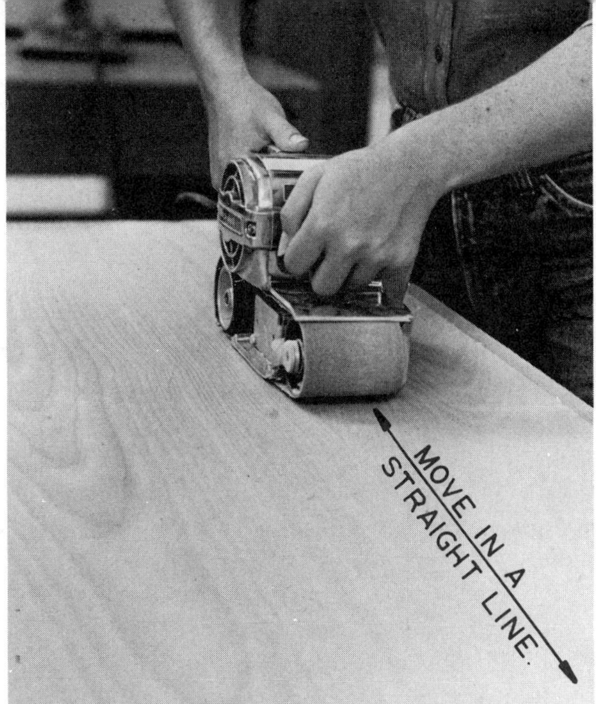

Figure 44-6
Hold the belt sander properly. Move it in a straight line.

Figure 44-7
To reduce sanding marks, keep the sander moving in the recommended pattern.

PORTABLE PAD SANDERS

Pad sanders, or finishing sanders, are simple to operate, Figure 44-8. The primary use of pad

Figure 44-8
Types of pad sanders.

sanders is for fine-finish sanding. But with coarse, abrasive paper you can also use them to remove material.

The three major types of pad sanders are the orbital, the vibrating and the straight-line, Figure 44-9. An *orbital pad sander* makes an elliptical motion on the pad. This sander removes material quickly, but part of the stroke goes across the grain. The sander scratches small circular marks into the surface. The marks will show when you apply a transparent finish. A *vibrating pad sander* moves sideways back and forth. This movement makes cross scratches in the surface. The sander removes the wood quickly, but the cross scratches are not desirable. A *straight-line pad sander* is the best of the three for producing a high-quality sanding job. The pad moves forward and backward with the grain. As long as you direct the sander parallel to the grain, you need not worry about cross scratches, Figure 44-10.

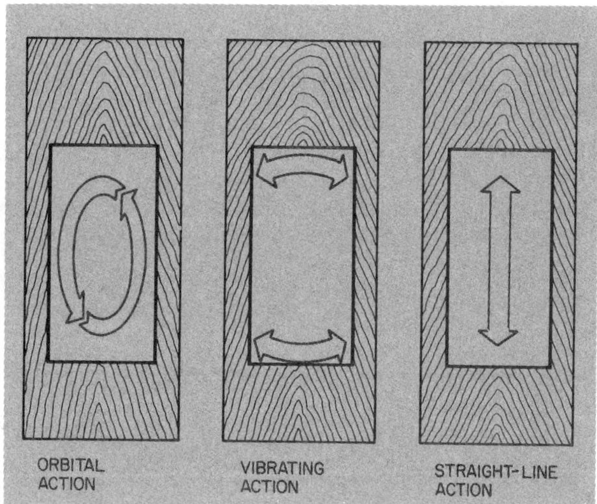

Figure 44-9
Pad sanders move in three different directions.

The three sanders are powered either by compressed air or by electricity. Electric sanders are convenient and inexpensive to operate. They require no special additional equipment. They tend to wear out easily, however, because they have many moving parts and because operators often overload the electric motors.

Compressed air sanders, or *pneumatic sanders*, are lightweight, compact and difficult to overpower, Figure 44-11. An air compressor is the power source. This type of sander usually is expensive because of its heavy construction. For efficient operation, use only clean air. Follow the manufacturer's suggestion for lubrication.

Most pad sanders have standard-size pads that use a fourth, a third or a half sheet of abrasive paper. The grit size of the paper depends on the sanding task. Insert the paper under the spring clips at the front and the rear of the sanding pad, Figure 44-12.

The size of the sander is determined by the size of the pad or by the strokes or oscillations per minute. These vary from 10,000 to 20,000 oscillations per minute.

Operation of the pad sander is simple. Place the sander flat on the surface and turn on the power. You can guide all but the straight-line sander in any direction. Cover the entire surface equally. Concentrating on one scratch or spot

Figure 44-10
A straight-line sander produces scratches with the grain.

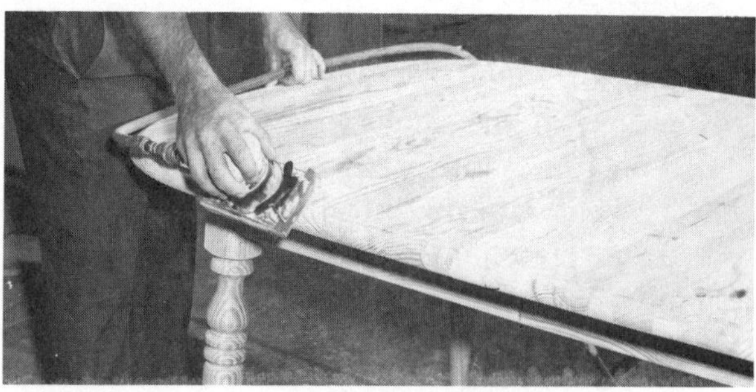

Figure 44-11
A pneumatic pad sander is compact. (The Aro Corporation)

will produce a low area. Let the weight of the sander supply the pressure. Pressing down on the machine will shorten the life of both the abrasive paper and the sander.

PORTABLE DISC SANDERS

Portable *disc sanders* are useful for rough shaping and sanding. The circular motion of the disc removes material quickly, Figure 44-13. This cross-sanding with coarse paper, however, makes deep cross scratches in the wood. Use the disc sander for sanding off old, thick paint and for rough shaping of complex shapes.

To use the sander properly, hold the pad at a slight angle so that only the outer half of the abrasive paper touches the wood. Holding the disc flat on the board will make it bounce out of control.

Figure 44-12
Spring clips hold the sandpaper on the pad of the sander.

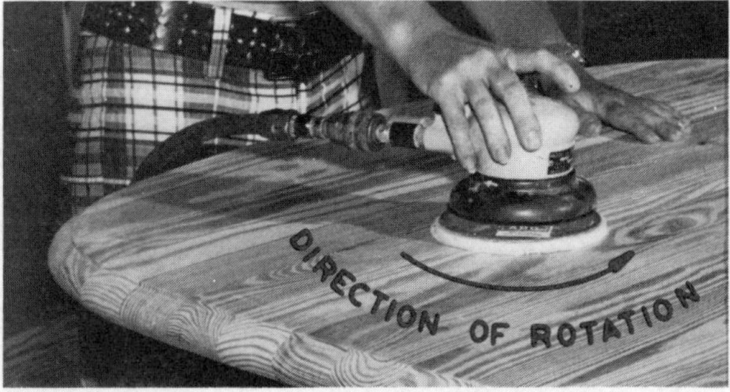

Figure 44-13
A disc sander removes material quickly. (The Aro Corporation)

REVIEW QUESTIONS

1. What determines the size of a portable belt sander?
2. What is meant by tracking?
3. Which size grit is a general-purpose size?
4. How should you move the belt sander over a horizontal surface?
5. Name the three types of pad sanders.
6. Which type of pad sander will leave no cross-scratch marks?
7. What types of surfaces should you sand with a disc sander?

SUGGESTED ACTIVITIES

1. Inspect your portable sanders and name all the parts.
2. Practice using the sanders in your shop. Dampen the sanded surface with a wet paper towel to see the scratch pattern.

SECTION

6

Construction Techniques

45
Furniture Construction

46
Kitchen Cabinets and Plastic Laminates

To make a piece of furniture you will use many joints and construction techniques. You need to understand how to select and make the various parts of a project such as a table or chest. All the parts must blend together to make a strong and attractive piece of furniture.

These techniques, combined with your skill in using hand and power tools, will result in successful projects. Section 6, Construction Techniques, will help you plan and construct a project. It will show you how to select joints and put together various parts. You will learn how to construct drawers, doors, cabinets and other major components.

UNIT

45

Furniture Construction

Objectives

After studying this unit you should be able to:

1 Identify the different types of furniture construction.

2 Construct doors and drawers.

3 Select from among joints and construction techniques.

Technical Terms

Leg and rail construction
Carcass construction
End panel
Dust panel
Lipped door
Facing
Flush door
Flush overlay door
Sliding door
Raised panel door
Wooden drawer slide
Kicker
Toeboard

You can choose from among many techniques to construct furniture. Some techniques are hundreds of years old. Others reflect recent technology.

You must select the techniques that best fit the piece of furniture you will be working on. Consider the techniques carefully. Using the wrong ones may produce a project that will not last or will be unattractive.

All furniture pieces fall into two categories. Pieces that have legs are built from *leg and rail construction*, Figure 45-1. Other pieces are made from *carcass construction*, Figure 45-2. Both types of construction have many combinations and variations.

Figure 45-1
The table and chairs are examples of leg and rail construction. (Crawford Furniture Mfg. Corp.)

Figure 45-2
A chest of drawers is an example of carcass construction. (Crawford Furniture Mfg. Corp.)

LEG AND RAIL CONSTRUCTION

Leg and rail construction requires some type of joinery. You will find a joint wherever a cross rail meets a leg. The area where the two members meet usually is small, so you will need a strong joint. Most furniture built from leg and rail construction is exposed to much force and weight. Good construction techniques will keep the legs from spreading.

The most common types of joints in leg and rail construction are the dowel and the mortise and tenon, Figure 45-3.

Legs and cross rails often are reinforced with a glue block or a metal corner brace, Figure 45-4. This strengthens the joinery. A chair seat or a tabletop often is attached by wood blocks. Usually a wood screw is driven through the block.

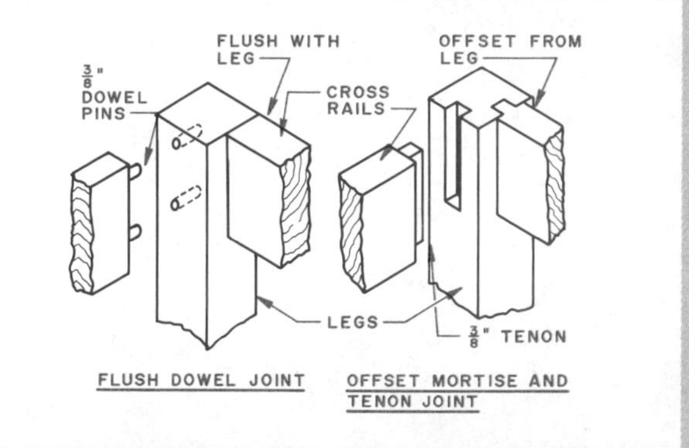

Figure 45-3
A dowel joint or mortise and tenon joint is used in leg and rail construction.

CARCASS CONSTRUCTION

An enclosed furniture piece usually is built by carcass construction. It may have drawers, doors or both. Typical examples include chests of drawers, stereo cabinets and dining room hutches. Carcass construction also is called casework. Figure 45-5 shows major parts of a piece of casework. Each part has many variations except for the carcass, or the boxed portion. The carcass essentially is the same. Doors and drawer fronts often vary to produce different styles.

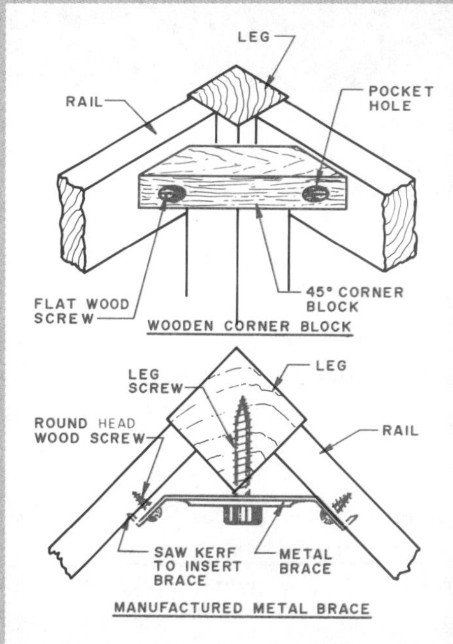

Figure 45-4
A corner block or metal brace reinforces the leg.

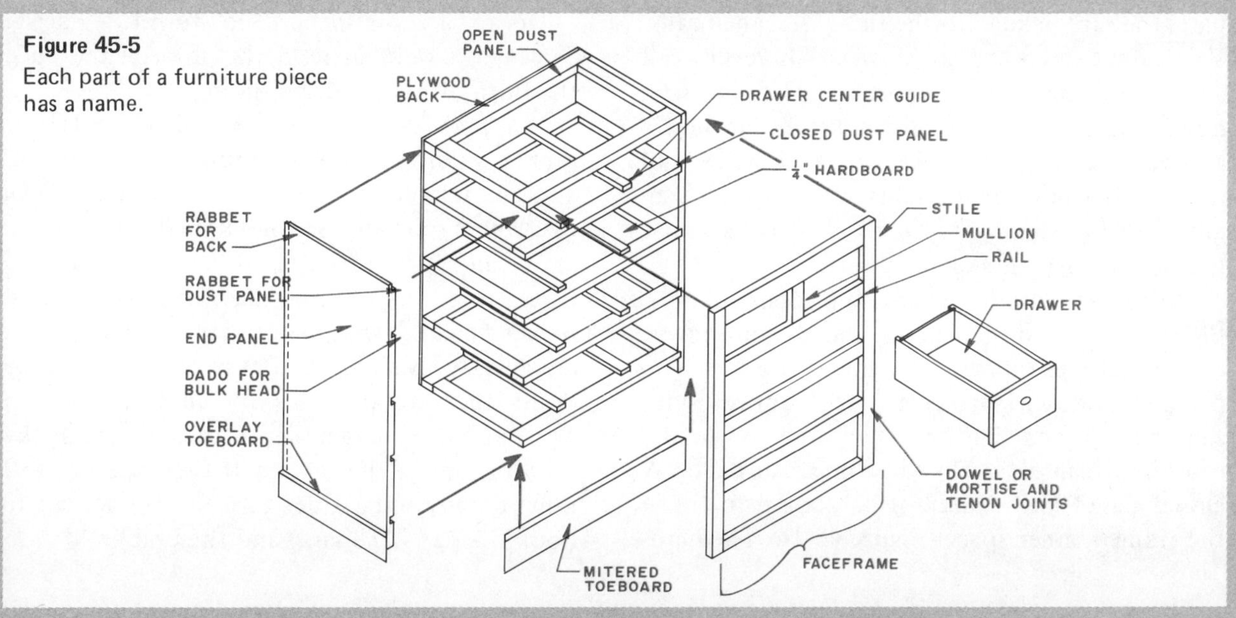

Figure 45-5
Each part of a furniture piece has a name.

Figure 45-6
This nightstand has a solid lumber end panel. Note the typical grain pattern of solid lumber.

Figure 45-7
An example of panel construction.

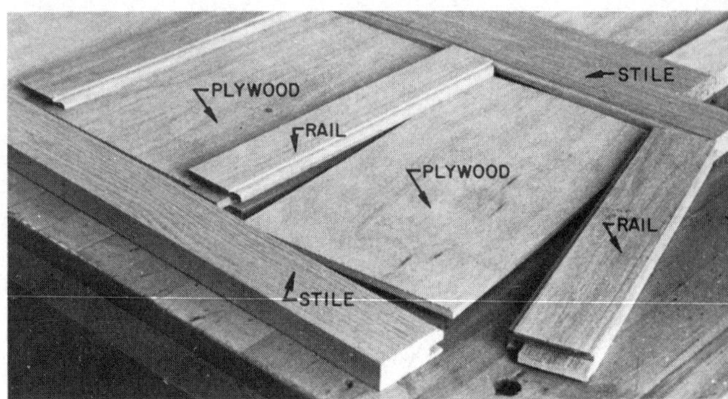

Figure 45-8
Major parts of an end panel include stile, rail and plywood panel.

End Panels

End panels have a solid lumber, a plywood or a panel construction. Solid lumber panels need the most material. The panels are made from narrow boards, Figure 45-6. Thus, it takes time to glue them. Large lumber panels may warp. Plywood end panels are easy to cut and do not warp. Usually they are more expensive. Sanding through their veneers, however, can be a problem.

End panels made from panel construction are used most often in commercial furniture, Figure 45-7. The end panels have a lumber frame around a plywood panel, Figure 45-8. Frame parts that are parallel to the floor are called rails. Vertical members are called stiles. Wherever a rail and a stile meet, use a mortise and tenon or a dowel joint. On the inside of the frame, cut a groove or a rabbet to hold the panel. Stiles and rails usually have high-quality wood. Panels usually are 1/4" (6 mm) plywood. You also can use hardboard, glass, metal and plastic.

Dust panels also have panel-type construction, Figure 45-9. A dust panel is under each drawer and sometimes immediately under the top. The panel provides a surface that the drawer sides can slide on and that can attach the top to the case. You can get a closed or an open panel. A closed panel has a piece of hardboard to fill in the frame's inner space, Figure 45-10. The hardboard provides reinforcement and a dirt-free compartment for the drawer. An open dust panel has only a frame with open spaces in between the frame members, Figure 45-11. Use an open panel when joining the top. Open and closed panels use inexpensive hardwood, such as poplar, for their dust panel frames.

Doors

Doors are important to furniture design. Types of doors include the lipped, the flush, the flush overlay and the sliding.

A *lipped door* has a 3/8" x 3/8" (10 x 10 mm) rabbet on either three or four edges, Figure 45-12. The rabbet and the front edge of the *facing* overlap. You can use the lipped door in just about any furniture style. It has two advantages. First, it covers an unsquare opening. Second, it can be used with many hardware styles that are readily available and easy to install. Lipped doors that are rabbeted on all four edges are 1/2" (13 mm) larger in width and length than the opening of the carcass. If there are 12" (305 mm) between the stiles of a faceframe, cut the door 12-1/2" (318 mm) and then rabbet it.

Figure 45-9
A closed dust panel is made from a lumber frame with a hardboard panel.

Figure 45-10
Use hardboard to enclose the dust panel that separates the drawers.

Figure 45-11
Use an open dust panel to hold the carcass together and attach the top.

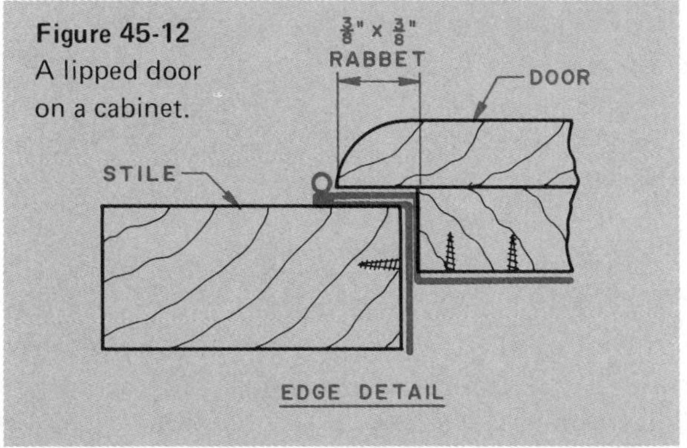

Figure 45-12
A lipped door on a cabinet.

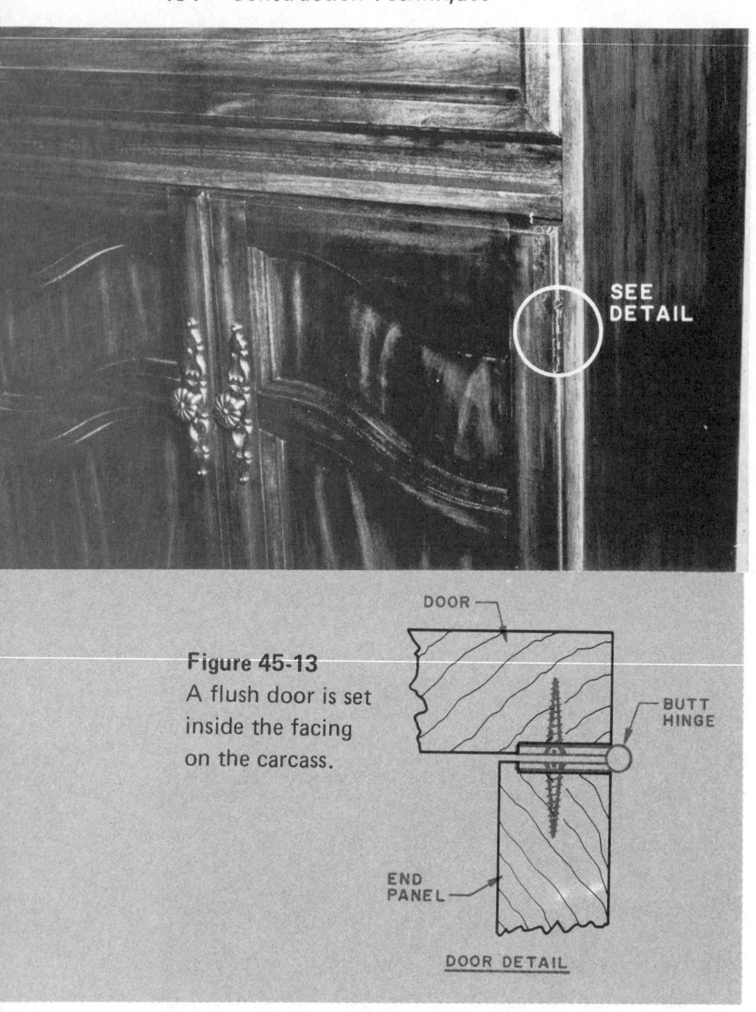

Figure 45-13
A flush door is set inside the facing on the carcass.

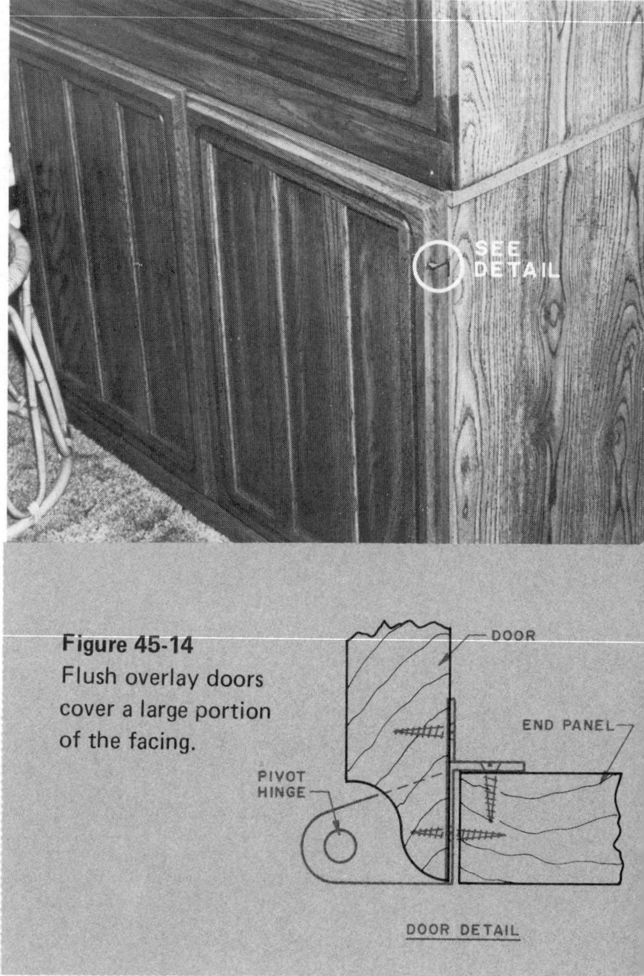

Figure 45-14
Flush overlay doors cover a large portion of the facing.

First, mount two semiconcealed hinges on the door. Then center the door on the carcass opening and install the remaining screws through the hinge and into the facing. The door must hang so that its edges are parallel to the surrounding lines of the furniture piece.

Mount a *flush door* so that the door's face is even with the front of the facing, Figure 45-13. A flush door lends itself to more traditional styles of furniture. The outside face of the door is even with the outer surface of the facing. It is one of the most difficult types of doors to install. The door is cut with a 1/16" (2 mm) space on all edges except the hinged side of the door. Both the door and the opening must be square to produce an attractive appearance. Use a butt hinge to hang the door. Cut a rectangular recess or gain into the door and the edge of the facing. Some woodworkers prefer to cut the gain only in the facing. This method is somewhat faster.

The third type of door is the *flush overlay door,* Figure 45-14. Apply this door to the front of the facing. Many woodworkers select the flush overlay for its plain appearance. It is used in contemporary styles of furniture. If a drawer is above the door, match the grain by cutting both the drawer and the door from the same panel. Leave edges square or shape them to a pattern. You will need special hardware.

Some pieces of furniture have *sliding doors,* Figure 45-15. Although 1/4" (6 mm) plywood is more common, hardboard, plastic or glass also can be used. You can make a wood track from hardwood or use commercial tracks. A sliding door made of wood slats is a tambour door. It is used on roll-top furniture, Figure 45-16.

Panel Door

Use a panel door with any of the door types described above. It is easy to construct, Figure

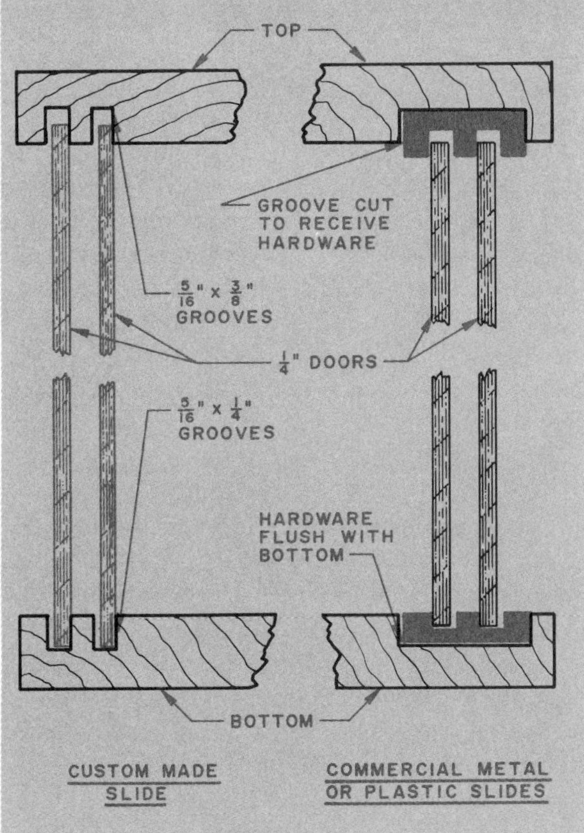

Figure 45-15
Sliding doors can have different kinds of slides.

Figure 45-17
A panel door is simple to make and offers a pleasing appearance.

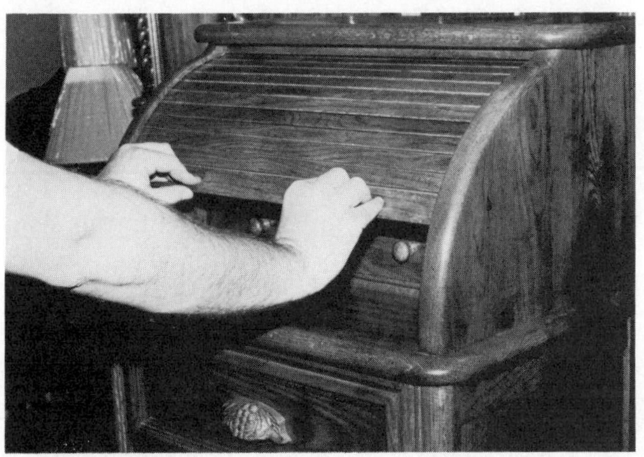

Figure 45-16
A tambour is a kind of sliding door.

45-17. The door has a framework of lumber with a matching 1/4" (6 mm) plywood panel in the center, Figure 45-18. Plastic, glass or other materials can replace the plywood. Cut a groove from end to end on the inside edges of the stiles and rails. Make a tenon at each end of the rails to match the groove in the stiles. Cut the plywood panel 1/8" (3 mm) smaller in width and length than the measurements from the bottom of the grooves. This will allow for expansion and

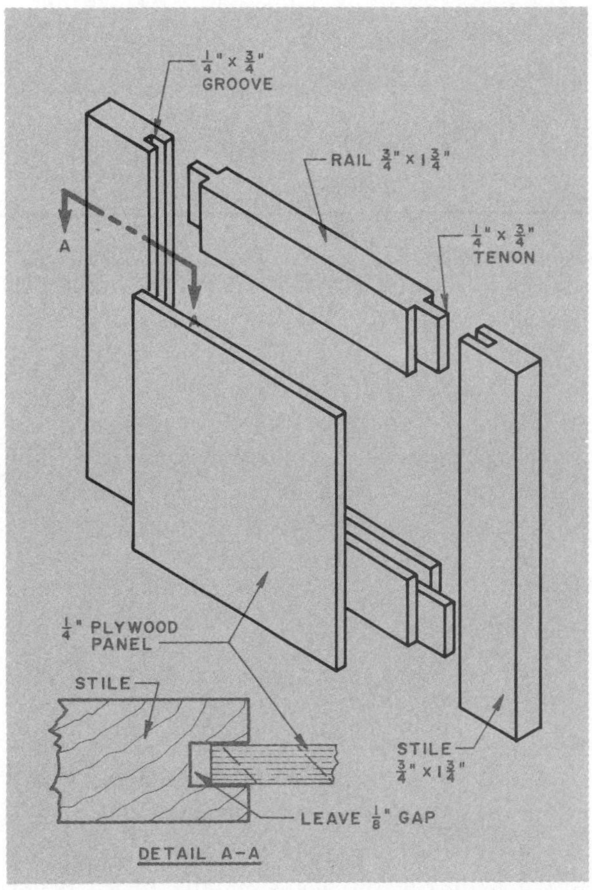

Figure 45-18
A panel door can be made from lumber and plywood.

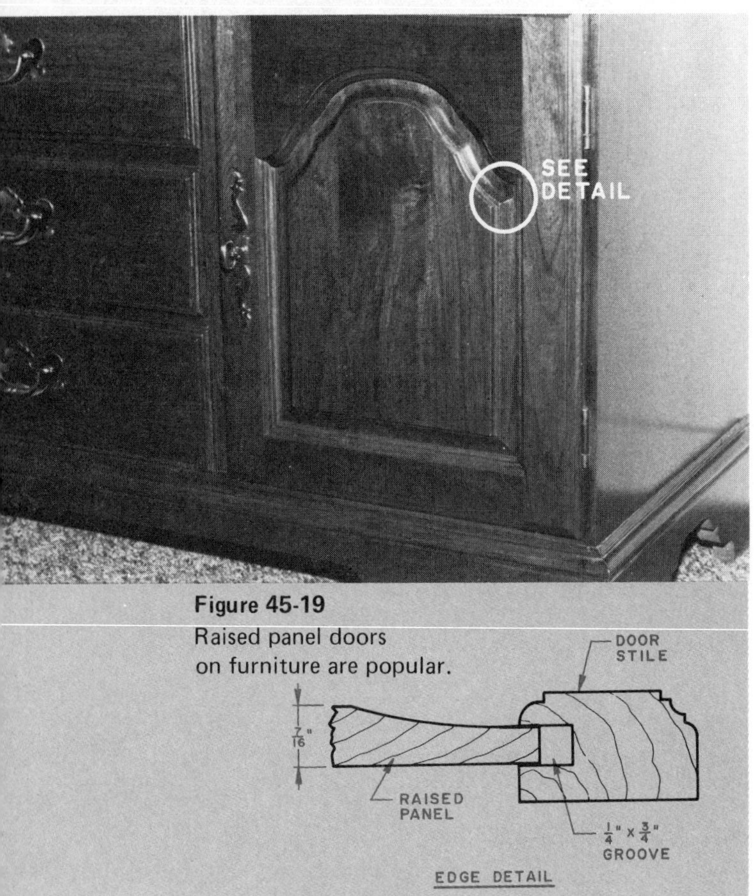

Figure 45-19
Raised panel doors on furniture are popular.

contraction. If possible, stain the entire panel before you assemble the door. This will prevent a light line of unstained wood from showing as the door swells and shrinks. On larger doors, use either a dowel joint or a haunched mortise and tenon joint to reinforce the corners. Apply glue to the joints and assemble. Do not glue the panel in place but allow it to float. Drive a few small brads from the back side of the door to hold it in position. You can shape the outside edges of the door to improve its appearance.

Raised Panel Door

A *raised panel door* is like a plain panel door with some exceptions, Figure 45-19. Make a stuck joint on the stiles and rails. Fill the center of the door with a solid panel. Shape all four edges of the panel with a concave cut to give a raised panel effect. Make the stuck joint and the raised panel on the shaper. Many raised panels have a crown top rail. You can make this arch cut on top of the raised panel. You need a shaper template and collar. Assemble the door following the same instructions as those for the panel door. Because the center panel is solid wood and not plywood, it is important to leave a space for expansion and contraction between the edge of the panel and the bottom of the groove.

Drawers

The major parts of a drawer are the front, sides, back and bottom, Figure 45-20. Each piece should be of durable, high-quality material. Make the drawer front of the same solid lumber as the doors and facing material. Solid hardwood is good for drawer sides and backs. Red oak, sycamore and poplar are typical choices. Softwood, plywood and hardboard are suitable for drawer bottoms.

Construct drawer sides and backs first. They should be 1/2" (13 mm) thick. The width of the side is equal to 1/8" (3 mm) less than the height of the drawer opening in the carcass. For most furniture pieces, the length of the drawer side is 1" (25 mm) shorter than the depth of the inside carcass measurement. It is important to shape the material square and flat. Cut a 1/4" x 1/4" (6 x 6 mm) groove on the inside of each side for the bottom, Figure 45-21. Position it 3/8" (10 mm) from the bottom edge of the drawer side. Cut a 1/4" x 1/2" (6 x 13 mm) dado on the same side as the groove for the back. Place it 1/2" (13 mm) from the back end. Round the top edges by using a 1/4" (6 mm) rounding over router bit. This gives the drawer a professional appearance.

Next, construct the drawer front. Decide whether you will use a lipped, flush or flush overlay edge style. The edge style usually is the same as that on the door.

The lipped drawer front has the same advantage as that of the lipped door. The size of the drawer front is 1/2" (13 mm) wider and longer than the opening of the carcass. For example, if the carcass opening is 4" x 12" (102 x 305 mm), the drawer front will be 4-1/2" x 12-1/2" (115 x 318 mm). The thickness is usually 3/4" (19 mm).

To complete the drawer front, make several cuts, Figure 45-22. Cut a 3/8" x 3/8" (10 x 10

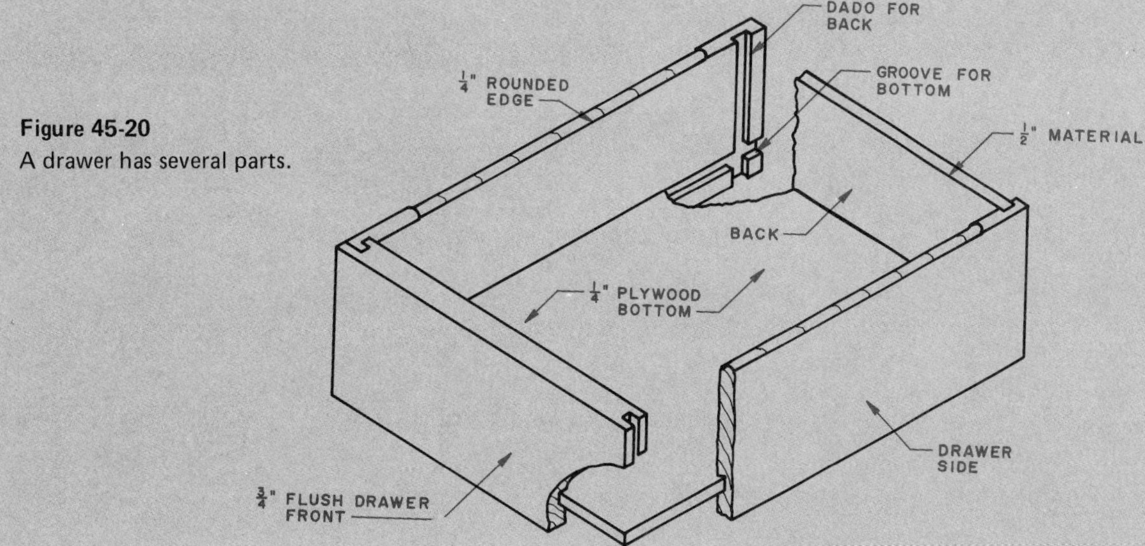

Figure 45-20
A drawer has several parts.

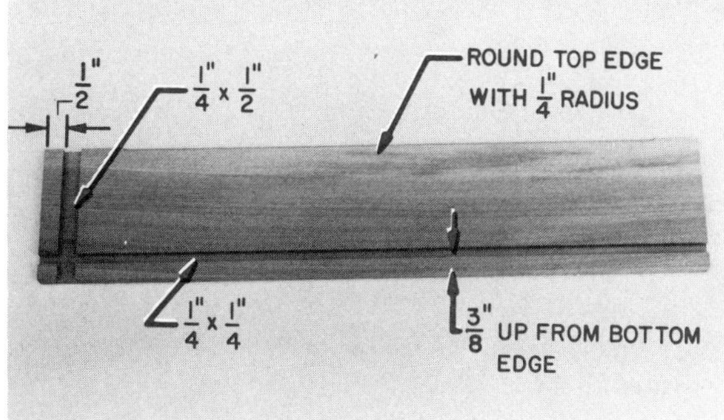

Figure 45-21
A drawer side has different cuts.

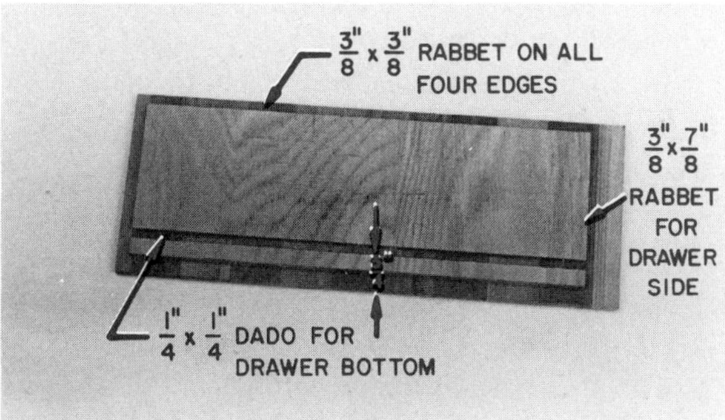

Figure 45-22
The back of a drawer front requires many cuts.

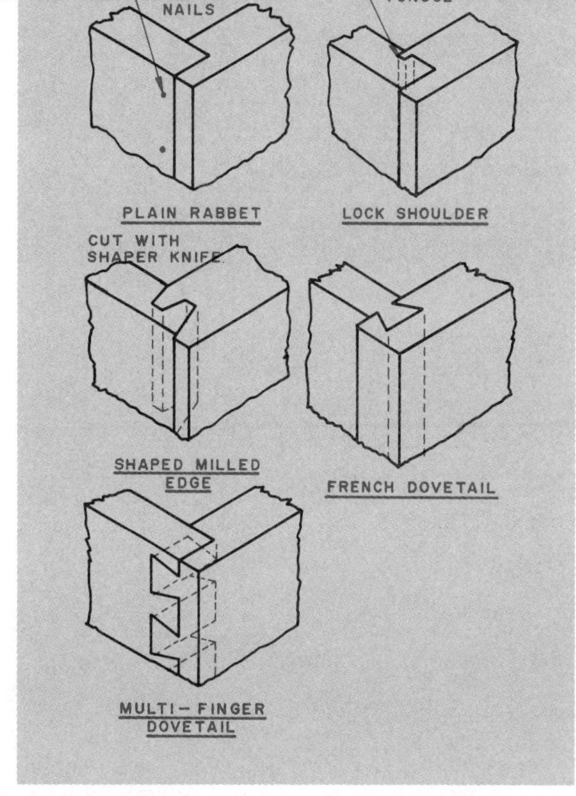

Figure 45-23
Different ways to attach drawer sides to drawer fronts.

mm) rabbet on all four edges. This will give the proper clearance for the drawer. Next, decide what type of joint you will use to attach the drawer sides to the drawer front. A plain rabbet is the simplest to make, but there are other possibilities, Figure 45-23. If you choose a plain rabbet, cut it the same width as the thickness of the drawer side.

In quality construction, drawers slide smoothly and easily. There are many methods of guiding a drawer, Figure 45-24. The selection of drawer slides depends on the design of the carcass and

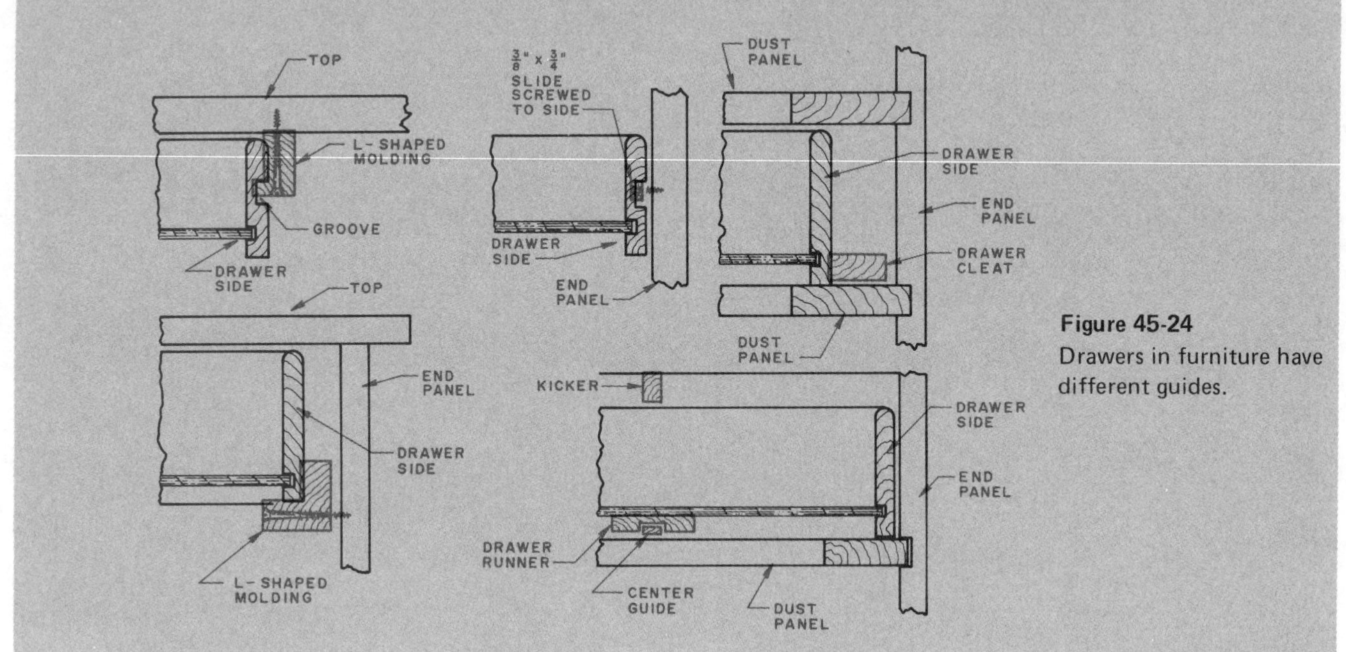

Figure 45-24
Drawers in furniture have different guides.

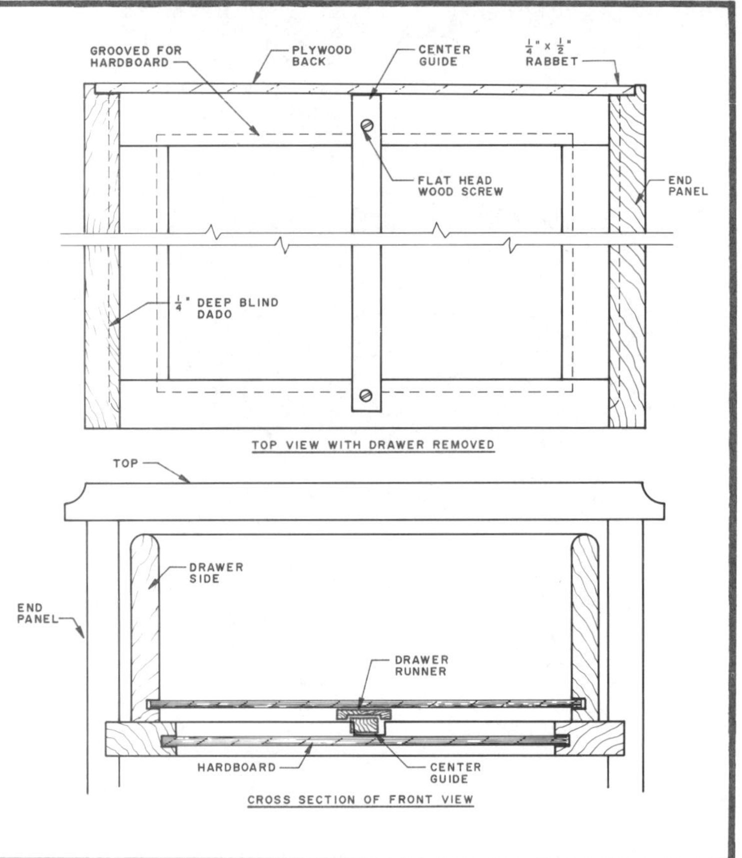

Figure 45-25
A center guide with a drawer runner is the most common method of guiding drawers.

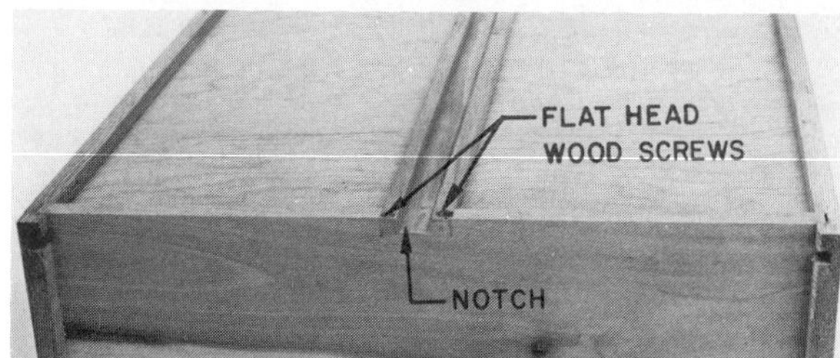

Figure 45-26
Cut a notch into the drawer back to allow the slide to be screwed to the bottom edge.

the preference of the woodworker. A *wooden drawer slide* usually is preferred for furniture, Figure 45-25. Use durable hardwood such as birch or hard maple. Cut the slide to fit into the dust panel and extend above the top surface 3/8″ (10 mm). Position the slide exactly in the middle of the carcass opening. Use wood screws to hold the ends in place.

Cut a notch along the bottom edge in the center of the drawer back. It should be 13/16″ (21 mm) wide by 7/16″ (11 mm) high. This notch moves along the 3/4″- (19 mm-) wide wooden drawer slide installed on the dust panel. After you apply the finish, rub paraffin wax on all mating surfaces. You may also install a wooden channel to slide along the drawer guide, Figure 45-26. This gives more bearing surface and longer life. When the drawer is pulled about halfway out, it tends to drop down as the back of the drawer rises off the dust panel. Install a *kicker* above the drawer to prevent this problem, Figure 45-27. Mount a piece of birch or maple behind the facing and attach it to the bottom of the dust panel or to the top immediately above the drawer. There should be a clearance of 1/16″ (2 mm) between the top of the back and the bottom edge of the kicker. Wood screws hold it in place.

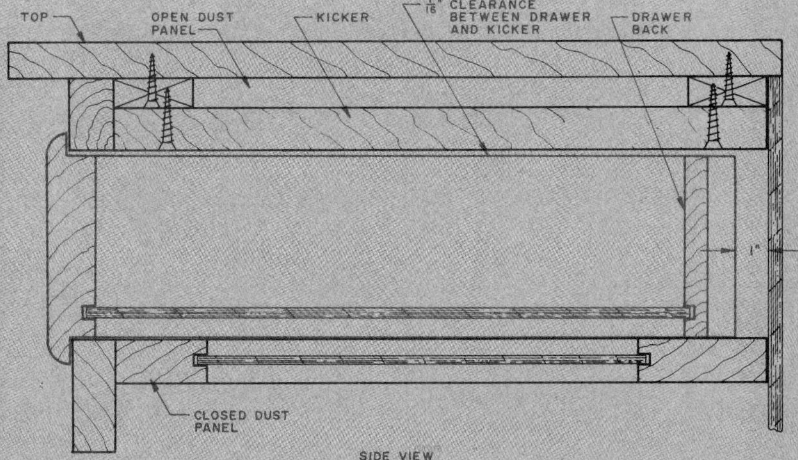

Figure 45-27
A kicker prevents the drawer from dropping down when it is pulled out.

Figure 45-28
A solid lumber top often has a shaped edge.

Figure 45-29
A piece of plywood has an edge band to cover the edge.

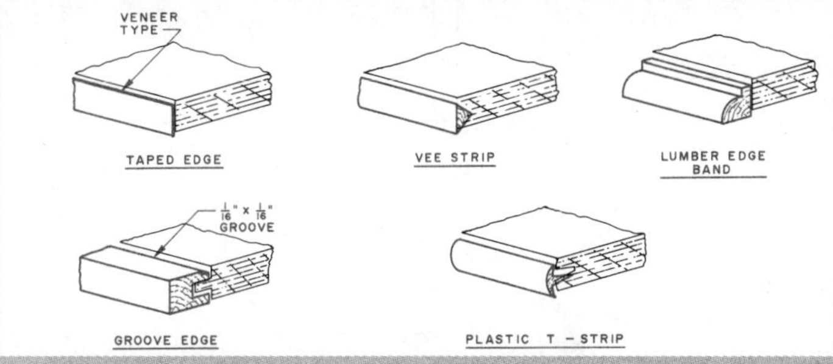

Figure 45-30
You can use different edgings for a veneered top.

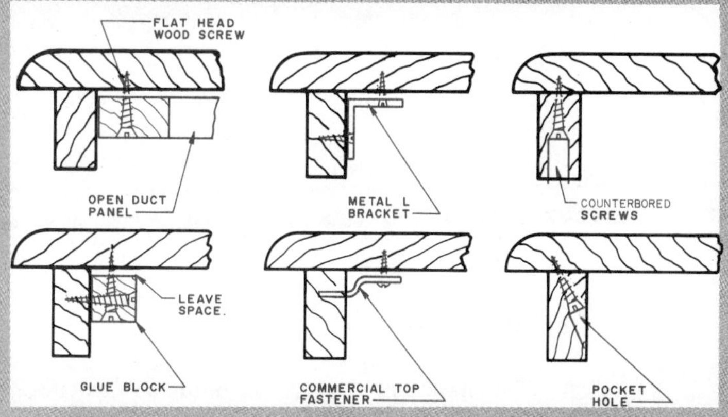

Figure 45-31
Fasten tops to the carcass in different ways.

OTHER FURNITURE CONSTRUCTION TECHNIQUES

Top construction. Furniture parts can be made either from solid lumber or edge-banded veneered material. The materials determine what assembly techniques to use. A solid lumber top should not have any type of edge band covering the ends and edges, Figure 45-28. Expansion and contraction of the top will break any joint at the corners. You may use some type of shaped edge to dress up the corners. If you use plywood or a veneered, covered particle board, apply an edge band, Figure 45-29. Different kinds of covering are shown in Figure 45-30. You can use a shaped edging on shelves, sides and other exposed edges of plywood or particle board. Use a miter or a butt joint at the corners. Reinforce the joint with a glue block, a spline or dowels.

Attaching top. Most furniture pieces have a top that must be attached to the carcass or legs. There are different ways to do this, Figure 45-31. If you rabbet an open dust panel into the top

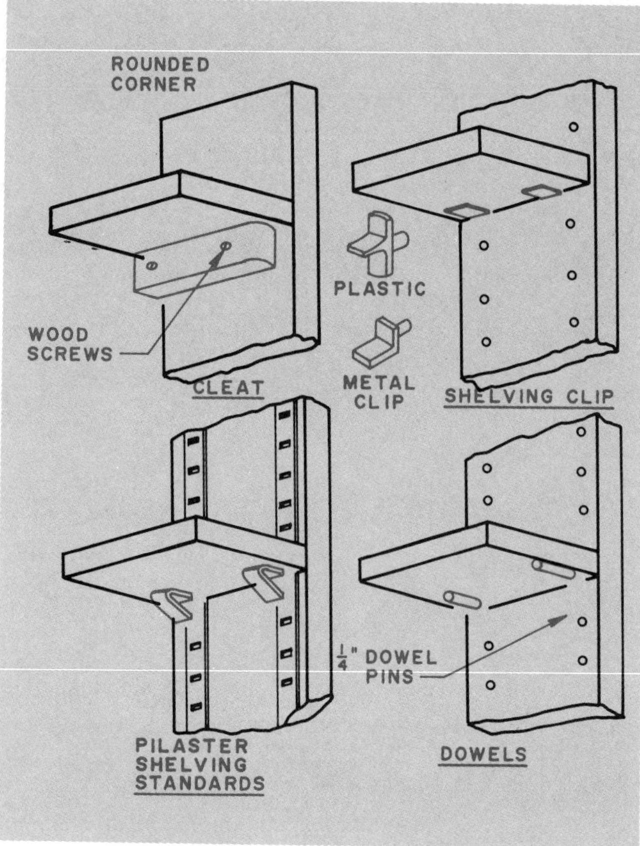

Figure 45-32
Attach shelving to the ends using one of the above techniques.

Figure 45-33
Apply a toeboard to the case and miter it at the corners.

of the ends, you can insert wood screws through the panel and into the top. This technique allows you to move the top anywhere on the carcass to compensate for a piece that is not exactly square. You also can remove the top easily.

Shelves. Shelves are stationary or adjustable, Figure 45-32. Attach stationary shelves to the sides with a blind dado. Adjustable shelves add storage flexibility inside the carcass.

Toeboards. Apply *toeboards* to the carcass and position them against the floor. They raise the carcass off the floor and provide more stability. Apply the toeboard to the outside of the carcass, Figure 45-33. Use a spline or other reinforcement to strengthen the miter joint at the corners.

REVIEW QUESTIONS

1. What are the two kinds of furniture construction? Sketch an example of each.
2. Name the two most common joints for leg and rail construction.
3. What two types of construction are used to make end panels?
4. What are the four types of door styles? Sketch an example of each.
5. Name two advantages of the lipped door.
6. Describe how to construct a raised panel.
7. Sketch the inside of a drawer side. Include the dados with their dimensions.
8. What should be the dimensions of a drawer front if the opening in the facing is 4-1/2" x 16-1/2" (115 x 419 mm)?
9. Sketch the parts of a wooden drawer slide. Give dimensions.
10. What is the purpose of a kicker?
11. Sketch four different methods of applying an edge band on plywood or particle board.
12. How is a top attached to the carcass using an open dust panel?
13. List four different methods for installing shelves.

SUGGESTED ACTIVITIES

1. Find a furniture piece constructed with leg and rail techniques and a piece constructed with carcass techniques. List the different types of joinery that you find.
2. Calculate and list the sizes of all parts of a drawer to be used in an opening 4" (102 mm) high by 14" (356 mm) wide. The inside carcass dimension is 21" (533 mm).
3. Visit a furniture store and see how many different materials and construction techniques you can find. How would you change them to make them better?

UNIT

46

Kitchen Cabinets and Plastic Laminates

Objectives

After studying this unit you should be able to:

1 Tell the difference between production and custom cabinets.

2 Name the major parts of cabinets and understand their functions.

3 Construct kitchen cabinets and plastic laminate tops.

Technical Terms

- Production cabinet
- Custom cabinet
- Lazy Susan
- Work triangle
- Faceframe
- Rail
- Stile
- Mullion
- Bulkhead
- Structural part
- Monorail
- Side-mounted rail
- Plastic laminate
- General purpose grade

Kitchen cabinet manufacturing is an important part of the woods industry. Each year, thousands of new cabinets go into many new and remodeled homes. The cabinets vary in both design and construction methods.

A typical kitchen has wooden base and wall cabinets and a plastic laminate countertop. They give beauty and usefulness to a room. Cabinets store silverware, pots and household appliances. The plastic laminate top provides a place to prepare food, put supplies and mount the sink.

KITCHEN CABINET

Manufactured kitchen cabinets are either production or custom. *Production cabinets* generally are made in large manufacturing plants that rely on mass-production techniques. Many workers are involved in producing cabinets. Each employee specializes in one job, for example, in assembling cabinet doors. *Custom cabinets* are made at a construction site or in a cabinet shop.

Production Cabinet

Production cabinets come in standard-width cabinets or modules, Figure 46-1. Most cabinet companies offer units that start at 9″ (230 mm) wide and increase in width by 3″ (76 mm) increments. They go up through 72″ (1829 mm). You can identify production cabinets by two vertical facing members or double stiles found wherever two cabinets or modules are attached, Figure 46-2.

Custom Cabinet

Custom cabinets are constructed differently, Figure 46-3. Usually, cabinetmakers complete the full set of cabinets and sometimes install the units. Custom workers must be able to do many types of jobs.

Custom units are unique. Once a cabinetmaker constructs a set of custom cabinets, another set exactly like it probably will never be built. Each set is designed and constructed for a particular kitchen. Double stiles are not necessary. Custom cabinets join to form a continuous unit.

Types of Cabinets

Custom and production cabinets have base and upper, or wall, units and specialized units,

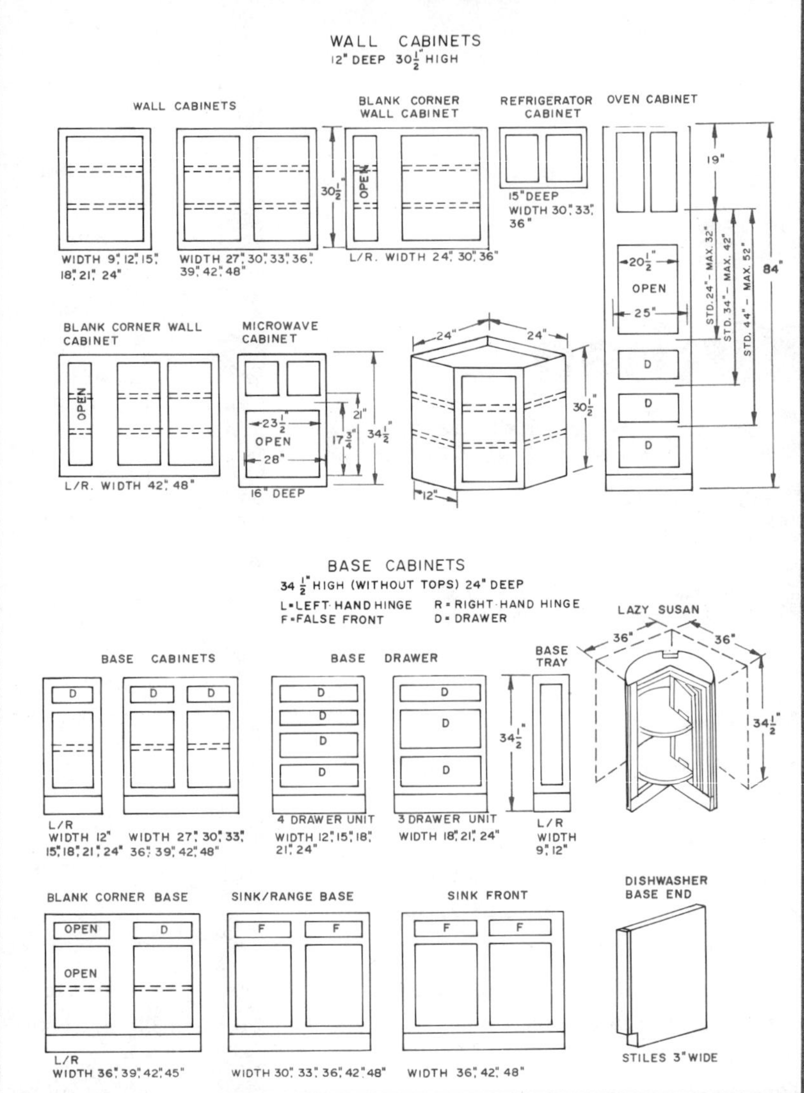

Figure 46-1
Production cabinets are made in standard-size modules.

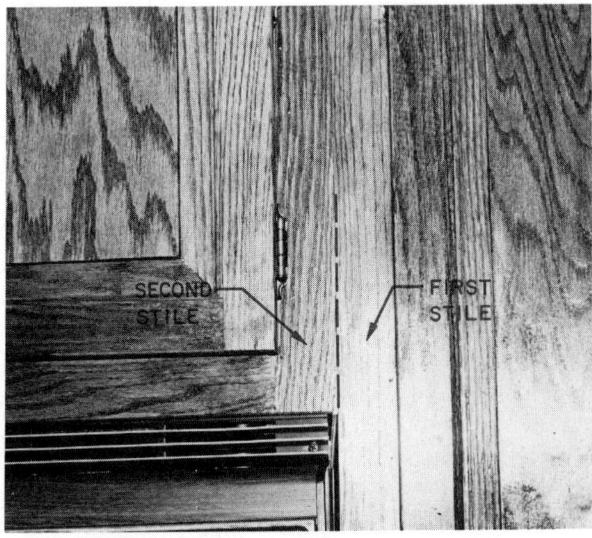

Figure 46-2
You can see stiles wherever two modules of production cabinets are attached.

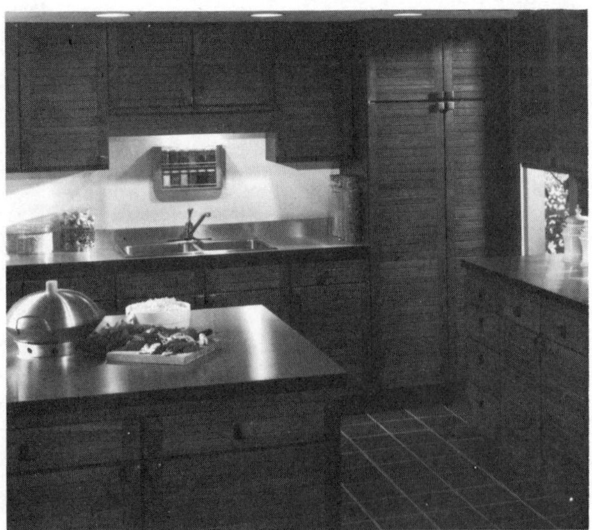

Figure 46-3
Custom cabinets are constructed specially for each kitchen. (Prestige Products Inc.)

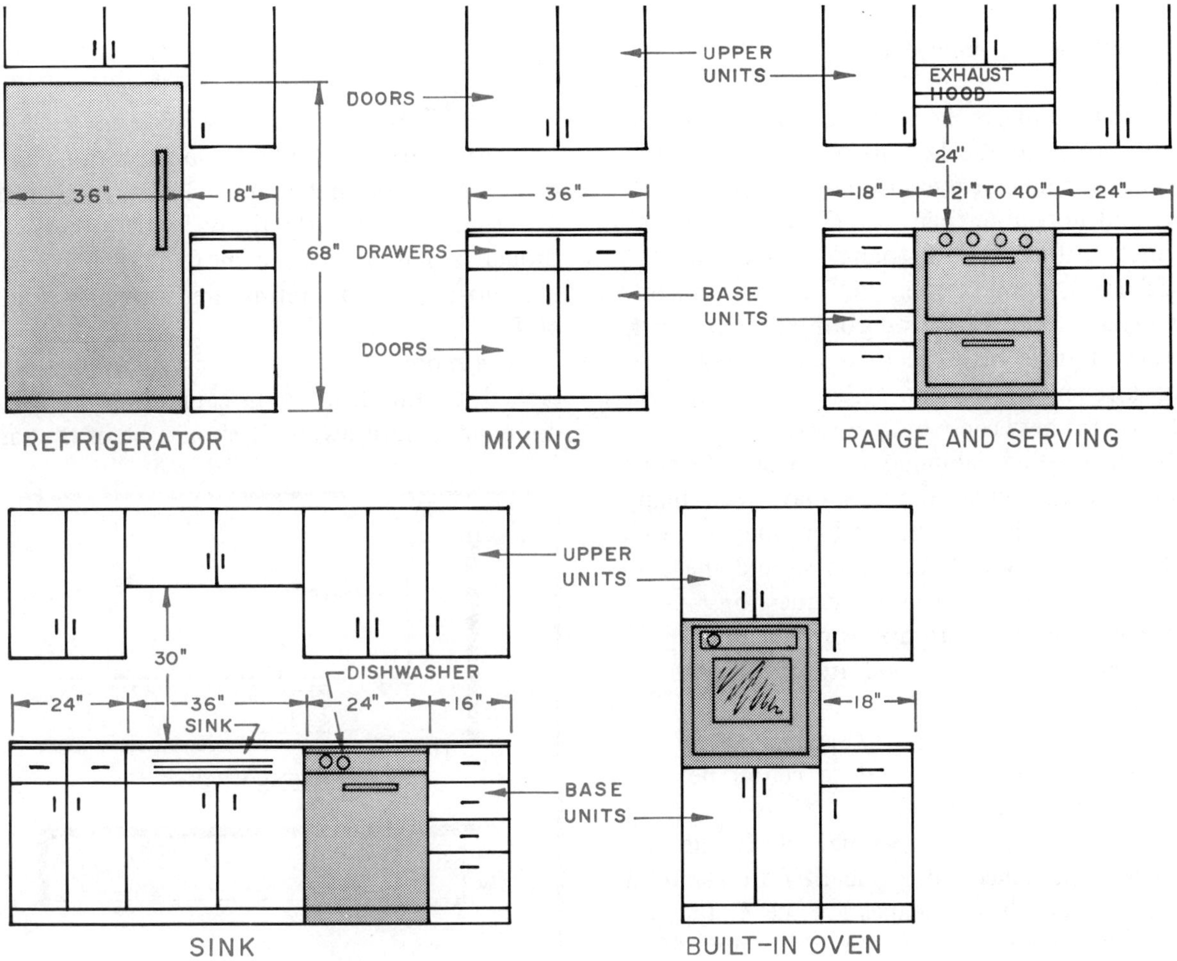

Figure 46-4
Kitchen work areas have both base and upper cabinet units.

Figure 46-4. A base unit has drawers and doors. It attaches to the wall and the floor. Upper cabinets have doors and fasten to the wall. Specialized cabinets are built for ovens and cleaning and china cabinets.

A *lazy Susan* often is used as a corner cabinet, Figure 46-5. It is a specialized cabinet. A lazy Susan comes as an upper or a base unit. It provides easy access to many items. It has revolving shelves that bring up front things in the back of the cabinet.

Planning Kitchen Cabinets

Cabinet construction requires a lot of planning. Cabinets that are not designed and positioned correctly will prove unsatisfactory no matter how well built they are.

In designing your kitchen's layout, locate your three major work centers with a *work triangle*, Figure 46-6. Your triangle should point to the range, the sink and the refrigerator. If you draw

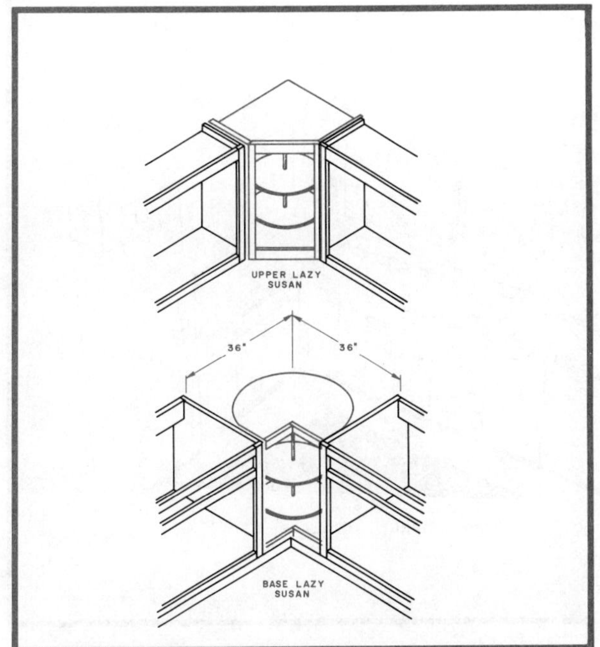

Figure 46-5
Lazy Susans have revolving shelves.

a line that connects the work centers, the perimeter, or total of the lengths of the sides of the triangle, should not measure less than 12′ (3658 mm) and not more than 22′ (6706 mm). If the perimeter of your work triangle is less than 12′ (3658 mm), your kitchen will be too compact. It will lack good floor and counter space. With a work triangle of more than 22′ (6706 mm), your kitchen will be too spread out. You will walk too far between work centers.

When locating cabinets, you must determine family needs. Some families may need many specialized cabinets, while others may do well with a simple layout. Cabinets should meet all family needs. Ask the following questions:

1. Do you need storage for portable appliances and other food-preparation equipment?
2. Do you want a desk or a sewing center?
3. Would you like an eating center next to the kitchen cabinets?

Generally, you as the planner will fit the cabinets and appliances into one of four standard kitchen shapes. These shapes are the *L*, the corridor, the one-wall, and the *U*, Figure 46-7. Kitchen shape depends on room shape and location of doors and windows.

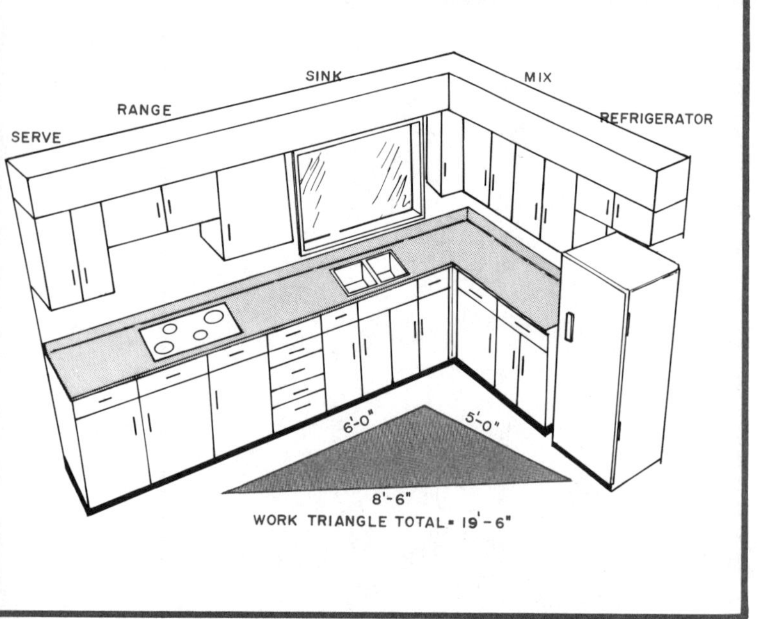

Figure 46-6
A work triangle is made up of the range, the sink and the refrigerator.

Cabinet Parts

Every part of kitchen construction has a name. A cabinetmaker must know these terms to communicate effectively with others. Although some parts have more than one name, the most common terms are shown in Figure 46-8.

Faceframe. A facing, or a *faceframe,* is attached to the front of a cabinet. It holds the doors and the drawers. It should be of the same

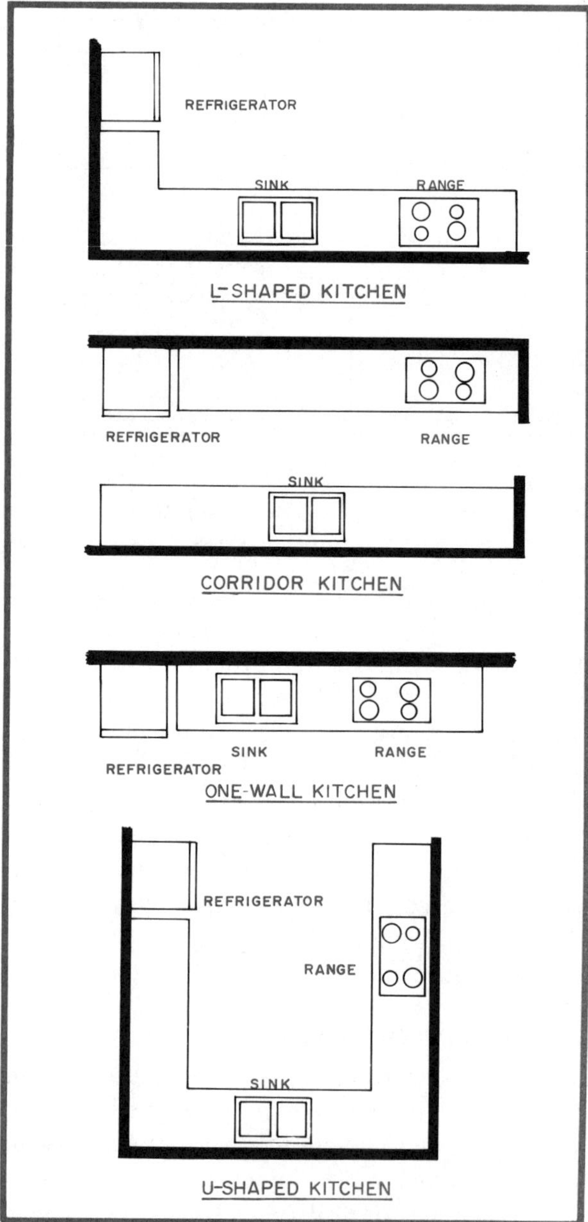

Figure 46-7
You should arrange kitchen cabinets in one of four shapes.

kind of lumber as the doors. Birch, oak and ash are common choices. Each faceframe has several parts, Figure 46-9. A piece running parallel with the floor is called a *rail*. A part perpendicular to rails or running vertically is a *stile*. Rails and stiles have other names that further identify where they are located. A *mullion* is a vertical part that is positioned between the right and the left stiles.

Rails and stiles form a joint at the point where they meet. Mortise and tenon and dowel joints make high-quality cabinet joints, Figure 46-10. Do not use simple butt joints. If you have enough time, glue the assembled faceframe to the cabinet. This eliminates the need for nails and for finishing the nail holes.

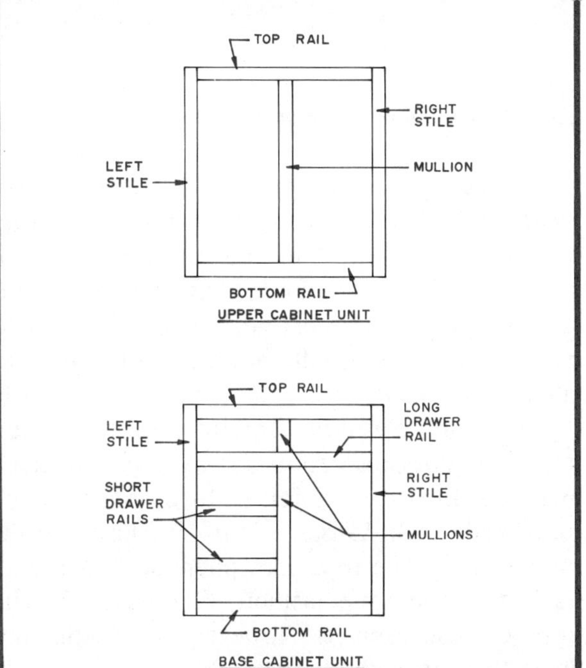

Figure 46-9
Each piece of the faceframe has a name.

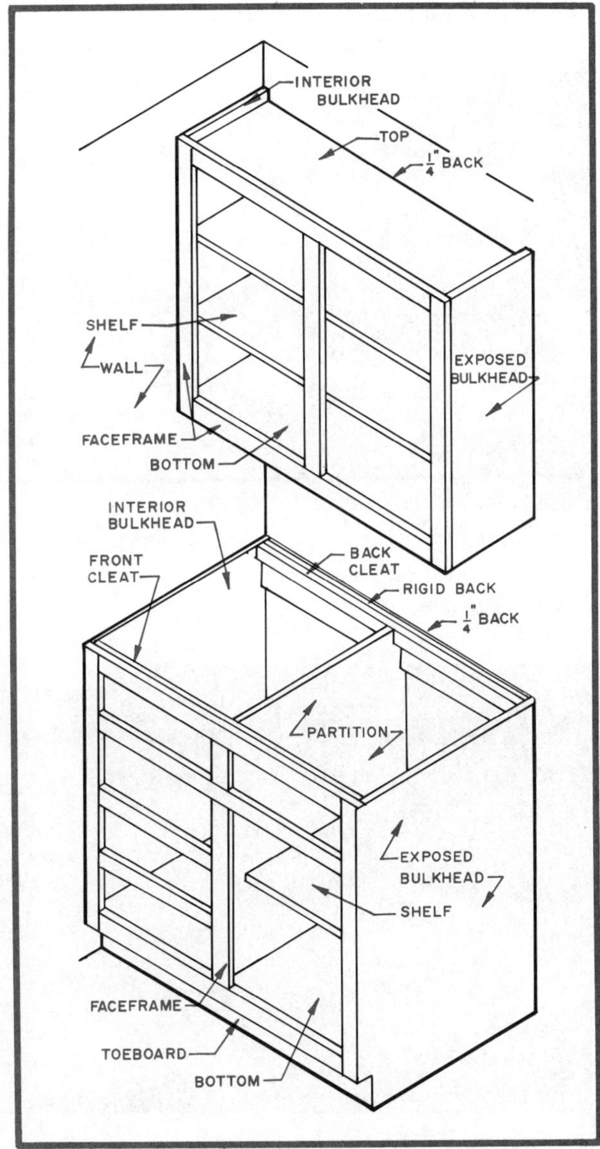

Figure 46-8
Each piece of a kitchen cabinet has a name.

Bulkheads. At each end of the cabinet is a *bulkhead*. There are exposed and interior bulkheads. Exposed bulkheads are visible after the cabinets and appliances are installed. Custom cabinet exposed bulkheads are made of 3/4" (19 mm) hardwood plywood to match the doors. Interior bulkheads are found against walls and appliances. These bulkheads are made of 3/4" (19 mm) fir plywood or particle board because they will not be visible.

Figure 46-10
Dowel joints assemble faceframes.

Bulkheads usually have a 1/4" (6 mm) deep dado to hold the 3/4" (19 mm) thick bottom, Figure 46-11. The dado positions the bottom and strengthens the cabinet. Interior bulkheads are nailed to the bottom, Figure 46-12. Exterior bulkheads usually are attached only with glue.

Tops and Bottoms. Interior bulkheads and tops and bottoms often are made of the same material. Bottoms are joined to the sides of the bulkheads with dadoes in both the base and the upper units. The tops for upper cabinets are attached in the same fashion, Figure 46-13. The tops of base cabinets, however, are plastic laminate that are applied separately.

Partitions. Partitions divide the cabinets. Without partitions, a long cabinet could not support shelves properly. Partitions usually are nailed into position through the bottom and the back.

Shelves. Most shelves are fir plywood with a solid lumber strip covering the front edge. You can use either adjustable or stationary shelves. You can move adjustable shelves to different levels easily by using commercial hardware. Use dadoes or nails to fasten stationary shelves on the bulkheads and partitions.

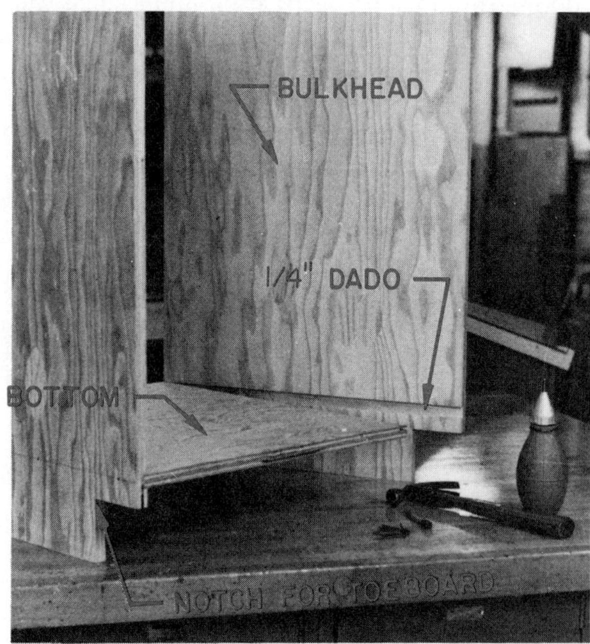

Figure 46-11
A 1/4" (6 mm) deep dado is cut into a bulkhead to hold the bottom.

Structural parts. To reinforce cabinets and to fasten them to the wall, use *structural parts*. Base units have a rigid back for strength and cleats for attaching the plastic laminate top, Figure 46-14. An upper unit has a nailing strip and a bottom cleat, Figure 46-15. A toeboard is in the recessed area under the base cabinet. The toeboard provides foot space. Without the toeboard, a person could not stand close to the cabinets.

Backs. A 1/4" (19 mm) piece of plywood is nailed or stapled to the back edge of the upper and the base cabinets to form a back, Figure 46-16. The back encloses the cabinet. Thus, the cabinet is not racked from side to side. A cabinet without a back is very weak.

Figure 46-12
Interior bulkheads are attached to the bottoms with 6d finish nails.

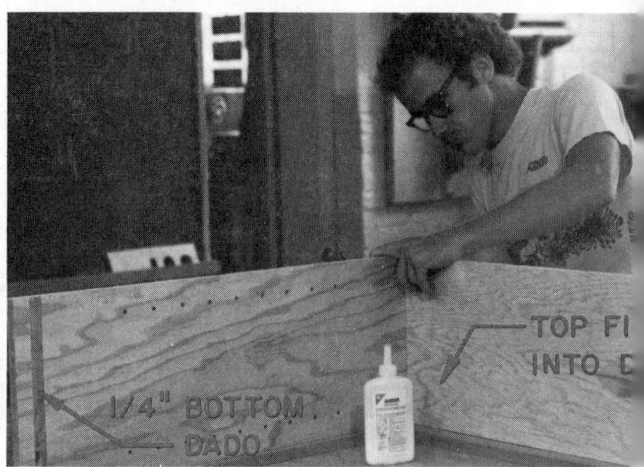

Figure 46-13
Tops and bottoms of upper cabinets are attached with 1/4" (6 mm) deep dadoes.

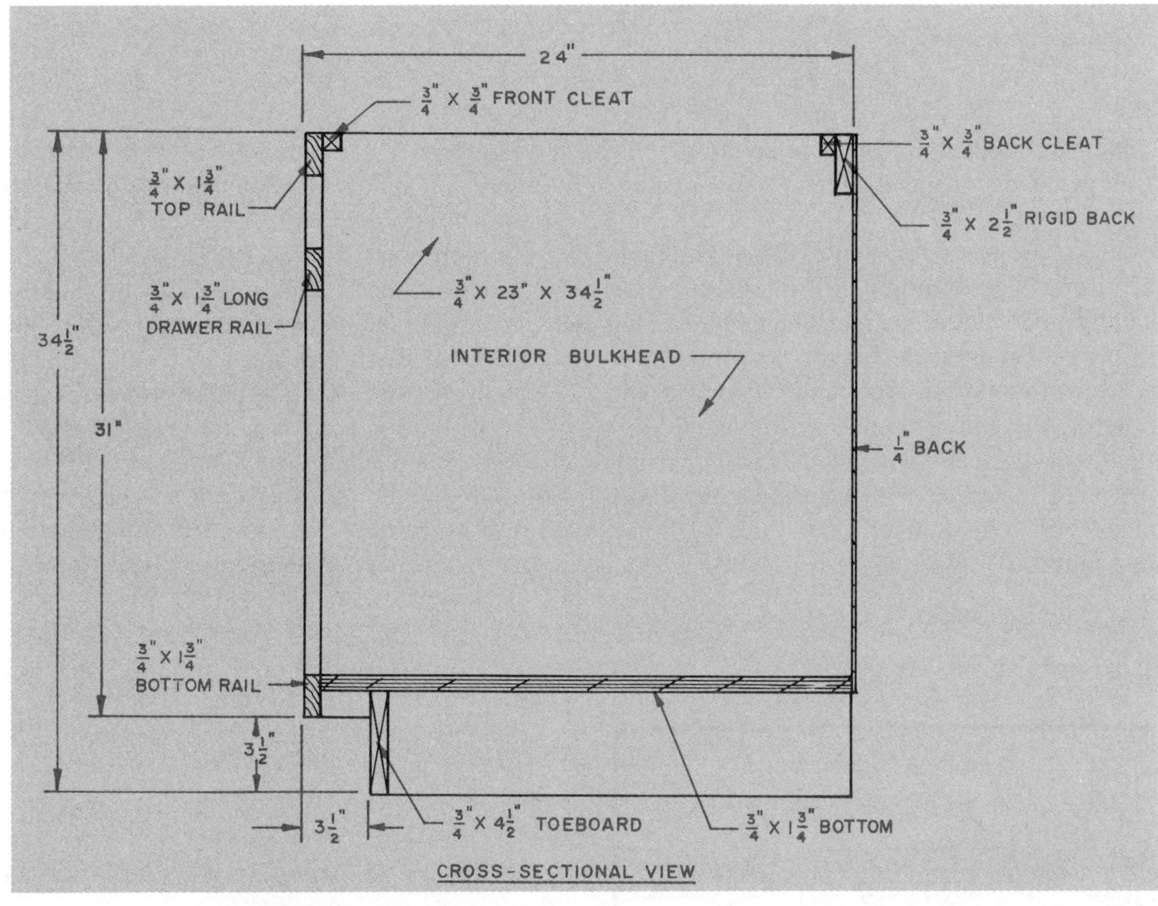

Figure 46-14
A front cleat, back cleat and rigid back add strength to the base cabinet.

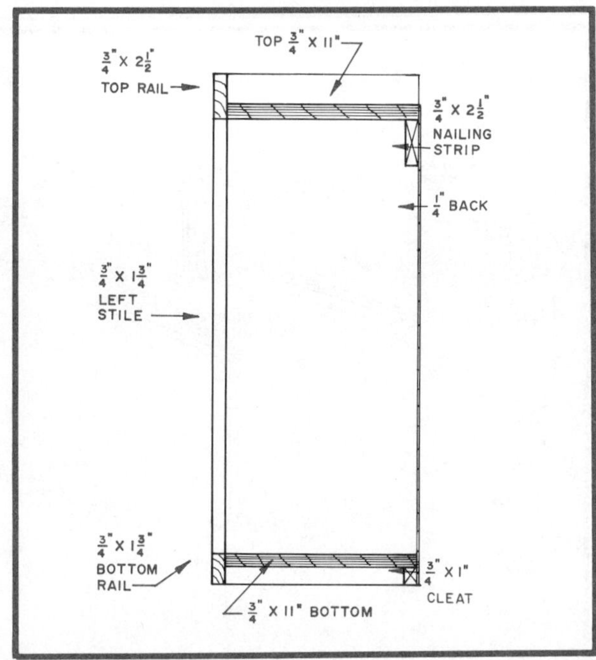

Figure 46-15
A cross-sectional view exposes the nailing strip and bottom cleat in an upper cabinet.

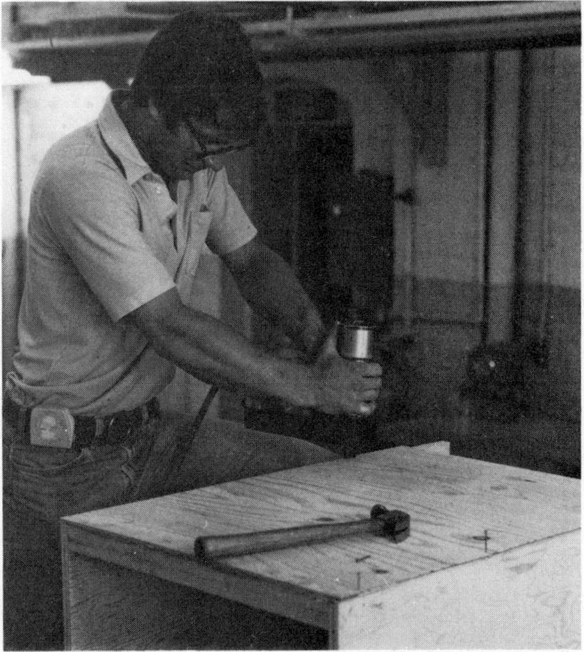

Figure 46-16
The plywood back can be attached with an air stapler or nailed on.

Door

Cabinet doors protect food and cooking utensils that are stored inside cabinets. Doors make a unit attractive.

Doors come in four major styles: lipped, flush, overlay, and sliding, Figure 46-17. For cabinets, lipped doors are preferable. The 3/8" (10 mm) rabbet around the door covers an unsquare opening in the faceframe. You can get many hinge patterns that are easy to install.

A plywood panel door is the most common. It is strong and easy to make. Raised panel doors are made of solid lumber. They are becoming more popular.

No door can be wider than 16" (406 mm) or taller than 48" (1219 mm). A larger door may warp and move away from the facing.

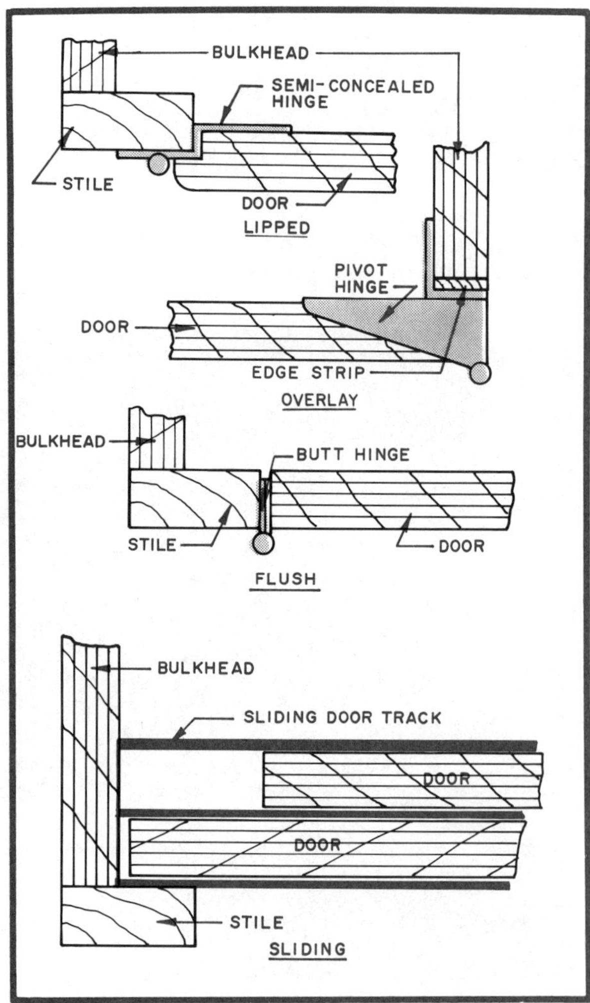

Figure 46-17
Cabinet doors can be any one of four styles.

Drawer

Drawers store spoons, forks and other small utensils. Single drawers are above each bottom door. A stack of four or more drawers offers even more storage areas.

Each drawer has two sides, a front, a back and a bottom, Figure 46-18. Drawer sides require a groove for the bottom and a dado for the back. The length of the back is determined by what type of sliding hardware is used. *Monorails* and *side-mounted rails* often are used for sliding drawer hardware, Figure 46-19. Each set of hardware contains mounting instructions to help you determine dimensions. The drawer-front style is usually the same as the doors.

PLASTIC LAMINATE

Kitchen cabinet tops usually are covered with *plastic laminate*. Some cabinets even have doors, drawer fronts and faceframes covered with this material. A plastic laminate often is known by its brand name, such as Formica®, Wilson Art®, Nevamar® and Textolite®.

A sheet of plastic laminate is five to seven layers of kraft paper that have been treated with phenolic resin. A printed layer of kraft paper

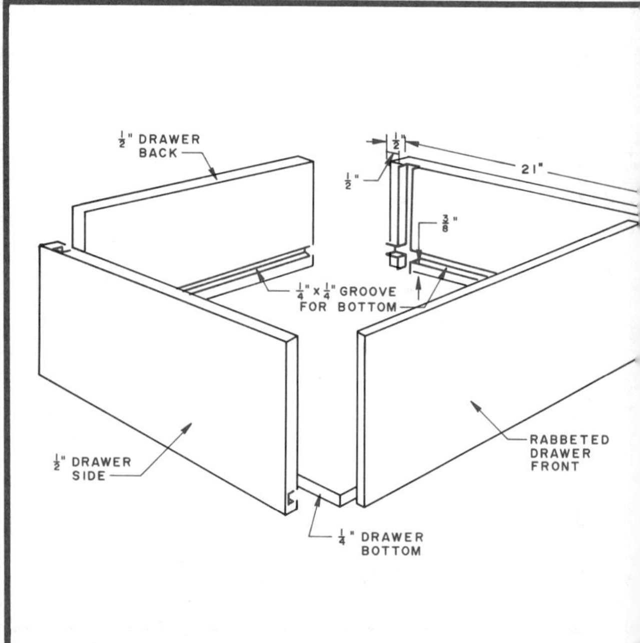

Figure 46-18
Kitchen cabinet drawers have several parts.

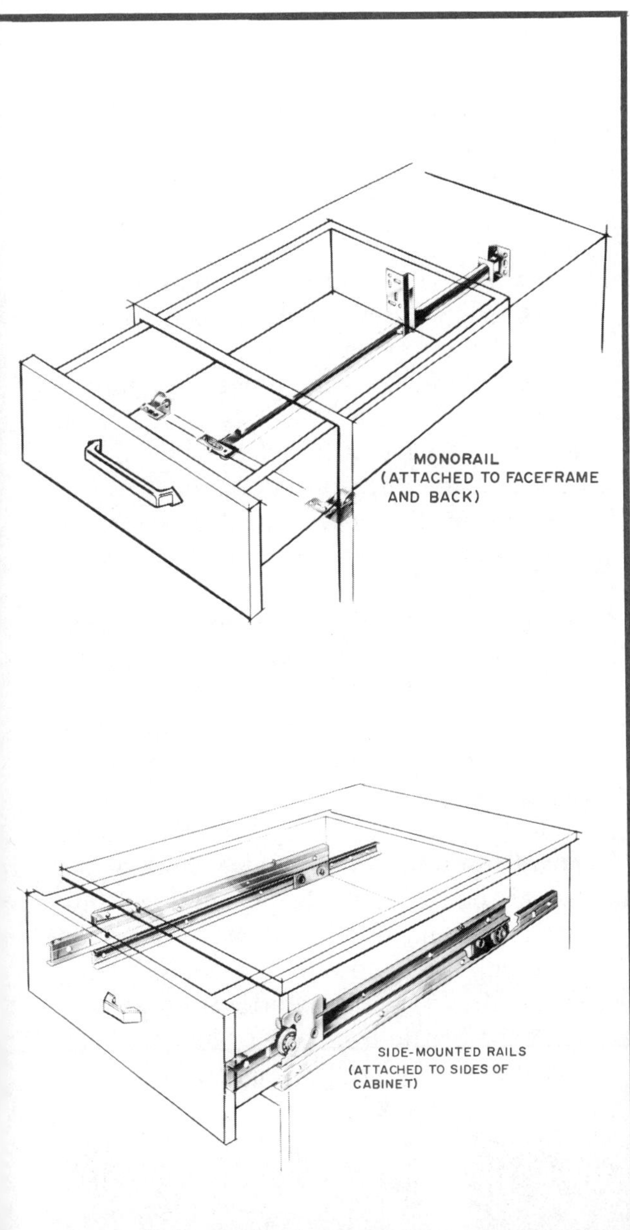

Figure 46-19
Drawers can be guided by monorails or side-mounted rails. (Knape & Vogt Manufacturing Co.)

applied to the top gives the sheet its color or pattern. Because this topmost layer can become scratched easily, a translucent topcoat of melamine is added for protection. All the layers are bonded in a press at 265° to 305° F at 800 to 1200 pounds per square inch. After baking for 60 to 90 minutes, the sheet is removed from the press and trimmed to finish size.

Plastic laminates are available in several patterns, finishes and grades. Companies that manufacture plastic laminate offer solid colors, wood grains and other patterns. With this range, a

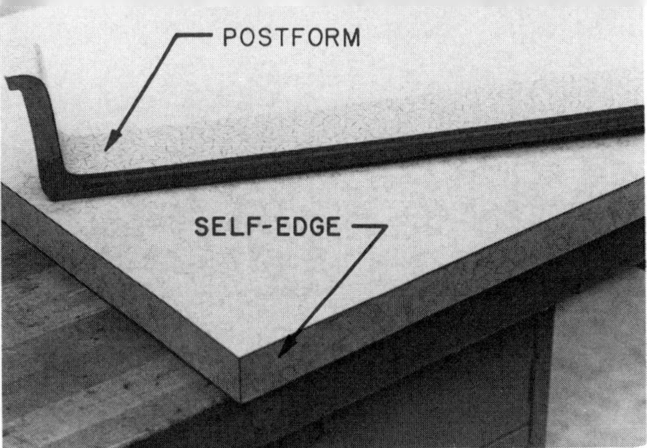

Figure 46-20
A self-edge top has square corners. A postform top has rounded corners.

kitchen designer can select a bright countertop that adds much color to a room or specify a laminate that will blend in with the cabinets.

Plastic laminate finishes are shiny, suede, embossed or wood grained. A shiny finish is known as a furniture finish. It looks highly polished but shows scratches easily. A suede finish is better because knife cuts and other surface marks blend in with it. Embossed and wood grain finishes produce special effects.

The grade of plastic laminates primarily applies to the thickness of the material. *General purpose grade* is 1/16″ (2 mm) thick. Mostly it is used on standard countertops. It comes in many colors, patterns and finishes. Because of its thickness, the general purpose grade is the most stable and has the greatest impact resistance. For tops that have rounded corners, a .050″ postforming grade is used, Figure 46-20. It is flexible and can be heated and bent to small radii. When you need additional strength, use 1/16″ (2 mm) balancing sheet grade on the underside of tops. Its dull brown color is not suitable for exposed surfaces. For walls and the fronts of cabinets, apply a 1/32″ (1 mm) vertical surface grade. Do not use it on countertops.

Plastic Laminate Tops

The two styles of cabinet tops are postform and self-edge, Figure 46-20. A postform top has a curved front edge and back. Specialized equipment rounds the corners. This cannot be done in a school. A self-edge top has square corners. It can be made easily on either a small or a large scale.

Procedures for Laminating Cabinet Tops

To laminate a cabinet top:

1. Construct the subtop, or substrate. The

best material for the substrate is 3/4" (19 mm) medium-density particle board. This material is very smooth and does not expand or contract very much.

Cut the subtop 25" (635 mm) wide and to the desired length. Many lumber suppliers sell particle board that is already cut to 25" (635 mm). You can determine the length by measuring the length of the face-frame. If your cabinet has exposed bulkheads cut the top 1" (25 mm) longer than the desired length for an overhang. To make the top 1 1/2" (38 mm) thick, glue and nail 3/4" x 2 1/2" (19 x 64 mm) strips to the bottom of a 3/4" x 25" (19 x 635 mm) piece, Figure 46-21.

2. Cut the plastic laminate to rough size from standard-size sheets. Select the sheet that will provide the least waste. Cut the edge band 1 3/4" (44 mm) wide and 1" (25 mm) longer than the finished length of the countertop. Cut pieces for the top at least 1" (25 mm) wider and longer than the substrate. A table saw with a combination carbide-tipped blade works well for sawing plastic laminates. If you use a table saw with the rip fence as a guide, attach an auxiliary fence to the inside of the rip fence, Figure 46-22. This will prevent the thin laminate from slipping under the fence and causing a crooked cut. On a table saw, cut with the good side facing up. You can use other tools, such as saber saws and hand saws, with some success.
3. Clean the bonding surfaces with pressurized air. Coat the back of the edge band and the edge of the top with contact cement. Use a small, disposable paint brush for applying cement, Figure 46-23. Apply an even coat first to the back of the edge band and then to the edge of the substrate.
4. Make sure that both glued surfaces are completely dry before bringing them together. After 15 minutes, you can test for dryness with a small piece of kraft paper. Lay the paper on the glued surface and apply pressure lightly, Figure 46-24. If the paper does not stick, you can apply the edging. If it does stick, wait 5 minutes and try again.
5. Hold the edge band away from the particle board to center it on the edge. Work with a helper, particularly when doing long tops. Bring one end of the laminate against the edge and work toward the opposite end, Figure 46-25. Apply additional pressure to stick the plastic laminate to the edge. You can use an edge roller, Figure 46-26, or a

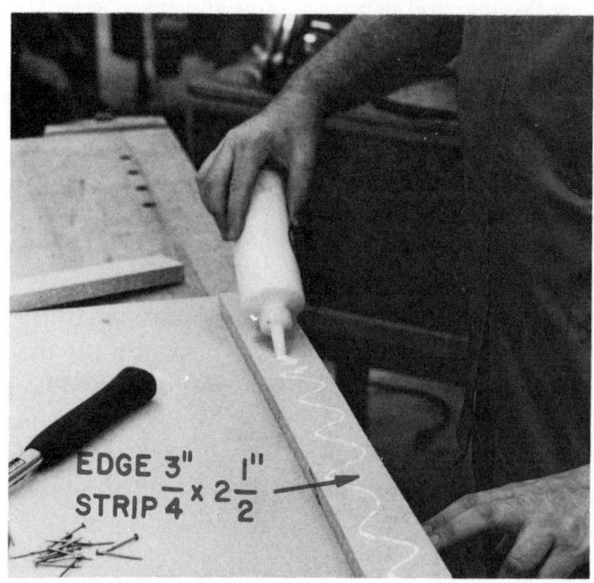

Figure 46-21
Glue and nail strips to the bottom of the top to make the 1-1/2" (38 mm) thickness.

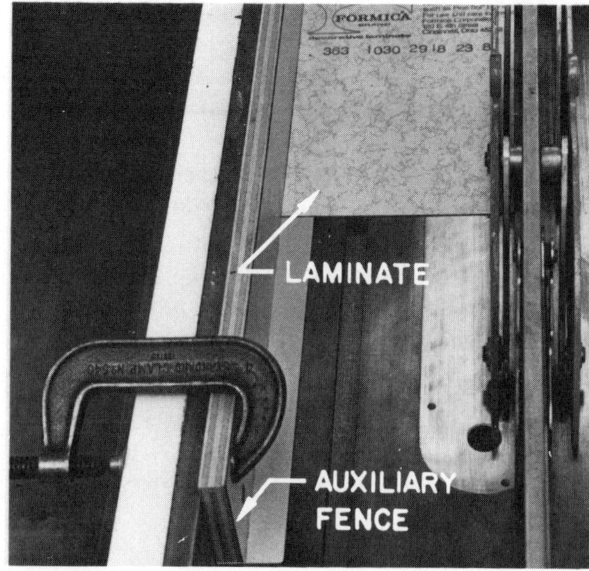

Figure 46-22
An auxiliary fence prevents plastic laminate from sliding under a rip fence.

Figure 46-23
A small paint brush works well for applying contact cement.

Figure 46-24
A piece of paper tests the dryness of contact cement.

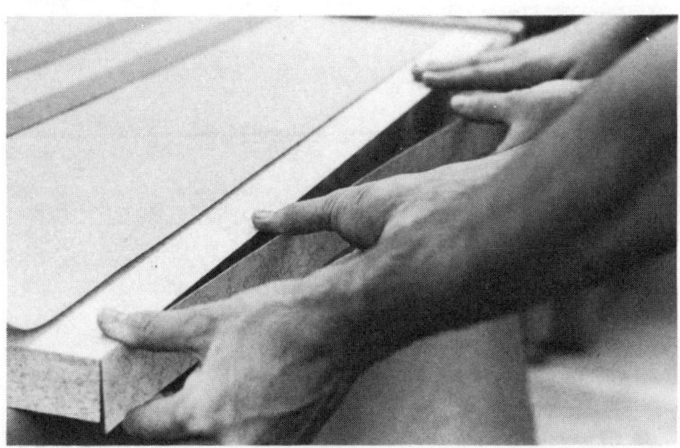

Figure 46-25
After the laminate is centered, stick the first end. Note that the opposite end is held away from the top.

wood block and mallet, Figure 46-27. Do not apply pressure too far out on the edge. Plastic laminates are brittle and can snap off easily.

6. Trim the excess plastic laminate with a router attachment that flush cuts plastic laminate or with a special router bit, Figure 46-28. A special router bit is better. Its ball-bearing pilot automatically determines the depth of cut, Figure 46-29.

Figure 46-26
An edge roller sticks the edge band.

Figure 46-27
A wooden block and mallet sticks the edge band.

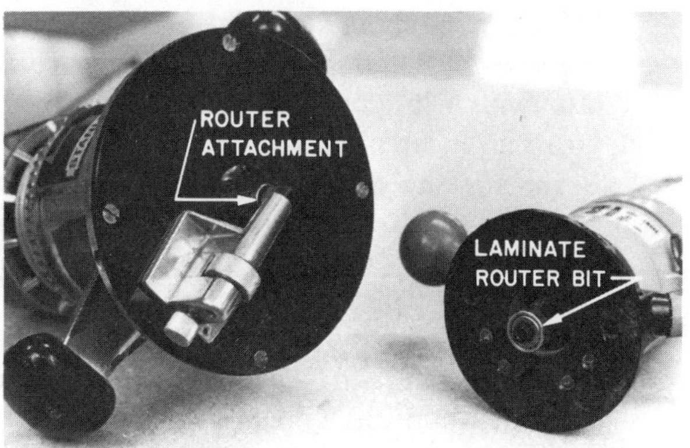

Figure 46-28
A router attachment or a laminate router bit trims the plastic laminate overhang.

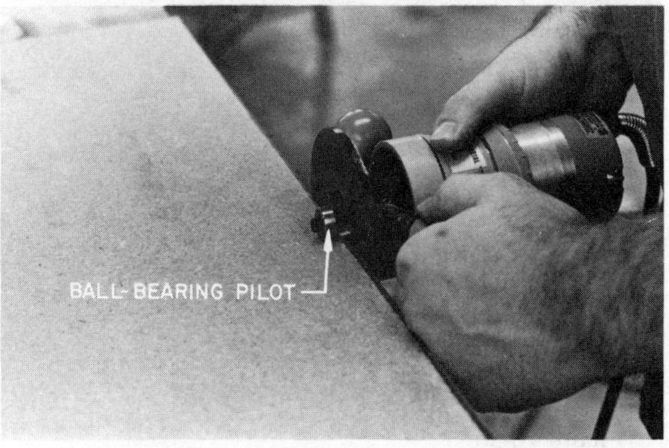

Figure 46-29
The overhang can be cut off quickly with a router.

Run the belt sander across the trimmed edges to even out the edges. You should run the sander with the belt rotating back toward the top. To prevent the sander from sanding too much and dishing out the particle board, keep moving it from side to side, Figure 46-30. Holding it in one spot will cause the belt to dig into the top. Be careful when handling the top. The edges are razor sharp.

7. Apply contact cement to the top and to the top piece of plastic laminate. As with the edge band, clean the bonding surfaces. Blow dirt off with pressurized air, Figure 46-31.

   Apply cement with a paint brush, a small roller (Figure 46-32) or a spray gun. Industry workers use the spray gun because it is fast. When the cement dries, apply the laminate.
8. Place 3/8" (10 mm) dowel pins every 12" (305 mm) along the top. The pins will keep the two glued surfaces from touching. They also will help you roll the laminate into position, Figure 46-33.
9. Begin sticking the top laminate from one end. Work to the opposite end by removing the dowel pins one at a time. Smooth the surface with light hand pressure.
10. Work out from the center, applying additional pressure with a laminate roller or a block of wood and a mallet, Figure 46-34.

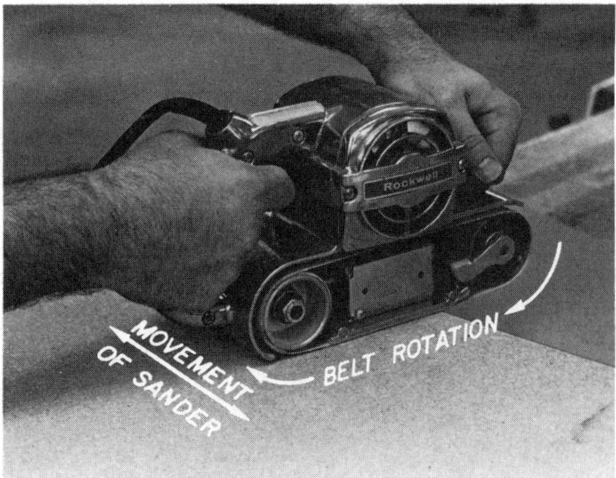

Figure 46-30
Move the sander from side to side with the belt rotating inward toward the top.

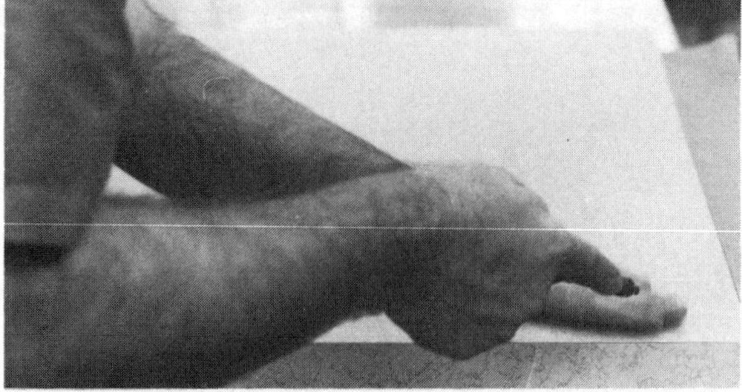

Figure 46-31
Blow off the top while moving your other hand over the surface.

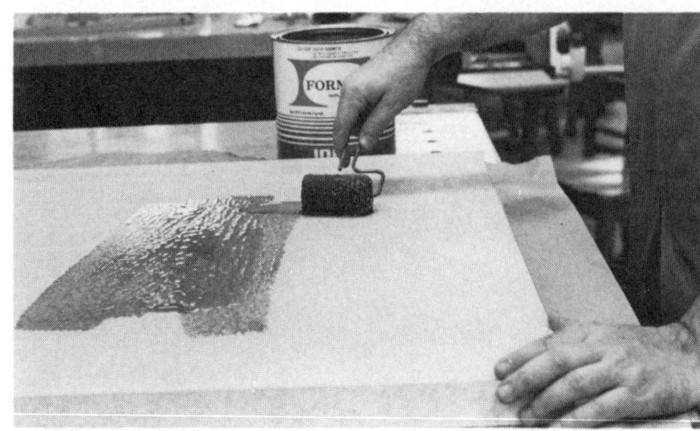

Figure 46-32
Contact cement can be applied with a small paint roller.

Figure 46-33
Dowel pins allow the laminate to be rolled into position.

Figure 46-34
A wide laminate roller applies the necessary pressure to the top.

11. Use a router with a bevel-cut bit to trim off the excess laminate, Figure 46-35. The top edge is beveled so that it looks finished and is not sharp. You must adjust the depth of cut carefully. Making too deep a cut removes the colored print from the laminate and creates a wide, dark line. This cannot be repaired.
12. File all exposed edges of the laminate so that they are smooth. You can use a special file or a single-cut mill bastard file. Clean the file with a file card. Always file downward so that the laminate will not lift off the top, Figure 46-36. Filing removes all mill marks created by the router. Remember, do not make too deep a cut. Working the file at a consistent angle produces a professional-looking top. Clean off the excess contact cement with a cloth that has been dipped in lacquer thinner.

Figure 46-35
A beveled router bit cuts the edge on an angle.

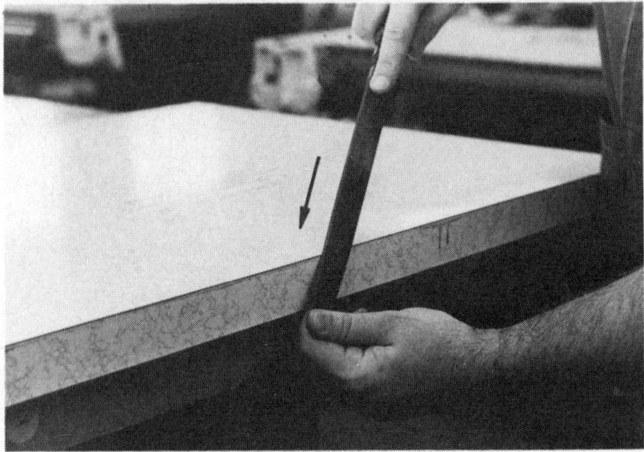

Figure 46-36
File downward to produce a smooth edge.

REVIEW QUESTIONS

1. How can you tell production cabinets from custom cabinets?
2. What type of shelves does a lazy Susan contain?
3. Sketch the top view of a set of kitchen cabinets. Include a work triangle.
4. Define *stile, rail* and *mullion.*
5. Where do you use interior and exterior bulkheads?
6. What is a *rigid back*? How do you use it?
7. A door should be no more than ____" wide and ____" tall.
8. List two types of metal sliding hardware used in kitchen cabinets.
9. Define *Formica®, kraft paper, suede finish* and *postforming.*
10. How wide is a standard countertop?
11. Which type of bonding agent glues plastic laminates?
12. Which machine is best for trimming the excess when applying plastic laminate?
13. What is the purpose of dowel pins when installing the top piece of plastic laminate?
14. A file is used for what purpose?

SUGGESTED ACTIVITIES

1. Inspect your set of kitchen cabinets. Are they custom or mass-produced? How many of the parts listed in this unit can you find on your cabinets?
2. Visit a lumber yard or a hardware store that sells kitchen cabinets. Make a list of all parts. Sketch any construction techniques that are different from what has been discussed in this unit.
3. Make a small plastic laminate top.

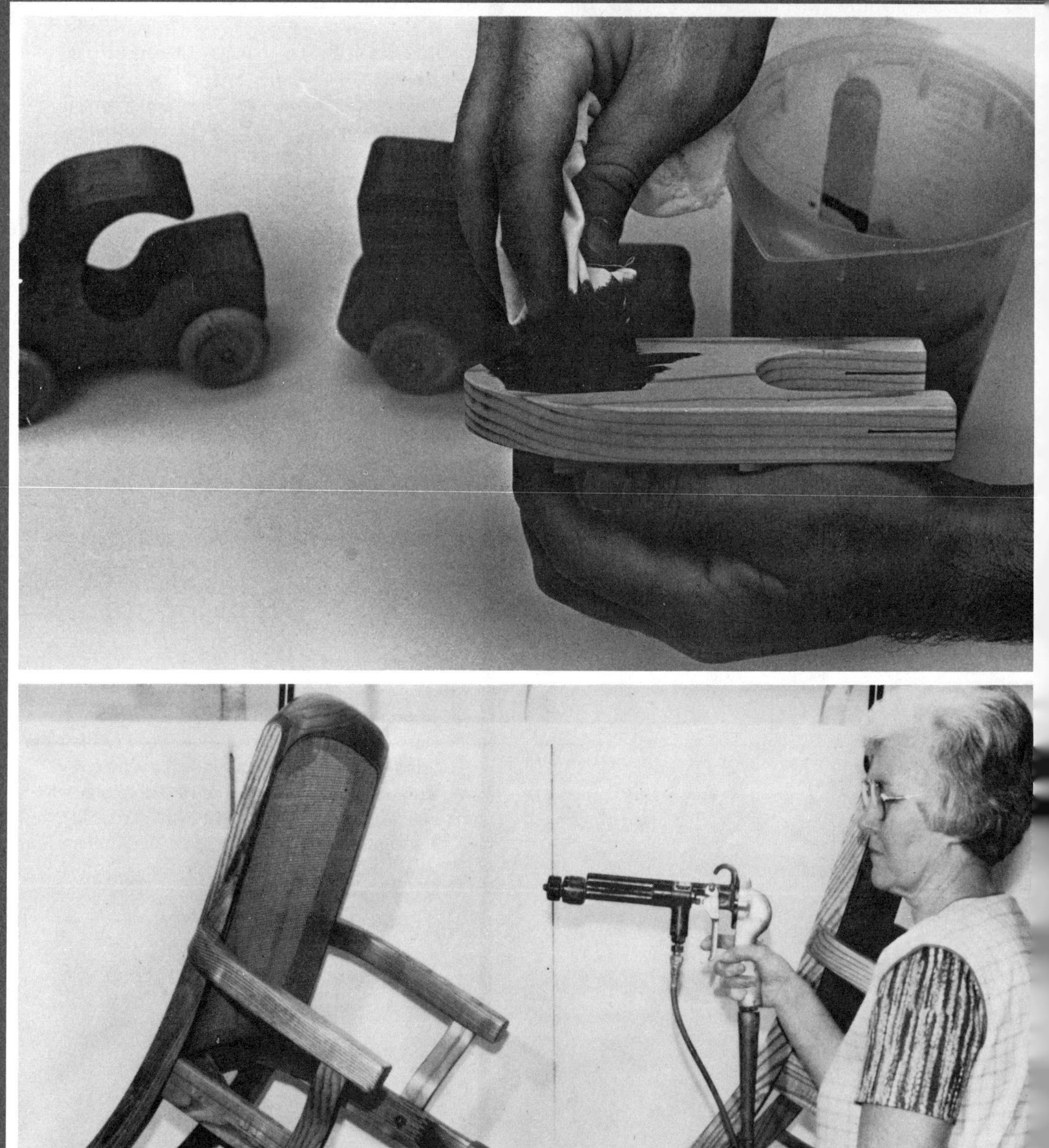

SECTION

7

Finishing

47
Abrasives

48
Preparing Surfaces for Finishing and Sanding

49
Filling Wood Surfaces

50
Wood Stains

51
Varnishes and Brushing Techniques

52
Lacquers and Spraying Techniques

53
Wipe-on Finishes

A project may be constructed with the highest skill. If the finish is not applied correctly, however, the appearance is ruined. Applying finish requires as much care as making and fitting accurate joints.

The purpose of Section 7, Finishing, is to give you the basics in applying a good finish. You will learn to select, from hundreds, the best finish for your project. Your choice will depend on appearance, amount of protection needed and equipment available. This section also will explain how to experiment with finishing samples to find the best procedure for finishing your project. By following the recommendations you should be able to complete your project with excellent results.

UNIT

47

Abrasives

Objectives

After studying this unit you should be able to:

1 Identify different abrasives and backing materials.

2 Describe the process for making abrasive paper.

3 Select grit sizes.

Technical Terms

Emery

Flint

Garnet

Electro-coated paper

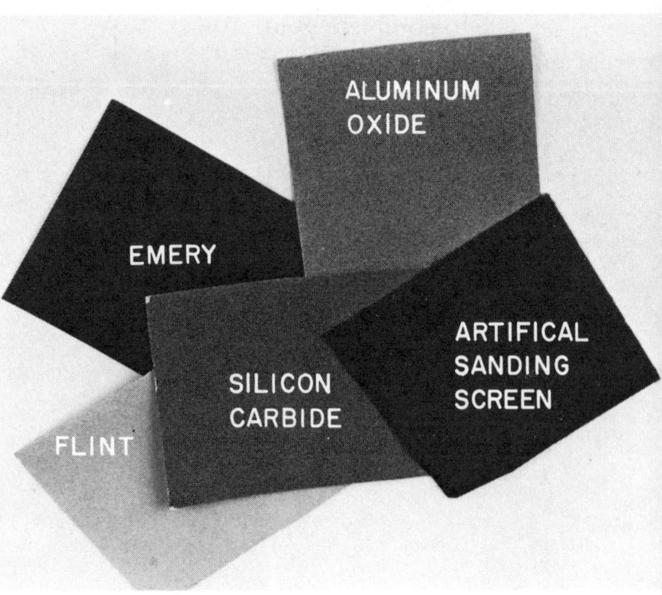

Figure 47-1
Many kinds of abrasives are available.

Coated abrasives come in many sizes, materials and degrees of coarseness. Coated abrasives generally are known as sandpaper. Abrasive paper is a more accurate name, however. Small pieces of abrasives, not sand, are glued to a backing material. These thousands of abrasive pieces smooth the wood.

TYPES OF ABRASIVES

There are several types of abrasives, Figure 47-1. Natural materials include emery, flint and garnet. Most abrasives sold today are synthetic. They include aluminum oxide and silicon carbide. A new abrasive is an artificial sanding screen. It is a cloth screen covered with small pieces of hard abrasive material. The screen lasts a long time and does not become clogged with resin and finish.

Each abrasive is different. *Emery* is black in color and primarily is used for polishing metal. *Flint* is an off-white color and is inexpensive. It does not maintain its cutting action for very long. Use it for sanding varnished or painted surfaces. A short cutting life is not important when sanding a finished surface. Many woodworkers prefer the reddish-brown *garnet*. As the abrasive paper is used, individual particles of garnet break off. This exposes sharp corners that continue to remove material. Use garnet abrasive paper for hand sanding. Natural aluminum oxide is brownish-gray. Often it is dyed red, gold or other colors. Aluminum oxide is the most widely used abrasive in the woods industry. Because it is tough and resistant to heat, it is used on sanding machine belts. Silicon carbide is bluish-black in color. Use it for sanding finishes with water as a lubricant.

Abrasives must be glued to backing material. Backing materials are either paper, cloth or fiber. Each is available in several thicknesses, or weights, Figure 47-2. Paper is available in A, B, C, D and E weights. A weight is the thinnest, and E weight is the thickest. Use C weight for most hand sanding and portable finishing sanders. C weight often is called cabinet paper. It is heavy enough to withstand hard use but fits most irregular shapes. Cloth backing is available in J or X weights. J weight is the lighter of the two. Use it with portable belt sanders. Use X weight for disc sanders and other heavy-duty applications. Fiber backing is made from toughened rag stock. Use fiber with stationary sanding machines. Synthetic fiber is becoming more popular. New synthetic backing materials are extremely tough and less expensive than cloth.

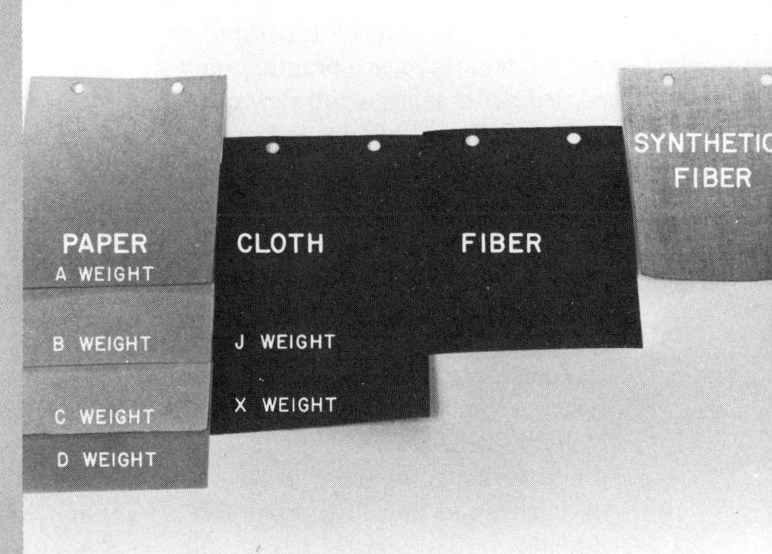

Figure 47-2
Abrasive backings come in different materials and weights.

MANUFACTURING OF ABRASIVE PAPER

After the abrasive and backing material have been selected, the abrasive paper or cloth is made, Figure 47-3. An adhesive is sprayed on the front side of the backing. This layer of bonding agent holds the abrasive to the backing. The abrasive is applied with an electro-coating method. In this process, the abrasive receives a negative electrical charge. The backing material receives a positive charge. As the abrasive is brought up to the backing, the difference in the

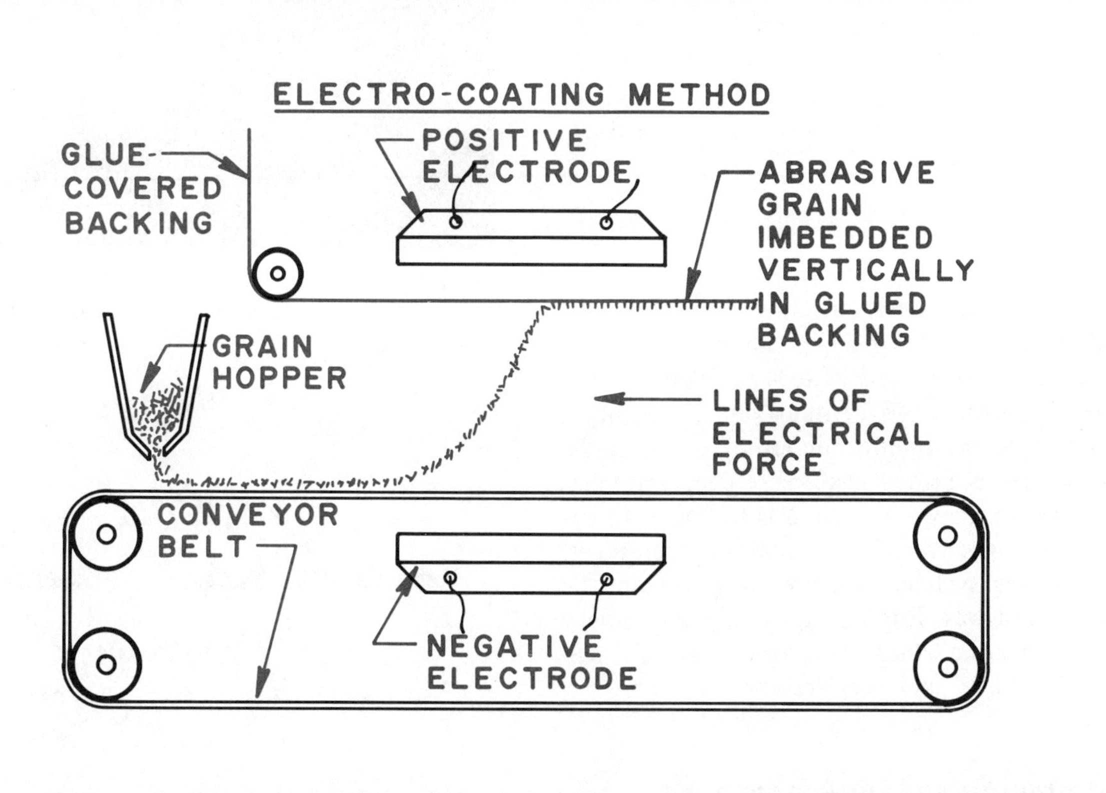

Figure 47-3
Most abrasive paper is made with an electro-coating process. (Norton Company)

electrical charges causes individual pieces of abrasive to stand on end. Because the sharp ends of the abrasive are pointing upward, *electro-coated paper* sands wood very quickly.

The first coat of adhesive applied to the backing is called the bond coat. It is responsible for bonding the bottom portion of each particle to the backing. This is not enough, however, to hold the abrasive. Another layer of glue, called the sizing coat, is applied over the abrasive to increase bonding strength.

The sizing coat makes the abrasive paper very rigid. To make it flexible, roll the backing over a sharp corner. This bends the sizing coat and prevents cracking. Flex the abrasive paper across its length and its width, Figure 47-4. The more directions the paper is flexed, the more easily it will sand small curves and irregular shapes.

The spacing of the abrasive particles is important, Figure 47-5. Closed-coat abrasive paper has little space between the abrasive particles. Use closed-coat abrasive paper for hardwood. It will sand quickly with few clogging problems. Use open-coat abrasive paper for softwoods. It has more space between particles than a closed-coat paper and sands more gently. About 50 to 70 percent of all abrasive papers are open-coat.

GRIT SIZES

Abrasives are rated by their grit size. The smaller the grit size or paper number, the larger the abrasive particles, Figure 47-6. Papers numbered 12 through 40 contain very large pieces of abrasive and remove material very quickly. Very coarse abrasives also make deep scratches in the wood. Papers with a 220 to 600 grit have very fine particles and make shallower scratches. Other rating systems also are used to state the size of abrasives. For example, flint and emery are sized by the words "very fine," "fine," "medium," "coarse" and "very coarse."

PURCHASING ABRASIVE PAPER

Abrasive paper is sold in sheets, belts, rolls, discs, and sleeves. For hand- and portable-sander use, use abrasive sheets. Standard sheet sizes include 9" x 11" and 4-1/2" x 5-1/2". Much information is given on the back of the abrasive, Figure 47-7. Belts, discs and sleeves also are made in standard sizes to fit sanding machines, Figure 47-8.

The price of abrasive paper is determined by several things. Buying a whole package of 50 or 100 sheets is the most economical. Lumber yards and hardware stores frequently sell packages of assorted papers. Smaller quantities generally will cost more. The coarser the grit, the more expensive the paper.

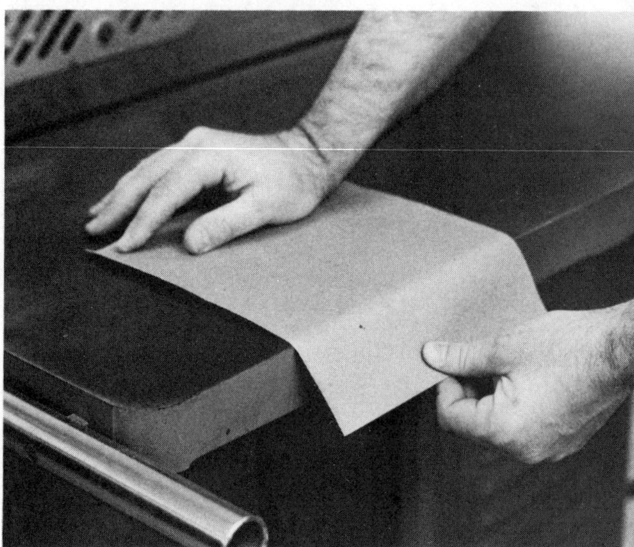

Figure 47-4
Flex the abrasive paper over a sharp edge to break the sizing coat.

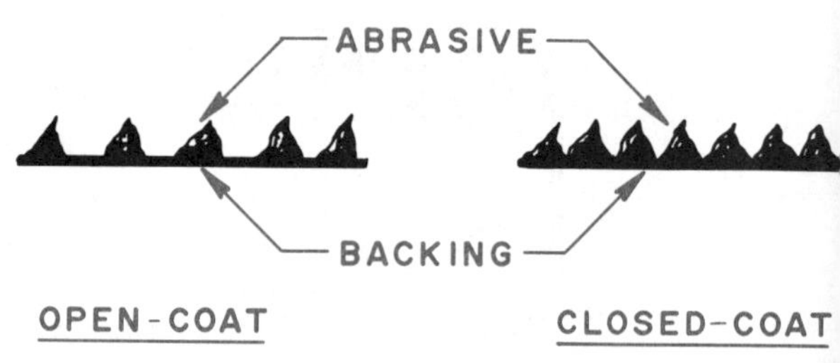

Figure 47-5
Open-coat abrasives have large spaces between the particles of abrasive. Closed-coat abrasives have very small spaces.

SIZES OF GRITS FOR DIFFERENT ABRASIVES

	Silicon Carbide	Aluminum Oxide	Garnet	Flint	Emery
Very Fine (Sanding between coats of finishing or polishing)	600	600-12/0	–	–	–
	500	500-11/0	–	–	–
	400	400-10/0	–	–	–
	360	–	–	–	–
	320	320-9/0	–	–	–
	280	280-8/0	280-8/0	–	–
	240	240-7/0	240-7/0	–	–
	220	220-6/0	220-6/0	Very Fine	–
Fine (Final sanding)	180	180-5/0	180-5/0	–	–
	150	150-4/0	150-4/0	–	Fine
	120	120-3/0	120-3/0	Fine	–
Medium (Rough sanding)	100	100-2/0	100-2/0	–	Medium
	80	80-1/0	80-1/0	Medium	–
	60	60-1/2	60-1/2	–	Coarse
Coarse (Abrasive planing)	50	50-1	50-1	Coarse	–
	40	40-1½	40-1½	–	–
Very Coarse (Grinding or rough shaping)	36	36-2	36-2	Very Coarse	Very Coarse
	30	30-2½	30-2½	–	–
	24	24-3	24-3	–	–
	20	20-3½	20-3½	–	–
	16	16-4	–	–	–
	12	12-4½	–	–	–

Figure 47-6
Sandpaper is available in a wide variety of grit sizes.

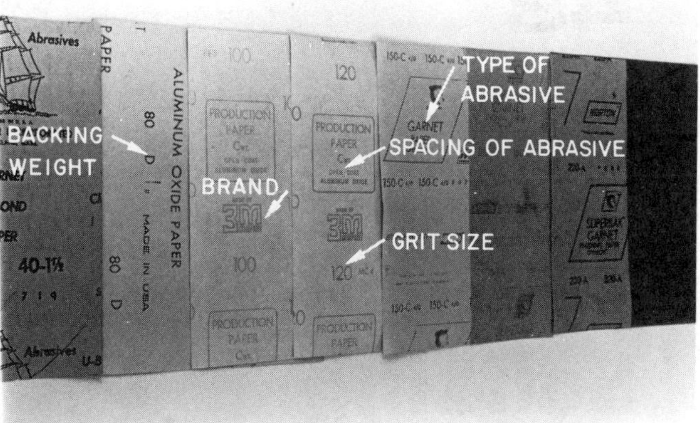

Figure 47-7
The backs of abrasive papers give much information.

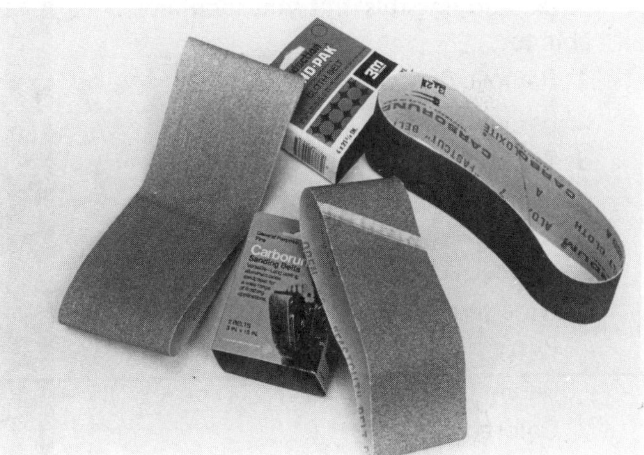

Figure 47-8
Sanding belts are sold in standard sizes.

REVIEW QUESTIONS

1. Name three natural abrasives.
2. Why do woodworkers often prefer garnet for hand sanding?
3. What advantage does aluminum oxide have?
4. Which paper weight should you use for hand sanding and portable finishing sanders?
5. What advantage does electro-coated paper have?
6. What is flexing?
7. The smaller the grit size, the ____ the abrasive particles will be.

SUGGESTED ACTIVITIES

1. Examine the abrasives in your shop. What types and grit sizes do you have?
2. Select the coarsest and finest pieces of abrasive paper in your shop. Sand one piece of wood with each. Sand another piece across the grain with each abrasive. Rub a stick of chalk across the surface of each board. How deep are the scratches? Which abrasive paper is better for finish sanding?

UNIT

48

Preparing Surfaces for Finishing and Sanding

Objectives

After studying this unit you should be able to:

1 Remove dents.

2 Fill in open defects.

3 Bleach wood to an even color.

4 Sand wood properly.

Technical Terms

Water Putty®

Putty filler

Cabinetmaker's putty

Colored sticks

Stick shellac

Bleach

Steel wool

Wet-or-dry abrasive paper

The first and most important step in finishing a product is to remove all defects from its surface. The most common defects include pencil marks, machine marks, glue, scratches, dents, chipped wood and sanding scratches. Too often, a finisher thinks that an applied finish will cover these defects. But the opposite is true. A finish brings out the wood's beauty, but it also makes any irregular markings more noticeable, Figure 48-1. A few minutes spent removing a surface defect before finishing will save hours of repairing the finish later.

REPAIRING MAJOR WOOD DEFECTS

Dents and open places in the wood are especially noticeable if left untouched. In most cases, these defects require more repair work than just sanding.

Dents

Dents should be fixed first. If the wood fibers are not broken, the dent can be removed easily. Many times you can raise a small dent by applying a drop of warm water in the spot, Figure 48-2. Use a clothes iron or soldering iron to steam deeper dents, Figure 48-3. To use an iron, first make a thin pad out of a piece of clean cloth. Dip the pad in water and wring it out.

Figure 48-1
A finish brings out the beauty of the wood. But it also makes surface defects more noticeable.

Place the wet pad over the dent and touch the top of the cloth with the heated iron. Keep the iron moving to prevent the wood from burning. Once the steam produced by the iron raises the dent, let the surface dry and sand it flat.

Figure 48-2
A small drop of water will raise a minor dent.

Open Defects

Open defects that should be filled include cracks, splits and open joints. These defects can be repaired with different types of fillers, colored sticks, plugs or stick shellac. After you apply any of these items, you must sand or clean the surface. Any filler left on the surface will prevent the stain from coloring the wood at that spot. Thus, any unwanted spots of filler will be visible.

Fillers come in several forms. One of them is a dry powder filler often called *Water Putty®*. Water is mixed with the powder to form a thick putty, Figure 48-4. You can mix powdered pigments with the filler to make a color that will match the final finish. Although vinegar can be added to slow the drying time, the mixed Water Putty® eventually will harden. Throw away any leftover filler.

Many woodworkers like *putty fillers* because they are premixed and easy to apply. Putty can be purchased in a variety of colors that closely match most woods. Keep the lid on the container whenever the filler is not being used, Figure 48-5. Otherwise, the solvents will evaporate, and the filler will dry out. Putty filler will not stain to the same color as the surrounding wood. As a result, it often will make a defect very noticeable when finish is applied.

Cabinetmaker's putty is a mixture of glue, water and fine sanding dust. It blends well with the surrounding wood. You can make the dust by sanding a board like the piece to be filled. Then mix the sanding dust with polyvinyl adhesive and a little water to form a paste, Figure 48-6. Use a lot of sanding dust so that the filler will accept stain. Apply the putty to the defect, and then let the putty dry for 24 hours. Afterwards, sand the surface thoroughly. Any glue left on the surface or worked into the wood will prevent the stain from penetrating.

After the stain and finish have been applied, you can use *colored sticks* to repair minor defects

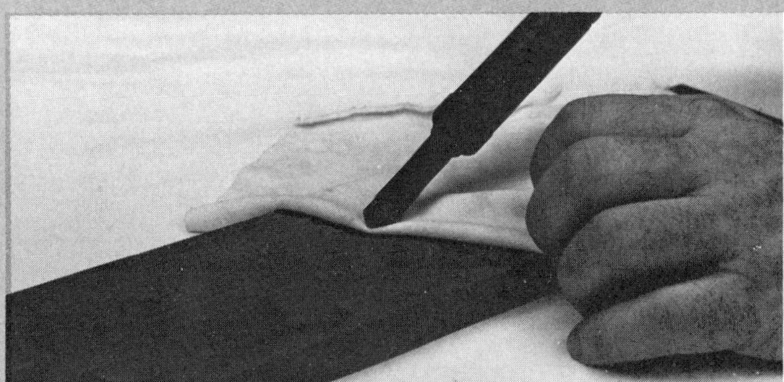

Figure 48-3
A soldering iron and dampened cloth will steam out major dents.

Figure 48-4
Water Putty® can repair major defects.

Figure 48-5
Putty filler containers should be closed when the filler is not being used.

Figure 48-6
Cabinetmaker's putty is a mixture of glue, sanding dust and water.

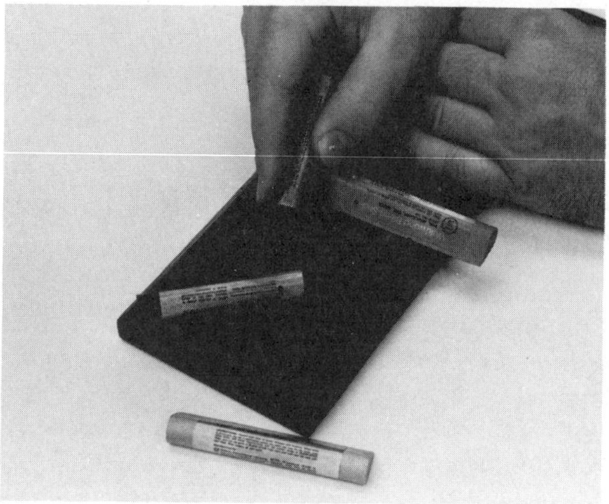

Figure 48-7
Colored sticks blend well with the surrounding wood.

such as nail holes and small cracks, Figure 48-7. You simply rub the stick into the defect. These sticks come in colors that will match nearly any application. Two colored sticks can be mixed to blend unusual colors. Remove any excess with fine abrasive paper.

Use a patch or plug to fill large open defects, Figure 48-8. This kind of work is the hardest way to fix a defect. First remove the defect with a chisel or drill. A Forstner bit that is the same diameter as the plug cutter often is used to remove the bad spot. Then cut a patch or plug that will fit exactly into the newly made opening. If you select the plug carefully, you probably can match both the grain pattern and color.

One of the oldest methods of repairing an open defect is to use *stick shellac* or lacquer

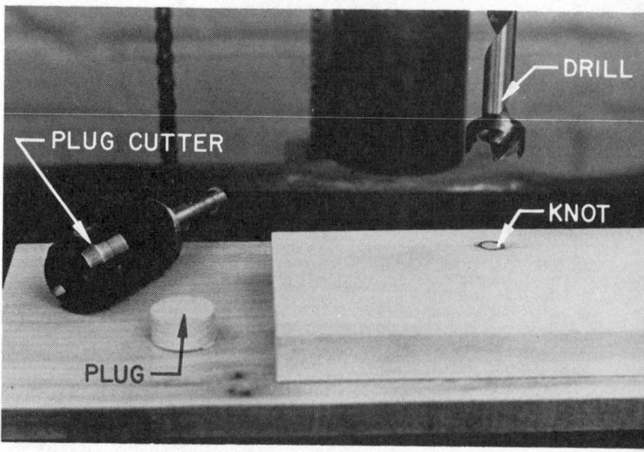

Figure 48-8
A plug made with a plug cutter can repair a knot.

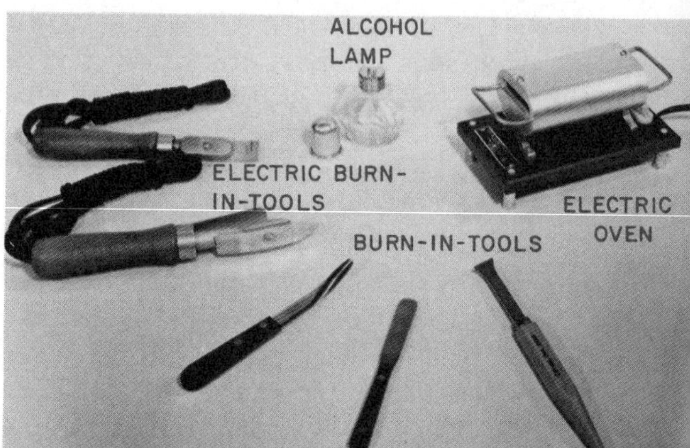

Figure 48-9
To apply stick shellac, use heated burn-in-tools or electric burn-in-tools.

sticks. This method requires special equipment and practice, Figure 48-9. First match a piece of stick shellac or a lacquer stick with the surrounding finished wood. Use shellac sticks on varnish-type finishes and lacquer sticks on lacquer finishes. Make a sample piece with the stain and finish applied to match the filler. Apply the filler with a knife called a *burn-in-tool*. Normally, you heat the burn-in-tool in a special electric oven or over an alcohol lamp. Some burn-in-tools come with electric heating elements and require no other form of heat. Place the shellac or lacquer on the defect and use the heated tool to melt the filler into the opening, Figure 48-10. Make sure that the melted filler is level with the surface. With practice, an exact match can be made with the surrounding wood. You may need to mix several colors to get a perfect match. After the filler cools, sand the wood to remove extra shellac or lacquer.

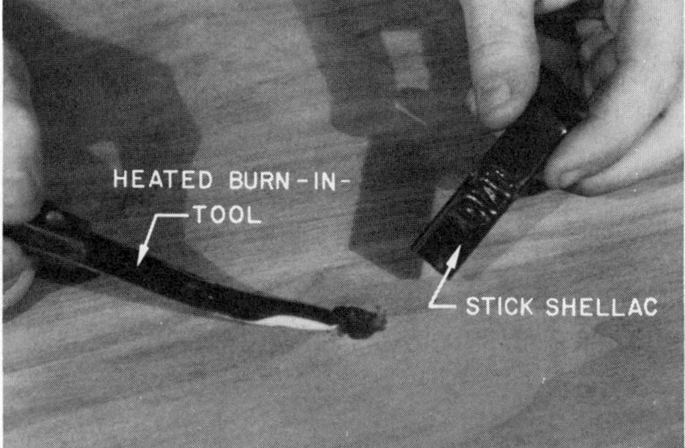

Figure 48-10
The heated burn-in-tool melts the shellac into the defect.

Figure 48-11
Wood bleach comes in several forms.

BLEACHING

Some woods vary widely in color. This creates staining problems. By using a two-part *bleach*, however, uneven color can be completely stripped from the stock, Figure 48-11. First wipe on the bleach with a rag or brush. After the bleach has dried, apply a material known as a neutralizer to stop the action of the bleach. If you want a lighter color, repeat the procedure. Because bleaches are strong chemicals, you should wear rubber gloves, protect your eyes and provide for adequate ventilation, Figure 48-12. If you need to remove only a small amount of color, use a liquid chlorine laundry bleach.

SANDING

Sanding, whether by hand or machine, is essential. A woodworker must remember to always sand with the grain, Figure 48-13. Scratches going across the grain that remain after sanding will be obvious after the finish has been applied.

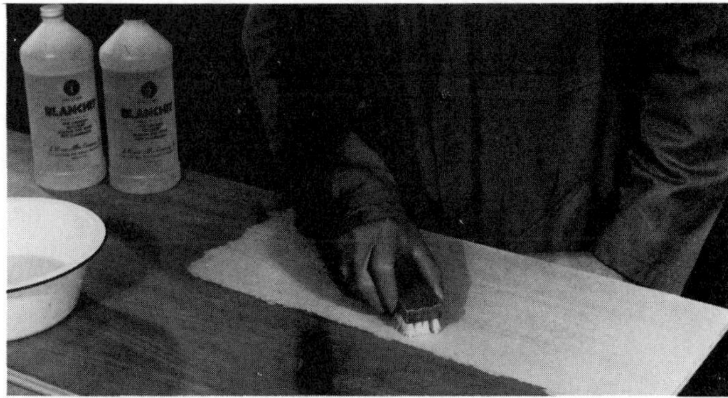

Figure 48-12
Have good ventilation and wear protective clothing when using bleach.

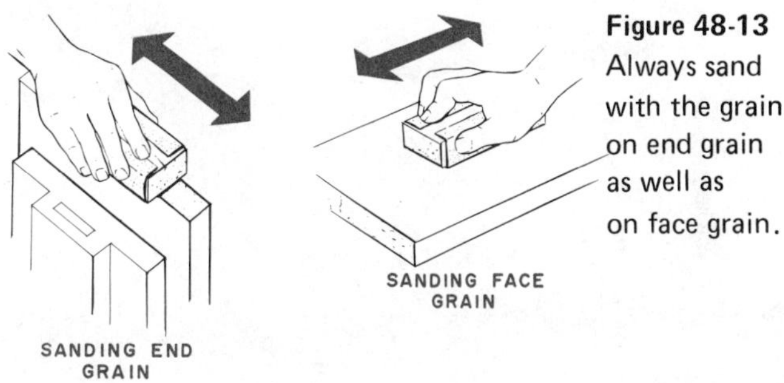

Figure 48-13
Always sand with the grain on end grain as well as on face grain.

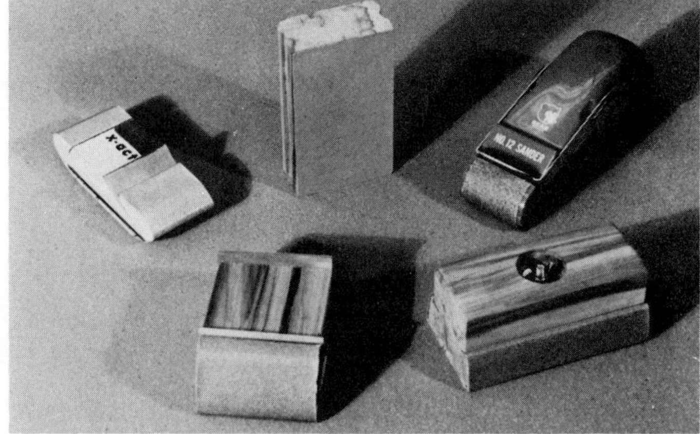

Figure 48-14
Always use some form of a sanding block when hand sanding.

Sanding by hand is the slowest way to sand wood. But this method gives excellent results. Always use a sanding block to keep the surface level, Figure 48-14. Wrapping abrasive paper around your hand and not using a sanding block will make high and low spots on the surface.

Garnet abrasive paper works the best for hand sanding because it does not glaze the surface.

A portable electric sander can remove wood faster than a hand sander. Both the orbital and vibrating styles of portable sanders, however, make cross scratches that are noticeable in the finished project. Straight-line portable sanders make scratches running with the grain, but these scratches will blend in with the surrounding grain. Aluminum oxide abrasive paper works the best for machine sanding because the heat produced by the sander does not wear down the paper.

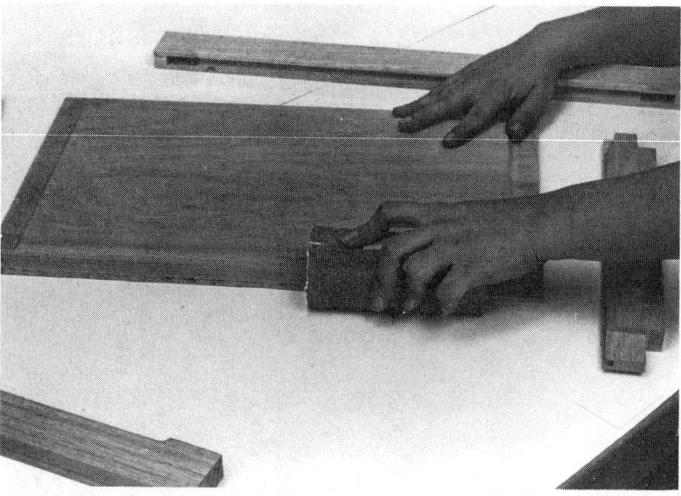

Figure 48-15
Sand as much of the project as possible before assembly.

PREPARING SURFACES FOR FINISHING

Wood must be worked down gradually from a planed surface to a fine sanded finish. The steps in working down a project are:

1. Plane all pieces down to the desired thickness and make any joints needed at exposed edges. You can use either hand tools or power equipment for these activities.
2. Determine which surfaces are to be on the inside of the project. Inside corners are difficult to sand, and so you should work them down before assembly, Figure 48-15. Do not remove too much material, however. Removing an excessive amount will make the joints fit poorly when assembled.
3. Remove any dents or other major defects. You may have to use filler. Some small knots and other small cracks may be left unfilled.

Figure 48-16
The hand scraper removes major mill marks.

4. Remove any other major defects that cause the surface to be uneven. To remove mill marks, use a cabinet scraper and then a hand scraper, Figure 48-16. In industry, woodworkers usually use power sanding machines to speed up this process.
5. Begin to sand the scraped surface with either a sanding block or a portable sander. Start with a 100-grit abrasive paper. Be sure to remove an equal amount of material from the total area. Attempting to sand only the defects will produce low spots.
6. Change to a 120-grit sandpaper after the whole area has been sanded. Clean the surface to remove old particles of abrasive. Continue sanding until you have removed all the deep sanding scratch marks.
7. Use smaller-grit abrasive paper in succession. In this way, you can remove scratches more quickly and get better results. Progress through 100-, 120-, 150- and 180-grit paper. A sander rarely completes a project with an abrasive finer than 180. Keep sanding until all mill marks and sanding scratches have been removed.
8. Be aware that any liquid finish applied to a piece of wood will raise the grain. To deal with this tendency, wipe the sanded piece with a wet sponge or cloth. Do not flood the surface but make certain the entire area becomes damp. After the surface has dried, lightly sand the raised wood fibers with 180-grit sandpaper. Failure to sand these

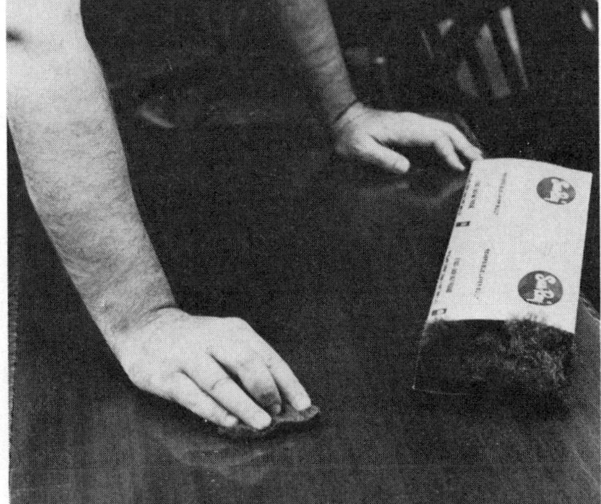

Figure 48-17
Use steel wool to rub down each coat of finish.

fibers will result in raised grain when the finish is applied.

9. Rub down lacquer, varnish or enamel finishes between coats. Use either *steel wood* or a special *wet-and-dry abrasive paper.* Steel wool is easy to use, but it leaves steel particles that are difficult to remove, Figure 48-17. You must remove these small pieces before applying a finish. Woodworkers also can use a special 320-grit wet-and-dry abrasive paper that works well when applied by hand, Figure 48-18. Apply water to keep the finish from filling up the abrasive paper. Sand with the grain and do not sand through the finish on the corners.
10. Use either pumice stone or rubbing compound to rub down the finish after all of it has been applied, Figure 48-19. You can use a felt pad and a rubbing oil to distribute the pumice stone evenly. Rubbing compound can be used without oil. Move the pad with the grain to prevent any noticeable cross scratches. Some woodworkers like to follow the pumice stone with a smoothing material known as rotten stone. This produces a finer finish and gives a deep hand-rubbed appearance.

Figure 48-18
Use a special wet-and-dry sandpaper with water to sand between coats of finish.

Figure 48-19
Pumice stone and rubbing oil give a project a hand-rubbed appearance.

REVIEW QUESTIONS

1 How can small dents be raised?
2 What can you use to steam out a large dent?
3 What do you mix with Water Putty® to make it into a thick putty?
4 Why should putty fillers be kept covered when not in use?
5 How is cabinetmaker's putty made?
6 When are colored sticks applied?
7 What is used to apply stick shellac?
8 What should be worn when working with bleaches?
9 Which abrasive should be used for hand sanding? For portable sanders?
10 List the recommended grit sizes that should be used to sand a surface.
11 What can be used to rub down a finish?

SUGGESTED ACTIVITIES

1 Visit your local lumberyard and make a list of the available fillers.
2 Practice steaming dents from a piece of scrap wood.
3 Make a set of sample boards with different finishes. Prepare the surfaces with different grits of abrasive paper. Leave some sanded to 100 grit and others sanded through 180 grit. Compare the results and see which gives the best finish.

UNIT

49

Filling Wood Surfaces

Objectives

After studying this unit you should be able to:

1 Identify woods that require filler.

2 List the ingredients of paste wood filler.

3 Apply wood filler properly.

Technical Terms

Paste wood filler
Silex
Vehicle
Barrier coat
Liquid filler

Figure 49-1
Paste wood filler is made of many ingredients.

You can see tiny, open pores in some woods. These small openings are called vessel elements. Vessel elements are found in ring-porous woods. Ring-porous woods include oak, ash, walnut and mahogany. (A more detailed explanation of ring-porous woods is found in the unit on wood science.) When a finish is applied to ring-porous woods, the open vessel elements become very distinct. It is necessary to fill these pores for a high-quality finish. You can do this by applying a wood filler to the vessel elements.

Some woods do not have large open pores. These are called diffuse-porous woods. They include maple, birch and cherry. In most cases, diffuse-porous woods do not require a thick wood filler. Some woodcutters, however, apply a very thin filler to fill any small pores.

PASTE WOOD FILLER

Paste wood filler is made from several materials, Figure 49-1. *Silex* is the major ingredient. Silex is mixed with a liquid *vehicle* made from boiled linseed oil, turpentine, benzine, Japan drier and sometimes a color pigment. These ingredients mixed together form a thick paste. Although woodworkers can mix their own filler, you can buy it in ready-to-apply form.

Paste wood filler is sold in a neutral color. Usually, it is a blonde color that matches unstained ashes and oaks very well. Darker woods or previously stained woods require a pigmented filler. You can color fillers by adding concentrated oil pigments, Figure 49-2. Mix carefully and thoroughly. Do not add too much pigment or the filler will be too dark. Start with a light color and gradually darken it by adding more pigment. You can lighten the tint by adding more filler.

Do not confuse paste wood filler with putty filler. Putty filler is used for major repair jobs. It is thicker than paste wood filler. Use it to fill nail holes, cracks and other defects.

APPLICATION OF THE FILLER

When you have mixed the filler to a creamy texture, apply it to the wood following this procedure:

1. Use a soft brush on the surface of the wood to remove dust and any loose or broken fragments of wood. Brush with the grain, Figure 49-3. A vacuum cleaner and a tack cloth also will help. A tack cloth has a sticky surface that removes dust.
2. Use a *barrier coat* to seal any previously stained wood. This will prevent the filler from lifting or changing the shade of the stain. Select a barrier coat that matches the color of the finish coat. Use shellac and lacquer sealer. Some woodworkers also apply a barrier coat to unstained wood to prevent the eventual graying of the filler.
3. Apply an even coat of filler to the surface. If you are filling a large surface area, work on a small section at a time. A 24" x 24" (610 x 610 mm) area is the largest that can be filled easily at one time. Work the filler into the pores with an old varnish brush. Brushing back and forth across the grain, Figure 49-4. You may want to rub the filler into the wood with your hands. This will stain your hands, so you may want to wear rubber gloves.

Figure 49-2
Tint filler to match dark woods or stain light-colored woods.

Figure 49-3
Use a soft brush to clean the pores of the wood.

Figure 49-4
Work the filler into the wood with a brush.

Figure 49-5
Remove excess filler when the pores are filled.

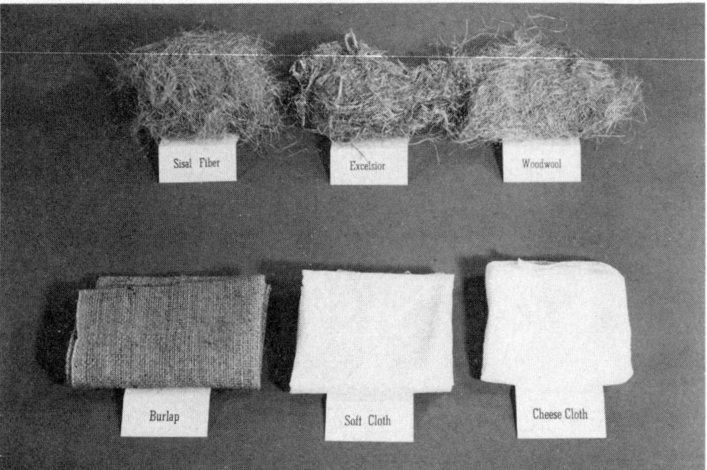

Figure 49-6
Although burlap is preferred, other materials can be used to wipe off the excess filler.

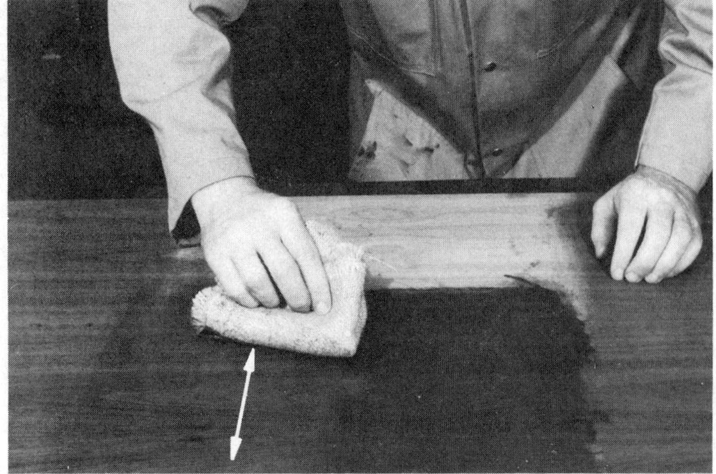

Figure 49-7
Using a pad of burlap, wipe across the grain.

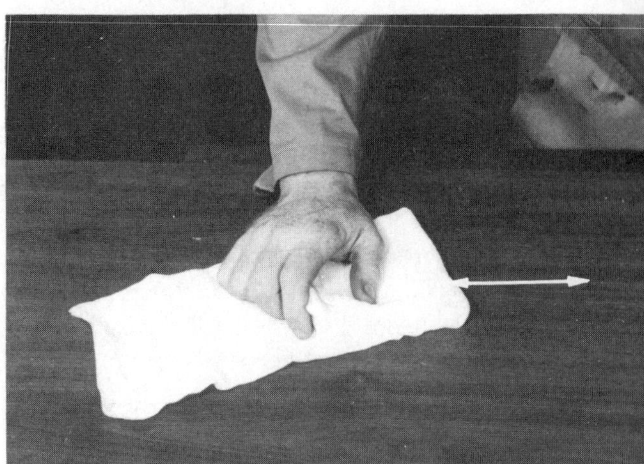

Figure 49-8
Remove all excess filler with a clean cloth.

4. Allow the filler to set for a few minutes. As it dries, the glossy, wet surface will become dull and flat. Rub your finger across the surface. The filler should stay in the pores, Figure 49-5. Do not leave the filler on the surface too long, or it will be very difficult to remove the excess.
5. Use burlap, woodwool, excelsior, sisal fiber, cloth or sawdust to remove the excess filler, Figure 49-6. Make a pad of any of these materials and wipe back and forth across the grain, Figure 49-7. This removes any filler on top of the wood and drives the mixture further into the pores. Change pads when they become dirty.
6. Continue wiping the surface with a clean cotton cloth, Figure 49-8. Rub with the grain. Any filler left on top of the surface of the wood will turn gray and be very noticeable.
7. Inspect inside corners and moldings very carefully. Use a sharp wooden stick that is wrapped with a soft cloth to clean these areas, Figure 49-9. Be careful not to mar the wood with the stick.
8. Dispose of used burlap and other materials properly. They are highly flammable. Throw them in an approved safety can. Do not pile them in an open container.
9. Allow the filler to dry at least 24 hours before you apply the finish. If the filler is too thin or is wiped out of the pores, apply a second coat. Repeat the same procedure, but thin the filler to 50 percent.

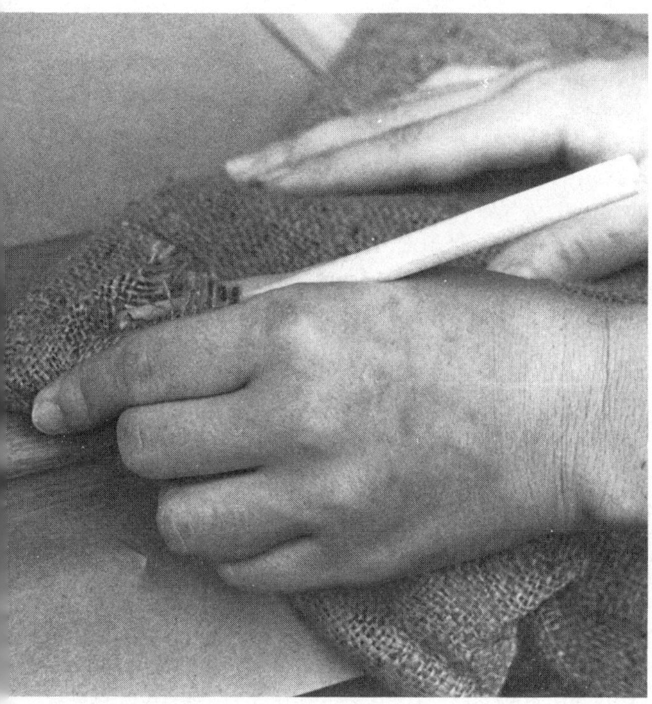

Figure 49-9
Clean corners with a cloth wrapped around a sharp, wooden stick.

Figure 49-10
Applying liquid filler to cherry wood.

OTHER FORMS OF FILLING

Sometimes, paste wood filler is not desirable. You may want to fill the pores with a clear finish. Varnish or lacquer produces a brighter, deeper appearance but requires many light coats of finish. If applying lacquer, fill the pores with several coats of sanding sealer. It is less costly and easier to sand than finishing lacquer. Sand each coat but do not sand through the finish. Eventually, the finish will fill the pores, producing a level surface. Transparent finishing requires a large amount of finish and much time. Wood filled with transparent finish does not look flat but keeps its natural appearance.

You also can use a *liquid filler* to fill pores. It is in a liquid form, so it is not as thick as paste wood filler. Because it is thin, you can use it for diffuse-porous woods. Use liquid filler for birch and cherry, Figure 49-10.

REVIEW QUESTIONS

1 What is the name of the tiny openings in wood?
2 Name three woods that usually require filling.
3 What is paste wood filler made of?
4 How can you tint filler?
5 What is a barrier coat?
6 How can you tell when filler is ready to be removed?
7 Why is sanding sealer sometimes used to fill in wood pores?
8 What is liquid filler?

SUGGESTED ACTIVITIES

1 Make a sample board out of oak or ash. Apply paste wood filler to one side. Fill the pores on the opposite face with sanding sealer. Which filler do you like better?
2 Select a piece of ring-porous wood and fill it with a red, blue or green filler. Use concentrated oil pigments to tint the filler. Do you like this special effect?

UNIT

50

Wood Stains

Objectives

After studying this unit you should be able to:

1 Identify the different types of wood stains.
2 Properly apply different stains.
3 Create special staining effects.

Technical Terms

Soluble dye
Insoluble pigment
Water stain
Penetrating oil stain
Pigmented oil stain
Nongrain-raising stain
Spraying extender
Spirit stain
Sap stain
Shading
Distressing

Figure 50-1
Water stains are sold in dry powder form.

Before finishing your wood project, you must decide what color it will be. Often you can leave the wood its natural color. Other times you might change the color by adding a stain to the wood surface. Stains can soften unpleasant colors in natural wood, highlight the wood grain, darken colors or imitate a more expensive wood.

A stain is a preparation of color suspended in a liquid. The liquid eventually evaporates out of the wood leaving only the colored stain. The color is provided either through soluble dyes or insoluble pigments. *Soluble dyes* penetrate into the wood fibers and modify the color of the wood. *Insoluble pigments* stay on the surface and partially cover the grain of the wood. You can use several different dyes and pigments to get particular colors.

You can apply stains in many ways. Normally, you put on liquid stains as a separate coat immediately after the final sanding. In certain cases you can add color to the wood surface by applying a mixture of stain and paste wood filler. You also can combine stain with the base coat of many finishes and then spray, brush or wipe both on the wood at the same time.

Always test the stain on a scrap piece before you use it on the project. Select a part of the project that will not be seen. Be sure you are satisfied with the results of your test scrap before you stain the rest of the piece.

TYPES OF STAIN

Stains are classified by the type of solvent, or vehicle, used to make the liquid. There are four major solvents – water, oil, nongrain-raising and spirit. All of these vehicles evaporate and leave the color close to or on the wood surface.

Water Stain

Water staining is one of the oldest methods of coloring wood. It is used today because of its many advantages. Water stain produces the clearest, most permanent tones. A water stain does not bleed into the finish as do other types of stains. In addition, water-stained wood fades the least when exposed to direct sunlight.

Mixing. Many shades of stain are available. You buy stain in dry powder form, Figure 50-1, and mix it with water. To make a small quantity

Figure 50-2
Use a dampened sponge to help raise the grain prior to staining.

Figure 50-3
A wash coat of shellac applied before using a water stain will keep the end grain from becoming too dark.

of water stain, stir 1/2 ounce of dye into 1 pint of warm water. Mix in additional dye to darken the stain. Add more water to lighten a shade. Surplus stain can be stored in a glass container and used at a later time.

Application. Water stain is difficult to apply evenly. If you do not apply the stain properly, the wood will be streaked with darker colors. To apply:

1. Prepare the wood by applying a light coat of water to all surfaces. Dark streaks occur on the surface because certain parts of unsealed wood absorb stain differently. A wet sponge rubbed over the wood raises the grain and equalizes the surface, Figure 50-2. After the wood dries, lightly sand the surface to remove all swelled wood fibers.
2. Pay special attention to the end grain. Even if you coat it with water before staining, the end grain will turn darker than the edges and faces of the board, Figure 50-3. To prevent this, brush the end grain with a wash coat of shellac and let it dry thoroughly before staining.

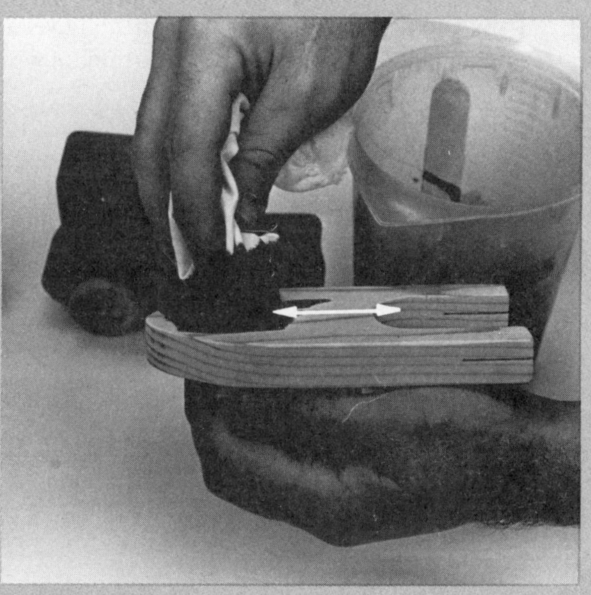

Figure 50-4
Wipe water stain on the wood with strokes running with the grain.

3. Select the method by which you will apply the stain. Spraying is preferable because you can get a consistent layer. The spray gun should have stainless steel passages to prevent rusting. But you can also dip or brush stain on the wood.
4. No matter what method you choose, be sure to apply the stain as evenly as possible. Try not to overlap the strokes of the cloth, brush or spray gun or you will cause dark streaks. If you apply stain with a soft cloth, use long, light strokes running with the grain, Figure 50-4.

5. Allow the stain to dry for 24 hours, then lightly sand the surface. Use 280-grit abrasive paper and sand with the grain of the wood. Sanding removes any raised grain caused by the water in the stain. Be careful not to sand through the stain and expose the raw wood.

If you think the surface is too light in color, after the first application, repeat the process.

Oil Stains

Oil staining is the common method of coloring wood for custom-made projects. Oil stains are available ready-to-use in many colors, Figure 50-5. They also are the easiest of all stains to apply. Even an inexperienced finisher can achieve an attractive stained surface that is not streaked with darker colors.

There are a few disadvantages to oil stain. Because linseed oil or another type of oil is its vehicle, oil stain does not penetrate as deeply as water stain. This causes oil stains to be less permanent and to fade when exposed to direct sunlight. In addition, most finishers believe that an oil stain does not produce a clear wood color and hides some of the features of the grain.

Kinds. The two types of oil stains are penetrating and pigmented. Each type uses a different kind of vehicle and coloring matter. A *penetrating oil stain* combines an oil-soluble dye with turpentine, naphtha, benzol or toluol as a vehicle. *Pigmented oil stain* mixes a pigment ground in oil with linseed oil.

Do not use penetrating oil stains on fine furniture because the stain may fade and bleed into the finish. Streaking is also a problem. To minimize the bleeding, apply a barrier coat. The barrier coat seals the stain and prevents the finish from attacking the stain.

Pigmented oil stain often is referred to as wiping stain because it produces a uniform color on furniture. Commonly used by students of woodworking, pigmented oil stain also is recommended for amateurs and hobbyists who want to stain furniture or cabinets.

Beginners also use gelled-pigmented oil and water-soluble stains because they are easy to apply and clean up, Figure 50-6. Gelled stain

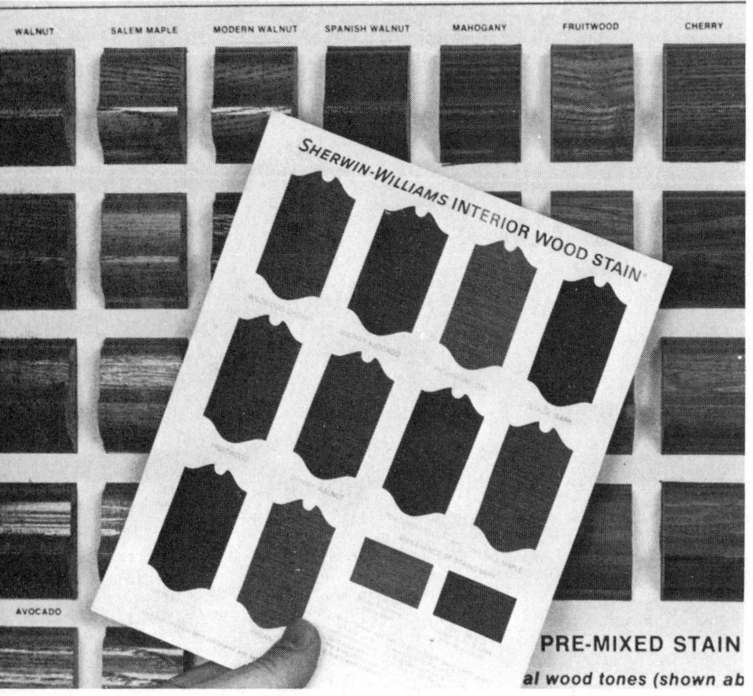

Figure 50-5
Oil stains are available in many colors.

Figure 50-6
Gelled wood stains and water-based stains are easy to apply and clean up.

Figure 50-7
Mix the pigment thoroughly by stirring the stain with a stick.

works well on vertical surfaces because it does not run easily. Water-soluble stains clean easily with soap and warm water.

Application. Oil stains are the easiest of all stains to apply. To apply:

1. Sand and clean the wood surface thoroughly. Also stir the stain well, Figure 50-7. If an oil stain is not mixed properly, you will get different degrees of color on the wood.
2. Stain may be wiped, dipped, brushed or sprayed. Use a brush on large surfaces. Dip the brush no more than one-third the length of the bristles into the stain. Brush the stain on by lightly stroking the surface, Figure 50-8. For small projects, use a lint-free cloth dipped in the stain. Wipe on the stain using short over-lapping strokes. On vertical surfaces, begin staining at the bottom edge. This will eliminate runs on unstained wood that may cause dark streaks.
3. Allow the surface to dry for 5 to 10 minutes. The longer the stain is left on the surface, the darker the color will be. But do not allow the end grain to dry as long as other surfaces, because stain darkens the end grain almost instantly. To keep the end grain from absorbing too much of an oil stain, coat the end grain lightly with boiled linseed oil or turpentine before staining.
4. Wipe off excess stain with a soft lint-free cloth. Rub across the grain to achieve the best results. Any stain that you do not remove will dry into a dark streak.
5. Allow the stain to dry for 24 hours. Repeat the staining process if you want a darker color.
6. Apply a sealer to prevent the oil stain from bleeding through the finish. A sanding sealer or wash coat of shellac works well.

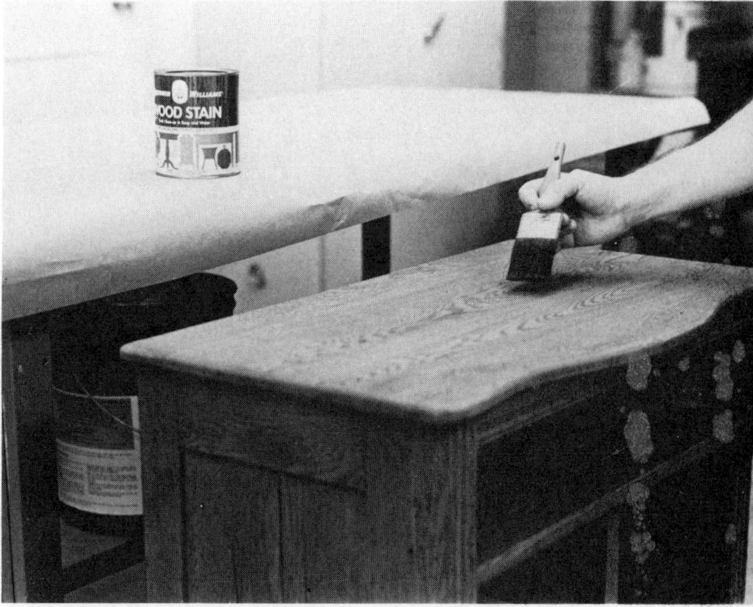

Figure 50-8
On large surfaces apply oil stain with a soft brush.

Nongrain-raising Stains

One of the newest types of stains is the *nongrain-raising stain* (NGR). This type of stain dries quickly, produces a transparent color and does not raise the grain, Figure 50-9. Lacquer sealer can be mixed with the stain so that you can combine staining and finishing in one operation. NGR stains are made from a dyebase. The dye mixes with either alcohol, glycol, acetone or toluol as a vehicle. This type of vehicle makes NGR stain dry quickly.

To apply a nongrain-raising stain:

1. Clean the wood surface and select the desired color of stain.
2. If possible, spray the stain lightly on the wood, Figure 50-10. Spraying gives the most consistent layer of stain. Be careful not to overlap the spray in the corners. You can cover more area with the stain if you add a *spraying extender* to the NGR. A spraying extender is a liquid that "waters down" the stain without affecting the color. Wiping or brushing the stain may produce dark streaks on big projects but can work fairly well on small projects. Do not overlap the strokes of the cloth or brush or you will get dark streaks.
3. Allow the surface to dry for 6 to 8 hours.

Figure 50-10
NGR stain and lacquer sealer can be mixed together and sprayed onto the surface.

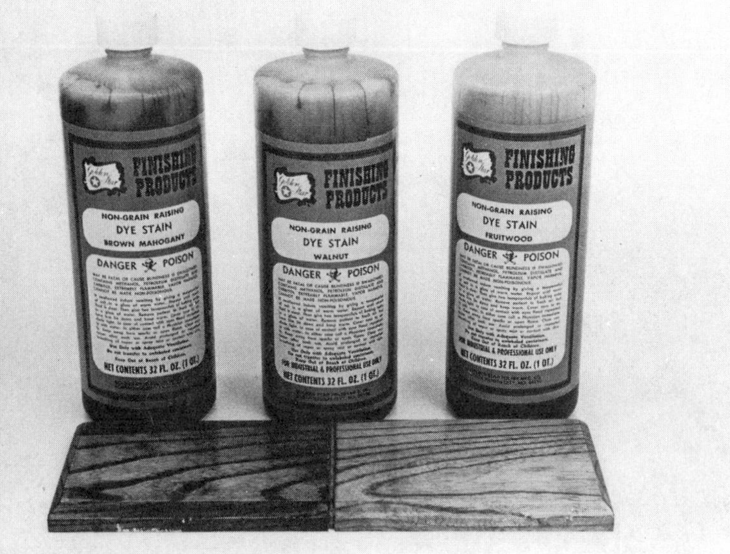

Figure 50-9
Nongrain-raising stains come in ready-to-use form.

Spirit Stains

Spirit stains are made from aniline dyes and alcohol. They are used primarily for furniture repair work because of their ability to penetrate materials easily. Spirit stains rarely are used to stain an entire project because they fade over the years.

STAINING FOR SPECIAL EFFECTS

Different treatments of stains can achieve special color effects. Some of these special effects are sap staining, shading and distressing.

Sap staining equalizes the color of furniture and cabinets. If you have a piece of light sapwood on an exposed surface, its color will contrast with the surrounding darker heartwood. To blend in this area, first apply a coat of stain only to the sapwood. Feather out the edges so that there will not be an abrupt change in color. Allow it to dry. Then apply the stain over the entire surface. Water stains and NGR stains work well for this type of sap staining.

Shading the outside edges of tops, ends, doors, and drawers gives a project an antique look. After you have stained the piece and applied the sanding sealer, use a darker shading lacquer to spray faintly over the corners. This shadow effect draws out these areas. Be careful, however. Too much lacquer makes the areas too dark. The shading lacquer should be feathered out to blend with the stained wood. Spray the remaining coats of lacquer after these areas have dried.

Distressing is a process of intentionally marring a piece of furniture to make it look antique. Mechanical distressing is done before finishing. Hitting the surface with a chain and boring angular holes are the most common methods. Surface distressing is done after you apply the sanding sealer. Surface distressing usually requires ground pigments and Japan drier, but many finishers use black or brown paint as a substitute. Select a dark contrasting color and dip a stiff bristle brush or toothbrush into the liquid. By rubbing your thumb across the bristles, you will speckle the wood with small, dark dots, Figure 50-11. You also can get this effect by using a commercial distressing aerosol spray.

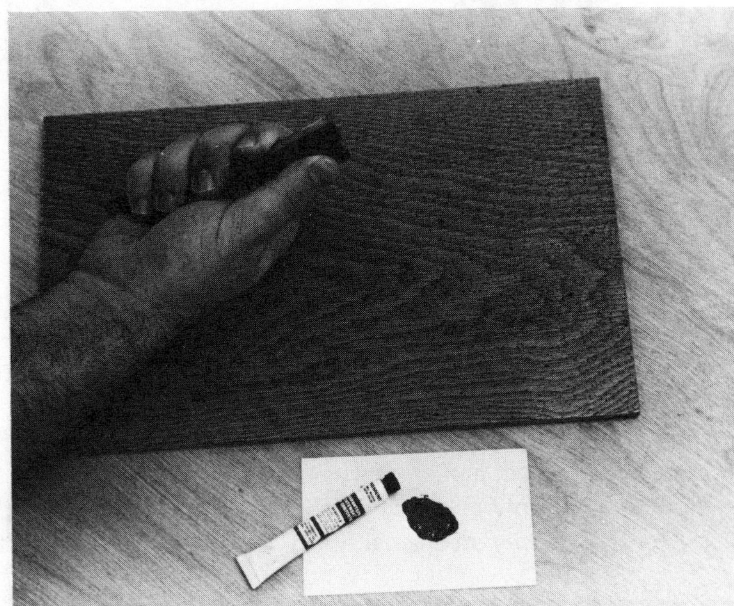

Figure 50-11
For surface distressing, rub the end of a brush covered with pigment.

REVIEW QUESTIONS

1 What three things can stain be used for?
2 What two ingredients make up a stain?
3 List the four major divisions of wood stains.
4 Name one advantage of water stains.
5 How should end grain be treated before applying a water stain?
6 What happens if you overlap water stain?
7 Name two disadvantages of oil stain.
8 What are the two types of oil stains?
9 How do you apply oil stains?
10 The longer the stain is left on the surface, the ____ the wood will be.
11 Name one advantage of nongrain-raising stains.
12 What are spirit stains primarily used for?
13 What is the difference between mechanical distressing and surface distressing?

SUGGESTED ACTIVITIES

1 Apply an oil stain on two scrap pieces of wood. Place one in a window where it will get direct sunlight most of the day. Keep the other inside a cabinet or drawer. What happens to the color after one month?
2 Try one of the special effects on a finishing sample. How would it look on a project you want to build?

UNIT

51

Varnishes and Brushing Techniques

Objectives

After studying this unit you should be able to:

1 List the major types of varnishes and their advantages.
2 Select a quality brush.
3 Apply a varnish finish.
4 Apply an enamel finish.

Technical Terms

Spirit varnish
Linseed oil varnish
Tung oil varnish
Synthetic oil varnish
Pure-bristle brush
Nylon-bristle brush
Brush keeper
Cross-brushing
Tipping-off
Enamel

Varnish is an excellent finish for wood. Varnishes are resinous coatings for wood that dry to a hard, lustrous film. Many pieces of furniture and cabinets are varnished.

There are more than 200 kinds of varnishes. You can select a specific type for each kind of project. Varnish provides a protective coating that has excellent body and depth. Certain types of varnishes are waterproof, alcohol-proof and, to a certain degree, heat-proof.

Varnish has few disadvantages. One problem is that it dries slowly. With certain types of varnishes, you may need six to nine days to finish a product. Another disadvantage is that dust sticks to the drying surface.

TYPES OF VARNISHES

All varnishes are made of three ingredients—the resin, the vehicle and the drier. The resin, or base, can be either natural or synthetic. A liquid vehicle is mixed with the resin to make the varnish easy to apply. A drier is added to shorten drying time. By varying the amounts of these materials, a varnish manufacturer can make an endless variety of varnishes.

You must use thinner or solvents to thin varnishes and to clean equipment used with varnishes. Varnishes with natural resins require the use

Figure 51-1
Thin varnishes with either mineral spirits or turpentine. Always read the label on the container for the proper choice.

Figure 51-2
Thin shellac with denatured alcohol.

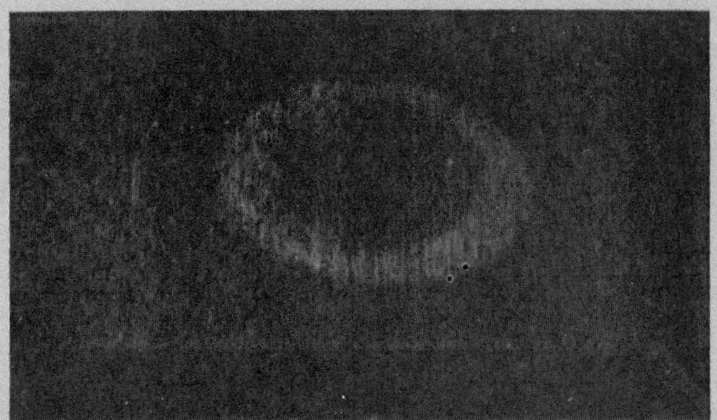

Figure 51-3
Placing a water glass on a shellac finish will create a water spot.

of turpentine or mineral spirits, Figure 51-1. Use mineral spirits or specialized solvents for synthetic resins. Most varnish containers have the recommended solvent printed on the label. The thinner must be compatible with the varnish.

The many kinds of varnishes are classified into four families. They are grouped by the type of film that develops when the varnish dries. They are spirit varnishes, linseed oil varnishes, tung oil varnishes and synthetic varnishes.

Spirit varnishes dry by evaporation of the solvent. Shellac is the most popular spirit varnish. It is a good barrier coat and sealer. The shellac should be thin so that it penetrates the wood. Orange shellac is the most common, but white shellac is used sometimes for light-colored woods. Both types of shellac are thinned (and brushes cleaned) with denatured alcohol, Figure 51-2. Most finishers do not consider shellac a good finish by itself. When used as a finish, shellac yellows with age and is subject to water spots, Figure 51-3. It also has a very short shelf life. It

Figure 51-4
Use a long-oil, or spar, varnish for exterior applications.

may spoil four to six months after the container is opened.

Linseed oil varnish is a common finish. These varnishes are divided into long-oil, medium-oil, or short-oil varnishes. Use long oils on exterior surfaces such as outside doors and boats, Figure 51-4. Long oils are frequently sold as spar varnish. Medium-oil varnishes dry much faster than long oils. They usually require about 24 hours to dry. Medium oils are used primarily on furniture and cabinets, Figure 51-5. Rubbing and polishing

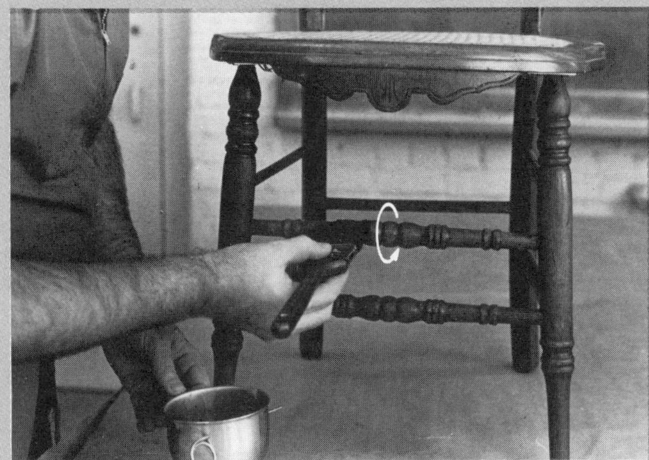

Figure 51-5
Medium-oil varnishes are excellent for furniture.

Figure 51-6
Polyurethane varnish develops an extremely hard finish.

varnishes are two types of medium-oil varnishes. Short-oil varnishes develop a very high shine but may crack and chip with age.

Tung oil varnish is a one-step, water-resistant finish. Use tung oil varnish for furniture and cabinets that will come in contact with water occasionally. When dry, this varnish resembles medium-oil linseed finish.

Synthetic varnishes are a new varnish type. They cure through polymerization, a chemical reaction that occurs when varnish is exposed to the air. Synthetic varnishes dry quickly. Synthetic varnishes are named for the specific plastic they contain. Some common types include alkyd, polyurethane and epoxy. Polyurethane is the most common kind and is used for small projects, Figure 51-6. It remains durable when exposed to water, chemicals and heat. Polyurethane requires a perfectly clean surface. All stains and fillers must be sealed completely. This synthetic varnish will break down when exposed to direct sunlight. Apply coats of polyurethane within 24 hours of each other. This varnish dries to such a hard smooth film that additional coats may not stick unless you roughen the surface by sanding it. Always use the same brand of varnish for all coats.

SELECTING A BRUSH

Apply varnishes and many other finishing materials with a brush. The brushing technique is popular because it is quick and inexpensive. However, it does take more time than spraying and a higher degree of skill than wiping techniques.

You first select a varnish brush for the job. Select a good brush if a high-quality finish is desired. A good brush will have flag ends, or bristles with split ends, Figure 51-7. The flag ends hold more and spread the finish into an even film. The bristles also should form a chisel edge. Long bristles toward the center of the brush form a natural angle for applying varnish, Figure 51-8. Inexpensive brushes do not have flag ends or chisel edges. If a chisel edge is formed on cheaper brushes, it usually is machine-cut rather than naturally formed.

When buying a brush, consider three things. First, consider the type of bristle, Figure 51-9. Use a *pure-bristle brush* for varnish. Top-quality varnish brushes are made of china-boar bristles. Other brushes have nylon or polyester bristles. Use these brushes to apply water-base finishes. Latex paints, for example, should be applied with a *nylon-bristle brush*. A brush with *XXX* on the handle contains the most rows of bristles. The more bristles in a brush, the more finish it will hold and the longer it will last.

Next, consider the width of the brush. Widths vary from 1/2" to 8" (13 to 203 mm). Use a narrow brush to do small projects and to get into small areas such as corners, Figure 51-10. Use

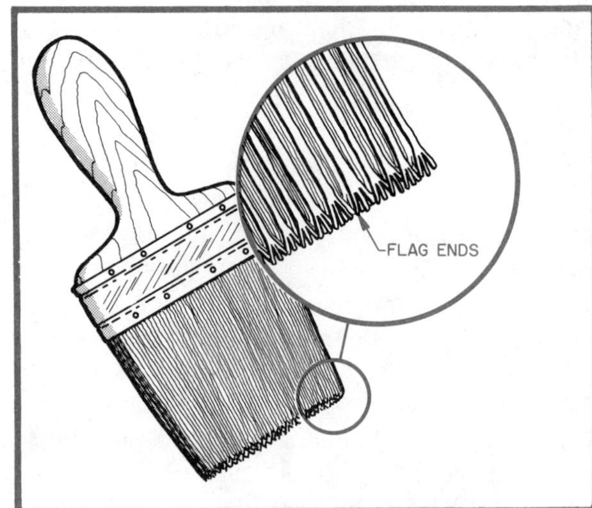

Figure 51-7
Bristles with flag ends will hold more finish and spread the liquid into an even film.

Figure 51-8
Hold a varnish brush at the same angle as the chisel edge of the bristles.

Figure 51-10
Use a narrow brush to reach into small areas.

wider brushes for large, flat areas, Figure 51-11. Use a 2" or 2-1/2" (51 or 64 mm) brush for most furniture and cabinets.

Finally, consider the shape of the handle and bristles, Figure 51-12. A flat handle is the most common style. Trim brushes have extra-long handles for reaching into small areas. Bristles can be flat, chisel-shaped or round. Most varnish brushes are chisel-shaped.

A good brush will last a long time if given proper care. Always clean the brush immediately after using it. Do not let the dirty brush stand

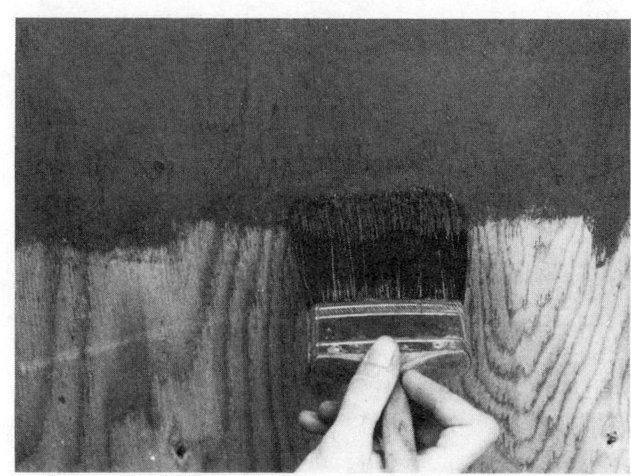

Figure 51-11
Use a wide brush on large, flat areas.

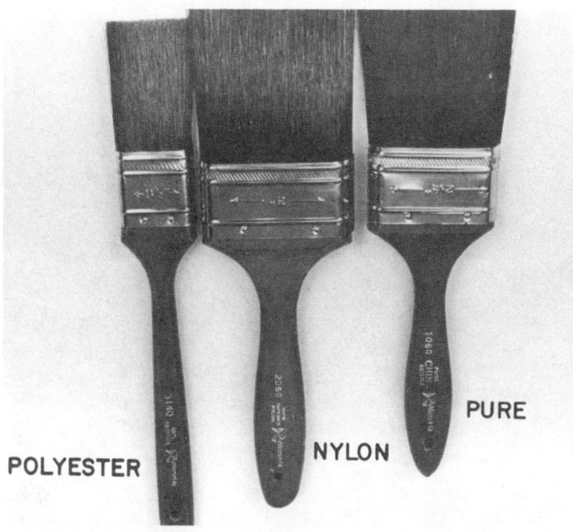

Figure 51-9
Finish brushes are available in polyester, nylon and pure-bristles.

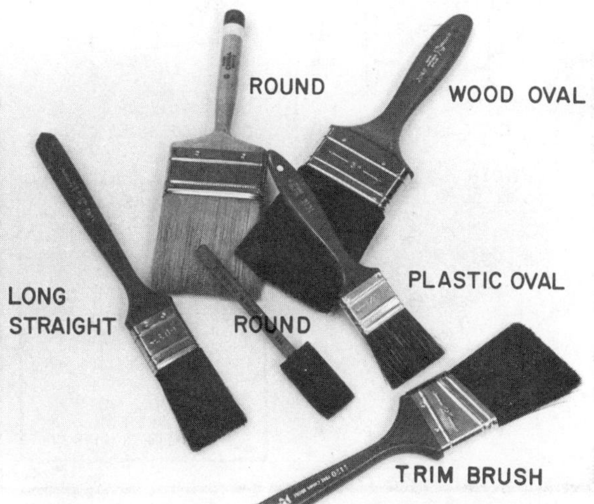

Figure 51-12
Brush handles are available in several styles.

Figure 51-13
Letting a brush stand in solvent will ruin the bristles.

in the solvent or you will ruin the bristles, Figure 51-13. If you are going to use a brush often, store it in a *brush keeper* after it has been cleaned, Figure 51-14. Use a mixture of half turpentine and half varnish in the keeper for varnish brushes.

To store brushes for a long time, clean them thoroughly in a three-container wash, Figure 51-15. Keep slightly dirty or old solvent in the first container. After bending the bristles back and forth several times in the first container, move the brush to the second container, filled with cleaner solvent. Wash the brush in this container. Finally, completely clean the brush in the third bath, filled with new solvent. As the solvent in the third container becomes dirty, use it to refill the first and second containers. Brushes cleaned in the three containers will be free from most finish. You may need to use a fourth or fifth wash to clean the brush completely. Clean the brush in new solvent until the solvent remains clear. Comb the bristles as they dry, Figure 51-16. Wrap dried brushes in paper to keep the bristles straight and clean. Store pure-bristle brushes with a small amount of turpentine worked into the bristles. Sprinkle moth crystals in the wrapping paper.

Figure 51-14
A brush keeper will store brushes properly for short periods of time.

Figure 51-15
Use a three-container wash to clean the brush thoroughly. Make certain that you use the correct solvent for each kind of finish.

Figure 51-16
Comb the bristles and wrap them with paper or in the original wrapper.

Figure 51-17
Carefully pour the varnish into a pan.

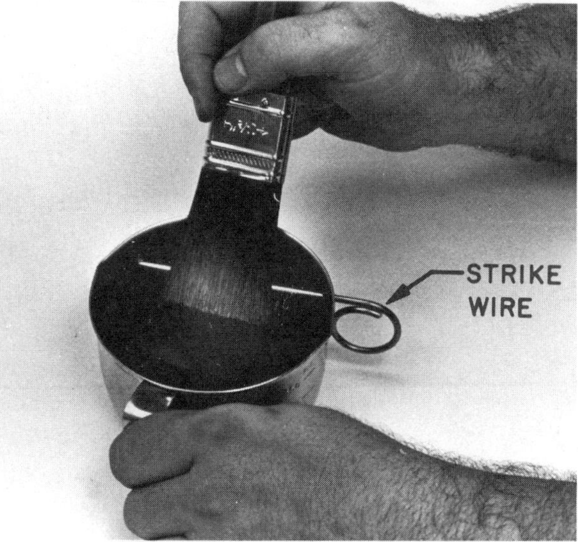

Figure 51-18
Wiping the brush on a strike wire.

BRUSHING ON A VARNISH FINISH

You must follow a specific procedure when brushing varnish on wood. The quality of the finish depends on correctly performing these steps:

1. Thoroughly clean and seal the surface of the project. Use pressurized air with a brush to clean. If you have stained or filled the wood, seal all surfaces with a barrier coat of shellac or similar material.
2. Do not use the varnish directly from the can it is sold in. The brush picks up dust particles from the wood and transfers them into the can. They will then be brushed back on the surface. Gently pour a small amount of the varnish from the can into a pan, Figure 51-17. Pouring the contents from a high level or splashing it against the sides of the pan produces air bubbles. You will see these bubbles in the final finish. Fit the pan with a strike wire for removing excess varnish from the brush, Figure 51-18. Wiping the brush against the side of the pan also can produce air bubbles. Do not pour unused varnish back into the original can.
3. Thin the first coat by 25 percent. Read the instructions on the varnish can for the recommended thinner. Stir the mixture carefully to prevent the formation of air bubbles. The thinned varnish will penetrate into the wood, forming a good base coat.
4. Apply varnish in a dust-free room. Do not dust or blow dust from your project in the finishing room. Remove as much dust and loose particles as possible. Use a tack rag to wipe off the remaining dust, Figure 51-19. Tack rags are available at most paint stores. They have a sticky surface that picks up dust. Wipe the rag over the entire area to be finished just before applying the varnish.
5. Flow the varnish onto the surface. Dip the brush into the finish between one-third and one-half the length of the bristles. Any more and the finish will soak the plug on the brush and make the brush difficult to clean.

Figure 51-19
Use a tack rag to remove leftover dust particles.

Figure 51-20
Cross-brushing across the grain.

Figure 51-21
Brushing with the grain is called tipping-off.

Brush the varnish across the grain, Figure 51-20. This is called *cross-brushing*. Set the brush in the center of the piece and move it toward the edge. If the surface is small, cover the entire area. Divide large surfaces into small sections and work each section separately.

6. Wipe off the brush on the strike wire immediately after cross-brushing each piece. Lightly brush with the grain, Figure 51-21. This is called *tipping-off*. Touch only the very tips of the bristles to the wet varnish. Start in one corner and work toward the center. Wipe the brush on the strike wire after each stroke. Overlap each stroke slightly. Inspect the newly applied finish very carefully. Any sags or runs must be removed before the surface of the varnish begins to dry. Remove dust particles from the wet finish with a pointed stick. By touching each individual particle, the stick will pick up pieces of dust, Figure 51-22.

Figure 51-22
Removing dust particles with a pointed stick. Attempt this only when the finish is wet.

7. Be sure the varnish is thoroughly dry before it is sanded. Use the following drying time schedule for applying the recommended four coats:

First coat	24 hours
Second coat	48 hours
Third coat	72 hours
Fourth coat	96 hours

8. Sand the first coat with wet-or-dry abrasive paper. Dip the abrasive paper in water and sand the surface lightly, Figure 51-23. Do not sand away the finish on the edges. By sanding, you will remove all lint and dust. Wipe the surface dry.
9. Wipe the surface with a tack cloth. Apply the second coat of varnish. Repeat steps 5, 6 and 7. Repeat for the third and fourth coats. Do not thin the varnish for the last three coats. Instead, apply the varnish full strength. Each coat of varnish adds another layer of finish and helps level the total sur-

Figure 51-23
Lightly sand the surface with wet-or-dry abrasive paper.

Figure 51-24
Rub the surface with pumice stone for a hand-rubbed appearance.

face. Fill all dips with varnish. Sand off any high spots. Do not sand through the varnish and into the wood. Do not sand all the varnish off of corners.

10. Rub down the final and fourth coat after it dries. Using linseed oil, sand the surface with 400-grit wet-or-dry abrasive paper. Then rub the finish with pumice stone and rubbing oil, Figure 51-24. Use a felt pad to apply the mixture. Always move the pad with the grain. Use rottenstone after the pumice to produce an even deeper finish.

ENAMELS

An *enamel* is a decorative, opaque varnish. When pigment is added to oil and resin, an enamel is produced. Enamel is more protective than transparent varnish because it is opaque. Pigments block out harmful ultraviolet rays from the sun that destroy most clear finishes. Enamel, however, covers the beauty of the wood. Enamels are available in flat, semigloss and gloss sheens. The higher the sheen, the more the surface defects will show. Poorly fitted joints and paint runs become obvious.

With most oil-base enamels and paints, it is very important first to apply a coat of primer, Figure 51-25. The label of the enamel container usually recommends a type of primer. Use a primer to increase the adhesion between the wood and the enamel. Without the primer coat, enamels may blister and peel. Do not thin regular enamel for use as a primer.

Apply enamels with the same brushing techniques used for transparent varnishes, Figure 51-26. Use a good pure-bristle varnish brush to spread the oil-base enamel on the surface. Use a nylon-bristle brush for latex enamels.

For most jobs, apply three coats. After you brush on one coat of primer and let it dry, apply a coat of enamel. You may need to sand the surface after the second coat dries, Figure 51-27. This will remove raised grain and dust particles.

Figure 51-25
Brush on a primer before applying oil-base enamel.

Figure 51-26
Apply enamel as you would apply varnish.

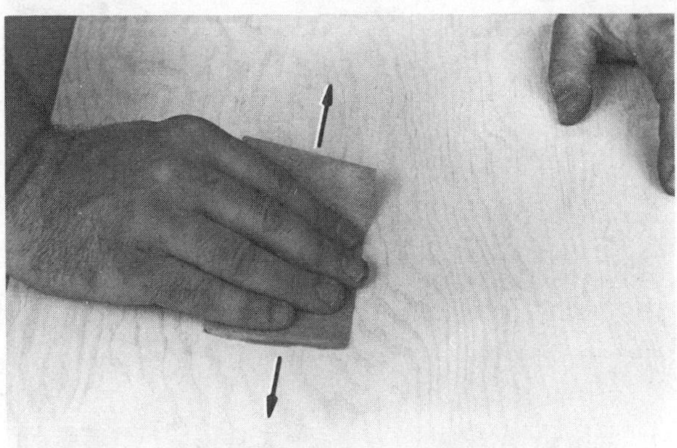

Figure 51-27
Sand between coats with a fine abrasive.

Figure 51-28
Latex enamels spread smoothly and form a protective coating.

Clean the surface after sanding. Apply the third coat, or finish coat, with a small amount of brushing. If you have prepared the surface properly, the finish coat will be very smooth. A properly prepared enamel surface is hard and durable.

Many woodworkers prefer latex enamel. It has the same qualities as oil-base enamels, plus some advantages, Figure 51-28. Check the label on the container for the recommended solvent. One advantage is that you can clean the brushes and other tools with warm water, Figure 51-29. Most latex paints are also self-priming, so you do not need to purchase primer. Instead, the first coat of latex serves as the primer coat.

Figure 51-29
Clean equipment with warm soapy water and rinse thoroughly.

REVIEW QUESTIONS

1 List three advantages and two disadvantages of varnishes.
2 What are the four kinds of varnishes?
3 What is the most popular spirit varnish?
4 Name three types of linseed oil varnishes.
5 Polyurethane varnishes should be applied on what type of a surface?
6 What advantages do flag-end bristles have?
7 Varnishes should be applied with what kind of bristles?
8 How should a varnish brush be cleaned and stored?
9 Why should varnish not be applied out of the can?
10 How much should you thin the first coat of varnish?
11 What is cross-brushing and tipping-off?
12 What is an enamel?
13 What is one advantage of latex paint?

SUGGESTED ACTIVITIES

1 Visit a local paint store and learn what varnishes are available. What does the salesperson recommend for your project?
2 See how many brushes your shop has. Are they properly cleaned and stored?
3 Practice applying a varnish to a sample board or project. Do you like the appearance?

UNIT

52

Lacquers and Spraying Techniques

Objectives

After studying this unit you should be able to:

1 Identify the different types of lacquers.
2 Identify the major pieces of spraying equipment.
3 Apply brushing and spraying lacquers properly.
4 Clean a spray gun.

Technical Terms

Nitrocellulose
Lacquer sealer
Clear gloss lacquer
Flattening agent
Dull lacquer
Water-white lacquer
Brushing lacquer
Hot spray lacquer
Water-reducible lacquer
Shading lacquer
Lacquer toner
Lacquer thinner
Regulator
Bleeder gun
Suction-feed gun
Pressure-feed gun
Internal mix
External mix
Triggering

Figure 52-1
Infrared lamps dry a lacquer finish in a few minutes. (Dry Clime Lamp Corporation)

Lacquer is a popular finish for cabinets and furniture. It dries quickly and forms a transparent to opaque protective film on the surface of the wood. Lacquer has a base of *nitrocellulose*, acrylic or other synthetic.

Lacquer has many advantages. You can apply several coats in a relatively short time. The lacquered product can be dried in a special oven, Figure 52-1. You can choose from many kinds of lacquers. Most lacquers are transparent. Shading lacquers, however, lightly tint the wood. Opaque lacquers hide the surface. Lacquers are available in many sheens or degrees of gloss. The sheen varies from a flat, dull surface to a super-high-gloss finish.

Lacquers have some disadvantages. All lacquers have a fast drying time. Brushing for too long a period will produce brush marks. Spray-type lacquers allow faster application but require special equipment. Regardless of the type of lacquer, it usually is not compatible with other finishes. Do not use lacquer over paint, varnish, wax or enamel. The solvents and thinners in the lacquer mixture will dissolve any of these finishes and mar your finish. When it is applied to a clean surface, lacquer dries to a hard finish. Because it has little flexibility, lacquer is subject to cracking and checking. This may happen when there are severe temperature or dimensional changes in the wood.

TYPES OF LACQUERS

Lacquers are sold in four basic sheens—gloss, semigloss, dull and flat. There are many variations of these. Lacquer can be purchased in containers of many sizes. These range from 16-ounce aerosol spray containers to 55-gallon barrels, Figure 52-2.

Lacquer sealers. Apply a *lacquer sealer* to the surface of the wood before you apply any other lacquer. The lacquer sealer forms a thick film in the pores of the wood. The film prevents stains and fillers from bleeding through the finish, Figure 52-3. Sealers provide adhesion for the remaining coats of lacquer. Use water-white sealer when the wood is to be as natural as possible. A sanding sealer costs less but will darken the wood. Neither type of sealer is as tough or as durable as gloss lacquer.

Clear gloss lacquers. These have a high sheen and solid content. Because of the high solid content, a few coats will create a thick film, Figure 52-4. *Clear gloss lacquers* build a thick film quickly. Flat or semigloss lacquer often is applied over the gloss coats. The flatter lacquer will cover the glossy surface and give the desired sheen.

Dull lacquers. These lacquers have a lower solid content than do gloss lacquers. The lack of sheen gives a hand-rubbed look, Figure 52-5. By adding a *flattening agent* to gloss lacquer, you can make *dull lacquer.* The flattening agent is a chemical that takes away the glossy appearance. To achieve dull finish, mix flat lacquer with gloss lacquer. Mixing one part of flat lacquer to four parts of clear gloss lacquer produces a semigloss finish.

Figure 52-2
Lacquer is available in different quantities.

Figure 52-3
Sanding sealer prevents stain or filler from bleeding through the finish.

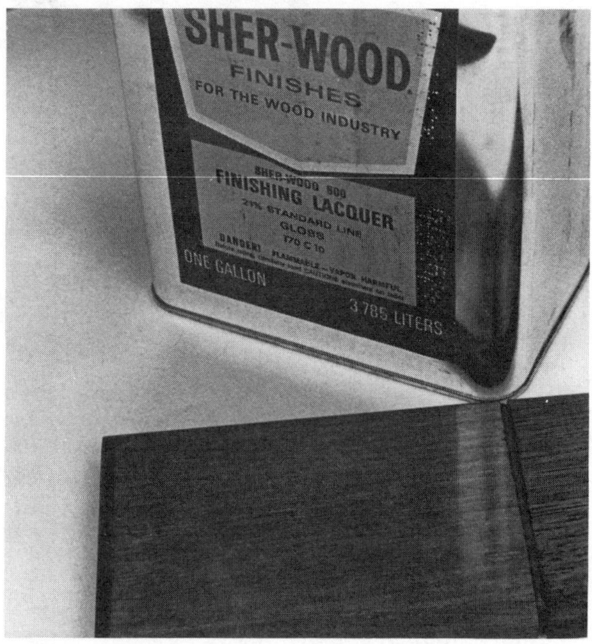

Figure 52-4
Gloss lacquer produces the highest degree of sheen.

Figure 52-5
Dull lacquer produces little or no sheen.

Figure 52-6
You can apply brushing lacquer with a brush.

Water-white lacquers. These are the clearest lacquers. They dry to an almost invisible film. *Water-white lacquer* is appropriate for wood that you want to look as natural as possible.

Brushing lacquers. These lacquers are slow drying. Apply them with a soft varnish brush, Figure 52-6. The longer drying time permits you to brush on the lacquer without leaving brush marks. Under normal drying conditions, *brushing lacquer* will dry in two hours.

Hot spray lacquers. You must use special heating equipment before you apply these lacquers. A special heater heats the lacquer to a very hot temperature, Figure 52-7. Hot spray reduces to a minimum most spraying defects. Because of the higher solid content, one coat of hot spray finish is equal to two coats of standard lacquer. Using *hot spray lacquer* saves time and labor.

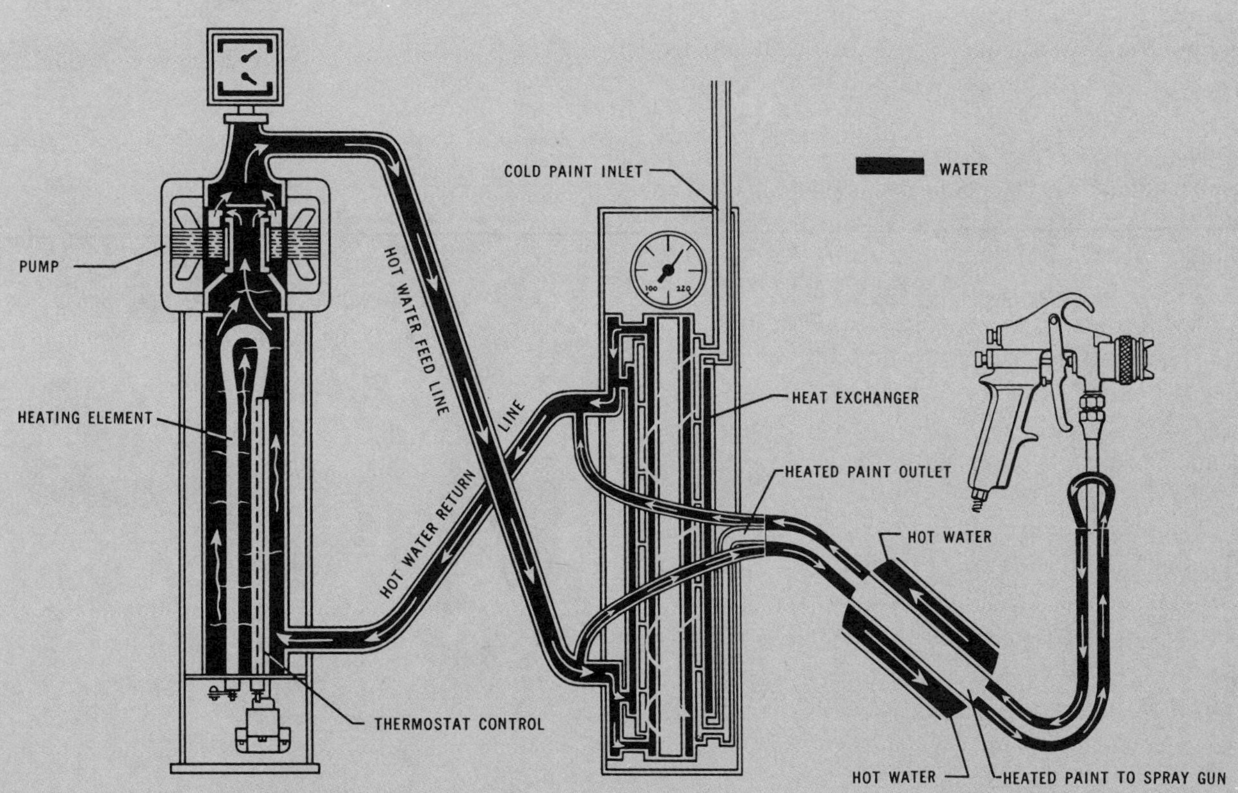

Figure 52-7
Heat hot spray lacquer with special equipment before applying it. (The DeVilbiss Co.)

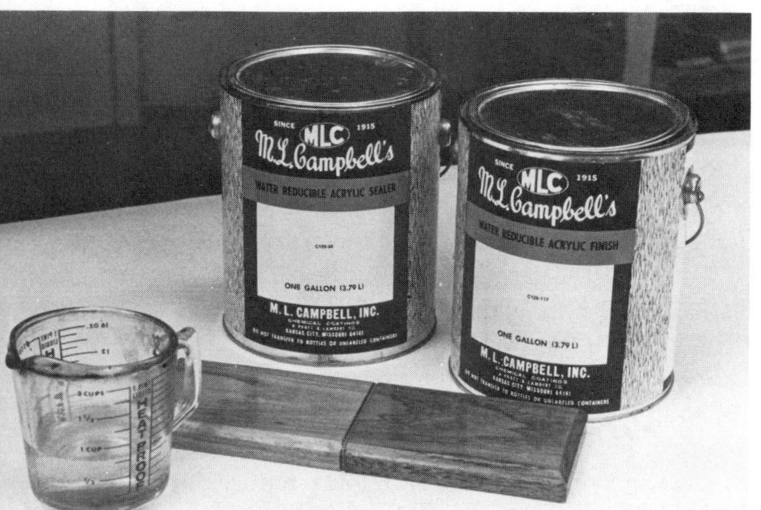

Figure 52-8
Use water to thin and clean equipment that you have used with water-reducible lacquers.

Water-reducible lacquers. These new acrylic lacquers are thinned with water, Figure 52-8. They are less flammable than nitrocellulose lacquers. They cause less pollution to the environment. *Water-reducible lacquers* give the same finish as nitrocellulose lacquers.

Shading lacquers and lacquer toners. Use these to add color to the surface of the wood. *Shading lacquers* are translucent. *Lacquer toners* are more opaque. They are useful when you want to conceal some of the texture of the product. Stir the pigmented lacquers thoroughly to mix the color completely. Furniture manufacturers often use this type of finish when plastic, solid wood and hardboard parts must all have the same color, Figure 52-9.

Colored lacquers. These lacquers are heavily pigmented to hide surface grain detail, Figure 52-10. They look like enamel paints after they have dried. They often are sold in aerosol containers. *Colored lacquers* have a faster drying time than enamels and produce a hard, durable finish.

BRUSHING LACQUER

Apply brushing type lacquers with a medium-soft, flat, pure-bristle or nylon-bristle varnish brush. Dip the brush into the container. Wipe the tip of the brush just enough to prevent dripping. Let the lacquer flow with the grain by

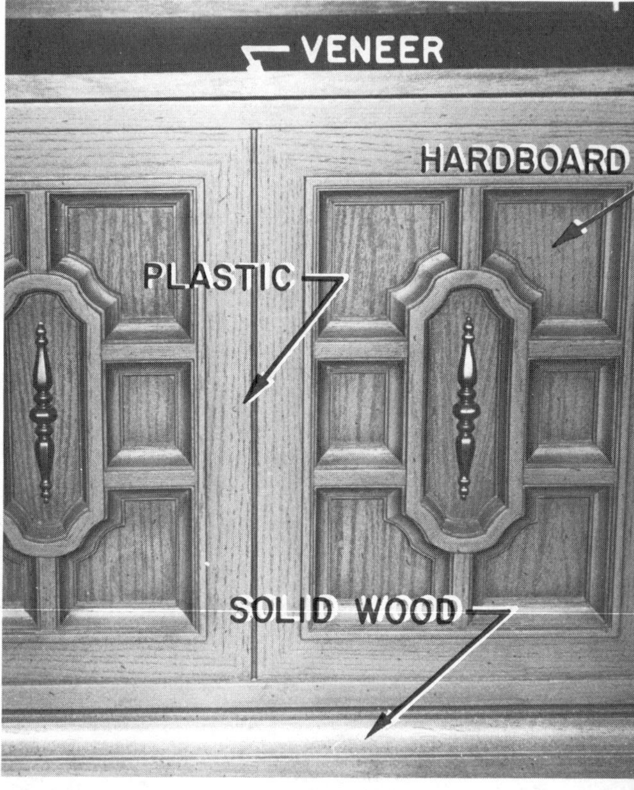

Figure 52-9
Use toners to give different materials the same finished appearance.

Figure 52-10
Colored lacquers look like paint.

holding the brush at a 45° angle, Figure 52-11. Keep the brush wet and do not try to spread the lacquer too much. Avoid overlapping the new coat to the partially set area. This will prevent roughness and brush marks. Any area you miss can be coated later.

Drying time is very important. Freshly applied lacquers dry to a dust-free finish in 30 minutes. Do not touch the project or expose it to dust during this time. Apply additional coats after a 2-hour period. Sand between coats with 320-grit wet-or-dry abrasive paper.

SPRAYING LACQUER SEALER

Apply one coat of lacquer sealer. More coats may cause checking or cracking of the finish. Thin the sealer to let it penetrate the wood. Apply lacquer sealers with a spray gun set at a high spraying pressure. A good starting pressure is 50 pounds per square inch. Although the sealer will raise the grain, sand it lightly with 320-grit wet-or-dry abrasive paper. Because the sealer is essentially in the wood and not on the surface, you easily can sand through the sealer and expose the raw wood.

SPRAYING LACQUERS

The best way to apply an even coat of lacquer is with a spray gun. Thin the lacquer before you shoot it through the spray gun. Mix a small quantity of *lacquer thinner* with the lacquer, or follow the instructions on the label of the container. Make a test spray on a sample piece. If the lacquer is too thick, it will not come out of the gun or will go on the surface unevenly. Too much thinner will reduce the solid content, and you will need to apply more coats. Use a lacquer thinner of good quality that is compatible with the lacquer, Figure 52-12. Lacquer thinners are classified as fast, medium or slow, depending on their drying time. The label on the lacquer container usually suggests what thinner to use.

Temperature and humidity will affect the lacquer finish. Too high or too low a temperature will shorten or lengthen the drying time. A favorable temperature is between 65° to 78° F (18° to 26° C). Allow at least two hours between coats for the lacquer to dry. High humidity may cause the finish to blush. This cloudy appearance will occur especially on rainy days. If the blushing is not too severe, it may disappear with time.

Figure 52-11
When you brush with lacquer, hold the brush at approximately a 45° angle.

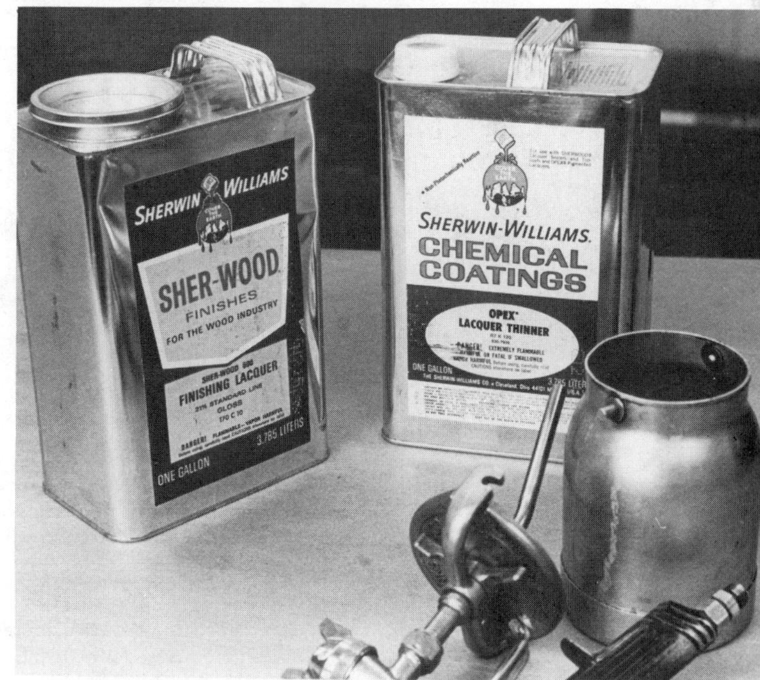

Figure 52-12
The lacquer and the lacquer thinner must be compatible.

COMMON SPRAY-GUN TROUBLES

Trouble	Possible Causes	Suggested Remedies
Sags and Runs	Material piled on too heavily.	Learn to judge correct depth of finish film.
	Dirty air cap and fluid tip.	Remove and clean air cap and fluid tip.
	Operation too slow.	Move gun more quickly.
	Fluid pressure too high.	Reduce fluid pressure.
	Gun too close to surface.	Hold gun 6" to 8" (152 to 203 mm) from surface.
	Material too thin.	Thin finish material correctly.
	Trigger not released at end of stroke.	Release trigger after each stroke.
	Gun at wrong angle to surface.	Hold gun at correct angle to surface.
Orange Peel	Gun strokes too rapid.	Take slower strokes.
	Gun too close to surface.	Hold gun 6" to 8" (152 to 203 mm) from surface.
	Poor thinner.	Use better grade of thinner.
	Overspray falling on previously sprayed surface.	Spray detailed parts first and finish with wet coat.
	Insufficient air pressure.	Increase atomizing pressure.
	Gun not spraying wet coat.	Check material, use correct stroke and overlap.
	Material not thinned properly.	Add correct amount of thinner.
	Gun stroke too far from surface.	Stroke gun 6" to 8" (152 to 203 mm) from surface.
Excessive Spray Fog	Fluid pressure too low.	Increase fluid pressure.
	Wrong air or fluid tip.	Choose correct tips.
	Atomizing air pressure too high.	Use least possible amount of air pressure.
	Material too thin.	Use correct amount of thinner.
	Gun stroke too far from surface.	Stroke gun 6" to 8" (152 to 203 mm) from surface.
Blushing	Lacquer dries too quickly.	Add retarder to lacquer.
	Finish absorbs moisture.	Avoid spraying in humid or cold weather.
Sputtering and Fluttering	Liquid cup tipped at acute angle.	When cup must be tipped, change fluid tube.
	Fluid passageway obstructed.	Clean fluid tip, needle and tube.
	Leaky connections (suction gun).	Lubricate and tighten connections.
	Fluid tip not tightened.	Tighten securely.
	Material too thick.	Thin material properly.
	Air vent in cup lid clogged.	Keep vent clean and clear of liquid.
	Fluid tube not tightened to pressure tank or pressure cup.	Keep tight and check for defects.
	Insufficient material in cup.	Refill cup with liquid.
Streaks	Tipping gun too much.	Spray should hit surface at right angles.
	Gun moved too quickly.	Slow gun strokes.
	Dirty air tip and fluid tip.	Clean air tip and fluid tip.
	Split spray.	Change air cap or reduce air.
	Gun held at wrong angle.	Hold gun at correct angle to surface.
	Strokes not overlapping sufficiently.	Follow parallel with previous strokes.
	Gun held too far from work.	Hold gun 6" to 8" (152 to 203 mm) from surface.
	Air pressure too high.	Use only as much air as is needed.
Faulty Spray Patterns:		
Spray Pattern Top-heavy	Dirt on air cap or fluid-tip seat.	Remove and clean thoroughly.
	Top side of fluid tip dirty.	Remove and clean.
	External mix horn holes partially plugged.	Remove air cap and clean.
Split Spray Pattern	Air and fluid not regulated properly.	Make spray pattern narrower.
	Dirty air tip or fluid tip.	Remove and clean.
Spray Pattern Bottom-heavy	Dirt on air cap or fluid-tip seat.	Remove and clean seat.
	Dirt on bottom side of fluid tip.	Remove and clean fluid tip.
	External mix horn holes partially clogged.	Remove and clean horn holes.
Spray Pattern Heavy at Center	Atomizing pressure too low.	Increase to proper pressure.
	Material too thick.	Thin material properly.
	Spreader adjustment valve not set properly.	Increase volume of air.
	Fluid tip too large for material.	Select proper fluid tip.
Spray Pattern Heavy to the Right	Dirt on right side of fluid tip.	Remove fluid tip and clean.
	Right side of horn holes partially clogged.	Remove air cap and clean.
Spray Pattern Heavy to the Left	Dirt on left side of fluid tip.	Remove fluid tip and clean.
	Left side of horn holes partially clogged.	Remove air cap and clean.

Figure 52-13
Common spray gun troubles, causes and remedies.

Problems can occur when you are spraying lacquer. They can be related either to spray-gun adjustments or to faulty spraying techniques. Figure 52-13 describes and analyzes these problems.

Spraying Equipment

Spraying equipment includes a compressor, a regulator, an air hose, a spray booth, a respirator and a spray gun. The compressor is an air pump that provides pressurized air, Figure 52-14. It must be adequate to supply enough dry, clean air to keep the spray gun operating properly.

Use a *regulator* to adjust the air pressure, Figure 52-15. Most high-pressure spray guns require 40 to 50 pounds per square inch to atomize the lacquer properly. This pressure may vary for different guns and different materials. Adjust the regulator until the right amount of pressure shows on the air gauge. Many regulators have a moisture trap to remove water. As air is pressurized in the compressor, it becomes warm and collects moisture. If this water is mixed with the lacquer, it will mar the finish.

The air hose connects the regulator and the spray gun. It usually is made of red rubber with brass fittings at each end, Figure 52-16. Keep the hose free of air leaks. Keep the length 8′ (2400 mm) or shorter.

The spray booth is an enclosure that keeps lacquer overspray confined and dust particles out. It usually is made of sheet metal and has a large exhaust system to remove the overspray

Figure 52-15
A regulator adjusts the air pressure and removes moisture from the air. (The DeVilbiss Co.)

Figure 52-14
A compressor pressurizes the air before the finish can be atomized. (The DeVilbiss Co.)

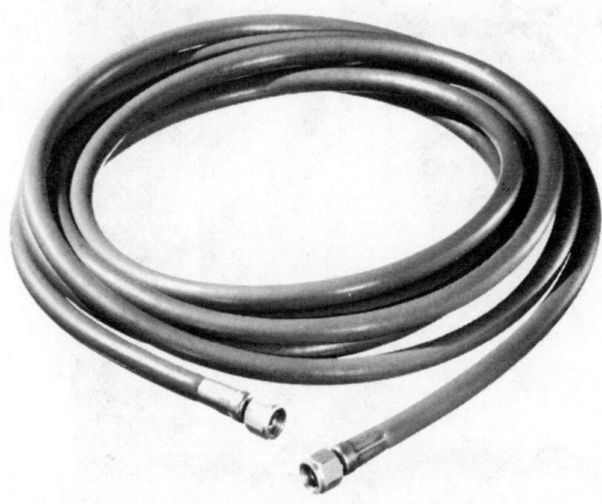

Figure 52-16
Air hoses must be free of leaks in both the brass fittings and the rubber portion. (The DeVilbiss Co.)

and any fumes. There are two types of exhaust systems. The dry exhaust system uses a paper filter, Figure 52-17. The exhaust sucks the overspray through the filter and then forces the air out. The exhaust system of the water-wash booth draws contaminated air through a series of water curtains to remove solids, Figure 52-18. Keep the booths clean and well-lighted with explosion-proof lights.

Wear a respirator when you are spraying lacquer. The mask covers your nose and mouth to prevent your breathing harmful vapors, Figure 52-19. Keep the mask clean and change the filter cartridges frequently.

Figure 52-17
A dry spray booth contains paper filters. (Binks Manufacturing Corporation)

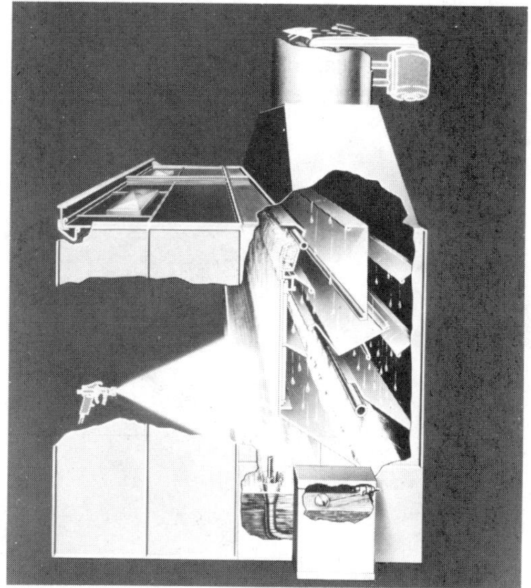

Figure 52-18
A water-wash booth removes finishing material in a water bath. (The DeVilbiss Co.)

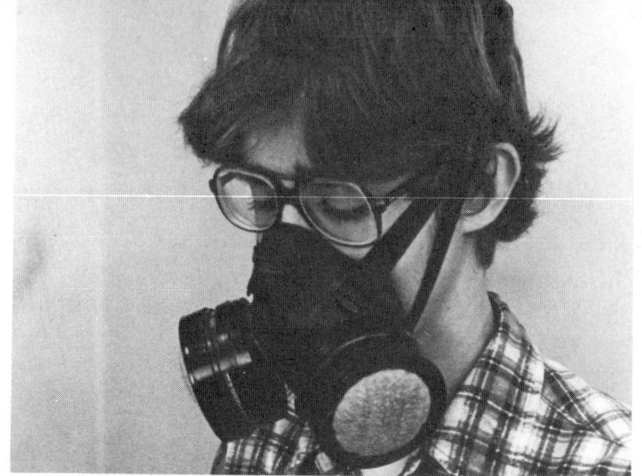

Figure 52-19
The respirator filters out harmful particles floating in the air.

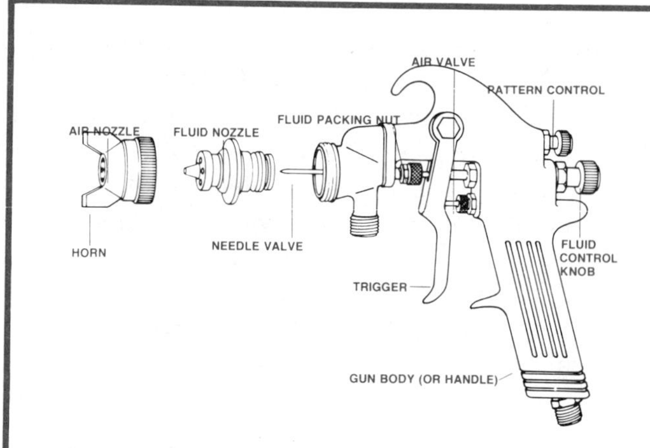

Figure 52-20
Major parts of a spray gun. (Binks Manufacturing Corporation)

The spray gun atomizes the liquid finish so that it can be sprayed onto the wood. Figure 52-20 shows the major parts of a spray gun. Finish enters the gun body and then enters the fluid nozzle when you pull back the needle valve with the trigger. Air enters through the fluid nozzle. Depending on the style of air nozzle, the air and the finish are mixed either inside or outside the nozzle.

Spray guns are of two types. A *bleeder gun* is constructed so that air passes through the gun at all times. It is used primarily on small compressors that would be overloaded if the flow of air were stopped. Pulling the trigger controls only the flow of finish. A *nonbleeder gun* is used on compressors that have a pressure regulator. When you first pull the trigger, air comes out of the nozzle of the gun. Pulling further back on the trigger releases the finish. The further back you pull the trigger, the more finish comes out.

Spray guns differ in the way the material is fed to the nozzle, Figure 52-21. The *suction-feed gun* has a nozzle designed to create a vacuum when air is forced through it. The vacuum sucks the liquid finish from the paint cup to the nozzle. Use the suction-feed gun for thinned lacquers and varnishes. It will not spray thick body materials, such as paints and enamels, properly. The *pressure-feed gun* feeds the finish to the nozzle through pressurized air. The airtight paint cup is under pressure that forces fluids up through the nozzle. This system is ideal for heavy enamels and house paints as well as for thinned materials.

The style of air cap mounted on the spray gun is another variable. It can be either an internal or an external mix, Figure 52-22. The *internal mix* has a long, narrow slot or other opening in the air cap. The fluid is atomized inside the air cap. Because of the low pressure the internal mix air cap requires, it is used primarily on small pressure-feed units. The major disadvantage of this style is that fast-drying materials dry in and around the slot. The *external mix* atomizes the air and finish outside the nozzle. The air is blown out of the two horns on each side of the nozzle. The fluid comes out the center hole in the middle of the nozzle. Either suction- or pressure-feed guns can use an external mix air cap.

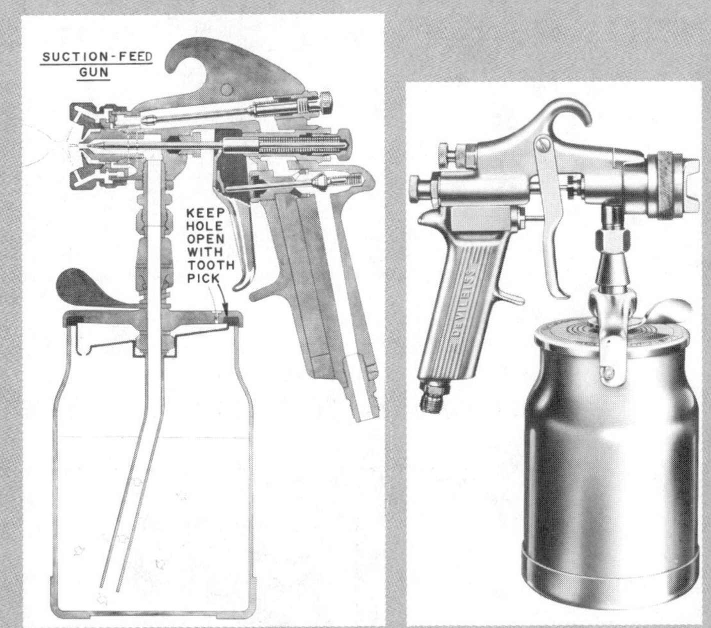

Figure 52-21
A suction system, *left,* or a pressure system, *right,* feeds the liquid finish to the nozzle. (The DeVilbiss Co.)

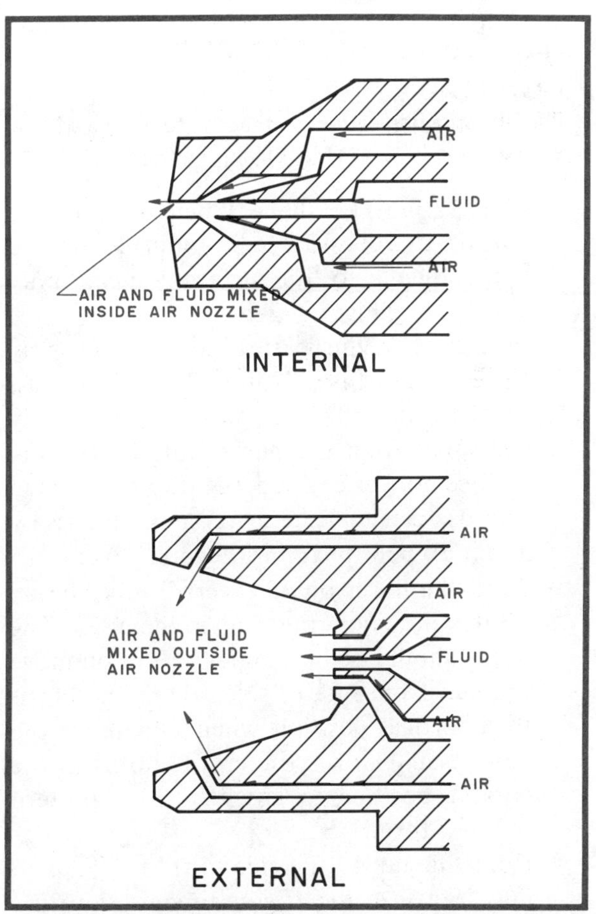

Figure 52-22
Internal mix guns atomize the finish inside the air nozzle. External mix guns atomize the finish outside the air nozzle.

Spraying Techniques

There are several important points to keep in mind when finishing a product. With much practice you will gain the skill to perform a superior spray job. Remember, finishes are flammable. Keep lighted cigarettes, sparks and flames away from the finishing area. Some spraying techniques are:

1. Learn how to adjust the gun. Refer to Figure 52-20. Adjust the fluid control valve to regulate the amount of material coming out of the nozzle. You can regulate the quantity of fluid by controlling the trigger or by applying more or less pressure to the paint cup. Use the pattern control valve to change the pattern of the spray. The valve adjusts from round to various oval-shaped fans. You can control this adjustment by regulating the amount of atomized air that goes through the nozzle. For most spraying, adjust the spray pattern until you achieve a

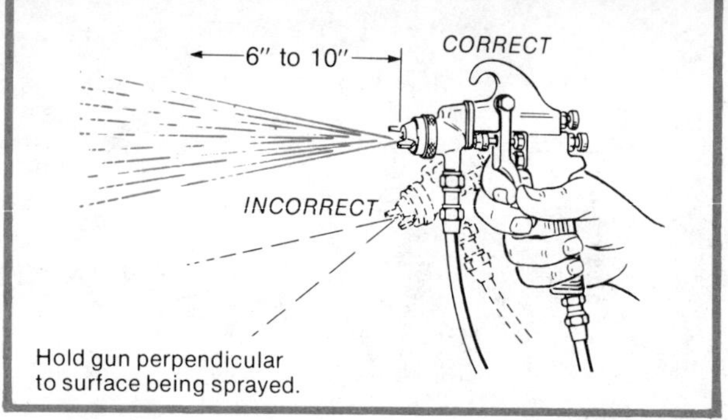

Figure 52-23
For a good spraying pattern, adjust the fan to a width of 6" to 10" (152 to 254 mm) and hold the gun in the proper position. (Binks Manufacturing Corporation)

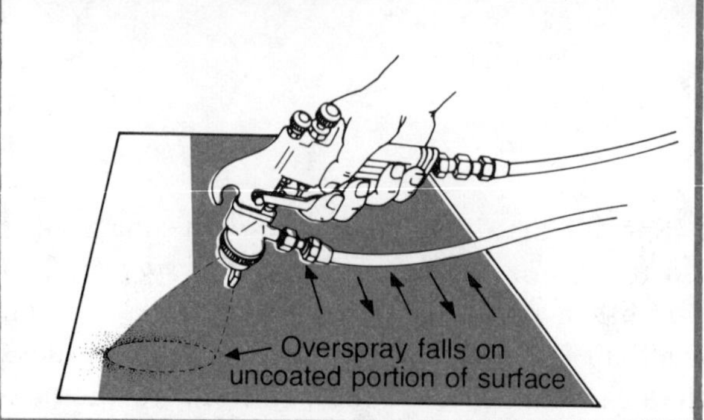

Figure 52-25
Overspray should fall on the uncoated surface. (Binks Manufacturing Corporation)

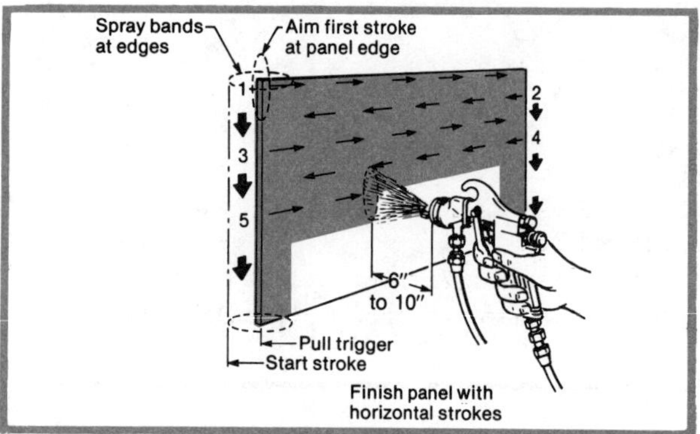

Figure 52-24
Plan the spraying pattern so that the total area will be evenly coated. (Binks Manufacturing Corporation)

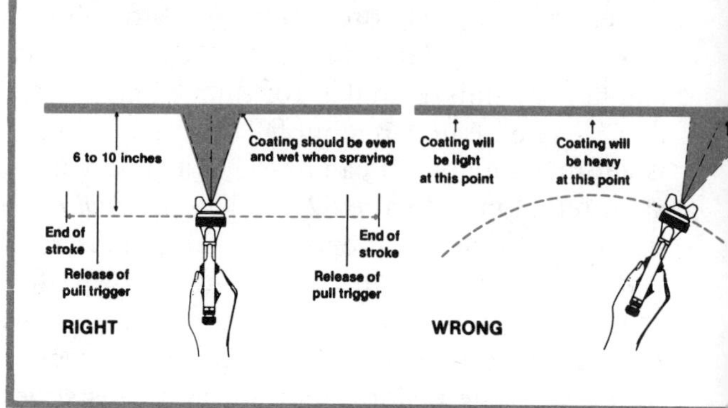

Figure 52-26
Move the gun straight across the surface. (Binks Manufacturing Corporation)

6" (152 mm) fan shape. When you hold the gun 6" to 10" (152 to 254 mm) from, and perpendicular to, the surface you can spray a wide area, Figure 52-23.

2. Plan the spraying pattern so that you spray the top edge first, Figure 52-24. Each pass of the gun will cover another area. Any overspray from the gun should fall on the surface not yet covered, Figure 52-25. When you use clear finishes, overlap each pass by about 50 percent to insure good coverage.
3. Turn the horns on an external mix air cap in the direction the gun is moving. The horns should be horizontal when you move the gun from side to side. Turn the horns to a vertical position when you move the gun up and down. Keep the horns in the correct position to give the spray pattern the best form.
4. Hold the gun to the side to start the spraying. Squeeze the trigger to start the fluid through the nozzle. Move the gun toward the surface in a straight line, keeping your wrist relatively stiff. Keep the gun as perpendicular to the surface as possible, Figure 52-26. If you swing the gun in a natural arc, the coating will not be even.
5. You can double-coat most surfaces. Apply the first coat by moving the gun with the grain. Spray a second coat across the grain. This technique will develop a smooth layer and build up film quickly.
6. Keep the gun moving at all times. If you allow it to stop, the finish will build up too quickly and cause sags and runs.
7. Learn *triggering*, or controlling the trigger action of the gun. When you pull the trigger all the way back, the flow of the finish will increase. Start the finish out of the gun before the spray reaches the edge of the stock. Release the trigger at the exact instant the spray reaches the opposite edge.

Cleaning the Spray Gun

Use lacquer thinner to clean the gun completely after each use. Otherwise the gun will become dirty and fail to function properly.

To clean the gun, follow this procedure:

1. Hold a clean rag over the nozzle of the gun

and pull the trigger. This will force most of the finish back into the paint cap. Do not do this with an airless spraying system. The high air pressure will cause serious damage.

2. Empty the paint cup and wash out any left-over finish. Place about 1" (25 mm) of lacquer thinner in the cup.
3. Reassemble the gun and spray about 1/4 cup of the thinner through the gun, Figure 52-27. To loosen any hardened finish, turn the nozzle in several positions as you spray. Squeeze and release the trigger several times. Aim the spray gun carefully toward the filters in the spray booth.
4. Unscrew the air cap and place it in the lacquer thinner to soak, Figure 52-28. With a rag dipped in lacquer thinner, wipe any left-over lacquer from the outside of the gun.
5. If the vent hole in the top of the paint cup lid becomes clogged, use a wooden toothpick soaked in lacquer thinner to clean it. Never use metal objects to remove the hardened finish. They will enlarge the hole and cause faulty spray patterns.

Do not submerge the gun in thinner. This will remove oil from the working parts and harden the packings. Disassemble the gun only if it needs major repair work. Spray guns will last a long time if you keep them clean.

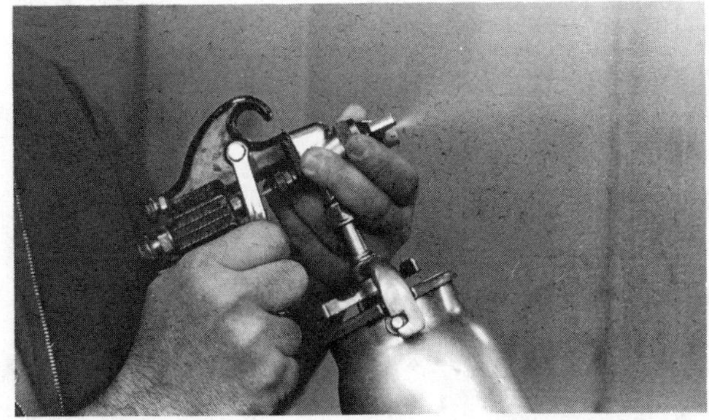

Figure 52-27
Spray the thinner through the gun as you turn the air nozzle.

Figure 52-28
Place the air cap in the lacquer thinner left in the paint cup.

REVIEW QUESTIONS

1 What is lacquer?
2 List three advantages and three disadvantages of lacquers.
3 What is the purpose of lacquer sealers? Which type gives a natural finish?
4 What is an advantage of using clear gloss lacquer as a base before applying a flatter lacquer?
5 How should you apply brushing lacquers?
6 What is the major advantage of water-reducible lacquers?
7 What is the purpose of the air hose?
8 Name the two types of spray booths.
9 What is the purpose of a respirator?
10 Define the following: bleeder, nonbleeder, suction feed, pressure feed, internal mix, external mix.
11 Sketch the body of a spray gun and label its major parts.
12 In which direction should the horns of an external mix air cap be turned when you are moving the gun from side to side?
13 List the steps in cleaning a spray gun.

SUGGESTED ACTIVITIES

1 Visit a paint store and make a list of the types of lacquers available. What are the uses of each type?
2 Prepare a finishing sample coated with lacquer. Compare it with a varnish sample and an oil sample. How are the three finishes different?
3 Inspect your spraying system. Identify the major parts.

UNIT

53

Wipe-on Finishes

Objectives

After studying this unit you should be able to:

1 Identify the different types of wipe-on finishes.
2 Apply wipe-on finishes properly.
3 Name the advantages and disadvantages of wipe-on finishes.

Technical Terms

Wax finishes
Oil finishes
Resin finishes
Rubbing waxes
Boiled linseed oil
FDA-approved oil
Danish oil

Wipe-on finishes have been used on furniture for centuries. Some museums have well-preserved pieces of furniture on which this type of finish was used. Although hundreds of years old, these finishes are still bright and have kept the furniture attractive.

Wipe-on finishes have many advantages and few disadvantages. One major advantage is that they can be applied with a cloth. They do not require expensive brushes or spraying equipment. Many schools and small shops select this finish because airborne dust does not interfere with wipe-on finishes. No special, clean finishing room is needed, Figure 53-1. Some woodworkers, however, believe a major disadvantage is that most wipe-on finishes do not build up any film thickness. With some of these finishes, a deep, high-gloss finish cannot be developed because of the lack of a thick, hard layer on the surface.

The Food and Drug Administration (FDA) has not approved most of these wipe-on finishes for use on food-storage or preparation products. You should finish such items as drinking mugs and fruit bowls only with an approved material, such as Behlen Salad Bowl Finish®.

There are three major types of wipe-on finishes. They are *wax finishes, oil finishes* and *resin finishes.* Of these three, the oil finishes are the most popular.

Figure 53-1
You can apply wipe-on finishes in the woodworking shop because they do not require a clean finishing room.

Figure 53-2
Paste wax can be used for a wipe-on finish.

Figure 53-3
A double boiler works well for melting paste wax. *Apply only enough heat to melt the wax.*

WAX FINISH

Waxes give a dull luster finish with a minimal effort. You can use special pigmented or unpigmented *rubbing waxes*. Regular paste wax often is a good choice, Figure 53-2. The only equipment you need is a soft cloth.

You may apply any type of wax either to bare wood or to a stained surface. The process is simple.

To produce a wax finish:

1. Remove all dust from the surface with a brush or pressurized air. Use tack cloth as a final cleaning process.
2. Place a small amount of the wax in a double boiler and heat, Figure 53-3. Be careful not to overheat the wax because it is extremely flammable. You must be able to work with the wax without burning yourself. Apply only enough heat to melt the wax. It must not boil. Once the wax has melted, you can apply it with a cloth pad. Use a circular motion to rub the melted wax into the wood, Figure 53-4. Work as much wax into the wood as possible without leaving a film on the surface. You can also apply the wax cold from the can. Wax applied cold will not penetrate the wood as deeply as warm wax will.

Figure 53-4
Rub the melted wax into the wood with a circular motion.

3. Buff the surface of the wood after the wax has dried 5 to 10 minutes, Figure 53-5. A soft, cotton cloth folded into a pad makes an excellent buffing cloth. Rub the surface in a back-and-forth motion. If you let the wax stay on the surface any longer without buffing, the wood will be difficult to polish.

Repeat the process two or three times. Make certain the surface is buffed completely after each coat. You may need to apply additional coats at a later time to restore the luster and provide more protection.

Once you have rubbed wax into the surface, you cannot apply another type of finish. The waxed surface will repel any other type of finish. There is no practical way of removing the wax.

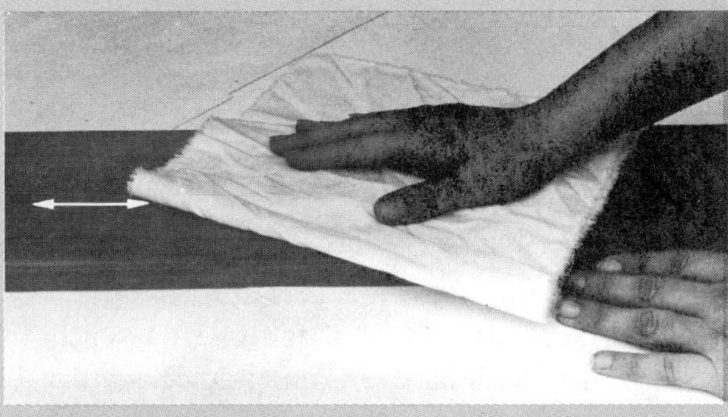

Figure 53-5
Buff the surface thoroughly with a soft cloth.

OIL FINISH

An oil finish has a beautiful, darkening effect. It usually is applied only to dark-colored woods, such as walnut, mahogany and cherry. The finish will never crack, chip or blister. When properly applied, the wood will repel water and resist heat and staining. Should the oil surface be scratched, you can easily retouch the scarred area with additional oil.

There are three major types of oil finishes. The three are *boiled linseed oil, FDA-approved oil* and *Danish oil.* Linseed oil is used seldom because of the odor.

Special FDA-approved oils are used for salad bowls and other eating utensils.

The oil finish preferred by woodworkers is Danish oil. You can apply it directly from the container. To apply Danish oil, follow this procedure:

1. Clean the surface thoroughly. If you are going to stain the article, apply the stain and allow it to dry. You can buy Danish oil with a stain already added. You can also mix pigmenting oil stains with the Danish oil to save a separate staining operation.
2. Soak a soft cloth in the oil. Then rub the oil into the wood. On horizontal surfaces you can flood the surface with the liquid oil and allow it to soak in, Figure 53-6.
3. Wipe the surface after 30 minutes and rub it dry with a clean cloth. If you leave any excess oil on top of the wood, the finish will be sticky. Allow the coat to dry for 1 hour. If you miss a spot of excess oil, you can soften and remove it by rubbing it with a rag soaked in oil.
4. Repeat the process three or four times. The more oil you rub into the surface, the better the wood will be preserved.
5. Wax the surface after the oil has completely dried. This will add luster to the finish.

NATURAL AND SYNTHETIC RESIN FINISHES

A surface treated with a natural or a synthetic resin finish will have an appearance similar to that of a varnished or lacquered surface, Figure 53-7. The major difference is that the resin finishes are wiped on with a cloth. The finishes often are called by their brand names, such as Sealacell® and Minwax®.

Figure 53-6
Flood the surface with as much oil as possible.

You apply either the natural or the synthetic resin finish in the following way:

1. Clean the surface completely. Any dust or wood particles will give a rough finish. Be sure to use a tack rag.
2. Apply a special sealer if the resin finish you use requires one. The sealer is relatively thin and penetrates the surface. It can be rubbed into the wood with a soft cloth. Leave no excess sealer on the surface, Figure 53-8. Allow the sealer to dry for the specified period of time, which will vary from 1/2 hour to 8 hours. If a sealer is not recommended

Figure 53-7
There are several different types of natural and synthetic resin finishes that give a dull sheen.

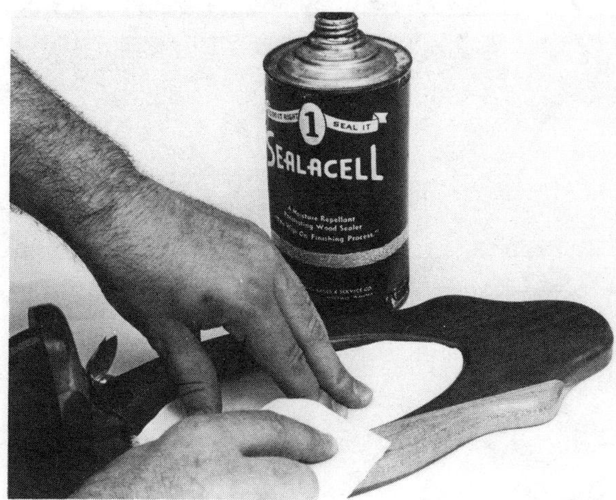

Figure 53-8
Rub the sealer coat deep into the wood.

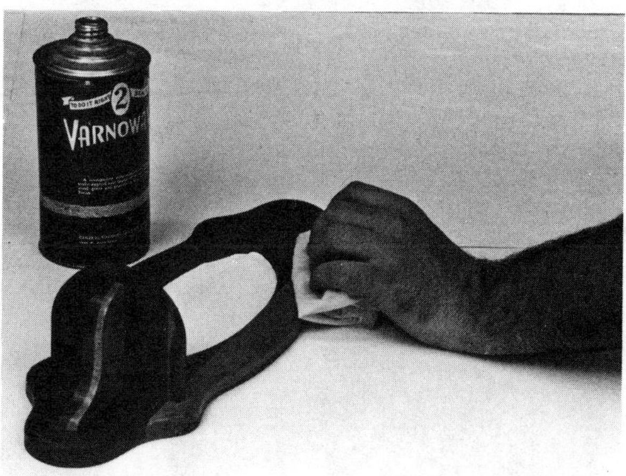

Figure 53-9
Additional coats will develop more sheen.

for use with a particular finish, the resin finish will be the first coat.

3. Lightly rub the surface with 320-grit wet-or-dry abrasive paper after the first coat has dried thoroughly. This will remove any raised grain.
4. Wipe the surface with a tack cloth. Then apply the resin finish, Figure 53-9. Soak a cloth with the finish, and wipe on the finish with a circular motion. Allow the liquid to soak in for 5 to 10 minutes. Wipe off any excess with a soft cloth. After the finish has dried, lightly sand the surface.

You can apply more than one coat of the resin. The number of coats you apply will depend on the amount of buildup desired. Additional coats of resin will give a deeper finish. Wipe on the last coat with strokes running with the wood grain. You can wax and polish the finished surface with paste wax.

REVIEW QUESTIONS

1. Name two advantages and one disadvantage of wipe-on finishes.
2. What are the three types of wipe-on finishes?
3. What do you use to apply a wax finish?
4. Why can no other finishes be applied over a waxed surface?
5. List the three types of oil finishes.
6. What will happen if excess oil is left on the surface?
7. How do natural and synthetic resin finishes differ from varnish or lacquer?
8. With what motion should you move the cloth when applying a resin finish?

SUGGESTED ACTIVITIES

1. Prepare a sample using an oil finish. Compare it with a lacquered and varnished sample. Which finish do you like the best?
2. Coat the bottom of a drinking glass with soda pop. Place it on top of your oil-finished sample. What happens after 24 hours? Would this be a good finish for a tabletop?

SECTION

The Woods Industry

54
Wood Science

55
Logging and Sawmill Industry

56
Grading Lumber

57
Veneers

58
Plywood

59
Particle Board

60
Hardboard

61
Curved Wood Members

62
Wood Preservatives and Fire Retardants

The woods industry includes many processes and materials. It begins with logging and ends with wood products such as lumber, plywood and particle board.

Section 8, The Woods Industry, will tell you more about wood materials. You will learn how wood materials are graded. This will help you better select and use wood materials. Section 8 also will explain the structure of wood and how wood is injected with chemicals. Studying this section will give you a better understanding of working with wood.

UNIT

54

Wood Science

Objectives

After studying this unit you should be able to:

1. Name the principal parts of a tree.
2. Name the simple wood cells.
3. Select the appropriate wood for a project.
4. Explain how moisture affects wood.
5. Identify wood defects.

Technical Terms

Pith
Heartwood
Springwood
Summerwood
Lignification
Tangential
Radial
Transverse
Longitudinal tracheid
Machinability
Nail-holding power
Deciduous
Coniferous
Equilibrium moisture content
Dry kiln
Moisture content
Oven-dry weight
Natural defect
Seasoning defect

An understanding of wood science is as important to a woodworker as a knowledge of woodworking techniques. It is essential to know about the structure of wood and how it reacts under different conditions. Without this knowledge, you might make decisions that could harm the appearance and construction of a product.

PRINCIPAL PARTS OF A TREE

Each part of a tree has a specific name and a particular function, Figure 54-1. At the center of the plant is the *pith*. It supports and feeds the stem, or trunk, during the first years of growth. Boards containing the pith are very unstable and will expand and contract a great deal. Surrounding the pith is the *heartwood*. The cells of heartwood are rigid, and the openings in the cells are filled with minerals from the soil. Heartwood provides strength to the tree. Heartwood is good for furniture and cabinet construction.

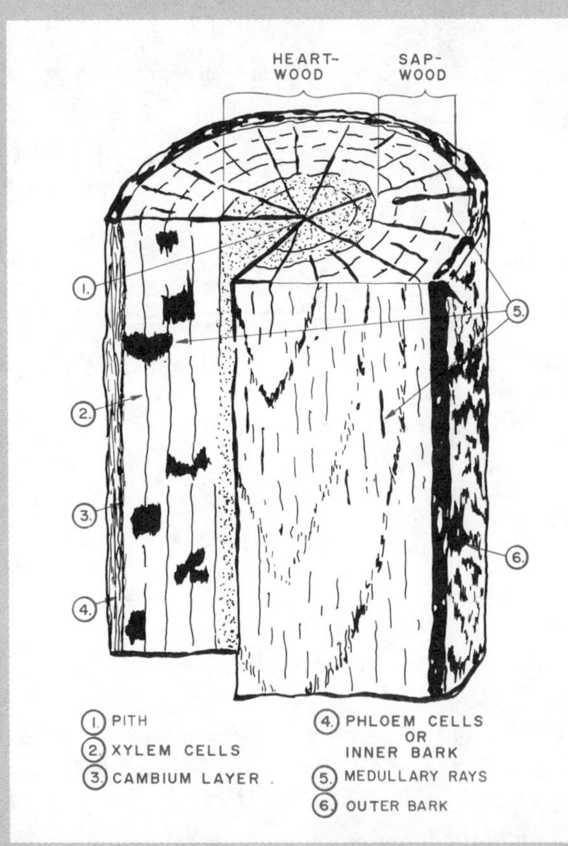

Figure 54-1
Each part of a tree has a specific name.

The *sapwood* is the layer of wood that surrounds the heartwood. It carries water and food throughout the height of the tree. Because the cell cavities are open, sapwood has much more moisture than heartwood. Raw, untreated sapwood is less decay resistant than heartwood, but it is easier to treat with preservatives. The band of sapwood is lighter in color than heartwood in many species of trees. Other woods will contain sapwood and heartwood that are the same color.

Both the sapwood and the heartwood contain growth rings, Figure 54-2. These circular bands of wood surround the pith. One growth ring is added each year to the outer surface of the sapwood. One part of the growth ring is light and one part is dark. The light ring is called *springwood,* or earlywood. It contains large cells. It develops early in the growing season when rain and sun are abundant. The narrow, dark band is *summerwood,* or latewood. The cells are much smaller. They develop slowly during the hot, dry months of the year. When the tree is cut down the growth rings can be counted to determine the approximate age of the tree.

Surrounding the sapwood is the cambium layer. The cambium layer forms new tree cells. These are either xylem or phloem cells. The sapwood and the heartwood are made entirely of xylem cells. Xylem cells in the sapwood are fairly soft, and the cavities within the cells are hollow. The sapwood cells have more water than the plugged cells in the heartwood. As the sapwood changes into heartwood, the cell walls harden and the wood becomes stiff. This process is called *lignification*.

To the outside of the cambium layer are bark cells, or phloem cells. This band of cells is the inner bark. These light tan cells carry food to the roots. As more phloem cells are added by the cambium layer, the tissue of the inner bark changes into outer bark, Figure 54-3. Bark protects and insulates the rest of the tree. It has little commercial value except as agriculture mulch.

The lines of cells that run perpendicular to the growth rings are called medullary rays, Figure 54-1. These rays carry food and water from the cambium layer to the interior of the tree. They also help hold the wood cells together. These rays add figure to the grain on certain cuts of lumber, Figure 54-4. Figure means the design

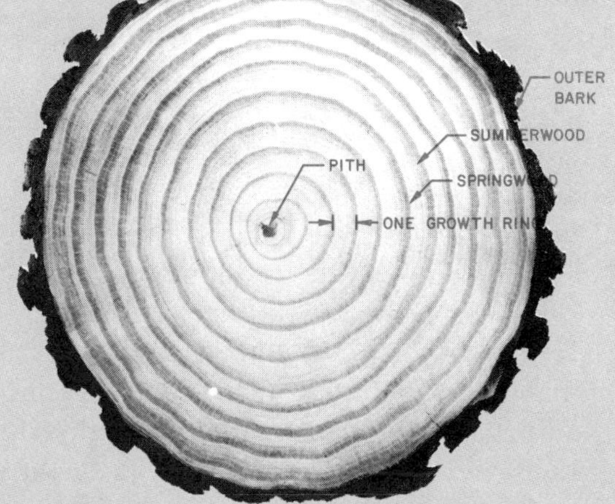

Figure 54-2
One layer of wood, the growth ring, is added each year. (U.S. Forest Service)

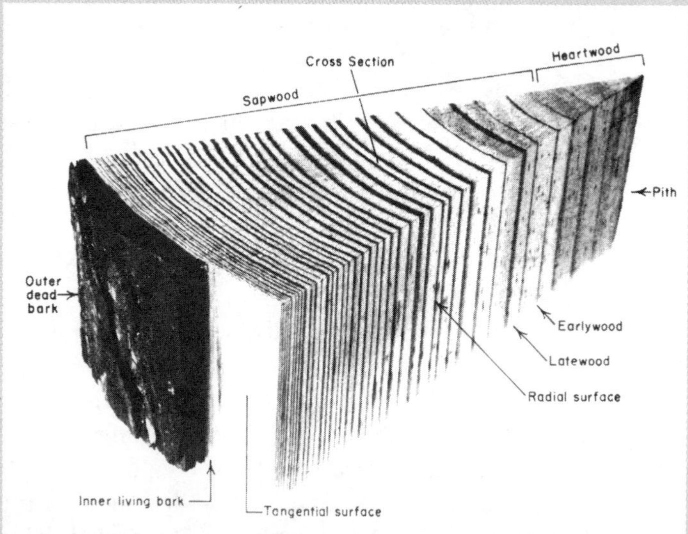

Figure 54-3
The light tan band of wood, or inner bark, eventually becomes the outer bark. (U.S. Forest Products Laboratory)

Figure 54-4
The medullary rays appear as large flecks on certain woods.

created in a wood surface by the arrangement of fibers, growth rings, knots and other details.

A board is made of thousands of tiny wood cells and lignin. Even the largest cells are no longer than 1/8" (3 mm). Lignin is a plasticlike material that holds the fibers together. Heat softens lignin. If you cut wood with a dull tool, the lignin becomes hot and flows to the surface of the board. This is a machine burn.

TANGENTIAL, RADIAL AND TRANSVERSE SURFACES

The surfaces of a board are faces, sides or ends. Depending on how a board is cut, the growth rings and the medullary rays will look different on each surface, Figure 54-5. On one board, the growth rings may lie tangent, or flat, to the surface. This is called the *tangential* surface. On another board the growth rings may be perpendicular to the surface. This is called a *radial* surface. Each board has different characteristics and properties.

A tangential surface displays the highest figure in its grain pattern. Look at the plain-sawed board shown in Figure 54-5. The reason for this appearance is that the growth rings lie tangent to the surface. Growth rings will form an angle of 0° to 35° to the face. Boards with this surface on the face are called plain-sawed or flat-sawed. This is the most economical method of cutting logs. Plain or flat sawing also produces the widest boards.

Other boards may have the tangential surface for the edge and the *radial* surface for the face. They are quarter-sawed. The face of quarter-sawed material is straight-grained. The growth rings are at 45° to 90° angles to the face. This material expands and contracts less than plain-sawed boards. Quarter sawing is the most stable of all cuts. The radial surface exposes the sides of the rays that run perpendicular to the growth rings, Figure 54-5. Woods with large rays have ray flecks on the radial surface. A rift-sawed board is a combination of a plain-sawed and quarter-sawed board, Figure 54-5. The growth rings will be at 45° to 35° angles to the face. The grain usually is straight, and the medullary rays appear as fine, light lines. Figure 54-6 shows how plain-sawed, quarter-sawed and rift-sawed

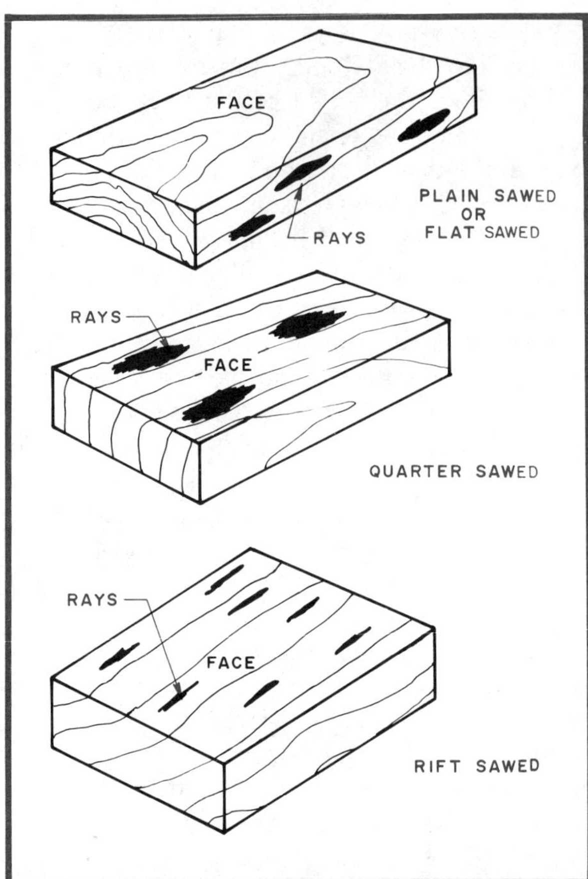

Figure 54-5
A board will look different depending on how it is cut.

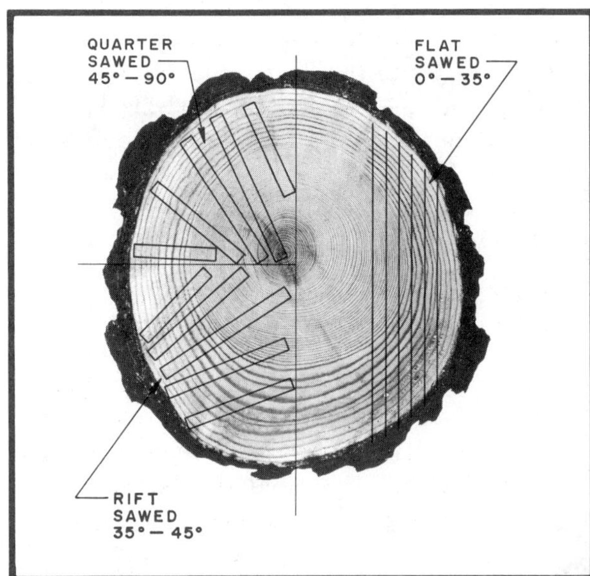

Figure 54-6
Cuts are made at different angles to the growth rings. (U.S. Forest Service)

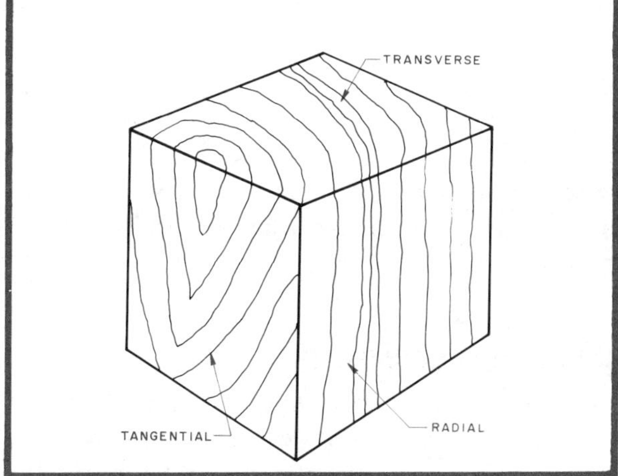

Figure 54-7
Each surface of a piece of wood has a name.

Figure 54-8
A magnified view of a piece of wood shows different cells clearly.

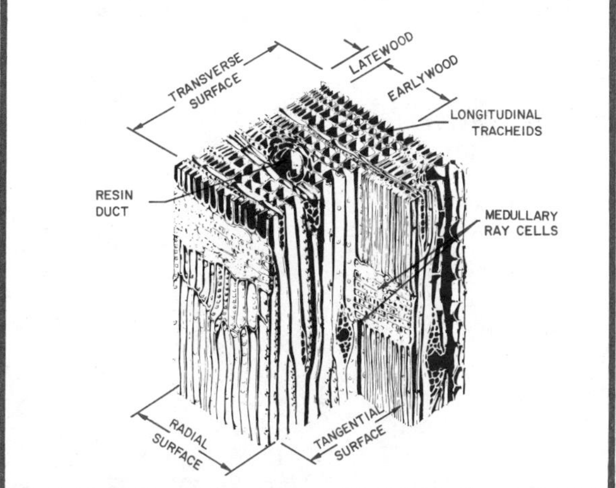

Figure 54-9
An enlarged cube of softwood. (U.S. Forest Products Laboratory)

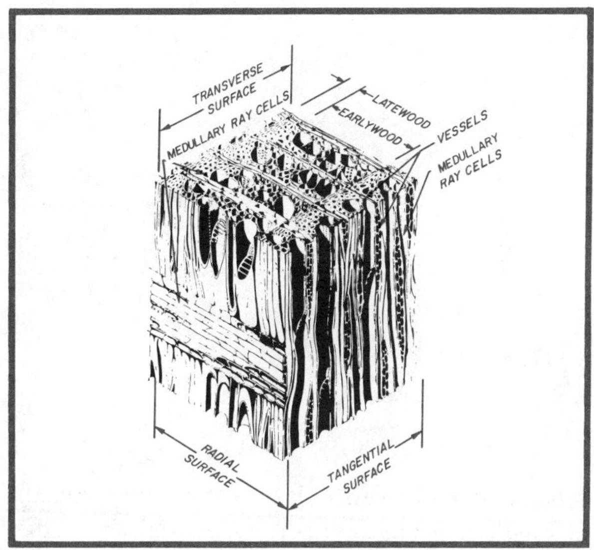

Figure 54-10
An enlarged cube of hardwood. (U.S. Forest Products Laboratory)

boards are cut from a log at different angles to the growth rings.

The end grain shows the growth rings clearly. This is the cross-sectional or *transverse* surface, Figure 54-7. Because most of the cells lie lengthwise along the length of the board, the ends of these cells are displayed on the transverse surface. The end grain of a board soaks up more stain and finish than the other surfaces because the ends of the woody fibers are exposed.

WOOD ANATOMY

If a cube of wood is magnified many times, it will show different features, Figure 54-8. Most of the cells in a board lie parallel to its length. These cells make the board strong and able to resist crushing. Because few of the cells lie perpendicular to its length, a board is relatively weak across the grain.

Softwoods are simpler in structure than hardwoods, Figure 54-9. About 90 to 95 percent of the cells in softwoods are long cells called *longitudinal tracheids*. Some softwoods have resin ducts. These contain pitch that may appear as streaks on the surface. The ducts conduct food to all parts of the tree. Rays are usually only one cell wide. The wood is weak where the rays join the longitudinal tracheids. Boards that lose moisture often crack along the rays.

Not all hardwoods are hard. Basswood, for example, is actually softer than most softwoods. Hardwoods have a complex structure because of the several different types of cells, Figure 54-10. The largest cells are called vessels, or pores. These

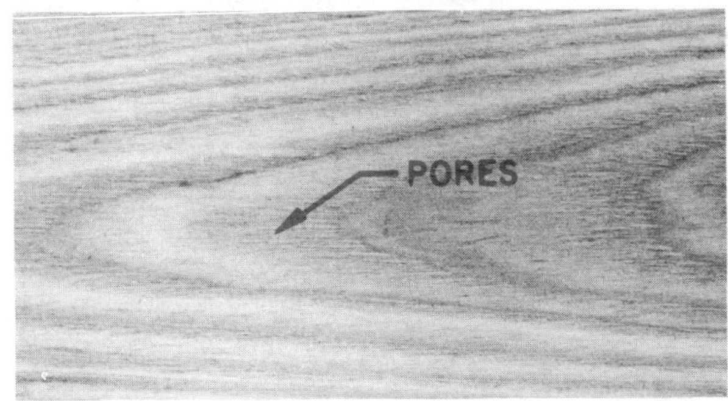

Figure 54-11
Ring-porous woods have large pores.

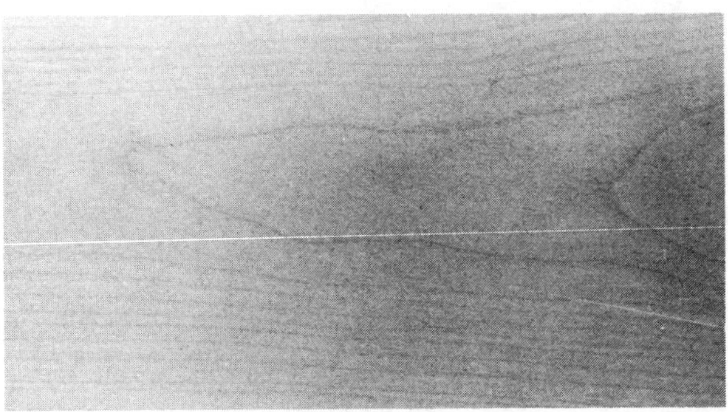

Figure 54-12
Diffuse-porous woods have small pores.

cells appear as small holes on the transverse surface and as grooves on the tangential and radial surfaces. Other longitudinal cells include strength and food-storage cells. Comparing the alignment of hardwood cells with that of softwood cells you can see how the vessels disrupt the arrangement of the other longitudinal cells. Rays on the various surfaces are similar to those in softwood, except in size. Rays in oaks may be more than 1" (25 mm) in diameter on the radial surface. Other woods such as sycamore, beech and maple also have ray flecks.

Knowing the different arrangement of these cells is helpful for wood identification. Hardwoods are either ring-porous or diffuse-porous. Wood that is ring-porous has large vessels in the springwood. This wood is open-grain, Figure 54-11. You may need to fill these pores with paste wood filler before finishing the wood. Vessels abruptly become smaller in the summerwood. Diffuse-porous wood has small vessels in the springwood, Figure 54-12. These cells gradually become smaller in the summerwood. Because the vessels are smaller, diffuse-porous woods are generally denser than ring-porous woods. This wood is closed-grain.

SELECTION OF WOODS

There are more than 99,000 different species of hardwood trees. But less than 200 of these are available in quantitites large enough for manufacturing purposes. This is still a sizable number for a woodworker to consider. There are also more than 25 commercial softwoods.

Each wood project or application has different requirements. For some projects, strength is the most important quality, Figure 54-13. For others, appearance is the first consideration, Figure 54-14. The cost and ease of machining are other factors, Figure 54-15.

A good furniture or cabinet designer always considers the physical properties of wood. These include hardness, weight, machinability, nail-holding power, compression strength and amount of figure, Figure 54-16. Many of these properties are interrelated.

Hickory, beech, hard maple and oak are known for their hardness. The harder the wood, the more resistant it is to denting and scratching. These woods wear well, resist crushing and polish easily. They are difficult to cut and shape and can split easily from nailing.

Weight helps to determine the strength of wood, Figure 54-17. Ash, birch, larch and southern pine are woods with a high weight. Density

Figure 54-13
Strength is important in construction. (Roseburg Lumber Company)

and specific gravity are related to weight. The heavier the weight and the higher the specific gravity, the more a wood will weigh.

Machinability means the ease with which a board can be sawed, planed, and shaped, Figure 54-18. Some woods do not chip and split easily. Soft maple, alder, basswood and cherry have good machinability.

The ability of wood to hold fasteners is its *nail-holding power*. Because a joint is often the weakest point on a project, a wood's ability to hold fasteners will determine the strength of

Figure 54-16
The excellent physical properties of oak make it suitable for a staircase.

Figure 54-14
The beauty of certain woods determines their use. (Crawford Furniture Manufacturing Corporation)

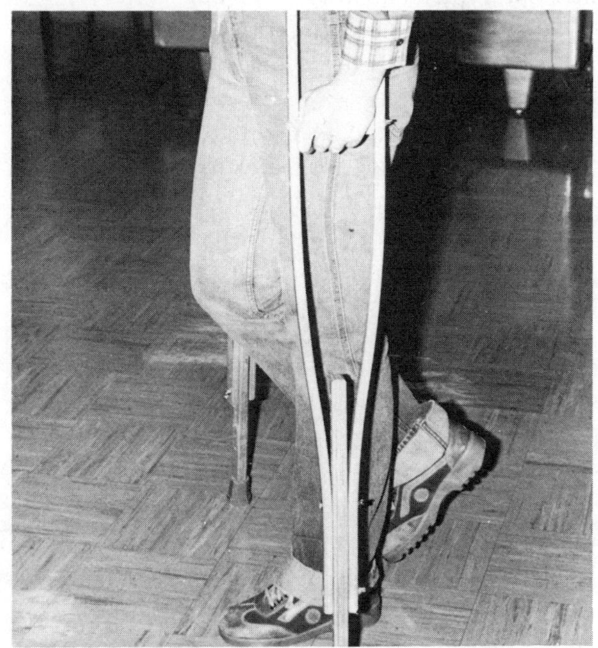

Figure 54-17
Ash is a good choice for crutches because of its strength.

Figure 54-15
Because of low cost and machinability, cedar commonly is used for pencils.

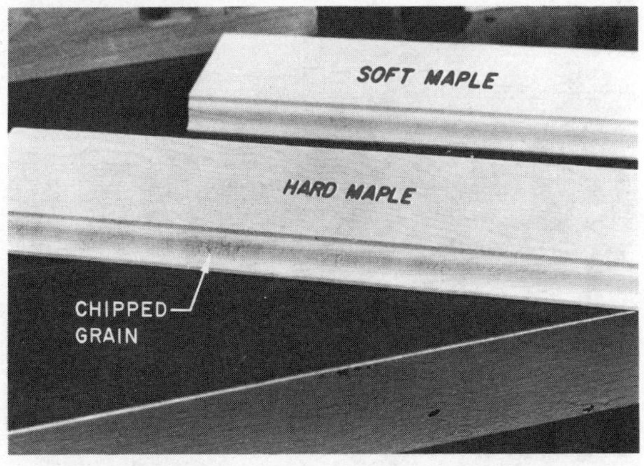

Figure 54-18
Hard maple lacks the machinability of soft maple.

these areas. The higher the nail-holding power, the stronger a piece of furniture or cabinet will be, Figure 54-19. Generally the denser the wood, the higher the nail-holding power. White ash, red oak, western larch and hard maples usually have high nail-holding power.

Certain members of a piece of furniture or a house support a great deal of weight. A leg on a bookcase or a stud in the wall of a house are examples. The ability to hold up a load is called compression strength, Figure 54-20. Woods with good compression strength include redwood, walnut, cherry, true hickory and Douglas fir.

When appearance is important, the amount of figure is a consideration, Figure 54-21. Figure is created in different ways. Color contrast adds to the amount of figure. Red gum, for example, has many colors varying from reds to browns. Differences between the growth rings also add figure. The color contrast between springwood and summerwood in yellow pine develops figure. Ray flecks on the face and edge of sycamore creates figure. Other types of woods are highly figured because of their wavy grain pattern. Curly maple, walnut butt, mahogany crotch and elm burl, for example, have unusual grain patterns, Figure 54-22.

Other considerations in selecting wood include amount of shrinkage and swelling, resistance to warping, bending ability and relative stiffness. Refer to the chart in Figure 54-23 for details on the properties of different woods.

Figure 54-19
Nail-holding power is essential to the strength of a wooden structure.

Figure 54-20
A universal testing machine tests compression strength.

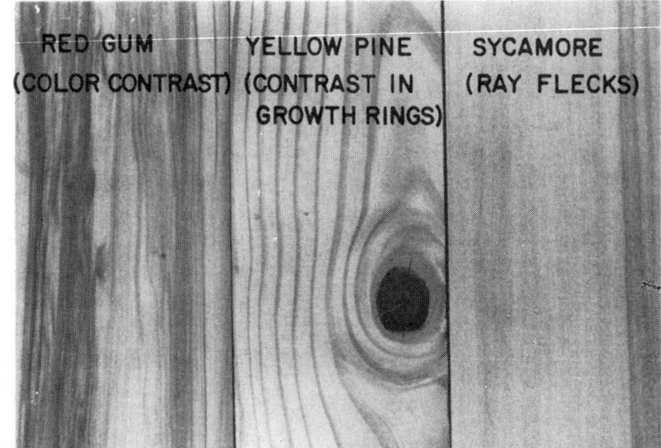

Figure 54-21
Color contrast, contrast in growth rings and ray flecks determine figure in wood.

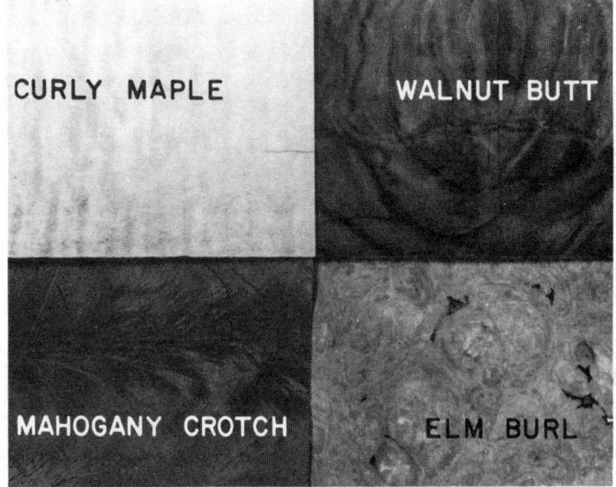

Figure 54-22
Unusual grain patterns develop figure.

Hardwoods	Relative Hardness	Relative Weight	Freedom from Shrinkage & Swelling	Freedom from Warping	Hand Tool Working	Nail-ability	Relative Bending Strength	Stiffness	Resistance to Decay	Amount of Figure	Ease of Finishing	Cost
Red Alder	Medium	Medium	Medium	Medium	Easy	Medium	Medium	Medium	Low	Medium	Easy	Medium
White Ash	High	Heavy	Medium	Medium	Hard	High	High	High	Low	High	Medium	Medium
Basswood	Low	Light	Poor	Medium	Easy	Low	Low	Medium	Low	Low	Hard	Medium
Beech	High	Heavy	Poor	Low	Hard	High	High	High	Low	Medium	Easy	Medium
Yellow Birch	High	Heavy	Poor	Medium	Hard	High	High	High	Low	Medium	Easy	Medium
Black Cherry	High	Medium	Medium	High	Hard	Medium	High	High	Medium	Medium	Easy	High
American Elm	High	Medium	Poor	Medium	Hard	High	High	High	Medium	High	Medium	Medium
Gum	Medium	Medium	Poor	Low	Medium	Medium	Medium	Medium	Medium	Medium	Medium	Medium
Hackberry	Medium	Medium	Poor	Low	Hard	Medium	Medium	Medium	Medium	High	Medium	Low
Hickory	High	Heavy	Poor	Medium	Hard	High	High	High	Low	Medium	Easy	Medium
Mahogany	Medium	Medium	Good	High	Medium	Medium	Medium	Medium	High	Medium	Medium	Medium
Hard Maple	High	Heavy	Poor	Medium	Hard	High	High	High	Low	Medium	Easy	High
Red Oak	High	Heavy	Poor	Medium	Hard	High	High	High	Low	High	Medium	Medium
White Oak	High	Heavy	Poor	Medium	Hard	High	High	High	High	High	Medium	Medium
Poplar	Low	Medium	Medium	High	Easy	Medium	Medium	Medium	Low	Medium	Easy	Low
Walnut	High	Heavy	Medium	High	Medium	Medium	High	High	High	Medium	Medium	High
American Sycamore	High	Medium	Poor	Low	Hard	High	Medium	Medium	Low	Medium	Easy	Medium
Cottonwood	Low	Medium	Poor	Low	Medium	Low	Low	Medium	Low	Low	Hard	Low
Softwoods												
Aromatic Cedar	Low	Light	Good	High	Hard	Medium	Low	Low	Medium	High	Medium	Medium
Douglas Fir	Medium	Medium	Medium	Medium	Hard	Medium	High	High	Medium	High	Medium	Medium
White Pine	Low	Medium	Medium	High	Easy	Medium	Medium	Medium	Medium	Low	Medium	Medium
Ponderosa Pine	Low	Medium	Medium	High	Easy	Medium	Low	Low	Low	Low	Medium	Medium
Yellow Pine	High	Heavy	Medium	Medium	Hard	High	High	High	Medium	High	Medium	Medium
Sugar Pine	Low	Low	Good	High	Easy	Medium	Low	Low	Low	Low	Hard	High
Western Red Cedar	Low	Light	Good	High	Easy	Low	Low	Low	High	Medium	Easy	Medium
Redwood	Medium	Medium	Good	High	Medium	Medium	Medium	Medium	High	Medium	Medium	High
Sitka Spruce	Low	Medium	Medium	High	Medium	Medium	Medium	High	Low	Medium	Medium	Medium
Western Larch	High	Heavy	Medium	Medium	Hard	High	High	High	Medium	High	Medium	Medium
Western Hemlock	Medium	Medium	Medium	Medium	Medium	Medium	Medium	High	Low	Medium	Medium	Medium

Figure 54-23
This chart provides a quick reference to the different properties of wood.

HARDWOODS

Hardwoods come from *deciduous* trees. These trees have broad leaves that fall off once a year. In the spring new leaves grow. Deciduous trees grow mostly in the northern and southern parts of the United States.

Hardwoods are selected principally for their appearance and hardness. These woods are commonly used in furniture, cabinets and millwork. Most hardwoods have a highly figured grain, resist abrasion and dents and are durable. The common hardwoods are shown in Figure 54-24

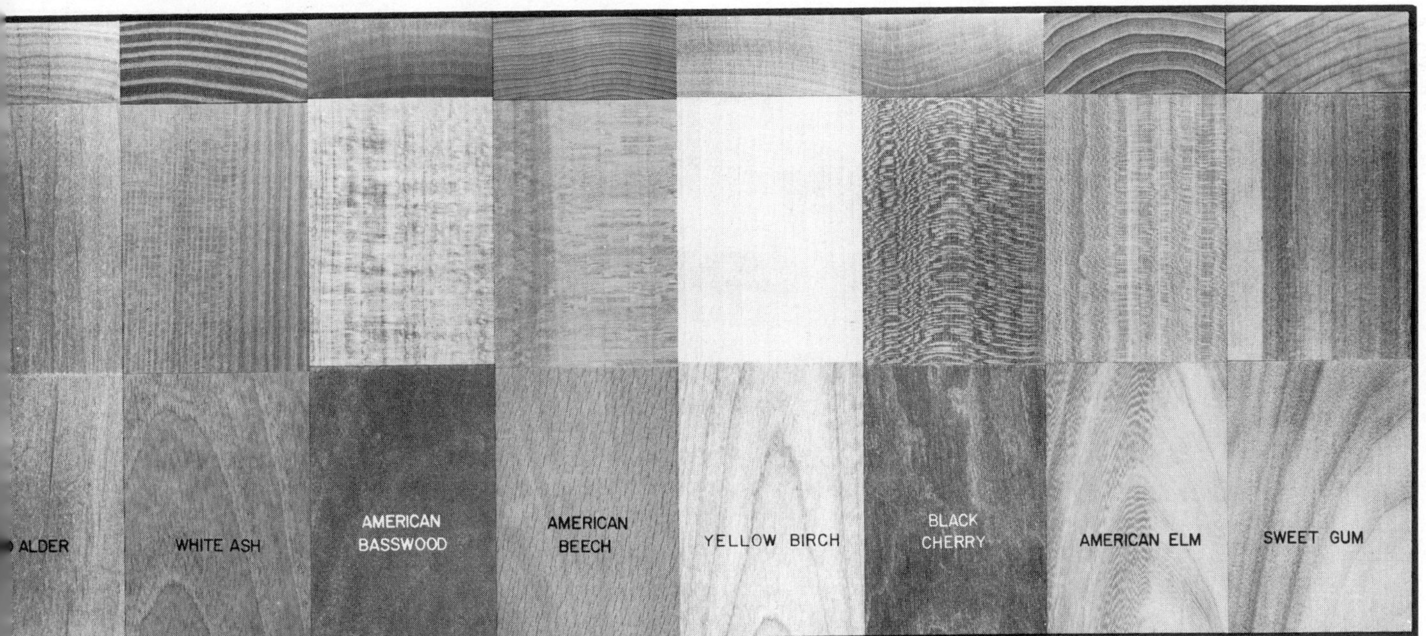

Figure 54-24
The three surfaces of various hardwoods. Each sample shows the transverse surface, *top*, radial surface, *center*, and tangential surface, *bottom*. (U.S. Forest Products Laboratory)

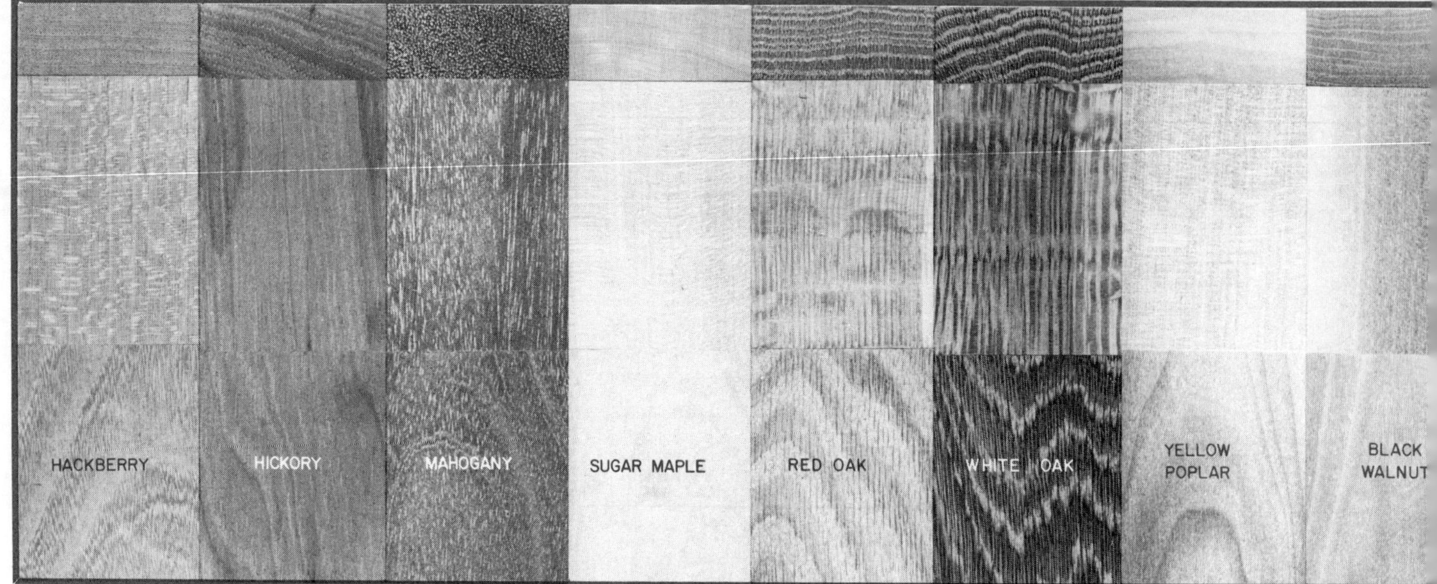

Figure 54-25
The three surfaces of various hardwoods. Each sample shows the transverse surface, *top,* radial surface, *center,* and tangential surface, *bottom.* (U.S. Forest Products Laboratory)

and Figure 54-25. They include the following.

Red alder. This wood is a pale, pinkish brown with a smooth texture. The surfaces have dark brown streaks. The wood is fairly lightweight and less expensive than many other hardwoods. The principal uses for red alder are in inexpensive furniture and millwork.

White ash. This is a common hardwood found in school shops. It has highly figured grain and a light blond color. Ash is highly resistant to shock. Because of this, it often is selected for baseball bats.

Basswood. This is one of the lightest hardwoods. Its pale, yellowish brown color is frequently interrupted by occasional dark mineral streaks. It is used for drafting boards and piano keys and in hand carving.

Beech. Heavy, hard and durable, beech is identified easily by its reddish brown color and the large ray flecks on the radial surface. Uses include cutting boards, flooring and handles.

Yellow birch. This wood varies in color from light tan to reddish brown. It is hard and shock-resistant. Birch is used for furniture, hardwood plywood and interior millwork. It is a popular wood for kitchen cabinets.

Black cherry. This wood is well known for its rich, warm, reddish brown color. It is fairly uniform in texture and has good machining properties. It is a popular furniture wood. Antiques are often made of cherry.

Elm. Elm is a furniture wood with open pores. It is light brown, sometimes with a red cast. It was once used for automobile parts. Cabinets and some furniture are now constructed of this wood.

Sweet gum. This multicolored wood contains reds, browns and other colors. Because of its even texture, this wood machines very well. Sweet gum often is selected for school projects and millwork.

Hackberry. This creamy white wood is used frequently in framework for upholstered furniture. It is often a substitute for ash in exposed furniture and cabinet parts. Hackberry is the best wood for steam bending.

Hickory. A tough hardwood, hickory is used for gymnasium equipment, ladders and some furniture. It is creamy white. Hickory often is combined with pecan in the same project.

Mahogany. This is a popular furniture wood. Philippine mahogany is the most common type. It varies from light blond to dark red. The grain has a straight or highly figured pattern.

Maple. There are two categories of maple—soft maple and hard maple. Both are hard, with a closed grain. Color varies from pure white to brown. Maple is used for flooring, bowling pins, furniture and sewing bobbins.

Oak. Oaks are also sold in two categories—red oak and white oak. Both have a highly figured grain and heavy weight. Red oak is reddish brown and is used for kitchen cabinets and furniture. White oak is light tan. Many schools use white oak for furniture projects in their woodworking shops.

Yellow poplar. This wood is often green and creamy white streaked with purple. Being rather soft, it works well with hand tools. Because it is inexpensive, woodworkers choose it for drawer slides, core stock for plywood and small pieces of furniture.

Black walnut. A favorite hardwood of many furniture makers, black walnut is a rich, chocolate brown. Most boards are highly figured and have open pores. Walnut is used for expensive furniture and gunstocks.

Exotic woods. Many hardwoods from foreign countries have interesting grain patterns, Figure 54-26. Their appearance and texture make them suitable for furniture. Zebrawood, rosewood and tulipwood are examples. Colors vary. Most exotic woods are expensive.

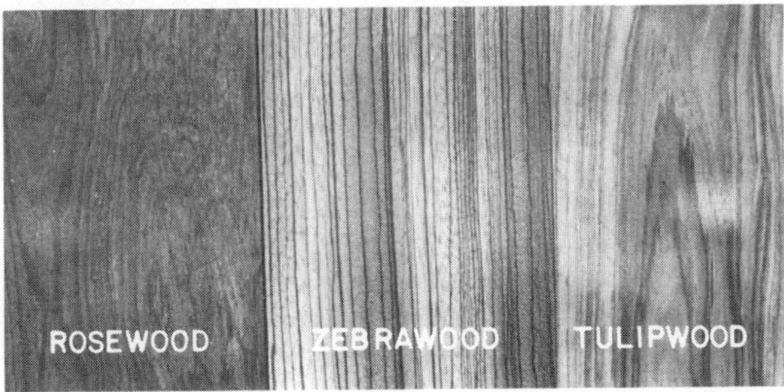

Figure 54-26
Exotic woods have unusual grain patterns or color.

SOFTWOOD

Softwoods come from *coniferous,* or cone-bearing, trees. These trees are called evergreens because they keep their leaves year-round. The leaves are needle-shaped. Coniferous trees grow primarily in the far western and southern parts of the United States.

Softwoods are strong and lightweight. Some softwoods are used for furniture and cabinets, but most are used in construction. Softwoods usually grow faster than hardwoods.

Major types of softwoods are shown in Figure 54-27. They include the following.

Aromatic cedar. This wood has a unique aroma. Color ranges from milky white to reddish brown. The wood has many knots. Many cedar chests are made from this wood.

Douglas fir. The major softwood used in construction is the Douglas fir. This reddish wood is exceptionally strong in compression. Its uses include wall studs, floor joists and plywood.

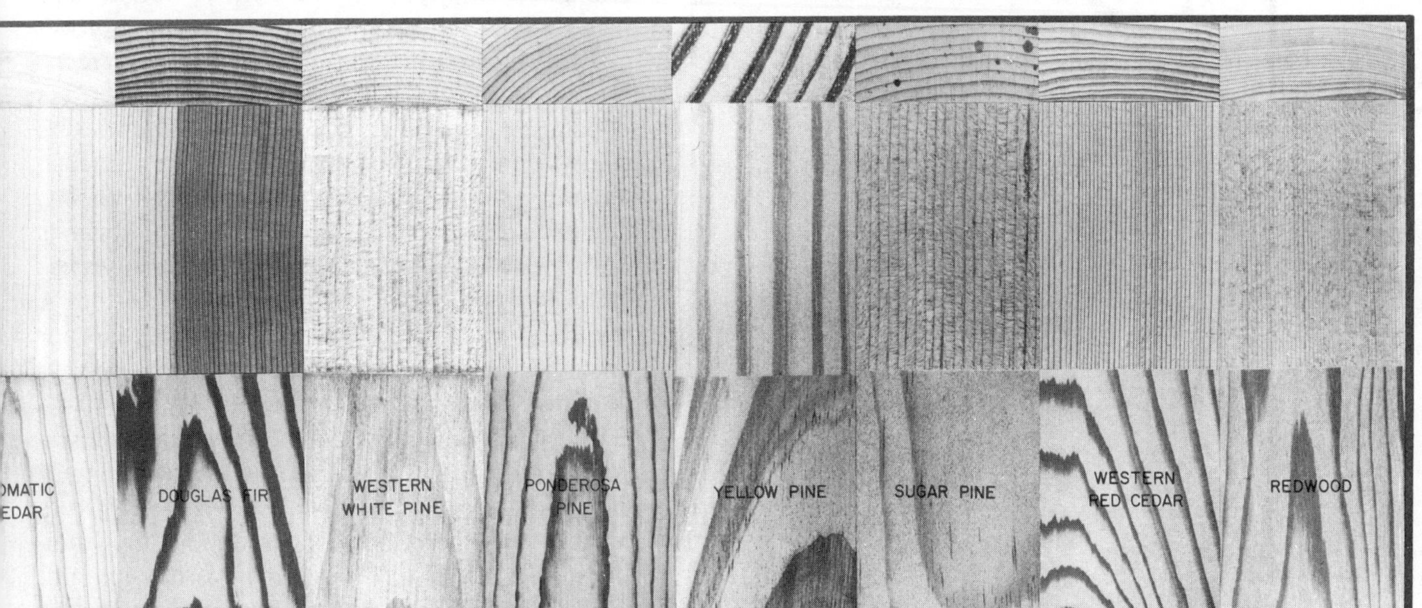

Figure 54-27
The three surfaces of various softwoods. Each sample shows the transverse surface, *top,* radial surface, *center,* and tangential surface, *bottom.* (U.S. Forest Products Laboratory)

Pines. Pines make up a large group of trees. They include white pine, ponderosa pine, yellow pine and sugar pine. Almost all white pine and ponderosa pine is used for furniture and structural parts of cabinets. Ponderosa pine also is used for moldings and trim. Sugar pine is a favorite wood of patternmakers. It has a smooth texture and is the easiest of all pines to work. Colors of pines range from pure white to pale yellow.

Western red cedar. This is a soft, decay-resistant wood. Because of its good weathering qualities, it is frequently used for fences and patios. The color ranges from light brown to reddish brown.

Redwood. One of the largest of all trees, redwoods have the highest resistance of all woods to decay and insects. The red color is in the heartwood. Redwood is excellent for outdoor use.

WOOD AND MOISTURE

The amount of moisture in wood changes constantly. When the temperature or the relative humidity changes, water evaporates or is absorped from the air. Evaporation makes wood shrink, Figure 54-28. Absorption of water makes wood expand. You should construct a wooden product with this change of size in mind. Otherwise, the joints will break apart. When trees first are cut into boards, the wood contains a great deal of moisture. A redwood tree, for example, may contain hundreds of gallons of water. At the time it first is cut, timber is said to be in the green state. It is very heavy when it is green. A green board may shrink as much as 1/2″ (13 mm) across the grain before all the moisture is lost.

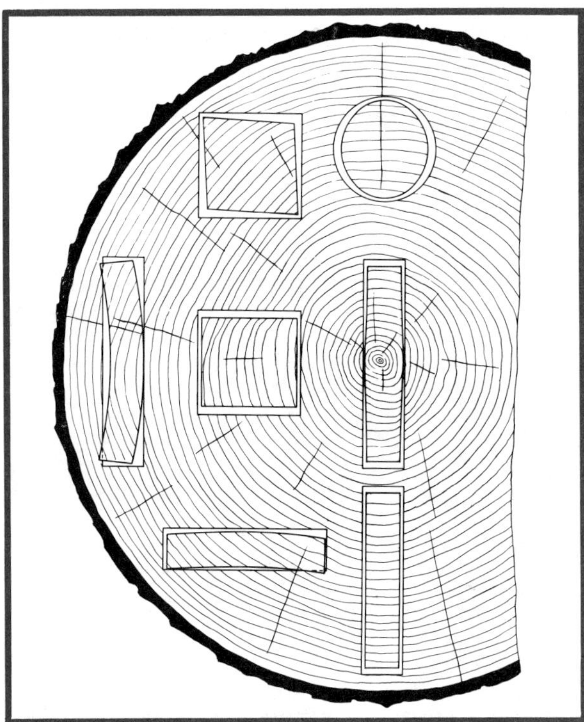

Figure 54-28
Different cuts of wood will shrink differently. (U.S. Forest Products Laboratory)

Green lumber has little value. When the moisture reaches a balance with the surrounding air, the wood is stable enough to use in furniture and cabinets. When wood agrees with its environment, it has reached the *equilibrium moisture content* (EMC). Until it reaches the EMC, the board will continue to shrink or swell. Different parts of the country have different average EMCs, Figure 54-29.

Seasoning Lumber

Drying wood from the green state to the recommended EMC is called seasoning. Different methods of seasoning lumber include air drying, kiln drying, dehumidification and solar drying. Each has advantages and disadvantages.

Air drying is the slowest and most natural process, Figure 54-30. Cool days with high relative humidity will dry the wood slightly. Hot, dry and windy days will season the material too quickly and cause checking and other seasoning defects. To air dry, stack boards with spacers or stickers separating each layer, Figure 54-31. The stickers allow the air to flow completely around each board. Proper stacking promotes fast drying. The minimum time for drying most hardwoods is one year for each inch of thickness. Many areas of the country may require a longer period. A two-inch board will need at least two years for drying. The major advantage of this method is its low cost. Disadvantages include the large amount of time needed, the likelihood of seasoning defects and the possibility that the material will not dry below 12 to 13 percent moisture content. Most areas of the country require furniture wood of 6 to 8 percent moisture content. Do not use air-dried material for interior projects.

Kiln drying is the most popular method of seasoning wood. Stack boards the same way as for air drying. Load the stack of wood, or charge,

6 PERCENT AVERAGE MOISTURE CONTENT

8 PERCENT AVERAGE MOISTURE CONTENT

11 PERCENT AVERAGE MOISTURE CONTENT

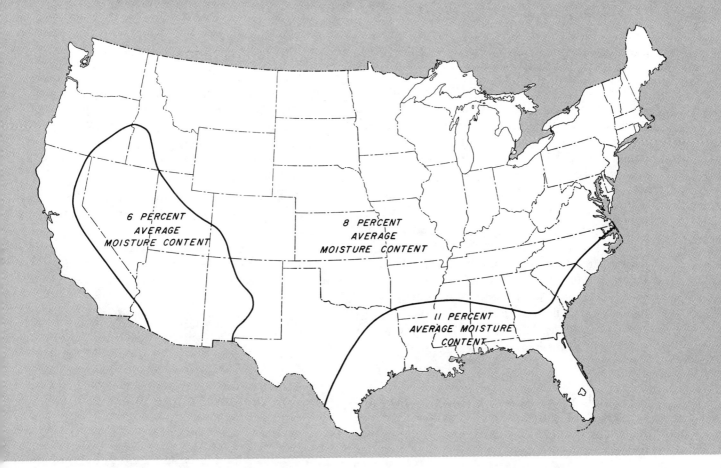

Figure 54-29
Parts of the country have different average equilibrium moisture contents. (U.S. Forest Products Laboratory)

Figure 54-30
Wood must be stacked properly for air drying. (Louisiana-Pacific Corporation)

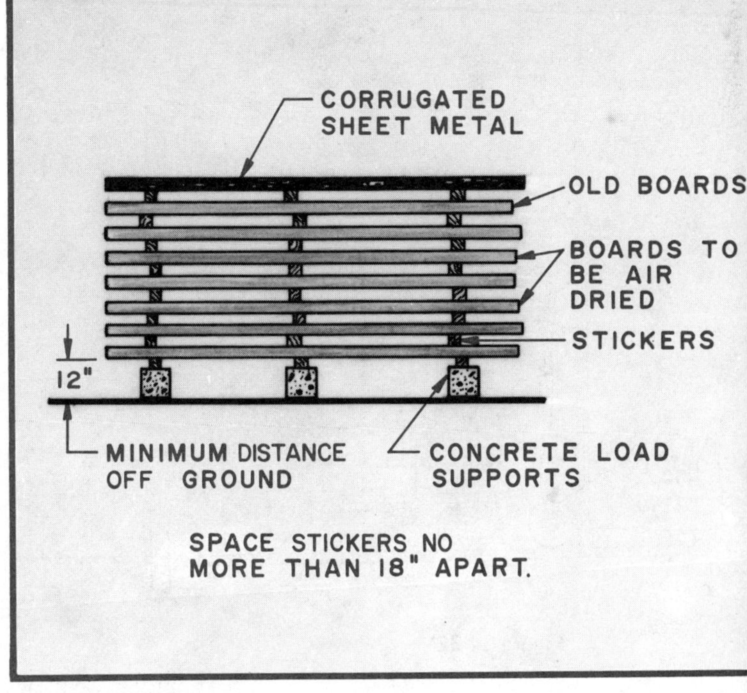

Figure 54-31
Stack boards properly.

inside an enclosed building. Drying conditions are controlled carefully throughout the building. Temperatures often reach 180° F (82° C) with an equally high relative humidity. Through steam supplied to the building, wet heat dries the material quickly, Figure 54-32. The kiln can dry the wood to any moisture content. You can dry most types of lumber in less than two weeks. Because of the controlled environment, seasoning defects are greatly reduced. Lumber dried in a kiln will not expand or contract as much as air-seasoned lumber.

A major disadvantage of the kiln process is the high cost. The natural gas that heats the water to steam is expensive. Many kilns, however, are fired with inexpensive wood waste.

Dehumidifcation and solar kilns are relatively new to this country. The dehumidification method uses electricity to dry the lumber. Solar kilns are the most economical, Figure 54-33. Solar kilns have a limited capacity of 500 board feet or less and are slow.

Measuring Moisture Content

Knowing the *moisture content* of lumber before you use it is important. If you use wood wetter than the recommended EMC, several things will occur. Many adhesives will not cure, producing a weak glue joint. Small cracks, called surface and end checks, will develop. Using stock that is too dry will make the boards swell eventually. Drawer slides will expand and stick. Joints may develop a crack.

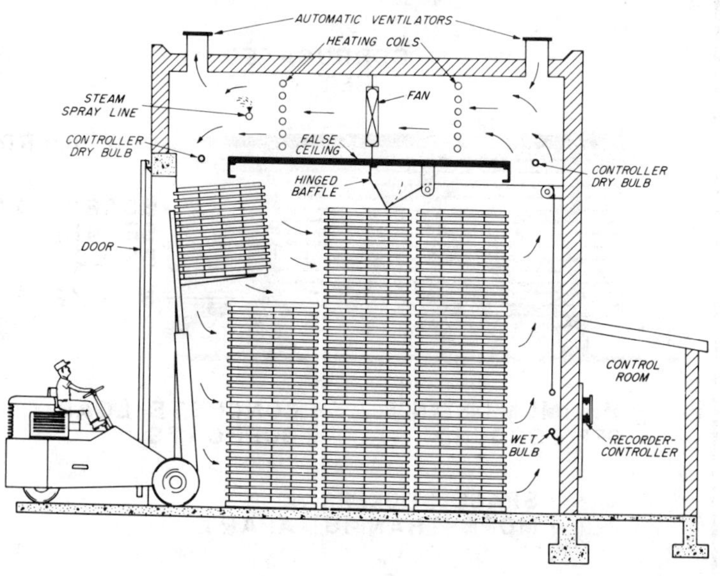

Figure 54-32
Steam heats a dry kiln while fans rapidly move the air throughout the structure. (U.S. Forest Products Laboratory)

Check moisture content with the oven-dry method or with a moisture meter. The oven-dry method of checking requires a one-inch section of wood, a gram scale and a laboratory oven. Select and cut the wood sample carefully, Figure 54-34. Weigh the piece of wood on the scale, Figure 54-35. Record this as the original weight. Then place the wood in an oven at 220° F (105° C). Reweigh the sample every 8 to 12 hours until it loses no more weight. This weight is the *oven-dry weight*. It means that the wood has a moisture content of 0 percent. Then you can work the following formula:

Moisture Content =

$$\frac{\text{Original Weight} - \text{Oven-dry Weight}}{\text{Oven-dry Weight}} \times 100$$

If the original weight of the sample was 100 grams and the oven-dry weight is 50 grams, then:

$$\text{Moisture Content} = \frac{100 - 50}{50} \times 100$$

Moisture Content = 1 x 100

Moisture Content = 100%

The result means that at the time the sample was cut, the moisture content of the board was 100 percent.

A faster way to calculate the moisture content is to use a moisture meter. This electronic device automatically measures the moisture content. A resistance meter has two probes. When you drive the probes into the wood, the meter measures the electrical resistance of the wood between the probes, Figure 54-36. You can tell the moisture content by reading the gauge on the meter. Most meters are accurate within 2 percent, and they register moisture content between 6 and 30 percent.

WOOD DEFECTS

Defects in wood are of two kinds. Natural defects occur within the tree while it is growing. *Seasoning defects* occur as the lumber loses or takes on moisture. These are easier to control and minimize than natural defects.

Knots make up 70 to 80 percent of all natural defects. Several types of knots are shown in Figure 54-37. They occur when a branch embedded in wood during the tree's growth is cut through. This defect is decorative, but it weakens the wood. A knot is sound when it is red and will not fall out of the board. Intergrown grain surrounds the knot. If a knot is brown and surrounded by a ring of bark, it is unsound and will eventually fall out. This is an encased knot. A knot that has fallen out will leave a knothole. A spiked knot may be sound or unsound. It occurs when a knot is cut through on its side.

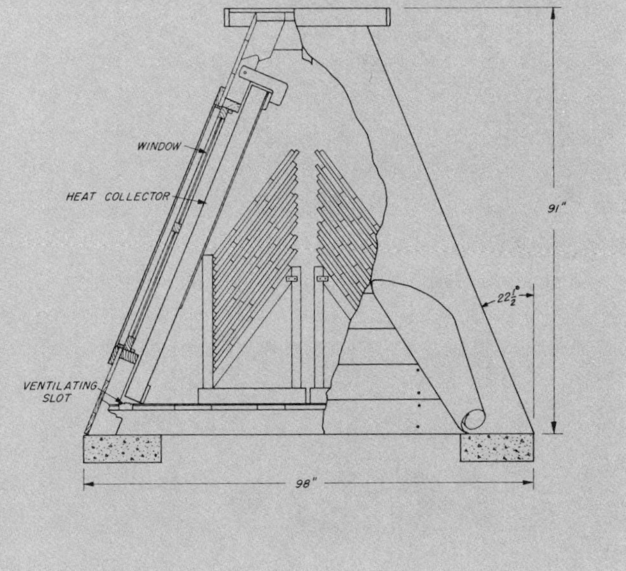

Figure 54-33
A solar kiln uses the sun to heat the wood. (U.S. Forest Products Laboratory)

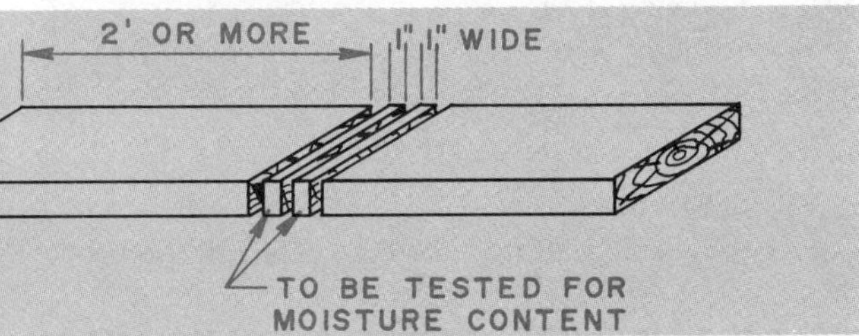

Figure 54-34
To check moisture content, cut samples carefully.

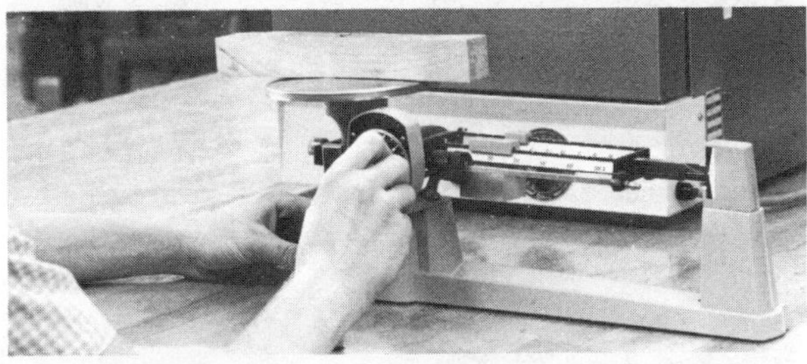

Figure 54-35
Weigh the sample on a scale to determine the original weight.

Figure 54-36
A resistance moisture meter has probes to be driven into the stock.

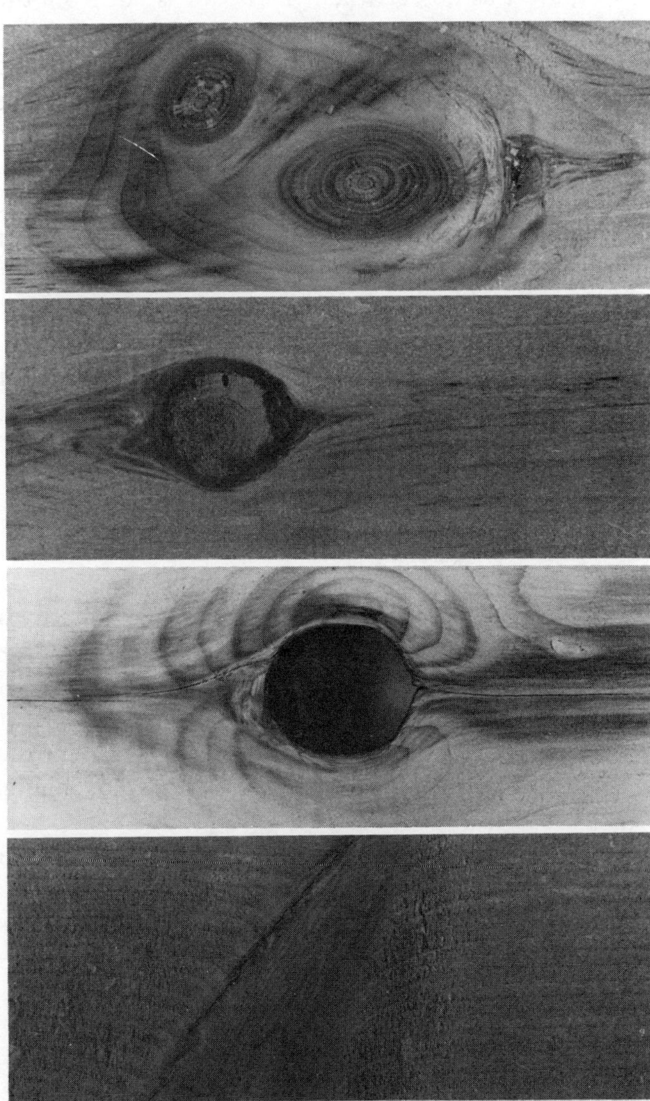

Figure 54-37
Types of knots.

Another natural defect that occurs only in softwood is pitch. Pitch is an accumulation of sap or resin. This defect causes refinishing and gluing problems. A pitch pocket is the most common form of pitch, Figure 54-38. If the boards containing these defects have been properly kiln-dried, the pockets will turn into a solid. This will minimize the problem.

Other natural defects include shake, wane and insect holes. Shake occurs in a tree when it is suddenly racked, or bent, as during a wind storm, Figure 54-39. Shake appears as small cracks running with or across the growth rings. Wane means the absence of wood or the presence of bark along an edge, Figure 54-40. Hardwoods often have this defect when the board is cut from the outer portion of the log. Insects boring holes in trees create another defect. Worms or grubs eat their way into the wood, leaving holes, Figure 54-41.

Seasoning defects in wood are warp, checks, stain, honeycombing and case hardening. All are serious problems that may lead to destruction of the board. Storing and drying logs and boards properly will reduce seasoning defects.

Warp is a seasoning defect that occurs in all types of woods, Figure 54-42. Any variation of shape from a true edge or surface is called warp. Warp develops as the board takes on or gives off moisture. The relaxing of stresses can also cause warp. One form of warp is cup. Cup is a curve from edge to edge on the face. Another form of warp is crook. It is a curve from end to end on the edge. A kink is a severe crook caused by a knot. A bowed board will not be flat on the face from end to end. Wind, or twist, is the most severe form of warp. A board in twist has one or more of its corners at a different level than the other corners. This causes serious machining problems.

Checks are small cracks on either the surface or the ends of boards, Figure 54-43. Those on the face or the edge are surface checks. Cracks on the end are end checks. Both kinds of checks occur along the medullary rays and develop because the outer surface of the boards dries faster than the core or inner section. End checks develop, for example, because moisture leaves the end of the boards 15 times faster than it leaves the remaining portion of the board. Painting the ends

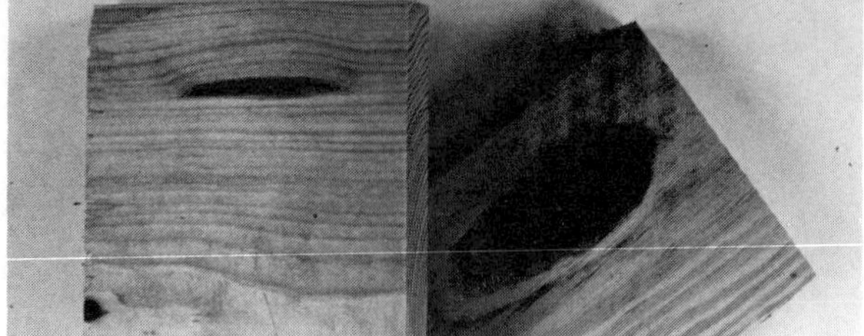

Figure 54-38
An accumulation of sap causes pitch pockets.

Figure 54-39
Shake appears as internal cracks.

Figure 54-40
Bark on the edge of the board is a defect called wane.

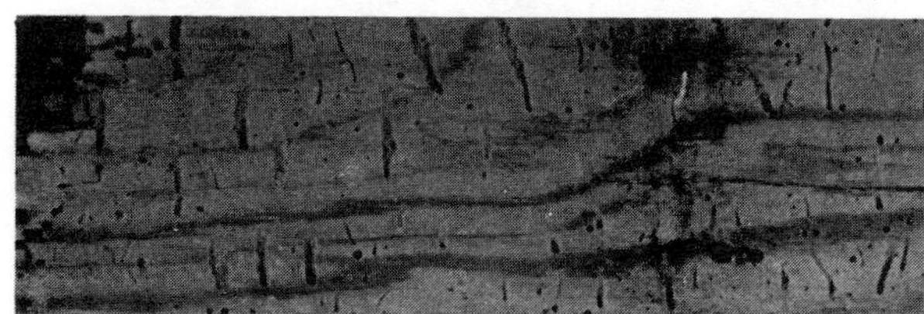

Figure 54-41
Insects can damage wood that has not been treated with preservatives.

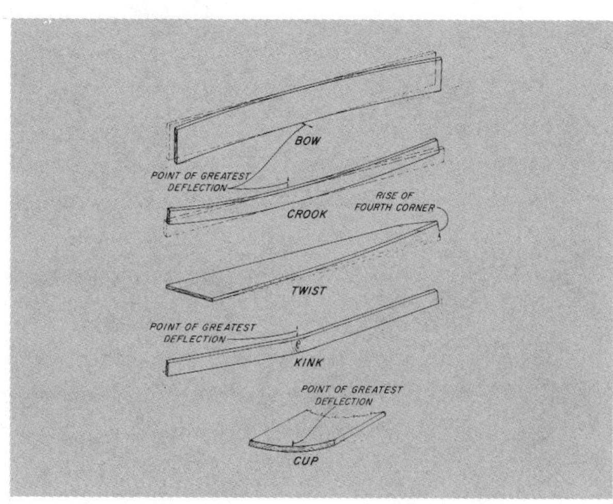

Figure 54-42
Forms of warp. (U.S. Forest Products Laboratory)

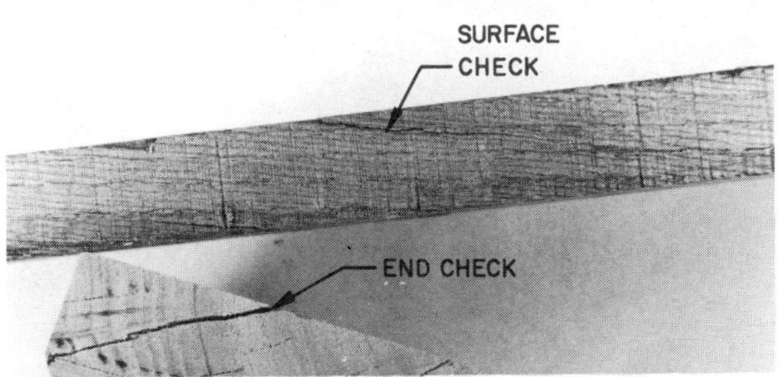

Figure 54-43
Checks appear on the edges, face and ends of boards.

Figure 54-44
Honeycombing occurs along the rays on the interior of the board.

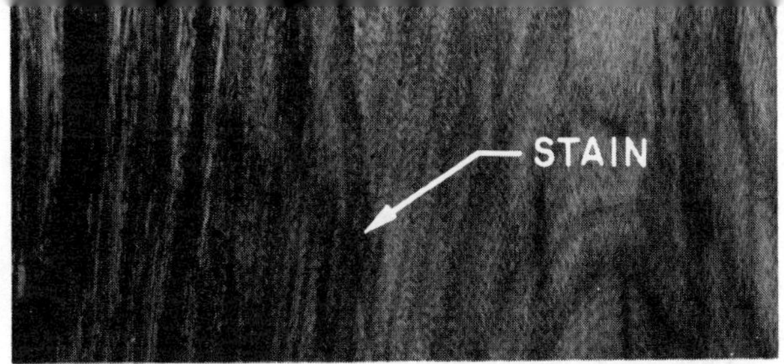

Figure 54-45
Stain changes the color of the wood.

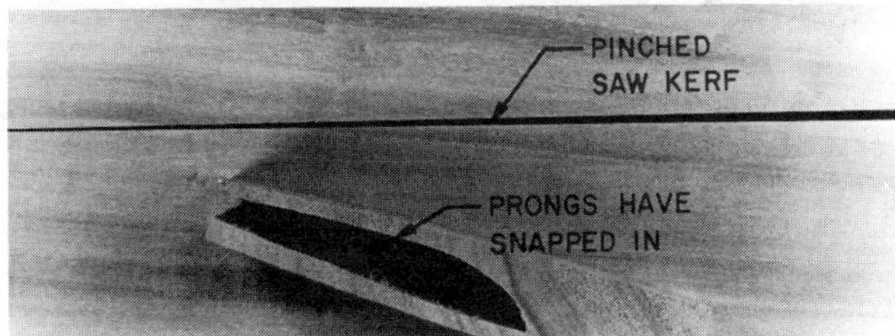

Figure 54-46
Case hardening makes the outer portion of the board pinch shut when the core is removed.

can reduce end checks. Once checks develop, you should not attempt to close the cracks by adding water to the defect. The swelling will cause the checks to close for a while. Upon drying, however, the cracks will widen even more.

Surface and end checks occur on the outer surface of a board. Honeycombing creates cracks on the interior section, Figure 54-44. If you cut into a board, you may find small cracks that do not appear on the surface. These openings are located along the medullary rays. Honeycombing is a seasoning defect. You can prevent it by drying the lumber properly.

Wood sometimes becomes stained after it is cut from the tree, Figure 54-45. Stain is caused by spores that float in the air. Depending on the spores, the wood may be colored green, brown or blue.

Case hardening is a serious seasoning defect that causes machining problems, Figure 54-46. This defect appears when the shell or outer portion of the board is drier and has more stresses than the core or inner section. By proper drying, you can prevent boards from case hardening. Case-hardened boards will cup when they are planed, and a crook will develop when they are sawed. They also may pinch the saw blade unless you use a saw splitter.

REVIEW QUESTIONS

1. What are the functions of pith, heartwood, sapwood and the cambium layer?
2. Sketch the transverse, tangential and radial surfaces of a board.
3. What are medullary rays?
4. List three advantages of hardness in wood.
5. Define compression strength, nail-holding power and figure.
6. Name six deciduous woods.
7. Name three coniferous woods.
8. What is equilibrium moisture content?
9. List four methods of seasoning lumber.
10. If the original weight of a board was 300 grams and the oven-dry weight is 250 grams, what was the moisture content at the start of the oven-dry test?
11. List three types of knots and define each.
12. What is shake?
13. Name three forms of warp. Make a sketch of each.

SUGGESTED ACTIVITIES

1. Sand the transverse surface of a piece of white oak with 280-grit abrasive paper. With a magnifying glass see how many different kinds of cells you can identify.
2. Cut from a tree branch a piece approximately 1" (25 mm) in diameter and 6" (76 mm) long. Weigh it immediately. After drying it to the oven-dry weight, determine the moisture content at the time it was cut.
3. Look through your scrap rack and identify the defects you find.

UNIT

55

Logging and Sawmill Industry

Objectives

After studying this unit you should be able to:

1 List the jobs done on a logging site.

2 Know how lumber is cut.

3 Name methods of seasoning lumber.

Technical Terms

Logger
Choker line
Headrig
Edger
Trim saw
Grader

It may be strange to think that the beginnings of fine furniture and cabinetry are small plants less than 3″ (76 mm) in height. Yet this is exactly how wood begins. The raw material for wood products begins in the nursery as small seedlings. The tender plants grow there until they are strong enough to endure a harsh outdoor environment, Figure 55-1. The trees are then planted, fertilized and tended to, much like a home gardener cares for fruit and vegetables. Because of careful attention, and new varieties of trees, the time from planting to harvesting has been reduced to 15 or 20 years.

After a tree develops to full size, it is harvested. Trees are cut in two ways. In clear cutting, whole sections of a forest are cut, Figure 55-2. This makes replanting and caring for the newly planted trees easier. Clear cutting is used primarily with softwoods, such as pines and Douglas fir. In selective cutting, only trees that have reached full maturity are harvested, Figure 55-3. Selective cutting primarily affects hardwoods, such as oaks and walnut.

A person who cuts trees is called a *logger.* A number of loggers make up a logging crew. Members of the logging crew have specialized jobs. After trees are marked for harvesting, they often are cut down with chain saws. This is called felling the tree. Then all the limbs are removed, and the usable logs are transferred to the loading site.

Figure 55-1
Foresters raise hybrid seedlings in a nursery. The seedlings are our future trees. (Western Wood Products Association)

Figure 55-2
Every tree is cut down in clear cutting. (Western Wood Products Association)

Figure 55-3
With selective cutting, only mature trees are cut. Others are left to grow. (Western Wood Products Association)

Frequently, logs are dragged from a steep mountainside with a *choker line* that is attached to a tall spar pole, Figure 55-4. A logger who specializes in wrapping cables around felled trees is called a choker setter. When the logs reach the loading site, a crane picks them up and puts them on a waiting truck. A trucker delivers the load of logs to the sawmill.

Logging operations are varied. Each lumber or logging company has its own methods. In

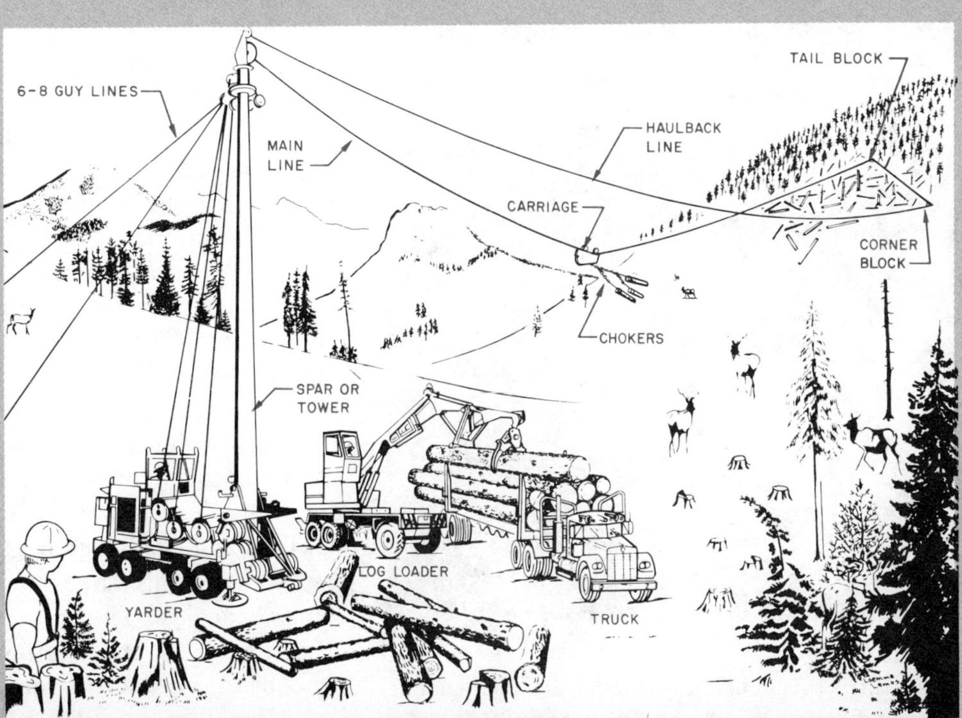

Figure 55-4
A choker line hauls logs up and down mountains to a loading site.

Figure 55-5
Hydraulic shears cut and remove the tree. (Morbard Industries, Inc.)

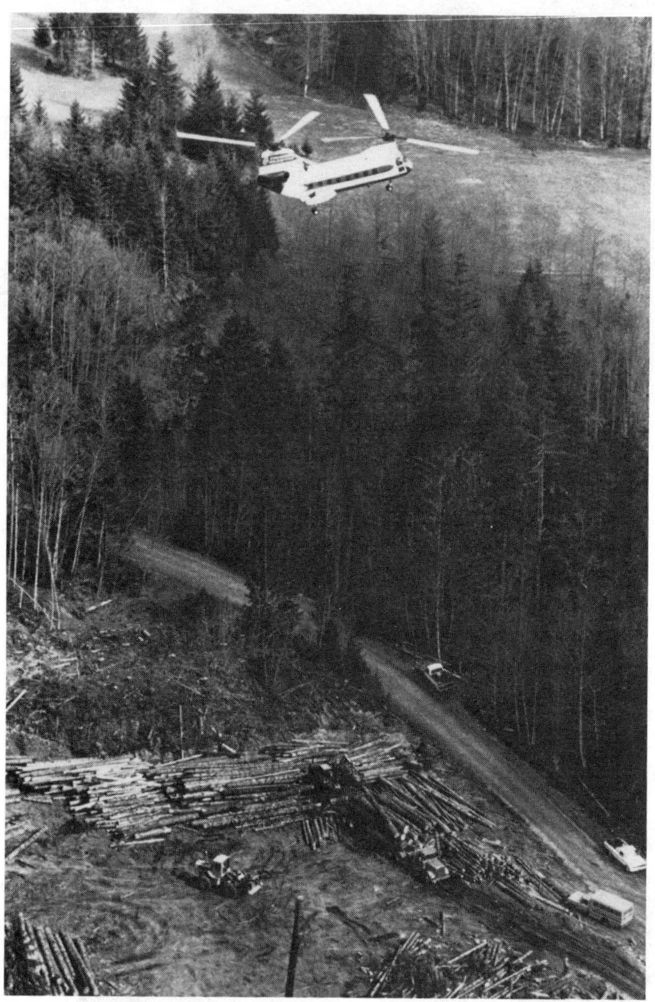

Figure 55-6
Helicopters sometimes remove logs from mountainous terrain. (Western Wood Products Association)

Figure 55-7
Logs go in the mill pond before the conveyor moves them into the sawmill. (Roseburg Lumber Company)

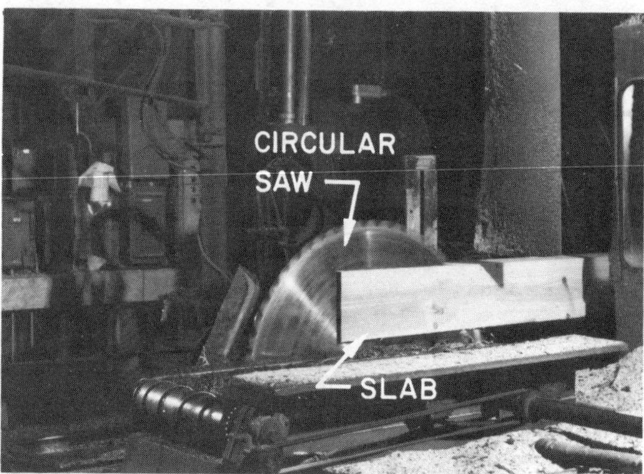

Figure 55-8
A circular saw headrig is used primarily in smaller mills that deal with hardwood.

southern forests large machines shear off trees at ground level, Figure 55-5. Some of these machines also remove the limbs and stack the logs on a rack that is mounted on one side of the machine. In mountainous western areas, helicopters often transport logs to trucks, Figure 55-6.

After logs are delivered to the mill, workers may stack them into large piles or put them in mill ponds. The mill pond keeps logs sorted and insects away from the wood, Figure 55-7. Then an elaborate conveyor system moves the logs through a debarking and washing station. Bark and dirt are removed because they are abrasive and cause undue wear on sawmill equipment.

One at a time, logs are sawed into boards with a *headrig*. This large machine has a saw blade and a carriage. The carriage moves the log back and forth past the rotating blade so that slabs of wood can be sawed from the log. A headrig uses two types of saw blades. Small, hardwood saw-

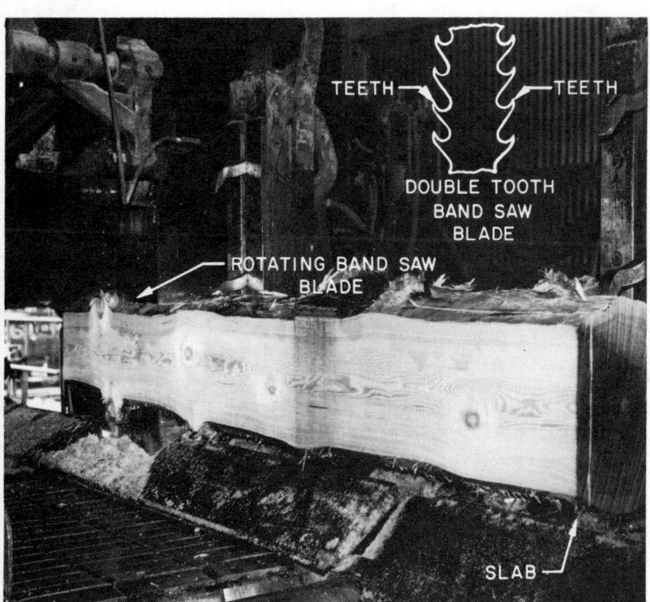

Figure 55-9
A band saw headrig cuts very large logs. Note that the log is clamped to the carriage. (Roseburg Lumber Company)

Figure 55-10
As boards come from the headrig, they are fed into an edger. The edger trims the rough edges. (Filer & Stowell Company)

mills use circular saw blades 3′ to 4′ in diameter, Figure 55-8. Larger mills use a wide-blade band saw, Figure 55-9. It has teeth on both edges of the blade. As the carriage passes back and forth, the teeth cut a slab of wood. This saw blade is used often with softwoods. Hardwood lumber is cut to boards as wide as possible. The wood is sold in random widths. Softwood lumber is cut to standard sizes.

Slabs usually go to the *edger* for the next cut, Figure 55-10. The edger cuts off any bark left on the slab's edges.

A *trim saw* cuts rough boards to standard lengths, Figure 55-11. Circular saw blades are spaced apart every 2′ (610 mm). A feed chain moves the board under the blades. The operator must move one of the many saw blades into the path of the approaching board. The operator tries to cut the board as long as possible.

Then a person called a *grader* marks rough boards, Figure 55-12. A grader quickly inspects each board as it comes from the trim saw and determines its grade. A grader works in the green chain. The green chain is a conveyor system that feeds each board past a grader.

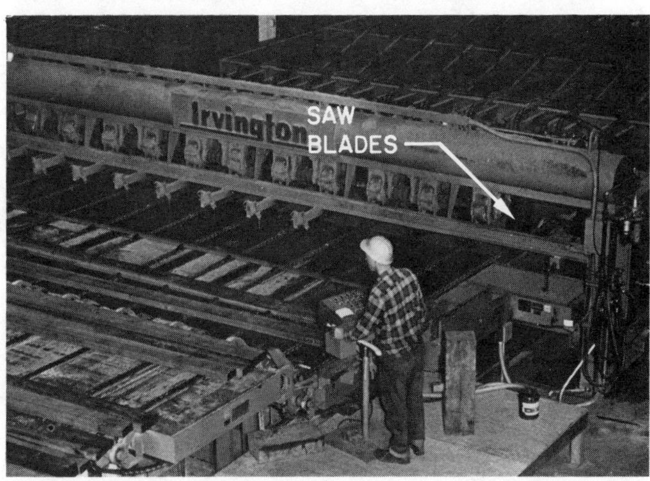

Figure 55-11
A worker cuts boards to length with a trim saw. (Louisiana-Pacific Corporation)

Figure 55-12
A grader determines the grade of each board. (Roseburg Lumber Company)

Figure 55-13
Strips of wood or stickers go between each layer of wood to provide better air circulation. (U.S. Forest Products Laboratory)

Workers stack graded material on stickers, Figure 55-13. Then seasoning starts. Seasoning is a process that removes moisture from wood. Most hardwoods first start to dry outdoors. There, moisture slowly evaporates from the stock. Next, the wood dries in a dry kiln, Figure 55-14. A dry kiln is a large building that has carefully controlled moist heat. Softwoods generally do not start to dry outdoors. They go immediately from the green chain into a dry kiln.

Figure 55-14
A dry kiln seasons large quantities of wood in a relatively short time. (U.S. Forest Products Laboratory)

REVIEW QUESTIONS

1 What is the difference between clear cutting and selective cutting?
2 What are people who cut trees called?
3 Which device drags logs from steep mountains?
4 What does the headrig do?
5 What cut does the edger make?
6 What is a trim saw?
7 Which process removes moisture from wood?
8 What is a dry kiln?

SUGGESTED ACTIVITIES

1 Find out what kinds of trees grow in your state. How far away from your area is a forest where trees are cut for lumber?
2 See if your class can visit a forest or a sawmill to learn more about the logging industry. Or have your instructor arrange for a movie or a slide show about the industry.

UNIT

56

Grading Lumber

Objectives

After studying this unit you should be able to:

1. Name major softwood and hardwood grains.
2. Name common applications for major grades of lumber.
3. List nominal and dressed sizes of softwood lumber.

Technical Terms

Western Wood Products Association
Southern Pine Inspection Bureau
National Hardwood Lumber Association
Scaling stick

Purchasing lumber can be very confusing. Lumber is available in a wide selection in many different grades. Woodworkers, however, should know the major grades of lumber to be able to measure wood quality and cost for a product. product.

SOFTWOOD GRADES

All softwood lumber grades are based upon the American Softwood Lumber Standard PS 20-70 established by the United States Department of Commerce. Other grading associations give additional specifications for the selling of individual boards.

Individual softwood associations grade lumber in a particular geographic area. The *Western Wood Products Association,* for example, covers most of the West. The *Southern Pine Inspection Bureau* grades the softwoods of the South.

Softwood lumber is divided into three size classifications–boards, dimension lumber and timbers.

Boards

A board is longer and wider than it is thick. Most boards in a lumberyard are 3/4" (19 mm) thick. Boards are divided into categories according to the appearance of the wood–select, common, factory and molding. Select and common boards are sometimes called appearance or yard lumber. There are several grades of wood within each category of board.

Select boards are top quality boards. All pieces must be a minimum of 4" (102 mm) wide. Different grades of select boards refer to the clearness of one side of the wood. Figure 56-1 shows the grades of select boards. The highest grade is

Figure 56-1
Select grades include B and Better, *left;* C Select, *center;* and D Select, *right.* (Western Wood Products Association)

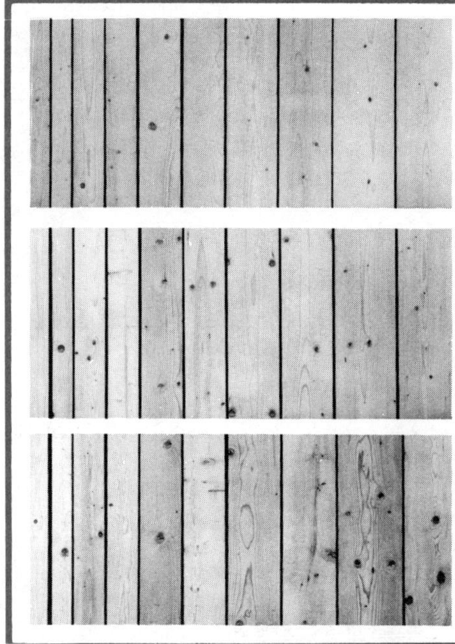

Figure 56-2
Common grades include No. 1 Common, *top;* No. 2 Common, *center;* and No. 3 Common, *bottom.* (Western Wood Products Association)

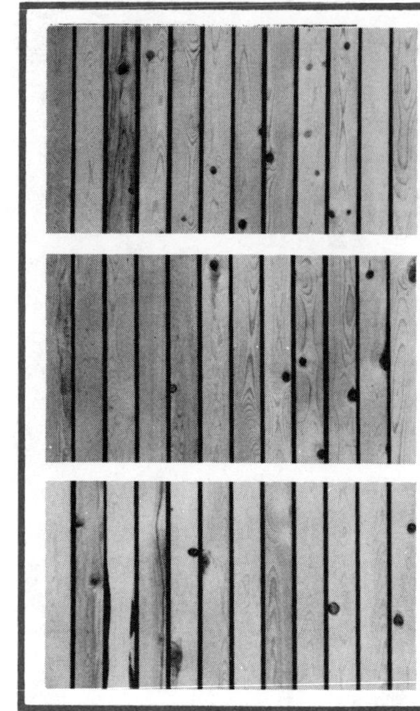

Figure 56-3
Dimension grades include No. 1 Structural, *top;* No. 2 Structural, *center;* and No. 3 Structural, *bottom.* (Western Wood Products Association)

B and Better, or sometimes called No. 1 and No. 2 clear. C Select is the second grade board and has only a few tight pin knots. Although C Select boards do take stain, they are considered top paint grade material. D Select is the lowest grade and may have serious defects on the poor face. But D Select boards have many short clear lengths. Although all select grades look good, they are not the strongest kind of board.

Common boards are suitable for general construction. They are available in sizes 1″ x 4″, 1″ x 6″, 1″ x 8″, 1″ x 10″ and 1″ x 12″. There are five grades of common boards numbered 1 through 5, Figure 56-2. No. 1 Common has the smallest sound red knots and is often sold as "knotty pine." The quality of common boards progressively decreases through the lowest grade numbers. No. 5 may contain any defect as long as it does not affect the structural strength of the board.

Factory, or shop, grades are determined by the amount of clear pieces of a certain size that can be cut from each board. The overall appearance of the board is not important. Factory Select is the highest quality shop board with the clearest material. It is used to make window and door parts. Other factory grades include Numbers 1, 2 and 3 Shop. All grades within this category have the rough, or nominal, thickness given by the quarter system. Sizes are: 4/4 = 1″, 5/4 = 1-1/4″, 6/4 = 1-1/2″ and 8/4 = 2″.

Molding boards are primarily for manufacturing trim or molding. Molding is stocked in strips 1″ and wider and 6′ and longer.

Dimension Lumber

Lumber between 2″ and 5″ thick and 2″ or more wide is called dimension lumber. It is designed for framing in houses and buildings. Typical uses include wall studs, floor joists and roof rafters. Dimension lumber is commonly called 2-bys and 4-bys.

Sometimes called structural lumber, dimension is graded for strength rather than appearance. Light framing grades are at least 2″ thick and numbered 1, 2 and 3 Structural, Figure 56-3. No. 1 is the strongest of these three. Some sawmills do not mark their lumber with this grading system. Instead, they label the grades in descending order of quality–construction, standard, utility and economy.

Studs only recently have been established as a lumber category. They are designed for wall support in houses. Structural joists and planks is a category of dimension lumber that comes in Select Structural No. 1, No. 2 and Economy grades. Joists and planks are used full length for support in floors and roofs.

Timbers

A timber is a large piece of wood cut to support much weight. Timbers come in thicknesses of 5″ or more and are used as beams, posts, girders and other supports.

HARDWOOD GRADES

Grading standards for hardwood are different from those for softwood. First of all, the grading system for hardwood is simpler. Instead of several softwood associations, the *National Hardwood Lumber Association* is the only group to set the grades for all hardwoods. Second, while softwood is graded by the best side of the board, hardwood is graded by the poor face. Finally, softwoods are used primarily for general building and construction. Builders utilize the whole board and rarely cut softwood into smaller pieces. Strength of the finished product is the prime consideration. Hardwoods, on the other hand, are judged more by appearance than by strength. Used primarily in furniture making and in exposed areas, hardwood is not as subject to the stress of heavy construction as softwood. Generally, hardwood is cut into clear, small pieces.

You can get an official booklet detailing the grading system of hardwoods from the National Hardwood Lumber Association. A general description follows.

Calculating Grades

To calculate the grade of hardwood, first determine the square feet of a board. Multiply the width in feet by the length in feet. This figure is called the surface measure in the grading of hardwood lumber. Then determine the poor face of the board or the side having the most defects. A grader visually marks out on this face the clear pieces, or cuttings. Each cutting must be free of all wane, knots, checks and other defects. The opposite side, or best face, must be sound. The wider and longer the individual cuttings, the higher the grade.

The clear pieces, or cuttings, actually are measured for the amount of wood contained in each

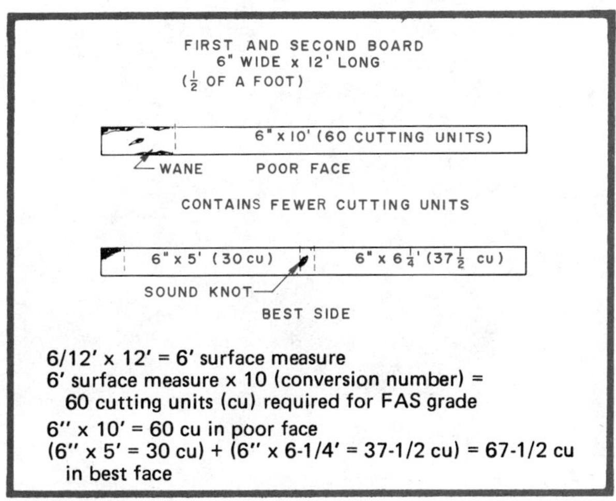

Figure 56-4
Marking a board into cutting units.
(National Hardwood Lumber Association)

piece. To determine the amount of material in a cutting, multiply the width in inches by the length in feet. Repeat this procedure for each cutting found on the board. Then add all the cuttings together for the total number of cutting units on the board., Figure 56-4.

Every grade of lumber must show a percentage of clear wood in each board. The individual percentage is then changed to a whole conversion number to make the calculation easier. Multiply this conversion number by the surface measure to determine the minimal number of cutting units necessary for a piece of lumber to make a particular grade. For example, grading rules state that to make the grade First and Second (FAS) each board must have at least 83-1/3 percent clear material. This percentage corresponds to the conversion number 10. For the minimal amount of clear material for grade FAS, the cutting units must be 10 times the surface measure of the board. With 60 cutting units, the board in Figure 56-4 is a FAS grade.

A grader also must consider the minimum sizes of the cuttings and the smallest width and length for the whole board. The smaller the sizes, the lower the grade of the board.

Standard Grades

Standard hardwood grades include–First, Second, Select, No. 1 Common, No. 2 Common, No. 3A Common and No. 3B Common. You can use a *scaling stick* to calculate the grade. A scaling stick quickly determines the surface measure

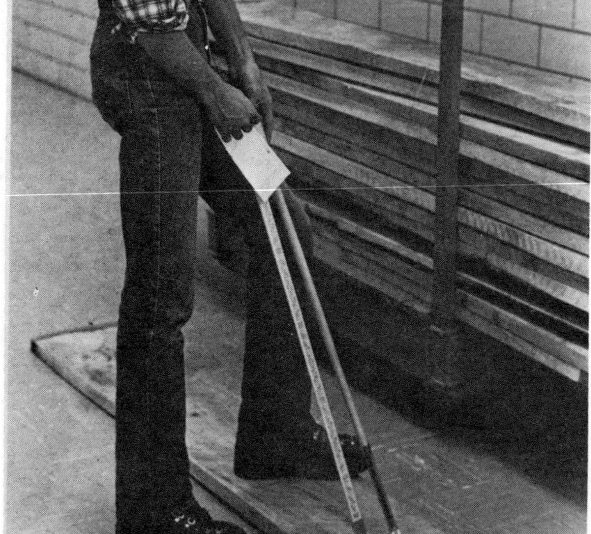

Figure 56-5
A scaling stick reduces the time it takes to determine the surface measure and the sizes of the cutting unit.

of a board and the sizes of the cutting units, Figure 56-5.

Although they are separate grades, First and Second are combined into one grade, FAS, for selling purposes. The high number of cutting units necessary for this grade causes the boards to be very wide and long, at least 6″ wide and 8′ long. For this reason, FAS boards often contain a great deal of sapwood.

Select grade is an unusual category of hardwood because both faces are graded. To qualify for Select grade the best face of the board must be a Second grade while the poor face must be No. 1 Common, Figure 56-6. Selects are a good choice for furniture and cabinets where only one side of the board is exposed. All Select hardwood boards must be at least 4″ wide and 6′ long. You can buy many small pieces at a reasonable price. Cuttings must be at least 3″ wide and 4′ long.

No. 1 Common is an excellent buy for use in school shops. More than 65 percent of the board must be clear, and the smallest cutting is 4″ by 2′ or 3″ x 3′. A No. 1 Common board has at least 8 times more cutting units than surface area, Figure 56-7. Often highly figured grain will be produced on this grade.

Cabinet and furniture companies frequently buy No. 2 Common, 3A Common and 3B Common hardwood. Such industries use mostly short pieces of wood and so they save money by buying one of these common hardwood grades. A minimum of 50 percent of the material must be clear on a No. 2 Common board, Figure 56-8. The cutting units should be 6 times larger than

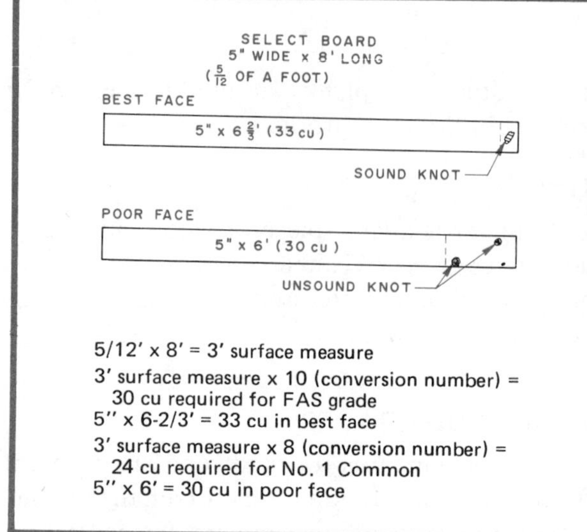

Figure 56-6
Grade both faces of a Select hardwood board. (National Hardwood Lumber Association)

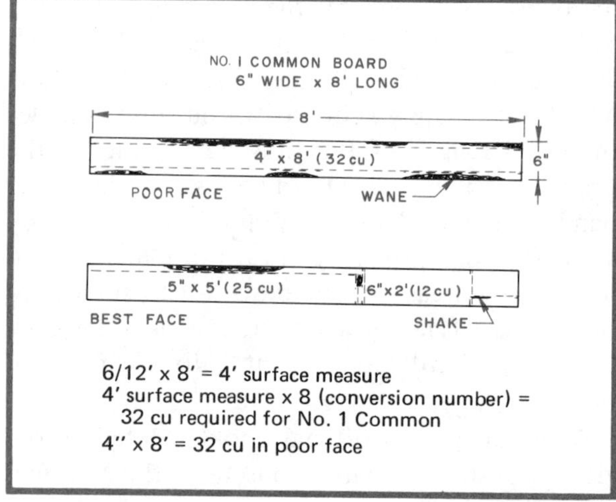

Figure 56-7
A No. 1 Common board has 32 cutting units. (National Hardwood Lumber Association)

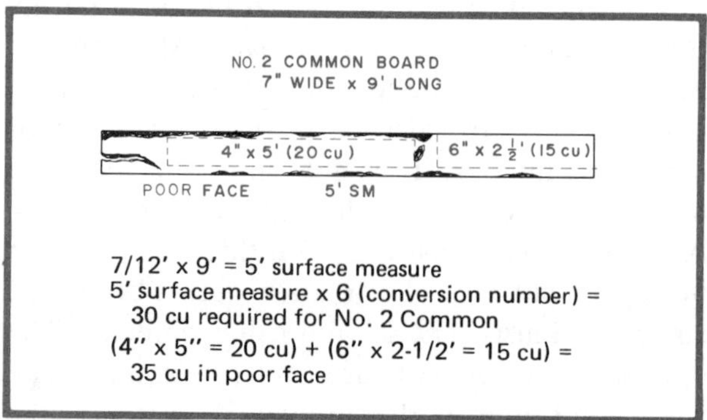

Figure 56-8
A No. 2 Common board has 30 cutting units. (National Hardwood Lumber Association)

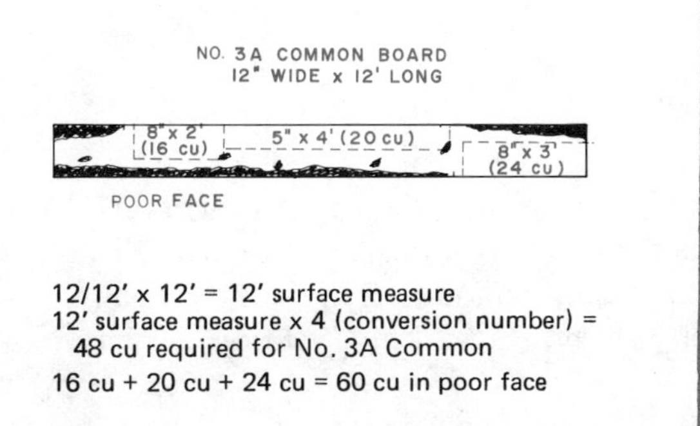

Figure 56-9
A No. 3A Common board has 48 cutting units. (National Hardwood Lumber Association)

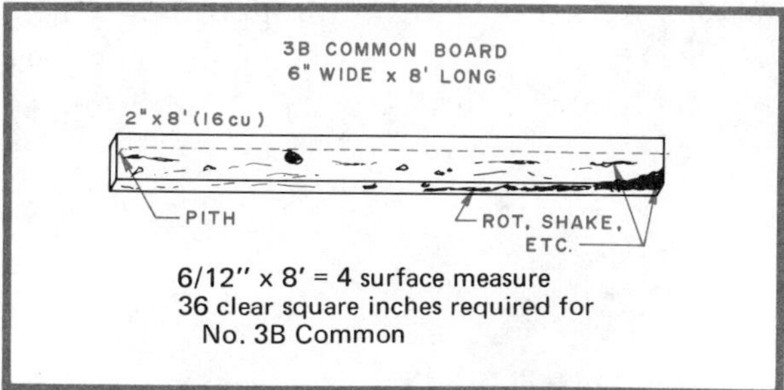

Figure 56-10
A No. 3B Common board contains only 36 square inches of clear materials. (National Hardwood Lumber Association)

the surface measure. No. 3A Common only comes in boards that are 3"wide and 2'long and larger, Figure 56-9. There must be at least 4 times more cutting units than the surface measure. A No. 3B Common board requires only 36 square inches of clear material, Figure 56-10. It can have any size of cuttings with no other requirements.

SIZES OF LUMBER

Softwood lumber is sold by standard nominal sizes, Figure 56-11. Although boards are called by the nominal size, they actually measure a little smaller. A 1" x 12" (25 x 305 mm) is approximately 3/4" x 11-1/4" (16 x 190 mm). This smaller size is called the dressed size. The reduction is caused by shrinkage during kiln drying and surfacing the rough boards.

Hardwood lumber is sold by random widths and lengths (RWL). Because hardwood is more valuable, the boards are left as large as possible when cut at the sawmill.

THICKNESS			WIDTH		
Nominal (in.)	**Dressed (in.)**	**Dressed (mm)**	**Nominal (in.)**	**Dressed (in.)**	**Dressed (mm)**
1	3/4	16	2	1-1/2	36
1-1/4	1-1/8	27	3	2-1/2	62
1-1/2	1-3/8	40	4	3-1/2	88
2	1-1/2	36	5	4-1/2	114
2-1/2	2	50	6	5-1/2	140
3	2-1/2	62	8	7-1/4	190
3-1/2	3	76	10	9-1/4	233
4	3-1/2	88	12	11-1/4	290

Figure 56-11
Nominal sizes and dressed sizes of softwood.

REVIEW QUESTIONS

1 What two grading associations establish the rules by which softwood lumber is sold?
2 List the standard softwood lumber grades.
3 What is another name for Nos. 1, 2 and 3 Dimension lumber?
4 What is molding grade primarily used for?
5 Which association grades hardwood lumber?
6 Define cutting, cutting units, surface measure.
7 List the standard hardwood lumber grades.
8 What are nominal and dressed sizes?

SUGGESTED ACTIVITIES

1 Visit a lumberyard. See what grades of lumber are available. If this is not possible, borrow a lumber catalog from your instructor. List all available grades.
2 Select a piece of hardwood lumber from the stock rack. See if you can determine the grade.

UNIT

57

Veneers

Objectives

After studying this unit you should be able to:

1 List the methods of varying the grain pattern of a veneered panel.
2 Identify different methods of slicing and matching veneer.
3 Veneer panels.

Technical Terms

Flitch
Rotary cut veneers
Flat sliced veneers
Quarter sliced veneers
Rift sliced veneers
Slip match
Book match
Butt match
Substrate
Telegraphing
Crossband
Balanced construction
Veneer saw
Veneer pins

Veneering was once considered an art practiced only by highly skilled woodworkers. Workers laminated very thin pieces of wood to furniture to accent and add to its beauty. Today, veneering is no longer just an art. It has become commonplace on such wood products as furniture and millwork.

Constructing the foundation or substructure is the first step in veneering a piece. This could be a plain piece of particle board for a chessboard or an entire piece of furniture made of an inexpensive hardwood. Uniformly thin sheets of veneer are then cut to width and length. Gluing the veneer to the surface completes the process, Figure 57-1.

Figure 57-1
This attractive veneered top has been made from a piece of particle board glued to a solid lumber edge band.

There are many advantages to veneering a product. Veneering is an economical way of covering a large area with expensive wood. You can use thin rosewood veneer, for example, to cover a tabletop. This would cost you much less than it would if you made the top of solid rosewood.

Particle board is a very stable base for veneer. Particle board expands and contracts less than solid lumber. You can create many interesting effects by selective cutting and matching of veneer strips. For example, the pattern shown in Figure 57-2 would be impossible to produce with other material.

Veneer is sold by the square foot. If you want to cover large panels or intend to use an unusual match, you may purchase a whole bundle. A bundle of veneer sliced from one tree is referred to as a *flitch,* Figure 57-3. The pieces of veneer in the flitch are stacked in the same order in which they were sliced. This order is important when you want to match veneer strips to make a wide panel.

Several factors determine the grain pattern of veneer. The first thing to consider is the part of the tree from which the veneer was cut, Figure 57-4. Most veneer is sliced from the straight trunk or large branches. This part of the tree produces a typical grain pattern.

Figure 57-2
You can develop unusual patterns by veneering.

Figure 57-3
A flitch is the entire bundle of veneer that was sliced from a single tree.

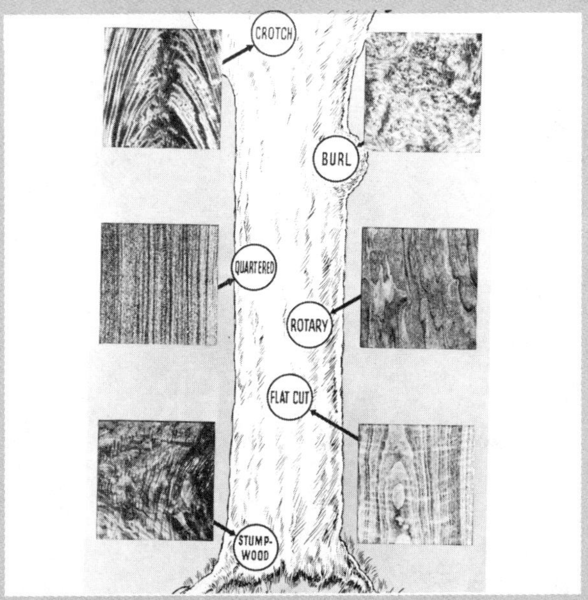

Figure 57-4
Cutting the veneer from various sections of the tree produces different grain patterns. (Fine Hardwoods/American Walnut Association)

Veneer also may be cut from the crotch of the tree, which is located just below the fork of the tree. Veneer from this section contains swirls and commonly is referred to as fire. Butt or stump wood comes from the junction of the roots and the stump. Its grain pattern usually is wavy. Wart-like cancerous growths, called burls, also are used for veneer. Veneer cut from burls has the most complex pattern of all. Burls are brittle and must be handled with great care.

The grain pattern of veneer can vary with the way the veneer is sliced, Figure 57-5. *Rotary cut veneer* makes up more than 90 percent of the veneer produced. This method of slicing produces a very wide grain pattern. A veneer lathe literally unwinds the log, Figure 57-6. This is similar to unrolling a roll of paper towels. Most hardwood veneers are *flat sliced veneers.* These veneers are cut by the flat slicing technique, in which a section of the log is clamped to a carriage and a large knife shaves off the veneer, Figure 57-7. The grain pattern is closely striped at the outer edges with a wide grain pattern toward the center. Other methods of producing veneer include quarter slicing, rift slicing and sawing. *Quarter sliced* and *rift sliced veneers* are produced to take advantage of straight grain and the medullary rays. Sawed veneers are not practical on a large scale because of the large amount of waste made by the saw kerf.

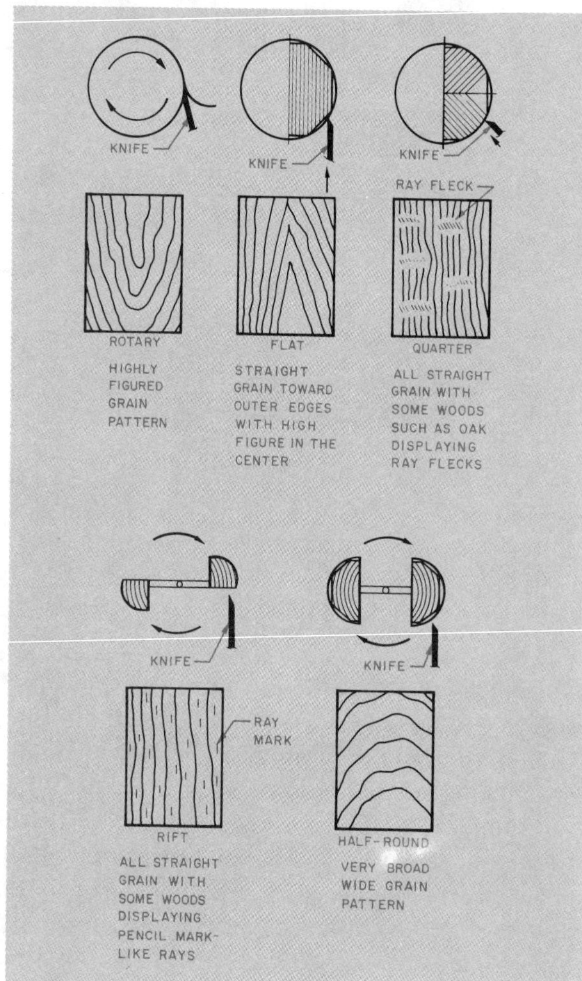

Figure 57-5
Different slicing methods produce different grain patterns.

Figure 57-6
A rotary veneering lathe unwinds a log. (U.S. Forest Products Laboratory)

Figure 57-7
Most hardwood veneer is produced with flat slicing. The log is clamped to the machine. A large knife slices strips of veneer from the log. (U.S. Forest Products Laboratory)

You can vary the grain pattern by matching in different ways. A woodworker can choose from a number of matching techniques, Figure 57-8. *Slip match* is the most common. You slide each piece of veneer off the top of the flitch and then glue the strips of veneer with the same side up. Another simple match is the *book match.* In this match you turn over every second piece of veneer, much like the pages of a book.

You can match veneer on the ends as well as on the edges. Diamond and reverse diamond are combinations of a *butt match* on the ends and a book match on the edges. The checkerboard and 4-way-center-and-butt patterns are two more ways of assembling veneer.

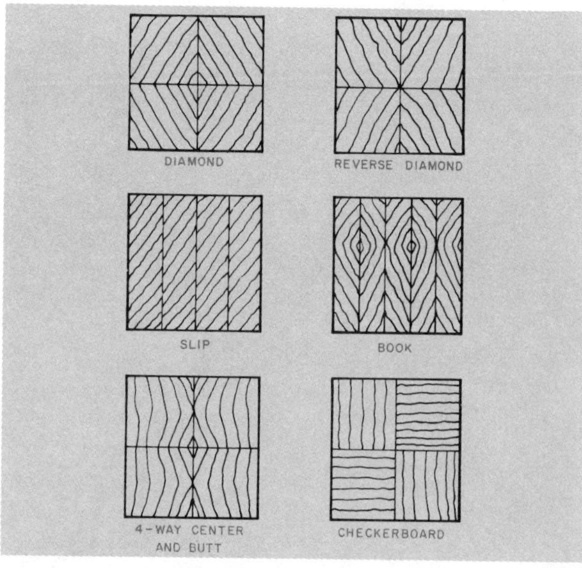

Figure 57-8
You can assemble veneer in different ways to develop many interesting patterns.

CONSTRUCTING A VENEERED PANEL

To make a veneered panel:

1. Start the veneering process by cutting the core or *substrate*. The material that you use must be as smooth as possible to prevent *telegraphing*. The term telegraphing describes a defect caused when the grain pattern of the substrate shows through the veneer. Particle board is the best material for a core or substrate, Figure 57-9. Sometimes you will want to veneer solid lumber or plywood. In these cases, first glue a *crossband* of an inexpensive tight grain veneer to the substrate with the grain going at a right angle to that of the substrate. Cover both faces of the substrate with an equal number of layers of veneer to prevent warping. This is called *balanced construction*. Then apply the finish veneer over the inexpensive layer with the grain at right angles to that of the crossband.
2. Select the veneer for the exposed surfaces. An ample supply must be available because there will be a great deal of waste. Carefully mark the places where the veneer is to be cut. Then rough out the lengths by cutting across the strip with an old pair of scissors, Figure 57-10. The length of the strip should be 1" (25 mm) longer than the panel to be veneered. Be careful not to split the veneer as you cut it.
3. Decide where the edge joint will fall on each piece of veneer. Lightly mark the joint with a straightedge and pencil. Position the line under a cutting fixture and clamp each end of the straightedge, Figure 57-11. With a sharp knife, a dovetail saw or a *veneer saw* cut the veneer along the straightedge. Follow this procedure for each edge of the joint.
4. Make sure that the grain pattern matches, and then join the edges. Use a trimming fixture and a block plane to work the edge down, Figure 57-12. Some woodworkers prefer to use a power jointer rather than a plane. For a perfect match, stack the two adjoining edges in the fixture side by side. Then plane the edges straight and smooth.

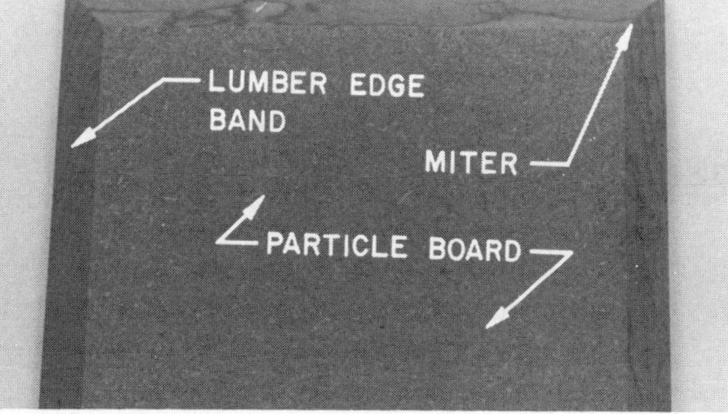

Figure 57-9
A piece of 3/4" (19 mm) particle board with a mitered lumber edge band makes an excellent surface for veneering.

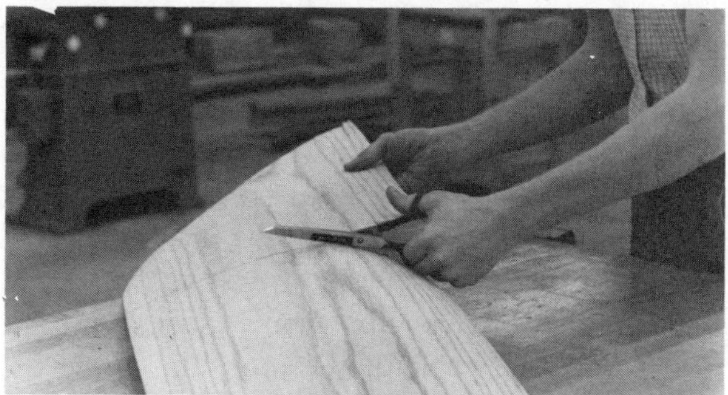

Figure 57-10
Cut pieces of veneer to rough length with scissors.

Figure 57-11
You can use a cutting fixture and veneering saw to cut the joint.

Figure 57-12
Place the two pieces of veneer together and clamp them in a fixture.

5. Place the pieces face side up on a layout board, such as a piece of plywood, Figure 57-13. Pin the strips of veneer in place with either *veneer pins* or small thumbtacks. Next place a piece of masking tape or veneer tape across the joint and at right angles to it every 6″ (152 mm). Finish the taping process by placing a strip of tape the full length of the joint, Figure 57-14. The special veneering tape is less likely to tear the veneer when it is removed.
6. Fold back the pieces of veneer to expose the edges of the joint. Use a small glue brush to apply polyvinyl glue along the edges, Figure 57-15. Then unfold the veneer and place the flat sheet on the layout board with the back up. Apply strips of tape across the back of the joint and allow the glue to dry.
7. Remove the tape from the back. Apply an even coat of adhesive to the substrate. Either polyvinyl or urea formaldehyde can be used, Figure 57-16. After the veneer is centered on the substrate, you must apply pressure immediately. Use a commercial press, Figure 57-17, or shopmade veneer clamps, Figure 57-18. No matter which method is selected, always use caul boards on each side of the veneered panel to give even pressure.

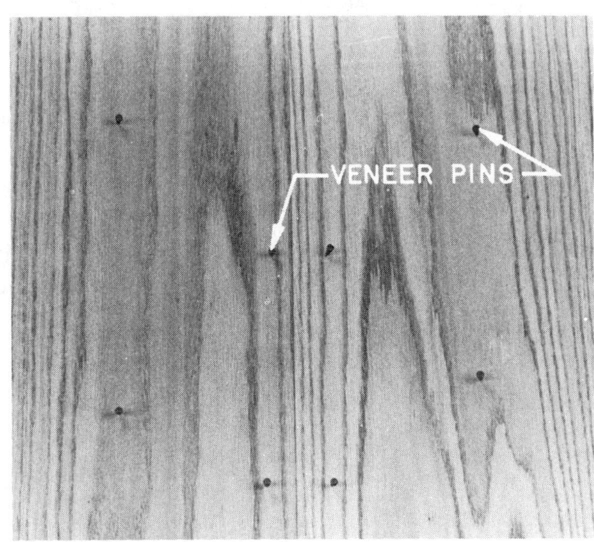

Figure 57-13
Fasten the trimmed veneer to a layout board to check the fit of the joint.

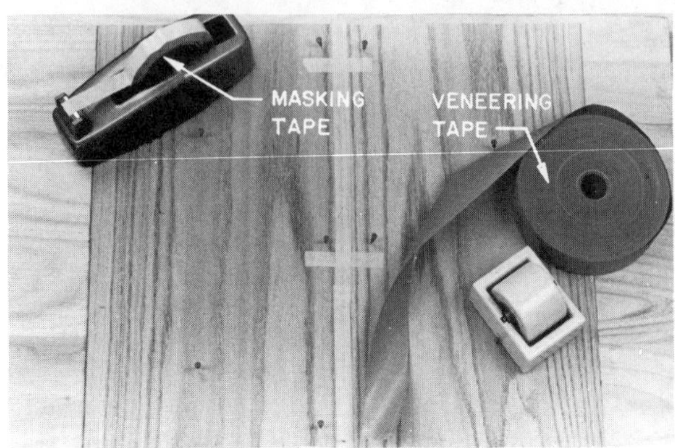

Figure 57-14
Tape the joint with either masking tape or veneering tape.

Figure 57-15
Apply adhesive to the edges with a small glue brush.

Figure 57-16
You can apply an even coat of adhesive to the substrate with either a glue spreader or a paintbrush.

You can glue small pieces of veneer, less than 24" x 24" (610 x 610 mm), in place with an electric clothes iron. No clamps are required. Spread polyvinyl on the substrate and center the veneer on it. Set the iron on "rayon" or "synthetic." Start in one corner and move the iron toward the center. Push downward and make short, overlapping strokes. Work across the panel, pushing the excess adhesive ahead of the iron.

8. After the adhesive has dried, you can trim away the excess veneer that extends over the edge of the core. Turn the panel over, and place it on a scrap piece of plywood. Carefully draw a sharp knife along the edge of the core while pushing down on the panel. Do not attempt to cut the veneer in one pass. Several passes will cut through the veneer slowly without chipping or tearing the face of the panel.

   Although the veneer is fairly smooth, some hand sanding is necessary. Because veneer is only 1/28" thick, sand carefully. Power sanders may cut through to the substrate. Remove the tape and sand as you would a piece of plywood.

Figure 57-17
A pod press quickly applies pressure to the veneered panel.

Figure 57-18
Shop-made clamps apply pressure with screwing devices.

REVIEW QUESTIONS

1. List three advantages of veneering.
2. What is "fire" in a piece of veneer?
3. Which is the most common method of slicing veneer?
4. Sketch a veneered panel that has been slip matched; a panel with a book match; and a panel with a diamond match.
5. What is telegraphing? How can it be prevented?
6. How can you make a veneered panel with balanced construction?
7. What kind of tape can you use to join two pieces of veneer?
8. Where should caul board be placed in a veneer press?

SUGGESTED ACTIVITIES

1. Visit a furniture store and list the different types of veneer slicing and matching methods used on furniture.
2. Build a small jewelry box and try different veneers and matches on the outside.

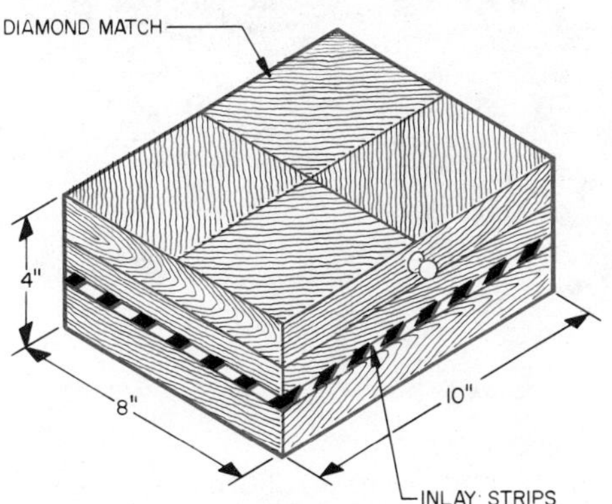

UNIT

58

Plywood

Objectives

After studying this unit you should be able to:

1 Identify the different types of plywood.

2 Explain the manufacturing process in making plywood.

3 Describe the major grades of plywood.

Technical Terms

Veneer core
Lumber core
Particle board core
Softwood plywood
Hardwood plywood
Marine plywood
Appearance grade
Engineering grade

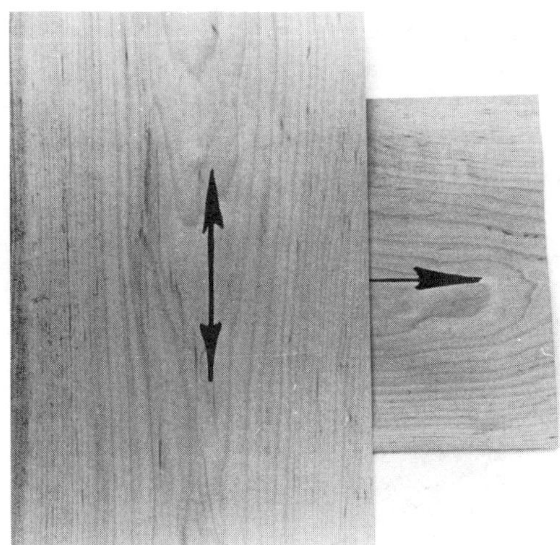

Figure 58-1
The grains of veneer in plywood are set at right angles to one another.

When plywood was introduced in the 1930s, most woodworkers considered it a cheap substitute for other woods. Since that time plywood has proved superior to many wood products. Today plywood is used in construction, cabinets and furniture. Plywood is a panel that has layers, or plies, of wood veneer. The grains of the layers are at right angles to one another, Figure 58-1. The layers are glued together.

Plywood has many advantages. It has a smooth, continuous surface that makes a joint-free panel. It is one of the strongest manufactured wood products. Workers often compare it to steel. It is equally strong with and across the grain because of its right-angled layers. Lumber is strong with the grain but relatively weak across it. Plywood is a good insulator. The insulating value of a piece of 3/4" (19 mm) softwood plywood is as high as that of 4-1/2" (114 mm) of brick, 7" (178 mm) of concrete or 80" (2032 mm) of steel.

PLYWOOD CONSTRUCTION

You can assemble plywood panels in several ways, Figure 58-2. A *veneer-core* panel has three to nine veneer layers. Veneer-core panel construction is the strongest and most popular. A *lumber-core* panel has many strips of lumber glued together. Its face and back are covered with veneer. Lumber-core panels often are used for cabinet doors that have an exposed edge. A *particle board-core* panel has one solid piece of particle board for its core. It is heavy and relatively weak but less expensive.

Workers manufacture plywood panels by first slicing logs or bolts into thin veneer, Figure 58-3. Slicing usually is done on a large veneering lathe, Figure 58-4. Veneers then dry and are graded before being cut to width and length. Major open defects in the face and the back are repaired with a plug, Figure 58-5. Frequently, small pieces are joined together to form wide sheets of veneer. This is done on a splicer that automatically spreads glue on the edges and bonds them. Veneer plies then are spread with an adhesive and stacked together before going into a laminating press, Figure 58-6. The press applies pressure while it heats the glue line in the panel, Figure 58-7. Then the glued-up panel is cut to size and sanded to finished size.

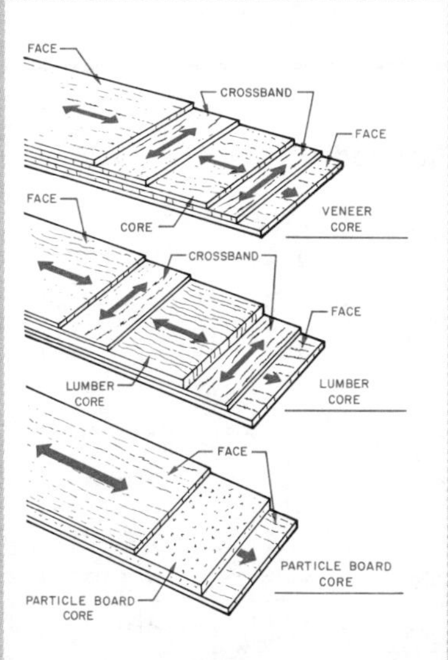

Figure 58-2
Plywood can be assembled in many ways.

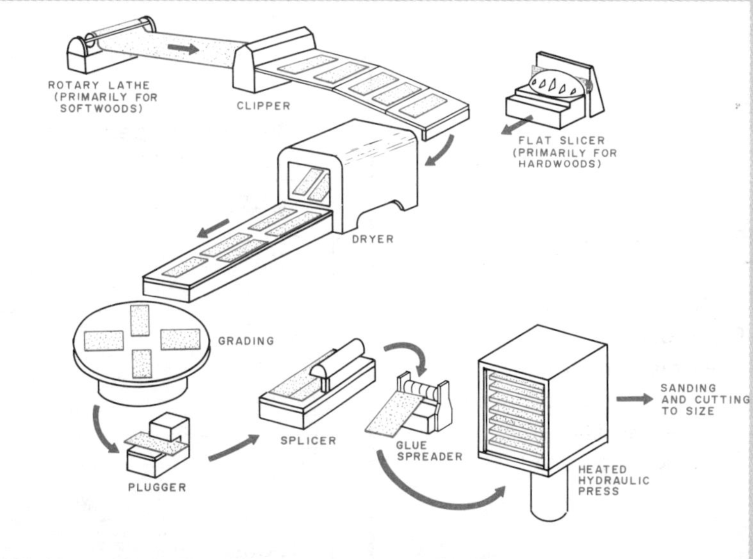

Figure 58-3
The procedure for manufacturing plywood.

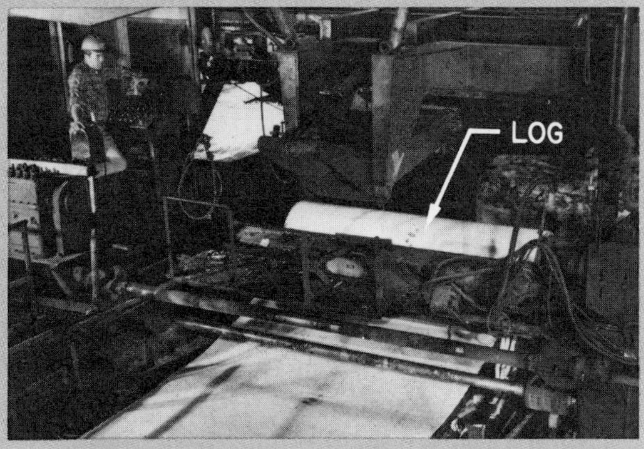

Figure 58-4
A veneering lathe peels a log to produce veneer. (American Plywood Association)

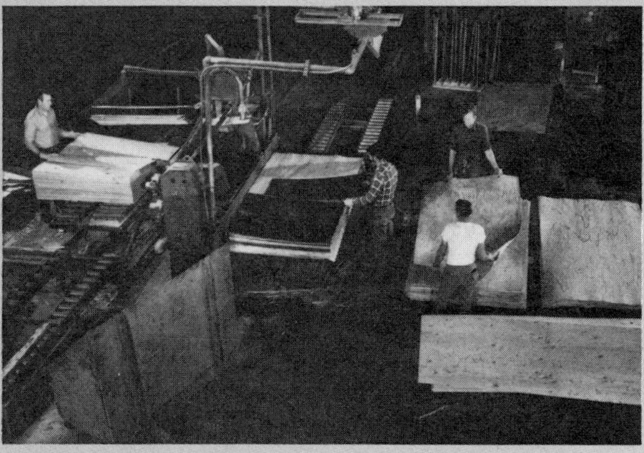

Figure 58-6
Workers apply adhesive to veneer with a glue spreader and then stack veneer to make the individual sheets. (American Plywood Association)

Figure 58-5
A worker plugs knot holes before veneer is used in a panel. (American Plywood Association)

Figure 58-7
A special hydraulic press applies pressure to freshly glued panels. (American Plywood Association)

Guide to Appearance Grades of Plywood(1)

SPECIFIC GRADES AND THICKNESSES MAY BE IN LOCALLY LIMITED SUPPLY.
SEE YOUR DEALER BEFORE SPECIFYING.

Type	Grade Designation(2)	Description and Most Common Uses	Typical(3) Grade-trademarks	Veneer Grade: Face	Veneer Grade: Inner Plies	Veneer Grade: Back	Most Common Thicknesses (inch)					
Interior Type	APA N-N, N-A, N-B INT	Cabinet quality. For natural finish furniture, cabinet doors, built-ins, etc. Special order items.	N-N G-1 INT-APA PS1-74 000 / N-A G-2 INT-APA PS1-74 000	N	C	N,A, or B						3/4
Interior Type	APA N-D INT	For natural finish paneling. Special order item.	N-D G-2 INT-APA PS1-74 000	N	D	D	1/4					
Interior Type	APA A-A INT	For applications with both sides on view, built-ins, cabinets, furniture, partitions. Smooth face; suitable for painting.	A-A G-1 EXT-APA PS1-74 000	A	D	A	1/4		3/8	1/2	5/8	3/4
Interior Type	APA A-B INT	Use where appearance of one side is less important but where two solid surfaces are necessary.	A-B G-1 EXT-APA PS1-74 000	A	D	B	1/4		3/8	1/2	5/8	3/4
Interior Type	APA A-D INT	Use where appearance of only one side is important. Paneling, built-ins, shelving, partitions, flow racks.	A-D GROUP 1 INTERIOR 000 APA	A	D	D	1/4		3/8	1/2	5/8	3/4
Interior Type	APA B-B INT	Utility panel with two solid sides. Permits circular plugs.	B-B G-2 INT-APA PS1-74 000	B	D	B	1/4		3/8	1/2	5/8	3/4
Interior Type	APA B-D INT	Utility panel with one solid side. Good for backing, sides of built-ins, industry shelving, slip sheets, separator boards, bins.	B-D GROUP 2 INTERIOR 000 APA	B	D	D	1/4		3/8	1/2	5/8	3/4
Interior Type	APA DECORATIVE PANELS	Rough-sawn, brushed, grooved, or striated faces. For paneling, interior accent walls, built-ins, counter facing, displays, exhibits.	DECORATIVE B-D GROUP 1 INTERIOR 000 APA	C or btr.	D	D		5/16	3/8	1/2	5/8	
Interior Type	APA PLYRON INT	Hardboard face on both sides. For countertops, shelving, cabinet doors, flooring. Faces tempered, untempered, smooth, or screened.	PLYRON -INT-APA 000		C & D					1/2	5/8	3/4
Exterior Type	APA A-A EXT	Use where appearance of both sides is important. Fences, built-ins, signs, boats, cabinets, commercial refrigerators, shipping containers, tote boxes, tanks, ducts. (4)	A-A G-1 INT-APA PS1-74 000	A	C	A	1/4		3/8	1/2	5/8	3/4
Exterior Type	APA A-B EXT	Use where the appearance of only one side is less important. (4)	A-B G-1 INT-APA PS1-74 000	A	C	B	1/4		3/8	1/2	5/8	3/4
Exterior Type	APA A-C EXT	Use where the appearance of only one side is important. Soffits, fences, structural uses, boxcar and truck lining, farm buildings. Tanks, trays, commercial refrigerators. (4)	A-C GROUP 1 EXTERIOR 000 APA	A	C	C	1/4		3/8	1/2	5/8	3/4
Exterior Type	APA B-B EXT	Utility panel with solid faces. (4)	B-B G-2 EXT-APA PS1-74 000	B	C	B	1/4		3/8	1/2	5/8	3/4
Exterior Type	APA B-C EXT	Utility panel for farm service and work buildings, boxcar and truck lining, containers, tanks, agricultural equipment. Also as base for exterior coatings for walls, roofs. (4)	B-C GROUP 3 EXTERIOR 000 APA	B	C	C	1/4		3/8	1/2	5/8	3/4
Exterior Type	APA HDO EXT	High Density Overlay. Has a hard, semi-opaque resin-fiber overlay both faces. Abrasion resistant. For concrete forms, cabinets, counter tops, signs, tanks. Also available with skid-resistant screen-grid surface. (4)	HDO A-A G-1 EXT-APA PS1-74 000	A or B	C or C plgd	A or B			3/8	1/2	5/8	3/4
Exterior Type	APA MDO EXT	Medium Density Overlay. Smooth, opaque, resin-fiber overlay one or both faces. Ideal base for paint, both indoors and outdoors. (4)(6)	MDO B-B G-2 EXT-APA PS1-74 000	B	C	B or C			3/8	1/2	5/8	3/4
Exterior Type	APA 303 SIDING EXT	Proprietary plywood products for exterior siding, fencing, etc. Special surface treatment such as V-groove, channel groove, striated, brushed, rough-sawn and texture-embossed MDO. Stud spacing (Span Rating) and face grade classification indicated on grade stamp.	303 SIDING 6-S GROUP 1 16 oc SPAN EXTERIOR 000 APA	(5)	C	C			11/32	15/32	19/32	
Exterior Type	APA T 1-11 EXT	Special 303 panel having grooves 1/4" deep, 3/8" wide, spaced 4" or 8" o.c. Other spacing optional. Edges shiplapped. Available unsanded, textured and MDO.	303 SIDING 6-S/W T1-11 GROUP 1 16oc SPAN EXTERIOR 000 APA	C or btr.	C	C					19/32	
Exterior Type	APA PLYRON EXT	Hardboard faces both sides, tempered, smooth or screened.	PLYRON EXT-APA 000		C					1/2	5/8	3/4
Exterior Type	APA MARINE EXT	Ideal for boat hulls. Made only with Douglas fir or western larch. Special solid jointed core construction. Subject to special limitations on core gaps and number of face repairs. Also available with HDO or MDO faces.	MARINE A-A EXT-APA PS1-74 000	A or B	B	A or B	1/4		3/8	1/2	5/8	3/4

(1) Sanded both sides except where decorative or other surfaces specified.
(2) Can be manufactured in Group 1, 2, 3, 4 or 5.
(3) The species groups, Identification Indexes and Span Ratings shown in the typical grade-trademarks are examples only. See "Group," "Identification Index" and "Span Rating" for explanations and availability.
(4) Can also be manufactured in Structural I (all plies limited to Group 1 species) and Structural II (all plies limited to Group 1, 2, or 3 species).
(5) C or better for 5 plies. C Plugged or better for 3 and 4 plies.
(6) Also available as a 303 siding.

Figure 58-8
The American Plywood Association has established many grades. (American Plywood Association)

There are two major kinds of plywood. *Softwood plywood* is the most common. It is used mostly in building construction. *Hardwood plywood* usually is chosen for its fine appearance. Cabinets and furniture often have hardwood plywood in their construction.

PLYWOOD GRADING

Each kind of plywood has a number of grades. In each case a different association establishes the grades.

Softwood Plywood

The American Plywood Association establishes the many grades of softwood plywood, Figure 58-8. The edge or the back of each panel has a grade stamp to help a customer, Figure 58-9. Each ply, or veneer, that makes up a sheet of softwood plywood is graded N, A, B, C, C plugged or D, Figure 58-10. The panel's face and back are graded. They do not always get the same grade. If a grading stamp has "interior" printed on it, the plywood's core contains veneers of D grade and better. If a stamp has "exterior" on it, the core has veneers of C and better. "Exterior glue" indicates that the veneer is usable for an exterior application. *Marine plywood* is of this type. It has no voids in its core.

All of the above terms apply to the appearance of softwood plywood. *Appearance grades* are used when strength is not a prime consideration. Cabinet sides and bottoms are good examples. When strength is a consideration, such as for construction purposes, look for *engineering grades,* Figure 58-11.

Hardwood Plywood

The Hardwood Plywood Association grades hardwood plywood. Because hardwood plywood is used for its appearance, its grading is concerned with only the face and the back. In order of quality, grades are premium, good, sound, utility and backing. Grades usually are abbreviated in a catalog. G1S/Snd tells you that the face of the panel is a good grade and the back is a sound grade. A listing of only one grade refers to the face. G1s tells you that the panel has a good grade for the face with any grade for the back. Usually, 1/4"- (6 mm) thick hardwood plywood is sold this way.

Hardwood is specified also by the type of adhesive it has and the quality of its core. Type I has exterior glue and is full-waterproof bond. Type II has interior glue. Type II accounts for 95 percent of all domestic hardwood plywood. When you need a core without any voids or holes, you can get a "solid core."

SIZES AND COST

A major advantage of plywood is its variety of sizes. Common thicknesses are 1/8", 1/4", 3/8", 1/2", 5/8", 3/4" and 1" (3, 6, 10, 13, 16, 19 and 25 mm). Although plywood is manufactured in many widths and lengths, 4' x 8' (1219 x 2438 mm) is the most common.

All plywood is sold by the square foot. A piece of 1/4" x 4' x 8' has 32 sq. ft. You can calculate the cost by first multiplying the width by the length in feet. Finish the problem by multiplying the number of square feet by the price per square foot. For example, 4' x 8' = 32 sq. ft.; 32 sq. ft. x 57¢ per square foot = $18.24.

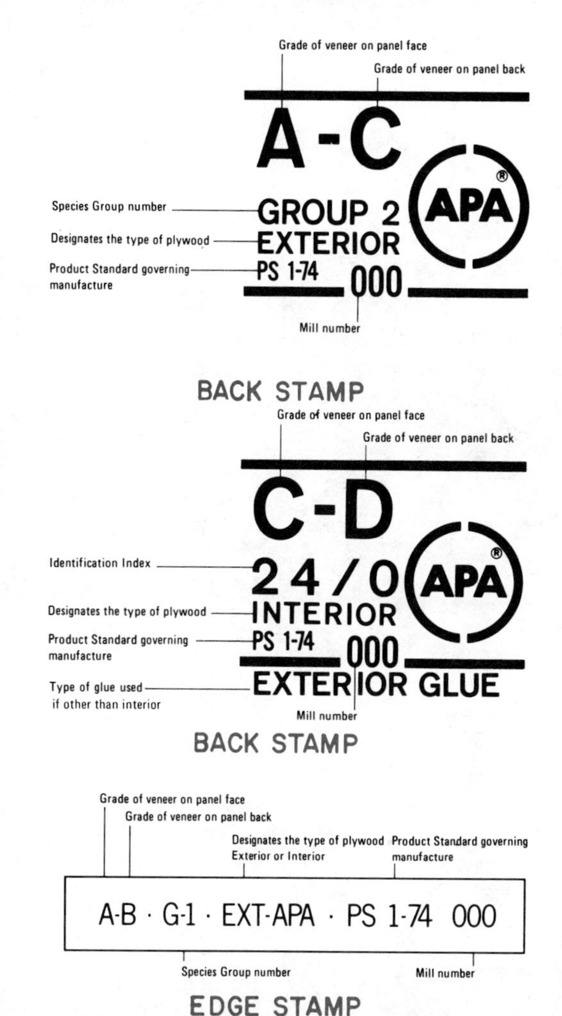

Figure 58-9
Grading stamps are on the back or the edge of a panel. (American Plywood Association)

Veneer Grades	
N	Smooth surface "natural finish" veneer. Select, all heartwood or all sapwood. Free of open defects. Allows not more than 6 repairs, wood only, per 4 x 8 panel, made parallel to grain and well matched for grain and color.
A	Smooth, paintable. Not more than 18 neatly made repairs, boat, sled, or router type, and parallel to grain, permitted. May be used for natural finish in less demanding applications.
B	Solid surface. Shims, circular repair plugs and tight knots to 1 inch across grain permitted. Some minor splits permitted.
C Plugged	Improved C veneer with splits limited to 1/8-inch width and knotholes and borer holes limited to 1/4 x 1/2-inch. Admits some broken grain. Synthetic repairs permitted.
C	Tight knots to 1-1/2-inch. Knotholes to 1 inch across grain and some to 1-1/2-inch if total width of knots and knotholes is within specified limits. Synthetic or wood repairs. Discoloration and sanding defects that do not impair strength permitted. Limited splits allowed. Stitching permitted.
D	Knots and knotholes to 2-1/2-inch width across grain and 1/2-inch larger within specified limits. Limited splits are permitted. Stitching permitted. Limited to Interior grades of plywood.

Figure 58-10
Standard veneer grades established by the American Plywood Association. (American Plywood Association)

Figure 58-11
Engineering grades for structural applications. (American Plywood Association)

Guide to Engineered Grades of Plywood

SPECIFIC GRADES AND THICKNESSES MAY BE IN LOCALLY LIMITED SUPPLY. SEE YOUR DEALER BEFORE SPECIFYING.

Type	Grade Designation	Description and Most Common Uses	Typical[1] Grade-trademarks	Veneer Grade: Face	Veneer Grade: Inner Plies	Veneer Grade: Back	Most Common Thicknesses (inch)				
Interior Type	APA C-D INT	For wall and roof sheathing, subflooring, industrial uses such as pallets. Most commonly available with exterior glue (CDX). Specify exterior glue where construction delays are anticipated and for treated-wood foundations. (7)	C-D 32/16 APA INTERIOR 000 C-D 24/0 APA INTERIOR 000 EXTERIOR GLUE	C	D	D	5/16	3/8	1/2	5/8	3/4
Interior Type	APA STRUCTURAL I C-D INT and APA STRUCTURAL II C-D INT	Unsanded structural grades where plywood strength properties are of maximum importance: structural diaphragms, box beams, gusset plates, stressed-skin panels, containers, pallet bins. Made only with exterior glue. See (6) for species group requirements. Structural I more commonly available. (7)	STRUCTURAL I C-D 24/0 APA INTERIOR 000 EXTERIOR GLUE	C(3)	D(3)	D(3)	5/16	3/8	1/2	5/8	3/4
Interior Type	APA STURD-I-FLOOR INT	For combination subfloor-underlayment. Provides smooth surface for application of resilient floor covering. Possesses high concentrated- and impact-load resistance during construction and occupancy. Manufactured with exterior glue only. Touch-sanded. Available square edge or tongue-and-groove. (7)	STURD-I-FLOOR 24oc T&G 23/32 INCH INTERIOR APA 000 EXTERIOR GLUE NRB 108/FHA-UM-66	C Plugged	(4)	D				19/32 5/8	23/32 3/4
Interior Type	APA STURD-I-FLOOR 48 O.C. (2·4·1) INT	For combination subfloor-underlayment on 32- and 48-inch spans. Provides smooth surface for application of resilient floor coverings. Possesses high concentrated- and impact-load resistance during construction and occupancy. Manufactured with exterior glue only. Unsanded or touch-sanded. Available square edge or tongue-and-groove. (7)	STURD-I-FLOOR 48oc 2·4·1 T&G 1·1/8 INCH INTERIOR APA 000 EXTERIOR GLUE NRB 108/FHA-UM-66	C Plugged	C(5) & D	D			1-1/8		
Interior Type	APA UNDERLAYMENT INT	For application over structural subfloor. Provides smooth surface for application of resilient floor coverings. Touch-sanded. Also available with exterior glue. (2)(6)	UNDERLAYMENT GROUP 1 INTERIOR APA 000	C Plugged	C(5) & D	D		3/8	1/2	19/32 5/8	23/32 3/4
Interior Type	APA C-D PLUGGED INT	For built-ins, wall and ceiling tile backing, cable reels, walkways, separator boards. Not a substitute for Underlayment or Sturd-I-Floor as it lacks their indentation resistance. Touch-sanded. Also made with exterior glue. (2)(6)	C-D PLUGGED GROUP 2 INTERIOR APA 000	C Plugged	D	D		3/8	1/2	19/32 5/8	23/32 3/4
Exterior Type	APA C-C EXT	Unsanded grade with waterproof bond for subflooring and roof decking, siding on service and farm buildings, crating, pallets, pallet bins, cable reels, treated-wood foundations. (7)	C-C 42/20 APA EXTERIOR 000	C	C	C	5/16	3/8	1/2	5/8	3/4
Exterior Type	APA STRUCTURAL I C-C EXT and APA STRUCTURAL II C-C EXT	For engineered applications in construction and industry where full Exterior type panels are required. Unsanded. See (6) for species group requirements. (7)	STRUCTURAL I C-C APA EXTERIOR 000	C	C	C	5/16	3/8	1/2	5/8	3/4
Exterior Type	APA STURD-I-FLOOR EXT	For combination subfloor-underlayment under resilient floor coverings where severe moisture conditions may be present, as in balcony decks. Possesses high concentrated- and impact-load resistance during construction and occupancy. Touch-sanded. Available square edge or tongue-and-groove. (7)	STURD-I-FLOOR 20oc 5/8 INCH EXTERIOR APA 000 NRB 108/FHA-UM-66	C Plugged	C(5)	C				19/32 5/8	23/32 3/4
Exterior Type	APA UNDERLAYMENT C-C PLUGGED EXT	For application over structural subfloor. Provides smooth surface for application of resilient floor coverings where severe moisture conditions may be present. Touch-sanded. (2)(6)	UNDERLAYMENT C-C PLUGGED GROUP 2 EXTERIOR APA 000	C Plugged	C(5)	C		3/8	1/2	19/32 5/8	23/32 3/4
Exterior Type	APA C-C PLUGGED EXT	For use as tile backing where severe moisture conditions exist. For refrigerated or controlled atmosphere rooms, pallet fruit bins, tanks, box car and truck floors and linings, open soffits. Touch-sanded. (2)(6)	C-C PLUGGED GROUP 2 EXTERIOR APA 000	C Plugged	C	C		3/8	1/2	19/32 5/8	23/32 3/4
Exterior Type	APA B-B PLYFORM CLASS I and CLASS II EXT	Concrete form grades with high reuse factor. Sanded both sides. Mill-oiled unless otherwise specified. Special restrictions on species. Available in HDO and Structural I. Class I most commonly available. (8)	B-B PLYFORM CLASS I EXTERIOR APA 000	B	C	B				5/8	3/4

(1) The species groups, Identification Indexes and Span Ratings shown in the typical grade-trademarks are examples only. See "Group," "Identification Index" and "Span Rating" for explanations and availability.
(2) Can be manufactured in Group 1, 2, 3, 4, or 5.
(3) Special improved grade for structural panels.
(4) Special veneer construction to resist indentation from concentrated loads, or other solid wood-base materials.
(5) Special construction to resist indentation from concentrated loads.
(6) Can also be manufactured in Structural I (all plies limited to Group 1 special species) and Structural II (all plies limited to Group 1, 2, or 3 species).
(7) Specify by Identification Index for sheathing and Span Rating for Sturd-I-Floor panels.
(8) Made only from certain wood species to conform to APA specifications.

REVIEW QUESTIONS

1 List three advantages of plywood.
2 What are the three types of cores used in plywood?
3 How are open defects repaired in the face and back veneers?
4 Which grading association establishes grades for softwood plywood? Name the grades.
5 Engineering grades are designed for what purposes?
6 Which grading association recommends grades for hardwood plywood?
7 Most hardwood plywood is glued with what type of adhesive?
8 Plywood is sold by what unit of measure?

SUGGESTED ACTIVITIES

1 Visit a lumber yard. See what grades of plywood are sold.
2 Look in your home to find applications for plywood.

UNIT

59

Particle Board

Objectives

After studying this unit you should be able to:

1 List the advantages and disadvantages of using particle board.
2 Describe how particle board is manufactured.
3 Work with particle board.

Technical Terms

Binder
Wood furnish
Hog
Density

The use of particle board is increasing in today's woods industry. It is used in many products, including furniture, toys, cabinets and homes, Figure 59-1. Particle board is made of wood chips pressed together with a *binder,* Figure 59-2. The binder glues the particles together when heat and pressure are applied.

Particle board is priced by the square foot. It is sold in sheets or panels. Widths range from 3′ to 8′ (914 to 2438 mm). Lengths range from 4′ to 24′ (1219 to 7315 mm). Thicknesses range from 1/10″ to 2″ (2.5 to 51 mm). The most frequently used panel sizes are 4′ x 8′ (1219 x 2438 mm). The most common thicknesses are 3/8″, 1/2″, 5/8″ and 3/4″ (10, 13, 16 and 19 mm).

Figure 59-1
Economical particle board is used in many products. (Willamette Industries)

Figure 59-2
Particle board is made of wood chips and an adhesive binder.

There are advantages and disadvantages to particle board. Advantages include a very smooth, grainless surface and little expansion and contraction. These advantages make particle board an ideal material for veneering and printing, Figure 59-3. In printing, wood grain is rolled onto the particle board surface. This is similar to the newspaper-printing process. Several ink colors and grain textures make printed particle board look like wood. Disadvantages of particle board include heaviness, weakness and unattractiveness.

Figure 59-3
These drawers are made of particle board. The sides are printed, and the fronts are veneered.

PARTICLE BOARD CONSTRUCTION

Manufacturing particle board takes many steps, Figure 59-4. The first step is the production of *wood furnish.* Furnish is made from small logs and wood shavings supplied by manufacturing plants. A large machine called a *hog* grinds

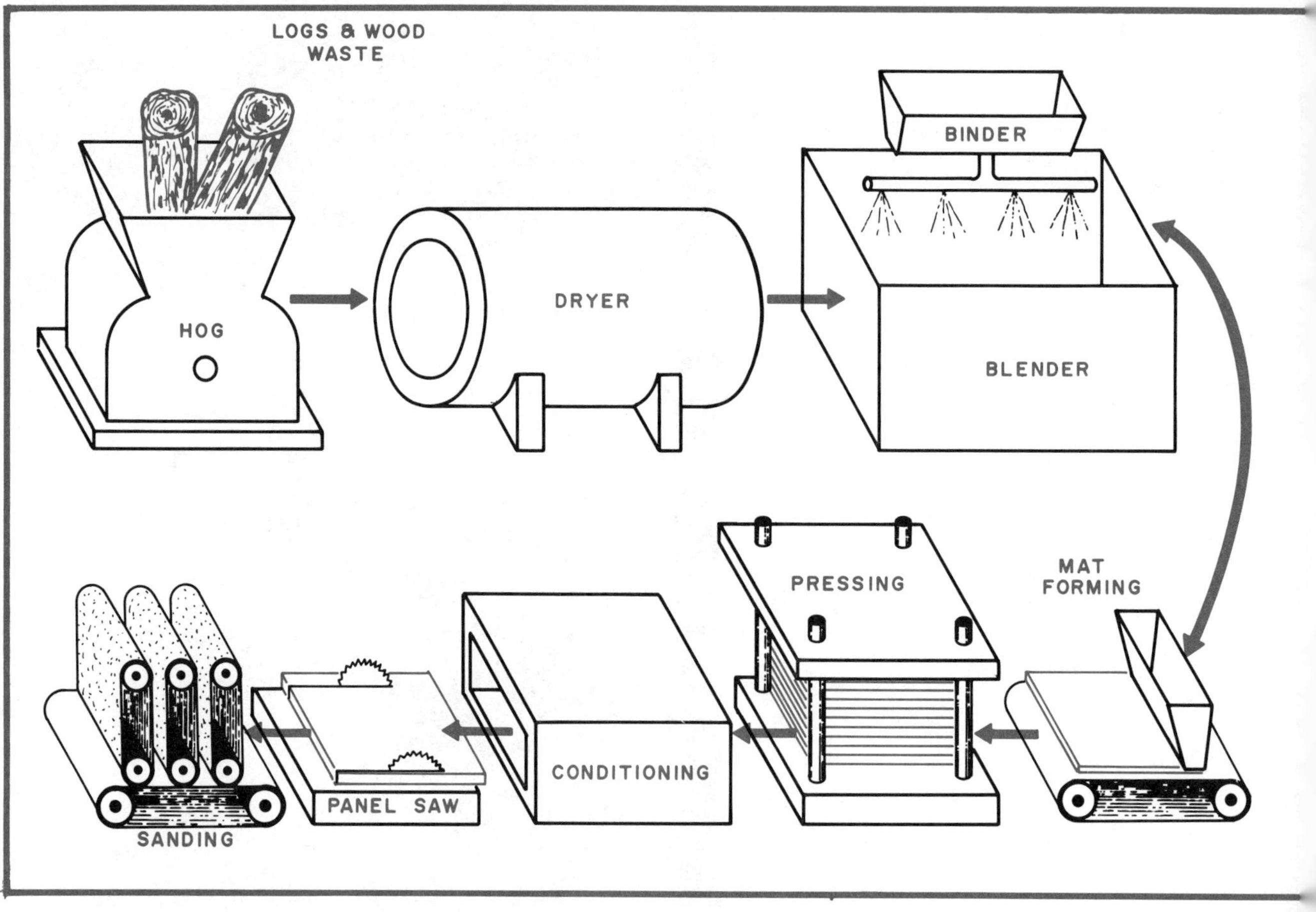

Figure 59-4
The steps in the production of particle board.

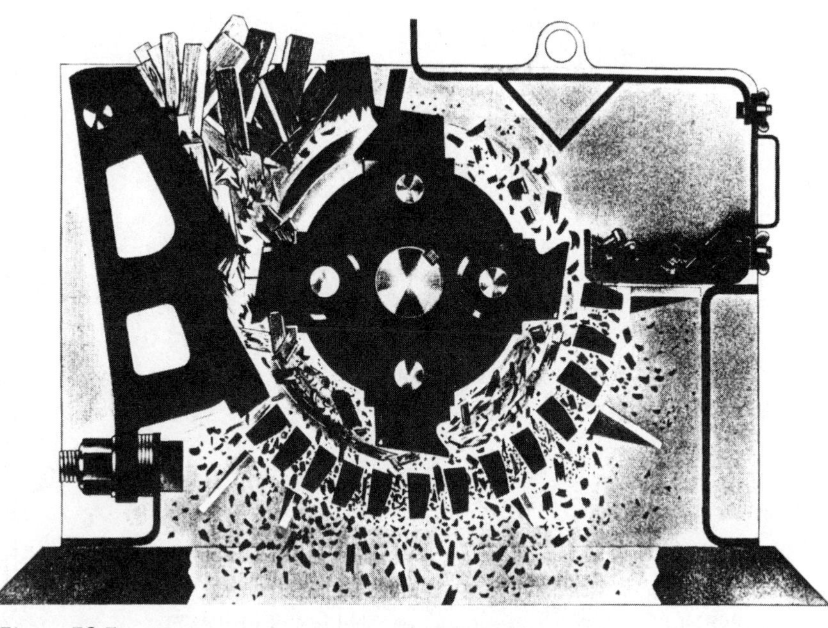

Figure 59-5
A hog grinds wood into furnish. The head chops up the raw material. (Williams Patent Crusher and Pulverizer Company)

TYPE	1 Particle board made with urea-formaldehyde, for interior use.			2 Particle board made with phenolic resin, for interior and exterior use.	
DENSITY	High Density 50 lbs/cu ft and over A	Medium Density 37 to 50 lbs/cu ft B	Low Density 37 lbs/cu ft and under C	High Density 50 lbs/cu ft and over A	Medium Density 37 to 50 lbs/cu ft B

Figure 59-6
Particle board is combined into several different grades.

the raw material into particles, Figure 59-5. The small pieces of wood are grouped by size. Water and a synthetic resin binder are added to the particles. The mixture is placed on a metal conveyor and cut to rough lengths. These thick mats of wood chips and binder are placed in a large, heated press. The press applies more than 1000 pounds of pressure. After pressing, the boards are sanded and cut to width and length.

PARTICLE BOARD GRADING

Particle board is made in many different grades. The grade varies by changing the size of the wood particles, adding different binders, and increasing or decreasing the density. *Density* can be defined as the weight of one cubic foot of particle board. The larger the particles in a panel, the lower the density. A large particle size also will reduce the strength and screw-holding power of the board. Urea formaldehyde is the most common binder for indoor particle board. Phenolic resin is the binder for panels to be used outdoors or in a damp environment.

There are three grades of particle board. Grade A has a high density and can be used for heavy, high-quality table tops. This grade is the strongest and most attractive when finished. Medium density, grade B, is used for common furniture parts. Medium density also is used for printed cabinet doors and sides. Entrance doors often are made of grade C, or low density. Figure 59-6 lists several possible combinations. All of these grades are approved by the National Particleboard Association, Figure 59-7.

WORKING WITH PARTICLE BOARD

Working with particle board requires a few special techniques. Because it is very abrasive to cutting tools, use carbide-tipped saw blades and router bits. Use type A-A sheet metal screws to increase holding power. Industry uses screws specially designed for particle board, Figure 59-8. Joining particle board requires special techniques. Figure 59-9 shows several joinery procedures.

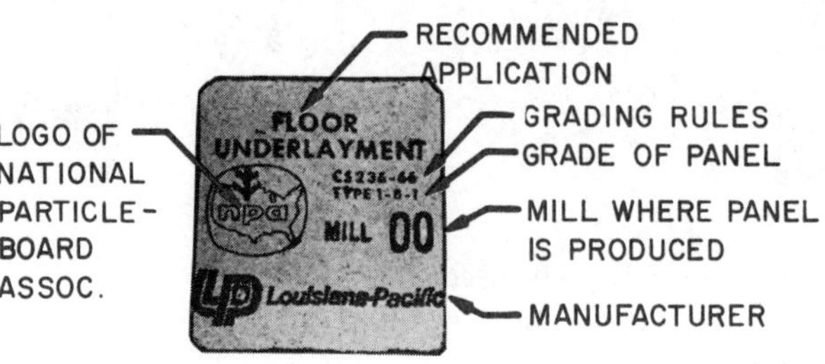

Figure 59-7
A grading stamp gives much information.

Figure 59-8
Specially designed particle board screws have a greater holding power than standard wood screws. Note the deep threads and thin heads.

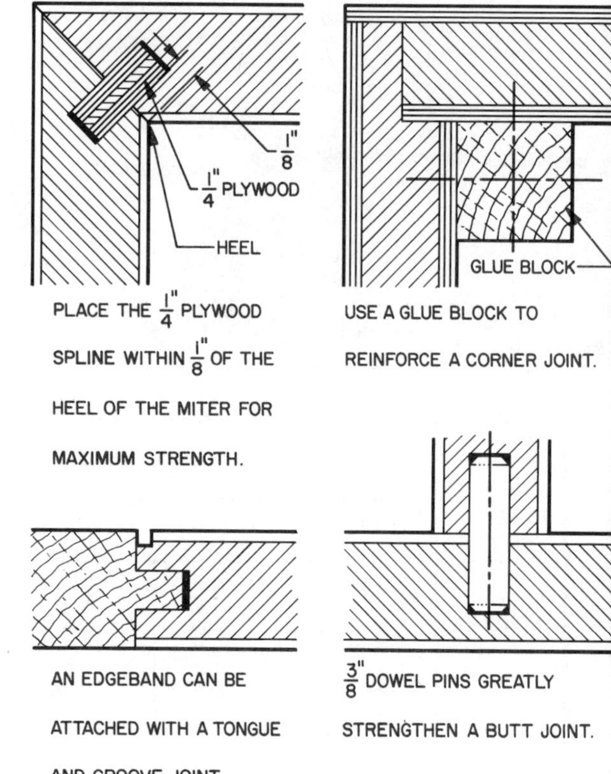

Figure 59-9
Special construction techniques used with particle board. (National Particleboard Association)

REVIEW QUESTIONS

1 What is a binder? What does it do?
2 List three advantages of particle board.
3 What is wood furnish?
4 What is density?
5 Which binder is used most for interior applications?
6 What kind of screws should you use with particle board?
7 Where should you place the spline in a miter joint?

SUGGESTED ACTIVITIES

1 Visit a lumberyard. What sizes and grades of particle board does it have?
2 Visit a furniture store. How many uses of particle board can you find?

UNIT

60

Hardboard

Objectives

After studying this unit you should be able to:

1. Identify major advantages of hardboard.
2. Describe the manufacturing process for hardboard.
3. Name the grades of hardboard.

Technical Terms

Lignin
Defiberized
Standard grade
Tempered grade
Service grade
Screened back
Pegboard

Figure 60-1
The construction industry uses hardboard as underlayment for floors.

Hardboard is another building material that provides a smooth, jointless panel. If you look closely at hardboard you will see a dark brown panel consisting of tiny wood fibers held together by *lignin.* Lignin is a naturally occurring adhesive found in all raw wood. No plastic binder is added.

Applications of hardboard vary. The construction industry uses the most hardboard as house siding, floor underlayment and wall paneling, Figure 60-1. Hardboard also is used as backing material in furniture and cabinets, as drawer bottoms and even as tabletops, Figure 60-2.

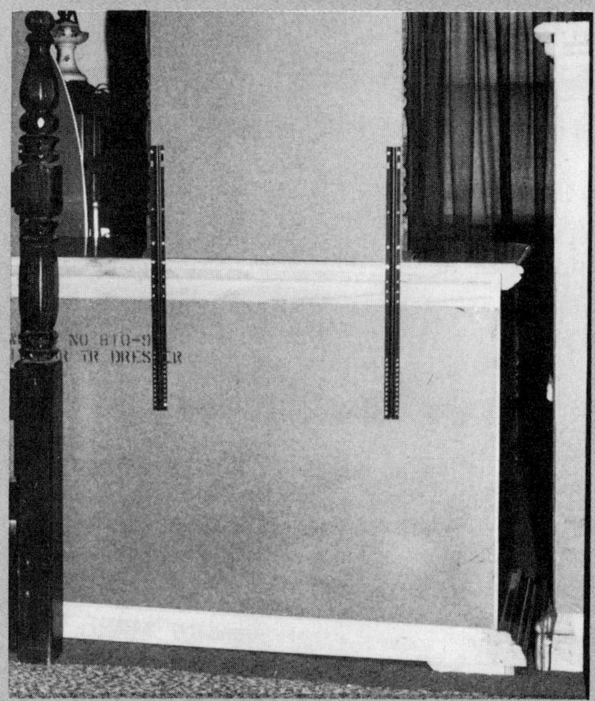

Figure 60-2
Because it is strong, hardboard serves as backing material for furniture.

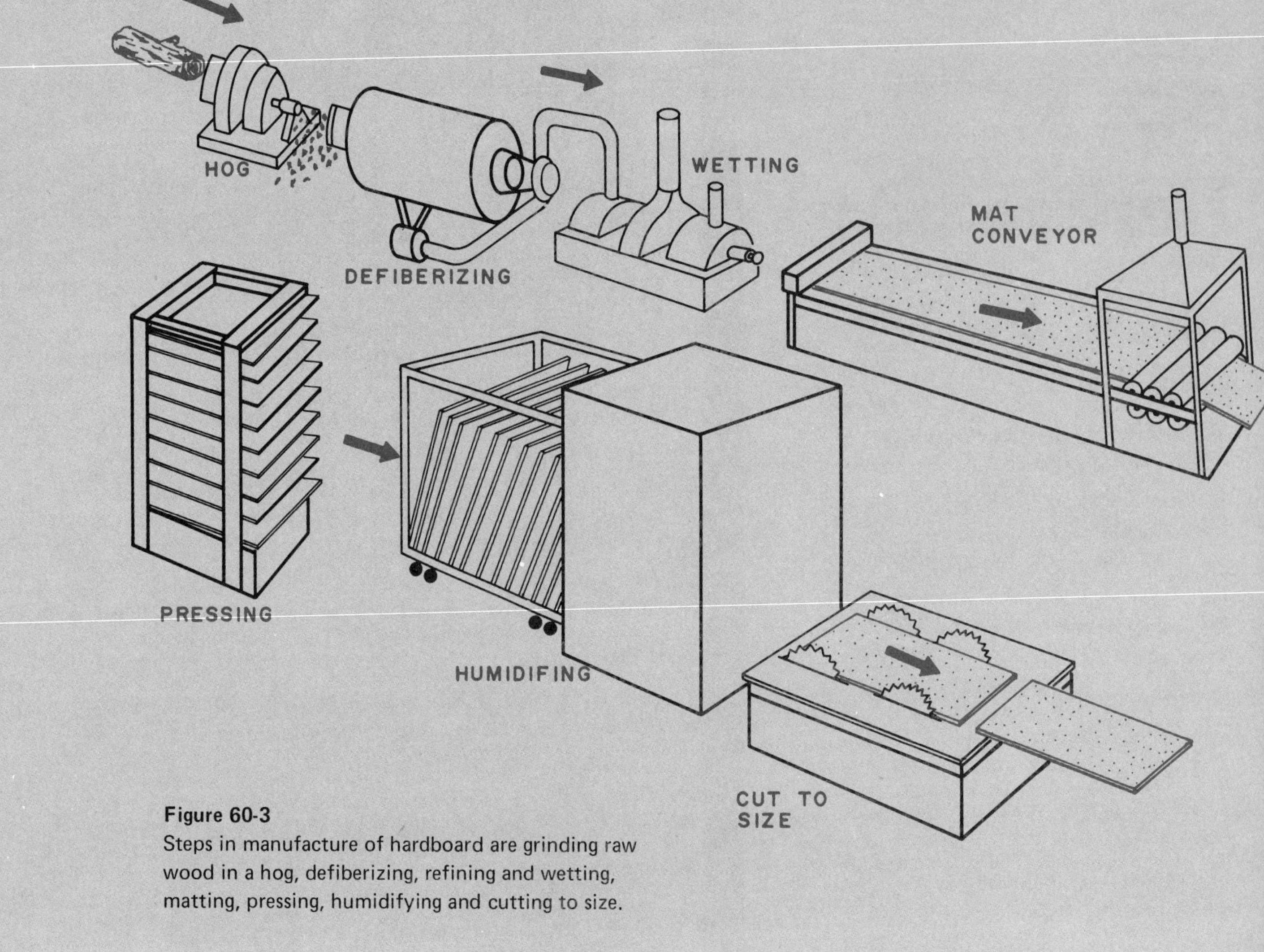

Figure 60-3
Steps in manufacture of hardboard are grinding raw wood in a hog, defiberizing, refining and wetting, matting, pressing, humidifying and cutting to size.

Hardboard has many advantages. It is priced reasonably. Its smooth hard surface resists denting and scratching. Because it has no grain pattern, hardboard is equally strong in any direction.

HARDBOARD CONSTRUCTION

A great deal of equipment is used to manufacture hardboard. The first step is grinding all raw wood in a hog, Figure 60-3. A hog grinds the material into chunks less than 1" (25 mm) in diameter. Depending on the hardboard manufacturer, the small pieces of wood are reduced further in size, or *defiberized,* by either one of two processes. One way, the explosion process, uses compressed air to blast the material into fine fibers. The other process uses fine abrasive wheels to grind the stock into fibers.

These fibers are then formed into a continuous mat. The mat of wood fibers is cut to rough lengths and are loaded into a hot press. When the press closes, the sheets bake at a very high temperature. This baking action dries all of the moisture from the panels. So that the sheets will not warp once removed from the press, they are placed in a humidity chamber to put moisture back into the hardboard. The product then is trimmed to a finished, standard size.

HARDBOARD GRADING

There are three grades of hardboard–Standard, Tempered and Service. Used primarily for making cabinets and furniture, *Standard grade* is produced in the greatest quantity. *Tempered grade* is the stiffest, hardest and most resistant to water and abrasion of all the grades. Added chemicals give this grade superior strength. Because of this high quality, builders often use tempered hardboard in exterior construction. The weakest and least water resistant grade is *Service*. Builders choose Service hardboard for interior applications where minimum weight is needed, such as for wall paneling.

All grades of hardboard come in either one or two smooth sides. A panel with one smooth side and a textured back is called a *screened back*, Figure 60-4. Hardboard also is available as *pegboard*—a board with series of holes uniformly spaced over the entire sheet. Storage hooks usually hang from the holes.

Like other wooden panels, hardboard is sold by the square foot. It is readily available in sheets 4′ x 8′ and in thicknesses of 1/8″, 3/10″ and 1/4″. For special applications, thicknesses are available from 1/16″ to 2″, widths from 2′ to 5′ and lengths from 4′ to 16′.

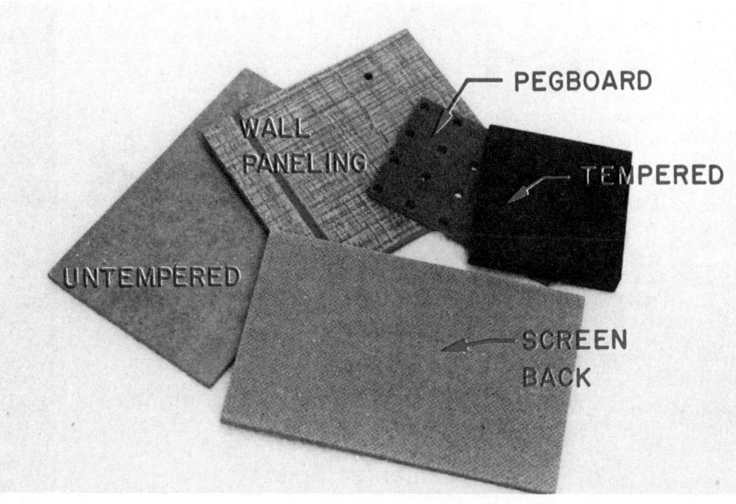

Figure 60-4
Hardboard comes in several forms.

WORKING WITH HARDBOARD

Hardboard is versatile and can be worked with common woodworking tools. It is recommended, however, that you use carbide-tipped cutting tools, especially when shaping the tempered grade, Figure 60-5. Hardboard works quite well to form a smooth, continuous, curved surface. Use a tempered grade for most curves. If you wet a standard grade, you can bend the panel over a heated form to a very sharp radius.

Figure 60-5
Use carbide-tipped tools to shape tempered hardboard.

REVIEW QUESTIONS

1. What holds the wood fibers together in hardboard?
2. List three advantages of hardboard.
3. Which two processes are used to break up wood chips into wood fibers?
4. What are the three grades of hardboard?
5. What is pegboard used for?

SUGGESTED ACTIVITIES

1. Visit your local lumberyard and see what sizes and grades of hardboard it sells.
2. Look around your school and see if you can find any applications of hardboard.

UNIT

61

Curved Wood Members

Objectives

After studying this unit you should be able to:

1 List the major methods of producing curved wood members.
2 Construct a simple laminate mold and produce a product.

Technical Terms

Anhydrous ammonia gas
Retort
Spring back
Fire-hose technique
Holding board

There are many curved members used in making wood products. Products that have curved members include furniture and sporting goods, Figure 61-1. Wood often is selected to make curved members because it is easy to form, is quite strong and, once finished, is very attractive.

You can produce curved members in many ways. Some techniques require specialized equipment and produce a very strong product. Other techniques use common woodworking equipment and produce pieces that have adequate strength for most applications.

BAND SAWING

Often school woodworking shops use a band saw to make curved members, Figure 61-2. Using a band saw requires a large piece of stock. Much of the stock is wasted. A pattern is cut using freehand techniques. The grain does not run parallel to the curved edges of the finished piece. Some people would find this objectionable. If the part has a sharp radius it will break easily.

SAW KERFS

You can use the saw kerf method to make a simple curve. A radial arm saw works best to make the closely spaced kerfs, Figure 61-3. Raise the blade so that only 1/16″ to 1/8″ (2 to 3 mm) of material will be left uncut on the bottom sur-

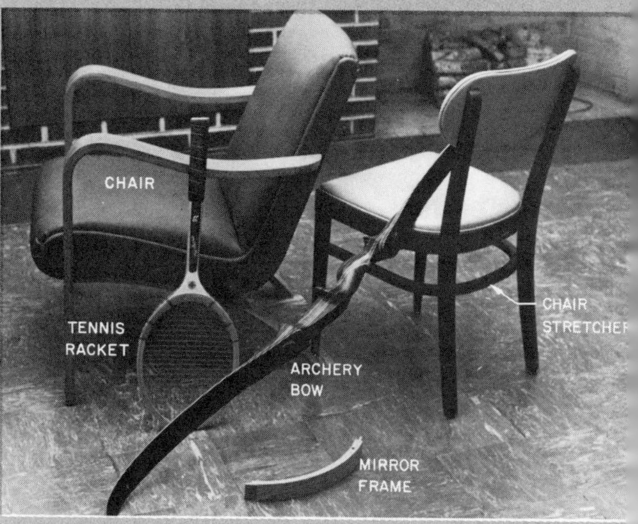

Figure 61-1
Examples of curved wood members.

Figure 61-2
You can use a band saw to cut a curved piece quickly.

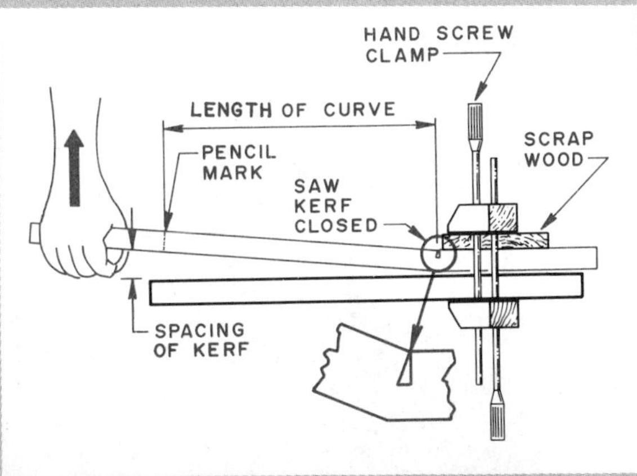

Figure 61-4
A way to determine the spacing between saw kerfs.

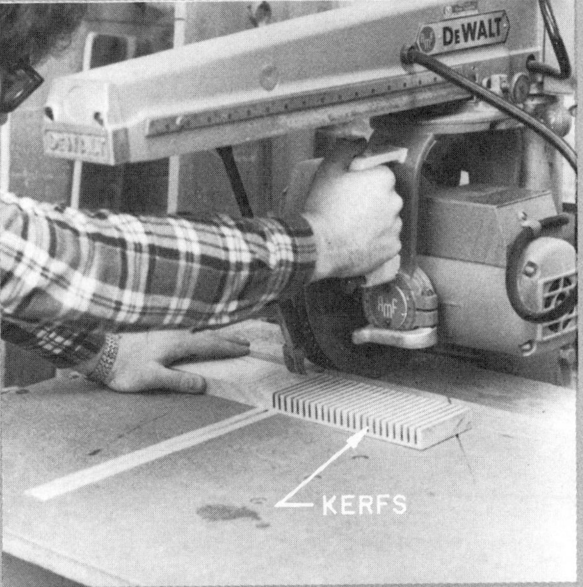

Figure 61-3
Multiple saw kerfs allow a thick board to bend into a curve.

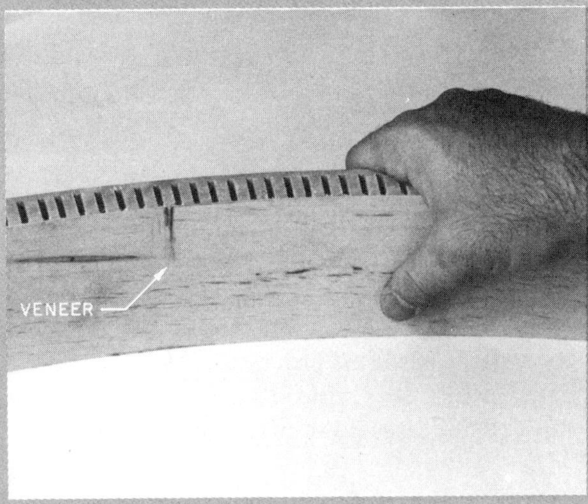

Figure 61-5
Glue a piece of veneer on the kerfed side of the curved member to reinforce the piece.

face of the board. Lay out the length of the curve on the stock. You can determine the distance between the kerfs in this way. First, make one cut on the first layout line. Next, clamp this end to a bench top, Figure 61-4. Then lift the opposite end of the stock until the top of the saw kerf closes. The distance between the bottom surface of the stock at the end of the curve and the bench top will equal the correct space between kerfs. Often a strip of veneer is glued with contact cement to the back (kerfed) side of the curved piece after it is bent into shape. The veneer reinforces the kerfed side and keeps the curved piece in its bent shape, Figure 61-5.

CHEMICAL BENDING

Another method of making curves is with chemical bending. Wood is placed in a special pressure chamber and soaked with *anhydrous ammonia gas*. The gas softens the hydrogen bonds between the wood and lignin. Lignin is the natural adhesive material that holds individual wood cells together. When the wood becomes soft and pliable, the gas is vented into a large container of water. After the wood is removed from the pressure chamber, it can be bent into shape, Figure 61-6. Wood normally is hand-held in the desired position until the ammonia has evaporated. Because the fumes are dangerous, the process must take place in a well-ventilated

Figure 61-6
An ammonia bending chamber softens the wood.

Figure 61-7
A steam retort steams and softens wood for bending.

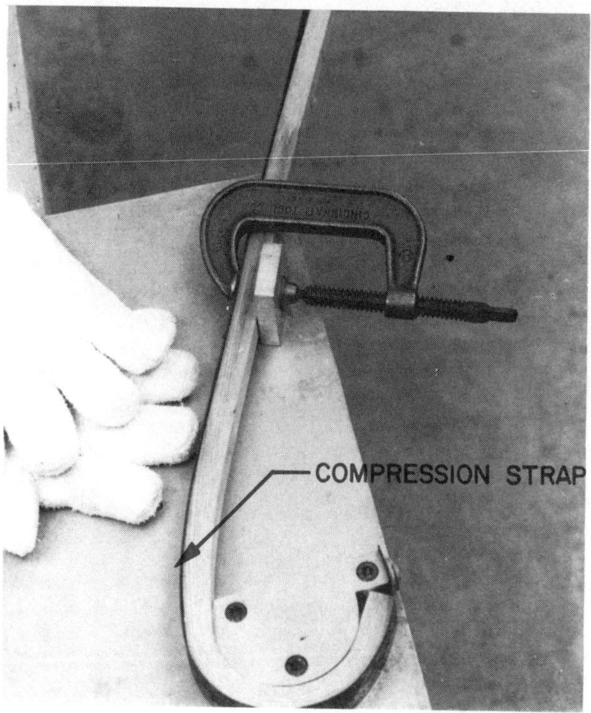

Figure 61-8
The steam-softened piece of stock is bent around a mold and clamped until dry.

area. You must wear asbestos gloves and other protective gear. This process should be used only under direct supervision. Because of the danger and expense, it is not a practical process.

STEAM BENDING

Industry usually uses steam bending to make furniture parts. Some schools also are equipped to steam wood. As with chemical bending, steam bending requires a pressure chamber. A chamber for steaming is called a *retort*, Figure 61-7. First, place the wood to be bent in the retort. Allow the steam to enter the chamber as quickly as possible. Steam softens the wood fibers and makes them easy to bend. Generally, you then bend the steamed wood around a mold. You must clamp the bent wood to the mold until it dries, Figure 61-8. Because wood fibers have a tendency to break out on the outside of curves, a metal compression strap is necessary. This metal scrap is kept stretched against the outside of the stock.

All steamed pieces have a tendency to return to their original shape. This tendency is called *spring back*. To compensate for this, make the mold to a smaller radius than that specified for the finished product. If you secure the wood to a metal mold and cook it until dry, there will be little or no spring back.

Certain woods steam bend more easily than others. Hackberry, white oak and walnut are considered the best. Even with these woods, which conform to a mold easily, some will fail occasionally because of irregular grain characteristics. Always cut and steam more straight grain pieces than you actually need. Ideally, wood to be steam bent is air dried to 20 percent moisture content before steaming.

Figure 61-9
A grand piano is a graceful musical instrument. The curved shape is produced by wood laminate.

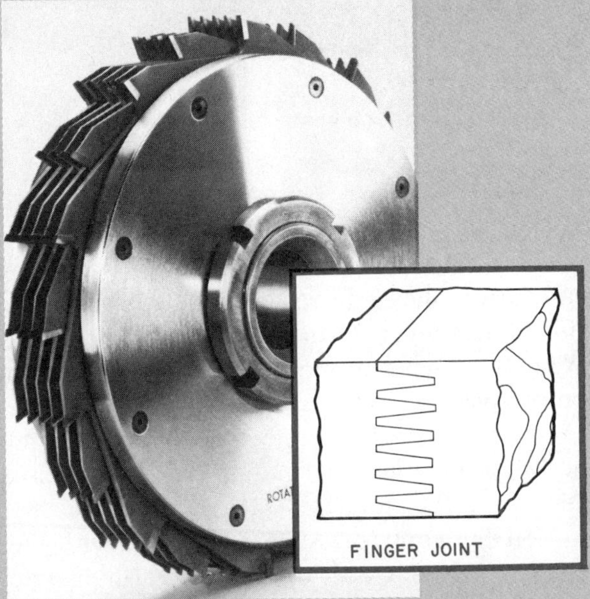

Figure 61-10
Finger joints are cut with a large cutter. The joints are glued together. (North American Products Corp.)

Figure 61-11
Finger joints form these beams that span 250 feet. (American Institute of Timber Construction)

WOOD LAMINATION

Wood lamination is the process of gluing several thin layers of wood together to form a bent shape. The grain of each layer is laid in the same direction. A grand piano with its laminated body not only achieves strength but also great beauty, Figure 61-9.

Quality materials are becoming more difficult to find. Laminates make good use of wood that contains large knots and other major defects. These defects can be cut out and the shorter boards reconnected with finger joints, Figure 61-10. This actually makes a stronger and better-looking product. Laminated products can be very large because of finger jointing unlimited lengths of wood, Figure 61-11. Once the mold is constructed, labor costs are low. Products can be made quickly.

When you make a laminate, use the thickest possible stock for each layer. The thinner the individual layers, the more clamping pressure is required. In addition, thinner stock warps more easily. To determine the thickest piece that can be used, bend a sample strip to the smallest curve of the finished product, Figure 61-12. If the strip of wood does not break, try thicker pieces until you determine the maximum thickness.

Most laminated products are made from a mold. In industrial plants the molds usually are made of metal and are heavy, Figure 61-13. For school shops, and other places where production is limited, molds can be made of wood, Figure 61-14.

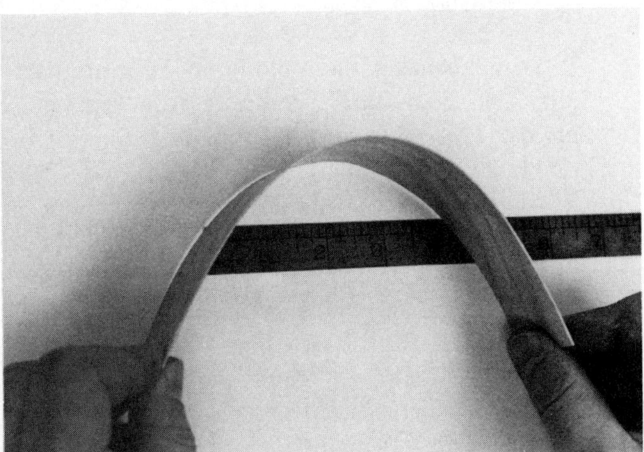

Figure 61-12
Bend a sample piece to the desired finished radius.

Figure 61-13
A commercial hydraulic laminating press with a large chair mold. (L & L Machinery)

Figure 61-14
Molds for limited production are made with lighter construction techniques.

You can make the mold in one or more parts. Most products are produced from two-piece molds. This style of mold usually is made from one large piece of material.

At least two alignment pins or dowels are necessary to help match the mold halves. Bore the holes on a drill press before cutting the mold, Figure 61-15. Lay out the curve of the laminated product on the stock. Carefully cut out the mold with a band saw. Many woodworkers cover the mating surfaces of the mold with a thin layer of cork. The soft material allows the mold to give around any high spots produced in the band sawing operation.

Figure 61-15
Use a drill press to bore the holes for the alignment pins.

Once the mold is constructed, cut the laminates to the same width and length as the mating surfaces of the mold. Apply an adhesive to one side of each layer. Then stack the layers together. Wrap wax paper around the laminate sandwich before placing it in the mold. Tape the two ends of the wax paper, Figure 61-16, to prevent adhesive from squeezing out of the laminate and sticking to the mold.

You can apply pressure to the mold with glue clamps, a bench vise or a special clamping device. Glue clamps and bench vises work well on small, simple molds, Figure 61-17.

Large complicated curves can be laminated with the *fire-hose technique*, Figure 61-18. Place a fire hose that has been sealed at both ends between the mold halves and the laminate. Then bolt together the mold halves with steel straps. Inflate the fire hose with air to apply pressure on the layers of wood. This technique works well because equal pressure is applied along the entire length of the laminate.

The mold should remain closed until the adhesive has cured completely. Taking the laminate out without fastening it to a straight *holding board* may cause the product to warp, Figure 61-19. The length of time it is taped to the holding board will vary with the product. The thicker the layers of veneer and the more there are of them, the longer it will take the adhesive to cure. To finish the product, cut the shape with a saw. Fill and hand sand rough edges.

Figure 61-16
Wrap the laminate sandwich with wax paper.

Figure 61-17
Apply pressure with glue clamps or a bench vise.

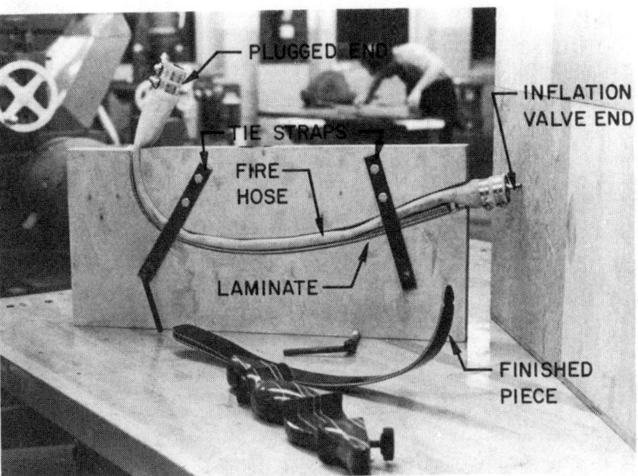

Figure 61-18
You can inflate a fire hose to apply pressure equally along the total length of the laminate.

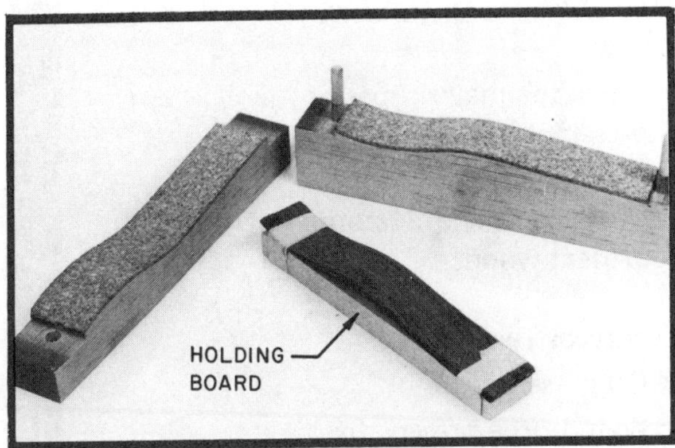

Figure 61-19
After removing the wax paper, tape the laminate to a holding board.

REVIEW QUESTIONS

1 How is a curved piece produced using a band saw?
2 What do you use to make multiple saw kerfs?
3 How does anhydrous ammonia gas soften the wood?
4 What is the name of the chamber used for steam bending?
5 Define spring back.
6 Name one application of wood lamination.
7 How are short pieces of wood joined end to end for a lamination?
8 Why should the laminate sandwich be wrapped in wax paper?
9 Sketch a fire hose laminate mold.

SUGGESTED ACTIVITIES

1 Visit a hardware store and see if any shovel handles or other wooden parts have curved parts. How do you think they were made?
2 Design a salad fork and spoon mold. Laminate a set of these utensils. Cut and sand them to finished shape.

UNIT

62

Wood Preservatives and Fire Retardants

Objectives

After studying this unit you should be able to:

1 Name the major types of preservatives and methods of application.

2 Describe how fire retardants protect wood.

Technical Terms

Oil preservatives

Waterborne preservatives

Nonpressure process

Pressure process

Full-cell process

Fire retardant

Wood is a beautiful and strong material with thousands of possible uses. Still more uses become possible when wood is injected with chemicals. Treated stock has properties that other building materials do not have.

Wood preservatives and fire retardants are two kinds of chemicals used to treat wood. Preservatives make the material poisonous to insects and fungus that destroy wood. If untreated wood is kept outdoors, it will be damaged, Figure 62-1. Fire retardants slow the burning rate of wood greatly, Figure 62-2. Both of these chemicals increase the market potential of wood. Treated

Figure 62-1
Insects and fungus attack untreated wood. (Western Wood Products Association)

Figure 62-2
This wooden beam, treated with fire retardant, lost less than 10 percent of its strength during a severe warehouse fire. (American Institute of Timber Construction)

wood is used in ways that would be too expensive for the use of steel, plastic and other building materials.

Figure 62-4
The stairs in the top photograph were treated with penta. The stairs in the bottom photograph were not treated and have decayed. (U.S. Forest Products Association)

PRESERVATIVES

Preservatives must meet certain requirements to be effective. The cost of the chemicals must be relatively low. Chemicals must penetrate the wood easily. Preservatives must not evaporate easily. If the wood cannot retain the preservative, it eventually will be destroyed. Finally, preservatives must not be harmful to people and animals.

There are two main classes of preservatives. Two chemicals, creosote and pentachlorophenol, are *oil preservatives.* Creosote changes the wood to a dark, oily color. This oily preservative easily rubs off and should not be painted. Railroad ties are impregnated with creosote, Figure 62-3. Pentachlorophenol, commonly called penta, is used on millwork such as windows and steps, Figure 62-4. Penta-treated wood is paintable.

Waterborne preservatives change the wood surface to a green color. Some people find this color objectionable and will not use a transparent finish on treated wood. The treated wood must be kiln-dried to reduce shrinkage. This chemical is not harmful to people. Waterborne preservatives often are used for wooden patios and all-weather foundations, Figure 62-5.

Figure 62-3
Railroad ties treated with creosote have a dark, oily appearance.

Figure 62-5
Wooden patios are frequently treated with waterborne preservatives. (Southern Forest Products Association)

Applying Preservatives

Preservatives are injected into wood by either a nonpressure or a pressure process. Brushing and dipping are examples of the *nonpressure process*. Home owners and carpenters often brush the preservative on the wood, Figure 62-6. Using a large paint brush, flood the surface with as much preservative as possible. Dipping is more efficient than brushing. Submerge preshaped boards in a large tank for two to three minutes, Figure 62-7. Apply penta by either of these techniques. You must have good ventilation and protective clothing when preserving wood. Some people are very sensitive to the chemicals and should not come in contact with preservatives.

The *pressure process* requires elaborate equipment, Figure 62-8. Most pressure treatments use the *full-cell process*, Figure 62-9. Stock is loaded in a large cylinder and a vacuum is applied. After all the air has been removed, the preservative is pumped into the cylinder. Pressure is applied to force the chemical into the wood. Wood treated with the full-cell process retains the most preservative. Creosotes and waterborne preservatives are injected using this technique.

Figure 62-7
Dipping wooden parts and allowing them to soak in the preservative provides good protection.

Figure 62-6
Brushing provides limited protection.

Figure 62-8
Wood is pressure-treated in a large chamber. (Koppers Incorporated)

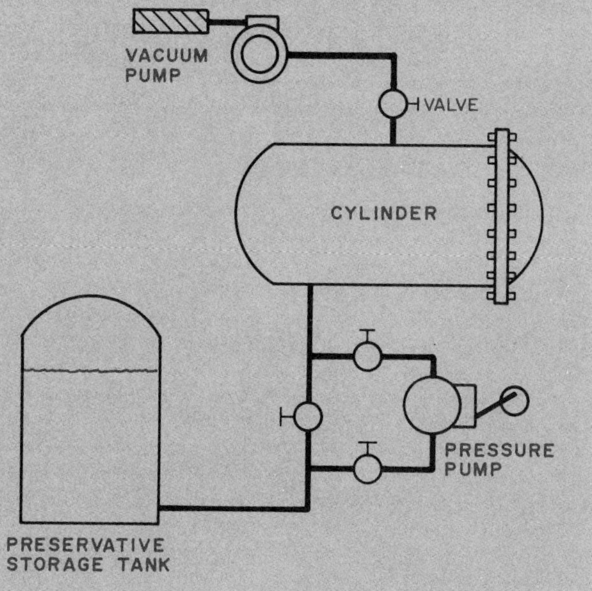

Figure 62-9
Equipment required in the full-cell process.

Figure 62-10
Although the steel beams have given way, the wooden beam has retained its strength. (American Institute of Timber Construction)

FIRE RETARDANTS

As raw wood burns, it forms a natural insulative layer that protects the inner core of the board, Figure 62-10. *Fire retardants* are injected into the wood to reduce the tendency to burn, Figure 62-11. Stock treated with these chemicals is used in wall paneling, doors and other exposed wooden parts of buildings.

Fire retardants are applied to wood by the full-cell process. Treated products must be less than 2″ (51 mm) thick. This chemical is abrasive to cutting tools such as shaper knives and saw blades. If possible, preshape stock to within 1/16″ (2 mm) of the size of the final shape. After the wood has been injected with retardant and kiln dried, shape the stock to final size. Removing only a small amount of the treated wood will prolong the life of your cutting tools.

Figure 62-11
The retardant-treated sample on the right does not burn when exposed to the same type of heat as the untreated sample on the left.

REVIEW QUESTIONS

1 List three characteristics of an effective preservative.
2 What are the two main classes of preservatives?
3 Name two oil preservatives.
4 Which type of preservative should be used if people come in close contact with the treated wood?
5 What are two nonpressure techniques?
6 Describe the full-cell process.
7 Which process is used to apply fire retardants?
8 Why should you preshape stock before applying fire retardants?

SUGGESTED ACTIVITIES

1 Look at a telephone post or railroad tie. What chemical was used to preserve the wood?
2 Ask members of your fire department what they know about fire retardants.

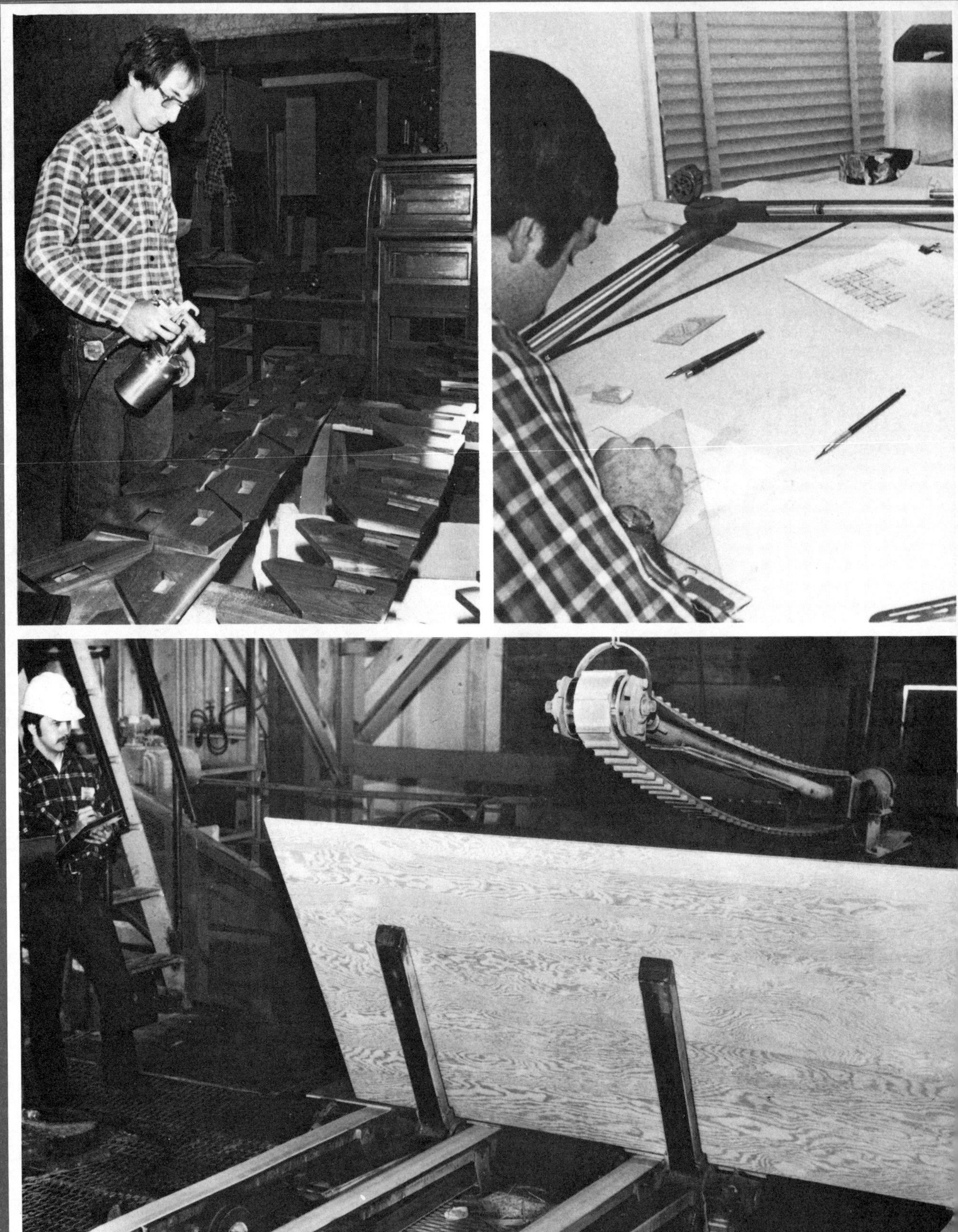

SECTION

9

Mass Production

63
Mass-production Manufacturing

Most furniture, doors and other wood products are made by mass production. When you understand how mass production works, you can buy wood products more intelligently.

Section 9, Mass Production, will show you how to set up a mass-production line. This section discusses in detail how products are manufactured. It might even give you some help in choosing a career.

UNIT

63

Mass-production Manufacturing

Objectives

After studying this unit you should be able to:

1 Explain the advantages of custom and mass-produced products.
2 List types of business ownership.
3 Describe the procedure for production planning.
4 Name the duties of major departments in a corporation.

Technical Terms

Custom production
Mass production
Specialization of labor
Interchangeable parts
Line organization
Line and staff organization
Stockholder
Mock-up
Tolerance
Prototype
Jig
Fixture
Quality control
Time and motion study

Mass production forms the base of our country's industry. Most of our products are produced in this way. More than 80 percent of all high school graduates will work directly or indirectly in mass production. It is not enough for a woodworker to know only how to perform operations on machines and with tools. An employee's position in a company is vital to the company's success. A knowledgeable worker not only helps the business but also advances and gets promotions.

CUSTOM PRODUCTION

Custom production is the oldest method of making products. In custom production, one skilled craftsperson makes the entire product, Figure 63-1. A cabinetmaker, for example, plans and makes scale drawings. The person then constructs the product, assembling one piece at a time. He or she even may apply the finish.

The cabinetmaker probably never makes two products exactly alike. The major advantage of custom production is that, in most cases, each product is unique. Usually, a craftsperson constructs a piece using high-quality material with technical expertise.

Custom production also has disadvantages. If workers used only custom-production techniques, they could not make all the goods we need. Custom-made products require many hours of labor. Thus, the products are expensive. Workers using mass-production techniques can make many goods in a relatively short time. Thus, the average consumer can afford to buy them.

MASS PRODUCTION

Mass production began in 1798. In that year Eli Whitney contracted with the United States Congress to produce 10,000 muskets in two years. Producing so many products in such a short time had never been tried before. Whitney had two ideas. One was about the *specialization of labor.* A worker would be trained to become efficient at one job. The other idea was of *interchangeable parts.* All the pieces for the muskets would be exactly alike. Thus, any piece could fit into any of the 10,000 muskets. Specialization of labor and interchangeable parts are still the basis of mass production.

Figure 63-1
In custom production, generally one person does all the work. First, the craftsperson makes drawings, *top left.* Next, the craftsperson assembles the product using custom techniques, *top right,* and then applies the finish, *bottom.*

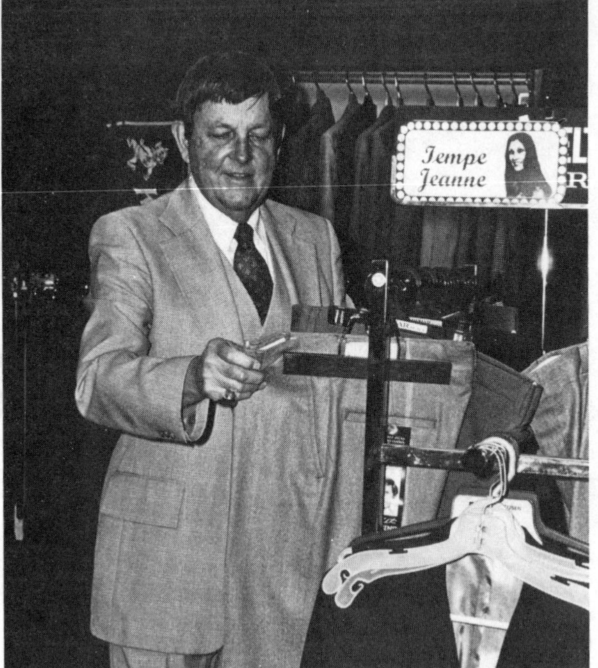

Figure 63-2
Many retail stores are sole proprietorships.

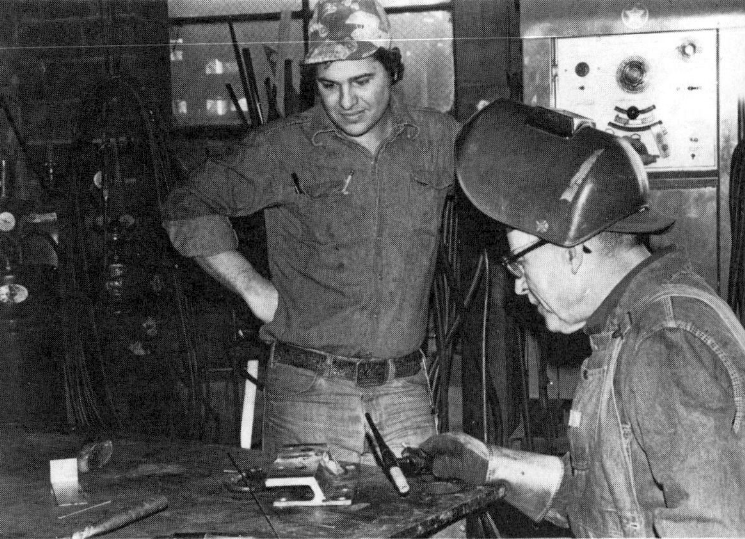

Figure 63-3
When a business is owned by two persons, it is a partnership.

TYPES OF BUSINESS ORGANIZATION

A business is organized into one of several forms. A business is a sole proprietorship, a partnership or a corporation. Which form a business takes has much to do with how it is run. Each type of organization has advantages and disadvantages.

Sole Proprietorship

Sole proprietorship is the oldest form of business organization. A sole proprietorship means that one person owns and controls the company, Figure 63-2. The owner alone is responsible for the company and receives all profits. This form of business is the simplest to run. Many small retail businesses are sole proprietorships.

The major disadvantages of this form are that the owner is liable for any debts and must raise all capital, or money, needed for business growth. Alone, the owner may not be able to get funds.

Partnership

A partnership is owned by two or more people, Figure 63-3. Generally, the partners equally share profits and debts. In some partnerships one person puts up most of the money while another person manages and supervises. The person who provides most of the money is called a silent partner. Because more than one person shares in responsibilities and decision making, a partnership often is preferred over a sole proprietorship. Disagreements, however, can end the business abruptly.

Corporation

Most businesses located in the United States are corporations. A corporation is organized in one of two ways–*line organization* or *line and staff organization,* Figure 63-4. The structure of both forms is called the chain of command. The chain of command is the path or route of company authority. In line organization each person is responsible to the person directly above. The military still uses line organization.

Businesses use line and staff organization more often. Throughout the chain of command, decisions are made in all levels and information is exchanged freely. Executives make major decisions. Staff persons assist executives.

Unlike a sole proprietorship or a partnership, a corporation is not privately owned. It is owned by *stockholders.* These are individuals who buy a percentage of the business, or shares, Figure 63-5. Stockholders usually are not active in company management and do not work for the company. Sometimes they are members of the board of directors. The board meets at least once a year and makes major decisions, Figure 63-6. The directors decide on such things as the purchase of new equipment, the expansion of a manufacturing plant or the addition of a new product line.

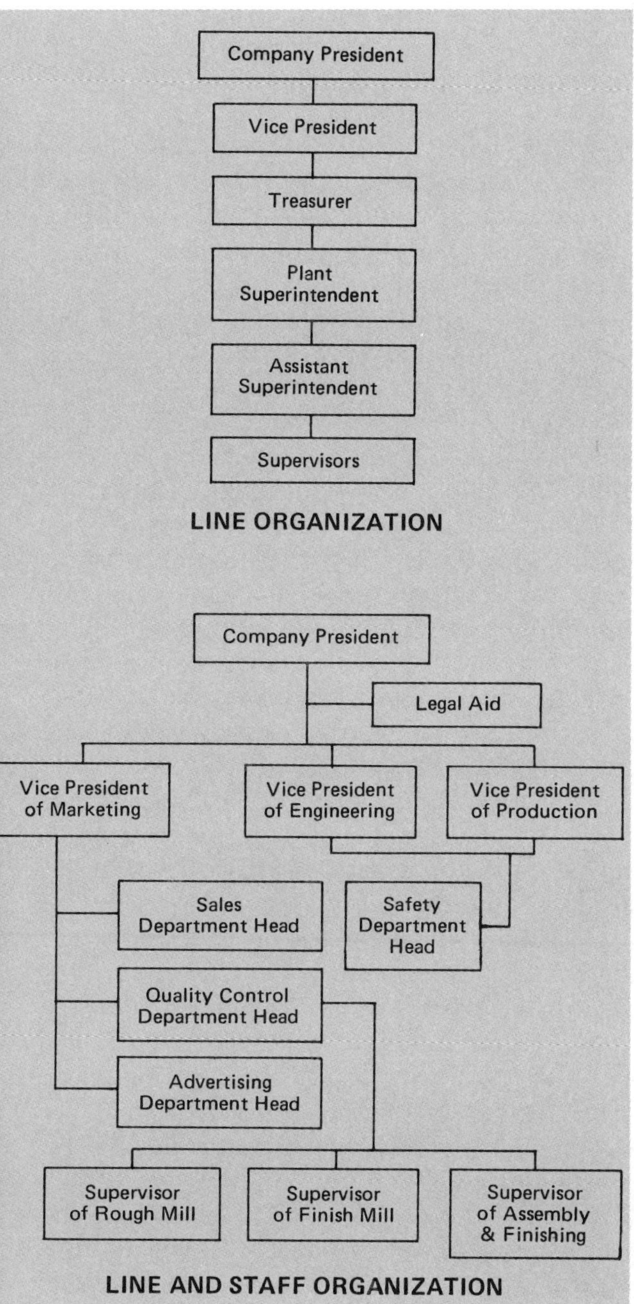

Figure 63-4
Corporations have either a line or a line and staff organization.

A corporation has many advantages. Capital and financing are easier to get. By selling shares of stock, the corporation can raise initial money. Also, many tax advantages are offered to a corporation. Because the corporation is considered an "artificial person," owners or stockholders are not legally responsible for debts.

INCORPORATED UNDER THE LAWS OF

No 7891 State of Kansas Shares -1-

Woodcraft Incorporated
Pittsburg, Kansas

Authorized Capital Stock $150,000.00
3,000 Shares Common Par Value $50.00 each

This Certifies that Lyle Duane Griffiths is the owner of ---- One ---- Shares of each of the Capital Stock of Woodcraft Incorporated transferable only on the books of the Corporation by the holder hereof in person or by Attorney upon surrender of this Certificate properly endorsed.

In Witness Whereof, the said Corporation has caused this Certificate to be signed by its duly authorized officers and to be sealed with the Seal of the Corporation this 10th day of May A.D. 1981

SHARES $50.00 EACH

Figure 63-5
A stock share is a piece of paper that tells how much of a corporation an individual owns.

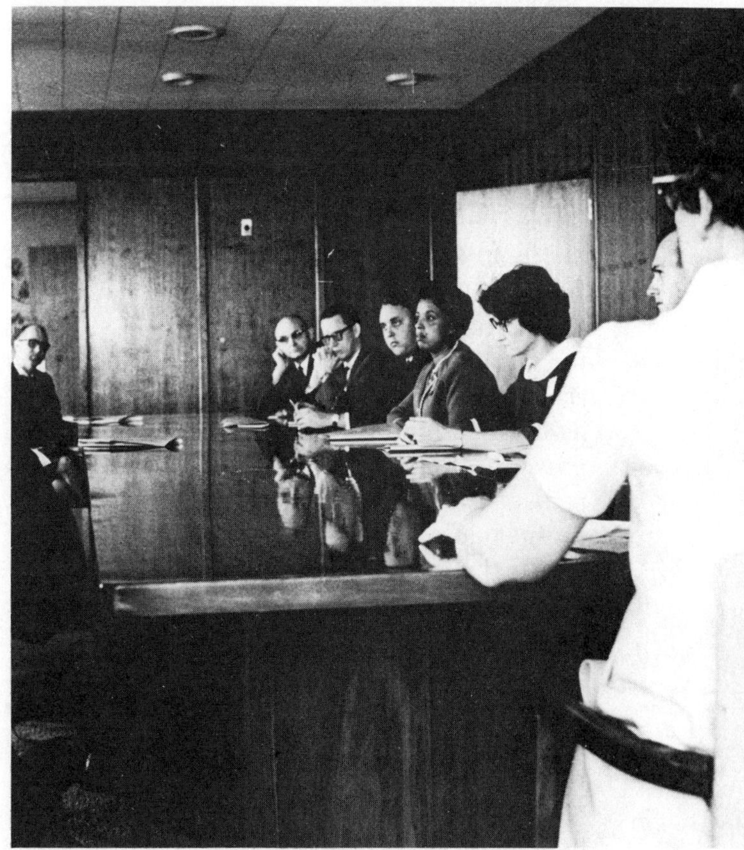

Figure 63-6
The board of directors governs a corporation. (Southern Furniture Manufacturers Association)

Figure 63-7
Persons working in the finance department should have an accounting background.

PLANNING A PRODUCT

Planning a product is probably the most important phase of mass production. Without thorough planning, the manufacturing process will fail. Planning includes all items related to finance, engineering, quality control and marketing. Often, these planning concerns become corporation departments, each supervised by a vice president.

Department of Finance

A finance department takes care of all company money matters. People in a finance department have received training in bookkeeping or accounting, Figure 63-7. They also understand manufacturing.

The finance department coordinates the sale of stock. Careful records are kept. Also, at the end of each year, the department calculates company profits and losses. The department reports the results to the board of directors. The board then decides how much profit goes to the stockholders and how much is kept to expand and improve the company. The more shares of stock a person owns, the larger the percentage of the profits that person will get.

The finance department also does a cost analysis. A cost analysis is a study you do to set the selling price for each product. In a cost analysis, you should figure total costs for raw materials, utilities, labor, machinery, rent, packaging and transportation. Add together all these costs and then divide by the number of products to be manufactured. You have now determined the unit price. The manufacturer sells new products to a wholesaler at this price. The wholesaler then stores and distributes the products to retailers. Consumers or direct customers buy the products in retail stores. Customers and consumers pay a higher price than the wholesalers because of transportation costs and wages.

Engineering Department

An engineering department has many responsibilities. It does initial product development and planning, keeps manufacturing records and improves existing products.

Research and development is an important area in the engineering department. People in this area evaluate design, material properties and production techniques. Product design comes from detailed sketches and mock-ups. A *mock-up* is a model that shows how a finished product will look. Mock-ups are made from simple materials, such as molding clay, foamed plastics, softwood and cardboard, Figure 63-8. Generally, the model does not have working parts.

Drafters use mock-ups to make final production drawings, Figure 63-9. Often, the drawings are not truly final. Further changes or revisions may be made before production.

While drawing, drafters keep tolerances in mind. A *tolerance* is the amount that a piece can vary from the design size and still be used in the product. Interchangeable parts not accurately made cannot be assembled. A tolerance is expressed as plus or minus a fractional part of an inch or a millimeter. For example, a tolerance of ± 1/16″ (± 2 mm) on a 2″ (51 mm) part will allow the part to be made 2-1/16″ (53 mm) or 1-15/16″ (49 mm). The closer the tolerances, the more difficult and expensive the part will be to manufacture.

Usually, a *prototype* is the final check on planning. A prototype is an actual, working product, Figure 63-10. Using custom techniques, a skilled worker carefully shapes and assembles each piece of the prototype.

The engineering department also designs and constructs special holding devices that locate and hold the part being shaped, position the cutting tool, or a combination of both. A *jig* is a holding device that supports a part being made and guides a cutting tool, Figure 63-11. A *fixture* usually clamps on a machine and locates work, Figure 63-12. It does not guide a cutting tool. Jigs and fixtures enable parts that are exactly alike to be mass produced.

Figure 63-8
This mock-up is made of cardboard.

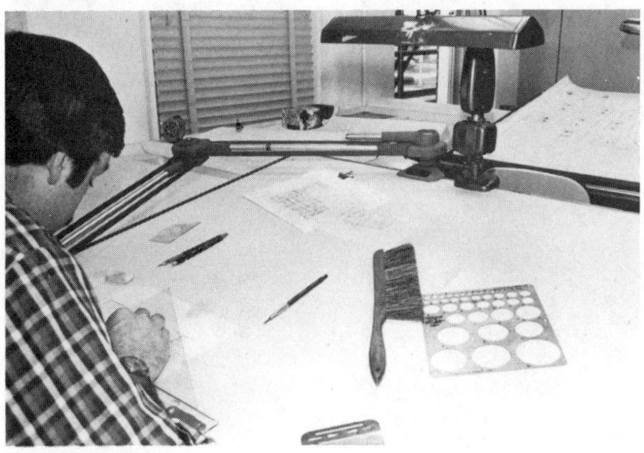

Figure 63-9
Production drawings are used in manufacturing the product.

Figure 63-11
This jig holds the part and guides the drill bit.

Figure 63-12
This fixture accurately locates the board so that the hole is bored in the exact place.

Figure 63-10
A prototype is a full-size product made with custom methods.

Jigs and fixtures must ensure safety. They must keep your hands a safe distance from the cutting tool, Figure 63-13. Keep in mind these other points about jigs and fixtures:

1. Make sure jigs and fixtures are made of durable materials. They will hold up during continuous use if made of such materials as hardwood, plywood and metal, Figure 63-14.
2. Hold pieces securely to keep them from loosening during shaping. You can use special fixture clamps, Figure 63-15.
3. Clean jigs and fixtures of waste and chips. Chips should fall away easily from the cutting area. Rabbeted fences and holes bored into the baseboard provide a place for chips, Figure 63-16. Thus, chips will not get in your way when you position the material. You can use pressurized air to blow away excess scraps.
4. Keep holding devices simple. You should be able to load and unload parts quickly.

Figure 63-13
This fixture keeps the operator's hands away from the cutting tool.

Figure 63-15
You must hold stock securely in place while it is being shaped.

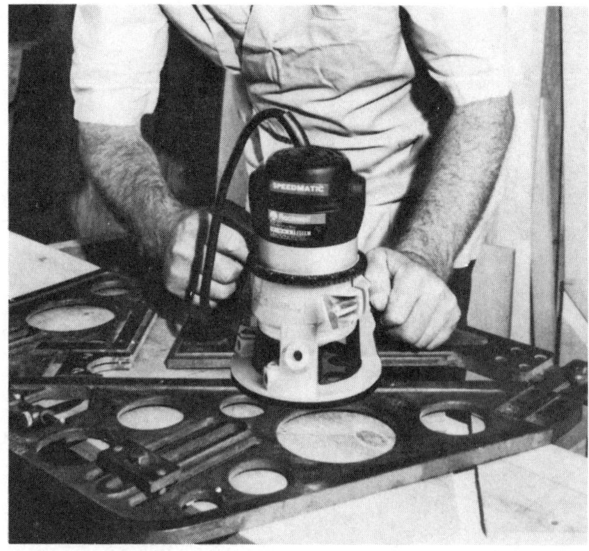

Figure 63-14
This metal jig will last a long time. (Rockwell International)

Figure 63-16
Rabbeted fences and holes in the baseboard provide a place for chips. Pressurized air blows away any excess.

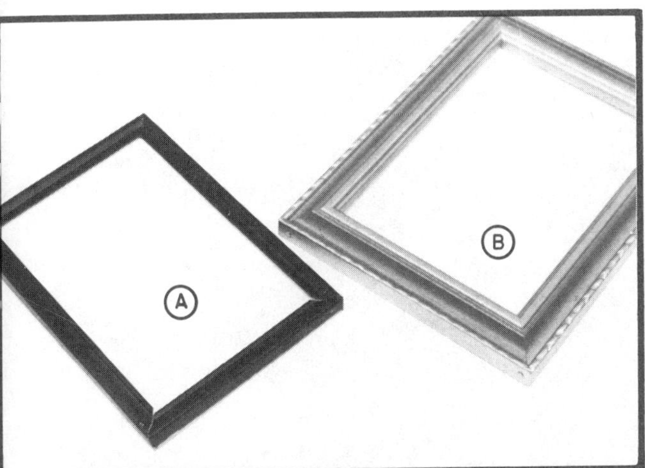

Figure 63-17
Frame *A* has poor fitting joints and a bad finish. Frame *B* is more desirable because of its high quality.

Figure 63-18
A quality control inspector checks to see that standards are maintained. (Roseburg Lumber Corporation)

Quality Control Department

When you purchase a product, you judge its quality. A well-constructed product of good materials has high quality. A sloppily constructed product of inferior materials has poor quality. Most often, consumers buy the better-made product, Figure 63-17.

A department in charge of *quality control* establishes quality guidelines that are approved by company executives. Members of the department and executives keep in mind that high quality standards cause higher production costs. For example, fine sanding requires a greater number of steps and more labor. The additional labor to perform this task costs more money.

After quality standards are established, they must be enforced. Quality control stations are set up at key points on the production line. Inspectors check pieces as they are manufactured to see that quality is maintained, Figure 63-18.

An inspector often uses a go-no-go gauge, Figure 63-19. This type of gauge has two slots, or holes, that are different sizes. A part is first inserted into the hole that is too large for it, or the go hole. If it fits, it is then tried in the smaller, or no-go, hole. Parts that do not fit into the no-go hole meet quality standards and are used in a product. Any parts that fit into the no-go hole are rejected and not used, Figure 63-20.

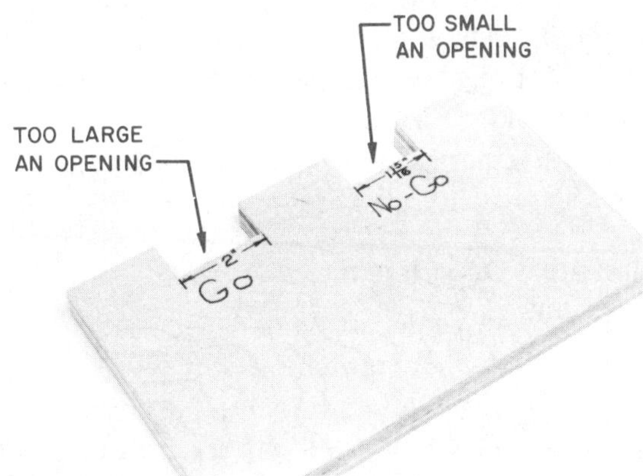

Figure 63-19
A go-no-go gauge checks the size of a piece.

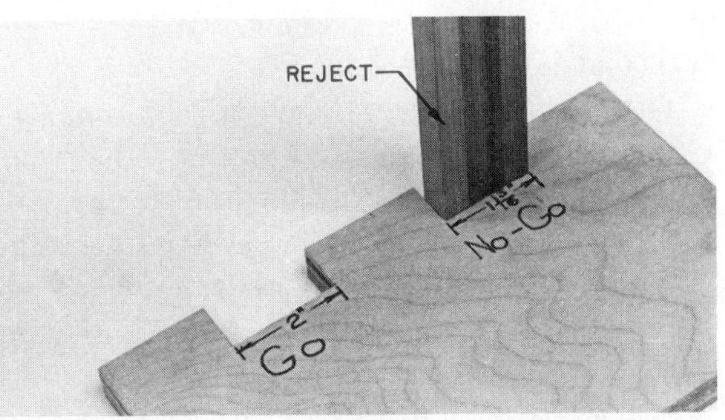

Figure 63-20
If a part fits into the no-go opening, it is a reject.

Figure 63-21
A remake being fixed with a new arm. (Southern Furniture Manufacturers Association)

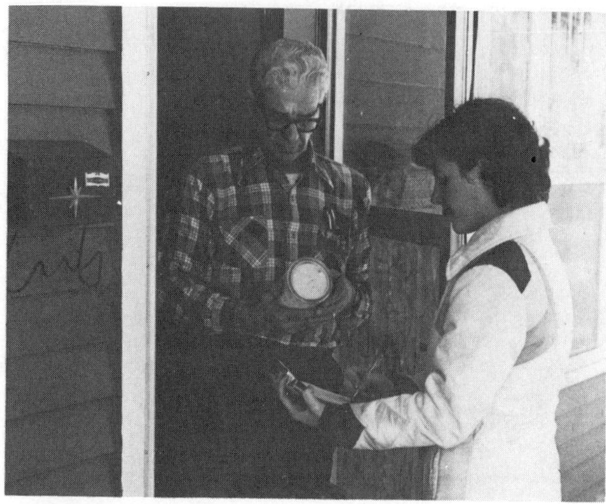

Figure 63-22
Questionnaires establish whether or not there is a demand for a product.

Rejects are those pieces that are poorly sanded and the incorrect size and have low-quality materials. They have been assembled and finished sloppily. Sometimes workers can correct the mistake, Figure 63-21. Thus, a reject becomes a remake. Some of the material and labor costs already invested are saved.

Marketing Department

A marketing department develops sales campaigns and conducts market surveys. A market survey should be conducted before any commitments are made or products are manufactured. A market survey has questionnaires that determine whether the product is needed, how much competition already exists and if the estimated price is realistic and attractive, Figure 63-22. The results of the survey are compiled and affect any decisions to be made.

Then the department designs a sales campaign. The campaign includes packaging, advertising and sales control. Packaging protects the item from damage and makes it appealing to the customer, Figure 63-23. Advertising acquaints the consumer with the product in a pleasing manner. Sales control predicts the number of products needed weekly, monthly or yearly. Sales control also coordinates the number of products manufactured with the demand for the product.

Figure 63-23
Packaging should be attractive and protect its contents.

Production Department

One important task of a production department is coordination between raw materials, machinery and worker training. The lack of any of the three will stop manufacturing.

A flow chart coordinates activities on a production line. A flow chart is a map that shows where machines are located and how the materials and parts move throughout a plant, Figure 63-24. The chart also shows where material is stored and where quality control stations are

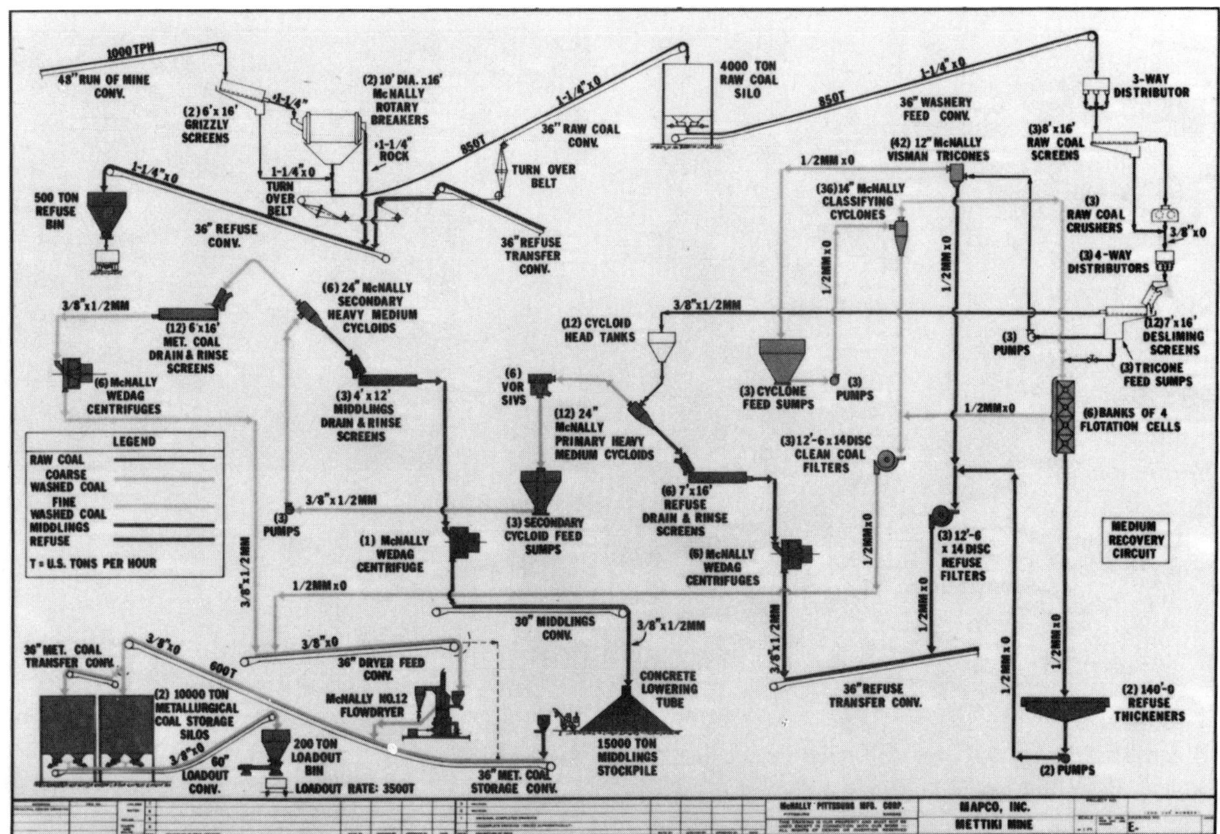

Figure 63-24
A flow chart shows how a product is produced. (McNally Pittsburg Manufacturing Corporation)

located. Each machine and location where a particular task is performed is called a work station. The chart shows the stations as symbols. A scale drawing of the manufacturing line can be used with the flow of materials drawn between the work stations. This type of flow chart shows any machines that are being overworked or any bottlenecks in moving materials.

PRODUCTION LINE

After the completion of planning and the arrival of raw materials, supervisors set up a production line. First, they tool up the machines. Ideally, they put machines into areas that best suit the flow of materials. Supervisors mount special cutting tools and jigs and fixtures to the machines. All the while, supervisors follow information on flow charts and production drawings, Figure 63-25.

Figure 63-25
A supervisor uses the flow chart and drawings to set up equipment.

Figure 63-26
A conveyor line helps to move products throughout a plant. (Dri-Quick)

Next, production workers learn how to run the machines. Workers learn some jobs quickly with little training. Other jobs require highly skilled workers.

Production begins with the first cut. If the departments have planned well, the parts will move smoothly down the line. Workers always should have raw materials and something to do. Often, a conveyor line delivers and takes away materials or finished goods, Figure 63-26.

After the production line runs smoothly, supervisors conduct *time and motion studies,* Figure 63-27. A supervisor studies a worker doing a job. The supervisor records how much time the worker takes. Through the study, the supervisor tries to improve operations for the worker so that tasks are done faster. The study also can determine a worker's efficiency and salary.

Safety inspectors oversee a production run. Accidents can cause painful injuries and cost a lot of money. An employee on sick leave can create manufacturing problems. A safety inspector sees that OSHA rules are followed and that no potential hazards exist. OSHA is the Occupational Safety and Health Act of the federal government. It establishes guidelines for safe working conditions.

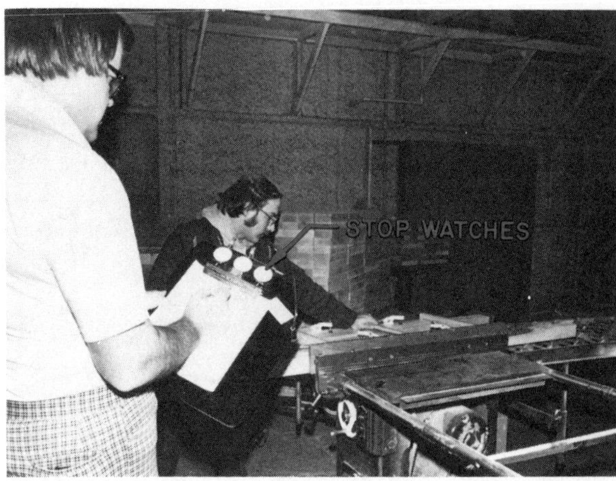

Figure 63-27
Stop watches time how long a worker takes to do a job.

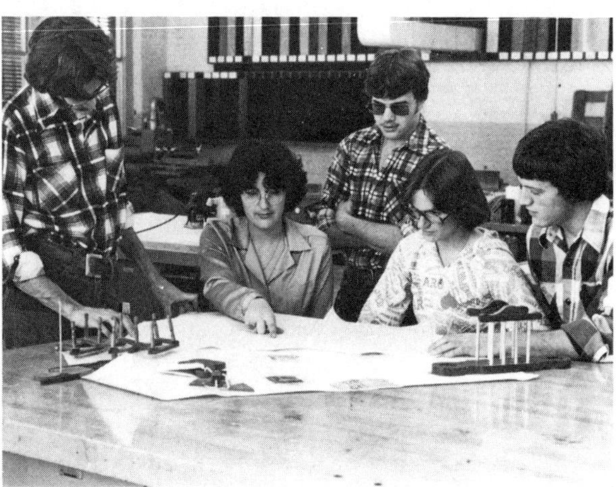

Figure 63-28
Students can learn about industry by developing and producing their own products.

Although each worker should maintain good quality, the quality control inspector checks to see that quality standards are kept. If quality falls below acceptable levels, sales will decrease. The company will lose money. Employees may be laid off.

LEARNING ABOUT MASS PRODUCTION

Understanding mass production will help you understand the industrial world. A woodworking shop is an excellent place to learn about mass production, Figure 63-28.

If your efforts are successful, your products could be sold at a profit. Your initial stockholders would be paid their dividends. Participating students also could share in the success. You will have done a good job and witnessed industry in action.

Your class can be organized like a company. You should follow the same form of organization outlined in this unit. Select a president and treasurer. Classmates who are creative may do well in research and development jobs. Everyone must participate in the production run.

REVIEW QUESTIONS

1 List two advantages and two disadvantages of custom-produced products.
2 What is specialization of labor?
3 Define *sole proprietorship, partnership* and *corporation.*
4 Which two forms of organization does a corporation have? Which is the more common?
5 Who owns a corporation?
6 Name two responsibilities of the finance department.
7 Name two responsibilities of the engineering department.
8 What is the difference between a mock-up and a prototype?
9 What is the difference between a jig and a fixture?
10 The quality control department has what responsibility?
11 A flow chart helps to show what about a manufacturing plant?
12 How are time and motion studies used in setting up a production line?

SUGGESTED ACTIVITIES

1 Visit a manufacturing plant. How many departments can you identify? Which type of jigs and fixtures do they use?
2 Organize your class into a company. Assign a position to everyone in the class. Mass produce a product.

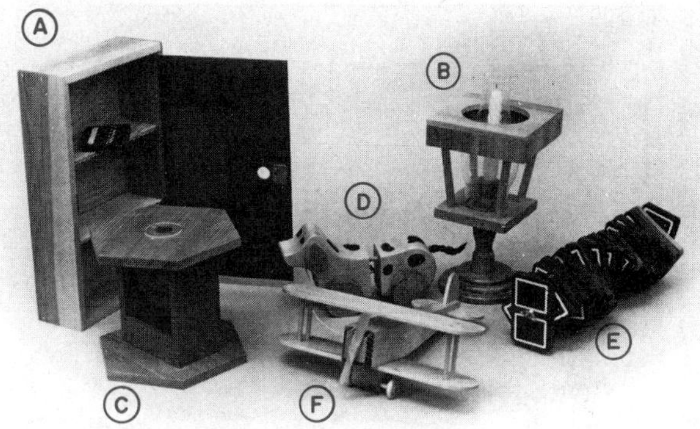

Possible mass-production projects: (A) tape cassette case, (B) decorative hurricane light, (C) bird feeder, (D) pull toy, (E) giant domino set, (F) wooden airplane.

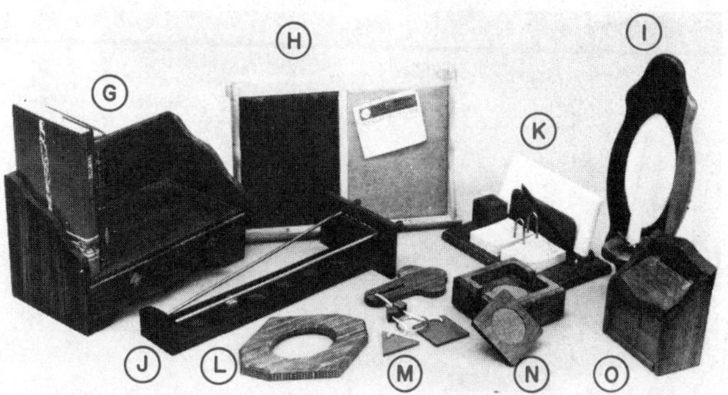

You also may want to make a (G) bookshelf, (H) message center, (I) wall sconce, (J) ball game, (K) desk set, (L) laminated picture frame, (M) string game, (N) coaster set, (O) recipe card box.

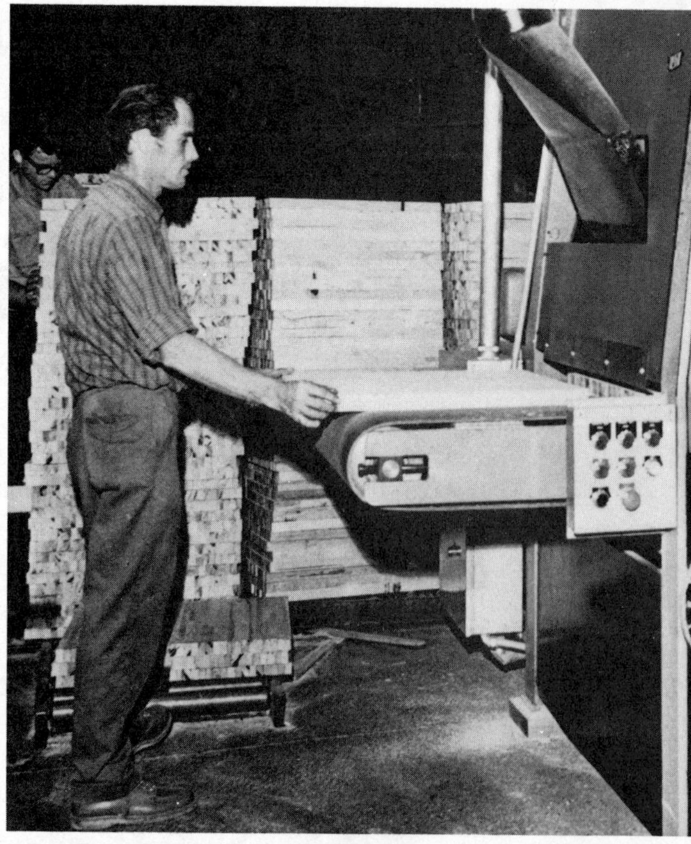

64
Careers

SECTION

10

Careers in Woodworking

As you study woodworking tools, processes and materials, you may find that certain topics interest you while others don't. This can help you choose a career in which you will be happy and successful. It also can help you find out which areas to avoid.

The woods industry includes a wide range of career activities. Those who appreciate fine skills and like working with their hands will find many opportunities. There are many related careers as well—designers, manufacturing managers and business people, for example.

It is the purpose of Section 10, Careers in Woodworking, to present information on a wide range of careers in the woods industry.

UNIT

64

Careers

Objectives

After studying this unit you should be able to:

1 Describe the steps necessary to succeed in industry.

2 Find detailed information on careers in the woods industry.

3 Explain the types of careers in the lumber industry.

4 Discuss the duties of various machine operators.

5 Describe the duties of assembly and finishing workers.

6 Explain the opportunities in careers related to the woods industry, such as design and sales.

7 Discuss career opportunities in construction.

8 Find information on professional careers in the woods industry.

The choice of an occupation determines a person's income and often where he or she lives. An occupation provides the money for food, housing, recreation and other necessities. It also provides a great deal of personal satisfaction.

When thinking of career possibilities in the woods industry, you should consider the current as well as the future demand for persons in each area. Consult *The Occupational Outlook Handbook* published by the U.S. Department of Labor, Bureau of Labor Statistics, Washington, D.C. You can purchase it from the Superintendent of Documents, U.S. Government Printing Office, Washington, D.C. 20402. Most school guidance counselors and libraries will have copies available.

Also, watch for changes in technology. Increased development of new products and tools opens new jobs and changes the nature of others. For example, the development of new glues and adhesives has expanded the uses for wood products in construction.

Consider your own interests and abilities. Choose an area of work that you enjoy and feel competent doing. If you enjoy your high school woodworking classes and perform well in them, then maybe a career in the woods industry is for you. You might want to take courses in plastics and metals to prepare for a job in furniture and cabinet construction, which uses materials other than wood. For a supervisory position, you would need a knowledge of drafting.

STEPS TO SUCCESS

Here are some essential points that will help you succeed on the job:

1. Be on time. For efficiency all employees should be present at the plant when work starts.
2. Come to work every day unless you are ill. Frequent absences leave vital operations undone.
3. Dress properly for the work to be performed. Wear regulation safety equipment as well as clothes that provide freedom of movement and comfort.
4. Get along with your fellow workers and the supervisory staff. One of the biggest causes of failure on the job is an inability to work well with others in the plant.

5. Look for ways to do your job better. Suggestions are appreciated and often rewarded.
6. Do your share of the work. Do not expect other people to make up for your lack of production.
7. Produce quality work. Craftsmanship is essential to the production of quality products.

CAREERS IN THE LUMBER INDUSTRY

In addition to growing and harvesting trees, the lumber industry manufactures lumber for construction and for remanufacturing into other products. (See Unit 1 for more information.)

Loggers harvest trees. Most loggers have no special training when they get their first job and must learn at the job site. Employers prefer high school graduates. The work is strenuous and continues out-of-doors in both hot and cold weather. Loggers live and work away from large cities.

There are many other kinds of jobs associated with the lumber industry. *Fallers* use power-operated saws to fell trees, Figure 64-1. After the tree is down, *buckers* cut off the limbs and cut up the trunk, Figure 64-2. A *choker setter* uses cables and tractors to skid the logs out of the woods.

Planing mill workers in sawmills convert the logs into lumber. The cut logs reach the mill usually by truck. *Log scalers* measure the logs, look for defects and estimate the amount and quality of lumber in the logs. *Pond workers* sort the logs to keep all of one kind together. The *bull-chain operator* runs a conveyor that pulls logs into the sawmill. A *barker operator* runs machinery that removes the bark. A *deck worker* and a *block setter* line up the logs on carriages to be sawed. The actual sawing is controlled by the *head sawyer*, who is the most experienced worker in the mill. A *pony edger* and a *trimmer saw operator* trim the lumber. *Graders* sort the boards according to quality, then *sorters* pull and stack the graded boards.

Dry kiln operators control the operation of the kiln, Figure 64-3. A kiln is a large, building-size oven that removes moisture from the boards.

Figure 64-2
Buckers saw the branches off the felled tree and cut the trunk into proper lengths. (Western Wood Products Association)

Figure 64-1
Fallers operate chain saws to fell trees marked for harvesting. (Western Wood Products Association)

Figure 64-3
A kiln removes moisture from the wood. (U.S. Forest Products Laboratory)

Figure 64-4
A planer operator adjusts and operates the planer that dresses the rough-cut lumber. (Louisiana-Pacific Corporation)

The dried lumber is dressed to size on a planer operated by a *planer operator,* Figure 64-4.

Most mill workers learn their skills on the job. They may start as laborers and work up to the jobs mentioned above. Usually, the major part of the operation is done out-of-doors.

For more information on mill work write International Woodworkers of America, 1622 N. Lombard St., Portland, Oregon 97217.

CAREERS IN WOODWORKING

In the production of wood products, such as furniture and cabinets, there are a variety of skilled and unskilled jobs. Most machine-operator and assembly jobs require little previous experience. A high school woodworking course and some on-the-job training are excellent preparation.

Machine-operator Positions

All machine-operator jobs present a certain amount of danger because of the high-speed cutting tools. Operators constantly must be aware of these dangers and the safety precautions. Following are some of the most common machine-operator jobs.

A *cut-out operator* begins the production process. He or she examines each piece of stock and cuts the necessary lengths on the chop saw. The operator also cuts out knots and other defects to ensure quality. A cut-out operator holds a responsible position that requires quick decision making, Figure 64-5.

Power saw operators feed stock through circular saws with power-feeding attachments. They must work quickly, keeping the stock tight against the fence so it is ripped accurately, Figure 64-6.

A *tenon machine operator* uses a machine

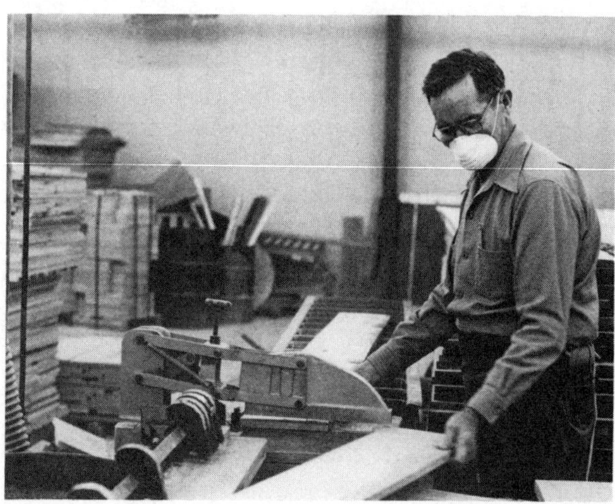

Figure 64-5
A cut-off operator cuts the wood into necessary sizes and also cuts out knots and defects. (Dawson Cabinet Company)

Figure 64-6
Power saw operators rip stock to the proper size. (Dawson Cabinet Company)

called a tenoner. It cuts tenons, notches, rabbets and grooves. The operator visually checks the parts being fed into the tenoner and rejects those with defects. The operator needs special instruction to operate the machine.

A *boring machine operator* works vertical and horizontal boring machines. No special preparation is necessary to run this machine.

A *spindle carver* operates a carving machine that has several spindles. The machine reproduces woodcarvings on furniture reproductions, Figure 64-7.

A *shaper operator* sets up and operates a wood shaper. This machine cuts grooves, rabbets, flutes and other shapes on the surface and edges of wood stock. The operator must know how to mount and line up knives, to set guides and stops on the machine and to shape work using rods and templates. These activities can be learned on the job by working with an experienced operator.

A *feeder* is a beginning position. This person places wood parts into machines that are set up and run by an experienced operator, Figure 64-8. An *off-bearer* removes stock as it is processed and stacks it to be moved to the next operation.

A *router operator* sets up, adjusts and feeds single- and multiple-spindle routers. Routers cut slots, bevels and designs in flat surfaces. The operator must be able to read drawings, set gauges and align work to the cutting devices.

A *molder operator* sets up, adjusts and operates high-speed molding machines. The molder has four cutter heads that can be set to cut into the edges of straight stock, Figure 64-9. Wood trim and moldings are examples of work from a molding machine. The operator must have considerable experience in woodworking before learning how to set up and operate a molder.

A *mortise machine operator* sets up and works on a mortiser to cut square and rectangular holes

Figure 64-7
A spindle carver uses a master pattern to carve several duplicates of the part. (Southern Furniture Manufacturers Association)

Figure 64-8
A feeder works stock into a power ripsaw. (Dawson Cabinet Company)

Figure 64-9
This molding machine quickly processes parts, using an automatic feeding device. (Mattison Manufacturing Company)

in wood parts. The operator works from instructions on a job route card. Ability to measure accurately is important. A beginner must work for some time with an experienced operator to learn the operation of this machine.

A *dovetail operator* mechanically cuts a dovetail joint in drawers and other furniture units.

A key person in wood manufacturing is the *setup specialist,* or *technician.* This person is responsible for setting up each machine to make the desired cuts or for checking the setups made by machine operators, Figure 64-10. Any setup made by an operator must be approved by the setup specialist before the job is run. This person must be thoroughly experienced on wood manufacturing machines. In addition, the person must read drawings, measure accurately and know how to adjust mechanical parts. Both a high school diploma and experience in wood manufacturing are essential for entry into this position. Some large companies prefer a college degree in an area such as wood technology.

Figure 64-10
This setup technician prepares a machine to make desired cuts so a machine operator can run it afterward. (Dawson Cabinet Company)

Figure 64-11
Furniture being assembled on an assembly-line conveyor.

A *machine room supervisor* is responsible for the total operation of all the machines. The supervisor oversees the work and helps plan production schedules. In addition, he or she is responsible for the quality of the parts and the efficiency of the workers. A supervisor must be thoroughly experienced in all areas of wood machining, safety and employee management. College graduates with majors in wood technology often fill this position.

Assembly Positions

After parts are cut to size and shape by a machine, they are assembled into the final product. Newcomers on the assembly line can learn quickly by working with an experienced worker. Normally only a few days of training are necessary. An assembly worker should know how to use common hand- and power-operated tools. Work on an assembly line must proceed quickly but carefully so the product is not damaged. Most assembly work is done on large tables or conveyors, Figure 64-11.

In wood product assembly jobs, workers begin by taking machine-cut parts from bins or storage carts and joining them together. Workers use a variety of tools such as hand- and air-operated clamps, gluing devices, air and electric drills, screwdrivers and staplers. An assembler must

Figure 64-12
To prepare a subassembly, this worker covers the joints of the frame with glue and places them together. (Dawson Cabinet Company)

Figure 64-13
An inspector checks the quality of the finished product before it is packed. (Dawson Cabinet Company)

place the parts in position, adjust the tools to their proper setting, and operate the clamps and tools, Figure 64-18. The assembler constantly looks for defective parts and discards them.

A *subassembler* joins several parts, Figure 64-12. The subassembler must see that all parts fit and are assembled according to directions.

The *subassembler helper* supplies the subassembler with wood parts and fastening devices. Sometimes this person helps hold or place parts in jigs. The helper also moves the assembled units to the next assembly station.

A *detail assembler* covers small, detail work. This includes gluing decorative overlays and installing glue blocks. The worker must be accurate and careful.

A *hardware trimmer* locates the hardware, drills the necessary holes if they were not drilled during production, and installs the hardware. A trimmer also sets locks and glass or mirrors. This work requires a variety of hand tools and some light power tools.

A key person in assembly is the *assembly setup technician.* This person sets up jigs and devices that hold the parts being joined. This is a responsible position because errors mean loss of parts. The setup technician checks alignment, proper fit and the expected dimensions of the product. The setup technician on an assembly may modify or repair a jig or holding device. He or she instructs all assemblers in their duties.

A setup technician must be able to measure accurately and to read drawings. A high school diploma plus the ability to supervise workers are essential. This position usually requires long experience in wood product manufacturing.

In any assembly operation the final product must be inspected. An *inspector* assures quality control of an assembled product. The inspection includes joints, the exposed surface, the finished dimensions and how parts, such as drawers, fit and operate, Figure 64-13. The inspector can reject products and demand their repair. He or she also can suggest changes in the assembly operation to improve quality.

After inspection the product is packed for shipment. Packing is done carefully so the product will not be damaged in shipping. Packing is an unskilled job that can be learned very quickly.

Figure 64-14
A machine sander dresses tabletops on a stroke belt sander. (Dawson Cabinet Company)

Figure 64-15
Sanding machine operators sand tabletops with an abrasive planer. (Dawson Cabinet Company)

Positions in Finishing

Finishing a wood product includes sanding, touching up minor defects, and coating with enamel, varnish or lacquer. Often parts are sanded before they are assembled.

A *machine sander* does the first sanding on external parts, Figure 64-14. This worker operates a variety of power sanders, including belt, pump, spool and flutter sanders, Figure 64-15. This person also makes a visual inspection of each part for defects.

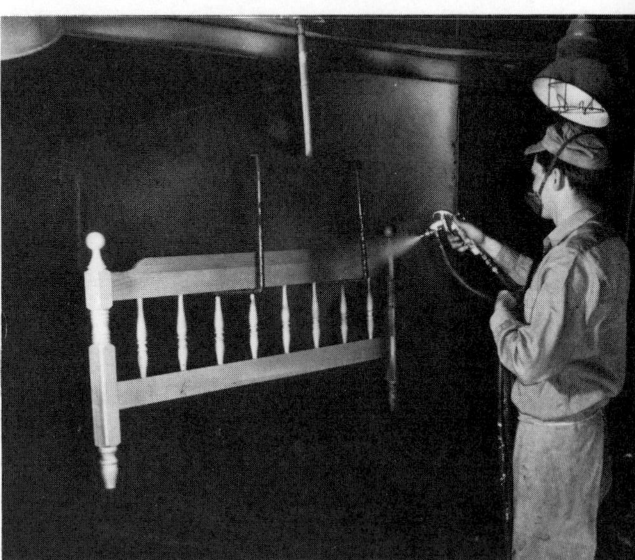

Figure 64-16
A finisher applies toner.

A *hand sander* puts a smooth finish on all final external surfaces. A worker can hand sand a raw wood surface or rub down another type of finish between coats. The hand sander must check for defects and work carefully so as not to have the surface irregular or grooved.

A *finisher* applies filler, stain, lacquer and other materials using a spray gun or brush, Figure 64-16. Sometimes the finisher rubs down the finish between coats. In a large company an individual finisher might specialize as a *finish wiper*, a *stainer*, a *spray operator* or a *machine and hand rubber*.

A *color technician* mixes and matches stains, lacquers, fillers, glazes and other finishing materials. These are matched to samples or mixed according to formulas. This color technician maintains the library of color formulas and develops new finish effects.

A *color shader and touch-up specialist* inspects the finished product for uniformity of finish and shading. He or she checks moldings, overlays, corners and edges. This person must be able to use a spray gun for touch-up work.

Jobs in Upholstery

Furniture units to be upholstered in a factory go to the upholstery section after the exposed parts are finished.

Upholstery workers specialize in just one part of the total trade. A *cutter* places patterns on the fabric and makes sure the pattern matches as desired. A cutter also cuts the fabric to shape with an electric cutting knife. A *cutter's helper* assists by spreading out fabric to be cut and marking it with the proper pattern.

A *sewer* sews all the parts for a particular piece of furniture. This work must be carefully and accurately done because the pattern must match at the seams and welts. A sewer also sews cushions and pillows, Figure 64-17. Experience as a seamstress is helpful in securing a job as a furniture production sewer.

Other jobs related to upholstery in a manufacturing plant include *tufting machine operator, quilting machine operator, cushion filler* and *seat, arm and back maker.*

You can learn the trade of upholstery and establish your own business. But an *upholsterer* in private business must understand thoroughly the field of upholstery. Upholsterers are expected to replace springs, padding, stuffing and fabrics. They also must measure accurately and figure necessary materials. In some cases they must repair broken furniture frames and refinish exposed wood parts. In addition, a knowledge of business practices such as paying taxes, collecting money, purchasing supplies and paying bills is necessary.

Design Positions

The design in furniture manufacture determines the sizes, proportions and materials used in a chair, cabinet, table or other wood product.

A *designer* is a creative person who can work with ideas, materials and people to produce a saleable product. The product designer must understand the processes of manufacturing wood products. In addition, some knowledge of marketing and the needs and tastes of the customer are essential. A designer presents sketches of various designs after consulting people in sales, production, market research, personnel and, in some cases, engineering. Designers employed by a manufacturing company work on the products

Figure 64-17
A sewer assembles fabric parts for upholstered furniture.

of that company. Those working for a consulting design firm may work on products for many companies.

Designers usually complete a four-year bachelor's degree program in a college or university. The study is balanced among science, art and humanities. Design students take several studio courses that stress two- and three-dimensional design. For more information write to The Industrial Designers Society of America, 1750 Old Meadow Road, McLean, Virginia 22101.

Sales Positions

Sales jobs in the wood products industry are in three areas–manufacturers' sales, wholesale sales and retail sales.

Manufacturers' sales representatives sell products made by their employer to other businesses. For example, a furniture manufacturer's sales representative sells to wholesale and retail furniture stores. Plywood manufacturers have sales representatives who visit sales outlets as well as architects, engineers and contractors. Part of their job is to explain to customers the many uses of plywood and encourage its use in building construction.

Manufacturers' sales representatives must be well informed about the products they sell and the needs of the customers. Often they give the customer technical information which helps them sell their product, Figure 64-18.

Manufacturers' sales representatives spend a lot of their week traveling. They have to schedule their time wisely and carry on extensive telephone and written contacts. They have to keep accurate records and write reports.

The best entrance into this field is to have a college degree in a major related to the industry. Beginning sales workers often receive special training from their employer before they work with customers. Advancing from sales into higher management positions in a company is possible. For more information write Sales and Marketing Executives International, Career Education Division, 380 Lexington Ave., New York, N.Y. 10017.

Wholesale sales representatives sell products made by many companies to other businesses. For example, a wholesale firm may handle many brands of furniture and cabinets and sell these to retail outlets that then sell to the public. The wholesale sales workers visit retail, industrial and commercial buyers. They distribute catalogs and other descriptive material to show the items they sell. Wholesale representatives usually do not emphasize any one brand, but describe the features of each. In addition, they advise customers on advertising, pricing and displays. For more information write National Association of Wholesale Distributors, 1725 K St., N.W., Washington, D.C. 20006.

Retail salespersons work directly with the public. They must understand the products and how they are used. Retail sales involves a knowledge of how the product works, colors and materials, and which product would do a particular job best. For example, a salesperson in retail building materials must know about lumber, paneling, cabinets, fasteners, plumbing, electrical supplies and many other construction materials.

The retail sales workers also help price items, stock shelves, prepare displays and take inventory. They write sales tickets and handle credit accounts.

Entry workers should have a high school education and some knowledge of the sales division where they are to work. They will have to learn by working with experienced employees. They can eventually move from retail sales into jobs as buyers, department managers or store managers. For more information write to the National Retail Merchants Association, 100 W. 31st St., New York, N.Y. 10001.

CONSTRUCTION

The construction industry employs many workers who use wood products. *Carpenters* are the largest group of building trade workers. Their work is divided into two groups, rough carpentry and finish carpentry. A highly skilled carpenter should be able to work in both areas.

Rough carpentry involves the erection of the wood framework in buildings. This includes the floors, walls, partitions, ceilings and roof. Rough carpenters also install heavy timbers in docks and bridges. They build concrete forms and scaffolding for heavy construction, Figure 64-19.

Finish carpentry includes the installation of molding, paneling, cabinets, windows, doors and

Figure 64-18
Sales representatives visit wood manufacturing company executives and keep them informed about their products. (Robert E. McKee, Inc.)

Figure 64-19
Rough carpentry includes building forms for poured concrete. (American Plywood Association)

hardware, Figûre 64-20. In addition, finish carpenters build stairs and lay hardwood floors.

Carpenters use a variety of hand and power tools, including hammers, saws, chisels, planes and drills.

Figure 64-20
This finish carpenter is installing vertical siding by a front entrance. (California Redwood Association)

Vocational schools and community colleges have programs to prepare carpenters. Many people train to be carpenters through an apprenticeship. An apprenticeship is a formal program in which a person learns skills on the job and attends special night classes. Most apprentice programs for carpenters last four years. For more information write the United Brotherhood of Carpenters and Joiners of America, 101 Constitution Ave., N.W., Washington, D.C. 20005.

Many carpenters become general contractors. A *general contractor* has the full responsibility for construction of a building. This includes securing the materials and the workers as well as the building of the structure.

The general contractor must know about all the trades involved in construction, such as architects, carpenters, plumbers, electricians and others, Figure 64-21. A contractor must be able to figure the cost of the building, estimate the necessary materials, oversee the work of others, collect money, order supplies and pay bills. For this reason, a sound knowledge of business practices is essential. For more information write the Associated General Contractors of America, Inc., 1957 E St., N.W., Washington, D.C. 20006.

Figure 64-21
A general contractor works with architects and others in the construction trades. (American Society of Civil Engineers)

PROFESSIONAL CAREERS IN RELATED AREAS

There are a number of career areas in which a knowledge of wood, wood processing and wood products is important. These include forestry, forestry technology, wood technology and architecture.

Foresters manage, develop and protect trees, land and wildlife. They oversee the planting and cutting of trees and protect them from disease, insects, fire and careless human acts, Figure 64-22. Foresters also ensure the preservation of wildlife and manage vast watershed areas, recreation camps and parks.

Some foresters who are involved in research provide technical information to those managing forests. A few find college and university teaching positions.

For an entry-level position in forestry, a minimum of a college bachelor's degree in forestry is required. Many complete master's degrees in this area. For more information write the Society of American Foresters, 5400 Grosvenor Lane, Washington, D.C. 20014.

A *forestry technician* assists the forester in the care and management of forest lands. The technician estimates the possible timber production of an area, supervises the cutting of roads into forest areas and measures logs harvested to determine how much lumber the trees will yield. He or she looks for disease and works to prevent soil erosion. The forestry technician also works to prevent and control fires.

Forestry technicians can take a one- or two-year course of study in a community college. Some learn by working directly with experienced foresters and technicians. For more information write the U.S. Department of Agriculture, Forest Service, Washington, D.C. 20250.

A career in *wood science and technology* is aimed at utilizing harvested wood in the most effective manner. This profession requires an understanding of the physical structure of wood

Figure 64-22
Foresters monitor the planting and growth of trees. (Western Wood Products Association)

and its behavior under stressful conditions. In addition, a wood scientist must know what properties of wood make it best for building and be able to develop new products using wood as the basic material. A major area of development is the manufacture of plywood furniture and cabinets. This work includes researching the proper design, utilizing the best manufacturing processes, and controlling the quality of the finished product.

Entry into the wood science field requires a bachelor's degree in wood science and technology. Some people go from wood science to manufacturers' sales.

An *architect* provides professional services to clients planning a building by designing a structure that is useful, attractive and safe. The architect carries through an idea for a building to the final construction. This involves working with both design and engineering. The architect begins a project with preliminary drawings. Eventually, the final working drawings show all details of a building, such as the size of structural members, wall design, location of plumbing and electrical fixtures and the exterior of the building.

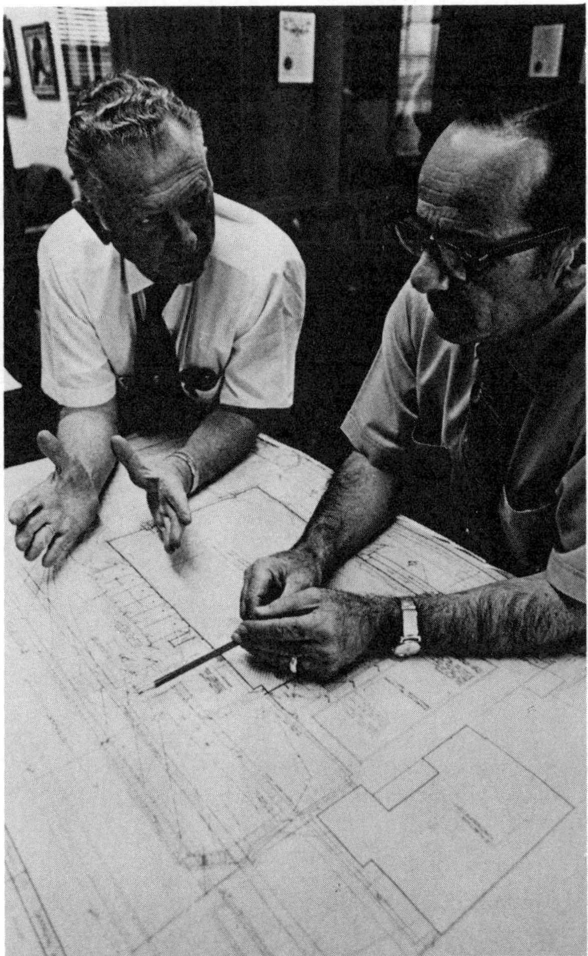

Figure 64-23
Architects work with contractors during the construction of a building. (Robert E. McKee, Inc.)

The architect works closely with the client in choosing the contractor to do the work. While the building is under construction, the architect, as the representative of the client, supervises the contractor's work, Figure 64-23.

Architects must complete a four- or five-year program at a college or university. After graduation, they work for a period under a licensed architect. After this service, they take the architectural licensing examination in the state where they work. For more information write the American Institute of Architects, 1735 New York Ave., N.W., Washington, D.C. 20006.

Figure 64-24
A plant manager handles the overall operation of the production facility. (Robert E. McKee, Inc.)

Figure 64-25
An advertising manager is responsible for all advertising of a company's products.

MANAGEMENT

In the wood manufacturing industry a well-prepared individual can progress into management positions within the company. Following are some positions commonly available.

A *plant manager* oversees operation of the plant, Figure 64-24. This includes receiving production materials, recruiting and training workers, producing the product and delivering the finished product to a customer. It is a difficult but well-paying position. A plant manager needs a college education in addition to industrial experience.

The *sales manager* is in charge of all aspects of the product's sale. Often this position is at the vice president's level. The sales manager promotes the product, hires the sales staff and handles the costs involved in selling the product. This person must have a college degree, usually in some area of business administration, and industrial experience.

The *purchasing agent* buys the materials to manufacture the product. In addition, he or she supervises a staff that processes the orders for tools and machinery as well as building materials. A degree in business administration is important.

The *advertising manager* promotes the sale of the product. This person might report to the vice president for sales or the sales manager. In addition to advertising manufacturers' sales, the advertising manager helps retail dealers promote the product, Figure 64-25. A college degree in advertising and industrial experience are necessary.

The *vice president for marketing* sees that the manufactured products move through the marketing channels to the consumer. This person works with the production staff to see that the products are made and shipped as required. District sales managers often report to the vice president for marketing. A master's degree in business administration and experience in the industry are required.

The position of *vice president* will vary depending on the size of the company. A large company will have a vice president for each of the major areas such as sales, manufacturing, purchasing, finance and engineering. All require college degrees and experience in the industry.

The *president* of a company holds the top administrative position. The president is responsible for the total operation of the company. He or she reports to a board of directors who are elected by the stockholders of the company.

TEACHING

Many people prefer to teach woodworking. Industrial arts teachers find positions in junior and senior high schools as well as junior and senior colleges. These persons are educated in several technical areas but may specialize in wood technology. Their degree programs have taught them how to plan and manage school shops, Figure 64-26. A bachelor's degree is a minimum requirement for teaching in public schools. Most teachers eventually earn a master's degree.

Vocational carpentry, cabinetmaking and upholstery are other teaching areas. These teachers must have complete training in the trade plus several years' full-time work experience. Some college work is also necessary to become certified as a teacher. Most of these teachers have bachelor's degrees.

You can get additional information on teaching vocational arts by contacting the nearest college or university that offers majors in industrial arts education and vocational technical education.

Figure 64-26
Industrial arts teachers show students the basic procedures for producing wood products. (Oliver Machinery Company)

REVIEW QUESTIONS

1 What are the basic factors that lead to success on the job?
2 What do lumber fallers do?
3 What is a kiln operator's main responsibility?
4 What are the basic machine-operator jobs in plants manufacturing wood products?
5 What tools do workers in product assembly use?
6 What special subjects do wood product designers need to know?
7 Where can you write to get information on sales and marketing?
8 What work does a finish carpenter perform?
9 What is a general contractor?
10 What education do you need to become a forester?
11 What professional management positions are available in the woods industry?

SUGGESTED ACTIVITIES

1 Invite persons with careers in the woods industry to visit the class and tell about their jobs.
2 Try to get a part-time or summer job in the area in which you are interested. Be alert on the job to learn as much as possible about the area.
3 Write to professional organizations that offer career information. Prepare a bulletin board display reporting what you found.

TRADITIONAL BOOKCASE

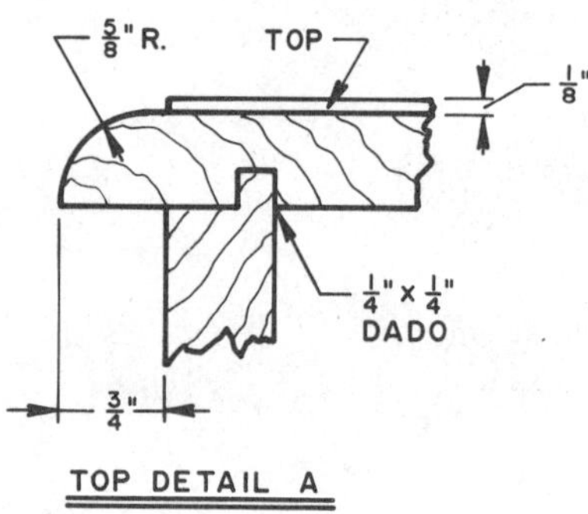

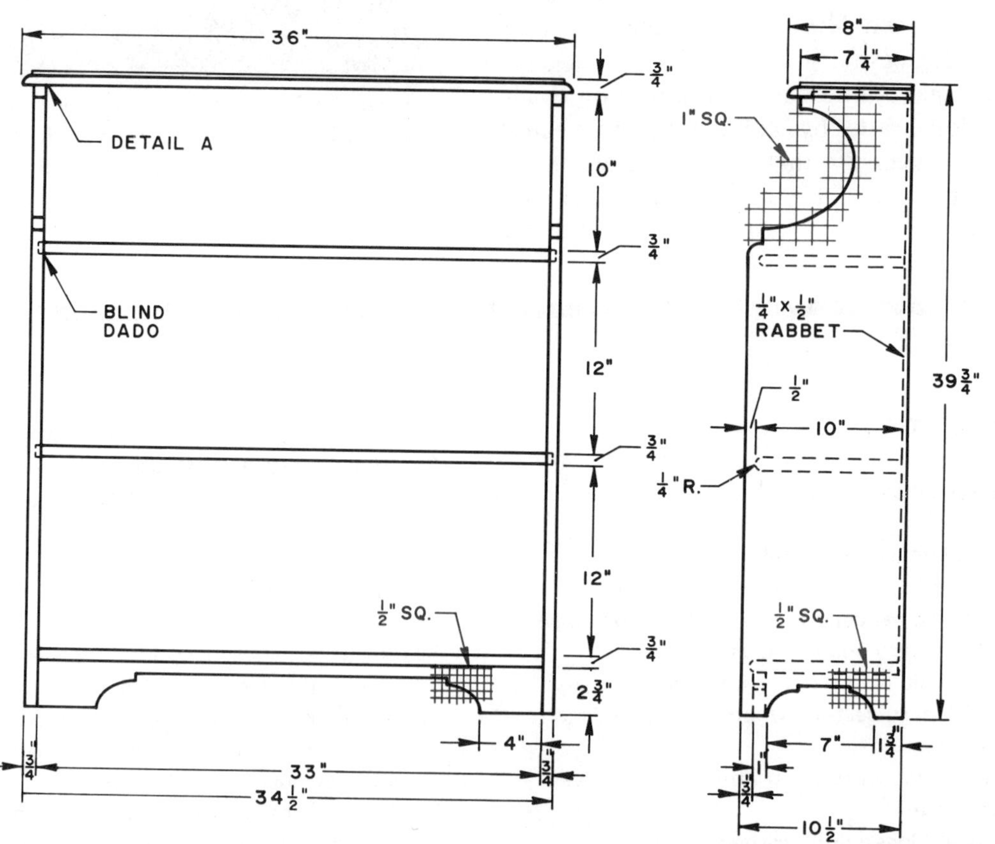

SECTION

11

Woodworking Projects

65
Projects

If you study and practice using the tools, techniques, processes and materials of the woods industry, you will be able to produce useful and pleasing wood products.

Section 11, Woodworking Projects, gives construction details for many such products. Some are simple and are good beginning projects. Others are more difficult and will challenge your skills.

UNIT

65

Projects

- Skill game
- Dart board
- Desk organizer
- Pool cue and ball rack
- Wishing well planter
- A nest of tables
- Colonial trinket cabinet
- Decorative trunks
- Colonial tray and stand
- Serving cart
- Drafting table
- Traditional bookcase
- Cedar chest
- Wall-hung desk
- Stereo/TV stand
- Wine and cheese rack
- Antique bench
- Contemporary chair
- Storage/appliance center
- Antique bread box
- Contemporary end table
- Bedside table
- Dining table
- Hexagonal commode
- Kitchen tools
- Pickets and shutters
- Jewelry box
- Gun rack
- Colonial recipe box
- Turnings

SKILL GAME

RULES FOR PLAYING THE SKILL GAME

1. PUSH THE TWO STEEL RODS TOGETHER.
2. PLACE THE 1" DIA. STEEL BALL BEARING ON TOP OF THE STEEL RODS.
3. GRIP THE HANDLES AND SLOWLY PULL THE RODS APART.
4. TRY TO GET THE BALL TO ROLL UP THE ROD AND FALL INTO THE FARTHEST HOLE. THE PLAYER WINS THE POINTS FOR THE HOLE THE BALL FALLS INTO.
5. EVERY PLAYER GETS THREE TRIES. KEEP TRACK OF YOUR OWN POINTS. WHOEVER HAS THE MOST POINTS AFTER THREE TURNS WINS.

DART BOARD

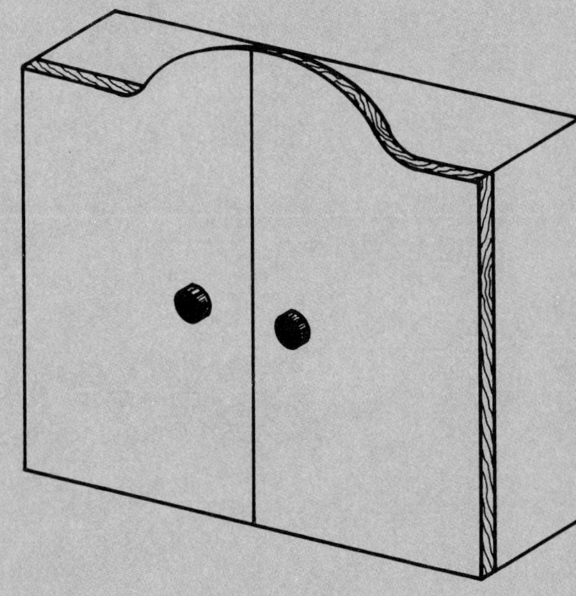

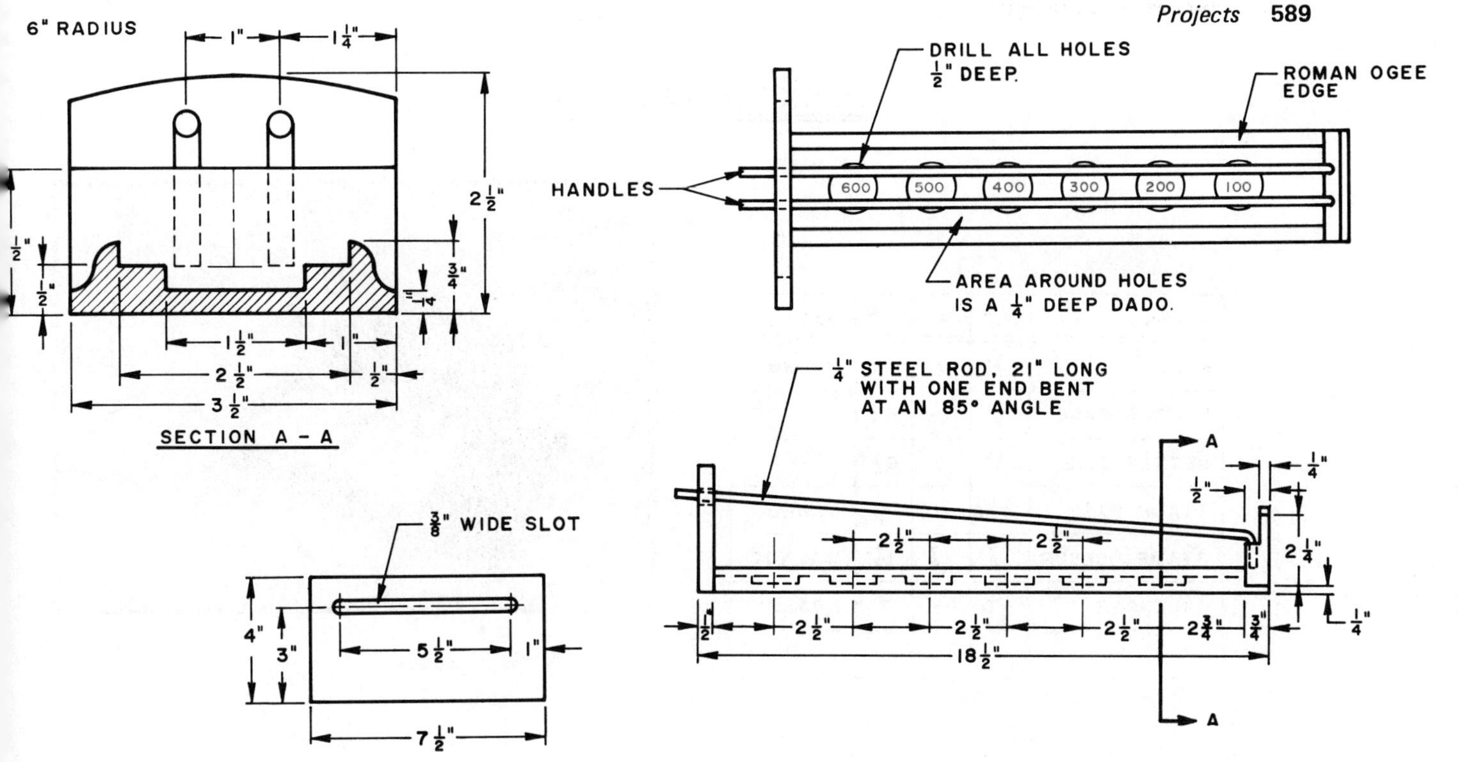

6" RADIUS
1"
1 1/4"
2 1/2"
1/2"
1/2"
3/4"
1/4"
1 1/2"
1"
2 1/2"
1/2"
3 1/2"
SECTION A - A
DRILL ALL HOLES
1/2" DEEP.
ROMAN OGEE
EDGE
HANDLES
600
500
400
300
200
100
AREA AROUND HOLES
IS A 1/4" DEEP DADO.
3/8" WIDE SLOT
4"
3"
5 1/2"
1"
7 1/2"
1/4" STEEL ROD, 21" LONG
WITH ONE END BENT
AT AN 85° ANGLE
A
A
1/4"
1/2"
2 1/2"
2 1/2"
2 1/4"
1/4"
1/2"
2 1/2"
2 1/2"
2 1/2"
2 3/4"
3/4"
18 1/2"

1 5/8"
5/8"
1/2"
1/4"
1/2"
1/4"
1/2"
1/4"
3/16"D.
1/2"D.
1 1/4"
8 x 1 3/4" R.H.B.
WOOD SCREW
DART AND CHALK RACK DETAIL
3/4"
5 x 3/4" R.H.B.
WOOD SCREW
1/2"
1/4"
1/4"
CHALKBOARD TRIM DETAIL
NOTE:
ALL STOCK 1/4" THICK
3/8" BEADING
CUT
1/4" x 1/2" RABBETED
BACK
1/4" PLYWOOD
BACK
CORK
BULLETIN
BOARD
MATERIAL
4"
3/4"
2"R.
6"R.
PAINTED HARDBOARD
TO SERVE AS
CHALKBOARD
SEE TRIM
DETAIL.
17"
13 1/4"
20"
6 1/2"
17"
SEE RACK
DETAIL.
1" BUTT
HINGE
HOLES FOR DARTS
1 1/4" C-C

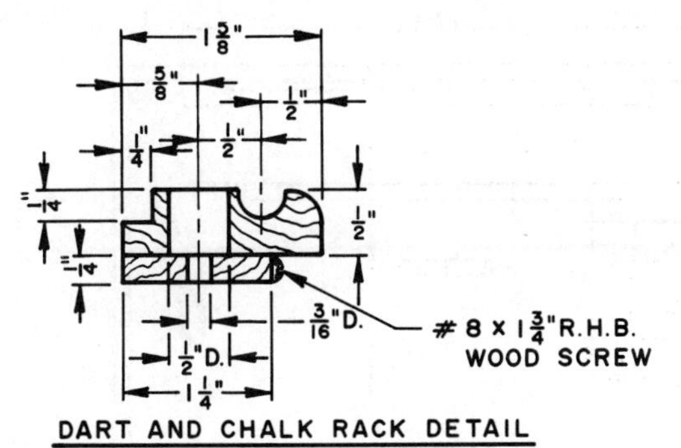

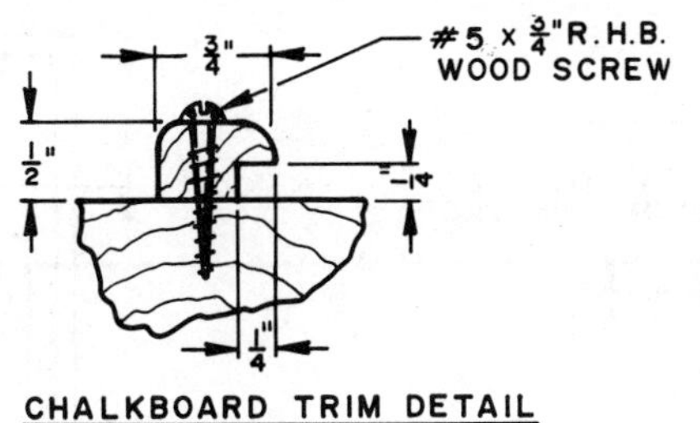

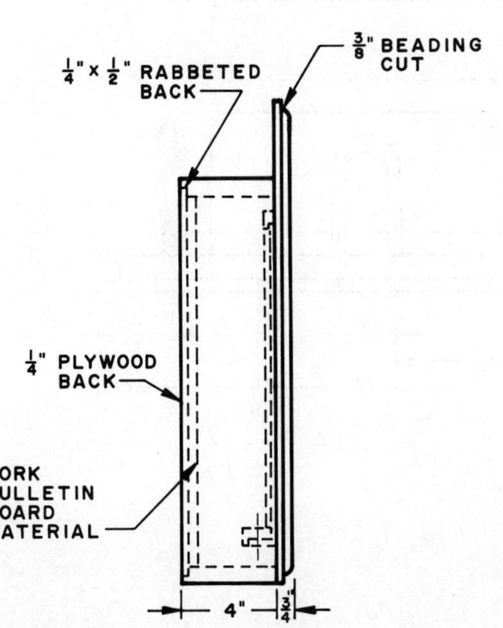

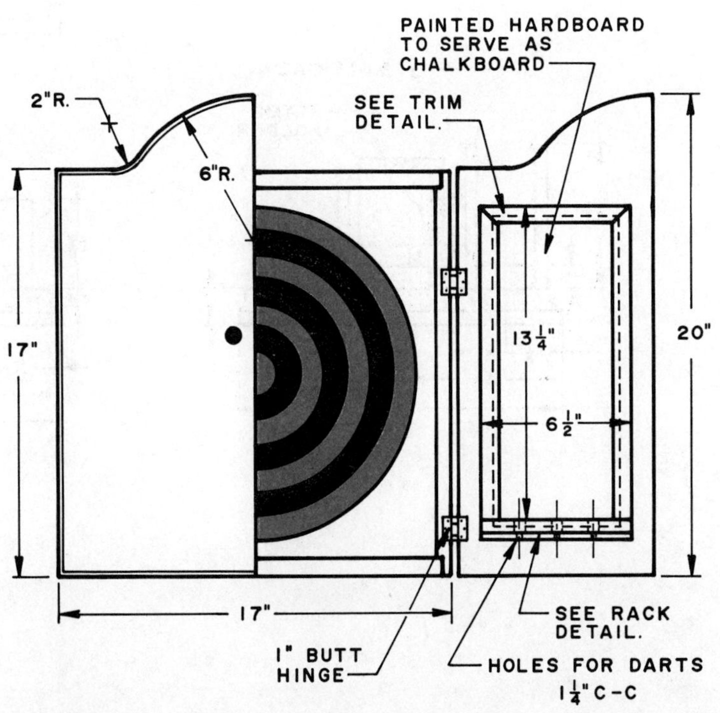

DESK ORGANIZER

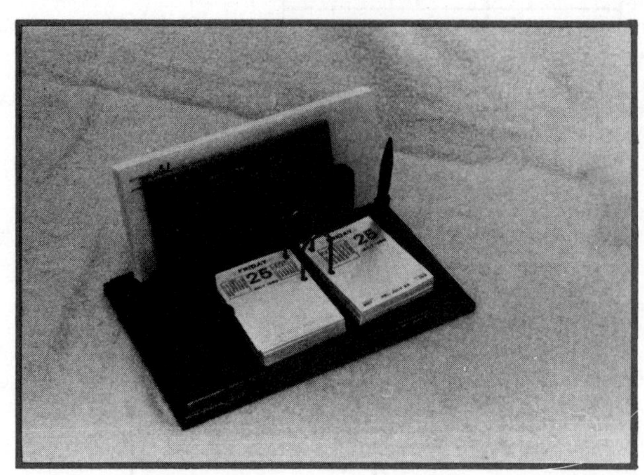

PARTS	T"	W"	L"	MATRL.
BASE	3/4"	7"	11"	WALNUT
LETTER BASE	1/2"	1 1/4"	8 3/4"	" "
LETTER SIDE	1/4"	3"	6 3/4"	" "
STAMP BASE	1 1/4"D	—	3/4"	DOWEL
STAMP HOLDER	1 7/8"	1 7/8"	1 7/8"	WALNUT
CALENDAR	1/4"D.	—	7"	BRASS

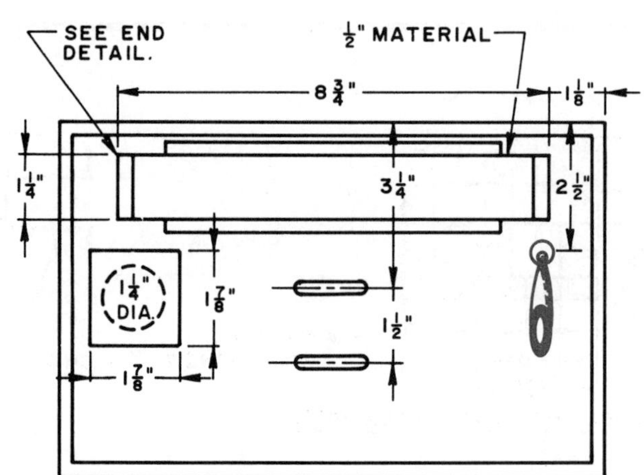

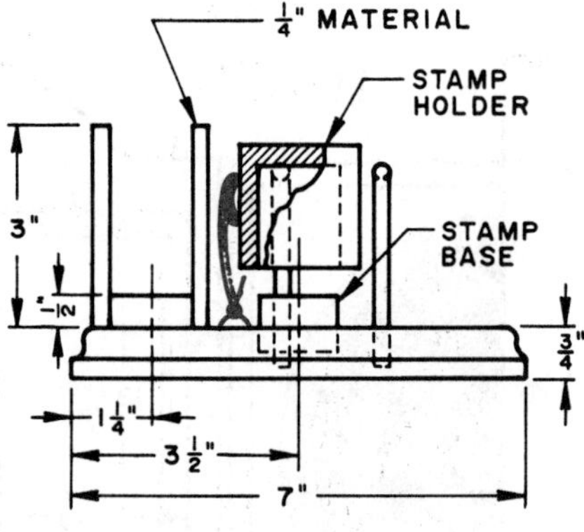

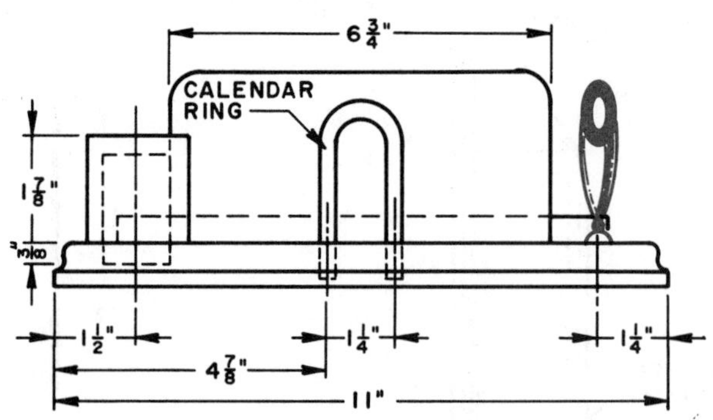

POOL CUE BALL RACK

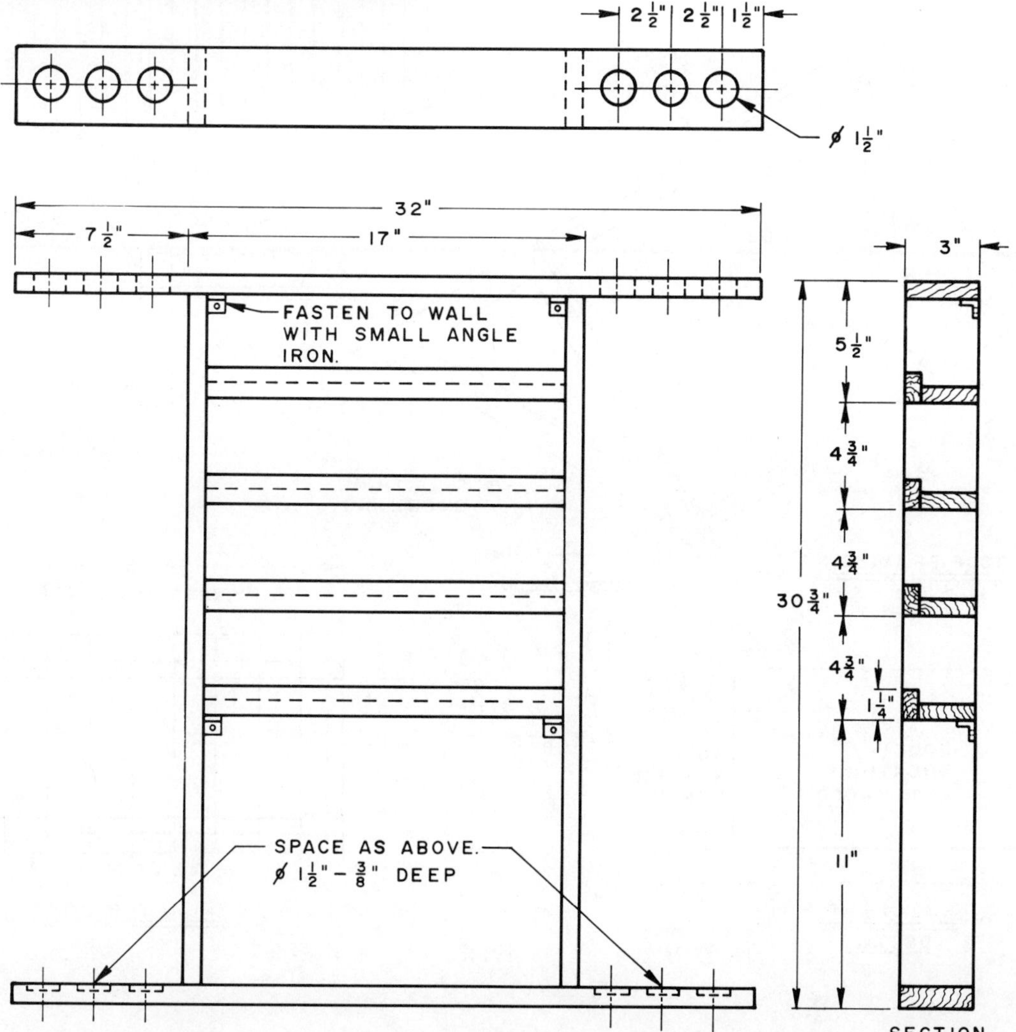

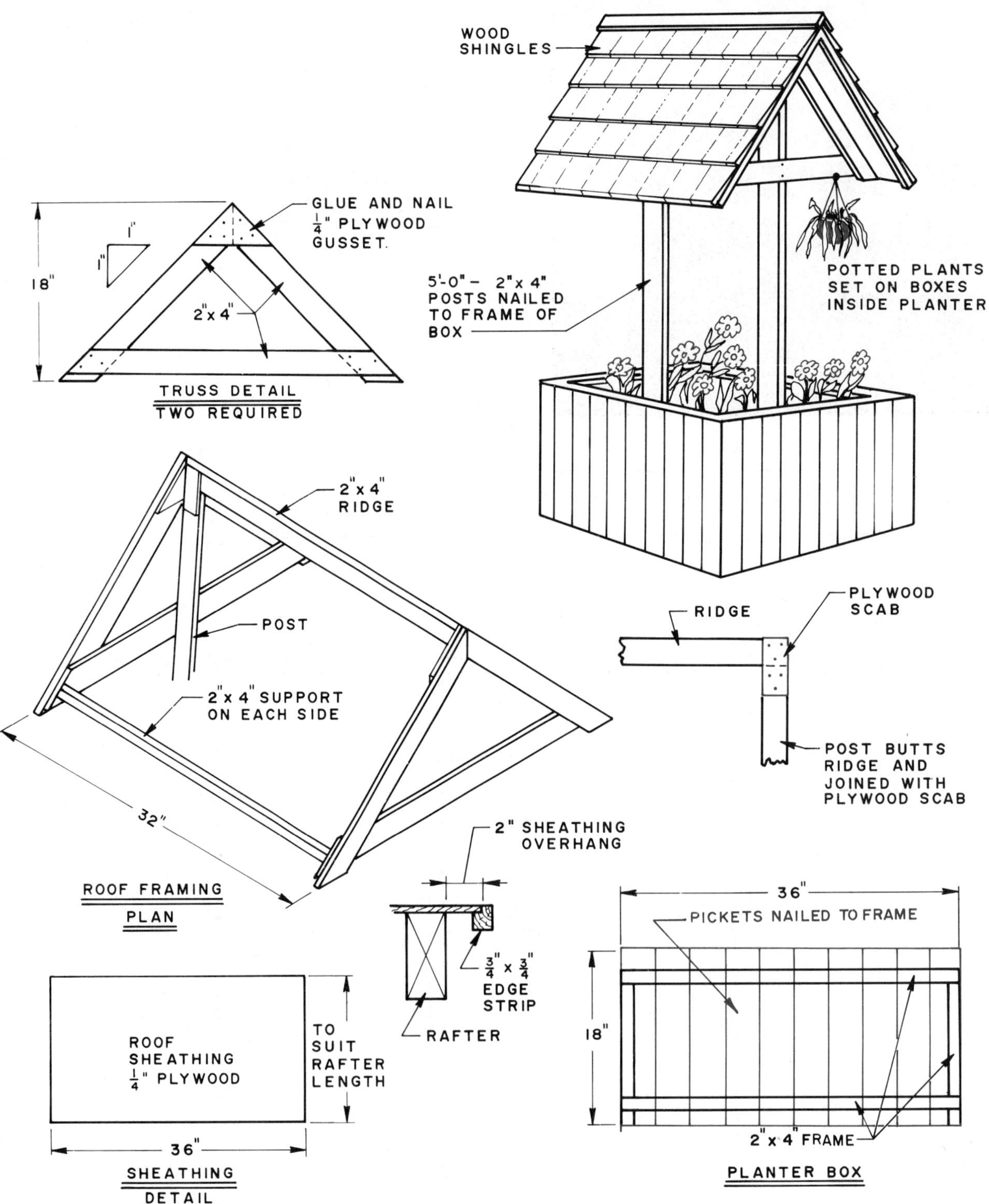
WISHING WELL
PLANTER
WOOD SHINGLES
GLUE AND NAIL 1/4" PLYWOOD GUSSET.
1"
1"
18"
2"x 4"
TRUSS DETAIL
TWO REQUIRED
5'-0" - 2"x 4" POSTS NAILED TO FRAME OF BOX
POTTED PLANTS SET ON BOXES INSIDE PLANTER
2"x 4" RIDGE
POST
2"x 4" SUPPORT ON EACH SIDE
32"
ROOF FRAMING
PLAN
RIDGE
PLYWOOD SCAB
POST BUTTS RIDGE AND JOINED WITH PLYWOOD SCAB
2" SHEATHING OVERHANG
3/4" x 3/4" EDGE STRIP
RAFTER
ROOF SHEATHING 1/4" PLYWOOD
TO SUIT RAFTER LENGTH
36"
SHEATHING
DETAIL
36"
PICKETS NAILED TO FRAME
18"
2"x 4" FRAME
PLANTER BOX

A NEST OF TABLES

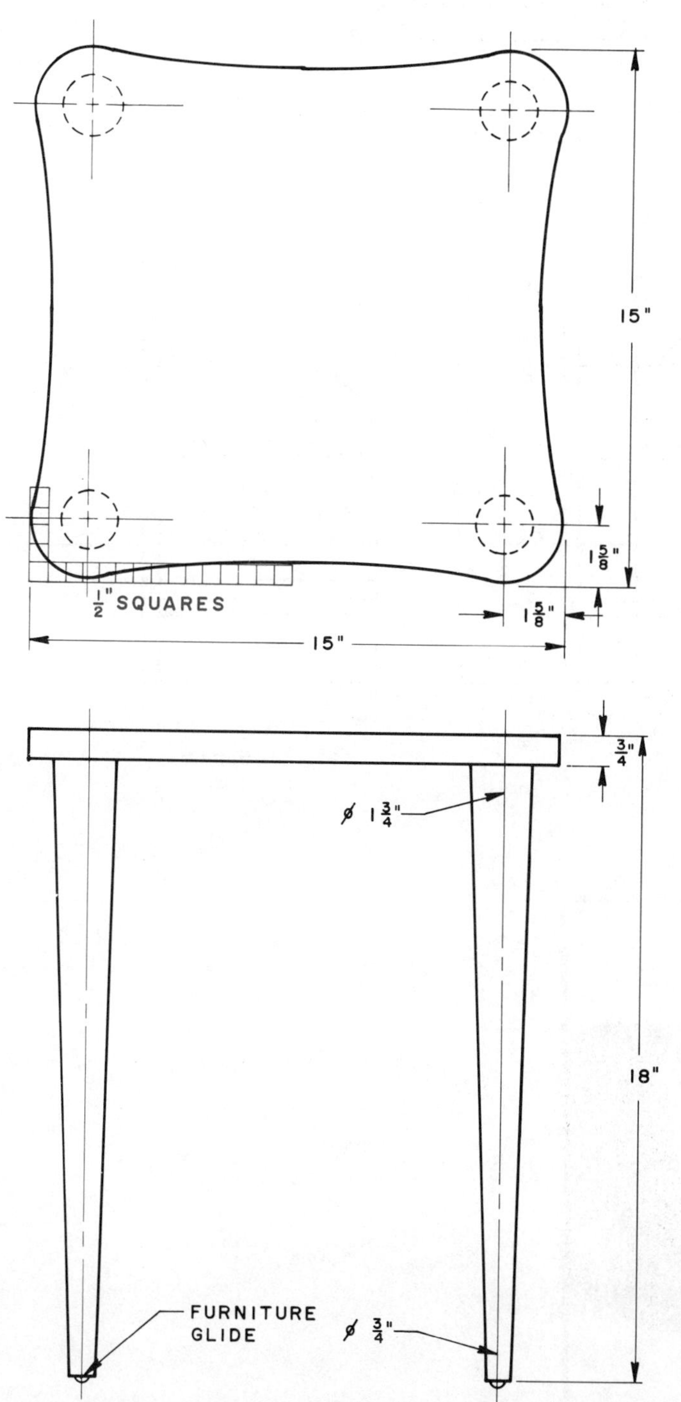

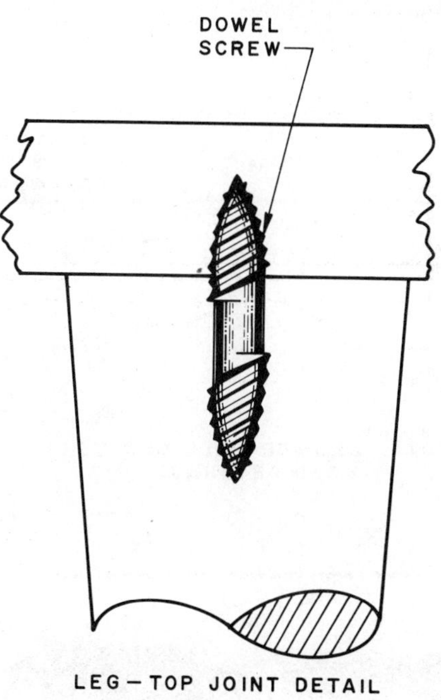

LEG—TOP JOINT DETAIL

COLONIAL TRINKET CABINET

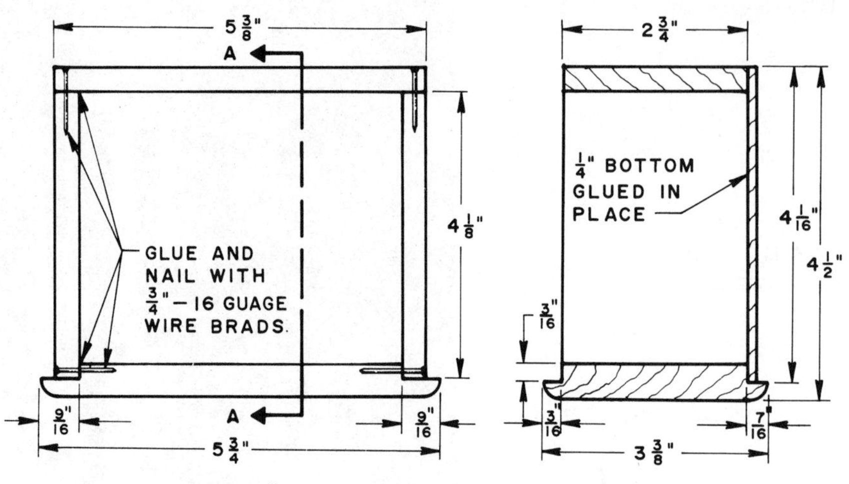

NOTE: ALL STOCK 3/8" THICK UNLESS OTHERWISE NOTED.

SECTION A–A

DRAWER DETAIL

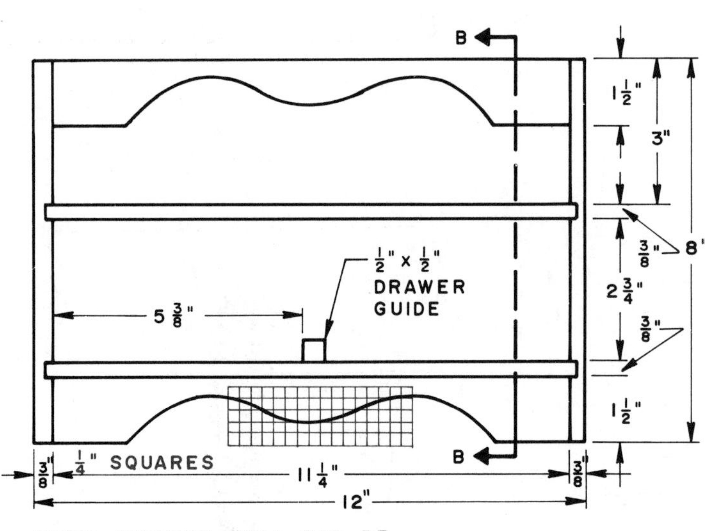

NOTE: DRAWER PULL CAN BE WOOD OR BRASS.

SECTION B–B

BODY DETAIL

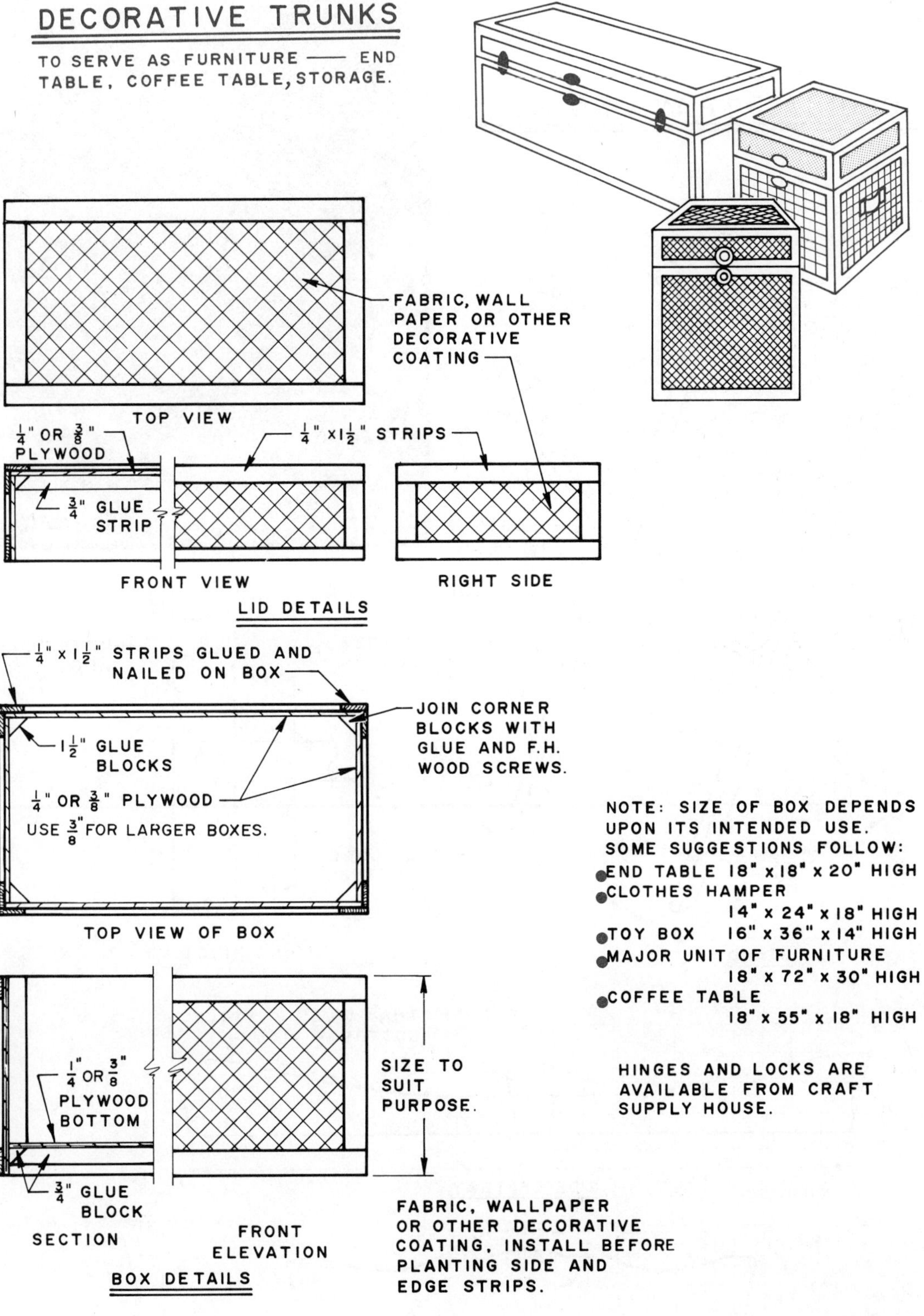

NOTE: SIZE OF BOX DEPENDS UPON ITS INTENDED USE. SOME SUGGESTIONS FOLLOW:

- END TABLE 18" x 18" x 20" HIGH
- CLOTHES HAMPER 14" x 24" x 18" HIGH
- TOY BOX 16" x 36" x 14" HIGH
- MAJOR UNIT OF FURNITURE 18" x 72" x 30" HIGH
- COFFEE TABLE 18" x 55" x 18" HIGH

HINGES AND LOCKS ARE AVAILABLE FROM CRAFT SUPPLY HOUSE.

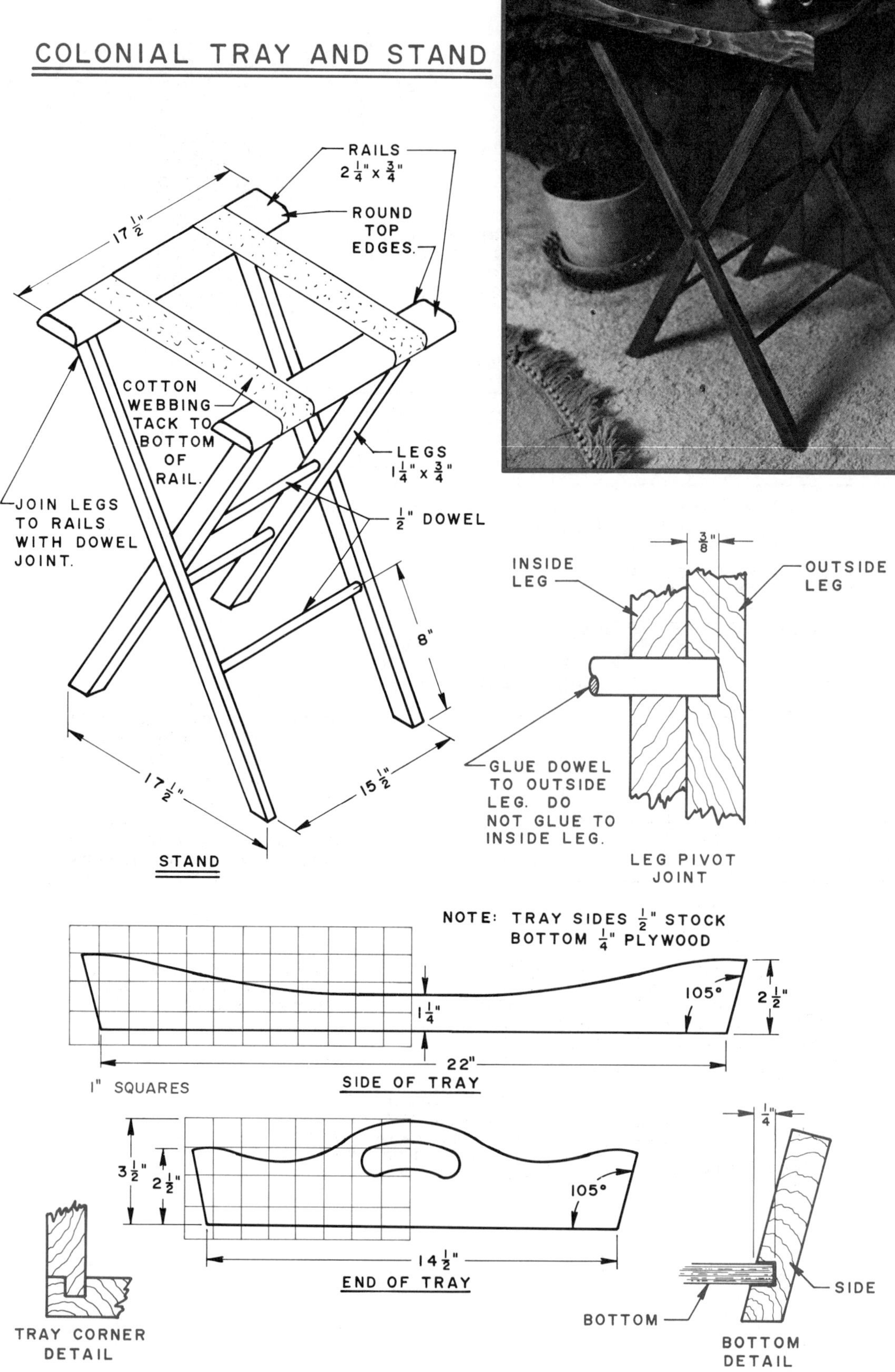
COLONIAL TRAY AND STAND
RAILS
2 1/4" x 3/4"
ROUND
TOP
EDGES.
17 1/2"
COTTON
WEBBING
TACK TO
BOTTOM
OF
RAIL.
LEGS
1 1/4" x 3/4"
JOIN LEGS
TO RAILS
WITH DOWEL
JOINT.
1/2" DOWEL
8"
17 1/2"
15 1/2"
STAND
3/8"
INSIDE
LEG
OUTSIDE
LEG
GLUE DOWEL
TO OUTSIDE
LEG. DO
NOT GLUE TO
INSIDE LEG.
LEG PIVOT
JOINT
NOTE: TRAY SIDES 1/2" STOCK
BOTTOM 1/4" PLYWOOD
105°
1 1/4"
2 1/2"
22"
1" SQUARES
SIDE OF TRAY
3 1/2"
2 1/2"
105°
14 1/2"
END OF TRAY
1/4"
SIDE
BOTTOM
TRAY CORNER
DETAIL
BOTTOM
DETAIL

SERVING CART

METRIC
ALL DIMENSIONS IN MILLIMETERS

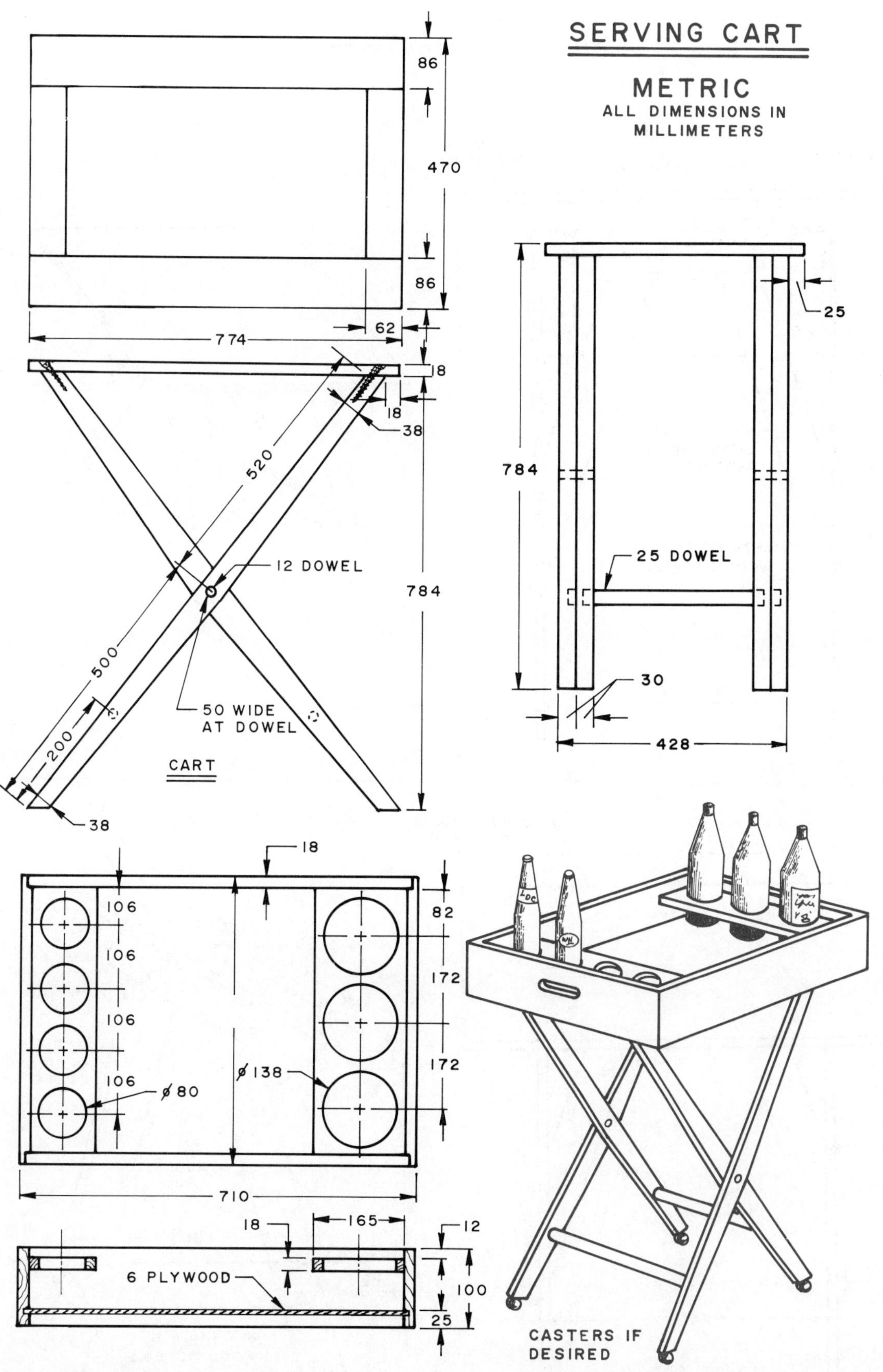

DRAFTING TABLE

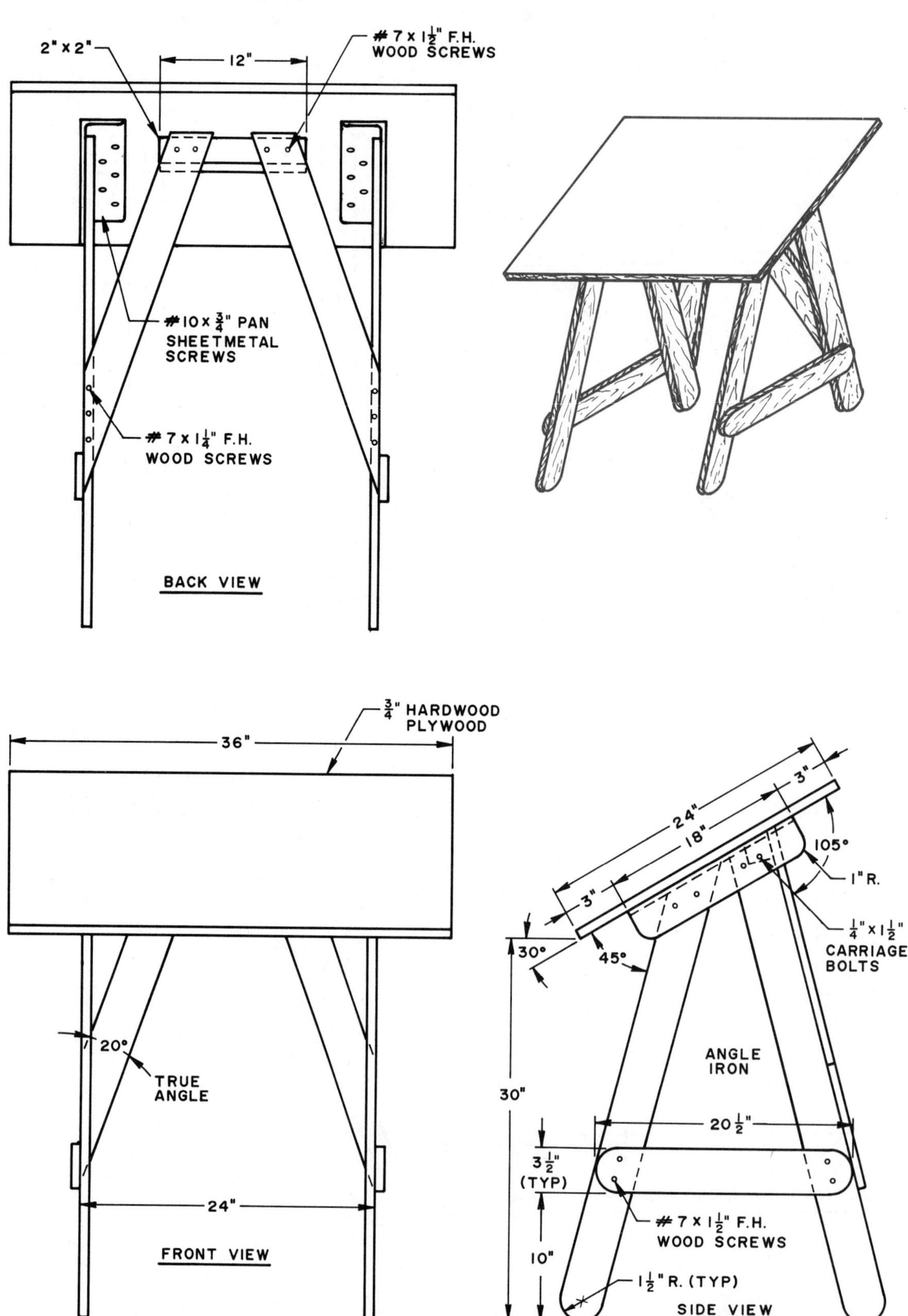
2" x 2"
12"
7 x 1½" F.H. WOOD SCREWS
10 x ¾" PAN SHEETMETAL SCREWS
7 x 1¼" F.H. WOOD SCREWS
BACK VIEW
¾" HARDWOOD PLYWOOD
36"
20°
TRUE ANGLE
24"
FRONT VIEW
24"
3"
18"
3"
105°
1" R.
¼" x 1½" CARRIAGE BOLTS
30°
45°
ANGLE IRON
30"
20½"
3½" (TYP)
7 x 1½" F.H. WOOD SCREWS
10"
1½" R. (TYP)
SIDE VIEW

TRADITIONAL BOOKCASE

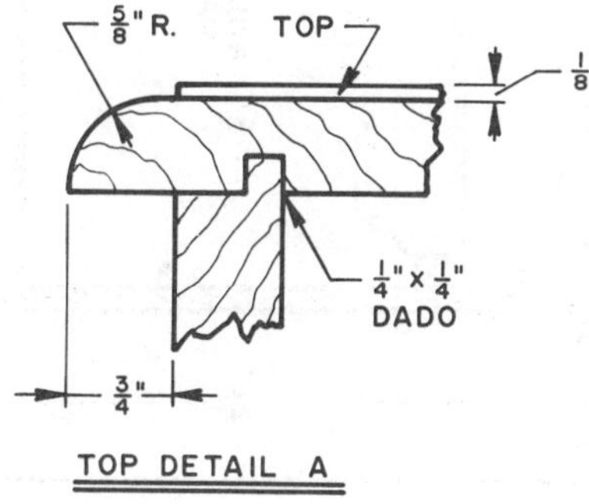

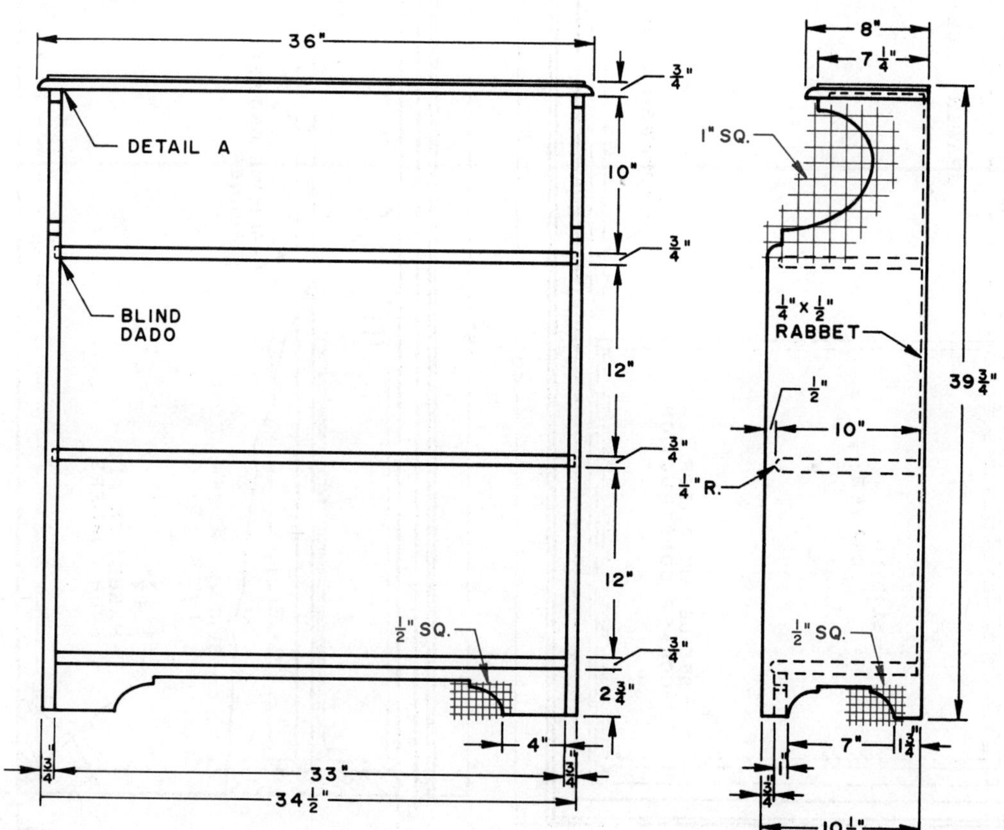

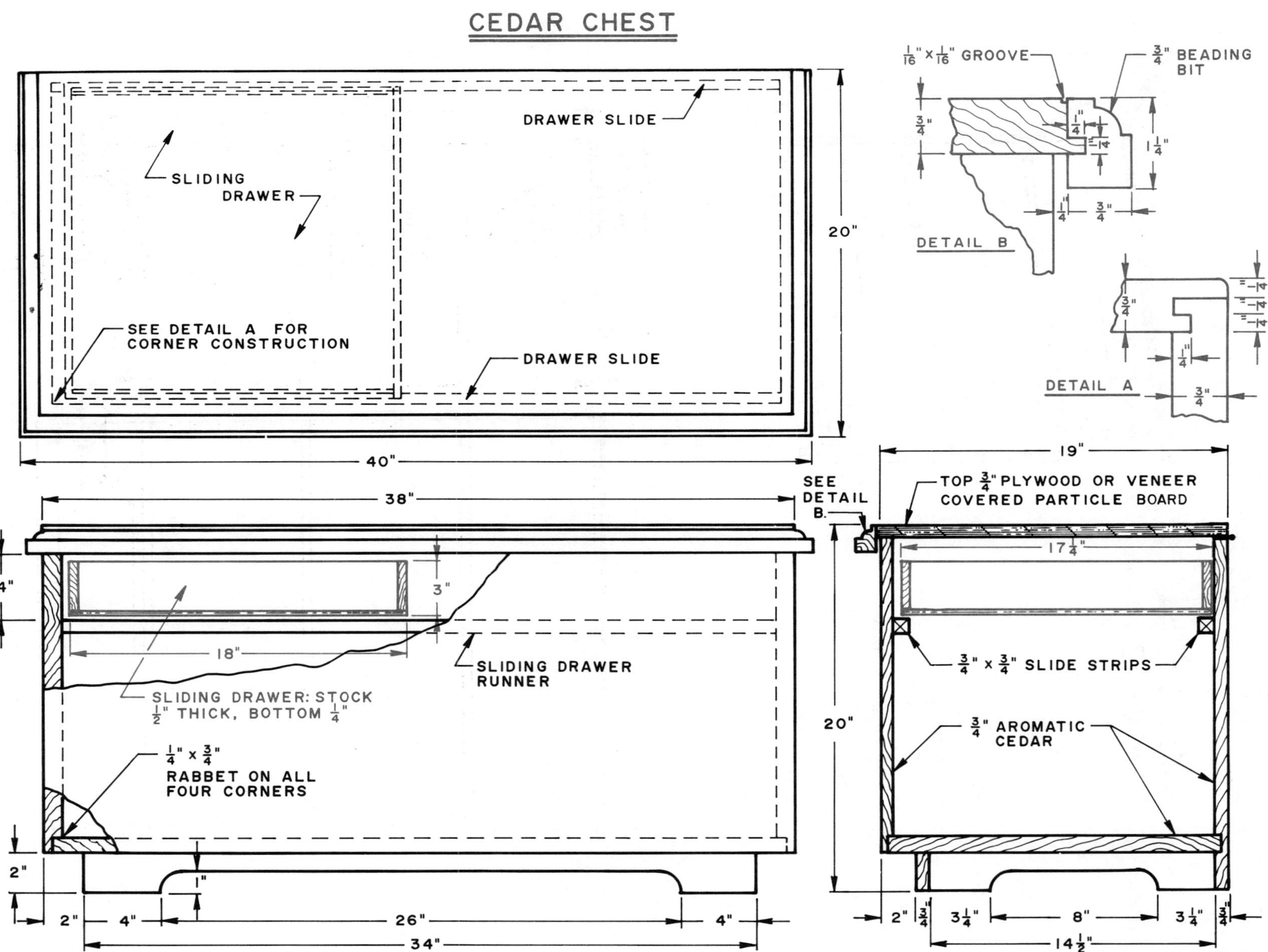
CEDAR CHEST
SLIDING DRAWER
DRAWER SLIDE
SEE DETAIL A FOR CORNER CONSTRUCTION
DRAWER SLIDE
20"
40"
1/16" x 1/16" GROOVE
3/4" BEADING BIT
DETAIL B
DETAIL A
38"
SEE DETAIL B.
4"
3"
18"
SLIDING DRAWER RUNNER
SLIDING DRAWER: STOCK 1/2" THICK, BOTTOM 1/4"
1/4" x 3/4"
RABBET ON ALL FOUR CORNERS
2"
1"
2"
4"
26"
4"
34"
19"
TOP 3/4" PLYWOOD OR VENEER COVERED PARTICLE BOARD
17 1/4"
3/4" x 3/4" SLIDE STRIPS
20"
3/4" AROMATIC CEDAR
2"
3 1/4"
8"
3 1/4"
14 1/2"

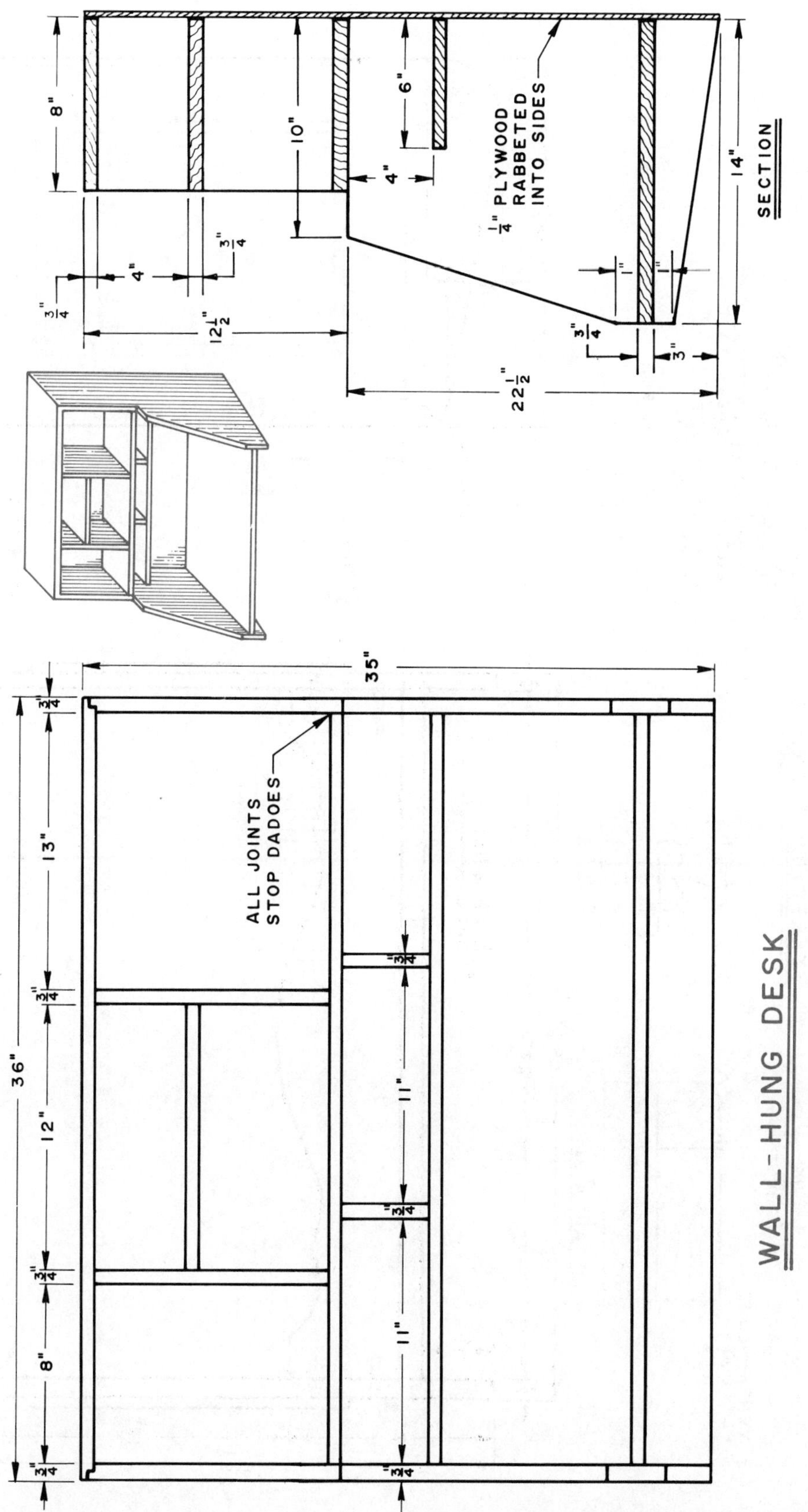
WALL-HUNG DESK
SECTION
1/4" PLYWOOD RABBETED INTO SIDES
ALL JOINTS STOP DADOES
35"
36"
22 1/2"
12 1/2"
14"
13"
12"
11"
10"
8"
6"
4"
3"
1"
3/4"

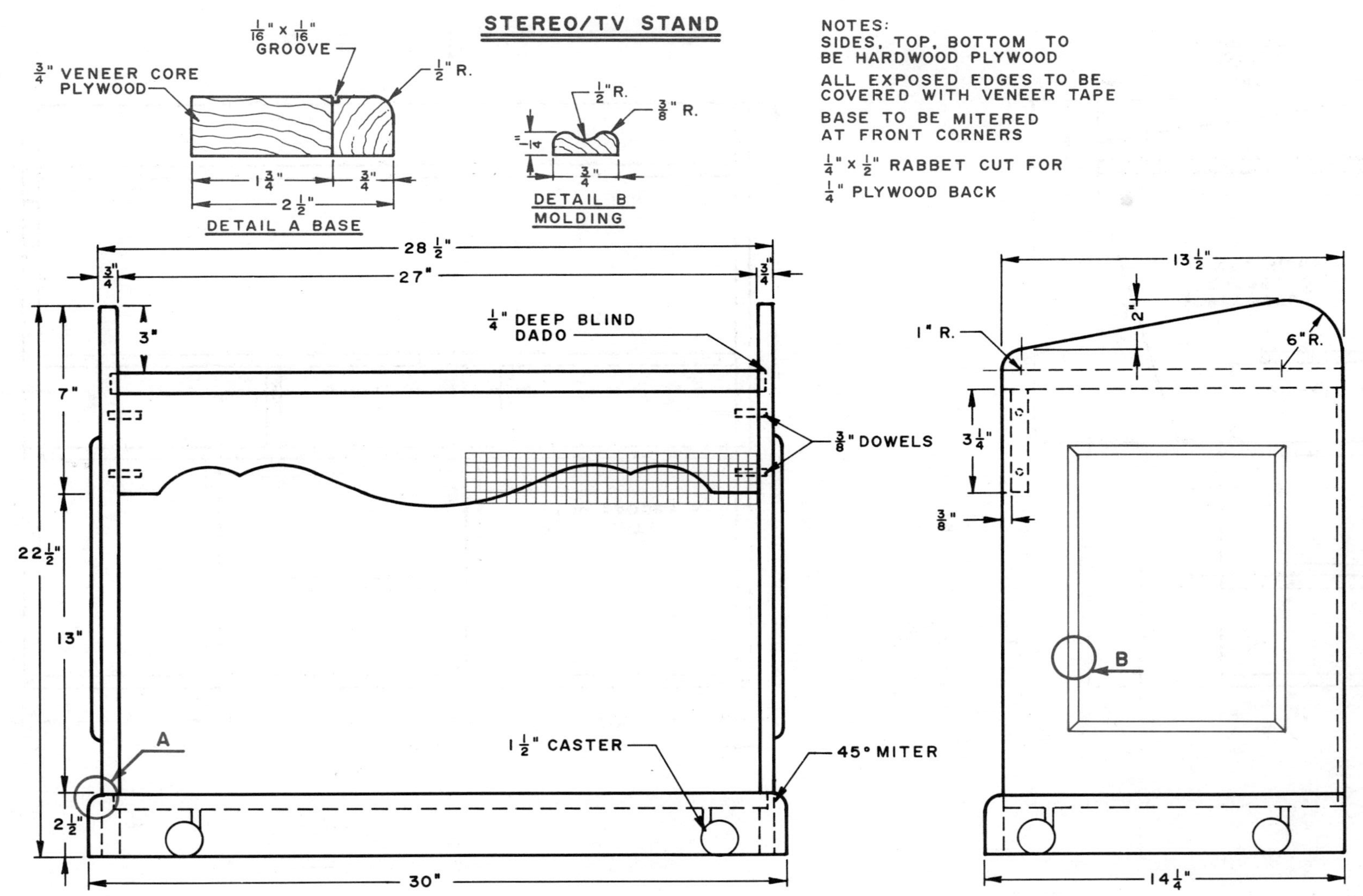
STEREO/TV STAND
3/4" VENEER CORE PLYWOOD
1/16" x 1/16" GROOVE
1/2" R.
1 3/4"
3/4"
2 1/2"
DETAIL A BASE
1/2" R.
3/8" R.
1/4"
3/4"
DETAIL B MOLDING
NOTES:
SIDES, TOP, BOTTOM TO BE HARDWOOD PLYWOOD
ALL EXPOSED EDGES TO BE COVERED WITH VENEER TAPE
BASE TO BE MITERED AT FRONT CORNERS
1/4" x 1/2" RABBET CUT FOR 1/4" PLYWOOD BACK
28 1/2"
3/4"
27"
3/4"
3"
1/4" DEEP BLIND DADO
7"
3/8" DOWELS
22 1/2"
13"
A
1 1/2" CASTER
45° MITER
2 1/2"
30"
13 1/2"
2"
1" R.
6" R.
3 1/4"
3/8"
B
14 1/4"

WINE & CHEESE RACK

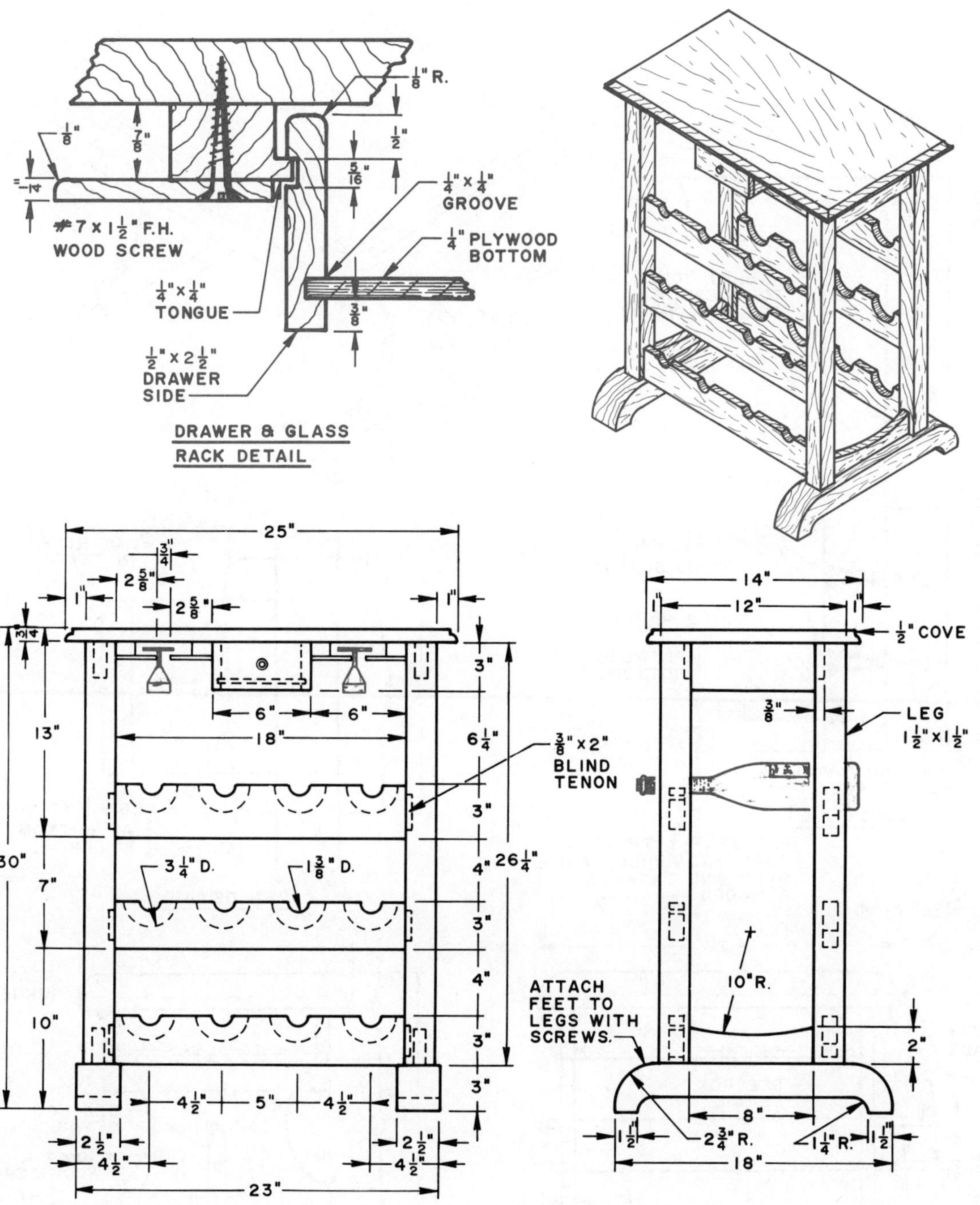

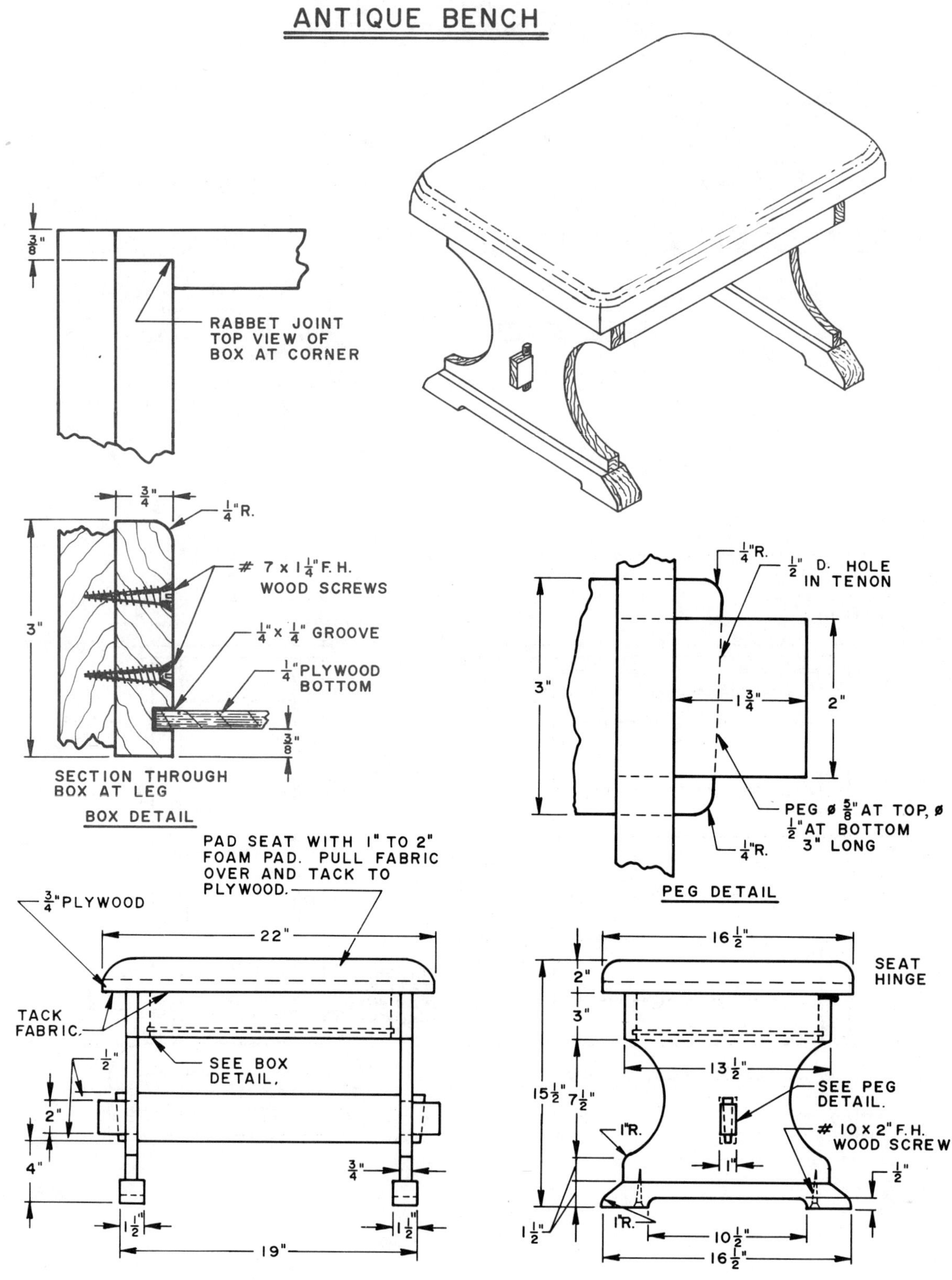
ANTIQUE BENCH
3/8"
RABBET JOINT
TOP VIEW OF
BOX AT CORNER
3/4"
1/4"R.
7 x 1 1/4" F.H.
WOOD SCREWS
3"
1/4" x 1/4" GROOVE
1/4" PLYWOOD
BOTTOM
3/8"
SECTION THROUGH
BOX AT LEG
BOX DETAIL
1/4"R.
1/2" D. HOLE
IN TENON
3"
1 3/4"
2"
PEG ø 5/8" AT TOP, ø
1/2" AT BOTTOM
3" LONG
1/4"R.
PEG DETAIL
PAD SEAT WITH 1" TO 2"
FOAM PAD. PULL FABRIC
OVER AND TACK TO
PLYWOOD.
3/4" PLYWOOD
22"
TACK
FABRIC.
SEE BOX
DETAIL.
1/2"
2"
4"
3/4"
1 1/2"
1 1/2"
19"
16 1/2"
SEAT
HINGE
2"
3"
13 1/2"
SEE PEG
DETAIL.
15 1/2"
7 1/2"
1"R.
10 x 2" F.H.
WOOD SCREW
1"
1/2"
1 1/2"
1"R.
10 1/2"
16 1/2"

CONTEMPORARY CHAIR

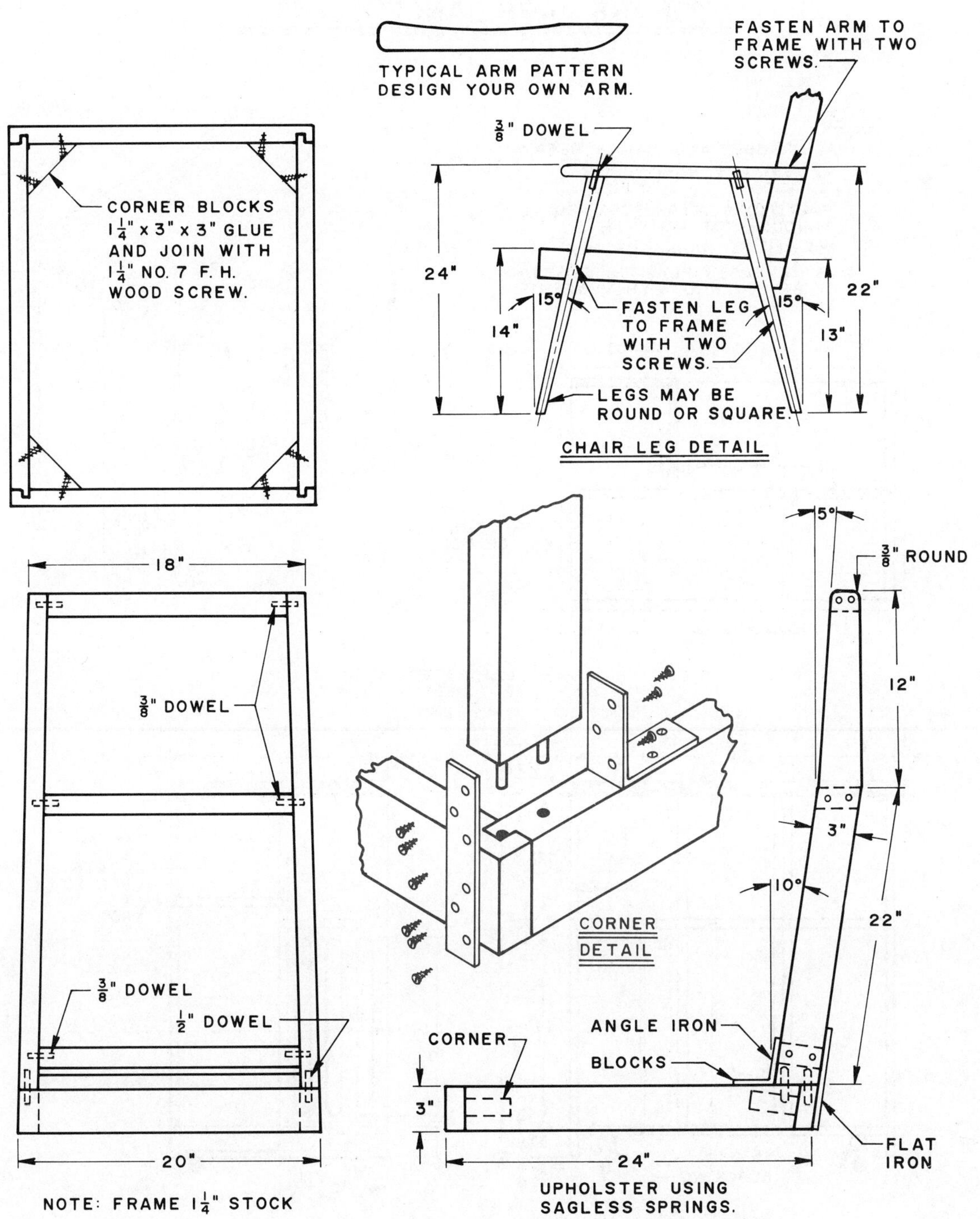
TYPICAL ARM PATTERN
DESIGN YOUR OWN ARM.
FASTEN ARM TO FRAME WITH TWO SCREWS.
3/8" DOWEL
24"
22"
14"
13"
15°
15°
FASTEN LEG TO FRAME WITH TWO SCREWS.
LEGS MAY BE ROUND OR SQUARE.
CHAIR LEG DETAIL
CORNER BLOCKS 1 1/4" x 3" x 3" GLUE AND JOIN WITH 1 1/4" NO. 7 F. H. WOOD SCREW.
18"
3/8" DOWEL
3/8" DOWEL
1/2" DOWEL
20"
NOTE: FRAME 1 1/4" STOCK
CORNER DETAIL
5°
3/8" ROUND
12"
3"
10°
22"
ANGLE IRON
CORNER
BLOCKS
3"
24"
FLAT IRON
UPHOLSTER USING SAGLESS SPRINGS.

CHAIR FRAME DETAILS

STORAGE / APPLIANCE CENTER

NOTES:

1. ALL RABBET AND DADO $\frac{1}{4}$" DEEP
2. MATERIAL: $\frac{3}{4}$" HARDWOOD PLYWOOD
3. PARTITIONS TO BE SCREWED THROUGH BOTTOM WITH # 7 x $1\frac{1}{4}$" F.H. WOOD SCREWS
4. ALL EXPOSED PLYWOOD EDGES TO BE COVERED WITH VENEER TAPE

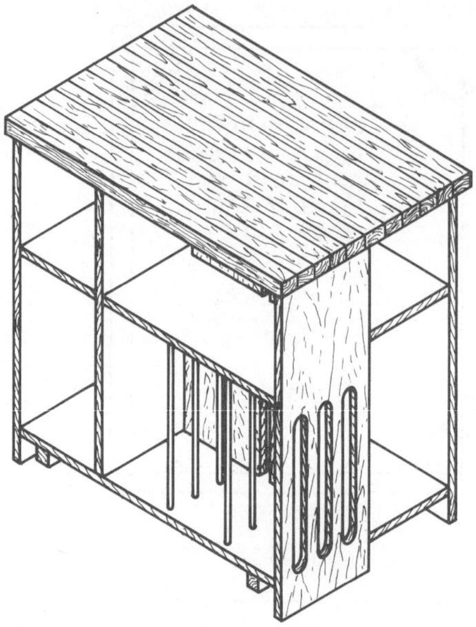

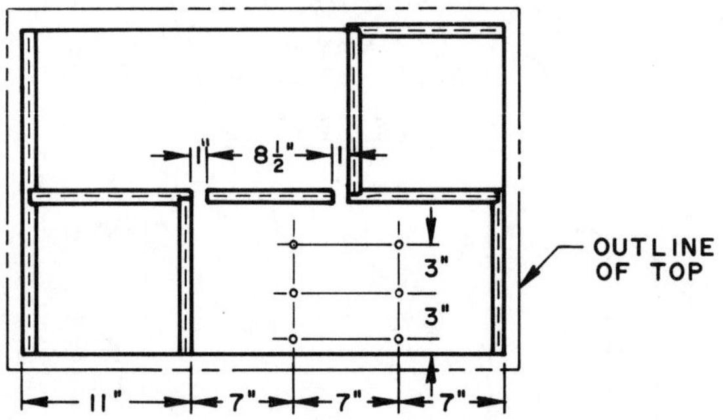

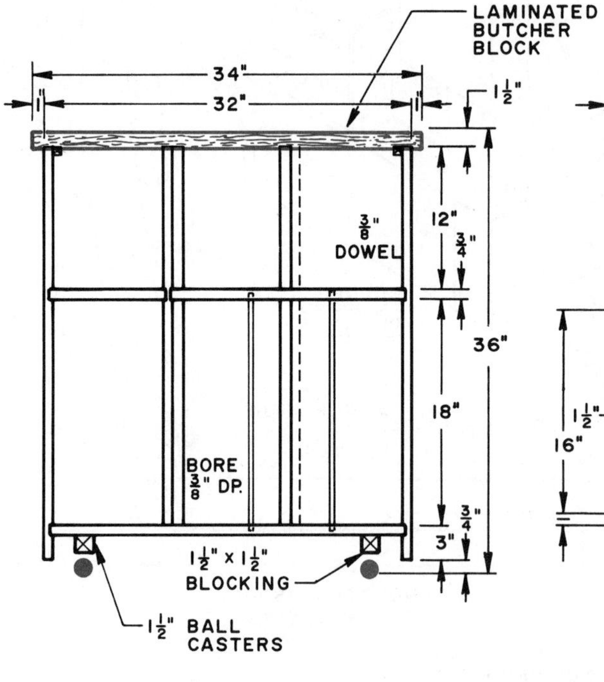

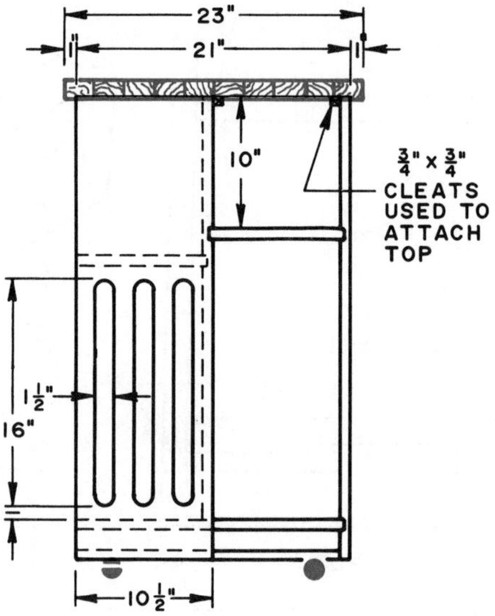

ANTIQUE BREAD BOX

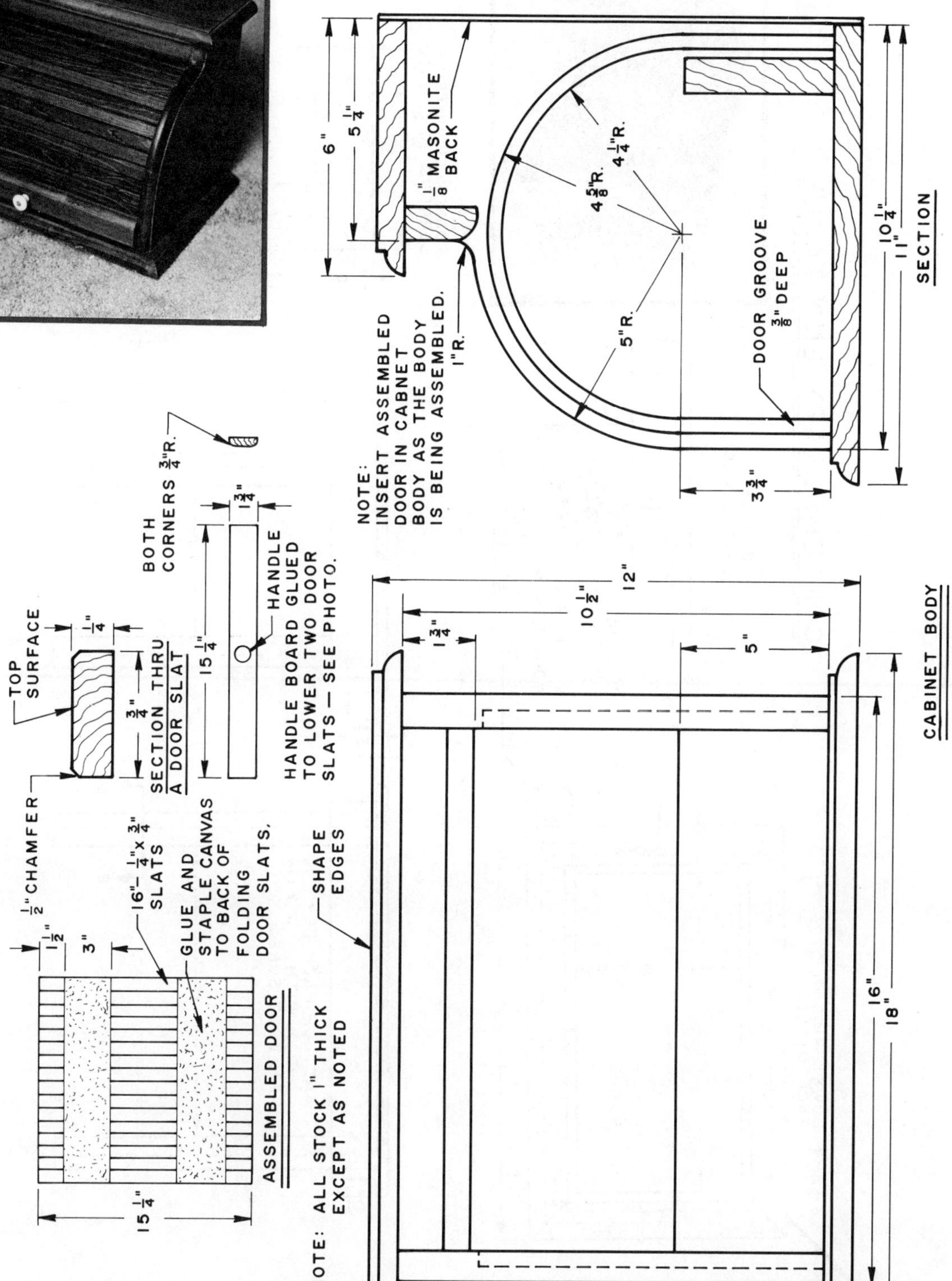

NOTE: INSERT ASSEMBLED DOOR IN CABINET BODY AS THE BODY IS BEING ASSEMBLED.

$\frac{1}{8}$" MASONITE BACK

6"

$5\frac{1}{4}$"

$4\frac{5}{8}$"R.

$4\frac{1}{4}$"R.

5"R.

1"R.

DOOR GROOVE $\frac{3}{8}$" DEEP

$3\frac{3}{4}$"

$10\frac{1}{4}$"

11"

SECTION

TOP SURFACE

$\frac{1}{4}$"

$\frac{3}{4}$"

SECTION THRU A DOOR SLAT

$\frac{1}{2}$" CHAMFER

BOTH CORNERS $\frac{3}{4}$"R.

$1\frac{3}{4}$"

$15\frac{1}{4}$"

HANDLE

HANDLE BOARD GLUED TO LOWER TWO DOOR SLATS — SEE PHOTO.

$1\frac{1}{2}$"

3"

16" - $\frac{1}{4}$" x $\frac{3}{4}$" SLATS

GLUE AND STAPLE CANVAS TO BACK OF FOLDING DOOR SLATS.

$15\frac{1}{4}$"

ASSEMBLED DOOR

SHAPE EDGES

12"

$10\frac{1}{2}$"

$1\frac{3}{4}$"

5"

16"

18"

1"

CABINET BODY

NOTE: ALL STOCK 1" THICK EXCEPT AS NOTED

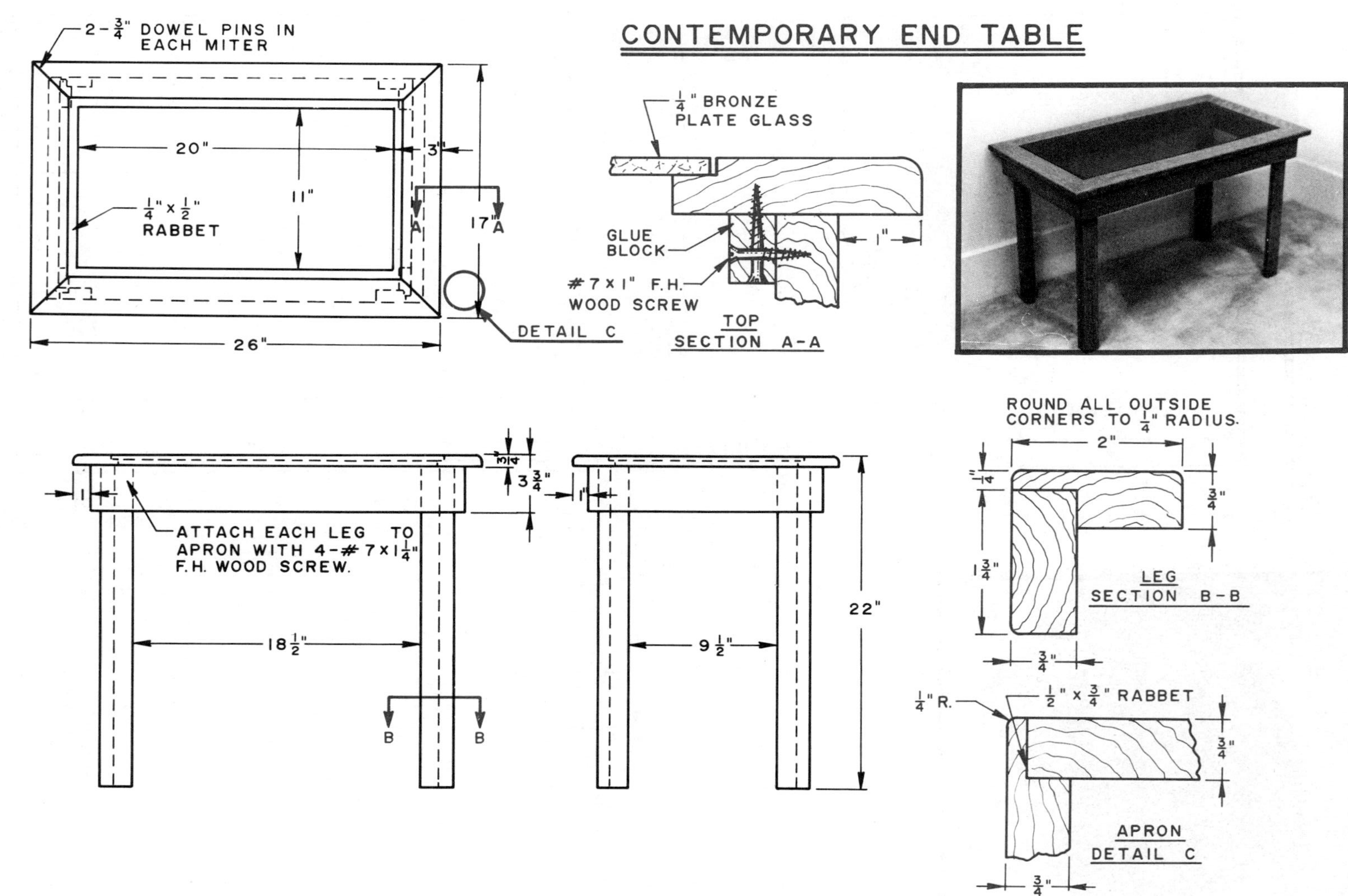
2-3/4" DOWEL PINS IN EACH MITER
CONTEMPORARY END TABLE
20"
3"
11"
1/4" x 1/2" RABBET
17"
A
26"
DETAIL C
1/4" BRONZE PLATE GLASS
GLUE BLOCK
#7 x 1" F.H. WOOD SCREW
1"
TOP SECTION A-A
ROUND ALL OUTSIDE CORNERS TO 1/4" RADIUS.
2"
3/4"
1 3/4"
1/4"
LEG SECTION B-B
3 3/4"
ATTACH EACH LEG TO APRON WITH 4-#7 x 1 1/4" F.H. WOOD SCREW.
18 1/2"
9 1/2"
22"
B
1/4" R.
1/2" x 3/4" RABBET
APRON DETAIL C

BEDSIDE TABLE

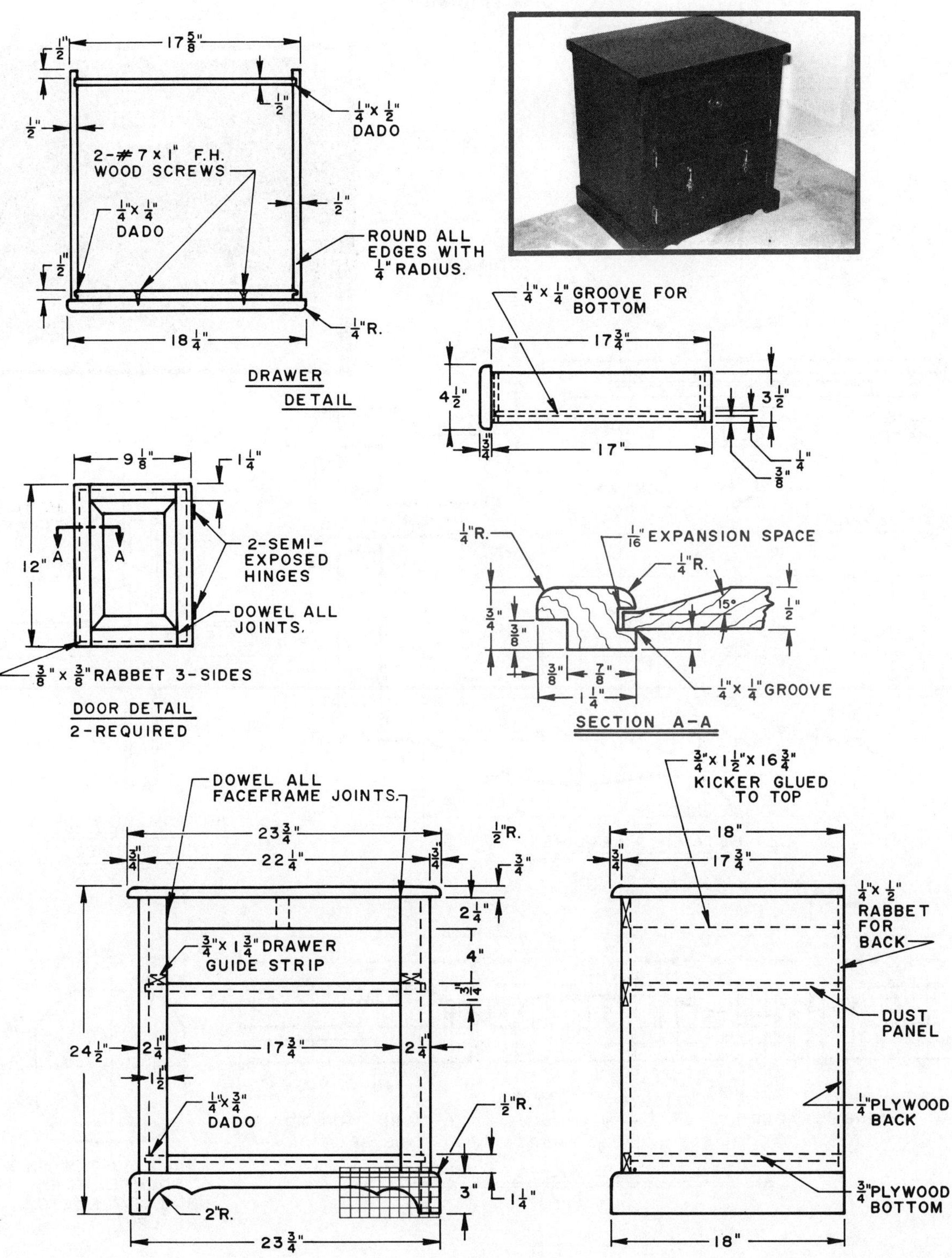

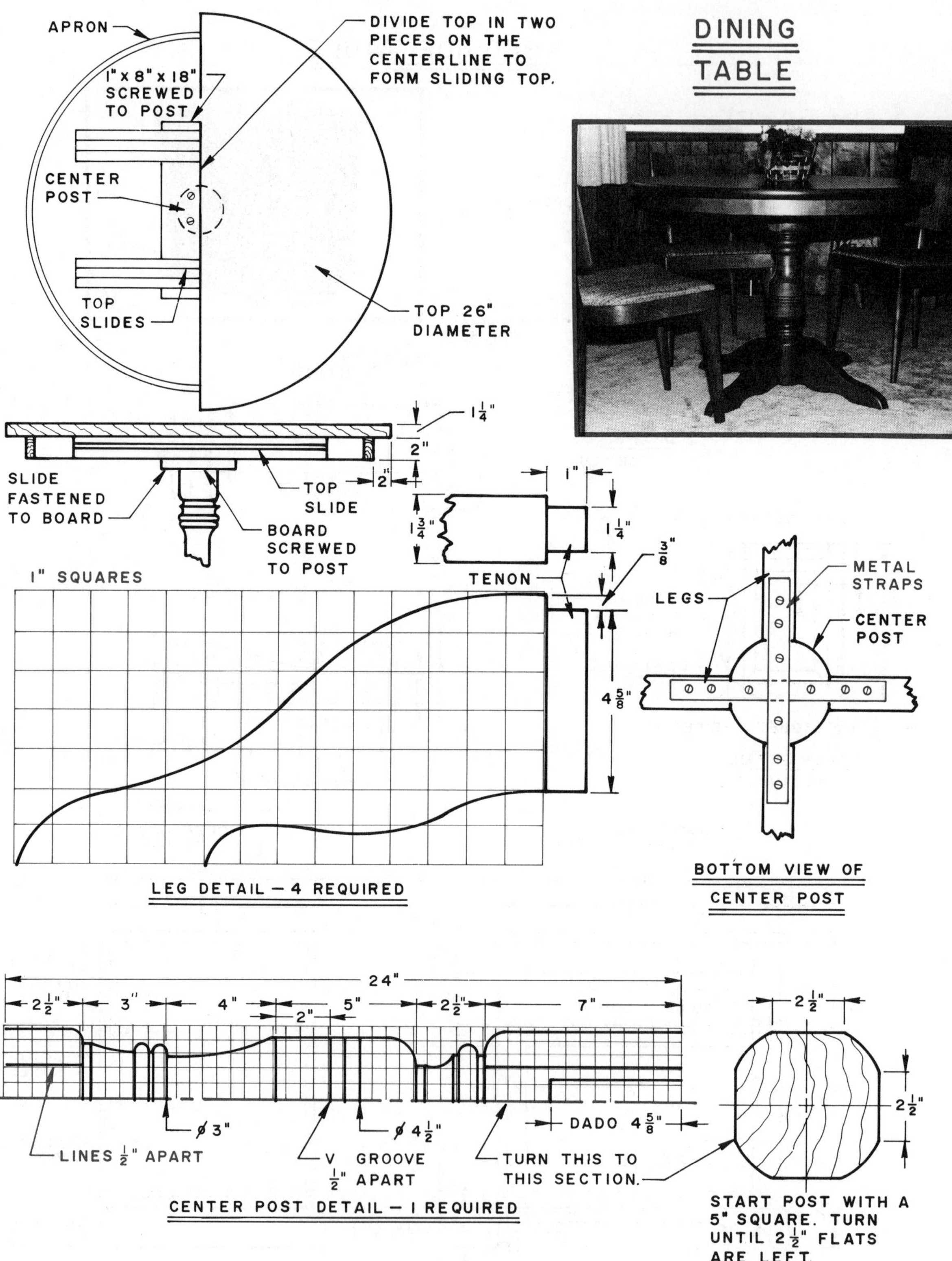

DINING TABLE
APRON
DIVIDE TOP IN TWO PIECES ON THE CENTERLINE TO FORM SLIDING TOP.
1" x 8" x 18" SCREWED TO POST
CENTER POST
TOP SLIDES
TOP 26" DIAMETER
1 1/4"
2"
2"
SLIDE FASTENED TO BOARD
TOP SLIDE
BOARD SCREWED TO POST
1"
1 3/4"
1 1/4"
3/8"
TENON
1" SQUARES
4 5/8"
LEG DETAIL — 4 REQUIRED
LEGS
METAL STRAPS
CENTER POST
BOTTOM VIEW OF CENTER POST
24"
2 1/2"
3"
4"
2"
5"
2 1/2"
7"
ø 3"
ø 4 1/2"
DADO 4 5/8"
LINES 1/2" APART
V GROOVE 1/2" APART
TURN THIS TO THIS SECTION.
CENTER POST DETAIL — 1 REQUIRED
2 1/2"
2 1/2"
START POST WITH A 5" SQUARE. TURN UNTIL 2 1/2" FLATS ARE LEFT.

HEXAGONAL COMMODE

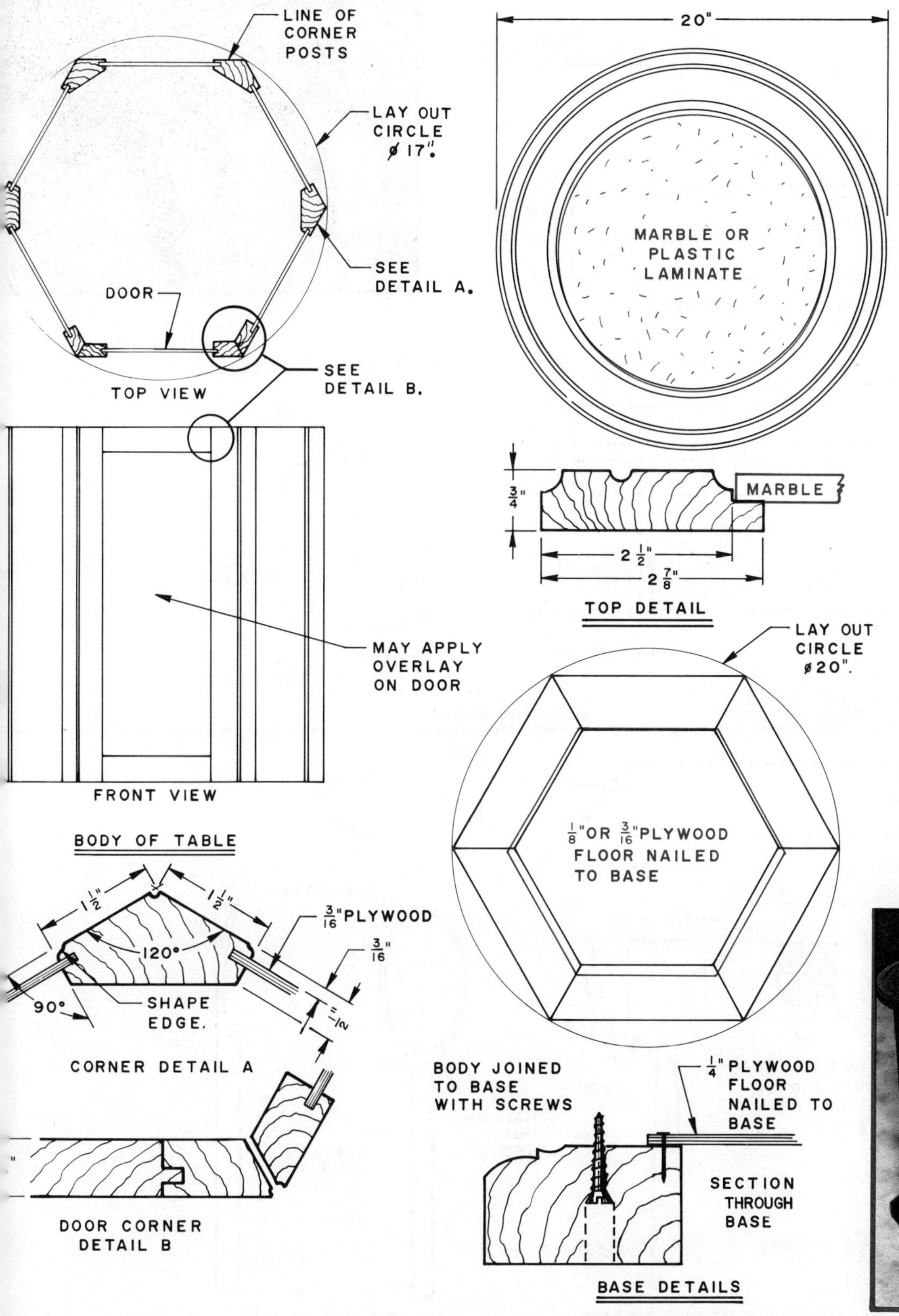

LINE OF CORNER POSTS

LAY OUT CIRCLE ⌀ 17".

SEE DETAIL A.

DOOR

SEE DETAIL B.

TOP VIEW

MAY APPLY OVERLAY ON DOOR

FRONT VIEW

BODY OF TABLE

$1\frac{1}{2}$" $1\frac{1}{2}$"

120°

$\frac{3}{16}$" PLYWOOD

$\frac{3}{16}$"

$\frac{1}{2}$"

90°

SHAPE EDGE.

CORNER DETAIL A

DOOR CORNER DETAIL B

20"

MARBLE OR PLASTIC LAMINATE

$\frac{3}{4}$"

MARBLE

$2\frac{1}{2}$"

$2\frac{7}{8}$"

TOP DETAIL

LAY OUT CIRCLE ⌀ 20".

$\frac{1}{8}$" OR $\frac{3}{16}$" PLYWOOD FLOOR NAILED TO BASE

BODY JOINED TO BASE WITH SCREWS

$\frac{1}{4}$" PLYWOOD FLOOR NAILED TO BASE

SECTION THROUGH BASE

BASE DETAILS

KITCHEN TOOLS

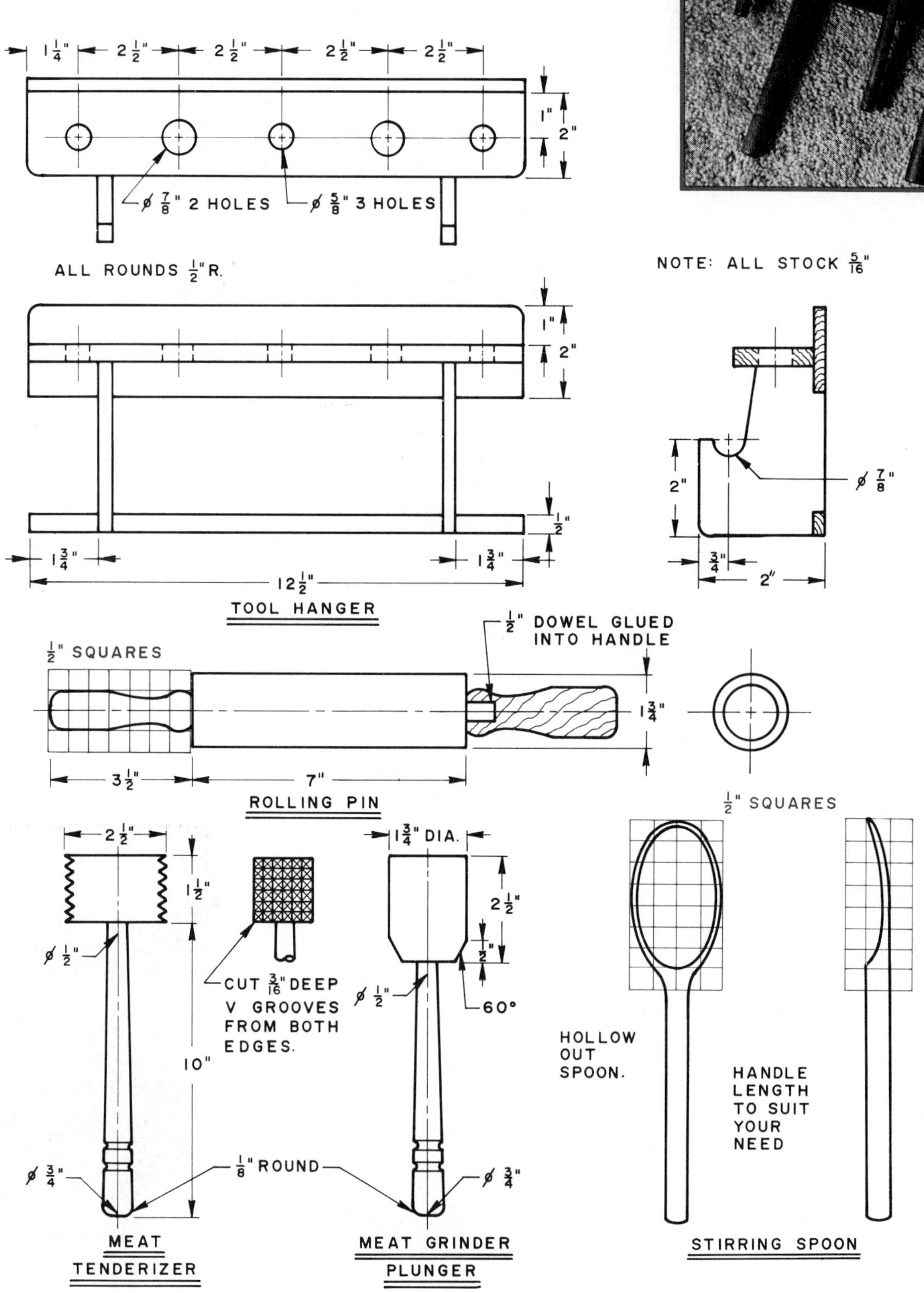

1 1/4" 2 1/2" 2 1/2" 2 1/2" 2 1/2"
1"
2"
ø 7/8" 2 HOLES
ø 5/8" 3 HOLES
ALL ROUNDS 1/2" R.
NOTE: ALL STOCK 5/16"
1"
2"
1/2"
1 3/4"
1 3/4"
12 1/2"
2"
ø 7/8"
3/4"
2"
TOOL HANGER
1/2" DOWEL GLUED INTO HANDLE
1/2" SQUARES
1 3/4"
3 1/2"
7"
ROLLING PIN
1/2" SQUARES
2 1/2"
1 1/2"
ø 1/2"
CUT 3/16" DEEP V GROOVES FROM BOTH EDGES.
10"
ø 3/4"
1/8" ROUND
MEAT TENDERIZER
1 3/4" DIA.
2 1/2"
1/2"
ø 1/2"
60°
ø 3/4"
MEAT GRINDER PLUNGER
HOLLOW OUT SPOON.
HANDLE LENGTH TO SUIT YOUR NEED
STIRRING SPOON

PICKETS AND SHUTTERS

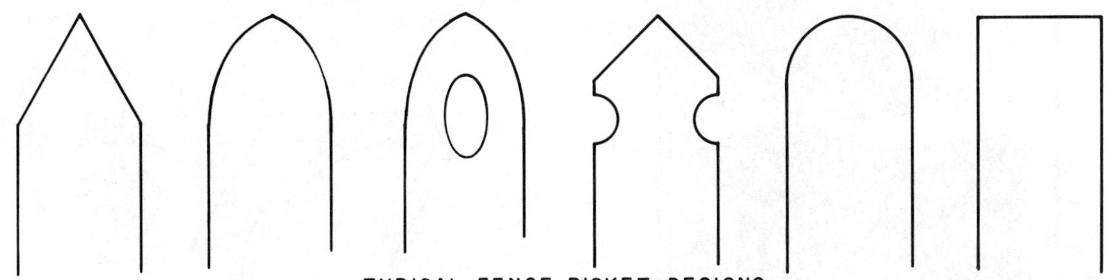

TYPICAL FENCE PICKET DESIGNS

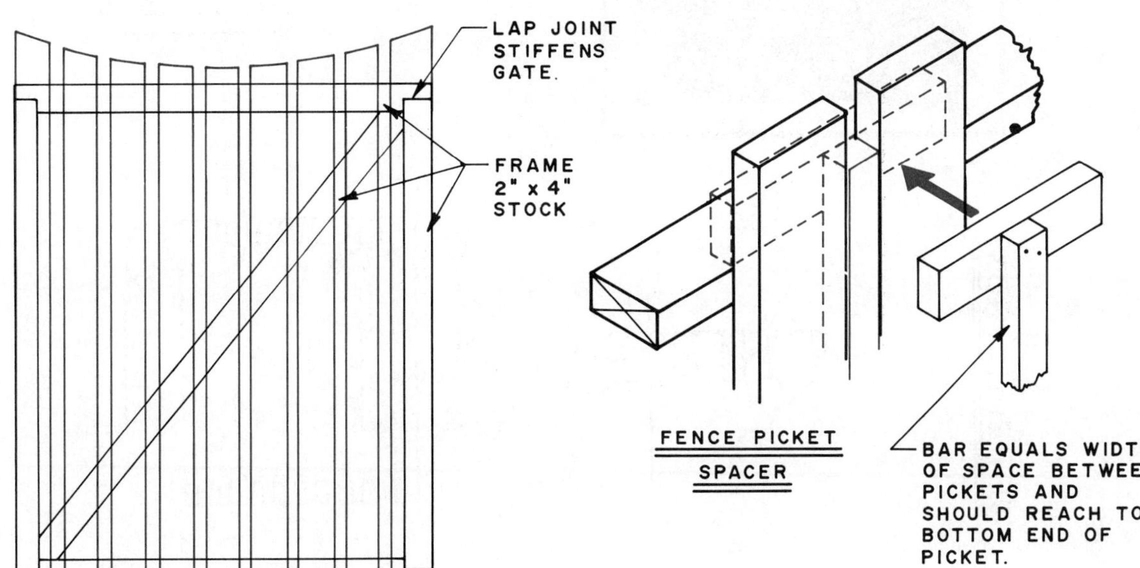
LAP JOINT STIFFENS GATE.
FRAME 2" x 4" STOCK
NAIL PICKETS TO FRAME AND DIAGONAL BRACE WITH GALVANIZED NAILS.
BAR EQUALS WIDTH OF SPACE BETWEEN PICKETS AND SHOULD REACH TO BOTTOM END OF PICKET.

TYPICAL GATE

FENCE PICKET SPACER

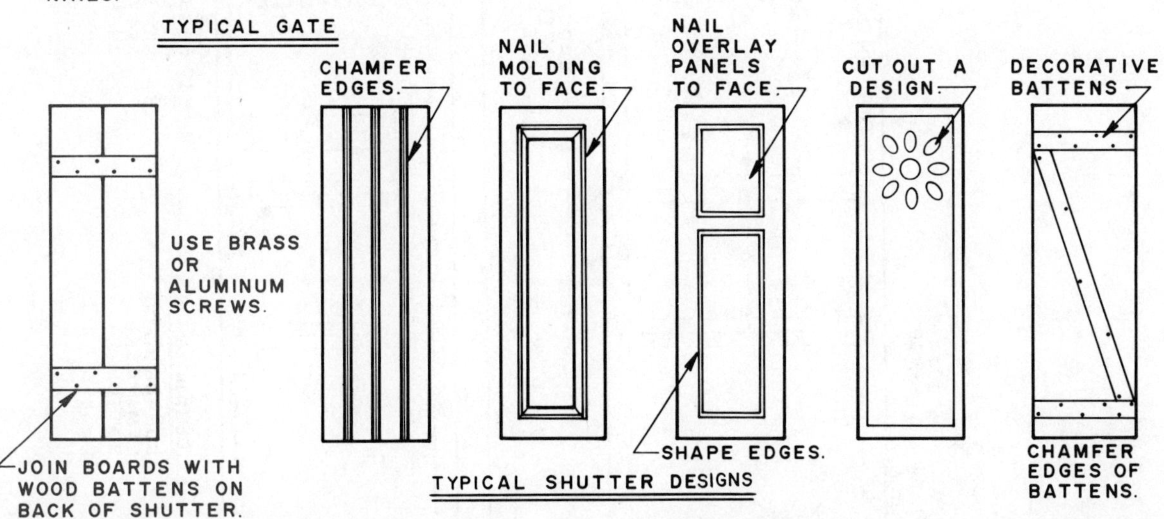
CHAMFER EDGES.
NAIL MOLDING TO FACE.
NAIL OVERLAY PANELS TO FACE.
CUT OUT A DESIGN.
DECORATIVE BATTENS
USE BRASS OR ALUMINUM SCREWS.
JOIN BOARDS WITH WOOD BATTENS ON BACK OF SHUTTER.
SHAPE EDGES.
CHAMFER EDGES OF BATTENS.

TYPICAL SHUTTER DESIGNS

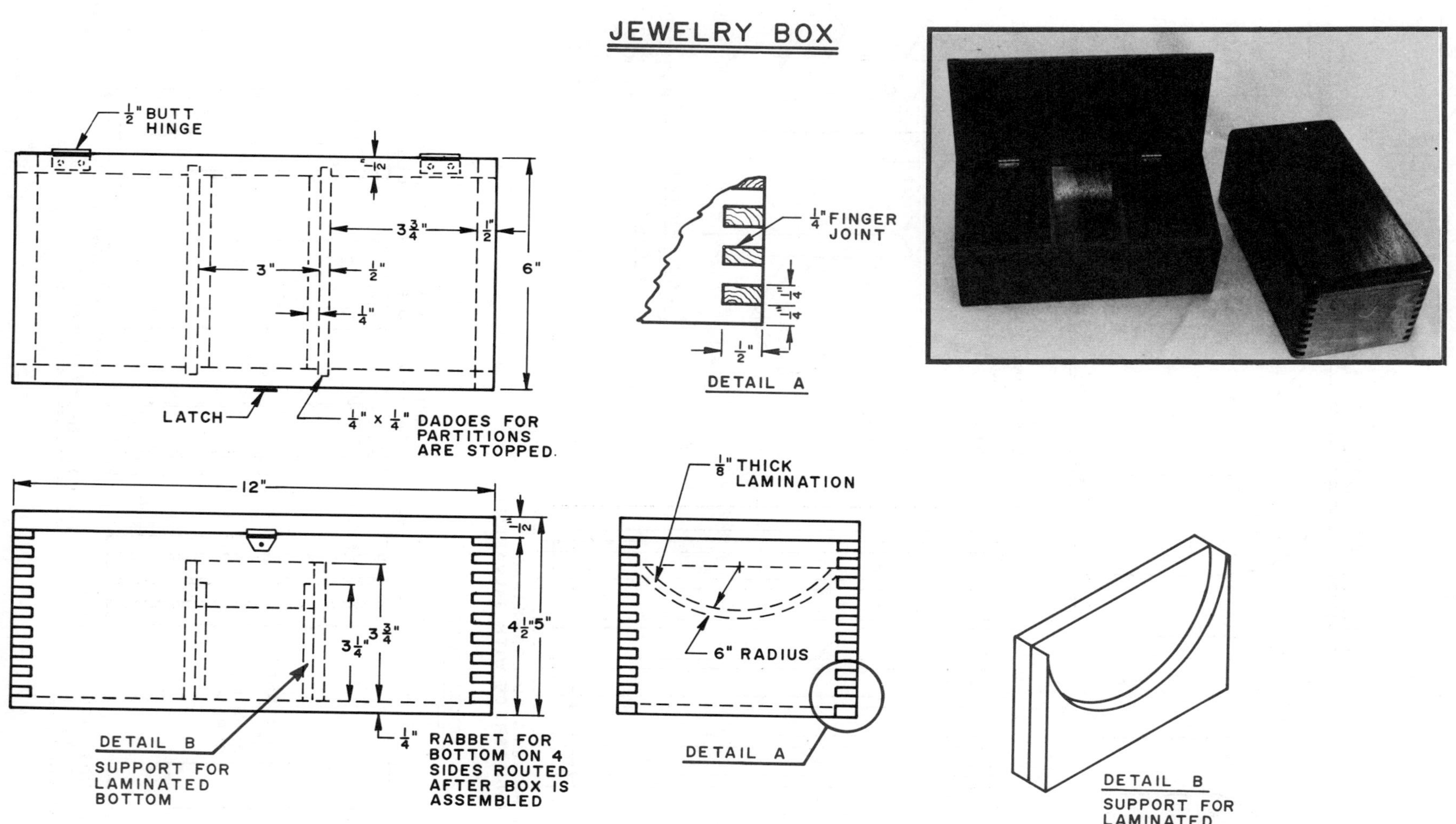
JEWELRY BOX
1/2" BUTT HINGE
1/2"
3 3/4"
1/2"
3"
1/2"
1/4"
6"
LATCH
1/4" x 1/4" DADOES FOR PARTITIONS ARE STOPPED.
1/4" FINGER JOINT
1/4"
1/4"
1/2"
DETAIL A
12"
1/2"
3 1/4"
3 3/4"
4 1/2"
5"
1/4" RABBET FOR BOTTOM ON 4 SIDES ROUTED AFTER BOX IS ASSEMBLED
DETAIL B
SUPPORT FOR LAMINATED BOTTOM
1/8" THICK LAMINATION
6" RADIUS
DETAIL A
DETAIL B
SUPPORT FOR LAMINATED BOTTOM.

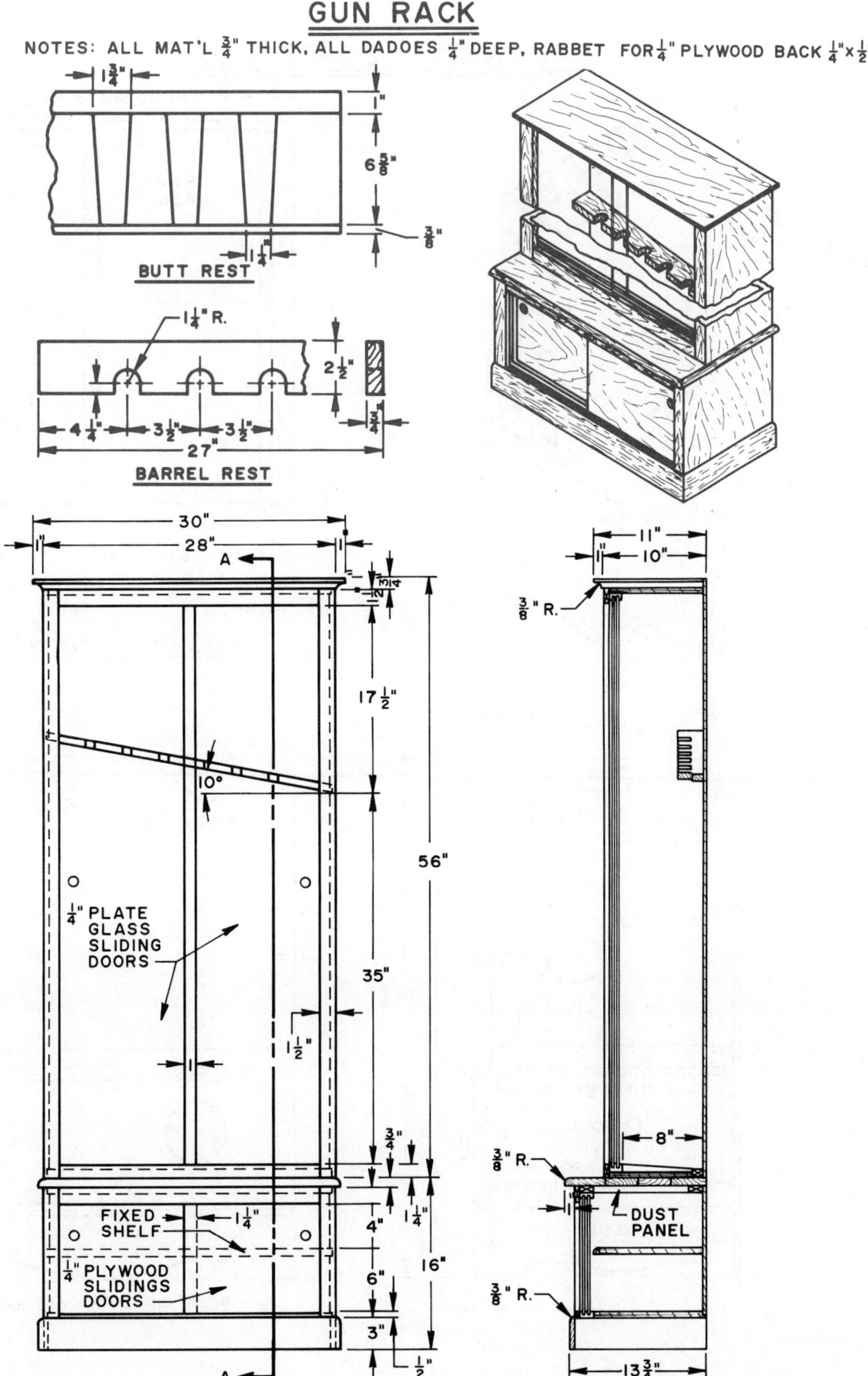
GUN RACK
NOTES: ALL MAT'L 3/4" THICK, ALL DADOES 1/4" DEEP, RABBET FOR 1/4" PLYWOOD BACK 1/4" x 1/2"
BUTT REST
BARREL REST
1 1/4" R.
27"
30"
28"
A
17 1/2"
10°
56"
1/4" PLATE GLASS SLIDING DOORS
35"
1 1/2"
FIXED SHELF
1/4" PLYWOOD SLIDINGS DOORS
4"
16"
6"
3"
11"
10"
3/8" R.
8"
DUST PANEL
13 3/4"
SECTION A-A

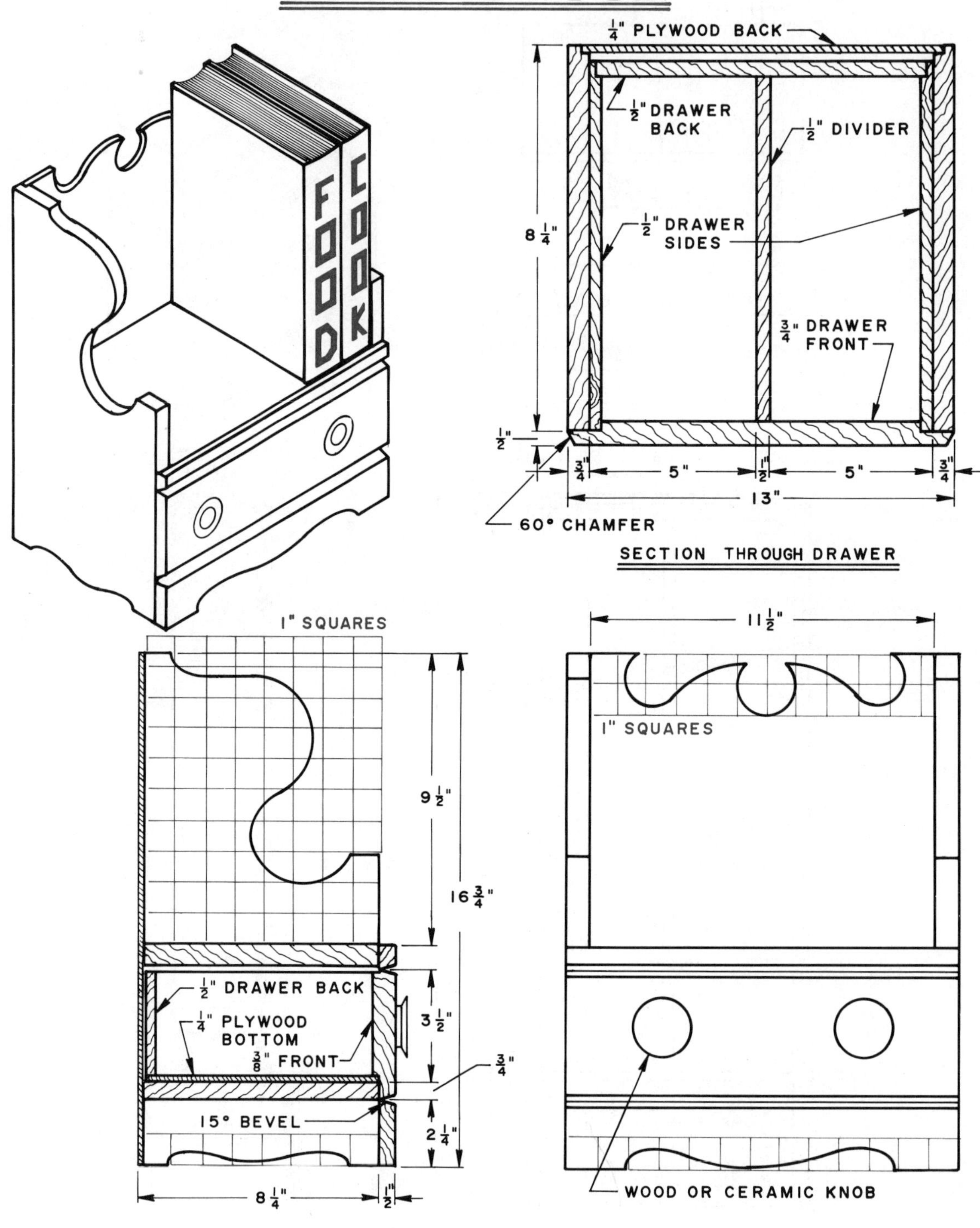
COLONIAL RECIPE BOX
FOOD
COOK
1/4" PLYWOOD BACK
1/2" DRAWER BACK
1/2" DIVIDER
1/2" DRAWER SIDES
3/4" DRAWER FRONT
8 1/4"
1/2"
3/4"
5"
1/2"
5"
3/4"
13"
60° CHAMFER
SECTION THROUGH DRAWER
1" SQUARES
9 1/2"
16 3/4"
1/2" DRAWER BACK
1/4" PLYWOOD BOTTOM
3/8" FRONT
3 1/2"
3/4"
15° BEVEL
2 1/4"
8 1/4"
1/2"
11 1/2"
1" SQUARES
WOOD OR CERAMIC KNOB

TURNINGS

THE FOLLOWING PROJECTS ARE BASED ON THE PURCHASE OF GLASS AND PLASTIC PARTS. BEFORE FINALIZING THE SIZE OF THE WOOD TURNING, BE CERTAIN THE PARTS ARE ON HAND SO THE WOOD CAN BE CUT TO FIT THEM. THE FOLLOWING ARE TYPICAL EXAMPLES OF UNITS AVAILABLE.

(Woodcraft Supply Corporation)

BUD VASE

GLASS BUD INSERT

VOID FOR WEIGHT

(Woodcraft Supply Corporation)

DISPLAY DOMES

(Woodcraft Supply Corporation)

HURRICANE LAMP

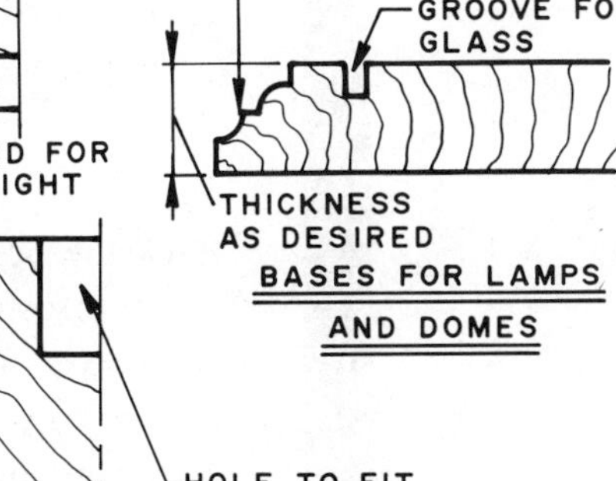

BASES FOR LAMPS AND DOMES

(Woodcraft Supply Corporation)

CHEESE SERVER

(Woodcraft Supply Corporation)

CANDLE HOLDER

HOLE TO FIT CANDLE OR CANDLE HOLDER

VOID FOR WEIGHT

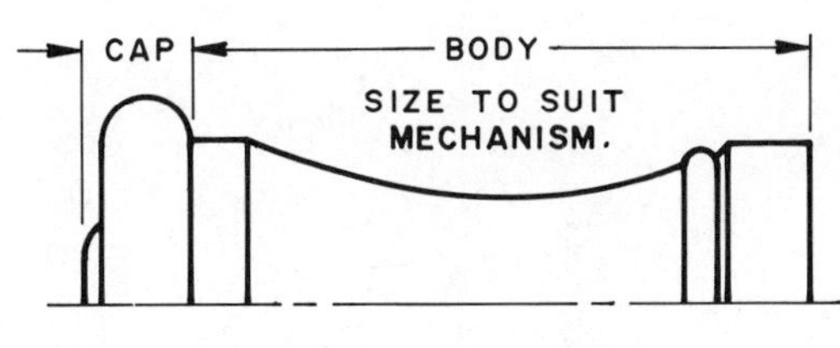

(Woodcraft Supply Corporation)

BOXES

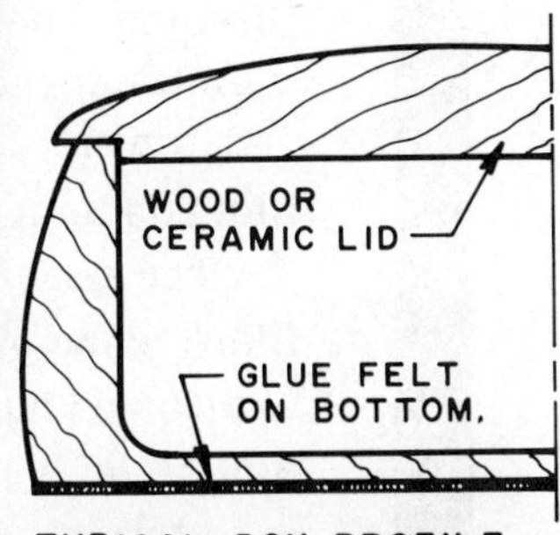

TYPICAL BOX PROFILE

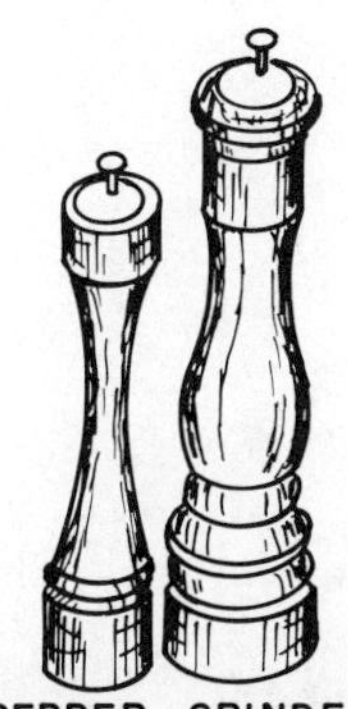

PEPPER GRINDER

Glossary

Abrasive A hard, sharp substance that smooths wood surfaces. Examples are flint, garnet, aluminum oxide and silicon carbide.

Adhesive An artificial material that holds two other materials together by surface attachment.

Air-dried lumber Lumber from which moisture has been removed by the heat and wind of the atmosphere.

Alcohol A thinner made from ethyl and wood alcohol, used in shellac.

Aluminum oxide An artificial abrasive used in abrasive paper and sharpening stones.

Annual growth ring A tree's growth layer, which is formed in one year. It contains springwood and summerwood.

Arbor A shaft in a woodworking machine on which a cutting tool is mounted.

Auger bit A tool used to bore holes in wood.

Backsaw A handsaw with a thin blade having a reinforced back and fine teeth.

Band saw An electric saw with an endless blade that runs over several large wheels. It is used for cutting curves.

Bark The outer layer of a tree.

Bayonet saw A portable electric jigsaw.

Belt sander An electric sander with an endless belt that runs over several wheels.

Benzene A solvent of coal tar used in finishing.

Bevel A sloping edge that runs from one face of a board to the other.

Bill of materials A statement listing the parts needed to make a product. It includes sizes and material details for each part.

Bleaching Removing the color from wood with a strong chemical solution.

Bleeding The soaking of a stain or other finishing material through the top layers of finish.

Blind dado A dado cut partway across a board. Once assembled, the joint cannot be seen.

Block plane A small hand plane useful for planing end grain.

Blue stain A fungus that causes certain woods to turn blue gray.

Blushing The changing of a lacquered finish to a whitish, cloudy color. It is caused by high humidity.

Board A piece of sawed lumber less than 2" (51 mm) thick.

Board foot A section of wood measuring 144 cubic inches.

Boiled linseed oil A natural oil finish that has been heated and mixed with metallic salts to shorten drying time.

Bonding agent An adhesive, glue or cement that fastens pieces of wood together.

Bore To make a round hole in wood.

Box nail A slender metal fastener with a large head on one end and a point on the other. It is used in heavy construction work.

Brace A crank-shaped hand tool used to turn an auger bit as it bores into wood.

Brad A small finishing nail available in lengths from 1/4" to 1-1/4" (6 to 32 mm).

Burl A bump that grows on the side of a tree. It is often sliced into highly figured veneer.

Burlap A coarse material woven of jute or hemp, used in upholstering.

Butt joint A joint made by fastening two boards end to end. The butt joint generally is the simplest but often the weakest joint, if it is not reinforced.

Cabinet clamp A clamp with a long bar, an adjustable jaw and a jaw operated by a screw. It is sometimes called a bar clamp.

Cabinet hinge A general term for any hinge used on cabinets.

Caliper A hand tool used to measure diameters of cylindrical and circular work.

Cambium The thin layer between the bark and the sapwood of a tree. It forms new wood and bark cells.

Carbide-tip circular saw blade A circular saw blade with a tungsten carbide tip on each tooth.

Casein glue A natural bonding agent made from milk curds.

Casing nail A slender metal fastener with a round, tapered head on one end and a point on the other.

C clamp A small, hand-operated clamp shaped like the letter C.

Cell A microscopic area enclosed in thin walls. Wood is made up of millions of cells.

Cellulose The substance forming the walls of wood cells.

Chamfer A slanted surface cut partway down an edge.

Check A lengthwise crack in a wood surface caused by loss of moisture.

Chisel A tool with a strong handle and a sharp cutting edge.

Chlorophyll The green coloring matter of plants.

Chuck A holding device designed to grip drill bits and other boring devices.

Circular saw An electrically driven saw with a circular blade sticking up through a flat, horizontal table.

Clamp A tool used to hold parts together.

Claw hammer A hammer with a pulling claw.

Combination blade A general-purpose, circular saw blade designed to crosscut and rip stock.

Common nail A metal fastener with a strong, flat head, a round body and a point on one end.

Compass saw A handsaw with a short, tapered blade.

Coniferous tree A cone-bearing, or evergreen, tree.

Conversion factor A figure used to convert dimensions, weights and other measures from customary to metric or metric to customary.

Coping saw A light saw with a C-shaped frame and a thin blade. It is used for cutting irregular curves in thin stock.

Core The center layer of a sheet of plywood.

Corrugated fastener A rectangular metal fastener with curved ridges and depressions on each side and teeth on one edge.

Counterboring Making one end of a hole larger so the head of a screw or bolt can fall below the surface and be covered from view. The sides of the hole are perpendicular to the surface.

Countersink A tool with a cone-shaped cutting edge used to cut a depression in the top of a hole. The cone-shaped hole is also called a countersink.

Cove A concave-shaped section in a piece of molding or lathe turning.

Crook The warping of a board along its edge.

Crossbands Thin veneer layers placed at right angles to the face and back.

Crosscut saw A saw designed to cut across the grain of a board.

Crotch The wood formed where two or more branches join together.

Cup The warping of a board across its width to make a rounded surface.

Dado A rectangular groove cut across the grain of a board.

Deciduous tree A tree with flat leaves that shed in the fall.

Defect Any irregularity in wood that lowers the grade of the material.

Diameter The straight line distance from a point on the circumference of a circle through the center to the circumference on the other side.

Diamond point chisel A narrow-bladed, wood-turning chisel with a cutting edge ending in a V-shaped point.

Dimension lumber Lumber more than 2″ (51 mm) but less than 5″ (127 mm) thick.

Double-cut file A file with a double set of teeth that cross each other at an angle.

Dovetail joint An interlocking joint with tapered pegs cut on the end of one board to fit into the matched recesses of the other.

Dowel A round wood pin used to align and strengthen a joint.

Dowel joint A butt joint reinforced with dowel pins.

Dressed size The size of lumber after it has been planed.

Drill To cut holes using straight shank twist drills.

Dry rot A form of decay that causes wood to fall apart. Dry rot occurs when the moisture content is higher than 20 percent.

Duplicate parts Parts that are the same size and shape.

Enamel An opaque finishing material made with colored pigments and a varnish.

End grain The surface of a board that exposes the ends of cells.

Equilibrium Moisture Content (EMC) The point at which wood does not take on or give off moisture when the surrounding air is at a given temperature and relative humidity.

Expansive bit A woodboring bit with an adjustable cutter that cuts holes of various diameters.

External-mix gun A type of spray gun that mixes the atomized finish air just in front of the air cap.

Feather board A wooden safety device containing several fingers to hold stock against the table or fence.

Fell To cut down a tree.

Fence A wood or metal guide that holds wood being processed on a machine.

Ferrule A metal sleeve placed over the bottom end of a chair or a table leg.

Fiber A long, narrow, tapering wood cell closed at both ends.

Fiber Saturation Point (FSP) The point at which the cell walls of a piece of wood are totally saturated with moisture, but none is contained within the cell cavity, or lumen. The FSP will occur between 25 and 32 percent moisture content.

Figure A pattern produced in a wood surface when the annual rings, medullary rays and knots are cut during sawing.

File A steel blade with rows of teeth used to smooth rough wood surfaces.

File card A brush with short, stiff bristles used to remove wood caught in the teeth of files.

Filler A paste preparation used to fill the pores of open-grained woods.

Finishing nail A round, slender metal fastener with a small, round head on one end and a point on the other. The head generally is set below the top surface of the wood.

Firsts and Seconds (FAS) The best commercial grades of hardwood lumber.

Flat head screw A wood screw with a flat, cone-shaped head.

Flint An inexpensive, natural abrasive, light tan in color, used in abrasive paper.

Flitch All the veneer sliced from one tree.

Foam rubber A padding material made of urethane, used as cushions in upholstered furniture.

Folding rule A rule that folds into a unit about 6″ (152 mm) long.

Forstner bit A wood bit without a feed screw, used to bore shallow holes close to the bottom side of a board.

Fraction A part of a whole, such as 1/4.

Framing square A large steel square used in carpentry and cabinetmaking.

French Polish A mixture of shellac and linseed oil used as a finish on lathe turnings.

Full-cell process The process of forcing preservatives or fire retardants into wood cells by means of a vacuum.

Fungi Microscopic plants in damp wood that cause mold, stain and decay.

Gain A rectangular notch cut into a piece of wood to receive a hinge.

Garnet A reddish abrasive used primarily in hand abrasive paper.

Gimp A braided cord used to trim the edges of an upholstered piece of furniture.

Glide A smooth, round, metal unit attached to the bottom of a leg of furniture. It helps the leg slide on the floor and keeps the leg from chipping.

Glue An organic material that joins objects together.

Gouge A concave woodcutting chisel.

Grade A designation of the quality of lumber or plywood.

Grain The arrangement, direction or pattern of the fibrous tissue in wood.

Green lumber Newly sawed lumber or wood with a large amount of moisture.

Grinder An electrically driven machine with rotating abrasive wheels, used to sharpen edge tools.

Groove A rectangular cut that runs parallel to the grain of a board.

Gullet The space between the tips of saw teeth.

Hand drill A hand-held drill with a chuck that holds straight shank twist drills.

Handsaw A steel blade with crosscut or rip teeth and a handle on one end.

Hand-screw clamp A clamp with two parallel wood jaws controlled by two hand-operated screws.

Hardboard A panel made by placing tiny wood fibers under heat and pressure.

Hardware Metal and plastic items, such as hinges, drawer slides, drawer pulls and sliding door channels.

Hardwood Wood cut from deciduous trees.

Heartwood The mature, dead wood forming the center of a tree. Often it is darker than the surrounding sapwood.

Hollow ground The sides of a saw blade made concave to reduce the width of the saw kerf and prevent binding of the blade.

Hone A hard stone that sharpens cutting tools.

Honeycombing Internal checking of wood along the wood rays.

Inlay An ornament set even with the top surface of a board.

Irregular curve A curve that does not have a fixed radius. Also a drafting tool used to draw irregular curves.

Jack plane A general-purpose plane that smooths the surface of boards.

Jig A device that positions a part or a tool for accurate machining.

Joint The setting of two pieces so that they can be secured together.

Jointer A power tool containing a circular cutterhead with knife blades. It is used primarily to make edges and faces of a board straight and smooth.

Jointer plane A plane with a long bed, used to smooth long edges and surfaces.

Kerf A slot made by the blade of a saw.

Kicker A strip of hardwood placed immediately above a drawer to keep it from tilting down as it is being pulled out.

Kiln drying Drying lumber with heat and controlled moisture in a closed room called a kiln.

Knot A hard, irregular area in a board, made by cutting through the place where a branch joins the trunk.

Lacquer A tough, durable, brittle finish.

Laminate To bond together several layers of material.

Lap joint A joint made by overlapping two boards and cutting them so they are flush when assembled.

Lathe An electrically driven machine used to form round parts, such as table legs and bowls.

Lazy Susan A specialized kitchen cabinet with revolving shelves.

Lignin A thermoplastic substance in a tree that serves as a bonding agent between the cells.

Lumber Wood cut to size at a sawmill and smoothed at a planing mill.

Lumber core plywood Plywood with a core of lumber.

Mallet A hammer with a head of wood or plastic.

Marking gauge A tool used to draw lines parallel to the edges of boards.

Medullary rays Rows of cells lying at right angles to the growth rings of a tree.

Meter The basic linear unit in the metric system of measurement, 39.37″.

Mill file A file with a single row of teeth.

Millimeter The smallest linear measurement in the metric system, 1/1000 of a meter.

Millwork The wood products made by millworking firms. Examples include finish woodwork, such as cabinets, windows, doors and trim.

Miter A joint formed by the meeting of two pieces at an angle, usually of 45°.

Miter box A tool that holds a board and a saw at a desired angle to each other while the board is being cut.

Moisture content The amount of water in a piece of wood, expressed as the percentage of oven-dry weight.

Molding A shaped piece of trim that adds decoration.

Mortise A rectangular hole cut to receive a tenon.

Muslin A coarse cotton cloth used in upholstering.

Nail A slender metal fastener that holds pieces of wood together.

Nail set A pointed tool that sets the head of a nail below the surface of a board.

Nib The cutting point on an auger bit that scores the wood in a circular pattern.

Nominal size The standard rough dimensions of lumber as it comes from the sawmill and before it is planed. These sizes are the way lumber is sold and not the actual finish dimensions.

Oil stain An oil-based stain used to color wood.

Oilstone A block of abrasive material that sharpens edge tools.

Open coat A type of abrasive paper with a large percentage of its surface uncovered by abrasive.

Open grain Ring-porous woods, such as oak and ash, that have many large pores on the surface.

Orange peel A pebbly lacquer finish caused by poor thinning or incorrect spraying methods.

Oval head screw A wood screw with an oval head.

Oven-dry wood Wood that has been dried in an oven to 0 percent moisture content.

Paint A pigment mixed with oil and used to coat wood.

Panel A large, flat sheet of material, such as plywood, hardboard or particle board.

Particle board A smooth, artificial panel formed by gluing wood chips together.

Parting tool A woodturning tool with a narrow cutting edge ending in a sharp V point.

Penny The term used to indicate the size of nails. The abbreviation for penny is *d.*

Perforated blade tool A forming tool with a thin steel blade that has holes punched through it to form teeth. It is used to smooth boards.

Phillips head screw A screw head with a cross-shaped slot.

Pigment A substance that gives color to material.

Pilot hole A hole drilled in the wood to receive the threaded portion of a wood screw. The screw's threads cut into the sides of the hole.

Pith The small, soft core of spongy tissue at the center of a tree.

Plain-sawed Lumber sawed in a plane perpendicular to the radius of a log. It is also called flat-sawed.

Plan of procedure A detailed listing of the steps to follow when building a product.

Plane A hand tool that smooths boards.

Planer An electrically powered machine that smooths the surface of boards.

Plastic laminate A thin plastic material used for covering countertops and cabinet fronts.

Plough A groove cut parallel to the direction of the grain.

Ply A single, thin layer of wood, usually about 1/28″ (.9 mm) thick.

Plywood A large panel made by gluing together thin layers of wood with the grains of adjoining layers perpendicular to each other.

Pocket cut A hole sawed completely inside the edges of the board.

Pore Minute opening in the surface of a board.

Preservative Chemical injected into boards to keep wood from decaying or being destroyed by insects.

Pressure-fed gun A spray-gun in which the liquid finish is forced by air pressure from the storage cup to the gun.

Primer A thin-bodied paint applied before other coats to penetrate the wood.

Protractor A tool that measures angles in degrees.

Pumice A white, finely ground, abrasive powder that polishes finishes. It comes from pulverized lava rock.

Push drill A hand-held drill using bits with flutes on each side. Pushing the handle up and down causes the bit to rotate clockwise and then counterclockwise.

Push stick A stick that pushes boards past a saw blade or other dangerous cutting device.

Quality control points Stages during the construction process at which the project is checked to see if it is within the specifications.

Quarter sawed Lumber sawed so that the annual rings are perpendicular to the face of the board.

Quill The sleeve that houses the drill press spindle and allows the drill chuck to be moved up or down.

Rabbet An L shape cut from the edge of a board.

Rabbet joint A joint made by fastening a piece of stock in an L-shaped recess cut along the edge of a board.

Rabbet plane A hand plane designed to cut rabbets in the edges of boards.

Raised panel door A door with a frame made of solid lumber with a concave cut around its edges.

Rasp A file with teeth on each surface. It is used for the rough filing of wood surfaces.

Relief cut A small cut made in the waste portion of the stock to make it easier to saw sharp curves.

Resawing Sawing lumber a second time to form thinner boards or dimension lumber.

Ripping Cutting in the direction of the grain of a board.

Ripsaw A saw designed to cut parallel to the grain of a board.

Rotary cutting Removing a thin layer of wood from a log by rotating it into a knife.

Rottenstone A fine, dark, polishing abrasive made from pulverized limestone.

Round head screw A wood screw with a half-round head.

Roundnose chisel A woodturning tool with a round cutting edge.

Router An electric machine that cuts grooves and shaped cuts into the surface or edge of boards.

Rubbing compound An abrasive that smooths the finish after it has dried.

Saber saw A portable electric saw with a small, straight blade that moves up and down. It cuts curves.

Sag A run in a wet film of finish when too much finish is applied.

Sand To rub the surface of a board with abrasive paper.

Sapwood The layer of a tree between the heartwood and the cambium. It is usually light in color and weight when dried.

Scarf A tapered joint used to join the ends of two pieces of wood.

Screw A metal fastening device that tapers to a point and has threads that cut into the wood.

Screwdriver A tool that drives screws into wood.

Sealer A layer of finish used to seal stain or other material that may bleed through the later coats of finish.

Season To remove the moisture from wood after it has been cut into lumber.

Section A drawing made along an imaginary plane through a product to show the interior details.

Set To bend the teeth of a saw right and left alternately so that the kerf is wider than the blade.

Shake Internal cracking of trees along the growth rings.

Shank hole A hole drilled in the wood to receive a wood screw.

Shellac A finishing material made of lac and alcohol.

Silicon carbide An artificial, black abrasive used in abrasive paper and sharpening stones.

Single-cut file A file with a single set of parallel teeth running diagonally across the face.

Skew chisel A woodturning tool with a slanted edge that makes shearing cuts.

Slip stone A small, wedge-shaped oilstone that sharpens gouges.

Smoothing plane A general-purpose plane slightly smaller than a jack plane.

Softwood Wood produced by conifers, or trees that have needles and cones.

Solvent A solution that dissolves a finishing material or cleans equipment.

Spar varnish A tough, waterproof, transparent finish.

Spirit stain An aniline dye mixed with alcohol that colors wood.

Spline A thin strip of wood set into grooves in two adjoining boards to help glue them together.

Springwood or earlywood The part of a growth ring that develops early in the growing season. It has thin-walled cells.

Square To produce surfaces at 90° angles to each other.

Square foot Equal to 144 square inches of surface area.

Starved joint A glue joint that lacks an adequate bonding agent.

Steel wool Fine strands of steel packed together to form a pad, used for rubbing down finishes.

Stick shellac Colored shellac in stick form. It melts into cracks of boards.

Sticker Wood strips placed between layers of wood that are stacked for seasoning.

Straight shank twist drill A drill with a round, straight shank and spiral flutes leading to the cutting edges.

Structural lumber Lumber that is 2″ (51 mm) or more thick and 4″ (102 mm) or more wide, intended for use where strength is required.

Suction-feed gun A spray gun that draws finish into the air cap by developing a vacuum in the storage container.

Summerwood or latewood The part of a growth ring that develops late in the growing season. It has thick-walled cells.

Tack Small, sharp-pointed nail with a large, flat head.

Tack rag A sticky rag that wipes down a project and picks up any dust.

Taper The gradual reducing of size toward one end.

T bevel A tool with an adjustable blade that lays out angles.

Template A full-size pattern that lays out a part.

Tenon A rectangular part designed to fit inside a mortise.

Thermosetting adhesive Bonding agent that undergoes a chemical change. Most types are waterproof and heat resistant.

Thinner A liquid added to a finishing material to reduce its thickness.

Timber Lumber 5″ (127 mm) or more in its smallest dimension.

Toenailing Driving a nail through one piece on a slant to enter a second piece on a slant.

Try square A tool that lays out and checks right angles.

Turpentine An oil from pine trees used as a thinner in oil-base paint and as a solvent in varnish.

Upholstering The technique of installing springs and applying padding and fabric to chairs and other covered furniture.

Upholstery spring Metal support made from steel wire that cushions seats and backs of chairs, sofas and other seating units.

Varnish A clear finishing material made from resin, drying oil and thinner.

Vehicle The liquid part of a finish bonding material.

Veneer A thin layer of wood glued over thicker wood to provide a more attractive surface.

Vise A holding tool with two jaws and a long screw to adjust them. It is fastened to a workbench and is used to hold materials.

Wane A defect in a board in which bark is present or part of the board is missing.

Warp The twisting of a board from a flat, true surface.

Wash coat A thin layer of finish that seals any finishing materials or wood pores.

Water stain A water-soluble dye that colors wood.

Water white The clearest lacquer or varnish.

Webbing Strips of jute fiber, plastic or metal suspended across the seat or back of a chair frame.

Webbing stretcher A tool that fastens webbing to the frame of a furniture piece.

Whet To sharpen a cutting edge on an oilstone.

Wind The twisting of a board into a shape like a propeller.

Working drawing A drawing showing the details needed to make a product.

Index

A
abrasives
  aluminum oxide, 374, 456, 464
  closed-coat paper, 458
  coated, 456
  electro-coated paper, 458
  emery, 456
  flint, 456
  garnet, 374, 456, 464
  grit sizes, 374, 458, 459
  manufacturing of, paper, 457
  natural, 456
  open-coat paper, 458
  purchasing of, 458
  sanding belts, 459
  sanding machine, 374
  sanding screen, artificial, 456
  sandpaper, 456
  silicon carbide, 456
  synthetic, 456
  synthetic fiber, 457
  thicknesses of, 456
  types of, 456
adhesives, 131, 132, 219, 221-223
  aliphatic thermoplastic resin, 221-222
  alpha cyanoacrylate, 222
  in assembling, 131, 132
  epoxy, 223
  hot melts, 222
  melamine-formaldehyde, 223
  phenol-formaldehyde, 223
  polyvinyl, 221
  resorcinol-formaldehyde, 223
  superglues, 222
  thermoplastics, 221-222
  thermosets, 221, 222-223
  white glue, 221
  yellow glue, 221
alkyd finish, 478
aluminum oxide abrasive, 374, 456, 464
American Plywood Association, 536, 537, 538
American Softwood Lumber Standard, 523
anchor, 186-189
  hollow wall, 186, 187
  lead calking, 188
  masonry, 186, 188
  Phillips nylon, 188, 189
  pin-grip masonry, 188
  plastic screw, 186, 188, 189
  plates, 186, 188, 189
angles, laying out of, 62
  protractors, 62
  T bevel, 62, 63
appearance, as design quality, 20
architect, 583
assembling devices, industrial, 124-129
  air-powered machines, 125
  case clamping machine, 127
  chair clamping machine, 127
  clamp carrier, 129
  clamping machines, 125
  door and sash clamping machine, 126
  drawer assembly machine, 126
  frame assembly machine, 127-128
  glue spreader, 129
  headboard and cabinet clamping machine, 125
  high-frequency assembly machine, 126
  panel-clamping device, 129
  pneumatic tools, 125
  upholstered-furniture machine, 127
assembly procedures, 120-137
  adhesive spreaders, 131, 132
  cabinet assembly, 137
  clamping, 133
  edge-to-edge assembly, 134
  face-to-face assembly, 133
  furniture frame assembly, 137
  glue joint cleaning, 134, 135
  subassemblies, 136, 137
  trial assembly, 131
auger bit, 102, 110-116
  bit gauge, 114
  boring with, 112-114
  counterbore, 114, 115
  countersink, 115
  double twist, 110, 111
  dowel bit, 111
  parts of, 110, 111
  single twist, 110, 111
  T bevel, 116
  types of, 110

B
backsaw, 73-75
band saw, 270-282, 546, 547
  blades, 272-275, 276
  circle cutting, 278-279
  compound sawing, 277-278
  crosscutting, 282
  curve cutting, 275-276
  curved wood members, 546, 547
  parts, 271
  resawing, 281
  ripping, 280
  safety rules, 270
  square inside corners, 281
  straight cuts, 280
  terminology, 270-272
  tracking, 270-271
bar clamp uses, 122, 123
belt sander, portable, 423-425
  dustbag attachments, 424
  parts of, 423, 424
  procedure for use, 425
  uses of, 423-424
belt sander, small stationary, 373, 378
  safety rules, 373
belt sander, wide, 374, 378-379
  parts, 378, 379
  safety rules, 374
bending wood, 546-551
  ammonia bending chamber, 548
  chemical, 548
  steam, 548
bevel
  cutting, 250
  jointing, 306
  making with hand plane, 82-84
  shaping with portable power planes, 399
bill of materials, 38
bits, drill, 363-365
  auger, 364
  Forstner, 364
  multi-spur, 364
  spade, 365
  spur, 363-364
  twist drills, 363
bits, portable router, 404-406
  beading, 404, 405
  carbide, 404
  carbon steel, 404
  chamfer, 405
  core box, 405
  cove, 405
  cutting edge, 404
  dovetail, 406, 407
  installation, 406
  pilot, 404
  rabbeting, 406, 407
  roman ogee, 405
  rounding over, 404, 405
  shank, 404
  straight, 406
  veining, 406
  V-grooving, 406
blades, band saw, 272-275, 276
blades, reciprocating saw, 392
blades, table saw, 236-241
  carbide 236, 237, 240, 241
  carbon steel, 236, 237, 238, 241
  changing of, 241
  combination, 238
  crosscut, 236
  flooring, 239
  hollow-ground body, 238
  plywood, 238, 239
  rip, 236, 237
  specialty, 238
  spring set, 238, 239
block plane, 85
boards, softwood grade, 523-524
  common, 524
  factory (shop), 524
  molding, 524
bolts, 184-185
  hanger, 184
  spring toggle, 187
  stove, 184
  toggle, 186, 187
bonding agents, 219-229. *See also* adhesives, cements, glues
boring on drill press, 366-371
  angular holes, 370-371
  circular stock, 371
  counterboring, 370-371
  deep holes, 368
  multiple holes, 369-370
  stopped holes, 368-369
  through holes, 366-367
boring tools, 110-119
  auger bit, 110
  boring fixture, shop-made, 113
  expansive bit brace, 110
  Forstner bit, 110
  safety rules, 110
box joints, 146-147, 175-178
  box pins, 173
  coping saw use, 176
  cutting with backsaw, 176
  cutting with dovetail saw, 176
  layout of, 175-176

template, 175
wood fixture use, 176
brace with auger bit, 111
brackets, 206
shelf, 206
table-leg, 206
brushing of varnish finish, 478-483
bristle, 478-479
brush keeper, 480
cleaning brushes, 480
cross-brushing, 482
handle shape, 479
nylon-bristle, 478
pumice stone, 483
pure-bristle, 478
rottenstone, 483
rubbing, 483
tack rag, 481
techniques of brushing, 481-483
tipping-off, 482
width, 478-479
bullnose rabbet plane, 85, 86
business organization, types of, 560-561
butt joint, 141, 150-152
clamp nails, 141, 150-152
corrugated fasteners, 141, 150-151
dowels, 141, 150
glue block, 141, 152
miter box, 150
nails, 141, 150
screws, 141, 150, 151
Skotch® fasteners, 152

C

cabinet assembly, 137, 227
cabinet clamp. *See* bar clamp
cabinet drawing, 39, 44
cabinetmaking industry drafting, 43-46
cabinets, kitchen, 441-453. *See also* kitchen cabinets
backs, 446
bottoms, 445
bulkheads, 445-446
cleat, 447
door, 448
drawer, 448, 449
faceframe, 444
joints, 445
mullion, 445
partitions, 446
shelves, 446
stile, 445
structural parts, 446
tops, 446, 449
cabinet scraper, 87-88
cabriole legs, 277
carcass construction, 430, 431-438
doors, 432-436
drawers, 436-438
dust panels, 423, 433
end panels, 432
careers, in woodworking, 7, 570-585
in construction, 580-582
in lumber industry, 573-574
in management, 584-585
in teaching, 585
in woodworking, 574-580
carriage clamps. *See* C clamps
carving tools, 89, 92, 99
casters, 202, 203
catches, door, 200, 201
bullet-type friction, 200
friction, 200
magnetic, 200
roller, 200, 201
C clamps, 120, 121, 122
double-C lever clamp, 122, 123
Lever Wrench®, 123
sizes of, 120
three-way, 122
uses of, 120
cements, 224
contact, 224
mastic, 224
chain mortiser, 350, 351
chamfer
cutting, 250
jointing, 306
making with hand plane, 82-84
making with portable power plane, 399
shaping with portable power plane, 399
use of marking gauge in layout, 83
chamfering, stopped, 306-307
chevrons, 185
chiseling, 90, 91
chisel mortiser, 350-354
chisels, 89-93, 98-99, 334-335
lathe, 334-335
shank, 90
sharpening of, 98-99
tang, 90
chop saw, 284
circles, cutting with band saw, 278-279
circle-cutting fixture, 278, 279
commercial fixture, 279
freehanding, 278
circles, laying out, 63-64
compass, 63
trammel points, 64
circular saw, portable, 384-390
blades, 386
commercial fixtures, 390
crosscutting, 386
panel saw, 390
parts, 384
plywood, cutting, 388-389
pocket cuts, 389
ripping, 387-388, 390
safety rules, 384
terminology, 385
uses, 384
clamping tools, hand-operated, 120-137
bar clamp, 122, 123
C clamp, 120, 121, 122, 123
corner clamp, 124
hand screw, 120, 121
miter vise, 124
piling clamp, 122, 123
press clamp, 124
spring clamp, 124
web clamp, 124
clothing, 50-51
collars, shaping on shaper, 328-330
ball bearing, 329
contact, 328, 329
procedure, 329-330
solid steel, 329
combination square, 60, 61
compass in layouts, 63, 64
compass saw, 72-73
compound sawing with band saw, 277-278
concave curve, smoothing with chisel, 91
construction careers, 580-582
construction techniques, 6, 428-499
contact cements, 224
convex curves, smoothing with chisel, 91
coping saw, 75-77
corner clamp, 124, 125
corrugated fastener, 184
countersink, dressing of, 103
filing, 103
honing, 103
cove cutting, 259-260
crosscut saw, 68, 69-70, 72
filing, 72
crosscutting, 69-70, 233, 242-244, 282
band saw, 282
circular stock, 282
clearance block, 243
cutting board, 242
duplicate parts, 242
long pieces, 244
with miter gauge, 242, 243, 282
safety rules, 233
stop rods, 244
with V block, 282
curved wood members, 546-551
ammonia bending chamber, 548
band sawing, 546-547
chemical bending, 547-548
lamination, 549-551
lignin, 547
products using, 546
radial arm saw, 546
retort, 548
saw kerfs, 546, 547
spring back, 548
steam bending, 548
veneer, 547, 551
curves
concave and convex, 91
external, 266
freehand, 275-276
internal, 267
large, 275
laying out, 63, 64
pattern layout, 275
relief cuts, 276
sharp, 276
small, 276
customary system, 8-9
cut-off saw. *See* radial arm saw
cuts, joinery. *See* joinery
cutters, shaper, 322-324
cylinder, turning on wood lathe, 339-341
calipers, 340
concave (cove) cuts, 342, 343
convex (bead) cuts, 342-343
gouge, 339
parting tool, 340
scraping method, 339
skew, 340, 343
square corner cutting, 341
taper cutting, 342
V cuts, 343

D

dado
blind, 143, 255
cutting with radial arm saw, 294
cutting with router, 410, 417

definition of, 143
dovetail, 143
groove, 255
joining, 144
joint, 143, 162-163
miter gauge use, 254
rabbet joint, 143
rip fence use, 254
stopped, 143
through, 143, 254

dado joints, 162-163
backsaw use, 163
cutting, 162
miter box use, 163
router plane use, 162, 163
try square use, 162
wood chisel use, 163

decorative cuts with radial arm saw, 296-297
cove, 296, 297
kerfs, 296
molding head use, 296
moldings, 297
saucer cut, 296, 297

design, elements of, 20-22
design, principles of, 22-24, 25
designer, industrial, 30
designing
furniture sizes, 24-25, 26, 27, 28
lettering, 25
materials, 24
measure, 30-32
project, 19-32

design sketch, 41-43
detail drawing, 44
dimension lumber, 523, 524-525
planks, 524-525
structural joists, 524-525
structural lumber, 524
studs, 524

dimensions, 37-38
disc sander, 373, 374-377, 427
abrasive replacement, 375
bevel and chamfer sanding, 376
cleaning stick use, 375
portable, 427
safety rules, 373
use of, 376-377

distressing, 474-475
door catches, 200, 201
doors, 432-436
flush, 434
flush overlay, 434
lipped, 432, 433
panel, 434, 435
raised panel, 436
sliding, 434, 435
tambour, 435

doors, rolling and sliding, hardware for, 198-199
metal door track, 198
plastic door track, 199

dovetail joints, 146-147, 175-178, 412-415
cutting with dovetail saw, 178
dovetail pins, 177
half-blind, 146
layout of, 177-178
with router, 412-415
through, 147, 178
try square use, 177

dovetail saw, 73-75
dowel joints, 165-169
auger bit use, 166
bit stop use, 167
depth stop, 166
dowel center use, 168
doweling jig use, 166, 167
dowel pins, 165
layout of, 166-168
long edge joints, 165
marking gauge use, 166
miter joint layout, 168, 169
rail and leg layout, 168
small butt joint, 165
square use, 166
twist drill use, 166

dowel screws, 184
drafter, 30
drafting, in cabinetmaking industry, 43-47
drawer guides, 201-202
drawer pulls, 190-191
drawers, 436-438
drawings, simple, 4
drawings, working, 33-47
bill of materials, 38
cabinetmaking industry, 43-47
design sketch, 41-43
dimensions, 37-38
line, 34-36
pictorial, 39-40
product notes, 38
scale, 36-37
section, 37
views, 33-34

drilling tools, 110-119, 359-372
drill press, 359-372
hand drill, 110, 118
push drill, 110, 118-119
safety rules, 110
twist drill, 100, 117

drill press, 359-372
angular holes boring, 370, 371
bits, 363-376
circular stock boring, 371
counterboring, 370, 371
deep hole boring, 368-369
fence, 360
function, 360
horizontal boring machine, 360
mortising on, 354
multiple hole boring, 369-370
multi-spindle boring machine, 360, 361
operation of, 362
router bit, 360
safety rules, 359
sanding, 372
stopped hole boring, 368
terminology, 361-362
through hole boring, 366-367
tools, drilling, 363, 365-366
variable speed, 362

drills, portable, 419-422
accessories, 419
awl, 419
boring holes, 420-422
chuck, 419, 420
fixture block, 421
parts, 419
pistol-grip handle, 419, 420
pneumatic drills, 422
reversing switch, 420
safety rules, 419
sizes, 420
terminology, 419
T handle, 420
variable speed, 420

E

economy, U.S., 2
edge, on shaper, 325-328
feather board use, 327

edge joint, 142, 150, 153-154
corrugated metal fasteners, 142
dowel, 142
edge lap type, 142
glue and, 142
milled glue joint, 142
planing edges, 153
rabbet-edge lap, 154
rabbet plane, 154
spline type, 142
tongue and groove type, 142

edge sander, 374, 380, 381
edge tools, sharpening of, 94-103
EMC. *See* equilibrium moisture content
emery, 456
enamel finish, 483-484
flat, 483
gloss, 483
latex, 484
oil-base, 483-484
primer, 483
semigloss, 483

end grain shaping, 328
end-to-end joints, 154
finger, 145
scarf, 145

enlarging designs, 65
epoxy, 223, 478
equilibrium moisture content (EMC), 512, 513, 514
expansive bit, 116

F

faceplate turning, 345-347
fasteners, 179-189
anchors, 186-189
bolts, 184
chevrons, 185
corrugated, 184
hook, 186
nails, 179-180, 185
power nailers, 179, 183-184
screw eyes, 186
screws, 179, 180-183, 184
selection of, 179
Skotch® fasteners, 184
staples, 179, 183-184
tacks, 185
toggle bolts, 186, 187

fastening devices, 141-149
metal, 147-149
nails, 214-218
plastic, 147-149

fastening techniques, 138-229
feed direction on shaper, 325
ferrules, 202, 203
files, 104-109
filling of wood surfaces, 466-469
finishes, varnish, 476-483
finishes, wipe-on, 496-499
oil, 496, 498
paste wax, 497
resin, 496, 498, 499

salad bowl finish, 496
wax, 496, 497
finishing, preparing surfaces for, 460-465
bleaching, 463
burn-in-tool, 462
cabinetmaker's putty, 461, 462
defects, 460
dent removal, 460-461
fillers, 461
lacquer sticks, 462
patch, 462
plug, 462
putty fillers, 461
stick shellac, 462
sticks, colored, 461, 462
Water Putty®, 461
finishing sander. *See* pad sander, portable
fire prevention, 51-52
fire retardants, 552-553, 555
flint, 456
flow chart, 566, 567
fore planes, 79-80
foresters, 582
Formica®, 448
forming tools, 104
Forstner bit, 110, 116, 364
framing square, 83
furniture construction, 430-446
carcass, 430, 431-438
doors, 432-436
drawers, 436-438
end panels, 432
leg and rail, 430
shelves, 439
toeboards, 446
top construction, 438
furniture frame assembly, 137
furniture sizes, 24-25, 26, 27, 28

G
gains with pin router, 417
garnet, 374, 456, 464
general contractor, 582
glides, furniture, 202, 203
glues
air stapler, 219
assembly procedures, 131, 132
blood albumin, 221
casein, 220-221
fish, 221
glue line, 219
glue pot, 220
hot animal, 220
liquid hyde, 220
mechanical adhesion, 219
specific adhesion, 219-220
vegetable, 221
glue welder, portable electronic, 227-229
gluing procedure, 224-229
gouges, 89, 92, 99
grades, hardboard, 544-545
pegboard, 545
screened back, 545
service, 544-545
standard, 544
tempered, 544
grades, particle board, 541, 542
grades, plywood, 536-538
engineering, 538
hardwood, 536, 537
softwood, 536-537, 538
stamps, grading, 537
standard veneer, 537
grading, lumber, 523-527
grinder, electric, 94-95
groove
chippers, 252, 254
dado, 252-258
dado head, 252, 253-254
definition of, 144
gain, 252
gouge, 92
plough, 252
rabbet, 252
router, 410
spline miter, 252
use of, 144
guides, 201-203

H
hacksaw, 75
hammer, 214
hand drill, 118
hand plane, 78-87
handsaw, 68-77
backsaw, 73-75
compass saw, 72-73
coping saw, 75-77
crosscut saw, 68, 69-70
dovetail saw, 73-75
hacksaw, 75
keyhole saw, 72-73
miter saw, 73-75
ripsaw, 68-69, 70, 71
hand scraper, 78, 87-88
hand screw, 120, 121
hand tools, 4, 5, 56-137
hardboard, 543-545
hardware, 190-207
brackets, shelf, 206
casters, 202-203
door catches, 200, 201
doors, rolling and sliding, 198-199
drawer guides, 201, 202
drawer pulls, 190-191
ferrules, 202-203
glides, 202-203
hinge, 191, 192
knobs, 190-191
legs, 206
locks, cabinet, 201
moldings, 206-207
supports, 204-205
hardwood grades, 525-527
appearance, 525
calculating grades, 525
clear pieces (cuttings), 525
common, 526, 527
scaling stick, 525, 526
second, 526
select, 526
standard grades, 525-527
strength, 525
hardwood plywood, 536, 537
hardwoods, 505-506, 509-511, 516-517
basswood, 510
beech, 510
black cherry, 510
black walnut, 511
closed-grain, 506
defects in, 516-517
diffuse-porous, 506
elm, 510
exotic woods, 511
hackberry, 510
hickory, 510
mahogany, 510
maple, 510
oak, 510
red alder, 510
sweet gum, 510
white ash, 510
yellow birch, 510
yellow poplar, 511
hexagon drawing, 66
hinges, 191, 192-199
butt, 192, 193, 194
cabinet, nonmortising, 195
center-mounted, 198
concealed, 198
continuous, 194
dado, 194, 195
lipped doors, 196, 197
overlay doors, 196, 197
piano, 194
pin, 197-198
pivot, 196, 197
semiconcealed, 195, 196-197
surface-mounted, 192, 193
wrap-around, concealed, 195
honesty, as design quality, 20
hook fasteners, 186
hopper joints. *See* miter, cutting of
hot melt adhesives, 222

I - J
isometric drawing, 39
isometric pictorial drawing, 39
jack plane, 78
jigsaw. *See* scroll saw
joinery
box joints, 296
lap joints, 295
miters, elaborate, 295
with radial arm saw, 295-297
with router, 410-415
tapers, 296
techniques, 6
tongue and groove joints, 295-296
jointer, 298-311
bevels and chamfers, 306-307
edge jointing, 303-304
face jointing, 303
facer, 299
operation, 301-302
parts, 299
plywood end grain and edges, 304-305
rabbets, cutting of, 308
safety rules, 298
squaring stock, 305-306
taper cutting, 308-310
terminology, 300
Uniplane®, 298, 299, 310-311
uses of, 298
jointer plane, 78, 79-80
joints
box, 146-147, 173-178
butt, 141, 150-152
dado, 162-163
dovetail, 146-147, 173-178
dowel, 165-169
edge, 142, 150, 153-154
end-to-end, 145
finger, 549
lap, 145, 160-161

miter, 142-143, 155-159
mortise and tenon, 146, 170-174
rabbet, 144-145, 163-165
wood, 140-149

K
kerf, 69, 546, 547
keyhole saw, 72-73
kitchen cabinets, 441-453. *See also* cabinets, kitchen
custom, 441, 442
parts of, 444-448
planning of, 443-444
plastic laminate, 448-453
production of, 441, 442
tops, 448-453
types of, 441-443
knife planer, 314-315
knobs, 190-191

L
lacquers, 485-495
brushing, 487, 488-489
clear gloss, 486
colored, 488
container size, 486
dull, 486, 487
flat, 486, 487
flattening agent, 486
gloss, 486, 487
hot spray, 487
sealers, 486
semigloss, 486
shading, 488
sheens, 486
toners, 488
water-reducible, 488
water-white, 487
lag screws, 184
laminates, plastic, 441, 448-453. *See also* plastic laminates
laminating kitchen cabinet tops, 449-453
lamination, wood, 549-551
lap joints, 145, 160-161
lathe
spindle, 334
wood, 332-348
lathe chisels, 334-335, 336
gouges, 334
parting tools, 335
round noses, 335
skews, 334
spear points, 335
square noses, 334
layout tools, 58-67
lazy Susan, 443
leg and rail construction, 430-431
legs, 206
length, measuring, 59-60
combination rule, 59
folding rule, 59
inch rule, 59
metric rule, 59
tape rule, 59-60
Lever Wrench®. *See* C clamps
line, 34-36
linseed oil varnish, 477-478
long-oil, 477
medium-oil, 477-478
short-oil, 477-478
locks, cabinet, 201
logging and sawmill industry, 518-522
clear cutting, 518-519
edger, 521
foresters, 518
grader, 521
logger, 518
logging operations, 519
lumber, cutting of, 520-521
nursery, 518
sawmill, 520
seasoning, 522
selective cutting, 518, 519
trim saw, 521
lumber, dimension, 523, 524-525
lumber, grading of, 523-527
hardwoods, 525-527
lumber, sizes of, 527
random widths and lengths (RWL), 527
softwoods, 523
lumber, seasoning of, 512-514, 515
air drying, 512, 513, 514
dehumidification, 512, 514
kiln drying, 512, 514
solar drying, 512
lumber, sizes of, 527
lumber industry, careers in, 573-574

M
machines, 4, 5
maintenance, safety, 51
mallet, use of, 90, 91, 92
manufacturing, 558-569
business organization, types of, 560-561
custom production, 558, 559
mass production, 558-569
product planning, 562-567
marking gauge, 83
marquetry, 268
mass production, 6, 558-569
mass products, 556-569
mastic cements, 224
materials
selection for designing, 24
for woodworking, 4
measure, 30-32
measurement
length, 59-60
width, 60-61
measuring devices for wood lathe, 335-336
calipers, inside, 335, 336
calipers, outside, 335, 336
ruler, steel, 336
measuring systems, 8-11
conversion factors, 10-11
customary system, 8-9
linear measure, 9-10
metal fastening devices, 147-149
clamp nail, 147
clips, 149
corrugated fastener, 147
hanger bolt, 148
Skotch® fastener, 147-148
Teenut® fastener, 148
metric design sizes, table of preferred, 32
metric system, 9-10
miter, cutting of, 250-252
compound, 250
flat, 250, 292-293
miter box, 74-75
miter gauge, 234-235
T-slotted, 235
miter joint
compound, 143
edge, 142
flat, 142
joining, 143
layout, 168, 169
making, 155-159
polygon, 143
use, 143
miter joint, reinforcing, 252
miter saw, 73-75
miter vise, 124, 125
mock-up, 563
moisture meter, 514, 515
molding, 206-207, 260-261
head, 260, 261
plywood auxiliary fence, 261
mortise and tenon joint, 146, 170-174, 349-358, 411-412
applications, 349
blind, 146
face, 171
function, 349
making, 349-358
mortise cutting, 171
mortise layout, 170-172
mortise, with router, 411-412
rail, 172-173
tenon cutting, 174
tenon layout, 172-174
mortisers, 349-354
bit, 352
chisel, 353
chisel and bit, 352-353
definition of, 349
drill press, mortising on, 354
parts, 350-352
safety rules, chisel mortiser, 349
terminology, chisel mortiser, 350-352
types, 350

N
nailing tools, 214-215
claw hammer, 214
hammer face, 214
nail set, 215
ripping claw, 214
nails, 179-180, 185, 216-218
aluminum, 179
annular, 181
box, 179
brads, 179-180
casing, 179-180, 215
clamp, 185
coated, 179, 180, 218
common, 179
diameters, 180
finishing, 179-180, 215
galvanized, 179, 218
grooved, 218
penny, in sizing of, 180
power-driven, 183-184
pulling, 217-218
sizes, 180
special-purpose, 180, 181
spiral, 181
threads, 180
types of, 179
wire gauge number, 180

nails, driving of, 215-216
casing, 215
finishing, 215
toenailing butt, 216
nails, placing of, 216-217
clinching, 213
face nailing, 213
finishing nail, use of, 216
staples, use of, 217
toenailing, 217
nails, power, 130
automatic nailing machine, 130
nailing machines, 130
National Particleboard Association, 541

O
oblique drawing, 39
Occupational Safety and Health Act (OSHA), 50
octagon, drawing of, 66
oil finish, 496, 498
application of, 498
boiled linseed oil, 498
Danish oil, 498
FDA-approved oil, 498
oilstone, 95-96, 97, 98

P
pad sander, portable, 425-427
panel router, 402, 403
panel saw, 390
particle board, 539-542
advantages, 539
construction, 539, 541, 542
disadvantages, 539
grading, 541, 542
hog, 539
manufacturing, 539-541
pricing, 539
screws, 542
uses, 539
wood furnish, 539
paste wax, 348
paste wood filler, 466-468
application of, 467
barrier coat, 467
silex, 466
vehicle, 466
pattern in sawing, 247-248
pattern shaping with shaper, 330-331
penny, in nail sizing, 180
pictorial drawings, 39-40
isometric, 39
oblique, 39
piling clamp, 122, 123
pin router, 401, 416-418
bits, 417
cuts, 417-418
parts, 416
pattern, 416
safety rules, 401
stationary routers, 402
uses, 402
plane iron sharpening, 96-98
block planes, 98
bullnose planes, 98
grinding, 96
honing, 96
rabbet planes, 98
planers, 312-319
abrasive, 312, 314, 315
defects, 318
double surfacer, 312, 313, 314
edge planing, 317
face planing, 316, 318
knife, 312
operation of, 319
safety rules, 312
single-head, 312
single planer parts, 313, 315
planes, hand, 78-87
bevel making, 82-84
block plane, 85
bullnose rabbet plane, 85-86
chamfer making, 82-84
fore planes, 79-80
jack planes, 78, 79-80
jointer planes, 79-80
parts, 79-80
rabbet planes, 85-86
smooth planes, 78, 79-80
spokeshave, 87
taper making, 82-84
trimming plane, 85
types, 79-80
use, 81-84
planes, portable power, 398-400
planning, 1-55
bill of materials, 12-13, 15
board feet, 16-17, 18
plan of procedure, 14, 15
project, 12-18
project-planning sheet, 14
square feet, 17
working drawing, 12, 13
plastic fastening devices, 147-149
plastic laminates, 441, 448-453
brand names, 448
cabinet tops, 449-453
grade, 449
postform top, 449
self-edge top, 449
plywood, 70-71, 534-538
advantages, 534
assembly, 534, 535
costs, 535
definition, 534
grades, 536, 537, 538
hardwood, 536, 537
kinds, 536
lumber core, 534
manufacture, 534, 535
particle board-core, 534
sawing, 70-71
sizes, 537
softwood, 536-537
uses, 534
veneer-core, 534
pneumatic drills, 422
pneumatic sanders, 380, 426-427
pneumatic tools, 125, 130
pocket knife sharpening, 100
polyurethane finish, 478
polyvinyl adhesives, 221, 228
portable power tools, 382-427
circular saw, 384-390
drill, 419-422
electric sander, 464
power plane, 398-400
sanders, 423-427
power nails, 130
power planes, portable, 398-400
bevel shaping, 399
carbide cutter use, 400
chamfer shaping, 399
operation, 399-400
parts, 398
safety rules, 398
terminology, 398
uses, 398
power tools, portable, 382-427
power tools, stationary, 230-381
preservatives, wood, 552-555
oil, 553-555
waterborne, 553-555
press clamps, 124
press screws, 124
production drawing, 45, 563
metric, 45
wood-cabinet, 45
production line, 567-568
product notes, 38
product planning in business organization, 562-567
professional careers, 582-583
architect, 583
foresters, 582
wood science and technology, 582-583
project designing, 19-32
project planning, 12-18
projects, woodworking, 586-617
antique bench, 604
appliance storage, 606
ball rack, pool, 591
bedside table, 609
bench, 604
bookcase, 599
box, bread, 607
box, jewelry, 614
box, recipe, 616
bread box, 607
cabinet, colonial trinket, 594
cart, serving, 597
cedar chest, 600
chair, 605
chest, cedar, 600
colonial recipe box, 616
colonial tray and stand, 596
colonial trinket cabinet, 594
commode, 611
contemporary chair, 605
dart board, 588-589
desk organizer, 590
desk, wall hung, 601
dining table, 610
drafting table, 598
end table, 608
game, skill, 588-589
gun rack, 615
hexagonal commode, 611
jewelry box, 614
kitchen tools, 612
organizer, desk, 590
pickets and shutters, 613
planter, 592
pool cue ball rack, 591
rack, gun, 615
rack, wine and cheese, 603
recipe box, 616
serving cart, 597
shutters, 613
skill game, 588-589
stereo/TV stand, 602
storage/appliance center, 606
table, bedside, 609
table, dining, 610

table, drafting, 598
table, end, 608
tables, nesting, 593
tools, kitchen, 612
tray and stand, 596
trinket cabinet, 594
trunks, 595
turnings, 617
TV/stereo stand, 602
wall hung desk, 601
wine rack, 603
wishing well planter, 592
prototype, 562, 563
pumice stone, 465, 483
push drill, 118-119

R

rabbet cutting, 256-257
with jointer, 308
with router, 410, 414, 415
rabbet joint, 144-145, 163-164
assembly, 144
making, 163-164
shouldered dado, 145
use, 144
rabbet plane, 85-86
radial arm saw, 283-297, 546
arm track, 284
attachments, 285
blades, 287
crosscutting, 288-289
curved wood members, 546
dadoing, 294
decorative cuts, 295-297
flat miter cutting, 292-293
joinery cuts, 295-297
ripping, 290, 291
safety rules, 283
single arm, 284
terminology, 284-287
radius, 64
rail and leg layout, 168
rasps, 104-109
cleaning and maintaining, 105
file card use, 106
safety rules, 104
shapes, 105
teeth, 105
use, 108
reciprocating chisel mortiser, 350, 351
reciprocating saw, 391-392, 393, 395-397
bevel making, 395
blades, 392
cutting, internal, 396
guiding methods, 395-396
parts of, 391
plunge cut, 396-397
safety rules, 391
slot method, 396
terminology, 392
use, 395-397
reducing designs, 65
resawing with band saw, 281
resawing stock, 246
feather board use, 246
resin finishes, natural and synthetic, 498-499
application, 498-499
Miniwax®, 498
Sealacell®, 498
sealer coat, 499
rip fence, 234, 235
rip guide, 395-396
ripping, 233
with band saw, 280
with handsaw, 70
with table saw, 245-246
ripsaw, 68-69, 70, 71, 72
rottenstone, 483
rounded corner layout, 64
router, 401-418
joinery, 410-415
numerically controlled (N.C.), 403
panel, 402, 403
pin, 401, 402
portable, 401-402
safety rules, 401
stationary, 402, 416-418
router joinery, 410-415
custom fence, 410, 411
dadoes, 410
dovetail joints, 412-415
grooves, 410
mortises, 411-412
rabbets, 411, 414, 415
tenons, 411-412
router, portable, 401, 402, 403-415
bits, 404-406
guiding, 407, 408-410
joinery, 410-415
operations, 407-408
parts, 402
power unit, 403
safety rules, 401
router, stationary, 402-403
numerically controlled (N.C.), 403
panel, 402, 403
pin, 402, 416-418
router plane use, 87
Royal 1-2-3®, 348
rubbing oil, 483

S

saber saw, 391-394
blades, 392, 393
parts, 391
safety rules, 391
terminology, 392
use, 394
safety. *See also names of individual tools*
finishing, 51-52
general, 5, 48-55
hand-tool, 52-53
machine, 53-55
sander, portable, 423-427
belt, 423-425
disc, 427
finishing, 425
pad, 425-427
pneumatic, 426-427
safety rules, 423
sanding, drill press, 372
sanding, preparing surfaces for, 463-465
aluminum oxide abrasive paper, 464
electric sander, portable, 464
garnet abrasive paper, 464
hand scraper, 464
pumice stone, 465
rubbing compound, 465
steel wool, 465
wet-and-dry abrasive paper, 465
sanding belts, 459
sanding drum for radial arm saw, 285
sanding machines, stationary, 373-381
abrasives, 374
belt, 373, 374, 378-379
disc, 373, 374-377
edge, 374, 380, 381
pneumatic-headed, 380, 381
safety rules, 373-374
spindle, 373, 377
stroke, 374, 380
sanding screen, artificial, 456
sap staining, 474-475
saw guards, 236
sawing
plywood, 70-71
with scroll saw, 267
sawing jig, 76, 77
sawmill industry, 518-522
saws
band, 270-282
crosscut, 68, 69-70
cut-off. *See* radial arm saw
hand, 68-77
hole, 365
jigsaw. *See* scroll saw
panel, 390
portable circular, 384-390
radial arm, 283-297
reciprocating, 391-392, 395-397
ripsaw, 68-69, 70, 71
saber, 391-394
scroll, 262-269
scale, 36-37
scrapers, 78, 87-88
burnisher, 102
cabinet, 87-88
hand, 88
sharpening, 102
screwdriver
cabinet, 212, 213
clutch head, 212, 213
dressing, 101
grinding wheel use, 101
Phillips, 212, 213
standard, 212, 213
screws, 210-211
bit, 210, 211
brass screw driving, 210
ratchet screwdriver, 210
spiral ratchet screwdriver, 211
steel screw driving, 210
screws, press, 124
screws, setting below surface, 211-212
counterbore, 212
plug cutter, 211
Screw-Mate® drill and countersink, 212
Screw-Sink® drill, 212
wood buttons, 212
screws, wood, 180-183
aluminum, 182
brass, 182
clutch head, 181
diameters, 181, 182
dowel, 184
face framing, 183
flat, 180
oval, 180, 182
Phillips, 180
Pozidriv®, 181
Robertson, 181
round, 180, 182
sizes, head and shank, 182

special purpose, 183
steel, mild, 182
wire gauge sizes, 181
scroll saw, 262-269
bench-type, 262
blades, 264, 265
commercial, 262
curves, external, 266
curves, internal, 267
filing of, 268, 269
marquetry sawing, 268
parts, 262
saber sawing, 267
safety rules, 262
sanding, 268, 269
terminology, 263
scroll saw device for radial arm saw, 285
section, 37
shading, 474-475
shapers, 320-331
collars, shaping with, 328-330
cuts, types of, 320
cutters, 322-324
double-spindle, 320, 321
edge, shaping entire, 326-328
end grain, shaping of, 328
feed direction, 325
fence, wooden, 322
machine parts, 320
molder, 321
pattern shaping, 330-331
safety rules, 320
shaper table, 321
single-spindle, 320
spindles, 322
terminology, 321-322
sharpening of edge tools, 94-103
shellac, 477
shelves, 439, 440
silicon carbide, 456
Skotch® fasteners, 184
smooth planes, 78
softwood, 505-506, 511-512, 516-517
aromatic cedar, 511
coniferous, 511
defects, 516-517
Douglas fir, 511
evergreens, 511
leaf types, 511
longitudinal tracheids, 505
pines, 511-512
red cedar, 512
redwood, 512
softwood grades, 523-527
American Softwood Lumber Standard, 523
associations, 523
boards, 523-524
dimension lumber, 523, 524-525
grades, 523
standard nominal sizes, 527
timbers, 523, 525
Western Wood Products Association, 523
softwood plywood grading, 536-537, 538
Southern Pine Inspection Bureau, 523
spindle lathe, 334
spindles, duplicating
duplicator, 344
pattern, 344
template, 344
spindle sander, 373, 377
inside curves, 377
oscillating, 377
safety rules, 373
spindles on shaper, 325
spirit varnish, 477
spokeshave, 87
spray guns, lacquer, 492-493
bleeder, 492
cleaning, 494-495
external mix, 493
internal mix, 493
nonbleeder, 492
pressure-feed, 493
suction-feed, 493
spraying equipment, lacquer, 491-493
air hose, 491
air pump, 491
compressor, 491
exhaust system, 492
regulator, 491
respirator, 491, 492
spray booth, 491, 492
spray gun, 491, 492-493
spraying techniques for lacquers, 485-495
equipment, 491
lacquer sealer, 489
spray gun troubles, 490
thinner, 489
spring clamps, 124
Spyral® blade, 76
square cut laying out, 62, 63
square inside corner cutting, 281
stains
nongrain-raising, 474
oil, 472-473
spirit, 474
water, 470-472
stains, wood, 470-475
application, 470
definition, 470
distressing, 474-475
insoluble pigments, 410
nongrain-raising, 474
sap staining, 474-475
shading, 474-475
soluble dyes, 470
special effects, 474-475
spirit, 474
types, 470-471
water stain, 470-472
staples, 130
portable pneumatic stapling machine, 130
power-driven, 183-184
power stapling machines, 130
stationary power tools, 230-381
steel wool, 465
stock removal for wood lathes
cutting, 337
gouge, 337
parting tool, 337
scraping, 337
skew, 337
stock selection, 58
stock share, 561
straight cuts with band saw, 280
radial arm saw, 280
ripping, 280
stroke sander, 374, 380
structure, 20
superglues, 222
supports, 204-205
drop-leaf, 204
hinge-and-leaf, 205
leg brace, 205
lid support, 205
wood wing, movable, 204
surfacer. *See* planers
surfaces, filling wood, 466-469. *See also* filling of wood surfaces
synthetic varnish, 478
alkyd, 478
epoxy, 478
polyurethane, 478
surfaces of trees, 504-505
cross-sectional, 505
cuts, 504
ends, 504
faces, 504
grain, 504
plain-sawed, 504
quarter-sawed, 504
radial, 504
rift-sawed, 504
sides, 504
tangential, 504
transverse, 504, 505

T

table saw, 232-261
bevels, 250
blade selection, 236, 237
chamfers, 250
commercial table saws, 234
cove cutting, 259-260
crosscutting, 233, 242-244
dadoes, 252-258
gang ripsaw, 232, 233, 234
grooves, 252-258
large panel and wide board cutting, 244-245
miters, 250
panel saw, 232, 233
parts, 233
pattern use, 247-248
resawing stock, 246
ripping, 233, 245-246
safety rules, 232
saw guards, 236
tenon, 258-259
terminology, 234-236
tacks, upholstery, 185
taper cutting
with hand plane, 82-84
with jointer, 308-310
with table saw, 248-249
tapering fixture, 248, 249
template, 64
tenon cutting, 258-259, 411-412
with circular saw, 258
dado head, 259
mortise, 258
with router, 411-412
tenoner, 258
tenoning fixture, commercial, 259
tenoner, 349, 350, 351-358
definition, 350
double-end, 355-356
radial arm saw, 355
safety rules, 349
single-end, 355, 356-358
table saw, 355

thermoset adhesives, 221, 222-223
timbers, 523, 525
  beams, 525
  girders, 525
  posts, 525
time and motion studies, 568
toeboards, 446
tolerance, 562
tools, carving, 89-93
tools. drilling, 363, 365-366
  circle cutters, 365
  counterbore, 366
  countersink, 366
  hole saws, 365
  plug cutters, 366
tools, edge, 94-103
tools, layout, 58-67
tools, nailing, 214-215
top construction, 438-439
tree parts, 502-504
  bark cells, 503
  cambium layer, 503
  earlywood, 503
  growth rings, 503, 504
  heartwood, 502
  inner bar, 503
  latewood, 503
  lignification, 503
  lignin, 504
  medullary rays, 503
  phloem cells, 503
  pith, 502
  sapwood, 503
  springwood, 503
  summerwood, 503
  xylem cells, 503
tree types
  hardwoods, 505-506, 509-511, 516-517
  softwoods, 511-512, 516-517
trimming plane, 85
try square, 83
tung oil varnish, 478
twist drill, 100, 117
  sharpening, 100

U-V

Uniplane®, 310-311
upholstery materials and fabrics, 6
variety saw. *See* table saw
varnish finish, 476-483
  brushing techniques, 481-403
  brush types, 478-480
  enamels, 483-484
  linseed oil, 477
  spirit, 477
  synthetic, 478
  tung oil, 478
  types, 476-478
veneered panel construction, 531-533
  adhesive application, 532, 533
  clamping, 531
  pod press, 533
  substrate cutting, 531
  taping joint, 532
  telegraphing, 531
  veneer saw, 531
veneers, 528-533, 547
  advantages, 528
  assembly, 530
  book match, 530
  butt match, 530
  checkerboard, 530
  diamond, 530
  flat sliced, 529
  flitch, 529
  four-way-center-and-butt, 530
  grain pattern, 529, 530
  laminate, 528
  quarter sliced, 529
  reverse diamond, 530
  rift sliced, 529
  rotary cut, 529, 530
  sawed, 529
  slip match, 530
  steps in veneering, 528
  veneered panel construction, 531-533

W-Y

wax finish, 496, 597
web clamp, 124
Western Wood Products Association, 523
whetstone, 95-96
white glue, 221
width measurement, 60-62
  combination square, 60, 61
  framing square, 60
  marking gauge, 60, 61
  straightedge, 60
wood
  growth, 6
  industry, 2, 500-555
  properties, 6
  quality and selection, 4, 506-508
  surface preparation, 5
woodcarving tools, 93
wood defects
  case hardening, 516, 517
  checks, 516-517
  honeycombing, 516-517
  insect holes, 516
  knots, 515
  natural, 514-516
  pitch, 516
  seasoning, 514-515, 517
  shake, 516
  stain, 516, 517
  wane, 516
  warp, 516
wood joints, 140-149
  box, 146-147
  butt, 141
  dadoes, 143-144
  dovetail, 146-147
  edge, 142
  end-to-end, 145
  grooves, 143-144
  lap, 145
  metal fastening devices, 147-149
  miter, 142-143
  mortise-and-tenon, 146
  rabbet, 144-145
  strength of, 140, 141
wood lathe equipment, 336-337
wood lathes, 332-348
  automatic, 333
  auxiliary equipment, 336-337
  chisel, 334-335
  cylinder, turning of, 339-343
  external turnings, 333
  faceplate turning, 345-347
  finishing turned pieces, 348
  internal turnings, 333
  lathe chisels, 334-335
  measuring devices, 335-336
  patternmaking, 333
  safety rules, 332
  spindle, 332, 333, 334, 344-345
  split turning, 344
  stock removal methods, 337
  terminology, spindle lathe, 334
wood members, curved, 546-551
wood moisture, 512-514, 515
  equilibrium moisture content (EMC), 512, 513, 514
  lumber seasoning, 512-514, 515
  measuring moisture, 514
wood preservatives, 552-555
wood properties, 506-508, 509
  beauty, 507
  bending ability, 508
  compression, 506, 508
  density, 506-507
  figure, amount of, 506, 508
  hardness, 506
  machinability, 506, 507
  nail-holding power, 506, 507, 508
  shrinkage, 508
  specific gravity, 507
  stiffness, 508
  strength, 506, 507
  swelling, 508
  warping, 508
  weight, 506
woods
  hardwoods, 505-506, 509-511, 516-517
  softwoods, 511-512, 516-517
wood science, 502-517
  anatomy, 505-506
  defects, 514-517
  hardwoods, 505-506, 509-511
  lumber seasoning, 512-514
  moisture, 512
  selection of woods, 506-508
  softwoods, 505-506
  surfaces, 504-505
  tree parts, 502-504
wood screw installation, 208-213
  countersink, 209
  drilling, 209
  drill sizes, 208
  oval head, 210
  pilot hole, 208, 209
  root diameter, 209
  screwdriver, 210
  screw starter, 210
  setting below surface, 211-212
  shank hole, 208, 209
wood stains, 470-475
  wood supplies, 4
  wood surface filling, 466-469
wood-turning tool sharpening, 98-99
woodworking careers, 574-580
  assembly, 576-577
  design, 579-580
  finishing, 578
  machine-operator, 574-576
  sales, 580
  upholstery, 578-579
working drawings, 33-47
work triangle, in kitchen cabinet planning, 443-444
yellow glue, 221